**U.S. Department of Justice**
Office of Information and Privacy

# Freedom of Information Act Guide & Privacy Act Overview

*May 2000 Edition*

Office of Information and Privacy
U.S. Department of Justice
Washington, D.C. 20530

**Co-Directors**
Richard L. Huff
Daniel J. Metcalfe

**Deputy Director**
Melanie Ann Pustay

**Associate Director**
Kirsten J. Moncada

**Editor**
Pamela Maida

For sale by the U.S. Government Printing Office
Superintendent of Documents, Mail Stop: SSOP, Washington, DC 20402-9328
ISBN 0-16-050388-4

# FREEDOM OF INFORMATION ACT GUIDE
# & PRIVACY ACT OVERVIEW

## MAY 2000 EDITION

The principal components of the <u>Freedom of Information Act Guide & Privacy Act Overview</u> are (1) the "Justice Department Guide to the Freedom of Information Act," which addresses the provisions of the Freedom of Information Act (FOIA), 5 U.S.C. § 552 (1994 & Supp. IV 1998), and (2) an overview of the provisions of the Privacy Act of 1974, 5 U.S.C. § 552a (1994 & Supp. IV 1998), which is prepared by the Office of Information and Privacy in coordination with the Office of Management and Budget. The full text of each access statute can be found at the end of this volume.

The history of cases cited in either the "Justice Department Guide to the FOIA" or the "Privacy Act Overview," including official and unofficial citations, can be found in the Department of Justice's <u>Freedom of Information Case List</u> (September 1998 edition). In a few instances, when no official citation exists, a decision is reported in Prentice-Hall's Government Disclosure Service ("Gov't Disclosure Serv."); such citations are provided in this edition for continued reference purposes even though that unofficial reporter has been discontinued.

This edition of the <u>Guide & Overview</u> was prepared by several members of the Office of Information and Privacy's attorney and paralegal staff. The "FOIA Guide" was prepared by Cynthia H. Anderson, Benjamin N. Bedrick, Kenneth Chason, Laura Denk, Brentin V. Evitt, Karen M. Finnegan, Lorraine Hartmann, Carol S. Hebert, Thomas P. Hester, Jr., Rosalind Kennedy, Janice Galli McLeod, Amber V. Matthews, Frank P. Menna, Melanie Ann Pustay, Tricia S. Wellman, Elizabeth Withnell, and Anne Davis Work--with the assistance of law clerks Donna J. Apostol, Graham L. Barron, William F. Benson, Joo Y. Chung, Shawn T. Noud, and Rachel E. Weir. The "Privacy Act Overview" was prepared by Kirsten J. Moncada, with the assistance of law clerk Joo Y. Chung. Additional copies of this volume are available through the Superintendent of Documents, U.S. Government Printing Office, Washington, D.C. 20402.

Both the "Justice Department Guide to the FOIA" and the "Privacy Act Overview" are available at the Justice Department's FOIA site on the World Wide Web (<u>www.usdoj.gov/04foia/04_7.html</u>).

# JUSTICE DEPARTMENT GUIDE TO THE FREEDOM OF INFORMATION ACT

The "Justice Department Guide to the Freedom of Information Act" is an overview discussion of the FOIA's exemptions, its law enforcement record exclusions, and its most important procedural aspects. Prepared by the attorney and paralegal staff of the Office of Information and Privacy, it is updated and revised each year. Any inquiry about the points addressed below, or regarding matters of FOIA administration or interpretation, should be made to the Office of Information and Privacy through its FOIA Counselor service, at (202) 514-3642 (514-FOIA), after initial consultation with an agency FOIA officer.

## TABLE OF CONTENTS

INTRODUCTION .................................................. 5

FOIA READING ROOMS ........................................ 16

PROCEDURAL REQUIREMENTS ................................ 23
    Entities Subject to the FOIA ...................................... 23
    Agency Records .................................................. 27
    FOIA Requesters ................................................. 32
    Proper FOIA Requests ........................................... 36
    Time Limits ...................................................... 47
    Searching for Records ........................................... 54
    "Reasonably Segregable" Obligation ............................. 59
    Referrals and Consultations ..................................... 62
    Responding to FOIA Requests .................................. 64

EXEMPTION 1 ..................................................... 70
    Standard of Review .............................................. 72
    Deference to Agency Expertise ................................... 77
    In Camera Submissions ......................................... 79
    Rejection of Classification Claims ............................... 83
    "Public Domain" Information .................................... 88
    Executive Order 12,958 .......................................... 93
    Duration of Classification and Declassification .................... 101
    Additional Considerations ....................................... 104

EXEMPTION 2 .................................................... 107
    "Low 2": Trivial Matters ........................................ 109
    "High 2": Risk of Circumvention ................................ 117

EXEMPTION 3 .................................................... 132
    Initial Considerations ........................................... 133
    Subpart (A) .................................................... 137
    Subpart (B) .................................................... 145
    Alternative Analyses ............................................ 151
    Additional Considerations ....................................... 159

| | |
|---|---:|
| EXEMPTION 4 | 163 |
|     Trade Secrets | 163 |
|     Commercial or Financial Information | 164 |
|     Obtained from a "Person" | 167 |
|     "Confidential" Information | 168 |
|     The <u>Critical Mass</u> Decision | 171 |
|     Applying <u>Critical Mass</u> | 173 |
|     Impairment Prong of <u>National Parks</u> | 187 |
|     Competitive Harm Prong of <u>National Parks</u> | 193 |
|     Third Prong of <u>National Parks</u> | 221 |
|     Privileged Information | 225 |
|     Interrelation with Trade Secrets Act | 227 |
| EXEMPTION 5 | 229 |
|     Initial Considerations | 230 |
|     Deliberative Process Privilege | 236 |
|     Attorney Work-Product Privilege | 258 |
|     Attorney-Client Privilege | 267 |
|     Other Privileges | 270 |
|     Applying the "Foreseeable Harm" Standard | 275 |
| EXEMPTION 6 | 280 |
|     Initial Considerations | 280 |
|     The <u>Reporters Committee</u> Decision | 283 |
|     Privacy Considerations | 285 |
|     Factoring in the Public Interest | 298 |
|     The Balancing Process | 313 |
| EXEMPTION 7 | 332 |
| EXEMPTION 7(A) | 349 |
| EXEMPTION 7(B) | 372 |
| EXEMPTION 7(C) | 373 |
| EXEMPTION 7(D) | 404 |
| EXEMPTION 7(E) | 434 |
| EXEMPTION 7(F) | 444 |
| EXEMPTION 8 | 448 |
| EXEMPTION 9 | 454 |
| EXCLUSIONS | 454 |
|     The (c)(1) Exclusion | 455 |
|     The (c)(2) Exclusion | 458 |
|     The (c)(3) Exclusion | 461 |
|     Procedural Considerations | 462 |
| DISCRETIONARY DISCLOSURE AND WAIVER | 465 |
|     Discretionary Disclosure | 467 |
|     Waiver | 477 |

## FEES AND FEE WAIVERS ... 490
- Fees ... 492
- Fee Waivers ... 502

## LITIGATION CONSIDERATIONS ... 519
- Jurisdiction and Venue ... 519
- Pleadings ... 532
- Exhaustion of Administrative Remedies ... 536
- "Open America" Stays of Proceedings ... 545
- Adequacy of Search ... 551
- Mootness and Other Grounds for Dismissal ... 563
- "Vaughn Index" ... 568
- "Reasonably Segregable" Requirements ... 582
- In Camera Inspection ... 584
- Summary Judgment ... 590
- Discovery ... 597
- Waiver of Exemptions in Litigation ... 602
- Attorney Fees and Litigation Costs ... 608
- Sanctions ... 628
- Considerations on Appeal ... 633

## "REVERSE" FOIA ... 640
- Standard of Review ... 645
- Executive Order 12,600 ... 651

## BASIC FOIA REFERENCES ... 655
- Congressional References ... 656
- Justice Department Materials ... 658
- Nongovernment Publications ... 659

# INTRODUCTION

The Freedom of Information Act[1] generally provides that any person has a right, enforceable in court, to obtain access to federal agency records, except to the extent that such records (or portions of them) are protected from disclosure by one of nine exemptions or by one of three special law enforcement record exclusions.

Enacted in 1966, the FOIA established for the first time an effective statutory right of access to government information. The principles of government openness and accountability underlying the FOIA, however, are inherent in the democratic ideal: "The basic purpose of [the] FOIA is to ensure an informed citizenry, vital to the functioning of a democratic society, needed to check against corruption and to hold the governors accountable to the governed."[2] The Supreme Court has emphasized that "[o]fficial information that sheds light on an agency's performance of its statutory duties falls squarely within that statutory purpose."[3]

This was emphasized also in the statement of FOIA policy issued by President Clinton on October 4, 1993, in which he called upon all federal agencies to renew their commitment to the Act and to enhance its effectiveness as a vital mechanism of government openness and accountability:

> For more than a quarter century now, the Freedom of Information Act has played a unique role in strengthening our democratic form of government. The statute was enacted based upon the fundamental principle that an informed citizenry is essential to the democratic process and that the more the American people know about their government the better they will be governed. Openness in government is essential to accountability and the Act has become an integral part of that process.[4]

To be sure, achieving an informed citizenry is a goal often counterpoised against other vital societal aims. Society's strong interest in an open government can conflict with other important interests of the general public--such as the public's interests in the effective and efficient operations of government; in the prudent governmental use of limited fiscal resources; and in the preservation of the confidentiality of sensitive personal, commercial, and governmental information. Though tensions among these competing interests are characteristic of a democratic society, their resolution lies in providing a workable formula that encompasses, balances, and appropriately protects all interests,

---

[1] 5 U.S.C. § 552 (1994 & Supp. IV 1998).

[2] NLRB v. Robbins Tire & Rubber Co., 437 U.S. 214, 242 (1978).

[3] United States Dep't of Justice v. Reporters Comm. for Freedom of the Press, 489 U.S. 749, 773 (1989).

[4] President's Memorandum for Heads of Departments and Agencies regarding the Freedom of Information Act, 29 Weekly Comp. Pres. Doc. 1999 (Oct. 4, 1993) [hereinafter President Clinton's FOIA Memorandum], reprinted in FOIA Update, Vol. XIV, No. 3, at 3.

# INTRODUCTION

while placing emphasis on the most responsible disclosure possible.[5] It is this accommodation of countervailing public concerns, with disclosure as the predominant objective, that the FOIA seeks to achieve.

The FOIA evolved after a decade of debate among agency officials, legislators, and public interest group representatives. It revised the public disclosure section of the Administrative Procedure Act;[6] which generally had been recognized as falling far short of its disclosure goals and had come to be looked upon as more a withholding statute than a disclosure statute.[7]

By contrast, under the thrust and structure of the FOIA, virtually every record possessed by a federal agency must be made available to the public in one form or another, unless it is specifically exempted from disclosure or specially excluded from the Act's coverage in the first place.[8] The nine exemptions of the FOIA ordinarily provide the only bases for nondisclosure,[9] and generally they are discretionary, not mandatory, in nature.[10] (For discussions of the discretionary nature of FOIA exemptions, and the making of discretionary disclosures as a matter of FOIA policy, see Discretionary Disclosure and Waiver, below.) Dissatisfied record requesters are given a relatively speedy remedy in the United States district courts, where judges determine the propriety of agency withholdings de novo and agencies bear the burden of proof in defending their nondisclosure actions.[11]

The FOIA contains seven subsections, the first two of which establish certain categories of information that must automatically be disclosed by federal agencies. Subsection (a)(1) of the FOIA[12] requires disclosure through publication in the Federal Register of information such as descriptions of agency organizations, functions, procedures; substantive rules; and statements of general policy.[13] This requirement provides automatic public access to very basic

---

[5] See S. Rep. No. 89-813, at 3 (1965).

[6] 5 U.S.C. § 1002 (1964) (amended 1966 and now codified at 5 U.S.C. § 552).

[7] See S. Rep. No. 89-813, at 5 (1965).

[8] See NLRB v. Sears, Roebuck & Co., 421 U.S. 132, 136 (1975).

[9] See 5 U.S.C. § 552(d).

[10] See Chrysler Corp. v. Brown, 441 U.S. 281, 293 (1979); see also, e.g., FOIA Update, Vol. VI, No. 3, at 3 ("OIP Guidance: Discretionary Disclosure and Exemption 4").

[11] See 5 U.S.C. § 552(a)(4)(B)-(C); see also FOIA Update, Vol. VI, No. 2, at 6.

[12] 5 U.S.C. § 552(a)(1).

[13] See, e.g., Aulenback, Inc. v. Federal Highway Admin., 103 F.3d 156, 168 (D.C. Cir. 1997); Hughes v. United States, 953 F.2d 531, 539 (9th Cir. 1992); NI Indus., Inc. v. United States, 841 F.2d 1104, 1107 (Fed. Cir. 1988); Bright v. INS, 837 F.2d 1330, 1331 (5th Cir. 1988); see also DiCarlo v. Commissioner,

(continued...)

# INTRODUCTION

information regarding the transaction of agency business.[14]

Subsection (a)(2) of the FOIA[15] requires that certain types of records--final opinions and orders rendered in the adjudication of cases, specific policy statements, certain administrative staff manuals, and some records previously processed for disclosure under the Act--be routinely made "available for public inspection and copying."[16] This is commonly referred to as the "reading room" provision of the FOIA,[17] and it requires that some such records be made available by agencies in "electronic reading rooms" as well.[18] (For a discussion of the operation of this FOIA subsection, see FOIA Reading Rooms, below.)

The courts have held that providing official notice and guidance to the general public is the fundamental purpose of the publication requirement of subsection (a)(1) and the "reading room" availability requirement of subsection (a)(2).[19] Failure to comply with the requirements of either subsection can result in invalidation of related agency action,[20] unless the complaining party

---

(...continued)
T.C. Memo 1992-280, slip op. at 9-10 (May 14, 1992) (publication in United States Government Manual, special edition of Federal Register, satisfies publication requirement of subsection (a)(1)(A) (citing 1 C.F.R. § 9 (1992))).

[14] See FOIA Update, Vol. XIII, No. 3, at 3-4 ("OIP Guidance: The 'Automatic' Disclosure Provisions of FOIA: Subsections (a)(1) & (a)(2)") (advising agencies to meet their subsection (a)(1) responsibilities on no less than quarterly basis).

[15] 5 U.S.C. § 552(a)(2).

[16] Id. § 552(a)(2)(A)-(D).

[17] See FOIA Update, Vol. XIII, No. 3, at 4; see also FOIA Update, Vol. XIX, No. 1, at 3-4; FOIA Update, Vol. XVIII, No. 1, at 3-5.

[18] See FOIA Update, Vol. XVII, No. 4, at 1-2 (discussing provisions of Electronic Freedom of Information Act Amendments of 1996, Pub. L. No. 104-231, 110 Stat. 3048); see also FOIA Update, Vol. XIX, No. 3, at 3-4 ("OIP Guidance: Recommendations for FOIA Web Sites"); FOIA Update, Vol. XVIII, No. 3, at 1-2 (describing early agency development of World Wide Web sites for "electronic reading room" purposes).

[19] See, e.g., Welch v. United States, 750 F.2d 1101, 1111 (1st Cir. 1985).

[20] See, e.g., Kennecott Utah Copper Corp. v. United States Dep't of the Interior, 88 F.3d 1191, 1203 (D.C. Cir. 1996) ("Congress has provided [a] means for encouraging agencies to fulfill their obligation to publish materials in the Federal Register" by "protect[ing] a person from being adversely affected" by an unpublished regulation.); Checkosky v. SEC, 23 F.3d 452, 459 (D.C. Cir. 1994); NI Indus., 841 F.2d at 1108; D&W Food Ctrs. v. Block, 786 F.2d 751, 757-58 (6th Cir. 1986); Anderson v. Butz, 550 F.2d 459, 462-63 (9th Cir. 1977); see also Texas Health Care Ass'n v. Bowen, 710 F. Supp. 1109, 1113-14, 1116 (W.D. Tex. 1989).

# INTRODUCTION

had actual and timely notice of the unpublished agency policy,[21] unless he is unable to show that he was adversely affected by the lack of publication,[22] or unless he fails to show that he would have been able to pursue "an alternative course of conduct" had the information been published.[23] However, unpublished interpretive guidelines that were available for copying and inspection in an agency program manual have been held not to violate subsection (a)(1),[24] and it also has been held that regulations pertaining solely to internal personnel matters that do not affect members of the public need not be published.[25]

---

[21] See, e.g., United States v. F/V Alice Amanda, 987 F.2d 1078, 1084-85 (4th Cir. 1993) (denying statutory defense of subsection (a)(1) when defendant had copy of unpublished regulations); United States v. Bowers, 920 F.2d 220, 222 (4th Cir. 1990) (finding that IRS's failure to publish tax forms did not preclude defendants' convictions for income tax evasion, as defendants had notice of duty to pay those taxes, duty is "manifest on face" of statutes, listing of places where forms can be obtained is published in Code of Federal Regulations, and defendants had filed tax returns before); Lonsdale v. United States, 919 F.2d 1440, 1447 (10th Cir. 1990); Tearney v. National Transp. Safety Bd., 868 F.2d 1451, 1454 (5th Cir. 1989); Bright, 837 F.2d at 1331; Mada-Luna v. Fitzpatrick, 813 F.2d 1006, 1018 (9th Cir. 1987); Sierra Club North Star Chapter v. Peña, 1 F. Supp. 2d 971, 980 (D. Minn. 1998) (holding organization subject to unpublished agency interpretation when it was "repeatedly informed" of agency's position); see also United States v. $200,000 in United States Currency, 590 F. Supp. 866, 874-75 (S.D. Fla. 1984) (alternative holding) (determining that published regulations adequately apprised individuals of obligation to use unpublished reporting form).

[22] See, e.g., Lake Mohave Boat Owners Ass'n v. National Park Serv., 78 F.3d 1360, 1368 (9th Cir. 1996); Alliance for Cannabis Therapeutics v. DEA, 13 F.3d 1131, 1136 (D.C. Cir. 1994); Bowers, 920 F.2d at 222; Sheppard v. Sullivan, 906 F.2d 756, 762 (D.C. Cir. 1990); Nguyen v. United States, 824 F.2d 697, 702 (9th Cir. 1987); Coos-Curry Elec. Coop., Inc. v. Jura, 821 F.2d 1341, 1347 (9th Cir. 1987).

[23] Alliance for Cannabis Therapeutics, 15 F.3d at 1136 (citing Zaharakis v. Heckler, 744 F.2d 711, 714 (9th Cir. 1984)).

[24] See McKenzie v. Bowen, 787 F.2d 1216, 1222-23 (8th Cir. 1986); see also Lake Mohave Boat Owners, 78 F.3d at 1368 (finding rate-setting guidelines to be "an agency staff manual governed by § 552(a)(2)," requiring only public availability, not Federal Register publication under subsection (a)(1)); Capuano v. National Transp. Safety Bd., 843 F.2d 56, 57-58 (1st Cir. 1988); Pagan-Astacio v. Department of Educ., No. 93-2173, slip op. at 9 (D.P.R. June 1, 1995) (determining that agency need not publish directory explaining existing regulation when it publishes Federal Register notice explaining where directory is available), aff'd, 81 F.3d 147 (1st Cir. 1996) (unpublished table decision); Medics, Inc. v. Sullivan, 766 F. Supp. 47, 52-53 (D.P.R. 1991); Sturm v. James, 684 F. Supp. 1218, 1223 n.6 (S.D.N.Y. 1988).

[25] See Hamlet v. United States, 63 F.3d 1097, 1103 (Fed. Cir. 1995) (holding that publication not required for personnel manuals "related solely to the [agency's] internal personnel rules and practices"); Pruner v. Department of

(continued...)

# INTRODUCTION

Of course, an agency is not required to publish substantive rules and policy statements of general applicability that it has not adopted.[26]

Under subsection (a)(3) of the FOIA--by far the most commonly utilized part of the Act--all records not made available to the public under subsections (a)(1) or (a)(2), or exempted from mandatory disclosure under subsection (b), or excluded under subsection (c), are subject to disclosure upon an agency's receipt of a proper FOIA request from any person.[27] (See the discussions of the

---

(...continued)
the Army, 755 F. Supp. 362, 365 (D. Kan. 1991) (holding that Army regulation governing procedures for applications for conscientious objector status concerned internal personnel matters and were not required to be published); see also Dilley v. National Transp. Safety Bd., 49 F.3d 667, 669-70 (10th Cir. 1995) (holding that publication of policy regarding FAA's authority to suspend pilot certificates not required when statute clearly grants agency broad disciplinary powers); Lonsdale, 919 F.2d at 1446-47 (holding that FOIA does not require publication of Treasury Department orders which internally delegate authority to enforce internal revenue laws). But see Smith v. National Transp. Safety Bd., 981 F.2d 1326, 1328-29 (D.C. Cir. 1993) (holding that unpublished policy bulletin regarding sanctions was not valid basis for suspension of license because sanctions policy affects public by altering public's behavior).

[26] See 5 U.S.C. § 552(a)(1); see, e.g., Xin-Chang Zhang v. Slattery, 55 F.3d 732, 749 (2d Cir. 1995) (reversing district court's order that agency give effect to unpublished rule after finding plaintiff adversely affected by lack of publication, when rule was to be effective only on date of publication and "[b]y its own terms, the [r]ule never became effective"); Clarry v. United States, 891 F. Supp. 105, 110-11 (E.D.N.Y. 1995) (stating that failure to publish notice of ban for reemployment of strikers did not violate FOIA's notice requirement when rule was not "formulated and adopted" by agency but was authorized by presidential directive and by statute); Peng-Fei Si v. Slattery, 864 F. Supp. 397, 405 (S.D.N.Y. 1994) ("The FOIA cannot be used to force an agency to adopt a new regulation that it withdrew from publication for the specific purpose of determining whether or not it should be adopted."); Xiu Qin Chen v. Slattery, 862 F. Supp. 814, 822 (E.D.N.Y. 1994) ("[A]n agency cannot be bound by [an un]published rule in a situation in which the agency never actually adopted the rule."); cf. Kennecott, 88 F.3d at 1202-03 (finding that FOIA does not authorize district court to order publication of regulation withdrawn by new Administration before it could be published).

[27] See 5 U.S.C. § 552(a)(3)(A) (stating that "FOIA request" under subsection (a)(3) cannot be made for any records "made available" under subsections (a)(1) or (a)(2)); United States Dep't of Justice v. Tax Analysts, 492 U.S. 136, 152 (1989); Schwarz v. United States Patent & Trademark Office, No. 95-5349, 1996 U.S. App. LEXIS 4609, at *1 (D.C. Cir. Feb. 22, 1996); Hardy v. ATF, 631 F.2d 653, 657 (9th Cir. 1980); Crews v. Internal Revenue, No. 99-8388, slip op. at 11-12 (C.D. Cal. Apr. 26, 2000); Reeves v. United States, No. 94-1291, 1994 WL 782235, at **1-2 (E.D. Cal. Nov. 16, 1994); see also FOIA Update, Vol. XVI, No. 1, at 2; FOIA Update, Vol. XIII, No. 3, at 4; FOIA Update, Vol. XII, No. 2, at 5. But see FOIA Update, Vol. XVIII, No. 1, at 3 (advising that while ordinary rule is that records placed in reading room under subsection (a)(2) cannot be

(continued...)

# INTRODUCTION

procedural aspects of subsection (a)(3) (including fees and fee waivers), the exemptions of subsection (b), and the exclusions of subsection (c), below.)

Subsection (c) of the FOIA,[28] which was added as part of the Freedom of Information Reform Act of 1986,[29] establishes three special categories of law enforcement-related records that have been entirely excluded from the coverage of the FOIA in order to safeguard against unique types of harm.[30] The extraordinary protection embodied in subsection (c) permits an agency to respond to a request for such records as if the records in fact did not exist. (See the discussion of the operation of these special provisions under Exclusions, below.)

Subsection (d) of the FOIA[31] makes clear that the Act was not intended to authorize any new withholding of information, including from Congress. While individual Members of Congress possess merely the same rights of access as those guaranteed to "any person" under subsection (a)(3), Congress as a body (or through its committees and subcommittees) cannot be denied access to information on the grounds of FOIA exemptions.[32]

Subsection (e) of the FOIA,[33] which was modified as part of the Electronic Freedom of Information Act Amendments of 1996,[34] requires an annual report from each federal agency regarding its FOIA operations, and an annual report from the Department of Justice to Congress regarding both FOIA litigation and the Department of Justice's efforts (primarily through the Office of Information and Privacy) to encourage agency compliance with the FOIA.[35]

---

(...continued)
subject of regular FOIA request, Congress made clear that that rule does not apply to new subsection (a)(2)(D) category of FOIA-processed records) (citing H.R. Rep. No. 104-795, at 21 (1996)).

[28] 5 U.S.C. § 552(c).

[29] Pub. L. No. 99-570, §§ 1801-1804, 100 Stat. 3207, 3207-48.

[30] See generally Attorney General's Memorandum on the 1986 Amendments to the Freedom of Information Act 18 (Dec. 1987).

[31] 5 U.S.C. § 552(d).

[32] See FOIA Update, Vol. V, No. 1, at 3-4 ("OIP Guidance: Congressional Access Under FOIA") (citing, e.g., H.R. Rep. No. 89-1497, at 11-12 (1966)); see also 5 U.S.C. § 552a(b)(9) (1994 & Supp. IV 1998) (counterpart provision of Privacy Act of 1974); cf. Leach v. RTC, 860 F. Supp. 868, 878-79 & n.13 (D.D.C. 1994) (treating contrary statements in Murphy v. Department of the Army, 613 F.2d 1151, 1156-58 (D.C. Cir. 1979), as "mere dicta"), appeal dismissed per stipulation, No. 94-5279 (D.C. Cir. Dec. 22, 1994).

[33] 5 U.S.C. § 552(e).

[34] Pub. L. No. 104-231, 110 Stat. 3048.

[35] See id. § 552(e)(5); see, e.g., FOIA Update, Vol. XIX, No. 3, at 6 (describ-
(continued...)

# INTRODUCTION

Agencies now prepare their annual reports for submission to the Department of Justice,[36] which in turn makes them available to the public through a single World Wide Web site.[37] Each agency also should make its annual FOIA report readily available on its own FOIA Web site.[38]

Subsection (f) of the FOIA[39] defines the term "agency" so as to subject the records of nearly all executive branch entities to the Act and defines the term "record" to include information maintained in an electronic format. (See the discussions of these terms under Procedural Requirements, Entities Subject to the FOIA, below, and Procedural Requirements, Agency Records, below.) Lastly, newly added subsection (g) of the FOIA[40] now requires agencies to prepare FOIA reference guides describing their information systems and their processes of FOIA administration, as an aid to potential FOIA requesters.[41]

\* \* \* \* \*

As originally enacted in 1966, the FOIA contained, in the views of many, several weaknesses that detracted from its ideal operation. In response, the courts fashioned certain procedural devices, such as the requirement of a "Vaughn Index"--a detailed index of withheld documents and the justification

---

(...continued)
ing range of OIP policy activities in connection with governmentwide implementation of Electronic FOIA amendments); FOIA Update, Vol. XIV, No. 3, at 8-9 (describing range of OIP policy activities, including its "ombudsman" function); see also FOIA Update, Vol. VIII, No. 3, at 2 (further description of same).

[36] See 5 U.S.C. § 552(e)(1); FOIA Update, Vol. XVIII, No. 3, at 3-7 ("OIP Guidance: Guidelines for Agency Preparation and Submission of Annual FOIA Reports"); see also FOIA Update, Vol. XIX, No. 3, at 2 (advising agencies further on preparation of annual FOIA reports).

[37] See FOIA Update, Vol. XIX, No. 3, at 2 (advising agencies on proper FOIA Web site treatment of annual FOIA reports in compliance with new electronic availability requirements of 5 U.S.C. § 552(e)(2)-(3), including through agency identification of Uniform Resource Locator (URL) for each report, and referencing Department of Justice's FOIA Web site at www.usdoj.gov/04foia).

[38] See 5 U.S.C. § 552(e)(2); see also FOIA Update, Vol. XIX, No. 3, at 4 (advising agencies to "clearly indicate the year of each of [their annual FOIA] reports" on their FOIA Web sites).

[39] 5 U.S.C. § 552(f).

[40] Id. § 552(g).

[41] See FOIA Update, Vol. XIX, No. 3, at 3 (referencing revised Office of Management and Budget guidance to agencies on contents of FOIA reference guides); see also FOIA Update, Vol. XVIII, No. 2, at 1 (discussing electronic availability of Justice Department's FOIA Reference Guide).

## INTRODUCTION

for their exemption, established in Vaughn v. Rosen[42]--and the requirement that agencies release segregable nonexempt portions of a partially exempt record, first established in EPA v. Mink.[43]

In an effort to further extend the FOIA's disclosure requirements, and also as a reaction to the abuses of the "Watergate era," the FOIA was substantially amended in 1974. The 1974 FOIA amendments considerably narrowed the overall scope of the Act's law enforcement and national security exemptions, and also broadened many of its procedural provisions--such as those relating to fees, time limits, segregability, and in camera inspection by the courts.[44] At the same time, Congress enacted the Privacy Act of 1974,[45] which supplements the FOIA when requests are made by individuals for records about themselves[46] and also contains a variety of separate privacy protections.[47] (For a discussion of the Privacy Act's provisions, see the Department of Justice's "Overview of the Privacy Act of 1974.")

In 1976, Congress again limited what could be withheld as exempt from disclosure under the FOIA, this time by narrowing its incorporation of the disclosure prohibitions of other statutes. (See the discussion of Exemption 3, below.) A technical change was made in 1978 to update the FOIA's provision for administrative disciplinary proceedings,[48] and in 1984 Congress repealed the expedited court-review provision previously contained in former subsection (a)(4)(D) of the Act.[49]

---

[42] 484 F.2d 820, 827 (D.C. Cir. 1973).

[43] 410 U.S. 73, 91 (1973); see 5 U.S.C. § 552(b) (sentence immediately following exemptions) (requiring disclosure of any "reasonably segregable" nonexempt information); see also FOIA Update, Vol. XIV, No. 3, at 11-12 ("OIP Guidance: The 'Reasonable Segregation' Obligation"); cf. FOIA Update, Vol. XVII, No. 1, at 1-2 (describing agency use of document imaging in automated FOIA processing).

[44] See, e.g., James T. O'Reilly, Federal Information Disclosure § 3.08 (2d ed. 1998) (summarizing provisions of 1974 FOIA amendments).

[45] 5 U.S.C. § 552a (1994 & Supp. IV 1998).

[46] See 5 U.S.C. § 552a(d); see, e.g., Martin v. Office of Special Counsel, 819 F.2d 1181, 1184 (D.C. Cir. 1987) (discussing relation between two acts); see also 5 U.S.C. § 552a(t) (addressing interrelationship of exemptions in two acts).

[47] See 5 U.S.C. § 552a; see also Memorandum on Privacy and Personal Information in Federal Records, 34 Weekly Comp. Pres. Doc. 870 (May 14, 1998), available in Westlaw, 1998 WL 241263 (May 14, 1998) (executive memorandum to heads of all federal departments and agencies on Privacy Act-related matters); FOIA Update, Vol. XIX, No. 2, at 1 (describing executive memorandum).

[48] 5 U.S.C. § 552(a)(4)(F).

[49] See Federal Courts Improvement Act of 1984, Pub. L. No. 98-620, § 402, 98 Stat. 3335, 3357 (codified at 28 U.S.C. § 1657 (1994)) (repealing provision
(continued...)

# INTRODUCTION

In 1986, after many years of administrative experience with the FOIA demonstrated that the Act was in need of both substantive and procedural reform,[50] Congress enacted the Freedom of Information Reform Act of 1986,[51] which amended the FOIA to provide broader exemption protection for law enforcement information, plus special law enforcement record exclusions, and also created a new fee and fee waiver structure.[52] The Department of Justice and other federal agencies took a number of steps to implement the provisions of the 1986 FOIA amendments.[53]

In October 1996, after several years of legislative consideration of "electronic record" issues,[54] Congress enacted the Electronic Freedom of Information Act Amendments of 1996,[55] which addressed the subject of electronic records, as well as the subject areas of FOIA reading rooms and agency backlogs of FOIA requests, among other procedural provisions.[56] All provisions of the

---

(...continued)
formerly codified at 5 U.S.C. § 552(a)(4)(D)); see also FOIA Update, Vol. VI, No. 2, at 6.

[50] See generally Freedom of Information Act: Hearings on S. 587, S. 1235, S. 1247, S. 1730, and S. 1751 Before the Subcomm. on the Constitution of the Senate Comm. on the Judiciary, 97th Cong., 1st Sess. (1981) (two volumes); see also FOIA Update, Vol. VII, No. 2, at 1; FOIA Update, Vol. V, No. 4, at 1; FOIA Update, Vol. V, No. 3, at 1, 4; FOIA Update, Vol. V, No. 1, at 1, 6; FOIA Update, Vol. IV, No. 3, at 1-2; FOIA Update, Vol. IV, No. 2, at 1; FOIA Update, Vol. III, No. 3, at 1-2; FOIA Update, Vol. III, No. 2, at 1-2; FOIA Update, Vol. III, No. 1, at 1-2, 3-8; FOIA Update, Vol. II, No. 4, at 1-2; FOIA Update, Vol. II, No. 3, at 1-2.

[51] Pub. L. No. 99-570, 100 Stat. 3207.

[52] See FOIA Update, Vol. VII, No. 4, at 1-2; see also id. at 3-6 (setting out statute in its amended form, interlineated to show exact changes made).

[53] See FOIA Update, Vol. VIII, No. 1, at 1-2; FOIA Update, Vol. IX, No. 3, at 1-14; FOIA Update, Vol. IX, No. 1, at 2.

[54] See, e.g., FOIA Update, Vol. XIII, No. 2, at 1, 3-10 (congressional testimony discussing need to modify FOIA to accommodate "electronic record" environment); see FOIA Update, Vol. XVII, No. 3, at 1-2 (describing electronic record legislative proposal); FOIA Update, Vol. XVII, No. 2, at 1 (same); see also FOIA Update, Vol. XV, No. 4, at 1-6; FOIA Update, Vol. XV, No. 3, at 1-2; FOIA Update, Vol. XV, No. 1, at 1; FOIA Update, Vol. XII, No. 4, at 1-2.

[55] Pub. L. No. 104-231, 110 Stat. 3048.

[56] See FOIA Update, Vol. XVII, No. 4, at 1-2, 10-11 (discussing statutory changes); see also id. at 3-9 (setting out statute in its amended form, interlineated to show exact changes made); President's Statement on Signing the Electronic Freedom of Information Act Amendments of 1996, 32 Weekly Comp. Pres. Doc. 1949 (Oct. 7, 1996), reprinted in FOIA Update, Vol. XVII, No. 4, at 9.

# INTRODUCTION

Electronic FOIA amendments are now effective.[57] (See the discussions of the provisions of the Electronic FOIA amendments under FOIA Reading Rooms, Procedural Requirements, Fees and Fee Waivers, and Litigation Considerations, below.) The Department of Justice and other federal agencies have taken a number of steps to implement the provisions of the Electronic FOIA amendments.[58]

Another significant Freedom of Information Act development was the issuance in October 1993 of statements of new FOIA policy by both President Clinton[59] and Attorney General Janet Reno,[60] which together established a

---

[57] See FOIA Update, Vol. XVII, No. 4, at 11 (including chart showing different effective dates for Electronic FOIA amendments' different provisions, ranging from March 31, 1997, to December 31, 1999).

[58] See Attorney General's Follow-Up Memorandum for Heads of Departments and Agencies regarding the Freedom of Information Act (Sept. 3, 1999) [hereinafter Attorney General Reno's Follow-Up FOIA Memorandum], reprinted in FOIA Update, Vol. XIX, No. 4, at 4-5 (emphasizing importance of "new partnership" between agency FOIA officers and agency Information Resources Management (IRM) personnel in Electronic FOIA amendment implementation); FOIA Update, Vol. XIX, No. 3, at 5-6 (Department of Justice congressional testimony describing agency's amendment implementation activities); id. at 3-4 ("OIP Guidance: Recommendations for FOIA Web Sites"); FOIA Update, Vol. XIX, No. 1, at 3-5 ("OIP Guidance: Electronic FOIA Amendments Implementation Guidance Outline"); FOIA Update, Vol. XVIII, No. 3, at 1-2 (describing agency amendment implementation activities involving development of World Wide Web sites); id. at 3-7 (Department of Justice guidelines on implementation of new annual reporting requirements); FOIA Update, Vol. XVIII, No. 2, at 1 (describing Justice Department's amendment implementation activities, including development of FOIA Reference Guide); FOIA Update, Vol. XVIII, No. 1, at 3-7 (addressing amendment implementation questions); FOIA Update, Vol. XVII, No. 4, at 1-11; see also FOIA Update, Vol. XIX, No. 3, at 2 (addressing additional amendment implementation questions); FOIA Update, Vol. XIX, No. 2, at 2 ("Web Site Watch" discussion of agency FOIA Web sites); FOIA Update, Vol. XIX, No. 1, at 2 (same); FOIA Update, Vol. XIX, No. 1, at 6 (addressing additional amendment implementation questions); FOIA Update, Vol. XVIII, No. 2, at 2 (same); Department of Justice FOIA Regulations, 28 C.F.R. pt. 16 (1999); cf. FOIA Update, Vol. XIX, No. 1, at 5 (advising agencies to implement amendments "without any disadvantage to FOIA requesters," regardless of status of implementing regulations). See generally FOIA Update, Vol. XIX, No. 3, at 1 (describing congressional hearing on agency amendment implementation activities).

[59] President Clinton's FOIA Memorandum, reprinted in FOIA Update, Vol. XIV, No. 3, at 3.

[60] Attorney General's Memorandum for Heads of Departments and Agencies regarding the Freedom of Information Act (Oct. 4, 1993) [hereinafter Attorney General Reno's FOIA Memorandum], reprinted in FOIA Update, Vol. XIV, No. 3, at 4-5.

# INTRODUCTION

strong new spirit of openness in government under the FOIA.[61] In conjunction with President Clinton's call upon all agencies to follow "the spirit" as well as the letter of the Act,[62] Attorney General Reno's FOIA Memorandum articulated the FOIA's "primary objective"--that of achieving "maximum responsible disclosure of government information."[63]

Among other things toward that disclosure objective, Attorney General Reno's FOIA Memorandum (1) rescinded the Department of Justice's previous standard for the defense of FOIA litigation; (2) established a new "foreseeable harm" standard applicable to the use of FOIA exemptions both in litigation and at the administrative level; and (3) strongly encouraged the making of discretionary disclosures of exempt information "whenever possible under the Act."[64] (See the further discussions of these FOIA policy principles under Exemption 5, Application of the "Foreseeable Harm" Standard, below, Discretionary Disclosure and Waiver, below, and Litigation Considerations, below.) These FOIA-disclosure policies are being implemented by agencies throughout the federal government as part of a range of related openness-in-government initiatives undertaken by the Department of Justice.[65]

In sum, the FOIA is a vital, continuously developing public disclosure mechanism which, with necessary refinements to accommodate both technological advancements and society's interests in an open and fully responsible government, can truly enhance our democratic way of life.

---

[61] See FOIA Update, Vol. XIV, No. 3, at 1-2.

[62] President Clinton's FOIA Memorandum, reprinted in FOIA Update, Vol. XIV, No. 3, at 3; see also FOIA Update, Vol. XIV, No. 3, at 1 (describing other aspects of President Clinton's FOIA Memorandum).

[63] Attorney General Reno's FOIA Memorandum, reprinted in FOIA Update, Vol. XIV, No. 3, at 4-5; see also FOIA Update, Vol. XIV, No. 3, at 5 (Attorney General memorandum to Justice Department employees urging "new institutional attitude toward FOIA administration").

[64] Attorney General Reno's FOIA Memorandum, reprinted in FOIA Update, Vol. XIV, No. 3, at 4-5; see also Attorney General Reno's Follow-Up FOIA Memorandum, reprinted in FOIA Update, Vol. XIX, No. 4, at 3-5 (reiterating importance of "foreseeable harm" standard to federal agencies in order to promote further discretionary disclosure in agency decisionmaking).

[65] See FOIA Update, Vol. XV, No. 2, at 1-2; see also FOIA Update, Vol. XIX, No. 3, at 5; FOIA Update, Vol. XVII, No. 3, at 7; FOIA Update, Vol. XVI, No. 3, at 1; FOIA Update, Vol. XVI, No. 1, at 1-2; FOIA Update, Vol. XV, No. 4, at 7; FOIA Update, Vol. XIV, No. 3, at 2, 10, 12; cf. FOIA Update, Vol. XV, No. 3, at 6 (describing National Performance Review FOIA activities at Justice Department).

## FOIA READING ROOMS

Subsection (a)(2) of the FOIA[1] provides for what is commonly referred to as "reading room" access.[2] It applies to certain basic agency records that, while not automatically published under subsection (a)(1) of the Act,[3] must routinely be made "available for public inspection and copying" in agency reading rooms.[4]

Historically under the FOIA, three categories of records--"final opinions [and] . . . orders" rendered in the adjudication of administrative cases,[5] specific agency policy statements,[6] and certain administrative staff manuals "that affect

---

[1] 5 U.S.C. § 552(a)(2) (1994 & Supp. IV 1998).

[2] See FOIA Update, Vol. XIII, No. 3, at 3-4 ("OIP Guidance: The 'Automatic' Disclosure Provisions of FOIA: Subsections (a)(1) & (a)(2)").

[3] 5 U.S.C. § 552(a)(1) (providing for Federal Register publication of very basic agency records, as discussed under Introduction, above).

[4] 5 U.S.C. § 552(a)(2); see Jordan v. United States Dep't of Justice, 591 F.2d 753, 756 (D.C. Cir. 1978) (en banc) (observing that subsection (a)(2) records must be made "automatically available for public inspection; no demand is necessary"); see also FOIA Update, Vol. XVIII, No. 1, at 4 (advising that large agencies with decentralized FOIA operations may maintain separate reading rooms for agency components).

[5] 5 U.S.C. § 552(a)(2)(A); see, e.g., NLRB v. Sears, Roebuck & Co., 421 U.S. 132, 155-59 (1975) (holding that NLRB advice and appeals memorandum deciding not to file unfair labor complaint was "final opinion" when decision not to file effectively put an end to formal complaint procedure); National Prison Project v. Sigler, 390 F. Supp. 789, 792-93 (D.D.C. 1975) (determining that parole board decisions denying inmate applications for parole were "reading room" records).

[6] 5 U.S.C. § 552(a)(2)(B); see, e.g., Bailey v. Sullivan, 885 F.2d 52, 62 (3d Cir. 1977) (stating that Social Security rule providing examples of medical conditions to be treated as "per se nonsevere" fell under subsection (a)(2)(B)); Tax Analysts v. IRS, No. 94-923, 1996 U.S. Dist. LEXIS 3259, at *9 (D.D.C. Mar. 15, 1996) (holding that IRS Field Service Advice Memoranda, even though not binding on IRS personnel, were "statements of policy"), aff'd on other grounds, 117 F.3d 607 (D.C. Cir. 1997); Public Citizen v. Office of United States Trade Representative, 804 F. Supp. 385, 387 (D.D.C. 1992) (concluding that agency submissions to trade panel containing agency's interpretation of U.S.'s international legal obligations were "statements of policy and interpretations adopted by the [agency]"); see also Vietnam Veterans of Am. v. Department of the Navy, 876 F.2d 164, 165 (D.C. Cir. 1989) (finding that opinions in which Judge Advocates General of Army and Navy have authority only to dispense legal advice--rendered in subject areas for which those officials do not have authority to act on behalf of agency--were not "statements of policy or interpretations adopted by" those agencies and were not required to be published or made available for public inspection).

# FOIA READING ROOMS

a member of the public'"[7]--have been made available in agency reading rooms.[8] Such records must be indexed by agencies in order to facilitate the public's convenient access to them.[9]

Routine public access to such records serves to guard against the development of agency "secret law" known to agency personnel but not to members of the public who deal with agencies, so records that have no precedential value and do not constitute the working law of the agency should not be required to be made available under this part of the Act.[10] Additionally, materials that are

---

[7] 5 U.S.C. § 552(a)(2)(C); see, e.g., Sladek v. Bensinger, 605 F.2d 899, 901 (5th Cir. 1979) (finding portions of DEA agents manual concerning treatment of confidential informants and search warrant procedures to be subsection (a)(2)(C) records); Stokes v. Brennan, 476 F.2d 699, 701 (5th Cir. 1973) (determining that "Training Course for Compliance Safety and Health Officers," including all instructor and student manuals, training slides, films, and visual aids, must be made available for public inspection and copying); Firestone Tire & Rubber Co. v. Coleman, 432 F. Supp. 1359, 1364-65 (N.D. Ohio 1976) (ruling that memoranda approved by Office of Standards Enforcement, which set forth agency's policy regarding sampling plans that office must follow when tire fails lab test under Federal Motor Vehicle Safety Standards were "reading room" records); see also Stanley v. DOD, No. 98-CV-4116, slip op. at 9-10 (S.D. Ill. June 22, 1999) (finding that administrative staff manuals pertaining to military hospital procedures did not "affect the public" and were not required to be given "reading room" treatment) (appeal pending).

[8] See FOIA Update, Vol. XIII, No. 3, at 4 (describing categories of records required to be placed in agency reading rooms); see also id. (noting that "an agency may withhold any record or record portion falling within subsection (a)(2) . . . if it is of such sensitivity as to fall within a FOIA exemption") (citing, e.g., Renegotiation Bd. v. Grumman Aircraft Eng'g Corp., 421 U.S. 168, 184 n.21 (1975)).

[9] See 5 U.S.C. § 522(a)(2); see, e.g., Irons & Sears v. Dann, 606 F.2d 1215, 1223 (D.C. Cir. 1979) (requiring agency to provide "reasonable index" of requested decisions); Taxation With Representation Fund v. IRS, 2 Gov't Disclosure Serv. (P-H) ¶ 81,028, at 81,080 (D.D.C. Apr. 22, 1980) (recognizing agency's "continuing duty" to make subsection (a)(2) records and indices available); Pennsylvania Dep't of Pub. Welfare v. United States, No. 99-175, 1999 WL 1051963, at *3 (W.D. Pa. Oct. 12, 1999) (permitting "limited discovery regarding the authenticity and completeness of the [index] produced by HHS, as well as the methodology used to compile it"); see also FOIA Update, Vol. XVII, No. 4, at 2 (discussing statutory indexing requirements under Electronic FOIA amendments). But cf. Tax Analysts v. IRS, No. 94-923, 1998 WL 419755, at *5 (D.D.C. May 1, 1998) (confusingly concluding that court has "no statutory authority for actually ordering . . . a remedy" regarding indexing requirement), appeal voluntarily dismissed, No. 94-5252 (D.C. Cir. Aug. 11, 1998).

[10] See Sears, 421 U.S. at 153-54 (observing that the reading room provision "represents a strong congressional aversion to 'secret [agency] law,' . . . and represents an affirmative congressional purpose to require disclosure of documents which have 'the force and effect of law'" (quoting H.R. Rep. No. 89-1497,

(continued...)

## FOIA READING ROOMS

published and offered for sale are not required to be placed in agency reading rooms.[11]

Agencies have made use of their FOIA reading rooms in achieving efficient "affirmative" disclosure of records that otherwise would be sought through less efficient FOIA requests.[12] In so doing, however, they must be mindful of the distinction between subsection (a)(2) records (i.e., "reading room" records) and subsection (a)(3) records (i.e., records subject to standard "FOIA requests") under the Act.[13]

---

[10](...continued) at 7 (1966))); Skelton v. Postal Serv., 678 F.2d 35, 41 (5th Cir. 1982) ("That requirement was designed to help the citizen find agency statements 'having precedential significance' when he becomes involved in 'a controversy with an agency.'" (quoting H.R. Rep. No. 89-1497, at 8)); Attorney General's Memorandum on the 1974 Amendments to the Freedom of Information Act 19 (Feb. 1975) (explaining that the "primary purpose of subsection (a)(2) was to compel disclosure of what has been called 'secret law,' or as the 1966 House Report put it, agency materials which have 'the force and effect of law in most cases'" (quoting H.R. Rep. No. 89-1497, at 7)); Attorney General's Memorandum on the Public Information Section of the Administrative Procedure Act 15 (June 1967) [hereinafter Attorney General's 1967 FOIA Memorandum] (advising that keeping "orders available in reading rooms . . . [that] have no precedential value, often would be impracticable and would serve no useful purpose"); see also Smith v. NTSB, 981 F.2d 1326, 1328 (D.C. Cir. 1993) (stating that the purpose of this "requirement is obviously to give the public notice of what the law is so that each individual can act accordingly"); Vietnam Veterans of Am., 876 F.2d at 165 (rejecting argument that legal opinions issued by Judge Advocates General of Army and Navy must be placed in agency reading room, because those opinions are not statements of policy which "operate as law"); Stanley, No. 98-CV-4116, slip op. at 9-10 (S.D. Ill. June 22, 1999) (finding that administrative staff manuals that do not have any "precedential significance" and would not assist members of the public in "tailor[ing] their behavior to the law" are not required to be made publicly available in agency reading room). But see National Prison Project, 390 F. Supp. at 793 (ruling otherwise prior to Supreme Court's emphasis on legislative history of subsection (a)(2) in Sears); Tax Analysts & Advocates v. IRS, 362 F. Supp. 1298, 1303 (D.D.C. 1973) (same), modified & remanded on other grounds, 505 F.2d 350 (D.C. Cir. 1974).

[11] See FOIA Update, Vol. XVII, No. 4, at 1 (noting that reading room obligation does not apply to any records that "are promptly published and [are] offered for sale") (quoting 5 U.S.C. § 552(a)(2)); Attorney General's 1967 FOIA Memorandum 15 (noting that "[t]his is to afford the agency 'an alternative means of making these materials available through publication'" (quoting S. Rep. No. 89-813, at 7 (1966))); see also FOIA Update, Vol. XIX, No. 1, at 3.

[12] See, e.g., FOIA Update, Vol. XIX, No. 1, at 1 (discussing Department of the Air Force affirmative electronic information disclosure program); see also FOIA Update, Vol. XVI, No. 1, at 1-2 (prompting "affirmative" agency disclosure practices through "reading room" access, among other means).

[13] See, e.g., FOIA Update, Vol. XVI, No. 1, at 2 (reminding that "an agency (continued...)

## FOIA READING ROOMS

The Electronic Freedom of Information Act Amendments of 1996[14] greatly modified the requirements of subsection (a)(2) by creating a fourth category of "reading room" records,[15] and by establishing a requirement for the electronic availability of "reading room" records in what may be regarded as "electronic reading rooms."[16]

First, in addition to the traditional three categories of "reading room" records discussed above, agencies must also include any records processed and disclosed in response to a FOIA request that "the agency determines have become or are likely to become the subject of subsequent requests for substantially the same records."[17] Under this provision, when records are disclosed in response to a FOIA request, an agency is required to determine whether they have become the subject of subsequent FOIA requests or, in the agency's best judgment based upon the nature of the records and the types of requests regularly received, are likely to be the subject of multiple requests in the future.[18] If either is the case, then those records in their FOIA-processed form become "reading room" records, which must automatically be made available to poten-

---

[13](...continued) cannot convert a subsection (a)(3) record into a subsection (a)(2) record (which cannot be the subject of a FOIA request under subsection (a)(3)) just by voluntarily placing it into its reading room"); FOIA Update, Vol. XII, No. 2, at 5 (advising that FOIA requesters may not be deprived of subsection (a)(3) access rights through voluntary "reading room" availability); see also Crews v. Internal Revenue, No. 99-8388, slip op. at 11-12 (C.D. Cal. Apr. 26, 2000) (declaring that policy statements and administrative staff manuals made available under subsection (a)(2) are not required to be made available in response to subsection (a)(3) requests); Reeves v. United States, No. 94-1291, 1994 WL 782235, at *1 (E.D. Cal. Nov. 16, 1994) (describing different treatment of subsection (a)(1), (a)(2), and (a)(3) records under Act). But see FOIA Update, Vol. XVIII, No. 1, at 3 (advising of exception to general rule for records in new fourth reading room category under Electronic FOIA amendments); cf. Tax Analysts, 1998 WL 419755, at *4 (failing to apprehend statutory distinction between records subject to subsections (a)(2) and (a)(3)).

[14] Pub. L. No. 104-231, 110 Stat. 3048.

[15] See 5 U.S.C. § 552(a)(2)(D).

[16] See id. § 552(a)(2); see also FOIA Update, Vol. XVII, No. 4, at 1-2 (discussing statutory changes); Attorney General's Follow-Up Memorandum for Heads of Departments and Agencies regarding the Freedom of Information Act (Sept. 3, 1999) [hereinafter Attorney General Reno's Follow-Up FOIA Memorandum], reprinted in FOIA Update, Vol. XIX, No. 4, at 4-5 (emphasizing importance of "electronic reading rooms" in satisfying FOIA obligations).

[17] 5 U.S.C. § 552(a)(2)(D). But see FOIA Update, Vol. XVIII, No. 2, at 2 (advising that agencies need not include records processed for contemporaneous multiple requests if they are not likely to be requested again, e.g., certain types of government contract submissions).

[18] See FOIA Update, Vol. XVIII, No. 1, at 3-4 (advising on processes for exercise of agency judgment under new reading room category).

## FOIA READING ROOMS

tial FOIA requesters.[19] Ideally, this availability will satisfy much of the future public demand for those processed records in a more efficient fashion.[20] Nevertheless, any subsequent FOIA request received for such records has to be responded to in the regular way as well, if the requester so chooses.[21]

Second, the Electronic FOIA amendments require agencies to use electronic information technology to enhance the availability of their "reading room" records: Agencies must make their newly created "reading room" records (i.e., records created by agencies on or after November 1, 1996,[22] in all four reading room categories) available to the public by "electronic means."[23] The Electronic FOIA amendments embody a strong statutory preference that this new electronic availability be provided by agencies in the form of online, Internet access--which can be most efficient for both agencies and the public alike.[24]

---

[19] See FOIA Update, Vol. XVII, No. 4, at 1-2; see also FOIA Update, Vol. XIX, No. 1, at 3-4 (compilation of OIP policy guidance regarding reading room matters); cf. Tax Analysts, 1998 WL 419755, at **4, 6 (requiring agency to place exceptionally large volume of FOIA-processed records in reading room on weekly basis, as they are processed, rather than all at once at conclusion of lengthy processing period). But see FOIA Update, Vol. XVIII, No. 1, at 3 (cautioning that any information about any first-party requester that would not be disclosed to any other FOIA requester, such as information protected by Privacy Act of 1974, 5 U.S.C. § 552a (1994 & Supp. IV 1998), or Trade Secrets Act, 18 U.S.C. § 1905 (1994 & Supp. IV 1998), would not be appropriate for automatic public disclosure under new reading room category).

[20] See FOIA Update, Vol. XVIII, No. 2, at 2 (citing H.R. Rep. No. 104-795, at 21 (1996)); see also FOIA Update, Vol. XVII, No. 4, at 1 (emphasizing connection between new reading room category and new "electronic reading room" mechanism in meeting public access demands); cf. President's Statement on Signing the Electronic Freedom of Information Act Amendments of 1996, 32 Weekly Comp. Pres. Doc. 1949 (Oct. 7, 1996), reprinted in FOIA Update, Vol. XVII, No. 4, at 9 (expressing "hope that there will be less need to use FOIA to obtain government information").

[21] See FOIA Update, Vol. XVIII, No. 1, at 3 (advising that while ordinary rule is that records placed in reading room under subsection (a)(2) cannot be subject of regular FOIA request, Congress made clear that such rule does not apply to new reading room category of FOIA-processed records) (citing H.R. Rep. No. 104-795, at 21 (1996)).

[22] See 5 U.S.C. § 552(a)(2); see also FOIA Update, Vol. XVIII, No. 1, at 4-5.

[23] 5 U.S.C. § 522(a)(2); see FOIA Update, Vol. XVIII, No. 1, at 3 (advising that records made available in "electronic reading rooms" must nevertheless be made available in conventional "paper" reading rooms as well) (citing H.R. Rep. No. 104-795, at 21 (1996)); see also id. (suggesting that computer terminals may be used to facilitate such reading room access).

[24] See 5 U.S.C. § 552(a)(2) (stressing use of "computer telecommunications" and establishing absolute requirement of Internet use by all agencies "by [no later than] December 31, 1999"); see also Attorney General Reno's Follow-Up

(continued...)

## FOIA READING ROOMS

Under the Electronic FOIA amendments, all federal agencies should have FOIA sites on the World Wide Web to serve this "electronic reading room" function,[25] as well as for other FOIA-related purposes.[26] This is a matter of great and growing importance to FOIA administration.[27] Agencies of such size that they contain sub-agencies or major agency components that administer the FOIA on a decentralized basis and have their own web sites may maintain multiple "electronic reading rooms," so long as they are linked together clearly and efficiently for web site users.[28]

Agencies must therefore place in their conventional "paper" reading rooms copies of any FOIA-processed records determined to fall within the new

---

[24](...continued)
FOIA Memorandum, reprinted in FOIA Update, Vol. XIX, No. 4, at 4-5 (emphasizing importance of "new partnership" between agency FOIA officers and agency Information Resources Management (IRM) personnel to achieve efficient disclosure through electronic means); FOIA Update, Vol. XVIII, No. 3, at 1-2 (describing efficiency of online public access).

[25] 5 U.S.C. § 552(a)(2); see FOIA Update, Vol. XIX, No. 3, at 3-4 ("OIP Guidance: Recommendations for FOIA Web Sites"); FOIA Update, Vol. XIX, No. 2, at 2 ("Web Site Watch" discussion of agency FOIA Web sites); FOIA Update, Vol. XIX, No. 1, at 2 (same); FOIA Update, Vol. XVIII, No. 3, at 1-2 (describing early agency development of World Wide Web sites for FOIA-related purposes, including "electronic reading rooms").

[26] See, e.g., 5 U.S.C. § 552(e)(2) (setting forth requirement that each agency make its annual FOIA report available to public electronically); see also FOIA Update, Vol. XIX, No. 3, at 3-4 (recommending basic elements and features of agency FOIA Web sites); cf. FOIA Update, Vol. XIX, No. 1, at 6 (encouraging agencies to consider as matter of administrative discretion establishing capability to receive FOIA requests via Internet).

[27] See FOIA Update, Vol. XIX, No. 3, at 1 (describing congressional interest in agency Web site development for purposes of FOIA administration); id. at 1, 3 (describing governmentwide attention to same); Attorney General Reno's Follow-Up FOIA Memorandum, reprinted in FOIA Update, Vol. XIX, No. 4, at 5 (declaring that "an agency's FOIA Web site has become an essential means by which its FOIA obligations are satisfied" so that FOIA Web site support "should be a primary mission of each agency's IRM staff").

[28] See FOIA Update, Vol. XIX, No. 3, at 3 (advising that "[c]larity to the web site user is essential to the effectiveness of the site"); FOIA Update, Vol. XIX, No. 1, at 6 (advising on use of FOIA Web sites by all agency components "once an agency has established its World Wide Web capability"); FOIA Update, Vol. XVIII, No. 1, at 4 (advising that agencies with separate "electronic reading rooms" for separate components "should ensure that [they] are linked together electronically so as to facilitate efficient user access"); see also FOIA Update, Vol. XIX, No. 3, at 4 (recommending that agencies check both accuracy and viability of their FOIA Web site links and text content of their FOIA home pages on regular basis).

**FOIA READING ROOMS**

fourth subsection (a)(2) category,[29] and must identify such records that were created by them on or after the November 1, 1996 cut-off date in order to make them available through their "electronic reading rooms" as well.[30] In doing so, they should be mindful that some of the records falling under this newer fourth category might not have been created by the agency and instead might have been generated elsewhere; while such records may be determined by the agency to fall within subsection (a)(2)(D), they are not "created" by the agency and should not be regarded as subject to the new electronic availability requirement.[31] However, an agency may as a matter of administrative discretion choose to make such records available electronically even though they were not generated by the agency, or not created after November 1, 1996, when to do so would be most cost-effective in serving public access needs under subsection (a)(2)(D).[32]

Agencies also should make clear to the users of their "electronic reading rooms" that while all of their subsection (a)(2) records are available in their conventional reading rooms, generally only those records created on or after November 1, 1996 are available in their electronic ones.[33] In addition, they should utilize indices to facilitate use of both types of reading rooms;[34] indeed, they are required by the Electronic FOIA amendments to maintain indexes of

---

[29] See FOIA Update, Vol. XVIII, No. 1, at 4 (advising that agencies may determine that records no longer fall within new reading room category after passage of time).

[30] See FOIA Update, Vol. XVIII, No. 1, at 5 (advising that redaction of record during FOIA processing does not amount to record "creation" for purposes of determining applicability of electronic availability requirement); see also FOIA Update, Vol. XVII, No. 4, at 2 (observing that in case of FOIA-processed records, very large proportion of those records will have been created prior to November 1, 1996 cut-off date, at least as of outset of Electronic FOIA amendments' implementation, and therefore will not be subject to electronic availability requirement).

[31] See FOIA Update, Vol. XVIII, No. 1, at 4-5 (citing United States Dep't of Justice v. Tax Analysts, 492 U.S. 136, 144 (1989)); see also 63 Fed. Reg. 29,591, 29,592 (1998) (discussing Justice Department regulation on point, currently at 28 C.F.R. § 16.2(c) (1999)).

[32] See FOIA Update, Vol. XIX, No. 1, at 4; see, e.g., FOIA Update, Vol. XIX, No. 3, at 5. But see FOIA Update, Vol. XVIII, No. 1, at 5 (cautioning agencies to guard against possibility that "electronic reading room" treatment of record generated by outside party might be regarded as copyright infringement by that party).

[33] See FOIA Update, Vol. XIX, No. 3, at 4; FOIA Update, Vol. XII, No. 4, at 2; see also FOIA Update, Vol. XVIII, No. 2, at 2 (advising agencies on practical treatment of written signatures on adjudicatory orders for "electronic reading room" purposes).

[34] See FOIA Update, Vol. XIX, No. 3, at 4 (recommending use of "visible links" for electronic indexing purposes); cf. FOIA Update, Vol. XVIII, No. 3, at 1-2 (describing early agency use of "home pages" and electronic "links" for FOIA-related purposes on agency World Wide Web sites).

## PROCEDURAL REQUIREMENTS

the FOIA-processed records in the newer fourth reading room category and to make them available on their FOIA Web sites.[35]

## PROCEDURAL REQUIREMENTS

The Freedom of Information Act requires federal agencies to make their records promptly available to any person who makes a proper request for them.[1] To provide a general overview of the Act's procedural requirements, this discussion will follow a rough chronology of how a typical FOIA request is processed--from the point of determining whether an entity in receipt of a request is subject to the FOIA in the first place to the review of an agency's initial decision regarding a FOIA request on administrative appeal. In administering the Act's procedural requirements, agencies should strive to do "everything possible to promote openness in the Government and to respond to citizens' requests for information in a customer-friendly manner."[2]

### Entities Subject to the FOIA

Agencies within the executive branch of the federal government, including the Executive Office of the President and independent regulatory agencies, are subject to the FOIA.[3] However, the FOIA does not apply to entities that "are neither chartered by the federal government [n]or controlled by it."[4]

---

[35] 5 U.S.C. § 552(a)(2)(E); cf. FOIA Update, Vol. XVIII, No. 3, at 3-7 (setting forth Justice Department guidelines for agency preparation and submission of revised form of annual FOIA reports, as required to be prepared by all agencies electronically and made available on FOIA Web sites as of February 1999); FOIA Update, Vol. XIX, No. 3, at 2 (advising agencies on proper FOIA Web site treatment of annual FOIA reports, in compliance with new electronic availability requirements of 5 U.S.C. § 552(e)(2)-(3), including through agency identification of Uniform Resource Locator (URL) for each report).

[1] 5 U.S.C. § 552(a)(3)(A) (1994 & Supp. IV 1998).

[2] Attorney General's Follow-Up Memorandum for Heads of Departments and Agencies regarding the Freedom of Information Act (Sept. 3, 1999), reprinted in FOIA Update, Vol. XIX, No. 4, at 3.

[3] Id. § 552(f).

[4] H.R. Rep. No. 93-1380, at 14 (1974), reprinted in House Comm. on Gov't Operations and Senate Comm. on the Judiciary, 94th Cong., 1st Sess., Freedom of Information Act and Amendments of 1974 (P.L. 93-502) Source Book: Legislative History, Texts, and Other Documents at 231-32 (1975); see Forsham v. Harris, 445 U.S. 169, 179-80 (1980) (holding that private grantee of federal agency is not itself subject to FOIA); Public Citizen Health Research Group v. HEW, 668 F.2d 537, 543-44 (D.C. Cir. 1981) (stating that medical peer review committees are not agencies under FOIA); Irwin Mem'l Blood Bank v. American Nat'l Red Cross, 640 F.2d 1051, 1057 (9th Cir. 1981) (determining that American National Red Cross is not an agency under FOIA); Gilmore v. United States Dep't of Energy, 4 F. Supp. 2d 912, 919-20 (N.D. Cal. 1998) (finding pri-
(continued...)

**PROCEDURAL REQUIREMENTS**

Thus, it is settled that state governments,[5] municipal corporations,[6] the courts,[7]

---

[4](...continued)
vately owned laboratory which developed electronic conferencing software, for which government owned nonexclusive license for its use, not "a government-controlled corporation" as it is not subject to day-to-day supervision by federal government nor are its employees or management considered government employees); Leytman v. New York Stock Exch., No. 95 CV 902, 1995 WL 761843, at *2 (E.D.N.Y. Dec. 6, 1995) (relying on Independent Investor Protective League v. New York Stock Exch., 367 F. Supp. 1376, 1377 (S.D.N.Y. 1973), finding that although "[t]he Exchange is subject to significant federal regulation, . . . it is not an agency of the federal government"); Rogers v. United States Nat'l Reconnaissance Office, No. 94-B-2934, slip op. at 7 (N.D. Ala. Sept. 13, 1995) (determining that "[t]he degree of government involvement and control over [private organizations which contracted with government to construct office facility is] insufficient to establish companies as federal agencies for purposes of the FOIA"); see also FOIA Update, Vol. XIX, No. 4, at 2 (noting FOIA's applicability to certain research data generated by private grantees of federal agencies, pursuant to the Omnibus Consolidated and Emergency Supplemental Appropriations Act for Fiscal Year 1999, Pub. L. No. 105-277, 112 Stat. 2681 (1998), as implemented by OMB Circular A-110, "Uniform Administrative Requirements for Grants and Agreements with Institutions of Higher Education, Hospitals, and Other Non-Profit Organizations," 64 Fed. Reg. 54,926 (1999)). But see Cotton v. Adams, 798 F. Supp. 22, 24 (D.D.C. 1992) (holding that Smithsonian Institution is an agency under FOIA on basis that it "performs governmental functions as a center of scholarship and national museum responsible for the safe-keeping and maintenance of national treasures"), holding questioned on appeal of award of attorney fees sub nom. Cotton v. Heyman, 63 F.3d 1115, 1123 (D.C. Cir. 1995) (noting that Smithsonian Institution could "reasonably interpret our precedent to support its position that it is not an agency under FOIA"); Association of Community Orgs. for Reform Now v. Barclay, No. 3-89-409T, slip op. at 8 (N.D. Tex. June 9, 1989) (holding that federal home loan banks are agencies under FOIA); cf. Dong v. Smithsonian Inst., 125 F.3d 877, 879 (D.C. Cir. 1997) (holding that Smithsonian Institution is not an agency for purposes of Privacy Act of 1974, 5 U.S.C. § 552a (1994 & Supp. IV 1998), as it is neither an "establishment of the executive branch" nor a "government-controlled corporation"), cert. denied, 524 U.S. 922 (1998).

[5] See, e.g., Lau v. Sullivan County Dist. Att'y, No. 99-7341, 1999 WL 1069966, at *2 (2d Cir. Nov. 12, 1999), cert. denied, 120 S. Ct. 1250 (2000); Martinson v. DEA, No. 96-5262, 1997 WL 634559, at *1 (D.C. Cir. July 3, 1997); Ortez v. Washington County, 88 F.3d 804, 811 (9th Cir. 1996); Davidson v. Georgia, 622 F.2d 895, 897 (5th Cir. 1980); see also McClain v. United States Dep't of Justice, No. 97-C-0385, 1999 WL 759505, at *2 (N.D. Ill. Sept. 1, 1999) (dismissing FOIA claims against state attorney general because "[p]laintiff may assert Privacy Act and Freedom of Information Act claims against . . . federal defendants only"); Beard v. Department of Justice, 917 F. Supp. 61, 63 (D.D.C. 1996) (holding District of Columbia Police Department to be "local" law enforcement agency not subject to FOIA); Gillard v. United States Marshals Serv., No. 87-0689, 1987 WL 11218, at *1 (D.D.C. May 11, 1987) (holding that District of Columbia Government records are not covered by FOIA).

## PROCEDURAL REQUIREMENTS

Congress,[8] and private citizens[9] are not subject to the FOIA. Nor does the FOIA apply to a presidential transition team.[10]

---

[6] See Lau, 1999 WL 1069966, at *2 (affirming dismissal of FOIA claims against county officials); McClain, 1999 WL 759505, at *2 (dismissing plaintiff's FOIA claims against county attorney); Rankel v. Town of Greensburgh, 117 F.R.D. 50, 54 (S.D.N.Y. 1987).

[7] See, e.g., Gaydos v. Mansmann, No. 98-5002, 1998 WL 389104, at *1 (D.C. Cir. June 24, 1998) (per curiam); Warth v. Department of Justice, 595 F.2d 521, 523 (9th Cir. 1979); United States v. Spain, No. 82-60-N, slip op. at 1 (E.D. Va. June 19, 1998) ("The courts of the United States are not agencies for the purposes of the Freedom of Information Act."), aff'd, 172 F.3d 865 (4th Cir.) (unpublished table decision), cert. denied, 119 S. Ct. 2029 (1999); see also Andrade v. United States Sentencing Comm'n, 989 F.2d 308, 309-10 (9th Cir. 1993) (Sentencing Commission, an independent body within judicial branch, is not subject to FOIA); United States v. Ford, No. 96-00271-01, 1998 U.S. Dist. LEXIS 16438, at *1 (E.D. Pa. Oct. 21, 1998) ("The Clerk of Court, as part of the judicial branch, is not an agency as defined by FOIA."); Butler v. United States Probation, No. 95-1705, 1996 U.S. Dist. LEXIS 5241, at *2 (D.D.C. Apr. 22, 1996) (U.S. Probation Office is not agency within meaning of FOIA); cf. Callwood v. Department of Probation of the V.I., 982 F. Supp. 341, 342 (D.V.I. 1997) ("[T]he Office of Probation is an administrative unit of [the] Court . . . [and] is not subject to the terms of the Privacy Act.").

[8] See, e.g., Smith v. United States Congress, No. 95-5281, 1996 WL 523800, at *1 (D.C. Cir. Aug. 28, 1996) (stating that FOIA does not apply to records held by Congress); Dow Jones & Co. v. Department of Justice, 917 F.2d 571, 574 (D.C. Cir. 1990) (holding that Congress is not an agency for any purpose under FOIA); see also Mayo v. United States Gov't Printing Office, 9 F.3d 1450, 1451 (9th Cir. 1994) (deciding that Government Printing Office is part of congressional branch and therefore is not subject to FOIA); Owens v. Warner, No. 93-2195, slip op. at 1 (D.D.C. Nov. 24, 1993) (ruling that office of Senator John Warner is not subject to FOIA), summary affirmance granted, No. 93-5415 (D.C. Cir. May 25, 1994).

[9] See, e.g., In re Olsen, BAP No. UT-98-088, 1999 Bankr. LEXIS 791, at *11 (B.A.P. 10th Cir. June 24, 1999) (holding that chapter seven bankruptcy trustee is not an agency under FOIA); Buemi v. Lewis, No. 94-4156, 1995 WL 149107, at *2 (6th Cir. Apr. 4, 1995) (concluding that the FOIA applies only to federal agencies and not to private individuals); Germosen v. Cox, No. 98-1294, 1999 WL 1021559, at *20 (S.D.N.Y. Nov. 9, 1999) (noting that "there is no authority in the FOIA or Privacy Act obligating . . . private individuals to maintain or make available documents to the public"); Allnutt v. United States Trustee, Region Four, No. 97-02414, slip op. at 6 (D.D.C. July 31, 1999) (holding private trustee of bankruptcy estates is not subject to FOIA even though trustee "cooperates [with] and submits regular reports to the United States Trustee," who is subject to FOIA), appeal dismissed for lack of jurisdiction, No. 99-5410 (D.C. Cir. Feb. 2, 2000).

[10] See Illinois Inst. for Continuing Legal Educ. v. United States Dep't of Labor, 545 F. Supp. 1229, 1231-33 (N.D. Ill. 1982); see also FOIA Update, Vol. IX,
(continued...)

**PROCEDURAL REQUIREMENTS**

Offices within the Executive Office of the President whose functions are limited to advising and assisting the President also do not fall within the definition of "agency";[11] such offices include the Office of the President and the President's personal staff.[12] The Court of Appeals for the District of Columbia Circuit illustrated this functional definition of "agency" when it held that the former Presidential Task Force on Regulatory Relief--chaired by the Vice President and composed of several cabinet members--was not an agency subject to the FOIA because the cabinet members acted not as heads of their departments "but rather as the functional equivalents of assistants to the President."[13]

Under this functional definition of "agency," however, executive branch entities whose responsibilities exceed merely advising and assisting the Presi-

---

[10](...continued)
No. 4, at 3-4 ("FOIA Counselor: Transition Team FOIA Issues"); cf. Wolfe v. HHS, 711 F.2d 1077, 1079 (D.C. Cir. 1983) (treating presidential transition team as not agency subject to FOIA and citing with approval Illinois Inst., 545 F. Supp. at 1231-33) (dicta).

[11] S. Conf. Rep. No. 93-1200, at 14 (1974), reprinted in 1974 U.S.C.C.A.N. 6285, 6293; see, e.g., Rushforth v. Council of Econ. Advisers, 762 F.2d 1038, 1042-43 (D.C. Cir. 1985) (ruling that Council of Economic Advisers is not an agency under FOIA); Nation Co. v. Archivist of the United States, No. 88-1939, slip op. at 5-6 (D.D.C. July 24, 1990) (finding that Tower Commission is not an agency under FOIA); National Sec. Archive v. Executive Office of the President, 688 F. Supp. 29, 31 (D.D.C. 1988) (concluding that Office of Counsel to President is not an agency under FOIA), aff'd sub nom. National Sec. Archive v. Archivist of the United States, 909 F.2d 541 (D.C. Cir. 1990); see also FOIA Update, Vol. XIV, No. 3, at 6-8 (Department of Justice memorandum specifying consultation process for agencies possessing White House-originated records or White House-originated information located in response to FOIA requests).

[12] See McDonnell v. Clinton, No. 97-1535, slip op. at 1 (D.D.C. July 3, 1997) (holding that "Office of the President, including its personal staff . . . whose sole function is to advise and assist the President, does not fall within the definition of agency" (citing Kissinger v. Reporters Comm. for Freedom of the Press, 445 U.S. 136, 150-55 (1980))), aff'd, 132 F.3d 1481 (D.C. Cir. 1997) (unpublished table decision); Sweetland v. Walters, 60 F.3d 852, 855-56 (D.C. Cir. 1995) (finding that Executive Residence staff, which is "exclusively dedicated to assisting the President in maintaining his home and carrying out his various ceremonial duties," is not an agency under FOIA).

[13] Meyer v. Bush, 981 F.2d 1288, 1294 (D.C. Cir. 1993); cf. Judicial Watch, Inc. v. Clinton, 76 F.3d 1232, 1234 (D.C. Cir. 1996) (holding that trust established to assist President Clinton with personal legal expenses is not subject to Federal Advisory Committee Act, 5 U.S.C. app. 2 (1994 & Supp. IV 1998), because "[a]dvice on the legal or ethical implications of presidential fund-raising for personal purposes . . . does not involve 'policy'"); Association of Am. Physicians & Surgeons v. Clinton, 997 F.2d 898, 911 (D.C. Cir. 1993) (declaring that President's Task Force on National Health Care Reform, composed of cabinet officials and chaired by First Lady, was not subject to Federal Advisory Committee Act).

## PROCEDURAL REQUIREMENTS

dent generally are considered "agencies" under the FOIA.[14] For example, the D.C. Circuit concluded that the Council on Environmental Quality (a unit within the Executive Office of the President) was an agency subject to the FOIA because its investigatory, evaluative, and recommendatory functions exceeded merely advising the President.[15] On the other hand, when the D.C. Circuit evaluated the structure of the National Security Council, its proximity to the President, and the nature of the authority delegated to it, the D.C. Circuit determined that the National Security Council is not an agency subject to the FOIA.[16]

### Agency Records

The Supreme Court has articulated a basic, two-part test for determining what constitutes "agency records" under the FOIA: "Agency records" are records that are (1) either created or obtained by an agency, and (2) under agency control at the time of the FOIA request.[17] Inasmuch as the "agency record" analysis usually hinges upon whether an agency has sufficient "control" over a record,[18] courts have identified four relevant factors for an agency to consider

---

[14] See Soucie v. David, 448 F.2d 1067, 1075 (D.C. Cir. 1971); see also Ryan v. Department of Justice, 617 F.2d 781, 784-89 (D.C. Cir. 1980).

[15] Pacific Legal Found. v. Council on Envtl. Quality, 636 F.2d 1259, 1263 (D.C. Cir. 1980) (holding that Council on Environmental Quality is an agency under FOIA); cf. Energy Research Found. v. Defense Nuclear Facilities Safety Bd., 917 F.2d 581, 584-85 (D.C. Cir. 1990) (determining that Defense Nuclear Facilities Safety Board is an agency because of its multiple functions).

[16] Armstrong v. Executive Office of the President, 90 F.3d 553, 559-65 (D.C. Cir. 1996).

[17] United States Dep't of Justice v. Tax Analysts, 492 U.S. 136, 144-45 (1989) (holding that court opinions in agency files are agency records).

[18] See, e.g., International Bhd. of Teamsters v. National Mediation Bd., 712 F.2d 1495, 1496 (D.C. Cir. 1983) (determining that submission of gummed-label mailing list as required by court order not sufficient to give "control" over record to agency); McErlean v. United States Dep't of Justice, No. 97-7831, 1999 WL 791680, at *11 (S.D.N.Y. Sept. 30, 1999) (finding that agency had no "control" over requested records because it assented to dissemination and use restrictions requested by confidential source who provided them); KDKA v. Thornburgh, No. 90-1536, 1992 U.S. Dist. LEXIS 22438, at **16-17 (D.D.C. Sept. 30, 1992) (concluding that Canadian Safety Board report of aircrash, although possessed by National Transportation Safety Board, is not under agency "control" because of restrictions imposed by Convention on International Civil Aviation); Teich v. FDA, 751 F. Supp. 243, 248-49 (D.D.C. 1990) (holding that documents submitted to FDA in "'legitimate conduct of its official duties'" are agency records notwithstanding FDA's presubmission review regulation allowing submitters to withdraw their documents from agency's files (quoting Tax Analysts, 492 U.S. at 145)); Rush v. Department of State, 716 F. Supp. 598, 600 (S.D. Fla. 1989) (finding that correspondence between former ambassador and Henry Kissinger (then Assistant to the President) were agency records of

(continued...)

**PROCEDURAL REQUIREMENTS**

when making such a determination: the intent of the record's creator to retain or relinquish control over the record; the ability of the agency to use and dispose of the record as it sees fit; the extent to which agency personnel have read or relied upon the record; and the degree to which the record was integrated into the agency's recordkeeping system or files.[19] Agency "control" is also the predominant consideration in determining the "agency record" status of records that are either generated[20] or maintained[21] by a government contractor.

---

[18](...continued)
Department of State as it exercised control over them); McCullough v. FDIC, 1 Gov't Disclosure Serv. (P-H) ¶ 80,194, at 80,494 (D.D.C. July 28, 1980) (concluding that reports transmitted to agency by state regulatory authorities were agency records because "it is questionable whether [state authorities] retained control" over them); see also FOIA Update, Vol. XIII, No. 3, at 5 (advising that records subject to "protective order" issued by administrative law judge remain within agency control and are subject to FOIA).

[19] See Tax Analysts v. United States Dep't of Justice, 845 F.2d 1060, 1069 (D.C. Cir. 1988) (citing Lindsey v. Bureau of Prisons, 736 F.2d 1462, 1465 (11th Cir. 1984)), aff'd, 492 U.S. 136 (1989); see, e.g., Katz v. NARA, 68 F.3d 1438, 1442 (D.C. Cir. 1995) (holding that autopsy x-rays and photographs of President Kennedy, created and handled as personal property of Kennedy estate, are presidential papers, not records of any agency); General Elec. Co. v. NRC, 750 F.2d 1394, 1400-01 (7th Cir. 1984) (determining that agency "use" of internal report submitted in connection with licensing proceedings renders report an agency record); Wolfe v. HHS, 711 F.2d 1077, 1079-82 (D.C. Cir. 1983) (holding that transition team records, although physically maintained within "four walls" of agency, were not agency records under FOIA); Judicial Watch, Inc. v. Clinton, 880 F. Supp. 1, 11-12 (D.D.C. 1995) (following Washington Post v. DOD, 766 F. Supp. 1, 17 (D.D.C. 1991), to find that transcript of congressional testimony provided "solely for editing purposes," with cover sheet restricting dissemination, is not an agency record), aff'd on other grounds, 76 F.2d 1232 (D.C. Cir. 1996); Marzen v. HHS, 632 F. Supp. 785, 801 (N.D. Ill. 1985) (declaring that records created outside federal government which "agency in question obtained without legal authority" are not agency records), aff'd on other grounds, 825 F.2d 1148 (7th Cir. 1987); Center for Nat'l Sec. Studies v. CIA, 577 F. Supp. 584, 586-90 (D.D.C. 1983) (holding that agency report, prepared "at the direct request of Congress" with intent that it remain secret and transferred to agency with congressionally imposed "conditions" of secrecy, is not an agency record); see also Holy Spirit Ass'n v. CIA, 636 F.2d 838, 841 (D.C. Cir. 1980) (warning that non-"agency record" status "can be lost" if record is "not designated" as such prior to agency's receipt of FOIA request); cf. SDC Dev. Corp. v. Mathews, 542 F.2d 1116, 1120 (9th Cir. 1976) (reaching "displacement-type" result for records governed by National Library of Medicine Act); Baizer v. United States Dep't of the Air Force, 887 F. Supp. 225, 228-29 (N.D. Cal. 1995) (holding that database of Supreme Court decisions, used for reference purposes or as research tool, is not an agency record); Waters v. Panama Canal Comm'n, No. 85-2029, slip op. at 5-6 (D.D.C. Nov. 26, 1985) (finding that Internal Revenue Code is not an agency record); FOIA Update, Vol. XI, No. 3, at 7-8 n.32.

[20] See Hercules, Inc. v. Marsh, 839 F.2d 1027, 1029 (4th Cir. 1988) (holding
(continued...)

## PROCEDURAL REQUIREMENTS

Courts have further refined the "agency record" concept by distinguishing "agency records" from "personal records," which are maintained by agency employees but are not subject to the FOIA.[22] In determining the "personal rec-

---

[20](...continued)
that army ammunition plant telephone directory prepared by contractor at government expense, bearing "property of the U.S." legend, is an agency record); Gilmore v. United States Dep't of Energy, 4 F. Supp. 2d 912, 922 (N.D. Cal. 1998) (finding that video conferencing software created by privately owned laboratory is not an agency record); Tax Analysts v. United States Dep't of Justice, 913 F. Supp. 599, 607 (D.D.C. 1996) (finding that electronic legal research database contracted by agency is not an agency record because licensing provisions specifically precluded agency control), aff'd, 107 F.3d 923 (D.C. Cir. 1997) (unpublished table decision); Lewisburg Prison Project, Inc. v. Federal Bureau of Prisons, No. 86-1339, slip op. at 4-5 (M.D. Pa. Dec. 16, 1986) (holding that training videotape provided by contractor is not an agency record).

[21] See, e.g., Burka, 87 F.3d at 515 (finding data tapes created and possessed by contractor to be agency records because of extensive supervision exercised by agency which evidenced "constructive control"); Los Alamos Study Group v. Department of Energy, No. 97-1412, slip op. at 4 (D.N.M. July 22, 1998) (determining that records created by contractor are agency records within meaning of FOIA because government contract "establishes [agency] intent to retain control over the records and to use or dispose of them as they see fit" and agency regulation "reinforces the conclusion that [the agency] intends to exercise control over the material"); Chicago Tribune Co. v. HHS, No. 95-C-3917, 1997 U.S. Dist. LEXIS 2308, at *33 (N.D. Ill. Feb. 26, 1997) (magistrate's recommendation) (finding that notes and audit analysis file created by independent contractor are agency records because they were created on behalf of and at request of agency and agency maintained "effective control" over them), adopted (N.D. Ill. Mar. 28, 1997); Rush Franklin Publ'g, Inc. v. NASA, No. 90-CV-2855, slip op. at 10 (E.D.N.Y. Apr. 13, 1993) (finding that computer tape maintained by contractor is not an agency record in absence of agency control); see also Sangre de Cristo Animal Protection, Inc. v. United States Dep't of Energy, No. 96-1059, slip op. at 3-6 (D.N.M. Mar. 10, 1998) (holding that records that agency neither possessed nor controlled and that were created by entity under contract with agency, although not agency records, are accessible under agency's regulation (10 C.F.R. § 1004.3 (1998)) that specifically provided for public availability of contractor records).

[22] See, e.g., Bureau of Nat'l Affairs, Inc. v. United States Dep't of Justice, 742 F.2d 1484, 1488-96 (D.C. Cir. 1984) (holding that appointment calendars and telephone message slips of agency official are not agency records); Spannaus v. United States Dep't of Justice, 942 F. Supp. 656, 658 (D.D.C. 1996) (finding that "'personal' files" of attorney no longer employed with agency were "beyond the reach of FOIA" if they were not turned over to agency at end of employment); Forman v. Chapotan, No. 88-1151, slip op. at 14 (W.D. Okla. Dec. 12, 1988) (rejecting contention that materials distributed to agency officials at privately sponsored seminar are agency records), aff'd, No. 89-6035 (10th Cir. Oct. 31, 1989); see also FOIA Update, Vol. IX, No. 4, at 3-4 (discussing circumstances under which presidential transition team documents can be regarded
(continued...)

## PROCEDURAL REQUIREMENTS

ord" status of a record, an agency should examine "the totality of the circumstances surrounding the creation, maintenance, and use" of the record.[23] Factors relevant to this inquiry include the purpose for which the document was created, the degree of integration of the record into the agency's filing system, and the extent to which the record's author or other employees used the record to conduct agency business.[24]

Agencies also should be mindful of the "agency record" status of research data generated through federal grants. The Omnibus Consolidated and Emergency Supplemental Appropriations Act for Fiscal Year 1999,[25] which partly overruled the longstanding Supreme Court precedent of Forsham v. Harris,[26] now makes certain research data generated through federal grants subject to

---

[22](...continued) as "personal records" when brought to federal agency); FOIA Update, Vol. V, No. 4, at 3-4 ("OIP Guidance: 'Agency Records' vs. 'Personal Records'").

[23] Bureau of Nat'l Affairs, 742 F.2d at 1492.

[24] See id. at 1492-93; FOIA Update, Vol. V, No. 4, at 3-4; see, e.g., Gallant v. NLRB, 26 F.3d 168, 171-72 (D.C. Cir. 1994) (stating that letters written on agency time on agency equipment by board member seeking renomination, which had been reviewed by other agency employees but not integrated into agency record system and over which author had not relinquished control, are not agency records); Inner City Press/Community on the Move v. Board of Governors of the Fed. Reserve Sys., No. 98-4608, 1998 U.S. Dist. LEXIS 15333, at *17 (S.D.N.Y. Sept. 30, 1998) (ruling that handwritten notes neither shared with other agency employees nor placed in agency files were not "agency records" even though they may have furthered their author's performance of his agency duties), aff'd, 182 F.3d 900 (2d Cir. 1999) (unpublished table decision); Clarkson, No. 97-2035, slip op. at 14 (D.D.C. June 30, 1998) (holding that notes taken by Federal Reserve Banks' employees are "personal" because they were maintained by authors for their own use, were not intended to be shared with other employees, and were not made part of Banks' filing systems); Judicial Watch, 880 F. Supp. at 11 (concluding that "telephone logs, calendar markings, [and] personal staff notes" not incorporated into agency recordkeeping system are not agency records); Dow Jones & Co. v. GSA, 714 F. Supp. 35, 39 (D.D.C. 1989) (determining that agency head's recusal list, shared only with personal secretary and chief of staff, is not an agency record); AFGE v. United States Dep't of Commerce, 632 F. Supp. 1272, 1277 (D.D.C. 1986) (finding that employee logs created voluntarily to facilitate work are not agency records even though containing substantive information), aff'd, 907 F.2d 203 (D.C. Cir. 1990). But cf. Grand Cent. Partnership, Inc. v. Cuomo, 166 F.3d 473, 481 (2d Cir. 1999) (rejecting agency affidavit concerning "personal" records as insufficient and remanding case for further development through affidavits by records' authors explaining their intended use of records in question); Ethyl Corp. v. EPA, 25 F.3d 1241, 1247-48 (4th Cir. 1994) (finding record search inadequate because employees "not properly instructed on how to distinguish personal records from agency records").

[25] Pub. L. No. 105-277, 112 Stat. 2681 (1998).

[26] 445 U.S. 169 (1980).

## PROCEDURAL REQUIREMENTS

the FOIA.[27] In Forsham, the Supreme Court held that data generated and maintained by private research institutions receiving federal grants are not "agency records" subject to the FOIA, and that a grantor agency is not obligated to demand such data in order to respond to any FOIA request for them.[28] This new statutory provision, however, required the Office of Management and Budget to revise its Circular A-110 (the regulatory publication by which OMB sets the rules governing grants from all federal agencies to institutions of higher education, hospitals, and nonprofit institutions) so that "all data produced under an award will be made available to the public through the procedures established under the Freedom of Information Act."[29] The final revised version of Circular A-110 requires agencies to respond to FOIA requests for certain grantee research findings by obtaining the requested data from the grantee and processing it for release to the requester.[30] In accordance with OMB's statutory authority over such matters, questions concerning the processing of FOIA requests for grantee research data should be directed to OMB's Office of Information and Regulatory Affairs, Information Policy and Technology Branch, at (202) 395-7856.

At a more fundamental level, the FOIA applies only to "records," not to tangible, evidentiary objects.[31] The courts initially defined "record" by relying on the traditional dictionary meaning of the term.[32] However, the Supreme Court subsequently broadened the meaning of "record" by incorporating the

---

[27] See FOIA Update, Vol. XIX, No. 4, at 2 (describing legislative change).

[28] Id. at 178-81.

[29] Omnibus Consolidated and Emergency Supplemental Appropriations Act for Fiscal Year 1999, Pub. L. No. 105-277, 112 Stat. 2681 (1998).

[30] See OMB Circular A-110, "Uniform Administrative Requirements for Grants and Agreements with Institutions of Higher Education, Hospitals, and Other Non-Profit Organizations," 64 Fed. Reg. 54,926 (1999); see also FOIA Update, Vol. XIX, No. 4, at 2 (discussing grantee records subject to FOIA under Circular A-110's definition of "research data").

[31] See Matthews v. United States Postal Serv., No. 92-1208, slip op. at 4 n.3 (W.D. Mo. Apr. 14, 1994) (holding that computer hardware is not "record"); Nichols v. United States, 325 F. Supp. 130, 135-36 (D. Kan. 1971) (holding that archival exhibits consisting of guns, bullets, and clothing pertaining to assassination of President Kennedy are not "records"), aff'd on other grounds, 460 F.2d 671 (10th Cir. 1972); see also FOIA Update, Vol. XIV, No. 1, at 1 (discussing implementation of President John F. Kennedy Assassination Records Collection Act of 1992, 44 U.S.C. § 2107 note (1994)); cf. FOIA Update, Vol. XIX, No. 4, at 2 (discussing provisions of "somewhat akin" FOIA-related statute, Nazi War Crimes Disclosure Act, 5 U.S.C.A. § 552 note (West Supp. 1999)).

[32] See DiViaio v. Kelley, 571 F.2d 538, 542 (10th Cir. 1978) ("[R]eliance may be placed on the dictionary meaning . . . as that which is written or transcribed to perpetuate knowledge."); Nichols, 325 F. Supp. at 135 (stating that reliance "placed on a dictionary of respected ancestry [Webster's]").

## PROCEDURAL REQUIREMENTS

more modern record media referenced in the Records Disposal Act[33] into its definition of the term.[34] With more recent technological advances, and consistent with the FOIA policy of encouraging widespread public access,[35] at least one court has included computer software in its definition of "record."[36] The Electronic Freedom of Information Act Amendments of 1996[37] define the term "record" as simply "includ[ing] any information that would be an agency record . . . when maintained by an agency in any format, including an electronic format."[38]

### FOIA Requesters

A FOIA request can be made by "any person," a broad term that encompasses individuals (including foreign citizens), partnerships, corporations, associations, and foreign or domestic governments;[39] requests may also be made

---

[33] 44 U.S.C. § 3301 (1994).

[34] See Forsham, 445 U.S. at 183 (treating "record" as including "'machine readable materials . . . regardless of physical form or characteristics'" (quoting Records Disposal Act)); see also New York Times Co. v. NASA, 920 F.2d 1002, 1005 (D.C. Cir. 1990) (holding that audiotape of Challenger astronauts is "record," as "FOIA makes no distinction between information in lexical and . . . non-lexical form"); Save the Dolphins v. United States Dep't of Commerce, 404 F. Supp. 407, 410-11 (N.D. Cal. 1975) (finding that motion picture film is "record" for purposes of FOIA).

[35] See President's Memorandum for Heads of Departments and Agencies regarding the Freedom of Information Act, 29 Weekly Comp. Pres. Doc. 1999 (Oct. 4, 1993), reprinted in FOIA Update, Vol. XIV, No. 3, at 3 (calling upon agencies to renew their commitment to "principles of government openness" underlying FOIA); accord FOIA Update, Vol. XVII, No. 4, at 9.

[36] Cleary, Gottlieb, Steen & Hamilton v. HHS, 844 F. Supp. 770, 782 (D.D.C. 1993) ("These [computer] programs preserve information and 'perpetuate knowledge.'" (quoting DiViaio, 571 F.2d at 542)); see also FOIA Update, Vol. XV, No. 4, at 4-5 (proposed electronic record FOIA principles); Department of Justice "Electronic Record" Report, reprinted in abridged form in FOIA Update, Vol. XI, No. 3, at 6-12 (discussing issue of "record" status of computer software). But see Gilmore, 4 F. Supp. 2d at 919-20 (holding alternatively that video conferencing software developed by privately owned laboratory may not be regarded as "record" on basis that such software "does not illuminate the structure, operation, or decisionmaking structure" of agency); Essential Info., Inc. v. USIA, 134 F.3d 1165, 1166 n.3 (D.C. Cir. 1998) (dictum) (suggesting, without authority, that Internet addresses "seem to be" not records, but "simply 'a means to access' records").

[37] Pub. L. No. 104-231, § 3, 110 Stat. 3048, 3049 (codified as amended at 5 U.S.C. § 552(f)(2) (1994 & Supp. IV 1998)).

[38] 5 U.S.C. § 552(f)(2); see also FOIA Update, Vol. XVII, No. 4, at 2 (discussing statutory amendment).

[39] 5 U.S.C. § 551(2) (1994).

## PROCEDURAL REQUIREMENTS

through an attorney or other representative on behalf of "any person."[40] Although the statute specifically excludes federal agencies from the definition of a "person,"[41] states and state agencies can make FOIA requests.[42] The only apparent exception of any significance to this broad "any person" standard is for those who flout the law, such as fugitives from justice, who may be denied judicial relief by the courts if the requested records relate to the requester's fugitive status.[43] This holds true also when the FOIA plaintiff is an agent acting on behalf of a fugitive.[44]

FOIA requests can be made for any reason whatsoever; because the purpose for which records are sought has no bearing upon the merits of the request, FOIA requesters do not have to explain or justify their requests.[45] As a

---

[40] See, e.g., Constangy, Brooks & Smith v. NLRB, 851 F.2d 839, 840 n.2 (6th Cir. 1988) (recognizing standing of attorney to request documents on behalf of client). But cf. Burka v. HHS, 142 F.3d 1286, 1290 (D.C. Cir. 1998) (holding when attorney makes request in his own name without disclosing that he is acting on behalf of a client, he may not later seek attorney fees for his legal work); McDonnell v. United States, 4 F.3d 1227, 1237-38 (3d Cir. 1993) (holding that person whose name does not appear on request does not have standing); MAXXAM, Inc. v. FDIC, No. 98-0989, slip op. at 5-6 (D.D.C. Jan. 21, 1999) (finding that corporate plaintiff whose name did not appear on FOIA request made by its attorney "'has not administratively asserted a right to receive [the requested records] in the first place'" (quoting McDonnell, 4 F.3d at 1237)). See generally Doherty v. United States Dep't of Justice, 596 F. Supp. 423, 427 n.4 (S.D.N.Y. 1984) (reviewing legislative history), aff'd on other grounds, 775 F.2d 49 (2d Cir. 1985).

[41] 5 U.S.C. § 551(2); see also FOIA Update, Vol. VI, No. 1, at 6 (advising that information requests from agencies within executive branch of federal government cannot be considered FOIA requests).

[42] See, e.g., Texas v. ICC, 935 F.2d 728, 728 (5th Cir. 1991); Massachusetts v. HHS, 727 F. Supp. 35, 35 (D. Mass. 1989).

[43] See Doyle v. United States Dep't of Justice, 668 F.2d 1365, 1365-66 (D.C. Cir. 1981) (holding that fugitive is not entitled to enforcement of FOIA's access provisions because he cannot expect judicial aid in obtaining government records related to sentence that he was evading). But cf. O'Rourke v. United States Dep't of Justice, 684 F. Supp. 716, 718 (D.D.C. 1988) (holding that convicted criminal, fugitive from his home country and undergoing U.S. deportation proceedings, qualified as "any person" for purpose of making FOIA request); Doherty, 596 F. Supp. at 424-29 (same).

[44] See Javelin Int'l, Ltd. v. United States Dep't of Justice, 2 Gov't Disclosure Serv. (P-H) ¶ 82,141, at 82,479 (D.D.C. Dec. 9, 1981).

[45] See United States Dep't of Justice v. Reporters Comm. for Freedom of the Press, 489 U.S. 749, 771 (1989); see also North v. Walsh, 881 F.2d 1088, 1096 (D.C. Cir. 1989) (rejecting requester's identity and intended use as factors for determining access rights under FOIA); Durns v. Bureau of Prisons, 804 F.2d 701, 706 (D.C. Cir. 1986) ("Congress granted the scholar and the scoundrel equal rights of access to agency records."), cert. granted, judgment vacated on

(continued...)

## PROCEDURAL REQUIREMENTS

result, and despite repeated Supreme Court admonitions for restraint,[46] requesters have invoked the FOIA successfully as a substitute for, or a supplement to, document discovery in the contexts of both civil[47] and criminal[48] litigation.

At the same time, as the Supreme Court has stated, a FOIA requester's basic rights to access are neither increased nor decreased because he or she has a greater interest in the records than an average member of the general pub-

---

[45](...continued)
other grounds & remanded, 486 U.S. 1029 (1988); Forsham v. Califano, 587 F.2d 1128, 1134 (D.C. Cir. 1978) (reasoning that while factors such as need, interest, or public interest may bear on agency's determination of order of processing, they have no bearing on individuals' rights of access under FOIA); see also FOIA Update, Vol. X, No. 2, at 5; FOIA Update, Vol. VI, No. 3, at 5.

[46] See United States v. Weber Aircraft Corp., 465 U.S. 792, 801-02 (1984); Baldrige v. Shapiro, 455 U.S. 345, 360 n.14 (1982); NLRB v. Robbins Tire & Rubber Co., 437 U.S. 214, 242 (1978); NLRB v. Sears, Roebuck & Co., 421 U.S. 132, 143 n.10 (1975); Renegotiation Bd. v. Bannercraft Clothing Co., 415 U.S. 1, 24 (1974).

[47] See, e.g., Jackson v. First Fed. Sav., 709 F. Supp. 887, 889 (E.D. Ark. 1989); see also FOIA Update, Vol. III, No. 1, at 10. But see Environmental Crimes Project v. EPA, 928 F. Supp. 1, 2 (D.D.C. 1995) (ordering stay of FOIA case "pending the resolution of the discovery disputes" in parties' related lawsuit to foreclose requester's attempt to "end run" or interfere with discovery); cf. Injex Indus. v. NLRB, 699 F. Supp. 1417, 1419 (N.D. Cal. 1986) (holding that FOIA cannot be used to circumvent nonreviewable decision to impound requested documents); Morrison-Knudsen Co. v. Department of the Army of the United States, 595 F. Supp. 352, 356 (D.D.C. 1984) ("[T]he use of FOIA to unsettle well established procedures governed by a comprehensive regulatory scheme must be . . . viewed not only 'with caution' but with concern."), aff'd, 762 F.2d 138 (D.C. Cir. 1985) (unpublished table decision).

[48] See, e.g., North, 881 F.2d at 1096. But cf. Jones v. FBI, 41 F.3d 238, 250 (6th Cir. 1994) ("FOIA's scheme of exemptions does not curtail a plaintiff's right to discovery in related non-FOIA litigation; but neither does that right entitle a FOIA plaintiff to circumvent the rules limiting release of documents under FOIA."); United States v. United States Dist. Court, Central Dist. of Cal., 717 F.2d 478, 480 (9th Cir. 1983) (holding that FOIA does not expand scope of criminal discovery permitted under Rule 16 of Federal Rules of Criminal Procedure); United States v. Agunbiade, No. 90-CR-610, 1995 WL 351058, at *7 (E.D.N.Y. May 10, 1995) (stating that FOIA requester "cannot employ the statute as a means to enlarge his right to discovery"); Johnson v. United States Dep't of Justice, 758 F. Supp. 2, 5 (D.D.C. 1991) ("Resort to Brady v. Maryland as grounds for waiving confidentiality is . . . outside the proper role of FOIA."); Stimac v. United States Dep't of Justice, 620 F. Supp. 212, 213 (D.D.C. 1985) ("Brady v. Maryland . . . provides no authority for releasing material under FOIA.").

## PROCEDURAL REQUIREMENTS

lic.[49] Such considerations, however, bear on certain procedural areas of the FOIA--such as expedited access, waiver or reduction of fees, and the award of attorney's fees and costs to a successful FOIA plaintiff--in which it is appropriate to examine a requester's need or purpose in seeking records. Moreover, as the Supreme Court has observed, a requester's identity can be significant in one substantive respect: "The fact that no one need show a particular need for information in order to qualify for disclosure under the FOIA does not mean that in no situation whatever will there be valid reasons for treating [an exemption] differently as to one class of those who make requests than as to another class."[50] In short, this means that an agency should not invoke a FOIA exemption to protect a requester from himself.[51]

Lastly, the Court of Appeals for the District of Columbia Circuit has held that under some circumstances a FOIA claim in litigation may survive even if the FOIA requester dies before the case is put to rest.[52]

---

[49] Sears, 421 U.S. at 143 n.10; see EPA v. Mink, 410 U.S. 73, 86 (1973) (declaring that FOIA "is largely indifferent to the intensity of a particular requester's need"); Lynch v. Department of the Treasury, No. 98-56368, 2000 WL 123236, at *4 (9th Cir. Jan. 28, 2000) (upholding district court's decision to not consider identity of requester in determining whether records were properly withheld under Exemption 7(A)), petition for cert. filed, 68 U.S.L.W. 3686 (U.S. Apr. 21, 2000) (No. 99-1697); Parsons v. Freedom of Info. Act Officer, No. 96-4128, 1997 WL 461320, at *1 (6th Cir. Aug. 12, 1997) (holding that plaintiff's argument of "legitimate need for the documents superior to that of the general public or the press" fails because identity of requester is irrelevant to determination of whether exemption applies); see also United Techs. v. FAA, 102 F.3d 688, 692 (2d Cir. 1996) ("'Congress[] created a scheme of categorical exclusion; it did not invite a judicial weighing of the benefits and evils of disclosure on a case-by-case basis.'" (quoting FBI v. Abramson, 456 U.S. 615, 631 (1982))); cf. Calder v. IRS, 890 F.2d 781, 783 (5th Cir. 1989) (holding that historian denied access under FOIA also has no "constitutional right of access" to Al Capone's tax records); Leach v. RTC, 860 F. Supp. 868, 871, 878-79 & n.13 (D.D.C. 1994) (individual Member of Congress granted no greater access to agency records than other FOIA requesters by virtue of position; issue held nonjusticiable), appeal dismissed per stipulation, No. 94-5279 (D.C. Cir. Dec. 22, 1994).

[50] United States Dep't of Justice v. Julian, 486 U.S. 1, 14 (1988); accord Reporters Comm., 489 U.S. at 771 (recognizing single exception to general FOIA-disclosure rule in case of "first-party" requester).

[51] See FOIA Update, Vol. X, No. 2, at 5 (advising agencies to treat first-party FOIA requesters in accordance with protectible interests that requesters can have in their own information, such as personal privacy information, and to treat third-party FOIA requesters differently).

[52] See Sinito v. United States Dep't of Justice, 176 F.3d 512, 513 (D.C. Cir. 1999) (holding that FOIA claim can survive death of original requester and remanding case for determination regarding who may properly be substituted for decedent); see also D'Aleo v. Department of the Navy, No. 89-2347, 1991 U.S. Dist. LEXIS 3884, at *4 (D.D.C. Mar. 21, 1991) (allowing decedent's execu-
(continued...)

**PROCEDURAL REQUIREMENTS**

Proper FOIA Requests

The FOIA specifies only two requirements for an access request: It must "reasonably describe" the records sought[53] and it must be made in accordance with the agency's published FOIA regulations.[54] Because "a person need not title a request for government records a 'FOIA request,'"[55] agencies should use sound administrative discretion when determining the nature of a request.[56] For example, a first-party access request that cites only the Privacy Act of 1974[57] should be processed under both that statute and the FOIA.[58] Toward this end, agencies should strive to follow not only the letter of the Act, but "its underlying spirit as well."[59]

---

[52](...continued)
utrix to be substituted as plaintiff). But see Hayles v. United States Dep't of Justice, No. H-79-1599, slip op. at 3 (S.D. Tex. Nov. 2, 1982) (dismissing case upon death of plaintiff when no timely motion for substitution was filed).

[53] 5 U.S.C. § 552(a)(3)(A) (1994 & Supp. IV 1998).

[54] Id. § 552(a)(3)(A)(ii); see, e.g., Borden v. FBI, No. 94-1029, slip op. at 2 (1st Cir. June 28, 1994) (per curiam) (affirming dismissal of case because requester failed to comply with agency's published regulations); McDonnell v. United States, 4 F.3d 1227, 1236-37 (3d Cir. 1993) ("[A] person whose name does not appear on [FOIA] request [as required by agency regulations] . . . has not made a formal request for documents within the meaning of the statute [and therefore] has no right to [the documents or to] sue in district court when the agency refuses to release requested documents."); Church of Scientology v. IRS, 792 F.2d 146, 150 (D.C. Cir. 1986) (stating that requesters must follow "the statutory command that requests be made in accordance with published rules"). But see Summers v. United States Dep't of Justice, 999 F.2d 570, 572-73 (D.C. Cir. 1993) (holding that 28 U.S.C. § 1746 (1994)--which requires that unsworn declarations be treated with "like force and effect" as sworn declarations--can be used in place of notarized-signature requirement of agency regulation for verification of FOIA privacy waivers).

[55] Newman v. Legal Servs. Corp., 628 F. Supp. 535, 543 (D.D.C. 1986). But see Blackwell v. EEOC, No. 2:98-38, 1999 U.S. Dist. LEXIS 3708, at *5 (E.D.N.C. Feb. 12, 1999) (finding request not properly made because plaintiff failed to follow agency regulation requiring that request be denominated explicitly as request for information under FOIA).

[56] See FOIA Update, Vol. VII, No. 1, at 6 (advising that "agencies are expected to honor a requester's obvious intent").

[57] 5 U.S.C. § 552a (1994 & Supp. IV 1998).

[58] See FOIA Update, Vol. VII, No. 1, at 6 (advising that it is "good policy for agencies to treat all first-party access requests as FOIA requests" regardless of whether FOIA is cited by requester).

[59] FOIA Update, Vol. XIV, No. 3, at 9; accord President's Memorandum for Heads of Departments and Agencies regarding the Freedom of Information Act, 29 Weekly Comp. Pres. Doc. 1999 (Oct. 4, 1993) [hereinafter President
(continued...)

## PROCEDURAL REQUIREMENTS

The legislative history of the 1974 FOIA amendments indicates that a description of a requested record that enables a professional agency employee familiar with the subject area to locate the record with a "reasonable amount of effort" is sufficient.[60] Courts have explained that "[t]he rationale for this rule is that FOIA was not intended to reduce government agencies to full-time investigators on behalf of requesters,"[61] or to allow requesters to conduct "fishing expeditions" through agency files.[62] Accordingly, one FOIA request was held invalid because it required an agency's FOIA staff either to have "clairvoyant capabilities" to discern the requester's needs or to spend "countless numbers of personnel hours seeking needles in bureaucratic haystacks."[63]

---

[59](...continued)
Clinton's FOIA Memorandum], reprinted in FOIA Update, Vol. XIV, No. 3, at 3; Attorney General's Memorandum for Heads of Departments and Agencies regarding the Freedom of Information Act (Oct. 4, 1993) [hereinafter Attorney General Reno's FOIA Memorandum], reprinted in FOIA Update, Vol. XIV, No. 3, at 4 (stressing "both the letter and the spirit" of FOIA); see also id. at 5 (calling for "new spirit of government openness" and "new institutional attitude toward FOIA administration" in follow-up Attorney General memorandum); FOIA Update, Vol. XVIII, No. 2, at 1 (urging continued commitment to "openness-in-government principles"); FOIA Update, Vol. XV, No. 2, at 1 (emphasizing importance of "better and more efficient communications with FOIA requesters").

[60] H.R. Rep. No. 93-876, at 6 (1974), reprinted in 1974 U.S.C.C.A.N. 6267, 6271; see, e.g., Brumley v. United States Dep't of Labor, 767 F.2d 444, 445 (8th Cir. 1985); Goland v. CIA, 607 F.2d 339, 353 (D.C. Cir. 1978); Marks v. United States Dep't of Justice, 578 F.2d 261, 263 (9th Cir. 1978).

[61] Assassination Archives & Research Ctr. v. CIA, 720 F. Supp. 217, 219 (D.D.C. 1989), aff'd in pertinent part, No. 89-5414 (D.C. Cir. Aug. 13, 1990); see Frank v. United States Dep't of Justice, 941 F. Supp. 4, 5 (D.D.C. 1996); Blakey v. Department of Justice, 549 F. Supp. 362, 366-67 (D.D.C. 1982), aff'd, 720 F.2d 215 (D.C. Cir. 1983) (unpublished table decision); see also Trenerry v. Department of the Treasury, No. 92-5053, 1993 WL 26813, at *3 (10th Cir. Feb. 5, 1993) (holding that agency not required to provide personal services such as legal research); Davis v. United States Dep't of Justice, 968 F.2d 1276, 1280-82 (D.C. Cir. 1992) (stating that burden is on requester, not agency, to show prior disclosure of otherwise exempt records); Lamb v. IRS, 871 F. Supp. 301, 304 (E.D. Mich. 1994) (finding requests outside scope of FOIA when they require legal research, are unspecific, or seek answers to interrogatories).

[62] Immanuel v. Secretary of the Treasury, No. 94-884, 1995 WL 464141, at *1 (D. Md. Apr. 4, 1995), aff'd, 81 F.3d 150 (4th Cir. 1996) (unpublished table decision); see also Freeman v. United States Dep't of Justice, No. 90-2754, slip op. at 3 (D.D.C. Oct. 16, 1991) ("The FOIA does not require that the government go fishing in the ocean for fresh water fish.").

[63] Devine v. Marsh, 2 Gov't Disclosure Serv. (P-H) ¶ 82,022, at 82,186 (E.D. Va. Aug. 27, 1981); see also Goldgar v. Office of Admin., 26 F.3d 32, 35 (5th Cir. 1994) (holding that agency not required to produce information sought by requester--"the identity of the government agency that is reading his mind"--
(continued...)

## PROCEDURAL REQUIREMENTS

However, the fact that a FOIA request is very broad or "burdensome" in its magnitude does not, in and of itself, entitle an agency to deny that request on the basis that it does not "reasonably describe" the records sought.[64] The key factor is the ability of an agency's staff to reasonably ascertain exactly which records are being requested and locate them.[65] The courts have held only that agencies are not required to conduct wide-ranging, "unreasonably burdensome" searches for records.[66] Agencies may nevertheless apply a "cut-

---

[63](...continued)
that does not exist in record form); Keenan v. United States Dep't of Justice, No. 94-1909, slip op. at 1 (D.D.C. Nov. 12. 1996) ("Plaintiff can not [sic] place a request for one search and then, when nothing is found, convert that request into a different search."); Graphics of Key West v. United States, 1996 WL 167861, at *7 (D. Nev. 1996) (finding plaintiff's request letters to be "more arguments than clear requests for information"); Kubany v. Board of Governors of the Fed. Reserve Sys., No. 93-1428, slip op. at 6-8 (D.D.C. July 19, 1994) (holding that request relying on exhibits containing "multiple, unexplained references to hundreds of accounts, and various flowcharts, and schematics" is "entirely unreasonable").

[64] See Ruotolo v. Department of Justice, 53 F.3d 4, 10 (2d Cir. 1995); Public Citizen v. FDA, No. 94-0018, slip op. at 2 (D.D.C. Feb. 9, 1996); see also FOIA Update, Vol. IV, No. 3, at 5. But see Domingues v. FBI, No. 98-74612, slip op. at 11 (E.D. Mich. July 24, 1999) (magistrate's recommendation) (determining that "a request directed to an agency's headquarters which does not request a search of its field offices, or which requests a blanket search of all field offices without specifying which offices should be searched, does not 'reasonably describe' any records which may be in those field offices, and an agency's search of just the headquarters records complies with the FOIA"), adopted (E.D. Mich. July 29, 1999); Massachusetts v. HHS, 727 F. Supp. 35, 36 n.2 (D. Mass. 1989) (holding that request for all records "relating to" particular subject is overbroad, "thus unfairly plac[ing] the onus of non-production on the recipient of the request and not where it belongs--upon the person who drafted such a sloppy request").

[65] See Yeager v. DEA, 678 F.2d 315, 322, 326 (D.C. Cir. 1982) (holding valid request encompassing over 1,000,000 computerized records: "The linchpin inquiry is whether the agency is able to determine 'precisely what records [are] being requested.'" (quoting legislative history)).

[66] See Nation Magazine v. United States Customs Serv., 71 F.3d 885, 892 (D.C. Cir. 1995) (agreeing that search which would require review of 23 years of unindexed files would be unreasonably burdensome, but disagreeing that search for dated memorandum through agency files indexed chronologically would be burdensome); Van Strum v. EPA, No. 91-35404, No. 91-35404, 1992 WL 197660, at *1 (9th Cir. Aug. 17, 1992) (accepting agency justification in denying or seeking clarification of overly broad requests which would place inordinate search burden on agency resources); AFGE v. United States Dep't of Commerce, 907 F.2d 203, 209 (D.C. Cir. 1990) (holding request which would require agency "to locate, review, redact, and arrange for inspection a vast quantity of material" to be "so broad as to impose an unreasonable burden upon the agency" (citing Goland, 607 F.2d at 353)); Marks, 578 F.2d at 263
(continued...)

## PROCEDURAL REQUIREMENTS

off" date for including records as responsive to requests,[67] and should notify requesters of such a practice through a published regulation or in the agency's letter to the requester.[68] (For further discussions of search requirements, see Procedural Requirements, Searching for Responsive Records, below, and Litigation Considerations, Adequacy of Search, below.)

By the same token, an agency also "must be careful not to read [a] request so strictly that the requester is denied information the agency well knows exists in its files, albeit in a different form from that anticipated by the re-

---

[66](...continued) (ruling that FBI is not required to search every one of its field offices); Gilbert v. United States Parole Comm'n, No. 97-2629, slip. op. at 7 (D.D.C. Mar. 23, 1999) ("Forcing the [agency] to search through over hundreds of thousands of files would impose an unreasonable burden on the agency."); O'Harvey v. Office of Workers' Compensation Programs, No. 95-0187, slip op. at 3 (E.D. Wash. Dec. 29, 1997) (finding request to be unreasonably burdensome because search would require agency "to review all of the case files maintained by the agency" and "would entail review of millions of pages of hard copies"), aff'd sub nom. O'Harvey v. Compensation Programs Workers, 188 F.3d 514 (9th Cir. 1999) (unpublished table decision); Spannaus v. United States Dep't of Justice, No. 92-372, slip op. at 6 (D.D.C. June 20, 1995) (finding agency is not required to determine all persons having ties to associations targeted in bankruptcy proceedings "and then search any and all civil or criminal files relating to those persons"), summary affirmance granted in pertinent part, No. 95-5267 (D.C. Cir. Aug. 16, 1996); see also Nolen v. Rumsfeld, 535 F.2d 890, 891-92 (5th Cir. 1976) ("[Plaintiff] is here seeking production of missing records, which is not within the purview of the Freedom of Information Act."). But see Ruotolo, F.3d at 9 (finding that request which required 803 files to be searched not "unreasonably burdensome"); Truitt v. Department of State, 897 F.2d 540, 544-46 (D.C. Cir. 1990) (requiring that subsequent search be conducted for responsive records that agency knew were removed from file); Peyton v. Reno, No. 98-1457, 1999 U.S. Dist. LEXIS 12125, at **4-5 (D.D.C. July 19, 1999) (finding that request for all records indexed under subject's name reasonably described records sought because agency failed to demonstrate that name search would be unduly burdensome).

[67] See, e.g., Blazy v. Tenet, 979 F. Supp. 10, 17 (D.D.C. 1997) (finding agency use of date of receipt as cut-off date for records search reasonable), summary affirmance granted, No. 97-5330 (D.C. Cir. May 12, 1998); Judicial Watch, 880 F. Supp. at 10 (observing that although agency provided plaintiff with document created after date of request letter, agency not required to do so because date of request can serve as "cut-off" for further search obligations under FOIA); Church of Scientology v. IRS, 816 F. Supp. 1138, 1148 (W.D. Tex. 1993) (holding documents generated subsequent to date specified in request outside of scope of request and need not be disclosed).

[68] See McGehee v. CIA, 697 F.2d 1095, 1105 (D.C. Cir.), vacated on other grounds on panel reh'g & reh'g en banc denied, 711 F.2d 1076 (D.C. Cir. 1983); see, e.g., 28 C.F.R. § 16.4 (1999) (Department of Justice FOIA regulation); see also FOIA Update, Vol. IV, No. 4, at 14.

## PROCEDURAL REQUIREMENTS

quester."[69] In liberally interpreting the intended scope of a FOIA request,[70] agencies should heed President Clinton's admonition to "handle requests for information in a customer-friendly manner [in order to] ensure compliance with both the letter and spirit of the Act."[71] To achieve this, agencies should be careful to undertake any "scoping" of documents found in response to a request only with full communication with the FOIA requester.[72]

When determining the scope of a FOIA request, however, agencies should remember that they are not required to create records in order to re-

---

[69] Hemenway v. Hughes, 601 F. Supp. 1002, 1005 (D.D.C. 1985); see also Miller v. Casey, 730 F.2d 773, 777 (D.C. Cir. 1984) (emphasizing that agency required to read FOIA request as drafted, "not as either [an] agency official or [the requester] might wish it was drafted"); Ferri v. Bell, 645 F.2d 1213, 1220 (3d Cir. 1981) (declaring that request "inartfully presented in the form of questions" cannot be dismissed, in toto, as too burdensome); Landes v. Yost, No. 89-6338, slip op. at 4-5 (E.D. Pa. Apr. 11, 1990) (finding that request was "reasonably descriptive" when it relied on agency's own outdated identification code), aff'd, 922 F.2d 832 (3d Cir. 1990) (unpublished table decision); FOIA Update, Vol. IV, No. 3, at 5.

[70] See FOIA Update, Vol. XVI, No. 3, at 3 (advising agencies to interpret terms of FOIA requests liberally (citing Nation Magazine v. United States Customs Serv., 71 F.3d 885, 890 (D.C. Cir. 1995))).

[71] President Clinton's FOIA Memorandum, reprinted in FOIA Update, Vol. XIV, No. 3, at 3; see Attorney General's Follow-Up Memorandum for Heads of Departments and Agencies regarding the Freedom of Information Act (Sept. 3, 1999) [hereinafter Attorney General Reno's Follow-Up FOIA Memorandum], reprinted in FOIA Update, Vol. XIX, No. 4, at 3 (encouraging agencies to do "everything possible to promote openness in the Government and to respond to citizens' requests for information in a customer-friendly manner"); Attorney General Reno's FOIA Memorandum, reprinted in FOIA Update, Vol. XIV, No. 3, at 4-5; FOIA Update, Vol. XV, No. 3, at 6 (describing National Performance Review FOIA activities at Justice Department); see also Horsehead Indus. v. EPA, No. 94-1299, slip op. at 4 n.2 (D.D.C. Jan. 3, 1997) (ruling that "[b]y construing the FOIA request narrowly, [agency] seeks to avoid disclosing information" and finds such approach to be "at odds with the Clinton Administration's policy of disclosure absent foreseeable harm"); FOIA Update, Vol. XIX, No. 1, at 6 (encouraging agencies to consider providing records in multiple forms if requested to do so, as a matter of "'customer-friendly' treatment of the requester"); cf. De Luca v. INS, No. 95-6240, 1996 U.S. Dist. LEXIS 2696, at *2 (E.D. Pa. Mar. 7, 1996) (noting that agency offered--as matter of administrative discretion--to create certification that it had no record that requester was naturalized citizen).

[72] See FOIA Update, Vol. XVI, No. 3, at 3-5 ("OIP Guidance: Determining the Scope of a FOIA Request") (advising of procedures and underlying considerations for document "scoping"); see also Halpern v. FBI, 181 F.3d 279, 289 (2d Cir. 1999) (holding cross-referenced files to be beyond scope of request because once agency "had requested clarification [about requester's interest in receiving such records], it could then in good faith ignore the cross-referenced files until it received an affirmative response" from requester).

## PROCEDURAL REQUIREMENTS

spond to FOIA requests,[73] nor are they required to answer questions posed as FOIA requests.[74] Similarly, agencies cannot be required by FOIA requesters to

---

[73] See, e.g., NLRB v. Sears, Roebuck & Co., 421 U.S. 132, 143 n.10 (1975) (holding that agency is not required to create explanatory materials); Poll v. United States Office of Special Counsel, No. 99-4021, 2000 WL 14422, at *5 n.2 (10th Cir. Jan. 10, 2000) (recognizing that "'FOIA neither requires an agency to answer questions disguised as a FOIA request, [nor] to create documents or opinions in response to an individual's request for information'" (quoting Hudgins v. IRS, 620 F. Supp. 19, 21 (D.D.C. 1985))); Sorrells v. United States, No. 97-5586, 1998 WL 58080, at *1 (6th Cir. Feb. 6, 1998) (advising that agency is not required to compile document that "contain[s] a full, legible signature"); Goldgar, 26 F.3d at 35 (stating that agency not required to produce information sought by requester that simply does not exist in record form); Krohn v. Department of Justice, 628 F.2d 195, 197-98 (D.C. Cir. 1980) (finding that agency "cannot be compelled to create the [intermediary records] necessary to produce" the information sought); Jones v. Runyon, 32 F. Supp. 2d 873, 875 (N.D. W. Va. 1998) (concluding that "because the FOIA does not obligate to create records or to make explanations, [agency] acted properly by providing access to those documents already created"), aff'd, 173 F.3d 850 (4th Cir. 1999) (unpublished table decision); Tax Analysts v. IRS, No. 94-923, 1998 WL 419755, at *2 (D.D.C. May 1, 1998) (declaring that "an agency need not add explanatory material to a document to make it more understandable in light of the redactions"); Bartlett v. United States Dep't of Justice, 867 F. Supp. 314, 316 (E.D. Pa. 1994) (ruling that agency not required to create handwriting analysis); Gabel v. Commissioner, 879 F. Supp. 1037, 1039 (N.D. Cal. 1994) (noting that FOIA does not require agency "to revamp documents or generate exegeses so as to make them comprehensible to a particular requestor"); Matthews, No. 92-1208, slip op. at 4 n.3 (W.D. Mo. Apr. 14, 1994) (declaring that agency not required to create "photocopy" of computer hardware); Cleary, 844 F. Supp. at 779 (holding that agency not required to recreate original database sought by requester); see also FOIA Update, Vol. V, No. 1, at 5; cf. Essential Info., Inc. v. USIA, 134 F.3d 1165, 1172 (D.C. Cir. 1998) (Tatel, J., dissenting) (observing that "FOIA contains no . . . translation requirement"). But cf. McDonnell, 4 F.3d at 1261 n.21 (suggesting, in dictum, that agency might be compelled to create translation of any disclosable encoded information); Schladetsch v. HUD, No. 99-0175, slip op. at 7 (D.D.C. Apr. 4, 2000) ("Because [the agency] has conceded that it possesses in its databases the discrete pieces of information which [plaintiff] seeks, extracting and compiling that data does not amount to the creation of a new record."); Jones v. OSHA, No. 94-3225, slip op. at 6 (W.D. Mo. June 6, 1995) (stating that agency must "retype," not withhold in full, documents required to be released by its own regulation, in order to delete FOIA-exempt information); International Diatomite Producers, 1993 WL 137286, at *5 (N.D. Cal. Apr. 28, 1993) (giving agency choice of compiling responsive list or redacting existing lists containing responsive information) FOIA Update, Vol. XVIII, No. 1, at 5-6 (advising of statutory obligations regarding electronic record searches and format of disclosure).

[74] See, e.g., Zemansky v. EPA, 767 F.2d 569, 574 (9th Cir. 1985); DiViaio v. Kelley, 571 F.2d 538, 542-43 (10th Cir. 1978); Carnessale v. Reno, No. 95-0279, slip op. at 2 (C.D. Cal. May 2, 1995) (finding request not proper under FOIA where it seeks answers to "a series of legal questions, some of them amounting

(continued...)

## PROCEDURAL REQUIREMENTS

seek the return of records over which they retain no "control"[75] (even records that were wrongfully removed from their possession);[76] to recreate records properly disposed of;[77] or to seek the delivery of records held by private enti-

---

[74](...continued)
to the rendition of a legal opinion"); Gillin v. Department of the Army, No. 92-325, slip op. at 10 (D.N.H. May 28, 1993) ("FOIA creates only a right of access to records, not a right to require an agency to disclose its collective reasoning behind agency actions, nor does FOIA provide a mechanism to challenge the wisdom of substantive agency decisions."); Patton v. United States R.R. Retirement Bd., No. ST-C-91-04, slip op. at 3 (W.D.N.C. Apr. 26, 1991) (stating that the FOIA "provides a means for access to existing documents and is not a way to interrogate an agency"), aff'd, 940 F.2d 652 (4th Cir. 1991) (unpublished table decision); Hudgins, 620 F. Supp. at 21 ("[The] FOIA creates only a right of access to records, not a right to personal services."); see also FOIA Update, Vol. V, No. 1, at 5.

[75] See Steinberg v. United States Dep't of Justice, 801 F. Supp. 800, 802 (D.D.C. 1992) (holding that agency is not obligated to retrieve law enforcement records transferred for use in criminal prosecutions to Commonwealth of Virginia).

[76] See Kissinger v. Reporters Comm. for Freedom of the Press, 445 U.S. 136, 150-55 (1980); cf. Spannaus v. United States Dep't of Justice, 942 F. Supp. 656, 658 (D.D.C. 1996) (finding that "personal files" of attorney no longer employed with agency were "beyond the reach of FOIA" if they were not turned over to agency at end of employment).

[77] See, e.g., Jones v. FBI, 41 F.3d 238, 249 (6th Cir. 1994); see also Laughlin v. Commissioner, No. 99-1258-K, 1999 U.S. Dist. LEXIS 16638, at *13 (S.D. Cal. Sept. 28, 1999) (refusing to order agency to recreate properly discarded document); Jones, 32 F. Supp. 2d at 875-76 (finding that agency did not improperly withhold requested report that was discarded in accordance with agency policies and practices); Rothschild v. Department of Energy, 6 F. Supp. 2d 38, 40 (D.D.C. 1998) (agreeing that because agency "is under no duty to disclose documents not in its possession," agency did not violate the FOIA by failing to provide discarded drafts of responsive documents); Green v. NARA, 992 F. Supp. 811, 817 (E.D. Va. 1998) (finding that agency met its FOIA obligation when it provided reasonable access to records sought by plaintiff prior to disposal of records under Records Disposal Act and noting that "FOIA . . . does not obligate agencies to retain all records [in its possession], nor does it establish specified procedures designed to guide disposal determinations"); cf. Folstad v. Board of Governors of the Fed. Reserve Sys., No. 1:99-124, 1999 U.S. Dist. LEXIS 17852, at *5 (W.D. Mich. Nov. 16, 1999) (recognizing that "[e]ven if the agency failed to keep documents that it should have kept, that failure would create neither responsibility under the FOIA to reconstruct those documents nor liability for the lapse") (appeal pending); FOIA Update, Vol. XVIII, No. 1, at 5-6 (advising that FOIA does not govern agency records-disposition practices). But cf. Valencia-Lucena v. United States Coast Guard, 180 F.3d 321, 328 (D.C. Cir. 1999) (rejecting agency's claim that it failed to locate requested records because they were type routinely destroyed and declaring that "generalized claims of destruction or non-preservation cannot sustain sum-
(continued...)

## PROCEDURAL REQUIREMENTS

ties.[78] Requesters also cannot use the FOIA as an "enforcement mechanism" to compel agencies to perform their missions.[79] Nor may requesters compel agencies to make automatic releases of records as they are created,[80] which means that requests cannot properly be made for "future" records not yet cre-

---

[77](...continued)
ment").

[78] See Folstad, 1999 U.S. Dist. LEXIS 17852, at *8 (finding that if agency "is no longer in possession of the documents, nothing in the FOIA requires the agency to obtain those documents from the private [banking] institution"); Rush Franklin Publ'g, Inc. v. NASA, No. 90-CV-2855, slip op. at 9-10 (E.D.N.Y. Apr. 13, 1993) (mailing list generated and held by federal contractor); Conservation Law Found. v. Department of the Air Force, No. 85-4377, 1986 U.S. Dist. LEXIS 24515, at *10 (D. Mass. June 6, 1986) (computer program generated and held by federal contractor); cf. United States v. Napper, 887 F.2d 1528, 1530 (11th Cir. 1989) (stating that FBI was entitled to return of documents loaned to city law enforcement officials, notwithstanding fact that copies of some documents had been disclosed) (non-FOIA case). But see Chicago Tribune Co. v. HHS, No. 95 C 3917, 1999 WL 299875, at *3 (N.D. Ill. May 4, 1999) (ordering nonparty government contractor to disclose audit data because "the government whole-handedly controls and blatantly influences [contractor's] action with respect to disclosure of the documents"), emergency stay denied, No. 99-2162 (7th Cir. June 9, 1999); Cal-Almond, Inc. v. USDA, No. 89-574, slip op. at 3-4 (E.D. Cal. Mar. 17, 1993) (ordering agency to reacquire records that mistakenly were returned to submitter upon closing of administrative appeal), appeal dismissed per stipulation, No. 93-16727 (9th Cir. Oct. 26, 1994); see also FOIA Update, Vol. XIX, No. 4, at 2 (discussing private grantee records made subject to FOIA under OMB Circular A-110, "Uniform Administrative Requirements for Grants and Agreements with Institutions of Higher Education, Hospitals, and Other Non-Profit Organizations," 64 Fed. Reg. 54,926 (1999)).

[79] See, e.g., Niagara Mohawk Power Corp. v. United States Dep't of Energy, No. 95-0952, transcript at 10 (D.D.C. Feb. 23, 1996) (bench order) (admonishing that FOIA is not to be used to force agency to obtain information from another agency), vacated & remanded on other grounds, 169 F.3d 16 (D.C. Cir. 1999); Gillin, No. 92-325, slip op. at 5 (D.N.H. May 28, 1993) (The "[r]equest focused primarily upon the decisions made by the [agency] in granting [the administrative permit], rather than the documentation upon which the [agency] relied."). But cf. National Ass'n of Criminal Defense Lawyers v. United States Dep't of Justice, slip op. at 8-10 (D.D.C. June 26, 1998) (concluding that plaintiff's FOIA suit caused agency to issue revised criminal prosecution policy and awarding interim attorney fees partly on such basis), interlocutory appeal dismissed for lack of juris., 182 F.3d 981 (D.C. Cir. 1999).

[80] See Mandel Grunfeld & Herrick v. United States Customs Serv., 709 F.2d 41, 43 (11th Cir. 1983) (determining that plaintiff not entitled to automatic mailing of materials as they are updated); Howard v. Secretary of the Air Force, No. SA-89-CA-1008, slip op. at 6 (W.D. Tex. Oct. 2, 1991) (concluding that plaintiff's request for records on continuing basis would "create an enormous burden, both in time and taxpayers' money"); see also FOIA Update, Vol. VI, No. 2, at 6.

## PROCEDURAL REQUIREMENTS

ated.[81]

In addition to reasonably describing the records sought, a FOIA requester must follow an agency's regulations in making a request.[82] Each federal agency must publish in the Federal Register its procedural regulations governing access to its records under the FOIA.[83] These regulations must inform the public of where and how to address requests; its schedule of fees for search, review, and duplication; its fee waiver criteria; and its administrative appeal procedures.[84] The Electronic Freedom of Information Act Amendments of 1996[85] affected several procedural aspects of FOIA administration[86] (including matters concerning the timing of processing FOIA requests, which are dis-

---

[81] See, e.g., Tuchinsky v. Selective Serv. Sys., 418 F.2d 155, 158 (7th Cir. 1969) (ordering that no automatic release required of material relating to occupational deferments until request in hand; "otherwise, [agency] would be required to 'run . . . loose-leaf service' for every draft counselor in the country"); Tax Analysts v. IRS, No. 94-923, 1998 WL 419755, at *4 (D.D.C. May 1, 1998) (recognizing that court could not order relief concerning documents not yet created and "for which a request for release has not even been made and for which administrative remedies have not been exhausted"); Lybarger v. Cardwell, 438 F. Supp. 1075, 1077 (D. Mass. 1977) (holding that "open-ended procedure" advanced by requester whereby records automatically disclosed not required by FOIA and "will not be forced" upon agency); cf. FOIA Update, Vol. XVI, No. 1, at 1 (citing OMB Circular A-130, "Management of Federal Information Resources," 59 Fed. Reg. 37,905 (1994) (prescribing policies to encourage agencies to affirmatively disseminate government information independent of FOIA context)). But cf. National Ass'n of Criminal Defense Lawyers, No. 97-372, slip op. at 17 (D.D.C. June 26, 1998) (granting interim attorney fees based in part upon novel finding that plaintiff prevailed when, during litigation, agency released report which was not yet in existence at time of plaintiff's request).

[82] 5 U.S.C. § 552(a)(3)(A); see, e.g., Blackwell v. EEOC, No. 2:98-38, 1999 U.S. Dist. LEXIS 3708, at *5 (E.D.N.C. Feb. 12, 1999) (finding request not properly made because plaintiff failed to follow agency regulation requiring that request be denominated explicitly as request for information under FOIA).

[83] See id. § 552(a)(4)(A), (a)(6)(A), (a)(6)(D), (a)(6)(E); see also id. § 552(g) (requiring agencies to make available "reference material or a guide for requesting records or information from the agency"); FOIA Update, Vol. XIX, No. 3, at 3 (discussing availability of agency reference guides through agency FOIA sites on World Wide Web); FOIA Update, Vol. XVIII, No. 2, at 1 (discussing electronic availability of Justice Department's FOIA Reference Guide).

[84] See, e.g., Department of Justice FOIA Regulations, 28 C.F.R. pt. 16 (1999).

[85] Pub. L. No. 104-231, 110 Stat. 3048 (codified as amended at 5 U.S.C. § 552 (1994 & Supp. IV 1998)).

[86] See FOIA Update, Vol. XIX, No. 1, at 3-5 ("OIP Guidance: Electronic FOIA Amendments Implementation Guidance Outline").

## PROCEDURAL REQUIREMENTS

cussed below).[87] Each federal agency is required to have published implementing regulations in the Federal Register that address these matters as well.[88]

Although an agency may occasionally waive some of its published procedures for reasons of public interest, speed, or simplicity, all agencies should remember that any "unnecessary bureaucratic hurdle has no place in [the Act's] implementation";[89] therefore, an agency may not impose any additional requirements on a requester beyond those prescribed in its regulations.[90] Of course, agencies should adhere strictly to their own regulations, especially when doing so would benefit the FOIA requester.[91] Conversely, a requester's failure to comply with an agency's procedural regulations governing access to records--such as those concerning properly addressed requests,[92] fees and fee

---

[87] See FOIA Update, Vol. XVII, No. 4, at 1-2, 10-11 (discussing statutory changes).

[88] 5 U.S.C. § 552(a)(6)(D), (a)(6)(E); see, e.g., 28 C.F.R. pt. 16 (1999); see also FOIA Update, Vol. XIX, No. 3, at 4 (discussing availability of agency regulations--including proposed implementing regulations--through agency FOIA Web sites); FOIA Update, Vol. XIX, No. 1, at 5 (advising agencies to be sure to apply all effective statutory provisions favoring requesters even if implementing regulations were delayed).

[89] President Clinton's FOIA Memorandum, reprinted in FOIA Update, Vol. XIV, No. 3, at 3; see, e.g., FOIA Update, Vol. XV, No. 3, at 6 (cautioning against practices that would cause unwarranted disadvantages to requesters in record-referral processes); see also Attorney General Reno's Follow-Up FOIA Memorandum, reprinted in FOIA Update, Vol. XIX, No. 4, at 3 (reiterating Attorney General's commitment to "principles of government openness" underlying FOIA).

[90] See Zemansky, 767 F.2d at 574; see also FOIA Update, Vol. X, No. 3, at 5 (addressing submission of FOIA requests by "fax" in relation to agency regulation); cf. FOIA Update, Vol. XIX, No. 1, at 6 (encouraging agencies to consider as matter of administrative discretion establishing capability to receive FOIA requests via Internet).

[91] See, e.g., Ruotolo, 53 F.3d at 10 (charging that agency failed to comply with its own regulation requiring it to assist requesters in reformulating requests determined not to reasonably describe records sought); Public Citizen v. FDA, No. 94-0018, slip op. at 2 (D.D.C. Feb. 9, 1996) (criticizing agency for asserting that request did not reasonably describe "records which could be located in the FDA's record keeping system without an unduly burdensome search" and ignoring plaintiff's concession to limit scope of request, court concluded that agency violated its own regulatory requirement to seek more specific information and to narrow scope of request); cf. FOIA Update, Vol. XIX, No. 1, at 5 (advising agencies to implement statutory provisions of Electronic FOIA amendments "without any disadvantage to FOIA requesters," regardless of status of implementing regulations).

[92] Stanley v. DOD, No. 93-4247, slip op. at 10 (S.D. Ill. July 28, 1998) (holding request not properly received when agency returned--unopened--improperly addressed request); Smith, 1996 U.S. Dist. LEXIS 5594, at *9 (N.D. Cal.
(continued...)

**PROCEDURAL REQUIREMENTS**

waivers,[93] proof of identity,[94] and administrative appeals[95]--may be held to

---

[92](...continued)
Apr. 23, 1996) (stating that "National Records Administration is not a HUD information center," and holding that plaintiff failed to exhaust administrative remedies by directing FOIA request to wrong agency); Sands v. United States, No. 94-0537, 1995 U.S. Dist. LEXIS 9252, at **10-12 (S.D. Fla. June 16, 1995) (noting clarity of agency's rules and reasonableness of agency's treatment of misdirected request, court found that plaintiff failed to exhaust administrative remedies by not directing request to appropriate office); United States v. Agunbiade, No. 90-CR-610, 1995 WL 351058, at *6 (E.D.N.Y. May 10, 1995) (ruling that plaintiff who did not direct request to "appropriate parties and agencies" in accordance with agency-specific rules failed to exhaust administrative remedies), aff'd sub nom. United States v. Osinowo, 100 F.3d 942 (2d Cir. 1996) (unpublished table decision). But see Coolman v. IRS, No. 98-6149, 1999 WL 675319, at *4 (W.D. Mo. July 12, 1999) (finding administrative remedies exhausted because "it cannot be said . . . that plaintiff's failure to use the address provided in [agency's] regulations prevented his request from arriving at the correct destination"), summary affirmance granted, 1999 WL 1419039 (8th Cir. Dec. 6, 1999); Raulerson v. Reno, No. 96-120, slip op. at 5 (D.D.C. Feb. 26, 1999) (finding search inadequate--notwithstanding agency regulations requiring that requests be addressed to individual offices maintaining records sought--because all offices likely to contain responsive records were not searched), summary affirmance granted, No. 99-5300 (D.C. Cir. Nov. 23, 1999), cert. denied, 68 U.S.L.W. 3685 (U.S. May 1, 2000) (No. 99-8595).

[93] See Pollack v. Department of Justice, 49 F.3d 115, 119 (4th Cir. 1995) (plaintiff's refusal to pay anticipated fees constitutes failure to exhaust administrative remedies); Grecco v. Department of Justice, No. 97-0419, slip op. at 5 (D.D.C. Apr. 1, 1999) (recognizing that requester's failure to pay fees or ask for fee waiver constitutes failure to exhaust administrative remedies) (motion for reconsideration pending); Smith v. IRS, No. 2:94-989, 1999 WL 357935, at *1 (D. Utah Mar. 24, 1999) (finding that plaintiff "failed to exhaust his administrative remedies in that he failed to pay the fees and costs in order to process his claims"); Patterson v. United States Dep't of Justice, No. 96-0095, slip op. at 1 (D.D.C. Mar. 23, 1999) (dismissing case because plaintiff failed to exhaust administrative remedies by not paying duplication fees); Stanley, No. 93-4247, slip op. at 9 (S.D. Ill. July 28, 1998) (finding request not properly received also because requester failed to follow agency regulations requiring agreement to pay fees).

[94] See Schwarz v. FBI, 31 F. Supp. 2d 540, 542 (N.D. W. Va. 1998) (recognizing that first-party requester's failure to follow agency regulations requiring her to submit fingerprints for positive identification constituted failure to exhaust administrative remedies), aff'd, 166 F.3d 334 (4th Cir. 1998) (unpublished table decision); cf. Martin v. United States Dep't of Justice, No. 96-2866, slip op. at 7-8 (D.D.C. Dec. 16, 1999) (ruling that requester who seeks law enforcement information about living third party and fails to provide subject's written authorization permitting disclosure of records has not failed to exhaust administrative remedies because agency regulations stated only that such authorization "will help the processing of [the] request") (motion for reconsideration pending). But cf. Pusa v. FBI, No. 99-04603, slip op. at 5 (C.D.
(continued...)

-46-

## PROCEDURAL REQUIREMENTS

constitute a failure to properly exhaust administrative remedies. (For a further discussion of exhaustion of administrative remedies, see Litigation Considerations, Exhaustion of Administrative Remedies, below.)

### Time Limits

Until an agency (or the proper component of that agency) receives a FOIA request, it is not obligated to search for responsive records, meet time deadlines, or release any records.[96] Requests not filed in accordance with pub-

---

[94](...continued)
Cal. Aug. 3, 1999) (holding that plaintiff who failed to submit third party's privacy waiver "has failed to exhaust administrative remedies under the FOIA by failing to comply with the agency's published procedures for obtaining third-party information").

[95] See, e.g., Lumarse v. HHS, No. 98-55880, 1999 WL 644355, at *5 (9th Cir. Aug. 24, 1999) (affirming dismissal of plaintiff's FOIA claim for failure to exhaust administrative remedies because plaintiff "does not allege that it [administratively] appealed the denials of its FOIA requests"); Teplitsky v. Department of Justice, No. 96-36208, 1997 WL 665705, at *1 (9th Cir. Oct. 24, 1997) (holding plaintiff had not exhausted administrative remedies when he did not administratively appeal denial of FOIA request even though agency notified him of procedure); RNR Enters. v. SEC, 122 F.3d 93, 98 (2d Cir. 1997) (ruling plaintiff had not exhausted his administrative remedies when he failed to appeal agency denial even though he was advised of his right to appeal and denial was issued during requisite time period); Comer v. IRS, No. 97-76329, 1999 U.S. Dist. LEXIS 16268, at *11 (E.D. Mich. Sept. 30, 1999) (finding that although plaintiff previously appealed agency's failure to promptly respond to his request, "[u]pon receiving the documents and the bill, and prior to filing suit, plaintiff was [again] obliged to administratively appeal whatever dissatisfactions he may have had with that result"); Patterson, No. 96-0095, slip op. at 1 (D.D.C. Mar. 23, 1999) (dismissing case because plaintiff failed to exhaust administrative remedies by not administratively appealing denial of fee waiver request); Blackwell v. EEOC, No. 2:98-38, 1999 U.S. Dist. LEXIS 3708, at *6 (E.D.N.C. Feb. 12, 1999) (stating that "the exhaustion of administrative remedies does not occur until the completion of an administrative appeal, unless the agency fails to comply [with] the applicable time limitations"); Thomas v. Office of United States Attorney, 171 F.R.D. 53, 54 (E.D.N.Y. 1997) (ruling that administrative remedies were not exhausted when plaintiff made further request for documents in appeal of agency's denial of plaintiff's initial request).

[96] See Brumley v. United States Dep't of Labor, 767 F.2d 444, 445 (8th Cir. 1985) (determining that agency complied with "FOIA's response time provisions" after advising plaintiff that routing of his request to appropriate office within agency would result in short delay "before the ten working day response period would begin running"); Blackwell v. EEOC, No. 2:98-38, 1999 U.S. Dist. LEXIS 3708, at *6 (E.D.N.C. Feb. 12, 1999) ("The time period for responding to a FOIA request . . . does not begin to run until the request is received by the appropriate office and officer in the agency, as set forth in the agency's published regulations."); see also Judicial Watch, Inc. v. United States Dep't of Justice, No. 97-2089, slip op. at 10-11 (D.D.C. July 14, 1998) (finding that the
(continued...)

## PROCEDURAL REQUIREMENTS

lished regulations are not deemed to have been received until they are identified as proper FOIA requests by agency personnel.[97] For example, under Department of Justice regulations,[98] a request is not considered received until the requester has promised to pay fees (above a minimum amount) or the receiving component has decided to waive all fees.[99] Moreover, if a requester agrees to pay properly assessed search, review, and/or duplication fees but later fails to pay those fees, an agency may refuse to process that requester's subsequent requests until the amount owed is paid.[100] (For a discussion of the assessment of fees, see Fees and Fee Waivers, below.)

Once an agency properly receives a FOIA request, it has twenty working days in which make a determination on the request.[101] Previously, once an agency was in receipt of a proper FOIA request, it was required to inform the requester of its decision to grant or deny access to the requested records within ten working days. The Electronic Freedom of Information Act Amendments of 1996 increased the Act's basic time limit for agency responses, lengthening it from ten to twenty working days.[102] Agencies are not necessarily required to release the records within the statutory time limit, but access to releasable rec-

---

[96] (...continued)
court was without jurisdiction when plaintiff filed complaint prior to lapse of statutory time limit); cf. Soghomonian v. United States, 82 F. Supp. 2d 1134, 1138 (E.D. Cal. 1999) (holding that 20-day time period for responding to administrative appeal begins when agency receives appeal, not when requester mails it).

[97] See, e.g., Lykins v. United States Dep't of Justice, 3 Gov't Disclosure Serv. (P-H) ¶ 83,092, at 83,637 (D.D.C. Feb. 28, 1983).

[98] 28 C.F.R. § 16.11(e) (1999).

[99] See Irons v. FBI, 571 F. Supp. 1241, 1243 (D. Mass. 1983), rev'd on other grounds, 811 F.2d 681 (1987); see also Pollack v. Department of Justice, 49 F.3d 115, 120 (4th Cir. 1995); cf. Oglesby v. United States Dep't of the Army, 920 F.2d 57, 66 (D.C. Cir. 1990); Loomis v. Department of Energy, No. 96-149, slip op. at 9-10 (N.D.N.Y. Mar. 9, 1999) (finding plaintiff's request properly received when he agreed to pay estimated fee that agency later revised upward), aff'd, 199 F.3d 1322 (2d Cir. 1999) (unpublished table decision).

[100] See Trenerry v. IRS, No. 95-5150, 1996 WL 88459, at *2 (10th Cir. Mar. 1, 1996); Atkin v. EEOC, No. 92-3275, slip op. at 5 (D.N.J. June 24, 1993); Crooker v. United States Secret Serv., 577 F. Supp. 1218, 1219-20 (D.D.C. 1983); FOIA Update, Vol. VII, No. 2, at 2; see also 5 U.S.C. § 552(a)(4)(A)(v).

[101] 5 U.S.C. § 552(a)(6)(A)(i) (1994 & Supp. IV 1998); see FOIA Update, Vol. XVII, No. 4, at 2, 10 (discussing Electronic FOIA amendments' modifications to FOIA's time-limit provisions); FOIA Update, Vol. XII, No. 3, at 5 (advising that merely acknowledging request within statutory time period is simply insufficient); cf. Judicial Watch, 880 F. Supp. at 10 (rejecting requester's claim that response in less than ten working days is evidence of "bad faith").

[102] Pub. L. No. 104-231, § 8(b), 110 Stat. 3048, 3052 (codified as amended at 5 U.S.C. § 552(a)(6)(A)(i) (1994 & Supp. IV 1998)).

## PROCEDURAL REQUIREMENTS

ords should, at a minimum, be granted promptly thereafter.[103]

In "unusual circumstances," an agency can extend the twenty-day time limit for processing a FOIA request if it tells the requester in writing why it needs the extension and when it will make a determination on the request.[104] The FOIA defines "unusual circumstances" as (1) the need to search for and collect records from separate offices; (2) the need to examine a voluminous amount of records required by the request; and (3) the need to consult with another agency or agency component.[105] If the required extension exceeds ten days, the agency must allow the requester an opportunity to modify his or her request, or to arrange for an alternative time frame for completion of the agency's processing.[106]

In many instances, though, agencies cannot meet these time limits for a variety of reasons, including the limitations on their resources.[107] Agencies therefore have adopted the court-sanctioned practice of generally handling backlogged FOIA requests on a "first-in, first-out" basis.[108] The Electronic FOIA amendments expressly authorized agencies to promulgate regulations providing for "multitrack processing" of their FOIA requests--which allows agencies to process requests on a first-in, first-out basis within each track, but also permits them to respond to relatively simple requests more quickly than

---

[103] See 5 U.S.C. § 552(a)(6)(C); see also Larson v. IRS, No. 85-3076, slip op. at 2-3 (D.D.C. Dec. 11, 1985) (finding that the FOIA "does not require that the person requesting records be informed of the agency's decision within ten days, it only demands that the government make [and mail] its decision within that time."). But see Manos v. United States Dep't of the Air Force, No. C-92-3986, 1993 U.S. Dist. LEXIS 1501, at **14-15 (N.D. Cal. Feb. 10, 1993) (holding, in exceptional decision, that mailing response within 10-day period not sufficient and that requester must actually receive response within 10-day period).

[104] 5 U.S.C. § 552(a)(6)(B)(i).

[105] Id. § 552(a)(6)(B)(iii).

[106] Id. § 552(a)(6)(B)(ii); see, e.g., 28 C.F.R. § 16.5(c) (1999) (Department of Justice FOIA regulation).

[107] See, e.g., Zuckerman v. FBI, No. 94-6315, slip op. at 8 (D.N.J. Dec. 6, 1995) (noting effects of resource limitations on complying with statutory time limits); see also FOIA Update, Vol. XV, No. 2, at 2; FOIA Update, Vol. XIV, No. 3, at 5, 8-9; FOIA Update, Vol. XIII, No. 2, at 8-10; FOIA Update, Vol. XI, No. 1, at 1-2; cf. FOIA Update, Vol. XVI, No. 1, at 1-2 (promoting practice of making agency records "affirmatively" available to public, rather than providing them only in response to particular FOIA requests, in order to benefit overall process of FOIA administration).

[108] See Open Am. v. Watergate Special Prosecution Force, 547 F.2d 605, 614-16 (D.C. Cir. 1976) (citing 5 U.S.C. § 552(a)(6)(C)); cf. Summers v. CIA, No. 98-1682, slip op. at 4 (D.D.C. July 26, 1999) (recognizing that agency need not adhere strictly to "first-in, first-out process[ing]" so long as "it is proceeding in a manner designed to be fair and expeditious").

## PROCEDURAL REQUIREMENTS

requests involving complex and/or voluminous records.[109]

A FOIA request may receive "expedited" treatment and be processed out of sequence if the requester can show an "exceptional need or urgency."[110] Courts have granted expedited access when exceptional circumstances surrounding a request, such as jeopardy to life or personal safety,[111] or a threatened loss of substantial due process rights,[112] warrant such treatment.

---

[109] Pub. L. No. 104-231, § 7(a), 110 Stat. 3048, 3050 (codified as amended at 5 U.S.C. § 552(a)(6)(D) (1994 & Supp. IV 1998)); see, e.g., FOIA Update, Vol. XVIII, No. 1, at 6 (discussing multitrack processing for agencies with decentralized FOIA operations); FOIA Update, Vol. XVII, No. 4, at 10 (discussing implementing regulations); see, e.g., 28 C.F.R. § 16.5(b) (Department of Justice implementing regulation); cf. FOIA Update, Vol. XVIII, No. 3, at 3-7 (advising agencies regarding reporting of multitrack-processing information in annual FOIA reports, beginning with annual report for Fiscal Year 1998).

[110] Open Am., 547 F.2d at 616 (D.C. Cir. 1976) (citing 5 U.S.C. § 552(a)(6)(C) (1976)); see also Whitehurst v. FBI, No. 96-572, slip op. at 5 (D.D.C. Feb. 5, 1997) (finding that expedited process is warranted where plaintiff's allegations regarding FBI crime laboratory potentially impact upon other criminal matters, where more than three years have elapsed, and where the agency has failed to release numerous documents it has already received and cleared for release to others); Schweihs v. FBI, 933 F. Supp. 719, 723 (N.D. Ill. 1996) (finding "no legal precedent or statutory or regulatory authority for prioritizing FOIA applicants by age or health status"); Gilmore v. FBI, No. 93-2117, slip op. at 3 (N.D. Cal. July 27, 1994) (ordering that request for information concerning government's key encryption and digital telephony initiative be expedited because material sought will "become less valuable if the FBI processes . . . on a first in-first out basis"); FOIA Update, Vol. IV, No. 3, at 3 ("OIP Guidance: When to Expedite FOIA Requests"); see also FOIA Update, Vol. XII, No. 3, at 5 (emphasizing need to promptly determine whether to expedite processing of request); cf. Fox v. United States Dep't of Justice, No. 94-4622, 1994 WL 923072, at *3 (C.D. Cal. Dec. 16, 1994) (ruling that agency is not required to disrupt its administrative routine unless requester has shown strong justification for obtaining documents in expedited manner), appeal dismissed, No. 94-56788 (9th Cir. Feb. 21, 1995).

[111] See, e.g., Exner v. FBI, 443 F. Supp. 1349, 1353 (S.D. Cal. 1978) (holding that plaintiff entitled to expedited access after leak of information exposed her to harm from organized crime figures), aff'd, 612 F.2d 1202 (9th Cir. 1980); Cleaver v. Kelley, 427 F. Supp. 80, 81 (D.D.C. 1976) (determining that exceptional circumstances existed when plaintiff faced multiple criminal charges carrying possible death penalty in state court).

[112] See, e.g., Neely v. FBI, No. 7:97-0786, slip op. at 9 (W.D. Va. July 27, 1998) (granting expedited processing of FOIA request for plaintiff with pending motion for new criminal trial when plaintiff had made specific allegations related to agency documents); Ferguson v. FBI, 722 F. Supp. 1137, 1141-43 (S.D.N.Y. 1989) (noting that "due process interest must be substantial" and holding that plaintiff's request for information regarding his particular postconviction proceeding required expedition); cf. Fiduccia v. United States
(continued...)

## PROCEDURAL REQUIREMENTS

Furthermore, the Electronic FOIA amendments require agencies to promulgate regulations providing for expedited processing of requests if the requester demonstrates a "compelling need" (as defined by the amended statute), or in any other case the agency deems appropriate under its regulations.[113] Under the amended statute, a requester can show "compelling need" in one of two ways: by establishing that his or her failure to obtain the records quickly "could reasonably be expected to pose an imminent threat to the life or physical safety of an individual;" or, if the requester is a "person primarily engaged in disseminating information," by demonstrating that an "urgency to inform the public concerning actual or alleged Federal Government activity"[114] exists. At their discretion, agencies may grant expedited treatment under additional circumstances as well.[115] Agencies must determine whether to grant a request for expedited access within ten calendar days of its receipt by the proper FOIA office.[116] (For a further discussion of expedited access, see Litigation Considerations, "Open America" Stays of Proceedings, below.)

---

[112](...continued)
Dep't of Justice, 185 F.3d 1035, 1041 (9th Cir. 1999) (rejecting argument that "requesters who sue agencies under the FOIA should have their requests handled before requesters who do not file lawsuits"); Raulerson v. Reno, 95-cv-2053, slip op. at 4-6 (D.D.C. Mar. 30, 1998) (denying FBI's motion to stay proceedings for nearly three years when plaintiff had asserted he had only two years to appeal criminal conviction and requested documents may aid in preparation of appeal), plaintiff's appeal dismissed, No. 98-5112 (D.C. Cir. May 5, 1998); Edmond v. United States Attorney, 959 F. Supp. 1, 6 (D.D.C. 1997) ("In the absence of some other urgency, Plaintiff cannot meet his burden by merely making a naked assertion that the Government is withholding Brady material in order to accelerate his FOIA processing.").

[113] Pub. L. No. 104-231, § 8(a), 110 Stat. 3048, 3051-52 (codified as amended at 5 U.S.C. § 552(a)(6)(E) (1994 & Supp. IV 1998)); see also FOIA Update, Vol. XIX, No. 1, at 5 (discussing significance of implementing regulations); FOIA Update, Vol. XVII, No. 4, at 10 (discussing new statutory provision).

[114] 5 U.S.C. § 552(a)(6)(E)(v); see, e.g., 28 C.F.R. § 16.5(d)(ii) (Department of Justice implementing regulation); see also FOIA Update, Vol. XIX, No. 4, at 2 (discussing Nazi War Crimes Disclosure Act, 5 U.S.C.A. § 552 note (West Supp. 1999), which does not directly amend the FOIA, but which does "impact[] directly on the FOIA [in that it provides] that any person who was persecuted by the Nazi government of Germany or its allies 'shall be deemed to have a compelling need' under 'section 552(a)(6)(E) of title 5, United States Code'" in making requests for access to classified Nazi war-criminal records (quoting 5 U.S.C.A. § 552 note, § 4)).

[115] See FOIA Update, Vol. XV, No. 2, at 2 (discussing establishment of Department of Justice policy of expediting requests that involve both widespread media interest and possible questions about government's integrity which affect public confidence); see also 28 C.F.R. § 16.5(d)(iv) (Department of Justice regulation codifying discretionary expedited-access policy).

[116] 5 U.S.C. § 552(a)(6)(C)(i); see, e.g., 28 C.F.R. § 16.5(d)(ii)(4) (Department of Justice implementing regulation).

**PROCEDURAL REQUIREMENTS**

An agency's failure to comply with the time limits for either an initial request or an administrative appeal may be treated as a "constructive exhaustion" of administrative remedies. A requester may immediately thereafter seek judicial review if he or she wishes to do so.[117] However, the D.C. Circuit has interpreted this rule of constructive exhaustion by requiring that once the agency responds to the FOIA request--after the statutory time limit but before the requester has filed suit--the requester must administratively appeal the denial before proceeding to court.[118] (For a discussion of this aspect of FOIA litigation, see Litigation Considerations, Exhaustion of Administrative Reme-

---

[117] See 5 U.S.C. § 552(a)(6)(C); see, e.g., Spannaus v. United States Dep't of Justice, 824 F.2d 52, 58 (D.C. Cir. 1987); Perdue Farms v. NLRB, 927 F. Supp. 897, 904 (E.D.N.C. 1996), vacated on other grounds, 108 F.3d 519 (4th Cir. 1997); see also McCall v. United States Marshals Serv., 36 F. Supp. 2d 3, 5 (D.D.C. 1999) (finding that plaintiff constructively exhausted his administrative remedies when court "provisionally filed" his FOIA complaint and application to proceed in forma pauperis before agency responded to his request, even though agency responded before court granted plaintiff's motion to proceed in forma pauperis); Information Acquisition Corp. v. Department of Justice, 444 F. Supp. 458, 462 (D.D.C. 1978) (concluding that administrative remedies were exhausted when agency failed to respond to request within statutory time limit); FOIA Update, Vol. IV, No. 1, at 6 (superseded in part). But see Pollack, 49 F.3d at 119 (holding that constructive exhaustion provision does not relieve requester of statutory obligation to pay fees which agency is authorized to collect); Teplitsky v. Department of Justice, No. 96-36208, 1997 WL 665705, at *1 (9th Cir. Oct. 24, 1997) (holding that plaintiff had not exhausted administrative remedies when he did not appeal denial of FOIA request even though agency notified him of procedure); RNR Enters. v. SEC, 122 F.3d 93, 98 (2d Cir. 1997) (ruling that plaintiff had not exhausted his administrative remedies when he failed to appeal agency denial even though he was advised of his right to appeal and denial was issued during requisite time period).

[118] See Oglesby, 920 F.2d at 61-65; accord Ruotolo v. Department of Justice, 53 F.3d 4, 9 (2d Cir. 1995) (finding administrative remedies exhausted when agency did not include notification of right to appeal its determination that request not reasonably described); Taylor v. Appleton, 30 F.3d 1365, 1370 (11th Cir. 1994) (stating that once party has waited for response from agency, actual exhaustion must occur before court has jurisdiction to review challenges); McDonnell v. United States, 4 F.3d 1227, 1240 (3d Cir. 1993) (upholding dismissal of claim as proper when plaintiff filed suit before filing appeal of denial received after exhaustion of statutory response period); see also Bryce v. Overseas Private Inv. Corp., No. A-96-595, slip op. at 12 (W.D. Tex. Sept. 28, 1998) (recognizing that although agency's failure to respond within statutory time limit constitutes constructive exhaustion, "if the agency responds with a determination prior to the requester filing suit, then the requirement to exhaust administrative review is revived"), appeal voluntarily dismissed, No. 99-50893 (5th Cir. Oct. 11, 1999); FOIA Update, Vol. XII, No. 2, at 3-4 ("OIP Guidance: Procedural Rules Under the D.C. Circuit's Oglesby Decision"). But see Mieras v. United States Forest Serv., No. 93-CV-74552, slip op. at 3 (E.D. Mich. Feb. 14, 1995) (misapplying D.C. Circuit rules on constructive exhaustion in declaring that plaintiff had not exhausted administrative remedies as he failed to file administrative appeal after agency response, even though he initiated lawsuit before agency response was made).

## PROCEDURAL REQUIREMENTS

dies, below.)

Under the law existing prior to the enactment of the Electronic FOIA amendments, an agency sued for not responding to a FOIA request could receive additional time to process that request if it could show that its failure to meet the statutory time limits resulted from "exceptional circumstances" and that it was applying "due diligence" in processing the request.[119] Previously, the need to process an extremely large volume of requests constituted "exceptional circumstances," and the commitment of large amounts of resources to process requests on a first-come, first-served basis was considered "due diligence."[120] The Electronic FOIA amendments, however, explicitly exclude "a predictable agency workload" of FOIA requests as "exceptional circumstances . . . unless the agency demonstrates reasonable progress in reducing its backlog of pending requests."[121] Nevertheless, a requester's refusal "to reasonably

---

[119] See 5 U.S.C. § 552(a)(6)(C) (1994); see also FOIA Update, Vol. IX, No. 4, at 5.

[120] See Open Am., 547 F.2d at 615-16; see also Gilmore v. NSA, No. 94-16165, 1995 WL 792079, at *1 (9th Cir. Dec. 11, 1995) (noting that even after agency's recent internal review of its FOIA operations to identify and correct deficiencies resulted in staff increase and implementation of "first-in/first-out" procedure, court determined it "unlikely that [agency] could process requests more quickly given that it must undertake a painstaking review of voluminous sensitive documents before disclosing requested information"); Jimenez v. FBI, 938 F. Supp. 21, 31 (D.D.C. 1996) ("In view of [the agency's] two-track system and the large volume of documents expected to be responsive to plaintiff's request, the Court finds that [the agency] has met the due diligence requirements for a stay."); Gilmore v. United States Dep't of State, No. 95-1098, slip op. at 27 (N.D. Cal. Feb. 9, 1996) (finding that in addition to other factors, "the recent and prolonged government shutdown provides a sufficient showing of exceptional circumstances"). See generally Attorney General's Memorandum for Heads of Departments and Agencies regarding the Freedom of Information Act (Oct. 4, 1993), reprinted in FOIA Update, Vol. XIV, No. 3, at 4-5 (recognizing that growing backlogs of agencies "dealing with high-volume demands for particularly sensitive records . . . appears to be a problem of too few resources in the face of too heavy a workload"); FOIA Update, Vol. XIV, No. 3, at 8-9 (discussing possible solutions to backlog problem); FOIA Update, Vol. XII, No. 2, at 8-10 (discussing agency difficulties with FOIA time limits and administrative backlogs); FOIA Update, Vol. XI, No. 1, at 1-2 (discussing effects of budgetary constraints upon agency FOIA operations). But see Matlack, Inc. v. EPA, 868 F. Supp. 627, 633 (D. Del. 1994) (deciding that agency's response that it has a "'large docket of Freedom of Information Act appeals and [is] working as quickly as possible to resolve them,' without more, is simply insufficient to demonstrate 'exceptional circumstances'").

[121] Pub. L. No. 104-231, § 7(c), 110 Stat. 3048, 3051 (codified as amended at 5 U.S.C. § 552(a)(6)(C)(ii) (1994 & Supp. IV 1998)); see, e.g., Fiduccia, 185 F.3d at 1042 (finding no exceptional circumstances when only "a slight upward creep in the caseload" caused backlog that agency claimed resulted from employee cutbacks and rejection of its budget requests); Emerson v. CIA, No. 99-0274, 1999 U.S. Dist. LEXIS 19511, at *3 (D.D.C. Dec. 16, 1999) (finding that

(continued...)

## PROCEDURAL REQUIREMENTS

modify the scope of a request or arrange for an alternative time frame for processing the request," may be used as evidence of "exceptional circumstances."[122] (For a discussion of the litigation aspects of the Act's "exceptional circumstances" provision, see Litigation Considerations, "Open America" Stays of Proceedings, below.)

### Searching for Records

The adequacy of an agency's search under the FOIA is determined by a test of "reasonableness," which may vary from case to case.[123] As a general rule, an agency must undertake a search that is "reasonably calculated to uncover all relevant documents."[124] The reasonableness of an agency's search de-

---

[121](...continued) agency was exercising due diligence in reducing backlog through use of new FOIA task force, new databases, and new document-scanning mechanisms); Judicial Watch of Florida, Inc. v. United States Dep't of Justice, No. 97-cv-2869, slip op. at 6 (D.D.C. Aug. 25, 1998) (granting stay of proceedings until year 2001 as FBI is processing FOIA requests on a "first-in/first out" basis, has hired additional employees to handle requests, and has reduced its backlog by 25 percent); Narducci v. FBI, No. 98-0130, slip op. at 1 (D.D.C. July 17, 1998) (observing that agency is "deluged with a volume of requests for information vastly in excess of that anticipated by Congress" and noting agency's "reasonable progress in reducing its backlog" of pending requests, court granted agency request to stay proceedings for 34 months); see also FOIA Update, Vol. XVIII, No. 3, at 3-7 (advising agencies regarding reporting of backlog-related information in annual FOIA reports, beginning with annual report for Fiscal Year 1998).

[122] 5 U.S.C. § 552(a)(6)(C)(iii); see also H.R. Rep. No. 104-795, at 24-25 (1996) (elaborating on circumstances).

[123] See Zemansky v. EPA, 767 F.2d 569, 571-73 (9th Cir. 1985) (observing that reasonableness of agency search depends upon facts of each case (citing Weisberg v. United States Dep't of Justice, 705 F.2d 1344, 1351 (D.C. Cir. 1983))).

[124] Weisberg, 705 F.2d at 1351; see, e.g., Mendoza v. Secretary of the Army, No. 98-5454, 1999 WL 515478, at *1 (D.C. Cir. June 23, 1999) (finding that "the government demonstrated that it had conducted a search reasonably calculated to uncover all relevant documents"); Schleeper v. Department of Justice, Nos. 98-5229, 98-5322, slip op. at 2 (D.C. Cir. Apr. 30, 1999) (granting government summary affirmance because agency affidavit established that "search was reasonably calculated to lead to the discovery of the documents sought"); Johnston v. United States Dep't of Justice, No. 97-2173, 1999 WL 518529, at *1 (8th Cir. Aug. 10, 1998) (concluding that agency demonstrated it conducted search reasonably calculated to uncover all responsive documents); Campbell v. United States Dep't of Justice, 164 F.3d 20, 27 (D.C. Cir. 1998) (noting that agency must search "'using methods which can be reasonably expected to produce the information requested'" (quoting Oglesby v. United States Dep't of the Army, 920 F.2d 57, 68 (D.C. Cir. 1990))); Miller v. United States Dep't of State, 779 F.2d 1378, 1383 (8th Cir. 1985) (recognizing that
(continued...)

-54-

## PROCEDURAL REQUIREMENTS

pends, in part, on how the agency conducted its search in light of the scope of the request[125] and the requester's description of the records sought.[126] The

---

[124](...continued)
search must be "'reasonably calculated to uncover all relevant documents'" (quoting Weisberg, 705 F.2d at 1351)).

[125] Voinche v. FBI, No. 96-5304, 1997 U.S. App. LEXIS 19089, at *3 (D.C. Cir. June 19, 1997) (ruling agency was not obliged to "search for records beyond the scope of the request"); Maynard v. CIA, 986 F.2d 547, 560 (1st Cir. 1993) (finding that agency search was properly limited to scope of FOIA request, with no requirement that secondary references or variant spellings be checked); Meeropol v. Meese, 790 F.2d 942, 956 (D.C. Cir. 1986) ("[A] search need not be perfect, only adequate, and adequacy is measured by the reasonableness of the effort in light of the specific request."); Adams v. FBI, No. 97-2861, slip op. at 7 (D.D.C. Mar. 3, 1999) (finding that requester cannot object to agency's failure to search under aliases not mentioned in request); Rothschild v. Department of Energy, 6 F. Supp. 2d 38, 39 (D.D.C. 1998) (declaring that agency is not required to search for records that "do not mention or specifically discuss" subject of request); cf. Kowalczyk v. Department of Justice, 73 F.3d 386, 389 (D.C. Cir. 1996) (finding search limited to agency headquarters files reasonable because plaintiff directed his request there); Russell v. Barr, No. 92-2546, slip op. at 4 (D.D.C. Aug. 28, 1998) (determining that agency searched "all reasonable terms" and "exceeded the call of duty" when "out of an abundance of caution," it searched using subject's maiden name, which was not provided in request). But see Summers v. United States Dep't of Justice, 934 F. Supp. 458, 461 (D.D.C. 1996) (notwithstanding fact that plaintiff's request specifically sought access to former FBI Director J. Edgar Hoover's "commitment calendars," finding agency search inadequate as agency did not use additional search terms such as "appointment" or "diary" to locate responsive records); cf. Canning v. United States Dep't of Justice, 919 F. Supp. 451, 460-61 (D.D.C. 1994) (when agency was aware that subject of request used two names, it should have conducted search under both names).

[126] See Domingues v. FBI, No. 98-74612, slip op. at 11 (E.D. Mich. July 24, 1999) (magistrate's recommendation) (determining that "a request directed to an agency's headquarters which does not request a search of its field offices, or which requests a blanket search of all field offices without specifying which offices should be searched, does not 'reasonably describe' any records which may be in those field offices, and an agency's search of just the headquarters records complies with the FOIA"), adopted (E.D. Mich. July 29, 1999); Malone v. Freeh, No. 97-3043, slip op. at 4 (D.D.C. Mar. 30, 1999) (rejecting argument that agency conducted inadequate search for records on third parties because requester sought information only about himself); Murphy v. IRS, 79 F. Supp. 2d 1180, 1185-86 (D. Haw. 1999) (holding that agency "conducted a reasonable search in light of the fact that Plaintiff gave no indication as to what types of files could possibly contain documents responsive to this request or where they might be located"); Bricker v. FBI, No. 97-2742, slip op. at 7 (D.D.C. Mar. 26, 1999) (approving agency search of "files where responsive information would likely be located" given limited information that requester provided about subject of request); Greenberg v. Department of Treasury, 10 F. Supp. 2d 3, 13 (D.D.C. 1998) (excusing agency's inability to locate materials "as written" in
(continued...)

-55-

**PROCEDURAL REQUIREMENTS**

reasonableness of a search also depends on the standards the agency used in determining where responsive records were likely to be found,[127] especially if the agency fails to locate records it has reason to know may exist,[128] or if the

---

[126](...continued)
request because agency records systems "are not indexed in a manner such that responsive records could have been located"); cf. Truitt v. Department of State, 897 F.2d 540, 544-46 (D.C. Cir. 1990) (stating that when request was "reasonably clear as to the materials desired," agency failed to conduct adequate search as it did not include file likely to contain responsive records).

[127] Oglesby 920 F.2d at 68 (holding agency may not limit search to one record system if others are likely to contain responsive records); Blanton v. United States Dep't of Justice, 63 F. Supp. 2d 35, 41 (D.D.C. 1999) (noting that even though agency did not search individual informant files for references to requester, any responsive information in such files would have been identified by agency's "cross-reference" search using requester's name) (motion for partial reconsideration pending); Hall v. United States Dep't of Justice, 63 F. Supp. 2d 14, 17-18 (D.D.C. 1999) (finding that agency need not search for records concerning subject's husband even though such records may have also included references to subject); Iacoe v. IRS, No. 98-C-0466, 1999 U.S. Dist. LEXIS 12809, at *11 (E.D. Wis. July 23, 1999) (recognizing that the agency "diligently searched for the records requested in those places where [the agency] expected they could be located"); Nation Magazine v. United States Customs Serv., No. 94-00808, slip op. at 8, 13-14 (D.D.C. Feb. 14, 1997) (stating that reasonable search did not require agency to search individual's personnel file in effort to locate substantive document drafted by him); cf. Bennett v. DEA, 55 F. Supp. 2d 36, 39-40 (D.D.C. 1999) (holding search inadequate when agency failed to search investigatory files for cases in which subject of request acted as informant, even though agency did not track informant activity by case name, number, or judicial district), appeal voluntarily dismissed, No. 99-5300 (D.C. Cir. Dec. 23, 1999).

[128] Valencia-Lucena v. United States Coast Guard, 180 F.3d 321, 328 (D.C. Cir. 1999) (finding that because requester provided agency with name of agency employee who possessed requested records during requester's criminal trial, "[w]hen all other sources fail to provide leads to the missing records, agency personnel should be contacted if there is a close nexus, as here, between the person and the particular record"); Campbell, 164 F.3d at 27 (declaring that search limited to agency's central records system was unreasonable because during search agency "discovered information suggesting the existence of documents that it could not locate without expanding the scope of its search"); Comer v. IRS, No. 97-76329, 1999 U.S. Dist. LEXIS 16268, at *3 (E.D. Mich. Sept. 30, 1999) (rejecting agency's assertion that it conducted reasonable search when plaintiff "listed a small number of specific persons who might have knowledge of [the requested documents] and specific places where they might be found" and agency did not indicate that it searched there); Loomis v. Department of Energy, No. 96-149, slip op. at 11-12 (N.D.N.Y. Mar. 9, 1999) (determining search inadequate in light of agency's admission that additional responsive records may exist in location not searched), aff'd, 199 F.3d 1322 (2d Cir. 1999) (unpublished table decision); Kronberg v. United States Dep't of Justice, 875 F. Supp. 861, 870-71 (D.D.C. 1995) (holding that search was inade-
(continued...)

## PROCEDURAL REQUIREMENTS

search requires agency employees to distinguish "personal" records from "agency" records.[129] Nevertheless, an agency's inability to locate every single responsive record does not undermine an otherwise reasonable search.[130]

---

[128](...continued)
quate when agency did not find records required to be maintained and plaintiff produced documents obtained by other FOIA requesters demonstrating that agency possessed files which may contain records sought); cf. Schrecker v. United States Dep't of Justice, 74 F. Supp. 2d 26, 36 (D.D.C. 1999) (finding that search was adequate because agency determined that records it failed to locate were type not required to be retained) (appeal pending); Juda v. United States Customs Serv., No. 98-0533, 1999 U.S. Dist. LEXIS 12536, at *13 (D.D.C. Aug. 3, 1999) (rejecting plaintiff's claims that agency failed to locate documents related to specific investigation in light of agency affidavits stating that no such investigation existed) (appeal pending); Vigneau v. O'Brien, No. 99-37ML, slip op. at 5 (D.R.I. Aug. 3, 1999) (magistrate's recommendation) (finding search adequate when agency employee who plaintiff alleged wrote requested records provided affidavit stating that no such records ever existed), adopted (D.R.I. Sept. 9, 1999).

[129] See Ethyl Corp. v. EPA, 25 F.3d 1241, 1247-48 (4th Cir. 1994) (citing agency failure to follow guidance concerning "personal record" considerations published in FOIA Update, Vol. V, No. 4, at 3-4); see also Kempker-Cloyd v. United States Dep't of Justice, No. 5:97-253, 1999 U.S. Dist. LEXIS 4813, at **12-13 (W.D. Mich. Mar. 12, 1999) (determining that agency acted in bad faith because it failed to review responsive records that agency official asserted were "personal"); cf. Grand Cent. Partnership, Inc. v. Cuomo, 166 F.3d 473, 481 (2d Cir. 1999) (rejecting agency affidavit concerning "personal" records as insufficient and remanding case for further development through affidavits by records' authors explaining their intended use of records in question).

[130] See Grand Cent. Partnership, 166 F.3d at 489 (declaring that fact that "some documents were not discovered until a second, more exhaustive, search was conducted does not warrant overturning the district court's ruling" that agency conducted reasonable search); Schwarz v. FBI, No. 98-4036, 1998 WL 667643, at *2 (10th Cir. Nov. 5, 1998) (concluding that "the fact that the [agency's] search failed to turn up three documents is not sufficient to contradict the reasonableness of the FBI's search without evidence of bad faith"), cert. denied, 525 U.S. 1053 (1998); Campbell, 164 F.3d at 28 n.6 (holding that "the inadvertent omission of three documents does not render a search inadequate when the search produced hundreds of pages that had been buried in archives for decades"); Citizens Comm'n on Human Rights v. FDA, 45 F.3d 1325, 1328 (9th Cir. 1995) (determining that search was adequate when agency spent 140 hours reviewing relevant files, notwithstanding fact that agency was unable to locate 137 of 1000 volumes of records); cf. Western Ctr. for Journalism v. IRS, No. 99-906, 2000 U.S. Dist. LEXIS 5073, at **7-9 (D.D.C. Mar. 31, 2000) (concluding that agency conducted reasonable search and acted in good faith by locating and releasing additional responsive records mistakenly omitted from its initial response, because "it is unreasonable to expect even the most exhaustive search to uncover every responsive file; what is expected of a law-abiding agency is that the agency admit and correct error when error is revealed") (motion for reconsideration pending). But see Oglesby v. United
(continued...)

## PROCEDURAL REQUIREMENTS

Prior to the enactment of the Electronic FOIA amendments, several courts held that agencies do not have to organize or reorganize file systems in order to respond to particular FOIA requests,[131] to write new computer programs to search for "electronic" data not already compiled for agency purposes,[132] or to aggregate computerized data files so as to effectively create new, releasable records.[133] More than one court ruled, though, that agencies may be required to perform relatively simple computer searches to locate requested records, or to demonstrate why such searches are unreasonable in a given case.[134]

---

[130](...continued) the Army, 79 F.3d 1172, 1185 (D.C. Cir. 1996) (acknowledging plaintiff's assertion that search was inadequate because of previous FOIA requester's claim that agency provided her with "well over a thousand documents," and holding that claim raises enough doubt to preclude summary judgment in absence of agency affidavit further describing its search); Accuracy in Media v. FBI, No. 97-2107, slip op. at 12 (D.D.C. Mar. 31, 1999) (directing agency to conduct further search for two unaccounted-for documents referenced in documents located by agency's otherwise reasonable search).

[131] See, e.g., Church of Scientology v. IRS, 792 F.2d 146, 150-51 (D.C. Cir. 1986); Miller v. United States Dep't of State, 779 F.2d 1378, 1385 (8th Cir. 1986); Neff v. IRS, No. 85-816, slip op. at 8 (S.D. Fla. Nov. 24, 1986); Auchterlonie v. Hodel, No. 83-C-6724, 1984 U.S. Dist. LEXIS 10911, at **5-6 (N.D. Ill. May 7, 1984).

[132] See Burlington N. R.R. v. EPA, No. 91-1636, slip op. at 4 (D.D.C. June 15, 1992); Clarke v. United States Dep't of the Treasury, No. 84-1873, 1986 WL 1234, at *1 (E.D. Pa. Jan. 24, 1986); see also FOIA Update, Vol. XIII, No. 2, at 3-7 (congressional testimony discussing "electronic record" FOIA issues).

[133] See Yeager v. DEA, 678 F.2d 315, 324 (D.C. Cir. 1982); see also "Department of Justice Report on 'Electronic Record' FOIA Issues" [hereinafter Department of Justice "Electronic Record" Report], reprinted in abridged form in FOIA Update, Vol. XI, No. 2, at 8-21 (discussing use of "computer programming" for FOIA search and processing purposes). But cf. International Diatomite Producers Ass'n v. United States Soc. Sec. Admin., No. 92-1634, 1993 WL 137286, at *5 (N.D. Cal. Apr. 28, 1993) (ordering agency to respond to request for specific information, portions of which were maintained in four separate computerized listings, by either compiling new list or redacting existing lists), appeal dismissed, No. 93-16723 (9th Cir. Nov. 1, 1993).

[134] See Thompson Publ'g Group, Inc. v. Health Care Fin. Admin., No. 92-2431, 1994 WL 116141, at *1 (D.D.C. Mar. 15, 1994) (finding that relatively simple computer searches and computer queries are reasonable for data that do not exist "in a single computer 'document' or 'file'"); Belvy v. United States Dep't of Justice, No. 94-923, slip op. at 7-9 (S.D. Fla. Dec. 15, 1994) (magistrate's recommendation) (rejecting agency's claim that it did not have to undertake computer search because it failed "to establish that the creation of such a [computer] program would be unreasonable"), adopted (S.D. Fla. Jan. 27, 1995); see also Department of Justice "Electronic Record" Report, reprinted in abridged form in FOIA Update, Vol. XI, No. 2, at 8-17 (discussing issue of com-
(continued...)

## PROCEDURAL REQUIREMENTS

Consistent with these latter cases, and to promote electronic database searches, the Electronic FOIA amendments now require agencies to make "reasonable efforts" to search for requested records in electronic form or format "except when such efforts would significantly interfere with the operation of the agency's automated information system."[135] The Electronic FOIA amendments now expressly define the term "search" as meaning "to review, manually or by automated means, agency records for the purpose of locating those records which are responsive to a request."[136] (For a discussion of the litigation aspects of adequacy of search, see Litigation Considerations, Adequacy of Search, below.)

### "Reasonably Segregable" Obligation

The FOIA requires that "any reasonably segregable portion of a record" must be released after appropriate application of the Act's nine exemptions.[137] Agencies should pay particularly close attention to this "reasonably segregable" requirement because courts may closely examine the propriety of agency segregability determinations,[138] even if the requester does not raise the issue of

---

[134](...continued) puter programming for search purposes).

[135] Pub. L. No. 104-231, § 5, 110 Stat. 3048, 3050 (codified as amended at 5 U.S.C. § 552(a)(3)(C) (1994 & Supp. IV 1998)); see Schladetsch v. HUD, No. 99-0175, slip op. at 10 (D.D.C. Apr. 4, 2000) (rejecting as insufficient agency affidavit that failed to show how creation and use of computer program to perform electronic database search for responsive information would require "unreasonable efforts" or would "substantially interfere" with agency's computer system); see also FOIA Update, Vol. XVII, No. 4, at 2 (discussing current electronic search requirements); cf. Hoffman v. United States Dep't of Justice, No. 98-1733-A, slip op. at 10-11 (W.D. Okla. Dec. 15, 1999) (finding agency not required to conduct physical search of records "if other computer-assisted search procedures available to an agency are more efficient and serve the same practical purpose of reviewing hard copies of documents").

[136] Pub. L. No. 104-231, § 5, 110 Stat. 3048, 3050 (codified as amended at 5 U.S.C. § 552(a)(3)(D) (1994 & Supp. IV 1998)); see Dayton Newspapers, Inc. v. Department of the Air Force, 35 F. Supp. 2d 1033, 1035 (S.D. Ohio 1998) (preliminary ruling without entry of judgment) (concluding that an estimated 51 hours required to "assemble" requested information from an agency database "is a small price to pay" in light of the FOIA's presumption favoring disclosure); see also Schladetsch, No. 99-0175, slip op. at 7 (D.D.C. Apr. 4, 2000) ("The programming necessary to conduct the [electronic database] search is a search tool and not the creation of a new record."); FOIA Update, Vol. XVIII, No. 1, at 6 (advising that search provisions of Electronic FOIA amendments do not involve record "creation" in Congress's eyes).

[137] 5 U.S.C. § 552(b) (1994 & Supp. IV 1998) (sentence immediately following exemptions).

[138] See, e.g., Patterson v. IRS, 56 F.3d 832, 840 (7th Cir. 1995) (finding agency certainly not entitled to withhold entire document if only "portions" contain

(continued...)

**PROCEDURAL REQUIREMENTS**

segregability at the administrative level or before the court.[139] Accordingly, an agency must adequately demonstrate to the court that all reasonably segregable, nonexempt information--perhaps even including individual numbers within multiple-digit codes[140]--was disclosed.[141]

---

[138](...continued) exempt information); Wightman v. ATF, 755 F.2d 979, 983 (1st Cir. 1985) (holding that detailed "process of segregation" is not unreasonable for request involving 36 document pages); Bristol-Myers Co. v. FTC, 424 F.2d 935, 938 (D.C. Cir. 1970) (stating that "statutory scheme does not permit a bare claim of confidentiality to immunize agency [records] from scrutiny" in their entireties); see also FOIA Update, Vol. XIV, No. 3, at 11-12 ("OIP Guidance: The 'Reasonable Segregation' Obligation") (citing, e.g., Schiller v. NLRB, 964 F.2d 1205 (D.C. Cir 1992)).

[139] See, e.g., Trans-Pac. Policing Agreement v. United States Customs Serv., 177 F.3d 1022, 1028 (D.C. Cir. 1999) (indicating that district court had affirmative duty to consider reasonable segregability even though requester never sought segregability finding administratively or before district court); Isley v. Executive Office for United States Attorneys, No. 98-5098, 1999 WL 1021934, at *7 (D.C. Cir. Oct. 21, 1999) (remanding case to district court for segregability finding even though neither party raised segregability issue in district court); see also Kimberlin v. Department of Justice, 139 F.3d 944, 951 (D.C. Cir.) (affirming application of exemption but nevertheless remanding case to district court for finding on segregability), cert. denied, 525 U.S. 891 (1998); Krikorian v. Department of State, 984 F.2d 461, 467 (D.C. Cir. 1993) (affirming general application of exemption but nevertheless remanding to district court for finding as to segregability); Schreibman v. United States Dep't of Commerce, 785 F. Supp. 164, 166 (D.D.C. 1991) (holding that segregation required for computer vulnerability assessment withheld under Exemption 2).

[140] See Trans-Pac., 177 F.3d at 1027-28 (going so far as to remand case to district court for determination of releasability of "four or six digits" of ten-digit numbers withheld in full); cf. Schrecker v. United States Dep't of Justice, 74 F. Supp. 2d 26, 32 (D.D.C. 1999) (finding that confidential informant "source codes and symbols are assigned in such a specific manner that no portion of the code is reasonably segregable") (appeal pending).

[141] See Davin v. United States Dep't of Justice, 60 F.3d 1043, 1052 (3d Cir. 1995) ("The statements regarding segregability are wholly conclusory, providing no information that would enable [plaintiff] to evaluate the FBI's decisions to withhold."); Schiller v. NLRB, 964 F.2d 1205, 1209-10 (D.C. Cir. 1992) (noting that agency's affidavit referred to withholding of "documents, not information," and remanding for specific finding as to segregability); Neely v. FBI, No. 7:97-0786, Order at 1 (W.D. Va. Jan. 25, 1999) (finding that agency applied exemptions "in a wholesale fashion" and without adequate explanation), vacated & remanded on other grounds, No. 99-1128, 2000 WL 331594 (4th Cir. Mar. 30, 2000); Carlton v. Department of the Interior, No. 97-2105, slip op. at 12 (D.D.C. Sept. 3, 1998) (requiring defendant agencies to provide further explanation of exemptions applied because agencies made "only a general statement that the withheld documents do not contain segregable portions"), appeal voluntarily dismissed, No. 98-5518 (D.C. Cir. Nov. 18, 1998); Church of (continued...)

**PROCEDURAL REQUIREMENTS**

If, however, an agency determines that nonexempt material is so "inextricably intertwined" that disclosure of it would "leave only essentially meaningless words and phrases," the entire record may be withheld.[142] In cases involving a large amount of records or an unreasonably high-cost "line-by-line" review, agencies may withhold small segments of nonexempt data "if the proportion of nonexempt factual material is relatively small and is so interspersed with exempt material that separation by the agency and policing by the courts would impose an inordinate burden."[143] Nevertheless, agencies should in all cases heed the Attorney General's admonition to consider making discretionary disclosures of exempt information in accordance with the "foreseeable

---

[141](...continued)
Scientology v. IRS, 816 F. Supp. 1138, 1162 (W.D. Tex. 1993) ("The burden is on the agency to prove the document cannot be segregated for partial release."); cf. Anderson v. CIA, 63 F. Supp. 2d 28, 30 (D.D.C. 1999) (declining, "especially in the highly classified context of this case," to "infer from the absence of the word 'segregable' [in the agency's affidavit] that segregability was possible"); Rockwell Int'l Corp. v. United States Dep't of Justice, No. 98-761, slip op. at 15-16 (D.D.C. Mar. 24, 1999) (rejecting plaintiff's unsupported assertion that documents withheld in full must contain segregable information, because "the documents at issue here are not of the type that are likely to contain" such information and "the agency made a good faith effort" to identify and release nonexempt information) (appeal pending).

[142] Neufeld v. IRS, 646 F.2d 661, 663 (D.C. Cir. 1981); see, e.g., Local 3, Int'l Bhd. of Elec. Workers v. NLRB, 845 F.2d 1177, 1179 (2d Cir. 1988); Mead Data Cent., Inc. v. United States Dep't of the Air Force, 566 F.2d 242, 261 (D.C. Cir. 1977); see also Yeager v. DEA, 678 F.2d 315, 322 n.16 (D.C. Cir. 1982) (concluding that it was appropriate to consider "intelligibility" of document and burden imposed by editing and segregation of nonexempt matters); Eagle Horse v. FBI, No. 92-2357, slip op. at 5-6 (D.D.C. July 28, 1995) (finding that release of polygraph examination, while protecting sensitive structure, pattern, and sequence of questions, was not feasible without reducing product to "unintelligible gibberish").

[143] Lead Indus. Ass'n v. OSHA, 610 F.2d 70, 86 (2d Cir. 1979); see, e.g., Solar Sources, Inc. v. United States, 142 F.3d 1033, 1039 (7th Cir. 1998) (finding that because agency would require eight work-years to identify all nonexempt documents in millions of pages of files, the very small percentage of documents that could be released were not "reasonably segregable"); Doherty v. United States Dep't of Justice, 775 F.2d 49, 53 (2d Cir. 1985) ("The fact that there may be some nonexempt matter in documents which are predominantly exempt does not require the district court to undertake the burdensome task of analyzing approximately 300 pages of documents, line-by-line."); Neufeld, 646 F.2d at 666 (holding that segregation not required when it "would impose significant costs on the agency and produce an edited document of little informational value"); Journal of Commerce v. United States Dep't of the Treasury, No. 86-1075, 1988 U.S. Dist. LEXIS 17610, at *21 (D.D.C. Mar. 30, 1988) (finding that segregation was "neither useful, feasible nor desirable" when it would compel agency "to pour through [literally millions of pages of documents] to segregate nonexempt material [and] would impose an immense administrative burden . . . that would in the end produce little in the way of useful nonexempt material").

## PROCEDURAL REQUIREMENTS

harm" standard.[144] (For discussions of discretionary disclosure, see Exemption 5, Applying the "Foreseeable Harm" Standard, below, and Discretionary Disclosure and Waiver, below; for a further discussion of segregability, see Litigation Considerations, "Reasonably Segregable" Requirements, below.)

### Referrals and Consultations

When an agency locates records responsive to a FOIA request, it should determine whether any of those records, or information contained in those records, originated with another agency or agency component.[145] As a matter of sound administrative practice, an agency should consult with any other agency or other agency component whose information appears in the responsive records, especially if that other agency or component is better able to determine whether the information is exempt from disclosure.[146] If the response to the consultation is delayed, the agency or component in receipt of the FOIA request should notify the requester that a supplemental response will follow when the consultation is completed.[147]

If an agency or component locates entire records originating with another agency or component, it should refer those records to their originator for its direct response to the requester.[148] The referring agency or component or-

---

[144] Attorney General's Memorandum for Heads of Departments and Agencies regarding the Freedom of Information Act (Oct. 4, 1993), reprinted in FOIA Update, Vol. XIV, No. 3, at 4-5 (noting connection between discretionary disclosure and satisfaction of "reasonable segregation" obligation); see also Attorney General's Follow-Up Memorandum for Heads of Departments and Agencies regarding the Freedom of Information Act (Sept. 3, 1999), reprinted in FOIA Update, Vol. XIX, No. 4, at 4 (emphasizing that under the "foreseeable harm" standard "a requested record or portion of a requested record . . . should be withheld from a FOIA requester only when it is not possible for an agency to disclose it as a matter of administrative discretion"); FOIA Update, Vol. XVIII, No. 2, at 1 (describing Attorney General's reiteration of importance of "foreseeable harm" standard to federal agencies in order to promote further discretionary disclosure in agency decisionmaking).

[145] Accord 5 U.S.C. § 552(a)(6)(B)(iii) (1994 & Supp. IV 1998).

[146] See, e.g., 28 C.F.R. § 16.4(c)(1) (1999) (Department of Justice regulation concerning consultations).

[147] See FOIA Update, Vol. XII, No. 3, at 3-4 ("OIP Guidance: Referral and Consultation Procedures"); see also FOIA Update, Vol. XIV, No. 3, at 6-8 (Department of Justice memorandum setting forth White House consultation process in which agency retains responsibility for responding to requester regarding White House-originated records or White House-originated information located within scope of FOIA request that agency has received).

[148] See FOIA Update, Vol. XII, No. 3, at 3-4; FOIA Update, Vol. IV, No. 3, at 5; see also, e.g., Rzeslawski v. United States Dep't of Justice, No. 97-1156, slip op. at 6 (D.D.C. July 23, 1998) (observing that an agency's "referral procedure is generally faster than attempting to make an independent determination re-
(continued...)

## PROCEDURAL REQUIREMENTS

dinarily should advise the requester of the referral and of the name of the agency FOIA office to which it was made.[149] Some agencies have streamlined their practices of continually referring certain routine records or classes of records to other agencies or components by establishing standard processing protocols and agreements between them.[150]

All agencies should remember, however, that even after they make such record referrals in response to FOIA requests, they retain the responsibility of defending any agency action taken on those records if the matter proceeds to litigation.[151] Additionally, agencies receiving referrals should handle them on a "first-in, first-out" basis among their other FOIA requests--but they should be sure to do so according to the date of the request's initial receipt at the referring agency, lest FOIA requesters be placed at a timing disadvantage through

---

[148](...continued) garding disclosure" and that "by placing the request in the hands of the originating agency, discretionary disclosure is more likely"); Stone v. Defense Investigative Serv., No. 91-2013, 1992 WL 52560, at *1 (D.D.C. Feb. 24, 1992) (recognizing that agencies may refer responsive records to originating agencies in responding to FOIA requests), aff'd, 978 F.2d 744 (D.C. Cir. 1992) (unpublished table decision); 28 C.F.R. § 16.4(c)(2) (Department of Justice regulation containing referral and consultation procedures).

[149] See FOIA Update, Vol. XII, No. 2, at 6. But see id. (warning agencies not to notify requesters of identities of other agencies to which record referrals are made, in any exceptional case in which so doing would reveal sensitive abstract fact about record's existence).

[150] See, e.g., 28 C.F.R. § 16.4(h) (Department of Justice regulation authorizing its components to make agreements with other components or agencies to eliminate need for consultations or referrals for particular types of records).

[151] See, e.g., Peralta v. United States Attorney's Office, 136 F.3d 169, 175 (D.C. Cir. 1998) (remanding case for further consideration of whether referral of FBI documents to FBI resulted in "improper withholding" of documents), on remand, 69 F. Supp. 2d 21, 29 (D.D.C. 1999) (holding that Executive Office for United States Attorneys' referral of documents to FBI was not improper); Williams v. FBI, No. 92-5176, 1993 WL 157679, at *1 (D.C. Cir. May 7, 1993) (illustrating that in litigation referring agency is nevertheless required to justify withholding of record that was referred to another agency); Hronek v. DEA, 16 F. Supp. 2d 1260, 1272 (D. Or. 1998) (noting that with respect to records referred to nonparty agencies "the ultimate responsibility for a full response lies with the [referring] agencies"); see also FOIA Update, Vol. XV, No. 3, at 6 (advising on proper litigation practice for defending referrals of records to other agencies); cf. Goldstein v. Office of Indep. Counsel, No. 87-2028, 1999 WL 570862, at *14 (D.D.C. July 29, 1999) (magistrate's recommendation) (requiring referring agency to ask agency receiving referral to provide court with its position concerning releasability of records referred); Grove v. Department of Justice, 802 F. Supp. 506, 518 (D.D.C. 1992) (declaring that agency may not use "'consultation' as its reason for a deletion, without asserting a valid exemption").

## PROCEDURAL REQUIREMENTS

agency referral practices.[152]

### Responding to FOIA Requests

The FOIA provides that each agency "shall make [its disclosable] records promptly available" upon request.[153] Although the D.C. Circuit has suggested that an agency is not required to make requested records available by mailing copies of them to a FOIA requester if the agency prefers to make the "responsive records available in one central location for [the requester's] perusal," such as in a "reading room,"[154] the Department of Justice strongly advises agencies to decline to follow such a practice unless the requester prefers it as well.[155] However, agencies certainly may require requesters to pay any fees owed before releasing the processed records; otherwise, agencies "would effectively be bankrolling search and review, and duplicating expenses because there would never be any assurance whatsoever that payment would ever be made once the requesters had the documents in their hands."[156]

---

[152] See FOIA Update, Vol. XV, No. 3, at 6 (observing that requester should "receive her rightful place in line as of the date upon which her request was received," and advising likewise regarding "consultation" practices (citing Freeman v. Department of Justice, 822 F. Supp. 1064, 1067 (S.D.N.Y. 1993))); cf. Williams v. United States, 932 F. Supp. 354, 357 & n.7 (D.D.C. 1996) (urging agency to set up "express lane" for referred records so as to not "tie up other agencies by taking an inordinate period of time to review referred rec-ords [and] unnecessarily inhibit the smooth functioning of the [other] agencies' well oiled FOIA processing systems").

[153] 5 U.S.C. § 552(a)(3)(A) (1994 & Supp. IV 1998).

[154] Oglesby v. United States Dep't of the Army, 920 F.2d 57, 70 (D.C. Cir. 1990); cf. Chamberlain v. United States Dep't of Justice, 957 F. Supp. 292, 296 (D.D.C.) (holding that FBI's offer to make "visicorder charts" available to requester for review at FBI Headquarters met FOIA requirements due to exceptional fact that charts could be damaged if photocopied), summary affirmance granted, 124 F.3d 1309 (D.C. Cir. 1997) (unpublished table decision).

[155] See FOIA Update, Vol. XII, No. 2, at 5 ("OIP Guidance: Procedural Rules Under the D.C. Circuit's Oglesby Decision") (recognizing that "the effective administration of the FOIA relies quite heavily upon agency transmittal of disclosable record copies to FOIA requesters by mail"); see also Comer v. IRS, No. 97-76329, 1999 U.S. Dist. LEXIS 16268, at *3 (E.D. Mich. Sept. 30, 1999) (observing that although "FOIA does not require agencies to provide members of the public with information they can access themselves . . . [t]he Court is perplexed . . . why [defendant] refuses to simply copy this information and send it to plaintiff so long as he is willing to pay for the copies"); accord President's Memorandum for Heads of Departments and Agencies regarding the Freedom of Information Act, 29 Weekly Comp. Pres. Doc. 1999 (Oct. 4, 1993), reprinted in FOIA Update, Vol. XIV, No. 3, at 3 ("[A]gencies should handle requests for information in a customer-friendly manner" and erect no "unnecessary bureaucratic hurdles.").

[156] Strout v. United States Parole Comm'n, 842 F. Supp. 948, 951 (E.D.

(continued...)

## PROCEDURAL REQUIREMENTS

Both agencies and requesters alike should remember to distinguish between the records that are made available in agency reading rooms (both conventional and "electronic") under subsection (a)(2) of the Act[157] and records that are sought through FOIA requests.[158] Agencies are not required to provide requesters with records that fall within subsection (a)(2) and are already available for "reading room" inspection and copying.[159] (For a discussion of "reading room" records, see FOIA Reading Rooms, above.)

The FOIA does not provide for limited disclosure; rather, it "speaks in terms of disclosure and nondisclosure [and] ordinarily does not recognize degrees of disclosure, such as permitting viewing, but not copying, of documents."[160] Moreover, providing exempt information to a requester and limiting his or her ability to further disclose it through a protective order is "not authorized by [the] FOIA."[161]

---

[156](...continued) Mich.), aff'd, 40 F.3d 136 (6th Cir. 1994); see also Taylor v. United States Dep't of the Treasury, No. A-96-CA-933, 1996 U.S. Dist. LEXIS 19909, at *5 (W.D. Tex. Dec. 17, 1996) (same); Trueblood v. United States Dep't of the Treasury, 943 F. Supp. 64, 68 (D.D.C. 1996) (recognizing that agency may require payment before sending processed records); Putnam v. United States Dep't of Justice, 880 F. Supp. 40, 42 (D.D.C. 1995) (allowing agency to require payment of current and outstanding fees before releasing records); Crooker v. ATF, 882 F. Supp. 1158, 1162 (D. Mass. 1995) (finding no obligation to provide records until current and past-due fees are paid).

[157] 5 U.S.C. § 552(a)(2); see FOIA Update, Vol. XVII, No. 3, at 1-2 (discussing maintenance of both conventional and "electronic" reading rooms under Electronic FOIA amendments).

[158] See 5 U.S.C. § 552(a)(3) (generally excluding "reading room" records from Act's regular "FOIA request" provisions).

[159] See Schwarz v. United States Patent & Trademark Office, No. 95-5349, 1996 U.S. App. LEXIS 4609, at **2-3 (D.C. Cir. Feb. 22, 1996) (per curiam); Crews v. Internal Revenue, No. 99-8388, slip op. at 11-12 (C.D. Cal. Apr. 26, 2000) (holding that "documents that are publicly available either in the [agency's FOIA] reading room or on the [I]nternet" are "not subject to production via FOIA requests"). But see FOIA Update, Vol. XVIII, No. 1, at 3 (advising that Congress made clear that newly established reading room category of FOIA-processed records would stand as exception to general rule and be subject to regular FOIA requests as well); see also FOIA Update, Vol. XVI, No. 1, at 2 (reminding that "an agency cannot convert a subsection (a)(3) record into a subsection (a)(2) record . . . just by voluntarily placing it into its reading room").

[160] Julian v. United States Dep't of Justice, 806 F.2d 1411, 1419 n.7 (9th Cir. 1986), aff'd, 486 U.S. 1 (1988); see Berry v. Department of Justice, 733 F.2d 1343, 1355 n.19 (9th Cir. 1984); see also Seawell, Dalton, Hughes & Timms v. Export-Import Bank, No. 84-241-N, slip op. at 2 (E.D. Va. July 27, 1984) (stating that there is no "middle ground between disclosure and nondisclosure").

[161] Schiffer v. FBI, 78 F.3d 1405, 1410 (9th Cir. 1996) (reversing district

(continued...)

## PROCEDURAL REQUIREMENTS

An agency must "provide the [requested] record in any form or format requested by the person if the record is readily reproducible by the agency in that form or format" and "make reasonable efforts to maintain its records in forms or formats that are reproducible" for such purposes.[162] Together, these two provisions require agencies to honor a requester's specific choice among existing forms of a requested record (assuming no exceptional difficulty in reproducing an existing record form)[163] and to make "reasonable efforts" to disclose a record in a different form or format when that is requested, if the record is "readily reproducible" in that new form or format.[164]

Given "that computer-stored records, whether stored in the central processing unit, on magnetic tape, or in some other form, are records for the purposes of the FOIA,"[165] agencies should endeavor to use advanced technology to satisfy existing or potential FOIA demands most efficiently--including through

---

[161](...continued) court's conditional disclosure order); see also Maricopa Audobon Soc'y v. United States Forest Serv., 108 F.3d 1082, 1088-89 (9th Cir. 1987) (rejecting plaintiff's offer to receive requested documents under confidentiality agreement because of rule that "FOIA does not permit selective disclosure of information to only certain parties, and that once the information is disclosed to [plaintiff], it must be made available to all members of the public who request it"); Swan v. SEC, 96 F.3d 498, 500 (D.C. Cir. 1996) ("Once records are released, nothing in the FOIA prevents the requester from disclosing the information to anyone else. The statute contains no provisions requiring confidentiality agreements or similar conditions."); cf. Arieff v. United States Dep't of the Navy, 712 F.2d 1462, 1469 (D.C. Cir. 1983) (refusing to grant protective order that would allow plaintiff's counsel and medical expert to review exempt information, lest anyone think that "even in the process of sustaining an exemption the secrets to which it pertains will be compromised").

[162] 5 U.S.C. § 552(a)(3)(B); see also FOIA Update, Vol. XVII, No. 4, at 2 (discussing statutory provisions); cf. Department of Justice "Electronic Record" Report, reprinted in abridged form in FOIA Update, Vol. XI, No. 3, at 3-6 (discussing "choice of format" issues regarding "electronic records").

[163] See, e.g., Chamberlain, 957 F. Supp. at 296 ("The substantial expense of reproducing the visicorder charts, as well as the possibility that the visicorder charts might be damaged if photocopied, make the Government's proposed form of disclosure [i.e., inspection] even more compelling.").

[164] See FOIA Update, Vol. XVIII, No. 1, at 5 (discussing agency obligations to produce records in requested forms or formats (citing H.R. Rep. No. 104-795, at 18, 21 (1996) (noting that amendments overrule Dismukes v. Department of the Interior, 603 F. Supp. 760, 761-63 (D.D.C. 1984), which previously allowed agency to chose format of disclosure if it chose "reasonably"))); see also FOIA Update, Vol. XIX, No. 1, at 6 (encouraging agencies to consider providing records in multiple forms as matter of administrative discretion if requested to do so).

[165] Yeager v. DEA, 678 F.2d 315, 321 (D.C. Cir. 1982); see Long v. IRS, 596 F.2d 362, 364-65 (9th Cir. 1979); see also FOIA Update, Vol. XVII, No. 4, at 2 (citing 5 U.S.C. § 552(f), as amended); FOIA Update, Vol. XI, No. 2, at 4 n.1.

## PROCEDURAL REQUIREMENTS

"affirmative" electronic disclosures.[166] To do so, and also to meet their "electronic reading room" obligations under the Electronic FOIA amendments as well,[167] all federal agencies must pay increasing attention to the design and development of their sites on the World Wide Web for purposes of FOIA administration.[168] Recognizing the importance of this, the Department of Justice has called upon all federal agencies to promote a "new partnership" between FOIA officers and agency Information Resources Management personnel.[169] (For a discussion of "electronic reading rooms," see FOIA Reading Rooms, above.)

When an agency denies an initial request in full or in part, it must provide the requester with certain specific information about the action taken on the request--including an estimate of the amount of denied information, unless doing so would undermine the protection provided by an exemption.[170] Addi-

---

[166] See FOIA Update, Vol. XIX, No. 3, at 1 (stressing congressional interest in "affirmative disclosures" of government information); id. at 5-6 (Department of Justice congressional testimony emphasizing same); FOIA Update, Vol. XIX, No. 1, at 1 (discussing Department of the Air Force affirmative electronic information disclosure program); FOIA Update, Vol. XVIII, No. 1, at 3 (advising that agencies may choose to meet their "paper" reading room responsibilities through placement of computer terminals in their "conventional" reading rooms); FOIA Update, Vol. XVI, No. 1, at 1-2 (promoting efficient agency disclosure through early Internet activity and other electronic means); FOIA Update, Vol. XV, No. 4, at 3 (proposed electronic record FOIA principles); see also FOIA Update, Vol. XVII, No. 1, at 1-2 (describing use of document imaging in automated FOIA processing).

[167] Pub. L. No. 104-231, § 4, 110 Stat. 3048, 3049 (codified as amended at 5 U.S.C. §§ 552(a)(2), (e)(2) (1994 & Supp. IV 1998)); see also FOIA Update, Vol. XIX, No. 1, at 3-5 ("OIP Guidance: Electronic FOIA Amendments Implementation Guidance Outline").

[168] See FOIA Update, Vol. XIX, No. 3, at 3-4 ("OIP Guidance: Recommendations for FOIA Web Sites"); FOIA Update, Vol. XIX, No. 2, at 2 ("Web Site Watch" discussion of agency FOIA Web sites); FOIA Update, Vol. XIX, No. 1, at 2 (same); FOIA Update, Vol. XVIII, No. 3, at 1-2 (describing early agency development of World Wide Web sites for FOIA purposes); see also FOIA Update, Vol. XIX, No. 3, at 2 (advising agencies on proper FOIA Web site treatment for annual FOIA reports, in compliance with new electronic availability requirements of 5 U.S.C. § 552(e)(2)-(3), including through agency identification of Uniform Resource Locator (URL) for each report).

[169] Attorney General's Follow-Up Memorandum for Heads of Departments and Agencies regarding the Freedom of Information Act (Sept. 3, 1999), reprinted in FOIA Update, Vol. XIX, No. 4, at 4 (emphasizing that assistance of agency IRM personnel in facilitating "the prompt and accurate disclosure of information through the agency's FOIA sites on the World Wide Web . . . is now vital to the full and proper administration of the Act").

[170] See 5 U.S.C. § 552(a)(6)(F); see, e.g., 28 C.F.R. § 16.6(c)(3) (1999); see also FOIA Update, Vol. XVIII, No. 2, at 2 (discussing alternative methods of satisfying obligation to estimate volume of deleted or withheld information,
(continued...)

## PROCEDURAL REQUIREMENTS

tionally, the Electronic FOIA amendments require agencies to indicate the amount of information excised at the point in the record where the excision was made, wherever it is "technically feasible" to do so.[171]

While "[t]here is no requirement that administrative responses to FOIA requests contain the same documentation necessary in litigation,"[172] a decision to deny an initial request must inform the requester of the reasons for denial; of the right to appeal; and of the name and title of each person responsible for the denial.[173] Agencies also must include administrative appeal notifications in

---

[170](...continued) including "forms of measurement" to be used); FOIA Update, Vol. XVII, No. 4, at 10-11 (discussing requirements of Electronic FOIA amendments).

[171] Pub. L. No. 104-231, § 4, 110 Stat. 3048, 3049 (codified as amended at 5 U.S.C. § 552(b) (concluding sentences) (1994 & Supp. IV 1998)); see, e.g., 28 C.F.R. § 16.6(c)(3); see also FOIA Update, Vol. XVIII, No. 1, at 6 (discussing use of "electronic markings to show the locations of electronic record deletions"); FOIA Update, Vol. XVII, No. 4, at 10 (advising that statutory obligation "also codifies the sound administrative practice of marking records to show all deletions when records are disclosed in conventional paper form"); cf. Tax Analysts v. IRS, No. 94-923, 1998 WL 419755, at *2 (D.D.C. May 1, 1998) (declaring that "an agency need not add explanatory material to a document to make it more understandable in light of the redactions").

[172] Crooker v. CIA, No. 83-1426, 1984 U.S. Dist. LEXIS 23177, at **3-4 (D.D.C. Sept. 28, 1984); see Judicial Watch, Inc. v. Clinton, 880 F. Supp. 1, 11-12 (D.D.C. 1995) (finding that agencies need not provide Vaughn Index until ordered by court after plaintiff has exhausted administrative process); Schaake v. IRS, No. 91-958, 1991 U.S. Dist. LEXIS 9418, at **9-10 (S.D. Ill. June 3, 1991) (ruling that court "lacks jurisdiction" to require agency to provide Vaughn Index at either initial request or administrative appeal stages); Safe-Card Servs. v. SEC, No. 84-3073, 1986 U.S. Dist. LEXIS 26467, at *5 (D.D.C. Apr. 21, 1986) (noting that requester has no right to Vaughn Index during administrative process), aff'd on other grounds, 926 F.2d 1197 (D.C. Cir. 1991); see also FOIA Update, Vol. VII, No. 3, at 6.

[173] 5 U.S.C. § 552(a)(6)(A)(i), (a)(6)(C)(i); see Mayock v. INS, 714 F. Supp. 1558, 1567 (N.D. Cal. 1989) (denying plaintiff's request for Vaughn Index at administrative level, but suggesting that agency regulations then in effect required "more information than just the number of pages withheld and an unexplained citation to the exemptions"), rev'd & remanded on other grounds sub nom. Mayock v. Nelson, 938 F.2d 1006 (9th Cir. 1991); Stanley v. DOD, No. 93-4247, slip op. at 14-15 (S.D. Ill. July 28, 1998) (finding constructive exhaustion when agency failed to provide requester with notice of administrative appeal rights regarding disputed fee estimate); Hudgins v. IRS, 620 F. Supp. 19, 20-21 (D.D.C. 1985) (suggesting that statements of appellate rights should be provided even when request was interpreted by agency as not reasonably describing records), aff'd, 808 F.2d 137 (D.C. Cir. 1987); see also FOIA Update, Vol. VI, No. 4, at 6 (discussing significance of apprising requesters of their rights to file administrative appeals of adverse FOIA determinations); cf. Kay v. FCC, 884 F. Supp. 1, 2-3 (D.D.C. 1995) (upholding notification that appeals were to

(continued...)

## PROCEDURAL REQUIREMENTS

all of their "no record" responses to FOIA requesters.[174]

Notifications to requesters should also contain other pertinent information: when and where records will be made available; what fees, if any, must be paid prior to the granting of access; what records are or are not responsive to the request; the date of receipt of the request or appeal; and the nature of the request or appeal and, when appropriate, the agency's interpretation of it.[175] Furthermore, because an agency is obligated to provide a FOIA requester with the "best copy available" of a record,[176] an agency should address in its correspondence any problem with the quality of its photocopy of a disclosed record.[177]

Finally, a requester has the right to administratively appeal any adverse determination an agency makes on his or her FOIA request.[178] Under Department of Justice regulations, for example, adverse determinations include: denials of records in full or in part; "no records" responses; denials of requests

---

[173](...continued) be filed with General Counsel even though Commission took final action on them).

[174] See Oglesby v. United States Dep't of the Army, 920 F.2d 57, 67 (D.C. Cir. 1990) (holding that an agency's "no record" response constitutes an "adverse determination" and therefore requires notification of appeal rights under 5 U.S.C. § 552(a)(6)(A)(i)); see also FOIA Update, Vol. XII, No. 2, at 5 ("OIP Guidance: Procedural Rules Under the D.C. Circuit's Oglesby Decision") (superseding FOIA Update, Vol. V, No. 3, at 2).

[175] See FOIA Update, Vol. XVI, No. 3, at 3-5 ("OIP Guidance: Determining the Scope of a FOIA Request") (emphasizing importance of communication with requester); see, e.g., Astley v. Lawson, No. 89-2806, 1991 WL 7162, at *2 (D.D.C. Jan. 11, 1991) (suggesting that the agency "might have been more helpful" to requester by "explaining why the information he sought would not be provided"); see also FOIA Update, Vol. XV, No. 2, at 1 (describing Department of Justice "FOIA Form Review" as example for other agencies to follow); accord Attorney General's Memorandum for Heads of Departments and Agencies regarding the Freedom of Information Act (Oct. 4, 1993), reprinted in FOIA Update, Vol. XIV, No. 3, at 4-5 (same).

[176] See McDonnell v. United States, 4 F.3d 1227, 1262 n.21 (3d Cir. 1993) ("Of course, we anticipate that [plaintiff] will receive the best possible reproduction of the documents to which he is entitled."); see also FOIA Update, Vol. XVI, No. 3, at 5 (advising agencies that "before providing a FOIA requester with a photocopy of a record that is a poor copy or is not entirely legible," they should "make reasonable efforts to check for any better copy of a record that could be used to make a better photocopy for the requester"); accord FOIA Update, Vol. XV, No. 2, at 1 (describing Attorney General's strong emphasis on "customer service objectives" in FOIA administration).

[177] See FOIA Update, Vol. XVI, No. 3, at 5 (advising of procedures to be used in cases involving poor photocopies of records).

[178] 5 U.S.C. § 552(a)(6)(A); see Oglesby, 920 F.2d at 63-71.

# EXEMPTION 1

for fee waivers; and denials of requests for expedited treatment.[179] An agency must make a determination on an administrative appeal within twenty working days after its receipt.[180] If an agency upholds a denial, it must inform the requester of the its reasons for upholding the denial and of the name and title of each person responsible for that administrative appeal decision.[181] An administrative appeal decision upholding an adverse determination must also inform the requester of the provisions for judicial review of that determination in the federal courts.[182] (For discussions of the various aspects of judicial review of agency action under the FOIA, see Litigation Considerations, below.)

## EXEMPTION 1

Exemption 1 of the FOIA protects from disclosure national security information concerning the national defense or foreign policy, provided that it has been properly classified in accordance with the substantive and procedural requirements of an executive order.[1] As of October 14, 1995, the executive order in effect is Executive Order 12,958.[2] It replaced Executive Order 12,356, which was issued in 1982.[3] Under Executive Order 12,958, limited classification is strongly emphasized and automatic declassification is a basic requirement.[4] Its provisions are discussed below.

The issuance of each new executive order raises the question of the applicability of successive executive orders to records that were in various stages of administrative or litigative handling as of the current executive order's ef-

---

[179] 28 C.F.R. § 16.6(c).

[180] Id. § 552(a)(6)(A)(ii).

[181] Id. § 552(a)(6)(A)(ii), (a)(6)(C)(i).

[182] Id. § 552(a)(6)(A)(ii).

[1] 5 U.S.C. § 552(b)(1) (1994 & Supp. IV 1998).

[2] 3 C.F.R. 333 (1996), reprinted in 50 U.S.C. § 435 note (Supp. II 1996), and reprinted in abridged form in FOIA Update, Vol. XVI, No. 2, at 5-10; see also Students Against Genocide (SAGE) v. Department of State, No. 96-667, 1998 WL 699074, at *7 n.13 (D.D.C. Aug. 24, 1998) (magistrate's recommendation), adopted, No. 96-667 (D.D.C. Sept. 29, 1998), subsequent magistrate's recommendation, 50 F. Supp. 2d 20, 23 (D.D.C. 1999), adopted, No. 96-667 (D.D.C. July 22, 1999) (appeal pending).

[3] 3 C.F.R. 166 (1983), reprinted in 50 U.S.C. § 435 note (1994); see also FOIA Update, Vol. III, No. 3, at 6-7; cf. FOIA Update, Vol. XVI, No. 2, at 11 (chart comparing major provisions of Exec. Order No. 12,356 with those of Exec. Order No. 12,958).

[4] See Exec. Order No. 12,958, §§ 1.2, 1.6, 3.4; see also FOIA Update, Vol. XVI, No. 2, at 1-2 (discussing major provisions of Exec. Order No. 12,958).

# EXEMPTION 1

fective date.[5] The appropriate executive order to apply, with its particular procedural and substantive standards, depends upon when the responsible agency official takes the final classification action on the record in question.[6]

Under the precedents established by the Court of Appeals for the District of Columbia Circuit, ordinarily the rule is that a reviewing court will assess the propriety of Exemption 1 withholdings under the executive order in effect when "the agency's ultimate classification decision is actually made."[7] Only when "a reviewing court contemplates remanding the case to the agency to correct a deficiency in its classification determination is it necessary" to comply with a superseding executive order.[8] It is also important to note that

---

[5] See FOIA Update, Vol. XVI, No. 2, at 3, 12 ("OIP Guidance: The Timing of New E.O. Applicability").

[6] See Halpern v. FBI, 181 F.3d 279, 289-90 (2d Cir. 1999); Campbell v. United States Dep't of Justice, 164 F.3d 20, 29 (D.C. Cir. 1998) (per curiam) (remanding for new declaration); Lesar v. United States Dep't of Justice, 636 F.2d 472, 480 (D.C. Cir. 1980); see also Bonner v. United States Dep't of State, 928 F.2d 1148, 1152 (D.C. Cir. 1991) (rejecting plaintiff's argument that court assess propriety of agency's classification determination at time of court's review because to do so would subject agencies and courts to "an endless cycle of judicially mandated reprocessing"); Weatherhead v. United States, No. 95-519, slip op. at 3 (E.D. Wash. Mar. 29, 1996) (holding that applicable executive order "is the one in effect at the time of classification"), reconsideration denied in pertinent part & granted in part, slip op. at 8 (E.D. Wash. Sept. 9, 1996) (upholding classification upon in camera inspection), rev'd on other grounds, 157 F.3d 735 (9th Cir. 1998), petition for cert. dismissed & appellate decision vacated, 120 S. Ct. 577 (1999); King v. Department of Justice, 830 F.2d 210, 217 (D.C. Cir. 1987); Hunsberger v. United States Dep't of Justice, No. 92-2587, slip op. at 4 n.5 (D.D.C. July 22, 1997) (finding agency properly applied Exec. Order No. 12,356 as that was order in effect at time classification determination made); Keenan v. Department of Justice, No. 94-1909, slip op. at 7-8 (D.D.C. Mar. 24, 1997) (rejecting argument that agency should apply Exec. Order No. 12,958 because it did not produce supporting affidavit until after effective date of new order), renewed motion for summary judgment granted in part & denied in part on other grounds (D.D.C. Dec. 16, 1997); cf. Summers v. Department of Justice, 140 F.3d 1077, 1082 (D.C. Cir. 1998) (remanding to district court because district court failed to articulate whether it was applying Exec. Order No. 12,356 or Exec. Order No. 12,958 to evaluate Exemption 1 withholdings, even though district court record made it clear), on remand, No. 87-3168, slip op. at 2 (D.D.C. Apr. 19, 2000) (applying Exec. Order No. 12,958 to uphold Exemption 1 withholdings).

[7] King, 830 F.2d at 217.

[8] Id.; see also Kern v. FBI, No. 94-0208, slip op. at 5-6 & n.2 (C.D. Cal. Sept. 14, 1998) (remanding due to lack of specificity of Vaughn Index; classified information to be reviewed under current Exec. Order No. 12,958); Greenberg v. United States Dep't of Treasury, 10 F. Supp. 2d 3, 12 (D.D.C. 1998) (applying Exec. Order No. 12,356 to records at issue, but noting that Exec. Order No. 12,958 would apply if court "[found] that the agencies im-

(continued...)

# EXEMPTION 1

agencies may, as a matter of discretion, reexamine their classification decisions under a newly issued executive order in order to take into account "changed international and domestic circumstances."[9]

Prior to examining the standard of review applied by courts in Exemption 1 cases, it is useful to review briefly the early decisions construing this exemption, as well as its legislative history. In 1973, the Supreme Court in EPA v. Mink[10] held that records classified under proper procedures were exempt from disclosure per se, without any further judicial review, thereby obviating the need for in camera review of information withheld under this exemption.[11] Responding in large part to the thrust of that decision, Congress amended the FOIA in 1974 to provide expressly for de novo review by the courts and for in camera review of documents, including classified documents, where appropriate.[12] In so doing, Congress apparently sought to ensure that national security records are properly classified by agencies and that reviewing courts remain cognizant of their authority to verify the correctness of agency classification determinations.[13]

## Standard of Review

After the FOIA was amended in 1974, numerous litigants challenged the sufficiency of agency affidavits in Exemption 1 cases, requesting in camera review by the courts and hoping to obtain disclosure of challenged documents. Nevertheless, courts initially upheld agency classification decisions in reliance upon agency affidavits, as a matter of routine, in the absence of evidence of

---

[8](...continued)
properly withheld information pursuant to Exemption 1"); cf. FOIA Update, Vol. XVI, No. 2, at 4, 12 (summarizing history of Exemption 1 disclosure orders and urging careful attention to classification determinations accordingly).

[9] Baez v. United States Dep't of Justice, 647 F.2d 1328, 1233 (D.C. Cir. 1980) (upholding agency's classification reevaluation under executive order issued during course of district court litigation); see, e.g., Miller v. United States Dep't of State, 779 F.2d 1378, 1388 (8th Cir. 1985) (agency chose to reevaluate under new Exec. Order No. 12,356); Military Audit Project v. Casey, 656 F.2d 724, 737 & n.41 (D.C. Cir. 1981) (agency chose to reevaluate under new Exec. Order No. 12,065); Keenan, No. 94-1909, slip op. at 7 (D.D.C. Mar. 24, 1997) (finding that although agency could "voluntarily reassess" its classification decision under Exec. Order No. 12,958, issued during pendency of lawsuit, agency not required to do so).

[10] 410 U.S. 73 (1973).

[11] Id. at 84.

[12] See 5 U.S.C. § 552(a)(4)(B).

[13] See H.R. Rep. No. 93-876, at 7-8 (1974), reprinted in 1974 U.S.C.C.A.N. 6267, 6272-73, and in House Comm. on Gov't Operations and Senate Comm. on the Judiciary, 94th Cong., 1st Sess., Freedom of Information Act and Amendments of 1974 (P.L. 93-502) Source Book: Legislative History, Texts, and Other Documents at 121, 127-28 (1975).

**EXEMPTION 1**

bad faith on the part of an agency.[14] In 1978, however, the Court of Appeals for the District of Columbia Circuit departed somewhat from such routine reliance on agency affidavits, prescribing in camera review to facilitate full de novo determinations of Exemption 1 claims, even when there was no showing of bad faith on the part of the agency.[15] This decision nevertheless recognized that the courts should "first 'accord substantial weight to an agency's affidavit concerning the details of the classified status of the disputed record.'"[16]

The D.C. Circuit further refined the appropriate standard for judicial review of national security claims under Exemption 1 (or under Exemption 3, in conjunction with certain national security protection statutes), finding that summary judgment is entirely proper if an agency's affidavits are reasonably specific and there is no evidence of bad faith.[17] Rather than conduct a de-

---

[14] See, e.g., Weissman v. CIA, 565 F.2d 692, 698 (D.C. Cir. 1977).

[15] Ray v. Turner, 587 F.2d 1187, 1194-95 (D.C. Cir. 1978).

[16] Id. at 1194 (quoting legislative history); see Students Against Genocide (SAGE) v. Department of State, No. 96-667, 1998 WL 699074, at *11 (D.D.C. Aug. 24, 1998) (magistrate's recommendation), adopted, No. 96-667 (D.D.C. Sept. 29, 1998) (appeal pending).

[17] See Halperin v. CIA, 629 F.2d 144, 148 (D.C. Cir. 1980); see, e.g., Schrecker v. United States Dep't of Justice, 74 F. Supp. 2d 26, 30 (D.D.C. 1999) (granting summary judgment when agency's "affidavits and indices pertaining to nondisclosure under Exemption 1 . . . [are] reasonably detailed and submitted in good faith") (appeal pending); Judicial Watch, Inc. v. Commission on United States-Pac. Trade & Inv. Policy, No. 97-0099, slip op. at 33 (D.D.C. Sept. 30, 1999) (finding that agency's "entries explain with substantial specificity what material it has withheld, why it withheld it, and the risk to U.S. foreign policy should the information be revealed," and that therefore there is no need for the court to "second guess the department's decision"); McErlean v. United States Dep't of Justice, No. 97-7831, 1999 WL 791680, at *6 (S.D.N.Y. Sept. 30, 1999) (holding that agency has "demonstrated the justification for each nondisclosure [under Exemption 1] with reasonable specificity"); Voinche v. FBI, 46 F. Supp. 2d 26, 29 (D.D.C. 1999) (declaring that agency properly invoked Exemption 1 when declaration "show[ed], with reasonable specificity, why the documents fall within the exemption" and when "there is no evidence of agency bad faith"); Billington v. Department of Justice, 11 F. Supp. 2d 45, 54, 58 (D.D.C. 1998) (applying Halperin standard generally and finding that plaintiff's evidence "whittles down to a string of if-then statements and suggestions of government conspiracy," which provide "no basis upon which to . . . warrant a probe of bad faith"); Canning v. United States Dep't of Justice, 848 F. Supp. 1037, 1042-43 (D.D.C. 1994) (applying Halperin standard); see also Hunt v. CIA, 981 F.2d 1116, 1119 (9th Cir. 1992) (Exemption 3); cf. Voinche v. FBI, 940 F. Supp. 323, 328 (D.D.C. 1996) (granting summary judgment despite "troubling" and "vague" affidavits in light of thoroughness of agency's other submissions and fact that Vaughn affidavits in Exemption 1 cases "inherently require a degree of generalization" to prevent compromise of national security interests), aff'd per curiam, No. 96-5304, 1997 U.S. App. LEXIS 19089 (D.C. Cir. June 19, 1997); Ajluni v. FBI,

(continued...)

# EXEMPTION 1

tailed inquiry, the court deferred to the expert opinion of the agency, noting that judges "lack the expertise necessary to second-guess such agency opinions in the typical national security FOIA case."[18] This review standard has been reaffirmed by the D.C. Circuit on a number of occasions,[19] and it has

---

[17](...continued)
947 F. Supp. 599, 607 (N.D.N.Y. 1996) (rejecting plaintiff's request for discovery of procedure by which documents are classified because Vaughn Index "sufficient"). But see Halpern v. FBI, 181 F.3d 279, 293 (2d Cir. 1999) (declaring that agency's "explanations read more like a policy justification" for Exec. Order No. 12,356, that the "affidavit gives no contextual description," and that it fails to "fulfill the functional purposes addressed in Vaughn"); Oglesby v. United States Dep't of the Army, 79 F.3d 1172, 1179-84 (D.C. Cir. 1996) (rejecting as insufficient certain Vaughn Indexes because agencies must itemize each document and adequately explain reasons for nondisclosure); Rosenfeld v. United States Dep't of Justice, 57 F.3d 803, 807 (9th Cir. 1995) (in affirming district court disclosure order, finding government failed to show with "any particularity" why classified portions of several documents should be withheld); Wiener v. FBI, 943 F.2d 972, 978-79 (9th Cir. 1991) (rejecting as inadequate agency justifications contained in coded Vaughn affidavits, based upon view that they consist of "boilerplate" explanations not "tailored" to particular information being withheld pursuant to Exemption 1); Oglesby v. United States Dep't of the Army, 920 F.2d 57, 66 n.12 (D.C. Cir. 1990) (noting degree of specificity required in public Vaughn affidavit in Exemption 1 case, especially with regard to agency's obligation to segregate and release nonexempt material); Greenberg v. United States Dep't of Treasury, 10 F. Supp. 2d 3, 15, 26-27 (D.D.C. 1998) (reserving judgment on Exemption 1 claims of CIA and FBI and ordering new affidavits because agencies' Vaughn Indexes found insufficient to permit court to engage in proper evaluation); Meeropol v. Reno, No. 75-1121, slip op. at 6-7 (D.D.C. Mar. 26, 1998) (finding, even after in camera review, FBI's declarations inadequate to justify withholdings in records relating to atomic bomb spies Julius and Ethel Rosenberg and ordering FBI to submit further Vaughn Indexes "in . . . substantiating [its] FOIA claims"); Keenan v. Department of Justice, No. 94-1909, slip op. at 8-11 (D.D.C. Mar. 24, 1997) (finding insufficient coded Vaughn Index which merely recites executive order's language without providing information about contents of withheld information), renewed motion for summary judgment denied in pertinent part (D.D.C. Dec. 16, 1997); Scott v. CIA, 916 F. Supp. 42, 44-49 (D.D.C. 1996) (finding CIA's affidavits "inadequate" because they "fail to provide any description of the nature or type of material redacted, much less justify the redaction by explaining how the . . . information withheld meets the requirements of the exemption").

[18] Halperin, 629 F.2d at 148; see also Bowers v. United States Dep't of Justice, 930 F.2d 350, 357 (4th Cir. 1991) (stating that "a court should hesitate to substitute its judgment of the sensitivity of the information for that of the agency"); Military Audit Project v. Casey, 656 F.2d 724, 738 (D.C. Cir. 1981) (emphasizing deference due agency's classification judgment).

[19] See, e.g., Krikorian v. Department of State, 984 F.2d 461, 464 (D.C. Cir. 1993); King v. United States Dep't of Justice, 830 F.2d 210, 217 (D.C. Cir. 1987) (concluding that "the court owes substantial weight to detailed agency
(continued...)

**EXEMPTION 1**

been adopted by other circuit courts as well.[20]

Indeed, if an agency affidavit passes muster under this standard, in camera review may be inappropriate because substantial weight must be accorded that affidavit.[21] In a 1996 decision, the D.C. Circuit stated that in a na-

---

[19](...continued)
explanations in the national security context"); Goldberg v. United States Dep't of State, 818 F.2d 71, 79-80 (D.C. Cir. 1987); see also Linn v. United States Dep't of Justice, No. 92-1406, 1995 WL 631847, at *26 (D.D.C. Aug. 22, 1995) (indicating that role of courts in reviewing Exemption 1 claims "is to determine whether the agency has presented a logical connection between its use of the exemption and the legitimate national security concerns involved; the Court does not have to ascertain whether the underlying facts of each specific application merit the agency's national security concerns"); Steinberg v. United States Dep't of Justice, 801 F. Supp. 800, 802-03 (D.D.C. 1992) (rejecting plaintiff's attack that coded Vaughn Index constituted inadequate "boilerplate," especially given "nature of underlying materials" which purportedly concern assassination of prime minister of friendly country), aff'd in pertinent part, 23 F.3d 548, 553 (D.C. Cir. 1994); Washington Post v. DOD, 766 F. Supp. 1, 6-7 (D.D.C. 1991) (declaring that judicial review of agency's classification decisions should be "quite deferential"); National Sec. Archive v. FBI, 759 F. Supp. 872, 875 (D.D.C. 1991) (explaining that government's burden to demonstrate proper withholding of material is "relatively light" in Exemption 1 context because court is required to "accord substantial weight to determination of [agency] officials"); cf. Department of the Navy v. Egan, 484 U.S. 518, 529-30 (1988) (allowing deference to agency expertise in granting of security clearances) (non-FOIA case).

[20] See, e.g., Maynard v. CIA, 986 F.2d 547, 555-56 & n.7 (1st Cir. 1993) (recognizing "substantial deference" so long as withheld information logically falls into exemption category cited and there exists no evidence of agency "bad faith"); Bowers, 930 F.2d at 357 (stating that "[w]hat fact or bit of information may compromise national security is best left to the intelligence experts"); Patterson v. FBI, 893 F.2d 595, 601 (3d Cir. 1990) (asserting that "courts are expected to accord 'substantial weight' to the agency's affidavit"); cf. Hunt, 981 F.2d at 1119 (applying similar deference in Exemption 3 case involving national security). But see Minier v. CIA, 88 F.3d 796, 800 (9th Cir. 1996) (providing for additional element to summary judgment analysis in FOIA cases by first requiring appeals court to determine whether district court had "adequate factual basis upon which to base its decision" before undertaking de novo review (citing Painting Indus. of Haw. Mkt. Recovery Fund v. United States Dep't of the Air Force, 26 F.3d 1479, 1482 (9th Cir. 1994), and Schiffer v. FBI, 78 F.3d 1405, 1409 (9th Cir. 1996))) (Exemption 3).

[21] See, e.g., Doherty v. United States Dep't of Justice, 775 F.2d 49, 53 (2d Cir. 1985) (adjudging that "the court should restrain its discretion to order in camera review"); Hayden v. NSA, 608 F.2d 1381, 1387 (D.C. Cir. 1979) (stating that "[w]hen the agency meets its burden by means of affidavits, in camera review is neither necessary nor appropriate"); Public Educ. Ctr., Inc. v. DOD, 905 F. Supp. 19, 22 (D.D.C. 1995) (declining in camera review of withheld videotapes after according substantial weight to agency's affidavit that public dis-
(continued...)

**EXEMPTION 1**

tional security case, a district court exercises "wise discretion" when it limits the number of documents it reviews in camera.[22] In upholding the district court's decision not to review certain documents in camera, the D.C. Circuit opined that limiting the number of documents examined by a court "makes it less likely that sensitive information will be disclosed" and, if there is an unauthorized disclosure of classified information, "makes it easier to pinpoint the source of the leak."[23]

In another case, the Court of Appeals for the Seventh Circuit analyzed the legislative history of the 1974 FOIA amendments and went so far as to conclude that "Congress did not intend that the courts would make a true de novo review of classified documents, that is, a fresh determination of the legitimacy of each classified document."[24] It is also noteworthy that the only Ex-

---

[21](...continued)
closure would harm national security); King v. United States Dep't of Justice, 586 F. Supp. 286, 290 (D.D.C. 1983) (characterizing in camera review as last resort), aff'd in part & rev'd in part on other grounds, 830 F.2d 210 (D.C. Cir. 1987); cf. Young v. CIA, 972 F.2d 536, 538-39 (4th Cir. 1992) (holding that district court did not abuse its discretion by refusing to review documents in camera--despite small number--because agency's affidavits found sufficiently specific to meet required standards for proper withholding). But see, e.g., Patterson, 893 F.2d at 599 (finding in camera review of two documents appropriate when agency description of records was insufficient to permit meaningful review and to verify good faith of agency in conducting its investigation); Allen v. CIA, 636 F.2d 1287, 1291 (D.C. Cir. 1980) (holding that conclusory affidavit by agency requires remand to district court for in camera inspection of 15-page document); Armstrong v. Executive Office of the President, No. 89-142, slip op. at 4-8 (D.D.C. July 28, 1995) (ordering in camera review of 4 of 17 documents at issue because government's explanation for withholdings insufficient, but denying plaintiff's request that court review documents merely because government subsequently released previously withheld material), aff'd on other grounds, 97 F.3d 575 (D.C. Cir. 1996); Moore v. FBI, No. 83-1541, 1984 U.S. Dist. LEXIS 18732, at *9 (D.D.C. Mar. 9, 1984) (finding in camera review particularly appropriate when only small volume of documents involved and government makes proffer), aff'd, 762 F.2d 138 (D.C. Cir. 1985) (unpublished table decision); cf. Jones v. FBI, 41 F.3d 238, 242-44 (6th Cir. 1994) (finding in camera inspection necessary, not because FBI acted in bad faith with regard to plaintiff's FOIA request, but due to evidence of illegality with regard to FBI's underlying investigation); Wiener, 943 F.2d at 979 & n.9 (noting that in camera review by district court cannot "replace" requirement for sufficient Vaughn Index and can only "supplement" agency's justifications contained in affidavits).

[22] Armstrong v. Executive Office of the President, 97 F.3d 575, 580 (D.C. Cir. 1996).

[23] Id.

[24] Stein v. Department of Justice, 662 F.2d 1245, 1253 (7th Cir. 1981).

**EXEMPTION 1**

emption 1 FOIA decision to find agency "bad faith,"[25] which initially held that certain CIA procedural shortcomings amounted to "bad faith" on the part of the agency, was subsequently vacated on panel rehearing.[26]

### Deference to Agency Expertise

While the standard of judicial review is often expressed in different ways, courts have generally deferred to agency expertise in national security cases.[27] Indeed, courts are usually reluctant to substitute their judgment in place of the agency's "unique insights" in the areas of national defense and foreign relations.[28]

---

[25] McGehee v. CIA, 697 F.2d 1095, 1113 (D.C. Cir. 1983).

[26] McGehee v. CIA, 711 F.2d 1076, 1077 (D.C. Cir. 1983); see also Washington Post Co. v. DOD, No. 84-2949, 1987 U.S. Dist. LEXIS 16108, at *12 (D.D.C. Feb. 25, 1987) (deciding that addition of second classification category at time of litigation "does not create an inference of 'bad faith' concerning the processing of plaintiff's request or otherwise implicating the affiant's credibility"); cf. Gilmore v. NSA, No. C92-3646, 1993 U.S. Dist. LEXIS 7694, at **28-30 (N.D. Cal. May 3, 1993) (holding that subsequent release by agency of some material initially withheld pursuant to Exemption 1 is not any indication of "bad faith").

[27] See, e.g., Young v. CIA, 972 F.2d 536, 538-39 (4th Cir. 1993) (finding district court properly deferred to agency affiant because no evidence of bad faith); Bowers v. United States Dep't of Justice, 930 F.2d 350, 357 (4th Cir. 1991) (observing that "[w]hat fact . . . may compromise national security is best left to the intelligence experts"); Doherty v. United States Dep't of Justice, 775 F.2d 49, 52 (2d Cir. 1985) (according "substantial weight" to agency declaration); Miller v. Casey, 730 F.2d 773, 776 (D.C. Cir. 1984) (same); Taylor v. Department of the Army, 684 F.2d 99, 109 (D.C. Cir. 1982) (holding that classification affidavits are entitled to "the utmost deference") (reversing district court disclosure order); Students Against Genocide (SAGE) v. Department of State, No. 96-667, 1998 WL 699074, at *11 (D.D.C. Aug. 24, 1998) (magistrate's recommendation) (declaring that plaintiff's arguments do not overcome "substantial weight accorded to DOS's classification decisions"), adopted, No. 96-667 (D.D.C. Sept. 29, 1998) (appeal pending); Badalementi v. Department of State, 899 F. Supp. 542, 546 (D. Kan. 1995) (according substantial weight to agency's affidavit and granting motion for summary judgment in light of agency's expertise in national security matters); Canning v. United States Dep't of Justice, 848 F. Supp. 1037, 1042 (D.D.C. 1994) (describing how in according such deference, courts "credit agency expertise in evaluating matters of national security by focusing attention primarily on whether affidavits are sufficiently specific and by ensuring that they are not controverted by contradictory evidence or evidence of bad faith"). But see FOIA Update, Vol. XVI, No. 2, at 4, 12 (summarizing history of Exemption 1 disclosure orders and urging careful attention to classification determinations accordingly).

[28] See, e.g., Miller v. United States Dep't of State, 779 F.2d 1378, 1387 (8th Cir. 1985); see also Maynard v. CIA, 986 F.2d 547, 556 n.9 (1st Cir. 1993)

(continued...)

**EXEMPTION 1**

Courts have demonstrated this general deference to agency expertise by according little or no weight to opinions of persons other than the agency classification authority when reviewing the propriety of agency classification determinations.[29] Persons whose opinions have been rejected by the courts in this context include a former ambassador who had personally prepared some

---

[28](...continued)
(stating that court "not in a position to 'second-guess'" agency's determination regarding need for continued classification of material); Krikorian v. Department of State, 984 F.2d 461, 464-65 (D.C. Cir. 1993) (acknowledging agency's "unique insights" in areas of national defense and foreign relations); Braslavsky v. FBI, No. 92 C 3027, slip op. at 4-5 (N.D. Ill. June 6, 1994) (indicating that courts "generally inclined" to accept agency positions in area of intelligence sources and methods; "[a] court has neither the experience nor expertise to determine whether a classification [determination] is substantively correct"), aff'd, 57 F.3d 1073 (7th Cir. 1995) (unpublished table decision); Willens v. NSC, 726 F. Supp. 325, 326-27 (D.D.C. 1989) (declaring that court cannot second-guess agency's national security determinations when they are "credible and have a rational basis"); cf. Aftergood v. CIA, No. 98-2107, 1999 U.S. Dist. LEXIS 18135, at *9 (D.D.C. Nov. 12, 1999) (declaring that "the law does not require certainty" in agency predictions of national security harm). But see King v. United States Dep't of Justice, 830 F.2d 210, 226 (D.C. Cir. 1987) (holding that trial court erred in deferring to agency's judgment that information more than 35 years old remained classified when executive order presumed declassification of information over 20 years old and agency merely indicated procedural compliance with order); Lawyers Comm. for Human Rights v. INS, 721 F. Supp. 552, 561 (S.D.N.Y. 1989) (reminding that such deference does not give agency "carte blanche" to withhold responsive documents without "valid and thorough affidavit"), subsequent decision, No. 87-Civ-1115, slip op. at 1-2 (S.D.N.Y. June 7, 1990) (upholding Exemption 1 excisions after in camera review of certain documents and classified CIA Vaughn affidavit).

[29] See, e.g., Van Atta v. Defense Intelligence Agency, No. 87-1508, 1988 WL 73856, at *1-2 (D.D.C. July 6, 1988) (rejecting opinion of requester who claimed that willingness of foreign diplomat to discuss issue indicated no expectation of confidentiality); Washington Post v. DOD, No. 84-2949, 1987 U.S. Dist. LEXIS 16108, at **19-20 (D.D.C. Feb. 25, 1987) (rejecting opinion of U.S. Senator who read document in official capacity as member of Committee on Foreign Relations); cf. Lawyers Alliance for Nuclear Arms Control v. Department of Energy, No. 88-CV-7635, 1991 WL 274860, at **1-2 (E.D. Pa. Dec. 17, 1991) (upholding Exemption 1 claim for Joint Verification Agreement records when requester provided no "admissible evidence" that officials of Soviet Union consented to release of requested nuclear test results); Alyeska Pipeline Serv. v. EPA, 856 F.2d 309, 315 (D.C. Cir. 1988) (emphasizing no "special deference to agency beyond Exemption 1 context"). But cf. Washington Post v. DOD, 766 F. Supp. 1, 13-14 (D.D.C. 1991) (adjudging that "nonofficial releases" contained in books by participants involved in Iranian hostage rescue attempt--including ground assault commander and former President Carter--have "good deal of reliability" and require government to explain "how official disclosure" of code names "at this time would damage national security").

**EXEMPTION 1**

of the records at issue,[30] a retired admiral,[31] a former agent of the CIA,[32] and a retired CIA staff historian.[33] And in a recent example of great deference to agency expertise, a court considering the sensitivity of disclosing for the third consecutive year the total budget request for all intelligence activities concluded that it "must defer to . . . [the agency's] decision that release . . . amidst the information already publicly-available, provides too much trend information and too great a basis for comparison and analysis for our adversaries."[34]

### In Camera Submissions

There are numerous instances in which courts have permitted agencies to submit explanatory in camera affidavits in order to protect certain national security information which could not be discussed in a public affidavit.[35] It is entirely clear, though, that agencies taking such a special step are under a duty to "create as complete a public record as is possible" before doing so.[36]

---

[30] See Rush v. Department of State, No. 88-8245, slip op. at 17-18 (S.D. Fla. Sept. 12, 1990) (magistrate's recommendation), adopted, 740 F. Supp. 1548, 1554 (S.D. Fla. 1990); cf. Goldberg v. United States Dep't of State, 818 F.2d 71, 79-80 (D.C. Cir. 1987) (accepting classification officer's determination even though more than 100 ambassadors did not initially classify information).

[31] See Hudson River Sloop Clearwater, Inc. v. Department of the Navy, 891 F.2d 414, 421-22 (2d Cir. 1989).

[32] See Gardels v. CIA, 689 F.2d 1100, 1106 n.5 (D.C. Cir. 1982).

[33] See Pfeiffer v. CIA, 721 F. Supp. 337, 340-41 (D.D.C. 1989).

[34] Aftergood, 1999 U.S. Dist. LEXIS 18135, at **11-12.

[35] See, e.g., Patterson v. FBI, 893 F.2d 595, 599-600 (3d Cir. 1990); Simmons v. United States Dep't of Justice, 796 F.2d 709, 711 (4th Cir. 1986); Ingle v. Department of Justice, 698 F.2d 259, 264 (6th Cir. 1983) (ruling that in camera review should be secondary to testimony or affidavits); Salisbury v. United States, 690 F.2d 966, 973 n.3 (D.C. Cir. 1982); Stein v. Department of Justice, 662 F.2d 1245, 1255-56 (7th Cir. 1981); Springmann v. United States Dep't of State, No. 93-1238, slip op. at 1 (D.D.C. Feb. 24, 2000) (granting motion for summary judgment upon in camera inspection); Greyshock v. United States Coast Guard, No. 94-00563, slip op. at 1 (D. Haw. May 9, 1995) (finding upon in camera examination of agency's classified declaration records at issue properly withheld), aff'd, 107 F.3d 16 (9th Cir. 1997) (unpublished table decision); cf. Armstrong v. Executive Office of the President, 97 F.3d 575, 580-81 (D.C. Cir. 1996) (finding that although district court may have erred by not explaining reasons for using in camera affidavit, any such error was "harmless" because agency adequately explained why it could not release withheld information).

[36] Phillippi v. CIA, 546 F.2d 1009, 1013 (D.C. Cir. 1976); see also Armstrong, 97 F.3d at 580 (holding that when district court uses an in camera affidavit, even in national security cases, "it must both make its reasons for doing so clear and make as much as possible of the in camera submission available to the opposing party" (citing Lykins v. United States Dep't of Justice, 725

(continued...)

# EXEMPTION 1

In this regard, it is reasonably well settled that counsel for plaintiffs are not entitled to participate in such in camera proceedings.[37] Several years ago, though, one court took the unprecedented step of appointing a special master to review and categorize a large volume of classified records.[38] In other instances involving large numbers of records, courts have on occasion ordered

---

[36](...continued)
F.2d 1455, 1465 (D.C. Cir. 1984)); Patterson, 893 F.2d at 600; Simmons, 796 F.2d at 710; Payne v. Minihan, No. 97-0266, slip op. at 49 & n.20 (D.N.M. Apr. 30, 1998) (ordering in camera affidavit upon finding that public record was "complete as possible") (appeal pending); Scott v. CIA, 916 F. Supp. 42, 48-49 (D.D.C. 1996) (denying request for in camera review until agency "creates as full a public record as possible"); Public Educ. Ctr., Inc. v. DOD, 905 F. Supp. 19, 22 (D.D.C. 1995) (ordering in camera review only after agency created "as full a public record as possible" (citing Hayden v. NSA, 608 F.2d 1381, 1384 (D.C. Cir. 1979)); National Sec. Archive v. Office of Indep. Counsel, No. 89-2308, 1992 U.S. Dist. LEXIS 13146, at **6-7 (D.D.C. Aug. 28, 1992) (applying Phillippi standards, refusing to review in camera affidavits until agency "has stated publicly 'in as much detail as possible' . . . reasons for nondisclosure"); Moessmer v. CIA, No. 86-948, slip op. at 9-11 (E.D. Mo. Feb. 17, 1987) (finding in camera review appropriate when record contains contradictory evidence), aff'd, 871 F.2d 1092 (6th Cir. 1988) (unpublished table decision). But see Public Citizen v. Department of State, No. 91-746, 1991 WL 179116, at *3 (D.D.C. Aug. 26, 1991) (ordering in camera review of records upon basis that public testimony of ambassador may have "waived" Exemption 1 protection), aff'd, 11 F.3d 198 (D.C. Cir. 1993).

[37] See Salisbury, 690 F.2d at 973 n.3; Weberman v. NSA, 668 F.2d 676, 678 (2d Cir. 1982); Hayden, 608 F.2d at 1385-86; Martin v. United States Dep't of Justice, No. 83-2674, slip op. at 1 (W.D. Pa. June 5, 1986) (requiring agency to release unclassified portions of transcript of in camera testimony), aff'd, 800 F.2d 1135 (3d Cir. 1986) (unpublished table decision); see also Ellsberg v. Mitchell, 709 F.2d 51, 61 (D.C. Cir. 1983) (holding that plaintiff's counsel not permitted to participate in in camera review of documents arguably covered by state secrets privilege); Pollard v. FBI, 705 F.2d 1151, 1154 (9th Cir. 1983) (finding no reversible error where court not only reviewed affidavit and documents in camera, but also received authenticating testimony ex parte); cf. Arieff v. United States Dep't of the Navy, 712 F.2d 1462, 1470-71 & n.2 (D.C. Cir. 1983) (denying participation by plaintiff's counsel even when information withheld was personal privacy information). But cf. Lederle Lab. v. HHS, No. 88-249, 1988 WL 47649, at *1 (D.D.C. May 2, 1988) (granting restrictive protective order in Exemption 4 case permitting counsel for requester to review contested business information).

[38] See Washington Post v. DOD, No. 84-3400, slip op. at 2 (D.D.C. Jan. 15, 1988), petition for mandamus denied sub nom. In re DOD, 848 F.2d 232 (D.C. Cir. 1988); cf. Bay Area Lawyers Alliance for Nuclear Arms Control v. Department of State, 818 F. Supp. 1291, 1301 (N.D. Cal. 1992) (holding that court "will not hesitate" to appoint special master to assist with in camera review of documents if agency fails to submit adequate Vaughn affidavits).

agencies to submit samples of the documents at issue for in camera review.[39]

In a decision which highlights some of the difficulties of Exemption 1 litigation practice, the Court of Appeals for the Fourth Circuit issued a writ of mandamus which required that court personnel who would have access to classified materials submitted in camera in an Exemption 1 case obtain security clearances prior to the submission of any such materials to the court.[40] On remand, the district court judge reviewed the disputed documents entirely on his own.[41] Consistent with the special precautions taken by courts in Exemption 1 cases, the government also has been ordered to provide a court reporter with the requisite security clearances to transcribe in camera proceedings, in order "to establish a complete record for meaningful appellate review."[42]

Agencies have in other cases been compelled to submit in camera affidavits when disclosure in a public affidavit would vitiate the very protection afforded by Exemption 1.[43] Such a procedure is sometimes employed when

---

[39] See, e.g., Wilson v. CIA, No. 89-3356, 1991 WL 226682, at *3 (D.D.C. Oct. 15, 1991) (ordering in camera submission of "sample" of 50 documents because "neither necessary nor practicable" for court to review all 1000 processed records).

[40] In re United States Dep't of Justice, No. 87-1205, slip op. at 4-5 (4th Cir. Apr. 7, 1988).

[41] Bowers v. United States Dep't of Justice, No. C-C-86-336, 1990 WL 41893, at *1 (W.D.N.C. Mar. 9, 1990), rev'd on other grounds, 930 F.2d 350 (4th Cir. 1991).

[42] Willens v. NSC, 720 F. Supp. 15, 16 (D.D.C. 1989); cf. Physicians for Soc. Responsibility, Inc. v. United States Dep't of Justice, No. 85-169, slip op. at 3-4 (D.D.C. Aug. 25, 1985) (transcript of in camera proceedings--from which plaintiff's counsel was excluded--placed under seal). But cf. Pollard, 705 F.2d at 1154 (finding no reversible error when no transcript made of ex parte testimony of FBI agent who merely "authenticated and described" documents at issue).

[43] See, e.g., Green v. United States Dep't of State, No. 85-0504, slip op. at 17-18 (D.D.C. Apr. 17, 1990) (determining that public Vaughn affidavit containing additional information could "well have the effect of prematurely letting the cat out of the bag"); cf. Maynard v. CIA, 986 F.2d 547, 557 (1st Cir. 1993) (reasoning that "a more detailed affidavit could have revealed the very intelligence sources and methods the CIA wished to keep secret"); Gilmore v. NSA, No. C92-3646, 1993 U.S. Dist. LEXIS 7694, at **18-19 (N.D. Cal. May 3, 1993) (ruling that agency has provided as much information as possible in public affidavit without "thwarting" purpose of Exemption 1 (citing King v. United States Dep't of Justice, 830 F.2d 210, 224 (D.C. Cir. 1987))); Center for Nat'l Sec. Studies v. Office of Indep. Counsel, No. 91-1691, slip op. at 4 (D.D.C. Mar. 2, 1993) (stating that "[i]n the national security context, the release of detailed information through discovery may render the FOIA exemption meaningless and compromise intelligence sources and methods"); Krikorian
(continued...)

# EXEMPTION 1

even the confirmation or denial of the existence of records at issue would pose a threat to national security--the so-called "Glomar" response.[44] (For a fur-

---

[43](...continued)
v. Department of State, No. 88-3419, 1990 WL 236108, at *3 (D.D.C. Dec. 19, 1990) (declaring agency's public affidavits sufficient because requiring more detailed descriptions of information would give foreign governments and confidential intelligence sources "reason to pause" before offering advice or useful information to agency officials in future), aff'd in pertinent part, 984 F.2d 461, 464-65 (D.C. Cir. 1993).

[44] See Phillippi, 546 F.2d at 1013 (regarding request for documents pertaining to Glomar Explorer submarine-retrieval ship; consequently, "neither confirm nor deny" response now known as "Glomar" response or "Glomarization"); see, e.g., Frugone v. CIA, 169 F.3d 772, 775 (D.C. Cir. 1999) (finding that CIA properly refused to confirm or deny whether plaintiff was ever employed by CIA when disclosure could cause "diplomatic tension between Chile and the United States" or could "lessen the burden facing a foreign intelligence agency attempting to track the CIA's covert activities abroad"); Miller v. Casey, 730 F.2d 773, 776 (D.C. Cir. 1984) (applying response to request for any record reflecting any attempt by western countries to overthrow Albanian government); Gardels v. CIA, 689 F.2d 1100, 1105 (D.C. Cir. 1982) (applying response to request for any record revealing any covert CIA connection with University of California); Arabian Shield Dev. Co. v. CIA, No. 3-98-0624, 1999 WL 118796, at *9 (N.D. Tex. Feb. 26, 1999) (holding that agency properly refused to confirm or deny whether it "has collected intelligence regarding specific individuals or corporations, or has an intelligence interest or a facility in a particular foreign location"), aff'd per curiam, No. 99-10327 (5th Cir. Jan. 28, 2000); Roman v. Dailey, No. 97-1164, 1998 U.S. Dist. LEXIS 6708, at **7-10 (D.D.C. May 11, 1998) (finding that agencies properly refused to confirm or deny existence of records about alleged satellite capabilities) (Exemptions 1 and 3); Earth Pledge Found. v. CIA, 988 F. Supp. 623, 627 (S.D.N.Y. 1996) (ruling that agency properly refused to confirm or deny existence of correspondence between CIA headquarters and alleged CIA station in Dominican Republic, because fact of station's existence itself was classified and disclosure would reveal agency's intelligence methods and could cause damage to U.S. foreign relations), aff'd per curiam, 128 F.3d 788 (2d Cir. 1997); Nayed v. INS, No. 91-805, 1993 WL 524541, at *2 (D.D.C. Nov. 29, 1993) (finding "Glomar" response appropriate for request for records on former Libyan national denied entry into United States because "confirmation that information exists would . . . be admission of identity of CIA intelligence interest . . . [while] denial . . . would allow interested parties to ascertain [such] interests based on their analysis of patterns of CIA answers in different FOIA cases"); D'Aleo v. Department of the Navy, No. 89-2347, 1991 U.S. Dist. LEXIS 3884, at **4-5 (D.D.C. Mar. 27, 1991) (holding that any confirmation or denial of existence of nondisclosure agreement allegedly signed by plaintiff would cause serious damage to national security); Marrera v. United States Dep't of Justice, 622 F. Supp. 51, 53-54 (D.D.C. 1985) (applying "Glomar" response to request for any record which would reveal whether requester was target of surveillance pursuant to Foreign Intelligence Surveillance Act); see also Exec. Order No. 12,958, § 3.7(a), 3 C.F.R. 333, 347 (1996), reprinted in 50 U.S.C. § 435 note (Supp. II 1996), and in FOIA Update, Vol. XVI, No. 2, at 9; Attorney General's Memo-
(continued...)

**EXEMPTION 1**

ther discussion of in camera review, see Litigation Considerations, In Camera Inspection, below.)

### Rejection of Classification Claims

Prior to 1986, no appellate court had ever upheld, on the substantive merits of the case, a decision to reject an agency's classification claim. In 1980, the Court of Appeals for the District of Columbia Circuit let stand, but on entirely procedural grounds, a district court determination that the CIA's affidavits were general and conclusory and that its Exemption 1 claims had to be rejected as "overly broad."[45] Moreover, that portion of the D.C. Circuit's decision was subsequently vacated by the Supreme Court.[46] Several years later, in an unprecedented and exceptionally complex case, a district court ordered the disclosure of classified records belatedly determined by it to be within the scope of the request and therefore not addressed in the agency's classification affidavits.[47] The government never had the opportunity to obtain appellate review of the merits of this adverse decision because the records were disclosed after stays pending appeal were denied, successively, by the district court, the Court of Appeals for the Ninth Circuit, and even by the Su-

---

[44](...continued) randum on the 1986 Amendments to the Freedom of Information Act 26 (Dec. 1987); FOIA Update, Vol. IV, No. 2, at 5; cf. Minier v. CIA, 88 F.3d 796, 801-02 (9th Cir. 1996) (finding "neither confirm nor deny" response proper for request seeking records on individual's employment relationship with CIA because to reveal such information would "provide a window into the [agency's] 'sources and methods'") (Exemption 3); Hunt v. CIA, 981 F.2d 1116, 1120 (9th Cir. 1992) (holding "Glomar" response proper for request for records on murdered Iranian national) (Exemption 3); Levy v. CIA, No. 95-1276, slip op. at 11-14 (D.D.C. Nov. 16, 1995) (finding "Glomar" response appropriate regarding request for CIA records on foreign national because "[c]onsistent treatment of all requests relating to foreign nationals is a critical element to the CIA's protective strategy to safeguard its intelligence sources and methods") (Exemption 3), summary affirmance granted, No. 96-5004 (D.C. Cir. Jan. 15, 1997). But cf. Payne, No. 97-0266, slip op. at 48-49 (D.N.M. Apr. 30, 1998) (ordering NSA to provide in camera affidavit justifying its "Glomar" response to request for records involving intercepted Iranian/Libyan messages and explaining "the nexus between [its response] . . . and the foreseeable harm to national security and/or impairment of NSA's communications intelligence" that confirmation or denial of existence of such cables would be expected to cause).

[45] Holy Spirit Ass'n v. CIA, 636 F.2d 838, 845 (D.C. Cir. 1980); see also FOIA Update, Vol. XVI, No. 2, at 4, 12 (providing summary of FOIA cases involving Exemption 1 disclosure orders).

[46] CIA v. Holy Spirit Ass'n, 455 U.S. 997 (1982); see also FOIA Update, Vol. III, No. 2, at 5.

[47] Powell v. United States Dep't of Justice, No. C-82-326, slip op. at 16 (N.D. Cal. Mar. 27, 1985); see also Powell v. United States Dep't of Justice, 584 F. Supp. 1508, 1517-18, 1530-31 (N.D. Cal. 1984).

# EXEMPTION 1

preme Court.[48] In addition, the district court ordered the disclosure of certain other segments of classified information because it was "convinced [that] disclosure of this information poses no threat to national security."[49] The district court did, however, grant a stay of this aspect of its disclosure order so the government could take an appeal.[50] Ultimately, the case was settled with the government being permitted to withhold this classified information.

In 1986, the Court of Appeals for the Second Circuit upheld a district court disclosure order in a case in which the district court found that the affidavit submitted by the FBI inadequately described the withheld documents and was unconvincing as to any potential harm which would result from disclosure.[51] This finding, coupled with in camera inspection of the documents by the district court, led the court of appeals to conclude that "it would be inappropriate . . . to give more deference to the FBI's characterization of the information than did the trial court."[52] The case was subsequently settled, however, and the plaintiff withdrew his request for the classified records ordered disclosed in exchange for the government's agreement not to seek to vacate the Second Circuit's opinion in the Supreme Court. The precedential value of the Second Circuit's decision is therefore questionable in light of the extraordinary procedural and factual nature of the case.

Also of note in this regard is a district court decision which required in camera affidavits on all records, most of which were classified, "not because the agencies' good faith had been controverted, but 'in order that the Court may be able to monitor the agencies' determinations'"; ultimately, the district court did order some classified information be disclosed.[53] However, the D.C. Circuit, on appeal, remanded the case for submission of briefs in light of the Supreme Court's decision in CIA v. Sims.[54] On remand, the district court found most of the information to be protected under Sims, but it affirmed its disclosure order with regard to some of the information that the CIA had sought to protect under Exemptions 1 and 3.[55] The D.C. Circuit subsequently reversed that part of the district court's order on remand that still required

---

[48] Powell, No. C-82-326, slip op. at 4-6 (N.D. Cal. June 14, 1985), stay denied, No. 85-1918 (9th Cir. July 18, 1985), stay denied, No. A-84 (U.S. July 31, 1985) (Rehnquist, Circuit Justice) (undocketed order).

[49] Powell, No. C-82-326, slip op. at 8 (N.D. Cal. Mar. 27, 1985).

[50] Powell, No. C-82-326, slip op. at 6 (N.D. Cal. June 14, 1985).

[51] Donovan v. FBI, 806 F.2d 55 (2d Cir. 1986); see also Donovan v. FBI, 625 F. Supp. 808, 811 (S.D.N.Y. 1986).

[52] 806 F.2d at 60.

[53] Fitzgibbon v. CIA, 578 F. Supp. 704, 709 (D.D.C. 1983), motion for reconsideration granted in part, No. 79-956 (D.D.C. July 5, 1984).

[54] 471 U.S. 159 (1985); see Fitzgibbon v. CIA, No. 84-5632 (D.C. Cir. Mar. 13, 1986).

[55] Fitzgibbon v. CIA, No. 79-956, slip op. at 14-15, 17-18 (D.D.C. May 19, 1989).

**EXEMPTION 1**

disclosure of certain CIA information, though it rested its decision upon Exemption 3 grounds alone.[56] It concluded that "whatever merits" there may have been to support disclosure of the information at issue in the case had been "vaporized by the unequivocal sweep of the Supreme Court's decision in Sims."[57]

Two significant D.C. Circuit decisions, each of which reversed a district court disclosure order, strongly reaffirmed the deference that is due an agency's classification judgment. In the first, the D.C. Circuit overturned a lower court conclusion that the existence of information in the public domain similar to the information at issue warranted the disclosure of that classified information.[58] Emphasizing that the least "bit" of classified information deserves protection, it observed that the "district court's finding . . . reveals a basic misunderstanding of the information withheld," and that the "district court did not give the required 'substantial weight' to the [agency's] uncontradicted affidavits."[59]

Similarly, in the second case, the D.C. Circuit vacated a district court determination that public statements by senior executive and legislative branch officials constituted sufficient official acknowledgment of "covert action" by the government against Nicaragua to warrant release of the sensitive documents at issue, specifically chastised the lower court for "refusing to consider in camera the confidential declaration and confidential memorandum of law offered by the government," and remanded the case for a more careful consideration of the government's classification judgment.[60] On remand, the district court found that the "Government's general acknowledgment of covert activities . . . is insufficient to require release" of its records.[61]

In 1995, the Court of Appeals for the Ninth Circuit affirmed a district court disclosure order of classified information.[62] In that case, involving a re-

___

[56] Fitzgibbon v. CIA, 911 F.2d 755, 757, 760, 764 (D.C. Cir. 1990).

[57] Id. at 760; see also Siminoski v. FBI, No. 83-6499, slip op. at 14-18 (C.D. Cal. Jan. 16, 1990) (rejecting magistrate's recommendation to disclose classified information).

[58] Abbotts v. NRC, 766 F.2d 604, 607-08 (D.C. Cir. 1985).

[59] Id. at 607 & n.3; see also Bowers v. United States Dep't of Justice, 930 F.2d 350, 352, 354-55 (4th Cir. 1991) (reversing district court order to disclose classified information because lower court was "clearly erroneous" in not applying proper standards in review of records and in not giving any weight to detailed explanations of FBI as to why undisclosed information in its counterintelligence files should be withheld).

[60] Peterzell v. Department of State, No. 84-5805, slip op. at 2 (D.C. Cir. Apr. 2, 1985).

[61] Peterzell v. Department of State, No. 82-2853, slip op. at 3 (D.D.C. Sept. 20, 1985).

[62] Rosenfeld v. United States Dep't of Justice, 57 F.3d 803, 807-08 (9th Cir. (continued...)

# EXEMPTION 1

quest to the FBI for records of its investigations into individuals and organizations associated with the Free Speech Movement at the University of California at Berkeley during the 1960s, the full Supreme Court previously had taken the extraordinary step of staying the district court's disclosure order pending a full review of the decision by the court of appeals.[63] In its ruling, the district court ignored the recommendation of a magistrate who had concluded that the information was properly classified by the FBI, and grounded its decision on its supposition that the information involved was "likely to have been public knowledge."[64]

Undertaking minimal appellate review, the Ninth Circuit held that the district court had "correctly concluded that the government did not carry its burden" as to the classified information contained in three documents because it had not demonstrated with sufficient "particularity" why classification was warranted.[65] It flatly rejected the FBI's argument that the lower court had failed to afford the government's classification determinations "substantial deference," summarily declaring that "[t]his contention does not persuade us [because] the FBI had failed to make an initial showing which would justify [such] deference."[66]

At the same time, the Ninth Circuit affirmed the district court's determination that a fourth document could be disclosed in part while "still accommodating the government's classification interest."[67] The district court had allowed the FBI to delete information identifying an informant, but ruled that the document as excised could be released to the requester.[68] In that instance, the Ninth Circuit held that the FBI had carried its burden with regard to the deleted portions of the document and permitted the agency to withhold them.[69]

Most recently, in a case that was watched closely because it was the first case decided under Executive Order 12,958, a district court initially ordered the disclosure of a letter sent by the British Home Office to the Department of

---

(...continued)
1995); see also FOIA Update, Vol. XVI, No. 2, at 13.

[63] Rosenfeld v. United States Dep't of Justice, 761 F. Supp. 1440, 1451 (N.D. Cal. 1991), emergency stay denied on juris. grounds, No. 91-15854 (9th Cir. June 12, 1991), stay pending appeal granted, 501 U.S. 1227 (1991); see also FOIA Update, Vol. XII, No. 3, at 1-2.

[64] 761 F. Supp. at 1451.

[65] 57 F.3d at 807.

[66] Id.

[67] Id. at 808.

[68] Id. at 807.

[69] Id. at 807-08.

**EXEMPTION 1**

Justice which was not classified until after receipt of the FOIA request.[70] The court first rejected the government's argument that the letter was properly classified as "foreign government information" because it found that the agency's affidavit failed to demonstrate a "contemporaneous expectation of confidentiality."[71] Furthermore, the court found that there was no showing by the government of a presumption of confidentiality under the prior executive order.[72] For purposes of its analysis, the court assumed that disclosure of the letter could "damage relations" between the United States and Great Britain.[73] Nonetheless, it determined that the government's affidavit was too "general" and "conclusory in nature" to permit the court to find that the letter was properly withheld pursuant to Exemption 1.[74]

On a motion for reconsideration, the court rejected the government's arguments that: (1) the court had failed to give the agency's determination of harm sufficient deference;[75] (2) the information constituted "foreign government information";[76] and (3) Executive Order 12,356 should have applied to the case because the letter was originated prior to the effective date of Executive Order 12,958.[77] With regard to the last argument, the court conceded that the prior order--which provided for a presumption of harm concerning the disclosure of "foreign government information"--would have applied "[h]ad the classification decision been made with reasonable dispatch."[78] After first rejecting the government's alternative motion that it undertake in camera inspection of the letter, the court "reluctantly" agreed to do so because "of the danger that highly sensitive . . . material might be released only because [the agency was] unable to articulate a factual basis for their concerns without giving away the information itself."[79] When this proved to be the case upon the court's in camera review of the document, the court granted the motion for reconsideration and upheld the letter's classification.[80]

---

[70] Weatherhead v. United States, No. 95-519, slip op. at 5-6 (E.D. Wash. Mar. 29, 1996), reconsideration granted in pertinent part (E.D. Wash. Sept. 9, 1996).

[71] Id. at 5-7; see also Exec. Order No. 12,958, § 1.1(d) (definition of "foreign government information").

[72] Weatherhead, No. 95-519, slip op. at 5-6 (E.D. Wash. Mar. 29, 1996).

[73] Id. at 7, 12.

[74] Id. at 10-11.

[75] Weatherhead, No. 95-519, slip op. at 3-4 (E.D. Wash. Sept. 9, 1996).

[76] Id. at 4-6.

[77] Id. at 6-7.

[78] Id. at 7.

[79] Id. at 7-8.

[80] Id. at 8. But see Keenan v. Department of Justice, No. 94-1909, slip op. at 8-9 (D.D.C. Dec. 16, 1997) (ordering upon in camera inspection release of (continued...)

**EXEMPTION 1**

On appeal, however, the Court of Appeals for the Ninth Circuit, in a 2-1 decision, flatly refused to defer to the State Department's judgment of foreign relations harm and ordered the letter disclosed.[81] The Solicitor General then petitioned the Supreme Court to grant certiorari review of the Ninth Circuit's ruling, which it did, and the case was scheduled for Supreme Court argument.[82] During the briefing of the case, however, the requester suddenly revealed that he was in possession of a subsequent letter from a local British Consul that addressed the same subject.[83] In response to this revelation, the State Department brought this new information to the attention of the British Government, which then decided to no longer insist on confidentiality for the letter.[84] Accordingly, and on an expedited basis, the letter was declassified, it was disclosed to the requester, and it became the basis for a successful motion by the Solicitor General to have the Supreme Court nullify the Ninth Circuit's adverse precedent on the ground that it no longer could be appealed.[85]

"Public Domain" Information

Several courts also have had occasion to consider whether agencies have a duty to disclose classified information which has purportedly found its way into the public domain. In this regard, it has been held that, in asserting a claim of prior public disclosure, a FOIA plaintiff bears "the initial burden of pointing to specific information in the public domain that appears to duplicate that being withheld."[86] Accordingly, Exemption 1 claims should not be

---

[80](...continued) document segments withheld by agency pursuant to Exemption 1 because agency "failed to demonstrate" how disclosure of information ranging from 32 to 46 years old could "continue to damage the national security"); Springmann v. United States Dep't of State, No. 93-1238, slip op. at 9-11 (D.D.C. Apr. 21, 1997) (initially ruling that disclosure of two paragraphs in embassy report about American employee engaging in religiously offensive behavior in Saudi Arabia would not harm national security), summary judgment granted to defendant upon reconsideration (D.D.C. Feb. 24, 2000) (ultimately ruling in agency's favor based upon in camera declaration).

[81] See Weatherhead v. United States, 157 F.3d 735, 742 (9th Cir. 1998).

[82] See Weatherhead v. United States, 527 U.S. 1063 (1999).

[83] See FOIA Update, Vol. XX, No. 1, at 1.

[84] See id.

[85] See United States v. Weatherhead, 120 S. Ct. 577 (1999) (vacating Ninth Circuit decision).

[86] Afshar v. Department of State, 702 F.2d 1125, 1130 (D.C. Cir. 1983); see Billington v. Department of Justice, 11 F. Supp. 2d 45, 54-56 (D.D.C. 1998), (rejecting plaintiff's unsubstantiated allegations that agency had previously released withheld information and finding fact that FBI "may have released similar types of information in one case does not warrant disclosure" in this case), summary judgment granted in pertinent part, 69 F. Supp. 2d 128, 135 (D.D.C. 1999) (appeal pending); Payne v. Minihan, No. 97-0266, slip op. at 44 (continued...)

**EXEMPTION 1**

undermined by generalized allegations that classified information has been leaked to the press or otherwise made available to members of the public.[87] Courts have carefully recognized the distinction between a bona fide declassification action or official release and unsubstantiated speculation lacking official confirmation, holding that classified information is not considered to be in the public domain unless it has been the subject of an official disclosure.[88]

---

[86](...continued)
(D.N.M. Apr. 30, 1998) (stating that plaintiff "failed to meet his burden of establishing that any of his proffered evidence represents an official governmental disclosure or acknowledgment or even that the published information . . . duplicates his requested information") (appeal pending); Steinberg v. United States Dep't of Justice, 179 F.R.D. 357, 361 (D.D.C. 1998) (finding plaintiff's bare claims that withheld information available in public domain not "credible"); Meeropol v. Reno, No. 75-1121, slip op. at 6-7 (D.D.C. Mar. 26, 1998) (ruling that plaintiffs failed to carry "burden of production" in asserting withheld information about atomic bomb spies Julius and Ethel Rosenberg available in public domain) (Exemptions 1 and 7(D)); Scott v. CIA, 916 F. Supp. 42, 50 (D.D.C. 1996) (ordering plaintiff to compile list of information allegedly in public domain "with specific documentation demonstrating the legitimacy of such claims" and requiring release of that information if actually in public domain unless government demonstrates its release "threatens the national security"); Pfeiffer v. CIA, 721 F. Supp. 337, 342 (D.D.C. 1989) (holding that plaintiff must do more than simply identify "information that happens to find its way into a published account" to meet this burden); cf. Davis v. United States Dep't of Justice, 968 F.2d 1276, 1279 (D.C. Cir. 1992) (stating that "party who asserts . . . material publicly available carries the burden of production on that issue . . . because the task of proving the negative--that the information has not been revealed--might require the government to undertake an exhaustive, potentially limitless search") (Exemptions 3, 7(C), and 7(D)). But see Washington Post v. DOD, 766 F. Supp. 1, 12-13 (D.D.C. 1991) (suggesting that agency has ultimate burden of proof when comparing publicly disclosed information with information being withheld, determining whether information is identical and, if not, determining whether release of slightly different information would harm national security).

[87] See Exec. Order No. 12,958, § 1.2(c), 3 C.F.R. 333, 335 (1996), reprinted in 50 U.S.C. § 435 note (Supp. II 1996), and in FOIA Update, Vol. XVI, No. 2, at 5 (stating that "[c]lassified information shall not be declassified automatically as a result of any unauthorized disclosure of identical or similar information"); see also Public Citizen v. Department of State, 11 F.3d 198, 201 (D.C. Cir. 1993) (holding that "an agency official does not waive FOIA exemption 1 by publicly discussing the general subject matter of documents which are otherwise properly exempt from disclosure under that exemption").

[88] See, e.g., Hoch v. CIA, No. 88-5422, 1990 WL 102740, at *1 (D.C. Cir. July 20, 1990) (concluding that without official confirmation, "clear precedent establishes that courts will not compel [an agency] to disclose information even though it has been the subject of media reports and speculation"); see also Simmons v. United States Dep't of Justice, 796 F.2d 709, 712 (4th Cir. 1986) (ruling that there had been no "widespread dissemination" of information in question); Abbotts v. NRC, 766 F.2d 604, 607-08 (D.C. Cir. 1985) (rea-
(continued...)

**EXEMPTION 1**

Another recurring issue is whether public statements by former government officials constitute such an "official disclosure," and thus prevent an agency from invoking Exemption 1 to withhold information that it determines still warrants national security protection. In this regard, the Court of Appeals for the Second Circuit has rejected the argument that a retired admiral's statements constituted an authoritative disclosure by the government.[89] It pointedly stated: "Officials no longer serving with an executive branch department cannot continue to disclose official agency policy, and certainly they cannot establish what is agency policy through speculation, no matter how

---

[88](...continued) soning that even if withheld data was same as estimate in public domain, not same as knowing NRC's official policy as to "proper level of threat a nuclear facility should guard against"); Afshar, 702 F.2d at 1130-31 (observing that foreign government can ignore "[u]nofficial leaks and public surmise . . . but official acknowledgment may force a government to retaliate"); Students Against Genocide (SAGE) v. Department of State, 50 F. Supp. 2d 20, 24-25 (D.D.C. May 25, 1999) (finding no official disclosure when United States Representative to United Nations shares document with representatives of other nations at United Nations Security Council meeting) (magistrate's recommendation), adopted, No. 96-667 (D.D.C. July 22, 1999) (appeal pending); Arabian Shield Dev. Co. v. CIA, No. 3-98-0624, 1999 U.S. Dist. LEXIS 2379, at *10 n.5 (N.D. Tex. Feb. 26, 1999) (rejecting plaintiff's citation to "unspecified public news reports" identifying individuals as CIA agents and holding that "public speculation and disclosure . . . is quite different from official disclosure"), aff'd per curiam, No. 99-10327, slip op. at 2 (5th Cir. 2000); Payne, No. 97-0266, slip op. at 44 (D.N.M. Apr. 30, 1998) (finding that "reason for such a high standard, and for devaluing the legal salience of prior publications or public statements which allegedly demonstrate that the requested information is in the public forum, is that even if the published information is true, the harm . . . may not be the information's dissemination in the media, . . . but the harm that will be caused by the official acknowledgment of the information"); Steinberg v. United States Dep't of Justice, 801 F. Supp. 800, 802 (D.D.C. 1992) (recognizing that "[p]assage of time, media reports and informed or uninformed speculation based on statements by participants cannot be used . . . to undermine [government's] legitimate interest in protecting international security [information]"), aff'd in pertinent part, 23 F.3d 548, 553 (D.C. Cir. 1994); Van Atta v. Defense Intelligence Agency, No. 87-1508, 1988 WL 73856, at **2-3 (D.D.C. July 6, 1988) (holding that disclosure of information to foreign government during diplomatic negotiations not "public disclosure"); cf. Frugone v. CIA, 169 F.3d 772, 775 (D.C. Cir. 1999) (holding that letter from OPM advising plaintiff that his employment records were in the custody of CIA is not "tantamount to an official statement of the CIA"); Hunt v. CIA, 981 F.2d 1116, 1120 (9th Cir. 1992) (fact that some information about subject of request may have been made public by other governmental agencies found not to defeat agency's "Glomar" response in Exemption 3 context). But see Lawyers Comm. for Human Rights v. INS, 721 F. Supp. 552, 569 (S.D.N.Y. 1989) (ruling that Exemption 1 protection is not available when same documents were disclosed by foreign government or when same information was disclosed to press in "off-the-record exchanges").

[89] See Hudson River Sloop Clearwater, Inc. v. Department of the Navy, 891 F.2d 414, 421-22 (2d Cir. 1989).

# EXEMPTION 1

reasonable it may appear to be."[90] Additionally, the Second Circuit affirmed the decision of the district court in holding that the congressional testimony of high-ranking Navy officials did not constitute official disclosure because it did not concern the specific information being sought.[91]

Similarly, courts have rejected the view that widespread reports in the media about the general subject matter involved are sufficient to overcome an agency's Exemption 1 claim for related records. Indeed, in one case, the court went so far as to hold that 180,000 pages of CIA records pertaining to Guatemala were properly classified despite the fact that the public domain contained significant information and speculation about CIA involvement in the 1954 coup in Guatemala: "CIA clearance of books and articles, books written by former CIA officials, and general discussions in Congressional publications do not constitute official disclosures."[92] In a subsequent case, one court went even further, holding that documents were properly classified even though disclosed "involuntarily as a result of [a] tragic accident such as an aborted rescue mission [in Iran], or used in evidence to prosecute espionage."[93]

In a 1990 decision, the Court of Appeals for the District of Columbia Circuit held that for information to be "officially acknowledged" in the context of Exemption 1, it must: (1) be as "specific" as the information previously released; (2) "match" the information previously disclosed; and (3) have been made public through an "official and documented" disclosure.[94] Applying these criteria, the D.C. Circuit reversed the lower court's disclosure order and held that information published in a congressional report did not constitute "official acknowledgment" of the purported location of a CIA station, because the information sought related to an earlier time period than that discussed in the report.[95] In so ruling, it did not address the broader question of whether congressional release of the identical information relating to intelligence

---

[90] Id. at 422.

[91] Id. at 421.

[92] Schlesinger v. CIA, 591 F. Supp. 60, 66 (D.D.C. 1984); see Pfeiffer v. CIA, 721 F. Supp. at 342; see also Washington Post, 766 F. Supp. at 11-12 (finding no "presumption of reliability" for facts contained in books subject to prepublication review by government agency); cf. McGehee v. Casey, 718 F.2d 1137, 1141 & n.9 (D.C. Cir. 1983) (determining that CIA cannot reasonably bear burden of conducting exhaustive search to prove that particular items of classified information have never been published) (non-FOIA case).

[93] Washington Post Co. v. DOD, No. 84-3400, slip op. at 3 (D.D.C. Sept. 22, 1986).

[94] Fitzgibbon v. CIA, 911 F.2d 755, 765 (D.C. Cir. 1990); see also Afshar, 702 F.2d at 1130, 1133-34. But see Krikorian v. Department of State, 984 F.2d 461, 467-68 (D.C. Cir. 1993) (remanding to district court to determine whether information excised in one document "officially acknowledged" by comparing publicly available record with record withheld; leaving to district court's discretion whether this could be better accomplished by supplemental agency affidavit or by in camera inspection).

[95] 911 F.2d at 765-66.

## EXEMPTION 1

sources and methods could ever constitute "official acknowledgment," thus requiring disclosure under the FOIA.[96] However, the D.C. Circuit had previously considered this broader question and had concluded that congressional publications do not constitute "official acknowledgment" for purposes of the FOIA.[97]

In 1993, the D.C. Circuit again had an opportunity to consider the issue of whether an agency had "waived" its ability to properly withhold records pursuant to Exemption 1. The case, Public Citizen v. Department of State,[98] involved the question of whether the public congressional testimony of the U.S. Ambassador to Iraq constituted such a "waiver" so as to prevent the agency from invoking the FOIA's national security exemption to withhold related records.[99] The district court had held--after reviewing the seven documents at issue in camera--that the public testimony had not "waived" Exemption 1 protection because the "context" of the information in the documents was sufficiently "different" so as to not "negate" their "confidentiality."[100] Terming this an "unusual FOIA case" because the requester did not challenge the district court's conclusion that the documents were properly exempt from disclosure under Exemption 1 and because the requester also conceded that it could not meet the strict test for "waiver," the D.C. Circuit rejected the requester's primary argument that the facts of this case distinguished it from the court's prior decisions on this question.[101]

The requester in Public Citizen contended first that the court's prior decisions concerned attempts by FOIA requesters to compel agencies to confirm or deny the truth of information that others had already publicly disclosed.[102] The plaintiff then argued that the Ambassador's public statements about her meeting with the Iraqi leader prior to the invasion of Kuwait were far more detailed than those that the D.C. Circuit had found did not constitute "waiver" in previous cases.[103] The D.C. Circuit repudiated both of the requester's points and, in affirming the district court's decision, grounded its own de-

---

[96] Id.

[97] See, e.g., Salisbury v. United States, 690 F.2d 966, 971 (D.C. Cir. 1982) (holding that inclusion of information in Senate report "cannot be equated with disclosure by the agency itself"); Military Audit Project v. Casey, 656 F.2d 724, 744 (D.C. Cir. 1981) (finding that publication of Senate report does not constitute official release of agency information); see also Earth Pledge Found. v. CIA, 988 F. Supp. 623, 628 (S.D.N.Y. 1996) (same), aff'd per curiam, 128 F.3d 788 (2d Cir. 1997).

[98] 11 F.3d at 199.

[99] Id.

[100] Public Citizen v. Department of State, 787 F. Supp. 12, 13, 15 (D.D.C. 1992).

[101] 11 F.3d at 201.

[102] Id. at 201-03.

[103] Id. at 203.

**EXEMPTION 1**

cision in the fact that the requester "conceded" it could not "meet [the] requirement that it show that [the Ambassador's] testimony was 'as specific as' the documents it [sought] in this case, or that her testimony 'matche[d]' the information contained in the documents."[104] Acknowledging that such a stringent standard is a "high hurdle for a FOIA plaintiff to clear," the D.C. Circuit concluded that the government's "vital interest in information relating to the national security and foreign affairs dictates that it must be."[105] To hold otherwise in a situation where the government had affirmatively disclosed some information about a classified matter would, in the court's view, give the agency "a strong disincentive ever to provide the citizenry with briefings of any kind on sensitive topics."[106] (For a further discussion of this issue, see Discretionary Disclosure and Waiver, below.)

A final, seemingly obvious point--but one nevertheless not accepted by all FOIA requesters--is that classified information will not be released under the FOIA even to a requester of "unquestioned loyalty."[107] In a case decided in 1990, a government employee with a current "Top Secret" security clearance was denied access to classified records pertaining to himself because Exemption 1 protects "information from disclosure based on the nature of the material, not on the nature of the individual requester."[108]

Executive Order 12,958

As with prior executive orders, Executive Order 12,958 recognizes both the right of the public to be informed about activities of its government and the need to protect national security information from unauthorized or untimely disclosure.[109] Accordingly, information may not be classified unless "its disclosure reasonably could be expected to cause damage to the national

---

[104] Id.

[105] Id.

[106] Id.

[107] Levine v. Department of Justice, No. 83-1685, slip op. at 6 (D.D.C. Mar. 30, 1984) (concluding that regardless of requester's loyalty, release of documents to him could "open the door to secondary disclosure to others").

[108] Martens v. United States Dep't of Commerce, No. 88-3334, 1990 U.S. Dist. LEXIS 10351, at *10 (D.D.C. Aug. 6, 1990) (Privacy Act case); see also Miller v. Casey, 730 F.2d 773, 778 (D.C. Cir. 1984) (determining that agency decision to deny historical research access is not reviewable by courts); cf. United States Dep't of Justice v. Reporters Comm. for Freedom of the Press, 489 U.S. 749, 771 (1989) (stating that "the identity of the requester has no bearing on the merits of his or her FOIA request") (Exemption 7(C)); FOIA Update, Vol. X, No. 2, at 5 (advising that as general rule all FOIA requesters should be treated alike).

[109] Exec. Order No. 12,958, 3 C.F.R. 333 (1996), reprinted in 50 U.S.C. § 435 note (Supp. II 1996), and reprinted in abridged form in FOIA Update, Vol. XVI, No. 2, at 5-10.

# EXEMPTION 1

security."[110] Courts grappling with the degree of certainty necessary to demonstrate the contemplated damage under this standard have recognized that an agency's articulation of the threatened harm must always be speculative to some extent and that to require a showing of actual harm would be judicial "overstepping."[111] In the area of intelligence sources and methods, courts are strongly inclined to accept the agency's position that disclosure of this type of information will cause damage to national security interests because this is "necessarily a region for forecasts in which [the agency's] informed judgment as to potential future harm should be respected."[112]

This standard is elaborated upon in Section 1.5 of the order, which specifies the types of information that may be considered for classification. The information categories identified as proper bases for classification in Executive Order 12,958 include: foreign government information;[113] vulnerabilities

---

[110] Exec. Order No. 12,958, § 1.2(a)(4); see also 32 C.F.R. § 2001.10(b) (1999) (directive of Information Security Oversight Office explaining that ability of agency classifier to identify and describe damage to national security caused by unauthorized disclosure is critical aspect of classification system); Attorney General's Memorandum for Heads of Departments and Agencies regarding the Freedom of Information Act (Oct. 4, 1993), reprinted in FOIA Update, Vol. XIV, No. 3, at 4-5 (establishing "foreseeable harm" standard governing use of FOIA exemptions); FOIA Update, Vol. XV, No. 2, at 3 (recognizing that harm standard is built into Exemption 1).

[111] Halperin v. CIA, 629 F.2d 144, 149 (D.C. Cir. 1980); see Aftergood v. CIA, No. 98-2107, 1999 U.S. Dist. LEXIS 18135, at *9 (D.D.C. Nov. 12, 1999) (declaring that "the law does not require certainty or a showing of harm" that has already occurred); cf. Snepp v. United States, 444 U.S. 507, 513 n.8 (1980) (articulating that "[t]he problem is to ensure, in advance, and by proper [CIA prepublication review] procedures, that information detrimental to the national interest is not published") (non-FOIA case).

[112] Gardels v. CIA, 689 F.2d 1100, 1106 (D.C. Cir. 1982); see also Washington Post v. DOD, 766 F. Supp. 1, 7 (D.D.C. 1991) (observing that disclosure of working files of failed Iranian hostage rescue attempt containing intelligence planning documents would "serve as a model of 'do's and don't's'" for future counterterrorist missions "with similar objectives and obstacles").

[113] See, e.g., Krikorian v. Department of State, 984 F.2d 461, 465 (D.C. Cir. 1993) (finding that telegram reporting discussion between agency official and high-ranking foreign diplomat regarding terrorism properly withheld as foreign government information; release would "jeopardize 'reciprocal confidentiality'" between governments) (decided under Exec. Order No. 12,356); McErlean v. United States Dep't of Justice, No. 97-7831, 1999 WL 791680, at *5 (S.D.N.Y. Sept. 30, 1999) (protecting identities and information obtained from foreign governments) (decided under Exec. Order No. 12,958); Ajluni v. FBI, No. 94-325, 1996 WL 776996, at *4 (N.D.N.Y. July 13, 1996) (rejecting plaintiff's assertion that to qualify as foreign government information agency "should be forced to identify at least which government supplied the information," because to do so would cause such sources of information "to dry up") (decided under Exec. Order No. 12,356); Badalementi v. Department of State,

(continued...)

**EXEMPTION 1**

or capabilities of systems, installations, projects, or plans relating to national security;[114] intelligence activities, sources or methods,[115] or cryptology;[116] for-

---

[113](...continued)
899 F. Supp. 542, 546-47 (D. Kan. 1995) (categorizing record reflecting negotiations among United States, Spain, and Italy regarding extradition of alleged drug smuggler as foreign government information) (decided under Exec. Order No. 12,356).

[114] See, e.g., Public Educ. Ctr., Inc. v. DOD, 905 F. Supp. 19, 21 (D.D.C. 1995) (identifying videotapes made during raid by U.S. forces in Somalia as relating to vulnerabilities or capabilities of projects concerning national security) (decided under Exec. Order No. 12,356); Gottesdiener v. Secret Serv., No. 86-576, slip op. at 5 (D.D.C. Feb. 21, 1989) (decided under Exec. Order No. 12,356); cf. U.S. News & World Report v. Department of the Treasury, No. 84-2303, 1986 U.S. Dist. LEXIS 27634, at *3 (D.D.C. Mar. 26, 1986) (providing protection for information regarding armored limousines for the President) (Exemptions 1 and 7(E)) (decided under Exec. Order No. 12,356).

[115] See, e.g., Jones v. FBI, 41 F.3d 238, 244 (6th Cir. 1994) (protecting "numerical designators" assigned to national security sources) (decided under Exec. Order No. 12,356); Patterson v. FBI, 893 F.2d 595, 597, 601 (3d Cir. 1990) (protecting information pertaining to intelligence sources and methods used by FBI in investigation of student who corresponded with 169 foreign nations) (decided under Exec. Order No. 12,356); Blazy v. Tenet, 979 F. Supp. 10, 23 (D.D.C. 1997) (finding that former CIA employee's polygraphs constitute "intelligence method") (Exemptions 1 and 3) (decided under Exec. Order No. 12,356), summary affirmance granted, No. 97-5330, 1998 WL 315583 (D.C. Cir. May 12, 1998); Tawalbeh v. United States Dep't of the Air Force, No. 96-6241, slip op. at 11 (C.D. Cal. Aug. 8, 1997) (protecting information which could enable hostile analysts to identify intelligence sources) (decided under Exec. Order No. 12,958); Voinche v. FBI, 940 F. Supp. 323, 327 (D.D.C. 1996) (protecting information that would reveal information about application of intelligence sources or methods) (decided under Exec. Order No. 12,958), aff'd per curiam, No. 96-5304, 1997 U.S. App. LEXIS 19089 (D.C. Cir. June 19, 1997); Nayed v. INS, No. 91-805, 1993 WL 524541, at *2 (D.D.C. Nov. 29, 1993) (determining that confirmation that records about plaintiff exist would reveal intelligence "method") (decided under Exec. Order No. 12,356); Allen v. DOD, 658 F. Supp. 15, 19-21 (D.D.C. 1986) (including deceased, potential, and unwitting intelligence sources) (decided under Exec. Order No. 12,356); cf. Knight v. CIA, 872 F.2d 660, 664 (5th Cir. 1989) (finding intelligence sources and methods protected under Exemption 3); Schrecker v. United States Dep't of Justice, 14 F. Supp. 2d 111, 117-18 (D.D.C. 1998) (observing, in context of requester's argument that agency is obligated to conduct research to determine if individuals mentioned in its files are alive, that identities of intelligence sources are protectible pursuant to Exemption 1 regardless of whether individuals are alive or deceased), summary judgment granted, 74 F. Supp. 2d 26 (D.D.C. 1999) (appeal pending).

[116] See McDonnell v. United States, 4 F.3d 1227, 1244 (3d Cir. 1993) (upholding classification of cryptographic information dating back to 1934 when release "could enable hostile entities to interpret other, more sensitive docu-

(continued...)

**EXEMPTION 1**

eign relations or foreign activities, including confidential sources;[117] military plans, weapons, or operations;[118] scientific, technological, or economic matters

---

[116](...continued) ments similarly encoded") (decided under Exec. Order No. 12,356); Gilmore v. NSA, No. C92-3646, 1993 U.S. Dist. LEXIS 7694, at **18-19, 22-23 (N.D. Cal. May 3, 1993) (finding mathematical principles and techniques in agency treatise protectible under this category of executive order) (decided under Exec. Order No. 12,356).

[117] See, e.g., Springmann v. United States Dep't of State, No. 93-1238, slip op. at 2-3 (D.D.C. Feb. 24, 2000) (upon renewed motion for summary judgment and after in camera review, accepting agency's judgment that disclosure of information about American employees' religiously offensive behavior in Saudi Arabia would have repercussions with respect to relations between United States and that country) (decided under Exec. Order No. 12,958); Linn v. United States Dep't of Justice, No. 92-1406, 1995 WL 631847, at *26 (D.D.C. Aug. 22, 1995) (finding Exemption 1 withholdings proper because agency demonstrated it has "a present understanding" with foreign government that any shared information will not be disclosed and that information concerning the relationship between the United States and that government will remain secret) (decided under Exec. Order No. 12,356); Armstrong v. Executive Office of the President, No. 89-142, slip op. at 2-3 (D.D.C. Aug. 11, 1995) (upon in camera review, finds documents properly withheld because disclosure would "damage relations with foreign countries"); Summers v. United States Dep't of Justice, No. 89-3300, slip op. at 8-9 (D.D.C. June 13, 1995) (ruling that disclosure of names of two foreign agents who visited FBI Director "could severely damage the delicate liaison established between the United States and this particular foreign government, as well as other governments that are similarly situated") (decided under Exec. Order No. 12,356); United States Comm. for Refugees v. Department of State, No. 91-3303, 1993 WL 364674, at *2 (D.D.C. Aug. 30, 1993) (holding that disclosure of withheld information could damage nation's foreign policy by jeopardizing success of negotiations with Haiti on refugee issues "[because] documents contain . . . frank assessments about the Haitian government") (decided under Exec. Order No. 12,356); St. Hilaire v. Department of Justice, No. 91-0078, 1992 WL 73545, at *4 (D.D.C. Mar. 18, 1992) (protecting portions of two cables between Department of State and its embassies because "[p]rotecting communications between . . . diplomatic instruments of sovereign states certainly is an appropriate reason for classifying documents") (decided under Exec. Order No. 12,356), aff'd, No. 92-5153 (D.C. Cir. Apr. 28, 1994); Van Atta v. Defense Intelligence Agency, No. 87-1508, 1988 WL 73856, at *2 (D.D.C. July 6, 1988) (protecting information compiled at request of foreign government for purpose of negotiations) (decided under Exec. Order No. 12,356). But see Keenan v. Department of Justice, No. 94-1909, slip op. at 9-11 (D.D.C. Dec. 16, 1997) (ordering release of document segments withheld by agency pursuant to Exemption 1 because agency failed to show that foreign governments named in documents more than 30 years old "still wish to maintain the secrecy of their cooperative efforts with" U.S.).

[118] See, e.g., Taylor v. Department of the Army, 684 F.2d 99, 109 (D.C. Cir. 1982) (protecting combat-ready troop assessments) (decided under Exec. Or-

(continued...)

-96-

**EXEMPTION 1**

relating to national security;[119] and government programs for safeguarding nuclear materials and facilities.[120]

It is important to note that, under Executive Order 12,958, there is no presumption that information in any of the above categories--such as foreign government information--is classified.[121] In addition, Executive Order 12,958 instructs that if there is any "significant doubt about the need to classify information, it should not be classified."[122]

Recently two judges of the United States District Court for the District of Columbia took opposing views as to what agencies must demonstrate to protect national security-related information exchanged with foreign governments.[123] In the first case, in which the agency's Vaughn Index contained no indication of an explicit promise of confidentiality between the agency and the foreign government, the court ordered the FBI to "disclose the circumstances from which it deduces, and from which the court might as well, that the information was shared in confidence."[124] The court subsequently granted the FBI's motion for summary judgment, though, after reviewing the agency's supplemental affidavit--which demonstrated that the FBI's relationship with the foreign government was based on an express understanding of confidenti-

---

[118](...continued) der No. 12,065); Tawalbeh, No. 96-6241, slip op. at 10-11 (C.D. Cal. Aug. 8, 1997) (protecting information about military readiness and operational security related to operations Desert Shield and Desert Storm) (decided under Exec. Order No. 12,958); Public Educ. Ctr., 905 F. Supp. at 21 (protecting videotapes made during U.S. military action in Somalia) (decided under Exec. Order No. 12,356); Washington Post Co. v. DOD, No. 84-2403, slip op. at 3 (D.D.C. Apr. 15, 1988) (foreign military information) (decided under Exec. Order No. 12,356); Hudson River Sloop Clearwater, Inc. v. Department of the Navy, 659 F. Supp. 674, 679 (E.D.N.Y. 1987) (NEPA/FOIA case) (decided under Exec. Order No. 12,356), aff'd, 891 F.2d 414, 417 (2d Cir. 1989).

[119] See Exec. Order No. 12,958, § 1.5(e).

[120] See id. § 1.5(f); see, e.g., Loomis v. United States Dep't of Energy, No. 96-149, slip op. at 14-16 (N.D.N.Y. Mar. 9, 1999) (nuclear containment layout plan and referenced document on propagation of radiological requirements and procedures) (decided under Exec. Order No. 12,958).

[121] See Exec. Order No. 12,958, § 1.5.

[122] Id. § 1.2(b).

[123] Compare Steinberg v. United States Dep't of Justice, 179 F.R.D. 357, 362-63 (D.D.C. 1998) (ordering FBI to submit further evidence to support confidentiality claim), with Billington v. Department of Justice, 11 F. Supp. 2d 45, 54-56 (D.D.C. 1998) (finding agency not required to demonstrate explicit confidentiality understanding), summary judgment granted in pertinent part, 69 F. Supp. 2d 128 (D.D.C. 1999) (appeal pending).

[124] Steinberg, 179 F.R.D. at 362-63.

-97-

## EXEMPTION 1

ality.[125] In the second case, the court specifically rejected the requester's argument that, in order to qualify for Exemption 1 protection, the agency's affidavit must demonstrate that there were explicit understandings of confidentiality between the agency and the foreign government regarding the information at issue.[126] In the court's view, "to compel the agency to supply more information would muddle the purpose of the exemption."[127] The latter view corresponds more closely to the deferential approach ordinarily taken by courts when reviewing cases involving Exemption 1. (For further discussions of the appropriate judicial standard in evaluating Exemption 1 claims, see Exemption 1, Standard of Review, above, and Exemption 1, Deference to Agency Expertise, above.)

As with prior orders, Executive Order 12,958 contains a number of distinct limitations on classification.[128] Specifically, information may not be classified to conceal violations of law, inefficiency, or administrative error,[129] to prevent embarrassment to a person or an agency,[130] to restrain competition,[131]

---

[125] Id. at 368-69.

[126] See Billington, 11 F. Supp. 2d at 57-58.

[127] Id.

[128] Exec. Order No. 12,958, § 1.8.

[129] Id. § 1.8(a)(1); see also Billington, 11 F. Supp. 2d at 57-58 (dismissing plaintiff's "unsubstantiated accusations" that information should be disclosed because FBI engaged in illegal "dirty tricks" campaign); Computer Prof'ls for Soc. Responsibility v. National Inst. of Standards & Tech., No. 92-0972, slip op. at 1-2 (D.D.C. Apr. 11, 1994) (finding no basis to conclude NSA improperly classified computer security guidelines in violation of law to "conceal its role" in developing such guidelines) (decided under Exec. Order No. 12,356), summary affirmance granted, No. 94-5153, 1995 WL 66803, at *1 (D.C. Cir. Jan. 13, 1995); Navasky v. CIA, 499 F. Supp. 269, 275-76 (S.D.N.Y. 1980) (rejecting as irrelevant requester's claim of illegality under similar provision in prior executive order so long as information properly classified pursuant to order's substantive requirements; likewise rejecting agency's claim of national security harm based upon possible loss of employment or damage to reputation for those persons cooperating with CIA's clandestine book-publishing activities) (decided under Exec. Order No. 12,065), aff'd, 679 F.2d 873 (2d Cir. 1981) (unpublished table decision).

[130] Exec. Order No. 12,958, § 1.8(a)(2); see also Billington, 11 F. Supp. 2d at 58-59 (rejecting plaintiff's argument that information was classified by FBI to shield agency and foreign government from embarrassment); Canning v. United States Dep't of Justice, 848 F. Supp. 1037, 1047-48 (D.D.C. 1994) (finding no credible evidence that FBI improperly withheld information to conceal existence of "potentially inappropriate investigation" of French citizen; "if anything, the agency released sufficient information to facilitate such speculation") (decided under Exec. Order No. 12,356); Wilson v. Department of Justice, No. 87-2415, 1991 WL 111457, at *2 (D.D.C. June 13, 1991) (rejecting requester's claim that information was classified to prevent embarrassment to foreign government official and holding that "even if some . . . information—

(continued...)

**EXEMPTION 1**

to prevent or delay the disclosure of information that does not require national security protection,[132] or to classify basic scientific research unrelated to the national security.[133] Moreover, Executive Order 12,958 specifically prohibits the reclassification of information "after it has been declassified and released to the public under proper authority."[134] Although Executive Order 12,958 authorizes the classification of a record after an agency has received a FOIA request for it, such agency action is permitted only through the "personal participation" of designated high-level officials and only on a "document-by-document basis."[135]

Executive Order 12,958 also contains a provision establishing a mechanism through which classification determinations can be challenged within the federal government.[136] Under this provision, "authorized holders of information"--individuals who are authorized to have access to such information--who, in good faith, believe that its classification is improper are "encouraged and expected" to challenge that classification.[137] Furthermore, agencies are required to set up internal procedures to implement this program, in order to ensure that holders are able to make such challenges without fear of retribution.[138]

In addition to the substantive criteria outlined in the applicable executive order, information must also adhere to the order's procedural require-

---

[130](...continued)
mation . . . were embarrassing to Egyptian officials, it would nonetheless be covered by Exemption 1 if, independent of any desire to avoid embarrassment, the information withheld [was] properly classified") (decided under Exec. Order No. 12,356).

[131] Exec. Order No. 12,958, § 1.8(a)(3).

[132] Id. § 1.8(a)(4).

[133] Id. § 1.8(b).

[134] Compare Exec. Order No. 12,958, § 1.8(c) (forbidding reclassification of information once officially disclosed), with Exec. Order No. 12,356, § 1.6(c) (permitting reclassification of information if it "may reasonably be recovered").

[135] Exec. Order No. 12,958, § 1.8(d); see, e.g., Council for a Livable World v. United States Dep't of State, No. 96-1807, slip op. at 8-9 (D.D.C. Nov. 23, 1998) (finding that the "State Department did not classify the documents . . . in accordance with proper procedure").

[136] Exec. Order No. 12,958, § 1.9.

[137] Id. § 1.9(a).

[138] Id. § 1.9(b); see also id. § 5.4(b) (authorizing Interagency Security Classification Appeals Panel to "decide on appeals by persons who have filed classification challenges"); 32 C.F.R. § 2001.13 (1999) (directive issued by Information Security Oversight Office describing procedures agencies must establish in order to consider classification challenges).

# EXEMPTION 1

ments in order to qualify for Exemption 1 protection.[139] Executive Order 12,958 prescribes the current procedural requirements to be employed by agencies; these include such matters as the proper markings to be applied to classified documents,[140] as well as the manner in which agencies designate officials to classify information in the first instance.[141]

With regard to the proper markings, Executive Order 12,958 requires, for the first time, that "a concise reason for classification" be stated on the face of each newly classified document.[142] It also requires that a date or event for declassification, a date ten years from the document's creation, or the relevant declassification exemption category, be specified on the document.[143] In addition, Executive Order 12,958 mandates the use of portion markings to indicate levels of classification within documents[144] and advocates the use of classified addenda in cases in which classified information comprises "a small portion of an otherwise unclassified document."[145] Governmentwide guidelines have been issued regarding these marking requirements.[146]

Executive Order 12,958 also establishes two government entities to provide oversight of agencies' classification determinations and their implementation of the order. The first, the Interagency Security Classification Appeals Panel, consists of senior-level representatives of the Secretaries of State and Defense, the Attorney General, the Director of Central Intelligence, the Archi-

---

[139] See, e.g., Tawalbeh, No. 96-6241, slip op. at 9 (C.D. Cal. Aug. 8, 1997) (noting that classification procedures set forth in Exec. Order No. 12,958 properly applied); Canning, 848 F. Supp. at 1048-49 (finding that agency adhered to appropriate classification procedures established by Exec. Order No. 12,356).

[140] Exec. Order No. 12,958, § 1.7; see also Cohen v. FBI, No. 93-1701, slip op. at 5-6 (D.D.C. Oct. 11, 1994) (rejecting plaintiff's argument that subsequent marking of two documents during agency's second classification review rendered FBI's classification action ineffective; to require agencies "to perform every classification review perfectly on the first attempt" would be "a very strict and unforgiving standard") (decided under Exec. Order No. 12,356).

[141] Exec. Order No. 12,958, § 1.4; see also Presidential Order of Oct. 13, 1995, 3 C.F.R. 513 (1996), reprinted in 50 U.S.C. § 435 note (Supp. II 1996) (designating those executive branch officials who are authorized to classify national security information in first instance).

[142] Exec. Order No. 12,958, § 1.7(a)(5) (requiring that such statements include, at a minimum, specifications of relevant classification categories).

[143] Id. § 1.7(a)(4).

[144] Id. § 1.7(c) (specifying that only Director of Information Security Oversight Office is authorized to grant portion-marking waivers).

[145] Id. § 1.7(g).

[146] See 32 C.F.R. § 2001.20-.24 (1999) (directive issued by Information Security Oversight Office providing detailed guidance on identification and marking requirements of Exec. Order No. 12,958).

**EXEMPTION 1**

vist of the United States, and the Assistant to the President for National Security Affairs.[147] Among other things, this body adjudicates classification challenges filed by agency employees and decides appeals from persons who have filed requests under the mandatory declassification review provisions of the order.[148] The second entity is the Information Security Policy Advisory Council, which is comprised of seven private-sector experts appointed by the President to serve as a formal Federal Advisory Committee for the purpose of advising the executive branch on matters of national security classification policy, such as "subject areas for systematic declassification review" and any "policy issues in dispute."[149]

Agencies with questions about the proper implementation of the substantive or procedural requirements of Executive Order 12,958 may consult with the Information Security Oversight Office (located within the National Archives and Records Administration, at (202) 219-5250), which holds governmentwide oversight responsibility for classification matters under the executive order.[150]

### Duration of Classification and Declassification

Perhaps the most significant provisions of Executive Order 12,958 establish (1) limitations on the length of time information may remain classified[151] and (2) enhanced procedures for the declassification of older government information.[152] In contrast to Executive Order 12,356, which mandated that "information . . . be classified as long as required by national security considerations,"[153] Executive Order 12,958 sets a ten-year limit on most new

---

[147] See Exec. Order No. 12,958, § 5.4(a)(1); see also 32 C.F.R. pt. 2001 app. A (1999) (bylaws of Interagency Security Classification Appeals Panel).

[148] See Exec. Order No. 12,958, § 5.4(b); see also id. § 3.6 (establishing mandatory declassification review program as non-FOIA mechanism for persons to seek access to classified information generated or maintained by agencies, including papers maintained by presidential libraries not accessible under FOIA).

[149] Id. § 5.5.

[150] See id. § 5.3; see also FOIA Update, Vol. XVI, No. 2, at 15 (describing responsibilities of current Information Security Oversight Office (ISOO) Director); FOIA Update, Vol. VI, No. 1, at 1-2 (describing responsibilities of ISOO under Exec. Order No. 12,356).

[151] Exec. Order No. 12,958, § 1.6, 3 C.F.R. 333, 337-38 (1996), reprinted in 50 U.S.C. § 435 note (Supp. II 1996), and in FOIA Update, Vol. XVI, No. 2, at 6.

[152] See id. § 3.4.

[153] Exec. Order No. 12,356, § 1.4(a), 3 C.F.R. 166 (1983), reprinted in 50 U.S.C. § 435 note (1994).

**EXEMPTION 1**

classification actions.[154] It is important to note that this ten-year rule applies only to information classified after Executive Order 12,958's effective date; it does not apply to information classified under prior executive orders.[155]

Executive Order 12,958 also establishes an automatic declassification mechanism that likewise did not exist under the prior one.[156] Under Executive Order 12,356 and the legal precedents established thereunder, the passage of time did not, by itself, require agencies to declassify information automatically upon the expiration of a specified time period.[157] In contrast, Executive Order 12,958 requires the automatic declassification of information that is more than twenty-five years old,[158] with exceptions limited to especially sen-

---

[154] Exec. Order No. 12,958, § 1.6(a) (setting forth general rule); see also id. § 1.6(d) (identifying categories of information which permit extension of classification beyond 10-year period).

[155] Id. § 1.6(e); see also 32 C.F.R. § 2001.12 (1999) (directive issued by Information Security Oversight Office providing further guidance on duration of classification, including information on extensions of 10-year rule).

[156] Compare Exec. Order No. 12,958, § 3.4(a) (mandating automatic declassification for 25-year-old information), with Exec. Order No. 12,356, § 3.1(a) (specifying that passage of time alone does not compel declassification); see also Exec. Order No. 12,937, 3 C.F.R. 949 (1994) (separate executive order issued by President Clinton automatically declassifying millions of pages of older records maintained by NARA).

[157] See, e.g., Oglesby v. United States Dep't of the Army, 79 F.3d 1172, 1183 (D.C. Cir. 1996) (stating that "passage of time alone is [not] enough to discredit an otherwise detailed and persuasive affidavit") (decided under Exec. Order No. 12,356); McDonnell v. United States, 4 F.3d 1227, 1243-45 (3d Cir. 1993) (rejecting plaintiff's argument that cryptographic information classified as exempt in 1934 is no longer entitled to protection because of passage of time) (decided under Exec. Order No. 12,356); Maynard v. CIA, 986 F.2d 547, 556 n.9 (1st Cir. 1993) (stating that "passage of some thirty years does not, by itself, invalidate [agency's] showing under Exemption 1") (decided under Exec. Order No. 12,356); Afshar v. Department of State, 702 F.2d 1125, 1138 n.18 (D.C. Cir. 1983) (ruling that change in circumstances does not require review of original classification) (decided under Exec. Order No. 12,356); Campbell v. United States Dep't of Justice, No. 89-3016, 1996 WL 554511, at *6 (D.D.C. Sept. 19, 1996) (finding, despite (unspecified) age of records, agency affidavits demonstrate that excised information was properly withheld) (decided under Exec. Order No. 12,356); Canning v. United States Dep't of Justice, 848 F. Supp. 1037, 1047 (D.D.C. 1994) (rejecting plaintiff's contention that collapse of Soviet Union "so drastically alter[s] international affairs as to render FBI's [current] security concerns somehow obsolete") (decided under Exec. Order No. 12,356); Siminoski v. FBI, No. 83-6499, slip op. at 17-18 (C.D. Cal. Jan. 16, 1990) (upholding classification of documents more than 40 years old because "age alone does not mandate release of otherwise sensitive documents") (decided under Exec. Order No. 12,356).

[158] Exec. Order No. 12,958, § 3.4(a) (applying 25-year rule to classified in-
(continued...)

**EXEMPTION 1**

sitive information designated as such by the heads of agencies.[159]

It is important to note that the effective date for the automatic declassification mechanism in Executive Order 12,958 has been extended by an additional eighteen months to October 17, 2001, generally, and by another eighteen months beyond that to April 17, 2003, for certain identified records.[160] This mechanism already has been addressed by several courts, all of which have refused to order disclosure of information more than twenty-five years old until the automatic disclosure provisions take effect.[161]

The automatic declassification mechanism applies to information currently classified under any predecessor executive order[162] and will lead to creation of a governmentwide declassification database.[163] For records that fall within any exception to Executive Order 12,958's automatic declassification mechanism, agencies are required to establish "a program for systematic declassification review" that focuses on any need for continued classification of such records.[164]

As did prior executive orders, Executive Order 12,958 provides for a

---

[158](...continued) formation determined by Archivist of United States to have "permanent historical value"); see also 32 C.F.R. § 2001.10(a) (1999) (directive issued by ISOO defining records of "permanent historical value").

[159] Exec. Order No. 12,958, § 3.4(b) (specifying categories of sensitive information qualifying for exception to 25-year rule--including, for example, information that would reveal identity of confidential human source, disclose U.S. military war plans still in effect, or violate statute or treaty); see also id. §§ 3.4(c), (d) (specifying manner in which agencies are to notify President of, and receive approval for, exceptions to automatic declassification).

[160] See Exec. Order No. 13,142, 64 Fed. Reg. 66089 (1999) (specifying that April 17, 2003, deadline pertains to "records otherwise subject to this paragraph for which a review or assessment conducted by the agency and confirmed by the Information Security Oversight Office has determined that they: (1) contain information that was created by or is under the control of more than one agency, or (2) are within file series containing information that almost invariably pertains to intelligence sources or methods").

[161] See Schrecker v. United States Dep't of Justice, 74 F. Supp. 2d 26, 30 (D.D.C. 1999) (appeal pending); Billington v. Department of Justice, 69 F. Supp. 2d 128, 134 (D.D.C. 1999) (appeal pending); Hall v. United States Dep't of Justice, 26 F. Supp. 2d 78, 80 (D.D.C. 1998).

[162] See Exec. Order No. 12,958, §§ 1.6(e), 3.4(a).

[163] See id. § 3.8 (directing Archivist to establish database of information that has been declassified by agencies and instructing agency heads to cooperate in this governmentwide effort).

[164] Id. § 3.5(a).

# EXEMPTION 1

"mandatory declassification review program."[165] This mechanism allows any person--entirely apart from the FOIA context--to request that an agency review its national security records for declassification.[166] Traditionally, the mandatory review program has been used by researchers interested in gaining access to papers maintained by presidential libraries, which are not accessible under the FOIA. However, under this provision any person may submit a mandatory review request to an agency.[167] Unlike under the FOIA, though, such requesters do not have the right to judicial review of the agency's action;[168] instead, Executive Order 12,958 authorizes persons to appeal an agency's final decision under this program to the Interagency Security Classification Appeals Panel.[169] To alleviate some of the burden of this program, Executive Order 12,958 contains a provision that allows an agency to deny a mandatory review request if it has already reviewed the information for declassification within the past two years.[170]

For declassification decisions, Executive Order 12,958 authorizes agencies to apply a balancing test--i.e., to determine "whether the public interest in disclosure outweighs the damage to national security that might reasonably be expected from disclosure."[171] Though Executive Order 12,958 specifies that this provision is implemented as a matter of administrative discretion and creates no new right of judicial review, it is significant that no such provision existed under Executive Order 12,356.[172]

### Additional Considerations

Two additional considerations addressed by Executive Order 12,958 already have been recognized by the courts. First, the "Glomar" response is explicitly incorporated into the order: "An agency may refuse to confirm or deny the existence or nonexistence of requested information whenever . . . its existence or nonexistence is itself classified under this order."[173] (For a further discussion of this point, see Exemption 1, In Camera Submissions, above.)

---

[165] Id. § 3.6.

[166] See id.

[167] See id.

[168] Id.; cf. Miller v. Casey, 730 F.2d 773, 778 (D.C. Cir. 1984) (refusing to review CIA decision to deny access to records under agency's discretionary "historical research program").

[169] See Exec. Order No. 12,958, §§ 3.6(b)(4), (d).

[170] Id. § 3.6(a)(3).

[171] Id. § 3.2(b).

[172] See FOIA Update, Vol. XVI, No. 2, at 11 (chart comparing provisions of Exec. Order No. 12,958 with those of Exec. Order No. 12,356).

[173] Exec. Order No. 12,958, § 3.7(a), 3 C.F.R. 333, 347 (1996), reprinted in 50 U.S.C. § 435 note (Supp. II 1996), and in FOIA Update, Vol. XVI, No. 2, at 9.

**EXEMPTION 1**

Second, the "mosaic" or "compilation" approach--the concept that apparently harmless pieces of information, when assembled together, could reveal a damaging picture--is recognized in Executive Order 12,958.[174] Compilations of otherwise unclassified information may be classified if the "compiled information reveals an additional association or relationship that: (1) meets the [order's classification] standards; and (2) is not otherwise revealed in the individual items of information."[175] This "mosaic" approach was presaged by a decision of the Court of Appeals for the District of Columbia Circuit in 1980[176] and has been endorsed by other courts.[177] The D.C. Circuit has also reaffirmed that even if there is other information that if released "would pose a greater threat to the national security," Exemption 1 "'bars the government from prying loose even the smallest bit of information that is properly classified.'"[178]

Another point to remember under Exemption 1 is the requirement that agencies segregate and release nonexempt information, unless the segregated

---

[174] See Exec. Order No. 12,958, § 1.8(e).

[175] Id.; see also Billington v. Department of Justice, 11 F. Supp. 2d 45, 55 (D.D.C. 1998) (applying cited provision of executive order to rule that "aggregate result" does not need to be "self-evident" to qualify for Exemption 1 protection) (appeal pending).

[176] Halperin v. CIA, 629 F.2d 144, 150 (D.C. Cir. 1980) (observing that "[e]ach individual piece of intelligence information, much like a piece of a jigsaw puzzle, may aid in piecing together other bits of information even when the individual piece is not of obvious importance in itself").

[177] See Loomis v. United States Dep't of Energy, No. 96-149, slip op. at 17 (N.D.N.Y. Mar. 9, 1999) (finding that safety measures regarding nuclear facilities set forth in manuals and lay-out plans contain highly technical information and that "such information in the aggregate could reveal sensitive aspects of operations") (decided under Exec. Order 12,958); Salisbury v. United States, 690 F.2d 966, 971 (D.C. Cir. 1982) (explicitly acknowledging "mosaic-like nature of intelligence gathering") (decided under Exec. Order No. 12,065); see also American Friends Serv. Comm. v. DOD, 831 F.2d 441, 444-45 (3d Cir. 1987) (recognizing "compilation" theory) (decided under Exec. Order No. 12,356); Taylor v. Department of the Army, 684 F.2d 99, 105 (D.C. Cir. 1982) (upholding classification of compilation of information on army combat units) (decided under Exec. Order No. 12,065); National Sec. Archive v. FBI, 759 F. Supp. 872, 877 (D.D.C. 1991) (adjudging that disclosure of code names and designator phrases could provide hostile intelligence analyst with "common denominator" permitting analyst to piece together seemingly unrelated data into snapshot of specific FBI counterintelligence activity) (decided under Exec. Order No. 12,356); Jan-Xin Zang v. FBI, 756 F. Supp. 705, 709-10 (W.D.N.Y. 1991) (upholding classification of any source-identifying word or phrase, which could by itself or in aggregate lead to disclosure of intelligence source) (decided under Exec. Order No. 12,356); cf. CIA v. Sims, 471 U.S. 159, 178 (1985) (Exemption 3).

[178] Abbotts v. NRC, 766 F.2d 604, 608 (D.C. Cir. 1985) (quoting Afshar v. Department of State, 702 F.2d 1125, 1130 (D.C. Cir. 1983)) (decided under Exec. Order No. 12,356).

# EXEMPTION 1

information would have no meaning.[179] The duty to release information that is "reasonably segregable"[180] applies in cases involving classified information as well as those involving nonclassified information.[181] During the past several years, the D.C. Circuit has reemphasized the FOIA's segregation requirement in a series of decisions,[182] two of which involved records withheld pursuant to Exemption 1.[183] In the first of these two decisions, the D.C. Circuit, although upholding the district court's substantive determination that the records contained information qualifying for Exemption 1 protection, nonethe-

---

[179] See, e.g., Doherty v. United States Dep't of Justice, 775 F.2d 49, 53 (2d Cir. 1985); Paisley v. CIA, 712 F.2d 686, 700 (D.C. Cir. 1983); Armstrong v. Executive Office of the President, 897 F. Supp. 10, 17 (D.D.C. 1995) (Vaughn Index and supporting affidavits demonstrate that limited number of country captions and source citations contained in intelligence summaries are so "inextricably intertwined" with text of summaries as to be exempt from disclosure); Bevis v. Department of the Army, No. 87-1893, slip op. at 2 (D.D.C. Sept. 16, 1988) (ruling that redaction not required when it would reduce balance of text to "unintelligible gibberish"); American Friends Serv. Comm. v. DOD, No. 83-4916, 1988 WL 82852, at *4 (E.D. Pa. Aug. 4, 1988) (very fact that records sought would have to be extensively "reformulated, re-worked and shuffled" prior to any disclosure established that nonexempt material was "inextricably intertwined" with exempt material), aff'd, 869 F.2d 587 (3d Cir. 1989) (unpublished table decision).

[180] 5 U.S.C. § 552(b) (sentence immediately following exemptions) (1994 & Supp. IV 1998).

[181] See, e.g., Oglesby v. United States Dep't of the Army, 920 F.2d 57, 66 n.12 (D.C. Cir. 1990) (dictum) (noting failure of Army affidavit to specify whether any reasonably segregable portions of 483-page document were withheld pursuant to Exemption 1); Ray v. Turner, 587 F.2d 1187, 1197 (D.C. Cir. 1978) (remanding for greater specificity in affidavit because agency may not rely on "exemption by document" approach even in Exemption 1 context); see also Harper v. DOD, No. 93-35876, 1995 WL 392032, at *2 (9th Cir. July 3, 1995) (reversing part of district court order which permitted agency to withhold entire report under Exemption 1, because district court failed to make "necessary findings" on segregability).

[182] See Trans-Pac. Policing Agreement v. United States Customs Serv., 177 F.3d 1022, 1028 (D.C. Cir. 1999); Kimberlin v. Department of Justice, 139 F.3d 944, 950 (D.C. Cir.), cert. denied, 525 U.S. 891 (1998); Army Times Publ'g Co. v. Department of the Air Force, 998 F.2d 1067, 1068, 1071-72 (D.C. Cir. 1993); PHE, Inc. v. Department of Justice, 983 F.2d 248, 252-53 (D.C. Cir. 1993); Schiller v. NLRB, 965 F.2d 1205, 1210 (D.C. Cir. 1992).

[183] See Oglesby v. United States Dep't of the Army, 79 F.3d 1172, 1180-81 (D.C. Cir. 1996); Krikorian v. Department of State, 984 F.2d 461, 466-67 (D.C. Cir. 1993); see also Canning v. United States Dep't of Justice, 848 F. Supp. 1037, 1049 n.2 (D.D.C. 1994) (applying Krikorian standard to specifically find that agency "carefully and methodically . . . respect[ed FOIA's segregation] principle"); Bay Area Lawyers Alliance for Nuclear Arms Control v. Department of State, No. C89-1843, slip op. at 7-8, 11-12 (N.D. Cal. June 4, 1993) (applying same standard).

# EXEMPTION 2

less remanded the case to the district court because it had failed to "make specific findings of segregability for each of the withheld documents."[184] In the second decision, the D.C. Circuit observed that although the agency might have been "aware of its duties under FOIA to disclose all nonsegregable information," it did not provide the court with an "adequate explanation" on which to base such a finding.[185] Accordingly, the D.C. Circuit also remanded the case to the district court for a more detailed description of the information withheld.[186]

As a final matter, agencies should be aware of the FOIA's "(c)(3) exclusion."[187] This special record exclusion applies to certain especially sensitive records maintained by the Federal Bureau of Investigation which pertain to foreign intelligence, counterintelligence or international terrorism matters. Where the existence of such records is itself a classified fact, the FBI may, so long as the existence of the records remains classified, treat the records as not subject to the requirements of the FOIA. (See the discussion of this provision under Exclusions, below.)

## EXEMPTION 2

Exemption 2 of the FOIA exempts from mandatory disclosure records that are "related solely to the internal personnel rules and practices of an agency."[1] Courts have interpreted the exemption to encompass two distinct categories of information:

(a) internal matters of a relatively trivial nature--sometimes referred to as "low 2" information; and

(b) more substantial internal matters, the disclosure of which would risk circumvention of a legal requirement--sometimes referred

---

[184] Krikorian, 984 F.2d at 467; see also Greenberg v. United States Dep't of Treasury, 10 F. Supp. 2d 3, 14-15 (D.D.C. 1998) (suggesting that CIA "more specifically" explain in subsequent Vaughn Index why portions of records withheld in full not reasonably segregable); FOIA Update, Vol. XIV, No. 3, at 11-12 ("OIP Guidance: The 'Reasonable Segregation' Obligation"); see also Attorney General's Memorandum for Heads of Departments and Agencies regarding the Freedom of Information Act (Oct. 4, 1993), reprinted in FOIA Update, Vol. XIV, No. 3, at 4-5 (stressing importance of segregation in connection with "foreseeable harm" standard); FOIA Update, Vol. XV, No. 2, at 3 (observing that harm element is "already built into" Exemption 1).

[185] Oglesby, 79 F.3d at 1181.

[186] Id.

[187] 5 U.S.C. § 552(c)(3); see also Attorney General's Memorandum on the 1986 Amendments to the Freedom of Information Act 24-25 (Dec. 1987).

[1] 5 U.S.C. § 552(b)(2) (1994 & Supp. IV 1998).

# EXEMPTION 2

as "high 2" information.[2]

For a long time, much confusion existed concerning the intended coverage of Exemption 2, due to the differing ways in which Exemption 2 was addressed in the Senate and House Reports when the FOIA was enacted. The Senate Report stated:

> Exemption No. 2 relates only to the internal personnel rules and practices of an agency. Examples of these may be rules as to personnel's use of parking facilities or regulation of lunch hours, statements of policy as to sick leave, and the like.[3]

The House Report provided a more expansive interpretation of Exemption 2's coverage, stating that it was intended to include:

> [o]perating rules, guidelines, and manuals of procedure for Government investigators or examiners . . . but [that] this exemption would not cover all "matters of internal management" such as employee relations and working conditions and routine administrative procedures which are withheld under present law.[4]

The Supreme Court confronted the conflict in Exemption 2's coverage of routine internal matters in a case in which a requester sought to obtain case summaries of Air Force Academy ethics hearings, and it found the Senate Report to be more authoritative. In Department of the Air Force v. Rose,[5] the Supreme Court construed Exemption 2's somewhat ambiguous language as protecting internal agency matters so routine or trivial that they could not be "subject to . . . a genuine and significant public interest."[6] The Court declared that Exemption 2 was intended to relieve agencies of the burden of assembling and providing access to any "matter in which the public could not reasonably be expected to have an interest."[7] At the same time, presaging the eventual development of "high 2," the Court also suggested in Rose that the policy enunciated by the House Report might permit an agency to withhold matters of some public interest "where disclosure may risk circumvention of agency regulation."[8]

---

[2] See FOIA Update, Vol. X, No. 3, at 3-4 ("OIP Guidance: Protecting Vulnerability Assessments Through Application of Exemption Two"); see, e.g., Schiller v. NLRB, 964 F.2d 1205, 1207 (D.C. Cir. 1992) (describing "low 2" and "high 2" aspects of exemption).

[3] S. Rep. No. 89-813, at 8 (1965).

[4] H. Rep. No. 89-1497, at 10 (1966), reprinted in 1966 U.S.C.C.A.N. 2418, 2427.

[5] 425 U.S. 352 (1976).

[6] Id. at 369.

[7] Id. at 369-70.

[8] Id. at 369.

## EXEMPTION 2

The Supreme Court's ruling in Rose helped to define the contours of Exemption 2, but it did not dispel all the confusion about its scope. Early judicial opinions, particularly in the Court of Appeals for the District of Columbia Circuit, showed that courts were unsure whether the exemption covered only internal personnel rules and personnel practices of an agency or, on the other hand, an agency's internal personnel rules and more general internal practices.[9] This confusion was finally laid to rest, at least in the D.C. Circuit, in Founding Church of Scientology v. Smith,[10] which articulated the following test for Exemption 2 coverage:

> First, the material withheld should fall within the terms of the statutory language as a personnel rule or internal practice of the agency. Then, if the material relates to trivial administrative matters of no genuine public interest, exemption would be automatic under the statute. If withholding frustrates legitimate public interest, however, the material should be released unless the government can show that disclosure would risk circumvention of lawful agency regulation.[11]

### "Low 2": Trivial Matters

Exemption 2 of the FOIA protects from disclosure internal matters of a

---

[9] Compare Jordan v. United States Dep't of Justice, 591 F.2d 753, 764 (D.C. Cir. 1978) (en banc) (exemption covers only internal personnel matters), and Allen v. CIA, 636 F.2d 1287, 1290 (D.C. Cir. 1980) (exemption covers nothing more than trivial administrative personnel rules), with Lesar v. United States Dep't of Justice, 636 F.2d 472, 485 (D.C. Cir. 1980) (exemption covers routine matters of merely internal interest), and Cox v. United States Dep't of Justice, 601 F.2d 1, 4 (D.C. Cir. 1979) (per curiam) (same). See generally DeLorme Publ'g Co. v. NOAA, 917 F. Supp. 867, 875-76 & n.10 (D. Me. 1996) (describing debate among various circuit courts on meaning of Exemption 2 language), appeal dismissed per stipulation, No. 96-1601 (1st Cir. July 8, 1996).

[10] 721 F.2d 828 (D.C. Cir. 1983).

[11] Id. at 830-31 n.4; see also Massey v. FBI, 3 F.3d 620, 622 (2d Cir. 1993) (holding that Exemption 2 applies to "non-employee information," such as informant symbol numbers and file numbers); Schiller, 964 F.2d at 1208 (finding Exemption 2 appropriate to withhold Equal Access to Justice Act litigation strategies); Dirksen v. HHS, 803 F.2d 1456, 1458-59 (9th Cir. 1986) (approving use of Exemption 2 to withhold Medicare claims-processing guidelines); Canning v. United States Dep't of the Treasury, No. 94-2704, slip op. at 15 (D.D.C. May 7, 1998) (concluding that Secret Service reliance on Exemption 2 for nondisclosure of internal office listing was proper). But see Abraham & Rose, P.L.C. v. United States, 138 F.3d 1075, 1080 (6th Cir. 1998) (declaring that Exemption 2 relates only to information about "an agency's internal 'rules and practices' for personnel"); Audubon Soc'y v. United States Forest Serv., 104 F.3d 1201, 1204 (10th Cir. 1997) (ruling that Exemption 2 may be applied only to documents related to "personnel practices" of agency); Thompson v. United States Dep't of Justice, No. 96-1118, slip op. at 28 (D. Kan. July 15, 1998) (same).

## EXEMPTION 2

relatively trivial nature.[12] As its legislative and judicial history make clear, in this "low 2" aspect Exemption 2 is the only exemption in the FOIA having a conceptual underpinning totally unrelated to any harm caused by disclosure per se.[13] Rather, this aspect of the exemption is based upon the unique rationale that the very task of processing and releasing some requested records would place an administrative burden on the agency that would not be justified by any genuine public benefit.[14] As such, this part of Exemption 2 is entirely subject to the policy of discretionary agency disclosure.[15]

For information to fall within Exemption 2, it must qualify as a personnel rule or internal practice of an agency or be sufficiently related to such a rule or practice.[16] Courts have included a variety of trivial administrative information within the "low 2" aspect of Exemption 2's coverage. For example, it has been held that routine internal personnel matters, such as performance standards and leave practices, are included within the scope of the exemption.[17] Personnel matters of greater public interest, however, such as the hon-

---

[12] See, e.g., Department of the Air Force v. Rose, 425 U.S. 352, 369-70 (1976); Lesar v. United States Dep't of Justice, 636 F.2d 472, 485 (D.C. Cir. 1980).

[13] See Rose, 425 U.S. at 369-70.

[14] See FOIA Update, Vol. 5, No. 1, at 10-11 ("FOIA Counselor: The Unique Protection of Exemption 2"); see, e.g., Martin v. Lauer, 686 F.2d 24, 34 (D.C. Cir. 1982) (Exemption 2 "serves to relieve the agency from the administrative burden of processing FOIA requests when internal matters are not likely to be the subject of public interest."); Fisher v. United States Dep't of Justice, 772 F. Supp. 7, 10 n.8 (D.D.C. 1991) (citing Martin, 686 F.2d at 34), aff'd, 968 F.2d 92 (D.C. Cir. 1992) (unpublished table decision).

[15] See FOIA Update, Vol. XV, No. 2, at 3 (emphasizing that agencies should apply discretionary disclosure policy to Exemption 2 "in its entire 'low 2' aspect").

[16] See Schwaner v. Department of the Air Force, 898 F.2d 793, 795 (D.C. Cir. 1990); see also Canning, No. 94-2704, slip op. at 15 (D.D.C. May 7, 1998) (finding description of circumstances that may trigger "an incident of interest to the Secret Service" to be "clearly 'practices of an agency'" and, therefore, properly protected); FOIA Update, Vol. XI, No. 2, at 2; cf. Goldstein v. Office of Indep. Counsel, No. 87-2028, 1999 WL 570862, at *6 (D.D.C. July 29, 1999) (magistrate's recommendation) (concluding that "a request of the [FBI] for hotel reservations does not implicate . . . any internal rule or practice of the FBI" and therefore "is not exempt under (b)(2)" even if it may be trivial or lacking in public interest).

[17] See, e.g., Small v. IRS, 820 F. Supp. 163, 168 (D.N.J. 1992) (employee service identification numbers); Pruner v. Department of the Army, 755 F. Supp. 362, 365 (D. Kan. 1991) (Army regulation concerning discharge of conscientious objectors); FBI Agents Ass'n v. FBI, 3 Gov't Disclosure Serv. (P-H) ¶ 83,058, at 83,566-67 (D.D.C. Jan. 13, 1983) (information relating to performance ratings, recognition and awards, leave practices, transfers, travel expenses, and allowances); NTEU v. United States Dep't of the Treasury, 487 F.

(continued...)

# EXEMPTION 2

or code proceedings at issue in Department of the Air Force v. Rose,[18] are not so covered.[19]

In the past, Exemption 2 was construed to permit the nondisclosure of mundane, yet far more pervasive administrative data--such as file numbers, mail routing stamps, initials, data processing notations, brief references to previous communications, and other similar administrative markings.[20] It

---

[17](...continued) Supp. 1321, 1324 (D.D.C. 1980) (bargaining history and IRS interpretation of labor contract provisions).

[18] 425 U.S. at 365-70.

[19] See, e.g., Vaughn v. Rosen, 523 F.2d 1136, 1140-43 (D.C. Cir. 1975) (evaluations of how effectively agency policies were being implemented); Globe Newspaper Co. v. FBI, No. 91-13257, 1992 WL 396327, at **2-3 (D. Mass. Dec. 29, 1992) (amount paid to FBI informant found to be personally involved in "ongoing criminal activities"); News Group Boston, Inc. v. National R.R. Passenger Corp., 799 F. Supp. 1264, 1266-68 (D. Mass. 1992) (disciplinary actions taken against Amtrak employees), appeal dismissed, No. 92-2250 (1st Cir. Dec. 4, 1992); North v. Walsh, No. 87-2700, slip op. at 3 (D.D.C. June 25, 1991) (travel vouchers of senior officials of Office of Independent Counsel); FBI Agents Ass'n, 3 Gov't Disclosure Serv. at 83,566-67 (standards of conduct, grievance procedures, and EEO procedures); Ferris v. IRS, 2 Gov't Disclosure Serv. (P-H) ¶ 82,084, at 82,363 (D.D.C. Dec. 23, 1981) (SES performance objectives).

[20] See, e.g., Hale v. United States Dep't of Justice, 973 F.2d 894, 902 (10th Cir. 1992) ("administrative markings and notations on documents; room numbers, telephone numbers, and FBI employees' identification numbers; a checklist form used to assist special agents in consensual monitoring; personnel directories containing the names and addresses of FBI employees; and the dissemination page of Hale's 'rap sheet'"), cert. granted, vacated & remanded on other grounds, 509 U.S. 918 (1993); Lesar, 636 F.2d at 485-86 (informant codes held "a matter of internal significance in which the public has no substantial interest [and which] bear no relation to the substantive contents of the records released"); Scherer v. Kelley, 584 F.2d 170, 175-76 (7th Cir. 1978) (protecting "file numbers, initials, signature and mail routing stamps, references to interagency transfers, and data processing references"), Hamilton v. Weise, No. 95-1161, 1997 U.S. Dist. LEXIS 18900, at *8 (M.D. Fla. Oct. 1, 1997) (finding purely administrative Customs Service codes concerning individual pilot properly protectible); Branch v. FBI, 658 F. Supp. 204, 208 (D.D.C. 1987) ("There is no question that [source symbol and file numbers are] trivial and may be withheld as a matter of law under Exemption 2."). But see Badalamenti v. United States Dep't of State, 899 F. Supp. 542, 547 (D. Kan. 1995) (agency's "bare assertion fails to demonstrate that the file and case numbers relate to an agency rule or practice or are otherwise encompassed within exemption 2"); Manna v. United States Dep't of Justice, 832 F. Supp. 866, 880 (D.N.J. 1993) ("DEA failed to describe or explain what these 'internal markings' are . . . [and if they] relate to internal rules or practice and whether these markings constitute trivial administrative matters of no public

(continued...)

**EXEMPTION 2**

also was held to justify the withholding of more extensive and substantive portions of administrative records and, most significantly, entire documents.[21]

One type of administrative record--federal personnel lists--caused the courts to struggle with the problem of determining when the threshold Exemption 2 requirement of being "related to" internal agency rules and practices is satisfied. The personal privacy protection of Exemption 6--successfully invoked to protect the names and home addresses of federal employees--is generally unavailable to protect the names and duty addresses of federal employees inasmuch as there ordinarily is no privacy interest in such information.[22]

In 1990, the Court of Appeals for the District of Columbia dispositively

---

[20](...continued) interest."); Fitzgibbon v. United States Secret Serv., 747 F. Supp. 51, 57 (D.D.C. 1990) (administrative markings do not "relate to" an agency rule or practice).

[21] See, e.g., Schiller v. NLRB, 964 F.2d 1205, 1208 (D.C. Cir. 1992) (internal time deadlines and procedures, recordkeeping directions, instructions on contacting agency officials for assistance and guidelines on agency decisionmaking); Nix v. United States, 572 F.2d 998, 1005 (4th Cir. 1978) (cover letters protected as matters of merely internal significance); Starkey v. IRS, No. C91-20040, slip op. at 10 (N.D. Cal. Dec. 6, 1991) (facsimile cover sheets, transcript, and employee travel information); Wilson v. Department of Justice, No. 87-2415, 1991 WL 11457, at *2 (D.D.C. June 13, 1991) (State Department transmittal slips from low-level officials); Barrett v. OSHA, No. C2-90-147, slip op. at 3-4 (S.D. Ohio Oct. 18, 1990) (administrative steps followed by OSHA prior to issuance of citation); KTVY-TV v. United States Postal Serv., No. 87-1432, slip op. at 15 (W.D. Okla. May 4, 1989) (computerized list of evidence gathered during investigation of shooting incident), aff'd on other grounds, 919 F.2d 1465 (10th Cir. 1990); Cox v. United States Dep't of Justice, No. 87-158, slip op. at 3 (D.D.C. Nov. 17, 1987) (investigation code name, supervising unit, details of property, and funding); Dickie v. Department of the Treasury, No. 86-649, slip op. at 3 (D.D.C. Mar. 31, 1987) (case-reporting procedures); Heller v. Marshals Serv., 655 F. Supp. 1088, 1092 (D.D.C. 1987) (brief and personal intra-agency memorandum labeled "trivial administrative detail[]"); Martinez v. FBI, No. 82-1547, slip op. at 10-11 (D.D.C. Dec. 19, 1985) (43 pages of postal inspector caseload management and timekeeping records).

[22] See, e.g., FLRA v. United States Dep't of the Treasury, 884 F.2d 1446, 1452-53 (D.C. Cir. 1989); FOIA Update, Vol. III, No. 4, at 3; FOIA Update, Vol. VII, No. 3, at 3-4 (recognizing exceptions for law enforcement and certain military personnel); see also 10 U.S.C.A. § 130b (West Supp. 2000); Department of Defense Freedom of Information Act Program Regulations, 32 C.F.R. § 286.12(f)(2)(ii) (1999) (restating express authority to withhold names and duty addresses for personnel assigned to sensitive, routinely deployable units); cf. Memorandum from Department of Defense Directorate for Freedom of Information and Security Review 1 (Oct. 26, 1999) (applying same delineation for electronic mail addresses, on privacy-protection grounds); id. (disclaiming "high 2" protection for nonsensitive electronic mail addresses).

# EXEMPTION 2

addressed the possible protection of federal personnel lists under Exemption 2 in <u>Schwaner v. Department of the Air Force</u>.[23] In a two-to-one decision, it held that a list of the names and duty addresses of military personnel stationed at Bolling Air Force Base does not meet the threshold requirement of being "related solely to the internal rules and practices of an agency."[24] The panel majority ruled that "the list does not bear an adequate relation to any rule or practice of the Air Force as those terms are used in exemption 2."[25] In so doing, it gave a new, stricter interpretation to the term "related to" under Exemption 2, holding that if the information in question is not itself actually a "rule or practice," then it must "shed significant light" on a "rule or practice" in order to qualify.[26] The D.C. Circuit concluded that "lists do not necessarily (or perhaps even normally) shed significant light on a rule or practice; insignificant light is not enough."[27] Thus, under <u>Schwaner</u>, Exemption 2 is not available to shield agencies from the burdens of processing requests for federal personnel lists.[28]

Furthermore, citing <u>Schwaner</u>, the Court of Appeals for the Sixth Circuit, has ruled that "information [contained in an IRS electronic database] that merely has a potential for shedding light on the practice of collecting and compiling information is not sufficiently related to a personnel rule or practice to satisfy . . . [the] Exemption 2 analysis."[29] The court concluded, however, that the requested information, contained in records of federal tax lien filings, may be protected by Exemptions 6 and 7(C).[30]

The second part of the "low 2" formulation concerns whether there "is a genuine and significant public interest" in disclosure of the records request-

---

[23] 898 F.2d 793 (D.C. Cir. 1990).

[24] <u>Id.</u> at 794.

[25] <u>Id.</u>

[26] <u>Id.</u> at 797; <u>see also</u> <u>Audubon Soc'y v. United States Forest Serv.</u>, 104 F.3d 1201, 1204 (10th Cir. 1997) (concluding that maps of habitats of owls deemed "threatened" under Endangered Species Act are not sufficiently related to internal personnel rules and practices).

[27] <u>Schwaner</u>, 898 F.2d at 797; <u>see also</u> <u>DeLorme Publ'g Co. v. NOAA</u>, 917 F. Supp. 867, 876 (D. Me. 1996) ("Nothing in Exemption 2 supports the proposition that government 'information may be withheld simply because it manifests an agency practice of <u>collecting</u> the information.'" (quoting <u>Schwaner</u>)), <u>appeal dismissed per stipulation</u>, No. 96-1601 (1st Cir. July 8, 1996).

[28] <u>See</u> <u>FOIA Update</u>, Vol. XI, No. 2, at 2 (modifying prior guidance in light of controlling nature of ruling by D.C. Circuit, as circuit of "universal venue" under FOIA).

[29] <u>Abraham & Rose, P.L.C. v. United States</u>, 138 F.3d 1075, 1081 (6th Cir. 1998).

[30] <u>Id.</u> at 1082-83.

**EXEMPTION 2**

ed.[31] An illustration of how this "public interest" delineation has been drawn can be found in a decision in which large portions of an FBI administrative manual were ruled properly withholdable on a "burden" theory under Exemption 2, but other portions, because of a discerned "public interest" in them, were not.[32] This decision is reflective of the D.C. Circuit's admonition in Founding Church of Scientology v. Smith[33] that "a reasonably low threshold should be maintained for determining when withheld administrative material relates to significant public interests."[34]

The nature of this "public interest" in "low 2" cases was affected by the Supreme Court's decision in United States Department of Justice v. Reporters Committee for Freedom of the Press.[35] In Reporters Committee, the Supreme Court held that the "public interest" depended on the nature of the document sought and its relationship to "the basic purpose [of the FOIA] 'to open agency action to the light of public scrutiny.'"[36] The Court concluded that the FOIA's "core purposes" would not be furthered by disclosure of a record about a private individual, even if it "would provide details to include in a news story, [because] this is not the kind of public interest for which Congress enacted the FOIA."[37] It also emphasized that a particular FOIA requester's intended use of the requested information "has no bearing on the merits of his or her FOIA

---

[31] Rose, 425 U.S. at 369.

[32] FBI Agents Ass'n, 3 Gov't Disclosure Serv. at 83,565-66; see also Berg v. Commodity Futures Trading Comm'n, No. 93-C6741, slip op. at 10 (N.D. Ill. June 23, 1994) (applying Rose and finding presence of public interest in "material dealing with how a public-funded agency handles inquiries from the public and responds to the public"); Church of Scientology v. IRS, 816 F. Supp. 1138, 1149 (W.D. Tex. 1993) (stating that "public is entitled to know how IRS is allocating" taxpayers' money as it pertains to IRS advance of travel funds to its employees), appeal dismissed per stipulation, No. 93-8431 (5th Cir. Oct. 21, 1993); News Group Boston, 799 F. Supp. at 1267 (finding legitimate public interest in disclosure of case-handling statements despite agency's stated fear that information may be misunderstood or misinterpreted by public); Globe Newspaper, 1992 WL 396327, at *2 (holding that amount paid to FBI informant personally involved in continuing criminal activity should be disclosed because it "falls squarely within the parameters set by Rose"); Singer v. Rourke, No. 87-1213, slip op. at 3-4 (D. Kan. Dec. 30, 1988) (holding Exemption 2 inapplicable to documents that relate to investigation of sexual and racial harassment at Air Force facility, because public has "genuine and significant interest" in learning whether the government has engaged in "such noxious activity" in agencies).

[33] 721 F.2d 828 (D.C. Cir. 1983).

[34] Id. at 830-31 n.4.

[35] 489 U.S. 749 (1989).

[36] Id. at 772 (quoting Rose, 425 U.S. at 372).

[37] Id. at 774.

**EXEMPTION 2**

request" and that FOIA requesters therefore should be treated alike.[38] (See the further discussion of this decision under Exemption 6, The Reporters Committee Decision, below.)

Although the Supreme Court's decision in Reporters Committee is based on an analysis of Exemption 7(C), its interpretation of what constitutes "public interest" under the FOIA logically may be applicable under Exemption 2 as well.[39] After Reporters Committee, courts increasingly focused upon the lack of any "legitimate public interest" when applying this aspect of the exemption to information found to be related to an agency's internal practices.[40] Indeed, a number of courts had already been taking such an approach in analyzing "low 2" cases before Reporters Committee.[41] Nevertheless, there remains the fact that this aspect of Exemption 2 simply does not cover any information in which there is "a genuine and significant public interest."[42]

---

[38] Id. at 771; see also FOIA Update, Vol. X, No. 2, at 5.

[39] See Schwaner, 898 F.2d at 800-01 (Revercomb, J., dissenting on issue not reached by majority) (relying on Reporters Committee "core purposes" analysis and finding no "meaningful" public interest in disclosure of names and duty addresses of military personnel).

[40] See Hale, 973 F.2d at 902 (finding no public interest in administrative markings and notations, personnel directories containing names and addresses of FBI employees, room and telephone numbers, employee identification numbers, consensual monitoring checklist form, and rap sheet-dissemination page); Germosen v. Cox, No. 98-1294, 1999 WL 1021559, at *12 (S.D.N.Y. Nov. 9, 1999) (finding "no legitimate [or genuine] public interest" in source symbol numbers and agent identification numbers, as well as in computer access codes, telephone and facsimile numbers, and numbers used to denote different categories of counterfeit currency) (appeal pending); Voinche v. FBI, 46 F. Supp. 2d 26, 30 (D.D.C. 1999) (applying Exemption 2 to telephone number of FBI's Public Corruption Unit as "trivial administrative matter of no genuine public interest"); News Group Boston, 799 F. Supp. at 1268 (holding that there is no public interest in payroll and job title codes); Buffalo Evening News, Inc. v. United States Border Patrol, 791 F. Supp. 386, 390-93 (W.D.N.Y. 1992) (declaring that there is no public interest in "soundex" encoding of alien's family name, in whether or not alien is listed in Border Patrol Lookout Book, in codes used to identify deportability, in narratives explaining circumstances of apprehension, or in internal routing information).

[41] See, e.g., Martin, 686 F.2d at 34 (Exemption 2 is "designed to screen out illegitimate public inquiries into the functioning of an agency."); Lesar, 636 F.2d at 485-86 (public has "no legitimate interest" in FBI's mechanism for internal control of informant identities); Struth v. FBI, 673 F. Supp. 949, 959 (E.D. Wis. 1987) (plaintiff offered no evidence of public interest in source symbol or source file numbers). But see Tax Analysts v. United States Dep't of Justice, 845 F.2d 1060, 1064 n.8 (D.C. Cir. 1988) (finding Exemption 2 inapplicable, without discussion, because of "public's obvious interest" in agency copies of court opinions), aff'd on other grounds, 492 U.S. 136 (1989).

[42] Rose, 425 U.S. at 369; see also FOIA Update, Vol. V, No. 1, at 11 (empha-
(continued...)

# EXEMPTION 2

Moreover, in October 1993, in conjunction with the President's call for more openness in government,[43] the Attorney General established new standards of government openness that strongly guide agency decisionmaking under the FOIA toward the Act's goal of maximum responsible disclosure.[44] The cornerstone of this FOIA policy is the "foreseeable harm" standard, which the Attorney General's FOIA Memorandum sets forth as follows:

> In short, it shall be the policy of the Department of Justice to defend the assertion of a FOIA exemption only in those cases where the agency reasonably foresees that disclosure would be harmful to an interest protected by that exemption. Where an item of information might technically or arguably fall within an exemption, it ought not to be withheld from a FOIA requester unless it need be.[45]

When "only a government interest would be affected" by a FOIA disclosure,[46] as is entirely the case with "low 2" information, there is a great potential for discretionary disclosure of such material.[47] Furthermore, as a matter of longstanding policy, agencies have been encouraged to release "low 2" information inasmuch as very often it is less burdensome, or of relatively negligible burden, for them to do so.[48] Accordingly, nearly all administrative information covered solely by the "low 2" part of Exemption 2 should now be appropriate for discretionary disclosure under Attorney General Reno's FOIA

---

[42](...continued)
sizing "low threshold" for disclosure of such information).

[43] President's Memorandum for Heads of Departments and Agencies regarding the Freedom of Information Act, 29 Weekly Comp. Pres. Doc. 1999 (Oct. 4, 1993), reprinted in FOIA Update, Vol. XIV, No. 3, at 3.

[44] Attorney General's Memorandum for Heads of Departments and Agencies regarding the Freedom of Information Act (Oct. 4, 1993) [hereinafter Attorney General Reno's FOIA Memorandum], reprinted in FOIA Update, Vol. XIV, No. 3, at 4-5.

[45] Id. at 4; see also Attorney General's Follow-Up Memorandum for Heads of Departments and Agencies regarding the Freedom of Information Act (Sept. 3, 1999), reprinted in FOIA Update, Vol. XIX, No. 4, at 3-5 (reiterating importance of "foreseeable harm" standard to federal agencies in order to promote further discretionary disclosure in agency decisionmaking).

[46] Attorney General Reno's FOIA Memorandum, reprinted in FOIA Update, Vol. XIV, No. 3, at 4.

[47] See FOIA Update, Vol. XV, No. 2, at 3 (discussing application of "foreseeable harm" standard through discretionary disclosure).

[48] See, e.g., Fonda v. CIA, 434 F. Supp. 498, 503 (D.D.C. 1977) (finding that where administrative burden is minimal and it would be easier to release material, policy underlying Exemption 2 does not permit withholding); see also FOIA Update, Vol. V, No. 1, at 11 (advising agencies to invoke exemption only where doing so truly avoids burden).

**EXEMPTION 2**

Memorandum.[49] In some cases, though, courts have continued to find that information is exempt under a "low 2" analysis, sometimes incorporating "high 2" circumvention language as well.[50] (For a further discussion of discretionary disclosure, see Discretionary Disclosure and Waiver, below.)

### "High 2": Risk of Circumvention

The second category of information covered by Exemption 2--internal matters of a more substantial nature the disclosure of which would risk the circumvention of a statute or agency regulation--has generated considerable controversy over the years. In Department of the Air Force v. Rose,[51] the Supreme Court specifically left open the question of whether such records fall within Exemption 2 coverage. Most of the cases first developed this aspect of the exemption in the context of law enforcement manuals containing sensitive staff instructions. For example, the position adopted by the Court of Appeals for the Eighth Circuit on this subject is that Exemption 2 does not relate to such matters, but that subsection (a)(2)(C) of the FOIA,[52] which arguably excludes law enforcement manuals from the automatic disclosure provisions of the FOIA, bars disclosure of manuals whose release to the public would significantly impede the law enforcement process.[53] Although tacitly approving the Eighth Circuit's argument, the Courts of Appeals for the Fifth and Sixth Circuits have an alternative rationale for withholding law enforcement manuals; disclosure would allow persons "simultaneously to violate the law and to avoid

---

[49] Attorney General Reno's FOIA Memorandum, reprinted in FOIA Update, Vol. XIV, No. 3, at 4-5; see also FOIA Update, Vol. XV, No. 2, at 3 (distinguishing between "low 2" and "high 2" information in connection with discretionary disclosure).

[50] See, e.g., Goldstein, 1999 WL 570862, at *5 (finding portions of FBI documents properly withheld as trivial information); Green v. DEA, No. 98-0728, slip op. at 6 (D.D.C. Sept. 30, 1998) (finding justified withholding by DEA of G-DEP numbers--codes describing classes of violators, types of drugs, and suspected locations of criminal activity--as protecting "information . . . both routine [and] internal [to the] agency and as . . . of little public interest where disclosure may risk circumvention of [law]"), summary affirmance granted in pertinent part, No. 99-5356, 2000 WL 271988 (D.C. Cir. Feb. 17, 2000); Coleman v. FBI, 13 F. Supp. 2d 75, 79 (D.D.C. 1998) (protecting FBI source symbol numbers and file numbers both as "low 2" "information [which] facilitates administrative operation and recordkeeping," and as "high 2" information because disclosure could allow "criminals to redirect their activities [to] avoid legal intervention"); Rosenberg v. Freeh, No. 97-0476, slip op. at 6 (D.D.C. May 12, 1998) (holding information properly protected "as both routine internal agency matters of no significant public interest and as matters of some public interest where disclosure may risk circumvention of statutes and agency regulations").

[51] 425 U.S. 352, 364, 369 (1976).

[52] 5 U.S.C. § 552(a)(2)(C) (1994 & Supp. IV 1998).

[53] See Cox v. Levi, 592 F.2d 460, 462-63 (8th Cir. 1979); Cox v. United States Dep't of Justice, 576 F.2d 1302, 1306-09 (8th Cir. 1978).

# EXEMPTION 2

detection"[54] by impeding law enforcement efforts.[55]

The majority of the courts in other circuits, however, have placed greater weight on the House Report[56] in this respect and accordingly have held that Exemption 2 is applicable to internal administrative and personnel matters, including law enforcement manuals, to the extent that disclosure would risk circumvention of an agency regulation or statute or impede the effectiveness of an agency's law enforcement activities.[57]

The Court of Appeals for the District of Columbia Circuit adopted this majority approach when the full court addressed the issue in Crooker v. ATF, a case involving a law enforcement agents' training manual.[58] Although not explicitly overruling its earlier en banc decision in Jordan v. United States Department of Justice, which held that guidelines for the exercise of prosecutorial discretion were not properly withholdable,[59] the en banc decision in Crooker specifically rejected the rationale of Jordan that Exemption 2 cannot protect law enforcement manuals or other documents whose disclosure would risk circumvention of the law.[60]

In Crooker, the D.C. Circuit fashioned a two-part test for determining which sensitive materials are exempt from mandatory disclosure under Exemption 2. This test requires both:

(1) that a requested document be "predominantly internal," and

(2) that its disclosure "significantly risks circumvention of agency regulations or statutes."[61]

Whether there is any public interest in disclosure is legally irrelevant under this "anti-circumvention" aspect of Exemption 2.[62] Rather, the concern

---

[54] Hawkes v. IRS, 467 F.2d 787, 795 (6th Cir. 1972).

[55] See id.; Sladek v. Bensinger, 605 F.2d 899, 902 (5th Cir. 1979).

[56] H. Rep. No. 89-1497, at 10 (1966), reprinted in 1966 U.S.C.C.A.N. 2418, 2427.

[57] See, e.g., Hardy v. ATF, 631 F.2d 653, 656 (9th Cir. 1980); Caplan v. ATF, 587 F.2d 544, 547 (2d Cir. 1978); Wilder v. IRS, 607 F. Supp. 1013, 1015 (M.D. Ala. 1985); Ferri v. Bell, No. 78-841, slip op. at 7-9 (M.D. Pa. Dec. 15, 1983); Fiumara v. Higgins, 572 F. Supp. 1093, 1102 (D.N.H. 1983).

[58] 670 F.2d 1051, 1074 (D.C. Cir. 1981) (en banc).

[59] 591 F.2d 753, 771 (D.C. Cir. 1978) (en banc).

[60] See 670 F.2d at 1074.

[61] Id. at 1073-74.

[62] See Voinche v. FBI, 940 F. Supp. 323, 328 (D.D.C. 1996), aff'd per curiam, No. 96-5304, 1997 U.S. App. LEXIS 19089 (D.C. Cir. June 19, 1997); In-
(continued...)

# EXEMPTION 2

under "high 2" is that a FOIA disclosure should not "benefit those attempting to violate the law and avoid detection."[63] Thus, this aspect of Exemption 2 fundamentally rests upon a determination of "foreseeable harm."[64]

In years past, it was often relatively easy to meet the first part of the Crooker test that the materials be "predominantly internal."[65] The D.C. Circuit established specific guidance on what constitutes an "internal" document in Cox v. United States Department of Justice, which held protectible information that

> does not purport to regulate activities among members of the public . . . [and] does [not] . . . set standards to be followed by agency personnel in deciding whether to proceed against or to take action affecting members of the public. Differently stated, the unreleased information is not "secret law," the primary target

---

[62](...continued)
stitute for Policy Studies v. Department of the Air Force, 676 F. Supp. 3, 5 (D.D.C. 1987). But see Kaganove v. EPA, 856 F.2d 884, 889 (7th Cir. 1988) (suggesting that document may not meet Crooker test if its purpose was not "legitimate"); Wilkinson v. FBI, 633 F. Supp. 336, 342 (C.D. Cal. 1986) (suggesting that charge that underlying investigation was conducted illegally might render exemption inapplicable); Oatley v. United States, 3 Gov't Disclosure Serv. (P-H) ¶ 83,274, at 84,065 (D.D.C. Aug. 16, 1983) (holding that civil service testing materials satisfy two-part Crooker test, but leaving open possibility that information would not be considered predominantly internal if grounds existed to suspect bias on the basis of race or sex in materials).

[63] Crooker, 670 F.2d at 1054.

[64] See Judicial Watch, Inc. v. United States Dep't of Commerce, 83 F. Supp. 2d 105, 110 (D.D.C. 1999) (applying "high 2" based upon determination that disclosure of government credit card numbers "would present an opportunity for misuse and fraud"); Attorney General's Memorandum for Heads of Departments and Agencies regarding the Freedom of Information Act (Oct. 4, 1993) [hereinafter Attorney General Reno's FOIA Memorandum], reprinted in FOIA Update, Vol. XIV, No. 3, at 4 (establishing "foreseeable harm" standard); see also Attorney General's Follow-Up Memorandum for Heads of Departments and Agencies regarding the Freedom of Information Act (Sept. 3, 1999) [hereinafter Attorney General Reno's Follow-Up FOIA Memorandum], reprinted in FOIA Update, Vol. XIX, No. 4, at 3-5; FOIA Update, Vol. XV, No. 2, at 3 (observing that harm element is "already built into" this Exemption 2 aspect).

[65] See Kaganove, 856 F.2d at 889 (finding that agency, like any employer, "reasonably would expect" applicant rating plan to be internal); NTEU v. United States Customs Serv., 802 F.2d 525, 531 (D.C. Cir. 1986) (maintaining that appointment of individual members of lower federal bureaucracy is primarily question of internal significance for agencies involved); Institute for Policy Studies, 676 F. Supp. at 5 ("[I]t is difficult to conceive of a document that is more 'predominantly internal' than a guide by which agency personnel classify documents.").

**EXEMPTION 2**

of [the FOIA's] disclosure provisions.[66]

Reflecting a measure of deference that is implicitly accorded law enforcement activities under this substantive aspect of Exemption 2,[67] courts have treated a wide variety of information pertaining to such activities as "internal," including:

(1) general guidelines for conducting investigations;[68]

(2) guidelines for conducting post-investigation litigation;[69]

---

[66] 601 F.2d 1, 5 (D.C. Cir. 1979) (per curiam); see also Sousa v. United States Dep't of Justice, No. 95-375, 1996 U.S. Dist. LEXIS 18627, at *11 (D.D.C. Dec. 9, 1996) (finding that "the exemption only applies to information 'used for a predominantly internal purpose'" (quoting Schiller v. NLRB, 964 F.2d 1205, 1207 (D.C. Cir. 1992))).

[67] See Schwaner v. Department of the Air Force, 898 F.2d 793, 796 (D.C. Cir. 1990) ("Judicial willingness to sanction a weak relation to 'rules and practices' may be greatest when the asserted government interest is relatively weighty."); Wiesenfelder v. Riley, 959 F. Supp. 532, 535 (D.D.C. 1997) (pointing out deference accorded law enforcement activities).

[68] See, e.g., PHE, Inc. v. United States Dep't of Justice, 983 F.2d 248, 251 (D.C. Cir. 1993) ("[R]elease of FBI guidelines as to what sources of information are available to its agents might encourage violators to tamper with those sources of information and thus inhibit investigative efforts."); Becker v. IRS, No. 91-C-1203, 1992 WL 67849, at *6 n.1 (N.D. Ill. Mar. 27, 1992) (exemption protects operational rules, guidelines, and procedures for law enforcement investigations and examinations), motion to amend denied (N.D. Ill. Apr. 12, 1993), aff'd in part & rev'd in part on other grounds, 34 F.3d 398 (7th Cir. 1994); Wilder v. Commissioner, 601 F. Supp. 241, 242-43 (M.D. Ala. 1984) (agreement between state and federal agencies concerning when to exchange information relevant to potential violations of tax laws held "predominantly internal" because it did not interpret substantive law, but instead governed exchange of information); Goldsborough v. IRS, No. 81-1939, 1984 WL 612, at *7 (D. Md. May 10, 1984) (protecting law enforcement manual setting out guidelines to be used in criminal investigation); Berkosky v. Department of Labor, No. 82-6464, slip op. at 3 (C.D. Cal. May 2, 1984) (holding that guidance for proper conduct of investigation of government contractor is designed solely to instruct investigators and does not "regulate the public").

[69] See, e.g., Schiller v. NLRB, 964 F.2d 1205, 1208 (D.C. Cir. 1992) (holding that exemption protects litigation strategy pertaining to Equal Access to Justice Act because disclosure would render information "operationally useless"); Silber v. United States Dep't of Justice, No. 91-876, transcript at 21 (D.D.C. Aug. 13, 1992) (bench order) (deciding that disclosure of agency's fraud litigation monograph would allow access to strategies and theories of government litigation and its efforts to enforce False Claims Act); see also Shumaker v. Commodity Futures Trading Comm'n, No. 97-7139, slip op. at 6-9 (N.D. Ohio May 27, 1997) (relying on Schiller to determine that agency settlement guidelines are similar to exempt litigation strategies and that disclosure would ren-
(continued...)

**EXEMPTION 2**

(3) guidelines for identifying law violators;[70]

(4) a study of agency practices and problems pertaining to undercover agents;[71] and

(5) sections of a Bureau of Prisons manual which summarize procedures for security of prison control centers, including escape prevention plans, control of keys and locks within a prison, instructions regarding transportation of federal prisoners, and the arms and defensive equipment inventories maintained in the facility.[72]

---

[69](...continued)
der those documents "operationally useless"). But see Dayton Newspapers, Inc. v. Department of the Air Force, No. C-3-97-78, slip op. at 15 (S.D. Ohio Mar. 26, 1999) (rejecting invocation of Exemption 2 for individual malpractice case settlement amounts, which court treated as not covered by "'internal personnel rules and practices'" and, therefore, "presumed to be subject to disclosure" absent any other applicable exemption).

[70] See, e.g., Dirksen v. HHS, 803 F.2d 1456, 1458-59 (9th Cir. 1986) (affirming nondisclosure of claims-processing guidelines that could be used by health care providers to avoid audits); Voinche, 940 F. Supp. at 328 (approving nondisclosure of manual describing techniques used by professional gamblers to evade prosecution); Church of Scientology Int'l v. IRS, 845 F. Supp. 714, 723 (C.D. Cal. 1993) (protecting "information about internal law enforcement techniques, practices, and procedures used by the IRS to coordinate the flow of information regarding Scientology"); Buffalo Evening News, Inc. v. United States Border Patrol, 791 F. Supp. 386, 393 (W.D.N.Y. 1992) (finding methods of apprehension and statement of ultimate disposition of case to be internal); Williston Basin Interstate Pipeline Co. v. Federal Energy Regulatory Comm'n, No. 88-592, 1989 WL 44655, at *2 (D.D.C. Apr. 17, 1989) (holding portions of audit report to be "functional equivalent" of investigative techniques manual, and thus protectible under Exemptions 2 and 7(E), because disclosure would reveal techniques used by agency personnel to ascertain whether plaintiff was in compliance with federal law); Fund for a Conservative Majority v. Federal Election Comm'n, No. 84-1342, slip op. at 4 (D.D.C. Feb. 26, 1985) (determining audit criteria not "secret law" because they merely provide "threshold requirements" for observing public behavior for illegal activity and do not define illegal activity); Windels, Marx, Davies & Ives v. Department of Commerce, 576 F. Supp. 405, 412 (D.D.C. 1983) (protecting computer program under Exemptions 2 and 7(E) because it merely instructs computer how to detect possible law violations, rather than modifying or regulating public behavior); Zorn v. IRS, 2 Gov't Disclosure Serv. (P-H) ¶ 82,240, at 82,664 (D.D.C. Mar. 19, 1982) (holding guidelines for identifying tax-protester churches not to be "secret law").

[71] See Cox v. FBI, No. 83-3552, slip op. at 1 (D.D.C. May 31, 1984) (holding that report concerning undercover agents had no effect on public and contained no "secret law"), appeal dismissed, No. 84-5364 (D.C. Cir. Feb. 28, 1985).

[72] See Miller v. Department of Justice, No. 87-533, 1989 WL 10598, at *1

(continued...)

## EXEMPTION 2

In what is perhaps the broadest application of this standard, a law enforcement document distributed to 1700 state, federal, and foreign law enforcement agencies was held to meet the test of "predominant internality" when its dissemination was necessary for maximum law enforcement effectiveness and any access by the general public was strictly denied.[73]

On the other hand, courts have been more reluctant to extend Exemption 2 protections in the non-law enforcement context without first finding that the records at issue are clearly predominantly internal. In 1992, the District Court for the District of Columbia held that a computer-calculating technique used by the Department of Transportation to determine the safety rating for motor carriers is not purely internal because it is used to determine "whether and to what extent certain violations will have any legal effect or carry any legal penalty."[74] In a second case that year, the same court held that documents relating to the procurement of telecommunications services by the federal government could not qualify as "primarily" internal because of the project's "massive" scale and significance.[75] In 1994, that court similarly ruled, after in camera review, that two FBI documents could not be withheld as "an internal 'rule or practice' of an agency," as such documents pertained to "planning, execution, and review of specific operations."[76] A year later, the United States District Court for the District of Oregon held that a daily diary used to verify contract compliance did not contain internal instructions to government officials and therefore could not be withheld under Exemption 2.[77]

In two decisions narrowly construing Exemption 2, the Courts of Appeals for the Ninth and Tenth Circuits have refused to protect maps showing nest site locations of two different species of birds because the documents

---

[72](...continued)
(D.D.C. Jan. 31, 1989); see also Linn v. United States Dep't of Justice, No. 92-1406, 1995 WL 417810, at *19 (D.D.C. June 6, 1995) (protecting numerical symbols used for identifying prisoners because release could assist others in breaching prisoners' security); Kuffel v. United States Bureau of Prisons, 882 F. Supp. 1116, 1123 (D.D.C. 1995) (same).

[73] See Shanmugadhasan v. United States Dep't of Justice, No. 84-0079, slip op. at 31-34 (C.D. Cal. Feb. 18, 1986) (portions of DEA periodical discussing drug-enforcement techniques and exchanges of information held protectible).

[74] Don Ray Drive-A-Way Co. v. Skinner, 785 F. Supp. 198, 200 (D.D.C. 1992).

[75] MCI Telecomms. Corp. v. GSA, No. 89-746, 1992 WL 71394, at *4 (D.D.C. Mar. 25, 1992).

[76] Butler v. United States Dep't of Justice, No. 86-2255, 1994 WL 55621, at *8 (D.D.C. Feb. 3, 1994) (finding that documents at issue did "not discuss the implementation of an existing agency procedure or practice, but instead contain[ed] discussions of plans apparently devised to respond to a particular set of circumstances"), appeal dismissed, No. 94-5078 (D.C. Cir. Sept. 8, 1994).

[77] Tidewater Contractors, Inc. v. USDA, No. 95-541, 1995 WL 604112, at *3 (D. Or. Oct. 4, 1995), appeal dismissed, No. 95-36238 (Mar. 14, 1996).

# EXEMPTION 2

failed the test of "predominant internality."[78] Declaring that the phrase "internal personnel" modified both "rules" and "practices" of an agency, the Tenth Circuit turned down arguments from the Forest Service that the maps related to agency practices in that they helped Forest Service personnel perform their management duties.[79] Refusing to consider the potential harm from disclosure of the maps,[80] the Tenth Circuit declared that it would "stretch[] the language of the exemption too far to conclude that owl maps 'relate' to personnel practices of the Forest Service."[81] In reaching this decision, though, the Tenth Circuit relied on an earlier opinion by the D.C. Circuit,[82] the rationale of which subsequently was specifically rejected by that court.[83]

Agreeing in a related case that such wildlife maps may not be protected from disclosure despite the potential risk of harm from their release, the Ninth Circuit did not explicitly accept the rationale of its circuit neighbor: Declaring that the maps bore "no meaningful relationship to the 'internal personnel rules and practices' of the Forest Service,"[84] it instead noted that the maps "do[] not tell the Forest Service how to catch lawbreakers [or] tell lawbreakers how to avoid the Forest Service's enforcement efforts," and it thereby specifically distinguished its previous Exemption 2 decisions involving law enforcement records.[85] The Ninth Circuit's decision, thus, leaves room for "high 2" protection of information bearing "law enforcement" significance.[86]

Often the "internality" of the documents is simply assumed; in those

---

[78] Maricopa Audubon Soc'y v. United States Forest Serv., 108 F.3d 1082 (9th Cir. 1997); Audubon Soc'y v. United States Forest Serv., 104 F.3d 1201 (10th Cir. 1997).

[79] Audubon Soc'y, 104 F.3d at 1204.

[80] But see Pease v. United States Dep't of Interior, No. 1:99CV113, slip op. at 2, 4 (D. Vt. Sept. 17, 1999) (finding, on basis of National Park Omnibus Management Act of 1998, 16 U.S.C. § 5937 (1994 & Supp. IV 1998), that agency properly withheld information pertaining to location of wildlife in Yellowstone National Park ecosystem).

[81] Id.; see also Thompson v. United States Dep't of Justice, No. 96-1118, slip op. at 30 (D. Kan. July 15, 1998) (following Audubon Soc'y to deny protection to file numbers found not to qualify under rigid application of "personnel practices" requirement).

[82] See Audubon Soc'y, 104 F.3d at 1204 (citing Jordan v. United States Dep't of Justice, 591 F.2d 753, 764 (D.C. Cir. 1978) (en banc)).

[83] See Crooker, 670 F.2d at 1074.

[84] Maricopa, 108 F.3d at 1086.

[85] Id. at 1087 (distinguishing Hardy, 631 F.2d at 653, and Dirksen, 803 F.2d at 1456).

[86] See id. at 1087 (emphasizing that nest-site information "does not constitute 'law enforcement material'" entitled to withholding under Exemption 2.)

# EXEMPTION 2

cases courts focus on what constitutes circumvention of legal requirements. Critically important are records that reveal the nature and extent of a particular investigation; these have been repeatedly held protectible on this "circumvention" basis.[87] On a point of increasing significance, the nondisclosure of computer codes used by law enforcement agencies that might provide the sophisticated requester with access to information concerning agency investigations stored in a computer system likewise has been upheld on this basis.[88] Nondisclosure of other sensitive computer-related information that might permit unauthorized access to agency communications systems has also been upheld under the same rationale.[89] However, in an exceptional decision, one

---

[87] See, e.g., Rosenberg v. Freeh, No. 97-0476, slip op. at 4-6 (D.D.C. May 12, 1998) (employing "high" and "low" 2 language to protect FBI source numbers, banking codes, and code name, disclosure of which would risk circumvention of the law); Wagner v. DEA, No. 93-2093, 1995 WL 350794, at *1 (D.D.C. May 26, 1995) (release of internal codes could "thwart DEA's investigative and enforcement efforts"); Augarten v. DEA, No. 93-2192, 1995 WL 350797, at *1 (D.D.C. May 22, 1995) (release of "drug codes, information identification codes, and violator identification codes" would reveal nature and extent of specific investigations); Manna v. United States Dep't of Justice, 832 F. Supp. 866, 872, 880 (D.N.J. 1993) (release of G-DEP and NADDIS numbers "would impede" investigative and enforcement efforts); Watson v. United States Dep't of Justice, 799 F. Supp. 193, 195 (D.D.C. 1992) (subjects could decode G-DEP and NADDIS numbers and change their activities "so as to evade detection"); Albuquerque Publ'g Co. v. United States Dep't of Justice, 726 F. Supp. 851, 854 (D.D.C. 1989) ("The public has no legitimate interest in gaining information [pertaining to violator and informant codes] that could lead to the impairment of DEA investigations."). But cf. KTVK-TV v. DEA, No. 89-379, 1989 U.S. Dist. LEXIS 10348, at *5 (D. Ariz. Aug. 29, 1989) (ordering disclosure of tape of speech by local police chief, given at seminar sponsored by DEA, which contained remarks on police department programs used or contemplated to discourage illegal drug use and finding that "disclosure of any of these programs would tend to discourage illegal use of drugs").

[88] See, e.g., Dirksen, 803 F.2d at 1459 (protecting instructions for computer coding); Prows v. United States Dep't of Justice, No. 90-2561, 1996 WL 228463, at *2 (D.D.C. Apr. 25, 1996) (protecting internal DEA markings and phrases that could, if released, facilitate improper access to sensitive information); Kuffel, 882 F. Supp. at 1123 (protecting computer and teletype routing symbols, access codes, and computer option commands); Beckette v. United States Postal Serv., No. 90-1246-N, 1993 WL 730711, at *4 (E.D. Va. Mar. 11, 1993) (protecting control file, which "is a set of instructions that controls the means by which data is entered and stored in the computer"), aff'd, 25 F.3d 1038 (4th Cir. 1994) (unpublished table decision); see also Windels, 576 F. Supp. at 412 (protecting computer program under Exemptions 2 and 7(E)); Kiraly v. FBI, 3 Gov't Disclosure Serv. (P-H) ¶ 82,465, at 83,135 (N.D. Ohio Feb. 17, 1982) (protecting computer codes under Exemptions 2 and 7(E)), aff'd, 728 F.2d 273 (6th Cir. 1984).

[89] See, e.g., Hall v. United States Dep't of Justice, No. 87-474, 1989 WL 24542, at *2 (D.D.C. Mar. 8, 1989) (protecting various items that "could facilitate unauthorized access to [agency] communications systems"); Institute for

(continued...)

**EXEMPTION 2**

court refused to apply this aspect of Exemption 2 to procedures that were designed to protect against states "circumventing" federal audit criteria for welfare reimbursement.[90]

Exemption 2's "circumvention" protection also should be readily applicable to vulnerability assessments, which are perhaps the quintessential type of record warranting protection on that basis; such records generally assess an agency's vulnerability (or that of another institution) to some form of outside interference or harm by identifying those programs or systems deemed the most sensitive and describing specific security measures that can be used to counteract such vulnerabilities.[91] A prime example of vulnerability assessments warranting protection under "high 2" are the computer security plans that all federal agencies are required by law to prepare.[92] In a decision involving such a document, Schreibman v. United States Department of Commerce,[93] Exemption 2 coverage was invoked to prevent unauthorized access to information which could result in "alternation [sic], loss, damage or destruction of data contained in the computer system."[94] It should be remembered, however, that even such a sensitive document must be reviewed to determine whether any "reasonably segregable" portion can be disclosed without harm.[95]

---

[89](...continued)
Policy Studies, 676 F. Supp. at 5 (according Exemption 2 protection to record revealing most sensitive portions of agency system which "could be used to seek out the [system's] vulnerabilities"); see also FOIA Update, Vol. X, No. 3, at 3-4. But see Linn, 1995 WL 417810, at **19, 21-22, 24-25 (refusing to protect agencies' access codes and routing symbols because risk of compromising the integrity of agencies' recordkeeping system found by the court to be "insufficient").

[90] See Massachusetts v. HHS, 727 F. Supp. 35, 42 (D. Mass. 1989) ("The Act simply cannot be interpreted in such a way as to presumptively brand a sovereign state as likely to circumvent federal law. The second prong of Exemption 2 does not apply when it is [the state] itself that seeks the information.").

[91] See FOIA Update, Vol. X, No. 3, at 3-4 ("OIP Guidance: Protecting Vulnerability Assessments Through Application of Exemption Two").

[92] See id. at 4 (citing Computer Security Act of 1987, Pub. L. No. 100-235, 101 Stat. 1724 (1988)).

[93] 785 F. Supp. 164 (D.D.C. 1991).

[94] Id. at 166.

[95] See id.; see, e.g., PHE, 983 F.2d at 252 (remanding for "high 2" segregation; "district court clearly errs when it approves the government's withholding of information under the FOIA without making an express finding on segregability" (citing Schiller, 964 F.2d at 1210)); Wightman v. ATF, 755 F.2d 979, 982-83 (1st Cir. 1985) (remanding for determination on segregability); see also FOIA Update, Vol. XIV, No. 3, at 11-12 ("OIP Guidance: The 'Reasonable Segregation' Obligation"); cf. Schrecker v. United States Dep't of Justice, 74 F. Supp. 2d 26, 32 (D.D.C. 1999) (finding that FBI properly "shield[ed] from disclosure [confidential informant] source codes [and] identifying data
(continued...)

**EXEMPTION 2**

(See the further discussions of this under Procedural Requirements, "Reasonably Segregable" Obligation, above, and Litigation Considerations, "Reasonably Segregable" Requirements, below.)

Release of various other categories of information also has been found likely to result in harmful circumvention:

(1) information that would reveal the identities of informants;[96]

(2) information that would reveal the identities of undercover agents;[97]

(3) sensitive administrative notations in law enforcement files;[98]

---

[95](...continued)
... no portion of [which] is reasonably segregable") (appeal pending); Archer v. HHS, 710 F. Supp. 909, 911 (S.D.N.Y. 1989) (upon in camera review, ordering disclosure of Medicare reimbursement-review criteria, but with specific audit trigger number segregated for protection).

[96] See, e.g., Davin v. United States Dep't of Justice, 60 F.3d 1043, 1065 (3d Cir. 1995) (informant codes); Jones v. FBI, 41 F.3d 238, 244 (6th Cir. 1994) (same); Massey v. FBI, 3 F.3d 620, 622 (2d Cir. 1993) (finding that disclosure of informant symbol numbers and source-identifying information "could do substantial damage to the FBI's law enforcement activities"); Jefferson v. O'Brien, No. 96-1365, slip op. at 6 (D.D.C. Feb. 22, 2000) (quoting extensively from FBI declaration to uphold protection for undercover activities and confidential source numbers, as well as related file numbers); Schrecker, 74 F. Supp. 2d at 32 (holding FBI data identifying confidential informants to be properly shielded from disclosure); Blanton v. United States Dep't of Justice, 63 F. Supp. 2d 35, 43 (D.D.C. 1999) (determining that "'informant codes plainly fall within the ambit of Exemption 2'" (quoting Lesar v. United States Dep't of Justice, 636 F.2d 472, 485 (D.C. Cir. 1980))); Accuracy in Media v. FBI, No. 97-2107, slip op. at 5 (D.D.C. Mar. 31, 1999) (crediting FBI's argument that informant symbol numbers are administrative tools used to protect actual identities of informants); Del Viscovo v. FBI, 903 F. Supp. 1, 2 (D.D.C. 1995) (agreeing that release of informant codes would frighten informants away), summary affirmance granted, No. 95-5388 (D.C. Cir. Jan. 24, 1997); Wickline v. FBI, No. 92-1189, 1994 WL 549756, at *2 n.5 (D.D.C. Sept. 30, 1994) (protection of informant codes held matter of "established law"). But cf. Globe Newspaper Co. v. FBI, No. 91-13257, 1992 WL 396327, at *3 (D. Mass. Dec. 29, 1992) (amount paid to FBI informant personally involved in continuing criminal activity ordered released).

[97] See Cox v. FBI, No. 83-3552, slip op. at 2 (D.D.C. May 31, 1984) (protecting report concerning FBI's undercover agent program because of potential for discovering identities of agents).

[98] See, e.g., Founding Church of Scientology v. Smith, 721 F.2d 828, 831 (D.C. Cir. 1983) (protecting sensitive instructions regarding administrative handling of document); Cappabianca v. Commissioner, United States Customs Serv., 847 F. Supp. 1558, 1563 (M.D. Fla. 1994) (protecting Customs Service file numbers "containing information such as the type and location of
(continued...)

**EXEMPTION 2**

(4) security techniques used in prisons;[99]

(5) agency audit guidelines;[100]

(6) agency testing materials;[101]

---

[98](...continued)
the case" because "if the code were cracked, [it] could reasonably lead to circumvention of the law"); Curcio v. FBI, No. 89-941, slip op. at 5 (D.D.C. Nov. 2, 1990) (protecting expense accounting in FBI criminal investigation).

[99] See, e.g., Cox v. United States Dep't of Justice, 601 F.2d at 4-5 (upholding nondisclosure of weapon, handcuff, and transportation security procedures); Jimenez v. FBI, 938 F. Supp. 21, 24 (D.D.C. 1996) (approving nondisclosure of criteria for classification of prison gang member); Hall, 1989 WL 24542, at *2 (reasoning that disclosure of teletype routing symbols, access codes, and data entry codes maintained by United States Marshals Service "could facilitate unauthorized access to information in law enforcement communications systems, and [thereby] jeopardize [prisoners' security]"); Miller, 1989 WL 10598, at *1 (disclosure of sections of Bureau of Prisons (BOP) Custodial Manual that describe procedures for security of prison control centers would "necessarily facilitate efforts by inmates to frustrate [BOP's] security precautions"); cf. Thornburgh v. Abbott, 490 U.S. 401, 417 (1989) (rejecting requester's constitutional challenge to BOP regulation excluding publications that, although not necessarily likely to lead to violence, are determined by warden "to create an intolerable risk of disorder . . . at a particular prison at a particular time") (non-FOIA case). But see Feshbach v. SEC, 5 F. Supp. 2d 774, 787-88 (N.D. Cal. 1997) (ordering disclosure of forms used to track status of SEC investigations based upon court's conclusion that agency provided only "conclusory and unsubstantiated statements in support of non-disclosure"); Linn, 1995 WL 631847, at **4-5 (rejecting as "conclusory" BOP's claim that release of case summary and internal memoranda would cause harm to safety of prisoners).

[100] See, e.g., Dirksen, 803 F.2d at 1458-59 (upholding protection of internal audit guidelines in order to prevent risk of circumvention of agency Medicare reimbursement regulations); Wiesenfelder, 959 F. Supp. at 535 (protecting benchmarks signifying when enforcement action taken, errors identifying agency's tolerance for mistakes, and dollar amounts of potential fines); Archer, 710 F. Supp. at 911 (ordering Medicare reimbursement-review criteria disclosed, but protecting specific number that triggers audit); Windels, 576 F. Supp. at 412-13 (withholding computer program containing anti-dumping detection criteria). But see Don Ray Drive-A-Way, 785 F. Supp. at 200 (knowing agency's regulatory priorities would allow regulated carriers to concentrate efforts on correcting most serious safety breaches).

[101] See, e.g., Patton v. FBI, 626 F. Supp. 445, 447 (M.D. Pa. 1985) (testing materials withheld under Privacy Act Exemption (k)(6), 5 U.S.C. § 552a(k)(6) (1994 & Supp. IV 1998), and FOIA Exemption 2 because release would impair effectiveness of system and give future applicants unfair advantage), aff'd, 782 F.2d 1030 (3d Cir. 1986) (unpublished table decision); Oatley, 3 Gov't Disclosure Serv. at 84,065 (civil service testing materials satisfy two-part Crooker
(continued...)

**EXEMPTION 2**

(7) codes that would identify intelligence targets;[102]

(8) agency credit card numbers;[103] and

(9) an agency's unclassified manual detailing the categories of information that are classified and their corresponding classification levels.[104]

With respect to file numbers of a sensitive nature, it is noteworthy that district courts in two very similar cases employed opposite legal approaches: In a decision that stands as an aberration, the District Court for the District of Kansas found that case file numbers used in the Department of Justice's Office of Professional Responsibility must be released because "the documents in question do[] not clear the [personnel practices] hurdle";[105] soon after, the District Court for the District of Columbia found that similar FBI file numbers "were properly withheld."[106]

---

[101](...continued)
test); see also Kaganove, 856 F.2d at 890 (disclosure of applicant rating plan would render it ineffectual and allow future applicants to "embellish" job qualifications); NTEU, 802 F.2d at 528-29 (disclosure of hiring plan would give unfair advantage to some future applicants); Samble v. United States Dep't of Commerce, No. 192-225, slip op. at 11 (S.D. Ga. Sept. 22, 1994) (release of evaluative criteria would compromise validity of rating process). But see Commodity News Serv. v. Farm Credit Admin., No. 88-3146, 1989 U.S. Dist. LEXIS 8848, at **12-15 (D.D.C. July 31, 1989) (holding steps to be taken in selecting receiver for liquidation of failed federal land bank, including sources agency might contact when investigating candidates, not protectible under "high 2" because agency did not demonstrate how disclosure would allow any applicant to "gain an unfair advantage in the . . . process").

[102] Tawalbeh v. United States Dep't of the Air Force, No. 96-6241, slip op. at 13 (C.D. Cal. Aug. 8, 1997) (finding that disclosure of Air Force internal intelligence collection codes "would allow unauthorized persons to decode classified . . . messages"); cf. Schrecker, 74 F. Supp. 2d at 32 (finding that disclosure of identity of "governmental unit that transmitted a particular document" could "risk circumvention of the ability of the [Defense Intelligence Agency] to collect or relay intelligence information").

[103] Judicial Watch, Inc. v. United States Dep't of Commerce, 83 F. Supp. 2d at 110 (upholding protection of government credit card numbers based upon "realistic possibility of . . . misuse and fraud").

[104] Institute for Policy Studies, 676 F. Supp. at 5. But see Wilkinson, 633 F. Supp. at 342 & n.13 (codes that identify law enforcement techniques not protectible under Exemption 2; instead must meet threshold requirement of compilation for law enforcement purposes for protection under Exemption 7(E)).

[105] Thompson, No. 96-1118, slip op. at 29-30 (D. Kan. July 15, 1998) (requiring release of Office of Professional Responsibility file numbers, even though recognizing their "sensitive and confidential" nature).

[106] Coleman v. FBI, 13 F. Supp. 2d 75, 79 (D.D.C. 1998) (Disclosing file
(continued...)

# EXEMPTION 2

Under some circumstances, Exemption 2 may be applied to prevent potential circumvention through a "mosaic" approach--information which would not by itself reveal sensitive law enforcement information can nonetheless be protected to prevent damage that could be caused by the assembly of different pieces of similar information by a requester.[107] This circumstance arose in a case involving a request for "Discriminant Function Scores" used by the IRS to select tax returns for examination.[108] Although the IRS conceded that release of any one individual's tax score would not disclose how returns are selected for audit, it took the position that the routine release of such scores would enable the sophisticated requester to discern, in the aggregate, its audit criteria, thus facilitating circumvention of the tax laws. The court accepted this rationale as an appropriate basis for affording protection under Exemption 2.[109] In a related case, one court upheld the denial of access to an IRS memorandum containing tolerance criteria used by the agency in its investigations, finding that disclosure would "undermine the enforcement of . . . internal revenue laws."[110]

---

[106](...continued)
numbers "could potentially reveal a sequence of information, including dates, times, and identities of . . . informant transactions thereby exposing the depth of FBI's informant coverage."); see also Pons v. United States Customs Serv., No. 93-2094, 1998 U.S. Dist. LEXIS 6084, at *11 (D.D.C. Apr. 23, 1998) (finding case numbers and filing codes to be predominantly internal and properly withheld); Davin v. United States Dep't of Justice, No. 92-1122, slip op. at 6 (W.D. Pa. Apr. 9, 1998) (finding "that the government is entitled to withhold . . . file numbers"), aff'd, 176 F.3d 471 (3d Cir. 1999) (unpublished table decision).

[107] See, e.g., Accuracy in Media, No. 97-2107, slip op. at 5 (D.D.C. Mar. 31, 1999) (finding persuasive FBI argument that, with release of informant symbol numbers, "over time an informant may be identified by revealing . . . connections with dates, times, places, events"); Jan-Xin Zang v. FBI, 756 F. Supp. 705, 712 (W.D.N.Y. 1991) (ruling that source symbol and administrative identifiers were properly withheld on basis that "accumulation of information" known to be from same source could lead to detection); cf. Davin, 60 F.3d at 1065 (remanding for agency to specify content of documents for which it raises "mosaic" argument).

[108] Ray v. United States Customs Serv., No. 83-1476, 1985 U.S. Dist. LEXIS 23091, at **9-10 (D.D.C. Jan. 28, 1985).

[109] Id.; see also Novotny v. IRS, No. 94-F-549, 1994 WL 722686, at *3 (D. Colo. Sept. 8, 1994); Wilder, 607 F. Supp. at 1015; accord Institute for Policy Studies, 676 F. Supp. at 5 (classification guidelines could reveal which parts of sensitive communications system are most sensitive and enable foreign intelligence services to gather related unclassified records and seek out system's vulnerabilities); cf. Halperin v. CIA, 629 F.2d 144, 150 (D.C. Cir. 1980) ("mosaic" analysis in Exemptions 1 and 3 context).

[110] O'Connor v. IRS, 698 F. Supp. 204, 206-07 (D. Nev. 1988). But cf. Archer, 710 F. Supp. at 911 (requiring careful segregation so that only truly sensitive portion of audit criteria is withheld).

# EXEMPTION 2

Although originally, as in <u>Crooker</u>, the "circumvention" protection afforded by Exemption 2 was applied almost exclusively to sensitive portions of criminal law enforcement manuals, it since has been extended to civil enforcement and regulatory matters, including some matters that are not law enforcement activities in the traditional sense.[111] In a pivotal case on this point, the National Treasury Employees Union sought documents known as "crediting plans," records used to evaluate the credentials of federal job applicants; the Customs Service successfully argued that disclosure of the plans would make it difficult to evaluate the applicants because they could easily exaggerate or even fabricate their qualifications, such falsifications would go undetected because the government lacked the resources necessary to verify each application, and unscrupulous future applicants could thereby gain an unfair competitive advantage.[112] The D.C. Circuit approved the withholding of such criteria under a refined application of <u>Crooker</u>, which focused directly on its second requirement, and held that the potential for circumvention of the selection program, as well as the general statutory and regulatory mandates to enforce applicable civil service laws, was sufficient to bring the information at issue within the protection of Exemption 2.[113] The agency demonstrated "circumvention" by showing that disclosure would either render the documents obsolete for their intended purpose, make the plan's criteria "operationally useless" or compromise the utility of the selection program.[114]

This approach was expressly followed by the Court of Appeals for the Seventh Circuit in <u>Kaganove</u> to withhold from an unsuccessful job applicant the agency's merit promotion rating plan on the basis that disclosure of the plan "would frustrate the document's objective [and] render it ineffectual" for the very reasons noted in the <u>NTEU</u> case.[115] Similarly, the District Court for

---

[111] See, e.g., Dirksen, 803 F.2d at 1458-59 (finding guidelines for processing Medicare claims properly withheld when disclosure could allow applicants to alter claims to fit them into certain categories and guidelines would thus "lose the utility they were intended to provide"); <u>Wiesenfelder</u>, 959 F. Supp. at 537-38 (finding trigger figures, error rate tolerances, and amounts of potential fines properly withheld because release would "substantially undermine" agency's regulatory efforts); <u>Archer</u>, 710 F. Supp. at 911 (protecting number of particular health procedures performed, which HHS contractor used to determine whether healthcare providers' claims for reimbursement under Medicare should be subjected to greater scrutiny; disclosure would allow providers "to avoid review and ensure automatic payment by submitting claims below the number . . . scrutinized").

[112] NTEU, 802 F.2d at 528-29.

[113] Id. at 529-31.

[114] Id. at 530-31; cf. United States Dep't of Justice v. FLRA, 988 F.2d 1267, 1269 (D.C. Cir. 1993) (crediting plans also held not subject to disclosure under Federal Service Labor-Management Relations Act, 5 U.S.C. § 7114(b)(4)(B) (1994)).

[115] Kaganove, 856 F.2d at 889; see also Samble, No. CV192-225, slip op. at 12 (S.D. Ga. Sept. 22, 1994) (citing <u>Kaganove</u>, 856 F.2d at 889, to protect cri-
(continued...)

**EXEMPTION 2**

the District of Columbia permitted the Department of Education to withhold information consisting of trigger figures, error rates, and potential fines that provide "internal guidance to staff about how, when, and why they should concentrate their regulatory oversight."[116] The court agreed with the agency that "[g]iving institutions the wherewithal to engage in a cost/benefit analysis in order to choose their level of compliance would substantially undermine [its] regulatory efforts and thwart its program oversight."[117]

It is noteworthy that the Seventh Circuit in Kaganove,[118] the Ninth Circuit in Dirksen,[119] and the D.C. Circuit in NTEU[120] all reached their results even in the absence of any particular agency regulation or statute to be circumvented. Thus, it seems likely that the second part of the Crooker test can properly be satisfied by a showing that disclosure would risk circumvention of general legal requirements,[121] so long as there is a specific determination of "foreseeable harm" in each instance.[122] In this regard, it is worth noting that the District Court for the District of Columbia has expressly ruled, in the context of Exemption 2, that the "passage of time" does not necessarily "reduce[]

---

[115](...continued)
teria used to evaluate job applicants).

[116] Wiesenfelder, 959 F. Supp. at 537.

[117] Id. at 537-38.

[118] 856 F.2d at 889.

[119] 803 F.2d at 1458-59.

[120] 802 F.2d at 529-31.

[121] See NTEU, 802 F.2d at 530-31 ("Where disclosure of a particular [record] would render [it] operationally useless, the Crooker analysis is satisfied whether or not the agency identifies a specific statute or regulation threatened by disclosure."); Knight v. DOD, No. 87-480, slip op. at 4 (D.D.C. Feb. 11, 1988) (memorandum detailing specific inventory audit guidelines held protectible because disclosure "would reveal Department of Defense rationale and strategy" for audit and would "create a significant risk that this information would be used by interested parties to frustrate ongoing or future audits"); Boyce v. Department of the Navy, No. 86-2211, slip op. at 2 (C.D. Cal. Feb. 17, 1987) (withholding routine hearing transcript under Exemption 2 where disclosure would circumvent terms of mere contractual agreement entered into under labor-relations statutory scheme); see also FOIA Update, Vol. X, No. 3, at 4.

[122] See Attorney General Reno's FOIA Memorandum, reprinted in FOIA Update, Vol. XIV, No. 3, at 4-5; see also Attorney General Reno's Follow-Up FOIA Memorandum, reprinted in FOIA Update, Vol. XIX, No. 4, at 4 (emphasizing that "information should be withheld from a FOIA requester only when it is not possible for an agency to disclose it as a matter of administrative discretion"); FOIA Update, Vol. XIV, No. 3, at 2 (advising that "foreseeable harm" standard requires process of particularized case-by-case review).

# EXEMPTION 3

the protections of a properly asserted exemption."[123]

Finally, under the Freedom of Information Reform Act of 1986,[124] many of the materials previously protectible only on a "high 2" basis may be protectible also under Exemption 7(E).[125] Several post-amendment cases have held such information to be exempt from disclosure under both Exemption 2 and Exemption 7(E).[126] While Exemption 2 must still be used if any information fails to meet Exemption 7's "law enforcement" threshold, Exemption 2's history and judicial interpretations should be helpful in applying Exemption 7(E). (See the discussion of Exemption 7(E), below.)

## EXEMPTION 3

Exemption 3 of the FOIA incorporates the disclosure prohibitions that are contained in various other federal statutes. As originally enacted in 1966, Exemption 3 was broadly phrased so as to simply cover information "specifically exempted from disclosure by statute."[1] Nearly a decade later, in FAA v. Robertson, the Supreme Court interpreted this language as evincing a con-

---

[123] Willis, No. 96-1455, slip op. at 7 (D.D.C. Aug. 6, 1997) (magistrate's recommendation), adopted (D.D.C. Feb. 14, 1998) (finding DEA numbers--G-DEP, NADDIS, and informant identifier codes--are protectible even after case is long closed), remanded on other grounds, 194 F.3d 175 (D.C. Cir. 1999) (unpublished table decision); cf. Buckner v. IRS, 25 F. Supp. 2d 893, 899 (N.D. Ind. 1998) ("Because DIF scores are investigative techniques . . . still used by the IRS in evaluating tax returns . . . the age of the scores is of no consequence" in determining their releasability.) (Exemption 7(E)).

[124] Pub. L. No. 99-570, § 1802, 100 Stat. 3207, 3207-48, 3207-49 (codified as amended at 5 U.S.C. § 552(b)(2) (1994 & Supp. IV 1998)).

[125] See Attorney General's Memorandum on the 1986 Amendments to the Freedom of Information Act 16-17 & n.32 (Dec. 1987); see also Kaganove, 856 F.2d at 888-89; Peralta v. United States Attorney's Office, No. 94-760, slip op. at 6 (D.D.C. 1999) (protecting radio channels used by FBI during physical surveillance, under both Exemptions 2 and 7(E)); Berg, No. 93-C6741, slip op. at 10 n.2 (N.D. Ill. June 23, 1994) ("[I]t would appear that exemption (b)(7)(E) is essentially a codification of the 'high 2' exemption.").

[126] See, e.g., PHE, 983 F.2d at 251 (release of "who would be interviewed, what could be asked, and what records or other documents would be reviewed" in FBI investigatory guidelines would risk circumvention of law); Voinche, 940 F. Supp. at 328, 331 (approving nondisclosure of information relating to security of Supreme Court building on basis of both Exemptions 2 and 7(E)); Silber, No. 91-876, transcript at 21 (D.D.C. Aug. 13, 1992) (disclosure of agency litigation tactics and strategy would create a significant risk of circumvention of agency regulations by enhancing adversary's posture); Williston Basin, 1989 WL 44655, at *2 (protecting identities of auditors, "purpose, source and conclusion" portions of audit reports, and section abstracts consisting of auditors' discussions of investigative techniques).

[1] Pub. L. No. 89-487, 80 Stat. 250, 251 (1966) (subsequently amended).

# EXEMPTION 3

gressional intent to allow statutes which permitted the withholding of confidential information, and which were enacted prior to the FOIA, to remain unaffected by the disclosure mandate of the FOIA; it accordingly held that a very broad withholding provision in the Federal Aviation Act which delegated almost unlimited discretion to agency officials to withhold specific documents in the "interest of the public" was incorporated within Exemption 3.[2] Fearing that this interpretation could allow agencies to evade the FOIA's disclosure intent, Congress in effect overruled the Supreme Court's decision by amending Exemption 3 in 1976.[3]

As amended, Exemption 3 allows the withholding of information prohibited from disclosure by another statute only if one of two disjunctive requirements are met: the statute either "(A) requires that the matters be withheld from the public in such a manner as to leave no discretion on the issue, or (B) establishes particular criteria for withholding or refers to particular types of matters to be withheld."[4] A statute thus falls within the exemption's coverage if it satisfies any one of its disjunctive requirements.[5]

## Initial Considerations

The Court of Appeals for the District of Columbia Circuit has held that records may be withheld under the authority of another statute pursuant to Exemption 3 "if--and only if--that statute meets the requirements of Exemption 3, including the threshold requirement that it specifically exempt matters from disclosure."[6] The D.C. Circuit emphasized that:

---

[2] 422 U.S. 255, 266 (1975).

[3] See Pub. L. No. 94-409, 90 Stat. 1241, 1247 (1976) (single FOIA amendment enacted together with Government in the Sunshine Act in 1976, 5 U.S.C. § 552b (1994 & Supp. IV 1998)); see also FOIA Update, Vol. XV, No. 2, at 6 (connecting disclosure policies of Government in the Sunshine Act and FOIA).

[4] 5 U.S.C. § 552(b)(3) (1994 & Supp. IV 1998) (emphasis added).

[5] See Long v. IRS, 742 F.2d 1173, 1178 (9th Cir. 1984); Irons & Sears v. Dann, 606 F.2d 1215, 1220 (D.C. Cir. 1979); American Jewish Congress v. Kreps, 574 F.2d 624, 628 (D.C. Cir. 1978). See generally 5 U.S.C. § 552(e)(1)(A)(ii) (provision of Electronic Freedom of Information Act Amendments of 1996 requiring agencies to list Exemption 3 statutes upon which they rely each year in their annual FOIA reports, beginning with reports for Fiscal Year 1998); FOIA Update, Vol. XVIII, No. 3, at 5 (provision of annual FOIA report guidelines issued by Department of Justice).

[6] Reporters Comm. for Freedom of the Press v. United States Dep't of Justice, 816 F.2d 730, 734 (D.C. Cir.), modified on other grounds, 831 F.2d 1124 (D.C. Cir. 1987), rev'd on other grounds, 489 U.S. 749 (1989); see also Essential Info., Inc. v. USIA, 134 F.3d 1165, 1168 (D.C. Cir. 1998) (ruling that statute that prohibits "dissemination" and "distribution" of certain information within U.S. is qualifying "nondisclosure" statute); Cal-Almond, Inc. v. USDA, 960 F.2d 105, 108 (9th Cir. 1992) (concluding that language must specifically prohibit disclosure, not merely prohibit expenditure of funds used in releasing

(continued...)

## EXEMPTION 3

a statute that is claimed to qualify as an Exemption 3 withholding statute must, on its face, exempt matters from disclosure. We must find a congressional purpose in the actual words of the statute (or at least in the legislative history of FOIA)--not in the legislative history of the claimed withholding statute, nor in an agency's interpretation of the statute.[7]

That is not to say that the breadth and reach of the disclosure prohibition must be found on the face of the statute, but that the statute must at least "explicitly deal with public disclosure."[8] (Previously, the D.C. Circuit had found legislative history probative on the issue of whether an enactment was intended to serve as a withholding statute within the meaning of Exemption 3.[9]) In any event, though, the legislative history of a newly enacted Exemption 3 statute may be considered in determining whether the statute is applicable to matters that are already pending.[10]

Exemption 3 generally is triggered only by federal statutes.[11] Federal rules of procedure, which are promulgated by the Supreme Court, ordinarily do not qualify under Exemption 3.[12] However, when a rule of procedure is subsequently modified and thereby specifically enacted into law by Congress,

---

(...continued)
information).

[7] Reporters Comm., 816 F.2d at 735; see also Anderson v. HHS, 907 F.2d 936, 951 n.19 (10th Cir. 1990) (holding that agency interpretation of statute not entitled to deference in determining whether statute qualifies under Exemption 3). But see Meyerhoff v. EPA, 958 F.2d 1498, 1501-02 (9th Cir. 1992) (looking to legislative history of withholding statute to determine that statutory amendment clarified rather than changed it); cf. Essential Info., 134 F.3d at 1165-67 (surveying legislative history of Smith-Mundt Act to bolster Exemption 3 ruling).

[8] Reporters Comm., 816 F.2d at 736; see, e.g., Cal-Almond, 960 F.2d at 108 (finding disclosure prohibition sought to be effectuated through appropriations limitation inadequate under Exemption 3); Belvy v. United States Dep't of Justice, No. 94-923, slip op. at 9-11 (S.D. Fla. Dec. 15, 1994) (determining that statute providing that exclusion hearings be "separate and apart from the public" does not explicitly forbid disclosure of asylum decisions emanating from those proceedings).

[9] See Public Citizen Health Research Group v. FDA, 704 F.2d 1280, 1284 (D.C. Cir. 1983).

[10] See Long v. IRS, 742 F.2d 1173, 1183-84 (9th Cir. 1984).

[11] See Washington Post Co. v. HHS, 2 Gov't Disclosure Serv. (P-H) ¶ 81,047, at 81,127 n.2 (D.D.C. Dec. 4, 1980) ("[A]n Executive Order . . . is clearly inadequate to support reliance on Exemption 3."), rev'd on other grounds, 690 F.2d 252 (D.C. Cir. 1982).

[12] See Founding Church of Scientology v. Bell, 603 F.2d 945, 952 (D.C. Cir. 1979) (holding that Rule 26(c) of Federal Rules of Civil Procedure, governing issuance of protective orders, is not statute under Exemption 3).

**EXEMPTION 3**

it may qualify under the exemption.[13] While the issue of whether a treaty can qualify as a statute under Exemption 3 has not yet been ruled on in any FOIA case, there is a sound policy basis for concluding that a treaty can so qualify.[14]

Once it is established that a statute is a nondisclosure statute and that it meets at least one of the disjunctive requirements of Exemption 3, an agency must also establish that the records in question fall within the withholding provision of the nondisclosure statute.[15] This, in turn, will often require an interpretation of the nondisclosure statute.[16] Courts have been somewhat divided over whether to construe the withholding criteria of the nondisclosure statute narrowly, consistent with the strong disclosure policies specifically embodied in the FOIA,[17] or broadly, pursuant to deferential standards of general administrative law.[18] Most recently, the Court of Appeals for the Second Cir-

---

[13] See, e.g., Fund for Constitutional Gov't v. National Archives & Records Serv., 656 F.2d 856, 867 (D.C. Cir. 1981) (concluding that Rule 6(e) of Federal Rules of Criminal Procedure, regulating disclosure of matters occurring before grand jury, satisfies Exemption 3's "statute" requirement because it was specially amended by Congress in 1977); Berry v. Department of Justice, 612 F. Supp. 45, 49 (D. Ariz. 1985) (determining that Rule 32 of Federal Rules of Criminal Procedure, governing disclosure of presentence reports, is "statute" for Exemption 3 purposes because it was affirmatively enacted into law by Congress in 1975).

[14] Cf. Whitney v. Robertson, 124 U.S. 190, 194 (1887) ("By the Constitution a treaty is placed on the same footing, and made of like obligation, with an act of legislation."); Public Citizen v. Office of the United States Trade Representative, 804 F. Supp. 385, 388 (D.D.C. 1992) (stating that trade agreement not ratified by Senate does not have status of "statutory law" and thus does not provide Exemption 3 protection).

[15] See A. Michael's Piano, Inc. v. FTC, 18 F.3d 138, 143 (2d Cir. 1994); Fund for Constitutional Gov't, 656 F.2d at 868; Public Citizen Health Research Group, 704 F.2d at 1284; Goland v. CIA, 607 F.2d 339, 350 (D.C. Cir. 1978); DeLorme Publ'g Co. v. NOAA, 917 F. Supp. 867, 870-71 (D. Me. 1996), appeal dismissed per stipulation, No. 96-1601 (1st Cir. July 8, 1996); see also Chesapeake Bay Found. v. USDA, 917 F. Supp. 64, 66 (D.D.C. 1996) (concluding that information requested did not fall within withholding statute), rev'd on other grounds, 108 F.3d 375 (D.C. Cir. 1997).

[16] See A. Michael's Piano, 18 F.3d at 143-45 (interpreting section 21(f) of FTC Act, 15 U.S.C. § 57b-2(f)); see also Aronson v. IRS, 973 F.2d 962, 965-66 (1st Cir. 1992) (giving deference to agency interpretation of withholding statute); Anderson v. HHS, 907 F.2d 936, 950-51 (10th Cir. 1990) (interpreting section 360j(c) of Medical Devices Act, 21 U.S.C.A. § 360j(c), and section 301(j) of Food, Drug, and Cosmetic Act, 21 U.S.C. § 331(j)); Grasso v. IRS, 785 F.2d 70, 74-75 (5th Cir. 1984) (interpreting section 6103 of Internal Revenue Code, 26 U.S.C. § 6103).

[17] See Anderson, 907 F.2d at 951; Grasso, 785 F.2d at 75; Currie, 704 F.2d 523, 526-27 (11th Cir. 1983); DeLorme Publ'g, 917 F. Supp. at 870-71.

[18] See Church of Scientology Int'l v. United States Dep't of Justice, 30 F.3d
(continued...)

# EXEMPTION 3

cuit observed that "the Supreme Court has never applied a rule of [either] narrow or deferential construction to withholding statutes."[19] Consequently, it adopted a pragmatic, and essentially neutral, stance regarding interpretation of Exemption 3 statutes, "looking to the plain language of the statute and its legislative history, in order to determine legislative purpose."[20]

With respect to subpart (B) statutes--which permit agencies some discretion to withhold or disclose records--review under the FOIA of agency action is limited to the determination that the withholding statute qualifies as an Exemption 3 statute and that the records fall within the statute's scope.[21] Beyond this determination, the agency's exercise of its discretion under the withholding statute is governed not by the FOIA, but by the withholding statute itself;[22] judicial review of that should not be within the FOIA's jurisdiction.[23]

Agencies and courts ordinarily specify the nondisclosure statute upon which Exemption 3 withholding is based. At least one court, however, found a need to conceal the nondisclosure statute that formed the basis for its ruling that the agency properly invoked Exemption 3, stating that "national security would be compromised and threats to the safety of individuals would arise" if it engaged in a specific discussion of the legal basis for Exemption 3's use in

---

(...continued)
224, 235 (1st Cir. 1994); Aronson, 973 F.2d at 967; White v. IRS, 707 F.2d 897, 900-01 (6th Cir. 1983) (holding that agency determination that documents in dispute fell within withholding provision of Internal Revenue Code was "neither arbitrary nor capricious"). But see DeLorme Publ'g, 917 F. Supp. at 871 (rejecting deferential review when statute at issue "ha[d] broad application and ha[d] been implemented by more than a dozen agencies").

[19] A. Michael's Piano, 18 F.3d at 144.

[20] Id.

[21] See Aronson, 973 F.2d at 967; Association of Retired R.R. Workers v. United States R.R. Retirement Bd., 830 F.2d 331, 335 (D.C. Cir. 1987). But see Long, 742 F.2d at 1181; DeLorme Publ'g, 917 F. Supp. at 871.

[22] See Aronson, 973 F.2d at 966; Association of Retired R.R. Workers, 830 F.2d at 336.

[23] Cf. Roley v. Assistant Attorney Gen., No. 89-2774, slip op. at 8 (D.D.C. Mar. 9, 1990) (determining that court's grant of permission to disclose grand jury records pursuant to Rule 6(e)(3)(C)(i) of Federal Rules of Criminal Procedure does not govern disposition of same records in FOIA suit); Garside v. Webster, 733 F. Supp. 1142, 1147 (S.D. Ohio 1989) (same). But cf. DeLorme Publ'g, 917 F. Supp. at 871 (proceeding de novo when statute at issue was administered by numerous federal agencies); Palmer v. Derwinski, No. 91-197, slip op. at 3-4 (E.D. Ky. June 10, 1992) (holding that disclosure order issued by court pursuant to 38 U.S.C. § 7332(b) (1994) requires VA to disclose records under FOIA).

**EXEMPTION 3**

that exceptional case.[24]

### Subpart (A)

Many statutes have been held to qualify as Exemption 3 statutes under the exemption's first subpart--which encompasses statutes that require information to be withheld and leave the agency no discretion on the issue. A primary example is Rule 6(e) of the Federal Rules of Criminal Procedure,[25] which regulates disclosure of matters occurring before a grand jury and which satisfies the basic "statute" requirement of Exemption 3 because it was specially amended by Congress in 1977.[26] It is well established that "Rule 6(e) embodies a broad sweeping policy of preserving the secrecy of grand jury material regardless of the substance in which the material is contained."[27] Yet, defining the parameters of Rule 6(e) protection is not always a simple task and has been the subject of much litigation. In Fund for Constitutional Government v. National Archives & Records Service, the Court of Appeals for the District of Columbia Circuit stated that the scope of the secrecy that must be afforded grand jury material "is necessarily broad" and, consequently, that "it encompasses not only the direct revelation of grand jury transcripts but also the disclosure of information which would reveal the 'identities of witnesses or jurors, the substance of the testimony, the strategy or direction of the investigation, the deliberations or questions of the jurors, and the like.'"[28]

---

[24] Simpson v. Department of State, No. 79-0674, 2 Gov't Disclosure Serv. (P-H) ¶ 81,280, at 81,798 (D.D.C. Apr. 30, 1981) (concluding, on remand, that Exemption 3 authorized withholding of State Department's entire "Biographic Register" of federal employees involved in foreign policy activities, even though court of appeals had already ruled in Simpson v. Vance, 648 F.2d 10, 17 (D.C. Cir. 1980), that Exemption 6 did not cover all such information).

[25] Fed. R. Crim. P. 6(e).

[26] See Fund for Constitutional Gov't v. National Archives & Records Serv., 656 F.2d 856, 867 (D.C. Cir. 1981); see also Watson v. United States Dep't of Justice, 799 F. Supp. 193, 195 (D.D.C. 1992).

[27] Iglesias v. CIA, 525 F. Supp. 547, 556 (D.D.C. 1981).

[28] 656 F.2d at 869 (quoting SEC v. Dresser Indus., 628 F.2d 1368, 1382 (D.C. Cir. 1980)); see also Church of Scientology Int'l v. United States Dep't of Justice, 30 F.3d 224, 235 (1st Cir. 1994) ("[D]ocuments identified as grand jury exhibits, and whose contents are testimonial in nature or otherwise directly associated with the grand jury process, such as affidavits and deposition transcripts, ordinarily may be withheld simply on the basis of their status as exhibits."); McDonnell v. United States, 4 F.3d 1227, 1246 (3d Cir. 1993) (protecting "[i]nformation and records presented to a federal grand jury . . . names of individuals subpoenaed . . . [and] federal grand jury transcripts of testimony"); Silets v. United States Dep't of Justice, 945 F.2d 227, 230 (7th Cir. 1991) (concluding that "identity of witness before grand jury and discussion of that witness's testimony . . . falls squarely within" Rule 6(e)'s prohibition); Germosen v. Cox, No. 98 Civ. 1294, 1999 WL 1021559, at *13 (S.D.N.Y. Nov. 9, 1999) (holding that identities of grand jury witnesses are protected by Rule 6(e))

(continued...)

**EXEMPTION 3**

(...continued)
(appeal pending); Peralta v. United States Attorney's Office, 69 F. Supp. 2d 21, 33 (D.D.C. 1999) (determining that Rule 6(e) prohibited the release of identities of grand jury witnesses and descriptions of information obtained by federal grand jury subpoenas); Anderson v. United States Dep't of Justice, No. 95-1880, 1999 U.S. Dist. LEXIS 5048, at *8 (D.D.C. Apr. 12, 1999) (finding local police department line-up record properly withheld as it contained Assistant United States Attorney's handwritten notes regarding witness reactions to viewing individuals in line-up and, if released, would reveal "identities of witnesses or jurors"); Telegraph Publ'g Co. v. United States Dep't of Justice, No. 95-521-M, slip op. at 16-18, 26-27 (D.N.H. Aug. 31, 1998) (citing Exemption 3 and Rule 6(e) as partial basis for protecting information related to grand jury, including correspondence between U.S. Attorney's Office and nongovernment attorneys pertaining to the grand jury, even where correspondence was not shown to grand jury and evidence notebooks were created by local police at direction of Assistant United States Attorney, because disclosure would "probably . . . reveal too much about evidence presented to the grand jury"); Greenberg v. United States Dep't of Treasury, 10 F. Supp. 2d 3, 27-28 (D.D.C. 1998) (permitting agency to withhold transcripts of conversations taped during course of FBI investigation and subsequently subpoenaed by grand jury); McQueen v. United States, 179 F.R.D. 522, 528-30 (S.D. Tex. May 6, 1998) (holding all matters before grand jury protected even if records predate grand jury investigation); Willis v. FBI, No. 96-1455, slip op. at 6 (D.D.C. Feb. 14, 1998) (declaring grand jury transcript properly withheld even though "at one time [requester's] counsel may have had a right of access to portions of the transcript for [witness impeachment purposes]"), aff'd in part on other grounds & remanded in part, 194 F.3d 175 (D.C. Cir. 1999) (unpublished table decision); Twist v. Reno, No. 95-258, 1997 U.S. Dist. LEXIS 8981, at *5 n.1 (D.D.C. May 12, 1997) (holding that agency properly withheld information that would reveal strategy or direction of grand jury investigation even though requester was previously on investigation team and had seen some of withheld information), summary affirmance granted, No. 97-5192, 1997 WL 811736 (D.C. Cir. Dec. 9, 1997); Jimenez v. FBI, 938 F. Supp. 21, 28 (D.D.C. 1996) (protecting notes written by Assistant United States Attorney in preparation for grand jury proceeding, records of third parties provided in course of proceeding, and notes concerning witnesses who testified); Voinche v. FBI, 940 F. Supp. 323, 329 (D.D.C. 1996) (holding that agency properly withheld name of witness subpoenaed to appear before grand jury, as well as time, place, and particular case), aff'd per curiam on other grounds, No. 96-5304, 1997 U.S. App. LEXIS 19089 (D.C. Cir. June 19, 1997); Spannaus v. United States Dep't of Justice, No. 92-372, slip op. at 7-8 (D.D.C. June 20, 1995) (permitting information identifying grand jury witnesses and testimony to be withheld, where plaintiff produced lists of news articles alleging much of information in public domain, but failed to point to specific prior disclosures); Canning v. United States Dep't of Justice, No. 92-0463, slip op. at 6 (D.D.C. June 26, 1995) (protecting "material that, while not directly mentioning the grand jury," nevertheless mentions witness names and describes witness testimony); Helmsley v. United States Dep't of Justice, No. 90-2413, slip op. at 4-6 (D.D.C. Sept. 25, 1992) (finding that Rule 6(e) protected records identifying witnesses who testified or were consulted, documents and evidence not presented but obtained through grand jury subpoenas, immunity applications

(continued...)

**EXEMPTION 3**

However, in its scrutiny of the scope of Rule 6(e) in <u>Senate of Puerto Rico v. United States Department of Justice</u>,[29] the D.C. Circuit firmly held that neither the fact that information was obtained pursuant to a grand jury subpoena, nor the fact that the information was submitted to the grand jury, is sufficient, in and of itself, to warrant the conclusion that disclosure is necessarily prohibited by Rule 6(e).[30] Rather, an agency must establish a nexus between the release of that information and "revelation of a protected aspect of the grand jury's investigation."[31] This requirement is particularly applicable to

---

(...continued)
and orders, exhibit lists, reports and memoranda discussing evidence, correspondence regarding compliance with subpoenas, documents, notes, and research relating to litigation regarding compliance with subpoenas, and letters among lawyers discussing grand jury proceedings).

[29] 823 F.2d 574 (D.C. Cir. 1987).

[30] <u>Id.</u> at 584; <u>see</u> <u>Washington Post Co. v. United States Dep't of Justice</u>, 863 F.2d 96, 100 (D.C. Cir. 1988) (same); <u>see also</u> <u>John Doe Corp. v. John Doe Agency</u>, 850 F.2d 105, 109 (2d Cir. 1988) ("A document that is otherwise available to the public does not become confidential simply because it is before a grand jury."), <u>rev'd on other grounds</u>, 493 U.S. 146 (1989); <u>Germosen</u>, 1999 WL 1021559, at *13 (stating that Rule 6(e) imposes "no requirement that materials actually be presented to the grand jury in order to fall within the rule's scope"); <u>Telegraph Publ'g</u>, No. 95-521-M, slip op. at 11 (D.N.H. Aug. 31, 1998) ("Exemption 3 . . . does not protect all information that is found in grand jury files since mere exposure to a grand jury does not, by itself, 'immunize' information from disclosure." (quoting <u>Church of Scientology Int'l</u>, 30 F.3d at 236)); <u>Isley v. Executive Office for United States Attorneys</u>, No. 96-0123, slip op. at 2-4 (D.D.C. Mar. 27, 1997) (ordering agency to provide further justification for withholding "transcripts, subpoenas, information provided in response to a grand jury subpoena, and information identifying who testified before a grand jury"), <u>appeal dismissed</u>, 203 F.3d 52 (D.C. Cir. 1997) (unpublished table decision); <u>Butler v. United States Dep't of Justice</u>, No. 86-2255, 1994 WL 55621, at *8 (D.D.C. Feb. 3, 1994) (holding descriptions of documents subpoenaed by grand jury not protected under Rule 6(e)), <u>appeal dismissed</u>, No. 94-5078 (D.C. Cir. Sept. 8, 1994); <u>Astley v. Lawson</u>, No. 89-2806, 1991 WL 7162, at *6 (D.D.C. Jan. 11, 1991) (ordering release of documents even though requester might have been able to deduce purpose for which records were subpoenaed, because records on their face did not reveal inner workings of grand jury).

[31] <u>Senate of P.R.</u>, 823 F.2d at 584; <u>see also</u> <u>Telegraph Publ'g</u>, No. 95-521-M, slip op. at 11 (D.N.H. Aug. 31, 1998) (stating that agencies must show nexus between disclosure of withheld information and impermissible revelation of grand jury matters to invoke protection of Exemption 3); <u>Burke v. DEA</u>, No. 96-1739, slip op. at 7 (D.D.C. Mar. 30, 1998) (determining that agency established nexus by showing that release of name of subpoenaed individual and information relating to subpoenaed insurance claims would reveal information about inner workings of grand jury); <u>Greenberg</u>, 10 F. Supp. 2d at 27-28 (finding nexus established because releasing transcripts of taped conversations would show "the direction or path the Grand Jury was taking"); <u>Karu v.</u>
(continued...)

# EXEMPTION 3

"extrinsic" documents that were created entirely independent of the grand jury process; for such a document, the D.C. Circuit emphasized in Washington Post Co. v. United States Department of Justice, the required nexus must be apparent from the information itself and "the government cannot immunize [it] by publicizing the link."[32] As a rule, an agency must be able to adequately document and support its determination that disclosure of the record in question would reveal a secret aspect of the grand jury proceeding.[33] And to do so,

---

(...continued)
United States Dep't of Justice, No. 86-771, slip op. at 4-5 (D.D.C. Dec. 1, 1987) (finding nexus established because "[w]ere this information to be released the very substance of the grand jury proceedings would be discernible"). But see Isley, No. 96-0123, slip op. at 4 (D.D.C. Mar. 27, 1997) (concluding agency "has not sufficiently linked the exemption to the contents of the withheld documents"); LaRouche v. United States Dep't of Justice, No. 90-2753, 1993 WL 388601, at *5 (D.D.C. June 25, 1993) (holding that letter prepared by government attorney discussing up coming grand jury proceedings did not reveal inner workings of grand jury).

[32] 863 F.2d at 100.

[33] See, e.g., Ashton v. VA, No. 99-6018, 1999 U.S. App. LEXIS 22957, at *3 (2d Cir. Sept. 3, 1999) (finding agency affidavit sufficient because it showed that withheld records revealed "confidential materials from grand jury proceedings" and that records were within scope of Rule 6(e) and Exemption 3); Rugiero v. United States Dep't of Justice, 35 F. Supp. 2d 977, 984 (E.D. Mich. 1998) (finding that agency affidavits, declarations, and portions of Vaughn Index sufficiently showed withheld records to be grand jury records, such as transcripts of witness testimony and "actual exhibits") (appeal pending); Hronek v. DEA, 16 F. Supp. 2d 1260, 1276 (D. Or. 1998) (requiring agency to resubmit Vaughn Index and explain how disclosure of subpoenas would "compromise the integrity of the grand jury process"); LaRouche v. United States Dep't of the Treasury, No. 91-1655, slip op. at 19-20 (D.D.C. May 22, 1998) (rejecting agency's withholding of entire category of documents and requiring agency to submit Vaughn Index sufficient to show that disclosure would reveal protected aspect of grand jury proceeding), summary judgment granted in part (D.D.C. Mar. 31, 2000) (holding that agency affidavit ultimately demonstrated nexus between disclosure and revelation of secret aspects of grand jury for most records withheld under 6(e), but ordering release where agency failed to demonstrate nexus); Kronberg v. United States Dep't of Justice, 875 F. Supp. 861, 867-68 (D.D.C. 1995) (ordering grand jury material released where prior disclosure was made to defense counsel and where government had not met burden of demonstrating that disclosure would reveal inner workings of grand jury); Linn v. United States Dep't of Justice, No. 92-1406, 1995 WL 417810, at *7 (D.D.C. June 6, 1995) ("[N]owhere in its affidavit does the DEA specifically link this exemption to the contents of the documents being withheld," but rather "merely states that it applied this exemption to withhold information that names witnesses and recounts testimony given to a federal grand jury."); Canning v. United States Dep't of Justice, 919 F. Supp. 451, 454-55 (D.D.C. 1994) (requiring government to produce affidavits "showing a basis for knowledge that the information came from grand jury" and explain how material is protected under Rule 6(e)); cf. Local 32B-

(continued...)

**EXEMPTION 3**

of course, agency FOIA personnel necessarily must be afforded unrestricted access to grand jury-protected information.[34]

A more recent, odd decision by the Court of Appeals for the First Circuit, Church of Scientology International v. United States Department of Justice, further clouds the precise contours of Rule 6(e).[35] Initially following Senate of Puerto Rico, the First Circuit rejected a position that the secrecy concerns protected by Rule 6(e) are automatically implicated for any materials "simply located in grand jury files."[36] Nevertheless, apparently operating under the premise that all grand jury exhibits constitute materials actually presented to the grand jurors, it further specified that, even with regard to "extrinsic documents," it would be "reasonable for an agency to withhold any document containing a grand jury exhibit sticker or that is otherwise explicitly identified on its face as a grand jury exhibit, as release of such documents reasonably could be viewed as revealing the focus of the grand jury investigation."[37] Thus, the First Circuit has seemingly placed itself in at least some degree of conflict with the D.C. Circuit's Senate of Puerto Rico interpretation of the grand jury rule.[38]

---

(...continued)
32J. Serv. Employees Int'l Union, AFL-CIO v. GSA, No. 97 Civ. 8509, 1998 WL 726000, at *7 (S.D.N.Y. Oct. 15, 1998) (concluding that agency's "[s]ealed declaration makes clear the existence of a grand jury investigation and sufficiently describes the relation of the requested materials to such investigation" and that agency properly withheld grand jury exhibits and identities of grand jury witnesses); Sousa v. United States Dep't of Justice, No. 95-375, 1997 U.S. Dist. LEXIS 9010, at **10-11 (D.D.C. June 19, 1997) (holding that supplemental Vaughn Index adequately demonstrated that disclosure of grand jury witness subpoenas, Assistant United States Attorney's handwritten notes discussing content of witness testimony, evidence used, and strategies would reveal protected aspects of grand jury investigation).

[34] Canning v. United States Dep't of Justice, No. 92-0463, slip op. at 4 (D.D.C. June 26, 1995) (finding that FOIA officers are "among those with approved access to grand jury material" and that FOIA officer properly reviewed withheld documents (citing Federal Grand Jury Practice 173 (Jan. 1993))); see also FOIA Update, Vol. XIX, No. 3, at 2 (advising agencies of same).

[35] 30 F.3d at 235-36.

[36] Id. at 236.

[37] Id. at 235 n.15 (dictum); cf. Rugiero, 35 F. Supp. 2d at 984 (distinguishing between grand jury information that is "completely exempt," such as exhibits and testimony, and documents that are not "completely exempt" because they were "created for purposes independent of grand jury investigations which have legitimate uses unrelated to the substance of the grand jury proceedings"); Foster v. United States Dep't of Justice, 933 F. Supp. 687, 691 (E.D. Mich. 1996) (protecting "final prosecution report" when "[e]ach page containe[d] a 'grand jury' secrecy label").

[38] See Senate of P.R., 823 F.2d at 584; see also Crooker v. IRS, No. 94-0755, 1995 WL 430605, at *9 n.2 (D.D.C. Apr. 27, 1995) (observing that withholding
(continued...)

## EXEMPTION 3

The Court of Appeals for the Ninth Circuit has held that a provision of the Ethics in Government Act of 1978,[39] protecting the financial disclosure reports of special government employees, meets the requirements of subpart (A).[40] While not actually distinguishing between the two subparts of Exemption 3, the Supreme Court in Baldrige v. Shapiro,[41] held that the Census Act[42] is an Exemption 3 statute because it requires that certain data be withheld in such a manner as to leave the Census Bureau with no discretion whatsoever.[43]

Sections 706(b) and 709(e) of Title VII of the Civil Rights Act of 1964[44] have also been held to meet the subpart (A) requirement because they allow the EEOC no discretion to publicly disclose matters pending before the Commission.[45] Similarly, the statute governing records pertaining to Currency Transaction Reports[46] has been found to meet the requirements of subpart

---

(...continued)
documents on the basis of grand jury exhibit labels "appears to be the type of per se withholding of grand jury material expressly rejected by the D.C. Circuit").

[39] 5 U.S.C. app. 4 § 107 (1994).

[40] Meyerhoff v. EPA, 958 F.2d 1498, 1502 (9th Cir. 1992) (construing 1978 version of statute). But see Church of Scientology v. IRS, 816 F. Supp. 1138, 1152 (W.D. Tex. 1993) (implying that Ethics in Government Act is subpart (B) Exemption 3 statute because FOIA disclosure can be made only if requester meets statute's disclosure requirements), appeal dismissed per stipulation, No. 93-8431 (5th Cir. Oct. 21, 1993).

[41] 455 U.S. 345 (1982).

[42] 13 U.S.C. §§ 8(b), 9(a) (1994 & Supp. IV 1998).

[43] 455 U.S. at 355.

[44] 42 U.S.C. §§ 2000e-5(b), 2000e-8(e) (1994).

[45] See Frito-Lay v. EEOC, 964 F. Supp. 236, 239-43 (W.D. Ky. 1997); Crump v. EEOC, No. 3:97-0275, slip op. at 5-6 (M.D. Tenn. May 30, 1997) (magistrate's recommendation), adopted (M.D. Tenn. June 18, 1997); American Centennial Ins. Co. v. EEOC, 722 F. Supp. 180, 183 (D.N.J. 1989); cf. EEOC v. City of Milwaukee, 54 F. Supp. 885, 893 (E.D. Wis. 1999) (noting that "any member of the public making a FOIA request" for materials at issue in this non-FOIA dispute "will be denied access, because Exemption 3 incorporates confidentiality provisions of sections 706(b) and 709(e) of Title VII) (non-FOIA case).

[46] 31 U.S.C. § 5319 (1994).

**EXEMPTION 3**

(A).[47] The International Investment Survey Act of 1976[48] has been held to be a subpart (A) statute[49] and certain portions of the overall public disclosure provisions of the Consumer Product Safety Act[50] likewise have been found to amply satisfy subpart (A)'s nondisclosure requirements.[51]

Additionally, the Hart-Scott-Rodino Antitrust Improvement Amendments to the Clayton Antitrust Act,[52] which prohibit disclosure of premerger notification materials submitted to the Department of Justice or the Federal Trade Commission, have been held to qualify as a subpart (A) statute,[53] as has a provision of the Antitrust Civil Process Act,[54] which explicitly exempts from the FOIA transcripts of oral testimony taken in the course of investigations under that Act.[55] Likewise, a provision of the now-expired Independent Counsel Reauthorization Act,[56] has been considered to qualify under Exemption 3, as the Department of Justice and the Independent Counsel have no discretion to disclose materials supplied under it to the court.[57]

Also, a section of the Transportation Safety Act of 1974,[58] which states that the National Safety Transportation Board shall withhold from public disclosure cockpit voice recordings associated with accident investigations, was found to fall within subsection (A) of Exemption 3.[59] Similarly, information

---

[47] See Linn v. United States Dep't of Justice, No. 92-1406, 1995 WL 631847, at *30 (D.D.C. Aug. 22, 1995); Small v. IRS, 820 F. Supp. 163, 166 (D.N.J. 1992); Vennes v. IRS, No. 5-88-36, slip op. at 6 (D. Minn. Oct. 14, 1988), aff'd, 890 F.2d 419 (8th Cir. 1989) (unpublished table decision).

[48] 22 U.S.C. § 3104(c) (1994).

[49] See Young Conservative Found. v. United States Dep't of Commerce, No. 85-3982, 1987 WL 9244, at **3-4 (D.D.C. Mar. 25, 1987).

[50] 15 U.S.C. § 2055(a)(2) (1994).

[51] See Mulloy v. Consumer Prod. Safety Comm'n, No. C-2-85-645, 1985 U.S. Dist. LEXIS 17194, at **2-5 (S.D. Ohio Aug. 2, 1985).

[52] 15 U.S.C. § 18a(h) (1994).

[53] See Lieberman v. FTC, 771 F.2d 32, 38 (2d Cir. 1985); Mattox v. FTC, 752 F.2d 116, 121 (5th Cir. 1985).

[54] 15 U.S.C. § 1314(g) (1994).

[55] See Motion Picture Ass'n of Am. v. United States Dep't of Justice, No. 80 Civ. 6612, slip op. at 1 (S.D.N.Y. Oct. 6, 1981).

[56] 28 U.S.C. § 592(e) (1994) (expired as of June 30, 1999).

[57] Cf. Public Citizen v. Department of Justice, No. 82-2909 (D.D.C. May 18, 1983) (construing 1978 version of statute).

[58] 49 U.S.C.A. § 1114 (West Supp. 1998).

[59] McGilvra v. National Transp. Safety Bd., 840 F. Supp. 100, 102 (D. Colo.
(continued...)

# EXEMPTION 3

contained in the Social Security Administration's "Numident system," which was obtained from death certificates provided by state agencies, has been held exempt on the basis of subpart (A) on the grounds that the language of the statute[60] "leaves no room for agency discretion."[61]

In a decision construing the application of the identical Exemption 3 language of the Government in the Sunshine Act[62] to the Defense Nuclear Facilities Safety Board Act[63] the D.C. Circuit has held that the latter statute allows no discretion with regard to the release of the Board's proposed recommendations, thus meeting the requirement of subpart (A).[64] By contrast, the D.C. Circuit found that the statute governing release by the FBI of criminal record information ("rap sheets")[65] fails to fulfill subpart (A)'s requirement of absolute withholding because the statute implies that the FBI has discretion to withhold records and, in fact, the FBI had exercised such discretion by its inconsistent manner of releasing "rap sheets" to the public.[66]

In an extraordinary decision, the Ninth Circuit held that language in an appropriations act specifying that "[n]one of the funds provided in this Act may be expended to release information acquired from any handler" under a particular agricultural program,[67] does not satisfy the requirement of subpart (A) because through such language Congress prohibited only "the expenditure of funds" for releasing the information, not release of the information under the FOIA itself.[68]

---

(...continued)
1993).

[60] 42 U.S.C. § 405(r) (1994).

[61] International Diatomite Producers Ass'n v. United States Soc. Sec. Admin., No. C-92-1634, 1993 WL 137286, at *3 (N.D. Cal. Apr. 28, 1993), appeal dismissed per stipulation, No. 93-16204 (9th Cir. Oct. 27, 1993).

[62] 5 U.S.C. § 552b (1994 & Supp. IV 1998).

[63] 42 U.S.C. § 2286 (1994 & Supp. III 1997).

[64] Natural Resources Defense Council v. Defense Nuclear Facilities Safety Bd., 969 F.2d 1248, 1249 (D.C. Cir. 1992).

[65] 28 U.S.C. § 534 (1994 & Supp. III 1997).

[66] See Reporters Comm. for Freedom of the Press v. United States Dep't of Justice, 816 F.2d 730, 736 n.9 (D.C. Cir.), modified on other grounds, 831 F.2d 1124 (D.C. Cir. 1987), rev'd on other grounds, 489 U.S. 749 (1989); see also Dayton Newspapers, Inc. v. FBI, No. C-3-85-815, slip op. at 6 (S.D. Ohio Feb. 9, 1993).

[67] Rural Development, Agriculture and Related Agencies Appropriations Act of 1989, Pub. L. No. 100-460, § 630, 102 Stat. 2229, 2262.

[68] Cal-Almond, Inc. v. USDA, 960 F.2d 105, 108 (9th Cir. 1992).

**EXEMPTION 3**

## Subpart (B)

Most Exemption 3 cases involve subpart (B)--which encompasses statutes that either provide criteria for withholding information or refer to particular matters to be withheld--either explicitly or implicitly. For example, a provision of the Consumer Product Safety Act[69] has been held to set forth sufficiently definite withholding criteria for it to fall within the scope of subpart (B),[70] and the provision which prohibits the Commission from disclosing any information that is submitted to it pursuant to section 15(b) of the Act[71] has been held to meet the requirements of subpart (B) by referring to particular types of matters to be withheld.[72]

Section 777 of the Tariff Act,[73] governing the withholding of "proprietary information," has been held to refer to particular types of information to be withheld and thus to be a subpart (B) statute.[74] Section 12(d) of the Railroad Unemployment Insurance Act[75] refers to particular types of matters to be withheld--information which would reveal employees' identities--and thus has been held to satisfy subpart (B).[76] Section 410(c)(2) of the Postal Reorganization Act,[77] governing the withholding of "information of a commercial nature . . . which under good business practice would not be publicly disclosed," has been held to refer to "particular types of matters to be withheld" and thus to be a subpart (B) statute.[78]

---

[69] 15 U.S.C. § 2055(b)(1) (1994).

[70] See Consumer Prod. Safety Comm'n v. GTE Sylvania, Inc., 447 U.S. 102, 122 (1980).

[71] 15 U.S.C. § 2055(b)(5) (1994).

[72] See Reliance Elec. Co. v. Consumer Prod. Safety Comm'n, No. 87-1478, slip op. at 16-17 (D.D.C. Sept. 19, 1989).

[73] 19 U.S.C. § 1677f (1994).

[74] See Mudge Rose Guthrie Alexander & Ferdon v. United States Int'l Trade Comm'n, 846 F.2d 1527, 1530 (D.C. Cir. 1988).

[75] 45 U.S.C. § 362(d) (1994).

[76] See Association of Retired R.R. Workers v. United States R.R. Retirement Bd., 830 F.2d 331, 334 (D.C. Cir. 1987); National Ass'n of Retired & Veteran Ry. Employees v. Railroad Retirement Bd., No. 87-117, slip op. at 5 (N.D. Ohio Feb. 20, 1991).

[77] 39 U.S.C. § 410(c)(2) (1994).

[78] Weres Corp. v. United States Postal Serv., No. 94-1984, slip op. at 3-6 (D.D.C. Sept. 23, 1996) (finding that agency properly withheld unit and total prices submitted by unsuccessful offerors for government contracts); cf. National W. Life Ins. Co. v. United States, 512 F. Supp. 454, 459, 462 (N.D. Tex. 1980) (concluding that list of names and duty stations of postal employees does not qualify as "commercial" information within scope of 39 U.S.C. § 410(c)(2)).

# EXEMPTION 3

Similarly, it has been held that section 12(c)(1) of the Export Administration Act, governing the disclosure of export licenses and applications,[79] authorizes the withholding of a sufficiently narrow class of information to satisfy the requirements of subpart (B) and thus qualifies as an Exemption 3 statute.[80] Likewise, the Collection and Publication of Foreign Commerce Act,[81] which explicitly provides for nondisclosure of shippers' export declarations, qualifies as an Exemption 3 statute under subpart (B).[82]

The Supreme Court has held that section 102(d)(3) of the National Security Act of 1947,[83] which requires the Director of the CIA to protect "intelligence sources and methods," clearly refers to particular types of matters to be withheld and thus comes within the ambit of subpart (B).[84] Likewise, section

---

[79] 50 U.S.C. app. § 2411(c)(1) (1994) (statute which expired on August 20, 1994, but has been reextended several times in past, in substantially identical form).

[80] See Armstrong v. Executive Office of the President, No. 89-142, slip op. at 30-35 (D.D.C. July 28, 1995) (protecting information from export license application under Export Administration Act as Exemption 3 statute even though statute had lapsed and its provisions were extended by executive order); Africa Fund v. Mosbacher, No. 92 Civ. 289, 1993 WL 183736, at *6 (S.D.N.Y. May 26, 1993) (holding that Export Administration Act protection applied to agency denial made after Act expired and before subsequent reextension); see also Lessner v. United States Dep't of Commerce, 827 F.2d 1333, 1336-37 (9th Cir. 1987) (construing statute as effective in 1987); cf. Council for a Livable World v. United States Dep't of State, No. 96-1807, slip op. at 11 (D.D.C. Jan. 21, 1998) (finding that Section 12(c)(1) of Export Administration Act, as specifically incorporated by reference into Arms Export Control Act (at 22 U.S.C. § 2778(e) (1994 & Supp. IV 1998)), is Exemption 3 statute that protects information concerning export-license applications, without acknowledging that Export Administration Act had lapsed), amended (D.D.C. Nov. 23, 1998).

[81] 13 U.S.C. § 301(g) (1994).

[82] See Africa Fund, 1993 WL 183736, at *5; Young Conservative Found. v. United States Dep't of Commerce, No. 85-3982, 1987 WL 9244, at **2-3 (D.D.C. Mar. 25, 1987).

[83] 50 U.S.C.A. § 403-3(c)(6) (West Supp. 1998).

[84] See CIA v. Sims, 471 U.S. 159, 167 (1985); see also Frugone v. CIA, 169 F.3d 772, 774-75 (D.C. Cir. 1999) (finding that CIA properly refused to confirm or deny existence of records concerning plaintiff's alleged employment relationship with CIA despite allegation that another government agency confirmed plaintiff's status as former CIA employee); Minier v. CIA, 88 F.3d 796, 801 (9th Cir. 1996) (finding that agency properly refused to confirm or deny existence of records concerning deceased person's alleged employment relationship with CIA); Maynard v. CIA, 986 F.2d 547, 554 (1st Cir. 1993) (stating that under § 403(d)(3) it is responsibility of Director of CIA to determine whether sources or methods should be disclosed); Krikorian v. Department of State, 984 F.2d 461, 465 (D.C. Cir. 1993) (same); Fitzgibbon v. CIA, 911 F.2d
(continued...)

**EXEMPTION 3**

6 of the Central Intelligence Agency Act of 1949[85]--protecting from disclosure "the organization, functions, names, official titles, salaries or numbers of per-

---

(...continued)
755, 761 (D.C. Cir. 1990) (same); <u>Hunt v. CIA</u>, 981 F.2d 1116, 1118 (9th Cir. 1992) (upholding agency's "Glomar" response to request on foreign national, because acknowledgement of any records would reveal sources and methods); <u>Knight v. CIA</u>, 872 F.2d 660, 663 (8th Cir. 1989) (same); <u>Levy v. CIA</u>, No. 95-1276, slip op. at 14-17 (D.D.C. Nov. 16, 1995) (same), <u>aff'd</u>, No. 96-5004 (D.C. Cir. Jan. 15, 1997); <u>Emerson v. CIA</u>, No. 99-00274, slip op. at 6-8 (D.D.C. May 8, 2000) (same); <u>Schrecker v. United States Dep't of Justice</u>, 74 F. Supp. 2d 26, 32-33 (D.D.C. 1999) (ruling that CIA properly refused to disclose identity of deceased intelligence sources, allegedly of historical significance, and noting that privacy concerns are not relevant) (appeal pending); <u>Aftergood v. CIA</u>, No. 98-2107, 1999 U.S. Dist. LEXIS 18135, at **12-15 (D.D.C. Nov. 12, 1999) (permitting CIA to withhold total budget request for all intelligence and intelligence-related activities where Director of Central Intelligence determined that disclosure would "tend to reveal" sources and methods); <u>Arabian Shield Dev. Co. v. CIA</u>, No. 3-98-CV-0624, 1999 WL 118796, at **4-5 (N.D. Tex. Feb. 26, 1999) (deferring to Director of CIA's determination that to confirm or deny existence of agency records pertaining to contract negotiations between U.S. oil company and foreign government would reveal sources and methods, while noting that the "Director [of Central Intelligence]'s determination in this regard is almost unassailable" and that "[a]bsent evidence of bad faith, the [CIA]'s determination 'is beyond the purview of the courts'"), <u>summary affirmance granted</u>, No. 99-10327 (5th Cir. 2000); <u>Students Against Genocide (SAGE) v. Department of State</u>, No. 96-667, 1998 WL 699074, at **7-8 (D.D.C. Aug. 24, 1998) (magistrate's recommendation) (finding that CIA properly refused to confirm or deny existence of photographs purportedly taken by U.S. spy planes and satellites, including photographs that allegedly were shown to members of United Nations Security Council by U.S. delegate to U.N.), <u>adopted</u> (D.D.C. Sept. 30, 1998) (appeal pending); <u>Blazy v. Tenet</u>, 979 F. Supp. 10, 23-24 (D.D.C. 1997) (protecting intelligence sources and methods located in requester's personnel file), <u>summary affirmance granted</u>, No. 97-5330 (D.C. Cir. May 12, 1998); <u>Andrade v. CIA</u>, No. 95-1215, 1997 WL 527347, at **3-5 (D.D.C. Aug. 18, 1997) (holding intelligence methods used in assessing employee fitness protectible); <u>Earth Pledge Found. v. CIA</u>, 988 F. Supp. 623, 627 (S.D.N.Y. 1996) (finding agency's "Glomar" response proper because acknowledgement of records would generate "danger of revealing sources"), <u>aff'd per curiam</u>, 128 F.3d 788 (2d Cir. 1997) (unpublished table decision); <u>Campbell v. United States Dep't of Justice</u>, No. 89-CV-3016, 1996 WL 554511, at *7 (D.D.C. Sept. 19, 1996) ("The CIA director is to be afforded 'great deference' by courts determining the propriety of nondisclosure of intelligence sources under 50 U.S.C. § 403."), <u>rev'd & remanded on other grounds</u>, 164 F.3d 20 (D.C. Cir. 1998); <u>cf.</u> <u>Linder v. DOD</u>, 133 F.3d 17, 25 (D.C. Cir. 1998) ("[C]ourts must give 'great deference' to the Director of Central Intelligence's determination that a classified document could reveal intelligence sources and methods and endanger national security.") (non-FOIA case).

[85] 50 U.S.C. § 403g (1994).

## EXEMPTION 3

sonnel" employed by the CIA--meets the requirements of subpart (B).[86] Similarly, section 6 of Public Law No. 86-36,[87] pertaining to the organization, functions, activities, and personnel of the NSA, has been held to qualify as a subpart (B) statute,[88] as has 18 U.S.C. § 798(a), which criminalizes the disclosure of any classified information "concerning the nature, preparation, or use of any code, cipher or cryptographic system of the United States."[89] A provision of the Atomic Energy Act, prohibiting the disclosure of "Restricted Data" to the public,[90] refers to particular types of matters and thus has been held to qualify as a subpart (B) statute as well.[91]

Section 7332 of the Veterans Health Administration Patient Rights Statute[92] generally prohibits disclosure of even the abstract fact that medical records on named individuals are maintained pursuant to that section, but it provides specific criteria under which particular medical information may be released, and thus has been found to satisfy the requirements of subpart (B).[93] Records created by the Department of Veterans Affairs as part of a medical

---

[86] See, e.g., Minier, 88 F.3d at 801; Roman, 1998 U.S. Dist. LEXIS 6708, at **10-11; Blazy, 979 F. Supp. at 23-24; Earth Pledge Found., 988 F. Supp. at 627-28; Campbell, 1996 WL 554511, at *6; Kronisch v. United States, No. 83-2458, 1995 WL 303625, at **4-6 (S.D.N.Y. May 18, 1995), aff'd on other grounds, 150 F.3d 112 (2d Cir. 1998); Hunsberger v. CIA, No. 92-2186, slip op. at 3 (D.D.C. Apr. 5, 1995); Rothschild v. CIA, No. 91-1314, 1992 WL 71393, at *2 (D.D.C. Mar. 25, 1992); Lawyers Comm. for Human Rights v. INS, 721 F. Supp. 552, 567 (S.D.N.Y. 1989); Pfeiffer v. CIA, 721 F. Supp. 337, 341-42 (D.D.C. 1989).

[87] 50 U.S.C. § 402 note (1994).

[88] See Founding Church of Scientology v. NSA, 610 F.2d 824, 828 (D.C. Cir. 1979); Hayden v. NSA, 452 F. Supp. 247, 252 (D.D.C. 1978), aff'd, 608 F.2d 1381 (D.C. Cir. 1979).

[89] Winter v. NSA, 569 F. Supp. 545, 548 (S.D. Cal. 1983); see also Gilmore v. NSA, No. C 92-3646, 1993 U.S. Dist. LEXIS 7694, at **26-27 (N.D. Cal. May 3, 1993) (finding information on cryptography currently used by NSA to be "integrally related" to function and activity of intelligence gathering and thus protected).

[90] 42 U.S.C.A. § 2162 (West Supp. 1998).

[91] See Meeropol v. Smith, No. 75-1121, slip op. at 53-55 (D.D.C. Feb. 29, 1984), aff'd in relevant part & remanded in part sub nom. Meeropol v. Meese, 790 F.2d 942 (D.C. Cir. 1986). But see General Elec. Co. v. NRC, 750 F.2d 1394, 1401 (7th Cir. 1984) (concluding that provision concerning technical information furnished by license applicants lacked sufficient specificity to qualify as Exemption 3 statute).

[92] 38 U.S.C. § 7332 (1994).

[93] See Palmer v. Derwinski, No. 91-197, slip op. at 3-4 (E.D. Ky. June 10, 1992).

**EXEMPTION 3**

quality-assurance program[94] have similarly been held to qualify for Exemption 3 protection.[95] Likewise, one court has suggested that section 5038 of the Juvenile Delinquency Records Statute,[96] which generally prohibits disclosure of the existence of records compiled pursuant to that section, but which does provide specific criteria for releasing the information, qualifies as a subpart (B) statute.[97] Similarly, another court has held that the recently enacted Section 207 of the National Park Omnibus Management Act of 1998,[98] which sets forth criteria for the Secretary of the Interior to apply when exercising discretion about release of "[i]nformation concerning the nature and specific location of [certain] National Park System resource[s]," including resources which are "endangered, threatened, rare, or commercially valuable," is within the scope of subpart (B).[99]

The Court of Appeals for the District of Columbia Circuit has held that a portion of the Patent Act[100] satisfies subpart (B) because it identifies the types of matters--patent applications and information concerning them--intended to be withheld.[101] As well, the portion of the Civil Service Reform Act concerning the confidentiality of certain labor relations training and guidance materi-

---

[94] See 38 U.S.C. § 5705(a) (1994).

[95] See Schulte & Sun-Sentinel Co. v. VA, No. 96-6251, slip op. at 3-4 (S.D. Fla. Feb. 2, 1996) (allowing agency to withhold mortality statistics); see also Dayton Newspapers, Inc. v. United States Dep't of the Air Force, No. C-3-97-78, slip op. at 8 (S.D. Ohio Mar. 26, 1999) (finding that 10 U.S.C. § 1102, equivalent medical quality-assurance statute for DOD, qualifies as Exemption 3 statute protecting "all 'medical quality assurance records,' regardless of whether the contents of such records originated within or outside of a medical quality assurance program").

[96] 18 U.S.C. § 5038 (1994 & Supp. IV 1998).

[97] See McDonnell v. United States, 4 F.3d 1227, 1251 (3d Cir. 1993) (holding that state juvenile delinquency records fall outside scope of statute).

[98] 16 U.S.C. § 5937 (1994 & Supp. IV 1998).

[99] Pease v. United States Dep't of Interior, No. 1:99CV113, slip op. at 2, 4 (D. Vt. Sept. 17, 1999) (finding that the agency properly withheld "certain information pertaining to the location, tracking and/or radio frequencies of grizzly bears" in the Yellowstone National Park ecosystem); cf. Maricopa Audubon Soc'y v. United States Forest Serv., 108 F.3d 1082, 1089 (9th Cir. 1997) (refusing to protect wildlife maps showing endangered species locations pursuant to Exemption 2); Audubon Soc'y v. United States Forest Serv., 104 F.3d 1201, 1204 (10th Cir. 1997) (same); FOIA Update, Vol. XVI, No. 3, at 2 (describing difficulty of protecting endangered species locations under Exemption 2 prior to legislative enactment qualifying under Exemption 3).

[100] 35 U.S.C. § 122 (1994).

[101] Irons & Sears v. Dann, 606 F.2d 1215, 1220 (D.C. Cir. 1979); accord Leeds v. Quigg, 720 F. Supp. 193, 194 (D.D.C. 1989).

## EXEMPTION 3

als,[102] has been held to qualify as a subpart (B) withholding statute.[103] In addition, the United States Information and Educational Exchange Act of 1948 (the "Smith-Mundt Act")[104] qualifies as a subpart (B) statute insofar as it prohibits the disclosure of certain overseas programming materials within the United States.[105] While the Smith-Mundt Act originally applied only to records prepared by the now-defunct United States Information Agency, the Foreign Affairs Reform and Restructuring Act of 1998 applied the relevant provisions of that statute to those programs within the Department of State that absorbed USIA's functions.[106]

The Commodity Exchange Act,[107] which prohibits the disclosure of business transactions, market positions, trade secrets, or customer names of persons under investigation under the Act, has been held to refer to particular types of matters and thus to satisfy subpart (B).[108] The D.C. Circuit has held that a provision of the Federal Aviation Act,[109] relating to security data the disclosure of which would be detrimental to the safety of airline travelers, similarly shields that particular data from disclosure under the FOIA.[110] It also has been held that the DOD's "technical data" statute,[111] which protects technical information with "military or space application" for which an export license is required, satisfies subpart (B) because it refers to sufficiently particular types of matters.[112]

---

[102] 5 U.S.C. § 7114(b)(4) (1994).

[103] See Dubin v. Department of the Treasury, 555 F. Supp. 408, 412 (N.D. Ga. 1981), aff'd, 697 F.2d 1093 (11th Cir. 1983) (unpublished table decision); NTEU v. OPM, No. 76-695, slip op. at 4 (D.D.C. July 9, 1979).

[104] 22 U.S.C. § 1461-1a (1994 & Supp. IV 1998).

[105] See Essential Info., Inc. v. USIA, 134 F.3d 1165, 1168-69 (D.C. Cir. 1998) (holding that Smith-Mundt Act qualifies as nondisclosure statute even though "it does not prohibit all disclosure of records but only disclosure to persons in this country").

[106] See Foreign Affairs Reform and Restructuring Act of 1998, 22 U.S.C. §§ 6501-6617 (Supp. IV 1998) (abolishing USIA (at 22 U.S.C. § 6531), transferring USIA functions to Department of State (at 22 U.S.C. § 6532), and applying Smith-Mundt Act to USIA functions that have been transferred to Department of State (at 22 U.S.C. § 6552(b))).

[107] 7 U.S.C. § 12 (1994).

[108] See Hunt v. Commodity Futures Trading Comm'n, 484 F. Supp. 47, 49 (D.D.C. 1979).

[109] 49 U.S.C. § 40119 (1994).

[110] Public Citizen, Inc. v. FAA, 988 F.2d 186, 194 (D.C. Cir. 1993).

[111] 10 U.S.C. § 130 (1994).

[112] See Chenkin v. Department of the Army, No. 93-494, 1994 U.S. Dist. LEXIS 20907, at *8 (E.D. Pa. Jan. 14, 1994), aff'd, 61 F.3d 894 (3d Cir. 1995)

(continued...)

**EXEMPTION 3**

Lastly, the Federal Transfer Technology Act,[113] which allows federal agencies the discretion to protect for five years any commercial and confidential information that results from a Cooperative Research And Development Agreement (CRADA) with a nonfederal party, has been held to qualify as an Exemption 3 statute.[114] Under a concurrent provision in that Act, the agency also is absolutely prohibited from disclosing any commercial and confidential information obtained from the CRADA's private-sector partner.[115] (See the discussion under Exemption 4, below.)

Alternative Analyses

Some statutes have been found to satisfy both Exemption 3 subparts. For example, while the Court of Appeals for the Third Circuit has held that section 222(f) of the Immigration and Nationality Act[116] sufficiently limits the category of information it covers--records pertaining to the issuance or refusal of visas and permits to enter the United States--to qualify as an Exemption 3 statute under subpart (B),[117] the Court of Appeals for the District of Columbia Circuit has specifically held that the section satisfies subpart (A) as well as subpart (B).[118]

Similarly, Exemption 3 protection for information obtained by law enforcement agencies pursuant to the statute governing court-ordered wiretaps, Title III of the Omnibus Crime Control and Safe Streets Act of 1968,[119] has been recognized by district courts on a variety of bases.[120] However, in Lam

---

(...continued)
(unpublished table decision); Colonial Trading Corp. v. Department of the Navy, 735 F. Supp. 429, 431 (D.D.C. 1990); see also American Friends Serv. Comm. v. DOD, No. 83-4916, 1986 WL 10659, at *4 (E.D. Pa. Sept. 25, 1986), rev'd on other grounds, 831 F.2d 441 (3d Cir. 1987).

[113] 15 U.S.C. § 3710a(c)(7) (1994).

[114] See DeLorme Publ'g Co. v. NOAA, 917 F. Supp. 867, 871 (D. Me. 1996), appeal dismissed per stipulation, No. 96-1601 (1st Cir. July 8, 1996).

[115] 15 U.S.C. § 3710a(c)(7)(B).

[116] 8 U.S.C. § 1202(f) (1994 & Supp. II 1996).

[117] DeLaurentiis v. Haig, 686 F.2d 192, 194 (3d Cir. 1982); accord Smith v. Department of Justice, No. 81-CV-813, 1983 U.S. Dist. LEXIS 10878, at **13-14 (N.D.N.Y. Dec. 13, 1983).

[118] Medina-Hincapie v. Department of State, 700 F.2d 737, 741-42 (D.C. Cir. 1983); accord Marulanda v. United States Dep't of State, No. 93-1327, slip op. at 4-6 (D.D.C. Jan. 31, 1996) (protecting documents relating to denial of plaintiff's visa even when agency previously released certain of those records that were determined not to breach confidentiality provision).

[119] See 18 U.S.C. §§ 2510-20 (1994 & Supp. IV 1998).

[120] See Gonzalez v. United States Dep't of Justice, No. 88-913, 1988 WL
(continued...)

## EXEMPTION 3

Lek Chong v. DEA,[121] the D.C. Circuit, finding that it "clearly identifies intercepted communications as the subject of its disclosure limitations," held that "Title III falls squarely within the scope of subsection (B)'s second prong, as a statute referring to <u>particular matters to be withheld</u>."[122] In one case, "pen register" applications and orders, obtained pursuant to Title III, mistakenly were held to be protected from disclosure by a provision of that statute,[123] and have been incorrectly found to fall under Exemption 3.[124] It should be noted that while "pen register" orders may be properly withheld pursuant to a sealing order issued by a court in accordance with the statute,[125] once the sealing

---

(...continued)
120841, at *2 (D.D.C. Oct. 25, 1988) (holding that 18 U.S.C. § 2511(2)(a)(ii), which regulates disclosure of existence of wiretap intercepts, meets requirements of subpart (A)); <u>Docal v. Bennsinger</u>, 543 F. Supp. 38, 43-44 (M.D. Pa. 1981) (relying upon entire statutory scheme of 18 U.S.C. §§ 2510-20 but not distinguishing between Exemption 3 subparts); <u>Carroll v. United States Dep't of Justice</u>, No. 76-2038, slip op. at 2-3 (D.D.C. May 26, 1978) (holding that 18 U.S.C. § 2518(8), which regulates disclosure of contents of wiretap intercepts, meets requirements of subpart (A)).

[121] 929 F.2d 729 (D.C. Cir. 1991).

[122] <u>Id.</u> at 733; <u>see also</u> <u>Willis v. FBI</u>, No. 98-5071, 1999 WL 236891, at *1 (D.C. Cir. Mar. 19, 1999) (finding that FBI properly withheld two electronic surveillance tapes under Title III and Exemption 3); <u>Payne v. United States Dep't of Justice</u>, No. 96-30840, slip op. at 5-6 (5th Cir. July 11, 1997) (holding that tape recordings obtained pursuant to Title III "fall squarely" within scope of Exemption 3); <u>Pray v. DEA</u>, No. 97-0134, slip op. at 3 (D.D.C. Feb. 3, 1998) (stating that information obtained through wiretap falls squarely within scope of Exemption 3), <u>summary affirmance granted in pertinent part & remanded in part on other grounds</u>, No. 98-5072 (D.C. Cir. Nov. 24, 1998); <u>Del Viscovo v. FBI</u>, 903 F. Supp. 1, 2 (D.D.C. 1995) (protecting "information relating to the lawful interception of communications"); <u>Manna v. United States Dep't of Justice</u>, No. 92-1840, slip op. at 3-4 (D.N.J. Aug. 25, 1993) (determining that analysis of audio tapes and identities of individuals conversing on tapes obtained pursuant to Title III is protected under Exemption 3), <u>aff'd on other grounds</u>, 51 F.3d 1158 (3d Cir. 1995); <u>Manchester v. DEA</u>, 823 F. Supp. 1259, 1267 (E.D. Pa. 1993) (ruling that wiretap applications and derivative information fall within broad purview of Title III), <u>aff'd</u>, 40 F.3d 1240 (3d Cir. 1994) (unpublished table decision); <u>cf.</u> <u>Cottone v. Reno</u>, 193 F.3d 550, 554-56 (D.C. Cir. 1999) (noting that wiretapped recordings obtained pursuant to Title III are ordinarily exempt from disclosure under Exemption 3, but holding that Exemption 3 protection was waived where FOIA requester precisely identified specific tapes that had been played in open court as evidence during public criminal trial).

[123] 18 U.S.C. § 3123(d) (1994).

[124] <u>McFarland v. DEA</u>, No. 94-620, slip op. at 4 (D. Colo. Jan. 3, 1995) (mistakenly protecting under Exemption 3 material "acquired through the use of a pen register").

[125] 18 U.S.C. § 3123(d)(1); <u>see, e.g.</u>, <u>Manna v. United States Dep't of Justice</u>,
(continued...)

**EXEMPTION 3**

order is lifted, the statute no longer prohibits release under the FOIA.[126]

The withholding of tax return information has been approved under three different theories. The United States Supreme Court and most appellate courts that have considered the matter have held either explicitly or implicitly that § 6103 of the Internal Revenue Code[127] satisfies subpart (B) of Exemption 3.[128] The Courts of Appeals for the D.C., Fifth, Sixth, and Tenth Circuits have further reasoned that § 6103 is a subpart (A) statute to the extent that a person is not entitled to access to tax returns or return information of other taxpayers.[129] It should be noted that pursuant to § 6103(b)(2), individuals are not

---

(...continued)
815 F. Supp. 798, 812 (D.N.J. 1993) (protecting under Exemption 3 sealed "pen register" applications and orders), aff'd on other grounds, 51 F.3d 1158 (3d Cir. 1995).

[126] See 18 U.S.C. § 3123(d). See generally Morgan v. United States Dep't of Justice, 923 F.2d 195, 197 (D.C. Cir. 1991) ("[T]he proper test for determining whether an agency improperly withholds records under seal is whether the seal, like an injunction, prohibits the agency from disclosing the records.").

[127] 26 U.S.C.A. § 6103 (West Supp. 1998).

[128] See, e.g., Church of Scientology v. IRS, 484 U.S. 9, 15 (1987); Aronson v. IRS, 973 F.2d 962, 964-65 (1st Cir. 1992) (finding that IRS lawfully exercised discretion to withhold street addresses pursuant to 26 U.S.C. § 6103(m)(1)); Long v. IRS, 891 F.2d 222, 224 (9th Cir. 1989) (holding that deletion of taxpayers' identification does not alter confidentiality of § 6103 information); DeSalvo v. IRS, 861 F.2d 1217, 1221 (10th Cir. 1988); Grasso v. IRS, 785 F.2d 70, 77 (3d Cir. 1986); Long v. IRS, 742 F.2d 1173, 1179 (9th Cir. 1984); Ryan v. ATF, 715 F.2d 644, 645 (D.C. Cir. 1983); Currie v. IRS, 704 F.2d 523, 527-28 (11th Cir. 1983); Willamette Indus. v. United States, 689 F.2d 865, 867 (9th Cir. 1982); Barney v. IRS, 618 F.2d 1268, 1274 n.15 (8th Cir. 1980) (dictum); Chamberlain v. Kurtz, 589 F.2d 827, 843 (5th Cir. 1979).

[129] D.C. Circuit: Stebbins v. Sullivan, No. 90-5361, 1992 WL 174542, at *1 (D.C. Cir. July 22, 1992); Fifth Circuit: Linsteadt v. IRS, 729 F.2d 998, 1000 (5th Cir. 1984); Sixth Circuit: Fruehauf Corp. v. IRS, 566 F.2d 574, 578 n.6 (6th Cir. 1977); Tenth Circuit: DeSalvo, 861 F.2d at 1221 n.4. See generally Lehrfeld v. Richardson, 132 F.3d 1463, 1467 (D.C. Cir. 1998) (protecting third-party "return information" submitted in support of application for tax-exempt status); Tax Analysts v. IRS, 117 F.3d 607, 611 (D.C. Cir. 1997) (holding that while Field Service Advice Memoranda contain some protectible "return information," they do not themselves constitute "return information" properly withholdable in their entireties under Exemption 3), on remand, No. 94-923, 1998 WL 419755, at **2-3 (D.D.C. May 1, 1998) (finding "true return information" withholdable from Field Service Advice Memoranda), appeal voluntarily dismissed, No. 98-5252 (D.C. Cir. Aug. 11, 1998), enforced, 1999 U.S. Dist. LEXIS 14950, at **8-16 (D.D.C. Sept. 2, 1999) (ordering certain information released because it does not qualify as "return information" as it does not include nongeneral information that can be associated with specific taxpayers); Kamman v. IRS, 56 F.3d 46, 49 (9th Cir. 1995) (holding appraisal of jewelry
(continued...)

**EXEMPTION 3**

entitled to obtain tax return information even regarding themselves if it is determined that release would impair enforcement by the IRS.[130] Information

---

(...continued)
seized from third-party taxpayer and auctioned to satisfy tax liability was not "return information"); Landmark Legal Found. v. IRS, 87 F. Supp. 2d 21, 25 (D.D.C. 2000) (deciding that "return information" includes information from third-party informants who complained to IRS about tax-exempt status of organizations as well as inquiries from individuals into tax-exempt status of organizations) (appeal pending); Allnutt v. United States Dep't of Justice, No. Y98-1722, 2000 U.S. Dist. LEXIS 4060, at **37-38 (D. Md. Mar. 6, 2000) (recognizing that § 6103 prohibits disclosure of third-party taxpayer information even though IRS collected such information as part of investigation of requester) (magistrate's recommendation); Murphy v. IRS 79 F. Supp. 2d 1180, 1183-84 (D. Haw. 1999) (upholding agency decision to withhold third-party return information despite requester's argument that he had "material interest" in information), appeal dismissed, No. 99-17325 (D.C. Cir. Apr. 24, 2000); Coolman v. IRS, No. 98-6149, 1999 WL 675319, at *5 (W.D. Mo. July 12, 1999) (holding that § 6103 prohibits disclosure of third-party tax return information), aff'd, No. 99-3963, 1999 WL 1419039 (8th Cir. Dec. 6, 1999); Tax Analysts v. IRS, 53 F. Supp. 2d 449, 451-53 (D.D.C. 1999) (declaring that "closing agreements" releasing tax-exempt organizations from tax liability constitute "tax return information" within scope of § 6103(a), and that because they are distinct from "applications" for tax-exempt status, which are open to public inspection under § 6104, they may not be disclosed); Barmes v. IRS, 60 F. Supp. 2d 896, 900-01 (S.D. Ind. 1998) (protecting "transcripts containing a variety of tax data concerning third party taxpayers"); Buckner v. IRS, 25 F. Supp. 2d 893, 899-900 (N.D. Ind. 1998) (ruling that information properly was withheld where disclosure would reveal identity of third-party taxpayer); Ginsberg v. IRS, No. 96-2265, 1997 WL 882913, at *4 (M.D. Fla. Dec. 23, 1997) (magistrate's recommendation) (holding that bulk of legal memorandum responding to Request for Technical Assistance was not protectible "return information"), adopted (M.D. Fla. Jan. 27, 1998); Crooker v. IRS, No. 94-0755, 1995 WL 430605, at *3 (D.D.C. Apr. 27, 1995) (requiring IRS to confirm that redactions were not taken for aliases plaintiff used in his tax-refund scheme); Gray, Plant, Mooty, Mooty & Bennett v. IRS, No. 4-90-210, 1990 U.S. Dist. LEXIS 18799, at *8 (D. Minn. Dec. 18, 1990) (ordering public report released because it does not qualify as "return information" as it does not include data in form which can be associated with particular taxpayer).

[130] See Youngblood v. Commissioner, No. 2:99-cv-9253, 2000 U.S. Dist. LEXIS 5083, at **26-29 (C.D. Cal. Mar. 6, 2000) (declaring that criminal tax investigation report was properly withheld where IRS demonstrated that disclosure would seriously impair federal tax administration); Anderson v. United States Dep't of Treasury, No. 98-1112, 1999 WL 282784, at **2-3 (W.D. Tenn. Mar. 24, 1999) (finding that disclosure to taxpayer of IRS-prepared "checkspread" charting all checks written by taxpayer over two-year period would seriously impair tax administration, notwithstanding IRS agent's disclosure of "checkspread" to taxpayer during interview); Brooks v. IRS, No. 96-6284, 1997 WL 718473, at *9 (E.D. Cal. Aug. 28, 1997) (upholding protection of revenue agent's notes because release "would permit Plaintiff to ascertain the extent of [IRS's] knowledge and predict the direction of [its] examina-

(continued...)

**EXEMPTION 3**

which would provide insights into how the IRS selects returns for audits has regularly been found to impair IRS's enforcement of tax laws.[131] Of course, it

---

(...continued)
tion"); Gibbs Int'l v. IRS, No. 7:96-996-13, slip op. at 1 (D.S.C. Oct. 8, 1996) (stating that "disclosure of the documents would chill future cooperation with foreign government treaty partners"), aff'd, 129 F.3d 116 (4th Cir. 1997) (unpublished table decision), cert. denied, 523 U.S. 1072 (1998); Holbrook v. IRS, 914 F. Supp. 314, 316-17 (S.D. Iowa 1996) (holding IRS agent's handwritten notes protectible because disclosure would interfere with enforcement proceedings and hence seriously impair tax administration); Pully v. IRS, 939 F. Supp. 429, 434-36 (E.D. Va. 1996) (holding documents relating to civil and criminal investigation of plaintiff protectible under Exemptions 3 and 7(A)); Fritz v. IRS, 862 F. Supp. 234, 236 (W.D. Wis. 1994) (finding that disclosure of name and address of purchaser of seized automobile would impair tax administration as "people would be less likely to purchase seized property" if their identities were revealed); Rollins v. United States Dep't of Justice, No. 90-3170, 1992 U.S. Dist. LEXIS 10884, at *19 (S.D. Tex. June 29, 1992) (stating that IRS memoranda revealing scope and direction of investigation properly withheld); Starkey v. IRS, No. 91-20040, 1991 WL 330895, at **2-3 (N.D. Cal. Dec. 6, 1991) (same); Church of Scientology v. IRS, No. 89-5894, 1991 U.S. Dist. LEXIS 3008, at *3 (C.D. Cal. Mar. 4, 1991) (concluding that release of document referring to information obtainable under various treaties would chill future cooperation of foreign governments and tax-treaty partners); Casa Investors, Ltd. v. Gibbs, No. 88-2485, 1990 WL 180703, at *4 (D.D.C. Oct. 11, 1990) (holding that recommendation for settlement of tax controversies prepared by low-level IRS employees requires protection). But see LeMaine v. IRS, No. 89-2914, 1991 U.S. Dist. LEXIS 18651, at **14-15 (D. Mass. Dec. 10, 1991) (deciding that release of information commonly revealed to public in tax enforcement proceedings would not "seriously impair Federal tax administration" overall).

[131] See Gillin v. IRS, 980 F.2d 819, 822 (1st Cir. 1992) (per curiam) (holding that differential function scores, used to identify returns most in need of examination or audit, are exempt from disclosure); Long v. IRS, 891 F.2d at 224 (finding that computer tapes used to develop discriminant function formulas protected); Coolman, 1999 WL 675319, at *5 (W.D. Mo. July 12, 1999) (holding that § 6103(b)(2) permits IRS to withhold discriminant function scores); Buckner, 25 F. Supp. 2d at 898-99 (concluding that discriminant function scores were properly withheld under § 6103(b)(2), even where scores were 17 years old, because IRS continued to use scores in determining whether to audit certain tax files); Wishart v. Commissioner, No. 97-20614, 1998 U.S. Dist. LEXIS 13306, at **17-18 (N.D. Cal. Aug. 6, 1998) (holding discriminant function scores protectible), aff'd, 199 F.3d 1334 (9th Cir. 1999) (unpublished table decision); Cujas v. IRS, No. 1:97CV00741, 1998 U.S. LEXIS 6466, at *16 (M.D.N.C. Apr. 15, 1998) (recognizing requester was likely to disseminate information about his discriminant function score, "thus making it easier for taxpayers to avoid an audit of their return[s]"), aff'd, 162 F.3d 1154 (4th Cir. 1998) (unpublished table decision); Inman v. Commissioner, 871 F. Supp. 1275, 1278 (E.D. Cal. 1994) (holding discriminant function scores properly exempt); Lamb v. IRS, 871 F. Supp. 301, 304 (E.D. Mich. 1994) (same); In re Church of Scientology Flag Serv. Org./IRS FOIA Litig., No. 91-423, slip op. at
(continued...)

**EXEMPTION 3**

also must be remembered that § 6103 applies only to tax return information obtained by the Department of the Treasury, not to such information maintained by other agencies which was obtained by means other than through the provisions of the Internal Revenue Code.[132]

At least one court of appeals and several district courts have explicitly embraced a third theory based upon the reasoning of Zale Corp. v. IRS.[133] These courts have held that it is not necessary to view § 6103 as an Exemption 3 statute in order to withhold tax return information because the provisions of this tax code section are intended to operate as the sole standard governing the disclosure or nondisclosure of such information, thereby "displacing" the FOIA.[134]

Viewing § 6103 as a "displacement" statute permits the courts to avoid the de novo review required by the FOIA and to apply instead less stringent standards of review pursuant to the Administrative Procedure Act,[135] and can relieve agencies from certain procedural requirements of the FOIA, such as the time limitations for responding to requests and the duty to segregate and release nonexempt information.[136] Nevertheless, even under this approach the government may be required to provide detailed Vaughn Indexes of the information being withheld, rather than general affidavits; the Sixth Circuit

---

(...continued)
3-4 (M.D. Fla. May 19, 1993) (determining that "tolerance criteria" and discriminant function scores were properly withheld) (multidistrict litigation case); Small v. IRS, 820 F. Supp. 163, 165-66 (D.N.J. 1992) (holding discriminant function scores protected under both Exemption 3 and Exemption 7(E)); Ferguson v. IRS, No. C-89-4048, 1990 U.S. Dist. LEXIS 15293, at *4 (N.D. Cal. Oct. 31, 1990) (finding that standards and data used in selection and examination of returns are exempt from disclosure where they would impair IRS enforcement).

[132] See FOIA Update, Vol. IX, No. 2, at 5.

[133] 481 F. Supp. 486, 490 (D.D.C. 1979).

[134] See, e.g., Cheek v. IRS, 703 F.2d 271, 271 (7th Cir. 1983) (noting that § 6103 also "displaces" Privacy Act of 1974, 5 U.S.C. § 552a (1994 & Supp. IV 1998)); King v. IRS, 688 F.2d 488, 495 (7th Cir. 1982); Kuzma v. IRS, No. 81-600E, slip op. at 7-8 (W.D.N.Y. Dec. 31, 1984); see also White v. IRS, 707 F.2d 897, 900 (6th Cir. 1983) (indicating approval of Zale).

[135] 5 U.S.C. §§ 701-706 (1994).

[136] See Grasso, 785 F.2d at 73-74; White, 707 F.2d at 900; Goldsborough v. IRS, No. Y-81-1939, 1984 WL 612, at **5-6 (D. Md. May 10, 1984); Green v. IRS, 556 F. Supp. 79, 84 (N.D. Ind. 1982), aff'd, 734 F.2d 18 (7th Cir. 1984) (unpublished table decision); Meyer v. Department of the Treasury, 82-2 U.S. Tax Cas. (CCH) ¶ 9678, at 85,448 (W.D. Mich. Oct. 2, 1982); see also Anderson v. United States Dep't of Treasury, 1999 WL 282784, at *3 (acknowledging that if § 6103 preempted FOIA, then Administrative Procedure Act standard of review, rather than more stringent FOIA standard of review, would apply, but concluding that case did not require choice because agency action satisfied more stringent FOIA standard).

# EXEMPTION 3

required this despite the fact that the court below had relied solely on the "displacement" theory for its decision.[137]

However, other courts have specifically refused to adopt this "displacement" analysis on the ground that to do so, once it is already evident that § 6103 is an Exemption 3 statute, "would be an exercise in judicial futility [requiring district courts] to engage in both FOIA and Zale analyses when confronted" with such cases.[138] Most significantly, the D.C. Circuit has squarely rejected the "displacement" argument on the basis that the procedures in § 6103 for members of the public to obtain access to IRS documents do not duplicate, and thus do not "displace," those of the FOIA.[139]

The D.C. Circuit's rejection of the "displacement" theory in relation to § 6103 is consistent with previous D.C. Circuit decisions involving similar "displacement" arguments. For example, it had previously rejected a "displacement" argument involving the Department of State's Emergency Fund statutes[140] when it held that inasmuch as Exemption 3 is not satisfied by these statutes, information cannot be withheld pursuant to them, even though they were enacted after the FOIA.[141]

Yet the D.C. Circuit has held that the procedures of the Presidential Recordings and Materials Preservation Act[142] exclusively govern the disclosure of transcripts of the tape recordings of President Nixon's White House conversa-

---

[137] Osborn v. IRS, 754 F.2d 195, 197-98 (6th Cir. 1985).

[138] Currie, 704 F.2d at 528; accord Grasso, 785 F.2d at 74; Long, 742 F.2d at 1177 (also rejecting section 701 of Economic Recovery Tax Act, 26 U.S.C. § 6103(b)(2) (1994), as "displacement" statute); Linsteadt, 729 F.2d at 1001-02; see also Britt v. IRS, 547 F. Supp. 808, 813 (D.D.C. 1982); Tigar & Buffone v. CIA, 2 Gov't Disclosure Serv. (P-H) ¶ 81,172, at 81,461 (D.D.C. Feb. 23, 1981).

[139] Church of Scientology v. IRS, 792 F.2d 146, 148-50 (D.C. Cir. 1986).

[140] 22 U.S.C. § 2671 (1994 & Supp. IV 1998); 31 U.S.C. § 3526 (1994).

[141] See Washington Post Co. v. United States Dep't of State, 685 F.2d 698, 703-04 & n.9 (D.C. Cir. 1982), cert. granted, 464 U.S. 812, vacated & remanded, 464 U.S. 979 (1983); see also FOIA Update, Vol. IV, No. 4, at 11 (noting that Supreme Court granted government's petition for certiorari, Washington Post Company withdrew its FOIA request, which had procedural effect of nullifying D.C. Circuit's decision, and that Supreme Court thus has never substantively reviewed issue); cf. United States Dep't of Justice v. Tax Analysts, 492 U.S. 136, 153-54 (1989) (holding that FOIA, not 28 U.S.C. § 1914 (1994), governs disclosure of court records in possession of government agencies); Paisley v. CIA, 712 F.2d 686, 697 (D.C. Cir. 1983) (stating that FOIA, not Speech or Debate Clause, is definitive word on disclosure of information within government's possession); Church of Scientology v. United States Postal Serv., 633 F.2d 1327, 1333 (9th Cir. 1980) (finding that postal statute does not displace more detailed and later-enacted FOIA absent specific indication of congressional intent to that effect).

[142] 44 U.S.C. § 2111 (1994 & Supp. III 1997).

**EXEMPTION 3**

tions, based upon that Act's comprehensive, carefully tailored procedure for releasing Presidential materials to the public.[143] Thus, the "displacement" theory may still be advanced for statutes which provide procedures for the release of information to the public that, in essence, duplicate the procedures provided by the FOIA,[144] or for statutes that comprehensively override the FOIA's access scheme.[145] In this connection, it should be noted that the FOIA's specific fee provision referring to other statutes that set fees for particular types of records[146] has the effect of causing those statutes to "displace" the FOIA's basic fee provisions.[147] (For a further discussion of this point, see Fees and Fee Waivers, below.)

---

[143] Ricchio v. Kline, 773 F.2d 1389, 1395 (D.C. Cir. 1985); cf. Katz v. NARA, 68 F.3d 1438, 1440-42 (D.C. Cir. 1995) (holding certain President John F. Kennedy autopsy material to be personal presidential papers not subject to FOIA).

[144] See Church of Scientology, 792 F.2d at 149 (dictum).

[145] See Ricchio, 773 F.2d at 1395; cf. Essential Info., Inc. v. USIA, 134 F.3d 1165, 1169-70 (D.C. Cir. 1998) (Henderson, J., concurring) (suggesting displacement theory as alternate ground for affirming agency withholding); SDC Dev. Corp. v. Mathews, 542 F.2d 1116, 1120 (9th Cir. 1976) (reaching "displacement-type" result for records governed by National Library of Medicine Act, 42 U.S.C. § 275 (1994)); Jones v. OSHA, No. 94-3225, slip op. at 7 (W.D. Mo. June 6, 1995) (requiring release of employee complaints where Occupational Safety and Health Act provided for disclosure); Gersh & Danielson v. EPA, 871 F. Supp. 407, 410 (D. Colo. 1994) (holding FOIA exemptions inapplicable where in conflict with disclosure provisions of Clean Water Act); FOIA Update, Vol. XI, No. 3, at 7-8 n.32. But cf. Minier v. CIA, 88 F.3d 796, 802 (9th Cir. 1996) ("[T]he JFK Act [President John F. Kennedy Assassination Records Collection Act, 44 U.S.C. § 2107 (1994 & Supp. III 1997)], by its own terms, is an entirely separate scheme from the FOIA"; however, "there is nothing to suggest that Congress intended the JFK Act to override the CIA's ability to claim proper FOIA exemptions." (citing Assassination Archives & Research Ctr. v. United States Dep't of Justice, 43 F.3d 1542, 1544 (D.C. Cir. 1995))); accord Winterstein v. United States Dep't of Justice, 89 F. Supp. 2d 79, 82-83 (D.D.C. 2000) (ruling that existence of Nazi War Crimes Disclosure Act, 5 U.S.C.A. § 552 note (West Supp. 1999), is not relevant to FOIA request for record pertaining to alleged Nazi war criminal except to extent that Congress's exclusion of particular class of records from Nazi War Crimes Disclosure Act was probative on question of whether Congress considered withholding of record to be in public interest).

[146] 5 U.S.C. § 552(a)(4)(A)(vi) (1994 & Supp. IV 1998).

[147] See Uniform Freedom of Information Act Fee Schedule and Guidelines, 52 Fed. Reg. 10,012-13 (1987) (implementing 5 U.S.C. § 552(a)(4)(A)(vi)); see also, e.g., Wade v. United States Dep't of Commerce, No. 96-0717, slip op. at 5-6 (D.D.C. Mar. 26, 1998) (recognizing that statute authorizing National Technical Information Service (NTIS) to establish its own fee schedule, 15 U.S.C. § 1153 (1994), supersedes standard FOIA fee provisions).

**EXEMPTION 3**

## Additional Considerations

Certain statutes fail to meet the requisites of either Exemption 3 prong. For instance, the Court of Appeals for the District of Columbia Circuit, in holding that provisions governing the FBI's sharing of "rap sheets"[148] do not qualify as an Exemption 3 statute because they do not expressly prohibit the disclosure of "rap sheets," explained that even if the provisions met the exemption's threshold requirement, they would not qualify as an Exemption 3 statute as they fail to satisfy either of its subparts.[149] Likewise, the Copyright Act of 1976[150] has been held to satisfy neither Exemption 3 subpart because, rather than prohibiting disclosure, it specifically permits public inspection of copyrighted documents.[151]

It has also been held that section 360j(h) of the Medical Device Amendments of 1976[152] is not an Exemption 3 statute because it does not specifically prohibit the disclosure of records,[153] nor is section 410(c)(6) of the Postal Reorganization Act,[154] because the broad discretion afforded the Postal Service to release or withhold records is not sufficiently specific.[155] Similarly, section 1106 of the Social Security Act[156] is not an Exemption 3 statute because it gives the Secretary of Health and Human Services wide discretion to enact regulations specifically permitting disclosure.[157] The Federal Insecticide, Fungicide,

---

[148] 28 U.S.C. § 534 (1994 & Supp. III 1997).

[149] Reporters Comm. for Freedom of the Press v. United States Dep't of Justice, 816 F.2d 730, 736 n.9 (D.C. Cir.), modified on other grounds, 831 F.2d 1124 (D.C. Cir. 1987), rev'd on other grounds, 489 U.S. 749 (1989).

[150] 17 U.S.C. § 705(b) (1994).

[151] See St. Paul's Benevolent Educ. & Missionary Inst. v. United States, 506 F. Supp. 822, 830 (N.D. Ga. 1980); see also FOIA Update, Vol. IV, No. 4, at 3-5 ("OIP Guidance: Copyrighted Materials and the FOIA") (emphasizing Copyright Act should not be treated as Exemption 3 statute and copyrighted records should be processed under Exemption 4 instead); accord Gilmore v. United States Dep't of Energy, 4 F. Supp. 2d 912, 922-23 (N.D. Cal. 1998) (alternate holding) (protecting copyrighted computer software pursuant to Exemption 4); FOIA Update, Vol. XVIII, No. 1, at 5-6 (cautioning agencies to "guard against the possibility that [Internet] dissemination of [reading room records] might be regarded as copyright infringement" in exceptional cases).

[152] 21 U.S.C. § 360j(h) (1994 & Supp. IV 1998).

[153] See Public Citizen Health Research Group v. FDA, 704 F.2d 1280, 1286 (D.C. Cir. 1983).

[154] 39 U.S.C. § 410(c)(6) (1994).

[155] See Church of Scientology v. United States Postal Serv., 633 F.2d 1327, 1333 (9th Cir. 1980).

[156] 42 U.S.C. § 1306 (1994).

[157] See Robbins v. HHS, No. 95-cv-3258, slip op. at 3-4 (N.D. Ga. Aug. 13, (continued...)

## EXEMPTION 3

and Rodenticide Act[158] also does not satisfy either prong of Exemption 3 because the withholding of certain information is entirely discretionary under that Act.[159]

A particularly difficult Exemption 3 issue was finally put to rest by the Supreme Court in 1988. In analyzing the applicability of Exemption 3 to the Parole Commission and Reorganization Act[160] and Rule 32 of the Federal Rules of Criminal Procedure, each of which governs the disclosure of presentence reports, the Supreme Court decisively held that they are Exemption 3 statutes only in part.[161] The Court found that they do not permit the withholding of an entire presentence report, but rather only those portions of a presentence report pertaining to a probation officer's sentencing recommendations, certain diagnostic opinions, information obtained upon a promise of confidentiality, and information which, if disclosed, might result in harm to any person, and that "the remaining parts of the reports are not covered by this exemption, and thus must be disclosed unless there is some other exemption which applies to them."[162]

Another Exemption 3 issue concerns the Trade Secrets Act[163] which prohibits the unauthorized disclosure of certain commercial and financial information. Although the Supreme Court has declined to decide whether the Trade Secrets Act is an Exemption 3 statute,[164] most courts confronted with the issue have held that it is not.[165]

---

(...continued)
1996), aff'd per curiam, No. 96-9000 (11th Cir. July 8, 1997).

[158] 7 U.S.C. § 136h(d) (1994).

[159] See Northwest Coalition for Alternatives to Pesticides v. Browner, 941 F. Supp. 197, 201 (D.D.C. 1996).

[160] 18 U.S.C. § 4208 (1994) (repealed as to offenses committed after November 1, 1987).

[161] United States Dep't of Justice v. Julian, 486 U.S. 1, 9 (1988).

[162] Id. at 11; see also FOIA Update, Vol. IX, No. 2, at 1-2.

[163] 18 U.S.C. § 1905 (1994 & Supp. IV 1998).

[164] Chrysler Corp. v. Brown, 441 U.S. 281, 319 n.49 (1979).

[165] See, e.g., Anderson v. HHS, 907 F.2d 936, 949 (10th Cir. 1990) ("[T]he broad and ill-defined wording of § 1905 fails to meet either of the requirements of Exemption 3."); Acumenics Research & Tech. v. United States Dep't of Justice, 843 F.2d 800, 805 n.6, 806 (4th Cir. 1988) (finding "no basis" for argument that Exemption 3 and § 1905 prevent disclosure of information that is outside scope of Exemption 4); General Elec. Co. v. NRC, 750 F.2d 1394, 1401-02 (7th Cir. 1984) (same); accord FOIA Update, Vol. VI, No. 3, at 3 ("OIP Guidance: Discretionary Disclosure and Exemption 4"); see also 9 to 5 Org. of Women Office Workers v. Board of Governors of the Fed. Reserve Sys., 721 F.2d 1, 12 (1st Cir. 1983) (specifically declining to address issue).

**EXEMPTION 3**

In 1987, the D.C. Circuit issued a decision that "definitively" resolved the issue by holding that the Trade Secrets Act does not satisfy either of amended Exemption 3's requirements and thus does not qualify as a separate withholding statute.[166] First, its prohibition against disclosure is not absolute, as it prohibits only those disclosures that are "not authorized by law."[167] Because duly promulgated agency regulations can provide the necessary authorization for release, the agency "possesses discretion to control the applicability" of the Act.[168] The existence of this discretion precludes the Trade Secrets Act from satisfying subpart (A) of Exemption 3.[169] Moreover, the court held that the Trade Secrets Act fails to satisfy the first prong of subpart (B) because it "in no way channels the discretion of agency decisionmakers."[170] Indeed, the court concluded, this utter lack of statutory guidance renders the Trade Secrets Act susceptible to invocation at the "whim of an administrator."[171] Finally, it was held that the Act also fails to satisfy the second prong of subpart (B) because of the "encyclopedic character" of the material within its scope and the absence of any limitation on the agencies covered or the sources of data included.[172] Given all these elements, the court held that the Trade Secrets Act simply does not qualify as an Exemption 3 statute.[173] This followed the Department of Justice's stated policy position on the issue.[174]

The D.C. Circuit's decision on this issue is entirely consistent with the legislative history of the 1976 amendment to Exemption 3, which states that the Trade Secrets Act was not intended to qualify as a nondisclosure statute under the exemption and that any analysis of trade secrets and commercial or financial information should focus instead on the applicability of Exemption 4.[175] However, some confidential business information now may be protected by the National Defense Authorization Act for Fiscal Year 1997.[176] This stat-

---

[166] See CNA Fin. Corp. v. Donovan, 830 F.2d 1132, 1137-43 (D.C. Cir. 1987).

[167] Id. at 1138.

[168] Id. at 1139.

[169] Id. at 1138.

[170] Id. at 1139.

[171] Id.

[172] Id. at 1140-41.

[173] Id. at 1141.

[174] See FOIA Update, Vol. VII, No. 3, at 6 (advising that Trade Secrets Act should not be regarded as Exemption 3 statute).

[175] See H.R. Rep. No. 94-880, at 23 (1976), reprinted in 1976 U.S.C.C.A.N. 2191, 2205; see also Anderson, 907 F.2d at 949-50; Acumenics, 843 F.2d at 805 n.6; CNA, 830 F.2d at 1142 n.70; General Elec., 750 F.2d at 1401-02; General Dynamics Corp. v. Marshall, 607 F.2d 234, 236-37 (8th Cir. 1979).

[176] See Pub. L. No. 104-201, § 821, 110 Stat. 2422 (containing parallel measures applicable to armed services and most civilian agencies) (codified at 10 (continued...)

## EXEMPTION 3

ute, enacted in 1996, provides blanket protection for the proposals of unsuccessful offerors submitted in response to a solicitation for a competitive proposal.[177] Under it, a successful offeror's proposal is also protected if it is not "set forth or incorporated by reference" in the final contract;[178] the key determinant of exempt status is whether the proposal was actually set forth in or incorporated into the contract.[179]

Lastly, a particularly controversial issue at one time was whether the Privacy Act of 1974[180] could serve as an Exemption 3 statute. The Privacy Act authorizes an individual to obtain access to those federal records maintained under the individual's name or personal identifier, subject to certain broad, system-wide exemptions.[181] If the Privacy Act had been regarded as an Exemption 3 statute, records exempt from disclosure to first-party requesters under the Privacy Act also would have been exempt under the FOIA; if not, requesters would have been able to obtain information on themselves under the FOIA notwithstanding that such information was exempt under the Privacy Act. In the early 1980s, the Department of Justice took the position that the Privacy Act was an Exemption 3 statute within the first-party requester context.[182] When a conflict subsequently arose among the circuits that considered the proper relationship between these two access statutes, the Supreme Court agreed to resolve the issue.[183] However, these cases became moot when Congress, upon enacting the Central Intelligence Agency Information Act in 1984, explicitly provided that the Privacy Act is not an Exemption 3 statute.[184] Thus, the Supreme Court dismissed the appeals in these cases and this issue has been placed entirely to rest.[185]

---

(...continued)
U.S.C. § 2305(g) (1994 & Supp. IV 1998), amended by Pub. L. No. 106-65, 113 Stat. 512 (Oct. 5, 1999) (extending coverage of statute to all agencies listed in 10 U.S.C. § 2303, notably NASA and Coast Guard), and at 41 U.S.C. § 253b(m) (1994 & Supp. III 1997)).

[177] Id.

[178] Id.; see FOIA Update, Vol. XVIII, No. 1, at 2 (describing provisions of relatively new statutes, which have not yet been subject to Exemption 3 litigation).

[179] See FOIA Update, Vol. XVIII, No. 1, at 2.

[180] 5 U.S.C. § 552a (1994 & Supp. IV 1998).

[181] See, e.g., 5 U.S.C. § 552a(j)(2).

[182] See FOIA Update, Vol. IV, No. 2, at 3.

[183] Provenzano v. United States Dep't of Justice, 717 F.2d 799 (3d Cir. 1983), cert. granted, 466 U.S. 926 (1984); Shapiro v. DEA, 721 F.2d 215 (7th Cir. 1983), cert. granted, 466 U.S. 926 (1984).

[184] Pub. L. No. 98-477, § 2(c), 98 Stat. 2209, 2212 (1984) (amending what is now subsection (t) of Privacy Act).

[185] United States Dep't of Justice v. Provenzano, 469 U.S. 14 (1984); FOIA
(continued...)

# EXEMPTION 4

Exemption 4 of the FOIA protects "trade secrets and commercial or financial information obtained from a person [that is] privileged or confidential."[1] This exemption is intended to protect the interests of both the government and submitters of information. Its existence encourages submitters to voluntarily furnish useful commercial or financial information to the government and it correspondingly provides the government with an assurance that such information will be reliable. The exemption also affords protection to those submitters who are required to furnish commercial or financial information to the government by safeguarding them from the competitive disadvantages that could result from disclosure. The exemption covers two broad categories of information in federal agency records: (1) trade secrets; and (2) information that is (a) commercial or financial, and (b) obtained from a person, and (c) privileged or confidential.

## Trade Secrets

For purposes of Exemption 4, the Court of Appeals for the District of Columbia Circuit in Public Citizen Health Research Group v. FDA,[2] has adopted a narrow "common law" definition of the term "trade secret" that differs from the broad definition used in the Restatement of Torts. The D.C. Circuit's decision in Public Citizen represented a distinct departure from what until then had been almost universally accepted by the courts--that "trade secret" is a broad term extending to virtually any information that provides a competitive advantage. In Public Citizen, the term "trade secret" was narrowly defined as "a secret, commercially valuable plan, formula, process, or device that is used for the making, preparing, compounding, or processing of trade commodities and that can be said to be the end product of either innovation or substantial effort."[3] This definition requires that there be a "direct relationship" between the trade secret and the productive process.[4]

The Court of Appeals for the Tenth Circuit has expressly adopted the D.C. Circuit's narrow definition of the term "trade secret," finding it "more consistent with the policies behind the FOIA than the broad Restatement definition."[5] In so doing, the Tenth Circuit noted that adoption of the broader Restatement definition "would render superfluous" the remaining category of

---

(...continued)
Update, Vol. V, No. 4, at 4. But see Hill v. Blevins, No. 92-0859 (M.D. Pa. Apr. 12, 1993) (incorrectly holding subsection (f)(3) of Privacy Act, which authorizes agency to establish procedures for disclosure of medical and psychological records, to be exempting statute under FOIA), aff'd, 19 F.3d 643 (3d Cir. 1994) (unpublished table decision).

[1] 5 U.S.C. § 552(b)(4) (1994 & Supp. IV 1998).

[2] 704 F.2d 1280, 1288 (D.C. Cir. 1983).

[3] Id.

[4] Id.

[5] Anderson v. HHS, 907 F.2d 936, 944 (10th Cir. 1990).

## EXEMPTION 4

Exemption 4 information "because there would be no category of information falling within the latter" category that would be "outside" the reach of the trade secret category.[6] Like the D.C. Circuit, the Tenth Circuit was "reluctant to construe the FOIA in such a manner."[7]

Trade secret protection has been recognized for product manufacturing and design information,[8] but has been denied for general information concerning a product's physical or performance characteristics or a product formula when release would not reveal the actual formula itself.[9]

### Commercial or Financial Information

The overwhelming bulk of Exemption 4 cases focus on whether the withheld information falls within its second, much larger category. To do so, the information must be commercial or financial, obtained from a person, and

---

[6] Id.

[7] Id.

[8] See, e.g., Center for Auto Safety v. National Highway Traffic Safety Admin., No. 99-1759, 2000 WL 359622, at **13-15 (D.D.C. Feb. 28, 2000) (tear pattern, fold pattern, number and location of tethers, type of inflator, gas generant used, number of inflation stages, tank tests used to measure inflator characteristics, and engineering specifications for automobile air bags) (appeal pending); Heeney v. FDA, No. 97-5461, slip op. at 12-13 & n.13 (C.D. Cal. Mar. 18, 1999) ("compliance testing" and "specification of the materials used in constructing" electrode catheter) (appeal pending); Sokolow v. FDA, No. 1:97-CV-252, slip op. at 7 (E.D. Tex. Feb. 19, 1998) (description of how drug is manufactured, including "analytical methods employed to assure quality and consistency" and "results of stability testing"), aff'd, 162 F.3d 1160 (5th Cir. 1998) (unpublished table decision); Citizens Comm'n on Human Rights v. FDA, No. 92-5313, slip op. at 14 (C.D. Cal. May 10, 1993) ("information about how a pioneer drug product is formulated, chemically composed, manufactured, and quality controlled"), aff'd in part & remanded in part on other grounds, 45 F.3d 1325 (9th Cir. 1995); Pacific Sky Supply, Inc. v. Department of the Air Force, No. 86-2044, 1987 WL 25456, at *1 (D.D.C. Nov. 20, 1987) (design drawings of airplane fuel pumps developed by private company and used by Air Force), modifying No. 86-2044, 1987 WL 18214 (D.D.C. Sept. 29, 1987), on motion to amend judgment, No. 86-2044, 1987 WL 28485 (D.D.C. Dec. 16, 1987); see also Yamamoto v. IRS, No. 83-2160, slip op. at 2 (D.D.C. Nov. 16, 1983) (report on computation of standard mileage rate prepared by private company and used by IRS); cf. Myers v. Williams, 819 F. Supp. 919 (D. Or. 1993) (preliminary injunction granted to prevent FOIA requester from disclosing trade secret acquired through mistaken, but nonetheless official, FOIA release) (non-FOIA case).

[9] See Center for Auto Safety, 2000 WL 359622, at *13 (air bag characteristics "not directly related to the production process"); Northwest Coalition for Alternatives to Pesticides v. Browner, 941 F. Supp. 197, 201-02 (D.D.C. 1996) ("common names and Chemical Abstract System (CAS) numbers of the inert ingredients" contained in pesticide formulas).

**EXEMPTION 4**

privileged or confidential.[10]

If information relates to business or trade, courts have little difficulty in considering it "commercial or financial."[11] The Court of Appeals for the District of Columbia Circuit has firmly held that these terms should be given their "ordinary meanings" and has specifically rejected the argument that the term "commercial" be confined to records that "reveal basic commercial operations," holding instead that records are commercial so long as the submitter has a "commercial interest" in them.[12] Similarly, in a case involving information submitted by a labor union, the Court of Appeals for the Second Circuit held that the term "commercial" includes anything "pertaining or relating to or dealing with commerce."[13] Indeed, commercial information can include

---

[10] See, e.g., Gulf & Western Indus. v. United States, 615 F.2d 527, 529 (D.C. Cir. 1979); Consumers Union v. VA, 301 F. Supp. 796, 802 (S.D.N.Y. 1969), appeal dismissed as moot, 436 F.2d 1363 (2d Cir. 1971).

[11] See, e.g., Lepelletier v. FDIC, 977 F. Supp. 456, 459 (D.D.C. 1997) ("identities of businesses having unclaimed deposits" deemed "financial information"), aff'd in part, rev'd in part & remanded on other grounds, 164 F.3d 37 (D.C. Cir. 1999); Cohen v. Kessler, No. 95-6140, slip op. at 9 (D.N.J. Nov. 25, 1996) ("rat study's raw data" submitted to support application for approval of new animal drug held "clearly commercial in nature" because data was "valuable to [submitter's] business activities"); Bangor Hydro-Elec. Co. v. United States Dep't of the Interior, No. 94-0173-B, slip op. at 7 (D. Me. Apr. 18, 1995) ("information relating to proposed [land] usage charges would be 'financial' as that term is commonly understood"); Allnet Communication Servs. v. FCC, 800 F. Supp. 984, 988 (D.D.C. 1992), aff'd, No. 92-5351 (D.C. Cir. May 27, 1994); RMS Indus. v. DOD, No. C-92-1545, slip op. at 6 (N.D. Cal. Nov. 24, 1992) ("interim pricing, type and quality of machines owned" and names and background of key employees and suppliers "is all financial because it directly reflects the financial capability of the companies to perform" government contract and was obtained "in the bidding and award process"); ISC Group v. DOD, No. 88-0631, 1989 WL 168858, at **2-3 (D.D.C. May 22, 1989) (investigative report concerning allegations of overcharging on government contract found "commercial or financial"); M/A-COM Info. Sys. v. HHS, 656 F. Supp. 691, 692 (D.D.C. 1986) (settlement negotiation documents reflecting "accounting and other internal procedures" deemed "commercial" as submitter had "commercial interest" in them); see also FOIA Update, Vol. VI, No. 1, at 3-4 ("OIP Guidance: Protecting Intrinsic Commercial Value"); FOIA Update, Vol. IV, No. 4, at 3-5 ("OIP Guidance: Copyrighted Materials and the FOIA"). But see Washington Research Project, Inc. v. HEW, 504 F.2d 238, 244-45 (D.C. Cir. 1974) (scientific research designs submitted in grant applications held not "commercial" absent showing that research itself had any commercial character).

[12] Public Citizen Health Research Group v. FDA, 704 F.2d 1280, 1290 (D.C. Cir. 1983) (citing Washington Post Co. v. HHS, 690 F.2d 252, 266 (D.C. Cir. 1982), and Board of Trade v. Commodity Futures Trading Comm'n, 627 F.2d 392, 403 (D.C. Cir. 1980)).

[13] American Airlines, Inc. v. National Mediation Bd., 588 F.2d 863, 870 (2d (continued...)

## EXEMPTION 4

even material submitted by a nonprofit entity.[14]

Despite the widely accepted breadth of the term, one court rejected an agency's determination that "factual information regarding the nature and frequency of in-flight medical emergencies"[15] qualified as "commercial information" for purposes of Exemption 4, finding that "medical emergencies detailed in the documents do not naturally flow from commercial flight operations, but rather are chance events which happened to occur while the airplanes were in flight."[16] In delimiting the scope of the term "commercial," the court opined that "[t]he mere fact that an event occurs in connection with a commercial operation does not automatically transform documents regarding that event into commercial information."[17]

Protection for financial information is not limited to economic data generated solely by corporations or other business entities, but rather has been held to apply to personal financial information as well.[18] Examples of items regarded as commercial or financial information include: business sales statistics; research data; technical designs; customer and supplier lists; profit and loss data; overhead and operating costs; and information on financial

---

(...continued)
Cir. 1978); see also Hustead v. Norwood, 529 F. Supp. 323, 326 (S.D. Fla. 1981) ("information relating to the employment and unemployment of workers constitutes commercial or financial information"); Brockway v. Department of the Air Force, 370 F. Supp. 738, 740 (N.D. Iowa 1974) (reports generated by a commercial enterprise "must generally be considered commercial information"), rev'd on other grounds, 518 F.2d 1184 (8th Cir. 1975).

[14] See Critical Mass Energy Project v. NRC, 975 F.2d 871, 880 (D.C. Cir. 1992) (en banc) (safety reports submitted by nonprofit consortium of nuclear power plants deemed "commercial in nature"); see also Sharyland Water Supply Corp. v. Block, 755 F.2d 397, 398 (5th Cir. 1985) (audit reports submitted by nonprofit water supply company deemed "clearly commercial"); American Airlines, 588 F.2d at 870 (employee "authorization cards" submitted by nonprofit union deemed "commercial").

[15] Chicago Tribune Co. v. FAA, No. 97 C 2363, 1998 WL 242611, at *3 (N.D. Ill. May 7, 1998).

[16] Id. at *2.

[17] Id.; see also Animal Legal Defense Fund, Inc. v. Department of the Air Force, 44 F. Supp. 2d 295, 303 (D.D.C. 1999) (denying summary judgment when agency's declaration merely "state[d]" that withheld documents "contain 'commercial and financial information,'" but failed to provide a "description of the documents to permit the [requester] or [the] Court to test the accuracy of that claim").

[18] See Washington Post, 690 F.2d at 266; FOIA Update, Vol. IV, No. 4, at 14. But see Washington Post, 690 F.2d at 266 (list of nonfederal employment positions held not "financial" within meaning of Exemption 4).

**EXEMPTION 4**

condition.[19]

## Obtained from a "Person"

The second of Exemption 4's specific criteria, that the information be "obtained from a person," is quite easily met in almost all circumstances. The term "person" refers to a wide range of entities,[20] including corporations, banks, state governments, agencies of foreign governments, and Native American tribes or nations.[21] The courts have held, however, that information generated by the federal government is not "obtained from a person" and is therefore excluded from Exemption 4's coverage.[22] Such information might possibly be protectible under Exemption 5, though, which incorporates a qualified privilege for sensitive commercial or financial information generated by the government.[23] (For a further discussion of the "commercial privilege," see

---

[19] See, e.g., Landfair v. United States Dep't of the Army, 645 F. Supp. 325, 327 (D.D.C. 1986).

[20] See, e.g., Nadler v. FDIC, 92 F.3d 93, 95 (2d Cir. 1996) (term "person" includes "'an individual, partnership, corporation, association, or public or private organization other than an agency'" (quoting definition found in Administrative Procedure Act, 5 U.S.C. § 551(2) (1994))); Goldstein v. HHS, No. 92-2013, slip op. at 4 (S.D. Fla. May 21, 1993) (magistrate's recommendation) ("term 'person' encompasses individuals, partnerships, corporations, and associations" (likewise quoting Administrative Procedure Act definition)), adopted (S.D. Fla. July 21, 1993).

[21] See, e.g., Stone v. Export-Import Bank, 552 F.2d 132, 137 (5th Cir. 1977) (foreign government agency); Lepelletier v. FDIC, 977 F. Supp. 456, 459 (D.D.C. 1997) (banks), aff'd in part, rev'd in part & remanded on other grounds, 164 F.3d 37 (D.C. Cir. 1999); Bangor Hydro-Elec. Co. v. United States Dep't of the Interior, No. 94-0173-B, slip op. at 7 (D. Me. Apr. 18, 1995) ("parties do not contest that the Penobscot Nation is a 'person' for purposes of exemption 4" (citing Indian Law Resource Ctr. v. Department of the Interior, 477 F. Supp. 144, 146 (D.D.C. 1979) ("The Hopi Tribe, as a corporation that is not part of the Federal Government, is plainly a person within the meaning of the Act."))); Hustead v. Norwood, 529 F. Supp. 323, 326 (S.D. Fla. 1981) (state government); Comstock Int'l, Inc. v. Export-Import Bank, 464 F. Supp. 804, 806 (D.D.C. 1979) (corporation); Neal-Cooper Grain Co. v. Kissinger, 385 F. Supp. 769, 776 (D.D.C. 1974) (foreign government or instrumentality).

[22] See Allnet Communication Servs. v. FCC, 800 F. Supp. 984, 988 (D.D.C. 1992) ("person" under Exemption 4 "refers to a wide range of entities including corporations, associations and public or private organizations other than agencies"), aff'd, No. 92-5351 (D.C. Cir. May 27, 1994); see also, e.g., Board of Trade v. Commodity Futures Trading Comm'n, 627 F.2d 392, 404 (D.C. Cir. 1980); Buffalo Evening News, Inc. v. SBA, 666 F. Supp. 467, 469 (W.D.N.Y. 1987); Consumers Union v. VA, 301 F. Supp. 796, 803 (S.D.N.Y. 1969), appeal dismissed as moot, 436 F.2d 1363 (2d Cir. 1971).

[23] See Federal Open Mkt. Comm. v. Merrill, 443 U.S. 340, 360 (1979); Morrison-Knudsen Co. v. Department of the Army of the United States, 595 F.
(continued...)

# EXEMPTION 4

Exemption 5, Other Privileges, below.)

Documents prepared by the government can still come within Exemption 4, however, if they simply contain summaries or reformulations of information supplied by a source outside the government.[24] Moreover, the mere fact that the government supervises or directs the preparation of information submitted by sources outside the government does not preclude that information from being "obtained from a person."[25]

## "Confidential" Information

The third requirement of Exemption 4 is met if information is "privileged or confidential." By far, most Exemption 4 litigation has focused on whether or not requested information is "confidential" for purposes of Exemption 4. In earlier years, courts based the application of Exemption 4 upon whether there was a promise of confidentiality by the government to the submitting party,[26] or whether the information was of the type not customarily released to the public by the submitter.[27]

---

(...continued)
Supp. 352, 354-56 (D.D.C. 1984), aff'd, 762 F.2d 138 (D.C. Cir. 1985).

[24] See, e.g., Gulf & Western Indus. v. United States, 615 F.2d 527, 529-30 (D.C. Cir. 1979) (contractor information contained in agency audit report); Matthews v. United States Postal Serv., No. 92-1208-CV-W-8, slip op. at 6 (W.D. Mo. Apr. 15, 1994) (technical drawings prepared by agency personnel, but based upon information supplied by computer company); Mulloy v. Consumer Prod. Safety Comm'n, No. 85-645, 1985 U.S. Dist. LEXIS 17194, at *2 (S.D. Ohio Aug. 2, 1985) (manufacturing and sales data compiled in Establishment Inspection Report prepared by Commission investigator after on-site visit to plant), aff'd, No. 85-3720 (6th Cir. July 22, 1986); BDM Corp. v. SBA, 2 Gov't Disclosure Serv. (P-H) ¶ 81,044, at 81,121 (D.D.C. Dec. 4, 1980) (contractor information contained in agency documents). But see Philadelphia Newspapers, Inc. v. HHS, 69 F. Supp. 2d 63, 67 (D.D.C. 1999) (characterizing agency audit as "not simply a summary or reformulation of information supplied by a source outside the government" and finding that an analysis "prepared by the government" is not "'obtained from a person'" and so "may not be withheld under Exemption 4"), appeal dismissed per stipulation, No. 99-5335 (D.C. Cir. Mar. 17, 2000).

[25] See Silverberg v. HHS, No. 89-2743, 1991 WL 633740, at *2 (D.D.C. June 14, 1991), appeal dismissed per stipulation, No. 91-5255 (D.C. Cir. Sept. 2, 1993); Daniels Mfg. Corp. v. DOD, No. 85-291, slip op. at 4 (M.D. Fla. June 3, 1986). But see Consumers Union, 301 F. Supp. at 803 (when product testing was actually performed by government personnel, using their expertise and government equipment, resulting data held not "obtained from a person" for purposes of Exemption 4).

[26] See, e.g., GSA v. Benson, 415 F.2d 878, 881 (9th Cir. 1969).

[27] See, e.g., Sterling Drug, Inc. v. FTC, 450 F.2d 698, 709 (D.C. Cir. 1971); M.A. Schapiro & Co. v. SEC, 339 F. Supp. 467, 471 (D.D.C. 1972).

# EXEMPTION 4

These earlier tests were then superseded by the rule of National Parks & Conservation Ass'n v. Morton,[28] long considered to be the leading case on the issue, which significantly altered the test for confidentiality under Exemption 4. In National Parks, the Court of Appeals for the District of Columbia Circuit held that the test for confidentiality was an objective one.[29] Thus, whether information would customarily be disclosed to the public by the person from whom it was obtained was not considered dispositive.[30] Likewise, an agency's promise that information would not be released was not considered dispositive.[31] Instead, the D.C. Circuit declared in National Parks that the term "confidential" should be read to protect governmental interests as well as private ones, according to the following two-part test:

> To summarize, commercial or financial matter is "confidential" for purposes of the exemption if disclosure of the information is likely to have either of the following effects: (1) to impair the Government's ability to obtain necessary information in the future; or (2) to cause substantial harm to the competitive position of the person from whom the information was obtained.[32]

These two principal Exemption 4 tests, which apply disjunctively, have often been referred to in subsequent cases as the "impairment prong" and the "competitive harm prong." In National Parks, the D.C. Circuit expressly reserved the question of whether any other governmental interests--such as compliance or program effectiveness--might also be embodied in a "third prong" of the exemption.[33] (For a further discussion of this point, see Exemption 4, Third Prong of National Parks, below.)

Seventeen years later, in a surprising development, D.C. Circuit Court Judge Randolph, joined by Circuit Court Judge Williams, suggested in a concurring opinion in Critical Mass Energy Project v. NRC, that if it were a question of first impression, they would "apply the common meaning of [the word] 'confidential' and [would] reject" the National Parks test altogether.[34] Judges Randolph and Williams contended that there was no "legitimate basis" for the D.C. Circuit's addition of "some two-pronged 'objective' test" for determining if material was "confidential" in light of the unambiguous language of the ex-

---

[28] 498 F.2d 765 (D.C. Cir. 1974).

[29] Id. at 766.

[30] Id. at 767.

[31] See Washington Post Co. v. HHS, 690 F.2d 252, 268 (D.C. Cir. 1982) (citing National Parks, 498 F.2d at 766).

[32] 498 F.2d at 770.

[33] Id. at 770 n.17.

[34] 931 F.2d 939, 948 (D.C. Cir.) (Randolph & Williams, JJ., concurring), vacated & reh'g en banc granted, 942 F.2d 799 (D.C. Cir. 1991), grant of summary judgment to agency aff'd en banc, 975 F.2d 871 (D.C. Cir. 1992).

# EXEMPTION 4

emption.[35] Nevertheless, they recognized that they "were not at liberty" to apply their "common sense" definition because the D.C. Circuit had "endorsed the National Parks definition many times," thus compelling them to follow it as well.[36] Thereafter, the government petitioned for, and was granted, an en banc rehearing in Critical Mass[37] so that the full D.C. Circuit could have an opportunity to consider whether the definition of confidentiality set forth in National Parks--and followed by the panel majority in Critical Mass--was indeed faithful to the language and legislative intent of Exemption 4.[38]

In August of 1992, the D.C. Circuit issued its en banc decision in Critical Mass. After examining the "arguments in favor of overturning National Parks, [the court] conclude[d] that none justifies the abandonment of so well established a precedent."[39] This ruling was founded on the principle of stare decisis--which counsels against the overruling of an established precedent.[40] The D.C. Circuit determined that "[i]n obedience to" stare decisis, it would not "set aside circuit precedent of almost twenty years' standing."[41] In so holding, it noted the "widespread acceptance of National Parks by [the] other circuits," the lack of any subsequent action by Congress that would remove the "'conceptual underpinnings'" of the decision, and the fact that the test had not proven to be "so flawed that [the court] would be justified in setting it aside."[42]

Although the National Parks test for confidentiality under Exemption 4 was thus reaffirmed, the full D.C. Circuit went on to "correct some misunderstandings as to its scope and application."[43] Specifically, the court "confined" the reach of National Parks and established an entirely new standard to be used for determining whether information "voluntarily" submitted to an agency is "confidential."[44] The United States Supreme Court declined to review the D.C. Circuit's en banc decision[45] and it now stands as the leading Exemption 4 case on this issue.[46]

---

[35] Id.

[36] Id.

[37] 942 F.2d 799 (D.C. Cir. 1991).

[38] See FOIA Update, Vol. XIII, No. 4, at 1.

[39] 975 F.2d 871, 877 (D.C. Cir. 1992).

[40] See id. at 875.

[41] Id.

[42] Id. at 876-77 (quoting Patterson v. McLean Credit Union, 491 U.S. 164, 173 (1989)).

[43] Id. at 875.

[44] Id. at 871, 879.

[45] 507 U.S. 984 (1993).

[46] See FOIA Update, Vol. XIV, No. 2, at 1.

**EXEMPTION 4**

## The Critical Mass Decision

Through its en banc decision in <u>Critical Mass Energy Project v. NRC</u>, a seven-to-four majority of the Court of Appeals for the District of Columbia Circuit established two distinct standards to be used in determining whether commercial or financial information submitted to an agency is "confidential" under Exemption 4.[47] Specifically, the tests for confidentiality set forth in <u>National Parks & Conservation Ass'n v. Morton</u>,[48] were confined "to the category of cases to which [they were] first applied; namely, those in which a FOIA request is made for financial or commercial information a person was obliged to furnish the Government."[49] The D.C. Circuit announced an entirely new test for the protection of information that is "voluntarily" submitted: Such information is now categorically protected provided it is not "customarily" disclosed to the public by the submitter.[50]

In reaching this result, the D.C. Circuit first examined the bases for its decision in <u>National Parks</u> and then identified various interests of both the government and submitters of information that are protected by Exemption 4.[51] By so doing, it found that different interests are implicated depending upon whether the requested information was submitted voluntarily or under compulsion.[52] As to the government's interests, the D.C. Circuit found that when submission of the information is "compelled" by the government, the interest protected by nondisclosure is that of ensuring the continued <u>reliability</u> of the information.[53] On the other hand, it concluded, when information is submitted on a "voluntary" basis, the governmental interest protected by nondisclosure is that of ensuring the continued and full <u>availability</u> of the information.[54]

The D.C. Circuit found that this same dichotomy between compelled and voluntary submissions applies to the submitter's interests as well: When submission of information is compelled, the harm to the submitter's interest is the "commercial disadvantage" that is recognized under the <u>National Parks</u>

---

[47] 975 F.2d 871, 879 (D.C. Cir. 1992).

[48] 498 F.2d 765, 770 (D.C. Cir. 1974).

[49] <u>Critical Mass</u>, 975 F.2d at 880.

[50] <u>Id.</u> at 879; <u>accord</u> <u>Bartholdi Cable Co. v. FCC</u>, 114 F.3d 274, 281 (D.C. Cir. 1997) ("The test for whether information is 'confidential' depends in part on whether the information was voluntarily or involuntarily disclosed to the government.") (non-FOIA case brought under Administrative Procedure Act, 5 U.S.C. § 706 (1994)).

[51] <u>Critical Mass</u>, 975 F.2d at 877-79.

[52] <u>Id.</u>

[53] <u>Id.</u> at 878.

[54] <u>Id.</u>

## EXEMPTION 4

"competitive injury" prong.[55] When information is volunteered, on the other hand, the exemption recognizes a different interest of the submitter--that of protecting information that "for whatever reason, 'would customarily not be released to the public by the person from whom it was obtained.'"[56]

Having delineated these various interests that are protected by Exemption 4, the D.C. Circuit then noted that the Supreme Court had "encouraged the development of categorical rules" in FOIA cases "whenever a particular set of facts will lead to a generally predictable application."[57] The court found that the circumstances of the Critical Mass case--which involved voluntarily submitted reports--lent themselves to such "categorical" treatment.[58]

Accordingly, the D.C. Circuit held that it was reaffirming the National Parks test for "determining the confidentiality of information submitted under compulsion," but was announcing a categorical rule for the protection of information provided on a voluntary basis.[59] It declared that such voluntarily provided information is "'confidential' for the purpose of Exemption 4 if it is of a kind that would customarily not be released to the public by the person from whom it was obtained."[60] It also emphasized that this categorical test for voluntarily submitted information is "objective" and that the agency invoking it "must meet the burden of proving the provider's custom."[61]

Applying this test to the information at issue in the Critical Mass case, the D.C. Circuit agreed with the district court's conclusion that the reports were commercial in nature, that they were provided to the agency on a voluntary basis, and that the submitter did not customarily release them to the public.[62] Thus, the reports were found to be confidential and exempt from disclo-

---

[55] Id.

[56] Id. (citing Sterling Drug, Inc. v. FTC, 450 F.2d 698, 709 (D.C. Cir. 1971)).

[57] Id. at 879 (citing United States Dep't of Justice v. Reporters Comm. for Freedom of the Press, 489 U.S. 749 (1989)).

[58] Id.

[59] Id.

[60] Id. But see Lee v. FDIC, 923 F. Supp. 451, 454 (S.D.N.Y. 1996) (misstating (and consequently misapplying) Critical Mass test for withholding voluntary submissions as including additional requirement that "disclosure would likely impair the government's ability to obtain necessary information in the future").

[61] Critical Mass, 975 F.2d at 879.

[62] Id. at 880 (citing first district court decision and first panel decision in Critical Mass, which recognized that submitter made reports available on confidential basis to individuals and organizations involved in nuclear power production process pursuant to explicit nondisclosure policy).

-172-

sure under this new test for Exemption 4.[63]

The D.C. Circuit concluded its opinion by observing the objection raised by the requester in the case that the new test announced by the court "may lead government agencies and industry to conspire to keep information from the public by agreeing to the voluntary submission of information that the agency has the power to compel."[64] The court dismissed this objection on the grounds that there is "no provision in FOIA that obliges agencies to exercise their regulatory authority in a manner that will maximize the amount of information that will be made available to the public through that Act" and that it did not "see any reason to interfere" with an agency's "exercise of its own discretion in determining how it can best secure the information it needs."[65]

### Applying Critical Mass

The pivotal issue that has arisen as a result of the decision in Critical Mass Energy Project v. NRC,[66] is the distinction that the court drew between information "required" to be submitted to an agency and information provided "voluntarily." Although the Court of Appeals for the District of Columbia Circuit never expressly articulated a definition of these two terms in its opinion in Critical Mass, the Department of Justice has issued policy guidance on this subject based upon an extensive analysis of the underlying rationale of the D.C. Circuit's decision, as well as several other indications of the court's intent.[67]

The Department of Justice has concluded that a submitter's voluntary participation in an activity--such as seeking a government contract or applying for a grant or a loan--does not govern whether any submissions made in

---

[63] Id.

[64] Id.

[65] Id.; see Animal Legal Defense Fund v. Secretary of Agric., 813 F. Supp. 882, 892 (D.D.C. 1993) (based upon this holding in Critical Mass, court found that there was "nothing" it could do, "however much it might be inclined to do so," to upset agency regulations that permitted regulated entities to keep documents "on-site," outside possession of agency, and thus unreachable under FOIA) (non-FOIA case brought under Administrative Procedure Act), vacated for lack of standing sub nom. Animal Legal Defense Fund, Inc. v. Espy, 53 F.3d 363 (D.C. Cir. 1994).

[66] 975 F.2d 871 (D.C. Cir. 1992) (en banc).

[67] See FOIA Update, Vol. XIV, No. 2, at 3-5 ("OIP Guidance: The Critical Mass Distinction Under Exemption 4"); see also id. at 6-7 ("Exemption 4 Under Critical Mass: Step-By-Step Decisionmaking"); accord McDonnell Douglas Corp. v. NASA, 895 F. Supp. 316, 317-18 (D.D.C. 1995) (noting that "[a]lthough no bright line rule exists for determining voluntariness, examination of the Critical Mass opinion sheds light on the type of information the D.C. Circuit Court contemplated as being voluntary") (reverse FOIA suit), aff'd on other grounds, No. 95-5290 (D.C. Cir. Sept. 17, 1996).

## EXEMPTION 4

connection with that activity are likewise "voluntary."[68] Rather than examining the nature of a submitter's participation in an activity, agencies are advised to focus on whether submission of the information at issue was required by those who chose to participate.[69] The Department of Justice's policy guidance also points out that information can be "required" to be submitted by a broad range of legal authorities, including informal mandates that call for submission as a condition of doing business with the government.[70] Furthermore, the existence of agency authority to require submission of information does not automatically mean such a submission is "required"; the agency authority must actually be exercised in order for a particular submission to be deemed "required."[71] The net effect under this guidance is that most submissions considered by agencies under Exemption 4 will be considered to be "required" and so will not qualify for the broader protection afforded to "voluntary" submissions under Critical Mass.[72]

There now have been numerous cases in which courts have applied the Critical Mass distinction between "voluntary" and "required" submissions. In one of the first such cases, involving an application for approval to transfer a contract, the District Court for the District of Columbia found that the submission had been required both by the agency's statute--which did not, on its face, apply to the submission at issue, but was found to apply based upon the agency's longstanding practice of interpreting the statute more broadly--and by the agency's letter to the submitters which required them to "submit the documents as a condition necessary to receiving approval of their applica-

---

[68] See FOIA Update, Vol. XIV, No. 2, at 5.

[69] See id.; see also id. at 1 (pointing to significance of this guidance to procurement process and its development in coordination with Office of Federal Procurement Policy).

[70] See id. at 5; accord Lepelletier v. FDIC, 977 F. Supp. 456, 460 n.3 (D.D.C. 1997) ("Information is considered 'required' if any legal authority compels its submission, including informal mandates that call for the submission of the information as a condition of doing business with the government."), aff'd in part, rev'd in part & remanded on other grounds, 164 F.3d 37 (D.C. Cir. 1999); see also Lykes Bros. S.S. Co. v. Pena, No. 92-2780, slip op. at 8-11 (D.D.C. Sept. 2, 1993) (submission "compelled" both by agency statute and by agency letter sent to submitters) (reverse FOIA suit).

[71] See FOIA Update, Vol. XIV, No. 2, at 5; accord Government Accountability Project v. NRC, No. 86-1976, slip op. at 12 (D.D.C. July 2, 1993) (dicta).

[72] See FOIA Update, Vol. XIV, No. 2, at 1; accord Attorney General's Memorandum for Heads of Departments and Agencies regarding the Freedom of Information Act (Oct. 4, 1993), reprinted in FOIA Update, Vol. XIV, No. 3, at 4-5 (establishing "foreseeable harm" standard governing FOIA exemptions); see also Attorney General's Follow-Up Memorandum for Heads of Departments and Agencies regarding the Freedom of Information Act (Sept. 3, 1999), reprinted in FOIA Update, Vol. XIX, No. 4, at 3-5 (reiterating importance of "foreseeable harm" standard); FOIA Update, Vol. XV, No. 2, at 3.

**EXEMPTION 4**

tion."[73] Using the same approach as the Department of Justice's <u>Critical Mass</u> guidance, the court specifically held that "[u]nder <u>Critical Mass</u>, submissions that are required to realize the benefits of a voluntary program are to be considered mandatory."[74] Similarly, when the FDA conditioned its approval of a new drug on the manufacturer's submission of a post-marketing study, the protocol for that study (i.e., its design, hypotheses, and objectives) was deemed a required submission (even in the absence of agency regulations requiring manufacturers to conduct such post-marketing studies) because submission for that particular manufacturer had, in fact, been "necessary in order to obtain FDA approval" for the drug and that rendered it "required."[75]

In another case which also used the same approach as the Department of Justice's <u>Critical Mass</u> guidance, the District Court for the District of New Jersey found that when a submitter provided documents to agency officials during a meeting concerning its tax status, it did so voluntarily, because "if the submission of the documents were obligatory, there would be a controlling statute, regulation or written order."[76] In the absence of any such "mandate," the court concluded that the submission was voluntary.[77]

In that case, the court rejected an argument advanced by the requester that despite the absence of a mandate requiring the submission, the court should "rule as a matter of law" that the documents were "required" to be submitted because submission was for the "benefit" of the submitter.[78] Finding that such an approach "results in putting the cart before the horse," the court noted that in <u>Critical Mass</u>, the D.C. Circuit decided first whether a submission was voluntary and only then did it apply the "less stringent standard for nondisclosure under the FOIA as an incentive for voluntary submitters to provide accurate and reliable information."[79] The requester's proposed test was "flawed," the court found, because it relied "too heavily on hindsight" and the court could "envision cases where someone at the time of submitting the doc-

---

[73] <u>Lykes</u>, No. 92-2780, slip op. at 9 (D.D.C. Sept. 2, 1993).

[74] <u>Id.</u>; <u>accord</u> <u>FOIA Update</u>, Vol. XIV, No. 2, at 3-5; <u>see also</u> <u>Lee v. FDIC</u>, 923 F. Supp. 451, 454 (S.D.N.Y. 1996) (when documents were "required to be submitted" in order to get government approval to merge two banks, court rejects agency's attempt to nonetheless characterize submission as "voluntary").

[75] <u>Public Citizen Health Research Group v. FDA</u>, 964 F. Supp. 413, 414 n.1 (D.D.C. 1997); <u>see, e.g.</u>, <u>Public Citizen Health Research Group v. FDA</u>, 997 F. Supp. 56, 61 n.3 (D.D.C. 1998) (information submitted in connection with New Drug Application deemed "required"), <u>aff'd in pertinent part</u>, 185 F.3d 898, 901, 903 (D.C. Cir. 1999); <u>Sokolow v. FDA</u>, No. 1:97-CV-252, slip op. at 6 (E.D. Tex. Feb. 19, 1998) (same), <u>aff'd</u>, 162 F.3d 1160 (5th Cir. 1998) (unpublished table decision).

[76] <u>AGS Computers, Inc. v. United States Dep't of Treasury</u>, No. 92-2714, slip op. at 10 (D.N.J. Sept. 16, 1993).

[77] <u>Id.</u> at 9-10.

[78] <u>Id.</u> at 10.

[79] <u>Id.</u>

## EXEMPTION 4

uments is clearly doing so on a voluntary basis, but when a benefit analysis... is performed thereafter, the incorrect result is reached that the submission was compulsory."[80]

This past year, the District Court for the District of Columbia found that several factors led to the conclusion that information submitted to an agency by automobile manufacturers regarding air bags was submitted voluntarily.[81] First, the court noted that the information had been "submitted to allow [the agency] to formulate its proposed rule on air bags . . . [and] was intended to aid [the agency] in developing a substantive policy position, and was not part of any [agency] proceeding, investigation, or compliance reporting where the submitter faced any risk of penalties or sanctions."[82] Moreover, the court noted, submission of "the information was not a condition precedent to gaining approval of some application, or receiving a government benefit."[83] The final factor considered by the court was whether the agency "could have required the manufacturers to submit responses, had they chosen to ignore" the agency's request for information.[84] On that point, the court held that although the agency had "broad information-gathering powers," in this instance it had "violated" the Paperwork Reduction Act[85] "in sending the information request to the manufacturers without obtaining pre-clearance from OMB, and thus could not have required the [manufacturers] to submit responses had they chosen to ignore" the agency's request for information.[86] For "all of these reasons," the court held that the submissions were "voluntary."[87]

The District Court for the Southern District of Texas has held that when a submitter promptly "cooperated with agency officials" and provided inspectors "all the information" they requested "prior to the issuance of any subpoenas or warrants," and when that cooperation ensured that the agency's investigation "was neither delayed nor impeded in any manner," all the information so provided was deemed to have been furnished voluntarily.[88] A submission was found to be "voluntary" in another case where the requester sought copies of the comments a submitter had provided the agency in response to

---

[80] Id. at 10-11.

[81] See Center for Auto Safety v. National Highway Traffic Safety Admin., No. 99-1759, 2000 WL 359622, at **15-17 (D.D.C. Feb. 28, 2000) (appeal pending).

[82] Id. at *16.

[83] Id.

[84] Id.

[85] 44 U.S.C. § 3502(3)(A)(i) (1994 & Supp. III 1997).

[86] Center for Auto Safety, 2000 WL 359622, at *16.

[87] Id. at *17.

[88] Shell Oil Co. v. United States Dep't of Labor, No. H-96-3113, slip op. at 13 (S.D. Tex. Mar. 30, 1998) (reverse FOIA suit), aff'd on other grounds, No. 98-20538 (5th Cir. Oct. 14, 1999).

**EXEMPTION 4**

the notice it had been given concerning a FOIA request that had been made for its information.[89] In finding that such comments had been "voluntarily submitted" to the agency, the court focused on the agency's submitter-notice regulations and found that they "clearly did not require . . . [the submitter] to provide any comments whatsoever."[90] The court noted that under those regulations, the failure to submit objections to the disclosure of requested information did "not constitute a waiver" and that the agency was still obligated to review the information to determine whether release was appropriate.[91] The court went on to note that "[t]he regulations do prescribe the content of any comments submitted, but they in no way require the submission of comments."[92] The court thus utilized, without reference to any authority, an approach that is inconsistent with the Department of Justice's Critical Mass guidance--perhaps because its ruling was primarily influenced by what the court perceived as the relatively weak "requirement" for submission embodied in the agency's submitter-notice regulations.[93]

In another case that turned on the wording of an agency's regulation, the same court found that the agency had demonstrated that the submission of information by kidney dialysis centers was voluntary and that the regulation relied on by the requester--in support of its contention that the submission was required--did not actually "require" the centers "to provide any particular information" and instead merely stated, "without further elaboration," that information "must be provided in the manner specified" by the agency's Secretary.[94] In that regard, the court found persuasive the agency's declaration that stated "unequivocally that the information was produced voluntarily and not subject to a statutory requirement."[95] By contrast, summary judgment was denied in another case when the agency's declaration entirely failed to indicate how the agency had received the requested documents.[96]

In a ruling that arguably takes the characterization of "voluntary" to its outermost reaches, the District Court for the Eastern District of Missouri held that a submission was voluntary even though the agency not only had the authority to issue a subpoena for the documents, but had in fact exercised that

---

[89] McDonnell Douglas Corp. v. NASA, No. 93-1540, 1993 WL 796612, at *1 (D.D.C. Nov. 17, 1993) (reverse FOIA suit).

[90] Id.

[91] Id. at *2 n.1.

[92] Id.

[93] See id. at **1, 2 & n.1.

[94] Minntech Corp. v. HHS, No. 92-2720, slip op. at 8 (D.D.C. Nov. 17, 1993).

[95] Id.

[96] See Animal Legal Defense Fund, Inc. v. Department of the Air Force, 44 F. Supp. 2d 295, 303 (D.D.C. 1999) (observing that "nowhere in his declaration does [the agency declarant] aver that [the submitter's] submissions came to the [agency] 'voluntarily'").

## EXEMPTION 4

authority by actually issuing such a subpoena.[97] The court flatly rejected the agency's argument that the issuance of the subpoena rendered the submission "required," finding that that "conclusion ignore[d] the fact that subpoenaed parties may challenge [the subpoena], both administratively and through objections to enforcement proceedings."[98] Although no challenge to the subpoena was actually brought, the court found it "highly likely" that such a challenge would have been successful given the fact that the court had previously ruled that the same documents were privileged and hence did not have to be disclosed to private parties who were in litigation with the submitter.[99] "This," the court declared, "shows that the production in fact was voluntary, not required."[100]

Significantly, the District Court for the District of Columbia has issued six decisions which all hold--consistent with the Department of Justice's policy guidance on this issue--that prices submitted in conjunction with a government contract are "required" submissions.[101] In the first of these decisions, the court held that the submitter "had no choice but to submit the unit price information once it chose to submit its proposal," as the terms of the Request for Proposals (RFP) "compelled [it] to submit its unit prices."[102] Relying on that decision, the court reiterated in the second case that a contract "bidder only provides confidential information because the agency requires it [and that] once a firm has elected to bid, it must submit the mandatory information if it hopes to win the contract."[103]

In the third decision (which was subsequently vacated when the FOIA

---

[97] McDonnell Douglas Corp. v. EEOC, 922 F. Supp. 235, 242 (E.D. Mo. 1996) (reverse FOIA suit), appeal dismissed, No. 96-2662 (8th Cir. Aug. 29, 1996).

[98] Id.

[99] Id.

[100] Id.

[101] McDonnell Douglas Corp. v. NASA, 981 F. Supp. 12, 15 (D.D.C. 1997) (reverse FOIA suit), reconsideration denied, No. 96-2611, slip op. at 7-8 (D.D.C. May 1, 1998), rev'd on other grounds, 180 F.3d 303 (D.C. Cir. 1999), reh'g en banc denied, No. 98-5251 (D.C. Cir. Oct. 6, 1999); Martin Marietta Corp. v. Dalton, 974 F. Supp. 37, 39 (D.D.C. 1997) (reverse FOIA suit); McDonnell Douglas, 895 F. Supp. at 317-18; McDonnell Douglas Corp. v. NASA, 895 F. Supp. 319, 325-26 (D.D.C. 1995) (reverse FOIA suit), vacated as moot, No. 95-5288 (D.C. Cir. Apr. 1, 1996); CC Distribs. v. Kinzinger, No. 94-1330, 1995 WL 405445, at *4 (D.D.C. June 28, 1995) (reverse FOIA suit); Chemical Waste Management, Inc. v. O'Leary, No. 94-2230, 1995 WL 115894, at *4 (D.D.C. Feb. 28, 1995) (reverse FOIA suit).

[102] Chemical Waste, 1995 WL 115894, at *4.

[103] CC Distribs., 1995 WL 405445, at *4.

# EXEMPTION 4

request was withdrawn while the case was on appeal),[104] the court again relied on the terms of the agency's RFP, which, it noted, "used language of compulsion in reference to pricing information."[105] There, the court also rejected as "temptingly simple" the submitter's argument that because it "did not have to enter into a contract, no information within the contract [should] be considered mandatory."[106] This "rather simplistic approach" was flatly rejected by the court as it "would result in classifying all government contractors as per se volunteers whose pricing information could easily be withheld from the public domain."[107]

In the fourth decision, after analyzing the Critical Mass decision, the court expressly concluded "as a matter of law" that "the price elements necessary to win a government contract are not voluntary."[108] Once again faced with an argument by the submitter that its submission of a proposal and its entry into a government contract were "obviously voluntary acts," the court found that such contentions were simply "inapposite."[109] Declaring that "no one disputes that the process of offer and acceptance giving rise to contractual obligations is voluntary," the court held that the "focal point" must be "the information itself" and that there was no question that the agency "required that the contract itemize the prices for specific services."[110] The court then went on to somewhat sarcastically note that the submitter was "not doing the government a favor by providing the most basic information in a contract--price," and observed that if "contractors want to win lucrative government contracts they must provide [agencies] with specific pricing elements for their goods and services."[111]

In the fifth decision, the court held that although the D.C. Circuit "has yet to address the issue, district court precedent in this Circuit uniformly and firmly points to the conclusion that the financial/commercial information found in the [submitter's] contracts was 'required' in the National Parks sense of the term by Federal Acquisition Regulations . . . and therefore [was] subject to the National Parks test."[112] In so holding, the district court again noted that "[w]hether to compete for [the agency's] business at all was, of course, [the submitter's] option, but having elected to do so it was required to submit the

---

[104] See McDonnell Douglas Corp. v. NASA, No. 95-5288 (D.C. Cir. Apr. 1, 1996) (reverse FOIA suit).

[105] McDonnell Douglas, 895 F. Supp. at 325.

[106] Id.

[107] Id.

[108] McDonnell Douglas, 895 F. Supp. at 318.

[109] Id.

[110] Id.

[111] Id.

[112] Martin Marietta, 974 F. Supp. at 39.

# EXEMPTION 4

information [the agency] insisted on having if it hoped to win the contract."[113]

Finally, in the most recent of these district court decisions, the court relied on this case law and held that "the relevant inquiry is whether the specific price elements and other information provided by [the submitter] were required to be submitted before [the agency] would award the contract."[114] Because the contract solicitation "included several statements indicating that bidders must submit certain information," the court determined that the agency "did not exceed the bounds of reasonableness in concluding that [the submitter] was 'required' to submit" the requested pricing information.[115]

The District Courts for the Eastern District of Missouri[116] and the District of Colorado[117] likewise have ruled that contract submissions were not provided voluntarily and that, as a consequence, the greater protection afforded by Critical Mass for voluntary submissions was not applicable. In so holding, the Colorado court also specifically rejected the argument advanced by the submitter that because it had "voluntarily entered into the contract with the Government" the contract submission should be considered "voluntary."[118] In contrast, two cases decided in the Eastern District of Virginia immediately after Critical Mass reached the opposite conclusion and held that contract submissions were voluntarily provided.[119] (As noted below, however, one of those cases was later expressly disclaimed by a subsequent court in that same district for failing to provide any justification whatsoever for its conclusion.[120])

Two years after the decision in Critical Mass, a case involving government contract prices reached the D.C. Circuit--after having been decided by

---

[113] Id.

[114] McDonnell Douglas, 981 F. Supp. at 15.

[115] Id.

[116] See TRIFID Corp. v. National Imagery & Mapping Agency, 10 F. Supp. 2d 1087, 1098 (E.D. Mo. 1998) (relying on case law from the District Court for the District of Columbia) (reverse FOIA suit).

[117] See Source One Management, Inc. v. United States Dep't of the Interior, No. 92-Z-2101, transcript at 6 (D. Colo. Nov. 10, 1993) (bench order) (reverse FOIA suit).

[118] Id. at 5.

[119] Environmental Tech., Inc. v. EPA, 822 F. Supp. 1226, 1229 (E.D. Va. 1993) (summarily declaring that unit price information provided in connection with government contract was voluntarily submitted) (reverse FOIA suit); Cohen, Dunn & Sinclair, P.C. v. GSA, No. 92-0057-A, transcript at 28 (E.D. Va. Sept. 10, 1992) (bench order) (same).

[120] Comdisco, Inc. v. GSA, 864 F. Supp. 510, 517 n.8 (E.D. Va. 1994) (denigrating Environmental Tech., 822 F. Supp. at 1229) (reverse FOIA suit); accord FOIA Update, Vol. XIV, No. 2, at 5 (same).

**EXEMPTION 4**

the lower court prior to the Critical Mass decision.[121] The D.C. Circuit, however, elected not to opine on the meaning of Critical Mass, or its applicability to government contract submissions, and instead remanded the case to the district court with instructions for that court to "reexamine the applicability of exemption 4 to the contract prices at issue under our holding in Critical Mass."[122] (On remand, the district court found Critical Mass to be inapplicable to a government contract submission.[123]) Similarly, another case was remanded back to the agency--which had made its Exemption 4 determination prior to the issuance of Critical Mass--so that any voluntarily submitted information could be identified and then analyzed under the Critical Mass standards.[124]

This past year, in McDonnell Douglas Corp. v. NASA, the D.C. Circuit once again eschewed an opportunity to analyze this issue.[125] Although the submitter argued that "its submission of bidding information [was] part and parcel of the voluntary act of submitting a bid," the D.C. Circuit found that it was not necessary to decide that issue because "assuming arguendo" that the submission was "required," the court "believe[d that] the disputed line item price information [was] confidential commercial or financial information under the National Parks test" in any event.[126]

In the first decision of its kind, the District Court for the District of Columbia differentiated between discrete items contained in a government contract and found that General and Administrative (G & A) rate ceilings were voluntarily provided to the government even though submission of actual G & A rates was "undisputed[ly] . . . a mandatory component" of an offeror's submission.[127] In so holding, the court rejected the agency's argument that because "submission of a cost proposal, including actual G & A rates was mandatory in order to compete for the contract," the G & A rate ceilings--which had been requested by the contracting officer during negotiations--"were also

---

[121] McDonnell Douglas Corp. v. NASA, No. 92-5342, slip op. at 2 (D.C. Cir. Feb. 14, 1994) (reverse FOIA suit).

[122] Id.

[123] McDonnell Douglas, 895 F. Supp. at 318.

[124] Alexander & Alexander Servs. v. SEC, No. 92-1112, 1993 WL 439799, at *12 (D.D.C. Oct. 19, 1993) (reverse FOIA suit), appeal dismissed, No. 93-5398 (D.C. Cir. Jan. 4, 1996).

[125] McDonnell Douglas Corp. v. NASA, 180 F.3d 303 (D.C. Cir. 1999) (reverse FOIA suit), reh'g en banc denied, No. 98-5251 (D.C. Cir. Oct. 6, 1999).

[126] Id. at 305-06 (mischaracterizing extensive Department of Justice guidance--set forth at FOIA Update, Vol. XIV, No. 2, at 3-7--that analyzed distinction between "voluntary" and "required" submissions).

[127] Cortez III Serv. Corp. v. NASA, 921 F. Supp. 8, 12 (D.D.C. 1996) (reverse FOIA suit), appeal dismissed voluntarily, No. 96-5163 (D.C. Cir. July 3, 1996).

**EXEMPTION 4**

a mandatory part of the cost proposal."[128] Because the contract solicitation was "silent as to G & A rate ceilings," and in the absence of any firm evidence that the submitter "was required to provide G & A rate ceilings in order to continue to compete for the contract," the court concluded that their submission had been voluntary.[129]

Other cases decided subsequent to Critical Mass have applied the new voluntary/required distinction, but they have done so without setting forth any rationale or analysis for their conclusions on this pivotal issue. Instead, the information at issue was summarily found either to have been voluntarily provided[130] or, conversely, to have been required to be submitted.[131] The D.C. Circuit had occasion to review one of these cases on appeal, but its unpublished opinion did not provide any further guidance on the Critical Mass distinction and instead merely affirmed the lower court's already terse decision on that point.[132]

---

[128] Id.

[129] Id. at 12-13.

[130] See Pentagen Techs. Int'l v. United States, No. 98CIV.4831, 2000 WL 347165, at *3 (S.D.N.Y. Mar. 31, 2000) (alternative holding) ("information may be viewed as having been produced voluntarily in order to supplement the Government's understanding of the IBM proposal"); Clarkson v. Greenspan, No. 97-2035, slip op. at 9 (D.D.C. June 30, 1998) (information "was voluntarily provided in confidence, and, according to [the agency] its release could jeopardize the continued availability of such information"), summary affirmance granted, No. 98-5349, 1999 WL 229017 (D.C. Cir. Mar. 2, 1999); Thomas v. Weise, No. 91-3278, slip op. at 6 (D.D.C. Oct. 7, 1994) (requester did "not dispute that the documents were voluntarily submitted"); Allnet Communication Servs. v. FCC, 800 F. Supp. 984, 990 (D.D.C. 1992) ("[t]o the extent that the information sought was submitted voluntarily, the material was properly withheld"), aff'd, No. 92-5351, slip op. at 3 (D.C. Cir. May 27, 1994).

[131] See Trans-Pac. Policing Agreement v. United States Customs Serv., No. 97-2188, 1998 U.S. Dist. LEXIS 7800, at *7 (D.D.C. May 14, 1998) (information provided on Import Declaration form "is supplied under compulsion"), rev'd & remanded for segregability determination, 177 F.3d 1022 (D.C. Cir. 1999); Garren v. United States Dep't of the Interior, No. CV-97-273, slip op. at 12 n.10 (D. Or. Nov. 17, 1997) (magistrate's recommendation) (information concerning purchase of river rafting concession contract required to be submitted), adopted (D. Or. Jan. 8, 1998); Africa Fund v. Mosbacher, No. 92-289, 1993 WL 183736, at **7 & 8 n.3 (S.D.N.Y. May 26, 1993) (information provided in export license applications required to be submitted); Citizens Comm'n on Human Rights v. FDA, No. 92-5313, slip op. at 15 (C.D. Cal. May 10, 1993) (information concerning New Drug Application required to be submitted), aff'd in part & remanded in part on other grounds, 45 F.3d 1325 (9th Cir. 1995).

[132] Allnet Communications Servs. v. FCC, No. 92-5351, slip op. at 3 (D.C. Cir. May 27, 1994) (finding no error in lower court first concluding that re-
(continued...)

**EXEMPTION 4**

In a case involving rather unusual factual circumstances, the District Court for the District of Columbia discussed the applicability of the <u>Critical Mass</u> distinction to documents that had been provided to the agency not by their originator, but as a result of the unauthorized action of a confidential source.[133] Although these documents were not actually at issue in the case, the court nevertheless elected to analyze their status under <u>Critical Mass</u>.[134] The court first noted that the decision in <u>Critical Mass</u> provided it with "little guidance" as those documents "had been produced voluntarily by the originator, without any intervening espionage."[135] The court nevertheless opined that in its case "the secret, unauthorized delivery" of the documents at issue made the submission "'involuntary' in the purest sense," but that application of the "more stringent standard for involuntary transfer would contravene the spirit" of <u>Critical Mass</u>.[136] Thus, the court declared that in such circumstances the proper test for determining the confidentiality of the documents should be the "more permissive standard" of <u>Critical Mass</u>, i.e., protection would be afforded if the information was of a kind that is not customarily released to the public by the submitter.[137]

Interestingly, the District Courts for the District of Maine and the Eastern District of Virginia both have expressly declined to consider the possible applicability of <u>Critical Mass</u> to the information at issue because the <u>Critical Mass</u> distinction has not yet been adopted by their respective courts of appeals.[138] In so holding, the District Court for the Eastern District of Virginia noted that although a previous decision arising out of that same district had, in fact, "adopted the <u>Critical Mass</u> test," that earlier opinion "provided little justification for its conclusion"; therefore, the court very pointedly "decline[d] to follow" it.[139]

Using a slightly different approach, the District Court for the Southern District of New York declared that it "need not decide whether <u>Critical Mass</u> is governing law in the Second Circuit" because the records at issue--which were

---

(...continued)
quested information was exempt under standard for required submissions and then also concluding that it would be exempt under standard for voluntary submissions).

[133] <u>Government Accountability</u>, No. 86-1976, slip op. at 2 (D.D.C. July 2, 1993).

[134] <u>Id.</u> at 10.

[135] <u>Id.</u> at 11-12.

[136] <u>Id.</u> at 12.

[137] <u>Id.</u>; <u>see also id.</u> at 11 (citing <u>Critical Mass</u>, 975 F.2d at 879).

[138] <u>See</u> <u>Bangor Hydro-Elec. Co. v. United States Dep't of the Interior</u>, No. 94-0173-B, slip op. at 9 n.3 (D. Me. Apr. 18, 1995); <u>Comdisco</u>, 864 F. Supp. at 517-19.

[139] <u>Comdisco</u>, 864 F. Supp. at 517 n.8 (referring to <u>Environmental Tech.</u>, 822 F. Supp. at 1226).

**EXEMPTION 4**

acquired by the FDIC by operation of law when it became receiver of a failed financial institution--were "not produced voluntarily [and so] the Critical Mass standard simply [did] not apply."[140] On appeal, the Court of Appeals for the Second Circuit agreed with the lower court on this point, stating that because the records at issue were not provided voluntarily, the Critical Mass test was "irrelevant to the issue presented" by the appeal.[141] Similarly, the Court of Appeals for the Ninth Circuit has observed that the Critical Mass distinction between voluntary and required submissions "becomes relevant only when information is submitted to the government voluntarily."[142] Finding that the records at issue in the case before it were required to be submitted by the terms of the agency's contract solicitation, the Ninth Circuit declared that in light of that fact, it "need not address" the Critical Mass distinction.[143]

Under Critical Mass, once information is determined to be voluntarily provided, it is afforded protection as "confidential" information "if it is of a kind that would customarily not be released to the public by the person from whom it was obtained."[144] The D.C. Circuit observed in Critical Mass that this test was "objective" and that the agency invoking it "must meet the burden of proving the provider's custom."[145] The subsequent cases that have applied this "customary treatment" standard to information found to have been voluntarily submitted typically contain only perfunctory discussions of the showing necessary to satisfy it.[146]

---

[140] Nadler v. FDIC, 899 F. Supp. 158, 161 (S.D.N.Y. 1995), aff'd, 92 F.3d 93 (2d Cir. 1996).

[141] Nadler v. FDIC, 92 F.3d 93, 96 n.1 (2d Cir. 1996).

[142] Frazee v. United States Forest Serv., 97 F.3d 367, 372 (9th Cir. 1996) (reverse FOIA suit).

[143] Id.

[144] 975 F.2d at 879.

[145] Id.; see Animal Legal Defense Fund, 44 F. Supp. 2d at 303 (noting that "unless [the agency declarant] would have personal knowledge about [the company's] customary practices, the [agency] will need an affidavit from an officer of [the company] to satisfy this final element of Critical Mass").

[146] See Cortez, 921 F. Supp. at 13 (submitter's "unrefuted sworn affidavits attest to the fact that G & A rate ceilings are the type of information that is not regularly disclosed to the public"); Thomas, No. 91-3278, slip op. at 6 (D.D.C. Oct. 7, 1994) ("uncontradicted affidavits reveal that the information is of a kind that the provider would not normally release to the public"); Minntech, No. 92-2720, slip op. at 8 n.3 (D.D.C. Nov. 17, 1993) ("The Court accepts HHS's declarations that the type of information provided is not the type that dialysis centers would release to the public."); Government Accountability, No. 86-1976, slip op. at 11 (D.D.C. July 2, 1993) (it "is not to be doubted" that documents are "unavailable to the public"); Environmental Tech., 822 F. Supp. at 1229 (it is "readily apparent that the information is of a kind that [the submitter] would not customarily share with its competitors or with the general public"); Harrison v. Lujan, No. 90-1512, slip op. at 1 (D.D.C. Dec. 8,

(continued...)

**EXEMPTION 4**

Nevertheless, there are a few decisions that contain some analysis of the standard. In one such case, the court identified the evidence that had been provided to demonstrate the submitter's customary treatment--specifically, a consulting contract, a protective order, and markings on the documents--and the court deemed that evidence "most persuasive."[147] Similarly, evidence given in another case to show customary treatment was identified as the submitter's practice of "carefully guard[ing]" disclosure of the documents "even within the corporate structure," the markings on the documents, and the fact that the company "strenuously, and successfully, opposed their production in discovery in multiple civil cases."[148] In yet another case, the court provided some useful elaboration on this issue by specifically noting and then rejecting as "vague hearsay," the requester's contention that there had been "prior, unrestricted disclosure" of the information at issue.[149] In so doing, the court expressly found the requester's evidence to be "nonspecific" and lacking precision "regarding dates and times" of the alleged disclosures; conversely, it noted that the submitter had "provided specific, affirmative evidence that no unrestricted disclosure" had occurred.[150] Accordingly, the court concluded that it had been "amply demonstrated" that the information satisfied the customary treatment standard of Critical Mass.[151]

A similar argument regarding public availability was advanced by a requester who contended that the submitters had "revealed" the requested information in "press releases, annual reports, and other such disclosures to the general public."[152] In each instance, however, the court found that the disclosures "have been limited, and have generally been accompanied by confidenti-

---

(...continued)
1992) (agency's "uncontradicted evidence . . . establishes that the documents at issue contain information that the provider would not customarily make available to the public"); Cohen, Dunn, No. 92-0057-A, transcript at 27 (E.D. Va. Sept. 10, 1992) (pricing information "is of a kind that would customarily not be released to the public by the entity from which it is obtained"); Allnet, 800 F. Supp. at 990 ("it has been amply demonstrated that [the submitters] would not customarily release the information to the public").

[147] AGS, No. 92-2714, slip op. at 11 (D.N.J. Sept. 16, 1993).

[148] McDonnell Douglas, 922 F. Supp. at 242.

[149] Allnet, 800 F. Supp. at 989.

[150] Id.

[151] Id. at 990. But cf. Atlantis Submarines Haw., Inc. v. United States Coast Guard, No. 93-00986, slip op. at 9 (D. Haw. Jan. 28, 1994) (although not expressly ruling on customary treatment standard, court upheld agency's decision to release voluntarily submitted safety report that was provided to agency in effort to "influence" its "regulatory decisions," finding that "after seeking to have its safety-related material incorporated into . . . [agency's] decision-making process," submitter could not then "have the report exempted from public disclosure") (denying motion for preliminary injunction in reverse FOIA suit), dismissed per stipulation (D. Haw. Apr. 11, 1994).

[152] Center for Auto Safety, 2000 WL 359622, at *17.

# EXEMPTION 4

ality agreements or protective orders."[153] In addition, the court noted that the information that was disclosed was "very general in nature and only an approximation of the information supplied" to the agency.[154] Finally, the court found that the requester was "unable to prove that the information it ha[d] uncovered [was] identical to the information provided" to the agency.[155] As a result, the court concluded that the customary treatment standard was satisfied.[156]

In creating this customary treatment standard, the D.C. Circuit in Critical Mass articulated the test as dependent upon the treatment afforded the information by the individual submitter and not the treatment afforded the information by an industry as a whole.[157] This approach has been followed by all the cases applying the customary treatment standard thus far, although one court also found it "relevant" that the requester--who was a member of the same industry as the submitters--had, "up until the eve of trial," taken the position that the type of information at issue ought not to be released.[158] Further, as applied by the D.C. Circuit in Critical Mass, the customary treatment standard allows for some disclosures of the information to have been made, provided that such disclosures were not made to the general public.[159]

As a matter of sound administrative practice, the Department of Justice has advised agencies to employ procedures analogous to those set forth in Executive Order 12,600[160] when making determinations under the customary

---

[153] Id. at *18.

[154] Id.

[155] Id.

[156] Id.

[157] 975 F.2d at 872, 878, 879, 880; accord Center for Auto Safety, 2000 WL 359622, at *17 (declaring that courts "must look at each manufacturer's customary treatment of [the requested] information, rather than how the industry as a whole treats it"); see also FOIA Update, Vol. XIV, No. 2, at 7 (advising agencies applying customary treatment standard to examine treatment afforded information by individual submitter).

[158] Cohen, Dunn, No. 92-0057-A, transcript at 27 (E.D. Va. Sept. 10, 1992).

[159] See 975 F.2d at 880 (specifically citing to lower court decision that noted records had been provided to numerous interested parties under nondisclosure agreements, but had not been provided to public-at-large); accord Center for Auto Safety, 2000 WL 359622, at *17 (emphasizing that "[l]imited disclosures, such as to suppliers or employees, do not preclude protection under Exemption 4, as long as those disclosures are not made to the general public"); see also FOIA Update, Vol. XIV, No. 2, at 7 (advising agencies that customary treatment standard allows submitter to have made some disclosures of information, provided such disclosures are not "public" ones).

[160] 3 C.F.R. 235 (1988), reprinted in 5 U.S.C. § 552 note (1994), and in FOIA Update, Vol. VIII, No. 2, at 2-3.

# EXEMPTION 4

treatment standard.[161] (For a further discussion of this executive order and its requirements, see Exemption 4, Competitive Harm Prong of National Parks, below, and "Reverse" FOIA, Executive Order 12,600, below.) Accordingly, whenever an agency is uncertain of a submitter's customary treatment of requested information, the submitter should be notified and given an opportunity to provide the agency with a description of its treatment of the information, including any disclosures that are customarily made and the conditions under which such disclosures occur.[162]

## Impairment Prong of National Parks

For information that is "required" to be submitted to an agency, the Court of Appeals for the District of Columbia Circuit has held that the tests for confidentiality originally established in National Parks & Conservation Ass'n v. Morton[163] continue to apply.[164] The first of these tests, the impairment prong, traditionally has been found to be satisfied when an agency demonstrates that the information at issue was provided voluntarily and that submitting entities would not provide such information in the future if it were subject to public disclosure.[165] Conversely, protection under the impairment prong traditionally has been denied when the court determines that disclosure

---

[161] See FOIA Update, Vol. XIV, No. 2, at 7.

[162] See id.

[163] 498 F.2d 765, 770 (D.C. Cir. 1974).

[164] See Critical Mass Energy Project v. NRC, 975 F.2d 871, 880 (D.C. Cir. 1992) (en banc).

[165] See, e.g., O'Harvey v. Compensation Programs Workers, No. 98-35106, 1999 WL 626633, at *1 (9th Cir. Aug. 16, 1999) (protecting information contained in Physician Directory Service database because disclosure "would impair the government's ability to purchase commercial data in the future" and to "obtain necessary medical information from physicians who would be unlikely to risk the dissemination of distorted data to the general public"); Bowen v. FDA, 925 F.2d 1225, 1228 (9th Cir. 1991) (protecting manufacturing formulas, processes, and quality control and internal security measures submitted voluntarily to FDA to assist with cyanide-tampering investigations because agencies relied heavily on such information and would be less likely to obtain it if businesses feared it would be made public); Heeney v. FDA, No. 97-5461, slip op. at 15-16 (C.D. Cal. Mar. 18, 1999) (protecting name of withdrawn medical device because, if disclosed, "manufacturers would be loathe to provide" such data in future applications and agency's "ability to carry out its regulatory objectives would be thwarted") (appeal pending); Gilmore v. United States Dep't of Energy, 4 F. Supp. 2d 912, 923 (N.D. Cal. 1998) (protecting video conferencing software provided to agency as part of joint venture, as there "can be no doubt that corporations will be less likely to enter into joint ventures with the government to develop technology if that technology can be distributed freely"); Klayman & Gurley v. United States Dep't of Commerce, No. 88-0783, 1990 WL 446704, at *2 (D.D.C. Apr. 17, 1990); ISC Group v. DOD, No. 88-0631, 1989 WL 168858, at *3 (D.D.C. May 22, 1989); Landfair v. United States Dep't of the Army, 645 F. Supp. 325, 328 (D.D.C. 1986).

## EXEMPTION 4

will not, in fact, diminish the flow of information to the agency[166]--for example, when it determines that the benefits associated with submission of particular information make it unlikely that the agency's ability to obtain future such submissions will be impaired.[167]

---

[166] See, e.g., Inter Ocean Free Zone, Inc. v. United States Customs Serv., 982 F. Supp. 867, 871 n.3 (S.D. Fla. 1997) (no impairment because "there can be no reasonable concern that those who are required by statute to submit [requested data] will risk violating the law"); Center to Prevent Handgun Violence v. United States Dep't of the Treasury, 981 F. Supp. 20, 23 (D.D.C. 1997) (same), appeal dismissed, No. 97-5357 (D.C. Cir. Feb. 2, 1998); Pentagon Fed. Credit Union v. National Credit Union Admin., No. 95-1475-A, slip op. at 4 (E.D. Va. June 7, 1996) (no impairment based on "merely speculative fear" that "disclosure might discourage future responses from credit unions"); Nadler v. FDIC, 899 F. Supp. 158, 161 (S.D.N.Y. 1995) (dicta) (no impairment possible when agency "gained access to [submitter's] information by operation of law when it became receiver"), aff'd on other grounds, 92 F.3d 93 (2d Cir. 1996); Key Bank of Me., Inc. v. SBA, No. 91-362-P, 1992 U.S. Dist. LEXIS 22180, at *11 (D. Me. Dec. 31, 1992) (no impairment based on speculative assertion that public disclosure of Dun & Bradstreet reports will adversely affect company's profits and thus make it "unlikely" that credit agencies will do business with government; this "intimation regarding impairment of profits in no way speaks to the ability of affected credit agencies to continue to exist and supply needed data"); Wiley Rein & Fielding v. United States Dep't of Commerce, 782 F. Supp. 675, 677 (D.D.C. 1992) (no impairment given fact that requested documents contained no "sensitive information" and there was "no reason to believe" that such information would not be provided in future), appeal dismissed as moot, No. 92-5122 (D.C. Cir. Mar. 8, 1993).

[167] See, e.g., McDonnell Douglas Corp. v. NASA, 981 F. Supp. 12, 15 (D.D.C. 1997) (no impairment from release of contract price information because "[g]overnment contracting involves millions of dollars and it is unlikely that release of this information will cause [agency] difficulty in obtaining future bids") (reverse FOIA suit), rev'd on other grounds, 180 F.3d 303 (D.C. Cir. 1999), reh'g en banc denied, No. 98-5251 (D.C. Cir. Oct. 6, 1999); Martin Marietta Corp. v. Dalton, 974 F. Supp. 37, 40 (D.D.C. 1997) (dictum) (no impairment from release of cost, pricing, and management information incorporated into government contract because contractors "will continue bidding for [agency] contracts despite the risk of revealing business secrets if the price is right") (reverse FOIA suit); Cohen v. Kessler, No. 95-6140, slip op. at 12 (D.N.J. Nov. 25, 1996) (no impairment from release of raw research data submitted in support of application for approval of new animal drug "in light of the enormous profits that drug manufacturers reap through product development and improvement"); Bangor Hydro-Elec. Co. v. United States Dep't of the Interior, No. 94-0173-B, slip op. at 9 (D. Me. Apr. 18, 1995) (no impairment because "it is in the [submitter's] best interest to continue to supply as much information as possible" in order to secure better usage charges for its lands); RMS Indus. v. DOD, No. C-92-1545, slip op. at 7 (N.D. Cal. Nov. 24, 1992) (no impairment from release of "contract bid prices, terms and conditions . . . since bids by nature are offers to provide goods and/or services for a price and under certain terms and conditions"); Buffalo Evening News, Inc. v. SBA, 666 F. Supp. 467, 471 (W.D.N.Y. 1987) (no impairment because it is un-

(continued...)

# EXEMPTION 4

Under the categorical test announced by the D.C. Circuit in Critical Mass Energy Project v. NRC, the voluntary character of an information submission is sufficient to render it exempt, provided the information would not be customarily released to the public by the submitter.[168] (For a further discussion of this point, see Exemption 4, Applying Critical Mass, above.) In this regard, the D.C. Circuit has made it clear that an agency's unexercised authority, or mere "power to compel" submission of information, does not preclude such information from being provided to the agency "voluntarily."[169] This holding was compatible with several decisions rendered prior to Critical Mass that had protected information under the impairment prong despite the existence of agency authority that could have been used to compel its submission.[170]

---

(...continued)
likely that borrowers would decline benefits associated with obtaining loans simply because status of loan was released); Daniels Mfg. Corp. v. DOD, No. 85-291, slip op. at 6 (M.D. Fla. June 3, 1986) (no impairment when submission "virtually mandatory" if supplier wished to do business with government); Badhwar v. United States Dep't of the Air Force, 622 F. Supp. 1364, 1377 (D.D.C. 1985) (same), aff'd in part & rev'd in part on other grounds, 829 F.2d 182 (D.C. Cir. 1987); Racal-Milgo Gov't Sys. v. SBA, 559 F. Supp. 4, 6 (D.D.C. 1981) (no impairment because "[i]t is unlikely that companies will stop competing for Government contracts if the prices contracted for are disclosed"). But see Orion Research, Inc. v. EPA, 615 F.2d 551, 554 (1st Cir. 1980) (finding impairment for technical proposals submitted in connection with government contract because release "would induce potential bidders to submit proposals that do not include novel ideas"); Pentagen Techs. Int'l v. United States, No. 98CIV.4831, 2000 WL 347165, at **2-3 (S.D.N.Y. Mar. 31, 2000) (alternative holding) (finding impairment for "highly proprietary technical solution proposed by IBM" that, if "viewed as being required by the Government in order to full[y] comprehend the IBM bid, . . . would impair the Government's ability to obtain necessary information from bidders in the future" if it were disclosed); RMS, No. C-92-1545, slip op. at 7 (N.D. Cal. Nov. 24, 1992) (finding impairment for equipment descriptions, employee, customer, and subcontractor names submitted in connection with government contract because "bidders only submit such information if it will not be released to their competitors"); Cohen, Dunn & Sinclair, P.C. v. GSA, No. 92-0057-A, transcript at 29 (E.D. Va. Sept. 10, 1992) (bench order) (finding impairment for detailed unit price information despite lack of "actual proof of a specific bidder being cautious in its bid or holding back").

[168] 975 F.2d at 879.

[169] Id. at 880; see FOIA Update, Vol. XIV, No. 2, at 5 ("OIP Guidance: The Critical Mass Distinction Under Exemption 4"); see also id. at 6-7 ("Exemption 4 Under Critical Mass: Step-By-Step Decisionmaking").

[170] See, e.g., Public Citizen Health Research Group v. FDA, 704 F.2d 1280, 1291 n.29 (D.C. Cir. 1983) (whether submissions are mandatory was a factor to be considered in an impairment claim, but was "not necessarily dispositive"); Washington Post Co. v. HHS, 690 F.2d 252, 268-69 (D.C. Cir. 1982). But see Teich v. FDA, 751 F. Supp. 243, 251 (D.D.C. 1990) (When "compelled
(continued...)

**EXEMPTION 4**

As a result of the D.C. Circuit's ruling in Critical Mass the significance of the impairment prong is undoubtedly diminished.[171] Nevertheless, the D.C. Circuit recognized that even when agencies require submission of information "there are circumstances in which disclosure could affect the reliability of such data."[172] Thus, after Critical Mass, the impairment prong of National Parks now applies to those limited situations in which information is required to be provided, but where disclosure of that information under the FOIA will result in a diminution of the "reliability" or "quality" of what is submitted.[173]

---

(...continued)
cooperation will obtain precisely the same results as voluntary cooperation, an impairment claim cannot be countenanced.") (decided prior to Critical Mass and thus now in conflict with that decision), appeal voluntarily dismissed, No. 91-5023 (D.C. Cir. July 2, 1992).

[171] See FOIA Update, Vol. XIV, No. 2, at 7.

[172] Critical Mass, 975 F.2d at 878 (citing Washington Post, 690 F.2d at 268-69); see Goldstein v. HHS, No. 92-2013, slip op. at 5 (S.D. Fla. May 21, 1993) (magistrate's recommendation) (rejecting argument that decision in Critical Mass "essentially did away" with impairment prong and noting that under that decision "it is appropriate to consider whether or not disclosure of the information would undermine the government's interest in insuring its reliability"), adopted (S.D. Fla. July 21, 1993).

[173] See Critical Mass, 975 F.2d at 878; accord Africa Fund v. Mosbacher, No. 92-289, 1993 WL 183736, at *7 (S.D.N.Y. May 26, 1993) (protecting information submitted with export license applications as it "fosters the provision of full and accurate information"); see also Goldstein, No. 92-2013, slip op. at 5, 7 (S.D. Fla. May 21, 1993) (protecting information concerning laboratory's participation in drug-testing program as it furthers agency's ability to continue to receive reliable information). But see Niagara Mohawk Power Corp. v. United States Dep't of Energy, 169 F.3d 16, 18 (D.C. Cir. 1999) (rejecting, as "inherently weak," claim of qualitative impairment when agency "secured the information under compulsion" and the data itself "appear[] to take the form of hard, cold numbers on energy use and production, the fudging of which may strain all but the deliberately mendacious"); Center to Prevent Handgun Violence, 981 F. Supp. at 23 (rejecting, as "speculative" and unreasonable, agency's claim that accuracy of information required to be reported on multiple sales reports "would be jeopardized by public disclosure"); Public Citizen Health Research Group v. FDA, 964 F. Supp. 413, 415 (D.D.C. 1997) (rejecting, as "unsupported, even by an assertion of agency experience on the point," agency's claim "that data submitted to the agency as part of its drug approval process 'would not be submitted as freely'" if requested document were disclosed (quoting agency declaration)); Silverberg v. HHS, No. 89-2743, 1991 WL 633740, at *4 (D.D.C. June 14, 1991) (rejecting, as "entirely speculative," claim of qualitative impairment based on contention that laboratory inspectors--who work in teams of three and whose own identities are protected--would fear litigation and thus be less candid if names of laboratories they inspected were released), appeal dismissed per stipulation, No. 91-5255 (D.C. Cir. Sept. 2, 1993); Teich, 751 F. Supp. at 252 (rejecting, as "absurd," submitter's contention that companies would be less likely to conduct and report

(continued...)

**EXEMPTION 4**

If an agency determines that release will not cause impairment, that decision should be given extraordinary deference by the courts.[174] In this regard there have been a few decisions addressing the feasibility of a submitter raising the issue of impairment on behalf of an agency. In one, the district court ruled that a submitter has "standing" to raise the issue of impairment.[175] Subsequently, however, the Court of Appeals for the Fourth Circuit refused to allow a submitter to make an impairment argument on the agency's behalf.[176] That appellate court decision was, in turn, subsequently relied on by a lower court which found that because "it is the government's interests that are protected" by the impairment prong, "it follows that it is the government that is best situated to make the determination of whether disclosure would inhibit future submissions."[177] That court reasoned that "it would be nonsense to block disclosure" of information "under the purported rationale of protecting government interests" when the government itself "wants to disclose" it.[178]

More than a decade ago, in Washington Post Co. v. HHS, the D.C. Circuit held that an agency must demonstrate that a threatened impairment is "significant," because a "minor" impairment is insufficient to overcome the general disclosure mandate of the FOIA.[179] Moreover, in Washington Post the D.C. Circuit held that the factual inquiry concerning the degree of impairment "necessarily involves a rough balancing of the extent of impairment and the

---

(...continued)
safety tests to FDA for fear of public disclosure because companies' own interests in engendering good will and in avoiding product liability suits is assurance that they will conduct "the most complete testing program" possible).

[174] See, e.g., General Elec. Co. v. NRC, 750 F.2d 1394, 1402 (7th Cir. 1984) (court observes that there is not "much room for judicial review of the quintessentially managerial judgment" that disclosure will not cause impairment) (reverse FOIA suit); McDonnell Douglas, 981 F. Supp. at 15-16 ("court should defer to the administrative agency's determination that release will not cause impairment"); CC Distribs. v. Kinzinger, No. 94-1330, 1995 WL 405445, at *4 (D.D.C. June 28, 1995) (same) (reverse FOIA suit); Chemical Waste Management, Inc. v. O'Leary, No. 94-2230, 1995 WL 115894, at *4 (D.D.C. Feb. 28, 1995) (same) (reverse FOIA suit); AT&T Info. Sys. v. GSA, 627 F. Supp. 1396, 1401 (D.D.C. 1986) (court finds that agency "'is in the best position to determine the effect of disclosure on its ability to obtain necessary technical information'" (quoting Orion, 615 F.2d at 554)) (reverse FOIA suit), rev'd on procedural grounds & remanded, 810 F.2d 1233 (D.C. Cir. 1987).

[175] United Techs. Corp. v. HHS, 574 F. Supp. 86, 89 (D. Del. 1983).

[176] Hercules, Inc. v. Marsh, 839 F.2d 1027, 1030 (4th Cir. 1988).

[177] Comdisco, Inc. v. GSA, 864 F. Supp. 510, 515 (E.D. Va. 1994) (reverse FOIA suit).

[178] Id. at 516.

[179] 690 F.2d at 269.

## EXEMPTION 4

importance of the information against the public interest in disclosure."[180] Because the case was remanded for further proceedings, the court found it unnecessary to decide the details of such a balancing test at that time.[181]

Five years later, in the first panel decision in Critical Mass, the D.C. Circuit cited Washington Post to reiterate that a threatened impairment must be significant, but it made no mention whatsoever of a balancing test.[182] The notion of a balancing test was resurrected in a subsequent decision of the D.C. Circuit in the Washington Post case.[183] This time the D.C. Circuit elaborated on the balancing test--even suggesting that it might apply to all aspects of Exemption 4, not just the impairment prong--and held that "information will be withheld only when the affirmative interests in disclosure on the one side are outweighed by the factors identified in National Parks I (and its progeny) militating against disclosure on the other side."[184] Because the case was remanded once again (and ultimately was settled), the court did not actually rule on the outcome of such a balancing process.[185]

The district court decision in Critical Mass, on remand from the first panel decision of the D.C. Circuit, was the first decision to explicitly apply a balancing test under the impairment prong of Exemption 4.[186] (Other district court decisions have utilized or made reference to a balancing test in ruling under the competitive harm prong.[187] For further discussion of this point, see Exemption 4, Competitive Harm Prong of National Parks, below.) In Critical Mass, the district court held that a consumer organization requesting information bearing upon the safety of nuclear power plants had "no particularized

---

[180] Id.

[181] Id.

[182] 830 F.2d 278, 286 (D.C. Cir. 1987), vacated en banc, 975 F.2d 871 (D.C. Cir. 1992).

[183] 865 F.2d 320, 326-27 (D.C. Cir. 1989).

[184] Id. at 327.

[185] Id. at 328.

[186] 731 F. Supp. 554, 555-56 (D.D.C. 1990), rev'd in part on other grounds & remanded, 931 F.2d 939 (D.C. Cir.), vacated & reh'g en banc granted, 942 F.2d 799 (D.C. Cir. 1991), grant of summary judgment to agency aff'd en banc, 975 F.2d 871 (D.C. Cir. 1992); see also Pentagon Fed. Credit Union v. National Credit Union Admin., No. 95-1475-A, slip op. at 4 (E.D. Va. June 7, 1996) (in course of rejecting agency's impairment claim as "merely speculative," court references requester's citation to Washington Post test and notes requester's assertion of public interest in documents).

[187] See, e.g., Teich, 751 F. Supp. at 243; see also Garren v. United States Dep't of the Interior, No. CV-97-273, slip op. at 13 (D. Or. Nov. 17, 1997) (magistrate's recommendation) (in rejecting competitive harm claim, court questioned what standard would be used in "balancing" under Exemption 4, but found it unnecessary "to resolve that question" because information at issue was not "within the scope of Exemption 4"), adopted (D. Or. Jan. 8, 1998).

**EXEMPTION 4**

need of its own" for access to the information and thus was "remitted to the general public interest in disclosure for disclosure's sake to support its request."[188] Although the court conceded that the public has an interest "of significantly greater moment than idle curiosity" in information concerning the safety of nuclear power plants, that same interest was shared by the NRC and the submitter of the information and their interest in preventing disclosure was deemed to be of "a much more immediate and direct nature."[189] Curiously, when this decision in Critical Mass was subsequently reviewed by both a second panel of the D.C. Circuit and then by the entire D.C. Circuit sitting en banc, no mention was made of any balancing test under Exemption 4.[190]

This issue was finally resolved by the D.C. Circuit last year in its decision in Public Citizen Health Research Group v. FDA.[191] There, the D.C. Circuit squarely rejected "a consequentialist approach to the public interest in disclosure" as "inconsistent with the '[b]alanc[e of] private and public interests' th[at] Congress struck in Exemption 4."[192] The court went on to state that "[t]hat balance is accurately reflected in the test of confidentiality" established by National Parks and that a requester cannot "bolster the case for disclosure by claiming an additional public benefit" in release.[193] "In other words," the D.C. Circuit declared, "the public interest side of the balance is not a function of the identity of the requester, . . . or of any potential negative consequences disclosure may have for the public, . . . nor likewise of any collateral benefits of disclosure."[194]

Competitive Harm Prong of National Parks

The great majority of Exemption 4 cases have involved the competitive harm prong of the test for confidentiality established in National Parks & Con-

---

[188] 731 F. Supp. at 556.

[189] Id.; see Gilmore, 4 F. Supp. 2d at 922-23 (declaring, for FOIA exemptions generally, that court "must balance the public interest in disclosure against the interest Congress intended the exemption to protect" and, upon determining that requested video conferencing software fell within protection of both prongs of Exemption 4, court balanced in favor of protection, finding "no countervailing public interest" in disclosure of the software inasmuch as it "sheds no light whatsoever on [agency's] performance of its duties").

[190] 931 F.2d 939, 945-47 (D.C. Cir.), vacated & reh'g en banc granted, 942 F.2d 799 (D.C. Cir. 1991), grant of summary judgment to agency aff'd en banc, 975 F.2d 871 (D.C. Cir. 1992).

[191] 185 F.3d 898, 904 (D.C. Cir. 1999) (ruling under competitive harm prong, but applying rationale applicable to all prongs of Exemption 4).

[192] Id.

[193] Id.

[194] Id.; accord Utah v. United States Dep't of the Interior, No. 2:98 CV 380, slip op. at 7 (D. Utah Nov. 3, 1999) (holding that "there is no balancing in applying Exemption 4 beyond the balancing that is inherent in the exemption itself").

## EXEMPTION 4

servation Ass'n v. Morton.[195] Information is "confidential" under this prong if disclosure "is likely . . . to cause substantial harm to the competitive position of the person from whom the information was obtained."[196] The Court of Appeals for the District of Columbia Circuit has "emphasize[d]" that the "'important point for competitive harm in the FOIA context . . . is that it be limited to harm flowing from the affirmative use of proprietary information by competitors'" and that this "'should not be taken to mean simply any injury to competitive position, as might flow from customer or employee disgruntlement.'"[197]

In order for an agency to make a determination under this prong it is essential that the submitter of the requested information be given an opportunity to provide the agency with its views on the possible competitive harm that would be caused by disclosure. While such an opportunity had long been voluntarily afforded submitters by several agencies and had been recommended by the Department of Justice,[198] for more than a decade now it has been expressly required by executive order.

Executive Order 12,600[199] provides for mandatory notification of submitters of confidential commercial information whenever an agency "determines that it may be required to disclose" such information under the FOIA.[200] Once submitters are notified, they must be given a reasonable period of time within which to object to disclosure of any of the requested infor-

---

[195] 498 F.2d 765, 770 (D.C. Cir. 1974).

[196] Id.

[197] Public Citizen Health Research Group v. FDA, 704 F.2d 1280, 1291 n.30 (D.C. Cir. 1983) (quoting Mark Q. Connelly, Secrets and Smokescreens: A Legal and Economic Analysis of Government Disclosures of Business Data, 1981 Wis. L. Rev. 207, 235-36); accord CNA Fin. Corp. v. Donovan, 830 F.2d 1132, 1152 & n.158 (D.C. Cir. 1987) (reiterating "policy behind Exemption 4 of protecting submitters from external injury" and rejecting submitter objections that did "not amount to 'harm flowing from the affirmative use of proprietary information by competitors'" (quoting Public Citizen, 704 F.2d at 1291 n.30)) (reverse FOIA suit). But see McDonnell Douglas Corp. v. NASA, 180 F.3d 303, 306-07 (D.C. Cir. 1999) (inexplicably accepting as legally valid--without any reference to (or seeming cognizance of) D.C. Circuit precedent to the contrary--submitter's claim that disclosure of government contract prices would cause submitter harm by permitting its "commercial customers to bargain down ('ratchet down') its prices more effectively") (reverse FOIA suit), reh'g en banc denied, No. 98-5251 (D.C. Cir. Oct. 6, 1999).

[198] See FOIA Update, Vol. III, No. 3, at 3.

[199] 3 C.F.R. 235 (1988), reprinted in 5 U.S.C. § 552 note (1994), and in FOIA Update, Vol. VIII, No. 2, at 2-3.

[200] Exec. Order No. 12,600, § 1. See generally OSHA Data/C.I.H., Inc. v. United States Dep't of Labor, No. 98-283, slip op. at 9-11 (D.N.J. June 11, 1998) (concluding that costs of notifying over 80,000 submitters are properly charged to requester seeking documents for commercial use) (appeal pending).

**EXEMPTION 4**

mation.[201] The executive order requires that agencies give careful consideration to the submitters' objections and provide them with a written statement explaining why any such objections are not sustained.[202] (For a further discussion of these procedures, see "Reverse" FOIA, Executive Order 12,600, below.)

As one court has emphasized, consultation with a submitter is "appropriate as one step in the evaluation process, [but it] is not sufficient to satisfy [an agency's] FOIA obligations."[203] Consequently, an agency is "required to determine for itself whether the information in question should be disclosed."[204] If an agency decides to invoke Exemption 4 and that decision is subsequently challenged in court by a FOIA requester, the submitter's objections to disclosure--usually provided in an affidavit filed in conjunction with the agency's papers--will, in turn, be evaluated and relied upon by the court in determining the propriety of the exemption claim.[205]

---

[201] Exec. Order No. 12,600, § 4.

[202] Id. § 5.

[203] Lee v. FDIC, 923 F. Supp. 451, 455 (S.D.N.Y. 1996).

[204] Id.; accord Exec. Order No. 12,600, § 5 (notification procedures specifically contemplate that agency makes ultimate determination concerning release); see also National Parks, 498 F.2d at 767 (in justifying nondisclosure, submitter's treatment of information held not to be "the only relevant inquiry"; rather, agency must be satisfied that harms underlying exemption are likely to occur).

[205] See, e.g., Public Citizen Health Research Group v. FDA, 997 F. Supp. 56, 64 n.4 (D.D.C. 1998) (noting with approval submitter's "recognition that some of the requested documents may be safely released" and considering it "evidence that their claims of exemption . . . are grounded in good faith--that the company is not reflexively resisting every request for disclosure"), aff'd in part, rev'd in part & remanded, 185 F.3d 898 (D.C. Cir. 1999); North Carolina Network for Animals v. USDA, No. 90-1443, slip op. at 8 (4th Cir. Feb. 5, 1991) (noting absence of sworn affidavits or detailed justification for withholding from submitters of information); Pentagon Fed. Credit Union v. National Credit Union Admin., No. 95-1475-A, slip op. at 4-5 (E.D. Va. June 7, 1996) (rejecting competitive harm argument advanced by agency which had no submitter objections to provide court due to its failure even to give notice to submitters who, in turn, ultimately provided sworn declarations to requester explicitly stating that disclosure would not cause them harm); Wiley Rein & Fielding v. United States Dep't of Commerce, 782 F. Supp. 675, 676 (D.D.C. 1992) (noting that "no evidence" was provided to indicate that submitters objected to disclosure), appeal dismissed as moot, No. 92-5122 (D.C. Cir. Mar. 8, 1993); Brown v. Department of Labor, No. 89-1220, 1991 U.S. Dist. LEXIS 1780, at *7 (D.D.C. Feb. 15, 1991), appeal dismissed, No. 91-5108 (D.C. Cir. Dec. 3, 1991); Teich v. FDA, 751 F. Supp. 243, 254 (D.D.C. 1990) (striking original declaration of submitter "on basic fairness grounds," and then finding submitter "not able to support its position"), appeal voluntarily dismissed, No. 91-5023 (D.C. Cir. July 2, 1992); Black Hills Alliance v. United
(continued...)

# EXEMPTION 4

The courts have tended to resolve issues of competitive harm on a case-by-case basis rather than by establishing general guidelines. For example, in some contexts customer names have been withheld because disclosure would cause substantial competitive harm[206] and in other contexts customer names have been ordered released because disclosure would not cause substantial competitive harm.[207] Similarly, in one case the table of contents and introductions to certain documents were withheld because the court found that their disclosure would "provide valuable descriptions of proprietary information,"[208] but in another case the court upheld an agency's decision to release a table of contents and other summary information because they revealed "only an outline" of the submitter's "operations and capabilities" and were "devoid of the detail which would be of value" to competitors.[209] The individualized and sometimes conflicting determinations indicative of competitive harm holdings is well illustrated in one case in which the D.C. Circuit originally affirmed a district court's decision which found that customer names of "CAT" scanner manufacturers were protected,[210] but subsequently vacated that decision upon the death of one of its judges.[211] On reconsideration, the newly constituted panel found that disclosure of the customer list raised a factual question as to the showing of competitive harm that precluded the granting of

---

(...continued)
States Forest Serv., 603 F. Supp. 117, 121 (D.S.D. 1984) (ordering disclosure and noting that "[i]t is significant that [the submitter] itself has not submitted an affidavit addressing" issue of competitive harm); see also Durnan v. United States Dep't of Commerce, 777 F. Supp. 965, 967 (D.D.C. 1991) (rejecting challenge to agency's reliance on submitter's declaration, finding it entirely "relevant" to competitive harm determination); cf. Silverberg v. HHS, No. 89-2743, 1990 WL 599452, at *1 (D.D.C. June 26, 1990) (when only some submitters made objections to disclosure, court permitted requester to obtain copies of those objections through discovery in order to enable him to substantiate his claim that not all submitters were entitled to Exemption 4 protection) (discovery order).

[206] See, e.g., RMS Indus. v. DOD, No. C-92-1545, slip op. at 7 (N.D. Cal. Nov. 24, 1992); Goldstein v. ICC, No. 82-1511, 1984 WL 3228, at **6-7 (D.D.C. July 31, 1985) (reopening case and protecting customer names); BDM Corp. v. SBA, 2 Gov't Disclosure Serv. (P-H) ¶ 81,044, at 81,120 (D.D.C. Dec. 4, 1980).

[207] See, e.g., Ivanhoe Citrus Ass'n v. Handley, 612 F. Supp. 1560, 1566 (D.D.C. 1985); Braintree Elec. Light Dep't v. Department of Energy, 494 F. Supp. 287, 290 (D.D.C. 1980).

[208] Allnet Communications Servs. v. FCC, No. 92-5351, slip op. at 5 (D.C. Cir. May 27, 1994).

[209] Dynalectron Corp. v. Department of the Air Force, No. 83-3399, 1984 WL 3289, at *5 (D.D.C. Oct. 30, 1984) (reverse FOIA suit).

[210] Greenberg v. FDA, 775 F.2d 1169, 1172-73 (D.C. Cir. 1985).

[211] Greenberg v. FDA, 803 F.2d 1213, 1215 (D.C. Cir. 1986).

**EXEMPTION 4**

summary judgment after all.[212]

Factual disputes concerning the likelihood that disclosure of requested information would cause competitive harm precluded a ruling on summary judgment motions in two cases decided three years ago by the District Court for the District of Columbia.[213] In the first case, after reviewing the "claims made by experts" representing both of the parties, the court concluded that because the claims were "contradictory," summary judgment was "an inappropriate vehicle" for resolution of the case, and the court instead scheduled a bench trial.[214] (The case was ultimately settled, however, and no trial took place.[215]) In the second case, the court found that the record did "not present a clear picture as to the competitive injury, if any, that would result from releasing" the requested document--a protocol (an outline of objectives and hypotheses) for a post-marketing study of a pharmaceutical drug.[216] Rather than proceeding to a trial, the court in that case ordered that the document and a memorandum supporting its withholding be submitted to the court in camera.[217] Thereafter, at the court's suggestion,[218] the document was also reviewed by "two experts identified by the parties and appointed by the court."[219] The experts then concluded, and the court agreed, that no competitive harm would "flow from the release" of the document and disclosure was ordered.[220]

Actual competitive harm need not be demonstrated for purposes of the competitive harm prong; evidence of "actual competition and a likelihood of

---

[212] Id. at 1219.

[213] Public Citizen Health Research Group v. FDA, 964 F. Supp. 413, 416 (D.D.C. 1997), review by expert witness suggested, No. 96-1650 (D.D.C. Mar. 18, 1997), summary judgment denied & document ordered released (D.D.C. Nov. 3, 1997); Public Citizen Health Research Group v. FDA, 953 F. Supp. 400, 402-03 (D.D.C. 1996), dismissed per stipulation, No. 94-0169, slip op. at 1 (D.D.C. Feb. 3, 1997).

[214] Public Citizen, 953 F. Supp. at 403.

[215] Public Citizen Health Research Group v. FDA, No. 94-0169, slip op. at 1 (D.D.C. Feb. 3, 1997) (agency agreed to release requested information as part of settlement).

[216] Public Citizen, 964 F. Supp. at 416.

[217] Id.

[218] See Public Citizen Health Research Group v. FDA, No. 96-1650, slip op. at 2 (D.D.C. Mar. 18, 1997) (because in camera submission "disabled" normal "adversary process," parties directed to recommend candidates for appointment as expert witnesses who, under protective order, could review material "and offer an opinion" as to likelihood of competitive harm).

[219] Public Citizen Health Research Group v. FDA, No. 96-1650, slip op. at 1 (D.D.C. Nov. 3, 1997).

[220] Id. at 1-2.

## EXEMPTION 4

substantial competitive injury" is all that need be shown.[221] The D.C. Circuit recently remanded a decision for further proceedings concerning the existence of "actual competition" and, in doing so, suggested that "a competitive injury is too remote for purposes of Exemption 4 if it can occur only in the occasional renegotiation of long-term contracts."[222] In this regard, a submitter's "admittedly weakened financial position" has been held "not [to] amount to a complete inability to suffer competitive harm," inasmuch as a "struggling, perhaps even failing, business remains entitled to the protections that Exemption Four affords to any company."[223]

In applying the competitive harm test, one court has gone so far as to order disclosure based upon a balancing test. Although it never expressly referred to it as such or cited to any supporting authority, the court found that disclosure of certain safety and effectiveness data pertaining to a medical device was "unquestionably in the public interest" and that the benefit of releasing this type of information "far outstrips the negligible competitive harm" alleged by the submitter.[224] In contrast, another court employed a balancing

---

[221] CNA, 830 F.2d at 1152 ; accord Frazee v. United States Forest Serv., 97 F.3d 367, 371 (9th Cir. 1996) (reverse FOIA suit); GC Micro Corp. v. Defense Logistics Agency, 33 F.3d 1109, 1113 (9th Cir. 1994); Gulf & Western Indus. v. United States, 615 F.2d 527, 530 (D.C. Cir. 1979); see, e.g., Utah v. United States Dep't of the Interior, No. 2:98 CV 380, slip op. at 4-5 (D. Utah Nov. 3, 1999) (rejecting requester's argument that submitter had "no viable competitors" and finding that agency had "met its burden of justification" on that issue); NBC v. SBA, 836 F. Supp. 121, 124 n.3 (S.D.N.Y. 1993) (noting that agency "should have provided more details" regarding possible competitive harm, but ruling nonetheless that generalized sworn declaration from submitter was sufficient); Journal of Commerce, Inc. v. United States Dep't of the Treasury, No. 86-1075, 1987 WL 4922, at *2 (D.D.C. June 1, 1987) (holding that submitter was not required to document or pinpoint actual harm, but need only show its likelihood) (partial grant of summary judgment), renewed motion for summary judgment granted, No. 86-1075, 1998 U.S. Dist. LEXIS 17610 (D.D.C. Mar. 30, 1988), aff'd, 878 F.2d 1446 (Fed. Cir. 1989) (unpublished table decision); HLI Lordship Indus. v. Committee for Purchase from the Blind & Other Severely Handicapped, 663 F. Supp. 246, 251 (E.D. Va. 1987) (concluding that competitive harm was likely, based upon fact that requester, who was a competitor of the submitter, had requested confidential treatment for its own similar submission).

[222] Niagara Mohawk Power Corp. v. United States Dep't of Energy, 169 F.3d 16, 18 (D.C. Cir. 1999); see also Hercules, Inc. v. Marsh, 659 F. Supp. 849, 854 (W.D. Va. 1987) (given fact that contract always awarded to submitter, protection under competitive harm prong unavailable as submitter failed to meet "threshold requirement" of facing competition) (reverse FOIA suit), aff'd, 839 F.2d 1027 (4th Cir. 1988).

[223] Inter Ocean Free Zone, Inc. v. United States Customs Serv., 982 F. Supp. 867, 872 (S.D. Fla. 1997).

[224] Teich, 751 F. Supp. at 253; see also Public Citizen, 964 F. Supp. at 415 (citing Teich and stating that "an additional factor that may be considered is

(continued...)

**EXEMPTION 4**

test under Exemption 4, but that court balanced in favor of protection--under both the impairment and competitive harm prongs--declaring that "there is no countervailing public interest in disclosure [of the requested video conferencing software] because [the software] sheds no light whatsoever on [the agency's] performance of its duties."[225]

The Court of Appeals for the Ninth Circuit has cited to National Parks and then declared that it "agree[d] with the D.C. Circuit" that in making an Exemption 4 determination it "must balance the strong public interest in favor of disclosure against the right of private businesses to protect sensitive information."[226] Although the Ninth Circuit thus used the term "balance," it did so in the context of holding that the agency had entirely failed to meet its burden of showing that disclosure of the very general information at issue was likely to cause "any potential for competitive harm, let alone substantial harm," and as a result, the court stated, rather colloquially, that the "FOIA's strong presumption in favor of disclosure trumps the contractors' right to privacy."[227]

This past year, the D.C. Circuit definitively resolved this issue by flatly rejecting a requester's proposal that the court "should gauge whether the competitive harm done to the sponsor of an [Investigational New Drug] by the public disclosure of confidential information 'is outweighed by the strong

---

(...continued)
whether there is a strong public interest in release of the information") (insufficient record precluded court from actually ruling on claim of competitive harm and in camera inspection ordered). But cf. Citizens Comm'n on Human Rights v. FDA, No. 92-5313, slip op. at 18 (C.D. Cal. May 10, 1993) (finding competitive harm and thus protecting research data used to support safety and effectiveness of pharmaceutical drug), aff'd in part & remanded in part on other grounds, 45 F.3d 1325 (9th Cir. 1995).

[225] Gilmore v. United States Dep't of Energy, 4 F. Supp. 2d 912, 923 (N.D. Cal. 1998); cf. Trans-Pac. Policing Agreement v. United States Customs Serv., No. 97-2188, 1998 U.S. Dist. LEXIS 7800, at *14 (D.D.C. May 14, 1998) (concluding, without actually using word "balancing," that agency's "proper application of Exemption 4 in this case does not offend the purposes of the FOIA"), rev'd & remanded for segregability determination, 177 F.3d 1022 (D.C. Cir. 1999).

[226] GC Micro, 33 F.3d at 1115.

[227] Id.; see Garren v. United States Dep't of the Interior, No. CV-97-273, slip op. at 13 n.11 (D. Or. Nov. 17, 1997) (magistrate's recommendation) (referring to GC Micro and questioning "nature" of public interest to be considered in Exemption 4 cases, but declining to resolve that issue inasmuch as requested information was outside Exemption 4's protection), adopted (D. Or. Jan. 8, 1998); cf. Martin Marietta Corp. v. Dalton, 974 F. Supp. 37, 41 (D.D.C. 1997) (in context of holding that submitter had failed to demonstrate that it would suffer competitive harm from release of information incorporated into government contract, court notes importance of opening government procurement process to public scrutiny) (reverse FOIA suit).

## EXEMPTION 4

public interest in safeguarding the health of human trial participants."[228] Declaring that a requester cannot "bolster the case for disclosure by claiming an additional public benefit" in release, the D.C. Circuit held that Congress has already struck the appropriate balance between public and private interests and that "[t]hat balance is accurately reflected in the test of confidentiality set forth in National Parks."[229] (For a further discussion of this point, see Exemption 4, Impairment Prong of National Parks, above.)

In assessing whether a submitter would suffer competitive harm, courts have held that "elaborate antitrust proceedings" are not required.[230] On the other hand, mere conclusory allegations of harm are unacceptable.[231] For example, the Ninth Circuit reversed a competitive harm determination made by the lower court which had protected, on a standard government form, the "percentage and dollar amount of work subcontracted out" to small disadvantaged businesses.[232] In so deciding, the Ninth Circuit rejected the contention advanced by the submitting contractors that disclosure would allow their competitors to "undercut future bids," holding that their "rather conclusory statements" to that effect were insufficient as the data was "made up of too many fluctuating variables for competitors to gain any advantage from the

---

[228] Public Citizen Health Research Group v. FDA, 185 F.3d 898, 903 (D.C. Cir. 1999).

[229] Id. at 904; accord Utah, No. 2:98 CV 380, slip op. at 7 (D. Utah Nov. 3, 1999) (holding that "there is no balancing in applying Exemption 4 beyond the balancing that is inherent in the exemption itself").

[230] National Parks & Conservation Ass'n v. Kleppe, 547 F.2d 673, 681 (D.C. Cir. 1976); accord GC Micro, 33 F.3d at 1115 ("law does not require [agency] to engage in a sophisticated economic analysis of the substantial competitive harm . . . that might result from disclosure"); Public Citizen, 704 F.2d at 1291.

[231] See, e.g., Public Citizen, 185 F.3d at 906 ("'[C]onclusory and generalized allegations of substantial competitive harm . . . cannot support an agency's decision to withhold requested documents.'"); Northwest Coalition for Alternatives to Pesticides v. Browner, 941 F. Supp. 197, 202 (D.D.C. 1996) (same); Lykes Bros. S.S. Co. v. Pena, No. 92-2780, slip op. at 13 (D.D.C. Sept. 2, 1993) (declaring that submitters are "required to make assertions with some level of detail as to the likelihood and the specific nature of the competitive harm they predict") (reverse FOIA suit); see also Public Citizen Health Research Group v. FDA, No. 99-0177, 2000 U.S. Dist. LEXIS 4108, at **6-9 (D.D.C. Jan. 19, 2000) (rejecting submitter's "conclusory" and "speculative" arguments regarding competitive harm); Heeney v. FDA, No. 97-5461, slip op. at 20 (C.D. Cal. Mar. 18, 1999) (rejecting competitive harm argument when submitter "provide[d] no reason" for seeking to withhold requested information) (appeal pending); Lee, 923 F. Supp. at 455 (rejecting competitive harm when submitter failed to provide "adequate documentation of the specific, credible, and likely reasons why disclosure of the document would actually cause substantial competitive injury").

[232] GC Micro, 33 F.3d at 1115.

**EXEMPTION 4**

disclosure."[233] Similarly, the District Court for the District of Columbia upheld an agency's decision to disclose three broad categories of information incorporated into a government contract--specifically, "cost and fee information, including material, labor and overhead costs, as well as target costs, target profits and fixed fees"; "component and configuration prices, including unit pricing and contract line item numbers"; and "technical and management information, including subcontracting plans, asset allocation charts, and statements of the work necessary to accomplish certain system conversions"--based upon the submitter's failure to specifically demonstrate that it would suffer competitive harm from their release.[234] In upholding release of this information, the court affirmed the agency's determination that "neither the revelation of cost and pricing data nor proprietary management strategies were likely to result in such egregious injury to [the submitter] as to disable it as an effective competitor for [the agency's] business in the future."[235]

Some courts have utilized a "mosaic" approach to sustain a finding of competitive harm, thereby protecting information that would not in and of itself cause harm, but which would be harmful when combined with information already available to the requester.[236] In one case--where it was found that a company's labor costs would be revealed by disclosure of its wage rate and manhour information--the court took the opposite approach, and disaggregated the requested information, ordering release of the wage rates without the manhour information, because release of one without the other would not cause the company competitive harm.[237] In denying a competitive harm claim, another court noted that because the requested information pertained

---

[233] Id. at 1114-15.

[234] Martin Marietta, 974 F. Supp. at 38, 40.

[235] Id. at 41.

[236] See, e.g., Trans-Pac., 1998 U.S. Dist. LEXIS 7800, at **10-11 (Harmonized Tariff Numbers, which are themselves publicly released, protected when linked to specific shipments of goods because "knowledgeable person can use [such] numbers to uncover information concerning the nature, cost, profit margin, and origin of shipments"); Lederle Lab. v. HHS, No. 88-0249, slip op. at 22-23 (D.D.C. July 14, 1988) (scientific tests and identities of agency reviewers withheld because disclosure would permit requester to "indirectly obtain that which is directly exempted from disclosure"); Timken Co. v. United States Customs Serv., 491 F. Supp. 557, 559 (D.D.C. 1980) (data reflecting sales between parent company and subsidiary withheld because even if disclosure of such data "would be insufficient, standing by itself, to allow computation of the cost of production, this cost would be ascertainable when coupled with other information").

[237] Painters Dist. Council Six v. GSA, No. 85-2971, slip op. at 8 (N.D. Ohio July 23, 1986); see also Lykes, No. 92-2780, slip op. at 15 (D.D.C. Sept. 2, 1993) (submitter failed to show any harm given fact that proposed disclosures would "redact all price terms, financial terms, rates and the like"); San Jose Mercury News v. Department of Justice, No. 88-20504, slip op. at 4-5 (N.D. Cal. Apr. 17, 1990) (no harm once company name and other identifying information deleted from requested forms).

## EXEMPTION 4

to every laboratory in a certain program, disclosure would not create a competitive advantage for any one of them because "each laboratory would have access to the same type of information as every other laboratory in the program."[238]

Many courts have held that if the information sought to be protected is itself publicly available through other sources, disclosure under the FOIA will not cause competitive harm and Exemption 4 is not applicable.[239] (The public availability of information has also defeated an agency's impairment claim.[240]) In addressing a claim of public availability, the District Court for the District of Columbia has declared that it is "[t]he party asserting public availability [who] must initially produce evidence to support its assertion, but the burden of persuasion remains on the opponent of disclosure."[241]

---

[238] Silverberg v. HHS, No. 89-2743, 1991 WL 633740, at *4 (D.D.C. June 14, 1991), appeal dismissed per stipulation, No. 91-5255 (D.C. Cir. Sept. 2, 1993); see also Carolina Biological Supply Co. v. USDA, No. 93CV00113, slip op. at 8 (M.D.N.C. Aug. 2, 1993) (competitive harm unlikely when all companies involved in same business will have equal access to information in question) (reverse FOIA suit).

[239] See, e.g., Niagara Mohawk Power Corp. v. United States Dep't of Energy, 169 F.3d at 19 (If the requester is correct that the sought-after information "is already in the public domain," then Exemption 4 cannot be used to protect it.); Anderson v. HHS, 907 F.2d 936, 952 (10th Cir. 1990) ("[N]o meritorious claim of confidentiality" can be made for documents which are in the public domain.); CNA, 830 F.2d at 1154 ("To the extent that any data requested under FOIA are in the public domain, the submitter is unable to make any claim to confidentiality--a sine qua non of Exemption 4."); Continental Stock Transfer & Trust Co. v. SEC, 566 F.2d 373, 375 (2d Cir. 1977); Lepelletier v. FDIC, 977 F. Supp. 456, 460 (D.D.C. 1997) (When state laws provide for publication of names of depositors of abandoned accounts, "it is clear that Exemption 4 is not applicable, because depositors who abandon their funds likewise relinquish their claims to confidentiality."), aff'd in part, rev'd in part & remanded on other grounds, 164 F.3d 37 (D.C. Cir. 1999); MCI Telecomms. Corp. v. GSA, No. 89-0746, 1992 WL 71394, at *6 (D.D.C. Mar. 25, 1992) ("publicly available documents cannot be considered confidential under Exemption 4"), defendants' subsequent motion for summary judgment granted on basis of collateral estoppel, No. 89-0746 (D.D.C. Feb. 27, 1995). Compare Lee, 923 F. Supp. at 455 (competitive injury claim rejected for information already available to public, albeit in different format), with Heeney, No. 97-5461, slip op. at 13-14 (C.D. Cal. Mar. 18, 1999) (competitive injury claim accepted when the "context of the information in agency records is different than that in the marketplace").

[240] See Farmworkers Legal Servs. v. United States Dep't of Labor, 639 F. Supp. 1368, 1371 (E.D.N.C. 1986).

[241] Northwest Coalition, 941 F. Supp. at 202 (citing Occidental Petroleum Corp. v. SEC, 873 F.2d 325, 342 (D.C. Cir. 1989)); see also Heeney, No. 97-5461, slip op. at 13 (C.D. Cal. Mar. 18, 1999) (observing that "[w]hile it may generally be known" that a certain company manufactures catheters, the re-

(continued...)

**EXEMPTION 4**

In applying this principle, one court has held that simply because individuals subject to a drug test had "a right of access to the performance and testing information" of the laboratory conducting their tests, that did "not make the [requested] information [concerning all certified laboratories] publicly available."[242] Similarly, release of a summary of a safety and effectiveness study was found not to waive Exemption 4 protection for the underlying raw data because the disclosed information did not "match the withheld information."[243] Significantly, when an agency had previously released data without the submitter's "knowledge or consent," the District Court for the District of Columbia rejected the agency's argument that that data was "now in the public domain and no longer entitled to confidential treatment."[244] In rebuffing that proposition, the court held that "[t]he prior release of information to a limited number of requesters does not necessarily make the information a matter of common public knowledge, nor does it lessen the likelihood that [the submitter] might suffer competitive harm if it is disclosed again."[245]

Confidentiality was also upheld in a case where the requester argued that some of the withheld material had been disclosed "collaterally."[246] First, the D.C. Circuit declared that "assuming that certain information is available publicly," it saw "little reason why the government must go through the expense and burden of producing the information now; there is no benefit to . . . [the requester] or to the public that can be gained by imposing such a duplicative function on the government."[247] As to the requester's argument that there was "value to be gained from the juxtaposition" of that "public information within" the submitter's materials, the D.C. Circuit found that the requester's own argument "concedes the confidentiality" of the material, because the requester clearly wanted "not only the collaterally disclosed information, but

---

(...continued)
quester failed to supply "evidence that the information redacted in fact concerns" that company).

[242] Silverberg, 1991 WL 633740, at *3.

[243] Cohen v. Kessler, No. 95-6140, slip op. at 12 (D.N.J. Nov. 25, 1996).

[244] Martin Marietta, 974 F. Supp. at 40.

[245] Id.; accord Trans-Pac., 1998 U.S. Dist. LEXIS 7800, at *13 (when "past release" of data "was isolated and unauthorized by" agency, such release found "not [to] affect the application of Exemption 4"); see Public Citizen, 953 F. Supp. at 401, 405 (when submitter's document "inadvertently released" to requester by agency and subsequently filed on public record, court noted absence of evidence that anyone had "taken advantage" of that public access and issued protective order sealing court record and precluding requester from publicly disseminating document pending court's determination of Exemption 4 applicability).

[246] Allnet, No. 92-5351, slip op. at 4 (D.C. Cir. May 27, 1994).

[247] Id.

## EXEMPTION 4

the proprietary manner with which" it had been utilized.[248]

The feasibility of "reverse engineering" (i.e., the process of independently recreating the requested information--for example, by obtaining a finished product and dismantling it to learn its constituent elements) has been considered in evaluating a showing of competitive harm because it "is germane to the question whether information is in the public domain (and thus whether a showing of competitive harm can be made)."[249] (Although in one case the court declined to even consider the requester's contention that reverse engineering was possible for information protected as a "trade secret" under Exemption 4,[250] in a more recent "trade secret" decision the court did consider such a claim.[251])

In Worthington Compressors, Inc. v. Costle,[252] the D.C. Circuit held that the cost of reverse engineering is a pertinent inquiry and that the test should be "whether release of the requested information, given its commercial value to competitors and the cost of acquiring it through other means, will cause substantial competitive harm to the business that submitted it."[253]

---

[248] Id.; see Public Citizen, 997 F. Supp. at 66 (recognizing that although some requested information "may be available because of overseas marketing," the "context provided by" agency release renders it "different," and competitive harm not "diminish[ed]").

[249] Northwest Coalition, 941 F. Supp. at 202.

[250] See Pacific Sky Supply, Inc. v. Department of the Air Force, No. 86-2044, 1997 WL 28485, at *1 (D.D.C. Dec. 16, 1987) (refusing to consider feasibility of reverse engineering for documents withheld as trade secrets because once trade secret determination is made, documents "'are exempt from disclosure, and no further inquiry is necessary'" (quoting Public Citizen, 704 F.2d at 1286)).

[251] See Center for Auto Safety v. National Highway Traffic Safety Admin., No. 99-1759, 2000 WL 359622, at *14 (D.D.C. Feb. 28, 2000) (considering, but rejecting, requester's argument that physical characteristics of air bags "are easily discernible" by "using simple hand tools to dismantle" them and finding instead that "[d]ismantling air bags to learn this information is dangerous, time-consuming, and expensive" and that therefore trade secret protection was appropriate) (appeal pending).

[252] 662 F.2d 45 (D.C. Cir.), supplemental opinion sub nom. Worthington Compressors, Inc. v. Gorsuch, 668 F.2d 1371 (D.C. Cir. 1981).

[253] Id. at 52; accord Greenberg, 803 F.2d at 1218; Northwest Coalition, 941 F. Supp. at 202; Daniels Mfg. Corp. v. DOD, No. 85-291, slip op. at 7-8 (M.D. Fla. June 3, 1986); Air Line Pilots Ass'n Int'l v. FAA, 552 F. Supp. 811, 814 (D.D.C. 1982); see also Zotos Int'l v. Young, 830 F.2d 350, 353 (D.C. Cir. 1987) (if commercially valuable information has remained secret for many years, it is incongruous to argue that it may be readily reverse-engineered) (non-FOIA case); Heeney, No. 97-5461, slip op. at 20 (C.D. Cal. Mar. 18, 1999) (rejecting the requester's claim that reverse engineering was possible, based on his failure to demonstrate "that he has the technical expertise to offer opin-

(continued...)

**EXEMPTION 4**

In that case, the D.C. Circuit pointed out that agency disclosures of information that benefit competitors at the expense of submitters deserve "close attention" by the courts.[254] As the court of appeals observed:

> Because competition in business turns on the relative costs and opportunities faced by members of the same industry, there is a potential windfall for competitors to whom valuable information is released under FOIA. If those competitors are charged only minimal FOIA retrieval costs for the information, rather than the considerable costs of private reproduction, they may be getting quite a bargain. Such bargains could easily have competitive consequences not contemplated as part of FOIA's principal aim of promoting openness in government.[255]

---

(...continued)
ions about reverse-engineering of the devices at issue," and finding that the documents requested revealed "more than could be learned through reverse-engineering" in any event).

[254] 662 F.2d at 51.

[255] Id.; see, e.g., Public Citizen, 185 F.3d at 905 (declaring that Exemption 4 "clearly" is designed to protect against disclosures that would permit competitors "to eliminate much of the time and effort that would otherwise be required to bring to market a [competitive] product" (citing Webb v. HHS, 696 F.2d 101, 103 (D.C. Cir. 1982) ("If a [drug] manufacturer's competitor could obtain all the data in the manufacturer's [New Drug Application (NDA)], it could utilize them in its own NDA without incurring the time, labor, risk, and expense involved in developing them independently."))); Public Citizen, 2000 U.S. Dist. LEXIS 4108, at **10-12 (protecting a company's investigators' names and the titles of unpublished articles because disclosure would permit competitors to "'eliminate much of the time and effort that would otherwise be required to bring to market'" a competitive product and because the company had "provid[ed] evidence that it would be costly for competitors to figure out through their own efforts all of the names and unpublished article titles at issue"); Sokolow v. FDA, No. 1:97-CV-252, slip op. at 7 (E.D. Tex. Feb. 19, 1998) (protecting drug safety and effectiveness information because it "could be used by competitors to develop clinical studies or other research toward a competing product"), aff'd, 162 F.3d 1160 (5th Cir. 1998) (unpublished table decision); Cohen, No. 95-6140, slip op. at 12 (D.N.J. Nov. 25, 1996) (protecting raw data contained in research study inasmuch as disclosure "would allow competitors to develop or refine their [own] products and avoid [incurring] the [corresponding] research and development costs because of the opportunity to piggy-back upon [the submitter's] development efforts," which "would therefore have [an] unwarranted deleterious impact on [the submitter's] competitive position"); Washington Psychiatric Soc'y v. OPM, No. 87-1913, 1988 U.S. Dist. LEXIS 17069, at *6 (D.D.C. Oct. 13, 1988); Pacific Sky Supply, Inc. v. Department of the Air Force, No. 86-2044, 1987 WL 18214, at **4-5 (D.D.C. Sept. 29, 1987), modified, No. 86-2044 (D.D.C. Nov. 20, 1987), motion to amend judgment denied, No. 86-2044 (D.D.C. Dec. 16, 1987); Air Line Pilots Ass'n v. FAA, 552 F. Supp. 811, 814 (D.D.C. 1982); see also Allnet, 800 F. Supp. at 988-89 (noting submitter's twenty-two million dollar investment and
(continued...)

# EXEMPTION 4

An agency's assertion of competitive harm for portions of a pesticide formula--which admittedly was capable of being reverse engineered--was rejected when the agency failed to explain "how difficult and costly" it would be to do so because, as the party "seeking to avoid disclosure," the agency was found not to have sustained its burden of "production and persuasion on that point."[256] Likewise, when information was found to be "freely or cheaply available from other sources," a court rejected a competitive harm claim, declaring that such information "cannot be considered protected confidential information."[257]

Neither the willingness of the requester to restrict circulation of the information[258] nor a claim by the requester that it is not a competitor of the submitter[259] should logically defeat a showing of competitive harm.[260] The question is whether "public disclosure" would cause harm; there is no "middle

---

(...continued)
rejecting requester's argument that receipt of seven million dollars in annual sales revenue is somehow "de minimis"); SMS Data Prods. Group, Inc. v. United States Dep't of the Air Force, No. 88-0481, 1989 WL 201031, at *3 (D.D.C. Mar. 31, 1989) (noting that release would allow competitors access to information that they would otherwise have to spend "considerable funds" to develop on their own).

[256] Northwest Coalition, 941 F. Supp. at 202.

[257] Frazee, 97 F.3d at 371 (upholding agency decision to release contractor's operating plan for managing recreational areas in national forest because "large portion of the [requested] information, such as details regarding collection and handling of fees, operating season dates, rules, and law enforcement, is available to anyone using or visiting the facilities" and other information, "such as employee uniforms, maintenance equipment, and signs, is in public view daily"--thereby making it unlikely that disclosure of operating plan would cause competitive harm); see also Atlantis Submarines Haw., Inc. v. United States Coast Guard, No. 93-00986, slip op. at 8 (D. Haw. Jan. 28, 1994) (finding that disclosure of admittedly "readily-observable" procedures in submarine operations manual would not afford competitors "any substantial 'windfall'" and so would not cause competitive harm) (denying motion for preliminary injunction in reverse FOIA suit), dismissed per stipulation (D. Haw. Apr. 11, 1994).

[258] See Seawell, Dalton, Hughes & Timms v. Export-Import Bank, No. 84-241, slip op. at 2 (E.D. Va. July 27, 1984); cf. Schiffer v. FBI, 78 F.3d 1405, 1411 (9th Cir. 1996) ("limited access" to exempt records, subject to protective order, "not authorized by FOIA") (Exemption 7(C) case).

[259] See, e.g., Burke Energy Corp. v. Department of Energy for the United States, 583 F. Supp. 507, 512 (D. Kan. 1984) (characterizing requester's "argument that it is not a competitor" as "totally without merit").

[260] Heeney, No. 97-5461, slip op. at 10 (C.D. Cal. Mar. 18, 1999) (explaining that the "identity of the requester is irrelevant . . . because once information has been released--even to a private, noncompeting individual such as [this particular requester]--the information has reached the public domain and cannot be withheld from subsequent requesters").

# EXEMPTION 4

ground between disclosure and nondisclosure."[261] Additionally, the passage of time, while sometimes eroding the likelihood of competitive injury,[262] does not necessarily defeat Exemption 4 protection, provided that disclosure of the material would still be likely to cause substantial competitive harm.[263] Finally, the D.C. Circuit has emphasized recently that it is incumbent upon the courts--and, logically, upon agencies in the first instance--to consider whether it is possible to redact requested information "in order to avoid application of Exemption 4."[264] (See the further discussions of this under Procedural Requirements, "Reasonably Segregable" Obligation, above, and Litigation Considerations, "Reasonably Segregable" Requirements, below.)

---

[261] Seawell, No. 84-241, slip op. at 2 (E.D. Va. July 27, 1984).

[262] See, e.g., Garren, No. CV-97-273, slip op. at 19-20 (D. Or. Nov. 17, 1997) (rejecting competitive harm claim for sales prices for concessions sold "seven or eight years" ago, finding that "price may be different for future transactions involving other parties and other companies and, potentially, a different operating environment"); Lee, 923 F. Supp. at 455 (rejecting competitive harm argument because "financial information in question is given for [a period two years previously] and any potential detriment which could be caused by its disclosure would seem likely to have mitigated with the passage of time"); Teich, 751 F. Supp. at 253 (rejecting competitive harm claim based partly upon fact that documents were as many as 20 years old); see also Africa Fund v. Mosbacher, No. 92-289, 1993 WL 183736, at *8 (S.D.N.Y. May 26, 1993) (rejecting argument that exemption permanently precludes release because passage of time might render later disclosures "of little consequence").

[263] See Center for Auto Safety, 2000 WL 359622, at *15 (declaring that "[i]nformation does not become stale merely because it is old" and protecting information that "represents years of research and development" which would "provide insights into a manufacturer's 'design concept and philosophy'"); see also, e.g., Burke, 583 F. Supp. at 514 (nine-year-old data protected); Timken Co. v. United States Customs Serv., 3 Gov't Disclosure Serv. (P-H) ¶ 83,234, at 83,976 (D.D.C. June 24, 1983) (ten-year-old data protected); see also FOIA Update, Vol. IV, No. 4, at 14.

[264] Trans-Pac. Policing Agreement v. United States Customs Serv., 177 F.3d 1022, 1029 (D.C. Cir. 1999) (holding that although "[t]here is certainly no doubt" that Exemption 4 was properly applied to ten-digit customs code, remand was necessary to determine whether "disclosure of redacted [codes] poses a likelihood of substantial harm"); see also Public Citizen, 185 F.3d at 907 (remanding to determine "whether the documents the agency has withheld contain information that can be segregated and disclosed"); Judicial Watch, Inc. v. United States Dep't of Commerce, 83 F. Supp. 2d 105, 111 (D.D.C. 1999) (deferring ruling on applicability of Exemption 4--despite finding that the affidavits "appear to support the withholding" of the documents--because they failed to provide sufficient detail "to permit the Court to conclude that documents withheld in their entirety do not contain any reasonably segregable information"); Attorney General's Memorandum for Heads of Departments and Agencies regarding the Freedom of Information Act (Oct. 4, 1993), reprinted in FOIA Update, Vol. XIV, No. 3, at 4-5 (reiterating importance of FOIA's "reasonable segregability" requirement).

# EXEMPTION 4

Numerous types of competitive injury have been identified by the courts as properly cognizable under the competitive harm prong, including the harms generally caused by disclosure of: detailed financial information such as a company's assets, liabilities, and net worth;[265] a company's actual costs, break-even calculations, profits and profit rates;[266] data describing a company's workforce which would reveal labor costs, profit margins and competitive vulnerability;[267] a company's selling prices, purchase activity and freight charges;[268] a company's purchase records, including prices paid for advertising;[269] technical and commercial data, names of consultants and subcontractors, performance, cost and equipment information;[270] shipper and importer names, type and quantity of freight hauled, routing systems, cost of raw materials, and information constituting the "bread and butter" of a manufacturing company;[271] currently unannounced and future products, proprietary technical information, pricing strategy and subcontractor information;[272] raw research data used to support a pharmaceutical drug's safety and effectiveness,

---

[265] See, e.g., National Parks, 547 F.2d at 684; Inner City Press/Community on the Move v. Board of Governors of the Fed. Reserve Sys., No. 98-4608, 1998 U.S. Dist. LEXIS 15333, at *14 (S.D.N.Y. Sept. 30, 1998) ("capital situation, [company's] assets, cash flow, investments, leverage ratios, 'cross-selling strategy,' pre-tax earnings by product line, dividend capacity, revenues, and rate changes for its insurance operations"), aff'd, 182 F.3d 900 (2d Cir. 1999) (unpublished table decision); Cleveland & Vicinity Dist. Council v. United States Dep't of Labor, No. 87CV2384, slip op. at 8-9 (N.D. Ohio Apr. 22, 1992) (magistrate's recommendation) (dollar volume of business), adopted (N.D. Ohio May 22, 1992).

[266] See, e.g., Gulf & Western, 615 F.2d at 530; see also Cortez III Serv. Corp. v. NASA, 921 F. Supp. 8, 12 (D.D.C. 1996) (General and Administrative (G & A) rate ceilings that are "nearly identical" to actual G & A rates) (alternative holding) (reverse FOIA suit), appeal dismissed voluntarily, No. 96-5163 (D.C. Cir. July 3, 1996).

[267] See, e.g., Westinghouse Elec. Corp. v. Schlesinger, 392 F. Supp. 1246, 1249 (E.D. Va. 1974), aff'd, 542 F.2d 1190 (4th Cir. 1976).

[268] See, e.g., Braintree, 494 F. Supp. at 289.

[269] See, e.g., Destileria Serralles, Inc. v. Department of the Treasury, No. 85-0837, slip op. at 9 (D.P.R. Sept. 22, 1988).

[270] See, e.g., RMS, No. C-92-1545, slip op. at 7 (N.D. Cal. Nov. 24, 1992); BDM Corp. v. SBA, 2 Gov't Disclosure Serv. (P-H) ¶ 81,189, at 81,495 (D.D.C. Mar. 20, 1981).

[271] Journal of Commerce, Inc. v. United States Dep't of the Treasury, No. 86-1075, 1988 U.S. Dist. LEXIS 17610, at **9-10 (D.D.C. Mar. 30, 1988), aff'd, 878 F.2d 1446 (Fed. Cir. 1989) (unpublished table decision); see, e.g., Inter Ocean Free Zone, 982 F. Supp. at 869, 873.

[272] See, e.g., SMS, 1989 WL 201031, at **3-4; see also Matthews v. United States Postal Serv., No. 92-1208-CV-W-8, slip op. at 6 (W.D. Mo. Apr. 15, 1994) (technical drawings relating to computer system sold to government, technology for which was still being sold to others).

**EXEMPTION 4**

information regarding an unapproved application to market the drug in a different manner, and sales and distribution data of a drug manufacturer;[273] and technical proposals which are submitted, or could be used, in conjunction with offers on government contracts.[274]

The District Court for the Southern District of New York has recognized protection under the competitive harm prong for documents pertaining to a proposed real estate venture, despite the fact that the harm that would flow from disclosure would come from a citizens group, rather than from competing real estate developers.[275] The court made its finding in light of the fact that the "avowed goal" of that group was "to drive the joint venture out of business."[276] The court found that irrespective of the identity of the requester, "the economic injury they may inflict on the joint venture is nonetheless a competitive injury" that would "jeopardize both the venture's relative position vis-a-vis other New York City real estate developers and its solvency."[277] This holding was affirmed by the Court of Appeals for the Second Circuit, which reiterated that "[t]he fact that [the] harm would result from active hindrance by the [requester] rather than directly by potential competitors does not affect the fairness considerations that underlie Exemption Four."[278]

The Second Circuit was faced with another "unusual question" concerning the applicability of the competitive harm prong when it decided a case involving a FOIA requester who "already [had] knowledge of the confidential information contained in the withheld documents."[279] The case concerned a request for design drawings that had been submitted by two companies seek-

---

[273] See Citizens Comm'n, No. 92-5313, slip op. at 18-20 (C.D. Cal. May 10, 1993); see also Heeney, No. 97-5461, slip op. at 14 (C.D. Cal. Mar. 18, 1999); Sokolow, No. 1:97-CV-252, slip op. at 7-8 (E.D. Tex. Feb. 19, 1998); Cohen, No. 95-6140, slip op. at 11-12 (D.N.J. Nov. 25 1996).

[274] See, e.g., Pentagen Techs. Int'l v. United States, No. 98CIV.4831, 2000 WL 347165, at *3 (S.D.N.Y. Mar. 31, 2000) (alternative holding); Joint Bd. of Control v. Bureau of Indian Affairs, No. 87-217, slip op. at 8 (D. Mont. Sept. 9, 1988); Landfair v. United States Dep't of the Army, 645 F. Supp. 325, 329 (D.D.C. 1986); Professional Review Org. v. HHS, 607 F. Supp. 423, 426 (D.D.C. 1985) (detailing manner in which professional services contract was to be conducted).

[275] Nadler v. FDIC, 899 F. Supp. 158, 163 (S.D.N.Y. 1995), aff'd, 92 F.3d 93 (2d Cir. 1996).

[276] Id.

[277] Id.

[278] Nadler v. FDIC, 92 F.3d 93, 97 (2d Cir. 1996). But cf. CNA, 830 F.2d at 1154 (in context of rejecting competitive harm argument based on "anticipated displeasure of [submitter's] employees" and on fear of "adverse public reaction," D.C. Circuit observed that such objections "simply do not amount to 'harm flowing from the affirmative use of proprietary information by competitors'" (quoting Public Citizen, 704 F.2d at 1291 n.30)).

[279] United Techs. Corp. v. FAA, 102 F.3d 688, 689 (2d Cir. 1996).

## EXEMPTION 4

ing approval to manufacture aircraft parts.[280] Those companies sought approval pursuant to "identicality" regulations, which permit a manufacturer to obtain approval for its parts based upon a showing that those parts are "identical" to parts which have already been approved; in this case, the approved parts were manufactured by the requester.[281] The requester argued that because the requested documents were "identical in all respects to the drawings" that it itself had previously submitted, they could not "be 'confidential' as to [the requester] within the meaning of FOIA Exemption 4."[282] In rejecting that contention, the Second Circuit first noted that "[i]t is a basic principle under [the] FOIA that the individuating circumstances of a requester are not to be considered in deciding whether a particular document should be disclosed."[283] Accordingly, the fact that the requester "already ha[d] knowledge of the information contained in the withheld documents" was found to be "irrelevant."[284] The Second Circuit also rejected the requester's argument that the Supreme Court's decision in United States Department of Justice v. Julian,[285] supported its contention "that confidentiality under Exemption 4 should be examined on a requester-specific basis," holding that because the requester was "not the party for whom the protections of Exemption 4 were intended, it ha[d] no claim of special access."[286] Inasmuch as the requester "'freely concede[d]' that it [could not] prevail if it must proceed" as if it were "any other member of the general public," the Second Circuit upheld the agency's decision to withhold the information.[287]

On the other hand, protection under the competitive harm prong has been denied when the prospect of injury is remote[288]--for example when a

---

[280] Id.

[281] Id.

[282] Id. at 690.

[283] Id.

[284] Id. at 691.

[285] 486 U.S. 1 (1988) (holding that presentence report privilege, which is designed to protect subjects of such reports, cannot be invoked against those same subjects when they seek access to their own reports).

[286] United Techs., 102 F.3d at 691-92 (noting that test for determining competitive harm "does not appear to contemplate its application on a requester-specific basis").

[287] Id.

[288] See, e.g., Carolina, No. 93CV00113, slip op. at 9 (M.D.N.C. Aug. 2, 1993) (finding that disclosure of the number of animals sold by companies supplying laboratory specimens "will be simply a small addition to information available in the marketplace" and thus will not cause competitive harm); Teich, 751 F. Supp. at 254 (concluding that disclosure of safety and effectiveness data pertaining to medical device at "this late date" in product approval process "could not possibly help" competitors of submitter); see also Brown,
(continued...)

# EXEMPTION 4

government contract is not awarded competitively[289]--or when the requested information is too general in nature.[290]

In addition, the D.C. Circuit, as well as several other courts, have held that the harms flowing from "embarrassing disclosure[s],"[291] or disclosures

---

(...continued)
1991 U.S. Dist. LEXIS 1780, at *7 (D.D.C. Feb. 15, 1991) (concluding that certain wage information is not protected because no showing was made that submitter would suffer "'substantial' injury" if information were disclosed).

[289] See Hercules, Inc. v. Marsh, 839 F.2d 1027, 1030 (4th Cir. 1988) (reverse FOIA suit); see also Garren, No. CV-97-273, slip op. at 22 (D. Or. Nov. 17, 1997) (ordering disclosure of sales price information for river rafting concessions in Grand Canyon National Park as there was "very little competition, and [a] built-in preference favors existing concessioners and allows them to match any competing bid, thereby negating the potential competitive harm from disclosure of the information"); U.S. News & World Report v. Department of the Treasury, No. 84-2303, 1986 U.S. Dist. LEXIS 27634, at *14 (D.D.C. Mar. 26, 1986) (ordering disclosure of aggregate contract price for armored limousines for the President because release would not be competitively harmful given unique nature of contract and agency's role in design of vehicles); cf. Cove Shipping, Inc. v. Military Sealift Command, No. 84-2709, slip op. at 8-10 (D.D.C. Feb. 27, 1986) (ordering release of contract's wage and benefit breakdown because it related to "one isolated contract, in an industry where labor contracts vary from bid to bid") (civil discovery case in which Exemption 4 case law applied).

[290] See, e.g., GC Micro, 33 F.3d at 1111 (general information on percentage and dollar amount of work subcontracted out to small disadvantaged businesses that does not reveal "breakdown of how the contractor is subcontracting the work, nor . . . the subject matter of the prime contract or subcontracts, the number of subcontracts, the items or services subcontracted, or the subcontractors' locations or identities"); North Carolina Network, No. 90-1443, slip op. at 9 (4th Cir. Feb. 5, 1991) (general information regarding sales and pricing that would not reveal submitters' costs, profits, sources, or age, size, condition, or breed of animals sold); SMS, 1989 WL 201031, at *4 (general information regarding publicly held corporation's management structure, financial and production capabilities, corporate history and employees, most of which would be found in corporation's annual report and SEC filings and would in any event be readily available to any stockholder interested in obtaining such information); Davis Corp. v. United States, No. 87-3365, 1988 U.S. Dist. LEXIS 17611, at **10-11 (D.D.C. Jan. 19, 1988) (information contained in letters from contractor to agency regarding performance of contract that did not reveal contractor's suppliers or costs) (reverse FOIA suit); EHE Nat'l Health Serv. v. HHS, No. 81-1087, slip op. at 5 (D.D.C. Feb. 24, 1984) ("mundane" information regarding submitter's operation) (reverse FOIA suit); American Scissors Corp. v. GSA, No. 83-1562, 1983 U.S. Dist. LEXIS 11712, at *11 (D.D.C. Nov. 15, 1983) (general description of manufacturing process with no details) (reverse FOIA suit).

[291] General Elec. Co. v. NRC, 750 F.2d 1394, 1402 (7th Cir. 1984) (reverse
(continued...)

## EXEMPTION 4

which could cause "customer or employee disgruntlement," are not cognizable under the competitive harm prong of Exemption 4.[292] (Moreover, such harms would not be cognizable under Exemption 6 either, for it is well established

---

[291](...continued)
FOIA suit).

[292] See, e.g., CNA, 830 F.2d at 1154 (declaring that "unfavorable publicity" and "demoralized" employees insufficient for showing of competitive harm); Public Citizen, 704 F.2d at 1291 n.30 (observing that competitive harm should "'be limited to harm flowing from the affirmative use of proprietary information by competitors'" and "'should not be taken to mean'" harms such as "'customer or employee disgruntlement'" or "'embarrassing publicity attendant upon public revelations concerning, for example, illegal or unethical payments to government officials'" (quoting law review article)); Center to Prevent Handgun Violence v. United States Dep't of the Treasury, 981 F. Supp. 20, 23 (D.D.C. 1997) (denying competitive harm claim for disclosure that would cause "unwarranted criticism and harassment" inasmuch as harm must "flow from competitors' use of the released information, not from any use made by the public at large or customers"), appeal dismissed, No. 97-5357 (D.C. Cir. Feb. 2, 1998); Daisy Mfg. Co. v. Consumer Prod. Safety Comm'n, No. 96-5152, 1997 WL 578960, at *4 (W.D. Ark. Feb. 5, 1997) (declaring that court "cannot condone" use of FOIA "as shield[] against potentially negative, or inaccurate, publicity") (reverse FOIA suit), aff'd, 133 F.3d 1081 (8th Cir. 1998); Public Citizen, 964 F. Supp. at 415 n.2 (opining that it is "questionable whether the competitive injury associated with 'alarmism' qualifies under Exemption 4" because competitive harm does not encompass "adverse public reaction"); Martech USA, Inc. v. Reich, No. C-93-4137, slip op. at 5 (N.D. Cal. Nov. 24, 1993) (maintaining that although "information could damage . . . [submitter's] reputation, this is not the type of competitive harm protected by" Exemption 4) (denying motion for temporary restraining order in reverse FOIA suit); Silverberg, 1991 WL 633740, at *4 (discounting possibility that competitors might "distort" requested information and thus cause submitter embarrassment as insufficient for showing of competitive harm); Badhwar v. United States Dep't of the Air Force, 622 F. Supp. 1364, 1377 (D.D.C. 1985) (concluding that "fear of litigation" insufficient for showing of competitive harm), aff'd in part & rev'd in part on other grounds, 829 F.2d 182 (D.C. Cir. 1987); cf. Playboy Enters. v. United States Customs Serv., 959 F. Supp. 11, 17 (D.D.C. 1997) (finding, in context of awarding attorney fees, that when agency initially withheld documents to protect "commercial interests of an alleged counterfeiter," that position was so unreasonable as to be "devoid of any merit"), appeal dismissed, No. 97-5128 (D.C. Cir. June 18, 1997). But see McDonnell Douglas, 180 F.3d at 306-07 (inexplicably accepting as legally valid submitter's claim that disclosure of government contract prices would cause submitter harm by permitting its "commercial customers to bargain down ('ratchet down') its prices more effectively"); Bauer v. United States, No. 92-0376, slip op. at 4 (D.D.C. Sept. 30, 1993) (inexplicably upholding deletion of name of corporation mentioned in investigatory report because release of name "in connection with a criminal investigation could cause undue speculation and commercial harm to that corporation"), remanded, No. 94-5205 (D.C. Cir. Apr. 14, 1995).

**EXEMPTION 4**

that businesses have no "corporate privacy."[293] For a further discussion of this point, see Exemption 6, Privacy Considerations, below.) Nevertheless, the D.C. Circuit skirted this issue and expressly did not decide whether an allegation of harm flowing only from the embarrassing publicity associated with disclosure of a submitter's illegal payments to government officials would be sufficient to establish competitive harm.[294] The court did go on to declare, however, that the submitter's "right to an exemption, if any, depends upon the competitive significance of whatever information may be contained in the documents" and that the submitter's motive for seeking confidential treatment, even if it was to avoid embarrassing publicity, was "simply irrelevant."[295]

Despite a wealth of case law supporting disclosure of government contract prices (as discussed below), the D.C. Circuit rendered a decision this past year in McDonnell Douglas Corp. v. NASA, that abruptly set aside NASA's disclosure determination for just such information.[296] The District Court for the District of Columbia had upheld NASA's decision to release contract prices based on the agency's thorough rebuttal of McDonnell Douglas's claims that release would cause it competitive harm.[297] The lower court reiterated the numerous grounds for NASA's disclosure decision, including the fact that release of contract pricing information "furthers the goals of [the] FOIA."[298] In addition, the court held that NASA had effectively disputed McDonnell Douglas's contentions regarding competitive harm when it determined that contractors "compete on a variety of factors other than price," that foreign competitors were "not likely to be substantially aided by release," and that "any difficulty" McDonnell Douglas "may face in future commercial contract negotiations [did] not qualify as a substantial competitive injury and should be viewed as the cost of doing business with the Government."[299]

The D.C. Circuit tersely reversed, however, dismissively characterizing NASA's responses to McDonnell Douglas as "silly," "mystifying," "convoluted," and "even astonishing."[300] Without reference to any of the prior appellate

---

[293] See, e.g., National Parks, 547 F.2d at 685 n.44.

[294] Occidental Petroleum Corp. v. SEC, 873 F.2d 325, 341 (D.C. Cir. 1989) (reverse FOIA suit).

[295] Id.

[296] 180 F.3d 303 (D.C. Cir. 1999) (reverse FOIA suit), reh'g en banc denied, No. 98-5251 (D.C. Cir. Oct. 6, 1999).

[297] McDonnell Douglas Corp. v. NASA, 981 F. Supp. 12, 16 (D.D.C. 1997) (reverse FOIA suit), reconsideration denied, No. 96-2611, slip op. at 7-8 (D.D.C. May 1, 1998), rev'd, 180 F.3d 303 (D.C. Cir. 1999), reh'g en banc denied, No. 98-5251 (D.C. Cir. Oct. 6, 1999).

[298] Id.

[299] Id.

[300] 180 F.3d at 306-07.

## EXEMPTION 4

court rulings on the issue,[301] or even to its own prior decisions limiting the type of harm recognized under the competitive harm prong to harm flowing from affirmative use of the information by competitors,[302] the D.C. Circuit perfunctorily declared McDonnell Douglas's arguments--that release "would permit its commercial customers to bargain down ('ratchet down') its prices more effectively" and "would help its domestic and international competitors to underbid it"--to be "indisputable."[303] As such, the opinion sets forth no new principle of law that should be applied in future such cases.[304] Because the cursory nature of the opinion and its lack of legal analysis make it difficult to draw conclusions from it, it is expected that further case law development on this issue will confine this decision to its particular facts and administrative record.[305]

Two years ago, at the same time that the lower court decision in McDonnell Douglas was handed down, another court upheld an agency's decision to disclose unit prices.[306] There, the submitter provided only "conclusory and generalized assertions" of harm, that "mainly detailed measures it took to guard and protect its pricing information," that the court found were "simply not relevant to the National Parks analysis."[307] An additional argument--that the submitter would suffer harm because the "contract contemplates option years and may be rebid," was not raised before the agency and so was considered to be "outside the scope of the administrative record."[308] Nonetheless, the court addressed it in the alternative, finding it "unpersuasive," as the precedent primarily relied on by the submitter concerned the possibility of "rebidding a contract for unperformed work," a situation deemed "factually and

---

[301] See Pacific Architects & Eng'rs v. United States Dep't of State, 906 F.2d 1345, 1347 (9th Cir. 1990) (upholding disclosure of contract unit prices) (reverse FOIA suit); Acumenics Research & Tech., Inc. v. United States Dep't of Justice, 843 F.2d 800, 808 (4th Cir. 1988) (same) (reverse FOIA suit).

[302] See CNA, 830 F.2d at 1154; Public Citizen, 704 F.2d at 1291 n.30.

[303] McDonnell Douglas, 180 F.3d at 306-07.

[304] See McDonnell Douglas Corp. v. NASA, No. 98-5251, slip op. at 2 (D.C. Cir. Oct. 6, 1999) (Silberman, J., concurring in denial of rehearing en banc) (clarifying that court's decision "did not" hold that protection of contract prices would "invariably" be called for and stressing that, rather, it held "only that the agency's explanation of its position" in that case was insufficient).

[305] See id.; see also Federal Acquisition Regulation (FAR), 48 C.F.R. §§ 15.503(b)(iv), 15.506(d)(2) (1999) (mandating disclosure of unit prices in post-award notices and debriefings for contracts solicited after January 1, 1998, and therefore providing the government with the "legal duty or authority . . . to publicize" prices, which the court twice stressed that it had found lacking in McDonnell Douglas, 180 F.3d at 306).

[306] TRIFID Corp. v. National Imagery & Mapping Agency, 10 F. Supp. 2d 1087, 1099-1101 (E.D. Mo. 1998) (reverse FOIA suit).

[307] Id. at 1099.

[308] Id.

# EXEMPTION 4

legally distinguishable from" the case at hand.[309]

A similar challenge to an agency's decision to disclose, among other things, a contractor's unit price information was soundly rejected in yet another decision by the District Court for the District of Columbia.[310] In upholding the agency's decision to release the information, the court rejected the submitter's contention that disclosure would enable its competitors "to predict its costs and profit margin, significantly enhancing their ability to underbid."[311] Declaring that "[t]he public, including competitors who lost the business to the winning bidder, is entitled to know just how and why a government agency decided to spend public funds as it did; to be assured that the competition was fair; and indeed, even to learn how to be more effective competitors in the future," the court upheld the agency's decision to release the information because the submitter had "simply failed to demonstrate" how it would be competitively harmed by its disclosure.[312] Although noting that the submitter "might prefer that less be known about its operations, and that the reasons for its past successes remain a mystery to be solved by the competitors on their own," the court held that the submitter had not shown "that it will in fact be unable to duplicate those successes unless [the agency] acquiesces in keeping the competition in the dark."[313]

The outcome of that case was consistent with four cases concerning contract price information that were decided previously--all of which were brought by submitters challenging agency decisions to disclose such information--and in which none of the submitters were able to convince the court that disclosure of the prices charged the government would cause them to suffer competitive harm.[314] One of the cases was remanded back to the agency for further factfinding on that issue,[315] but in the remaining three cases the com-

---

[309] Id. at 1100.

[310] Martin Marietta, 974 F. Supp. at 38 (specifically, "cost and fee information," and "component and configuration prices"--including unit pricing and contract line item numbers--and "technical and management information").

[311] Id. at 40.

[312] Id. at 41.

[313] Id.

[314] McDonnell Douglas Corp. v. NASA, 895 F. Supp. 319, 326 (D.D.C. 1995) (reverse FOIA suit), vacated as moot, No. 95-5288 (D.C. Cir. Apr. 1, 1996); CC Distribs. v. Kinzinger, No. 94-1330, 1995 WL 405445, at **5-6 (D.D.C. June 28, 1995) (reverse FOIA suit); Chemical Waste Management, Inc. v. O'Leary, No. 94-2230, 1995 WL 115894, at **4-5 (D.D.C. Feb. 28, 1995) (reverse FOIA suit); Comdisco, Inc. v. GSA, 864 F. Supp. 510, 516 (E.D. Va. 1994) (reverse FOIA suit).

[315] Chemical Waste, 1995 WL 115894, at *5 (agency required to correct administrative record by addressing submitter's "actual complaints of [competitive] harm," i.e., that when contract was rebid, new contractor "will be asked to perform the exact same--and, as yet, unrendered--services that were ex-
(continued...)

## EXEMPTION 4

petitive harm arguments were rejected outright by the court.[316] (One of these cases subsequently was vacated after the FOIA request was withdrawn while the case was on appeal.[317])

Additionally, there are three other cases which contain a thorough analysis of the possible effects of disclosure of unit prices--including two appellate decisions--and in all three of these cases the courts likewise denied Exemption 4 protection, finding that disclosure of the prices would not directly reveal confidential proprietary information, such as a company's overhead, profit rates, or multiplier, and that the possibility of competitive harm was thus too speculative.[318] For example, the Court of Appeals for the Ninth Circuit denied Exemption 4 protection for the unit prices provided by a successful offeror despite the offeror's contention that competitors would be able to determine its profit margin by simply subtracting from the unit price the other component parts which are either set by statute or standardized within the industry.[319] The Ninth Circuit upheld the agency's determination that competitors would not be able to make this type of calculation because the component figures making up the unit price were not, in fact, standardized, but instead were subject to fluctuation.[320]

Almost twenty years ago, in the absence of a showing of competitive

---

(...continued)
pected to be performed under" existing contract).

[316] McDonnell Douglas, 895 F. Supp. at 326 (submitter "failed to show with any particularity how a competitor could use the information at issue to cause competitive injury"); CC Distribs., 1995 WL 405445, at *5 (submitter failed "to explain how its competitors could reverse-engineer its pricing methods and deduce its concessions from suppliers," which it had conclusorily claimed would occur if its unit prices were disclosed); Comdisco, 864 F. Supp. at 516 (submitter failed to satisfy standard that it "present persuasive evidence that disclosure of the unit prices would reveal some confidential piece of information, such as a profit multiplier or risk assessment, that would place the submitter at a competitive disadvantage").

[317] See McDonnell Douglas Corp. v. NASA, No. 95-5288 (D.C. Cir. Apr. 1, 1996).

[318] Pacific Architects, 906 F.2d at 1347; Acumenics, 843 F.2d at 808; J.H. Lawrence Co. v. Smith, No. 81-2993, slip op. at 8-9 (D. Md. Nov. 10, 1982). But see Sperry Univac Div. v. Baldrige, 3 Gov't Disclosure Serv. (P-H) ¶ 83,265, at 84,052 (E.D. Va. June 16, 1982) (protecting unit prices on finding that they revealed submitter's pricing and discount strategy), appeal dismissed, No. 82-1723 (4th Cir. Nov. 22, 1982).

[319] Pacific Architects, 906 F.2d at 1347.

[320] Id. at 1347-48; see RMS, No. C-92-1545, slip op. at 7 (N.D. Cal. Nov. 24, 1992) (court "unconvinced based on the evidence that the release of contract bid prices, terms and conditions whether interim or final will harm the successful bidders"); see also GC Micro, 33 F.3d at 1114-15 (relying on Pacific Architects, court orders disclosure of percentage and dollar amount of work subcontracted out by defense contractors).

**EXEMPTION 4**

harm, the District Court for the District of Columbia denied Exemption 4 protection for the prices charged the government for computer equipment, and in so doing stated that "[d]isclosure of prices charged the Government is a cost of doing business with the Government."[321] This "cost of doing business" principle was later expressly recognized by the District Court for the District of Columbia as a "general proposition" that agencies may reasonably follow.[322] Although it is not applicable "to every case that arises,"[323] the court nevertheless found that it is "incumbent upon" a submitter challenging a contract price disclosure decision to "demonstrate that [an agency's] decision to follow this general proposition"--namely, that disclosure of contract prices is a cost of doing business with the government--is somehow arbitrary or capricious.[324] This ruling comports with the court's decision in an earlier unit price case in which it had recognized the "strong public interest in release of component and aggregate prices in Government contract awards."[325] Although the D.C. Circuit in its recent decision in McDonnell Douglas noted that NASA had advised the submitter "that publication of line item prices is the 'price of doing business' with the government," the court inexplicably took the view that such a statement "either assumes the conclusion, or else assumes a legal duty or authority on the government to publicize these prices," something that NASA did not assert in that case.[326]

Such a "legal authority" can be found in the Federal Acquisition Regulation (FAR)--the governmentwide regulation that governs agency contracting--which specifically provides that the unit prices of each contract award are to be disclosed to unsuccessful offerors during the postaward notice and debriefing process; most significantly, the FAR expressly provides that "any stated unit prices of each award shall be made publicly available, upon request."[327]

---

[321] Racal-Milgo Gov't Sys. v. SBA, 559 F. Supp. 4, 6 (D.D.C. 1981); accord CC Distribs., 1995 WL 405445, at *6; JL Assocs., 90-2 CPD 261, B-239790 at 4 (Oct. 1, 1990) (Comptroller General decision noting that "disclosure of prices charged the government is ordinarily a cost of doing business with the government"); see also EHE, No. 81-1087, slip op. at 4 (D.D.C. Feb. 24, 1984) ("[O]ne who would do business with the government must expect that more of his offer is more likely to become known to others than in the case of a purely private agreement.").

[322] CC Distribs., 1995 WL 405445, at *6.

[323] Id. (referring to Chemical Waste, 1995 WL 115894, at *5, where prices at issue were those of a subcontractor who was "not in privity of contract" with agency and thus was not, in fact, "doing business with the government").

[324] Id.

[325] AT&T Info. Sys. v. GSA, 627 F. Supp. 1396, 1403 (D.D.C. 1986) (reverse FOIA suit); rev'd on other grounds & remanded, 810 F.2d 1233, 1236 (D.C. Cir. 1987).

[326] McDonnell Douglas, 180 F.3d at 306.

[327] 48 C.F.R. §§ 15.503(b)(iv), 15.506(d)(2) (establishing disclosure mandate for all contracts solicited after January 1, 1998); see FOIA Update, Vol.

(continued...)

# EXEMPTION 4

Because Exemption 4 protection is vitiated if the information is publicly available elsewhere, all unit prices of successful offerors that are required to be disclosed under the FAR should not be considered to fall under Exemption 4.[328]

Several years ago, and prior to the decision by the D.C. Circuit in Critical Mass Energy Project v. NRC,[329] three cases involving unit prices were decided by the District Court for the District of Columbia, with each case reaching a different result. In one, the court ordered disclosure of the unit prices, rejecting as "highly speculative" the argument that their release would allow competitors to calculate the submitter's profit margin and thus be able to underbid it in future procurements.[330] In another case, the court determined that the submitter's competitive harm arguments were not speculative and it even

---

(...continued)
XVIII, No. 4, at 1 (advising agencies that due to FAR's authorization to publicly release unit prices, they need not give formal submitter notice prior to releasing such prices (but they are best advised as a matter of agency discretion and courtesy to inform the submitter of an imminent disclosure)).

[328] See FOIA Update, Vol. XVIII, No. 4, at 1; FOIA Update, Vol. V, No. 4, at 4; FOIA Update, Vol. VII, No. 1, at 6; accord Comdisco, 864 F. Supp. at 516 (noting that unit prices are "the sort of pricing information routinely disclosed under the [FAR]" (citing Acumenics, 843 F.2d at 807-08)); JL Assocs., 90-2 CPD 261, B-239790 at 4 n.2 (Oct. 1, 1990) (Comptroller General decision rejecting argument that disclosure of option prices would cause submitter competitive harm by revealing pricing strategy and decisionmaking process and noting that FAR "expressly advises awardees that the unit prices of awards will generally be disclosed to unsuccessful offerors"); see also McDonnell Douglas, 180 F.3d at 306 (emphasizing that its decision to overturn agency's disclosure decision was reached in absence of agency reliance on "any independent legal authority to release" requested information); cf. McDonnell Douglas Corp. v. Widnall, No. 94-0091, slip op. at 13 (D.D.C. Apr. 11, 1994) (in ruling on different FAR disclosure provision, court held that provision served as legal authorization for agency to release exercised option prices and thus such prices were "not protected from disclosure by the Trade Secrets Act," 18 U.S.C. § 1905 (1994 & Supp. IV 1998), and court need not reach issue of applicability of Exemption 4), and McDonnell Douglas Corp. v. Widnall, No. 92-2211, slip op. at 8 (D.D.C. Apr. 11, 1994) (same), cases consolidated on appeal & remanded for further development of the record, 57 F.3d 1162, 1167 (D.C. Cir. 1995) (because agency's FAR "authorization argument is intertwined analytically" with Exemption 4 coverage issue, remand to agency ordered so that court "can have one considered and complete statement of the Air Force's position" on submitter's claim that its prices were protected by Exemption 4) (non-FOIA cases brought under Administrative Procedure Act, 5 U.S.C. § 706 (1994)). But see Environmental Tech., Inc. v. EPA, 822 F. Supp. 1226, 1229 n.4 (E.D. Va. 1993) (interpreting less specific, pre-1998 version of unit price FAR provision to somehow prohibit release of unit prices if such information "constitutes 'confidential business information'") (reverse FOIA suit).

[329] 975 F.2d 871 (D.C. Cir. 1992) (en banc).

[330] Brownstein Zeidman & Schomer v. Department of the Air Force, 781 F. Supp. 31, 33 (D.D.C. 1991).

**EXEMPTION 4**

went so far as to issue an injunction permanently prohibiting the agency from releasing those unit prices to the public.[331] In the third such case, the court found that it was a "fact-intensive question" whether the submitter would suffer competitive harm from release of its "price information" and it therefore declined to rule on the applicability of Exemption 4 in the context of a summary judgment motion.[332] (That case was never resolved on the merits by the District of Columbia court as the issue was first litigated by a party acting on behalf of the plaintiff in the Eastern District of Virginia[333] and the principle of collateral estoppel was then found to prevent the plaintiff from relitigating the issue in the District of Columbia.[334])

The District Court for the District of Columbia issued another decision during that same time period in a case involving unexercised option prices rather than "ordinary" unit prices.[335] In that case, the court expressly stated that it "generally agrees that '[d]isclosure of prices charged the Government is a cost of doing business with the Government.'"[336] It then upheld the agency's decision to release the option prices because "competitively sensitive information such as cost, overhead, or profit identifiers would not be revealed."[337] This decision was subsequently vacated by the D.C. Circuit, however,[338] after the FOIA requester withdrew its request while the case was pending on appeal. In the absence of a FOIA requester seeking access to the information, the court held that the case had become moot.[339]

In the immediate wake of Critical Mass, two decisions somewhat

---

[331] McDonnell Douglas Corp. v. NASA, No. 91-3134, transcript at 10 (D.D.C. Jan. 24, 1992) (bench order) (reverse FOIA suit), remanded for further consideration in light of Critical Mass, No. 92-5342 (D.C. Cir. Feb. 14, 1994), on remand, 895 F. Supp. 316, 319 (D.D.C. 1995) (Critical Mass found inapplicable; agency denied opportunity to remedy "inadequacies" in record; court held that permanent injunction "remains in place"), aff'd for agency failure to timely raise argument, No. 95-5290 (D.C. Cir. Sept. 17, 1996).

[332] MCI, 1992 WL 71394, at *6.

[333] Cohen, Dunn & Sinclair, P.C. v. GSA, No. 92-0057-A (E.D. Va. Sept. 10, 1992) (bench order).

[334] MCI Telecomms. Corp. v. GSA, No. 89-0746, slip op. at 4-9 (D.D.C. Feb. 27, 1995).

[335] General Dynamics Corp. v. United States Dep't of the Air Force, 822 F. Supp. 804, 807 (D.D.C. 1992) (reverse FOIA suit), vacated as moot, No.92-5186 (D.C. Cir. Sept. 23, 1993).

[336] Id. at 807 (quoting Racal-Milgo, 559 F. Supp. at 6).

[337] Id.; see RMS, No. C-92-1545, slip op. at 7 (N.D. Cal. Nov. 24, 1992) (rejecting competitive harm claim for "interim" prices).

[338] General Dynamics Corp. v. Department of the Air Force, No. 92-5186, slip op. at 1 (D.C. Cir. Sept. 23, 1993) (reverse FOIA suit).

[339] Id.

## EXEMPTION 4

reflexively afforded protection to unit prices premised on the theory that contract submissions are "voluntary" and that such pricing terms are not customarily disclosed to the public.[340] These decisions appear to implicitly define voluntary submissions according to the nature of the activity to which they are connected and thus are contrary to the policy guidance issued by the Department of Justice concerning the voluntary/required distinction.[341] Indeed, one of these decisions[342] was expressly disclaimed by another judge in that same judicial district for failing to identify any justification whatsoever for its conclusion.[343] (For a further discussion of Critical Mass and its "voluntariness" standard, see Exemption 4, Applying Critical Mass, above.) In addition to affording protection to contract pricing information under Critical Mass, the other decision, in a rather cursory order issued from the bench, went on to alternatively afford protection under the competitive harm prong.[344]

None of the above cases concerning unit prices involved a request for pricing information submitted by an unsuccessful offeror. In the first decision to touch on this point, the court considered a situation in which the requester did not actually seek unit prices, but instead had requested the bottom-line price (total cumulative price) that an unsuccessful offeror had proposed for a government contract, as well as the bottom-line prices it had proposed for four years' worth of contract options.[345] Accepting the submitter's contention that disclosure of these bottom-line prices would cause it to suffer competitive harm by enabling competitors to deduce its pricing strategy, the court found that unsuccessful offerors had a different expectation of confidentiality than successful offerors, that the public interest in disclosure of pricing information concerning unawarded contracts was slight, and most importantly, that the unsuccessful offeror--who would be competing with the successful offeror on the contract options as well as on future related contracts--had demonstrated factually how the contract and option prices could be used by its competitors to derive data harmful to its competitive position.[346]

Congress has now addressed this issue with a statute that prohibits

---

[340] Environmental Tech., 822 F. Supp. at 1229; Cohen, Dunn, No. 92-0057-A, transcript at 28 (E.D. Va. Sept. 10, 1992).

[341] See FOIA Update, Vol. XIV, No. 2, at 3-5 ("OIP Guidance: The Critical Mass Distinction Under Exemption 4"); id. at 6-7 ("Exemption 4 Under Critical Mass: Step-By-Step Decisionmaking").

[342] Environmental Tech., 822 F. Supp. at 1229.

[343] Comdisco, 864 F. Supp. at 517 n.8.

[344] Cohen, Dunn, No. 92-0057-A, transcript at 29; Findings of Fact at 7-8 (E.D. Va. Sept. 10, 1992) (accepting argument that disclosure of detailed unit price information would reveal pricing strategy and permit future bids to be predicted and undercut).

[345] Raytheon Co. v. Department of the Navy, No. 89-2481, 1989 WL 550581, at *1 (D.D.C. Dec. 22, 1989).

[346] Id. at **5-6; see also FOIA Update, Vol. XI, No. 2, at 2; FOIA Update, Vol. IV, No. 4, at 10-11.

# EXEMPTION 4

most agencies from disclosing solicited contract proposals--which would contain proposed price information--if those proposals have not become incorporated into an ensuing government contract.[347] This Exemption 3 statute has the practical effect of providing statutory protection for the prices proposed by unsuccessful offerors because, by definition, that information is not incorporated into the resulting government contract.[348]

## Third Prong of National Parks

In addition to the impairment prong and the competitive harm prong of the test for confidentiality established in National Parks & Conservation Ass'n v. Morton, the decision specifically left open the possibility of a third prong that would protect other governmental interests, such as compliance and program effectiveness.[349] Several subsequent decisions reaffirmed this possibility in dicta[350] and, as discussed below, with its en banc decision in Critical Mass Energy Project v. NRC, the Court of Appeals for the District of Columbia Circuit conclusively recognized the existence of a "third prong" under National Parks.[351]

The third prong received its first thorough appellate court analysis and acceptance by the Court of Appeals for the First Circuit.[352] In 9 to 5 Organization for Women Office Workers v. Board of Governors of the Federal Reserve System, the First Circuit expressly admonished against using the two primary

---

[347] National Defense Authorization Act for Fiscal Year 1997, Pub. L. No. 104-201, § 821, 110 Stat. 2422 (containing parallel measures applicable to armed services and most civilian agencies) (codified at 10 U.S.C. § 2305(g) (1994 & Supp. IV 1998), amended by Pub. L. No. 106-65, 113 Stat. 512 (Oct. 5, 1999) (extending coverage of statute to all agencies listed in 10 U.S.C. § 2303, notably NASA and Coast Guard), and at 41 U.S.C. § 253b(m) (1994 & Supp. III 1997)).

[348] See FOIA Update, Vol. XVIII, No. 1, at 2 (discussing new statute and fact that key determinant of exempt status under it is whether proposal was incorporated into or otherwise set forth in resulting contract).

[349] 498 F.2d 765, 770 n.17 (D.C. Cir. 1974).

[350] Washington Post Co. v. HHS, 690 F.2d 252, 268 n.51 (D.C. Cir. 1982); National Parks & Conservation Ass'n v. Kleppe, 547 F.2d 673, 678 n.16 (D.C. Cir. 1976); Public Citizen Health Research Group v. FDA, 539 F. Supp. 1320, 1326 (D.D.C. 1982), rev'd & remanded on other grounds, 704 F.2d 1280 (D.C. Cir. 1983).

[351] 975 F.2d 871, 879 (D.C. Cir. 1992); see also FOIA Update, Vol. XIV, No. 2, at 7 ("Exemption 4 Under Critical Mass: Step-By-Step Decisionmaking").

[352] 9 to 5 Org. for Women Office Workers v. Board of Governors of the Fed. Reserve Sys., 721 F.2d 1 (1st Cir. 1983); accord Africa Fund v. Mosbacher, No. 92-289, 1993 WL 183736, at *7 (S.D.N.Y. May 26, 1993) (finding third prong satisfied when agency "submitted extensive declarations that explain why disclosure of documents . . . would interfere with the export control system" (citing Durnan v. United States Dep't of Commerce, 777 F. Supp. 965, 967 (D.D.C. 1991))).

## EXEMPTION 4

prongs of National Parks as "the exclusive criteria for determining confidentiality" and held that the pertinent inquiry is whether public disclosure of the information will harm an "identifiable private or governmental interest which the Congress sought to protect by enacting Exemption 4 of the FOIA."[353]

Thereafter, the Department of Justice issued policy guidance regarding Exemption 4 protection for "intrinsically valuable" records--records that are significant not for their content, but as valuable commodities which can be sold in the marketplace.[354] Because protection for such documents is well rooted in the legislative history of Exemption 4, the third prong of the National Parks test should permit the owners of such records to retain their full proprietary interest in them when release through the FOIA would result in a substantial loss of their market value.[355] Of course, this protection would be

---

[353] 9 to 5, 721 F.2d at 10; see, e.g., Nadler v. FDIC, 899 F. Supp. 158, 161-63 (S.D.N.Y. 1995) (protecting joint venture agreement acquired when FDIC became receiver of failed bank under third prong because disclosure could "hurt the venture's prospects for financial success," which in turn would "reduce returns to the FDIC," and thereby "interfere significantly with the FDIC's receivership program, which aims to maximize profits on the assets acquired from failed banks"), aff'd on other grounds, 92 F.3d 93 (2d Cir. 1996); Allnet Communication Servs. v. FCC, 800 F. Supp. 984, 990 (D.D.C. 1992) (protecting computer models under third prong because disclosure would make providers of proprietary input data reluctant to supply such data to submitter, and without that data computer models would become ineffective, which, in turn, would reduce effectiveness of agency's program), aff'd on other grounds, No. 92-5351 (D.C. Cir. May 27, 1994); Clarke v. United States Dep't of the Treasury, No. 84-1873, 1986 WL 1234, at **2-3 (E.D. Pa. Jan. 24, 1986) (protecting identities of Flower Bond owners under third prong because government had legitimate interest in fulfilling "pre-FOIA contractual commitments of confidentiality" given to investors in order to ensure that pool of future investors willing to purchase government securities was not reduced; if that occurred, the pool of money from which government borrows would correspondingly be reduced, thereby harming national interest); Comstock Int'l, Inc. v. Export-Import Bank, 464 F. Supp. 804, 808 (D.D.C. 1979) (protecting loan applicant information under third prong on showing that disclosure would impair Bank's ability to promote U.S. exports); see also FOIA Update, Vol. IV, No. 4, at 15; cf. M/A-COM Info. Sys. v. HHS, 656 F. Supp. 691, 692 (D.D.C. 1986) (protecting settlement negotiation documents upon finding that "it is in the public interest to encourage settlement negotiations in matters of this kind and it would impair the ability of HHS to carry out its governmental duties if disclosure . . . were required"). But see News Group Boston, Inc. v. National R.R. Passenger Corp., 799 F. Supp. 1264, 1269 (D. Mass. 1992) (recognizing existence of third prong, but declining to apply it based on lack of specific showing that agency effectiveness would be impaired), appeal dismissed, No. 92-2250 (1st Cir. Dec. 4, 1992).

[354] See FOIA Update, Vol. VI, No. 1, at 3-4 ("OIP Guidance: Protecting Intrinsic Commercial Value").

[355] See id.; see also FOIA Update, Vol. IV, No. 4, at 3-5 (setting forth similar basis for protecting copyrighted materials against substantial adverse market

(continued...)

# EXEMPTION 4

available only if there were sufficient evidence to demonstrate factually that potential customers would actually utilize the FOIA as a substitute for directly purchasing the records from the submitter.[356]

Such a showing was made in a case decided two years ago concerning a request for copyrighted video conferencing software that the requester wanted to distribute on the Internet.[357] The court readily held that in such a situation "[t]here can be no doubt" that disclosure would cause "substantial commercial harm,"[358] because if the "technology is freely available on the Internet, there is no reason for anyone to license [it] from [its owner], and the value of [the owner's] copyright effectively will have been reduced to zero."[359]

The third prong was at issue in a case decided several years ago that concerned an agency that had the authority--but had not yet had the time and resources--to promulgate a regulation that would require submission of certain data.[360] During this interim period the agency was relying on companies to voluntarily submit the desired information.[361] In that case the court rejected the agency's argument that under these circumstances disclosure would impair its efficiency and effectiveness, holding instead that because Congress had "announced a preference for mandatory over voluntary submissions," the

---

(...continued)
effect caused by FOIA disclosure).

[356] See Brittany Dyeing & Printing Corp. v. EPA, No. 91-2711, slip op. at 10-12 (D.D.C. Mar. 12, 1993) (rejecting argument that FOIA disclosure of Dun & Bradstreet report would cause "loss of potential customers" because no evidence was presented to support contention that potential customers would use FOIA in such a manner, particularly in light of time involved in receiving information through FOIA process; nor was it shown how many such reports would be available through FOIA and court would not assume that majority, or even substantial number, could be so obtained); Key Bank of Me., Inc. v. SBA, No. 91-362-P, 1992 U.S. Dist. LEXIS 22180, at **11-12 (D. Me. Dec. 31, 1992) (denying protection for Dun & Bradstreet reports because "the notion that those who are in need of credit information will use the government as a source in order to save costs belies common sense").

[357] Gilmore v. United States Dep't of Energy, 4 F. Supp. 2d 912, 922-23 (N.D. Cal. 1998).

[358] Id. at 922 (protecting software, but not expressly doing so under "third prong").

[359] Id. at 923 (discounting requester's argument that owner had "received only relatively meager royalties" and declaring that "there is a presumption of irreparable harm when a copyright is infringed"); see also FOIA Update, Vol. XVIII, No. 1, at 5-6 (cautioning agencies to "guard against the possibility that [Internet] dissemination of [reading room records] might be regarded as copyright infringement" in exceptional cases).

[360] Teich v. FDA, 751 F. Supp. 243, 251 (D.D.C. 1990), appeal voluntarily dismissed, No. 91-5023 (D.C. Cir. July 2, 1992).

[361] Id. at 251.

## EXEMPTION 4

agency was "hard-pressed to support its claim that voluntary submissions are somehow more efficient."[362]

Thirteen years after the National Parks decision first raised the possibility that Exemption 4 could protect interests other than those reflected in the impairment and competitive harm prongs, a panel of the Court of Appeals for the District of Columbia Circuit embraced the third prong in the first appellate decision in Critical Mass.[363] There, the panel adopted what it termed the "persuasive" reasoning of the First Circuit and expressly held that an agency may invoke Exemption 4 on the basis of interests other than the two principally identified in National Parks.[364]

Upon remand from the D.C. Circuit, the district court in Critical Mass found the requested information to be properly withheld pursuant to the third prong.[365] The court reached this decision based on the fact that if the requested information were disclosed, future submissions would not be provided until they were demanded under some form of compulsion--which would then have to be enforced, precipitating "acrimony and some form of litigation with attendant expense and delay."[366] On appeal for the second time, a panel of the D.C. Circuit reversed the lower court on this point, but that decision was itself vacated when the D.C. Circuit decided to hear the case en banc.[367]

In its en banc decision in Critical Mass, the D.C. Circuit conducted an extensive review of the interests sought to be protected by Exemption 4 and expressly held that "[i]t should be evident from this review that the two interests identified in the National Parks test are not exclusive."[368] In addition, the D.C. Circuit went on to state that although it was overruling the first panel decision in Critical Mass, it "note[d]" that that panel had adopted the First Circuit's conclusion in 9 to 5 that Exemption 4 protects a "governmental interest in administrative efficiency and effectiveness."[369] Moreover, the D.C. Circuit specifically recognized yet another Exemption 4 interest--namely, "a private

---

[362] Id. at 252-53.

[363] 830 F.2d 278, 282, 286 (D.C. Cir. 1987), vacated en banc, 975 F.2d 871 (D.C. Cir. 1992).

[364] Id. at 286.

[365] 731 F. Supp. 554, 557 (D.D.C. 1990), rev'd in part & remanded, 931 F.2d 939 (D.C. Cir.), vacated & reh'g en banc granted, 942 F.2d 799 (D.C. Cir. 1991), grant of summary judgment to agency aff'd en banc, 975 F.2d 871 (D.C. Cir. 1992).

[366] Id.

[367] 931 F.2d 939, 944-45 (D.C. Cir.), vacated & reh'g en banc granted, 942 F.2d 799 (D.C. Cir. 1991), grant of summary judgment to agency aff'd en banc, 975 F.2d 871 (D.C. Cir. 1992).

[368] 975 F.2d at 879.

[369] Id.; see also Allnet, 800 F. Supp. at 990 (recognizing, after Critical Mass, third-prong protection to prevent agency effectiveness from being impaired).

# EXEMPTION 4

interest in preserving the confidentiality of information that is provided the Government on a voluntary basis."[370] It declined to offer an opinion as to whether any other governmental or private interests might also fall within Exemption 4's protection.[371]

The Court of Appeals for the Second Circuit--in the course of reviewing a decision of the District Court for the Southern District of New York which had afforded protection to documents based upon application of the third prong--expressly declined to consider whether that application was "properly afforded."[372] In so doing, the Second Circuit noted that while it had previously "adopted the National Parks formulation of Exemption 4," that "adoption did not encompass the speculation regarding 'program effectiveness'" that was set forth in National Parks.[373]

## Privileged Information

The term "privileged" in Exemption 4 has been utilized by some courts as an alternative for protecting nonconfidential commercial or financial information. Indeed, the Court of Appeals for the District of Columbia Circuit has indicated that this term should not be treated as being merely synonymous with "confidential," particularly in light of the legislative history's explicit reference to certain privileges, e.g., the attorney-client and doctor-patient privileges.[374] Nevertheless, during the FOIA's first two decades, only two district court decisions discussed "privilege" in the Exemption 4 context.

In one case, a court upheld the Department of the Interior's withholding of detailed statements by law firms of work that they had done for the Hopi Indians on the ground that they were "privileged" because of their work-product nature within the meaning of Exemption 4: "The vouchers reveal strategies developed by Hopi counsel in anticipation of preventing or preparing for legal action to safeguard tribal interests. Such communications are entitled to protection as attorney work product."[375] In the second case, a legal memorandum prepared for a utility company by its attorney qualified as legal advice protectible under Exemption 4 as subject to the attorney-client privilege.[376] In both of these cases the information was also withheld as "confidential."

It was not until another five years had passed that a court protected ma-

---

[370] 975 F.2d at 879.

[371] Id.

[372] Nadler v. FDIC, 92 F.3d 93, 96 (2d Cir. 1996).

[373] Id. at n.2 (citing Continental Stock Transfer & Trust Co. v. SEC, 566 F.2d 373, 375 (2d Cir. 1977)).

[374] Washington Post Co. v. HHS, 690 F.2d 252, 267 n.50 (D.C. Cir. 1982).

[375] Indian Law Resource Ctr. v. Department of the Interior, 477 F. Supp. 144, 148 (D.D.C. 1979).

[376] Miller, Anderson, Nash, Yerke & Wiener v. United States Dep't of Energy, 499 F. Supp. 767, 771 (D. Or. 1980).

## EXEMPTION 4

terial relying solely on the "privilege" portion of Exemption 4--specifically, by recognizing protection for documents subject to the "confidential report" privilege.[377] In a brief opinion, one court recognized Exemption 4 protection for settlement negotiation documents, but did not expressly characterize them as "privileged."[378] Another court subsequently recognized Exemption 4 protection for documents subject to the critical self-evaluative privilege.[379]

Sixteen years after the first decision that protected attorney-client information under Exemption 4, the District Court for the Eastern District of Missouri issued the second such decision.[380] The court held that a company's "adverse impact analyses, [prepared] at the request of its attorneys, for the purpose of obtaining legal advice about the legal ramifications of [large scale] reductions in force,"[381] were protected by the attorney-client privilege.[382] In so holding, the court found that disclosure of the documents to the agency "constituted only a limited waiver and did not destroy the privilege."[383]

On the other hand, the Court of Appeals for the Tenth Circuit has held that documents subject to a state protective order entered pursuant to the State of Utah's equivalent of Rule 26(c)(7) of the Federal Rules of Civil Procedure--which permits courts to issue orders denying or otherwise limiting the manner in which discovery is conducted so that a trade secret or other confidential commercial information is not disclosed or is only disclosed in a certain way--were not "privileged" for purposes of Exemption 4.[384] While observing that discovery privileges "may constitute an additional ground for nondisclosure" under Exemption 4, the Tenth Circuit noted that those other privi-

---

[377] Washington Post Co. v. HHS, 603 F. Supp. 235, 237-39 (D.D.C. 1985), rev'd on procedural grounds & remanded, 795 F.2d 205 (D.C. Cir. 1986).

[378] M/A-COM Info. Sys. v. HHS, 656 F. Supp. 691, 692 (D.D.C. 1986); see also FOIA Update, Vol. VI, No. 4, at 3-4 ("OIP Guidance: Protecting Settlement Negotiations").

[379] Washington Post Co. v. United States Dep't of Justice, No. 84-3581, 1987 U.S. Dist. LEXIS 14936, at *21 (D.D.C. Sept. 25, 1987) (magistrate's recommendation), adopted, No. 84-3581 (D.D.C. Dec. 15, 1987), rev'd in part on other grounds & remanded, 863 F.2d 96, 99 (D.C. Cir. 1988). But cf. Kansas Gas & Elec. Co. v. NRC, No. 87-2748, slip op. at 4 (D.D.C. July 2, 1993) (because self-critical analysis privilege was previously rejected in state court proceeding brought to suppress disclosure of documents, "doctrine of collateral estoppel" precluded "relitigation" of that claim in federal court) (reverse FOIA suit).

[380] McDonnell Douglas Corp. v. EEOC, 922 F. Supp. 235, 237, 242-43 (E.D. Mo. 1996) (alternative holding) (reverse FOIA suit), appeal dismissed, No. 96-2662 (8th Cir. Aug. 29, 1996).

[381] Id. at 237.

[382] Id. at 242-43.

[383] Id. at 243.

[384] Anderson v. HHS, 907 F.2d 936, 945 (10th Cir. 1990).

# EXEMPTION 4

leges were for information "not otherwise specifically embodied in the language of Exemption 4."[385] By contrast, it concluded, recognition of a privilege for materials protected by a protective order under Rule 26(c)(7) "would be redundant and would substantially duplicate Exemption 4's explicit coverage of 'trade secrets and commercial or financial information.'"[386] Additionally, the Court of Appeals for the Fifth Circuit has "decline[d] to hold that the [FOIA] creates a lender-borrower privilege," despite the express reference to such a privilege in Exemption 4's legislative history.[387]

## Interrelation with Trade Secrets Act

Finally, it should be noted that the Trade Secrets Act[388]--an extraordinarily broadly worded criminal statute--prohibits the disclosure of much more than simply "trade secret" information and instead prohibits the unauthorized disclosure of all data protected by Exemption 4.[389] (See the discussion of this statute under Exemption 3, Additional Considerations, above.) Indeed, virtually every court that has considered the issue has found the Trade Secrets Act and Exemption 4 to be "coextensive."[390] In 1987, the Court of Appeals for the District of Columbia Circuit issued a long-awaited decision which contains an extensive analysis of the argument advanced by several commentators that the scope of the Trade Secrets Act is narrow, extending no more broadly than the scope of its three predecessor statutes.[391] The D.C. Circuit rejected that argument and held that the scope of the Trade Secrets Act is "at least co-extensive with that of Exemption 4."[392] Thus, the court held that if information

---

[385] Id.

[386] Id.

[387] Sharyland Water Supply Corp. v. Block, 755 F.2d 397, 400 (5th Cir. 1985).

[388] 18 U.S.C. § 1905 (1994 & Supp. IV 1998).

[389] See CNA Fin. Corp. v. Donovan, 830 F.2d 1132, 1140 (D.C. Cir. 1987) (noting that Trade Secrets Act "appears to cover practically any commercial or financial data collected by any federal employee from any source" and that "comprehensive catalogue of items" listed in Act "accomplishes essentially the same thing as if it had simply referred to 'all officially collected commercial information' or 'all business and financial data received'") (reverse FOIA suit).

[390] See, e.g., General Elec. Co. v. NRC, 750 F.2d 1394, 1402 (7th Cir. 1984) (reverse FOIA suit).

[391] CNA, 830 F.2d at 1144-52.

[392] Id. at 1151; accord Bartholdi Cable Co. v. FCC, 114 F.3d 274, 281 (D.C. Cir. 1997) (citing CNA, court declares: "[W]e have held that information falling within Exemption 4 of [the] FOIA also comes within the Trade Secrets Act.") (non-FOIA case brought under Administrative Procedure Act, 5 U.S.C. § 706 (1994)). But see McDonnell Douglas Corp. v. Widnall, 57 F.3d 1162, 1165 n.2 (D.C. Cir. 1995) (noting in dicta that court "suppose[s] it is possible that this statement [from CNA] is no longer accurate in light of [the court's]

(continued...)

## EXEMPTION 4

falls within the scope of Exemption 4, it also falls within the scope of the Trade Secrets Act.[393]

The Trade Secrets Act, however, does not preclude disclosure of information "otherwise protected" by that statute, if the disclosure is "'authorized by law.'"[394] (For a further discussion of this point, see "Reverse" FOIA, below.) For that reason, the D.C. Circuit has concluded that it need not "attempt to define the outer limits" of the Trade Secrets Act, i.e., whether information falling outside the scope of Exemption 4 was nonetheless still within the scope of the Trade Secrets Act, because the FOIA itself would provide authorization for release of any information falling outside the scope of an exemption.[395]

The practical effect of the Trade Secrets Act is to limit an agency's ability to make a discretionary release of otherwise-exempt material, because to do so in violation of the Trade Secrets Act would not only be a criminal offense, it would also constitute "a serious abuse of agency discretion" redressable through a reverse FOIA suit.[396] Thus, in the absence of a statute or properly promulgated regulation giving the agency authority to release the information--which would remove the disclosure prohibition of the Trade Secrets Act[397]--a determination by an agency that information falls within Exemp-

---

(...continued)
recently more expansive interpretation of the scope of Exemption 4" in Critical Mass Energy Project v. NRC, 975 F.2d 871, 879 (D.C. Cir. 1992)) (non-FOIA case brought under Administrative Procedure Act).

[393] CNA, 830 F.2d at 1151-52; see also Bartholdi, 114 F.3d at 281 (when information shown to be protected by Exemption 4, government is generally "precluded from releasing" it due to provisions of Trade Secrets Act).

[394] Bartholdi, 114 F.3d at 281 (quoting Trade Secrets Act).

[395] CNA, 830 F.2d at 1152 n.139; see also Frazee v. United States Forest Serv., 97 F.3d 367, 373 (9th Cir. 1996) (holding that because requested document was "not protected from disclosure under Exemption 4," it also was "not exempt from disclosure under the Trade Secrets Act") (reverse FOIA suit).

[396] National Org. for Women v. Social Sec. Admin., 736 F.2d 727, 743 (D.C. Cir. 1984) (Robinson, J., concurring); accord McDonnell Douglas, 57 F.3d at 1164 (Trade Secrets Act "can be relied upon in challenging agency action that violates its terms as 'contrary to law' within the meaning of the Administrative Procedure Act"); Pacific Architects & Eng'rs v. United States Dep't of State, 906 F.2d 1345, 1347 (9th Cir. 1990) (reverse FOIA suit); Charles River Park "A," Inc. v. HUD, 519 F.2d 935, 942 (D.C. Cir. 1975) (reverse FOIA suit); see also FOIA Update, Vol. VI, No. 3, at 3 ("OIP Guidance: Discretionary Disclosure and Exemption 4"); accord FOIA Update, Vol. XV, No. 2, at 3.

[397] See, e.g., McDonnell Douglas Corp. v. Widnall, No. 94-0091, slip op. at 13 (D.D.C. Apr. 11, 1994) (FAR disclosure provision served as legal authorization for agency to release exercised option prices and thus such prices were "not protected from disclosure by the Trade Secrets Act"), and McDonnell Douglas Corp. v. Widnall, No. 92-2211, slip op. at 8 (D.D.C. Apr. 11, 1994) (same) (non-FOIA cases brought under Administrative Procedure Act), cases
(continued...)

tion 4 is "tantamount" to a decision that it cannot be released.[398]

## EXEMPTION 5

Exemption 5 of the FOIA protects "inter-agency or intra-agency memorandums or letters which would not be available by law to a party other than an agency in litigation with the agency."[1] The courts have construed this somewhat opaque language to "exempt those documents, and only those documents that are normally privileged in the civil discovery context."[2]

Although originally it was "not clear that Exemption 5 was intended to incorporate every privilege known to civil discovery,"[3] the Supreme Court subsequently made it clear that the coverage of Exemption 5 is quite broad, encompassing both statutory privileges and those commonly recognized by case law, and that it is not limited to those privileges explicitly mentioned in its legislative history.[4] Accordingly, the Court of Appeals for the District of Columbia Circuit has stated that the statutory language "unequivocally" incorporates "all civil discovery rules into FOIA [Exemption 5]."[5] However, this incorporation of discovery privileges requires that a privilege be applied in the FOIA context as it exists in the discovery context.[6] Thus, the precise contours of a privilege, with regard to applicable parties or types of information which are protectible, are also incorporated into the FOIA.[7]

---

(...continued)
consolidated on appeal & remanded for further development of the record, 57 F.3d 1162 (D.C. Cir. 1995).

[398] CNA, 830 F.2d at 1144.

[1] 5 U.S.C. § 552(b)(5) (1994 & Supp. IV 1998).

[2] NLRB v. Sears, Roebuck & Co., 421 U.S. 132, 149 (1975); see also FTC v. Grolier Inc., 462 U.S. 19, 26 (1983); Martin v. Office of Special Counsel, 819 F.2d 1181, 1184 (D.C. Cir. 1987).

[3] Federal Open Mkt. Comm. v. Merrill, 443 U.S. 340, 354 (1979).

[4] See United States v. Weber Aircraft Corp., 465 U.S. 792, 800 (1984); see also FOIA Update, Vol. V, No. 4, at 6. But see Burka v. HHS, 87 F.3d 508, 517 (D.C. Cir. 1996) (ruling that before material may be found privileged, agency must show that it is protected in discovery for reasons similar to those used by agency in FOIA context).

[5] Martin, 819 F.2d at 1185; see also Badhwar v. United States Dep't of the Air Force, 829 F.2d 182, 184 (D.C. Cir. 1987) ("Exemption 5 requires the application of existing rules regarding discovery.").

[6] See United States Dep't of Justice v. Julian, 486 U.S. 1, 13 (1988) (holding that presentence report privilege, designed to protect report subjects, cannot be invoked against them as first-party requesters).

[7] See id.

# EXEMPTION 5

The three primary, most frequently invoked privileges that have been held to be incorporated into Exemption 5 are the deliberative process privilege (referred to by some courts as "executive privilege"), the attorney work-product privilege, and the attorney-client privilege.[8]

## Initial Considerations

The threshold issue under Exemption 5 is whether a record is of the sort intended to be covered by the phrase "inter-agency or intra-agency memorandums," a phrase which would seem to contemplate only those documents generated by an agency and not circulated beyond the executive branch.[9] In fact, however, in recognition of the necessities and practicalities of agency operations, the courts have construed the scope of Exemption 5 far more expansively and have included documents generated outside of an agency.[10] This pragmatic approach has been characterized as the "functional test" for assessing the applicability of Exemption 5 protection.[11] However, some documents generated within an agency, but directed outside of the executive branch, have been found to fail this threshold test and thus not qualify for Exemption 5 protection.[12]

---

[8] See Sears, 421 U.S. at 149; see also FOIA Update, Vol. XV, No. 2, at 3-7 ("OIP Guidance: Applying the "Foreseeable Harm" Standard Under Exemption Five").

[9] See United States Dep't of Justice v. Julian, 486 U.S. 1, 11 n.9 (1988) (Scalia, J., dissenting) (observing that "the most natural meaning of the phrase 'intra-agency memorandum' is a memorandum that is addressed both to and from employees of a single agency-as opposed to an 'inter-agency memorandum,' which would be a memorandum between employees of two different agencies").

[10] See Burt A. Braverman & Francis J. Chetwynd, Information Law § 9-3.1 (1985 & Supp. 1990).

[11] See Durns v. Bureau of Prisons, 804 F.2d 701, 704 n.5 (D.C. Cir.) (employing "a functional rather than a literal test in assessing whether memoranda are 'inter-agency or intra-agency'"), cert. granted, judgment vacated on other grounds & remanded, 486 U.S. 1029 (1988).

[12] See, e.g., Dow Jones & Co. v. Department of Justice, 917 F.2d 571, 575 (D.C. Cir. 1990) (holding agency records transmitted to Congress for purposes of congressional inquiry not "inter-agency" records under Exemption 5 on basis that Congress is not an "agency" under FOIA); see also Paisley v. CIA, 712 F.2d 686, 699 n.54 (D.C. Cir. 1983) (presaging Dow Jones by suggesting that agency responses to congressional requests for information may not constitute protectible "inter-agency" communications). But cf. Rashid v. HHS, No. 98-0898, slip op. at 6-7 (D.D.C. Mar. 2, 2000) (holding correspondence sent by Assistant United States Attorney to expert witness, requesting evaluation of evidence in case, protectible under attorney work-product privilege); General Electric Co. v. EPA, 18 F. Supp. 2d 138, 142 (D. Mass. 1998) ("[L]etters from a federal agency to a state agency that solicit or respond to the state agency's input in an effort to coordinate and tailor joint regulatory efforts may

(continued...)

**EXEMPTION 5**

Regarding documents generated outside of an agency but created pursuant to agency initiative, whether purchased or provided voluntarily without compensation, it has been held that "Congress apparently did not intend 'inter-agency and intra-agency' to be rigidly exclusive terms, but rather to include any agency document that is part of the deliberative process."[13] Thus, recommendations from Congress may be protected,[14] as well as advice from a state agency.[15] Similarly, the Court of Appeals for the District of Columbia Circuit has held that Exemption 5 likewise applies to documents originating with a court.[16] Under this "functional" approach, documents generated by consultants outside of an agency are typically found to qualify for Exemption 5 protection because agencies, in the exercise of their functions, commonly have "a special need for the opinions and recommendations of temporary consultants."[17] Indeed, it has been recognized that such advice can "play[] an integral function in the government's decision[making]."[18]

---

[12](...continued)
be no less a part of the federal agency's deliberative processes than the state agency's recommendations or advice when acted upon at the federal level.").

[13] Ryan v. Department of Justice, 617 F.2d 781, 790 (D.C. Cir. 1980); see also Hooper v. Bowen, No. 88-1030, slip op. at 18 (C.D. Cal. May 24, 1989) ("courts have regularly construed this threshold test expansively rather than hypertechnically"); FOIA Update, Vol. III, No. 3, at 10 ("FOIA Counselor: Protecting 'Outside' Advice"); cf. National Ass'n of Criminal Defense Lawyers v. United States Dep't of Justice, No. 97-372, slip op. at 7-8 (D.D.C. July 22, 1998) (protecting agency-generated draft report circulated to nongovernmental parties for review and comment).

[14] See Ryan, 617 F.2d at 790 (protecting judicial recommendations from senators to Attorney General).

[15] See Mobil Oil Corp. v. FTC, 406 F. Supp. 305, 315 (S.D.N.Y. 1976) ("[T]he rationale applies with equal force to advice from state as well as federal agencies.").

[16] Durns, 804 F.2d at 704 & n.5 (applying Exemption 5 to presentence report prepared by probation officer for sentencing judge, with copies provided to Parole Commission and Bureau of Prisons); cf. Badhwar v. United States Dep't of the Air Force, 829 F.2d 182, 184-85 (D.C. Cir. 1987) (upholding application of Exemption 5--without discussing "inter-agency and intra-agency" threshold--to material supplied by outside contractors).

[17] Soucie v. David, 448 F.2d 1067, 1078 n.44 (D.C. Cir. 1971); cf. CNA Fin. Corp. v. Donovan, 830 F.2d 1132, 1161 (D.C. Cir. 1987) (recognizing importance of outside consultants in deliberative process privilege context).

[18] Hoover v. United States Dep't of the Interior, 611 F.2d 1132, 1138 (5th Cir. 1980); see also, e.g., Lead Indus. Ass'n v. OSHA, 610 F.2d 70, 83 (2d Cir. 1979); Wu v. National Endowment for the Humanities, 460 F.2d 1030, 1032 (5th Cir. 1972) (protecting recommendations of volunteer consultants); Judicial Watch, Inc. v. Commission on United States-Pac. Trade & Inv. Policy, No. 97-0099, slip op. at 9 (D.D.C. Sept. 30, 1999) (protecting recommendations from individuals outside government regarding proposed executive branch
(continued...)

# EXEMPTION 5

Several years ago, the D.C. Circuit made broad use of the "functional" test, holding that Exemption 5's "inter-agency or intra-agency" threshold requirement was satisfied even where no "formal relationship" existed between HHS and an outside scientific journal reviewing an article submitted by an HHS scientist for possible publication.[19] The D.C. Circuit held that the deciding factor is the "role" the evaluative comments from the journal's reviewers play in the process of agency deliberations--that is, they are regularly relied upon by agency authors and supervisors in making the agency's decisions.[20] Most recently, the D.C. Circuit has found the consultative relationship between former Presidents and agencies under the Presidential Records Act[21] to fall within the "functional" test framework.[22] While courts ordinarily require that there be some formal or informal relationship between the "consultant" and the agency, some courts have accorded Exemption 5 protection even absent such a relationship.[23]

---

[18](...continued) appointees); S.A. Ludsin & Co. v. SBA, No. 96 CV 5972, 1998 WL 355394, at **2-3 (E.D.N.Y. Apr. 2, 1998) (protecting documents prepared by paid outside consultants); Hooper, No. 88-1030, slip op. at 17-19 (C.D. Cal. May 24, 1989) (protecting records originating with private insurance companies which acted as "fiscal intermediaries" for Health Care Financing Administration); American Soc'y of Pension Actuaries v. Pension Benefit Guar. Corp., 3 Gov't Disclosure Serv. (P-H) ¶ 83,182, at 83,846 (D.D.C. June 14, 1983) (protecting documents prepared by paid outside consultants).

[19] Formaldehyde Inst. v. HHS, 889 F.2d 1118, 1123-24 (D.C. Cir. 1989).

[20] Id. at 1123-24 (citing CNA, 830 F.2d at 1161); see also Weinstein v. HHS, 977 F. Supp. 41, 44-45 (D.D.C. 1997) (protecting evaluations by outside scientific experts utilized in "NIH's competitive grant application process"). But see Texas v. ICC, 889 F.2d 59, 62 (5th Cir. 1989) (embracing "functional test" but finding it not satisfied for documents submitted by private party not standing in any consultative or advisory role with agency); Bangor Hydro-Elec. Co. v. United States Dep't of the Interior, No. 94-0173-B, slip op. at 5 (D. Me. Apr. 18, 1995) (concluding that, even assuming agency and Indian Nation "enjoy a trust relationship," intra-agency threshold not satisfied where agency "did not 'call upon' the Nation to 'assist in internal decision-making'"; instead, "the Nation 'approached the government with their own interest in mind'" (quoting County of Madison v. United States Dep't of Justice, 641 F.2d 1036, 1042 (1st Cir. 1981))).

[21] 44 U.S.C. §§ 2201-07 (1994).

[22] Public Citizen, Inc. v. United States Dep't of Justice, 111 F.3d 168, 170-72 (1997) ("Consultations under the Presidential Records Act are precisely the type that Exemption 5 was designed to protect.").

[23] See Weinstein, 977 F. Supp. at 45 (finding grant applicant's rebuttal letter not to be "intra-agency" but protecting it nevertheless because disclosure "would effectively expose the substance" of agency's underlying intra-agency recommendation (citing FBI v. Abramson, 456 U.S. 615 (1982))); Destileria Serralles, Inc. v. Department of the Treasury, No. 85-837, slip op. at 10 (D.P.R. Sept. 22, 1988) (protecting confidential business information fur-

(continued...)

# EXEMPTION 5

However, a minority of courts, particularly in the context of witness statements taken in NLRB investigations, have not embraced the "functional test" and have rigidly applied the "inter-agency or intra-agency" language of Exemption 5's threshold to find that documents submitted by nonagency personnel are not protectible under the exemption.[24]

In 1990, the D.C. Circuit held in Dow Jones & Co. v. Department of Justice,[25] that documents transmitted to Congress do not qualify for Exemption 5 protection, based upon the simple fact that Congress is not an "agency" under the terms of the statute.[26] Nevertheless, the D.C. Circuit stated that agencies may "protect communications outside the agency so long as those communi-

---

[23](...continued) nished to agency by business competitor); Information Acquisition Corp. v. Department of Justice, No. 77-839, slip op. at 4 (D.D.C. May 23, 1979) (protecting unsolicited comments from members of public on presidential nomination); see also FOIA Update, Vol. VIII, No. 2, at 4-5 ("OIP Guidance: Broad Protection for Witness Statements"); FOIA Update, Vol. III, No. 3, at 10.

[24] See Klamath Water Users Protective Ass'n v. Department of the Interior, 189 F.3d 1034, 1038 (9th Cir. 1999) (declining to "address the reach" of Exemption 5 threshold and ordering disclosure of records based upon conclusion that Indian Tribes with whom agency had consultative relationship also had disqualifying "direct interest" in subject matter), petition for cert. filed, No. 99-1871 (U.S. May 22, 2000); Grand Cent. Partnership, Inc. v. Cuomo, 166 F.3d 473, 484 (2d Cir. 1999) (refusing to extend privilege to letter from New York City Council member to federal agency on basis that FOIA "applies only to federal and not to state agencies"); Thurner Heat Treating Corp. v. NLRB, 839 F.2d 1256, 1259-60 (7th Cir. 1988) (holding witness statements taken from nonagency employees in contemplation of litigation not intra-agency); Van Bourg, Allen, Weinberg & Roger v. NLRB, 751 F.2d 982, 985 (9th Cir. 1985) (construing Exemption 5 narrowly to apply "only to internal agency documents or documents prepared by outsiders who have a formal relationship with the agency"); Poss v. NLRB, 654 F.2d 659, 659 (10th Cir. 1977) (same); Aircraft Gear Corp. v. NLRB, No. 92-C-6023, slip op. at 6-10 (N.D. Ill. Mar. 14, 1994) (explicitly following Thurner); Kilroy v. NLRB, 633 F. Supp. 136, 140 (S.D. Ohio 1985) (finding witness statements taken from nonagency employees not intra-agency), aff'd, 823 F.2d 553 (6th Cir. 1987) (unpublished table decision); see also Southam News v. INS, No. 85-2721, slip op. at 17 (D.D.C. May 18, 1989) (holding that letters to and from private parties did not meet threshold); Knight v. DOD, No. 87-480, slip op. at 2-3 (D.D.C. Dec. 7, 1987) (holding correspondence to contractors not intra-agency); American Soc'y of Pension Actuaries v. Pension Benefit Guar. Corp., No. 82-2806, slip op. at 3 (D.D.C. July 22, 1983) (holding that advice of professional advisory committees does not merit protection as disclosure would not chill outsiders' candor).

[25] 917 F.2d 571 (D.C. Cir. 1990).

[26] Id. at 574 (citing 5 U.S.C. § 551(1) (1994)).

# EXEMPTION 5

cations are part and parcel of the agency's deliberative process."[27]

The issue remains unsettled as to documents generated in the course of settlement negotiations. Communications reflecting settlement negotiations between the government and an adverse party, which are of necessity exchanged between the parties, have been held not to constitute "intra-agency" memoranda under Exemption 5.[28] However, certain of those courts recognized the great difficulties inherent in such a harsh Exemption 5 construction, especially in light of the "logic and force of [the] policy plea"[29] that the government's indispensable settlement mechanism can be impeded by such a result.[30]

Accordingly, one court has held that notes of an agency employee which reflected positions taken and issues raised in treaty negotiations were properly withheld pursuant to Exemption 5 because their release would harm the agency deliberative process.[31] Other courts have found the attorney work-product and deliberative process privileges to be properly invoked for documents prepared by agency personnel which reflected the substance of meetings between adverse parties and agency personnel in preparation for eventual settlement of a case.[32] Furthermore, Justice Brennan, noting the need for

---

[27] Id. at 575.

[28] See County of Madison, 641 F.2d at 1042; M/A-COM Info. Sys. v. HHS, 656 F. Supp. 691, 692 (D.D.C. 1986) (applying privilege under Exemption 4 but not under Exemption 5); NAACP Legal Defense & Educ. Fund, Inc. v. United States Dep't of Justice, 612 F. Supp. 1143, 1145-46 (D.D.C. 1985); Norwood v. FAA, 580 F. Supp. 994, 1002-03 (W.D. Tenn. 1984) (on motion for clarification and reconsideration); Center for Auto Safety v. Department of Justice, 576 F. Supp. 739, 747-49 (D.D.C. 1983).

[29] County of Madison, 641 F.2d at 1040.

[30] Id.; see also Center for Auto Safety, 576 F. Supp. at 746 n.18 (quoting County of Madison, 641 F.2d at 1040); Murphy v. TVA, 571 F. Supp. 502, 506 (D.D.C. 1983) (observing that public policy favoring compromise over confrontation would be "seriously undermined" if internal documents reflecting employees' thoughts during course of negotiations were released).

[31] Fulbright & Jaworski v. Department of the Treasury, 545 F. Supp. 615, 620 (D.D.C. 1982).

[32] See Coastal States Gas Corp. v. Department of Energy, 617 F.2d 854, 866 (D.C. Cir. 1980) (deliberative process privilege); Finkel v. HUD, No. 90-3106, 1995 WL 151790, at **3-4 (E.D.N.Y. Mar. 28, 1995) (deliberative process privilege), aff'd, No. 95-6112, 1996 U.S. App. LEXIS 2895, at *1 (2d Cir. Feb. 21, 1996); Wilson v. Department of Justice, No. 87-2415, slip op. at 8-11 (D.D.C. June 14, 1992) (attorney work-product privilege); Cities Serv. Co. v. FTC, 627 F. Supp. 827, 832 (D.D.C. 1984) (attorney work-product privilege), aff'd, 778 F.2d 889 (D.C. Cir. 1985) (unpublished table decision); see also FOIA Update, Vol. III, No. 3, at 10; cf. United States v. Metropolitan St. Louis Sewer Dist., 952 F.2d 1040, 1045 (8th Cir. 1992) (holding draft consent decrees covered by both deliberative process and attorney work-product privileges; remanded for

(continued...)

**EXEMPTION 5**

protecting attorney work-product information, specifically cited as a particular disclosure danger the ability of adverse parties to "gain insight into the agency's general strategic and tactical approach to deciding when suits are brought . . . and on what terms they may be settled."[33]

Thus, the law with respect to settlement documents stands in a state of flux, with repeated judicial suggestions underscoring the dangers of their disclosure, but with substantial case precedents standing as obstacles to Exemption 5 protection for those documents that have been shared with opposing parties. All of the adverse decisions in this area, though, have failed to take cognizance of the more recent development of a distinct "settlement negotiation" privilege outside of the FOIA.[34] In addition, settlement information may qualify for protection under Exemption 4 where the information meets the "commercial or financial" threshold,[35] as well as under the more traditional Exemption 5 privileges. Accordingly, while such information may be withheld by agencies at the administrative level pursuant to Exemption 5 where there is a "foreseeable harm" in disclosure,[36] special care should be taken to maximize the prospects of favorable case law development on this delicate issue.

Additionally, it is not the "hypothetical litigation" between particular parties (in which relevance or need are appropriate factors) which governs the

---

[32](...continued) determination of whether privileges waived); Greenberg v. United States Dep't of Treasury, 10 F. Supp. 2d 3, 17 (D.D.C. 1998) (remanding to agency for determination of whether document contained "evaluations" of settlement negotiation process covered by deliberative process privilege or merely non-protectible "factual" descriptions). But see Mead Data Cent., Inc. v. United States Dep't of the Air Force, 566 F.2d 242, 257-58 (D.C. Cir. 1977) (finding that certain documents prepared by agency concerning negotiations failed to reveal any inter-agency deliberations and therefore were not withholdable).

[33] FTC v. Grolier Inc., 462 U.S. 19, 31 (1983) (Brennan, J., concurring) (emphasis added).

[34] See, e.g., Butta-Brinkman v. FCA Int'l, 164 F.R.D. 475, 477 (N.D. Ill. 1995); Olin Corp. v. Insurance Co. of N. America, 603 F. Supp. 445, 449-50 (S.D.N.Y. 1985); Bottaro v. Hatton Assocs., 96 F.R.D. 158, 159-60 (E.D.N.Y. 1982); see also FOIA Update, Vol. VI, No. 4, at 3-4 ("OIP Guidance: Protecting Settlement Negotiations"). But see Burka v. HHS, 87 F.3d 508, 517 (D.C. Cir. 1996) (ruling that before certain material may be found privileged, agency must show that it is protected in discovery for reasons similar to those used by agency in FOIA context).

[35] See M/A-COM, 656 F. Supp. at 692 (applying privilege under Exemption 4).

[36] Accord Attorney General's Memorandum for Heads of Departments and Agencies regarding the Freedom of Information Act (Oct. 4, 1993), reprinted in FOIA Update, Vol. XIV, No. 3, at 4-5 (establishing "foreseeable harm" standard governing use of FOIA exemptions); cf. 5 U.S.C. § 574(j) (1994 & Supp. IV 1998) (providing statutory protection for some alternative dispute resolution communications).

**EXEMPTION 5**

Exemption 5 inquiry;[37] rather, it is the circumstances in private litigation in which memoranda would "routinely be disclosed."[38] Therefore, whether the privilege invoked is absolute or qualified is of no significance.[39] Accordingly, no requester is entitled to greater rights of access under Exemption 5 by virtue of whatever special interests might influence the outcome of actual civil discovery to which he is a party.[40] Indeed, such an approach, combined with a pragmatic application of Exemption 5's threshold language, is the only means by which the Supreme Court's firm admonition against use of the FOIA to circumvent discovery privileges can be given full effect.[41] Nevertheless, the mere fact that information may not generally be discoverable does not necessarily mean that it is not discoverable by a specific class of parties in civil litigation. Just as the FOIA's privacy exemptions are not used against a first-party requester,[42] a privilege that is designed to protect a certain class of persons cannot be invoked against those persons as FOIA requesters.[43]

### Deliberative Process Privilege

The most commonly invoked privilege incorporated within Exemption 5 is the deliberative process privilege, the general purpose of which is to "prevent injury to the quality of agency decisions."[44] Specifically, three policy purposes consistently have been held to constitute the bases for this privilege: (1)

---

[37] NLRB v. Sears, Roebuck & Co., 421 U.S. 132, 149 n.16 (1975).

[38] H.R. Rep. No. 89-1497, at 10 (1966), reprinted in 1966 U.S.C.C.A.N. 2418.

[39] See Grolier, 462 U.S. at 27; see also FOIA Update, Vol. V, No. 4, at 6.

[40] See Grolier, 462 U.S. at 28; Sears, 421 U.S. at 149; see also, e.g., Martin v. Office of Special Counsel, 819 F.2d 1181, 1184 (D.C. Cir. 1987) ("the needs of a particular plaintiff are not relevant to the exemption's applicability"); Swisher v. Department of the Air Force, 660 F.2d 369, 371 (8th Cir. 1981) (observing that applicability of Exemption 5 is in no way diminished by fact that privilege may be overcome by showing of "need" in civil discovery context).

[41] See United States v. Weber Aircraft Corp., 465 U.S. 792, 801-02 (1984) ("We do not think that Congress could have intended that the weighty policies underlying discovery privileges could be so easily circumvented."); see also Martin, 819 F.2d at 1186 (Where a requester is "unable to obtain those documents using ordinary civil discovery methods, . . . FOIA should not be read to alter that result."); cf. National Ass'n of Criminal Defense Lawyers, No. 97-372, slip op. at 8-10 (D.D.C. July 22, 1998) (although agency made limited disclosures pursuant to criminal discovery rules, report held protectible because not "normally available by law" to party in litigation with agency).

[42] See H.R. Rep. No. 93-1380, at 13 (1974); see also FOIA Update, Vol. X, No. 2, at 4.

[43] See Julian, 486 U.S. at 13 (holding that presentence report privilege, designed to protect reports' subjects, cannot be invoked against them as first-party requesters).

[44] NLRB v. Sears, Roebuck & Co., 421 U.S. 132, 151 (1975).

# EXEMPTION 5

to encourage open, frank discussions on matters of policy between subordinates and superiors; (2) to protect against premature disclosure of proposed policies before they are finally adopted; and (3) to protect against public confusion that might result from disclosure of reasons and rationales that were not in fact ultimately the grounds for an agency's action.[45]

Logically flowing from the foregoing policy considerations is the privilege's protection of the "decision making processes of government agencies."[46] In concept, the privilege protects not merely documents, but also the integrity of the deliberative process itself where the exposure of that process would result in harm.[47]

Indeed, in a major en banc decision, the Court of Appeals for the Dis-

---

[45] See, e.g., Russell v. Department of the Air Force, 682 F.2d 1045, 1048 (D.C. Cir. 1982); Coastal States Gas Corp. v. Department of Energy, 617 F.2d 854, 866 (D.C. Cir. 1980); Jordan v. United States Dep't of Justice, 591 F.2d 753, 772-73 (D.C. Cir. 1978) (en banc); AFGE v. HHS, 63 F. Supp. 2d 104, 108 (D. Mass. 1999) (holding that release of predecisional documents "could cause harm by providing the public with erroneous information"). But see ITT World Communications, Inc. v. FCC, 699 F.2d 1219, 1237-38 (D.C. Cir. 1983) (dictum) (suggesting that otherwise exempt predecisional material "may" be ordered released so as to explain actual agency positions), rev'd on other grounds, 466 U.S. 463 (1984).

[46] Sears, 421 U.S. at 150; see also Missouri ex rel. Shorr v. United States Army Corps of Eng'rs, 147 F.3d 708, 710 (8th Cir. 1998) ("The purpose of the deliberative process privilege is to allow agencies freely to explore alternative avenues of action and to engage in internal debates without fear of public scrutiny.").

[47] See, e.g., National Wildlife Fed'n v. United States Forest Serv., 861 F.2d 1114, 1119 (9th Cir. 1988) ("[T]he ultimate objective of exemption 5 is to safeguard the deliberative process of agencies, not the paperwork generated in the course of that process."); Schell v. HHS, 843 F.2d 933, 940 (6th Cir. 1988) ("Because Exemption 5 is concerned with protecting the deliberative process itself, courts now focus less on the material sought and more on the effect of the material's release."); Dudman Communications Corp. v. Department of the Air Force, 815 F.2d 1565, 1568 (D.C. Cir. 1987) ("Congress enacted Exemption 5 to protect the executive's deliberative processes--not to protect specific materials."); Greenberg v. United States Dep't of Treasury, 10 F. Supp. 2d 3, 16 n.19 (D.D.C. 1998) (Exemption 5 "is not limited to preventing embarrassment or 'chilling' of the individual authors of deliberative documents" but is designed to prevent chilling of agency deliberations.); Chemical Mfrs. Ass'n v. Consumer Prod. Safety Comm'n, 600 F. Supp. 114, 117 (D.D.C. 1984) (ongoing regulatory process would be subject to "delay and disrupt[ion]" if preliminary analyses were prematurely disclosed); cf. Hennessey v. United States Agency for Int'l Dev., No. 97-1133, 1997 WL 537998, at *3 (4th Cir. Sept. 2, 1997) (finding no "intra-agency 'deliberative process,'" as agency intended all interested parties to be involved in decision); Bangor Hydro-Elec. Co. v. United States Dep't of the Interior, No. 94-0173-B, slip op. at 6, (D. Me. Apr. 18, 1995) (deliberative process privilege inapplicable when by regulation entire decisionmaking process is open to all interested parties) (alternative holding).

# EXEMPTION 5

trict of Columbia Circuit emphasized that even the mere status of an agency decision within an agency decisionmaking process may be protectible if the release of that information would have the effect of prematurely disclosing "the recommended outcome of the consultative process . . . as well as the source of any decision."[48] This is particularly important to agencies involved in a regulatory process that specifically mandates public involvement in the decision process once the agency's deliberations are complete.[49] Moreover, the predecisional character of a document is not altered by the fact that an agency has subsequently made a final decision[50] or even has decided to not make a final decision.[51] Nor is it altered by the passage of time in general.[52]

Traditionally, the courts have established two fundamental requirements, both of which must be met, for the deliberative process privilege to be invoked.[53] First, the communication must be predecisional, i.e., "antecedent to the adoption of an agency policy."[54] Second, the communication must be deliberative, i.e., "a direct part of the deliberative process in that it makes rec-

---

[48] Wolfe v. HHS, 839 F.2d 768, 775 (D.C. Cir. 1988) (en banc).

[49] See id. at 776; see also Missouri, 147 F.3d at 710-11 (protecting intra-agency memorandum commenting on draft environmental impact statement and finding that "[a]lthough [the National Environmental Policy Act] contemplates public participation . . . NEPA's statutory language specifically indicates that disclosure to the public is to be in accord with FOIA, which includes Exemption 5"); National Wildlife, 861 F.2d at 1120-21 (draft forest plans and preliminary draft environmental impact statements protected); Chemical Mfrs., 600 F. Supp. at 118 (preliminary scientific data generated in connection with study of chemical protected).

[50] See, e.g., Federal Open Mkt. Comm. v. Merrill, 443 U.S. 340, 360 (1979); May v. Department of the Air Force, 777 F.2d 1012, 1014-15 (5th Cir. 1985); Cuccaro v. Secretary of Labor, 770 F.2d 355, 357 (3d Cir. 1985); Judicial Watch of Fla., Inc. v. United States Dep't of Justice, No. 97-2869, slip op. at 13 (D.D.C. Feb. 22, 2000) (rejecting specious assertion that deliberative process privilege "expires" after deliberations have ended and relevant decision has been made) (motion for reconsideration pending); see also FOIA Update, Vol. XVI, No. 3, at 5.

[51] See Judicial Watch, Inc. v. Clinton, 880 F. Supp. 1, 13 (D.D.C. 1995), aff'd on other grounds, 76 F.3d 1232 (D.C. Cir. 1996).

[52] See, e.g., AGS Computers, Inc. v. United States Dep't of Treasury, No. 92-2714, slip op. at 13 (D.N.J. Sept. 16, 1993) (holding that predecisional character not lost through passage of time); Founding Church of Scientology v. Levi, 1 Gov't Disclosure Serv. (P-H) ¶ 80,155, at 80,374 (D.D.C. Aug. 12, 1980). But see FOIA Update, Vol. XV, No. 2, at 4 (advising that deliberative process sensitivity "fades with the passage of time").

[53] See Mapother v. Department of Justice, 3 F.3d 1533, 1537 (D.C. Cir. 1993) ("The deliberative process privilege protects materials that are both predecisional and deliberative." (citing Petroleum Info. Corp. v. United States Dep't of the Interior, 976 F.2d 1429, 1434 (D.C. Cir. 1992))).

[54] Jordan, 591 F.2d at 774.

# EXEMPTION 5

ommendations or expresses opinions on legal or policy matters."[55] The burden is upon the agency to show that the information in question satisfies both requirements.[56]

In determining whether a document is predecisional, an agency does not necessarily have to point specifically to an agency final decision, but merely establish "what deliberative process is involved, and the role played by the documents in issue in the course of that process."[57] On this point, the Supreme Court has been very clear:

> Our emphasis on the need to protect pre-decisional documents does not mean that the existence of the privilege turns on the ability of an agency to identify a specific decision in connection with which a memorandum is prepared. Agencies are, and properly should be, engaged in a continuing process of examining their policies; this process will generate memoranda containing recommendations which do not ripen into agency decisions; and the lower courts should be wary of interfering with this process.[58]

---

[55] Vaughn v. Rosen, 523 F.2d 1136, 1143-44 (D.C. Cir. 1975).

[56] See Coastal States, 617 F.2d at 866.

[57] Coastal States, 617 F.2d at 868; see also Providence Journal Co. v. United States Dep't of the Army, 981 F.2d 552, 559 (1st Cir. 1992) (protecting Inspector General's recommendations even though decisionmakers were not obligated to follow them); Formaldehyde Inst. v. HHS, 889 F.2d 1118, 1123 (D.C. Cir. 1989) (protecting recommendations on suitability of article for publication, though decision on "whether and where" to publish article had not yet been made); Greenberg, 10 F. Supp. 2d at 17 (A document that is "an evaluation of the legal status" of a case would be protected; an "instruction from a senior to a junior official as to what legal action should be taken--a final decision . . . does not merit Exemption 5 protection."); Horsehead Industries v. EPA, No. 94-1299, slip op. at 14 (D.D.C. Oct. 1, 1996) ("In determining whether material is predecisional in nature, courts must look to see what role the material played in the decisionmaking process. . . . A statement of an opinion by an agency official or preliminary findings reported by a public affairs official do not necessarily constitute a statement of EPA policy or final opinion that has the force of law."); Knowles v. Thornburgh, No. 90-1294, slip op. at 5-6 (D.D.C. Mar. 11, 1992) (holding information generated during process preceding President's ultimate decision on application for clemency was predecisional); cf. Animal Legal Defense Fund, Inc. v. Department of the Air Force, 44 F. Supp. 2d 295, 299 (D.D.C. 1999) (rejecting privilege claim because agency "utterly failed to specify the role played by each withheld document" in policy-formulation process).

[58] Sears, 421 U.S. at 151 n.18; see also Schell, 843 F.2d at 941 ("When specific advice is provided, . . . it is no less predecisional because it is accepted or rejected in silence, or perhaps simply incorporated into the thinking of superiors for future use."); Greenberg, 10 F. Supp. 2d at 16 (rejecting argument that documents were not deliberative because not actually relied upon, observing that "[i]f the author had known that the notes discussing the proposed ques-
(continued...)

**EXEMPTION 5**

Thus, so long as a document is generated as part of such a continuing process of agency decisionmaking, Exemption 5 can be applicable.[59] In a par-

---

[58](...continued)
tions and issues would be subject to FOIA disclosure if not actually used, the author likely would have been more cautious in what he or she recommended"); Brooks v. IRS, No. CV-F-96-6284, 1997 U.S. Dist LEXIS 21075, at **23-24 (E.D. Cal. Nov. 17, 1997) ("governmental privilege does not hinge on whether or not the District Counsel relied on or accorded any weight to the information at issue in rendering its final decision"); Perdue Farms, Inc. v. NLRB, No. 2:96-CV-27-BO(1), 1997 U.S. Dist. LEXIS 14579, at *17 (E.D.N.C. Aug. 5, 1997) ("Although some [deliberative] processes do not ripen into agency decisions, this does not preclude application of the deliberative process privilege."); Hunt v. United States Marine Corp., 935 F. Supp. 46, 51 (D.D.C. 1996) (agency need not point specifically to final decision made); Chemical Mfrs., 600 F. Supp. at 118 ("[t]here should be considerable deference to the [agency's] judgment as to what constitutes . . . 'part of the agency give-and-take--of the deliberative process--by which the decision itself is made'" (quoting Vaughn, 523 F.2d at 1144)); Pfeiffer v. CIA, 721 F. Supp. 337, 340 (D.D.C. 1989) (court "must give considerable deference to the agency's explanation of its decisional process, due to agency's expertise"). But cf. Maricopa Audubon Soc'y v. United States Forest Serv., 108 F.3d 1089, 1094 (9th Cir. 1997) (oddly declaring Supreme Court pronouncement to be merely "cautionary dictum").

[59] See, e.g., Felsen v. HHS, No. 95-975, slip op. at 90 (D. Md. Sept. 30, 1998) ("agency need not identify any specific decision, but merely must establish 'what deliberative process is involved, and the role played by the documents in issue in the course of that process'" (quoting Coastal States, 617 F.2d at 868)); Maryland Coalition for Integrated Educ. v. United States Dep't of Educ., No. 89-2851, slip op. at 6 (D.D.C. July 20, 1992) (finding material prepared during compliance review that goes beyond critique of reviewed program to discuss broader agency policy to be part of deliberative process), appeal voluntarily dismissed, No. 92-5346 (D.C. Cir. Dec. 13, 1993); Washington Post Co. v. DOD, No. 84-2949, 1987 U.S. Dist LEXIS 16108, at *29 (D.D.C. Feb. 25, 1987) (document generated in continuing process of examining agency policy falls within deliberative process); Ashley v. United States Dep't of Labor, 589 F. Supp. 901, 908-09 (D.D.C. 1983) (holding that documents containing agency self-evaluations need not be shown to be part of clear process leading up to "assured" final decision so long as agency can demonstrate that documents were part of some deliberative process). But see Maricopa, 108 F.3d at 1094 (dictum) ("agency must identify a specific decision where document is pre-decisional"); Senate of P.R. v. United States Dep't of Justice, 823 F.2d 574, 585 (D.C. Cir. 1987) (suggesting agency must specify final "decisions to which the advice or recommendations . . . contributed"); LaRouche v. United States Dep't of the Treasury, No. 91-1655, slip op. at 28-29 (D.D.C. May 22, 1998) (citing Senate of P.R. for proposition that court must be able to pinpoint specific agency decision to which document relates); Canning v. Department of the Treasury, No. 94-2704, slip op. at 19-20 (D.D.C. May 7, 1998) ("[T]o accept an agency's nondisclosure of a document because it is predecisional, 'a court must be able to pinpoint an agency decision or policy to which the document contributed.'" (quoting Senate of P.R., 823 F.2d at 585)); Cook v. Watt, 597 F. Supp. 545, 550-52 (D. Alaska 1983) (confusingly refusing to extend

(continued...)

# EXEMPTION 5

ticularly instructive decision, <u>Access Reports v. Department of Justice</u>,[60] the D.C. Circuit emphasized the importance of identifying the larger process to which a document sometimes contributes. Further, "predecisional" documents are not only those circulated within the agency, but can also be those from an agency lacking decisional authority which advises another agency possessing such authority.[61]

In contrast, however, are postdecisional documents. They generally embody statements of policy and final opinions that have the force of law,[62] that implement an established policy of an agency,[63] or that explain actions that an agency has already taken.[64] Exemption 5 ordinarily does not apply to postdecisional documents, as "the public is vitally concerned with the reasons which did supply the basis for an agency policy actually adopted."[65] However, if a document is postdecisional in form but predecisional in its content, it may be protectible. For example, one court recently held that an "e-mail message" generated after the relevant agency decision had been made, but which merely

---

[59](...continued)
privilege to documents originating in deliberative process merely because process held in abeyance and no decision reached). <u>Compare</u> <u>Parke, Davis & Co. v. Califano</u>, 623 F.2d 1, 6 (6th Cir. 1980) (holding document must be "essential element" of deliberative process), <u>with</u> <u>Schell</u>, 843 F.2d at 939-41 (appearing to reject, at least implicitly, "essential element" test), <u>and</u> <u>AFGE</u>, 63 F. Supp. at 108-09 (rejecting proposed "essential functions" test).

[60] 926 F.2d 1192, 1196 (D.C. Cir. 1991); see also <u>Taylor v. Department of the Treasury</u>, No. C90-1928, slip op. at 3-4 (N.D. Cal. Jan. 20, 1991) (stating that deliberative process privilege covers "communications leading to the actual enactment of a law, not merely communications preceding a decision to commence the process of amending a law").

[61] See <u>Renegotiation Bd. v. Grumman Aircraft Eng'g Corp.</u>, 421 U.S. 168, 188 (1975); <u>Bureau of Nat'l Affairs, Inc. v. United States Dep't of Justice</u>, 742 F.2d 1484, 1497 (D.C. Cir. 1984); <u>Blazar v. OMB</u>, No. 92-2719, slip op. at 14 (D.D.C. Apr. 15, 1994) (finding recommendations from OMB to the President to be predecisional).

[62] See, e.g., <u>Taxation With Representation Fund v. IRS</u>, 646 F.2d 666, 677-78 (D.C. Cir. 1981).

[63] See, e.g., <u>Brinton v. Department of State</u>, 636 F.2d 600, 605 (D.C. Cir. 1980); <u>Nissei Sangyo America, Ltd. v. IRS</u>, No. 95-1019, 1997 U.S. Dist. LEXIS 22473, at **23-24 (D.D.C. May 8, 1997) (magistrate's recommendation) (declining to apply deliberative process privilege to results of tax audit in which agency was merely "applying published tax laws to factual information regarding a taxpayer"), <u>adopted</u> (D.D.C. Jan. 28, 1998).

[64] See, e.g., <u>Sears</u>, 421 U.S. at 153-54; <u>Judicial Watch, Inc. v. HHS</u>, 27 F. Supp. 2d 240, 245 (D.D.C. 1998) ("deliberative process privilege does not protect documents that merely state or explain agency decisions"). <u>But cf.</u> <u>Murphy v. TVA</u>, 571 F. Supp. 502, 505 (D.D.C. 1983) (protection afforded to "interim" decisions which agency retains option of changing).

[65] <u>Sears</u>, 421 U.S. at 152.

# EXEMPTION 5

reiterated the agency's predecisional deliberations and the author's own recommendations, was essentially predecisional and thus protectible under Exemption 5.[66]

Indeed, many courts have questioned whether certain documents at issue were tantamount to agency "secret law," i.e., "orders and interpretations which [the agency] actually applies to cases before it,"[67] and which are "routinely used by agency staff as guidance."[68] Such documents should be disclosed because they are not in fact predecisional, but rather "discuss established policies and decisions."[69] Only those portions of a postdecisional document that discuss predecisional recommendations not expressly adopted can be protected.[70]

Several criteria have been fashioned to clarify the "often blurred" distinction between predecisional and postdecisional documents.[71] First, an

---

[66] North Dartmouth Properties, Inc. v. HUD, 984 F. Supp. 65, 69 (D. Mass. 1997) (noting that author may not have known that final decision had been reached at time he composed message because "[n]o one would waste time preparing an e-mail message in an attempt to persuade someone to reach a conclusion if he knew that the conclusion he was advocating had already been reached").

[67] Sterling Drug, Inc. v. FTC, 450 F.2d 698, 708 (D.C. Cir. 1971).

[68] Coastal States, 617 F.2d at 869; see also Schlefer v. United States, 702 F.2d 233, 243-44 (D.C. Cir. 1983).

[69] Coastal States, 617 F.2d at 868; Hansen v. United States Dep't of the Air Force, 817 F. Supp. 123, 124-25 (D.D.C. 1992) (draft document used by agency as final product ordered disclosed); see also Carlton v. Department of Interior, No. 97-2105, slip op. at 15 n.7 (D.D.C. Sept. 3, 1998) (observing that court "need not find that the agency is withholding secret law . . . to conclude that the government has nevertheless failed to justify its withholdings under FOIA Exemption 5").

[70] See Sears, 421 U.S. at 151 (holding postdecisional documents subject to deliberative process privilege "as long as prior communications and the ingredients of the decisionmaking process are not disclosed"); see also Mead Data Cent., Inc. v. United States Dep't of the Air Force, 566 F.2d 242, 257 (D.C. Cir. 1977) ("It would exalt form over substance to exempt documents in which staff recommend certain action or offer their opinions on given issues but require disclosure of documents which only 'report' what those recommendations and opinions are."); Blazar, No. 92-2719, slip op. at 15 (D.D.C. Apr. 15, 1994) (deciding that President's indication of which alternative he adopted does not waive privilege for unadopted recommendations); cf. Steinberg v. United States Dep't of Justice, No. 91-2740, 1993 WL 385820, at *3 (D.D.C. Sept. 13, 1993) (holding that protection of exemption not lost where decision to conduct particular type of investigation was only intermediate step in larger process).

[71] See Schlefer, 702 F.2d at 237. See generally ITT, 699 F.2d at 1235; Arthur Andersen & Co. v. IRS, 679 F.2d 254, 258-59 (D.C. Cir. 1982); Tax Analysts v.

(continued...)

**EXEMPTION 5**

agency should determine whether the document is a "final opinion" within the meaning of one of the two "automatic" disclosure provisions of the FOIA, subsection (a)(2)(A).[72] In an extensive consideration of this point, the Court of Appeals for the Fifth Circuit held that, as subsection (a)(2)(A) specifies "the adjudication of [a] case[]," Congress intended "final opinions" to be only those decisions resulting from proceedings (such as that in Sears) in which a party invoked (and obtained a decision concerning) a specific statutory right of "general and uniform" applicability.[73] However, the D.C. Circuit recently stated that field service advice memoranda issued by the Internal Revenue Service's Office of Chief Counsel are not predecisional documents as they are solely "statements of an agency's legal position."[74] This conclusion was reached even though the opinions were found to be "non-binding" on the ultimate decisionmakers.[75]

Second, the nature of the decisionmaking authority vested in the office or person issuing the document must be considered.[76] If the author lacks "legal decision authority," the document is far more likely to be predecisional.[77]

---

[71](...continued)
IRS, No. 94-923, 1996 U.S. Dist. LEXIS 3259, at **4-8 (D.D.C. Mar. 15, 1996), aff'd, 117 F.3d 607 (D.C. Cir. 1997).

[72] 5 U.S.C. § 552(a)(2)(A) (1994 & Supp. IV 1998); see Federal Open Mkt. Comm., 443 U.S. at 360-61 n.23.

[73] Skelton v. United States Postal Serv., 678 F.2d 35, 41 (5th Cir. 1982). But see Afshar v. Department of State, 702 F.2d 1125, 1142-43 (D.C. Cir. 1983) (holding even single recommendation of no precedential value or applicability to rights of individual members of public loses protection if specifically adopted as basis for final decision).

[74] Tax Analysts v. IRS, 117 F.3d 607, 617 (D.C. Cir. 1997); cf. Ginsberg v. IRS, No. 96-2265-CIV-T-26E, 1997 WL 882913, at **4 & n.4, 5 (M.D. Fla. Dec. 23, 1997) (magistrate's recommendation) ("Although the opinions of District Counsel may not represent final opinions or policy statements of the IRS . . . [they were] relied upon and specifically referenced" by the IRS agent in the conduct of the examination.), adopted (M.D. Fla. Jan. 27, 1998), appeal dismissed, No. 98-2384 (11th Cir. June 5, 1998).

[75] Tax Analysts, 117 F.3d at 617.

[76] See Pfeiffer, 721 F. Supp. at 340 ("What matters is that the person who issues the document has authority to speak finally and officially for the agency.").

[77] Grumman, 421 U.S. at 184-85; see also A. Michael's Piano, Inc. v. FTC, 18 F.3d 138, 147 (2d Cir. 1994) (finding staff attorney's recommendation predecisional as she had no authority to close investigation); Badhwar v. United States Dep't of the Air Force, 615 F. Supp. 698, 702-03 (D.D.C. 1985) (concluding that Air Force safety board does not make decisions, only recommendations), aff'd in part & remanded in part on other grounds, 829 F.2d 182 (D.C. Cir. 1987); American Postal Workers Union v. Office of Special Counsel, No. 85-3691, slip op. at 6 (D.D.C. June 24, 1986) (protecting prosecutorial
(continued...)

# EXEMPTION 5

A crucial caveat in this regard, however, is that courts often look "beneath formal lines of authority to the reality of the decisionmaking process."[78] Hence, even an assertion by the agency that an official lacks ultimate decisionmaking authority might be "superficial" and unavailing if agency "practices" commonly accord decisionmaking authority to that official.[79] Conversely, an agency official who appears to have final authority may in fact not have such authority or may not be wielding that authority in a particular situation.[80]

Careful analysis of the decisionmaking process is sometimes required to determine whether the records reflect an earlier preliminary decision or recommendations concerning follow-up issues,[81] or whether the document

---

[77](...continued) recommendations to special counsel which were not binding or dispositive). But see Tax Analysts, 117 F.3d at 617 (finding chief counsel's "non-binding" opinions to field offices not predecisional).

[78] Schlefer, 702 F.2d at 238; see also National Wildlife, 861 F.2d at 1123; cf. Goldstein v. Office of Indep. Counsel, No. 87-2028, 1999 WL 570862, at *7 (D.D.C. July 29, 1999) (protecting recommendations on possible criminal investigations from head of Department of Justice's Criminal Division to Director of FBI).

[79] Schlefer, 702 F.2d at 238, 241; see, e.g., Badran v. United States Dep't of Justice, 652 F. Supp. 1437, 1439 (N.D. Ill. 1987) (concluding that INS decision on plaintiff's bond was final, even though it was reviewable by immigration judge, because "immigration judges are independent from the INS, and no review of plaintiff's bond occurred within the INS").

[80] See, e.g., National Wildlife, 861 F.2d at 1122-23 (finding that headquarters' comments on regional plans were opinions and recommendations); Judicial Watch, No. 97-2869, slip op. at 10-12 (D.D.C. Feb. 22, 2000) (protecting predecisional notes made by Attorney General at campaign finance task force meeting); National Ass'n of Criminal Defense Lawyers v. United States Dep't of Justice, No. 97-372, slip op. at 10-13 (D.D.C. July 22, 1998) (deciding that predecisional character of draft inspector general report is not affected by fact that FBI took adverse personnel action against investigated employees after reviewing it); Jowett, Inc. v. Department of the Navy, 729 F. Supp. 871, 874 (D.D.C. 1989) (protecting audit reports prepared by entity lacking final decisionmaking authority).

[81] See, e.g., City of Va. Beach v. United States Dep't of Commerce, 995 F.2d 1247, 1254 (4th Cir. 1993) (protecting documents discussing past decision as it impacts on future decision); Access Reports, 926 F.2d at 1196 (finding that staff attorney memo on how proposed FOIA amendments would affect future cases not postdecisional working law but opinion on how to handle pending legislative process); Hamrick v. Department of the Navy, No. 90-283, 1992 WL 739887, at *2 (D.D.C. Aug. 28, 1992) ("[D]ocuments prepared after [agency's] decision to dual source the F404 engines are not 'formal agency policy,' but, recommendations for future decisions relating to F404 procurement based upon lessons learned from the dual sourcing decisionmaking process."), appeal voluntarily dismissed, No. 92-5376 (D.C. Cir. Aug. 4, 1995); Dow,

(continued...)

**EXEMPTION 5**

sought reflects a final decision or merely advice to a higher authority.[82] Thus, agency recommendations to OMB concerning the development of proposed legislation to be submitted to Congress are predecisional,[83] but descriptions of "agency efforts to ensure enactment of policies already established" are postdecisional.[84]

Third, it is useful to examine the direction in which the document flows along the decisionmaking chain. Naturally, a document "from a subordinate to a superior official is more likely to be predecisional"[85] than is the contrary case: "[F]inal opinions . . . typically flow from a superior with policymaking authority to a subordinate who carries out the policy."[86] However, under cer-

---

[81](...continued)
Lohnes & Albertson v. Presidential Comm'n on Broad. to Cuba, 624 F. Supp. 572, 574-75 (D.D.C. 1984) (holding records predecisional because, although documents discussed implementation of previous decision, issues discussed were "not mere details to be worked out but rather matters requiring further study and generating debate which culminated in the making of new policy").

[82] See, e.g., AFGE v. United States Dep't of Commerce, 907 F.2d 203, 208 (D.C. Cir. 1990); Bureau of Nat'l Affairs, 742 F.2d at 1497.

[83] See Bureau of Nat'l Affairs, 742 F.2d at 1497.

[84] Dow, Lohnes & Albertson v. USIA, No. 82-2569, slip op. at 15-16 (D.D.C. June 5, 1984), vacated in part, No. 84-5852 (D.C. Cir. Apr. 17, 1985); see also Badhwar v. United States Dep't of Justice, 622 F. Supp. 1364, 1372 (D.D.C. 1985) ("There is nothing predecisional about a recitation of corrective action already taken.").

[85] Coastal States, 617 F.2d at 868; see also Nadler v. United States Dep't of Justice, 955 F.2d 1479, 1491 (11th Cir. 1992) ("[A] recommendation to a supervisor on how to proceed is predecisional by nature."); Students Against Genocide (SAGE) v. Department of State, No. 96-667, 1999 WL 699074, at *12 (D.D.C. Aug. 24, 1998) (magistrate's recommendation) (holding field notes of official analyzing factual information and making recommendations on U.S. foreign policy exempt), adopted (D.D.C. Sept. 29, 1998) (appeal pending); Hayes v. Department of Labor, No. 96-1149-P-M, 1998 U.S. Dist. LEXIS 14120, at *18 (S.D. Ala. June 18, 1998) (magistrate's recommendation) ("[A] recommendation from a lower-level employee to a higher-level manager qualifies as a predecisional, deliberative document for purposes of exemption 5."), adopted (S.D. Ala. Aug. 10, 1998); Burke v. DEA, No. 96-1739, slip op. at 8 (D.D.C. Mar. 31, 1998) (protecting correspondence from postal inspector to Assistant United States Attorney who he was assisting in prosecution), appeal dismissed, No. 98-5113 (D.C. Cir. Mar. 31, 2000); MCI Telecomms. Corp. v. GSA, No. 89-746, 1992 WL 71394, at *3 (D.D.C. Mar. 25, 1992) (finding guidelines developed by panel members making recommendations to be predecisional); Ginsberg, 1997 WL 882913, at **4-5 (holding protectible IRS agent's "request for technical assistance" and supervisor's addendum revealing "areas of concern of the two authors" during conduct of examination).

[86] Brinton, 636 F.2d at 605; see also AFGE v. United States Dep't of Commerce, 632 F. Supp. 1272, 1276 (D.D.C. 1986); Ashley, 589 F. Supp. at 908; cf.
(continued...)

## EXEMPTION 5

tain circumstances, recommendations can flow from the superior to the subordinate.[87] Moreover, even a policymaker's own predecisional notes may be protectible.[88] Perhaps the most important factor to consider is the "'role, if any, that the document plays in the process of agency deliberations.'"[89]

Finally, even if a document is clearly protected from disclosure by the deliberative process privilege, it may lose this protection if a final decisionmaker "chooses expressly to adopt or incorporate [it] by reference."[90] Some courts, though, have suggested a less stringent standard of "formal or informal adoption."[91] Also, although mere "approval" of a predecisional docu-

---

[86](...continued)
Shumaker, Loop & Kendrick v. Commodity Futures Trading Comm'n, No. 97-7139, slip op. at 14 (N.D. Ohio Nov. 27, 1997) (protecting advisory document where there was "no indication that the author of the document had authority to establish agency policy").

[87] See National Wildlife, 861 F.2d at 1123 (finding comments from headquarters to regional office, under circumstances presented, to be advisory rather than directory); North Dartmouth Properties, 984 F. Supp. at 70 (dictum) ("Conversation is, after all, a two-way street. A superior would be willing to engage a subordinate in candid debate only if he knows that his opinions will also be protected by the 'deliberative process' privilege.")

[88] See Judicial Watch, No. 97-2869, slip op. at 10-12 (D.D.C. Feb. 22, 2000); cf. Conoco Inc. v. United States Dep't of Justice, 687 F.2d 724, 727 (3d Cir. 1982) (rejecting contention that only records "'circulated within the agency'" may be withheld under Exemption 5).

[89] Formaldehyde, 889 F.2d at 1122 (quoting CNA Fin. Corp. v. Donovan, 830 F.2d 1132, 1161 (D.C. Cir. 1987)).

[90] Sears, 421 U.S. at 161; see, e.g., Afshar, 702 F.2d at 1140 (finding recommendation expressly adopted in postdecisional memorandum); Shumaker, No. 97-7139, slip op. at 14 (ordering disclosure of advisory document written by agency general counsel and "thereafter adopted as the official position of the agency"); Brotherhood of Locomotive Eng'rs v. Surface Transp. Bd., No. 96-1153, 1997 WL 446261, at **4-5 (D.D.C. July 31, 1997) (finding staff recommendation adopted in both written decision and commission vote); Burkins v. United States, 865 F. Supp. 1480, 1501 (D. Colo. 1994) (holding that final report's statement that findings are same as those of underlying memorandum constituted adoption of that document); Atkin v. EEOC, No. 91-2508, slip op. at 23-24 (D.N.J. July 14, 1993) (holding recommendation to close file not protectible where contained in agency's actual decision to close file); cf. Tax Analysts, 117 F.3d at 617 (finding that documents "routinely used" and "relied upon by agency personnel," in particular factual setting, were "statements of the agency's legal position" and accordingly not protectible).

[91] Coastal States, 617 F.2d at 866; see also Pentagon Fed. Credit Union v. National Credit Union Admin., No. 95-1475, slip op. at 5-8 (E.D. Va. June 7, 1996) (finding that board of directors' action "embracing" recommendations in "substantially same language" made documents postdecisional); American Soc'y of Pension Actuaries v. IRS, 746 F. Supp. 188, 192 (D.D.C. 1990) (order-
(continued...)

**EXEMPTION 5**

ment does not necessarily constitute adoption of it,[92] an inference of incorporation or adoption has twice been found to exist where a decisionmaker accepted a staff recommendation without giving a statement of reasons.[93] Where it is unclear whether a recommendation provided the basis for a final decision, the recommendation should be protectible.[94]

A second primary limitation on the scope of the deliberative process privilege is that of course it applies only to "deliberative" documents and it ordinarily is inapplicable to purely factual matters, or to factual portions of otherwise deliberative memoranda.[95] Not only would factual material "gener-

---

[91](...continued) ing disclosure after finding that IRS's budget assumptions and calculations were "relied upon by government" in making final estimate for President's budget); cf. Skelton, 678 F.2d at 39 n.5 (declining to express opinion on whether reference must be to specific portion of document for express incorporation of that portion to occur).

[92] See, e.g., Rockwell Int'l v. United States Dep't of Justice, No. 98-761, slip op. at 8-9, 15 (D.D.C. Mar. 24, 1999) (finding no adoption where public memorandum merely referred to underlying documents as evidence supporting its conclusions and observing that "the memorandum is itself a discussion and statement of reasons [that] stands alone, independent of its supporting documents") (appeal pending); North Dartmouth Properties, 984 F. Supp. at 69-70 (holding that fact that agency ultimately reached conclusion advocated by author of withheld document did not constitute adoption of author's reasoning); AFGE v. Department of the Army, 441 F. Supp. 1308, 1311 (D.D.C. 1977) (holding that decisionmaker's letter setting forth reasons for decision, not underlying report, constituted final agency decision).

[93] See American Soc'y of Pension Actuaries, 746 F. Supp. at 191; Martin v. MSPB, 3 Gov't Disclosure Serv. (P-H) ¶ 82,416, at 83,044 (D.D.C. Sept. 14, 1982). But see American Postal Workers Union, No. 85-3691, slip op. at 7-9 (D.D.C. June 24, 1986) (declining to infer incorporation).

[94] See Grumman, 421 U.S. at 184-85; Afshar, 702 F.2d at 1143 n.22; see also Perdue Farms, 1997 U.S. Dist. LEXIS 14579, at **20-23 (holding fact that document was created only two days before issuance of final decision insufficient to give rise to inference of adoption); Greyson v. McKenna & Cuneo, 879 F. Supp. 1065, 1069 (D. Colo. 1995) (deciding that use of phrase "the evidence shows" not enough for inference of adoption); Africa Fund v. Mosbacher, No. 92-289, 1993 WL 183736, at *7 (S.D.N.Y. May 26, 1993) (concluding that record did not suggest either "adoption" or "final opinion" of agency); Wiley Rein & Fielding v. United States Dep't of Commerce, No. 90-1754, slip op. at 6 (D.D.C. Nov. 27, 1990) ("Denying protection to a document simply because the document expresses the same conclusion reached by the ultimate agency decision-maker would eviscerate Exemption 5."); Ahearn v. United States Army Materials & Mechanics Research Ctr., 580 F. Supp. 1405, 1407 (D. Mass. 1984) (holding that fact that general officer reached same conclusion as report of investigation did not constitute adoption of report's reasoning).

[95] See, e.g., Coastal States, 617 F.2d at 867; Rashid v. HHS, No. 98-0898,
(continued...)

## EXEMPTION 5

ally be available for discovery,"[96] but its release usually would not threaten consultative agency functions.[97] This seemingly straightforward distinction between deliberative and factual materials can blur, however, where the facts themselves reflect the agency's deliberative process[98]--which has prompted the D.C. Circuit to observe that "the use of the factual matter/deliberative matter distinction produced incorrect outcomes in a small number of cases."[99] In fact, the full D.C. Circuit has firmly declared that factual information should be examined "in light of the policies and goals that underlie" the privilege and in "the context in which the materials are used."[100]

Recognizing the shortcomings of a rigid factual/deliberative distinction, courts generally allow agencies to withhold factual material in an otherwise "deliberative" document under two general types of circumstances.[101] The first circumstance occurs when the author of a document selects specific facts out of a larger group of facts and this very act is deliberative in nature. In Montrose Chemical Corp. v. Train, for example, the summary of a large volume of public testimony compiled to facilitate the EPA Administrator's decision on a particular matter was held to be part of the agency's internal deliberative process.[102] The very act of distilling the testimony, of separating the significant facts from the insignificant facts, constituted an exercise of judgment by agency personnel.[103] Such "selective" facts are therefore entitled to the

---

[95](...continued)
slip op. at 11-12 (D.D.C. Mar. 2, 2000) (declining to extend privilege to agency requests for outside experts' evaluations on basis that although "[t]he requests were predecisional, . . . they were not deliberative in that they did not 'reflect the give-and-take of the consultative process'" (quoting Coastal States, 617 F.2d at 866)).

[96] EPA v. Mink, 410 U.S. 73, 87-88 (1973).

[97] See Montrose Chem. Corp. v. Train, 491 F.2d 63, 66 (D.C. Cir. 1974); see also D.C. Technical Assistance Org. v. HUD, No. 98-0280, slip op. at 4-5 (D.D.C. July 29, 1999) (ordering release of factual portion of otherwise deliberative record because it "does not evaluate the actions taken, but only describes them"); Horsehead, No. 94-1299, slip op. at 16 (D.D.C. Oct. 1, 1996) ("EPA has not demonstrated how the disclosure of either the testing processes . . . or the data from that testing involves [sic] its deliberative process.").

[98] See, e.g., Skelton, 678 F.2d at 38-39.

[99] Dudman, 815 F.2d at 1568.

[100] Wolfe, 839 F.2d at 774; see also National Wildlife, 861 F.2d at 1119 ("ultimate objective" of Exemption 5 is to safeguard agency's deliberative process).

[101] See FOIA Update, Vol. VII, No. 3, at 6.

[102] 491 F.2d at 71.

[103] Id. at 68; see, e.g., Poll v. United States Office of Special Counsel, No. 99-4021, 2000 WL 14422, at *3 (10th Cir. Oct. 14, 1999) (protecting factual "dis-
(continued...)

**EXEMPTION 5**

same protection as that afforded to purely deliberative materials, as their release would "permit indirect inquiry into the mental processes,"[104] and so "expose" predecisional agency deliberations.[105] Thus, to protect the factual materials, an agency must identify a process which "could reasonably be construed as predecisional and deliberative."[106]

---

[103](...continued) tillation" which revealed significance that examiner attributed to various aspects of case); Melius v. National Indian Gaming Comm'n, No. 98-2210, 1999 U.S. Dist. LEXIS 17537, at *12 (D.D.C. Nov. 3, 1999) (affirming agency denial of "fact summaries that show the investigators' deliberation in determining [plaintiff's] suitability" for federal appointment); Mace, 37 F. Supp. 2d at 1150 (protecting factual "distillation" in otherwise deliberative EEOC report), aff'd, 197 F.3d 329 (8th Cir. 1999); Means v. Segal, No. 97-1301, slip op. at 10-11 (D.D.C. Mar. 18, 1998) (magistrate's recommendation) (holding that factual material "could not be released as segregable from the remainder, as the facts discussed in the investigative report reflect the value placed on each in forming the recommendation"), adopted (D.D.C. Apr. 15, 1998), aff'd per curiam, No. 98-5170 (D.C. Cir. Oct. 6, 1998), cert. denied, 525 U.S. 1183 (1999); Atkin, No. 91-2508, slip op. at 21 (D.N.J. July 14, 1993) (holding exempt staff selection of certain factual documents to be used for report preparation); Bentson Contracting Co. v. NLRB, No. 90-451, slip op. at 3 (D. Ariz. Dec. 28, 1990) (finding that agency properly withheld document characterizing issues most important to parties and discussing how facts were analyzed in decisional process).

[104] Williams v. United States Dep't of Justice, 556 F. Supp. 63, 65 (D.D.C. 1982).

[105] Mead Data, 566 F.2d at 256; see also Providence Journal, 981 F.2d at 562 (revealing Inspector General's factual findings would divulge substance of related recommendations); Lead Indus., 610 F.2d at 85 (disclosing factual segments of summaries would reveal deliberative process by "demonstrating which facts in the massive rule-making record were considered significant to the decisionmaker"); Farmworkers Legal Servs. v. United States Dep't of Labor, 639 F. Supp. 1368, 1373 (E.D.N.C. 1986) (list of farmworker camps was "selective fact" and thus protected).

[106] City of Va. Beach, 995 F.2d at 1255; see also ITT, 699 F.2d at 1239 (holding that notes must be more than "straightforward factual narrations" to be protected); Playboy Enters. v. Department of Justice, 677 F.2d 931, 936 (D.C. Cir. 1982) (concluding that factual materials must be generated in course of agency's decisionmaking process to be protectible); Bryce v. OPIC, No. 96-595, slip op. at 17 (W.D. Tex. Sept. 28, 1998) (finding set of photographs to be "factual in nature" and rejecting argument that photographs are deliberative in that they embody agency consultant's "determination of those aspects of [a mining site] that it determined were of sufficient significance to bring to OPIC's attention"), appeal withdrawn, No. 99-50893 (5th Cir. Oct. 14, 1999) ; Lacy v. United States Dep't of the Navy, 593 F. Supp. 71, 78 (D. Md. 1984) (holding that photographs attached to deliberative report "do not become part of the deliberative process merely because some photographs were selected and others were not").

# EXEMPTION 5

A D.C. Circuit opinion concerning a report consisting of factual materials prepared for an Attorney General decision on whether to allow former U.N. Secretary General Kurt Waldheim to enter the United States provides an illustration of this factual/deliberative distinction and of the breadth of deliberative process privilege coverage under existing case law.[107] The D.C. Circuit found that "the majority of [the report's] factual material was assembled through an exercise of judgment in extracting pertinent material from a vast number of documents for the benefit of an official called upon to take discretionary action," and that it therefore fell within the deliberative process privilege.[108] By contrast, it also held that a chronology of Waldheim's military career was not deliberative, as it was "neither more nor less than a comprehensive collection of the essential facts" and "reflect[ed] no point of view."[109] Significantly, this entire report was found to be appropriate for discretionary disclosure pursuant to the litigation review instituted by Attorney General Reno's FOIA Memorandum of October 4, 1993,[110] and it was subsequently released in full.[111]

The second such circumstance is when factual information is so inextricably connected to the deliberative material that its disclosure would expose or cause harm to the agency's deliberations. If revealing factual information is tantamount to revealing the agency's deliberations, then the facts may be withheld.[112] For example, the D.C. Circuit has held that the deliberative proc-

---

[107] Mapother, 3 F.3d at 1538-40.

[108] Id. at 1539 (distinguishing and confining Playboy as involving report designed only to inform Attorney General of facts he would make available to Member of Congress, rather than one involving any decision he would have to make); see also City of Va. Beach, 995 F.2d at 1255 (similarly observing that in Playboy "[the] agency identified no decision in relation to the withheld investigative report").

[109] Mapother, 3 F.3d at 1539-40; see also D.C. Technical Assistance Org., No. 98-0280, slip op. at 5 (D.D.C. July 29, 1999) ("The order in which the [factual portions] are listed is apparently random, so that disclosing them reveals nothing of the decision making process or of the subjective assessment that follows.").

[110] Attorney General's Memorandum for Heads of Departments and Agencies regarding the Freedom of Information Act (Oct. 4, 1993) [hereinafter Attorney General Reno's FOIA Memorandum], reprinted in FOIA Update, Vol. XIV, No. 3, at 4-5 (establishing "foreseeable harm" standard governing use of FOIA exemptions).

[111] See FOIA Update, Vol. XV, No. 2, at 1; see also FOIA Update, Vol. XV, No. 4, at 7 (listing additional such examples).

[112] See, e.g., Wolfe, 839 F.2d at 774-76 ("fact" of status of proposal in deliberative process protected); Brownstein Zeidman & Schomer v. Department of the Air Force, 781 F. Supp. 31, 36 (D.D.C. 1991) (release of summaries of negotiations would inhibit free flow of information as "summaries are not simply the facts themselves"); Jowett, 729 F. Supp. at 877 (manner of selecting and presenting even most factual segments of audit reports would reveal process

(continued...)

**EXEMPTION 5**

ess privilege covers construction cost estimates, which the court characterized as "elastic facts," finding that their disclosure would reveal the agency's deliberations.[113]

Similarly, when factual or statistical information is actually an expression of deliberative communications, it may be withheld on the basis that to reveal that information would reveal the agency's deliberations.[114] Exemption 5 thus covers scientific reports that constitute the interpretation of technical data, insofar as "the opinion of an expert reflects the deliberative process of decision or policy making."[115] It has even been extended to cover successive reformulations of computer programs that were used to analyze scientific

---

[112](...continued) by which agency's final decision is made); Washington Post Co. v. DOD, No. 84-2403, slip op. at 5 (D.D.C. Apr. 15, 1988) (factual assertions in briefing documents found "thoroughly intertwined" with opinions and impressions); Washington Post, 1987 U.S. Dist. LEXIS 16108, at *33 (summaries and lists of materials relied upon in drafting report found "inextricably intertwined with the policymaking process"). But see Army Times Publ'g Co. v. Department of the Air Force, No. 90-1383, slip op. at 8 (D.D.C. Feb. 28, 1995) (finding aggregate results of surveys to be merely basis for opinions and not themselves deliberative in nature).

[113] Quarles v. Department of the Navy, 893 F.2d 390, 392-93 (D.C. Cir. 1990).

[114] See, e.g., Kennecott Utah Copper Corp. v. EPA, No. 94-162, slip op. at 4 (D.D.C. Sept. 11, 1995) (holding material relating to preparation of Hazard Ranking Scores part of deliberative process); SMS Data Prods. Group, Inc. v. United States Dep't of the Air Force, No. 88-481, 1989 WL 201031, at **1-2 (D.D.C. Mar. 31, 1989) (holding technical scores and technical rankings of competing contract bidders predecisional and deliberative); National Wildlife Fed'n v. United States Forest Serv., No. 86-1255, slip op. at 9 (D.D.C. Sept. 26, 1987) (protecting variables reflected in computer program's mathematical equation); American Whitewater Affiliation v. Federal Energy Regulatory Comm'n, No. 86-1917, 1986 U.S. Dist. LEXIS 17067, at *10 (D.D.C. Dec. 2, 1986) ("the cost and energy comparisons involved in this case are deliberative"); Brinderson Constructors, Inc. v. United States Army Corps of Eng'rs, No. 85-905, 1986 WL 293230, at *5 (D.D.C. June 11, 1986) ("computations are certainly part of the deliberative process"); Professional Review Org., Inc. v. HHS, 607 F. Supp. 423, 427 (D.D.C. 1985) (observing that scores used to rate procurement proposals may be "numerical expressions of opinion rather than 'facts'").

[115] Parke, Davis, 623 F.2d at 6; see also Quarles, 893 F.2d at 392-93 (protecting cost estimates as "elastic facts"); National Wildlife, 861 F.2d at 1120 ("opinions on facts and their [sic] consequences of those facts form the grist for the policymaker's mill"); Horsehead, No. 94-1299, slip op. at 15-20 (D.D.C. Oct. 1, 1996) (finding that agency scientists' "open discussion of the effectiveness of . . . testing results and frank exchanges of view regarding the interpretation of those results reside near the core of an agency's deliberative process"). But see Ethyl Corp. v. EPA, 478 F.2d 47, 50 (4th Cir. 1973) (characterizing such material as "technological data of a purely factual nature").

# EXEMPTION 5

data.[116] The government interest in withholding technical data is heightened if such material is requested at a time when disclosure of a scientist's "nascent thoughts . . . would discourage the intellectual risktaking so essential to technical progress."[117] Moreover, it is noteworthy that the D.C. Circuit has stated that the "results of . . . factual investigations" may be within the protective scope of Exemption 5.[118] However, the D.C. Circuit also has emphasized that agencies bear the burden of demonstrating that disclosure of such information "would actually inhibit candor in the decision-making process."[119]

Documents that are commonly encompassed by the deliberative process privilege include "advisory opinions, recommendations, and deliberations comprising part of a process by which governmental decisions and policies are formulated,"[120] the release of which would likely "stifle honest and frank com-

---

[116] See Cleary, Gottlieb, Steen & Hamilton v. HHS, 884 F. Supp. 770, 782-83 (D.D.C. 1993).

[117] Chemical Mfrs., 600 F. Supp. at 118.

[118] Paisley v. CIA, 712 F.2d 686, 698 n.53 (D.C. Cir. 1983) (dictum). But see Rashid, No. 98-0898, slip op. at 13-14 (D.D.C. Mar. 2, 2000) (opining without authority that "[t]he results of research are factual and not deliberative information").

[119] Army Times Publ'g Co. v. Department of the Air Force, 998 F.2d 1067, 1070 (D.C. Cir. 1993) (holding that agencies must show how process would be harmed where some factual material was released and similar factual material was withheld); see also American Petroleum Inst. v. EPA, 846 F. Supp. 83, 90-91 (D.D.C. 1994) (ordering agency to show how factual information could reveal deliberative process).

[120] Sears, 421 U.S. at 150; see also Jernigan v. Department of the Air Force, 1998 WL 658662, at *2 (9th Cir. Sept. 17, 1998) (protecting "opinions and recommendations" of agency investigating officer); National Wildlife, 861 F.2d at 1121 ("Recommendations on how to best deal with a particular issue are themselves the essence of the deliberative process."); Judicial Watch, No. 97-2869, slip op. at 10-12 (D.D.C. Feb. 22, 2000) (protecting notes taken by Attorney General at campaign finance task force meeting, but not shared with any other person, because their release "could reveal how the [Attorney General] prioritized different facts and considerations in deliberating whether or not to appoint an independent counsel . . . [and] reveal her interpretation of public policies which she deemed relevant" to decision whether to appoint independent counsel) (motion for reconsideration pending); Judicial Watch, Inc. v. Department of Commerce, 90 F. Supp. 2d 9, 14 (D.D.C. 1999) (protecting memoranda weighing reasons for and against including various companies on trade missions); Clarkson v. Greenspan, No. 97-2035, slip op. at 10-11 (D.D.C. June 30, 1998) (protecting transcripts and briefing materials from Federal Open Market Committee meetings at which monetary policy is formulated), aff'd, No. 98-5349 (D.C. Cir. Mar. 2, 1999); Perdue Farms, 1997 U.S. Dist. LEXIS 14579, at **30-36 (protecting preliminary recommendations, personal assessments, legal analyses, and routine inter- and intra-agency consultations by and among agency personnel in course of NLRB investigation); Four Corners
(continued...)

# EXEMPTION 5

munication within the agency."[121] Accordingly, though the case law is not yet entirely settled on the point, "briefing materials"--such as reports or other documents which summarize issues and advise superiors--should be protectible under the deliberative process privilege.[122]

A category of documents particularly likely to be found exempt under the deliberative process privilege is "drafts,"[123] although it has been observed

---

[120](...continued) Action Coalition v. United States Dep't of the Interior, No. 92-Z-2106, transcript at 4-5 (D. Colo. Dec. 9, 1992) (bench order) (holding marginal notes and editorial comments reflect deliberative process); Fine v. United States Dep't of Energy, No. 88-1033, slip op. at 9 (D.N.M. June 22, 1991) (finding that notes written in margins of documents constitute deliberations of documents' recipient); Jowett, 729 F. Supp. at 875 (protecting documents that are "part of the give-and-take between government entities"); Strang v. Collyer, 710 F. Supp. 9, 12 (D.D.C. 1989) (approving withholding of meeting notes that reflect the exchange of opinions between agency personnel or divisions of agency), aff'd sub nom. Strang v. DeSio, 899 F.2d 1268 (D.C. Cir. 1990) (unpublished table decision).

[121] Coastal States, 617 F.2d at 866; see also Missouri, 147 F.3d at 711 ("Perhaps a fuller description [of the record] and why it is exempt might have avoided this litigation, but it was not improper for the [agency] to conclude that open and frank intra-agency discussion would be 'chilled' by public disclosure."); Schell, 843 F.2d at 942 ("It is the free flow of advice, rather than the value of any particular piece of information, that Exemption 5 seeks to protect.").

[122] See Thompson v. Department of the Navy, No. 97-5292, 1998 WL 202253, at *1 (D.C. Cir. Mar. 11, 1998) (per curiam), cert. denied, 525 U.S. 982 (1998) (holding materials created to brief senior officials who were preparing to respond to media inquiries protectible); Access Reports, 926 F.2d at 1196-97 (dictum); Klunzinger v. IRS, No. 5:96-CV-209, 1998 U.S. Dist. LEXIS 3226, at *31 (W.D. Mich. Mar. 3, 1998) (holding paper prepared to brief Commissioner for meeting protectible); Hunt, 935 F. Supp. at 52 (holding "point papers" compiled to assist officers in formulating decision protectible); Washington Post, 1987 U.S. Dist. LEXIS 16108, at *33 (holding summaries and lists of material compiled for general's report preparation protectible); Williams, 556 F. Supp. at 65 (holding "briefing papers prepared for the Attorney General prior to an appearance before a congressional committee" protectible); see also FOIA Update, Vol. IX, No. 4, at 5. But see National Sec. Archive v. FBI, No. 88-1507, 1993 WL 128499, at **2-3 (D.D.C. Apr. 15, 1993) (finding briefing papers not protectible).

[123] See, e.g., City of Va. Beach, 995 F.2d at 1253; Town of Norfolk v. United States Corps of Eng'rs, 968 F.2d 1438, 1458 (1st Cir. 1992); Dudman, 815 F.2d at 1569; Russell, 682 F.2d at 1048; Lead Indus., 610 F.2d 70, of 85-86 (2d Cir. 1979); Snoddy v. Hawke, No. 99-1636, slip op. at 1-2 (D. Colo. Dec. 20, 1999); LaRouche, No. 91-1655, slip op. at 30 (May 22, 1998) (protecting draft search warrant affidavits and stating that "it is axiomatic that draft documents reflect some give and take on the part of those involved in the drafts").

## EXEMPTION 5

that such a designation "does not end the inquiry."[124] It should be remembered, though, that the very process by which a "draft" evolves into a "final" document can itself constitute a deliberative process warranting protection.[125] As a result, Exemption 5 protection can be available to a draft document re-

---

[124] Arthur Andersen, 679 F.2d at 257 (citing Coastal States, 617 F.2d at 866); see also Petroleum Info., 976 F.2d at 1436 n.8 (suggesting new harm standard for "mundane," nonpolicy-oriented documents, which can include drafts); see also Law Firm of Tidwell Swaim & Assocs., P.C. v. Herrmann, No. 97-2097, 1998 WL 740765, at *3 (N.D. Tex. Oct. 16, 1998) (declining to hold drafts privileged based on agency affidavit and ordering in camera review), dismissed, (N.D. Tex. May 4, 1999); Lee v. FDIC, 923 F. Supp. 451, 458 (S.D.N.Y. 1996) (holding document's draft status not sufficient reason for automatic exemption from disclosure); Hansen, 817 F. Supp. at 124-25 (concluding that unpublished internal document lost draft status when consistently treated by agency as finished product over many years).

[125] See, e.g., National Wildlife, 861 F.2d at 1122 ("To the extent that [the requester] seeks through its FOIA request to uncover any discrepancies between the findings, projections, and recommendations between the draft[s] prepared by lower-level [agency] personnel and those actually adopted, . . . it is attempting to probe the editorial and policy judgments of the decisionmakers."); Marzen v. HHS, 825 F.2d 1148, 1155 (7th Cir. 1987) ("[E]xemption protects not only the opinions, comments and recommendations in the draft, but also the process itself."); Dudman, 815 F.2d at 1568-69; Russell, 682 F.2d at 1048-50; Pies v. IRS, 668 F.2d 1350, 1353-54 (D.C. Cir. 1981); AFGE v. HHS, 63 F. Supp. 2d 104, 109 (D. Mass. 1999) (holding draft indoor air quality survey protectible because release would "enable a careful reader to determine the substance of HHS' proposed and adopted changes" and thereby "discourage candid discussion within the agency") (appeal pending); National Ass'n of Criminal Defense Lawyers, No. 97-372, slip op. at 13-14 (D.D.C. July 22, 1998) (holding draft inspector general report protectible because release "would uncover the [Office of the Inspector General's] deliberations regarding what should and should not have been included in the final report"); Horsehead, No. 94-1299, slip op. at 19 (D.D.C. Oct. 1, 1996) ("Comparing the draft with the final version ultimately adopted by the agency would provide the requester with a picture window view into the agency's deliberations, the precise danger that Exemption 5 was crafted to avoid."); Rothschild v. CIA, No. 91-1314, slip op. at 6-7 (D.D.C. Mar. 25, 1992) (extending protection to "marginalia consisting of comments, opinions, further relevant information and associated notes" on drafts); Oxy USA Inc. v. United States Dep't of Energy, No. 88-C-541-B, slip op. at 5 (N.D. Okla. July 13, 1989) (agency need not show extent to which draft differs from final document, because to do so would itself expose what occurred in deliberative process); Strang, 710 F. Supp. at 12 (holding drafts protectible because "they reflect the agency's decision-making process and their disclosure would injure the quality of agency decisions"); Exxon, 585 F. Supp. at 698 (rejecting argument that agency must show how draft differs from final document, because such a requirement would "expose what occurred in the deliberative process between the draft's creation and the final document's issuance"); see also FOIA Update, Vol. VII, No. 2, at 2; FOIA Update, Vol. IV, No. 1, at 6.

**EXEMPTION 5**

gardless of whether it differs from its final version.[126]

Several years ago, the factual/deliberative distinction led to sharply contrasting decisions by two circuit courts of appeal, where the issue was the Commerce Department's withholding of numeric material.[127] Both the Assembly of the State of California and the Florida House of Representatives sought "adjusted" census figures for their respective states that were developed in the event that the Secretary of Commerce decided to adjust the 1990 census, an event that did not occur.[128] The Court of Appeals for the Eleventh Circuit applied a rigid "fact or opinion" test in determining whether such numerical data are protectible.[129] It viewed the census data as "opinion" that was ultimately rejected by the decisionmaker and therefore held them to be withholdable pursuant to the deliberative process privilege.[130] The Court of Appeals for the Ninth Circuit, on the other hand, applied a "functional" test under which it found that the data, on "the continuum of deliberation and fact . . . fell closer to fact."[131] The Ninth Circuit ordered the California data released on the basis that disclosure would not reveal any of the Department of Commerce's deliberative processes.[132] Since neither case went to the Supreme Court, this narrow conflict remains.

More recently, in a case involving purely factual data found not to fall within the deliberative process privilege, Petroleum Information Corp. v. United States Department of the Interior, the D.C. Circuit strongly indicated that such information should be shielded by the privilege or not according to whether it involves "some policy matter."[133] It focused on "whether the agency has plausibly demonstrated the involvement of a policy judgment in the decisional process relevant to the requested documents,"[134] while at the same time suggesting that more "mundane" documents should be protected when "dis-

---

[126] See Mobil Oil Corp. v. EPA, 879 F.2d 698, 703 (9th Cir. 1989) (dicta); Lead Indus., 610 F.2d at 86; see also Exxon, 585 F. Supp. at 698; City of W. Chicago v. NRC, 547 F. Supp. 740, 751 (N.D. Ill. 1982); FOIA Update, Vol. VII, No. 2, at 2. But see Texaco, Inc. v. United States Dep't of Energy, 2 Gov't Disclosure Serv. (P-H) ¶ 81,296, at 81,833 (D.D.C. Oct. 13, 1981) (aberrational ruling, without analysis, to the contrary).

[127] Assembly of Cal. v. United States Dep't of Commerce, 968 F.2d 916 (9th Cir. 1992); Florida House of Representatives v. United States Dep't of Commerce, 961 F.2d 941 (11th Cir. 1992).

[128] Assembly of Cal., 968 F.2d at 917-18; Florida House of Representatives, 961 F.2d at 943-44.

[129] Florida House of Representatives, 961 F.2d at 950.

[130] Id.

[131] Assembly of Cal., 968 F.2d at 921-22.

[132] Id. at 923.

[133] 976 F.2d at 1435.

[134] Id. at 1436.

## EXEMPTION 5

closure genuinely could be thought likely to diminish the candor of agency deliberations in the future."[135] This emerging "policy" focus has been adopted by other courts,[136] and it provides a useful focal point for the exercise of sound administrative discretion in the application of the deliberative process privilege on a case-by-case basis--especially in accordance with current discretionary disclosure policy standards.[137] (See Exemption 5, Applying the "Foreseeable Harm" Standard, below, and Discretionary Disclosure and Waiver, below, for discussions of discretionary disclosure in connection with Exemption 5.)

Lastly, the protection of the very integrity of the deliberative process can, in some contexts, be the basis for protecting factual information.[138] It

---

[135] Id. at 1436 n.8; accord Army Times, 998 F.2d at 1071, 1072 (concluding that "potentially harmful" factual information could be withheld if it were determined that it "would actually inhibit candor in the decision-making process if made available to the public").

[136] See Hennessey, 1997 WL 537998, at *5 ("report does not bear on a policy-oriented judgment of the kind contemplated by Exemption 5" (citing Petroleum Info., 976 F.2d at 1437)); Ethyl Corp. v. EPA, 25 F.3d 1241, 1248-49 (4th Cir. 1994) ("privilege does not protect a document which is merely peripheral to actual policy formulation"); Chicago Tribune, Co. v. HHS, No. 95-C-3917, 1997 U.S. Dist. LEXIS 2308, at *50 (N.D. Ill. Feb. 26, 1997) (magistrate's recommendation) (holding scientific judgments not protectible when they do not address agency policymaking), adopted (N.D. Ill. Mar. 28, 1997); Horsehead, No. 94-1299, slip op. at 19 (D.D.C. Oct. 1, 1996) (documents containing descriptions of scientific test results not protectible because they are "simply barren of any suggestion of advice or recommendations regarding policy judgments, and the factual information is easily segregated"); Larue v. IRS, No. 3-93-423, 1994 WL 315750, at *2 (E.D. Tenn. Jan. 27, 1994) (privilege covers documents "actually related to the process by which policy is formed"); Maryland Coalition, No. 89-2851, slip op. at 5-6 (D.D.C. July 20, 1992) (holding agency's "routine review" of state compliance and "assess-[ment of] how well existing policies are being implemented by the state" not protectible because they "do not suggest or recommend future agency policy"), appeal voluntarily dismissed, No. 92-5346 (D.C. Cir. Dec. 13, 1993); Maryland Coalition for Integrated Educ. v. United States Dep't of Educ., No. 92-2178, slip op. at 2 (D.D.C. June 30, 1993) (same); see also Mapother, 3 F.3d at 1537-39 (discussing and harmonizing existing D.C. Circuit case law); Army Times, 998 F.2d at 1070 (pointing to "process by which decisions and policies" are formulated).

[137] See Attorney General Reno's FOIA Memorandum, reprinted in FOIA Update, Vol. XIV, No. 3, at 4-5; see also Attorney General's Follow-Up Memorandum for Heads of Departments and Agencies regarding the Freedom of Information Act (Sept. 3, 1999), reprinted in FOIA Update, Vol. XIX, No. 4, at 3-5 (reiterating importance of "foreseeable harm" standard to federal agencies in order to promote further discretionary disclosure in agency decisionmaking); FOIA Update, Vol. XV, No. 2, at 3-6 ("OIP Guidance: Applying the 'Foreseeable Harm' Standard Under Exemption Five").

[138] See, e.g., Wolfe, 839 F.2d at 776 (revealing status of proposal in delibera-
(continued...)

**EXEMPTION 5**

also should be noted that under some circumstances disclosure of even the identity of the author of a deliberative document could chill the deliberative process, thus warranting protection of that identity under Exemption 5.[139] One court has noted that the danger of revealing the agency's deliberations by disclosing facts is particularly acute when the document withheld is "short."[140] Factual information within a deliberative document may be withheld also when it is impossible to reasonably segregate meaningful portions of that factual information from the deliberative information.[141]

---

[138](...continued) tive process "could chill discussions at a time when agency opinions are fluid and tentative"); Dudman, 815 F.2d at 1568 (revealing editorial judgments would stifle creative thinking).

[139] See, e.g., Brinton v. Department of State, 636 F.2d 600, 604 (D.C. Cir. 1980) (protecting identities of attorneys providing legal advice to Secretary of State); Cofield v. City of LaGrange, No. 95-179, 1996 WL 32727, at *6 (D.D.C. Jan. 24, 1996) (finding internal routing notations possibly leading to identification of employees involved in decisionmaking protectible); Miscavige v. IRS, No. 91-1638, 1993 WL 389808, at *3 (N.D. Ga. June 15, 1992) (handwritten signatures of agency employees involved in ongoing examination of church's claim of exempt status), aff'd on other grounds, 2 F.3d 366 (11th Cir. 1993); City of W. Chicago v. NRC, 547 F. Supp 740, 750 (N.D. Ill. 1982) (holding list of contributors to preliminary draft protectible even if names are in public version); Tax Reform Research Group v. IRS, 419 F. Supp. 415, 423-24 (D.D.C. 1976) (protecting identities of persons giving advice on policy matters when substance of policy discussions released); see also FOIA Update, Vol. VI, No. 2, at 6; cf. Wolfe, 839 F.2d at 775-76 (discussing how particularized disclosure can chill agency discussions); cf. Greenberg, 10 F. Supp. 2d at 16 n.19 (mere redaction of authors' names would not remove chilling effect on decisionmaking process).

[140] Nadler, 955 F.2d at 1491 (dicta) (considering document "one and one-half pages in length").

[141] See Local 3, Int'l Bhd. of Elec. Workers v. NLRB, 845 F.2d 1177, 1180 (2d Cir. 1988) (concluding that short document would be rendered "nonsensical" by segregation); see also Lead Indus., 610 F.2d at 86 ("Instead of merely combing the documents for 'purely factual' tidbits, the court should have considered the segments in the context of the whole document and that document's relation to the administrative process."); Linn v. United States Dep't of Justice, No. 92-1406, 1995 WL 631847, at **30-31 (D.D.C. Aug. 22, 1995) (holding agency met burden in showing that in some instances factual material could not be segregated); Badhwar, 622 F. Supp. at 1375 (finding it impossible to "reasonably" segregate nondeliberative material from autopsy report); Morton-Norwich Prods., Inc. v. Mathews, 415 F. Supp. 78, 82 (D.D.C. 1976). But see Army Times, 998 F.2d at 1070 (emphasizing agency obligation to specifically address possible segregability and disclosure of factual information); accord FOIA Update, Vol. XIV, No. 3, at 10-11 ("OIP Guidance: The 'Reasonable Segregation' Obligation").

# EXEMPTION 5

## Attorney Work-Product Privilege

The second traditional privilege incorporated into Exemption 5 is the attorney work-product privilege, which protects documents and other memoranda prepared by an attorney in contemplation of litigation.[142] As its purpose is to protect the adversarial trial process by insulating the attorney's preparation from scrutiny,[143] the work-product privilege ordinarily does not attach until at least "some articulable claim, likely to lead to litigation," has arisen.[144] The privilege is not limited to civil proceedings, but rather extends to administrative proceedings[145] and to criminal matters as well.[146] Similarly, the privi-

---

[142] See Hickman v. Taylor, 329 U.S. 495, 509-10 (1947); Fed. R. Civ. P. 26(b)(3).

[143] See Jordan v. United States Dep't of Justice, 591 F.2d 753, 775 (D.C. Cir. 1978) (en banc).

[144] Coastal States Gas Corp. v. Department of Energy, 617 F.2d 854, 865 (D.C. Cir. 1980).

[145] See, e.g., McErlean v. United States Dep't of Justice, No. 97-7831, 1999 WL 791680, at *7 (S.D.N.Y. Sept. 30, 1999) (INS deportation proceeding), amended (S.D.N.Y. Oct. 29, 1999); Means v. Segal, No. 97-1301, slip op. at 11-12 (D.D.C. Mar. 18, 1998) (magistrate's recommendation) (unfair labor practice determination), adopted (D.D.C. Apr. 15, 1998), aff'd per curiam, No. 98-5170 (D.C. Cir. Oct. 6, 1998), cert. denied, 525 U.S. 1183 (1999); Williams v. McCausland, No. 90-Civ-7563, 1994 WL 18510, at *10 (S.D.N.Y. Jan. 18, 1994) (MSPB proceeding); Exxon Corp. v. Department of Energy, 585 F. Supp. 690, 700 (D.D.C. 1983) (regulatory audits and investigations); cf. Martin v. Office of Special Counsel, 819 F.2d 1181, 1187 (D.C. Cir. 1987) (reaching same result under Exemption (d)(5) of Privacy Act, 5 U.S.C. § 552a(d)(5) (1994 & Supp. IV 1998)).

[146] See, e.g., Nadler v. United States Dep't of Justice, 955 F.2d 1479, 1491 (11th Cir. 1992); Antonelli v. Sullivan, 732 F.2d 560, 561 (7th Cir. 1983); Spannaus v. United States Dep't of Justice, No. 92-0372, slip op. at 4 (D.D.C. Sept. 30, 1999) (holding privilege applicable to document prepared by Assistant United States Attorney that discusses grand jury procedures in criminal case, and stating that "[i]t is difficult to imagine a more direct application of the work product privilege"); Slater v. Executive Office for United States Attorneys, No. 98-1663, 1999 U.S. Dist. LEXIS 8399, at *9 (D.D.C. May 24, 1999) (protecting portions of letter from Assistant United States Attorney to FBI revealing investigative strategy in criminal case); Telegraph Publ'g Co. v. United States Dep't of Justice, No. 95-521, slip op. at 19-20 (D.N.H. Aug. 31, 1998) (holding privilege applicable to materials prepared by Assistant United States Attorney in preparation for criminal prosecution); Rzeslawski v. United States Dep't of Justice, No. 97-1156, slip op. at 9 (D.D.C. July 23, 1998) (affirming use of privilege for Assistant United States Attorney's handwritten notes reflecting trial preparation in criminal case), appeal dismissed, No. 00-5029 (D.C. Cir. Apr. 11, 2000); see also FOIA Update, Vol. V, No. 2, at 7. But cf. Powell v. Department of Justice, 584 F. Supp. 1508, 1520 (N.D. Cal. 1984) (suggesting, but not deciding, that attorney work-product materials generated

(continued...)

**EXEMPTION 5**

lege has also been held applicable to documents generated in preparation of an amicus brief.[147]

The privilege sweeps broadly in several respects.[148] First, litigation need never have actually commenced, so long as specific claims have been identified which make litigation probable.[149] Significantly, the Court of Appeals for the District of Columbia Circuit has ruled that the privilege "extends to documents prepared in anticipation of foreseeable litigation, even if no specific claim is contemplated."[150] The privilege also has been held to attach to records of law enforcement investigations, when the investigation is "based upon a specific wrongdoing and represent[s] an attempt to garner evidence and build a case against the suspected wrongdoer."[151]

---

[146](...continued) in criminal case should be subject to disclosure under criminal discovery provisions).

[147] See Strang v. Collyer, 710 F. Supp. 9, 12-13 (D.D.C. 1989), aff'd sub nom. Strang v. DeSio, 899 F.2d 1268 (D.C. Cir. 1990) (unpublished table decision).

[148] See generally FOIA Update, Vol. IV, No. 3, at 6.

[149] See Kent Corp. v. NLRB, 530 F.2d 612, 623 (5th Cir. 1976); see, e.g., Blazy v. Tenet, 979 F. Supp. 10, 24 (D.D.C. 1997) (observing that communication between agency employee review panel and agency attorney throughout process of deciding whether to retain plaintiff "at the very least demonstrates that the [panel] was concerned about potential litigation"), summary affirmance granted, No. 97-5330 (D.C. Cir. May 12, 1998); Chemcentral/Grand Rapids Corp. v. EPA, No. 91-C-4380, 1992 WL 281322, at **3-4 (N.D. Ill. Oct. 6, 1992) (holding that privilege applies to legal advice given for specific agency clean-up sites); Savada v. DOD, 755 F. Supp. 6, 7 (D.D.C. 1991) (finding threat of litigation by counsel for adverse party sufficient); cf. Means, No. 97-1301, slip op. at 11-12 (D.D.C. Mar. 18, 1998) (holding privilege applicable to records prepared for unfair labor practice complaint that agency later dropped).

[150] Schiller v. NLRB, 964 F.2d 1205, 1208 (D.C. Cir. 1992); see also Delaney, Migdail & Young, Chartered v. IRS, 826 F.2d 124, 127 (D.C. Cir. 1987) (privilege extends to documents prepared when identity of prospective litigation opponent unknown).

[151] SafeCard Servs. v. SEC, 926 F.2d 1197, 1202 (D.C. Cir. 1991); see, e.g., Winterstein v. United States Dep't of Justice, 89 F. Supp. 2d 79, 81 (D.D.C. 2000) (protecting prosecution memorandum "prepared for the purpose of pursuing a specific claim--namely, the contemplated prosecution of Arthur Rudolph"); Germosen v. Cox, No. 98-1294, 1999 WL 1021559, at *14 (S.D.N.Y. Nov. 9, 1999) (protecting correspondence between United States Attorney's Office and Postal Inspection Service regarding criminal investigative and prosecutive strategy) (appeal pending); Pentagen Techs. Int'l v. United States, No. 98-4831, 1999 WL 378345, at *3 (S.D.N.Y. June 9, 1999) (upholding application of privilege to attorney notes regarding qui tam suit in which government ultimately declined to intervene); LaRouche v. United States Dep't of the Treasury, No. 91-1655, slip op. at 24-26 (D.D.C. May 22, 1998) (holding that privilege covers letter from Assistant United States Attorney to IRS official
(continued...)

## EXEMPTION 5

However, the mere fact that it is conceivable that litigation might occur at some unspecified time in the future will not necessarily be sufficient to protect attorney-generated documents; it has been observed that "the policies of the FOIA would be largely defeated" if agencies were to withhold any documents created by attorneys "simply because litigation might someday occur."[152] But when litigation is reasonably regarded as inevitable, a specific claim need not yet have arisen.[153]

Further, it has been held that a document prepared for two disparate purposes was compiled in anticipation of litigation if "litigation was a major factor" in the decision to create it.[154] However, documents prepared in an

---

[151](...continued) requesting IRS participation in ongoing grand jury investigation of plaintiff); Rosenberg v. Freeh, No. 97-0476, slip op. at 7-8 (D.D.C. May 13, 1998) (protecting documents generated by United States Attorney's Office in considering prosecutive action against subjects of undercover operation); Sousa v. United States Dep't of Justice, No. 95-375, 1997 U.S. Dist. LEXIS 9010, at *20 (D.D.C. June 19, 1997) (holding that documents were described sufficiently to show that murder investigation, leading to potential prosecution, was underway); Feshbach v. SEC, 5 F. Supp. 2d 774, 783 (N.D. Cal. 1997) (protecting documents pertaining to preliminary examination "based upon a suspicion of specific wrongdoing and represent[ing] an effort to obtain evidence and to build a case against the suspected wrongdoer").

[152] Senate of P.R. v. United States Dep't of Justice, 823 F.2d 574, 587 (D.C. Cir. 1987) (citing Coastal States, 617 F.2d at 865).

[153] See Schiller, 964 F.2d at 1208 (holding documents that provide tips and instructions for handling future litigation protectible); Delaney, 826 F.2d at 127 (holding memoranda that "advise the agency of the types of legal challenges likely to be mounted against a proposed program, potential defenses available to the agency and the likely outcome" protectible); Brotherhood of Locomotive Eng'rs v. Surface Transp. Bd., No. 96-1153, 1997 WL 446261, at *6 (D.D.C. July 31, 1997) (finding future litigation "probable" when agency aware that interpretation will be contested in court); Direct Response Consulting Serv. v. IRS, No. 94-1156, 1995 WL 623282, at *2 (D.D.C. Aug. 21, 1995) (holding that articulable claim arose when agency became aware that its position was not accepted by taxpayers); Lacefield v. United States, No. 92-N-1680, 1993 WL 268392, at *8 (D. Colo. Mar. 10, 1993) (holding that knowledge that adversary plans to challenge agency position constitutes articulable claim); Silber v. United States Dep't of Justice, No. 91-876, transcript at 23-24 (D.D.C. Aug. 13, 1992) (bench order) (deciding that privilege covers monograph written to assist attorneys in prosecuting cases); Anderson v. United States Parole Comm'n, 3 Gov't Disclosure Serv. (P-H) ¶ 83,055, at 83,557 (D.D.C. Jan. 6, 1983) (deciding that privilege covers case digest of legal theories and defenses frequently used in litigation).

[154] Wilson v. Department of Energy, No. 84-3163, slip op. at 7 n.1 (D.D.C. Jan. 28, 1985); see also Brotherhood, 1997 WL 446261, at *6 (holding that privilege applies where document created "in part" for litigation). But see United States v. Gulf Oil Corp., 760 F.2d 292, 296-97 (Temp. Emer. Ct. App.

(continued...)

**EXEMPTION 5**

agency's ordinary course of business, not sufficiently related to litigation, may not be accorded protection.[155]

The attorney work-product privilege also has been held to cover documents "relat[ing] to possible settlements" of litigation.[156] Logically, it can also protect the recommendation to close litigation,[157] and even the final agency decision to terminate litigation.[158] But documents prepared subsequent to the closing of a case are presumed, absent some specific basis for concluding otherwise, not to have been prepared in anticipation of litigation.[159]

---

[154](...continued) 1985) (holding that anticipation of litigation must be "the primary motivating purpose behind the creation of the document") (non-FOIA case).

[155] See Hennessey v. United States Agency for Int'l Dev., No. 97-1113, 1997 WL 537998, at *6 (4th Cir. Sept. 2, 1997) (deciding that report commissioned to complete project not prepared "because of the prospect of litigation," despite threat of suit); Hill Tower, Inc. v. Department of the Navy, 718 F. Supp. 562, 567 (N.D. Tex. 1988) (concluding that aircraft accident investigation information in JAG Manual report not created in anticipation of litigation).

[156] United States v. Metropolitan St. Louis Sewer Dist., 952 F.2d 1040, 1045 (8th Cir. 1992) (remanding to determine if privilege was waived); see also Cities Serv. Co. v. FTC, 627 F. Supp. 827, 832 (D.D.C. 1984), aff'd, 778 F.2d 889 (D.C. Cir. 1985) (unpublished table decision); Church of Scientology v. IRS, No. 90-11069, slip op. at 20 (D. Mass. Apr. 22, 1992) (magistrate's recommendation) (holding that fact that parties were contemplating settlement does not foreclose application of attorney work-product privilege); cf. Carey-Canada, Inc. v. Aetna Cas. & Sur. Co., 118 F.R.D. 250, 251-52 (D.D.C. 1987) (civil discovery context).

[157] See, e.g., A. Michael's Piano, Inc. v. FTC, 18 F.3d 138, 146-47 (2d Cir. 1994) (concluding that exemption still applicable, even if staff attorney was considering or recommending closing investigation); cf. Tax Analysts v. IRS, No. 94-923, slip op. at 6 (D.D.C. Sept. 3, 1999) (protecting record containing "mental impressions" of agency attorney as to whether agency should continue to contest certain matters in litigation, or cease litigating case altogether) (appeal pending); Grecco v. Department of Justice, No. 97-0419, slip op. at 12 (D.D.C. Apr. 1, 1999) (holding exemption applicable to records concerning determination whether to appeal lower court decision).

[158] See FOIA Update, Vol. VI, No. 3, at 5.

[159] See Senate of P.R., 823 F.2d at 586; Canning v. Department of the Treasury, No. 94-2704, slip op. at 12 (D.D.C. May 7, 1998) (holding prosecutor's letter setting forth reasons relied upon in declining to prosecute case and "written after the conclusion of the investigation and after the decision to forgo litigation was made," not covered by privilege); Grine v. Coombs, No. 95-342, 1997 U.S. Dist. LEXIS 19578, at *10 (W.D. Pa. Oct. 10, 1997) (finding privilege not applicable where no further agency enforcement action was contemplated at time of document's creation). But see Senate of P.R. v. United States Dep't of Justice, No. 84-1829, 1992 WL 119127, at *8 (D.D.C. May 13, 1992) (finding reasonable anticipation of litigation when case was closed but
(continued...)

# EXEMPTION 5

Moreover, one court has even held that documents not originally prepared in anticipation of litigation cannot assume the protection of the work-product privilege merely through their later placement in a litigation-related document.[160]

Second, Rule 26(b)(3) of the Federal Rules of Civil Procedure allows the privilege to be used to protect documents prepared "by or for another party or by or for that other party's representative." Not only do documents prepared by agency attorneys who are responsible for the litigation of a case which is being defended or prosecuted by the Department of Justice qualify for the privilege,[161] but also documents prepared by an attorney "not employed as a litigator."[162] Courts have looked at the plain meaning of the rule and have extended work-product protection to materials prepared by nonattorneys who are supervised by attorneys.[163] The unstated premise in such cases is that

---

[159](...continued)
agency was carefully reevaluating it in light of new evidence).

[160] Dow Jones & Co. v. Department of Justice, 724 F. Supp. 985, 989 (D.D.C. 1989), aff'd on other grounds, 917 F.2d 571 (D.C. Cir. 1990).

[161] See, e.g., Cook v. Watt, 597 F. Supp. 545, 548 (D. Alaska 1983).

[162] Illinois State Bd. of Educ. v. Bell, No. 84-337, slip op. at 9-10 (D.D.C. May 31, 1985).

[163] See, e.g., Davis v. FTC, No. 96-CIV-9324, 1997 WL 73671, at *2 (S.D.N.Y. Feb. 20, 1997) (protecting material prepared by economists for administrative hearing); Creel v. United States Dep't of State, No. 6:92CV559, 1993 U.S. Dist. LEXIS 21187, at *27 (E.D. Tex. Sept. 29, 1993) (magistrate's recommendation) (protecting special agent's notes made while assisting attorney in investigation), adopted (E.D. Tex. Dec. 30, 1993), aff'd, 42 F.3d 641 (5th Cir. 1995) (unpublished table decision); Durham v. United States Dep't of Justice, 829 F. Supp. 428, 432-33 (D.D.C. 1993) (protecting material prepared by government personnel under prosecuting attorney's direction), appeal dismissed for failure to timely file, No. 93-5354 (D.C. Cir. Nov. 29, 1994); Taylor v. Office of Special Counsel, No. 91-N-734, slip op. at 17 (D. Colo. Mar. 22, 1993) (holding that privilege covers telephone interview conducted by examiner at request of attorney); Joint Bd. of Control v. Bureau of Indian Affairs, No. 87-217, slip op. at 9-10 (D. Mont. Sept. 9, 1988) (protecting water studies produced by contract companies); Nishnic v. United States Dep't of Justice, 671 F. Supp. 771, 772-73 (D.D.C. 1987) (holding historian's research and interviews privileged); Wilson, No. 84-3163, slip op. at 8 (D.D.C. Jan. 28, 1995) (holding consultant's report privileged); Exxon Corp. v. FTC, 466 F. Supp. 1088, 1099 (D.D.C. 1978) (protecting economist's report), aff'd, 663 F.2d 120 (D.C. Cir. 1980). But cf. Richman v. United States Dep't of Justice, No. 90-C-19-C, slip op. at 3 (W.D. Wis. Mar. 2, 1994) (confusing subtleties of privileges to hold that information not prepared "by a lawyer in preparation for litigation" not entitled to any protection under Exemption 5 whatsoever); Brittany Dyeing & Printing Corp. v. EPA, No. 91-2711, slip op. at 7-8 (D.D.C. Mar. 12, 1993) (confusing attorney work-product privilege and deliberative process privilege to hold that witness statements taken by investigator at behest of counsel cannot be protected be-

(continued...)

# EXEMPTION 5

work-product protection is appropriate when the nonattorney acts as the agent of the attorney; when that is not the case, the work-product privilege as incorporated by the FOIA has not been extended to protect the material prepared by the nonattorney.[164]

Third, the work-product privilege has been held to remain applicable when the information has been shared with a party holding a common interest with the agency.[165] The privilege remains applicable also when the document has become the basis for a final agency decision.[166]

In NLRB v. Sears, Roebuck & Co.,[167] the Supreme Court allowed the withholding of a final agency decision on the basis that it was shielded by the work-product privilege,[168] but it also stated that Exemption 5 can never apply to final decisions and it expressed reluctance to "construe Exemption 5 to ap-

---

[163](...continued) cause they would "not expose agency decisionmaking process").

[164] See Hall v. Department of Justice, No. 87-474, 1989 WL 24542, at **7-8 (D.D.C. Mar. 8, 1989) (magistrate's recommendation) (concluding that agency's affidavit failed to show that prosecutorial report of investigation was prepared by Marshals Service personnel under direction of attorney), adopted (D.D.C. July 31, 1989); Nishnic, 671 F. Supp. at 810-11 (holding summaries of witness statements taken by USSR officials for United States Department of Justice not protectible).

[165] See, e.g., Gulf Oil, 760 F.2d at 295-96 (protecting documents shared between two companies contemplating merger); Chilivis v. SEC, 673 F.2d 1205, 1211-12 (11th Cir. 1982); Nishnic v. United States Dep't of Justice, 671 F. Supp. 771, 775 (D.D.C. 1987) (documents shared with foreign nation). But see Texas v. ICC, 889 F.2d 59, 62 (5th Cir. 1989) (holding communications between agency and interested nonagency not protectible because nonagency "did not stand in any consultative or advisory role" to agency).

[166] See Uribe v. Executive Office for United States Attorneys, No. 87-1836, 1989 U.S. Dist. LEXIS 5691, at **6-7 (D.D.C. May 23, 1989) (protecting criminal "prosecution declination memorandum") (citing FTC v. Grolier Inc., 462 U.S. 19 (1983)); Iglesias v. CIA, 525 F. Supp. 547, 559 (D.D.C. 1981) ("[A]ny argument to the effect that the attorney's opinions in question may have become the basis for final agency action is irrelevant [to the applicability of] the work-product privilege."); FOIA Update, Vol. VI, No. 3, at 5; see also Federal Open Mkt. Comm. v. Merrill, 434 U.S. 340, 360 n.23 (1979) (protecting final determination under commercial privilege); cf. NLRB v. Sears, Roebuck & Co., 421 U.S. 132, 160 (1975) (holding that memoranda reflecting agency decision to prosecute party do not constitute "final disposition" of "case" within the meaning of subsection (a)(2) of FOIA). But see Grolier, 462 U.S. at 32 n.4 (Brennan, J., concurring) ("[I]t is difficult to imagine how a final decision could be 'prepared in anticipation of litigation or for trial.'").

[167] 421 U.S. 132 (1975).

[168] Id. at 160.

## EXEMPTION 5

ply to documents described in 5 U.S.C. § 552(a)(2),"[169] the "reading room" provision of the FOIA.[170] This result inevitably led to no small amount of confusion,[171] which was cleared up by the Supreme Court in Federal Open Market Committee v. Merrill.[172] In Merrill, the Court explained its statements in Sears,[173] and plainly stated that even if a document is a final opinion, and therefore falls within subsection (a)(2)'s mandatory disclosure requirements, it still may be withheld if it falls within the work-product privilege.[174] (For a discussion of the automatic disclosure requirements of subsection (a)(2), see FOIA Reading Rooms, above.)

Fourth, the Supreme Court's decisions in United States v. Weber Aircraft Corp.[175] and FTC v. Grolier Inc.,[176] viewed in light of the traditional contours of the attorney work-product doctrine, afford sweeping attorney work-product protection to factual materials. Because factual work-product enjoys qualified immunity from civil discovery, such materials are discoverable "only upon a showing that the party seeking discovery has substantial need" of materials which cannot be obtained elsewhere without "undue hardship."[177] In Grolier, the Supreme Court held that the "test under Exemption 5 is whether the documents would be 'routinely' or 'normally' disclosed upon a showing of relevance."[178] Because the rules of civil discovery require a showing of "substantial need" and "undue hardship" in order for a party to obtain any factual

---

[169] Id. at 153-54.

[170] See FOIA Update, Vol. XIII, No. 3, at 3-4 ("OIP Guidance: The 'Automatic' Disclosure Provisions of FOIA: Subsections (a)(1) & (a)(2)"); see also FOIA Update, Vol. XVII, No. 4, at 1-2 (describing amendments to subsection (a)(2)).

[171] See, e.g., Bristol-Meyers Co. v. FTC, 598 F.2d 18, 24 n.11, 29 (D.C. Cir. 1978).

[172] 443 U.S. 340 (1979).

[173] Id. at 360 n.23 (clarifying that Sears observations were made in relation to privilege for predecisional communications only).

[174] Id. ("It should be obvious that the kind of mutually exclusive relationship between final opinions and statements of policy, on one hand, and predecisional communications, on the other, does not necessarily exist between final statements of policy and other Exemption 5 privileges."). But see Safe-Card, 926 F.2d at 1203-05, 1206 (mistakenly applying Bristol-Meyers, a pre-Merrill decision, in requiring release of work product that memorializes final decision); Richman v. United States Dep't of Justice, No. 90-C-19-C, slip op. at 9 (W.D. Wis. Feb. 2, 1994) (mistakenly concluding that privilege applies only when material is predecisional).

[175] 465 U.S. 792 (1984).

[176] 462 U.S. 19 (1983).

[177] Fed. R. Civ. P. 26(b)(3).

[178] 462 U.S. at 26; see also Sears, 421 U.S. at 149 & n.16.

# EXEMPTION 5

work-product,[179] such materials are not "routinely" or "normally" discoverable. This "routinely or normally discoverable" test was unanimously reaffirmed by the Supreme Court in Weber Aircraft.[180]

Although several pre-Weber Aircraft circuit court decisions mistakenly limited attorney work-product protection to "deliberative" material,[181] no distinction between factual and deliberative work-product should be applied. This broad view of the privilege has been expressed by several courts, including the D.C. Circuit, to clarify once and for all that factual information is fully entitled to work-product protection.[182] However, it should be remembered

---

[179] Fed. R. Civ. P. 26(b)(3).

[180] 465 U.S. at 799.

[181] See Robbins Tire & Rubber Co. v. NLRB, 563 F.2d 724, 735 (5th Cir. 1977), rev'd on other grounds, 437 U.S. 214 (1978); Deering Milliken, Inc. v. Irving, 548 F.2d 1131, 1138 (4th Cir. 1977); Title Guar. Co. v. NLRB, 534 F.2d 484, 492-93 n.15 (2d Cir. 1976).

[182] See Martin, 819 F.2d at 1187 ("The work-product privilege simply does not distinguish between factual and deliberative material."); see also Tax Analysts v. IRS, 117 F.3d 607, 620 (D.C. Cir. 1997) (holding that district court was in error to limit protection to "the mental impressions, conclusions, opinions, or legal theories of an attorney"); Norwood v. FAA, 993 F.2d 570, 576 (6th Cir. 1993) (holding that work-product privilege protects documents regardless of status as factual or deliberative); Nadler, 955 F.2d at 1492 ("[U]nlike the deliberative process privilege, the work-product privilege encompasses factual materials."); May v. IRS, 85 F. Supp. 2d 939 (W.D. Mo. 1999) (protecting both "the factual basis for [a] potential prosecution and an analysis of the applicable law"); Rugiero v. United States Dep't of Justice, 35 F. Supp. 2d 977, 984 (E.D. Mich. 1998) ("[T]he law is clear that . . . both factual and deliberative work product are exempt from release under FOIA.") (appeal pending); Manchester v. DEA, 823 F. Supp. 1259, 1269 (E.D. Pa. 1993) (deciding that segregation not required where "factual information is incidental to, and bound with, privileged" information); Manna v. United States Dep't of Justice, 815 F. Supp. 798, 814 (D.N.J. 1993) (following Martin), aff'd on other grounds, 51 F.3d 1158 (3d Cir. 1995); Spannaus v. United States Dep't of Justice, No. 85-1015, slip op. at 21-22 (D. Mass. Nov. 12, 1992) (concluding documents need not show litigative strategy to be withheld in full); United Techs. Corp. v. NLRB, 632 F. Supp. 776, 781 (D. Conn. 1985) ("[i]f a document is attorney work product the entire document is privileged."), aff'd on other grounds, 777 F.2d 90 (2d Cir. 1985); accord FOIA Update, Vol. V, No. 4, at 6. But see Nickerson v. United States, 95-C-7395, 1996 WL 563465, at *3 (N.D. Ill. Oct. 1, 1996) (mistakenly ruling that facts must be segregated under privilege); Fine v. United States Dep't of Energy, 830 F. Supp. 570, 574-76 (D.N.M. 1993) (refusing to follow Martin); cf. Tax Analysts v. IRS, No. 94-923, 1998 WL 419755, at *3 (D.D.C. May 1, 1998) (requiring agency to disclose "agency working law, legal analysis, and conclusions, so long as the 'mental impressions, conclusions, opinions, or legal theories of an attorney' are protected" (quoting Tax Analysts v. IRS, 117 F.3d 607, 619 (D.C. Cir. 1997)), because to allow otherwise would "eviscerate" the court of appeals' ruling that agency

(continued...)

## EXEMPTION 5

that the agency always has the burden of showing that the privilege applies to all withheld information.[183]

A collateral issue is the applicability of the attorney work-product privilege to witness statements. Within the civil discovery context, the Supreme Court has recognized at least a qualified privilege from civil discovery for such documents, i.e., such material was held discoverable only upon a showing of necessity and justification.[184] Applying the "routinely and normally discoverable" test of Grolier and Weber Aircraft, the D.C. Circuit has firmly held that witness statements are protectible under Exemption 5.[185] Despite the weight of law that supports the proposition that the contours of Exemption 5 are co-extensive with the protections of the work-product privilege, though, some courts have held that witness statements are not protectible, either on the theory that they fail to meet Exemption 5's threshold requirement,[186] or that the witness statements are merely unprivileged factual information which must be segregated for disclosure.[187]

Any such differences over the traditional protection accorded witness statements do not in any event affect the viability of protecting aircraft accident witness statements; such statements are protected under a distinct com-

---

[182](...continued)
must release its field service advice memoranda to requester), appeal voluntarily dismissed, No. 94-00923 (D.C. Cir. Aug. 11, 1998).

[183] See, e.g., Linn v. United States Dep't of Justice, No. 92-1406, 1995 WL 417810, at **19, 29-30 (D.D.C. June 6, 1995) (requiring that agency specifically explain why material protected by privilege); Kronberg v. United States Dep't of Justice, 875 F. Supp. 861, 869 (D.D.C. 1995) (requiring agency to show how privilege applies).

[184] See Hickman, 329 U.S. at 511.

[185] See Martin, 819 F.2d at 1187.

[186] See Thurner Heat Treating Corp. v. NLRB, 839 F.2d 1256, 1259-60 (7th Cir. 1988) (holding witness statements taken from nonagency employees held not "intra-agency"); Van Bourg, Allen, Weinberg & Roger v. NLRB, 751 F.2d 982, 985 (9th Cir. 1985) (construing Exemption 5 narrowly so as to apply only to "internal agency documents or documents prepared by outsiders who have a formal relationship with the agency"); Poss v. NLRB, 565 F.2d 654, 659 (10th Cir. 1977) (same); Aircraft Gear Corp. v. NLRB, No. 92-C-6023, slip op. at 6-10 (N.D. Ill. Mar. 14, 1994) (explicitly following Thurner); Kilroy v. NLRB, 633 F. Supp. 136, 142 (S.D. Ohio 1985) (rejecting application of Weber Aircraft to witness statements), aff'd, 823 F.2d 553 (6th Cir. 1987) (unpublished table decision).

[187] See, e.g., Uribe, 1989 U.S. Dist. LEXIS 5691, at *7 (statements made by plaintiff during interrogation did not "represent the attorney's conclusions, recommendations and opinions"); Wayland v. NLRB, 627 F. Supp. 1473, 1476 (M.D. Tenn. 1986) (witness statements not shown to be other than objective reporting of facts and "thus do not reflect the attorney's theory of the case and his litigation strategy"). But see FOIA Update, Vol. VIII, No. 2, at 4-5 ("OIP Guidance: Broad Protection for Witness Statements").

# EXEMPTION 5

mon law privilege that was first enunciated in Machin v. Zuckert[188] and then was applied under the FOIA in Weber Aircraft.[189] (See the discussion under Exemption 5, Other Privileges, below.)

As a final point, it should be noted that the Supreme Court's decision in Grolier resolved a split in the circuits by ruling that the termination of litigation does not vitiate the protection for material otherwise properly categorized as attorney work-product.[190] Thus, there exists no temporal limitation on work-product protection under the FOIA, as a matter of law.[191] Consequently, although there is no "public interest" exception to the application of the work-product privilege,[192] this is an area in which there exists an exceptionally large potential for the exercise of sound administrative discretion to disclose technically exempt information in accordance with Attorney General Reno's FOIA Memorandum of October 4, 1993.[193] (See the discussions of such discretionary disclosure under Exemption 5, Applying the "Foreseeable Harm" Standard, below, and Discretionary Disclosure and Waiver, below.)

### Attorney-Client Privilege

The third traditional privilege incorporated into Exemption 5 concerns "confidential communications between an attorney and his client relating to a legal matter for which the client has sought professional advice."[194] Unlike the attorney work-product privilege, the attorney-client privilege is not limited to the context of litigation. Moreover, although it fundamentally applies to facts

---

[188] 316 F.2d 336, 338 (D.C. Cir. 1963).

[189] 465 U.S. at 799; see also Badhwar v. United States Dep't of the Air Force, 829 F.2d 182, 185 (D.C. Cir. 1987) ("[T]he disclosure of 'factual' information that may have been volunteered would defeat the policy on which the Machin privilege is based.").

[190] 462 U.S. at 28; cf. Clark-Cowlitz Joint Operating Agency v. Federal Energy Regulatory Comm'n, 798 F.2d 499, 502-03 (D.C. Cir. 1986) (en banc) (same result under Government in the Sunshine Act, 5 U.S.C. § 552b (1994 & Supp. IV 1998)).

[191] See FOIA Update, Vol. IV, No. 3, at 1-2.

[192] See Winterstein, 89 F. Supp. 2d at 82.

[193] Attorney General's Memorandum for Heads of Departments and Agencies regarding the Freedom of Information Act (Oct. 4, 1993); see also Attorney General's Follow-Up Memorandum for Heads of Departments and Agencies regarding the Freedom of Information Act (Sept. 3, 1999), reprinted in FOIA Update, Vol. XIX, No. 4, at 3-5 (reiterating importance of "foreseeable harm" standard to federal agencies in order to promote further discretionary disclosure in agency decisionmaking); FOIA Update, Vol. XV, No. 2, at 3-6 ("OIP Guidance: Applying the 'Foreseeable Harm' Standard Under Exemption Five"); FOIA Update, Vol. VI, No. 3, at 5 (suggesting that consideration be given to discretionary disclosure of work-product information).

[194] Mead Data Cent., Inc. v. United States Dep't of the Air Force, 566 F.2d 242, 252 (D.C. Cir. 1977).

# EXEMPTION 5

divulged by a client to his attorney, this privilege also encompasses any opinions given by an attorney to his client based upon those facts,[195] as well as communications between attorneys which reflect client-supplied information.[196]

The Supreme Court, in the civil discovery context, has emphasized the public policy underlying the attorney-client privilege--"that sound legal advice or advocacy serves public ends and that such advice or advocacy depends upon the lawyer's being fully informed by the client."[197] As is set out in greater

---

[195] See, e.g., Jernigan v. Department of the Air Force, No. 97-35930, 1998 WL 658662, at *2 (9th Cir. Sept. 17, 1998) (holding that privilege covers agency attorney's legal review of internal "Social Action" investigation); Schlefer v. United States, 702 F.2d 233, 244 n.26 (D.C. Cir. 1983) (observing that privilege "permits nondisclosure of an attorney's opinion or advice in order to protect the secrecy of the underlying facts"); Barmes v. IRS, 60 F. Supp. 2d 896, 901 (S.D. Ind. 1998) (protecting material "prepared by an IRS attorney in response to a request by a revenue officer to file certain liens pursuant to collection efforts against the plaintiffs"); Wishart v. Commissioner, No. 97-20614, 1998 U.S. Dist. LEXIS at *16 (N.D. Cal. Aug. 6, 1998) (stating that privilege protects documents "created by attorneys and by the individually-named [defendant] employees for purposes of obtaining legal representation from the government"), aff'd, 1999 WL 985142 (9th Cir. Oct. 18, 1999); Cujas v. IRS, No. 1:97CV00741, 1998 U.S. Dist. LEXIS 6466, at *19 (M.D.N.C. Apr. 15, 1998) (holding that privilege encompasses "notes of a revenue officer . . . reflecting the confidential legal advice that the agency's District Counsel orally gave the officer in response to a proposed course of action"), aff'd, No. 98-1641 (4th Cir. Aug. 25, 1998); Ludsin v. SBA, No. 96-2865, slip op. at 3 (D.D.C. Apr. 24, 1997) (holding that privilege covers intra-agency memoranda containing agency attorney's "legal conclusions and reasoning"); Linn v. United States Dep't of Justice, No. 92-1406, 1995 WL 631847, at **32-33 (D.D.C. Aug. 22, 1995) (protecting confidential legal advice given in course of grand jury investigation covered by privilege); NBC v. SBA, 836 F. Supp. 121, 124-25 (S.D.N.Y. 1993) (holding that privilege covers "professional advice given by attorney that discloses" information given by client); cf. Direct Response Consulting Serv. v. IRS, No. 94-1156, 1995 WL 623282, at *3 (D.D.C. Aug. 21, 1995) (finding privilege inapplicable to attorney's memoranda to file which were never communicated to client). But see Lee v. FDIC, 923 F. Supp. 451, 457-58 (S.D.N.Y. 1996) (declaring, without authority, that documents containing only "standard legal analysis" are not covered by privilege); cf. Brinton v. Department of State, 636 F.2d 600, 605 (D.C. Cir. 1980) (holding district court record insufficient to support claim of privilege because it contained "no finding that the communications are based on or related to confidences from the client").

[196] See, e.g., McErlean v. United States Dep't of Justice, No. 97-7831, 1999 WL 791680, at *7 (S.D.N.Y. Sept. 30, 1999); Buckner v. IRS, No. 1:97-CV-414, 1998 U.S. Dist. LEXIS 12449, at *19 (N.D. Ind. July 24, 1998); Green v. IRS, 556 F. Supp. 79, 85 (N.D. Ind. 1982), aff'd, 734 F.2d 18 (7th Cir. 1984) (unpublished table decision).

[197] Upjohn Co. v. United States, 449 U.S. 383, 389 (1981); see also FOIA
(continued...)

**EXEMPTION 5**

detail in the discussion of the attorney work-product above, the Supreme Court held in United States v. Weber Aircraft Corp.[198] and in FTC v. Grolier Inc.[199] that the scopes of the various privileges are coextensive in the FOIA and civil discovery contexts.[200] Thus, those decisions that expand or contract the privilege's contours according to whether it is presented in a civil discovery or a FOIA context[201] do not accurately reflect the law.[202]

The parallelism of a civil discovery privilege and Exemption 5 protection is particularly significant with respect to the concept of a "confidential communication" within the attorney-client relationship. To this end, one court has held that confidentiality may be inferred when the communications suggest that "'the government is dealing with its attorneys as would any private party seeking advice to protect personal interests.'"[203] In Upjohn Co. v. United States, the Supreme Court held that the attorney-client privilege covers attorney-client communications when the specifics of the communication are confidential, even though the underlying subject matter is known to third parties.[204] Accordingly, the line of FOIA decisions in the Court of Appeals for the District of Columbia Circuit that squarely conflicts with the Upjohn analy-

---

[197](...continued) Update, Vol. VI, No. 2, at 3-4 ("OIP Guidance: The Attorney-Client Privilege"); cf. Swidler & Berlin v. United States, 524 U.S. 399, 407 (1998) (addressing privilege in context of criminal investigation; observing that "there is no case authority for the proposition that the privilege applies differently [with respect to applicability after client's death] in criminal and civil cases").

[198] 465 U.S. 792 (1984).

[199] 462 U.S. 19 (1983).

[200] 465 U.S. at 799-800; 462 U.S. at 26-28. But cf. In re Lindsey, 148 F.3d 1100, 1114 (D.C. Cir. 1998) (stating that, in criminal context, "government attorney-client privilege" does not shield "information related to criminal misconduct") (non-FOIA case); In re Grand Jury Subpoena Duces Tecum, 112 F.3d 910, 921 (8th Cir.) (same) (non-FOIA case).

[201] See, e.g., Mead Data, 566 F.2d at 255 & n.28.

[202] See FOIA Update, Vol. VI, No. 2, at 3-4.

[203] Alamo Aircraft Supply, Inc. v. Weinberger, No. 85-1291, 1986 U.S. Dist. LEXIS 29010, at *5 (D.D.C. Feb. 21, 1986) (quoting Coastal States Gas Corp. v. Department of Energy, 617 F.2d 854, 863 (D.C. Cir. 1980)). But see Dow, Lohnes & Albertson v. Presidential Comm'n on Broad. to Cuba, 624 F. Supp. 572, 578 (D.D.C. 1984) (holding that confidentiality must be shown in order to invoke Exemption 5).

[204] 449 U.S. at 395-96; see also United States v. Cunningham, 672 F.2d 1064, 1073 n.8 (2d Cir. 1982); Judicial Watch, Inc. v. Commission on United States-Pac. Trade & Inv. Policy, No. 97-0099, slip op. at 17 (D.D.C. Sept. 30, 1999) (citing Upjohn); In re Ampicillin Antitrust Litig., 81 F.R.D. 377, 388-90 (D.D.C. 1978).

**EXEMPTION 5**

sis[205] should not be followed.[206]

The Supreme Court in Upjohn concluded that the privilege encompasses confidential communications made to the attorney not only by decisionmaking "control group" personnel, but also by lower-echelon employees.[207] This broad construction of the attorney-client privilege acknowledges the reality that such lower-echelon personnel often possess information relevant to an attorney's advice-rendering function.[208] However, the D.C. Circuit has recently held that otherwise confidential agency memoranda are not protected under the privilege if they are merely interpretations of agency law.[209]

The nature of this privilege, and its partial overlap with the deliberative process privilege and attorney work-product privilege under Exemption 5, make it no less subject to potential discretionary disclosure under current policy standards.[210] (See the discussions of such discretionary disclosure under Exemption 5, Applying the "Foreseeable Harm" Standard, below, and Discretionary Disclosure and Waiver, below.)

### Other Privileges

The FOIA neither expands nor contracts existing privileges, nor does it create any new privileges.[211] However, the Supreme Court has indicated that Exemption 5 may incorporate virtually all civil discovery privileges; if a document is immune from civil discovery, it is similarly protected from mandatory

---

[205] See, e.g., Tax Analysts v. IRS, 117 F.3d 607, 618-20 (D.C. Cir. 1997); Schlefer, 702 F.2d at 245; Brinton, 636 F.2d at 604; Mead Data, 566 F.2d at 255.

[206] See FOIA Update, Vol. VI, No. 2, at 4.

[207] 449 U.S. at 392-97.

[208] See id.; see also Sherlock v. United States, No. 93-0650, 1994 WL 10186, at *3 (E.D. La. Jan. 12, 1994) (holding privilege applicable to communications from collection officer to district counsel); Murphy v. TVA, 571 F. Supp. 502, 506 (D.D.C. 1983) (holding that circulation of information within agency to employees involved in matter for which advice sought does not breach confidentiality); LSB Indus. v. Commissioner, 556 F. Supp. 40, 43 (W.D. Okla. 1982) (protecting information provided by agency investigators and used by agency attorneys).

[209] Tax Analysts, 117 F.3d at 619-20.

[210] See FOIA Update, Vol. XV, No. 2, at 3-6 ("OIP Guidance: Applying the 'Foreseeable Harm' Standard Under Exemption Five") (pointing out that attorney-client privilege can be waived with consent of client agency).

[211] See Association for Women in Science v. Califano, 566 F.2d 339, 342 (D.C. Cir. 1977); see also Badhwar v. United States Dep't of the Air Force, 829 F.2d 182, 184 (D.C. Cir. 1987) ("To decide [whether a recognized privilege should be abandoned] in a FOIA case would be inappropriate, as Exemption 5 requires the application of existing rules regarding discovery, not their reformulation.").

**EXEMPTION 5**

disclosure under the FOIA.[212] Because Rule 501 of the Federal Rules of Evidence allows courts to create privileges as necessary,[213] there exists the potential for "new" privileges to be applied under Exemption 5.[214] However, one major caveat should be noted in the application of any discovery privilege under the FOIA: A privilege should not be used against a requester who would routinely receive such information in civil discovery.[215]

Nearly twenty years ago, the Supreme Court in Federal Open Market Committee v. Merrill[216] found an additional privilege incorporated within Exemption 5 based upon Federal Rule of Civil Procedure 26(c)(7), which provides that "for good cause shown . . . a trade secret or other confidential research, development or commercial information" is protected from discovery. This qualified privilege is available "at least to the extent that this information is generated by the Government itself in the process leading up to the awarding of a contract" and expires upon the awarding of the contract or upon the withdrawal of the offer.[217] The theory underlying the privilege is that early release of such information would likely put the government at a competitive disadvantage by endangering consummation of a contract; consequently, "the sensitivity of the commercial secrets involved, and the harm that would be inflicted upon the Government by premature disclosure should . . . serve as rele-

---

[212] See United States v. Weber Aircraft Corp., 465 U.S. 792, 799-800 (1984); FTC v. Grolier Inc., 462 U.S. 19, 26-27 (1983).

[213] See Trammel v. United States, 445 U.S. 40, 47 (1980); see, e.g., Dellwood Farms, Inc. v. Cargill, Inc., 128 F.3d 1122, 1124-25 (7th Cir. 1997) (recognizing judge-fashioned "law enforcement investigatory privilege") (non-FOIA case); Kientzy v. McDonnell Douglas Corp., 133 F.R.D. 570, 571-73 (E.D. Mo. 1991) (recognizing "ombudsman privilege" under Rule 501 of Federal Rules of Evidence) (non-FOIA case); Shabazz v. Scurr, 662 F. Supp. 90, 92 (S.D. Iowa 1987) (same) (non-FOIA case); see also In re Sealed Case, 121 F.3d 729, 751-52 (D.C. Cir. 1997) (recognizing "presidential communications privilege" that applies to "communications made by presidential advisers in the course of preparing advice for the President . . . even when these communications are not made directly to the President") (non-FOIA case). But cf. In re Sealed Case, No. 98-3069, 1998 WL 370584, at *1 (D.C. Cir. July 7, 1998) (declining to recognize proposed "protective function privilege") (non-FOIA case).

[214] See, e.g., FOIA Update, Vol. VI, No. 4, at 3-4 (suggesting that new privilege for settlement negotiations records should be recognized under Exemption 5). But see Burka v. HHS, 87 F.3d 508, 517 (D.C. Cir. 1996) (holding that for record to be found privileged, agency must show that it is protected in discovery for reasons similar to those used by agency in FOIA context).

[215] See, e.g., United States Dep't of Justice v. Julian, 486 U.S. 1, 9 (1988) (holding that presentence report privilege, designed to protect report subjects, cannot be invoked against them as first-party requesters); cf. Badhwar, 829 F.2d at 184 ("Exemption 5 requires application of existing rules regarding discovery, not their reformulation.").

[216] 443 U.S. 340 (1979).

[217] Id. at 360.

# EXEMPTION 5

vant criteria."[218]

This harm rationale has led one court to hold that the commercial privilege may be invoked when a contractor who has submitted proposed changes to the contract requests sensitive cost estimates.[219] Based upon this underlying theory, there is nothing in Merrill to prevent it from being read more expansively to protect the government from competitive disadvantage outside of the contract setting, as the issue in Merrill was not presented strictly within such a setting.[220] However, the Court of Appeals for the District of Columbia Circuit recently declined to extend this privilege to scientific research, holding that the agency had failed to show that such material is "generally protected in civil discovery for reasons similar to those asserted in the FOIA context."[221]

While the breadth of this privilege is still not fully established, a realty appraisal generated by the government in the course of soliciting buyers for its property has been held to fall squarely within it,[222] as have documents containing communications between agency personnel, potential buyers, and real estate agents concerning a proposed sale of government-owned real estate,[223] an agency's background documents which it used to calculate its bid in a "contracting out" procedure,[224] and portions of inter-agency cost estimates prepared by the government for use in the evaluation of construction proposals submitted by private contractors.[225] Quite clearly, however, purely legal memoranda drafted to assist contract award deliberations are not encompassed by

---

[218] Id. at 363.

[219] Taylor Woodrow Int'l v. United States, No. 88-429, slip op. at 5-7 (W.D. Wash. Apr. 6, 1989) (concluding that disclosure would permit requester to take "unfair commercial advantage" of agency).

[220] See 443 U.S. at 360.

[221] Burka, 87 F.3d at 517.

[222] See Government Land Bank v. GSA, 671 F.2d 663, 665-66 (1st Cir. 1982) ("FOIA should not be used to allow the government's customers to pick the taxpayers' pockets.").

[223] See Marriott Employees' Fed. Credit Union v. National Credit Union Admin., No. 96-478-A, slip op. at 3 (E.D. Va. Dec. 24, 1996).

[224] See Morrison-Knudsen Co. v. Department of the Army of the United States, 595 F. Supp. 352, 354-56 (D.D.C. 1984), aff'd, 762 F.2d 138 (D.C. Cir. 1985) (unpublished table decision).

[225] See Hack v. Department of Energy, 538 F. Supp. 1098, 1100 (D.D.C. 1982); see also FOIA Update, Vol. IV, No. 4, at 14-15. But see American Soc'y of Pension Actuaries v. Pension Benefit Guar. Corp., No. 82-2806, slip op. at 3-4 (D.D.C. July 22, 1983) (distinguishing Merrill). See generally Feldman, The Government's Commercial Data Privilege Under Exemption Five of the Freedom of Information Act, 105 Mil. L. Rev. 125 (1984); Belazis, The Government's Commercial Information Privilege: Technical Information and the FOIA's Exemption 5, 33 Admin. L. Rev. 415 (1981).

**EXEMPTION 5**

this privilege.[226]

The Supreme Court in United States v. Weber Aircraft Corp.[227] held that Exemption 5 incorporates the special privilege protecting witness statements generated during Air Force aircraft accident investigations. Broadening the holding of Merrill that a privilege "mentioned in the legislative history of Exemption 5 is incorporated by the exemption,"[228] the Court ruled in Weber Aircraft that this long-recognized civil discovery privilege, even though not specifically mentioned there, nevertheless falls within Exemption 5.[229] The "plain statutory language"[230] and the clear congressional intent to sustain claims of privilege when confidentiality is necessary to ensure efficient governmental operations[231] support this result.[232] This privilege has been applied also to protect statements made in Inspector General investigations.[233]

Similarly, in Hoover v. Department of the Interior, the Court of Appeals for the Fifth Circuit recognized an Exemption 5 privilege based on Federal Rule of Civil Procedure 26(b)(4), which limits the discovery of reports prepared by expert witnesses.[234] The document at issue in Hoover was an appraiser's report prepared in the course of condemnation proceedings.[235] In support of its conclusions, the Fifth Circuit stressed that such a report would not have been routinely discoverable and that premature release would jeopardize the

---

[226] See Shermco Indus. v. Secretary of the Air Force, 613 F.2d 1314, 1319-20 n.11 (5th Cir. 1980); see also News Group Boston, Inc. v. National R.R. Passenger Corp., 799 F. Supp. 1264, 1270 (D. Mass. 1992) (finding affidavits insufficient to show why Amtrak payroll information covered by privilege), appeal voluntarily dismissed, No. 92-2250 (1st Cir. Dec. 4, 1992).

[227] 465 U.S. at 799.

[228] Id. at 800.

[229] Id. at 804; see also FOIA Update, Vol. V, No. 2, at 12-13.

[230] 465 U.S. at 802.

[231] See id.

[232] See also Badhwar, 829 F.2d at 185 (privilege applied to contractor report).

[233] See Ahearn v. United States Army Materials & Mechanics Research Ctr., 583 F. Supp. 1123, 1124 (D. Mass. 1984); see also Walsh v. Department of the Navy, No. 91-C-7410, 1992 WL 67845, at *4 (N.D. Ill. Mar. 23, 1992); AFGE v. Department of the Army, 441 F. Supp. 1308, 1313 (D.D.C. 1977). But see Nickerson v. United States, No. 95-C-7395, 1996 WL 563465, at *3 (N.D. Ill. Oct. 1, 1996) (holding privilege not applicable to statements made in course of medical malpractice investigation); Washington Post Co. v. United States Dep't of the Air Force, 617 F. Supp. 602, 606-07 (D.D.C. 1985) (finding privilege inapplicable when report format provided anonymity to witnesses).

[234] 611 F.2d 1132, 1141 (5th Cir. 1980).

[235] Id. at 1135.

**EXEMPTION 5**

bargaining position of the government.[236]

Because Exemption 5 incorporates virtually all civil discovery privileges, courts have recognized the applicability of other privileges, whether traditional or new, in the FOIA context.[237] Among those other privileges now recognized for purposes of the FOIA are the confidential report privilege,[238] the presentence report privilege,[239] the critical self-evaluative privilege,[240] the settlement negotiations privilege,[241] and the expert materials privilege.[242] (For a detailed discussion of the settlement negotiations privilege, see Exemption 5, Initial Considerations, above.)

Lastly, while it is evident that courts will continue to apply such civil discovery privileges under Exemption 5 of the FOIA, the mere fact that a particular privilege has been recognized by state law will not necessarily mean

---

[236] Id. at 1142; cf. Chemical Mfrs. Ass'n v. Consumer Prod. Safety Comm'n, 600 F. Supp. 114, 118-19 (D.D.C. 1984) (observing that Rule 26(b)(4) provides parallel protection in civil discovery for opinions of expert witnesses who will not testify at trial).

[237] See Martin v. Office of Special Counsel, 819 F.2d 1181, 1185 (D.C. Cir. 1987) (stating that Exemption 5 "unequivocally" incorporates "all civil discovery rules into FOIA"). But see Burka v. HHS, 87 F.3d 508, 521 (D.C. Cir. 1996) (refusing to recognize "confidential research information" privilege because such privilege is not yet "established or well-settled . . . in the realm of civil discovery"); cf. Melendez-Colon v. Department of the Navy, 56 F. Supp. 2d 142, 145 (D.P.R. 1999) (rejecting argument that FOIA "creates a separate discovery or evidentiary privilege" that would bar plaintiff from using document at evidentiary hearing in particular litigation).

[238] See Washington Post Co. v. HHS, 603 F. Supp. 235, 238-39 (D.D.C. 1985) ("confidential report" privilege applied under Exemption 4), rev'd on other grounds, 795 F.2d 205 (D.C. Cir. 1986).

[239] See Julian, 486 U.S. at 9 (recognizing privilege, but finding it applicable to third-party requesters only).

[240] See Washington Post Co. v. United States Dep't of Justice, No. 84-3581, slip op. at 18-21 (D.D.C. Sept. 25, 1987) (magistrate's recommendation) (applying privilege under Exemption 4), adopted (D.D.C. Dec. 15, 1987), rev'd & remanded on other grounds, 863 F.2d 96 (D.C. Cir. 1988). But see Sangre de Cristo Animal Protection, Inc. v. Department of Energy, No. 96-1059, slip op. at 7-9 (D.N.M. Mar. 10, 1998) (declining to apply privilege to records of animal research facility, citing Tenth Circuit's "cautious approach to expanding common law privileges").

[241] See M/A-COM Info. Sys. v. HHS, 656 F. Supp. 691, 692 (D.D.C. 1986) (applying privilege under Exemption 4, not under Exemption 5).

[242] See Nissei Sangyo Am., Ltd. v. IRS, No. 95-1019, 1998 U.S. Dist. LEXIS 2966, at **2-3 (D.D.C. Jan. 28, 1998) (holding that because Federal Rules of Civil Procedure "established a separate exception to discovery for expert materials . . . Exemption 5 of the FOIA . . . incorporates" it).

**EXEMPTION 5**

that it will be recognized by a federal court.[243]

### Applying the "Foreseeable Harm" Standard

In her FOIA Memorandum of October 4, 1993, Attorney General Janet Reno established new standards of government openness that strongly guide agency decisionmaking under the FOIA, the cornerstone of which is the "foreseeable harm" standard governing the use of FOIA exemptions.[244] This standard applies together with its corollary emphasis on discretionary FOIA disclosure, based upon the touchstone principle that exempt information "ought not be withheld from a FOIA requester unless it need be."[245] The wide range of agency information that is covered by the three major privileges of Exemption 5--the deliberative process privilege, the attorney work-product privilege, and the attorney-client privilege--warrants especially close attention in connection with the "foreseeable harm" standard.[246]

Of the three major privileges incorporated into Exemption 5, the traditional privilege protecting the processes of institutional deliberations is the one most commonly applicable to the records maintained at all federal agencies. Over the years, the courts have applied the deliberative process privilege under Exemption 5 to the entire gamut of records that are created during the processes of agency decisionmaking. (See Exemption 5, Deliberative Process Privilege, above, for a discussion of the breadth of records covered by this privilege.) Thus, there is much room for agencies to apply the "foreseeable harm" standard within the realm of the deliberative process privilege under Exemption 5 and to disclose information that, in the words of Attorney General Reno's FOIA Memorandum, "might technically or arguably fall within"

---

[243] See, e.g., Sneirson v. Chemical Bank, 108 F.R.D. 159, 162 (D. Del. 1985) (non-FOIA case); Cincotta v. City of N.Y., No. 83-7506, 1984 WL 1210, at \*\*1-2 (S.D.N.Y. Nov. 14, 1984) (non-FOIA case).

[244] Attorney General's Memorandum for Heads of Departments and Agencies regarding the Freedom of Information Act (Oct. 4, 1993) [hereinafter Attorney General Reno's FOIA Memorandum], reprinted in FOIA Update, Vol. XIV, No. 3, at 4-5; see also FOIA Update, Vol. XV, No. 2, at 3-6 ("OIP Guidance: Applying the 'Foreseeable Harm' Standard Under Exemption 5").

[245] Attorney General Reno's FOIA Memorandum, reprinted in FOIA Update, Vol. XIV, No. 3, at 4-5; see also Nationwide Bldg. Maintenance, Inc. v. Sampson, 559 F.2d 704, 712 n.34 (D.C. Cir. 1977) (observing that some information, "while arguably exempt[,] need not be withheld").

[246] See, e.g., FOIA Update, Vol. XV, No. 4, at 7 (summarizing cases in which much information previously withheld under Exemption 5 was disclosed upon application of "foreseeable harm" standard during process of litigation review); see also FOIA Update, Vol. XVIII, No. 2, at 1 (describing Attorney General's reiteration of importance of "foreseeable harm" standard to federal agencies in order to promote further discretionary disclosure in agency decisionmaking).

# EXEMPTION 5

it.[247] In doing so, they should be mindful that the "foreseeable harm" standard, by its very nature, requires FOIA officers to consider the applicability of an exemption on a case-by-case basis--i.e., through "consideration of the reasonably expected consequences of disclosure in each particular case."[248]

In each case, a FOIA officer should now determine whether disclosure of the information in question would foreseeably harm the basic institutional interests that underlie the deliberative process privilege in the first place.[249] In other words, he or she must consider whether it "would actually inhibit candor in the decision-making process" to disclose that particular information to the public at that particular time.[250]

In making these harm determinations--which can be difficult ones inasmuch as they must be reached individually and no longer can be made on any categorical basis--agency FOIA officers can be guided by their analyses of a number of primary factors that logically come into play:

(1) The nature of the decision involved. Some agency decisions are highly sensitive and perhaps even controversial; most of them are far less so.

(2) The nature of the decisionmaking process. Some agency decision-making processes require total candor and confidentiality; many others are not nearly so dependent.

(3) The status of the decision. If the decision is not yet made, then there is a far greater likelihood of harm from disclosure; conversely, with decisions already made there is certainly less likelihood.[251]

(4) The status of the personnel involved. Are the same agency employees, or other employees who are similarity situated, likely to be affected by the disclosure?[252]

---

[247] Id.

[248] FOIA Update, Vol. XIV, No. 3, at 2. But cf. Missouri ex rel. Shorr v. United States Army Corps of Eng'rs, 147 F.3d 708, 710-11 (8th Cir. 1998) (addressing Council on Environmental Quality regulation (40 C.F.R. § 1506.6(f) (1997)) that mandates categorical disclosure of inter-agency comments pertaining to environmental impact statements, but finding it inapplicable because of intra-agency character of document at issue).

[249] See Attorney General's Follow-Up Memorandum for Heads of Departments and Agencies regarding the Freedom of Information Act (Sept. 3, 1999), reprinted in FOIA Update, Vol. XIX, No. 4, at 3-5 (reiterating importance of "foreseeable harm" standard to federal agencies).

[250] Army Times Publ'g Co. v. Department of the Air Force, 998 F.2d 1067, 1072 (D.C. Cir. 1993).

[251] See FOIA Update, Vol. I, No. 1, at 4; see also FOIA Update, Vol. XVI, No. 3, at 5.

[252] See FOIA Update, Vol. I, No. 1, at 4; see also FOIA Update, Vol. XVI, No.
(continued...)

# EXEMPTION 5

(5) <u>The potential for process impairment</u>. How much room is there for actual diminishment of deliberative quality if the personnel involved do feel inhibited by potential disclosure?[253]

(6) <u>The significance of any process impairment</u>. In some cases, any anticipated "chilling effect" on the agency's decisionmaking process might be so minimal as to be practically negligible.

(7) <u>The age of the information</u>. While there is no universally applicable age-based litmus test, the sensitivity of information tends to fade with the passage of time.[254]

(8) <u>The sensitivity of individual record portions</u>. Apart from any other factor or consideration, FOIA officers ultimately must focus on "the individual sensitivity of each item of information."[255]

Similarly, the application of the "foreseeable harm" standard to records falling within Exemption 5's attorney work-product privilege holds enormous potential for increased agency disclosure. This is due in large part to the fact that the privilege, as it operates under the FOIA, is extremely broad in multiple respects. Its substantive scope is so broad as to cover literally every bit of information that is prepared in connection with a case.[256] Moreover, under the Supreme Court's <u>Grolier</u> decision, the privilege can apply under Exemption 5 "in perpetuity," without any temporal limitation whatsoever.[257] (See Exemption 5, Attorney Work-Product Privilege, above, for a further discussion of this privilege.)

Thus, the attorney work-product privilege technically applies to a very wide and very deep range of litigation-related records that may be requested under the FOIA. A proper application of Attorney General Reno's "foreseeable harm" standard should proceed with full appreciation of the privilege's exceptional breadth in this regard and of the corresponding FOIA-policy obli-

---

[252](...continued)
3, at 5; <u>United States v. Nixon</u>, 418 U.S. 683, 705 (1974) (focusing on "expect[ation]" of personnel in determining whether disclosure may be "detriment[al to] the decision making process").

[253] <u>See, e.g.</u>, FOIA Update, Vol. IX, No. 4, at 4 (observing that some presidential transition advice "simply would not be given--or at least not so candidly--if it were not protectible under the FOIA").

[254] <u>See</u> FOIA Update, Vol. XIV, No. 3, at 2; <u>cf.</u> <u>Craig v. United States</u>, 131 F.3d 99, 107 (2d Cir. 1997) ("[T]he passage of time erodes many of the justifications for continued secrecy.") (grand jury secrecy case).

[255] <u>Id.</u>

[256] <u>See</u> FOIA Update, Vol. V, No. 4, at 6; <u>see also</u> FOIA Update, Vol. VIII, No. 2, at 5 (covering "entireties of witness statements").

[257] <u>FTC v. Grolier Inc.</u>, 462 U.S. 19, 25 (1983); <u>see also</u> FOIA Update, Vol. IV, No. 3, at 1-2.

## EXEMPTION 5

gation to eschew it to the maximum extent possible.[258]

First and foremost, when the related litigation has ended, an agency should no longer assert the privilege under the FOIA unless it determines that because of some special continuing sensitivity, disclosure would "cause real harm to the interests of the attorney and his client even after the controversy in the prior litigation is resolved."[259] While there can be no hard and fast rule on such matters, it is not hard to imagine even any such lingering sensitivity beginning to fade after a period of just a few months or years beyond a case's conclusion.[260]

Furthermore, regardless of whether the passage of time alone is sufficient to allow disclosure of an entire work-product file, the "foreseeable harm" requirement should yield disclosure of the bulk of material found within the broad, fact-laden scope of the privilege in any event. This is information that is, after all, by definition subject to discovery disclosure based upon mere showings of litigation relevance and need.[261] There will be little need for an agency to assert the work-product privilege for such information in many instances, even during the pendency of litigation, if it has no inherent sensitivity in connection with any current or prospective litigation process. And even if there is such sensitivity to some portion of a litigation file,[262] agencies should take pains to segregate that information from all nonsensitive information in order to achieve a maximum disclosure result.[263]

In sum, the nature of the attorney work-product privilege is such that an agency should always bear in mind the following primary elements when applying the "foreseeable harm" standard to information covered by it:

(1) <u>The time element</u>. Is the case still pending, or is it sufficiently past that the sensitivity of even the core information covered by the privilege's first tier has faded?

(2) <u>The litigation connection element</u>. If the case itself is at an end,

---

[258] See FOIA Update, Vol. XVIII, No. 2, at 1; FOIA Update, Vol. XV, No. 2, at 5-6; see, e.g., FOIA Update, Vol. VI, No. 3, at 5 (encouraging discretionary disclosure of certain attorney work-product records absent any harm).

[259] Grolier, 462 U.S. at 28, 30 (Brennan, J., concurring).

[260] See FOIA Update, Vol. XIV, No. 3, at 2.

[261] See Fed. R. Civ. P. 26(b)(3).

[262] See, e.g., Grolier, 462 U.S. at 30-31 (recounting circumstances in "recurring" litigation that can amount to such sensitivity).

[263] See FOIA Update, Vol. XIV, No. 3, at 11-12 ("OIP Guidance: The 'Reasonable Segregation' Obligation") (advising agencies to undertake processes of "more particularized record review" in implementing both new "foreseeable harm" standard and also their related statutory obligation to segregate all nonexempt record portions for FOIA disclosure); see also id. at 4 (Attorney General's FOIA Memorandum tying both obligations to new emphasis on discretionary disclosure, toward objective of "maximum responsible disclosure").

**EXEMPTION 5**

does the information truly remain sensitive due to its connection to similar or recurring litigation?[264]

(3) The substantive scope element. Critical distinctions should be drawn between the "attorney thought process" information within the privilege's inner core, and information that could include even "pure facts" that are covered by its outer scope.[265]

(4) The inherent sensitivity element. Regardless of any other consideration, some portions of litigation files simply have no inherent sensitivity in any event.

Lastly, agencies also should be alert to the potential for making discretionary disclosures through application of the "foreseeable harm" standard even to information that falls within the traditional attorney-client privilege. This privilege is designed to protect all "confidential communications between an attorney and his client relating to a legal matter for which the client has sought professional advice."[266] (See Exemption 5, Attorney-Client Privilege, above, for a discussion of this privilege.) With the exception of the narrow circumstance in which a government attorney represents an agency employee who is sued individually in a federal case, federal government attorneys represent their own agencies--or sometimes other federal agencies--when acting in a legal capacity. This means that, almost invariably, the privilege that attaches to an attorney's legal work will be one that his or her agency (perhaps in consultation with another agency) is free to invoke or not to invoke, as a matter of its administrative discretion. In other words, it is the agency's own privilege to waive if it chooses to do so.

As a matter of policy in the implementation of Attorney General Reno's FOIA Memorandum, bolstered by President Clinton's call upon all agencies to heed "both the letter and spirit of the Act,"[267] all agencies should consider making liberal waivers of the attorney-client privilege under the FOIA. Often, there is a good deal of overlap between this privilege and the attorney work-product privilege already discussed.[268] It will do little good for an agency to pursue discretionary waiver of its attorney work-product privilege, through rigorous application of the "foreseeable harm" elements outlined above, if it does not waive any applicable attorney-client privilege in like fashion.

---

[264] See, e.g., Winterstein, 89 F. Supp. 2d at 82 (withholding 16-year-old prosecution memorandum because of its connection to other "still pending investigations" of persons involved in Nazi atrocities).

[265] See FOIA Update, Vol. V, No. 4, at 6.

[266] Mead Data Cent., Inc. v. United States Dep't of the Air Force, 566 F.2d 242, 252 (D.C. Cir. 1977).

[267] President's Memorandum for Heads of Departments and Agencies regarding the Freedom of Information Act, 29 Weekly Comp. Pres. Doc. 1999 (Oct. 4, 1993), reprinted in FOIA Update, Vol. XIV, No. 3, at 3.

[268] See FOIA Update, Vol. VI, No. 2, at 3.

# EXEMPTION 6

Similarly, all agency FOIA officers should be mindful that there are strong connections between the attorney-client privilege and the deliberative process privilege as they apply to federal agencies.[269] When a government attorney is asked to give legal advice, that advice nearly always is sought in connection with an agency action that is subject to legal review or some other active decisionmaking process. Therefore, the same strong policy considerations that can compel discretionary disclosure in relation to the deliberative process privilege, discussed above, should compel likewise insofar as this privilege applies to the same information.

Federal agencies should strive to implement President Clinton's and Attorney General Reno's "strong new spirit of openness in government"[270] through a conscientious application of the "foreseeable harm" standard and the making of discretionary disclosures under Exemption 5.[271] This exemption, more than any other of the Act, is at the very core of federal government operations; no information covered by its broad privileges should be withheld from public scrutiny unless there is an identified need for doing so. As Congress has stated in a comparable context, it should be "the policy of the United States that the public is entitled to the fullest practicable information regarding the decisionmaking processes of the Federal Government."[272]

## EXEMPTION 6

Personal privacy interests are protected by two provisions of the FOIA, Exemptions 6 and 7(C). While the application of Exemption 7(C), discussed below, is limited to information compiled for law enforcement purposes, Exemption 6 permits the government to withhold all information about individuals in "personnel and medical files and similar files" when the disclosure of such information "would constitute a clearly unwarranted invasion of personal privacy."[1] Of course, these exemptions cannot be invoked to withhold from a requester information pertaining only to himself.[2]

### Initial Considerations

To warrant protection under Exemption 6, information must first meet its threshold requirement; in other words, it must fall within the category of

---

[269] See id. (pointing to "significant overlap" between privileges).

[270] FOIA Update, Vol. XIV, No. 3, at 1.

[271] See, e.g., FOIA Update, Vol. XV, No. 4, at 7 (citing examples of such discretionary disclosure); see also FOIA Update, Vol. XVIII, No. 2, at 1 (emphasizing importance of discretionary disclosure).

[272] 5 U.S.C. § 552b note (1994 & Supp. IV 1998) (policy statement enacted as part of Government in the Sunshine Act in 1976).

[1] 5 U.S.C. § 552(b)(6) (1994 & Supp. IV 1998).

[2] See H.R. Rep. No. 93-1380, at 13 (1974); see also FOIA Update, Vol. X, No. 2, at 5.

# EXEMPTION 6

"personnel and medical files and similar files."[3] Personnel and medical files are easily identified. However, there has not always been complete agreement about the meaning of the term "similar files." Prior to 1982, judicial interpretations of that phrase varied considerably and included a troublesome line of cases in the Court of Appeals for the District of Columbia Circuit, commencing with Board of Trade v. Commodity Futures Trading Commission,[4] which narrowly construed the term to encompass only "intimate" personal details.

In 1982, the Supreme Court acted decisively to resolve this controversy. In United States Department of State v. Washington Post Co.,[5] it firmly held, based upon a review of the legislative history of the FOIA, that Congress intended the term to be interpreted broadly, rather than narrowly.[6] The Court stated that the protection of an individual's privacy "surely was not intended to turn upon the label of the file which contains the damaging information."[7] Rather, the Court made clear that all information that "applies to a particular individual" meets the threshold requirement for Exemption 6 protection.[8]

The D.C. Circuit, sitting en banc, subsequently reinforced the Supreme Court's broad interpretation of this term by holding that a tape recording of the last words of the space shuttle Challenger crew, which "reveal[ed] the sound and inflection of the crew's voices during the last seconds of their lives . . . contains personal information the release of which is subject to the balancing of the public gain against the private harm at which it is purchased."[9] Not only did the D.C. Circuit determine that "lexical" and "non-lexical" information are subject to identical treatment under the FOIA,[10] it also concluded that

---

[3] 5 U.S.C. § 552(b)(6).

[4] 627 F.2d 392, 400 (D.C. Cir. 1980).

[5] 456 U.S. 595 (1982).

[6] Id. at 599-603 (citing H.R. Rep. No. 89-1497, at 11 (1966); S. Rep. No. 89-813, at 9 (1965); S. Rep. No. 88-1219, at 14 (1964)).

[7] Id. at 601 (citing H.R. Rep. No. 89-1497, at 11 (1966)).

[8] Id. at 602. But see Providence Journal Co. v. United States Dep't of the Army, 781 F. Supp. 878, 883 (D.R.I. 1991) (finding investigative report of criminal charges not to be "similar file" because it was "created in response to specific criminal allegations" rather than as "regularly compiled administrative record"), modified & aff'd on other grounds, 981 F.2d 552 (1st Cir. 1992).

[9] New York Times Co. v. NASA, 920 F.2d 1002, 1005 (D.C. Cir. 1990) (en banc). But see Greenpeace USA, Inc. v. EPA, 735 F. Supp. 13, 14 (D.D.C. 1990) (concluding that information pertaining to employee's compliance with agency regulations regarding outside employment "does not go to personal information . . . [e]ven in view of the broad interpretation [of Exemption 6] enunciated by the Supreme Court").

[10] 920 F.2d at 1005.

## EXEMPTION 6

Exemption 6 is equally applicable to the "author" and the "subject" of a file.[11]

It is also important to note that, in order to qualify for protection under Exemption 6, information must be identifiable to a specific individual. Information pertaining to a large group of individuals is not identifiable to any specific individual, unless that bit of information is attributable to members of the group as a whole.[12] Likewise, information pertaining to a single individual whose identity cannot be determined after deletion of his name from the records does not qualify for Exemption 6 protection.[13]

Once it has been established that information meets the threshold requirement of Exemption 6, the focus of the inquiry turns to whether disclosure of the records at issue "would constitute a clearly unwarranted invasion of personal privacy." This requires a balancing of the public's right to disclosure against the individual's right to privacy.[14] First, it must be ascertained whether a protectible privacy interest exists that would be threatened by disclosure. If no privacy interest is found, further analysis is unnecessary and the information at issue must be disclosed.[15]

On the other hand, if a privacy interest is found to exist, the public in-

---

[11] Id. at 1007-08.

[12] See, e.g., Arieff v. United States Dep't of the Navy, 712 F.2d 1462, 1467-68 (D.C. Cir. 1983) (list of drugs ordered for use by some members of group of over 600 individuals); Na Iwi O Na Kupuna v. Dalton, 894 F. Supp. 1397, 1413 (D. Haw. 1995) (records pertaining to large group of Native Hawaiian human remains) (reverse FOIA case).

[13] See Chicago Tribune Co. v. HHS, No. 95 C 3917, 1997 U.S. Dist. LEXIS 2308, at **43-46 (N.D. Ill. Feb. 26, 1997) (magistrate's recommendation) (ordering release of breast cancer patient data forms that identify patients only by 9-digit encoded "Study Numbers"), adopted (N.D. Ill. Mar. 28, 1997); Citizens for Envtl. Quality v. USDA, 602 F. Supp. 534, 538-39 (D.D.C. 1984) (ordering disclosure of health test results because identity of only agency employee tested could not, after deletion of his name, be ascertained from information known outside agency) (citing Department of the Air Force v. Rose, 425 U.S. 352, 380 n.19 (1976) (dicta)); see also Senate of P.R. v. United States Dep't of Justice, No. 84-1829, 1993 U.S. Dist. LEXIS 12162, at *32 (D.D.C. Aug. 24, 1993) (ordering release of information about inmate's cooperation after redaction of name and identifying details); cf. United States Dep't of State v. Ray, 502 U.S. 154, 176 (1991) ("Although disclosure of [highly] personal information constitutes only a de minimis invasion of privacy when the identities of the interviewees are unknown, the invasion of privacy becomes significant when personal information is linked to particular interviewees.").

[14] See Rose, 425 U.S. at 372; Fund for Constitutional Gov't v. National Archives & Records Serv., 656 F.2d 856, 862 (D.C. Cir. 1981).

[15] See Ripskis v. HUD, 746 F.2d 1, 3 (D.C. Cir. 1984); Holland v. CIA, No. 91-1233, 1992 WL 233820, at *16 (D.D.C. Aug. 31, 1992) (stating that information must be disclosed when there is no significant privacy interest, even if public interest is also de minimis).

**EXEMPTION 6**

terest in disclosure, if any, must be weighed against the privacy interest in nondisclosure.[16] If no public interest exists, the information should be protected; as the D.C. Circuit has observed, "something, even a modest privacy interest, outweighs nothing every time."[17] Similarly, if the privacy interest outweighs the public interest, the information should be withheld; if the opposite is found to be the case, the information should be released.[18]

### The Reporters Committee Decision

In 1989, the Supreme Court issued a landmark FOIA decision in United States Department of Justice v. Reporters Committee for Freedom of the Press,[19] which greatly affects all privacy-protection decisionmaking under the Act. The Reporters Committee case involved FOIA requests from members of the news media for access to any criminal history records--known as "rap sheets"--maintained by the FBI regarding certain persons alleged to have been involved in organized crime and improper dealings with a corrupt Congressman.[20] In holding "rap sheets" entitled to protection under Exemption 7(C), the Supreme Court set forth five guiding principles that now govern the process by which determinations are made under both Exemptions 6 and 7(C) alike:

First, the Supreme Court made clear in Reporters Committee that substantial privacy interests can exist in personal information even though the information has been made available to the general public at some place and point in time. Establishing a "practical obscurity" standard,[21] the Court observed that if such items of information actually "were 'freely available,' there would be no reason to invoke the FOIA to obtain access to" them.[22]

Second, the Court articulated the rule that the identity of a FOIA requester cannot be taken into consideration in determining what should be released under the Act. With the single exception that of course an agency will not invoke an exemption when the particular interest to be protected is the requester's own interest, the Court declared, "the identity of the request-

---

[16] See Ripskis, 746 F.2d at 3.

[17] National Ass'n of Retired Fed. Employees v. Horner, 879 F.2d 873, 879 (D.C. Cir. 1989); see also International Bhd. of Elec. Workers Local No. 5 v. HUD, 852 F.2d 87, 89 (3d Cir. 1988) (perceiving no public interest in disclosure of employees' social security numbers).

[18] See FOIA Update, Vol. X, No. 2, at 7 (outlining mechanics of balancing process).

[19] 489 U.S. 749 (1989); see also FOIA Update, Vol. X, No. 2, at 3-6 ("OIP Guidance: Privacy Protection Under the Supreme Court's Reporters Committee Decision").

[20] 489 U.S. at 757.

[21] Id. at 762, 780.

[22] Id. at 764.

## EXEMPTION 6

ing party has no bearing on the merits of his or her FOIA request."[23]

Third, the Court declared that in determining whether any public interest would be served by a requested disclosure, one should no longer consider "the purposes for which the request for information is made."[24] Rather than turn on a requester's "particular purpose," circumstances, or proposed use, the Court ruled, such determinations "must turn on the nature of the requested document and its relationship to" the public interest generally.[25]

Fourth, the Court narrowed the scope of the public interest to be considered under the Act's privacy exemptions, declaring for the first time that it is limited to "the kind of public interest for which Congress enacted the FOIA."[26] This "core purpose of the FOIA," as the Court termed it,[27] is to "shed[] light on an agency's performance of its statutory duties."[28]

Fifth, the Court established the proposition, under Exemption 7(C), that agencies may engage in "categorical balancing" in favor of nondisclosure.[29] Under this approach, which builds upon the above principles, it may be determined, "as a categorical matter," that a certain type of information always is protectible under an exemption, "without regard to individual circumstances."[30]

---

[23] Id. at 771.

[24] Id.

[25] Id. at 772.

[26] Id. at 774.

[27] Id. at 775.

[28] Id. at 773; see also O'Kane v. United States Customs Serv., 169 F.3d 1308, 1310 (11th Cir. 1999) (affirming that Electronic Freedom of Information Act Amendments of 1996, Pub. L. No. 104-231, 110 Stat. 3048, do not overrule Reporters Committee definition of public interest) (per curiam); Lissner v. United States Customs Serv., No. 98-7438, slip op. at 11-15 (C.D. Cal. June 15, 1999) (same) (appeal pending).

[29] Reporters Comm., 489 U.S. at 776-80 & n.22.

[30] Id. at 780; see, e.g., Reed v. NLRB, 927 F.2d 1249, 1252 (D.C. Cir. 1991) ("Exemption 6 protects 'Excelsior' lists [names and addresses of employees eligible to vote in union representation elections] as a category."); Grove v. Department of Justice, 802 F. Supp. 506, 511 (D.D.C. 1992) (Categorical balancing is appropriate for "information concerning criminal investigations of private citizens.") (Exemption 7(C)). But cf. Armstrong v. Executive Office of the President, 97 F.3d 575, 581-82 (D.C. Cir. 1996) (finding that agency had not adequately established basis for categorical rule for withholding identities of low-level FBI agents); Nation Magazine v. United States Customs Serv., 71 F.3d 885, 893-96 (D.C. Cir. 1995) (rejecting categorical issuance of "Glomar" response in case involving request for information concerning presidential candidate H. Ross Perot's offer "to help a federal agency fulfill its statutory

(continued...)

**EXEMPTION 6**

## Privacy Considerations

The first step in the Exemption 6 balancing process requires an assessment of the privacy interests at issue.[31] The relevant inquiry is whether public access to the information at issue would violate a viable privacy interest of the subject of such information.[32] In its Reporters Committee decision, the Supreme Court stressed that "both the common law and the literal understandings of privacy encompass the individual's control of information concerning his or her person."[33] Thus, in Reporters Committee, the Court found a "strong privacy interest" in the nondisclosure of records of a private citizen's criminal history, "even where the information may have been at one time public."[34] Of course, information need not be intimate or embarrassing to qualify for Exemption 6 protection.[35]

As a general rule, the threat to privacy must be real rather than speculative.[36] In some cases, this principle formerly was interpreted to mean that the privacy interest must be threatened by the very disclosure of information and not by any possible "secondary effects" of such release.[37] The Court of Appeals for the District of Columbia Circuit, however, subsequently clarified its holding in Arieff v. United States Department of the Navy,[38] which had been read as stating that "secondary effects" were not cognizable under Exemption 6. In National Association of Retired Federal Employees v. Horner [hereinafter NARFE], the D.C. Circuit explained that the point in Arieff was that Exemp-

---

[30](...continued) duties to interdict drugs") (Exemption 7(C)); see also FOIA Update, Vol. XVII, No. 2, at 3-4 ("OIP Guidance: The Bifurcation Requirement for Privacy 'Glomarization'").

[31] See FOIA Update, Vol. X, No. 2, at 7.

[32] See Schell v. HHS, 843 F.2d 933, 938 (6th Cir. 1988); Ripskis v. HUD, 746 F.2d 1, 3 (D.C. Cir. 1984).

[33] 489 U.S. 749, 763 (1989).

[34] Id. at 767; see also DOD v. FLRA, 510 U.S. 487, 500 (1994) (finding privacy interest in federal employees' home addresses even though they "often are publicly available through sources such as telephone directories and voter registration lists"); FOIA Update, Vol. X, No. 2, at 4.

[35] See United States Dep't of State v. Washington Post Co., 456 U.S. 595, 600 (1982); National Ass'n of Retired Fed. Employees v. Horner, 879 F.2d 873, 875 (D.C. Cir. 1989).

[36] See Department of the Air Force v. Rose, 425 U.S. 352, 380 n.19 (1976); Carter v. United States Dep't of Commerce, 830 F.2d 388, 391 (D.C. Cir. 1987); Arieff v. United States Dep't of the Navy, 712 F.2d 1462, 1467-68 (D.C. Cir. 1983).

[37] See, e.g., Southern Utah Wilderness Alliance, Inc. v. Hodel, 680 F. Supp. 37, 39 (D.D.C. 1988), vacated as moot, No. 88-5142 (D.C. Cir. Nov. 15, 1988).

[38] 712 F.2d at 1468.

## EXEMPTION 6

tion 6 was inapplicable because there was only "mere speculation" of a privacy invasion, i.e., only a slight possibility that the information, if disclosed, would be linked to a specific individual.[39] It has now explicitly been recognized that "[w]here there is a substantial probability that disclosure will cause an interference with personal privacy, it matters not that there may be two or three links in the causal chain."[40] Even prior to that clarification, one court pragmatically observed that to distinguish between the initial disclosure and unwanted intrusions as a result of that disclosure would be "to honor form over substance."[41]

In some instances, the disclosure of information may involve no invasion of privacy because no expectation of privacy exists. For example, civilian federal employees have no expectation of privacy regarding their names, titles, grades, salaries, and duty stations.[42] Likewise, the Department of the Army discloses the name, rank, date of rank, gross salary, duty assignments, office telephone number, source of commission, promotion sequence number, awards and decorations, educational level, and duty status of its military personnel in most circumstances.[43]

---

[39] 879 F.2d at 878; see also Dayton Newspapers, Inc. v. Department of the Air Force, No. C-3-97-78, slip op. at 13-14 (S.D. Ohio Mar. 26, 1999) (declining to protect medical malpractice settlement figures based upon "mere possibility that factual information might be pieced together to supply 'missing link' and lead to personal identification" of claimants); Chicago Tribune Co. v. HHS, No. 95 C 3917, 1997 U.S. Dist. LEXIS 2308, at **43-46 (N.D. Ill. Feb. 26, 1997) (magistrate's recommendation) (finding "speculative at best" agency's argument that release of breast cancer patient data forms that identify patients only by nine-digit encoded "Study Numbers" could result in identification of individual patients), adopted (N.D. Ill. Mar. 28, 1997).

[40] NARFE, 879 F.2d at 878; see, e.g., Hougan & Denton v. United States Dep't of Justice, No. 90-1312, slip op. at 3 (D.D.C. July 3, 1991) (concluding that solicitation by employers would invade privacy of participants in union's training program). But see United States Dep't of State v. Ray, 502 U.S. 164, 179-82 (1991) (Scalia, J., concurring in part).

[41] Hudson v. Department of the Army, No. 86-1114, 1987 WL 46755, at *3 (D.D.C. Jan. 29, 1987) (protecting personal information on basis that disclosure could ultimately lead to physical harm), aff'd, 926 F.2d 1215 (D.C. Cir. 1991) (unpublished table decision); see also, e.g., Hemenway v. Hughes, 601 F. Supp. 1002, 1006-07 (D.D.C. 1985) (same).

[42] See 5 C.F.R. § 293.311 (2000); see also Core v. United States Postal Serv., 730 F.2d 946, 948 (4th Cir. 1984) (finding no substantial invasion of privacy in information identifying successful federal job applicants); National W. Life Ins. v. United States, 512 F. Supp. 454, 461 (N.D. Tex. 1980) (discerning no expectation of privacy in names and duty stations of Postal Service employees).

[43] See Army Reg. 340-21, ¶ 3-3a(1), 5 July 1985; see also Army Reg. 25-55, ¶ 3-200, No. 6(b), 14 May 1997 (providing for withholding of names and duty addresses of military personnel assigned to units that are "sensitive, routinely (continued...)

**EXEMPTION 6**

    Furthermore, if the information at issue is particularly well known or is widely available within the public domain, there generally is no such expectation of privacy.[44] Nor does an individual have any expectation of privacy with respect to information that he himself has made public.[45] On the other hand, if the information in question was at some time or place available to the public, but is now "hard-to-obtain information," the individual to whom it pertains may have a privacy interest in maintaining its "practical obscurity."[46] Similarly, the mere fact that some of the information may be known to some

---

[43](...continued) deployable or stationed in foreign territories"); Memorandum from Department of Defense Directorate for Freedom of Information and Security Review 1 (Oct. 26, 1999) (applying same delineation for electronic mail addresses, on privacy-protection grounds); cf. 10 U.S.C.A. § 130b (West Supp. 2000) (Department of Defense-wide provision); Department of Defense Freedom of Information Act Program Regulations, 32 C.F.R. § 286.12(f)(2)(ii) (1999) ("Names and duty addresses (postal and/or e-mail) . . . for personnel assigned to units that are sensitive, routinely deployable, or stationed in foreign territories are withholdable under [Exemption 6].").

[44] See, e.g., Avondale Indus. v. NLRB, 90 F.3d 955, 961 (5th Cir. 1996) (finding that names and addresses of voters in union election were already disclosed in voluminous public record and that there was no showing that public record was compiled in such a way as to effectively obscure that information); Detroit Free Press, Inc. v. Department of Justice, 73 F.3d 93, 96-97 (6th Cir. 1996) (finding no privacy rights in mug shots of defendants in ongoing criminal proceedings when names are public and defendants have appeared in open court); Blanton v. United States Dep't of Justice, No. 93-2398, 1994 U.S. Dist. LEXIS 21444, at **11-12 (W.D. Tenn, July 14, 1994) ("The fact of [requester's former counsel's] representation is a matter of public record . . . . Whether an individual possesses a valid license to practice law is also a matter of public record and cannot be protected by any privacy interest."); National W. Life Ins., 512 F. Supp. at 461 (noting that names and duty stations of most federal employees are routinely published and available through Government Printing Office).

[45] See Nation Magazine v. United States Customs Serv., 71 F.3d 885, 896 (D.C. Cir. 1995) (finding no privacy interest in documents concerning presidential candidate H. Ross Perot's offer to aid federal government in drug interdiction, a subject about which Perot had made several public statements).

[46] Reporters Comm., 489 U.S. at 780; see also Washington Post, 456 U.S. at 603 n.5; Fiduccia v. United States Dep't of Justice, 185 F.3d 1035, 1046-47 (9th Cir. 1999) (protecting information about two individuals whose homes were searched ten years previously despite publicity at that time and fact that some information might be public in various courthouses) (Exemption 7(C)); Abraham & Rose, P.L.C. v. United States, 138 F.3d 1075, 1083 (6th Cir. 1998) (noting that there may be privacy interest in personal information even if "available on publicly recorded filings"); Linn v. United States Dep't of Justice, No. 92-1406, 1995 WL 417810, at *31 (D.D.C. June 6, 1995) (declaring that even if "some of the names at issue were at one time released to the general public, individuals are entitled to maintaining the 'practical obscurity' of personal information that is developed through the passage of time").

# EXEMPTION 6

members of the public does not negate the individual's privacy interest in preventing further dissemination to the public at large.[47] And one court has found that the subject of a photograph introduced into the court record "retained at least some privacy interest in preventing the further dissemination of the photographic image" when "[t]he photocopy in the Court record was of such poor quality as to severely limit its dissemination."[48]

As another example, FOIA requesters, except when they are making first-party requests, do not ordinarily expect that their names will be kept private; therefore, release of their names would not cause even the minimal invasion of privacy necessary to trigger the balancing test.[49] Personal information about FOIA requesters, however, such as home addresses and home telephone numbers, should not be disclosed.[50] In addition, the identities of first-party requesters under the Privacy Act of 1974[51] should be protected because, unlike under the FOIA, an expectation of privacy can fairly be inferred from the personal nature of the records involved in those requests.[52]

The majority of courts to have considered the issue have held that individuals who write to the government expressing personal opinions generally do so with some expectation of confidentiality; their identities, but not neces-

---

[47] See Isley v. Executive Office for United States Attorneys, No. 98-5098, 1999 WL 1021934, at *4 (D.C. Cir. Oct. 21, 1999) (finding no evidence that previously disclosed documents "continue to be 'freely available' in any 'permanent public record'") (Exemption 7(C)); Mueller v. United States Dep't of the Air force, 63 F. Supp. 2d 738, 743 (E.D. Va. 1999) (stating that existence of publicity surrounding events does not eliminate privacy interest) (Exemptions 6 and 7(C)); Chin v. United States Dep't of the Air Force, No. 97-2176, slip op. at 5 (W.D. La. June 24, 1999) (concluding that although "some of the events are known to certain members of the public . . . this fact is insufficient to place this record for dissemination into the public domain") (appeal pending); cf. Schiffer v. FBI, 78 F.3d 1405, 1411 (9th Cir. 1996) (treating requester's personal knowledge as irrelevant in assessing privacy interests).

[48] Baltimore Sun Co. v. United States Customs Serv., No. 97-1991, slip op. at 5 (D. Md. Nov. 21, 1997) (Exemption 7(C)); see also Times Picayune Publ'g Corp. v. United States Dep't of Justice, 37 F. Supp. 2d 472, 477-82 (E.D. La. 1999) (protecting mug shot of prominent individual despite wide publicity prior to guilty plea, observing that "mug shot is more than just another photograph of a person") (Exemption 7(C)).

[49] See FOIA Update, Vol. VI, No. 1, at 6; see also Holland v. CIA, No. 91-1233, 1992 WL 233829, at **15-16 (D.D.C. Aug. 31, 1992) (holding that researcher who sought assistance of presidential advisor in obtaining CIA files he had requested is comparable to FOIA requester whose identity is not protected by Exemption 6); Martinez v. FBI, No. 82-1547, slip op. at 7 (D.D.C. Dec. 19, 1985) (denying protection for identities of news reporters seeking information concerning criminal investigation) (Exemption 7(C)).

[50] See FOIA Update, Vol. VI, No. 1, at 6.

[51] 5 U.S.C. § 552a (1994 & Supp. IV 1998).

[52] See FOIA Update, Vol. VI, No. 1, at 6.

**EXEMPTION 6**

sarily the substance of their letters, ordinarily should be withheld.[53] Nevertheless, in some circumstances courts have refused to accord privacy protection to such government correspondents.[54]

---

[53] See Strout v. United States Parole Comm'n, 40 F.3d 136, 139 (6th Cir. 1994) (articulating public policy against disclosure of names and addresses of people who write Parole Commission opposing convict's parole); Save Our Springs Alliance v. Babbitt, No. A-97-CA-259, slip op. at 7-8 (W.D. Tex. Nov. 19, 1997) (concluding that release of home addresses and telephone numbers of government correspondents would not shed light on whether agency improperly considered writers' comments); Voinche v. FBI, 940 F. Supp. 323, 329-30 (D.D.C. 1996) ("There is no reason to believe that the public will obtain a better understanding of the workings of various agencies by learning the identities of . . . private citizens who wrote to government officials . . . ."), aff'd per curiam, No. 96-5304, 1997 U.S. App. LEXIS 19089 (D.C. Cir. June 19, 1997); Wilson v. Department of Justice, No. 87-2415, 1991 WL 111457, at *6 (D.D.C. June 14, 1991) (protecting identity of individual who wrote to Senator about matter of public interest); Holy Spirit Ass'n v. United States Dep't of State, 526 F. Supp. 1022, 1032-34 (S.D.N.Y. 1981) (finding that "strong public interest in encouraging citizens to communicate their concerns regarding their communities" is fostered by protecting identities of writers); see also Holy Spirit Ass'n v. FBI, 683 F.2d 562, 564 (D.C. Cir. 1982) (concurring with nondisclosure of correspondence because communications from citizens to their government "will frequently contain information of an intensely personal sort") (MacKinnon, J., concurring) (Exemptions 6 and 7(C)); cf. Ortiz v. HHS, 874 F. Supp. 570, 573-75 (S.D.N.Y.) (protecting letter to HHS alleging social security fraud) (Exemptions 7(C) and 7(D)), aff'd on Exemption 7(D) grounds, 70 F.3d 729 (2d Cir. 1995).

[54] See Landmark Legal Found. v. IRS, 87 F. Supp. 2d 21, 27-28 (D.D.C. 2000) (declining to protect citizens who wrote to IRS to express opinions or provide information; noting that "IRS has suggested no reason why existing laws are insufficient to deter any criminal or tortious conduct targeted at persons who would be identified") (appeal pending); Judicial Watch of Fla., Inc. v. United States Dep't of Justice, No. 97-2869, slip op. at 16-17 (D.D.C. Feb. 22, 2000) (allowing deletion of home addresses and telephone numbers but ordering release of identities of individuals who wrote to Attorney General about campaign finance or Independent Counsel issues) (motion for reconsideration pending); Alliance for the Wild Rockies v. Department of the Interior, 53 F. Supp. 2d 32, 36-37 (D.D.C. 1999) (concluding that agency "made it abundantly clear in its notice that the individuals submitting comments to its rulemaking would not have their identities concealed" when rulemaking notice "specified that '[t]he complete file for this proposed rule is available for inspection'"), remanded for further action in accordance with settlement, No. 99-5292 (D.C. Cir. Apr. 19, 2000); Cardona v. INS, No. 93-3912, 1995 WL 68747, at *3 (N.D. Ill. Feb. 15, 1995) (finding only "de minimis invasion of privacy" in release of name and address of individual who wrote letter to INS complaining about private agency that offered assistance to immigrants); Powell v. United States Dep't of Justice, No. C-82-326, slip op. at 5 (N.D. Cal. Mar. 27, 1985) (ordering disclosure of names of private citizens who wrote to Members of Congress and to Attorney General expressing views on McCarthy-era prosecution).

# EXEMPTION 6

Additionally, neither corporations nor business associations possess protectible privacy interests.[55] The closely held corporation or similar business entity, however, is an exception to this principle: "While corporations have no privacy, personal financial information is protected, including information about small businesses when the individual and corporation are identical."[56] Such an individual's expectation of privacy is, however, diminished with regard to matters in which he or she is acting in a business capacity.[57]

The right to privacy of deceased persons is not entirely settled, but the majority rule is that death extinguishes their privacy rights.[58] The Depart-

---

[55] See, e.g., Sims v. CIA, 642 F.2d 562, 572 n.47 (D.C. Cir. 1980); National Parks & Conservation Ass'n v. Kleppe, 547 F.2d 673, 685 n.44 (D.C. Cir. 1976); Ivanhoe Citrus Ass'n v. Handley, 612 F. Supp. 1560, 1567 (D.D.C. 1985).

[56] Providence Journal Co. v. FBI, 460 F. Supp. 778, 785 (D.R.I. 1978), rev'd on other grounds, 602 F.2d 1010 (1st Cir. 1979); see also Beard v. Espy, No. 94-16748, 1995 U.S. App. LEXIS 38269, at *3 (9th Cir. Dec. 11, 1995); National Parks, 547 F.2d at 685-86; FOIA Update, Vol. III, No. 4, at 5.

[57] See, e.g., Oregon Natural Desert Ass'n v. United States Dep't of the Interior, 24 F. Supp. 2d 1088, 1089 (D. Or. 1998) (concluding that cattle owners found to have violated federal grazing laws have "diminished expectation of privacy" in names when information relates to commercial interests); Washington Post Co. v. USDA, 943 F. Supp. 31, 34-36 (D.D.C. Oct. 18, 1996) (finding that farmers who received subsidies under cotton price support program have only minimal privacy interest in home addresses from which they also operate businesses), appeal voluntarily dismissed, No. 96-5373 (D.C. Cir. May 19, 1997); Ackerson & Bishop Chartered v. USDA, No. 92-1068, slip op. at 1 (D.D.C. July 15, 1992) (concluding that commercial mushroom growers operating under individual names have no expectation of privacy); Lawyers Comm. for Human Rights v. INS, 721 F. Supp. 552, 569 (S.D.N.Y. 1989) (stating that "disclosure [of names of State Department's officers and staff members involved in highly publicized case] merely establishes State [Department] employees' professional relationships or associates these employees with agency business"). But see Campaign for Family Farms v. Glickman, 200 F.3d 1180, 1187-89 (8th Cir. 2000) (protecting identities of pork producers who signed petition calling for abolishment of mandatory contributions to fund for marketing and advertising pork, because release would reveal position on referendum and "would vitiate petitioners' privacy interest in secret ballot") ("reverse" FOIA suit); Hill v. USDA, 77 F. Supp. 2d 6, 8 (D.D.C. 1999) (finding privacy interest in records of business transactions between borrowers and partly owned family corporation relating to loans made by Farmers Home Administration to individual borrowers), summary affirmance granted, No. 99-5365, 2000 WL 520724, at *1 (D.C. Cir. Mar. 7, 2000).

[58] See, e.g., Na Iwi O Na Kupuna v. Dalton, 894 F. Supp. 1397, 1413 (D. Haw. 1995) ("reverse" FOIA suit); Tigar & Buffone v. United States Dep't of Justice, No. 80-2382, slip op. at 9-10 (D.D.C. Sept. 30, 1983) (Exemption 7(C)); Diamond v. FBI, 532 F. Supp. 216, 227 (S.D.N.Y. 1981), aff'd on other grounds, 707 F.2d 75 (2d Cir. 1983); cf. United States v. Schlette, 842 F.2d 1574, 1581 (9th Cir.) (disclosure of presentence report of deceased person pur-
(continued...)

# EXEMPTION 6

ment of Justice has long followed this general rule as a matter of policy.[59] However, particularly sensitive, often graphic, personal details about the circumstances surrounding an individual's death may be withheld when necessary to protect the privacy interests of surviving family members.[60] Even information that is not particularly sensitive in itself may be withheld to protect the privacy of surviving family members if disclosure would cause "a disruption of their peace of minds."[61] And the D.C. Circuit has expressly recognized

---

[58](...continued)
suant to Rule 32(c) of Federal Rules of Criminal Procedure), amended, 854 F.2d 359 (9th Cir. 1988). But see Kiraly v. FBI, 728 F.2d 273, 277-78 (6th Cir. 1984) (adopting district court rationale, "which held: '. . . that the right to recovery for invasion of privacy lapses upon the person's death does not mean that the government must disclose inherently private information as soon as the individual dies'") (Exemption 7(C)).

[59] See FOIA Update, Vol. III, No. 4, at 5.

[60] See, e.g., Hale v. United States Dep't of Justice, 973 F.2d 894, 902 (10th Cir. 1992) (perceiving "no public interest in photographs of the deceased victim, let alone one that would outweigh the personal privacy interests of the victim's family") (Exemption 7(C)), cert. granted, vacated & remanded on other grounds, 509 U.S. 918 (1993); Bowen v. FDA, 925 F.2d 1225, 1228 (9th Cir. 1991) (affirming nondisclosure of autopsy reports of individuals killed by cyanide-contaminated products); Badhwar v. United States Dep't of the Air Force, 829 F.2d 182, 186 (D.C. Cir. 1987) (noting that some autopsy reports might "shock the sensibilities of surviving kin"); Marzen v. HHS, 825 F.2d 1148, 1154 (7th Cir. 1987) (holding deceased infant's medical records exempt because their release "would almost certainly cause . . . parents more anguish"); Isley v. Executive Office for United States Attorneys, No. 96-0123, slip op. at 3-4 (D.D.C. Feb. 25, 1998) (approving withholding of "medical records, autopsy reports and inmate injury reports pertaining to a murder victim as a way of protecting surviving family members"), aff'd on other grounds, 203 F.3d 52 (D.C. Cir. 1999) (unpublished table decision); Katz v. NARA, 862 F. Supp. 476, 483-86 (D.D.C. 1994) (holding that Kennedy family's privacy interests would be invaded by disclosure of "graphic and explicit" JFK autopsy photographs), aff'd on other grounds, 68 F.3d 1438 (D.C. Cir. 1995). But see Outlaw v. United States Dep't of the Army, 815 F. Supp. 505, 506 (D.D.C. 1993) (ordering disclosure in absence of evidence of existence of any survivor who would be offended by release of murder-scene photographs of man murdered 25 years earlier); Journal-Gazette Co. v. United States Dep't of the Army, No. F89-147, slip op. at 8-9 (N.D. Ind. Jan. 8, 1990) (holding that because autopsy report of Air National Guard pilot killed in training exercise contained "concise medical descriptions of the cause of death," not "graphic, morbid descriptions," survivors' minimal privacy interest outweighed by public interest).

[61] New York Times Co. v. NASA, 782 F. Supp. 628, 631-32 (D.D.C. 1991) (withholding audiotape of voices of Challenger astronauts recorded immediately before their deaths, to protect family members from pain of hearing final words of loved ones); see also Katz, 862 F. Supp. at 485 ("[T]here can be no mistaking that the Kennedy family has been traumatized by the prior publica-
(continued...)

## EXEMPTION 6

that certain "reputational" and "family-related" interests survive death.[62]

Public figures do not surrender all rights to privacy by placing themselves in the public eye, though their expectations of privacy certainly may be diminished. In some instances, "[t]he degree of intrusion is indeed potentially augmented by the fact that the individual is a well known figure."[63] It has been held that disclosure of sensitive personal information contained in investigative records about a public figure is appropriate "only where exceptional interests militate in favor of disclosure."[64] Thus, although one's status

---

[61](...continued) tion of the unauthorized records and that further release of the [JFK] autopsy materials will cause additional anguish."); Cowles Publ'g Co. v. United States, No. 90-349, slip op. at 6-7 (E.D. Wash. Dec. 20, 1990) (withholding identities of individuals who became ill or died from radiation exposure in order to protect living victims and family members of deceased persons from intrusive contacts and inquiries); FOIA Update, Vol. III, No. 4, at 5.

[62] See Accuracy in Media, Inc. v. National Park Serv., 194 F.3d 120, 123 (D.C. Cir. 1999) (recognizing that some privacy interest may survive death, but finding it unnecessary in this case to "explore whether the interest belongs to living close survivors (in which case it might end at their deaths), or alternatively may inhere posthumously in the subject himself (in which case it would seem to be of indefinite duration), or both") (Exemption 7(C)), cert. denied, 68 U.S.L.W. 3711 (U.S. May 15, 2000) (No. 99-1578); Campbell v. United States Dep't of Justice, 164 F.3d 20, 33-34 (D.C. Cir. 1998) (stating that although "death clearly matters, as the deceased by definition cannot personally suffer the privacy-related injuries that may plague the living . . . [t]he court must also account for the fact that certain reputational interests and family-related privacy expectations survive death," but concluding that "[t]he scope and weight of these interests need not be resolved" in this case) (Exemption 7(C)); cf. Schrecker v. United States Dep't of Justice, 74 F. Supp. 2d 26, 33-34 (D.D.C. 1999) (finding no public interest to outweigh privacy interests that, although diminished with death, survive in form of "reputational" and "family-related" privacy interests) (appeal pending).

[63] Fund for Constitutional Gov't v. National Archives & Records Serv., 656 F.2d 856, 865 (D.C. Cir. 1981) (Exemption 7(C)); see Times Picayune, 37 F. Supp. 2d at 478-79 (noting that prominence of person "may well exacerbate the privacy intrusions") (Exemption 7(C)); cf. Wichlacz v. United States Dep't of Interior, 938 F. Supp. 325, 333-34 (E.D. Va. 1996) (recognizing that intense media scrutiny of death of White House Deputy Counsel Vincent Foster enhances privacy interest of individuals connected even remotely with investigation), aff'd, 114 F.3d 1178 (4th Cir. 1997) (unpublished table decision).

[64] Fund, 656 F.2d at 866; see also Nation Magazine v. Department of State, No. 92-2303, slip op. at 20-24 & n.15 (D.D.C. Aug. 18, 1995) (holding that public interest in information about presidential candidate H. Ross Perot's dealings with government or whether he was ever investigated by FBI is not kind of public interest recognized by FOIA); Wilson, 1991 WL 111457, at *6 (stating that even Iran-Contra figure Richard Secord would have privacy interest in fact that he was investigated; such investigation would reveal "little

(continued...)

**EXEMPTION 6**

as a public figure might in some circumstances tip the balance in favor of disclosure, a public figure does not, by virtue of his status, forfeit all rights of privacy.[65] Nor does a candidate for federal political office forfeit all rights to privacy.[66] It also should be noted that, unlike under the Privacy Act, foreign nationals are entitled to the same privacy rights under the FOIA as are U.S. citizens.[67]

Individuals do not waive their privacy rights merely by signing a document that states that information may be released to third parties under the FOIA.[68] As one court has observed, such a statement is not a waiver of the right to confidentiality, it is merely a warning by the agency and corresponding acknowledgment by the signers "that the information they were providing could be subject to release."[69] Similarly, individuals who sign a petition,

---

[64](...continued)
about 'what government is up to'"). But see Wilson v. Department of Justice, 87-2415, 1991 WL 120052, at *4 (D.D.C. June 17, 1991) (ordering further declarations to determine whether any of the individuals investigated "are 'public figures' like the plaintiff whose involvement in Government operations would be of interest to the public").

[65] See Fund, 656 F.2d at 865; Billington v. Department of Justice, 11 F. Supp. 2d 45, 62 (D.D.C. 1998) (finding that although public officials in some circumstances have diminished privacy, residual privacy interests militate against disclosure of nonpublic details); cf. Strassman v. United States Dep't of Justice, 792 F.2d 1267, 1268 (4th Cir. 1986) (Exemption 7(C)); McNamera v. United States Dep't of Justice, 974 F. Supp. 946, 959 (W.D. Tex. Aug. 12, 1997) (stating that "[s]imply because an individual was once a public official does not mean that he retains that status throughout his life" and holding that three years after a disgraced sheriff resigned he was "a private, not a public figure") (Exemption 7(C)); Steinberg v. United States Dep't of Justice, No. 93-2409, slip op. at 11 (D.D.C. July 14, 1997) ("[E]ven widespread knowledge about a person's business cannot serve to diminish his or her privacy interests in matters that are truly personal.") (Exemption 7(C)); see also FOIA Update, Vol. III, No. 4, at 5.

[66] See Nation Magazine, 71 F.3d at 894 & n.9 ("Although candidacy for federal office may diminish an individual's right to privacy . . . it does not eliminate it . . . ."); Hunt v. United States Marine Corps, 935 F. Supp. 46, 54 (D.D.C. 1996) (finding that senatorial candidate Oliver North has unquestionable privacy interest in his military service personnel records and medical records); Nation Magazine, No. 92-2303, slip op. at 20-23 (D.D.C. Aug. 18, 1995) (upholding refusal to confirm or deny existence of investigative records pertaining to presidential candidate H. Ross Perot).

[67] See Shaw v. United States Dep't of State, 559 F. Supp. 1053, 1067 (D.D.C. 1983); see also United States Dep't of State v. Ray, 502 U.S. 164 (1991) (applying traditional analysis of privacy interests under FOIA to Haitian nationals); FOIA Update, Vol. VI, No. 3, at 5.

[68] See Hill, 77 F. Supp. 2d at 8.

[69] Id. (rejecting argument that borrowers of Farmers Home Administration
(continued...)

## EXEMPTION 6

knowing that those who sign afterward will observe their signatures, do not waive their privacy interests.[70] While such persons "would have no reason to be concerned that a limited number of like-minded individuals may have seen their names," they may well be concerned "that the petition not become available to the general public, including those opposing [the petitioners' position]."[71]

In addition, individuals who testify at criminal trials do not forfeit their rights to privacy except on those very matters that become part of the public record.[72] Nor do individuals who plead guilty to criminal charges lose all rights to privacy with regard to the proceedings against them.[73] Similarly, individuals who provide law enforcement agencies with reports of illegal conduct have well-recognized privacy interests, particularly when such persons reasonably fear reprisals for their assistance.[74] Even absent any evidence of

---

[69] (...continued) loans waived privacy interests by signing loan-application documents that warned that information supplied could be subject to release to third parties)

[70] See Campaign for Family Farms, 200 F.3d at 1188.

[71] Id.

[72] See Isley, 1999 WL 1021934, at *4; Kiraly, 728 F.2d at 279; Brown v. FBI, 658 F.2d 71, 75 (2d Cir. 1981); Coleman v. FBI, 13 F. Supp. 2d 75, 80 (D.D.C. 1998); cf. Irons v. FBI, 880 F.2d 1446, 1454 (1st Cir. 1989) (en banc) (holding that disclosure of any source information beyond that actually testified to by confidential source is not required) (Exemption 7(D)).

[73] See Times Picayune, 37 F. Supp. 2d at 477-78 (refusing to order release of mug shot, which with its "unflattering facial expressions" and "stigmatizing effect [that] can last well beyond the actual criminal proceedings . . . preserves, in its unique and visually powerful way, the subject individual's brush with the law for posterity"); see also McNamera, 974 F. Supp. at 959 (holding that convict's privacy rights are diminished only with respect to information made public during criminal proceedings against him) (Exemption 7(C)).

[74] See McCutchen v. HHS, 30 F.3d 183, 189 (D.C. Cir. 1994) ("The complainants [alleging scientific misconduct] have a strong privacy interest in remaining anonymous because, as 'whistle-blowers,' they might face retaliation if their identities were revealed.") (Exemption 7(C)); Holy Spirit, 683 F.2d at 564-65 (concurring opinion) (Exemptions 6 and 7(C)); Summers v. United States Dep't of Justice, No. 87-3168, slip op. at 4-15 (D.D.C. Apr. 19, 2000) (protecting identities of individuals who provided information to FBI Director J. Edgar Hoover concerning well-known people "because persons who make allegations against public figures are often subject to public scrutiny"); Ortiz, 874 F. Supp. at 573-75 (probable close relationship between plaintiff and author of letter about her to HHS likely to lead to retaliation); Cappabianca v. Commissioner, United States Customs Serv., 847 F. Supp. 1558, 1564-65 (M.D. Fla. 1994) ("opportunity for harassment or embarrassment is very strong" in case involving investigation of "allegations of harassment and retaliation for cooperation in a prior investigation") (Exemptions 6 and 7(C)); Manna v. United States Dep't of Justice, 815 F. Supp. 798, 809 (D.N.J. 1993)

(continued...)

# EXEMPTION 6

fear of reprisals, however, witnesses who provide information to investigative bodies--administrative and civil, as well as criminal--ordinarily are accorded privacy protection.[75] (For a more detailed discussion of the privacy protection accorded such law enforcement sources, see Exemption 7(C), below.)

An agency ordinarily is not required to conduct research to determine whether an individual has died or whether his activities have sufficiently become the subject of public knowledge so as to bar the application of Exemption 6.[76] This is further strengthened by the Supreme Court's observations in

---

[74](...continued)
(Because La Cosa Nostra "is so violent and retaliatory, the names of interviewees, informants, witnesses, victims and law enforcement personnel must be safeguarded.") (Exemption 7(C)), aff'd, 51 F.3d 1158 (3d Cir. 1995).

[75] See, e.g., Ford v. West, No. 97-1342, 1998 WL 317561, at **1-2 (10th Cir. June 12, 1998) (finding thoughts, sentiments, and emotions of coworkers questioned in investigation of racial harassment claim within protections of Exemptions 6 and 7(C)); Hayes v. United States Dep't of Labor, No. 96-1149, slip op. at 9-10 (S.D. Ala. June 18, 1998) (magistrate's recommendation) (protecting information that "would have divulged personal information or disclosed the identity of a confidential source" in OSHA investigation) (Exemption 7(C)), adopted (S.D. Ala. Aug. 10, 1998); Tenaska Washington Partners v. United States Dep't of Energy, No. 8:96-128, slip op. at 6-8 (D. Neb. Feb. 19, 1997) (protecting information that would "readily identify" individuals who provided information during routine Inspector General audit); McLeod v. Pena, No. 94-1924, slip op. at 4 (D.D.C. Feb. 9, 1996) (protecting in their entireties memoranda and witness statements concerning investigation of plaintiff's former commanding officer when unit consisted of 8 officers and 20 enlisted personnel) (Exemption 7(C)), summary affirmance granted sub nom. McLeod v. United States Coast Guard, No. 96-5071, 1997 U.S. App. LEXIS 6000 (D.C. Cir. Feb. 10, 1997). But see Summers, No. 87-3168, slip op. at 5-6 (D.D.C. Apr. 19, 2000) (ordering disclosure of identities of individuals who provided information to former FBI Director J. Edgar Hoover about certain organizations or events because "no danger of reprisal is mentioned" and act of supplying such information "does not appear to be embarrassing or likely to lead to invasive inquiries into the person's private life"); cf. Steinberg v. United States Dep't of Justice, 179 F.R.D. 366, 371-72 (D.D.C. 1998) (privacy interest in substance of information furnished to government by known informant "[a]s a general proposition . . . cannot outweigh a substantial public interest in disclosure"); Fine v. United States Dep't of Energy, 823 F. Supp. 888, 896 (D.N.M. 1993) (ordering disclosure based in part upon fact that plaintiff no longer employed by agency and "not in a position on-the-job to harass or intimidate employees of DOE/OIG and/or its contractors").

[76] See FOIA Update, Vol. V, No. 1, at 5; see also, e.g., Schrecker v. United States Dep't of Justice, 14 F. Supp. 2d 111, 118 (D.D.C. 1998) (refusing to require agency to search all available public sources to determine whether individuals mentioned in documents over 25 years old are alive or dead) (appeal pending); Manna v. United States Dep't of Justice, No. 92-1840, slip op. at 8 (D.N.J. Aug. 27, 1993) (finding government's obligation fulfilled by search of computerized index system and index cards for evidence of death of witness
(continued...)

## EXEMPTION 6

Reporters Committee that "without regard to individual circumstances" certain categories of records will always warrant privacy protection and that "the standard virtues of bright-line rules are thus present, and the difficulties attendant to ad hoc adjudication may be avoided."[77]

Nevertheless, several courts, when faced with very old documents, have refused to accept the presumption that all individuals mentioned in such documents are alive.[78] In one such case, the Court of Appeals for the Third Circuit ruled that "after a sufficient passage of time . . . it would be unreasonable . . . not to assume that many of the individuals named in the requested records have died."[79] It held that it was "within the discretion of the district court to

---

[76](...continued)
relocated more than 20 years ago), aff'd, 51 F.3d 1158 (3d Cir. 1995); Williams v. United States Dep't of Justice, 556 F. Supp. 63, 66 (D.D.C. 1982) (finding agency's good-faith processing, rather than extensive research for public disclosures, sufficient in lengthy, multifaceted judicial proceedings); cf. McGehee v. Casey, 718 F.2d 1137, 1141 n.9 (D.C. Cir. 1983) (recognizing that CIA cannot reasonably bear burden of conducting exhaustive search to prove that particular items of classified information have never been published) (non-FOIA case).

[77] 489 U.S. at 780; accord Halloran v. VA, 874 F.2d 315, 322 (5th Cir. 1989); see also FOIA Update, Vol. X, No. 2, at 4.

[78] See Diamond, 707 F.2d at 77 (requiring agency to review 200,000 pages outside scope of request to search for evidence as to whether subjects' privacy had been waived through death or prior public disclosure) (Exemption 7(C)); Outlaw, 815 F. Supp. at 506 (declining to withhold photographs of victim murdered 25 years ago to protect privacy of relatives when "[d]efendant's concern for the privacy of the decedent's surviving relatives has not extended to an effort to locate them . . . [and] there is no showing by defendant that, as of now, there are any surviving relatives of the deceased, or if there are, that they would be offended by the disclosure"); Wilkinson v. FBI, No. 80-1048, slip op. at 12-13 (C.D. Cal. June 17, 1987) (holding Exemption 7(C) inapplicable to documents more than 30 years old because government relied on presumption that "all persons [who are] the subject of FOIA requests are . . . living"); cf. Summers v. Department of Justice, 140 F.3d 1077, 1085 (D.C. Cir. 1998) (Williams, J., concurring) (suggesting that "taking death into account only if the fact has happened to swim into their line of vision" might not be adequate if FBI has access to "data bases that could resolve the issue") (Exemptions 6 and 7(C)); Rosenfeld v. United States Dep't of Justice, 57 F.3d 803, 813 (9th Cir. 1995) (ordering disclosure of information based upon belief that it was not likely that anyone could be identified 25 years later) (Exemption 7(C)). But see Assassination Archives & Research Ctr. v. CIA, 903 F. Supp. 131, 133 (D.D.C. 1995) (protecting identities of third parties in 30- to 40-year-old records based upon finding "that the passage of time may actually increase privacy interests") (Exemption 7(C)).

[79] Davin v. United States Dep't of Justice, 60 F.3d 1043, 1059 (3d Cir. 1995); see also Davin v. United States Dep't of Justice, No. 92-1122, slip op. at 9 (W.D. Pa. Apr. 9, 1998) (finding, on remand, diminished privacy interests due
(continued...)

**EXEMPTION 6**

require an agency to demonstrate that the individuals upon whose behalf it claims the privacy exemption are, in fact, alive," considering "such factors as the number of named individuals that must be investigated, and the age of the requested records."[80]

Faced with "reverse" FOIA challenges, several courts have had to consider whether to order agencies *not* to release records pertaining to individuals that agencies had determined should be disclosed. In a case that reached the Court of Appeals for the Eighth Circuit, the signers of a petition requesting a referendum to abolish a mandatory payment by pork producers sued to prevent the Department of Agriculture from releasing their names pursuant to a FOIA request.[81] The Eighth Circuit agreed that, under the standards of the Administrative Procedure Act,[82] the Department of Agriculture's initial disclosure determination was not in accordance with law and the names must be withheld.[83] By contrast, a Native Hawaiian group brought suit to enjoin the Department of the Navy from making public certain information concerning a large group of Native Hawaiian human remains that had been inventoried pursuant to the Native American Graves Protection and Repatriation Act.[84] The court in that case held that the agency properly had determined that the information did not qualify for Exemption 6 protection and that it could be released.[85] These privacy "reverse" FOIA cases are similar in posture to the

---

[79](...continued)
to passage of time and likelihood that obsolescence of majority of addresses would render individuals difficult to locate), aff'd, 176 F.3d 471 (3d Cir. 1999) (unpublished table decision).

[80] Davin, 60 F.3d at 1059 (considering records of 1930s and 1940s investigations of Workers Alliance of America); see also McDonnell v. United States, 4 F.3d 1227, 1254 (3d Cir. 1993) (requiring agency to determine whether individual whose medical records were contained in file regarding 1934 fire on ocean liner Morro Castle was living or dead); Hall v. United States Dep't of Justice, 26 F. Supp. 2d 78, 81-82 (D.D.C. 1998) (employing rebuttable presumption that "if 50 years have passed since the date of the document or the event it describes, whichever is earlier, it will be presumed that the informant is deceased") (Exemption 7(C)); cf. Samuel Gruber Educ. Project v. United States Dep't of Justice, 24 F. Supp. 2d 1, 2 (D.D.C. 1998) (ordering plaintiff to obtain from Social Security Administration records establishing deaths of individuals whose deaths were not yet known and ordering agency to process records pertaining to those individuals for whom plaintiff has thus established deaths).

[81] Campaign for Family Farms, 200 F.3d at 1182-84.

[82] 5 U.S.C. §§ 701-06 (1994).

[83] Campaign for Family Farms, 200 F.3d at 1184-89.

[84] Na Iwi O Na Kupuna v. Dalton, 894 F. Supp. 1397, 1402-04 (D. Haw. 1995).

[85] Id. at 1412-13 (concluding that Exemption 6 was not intended to protect information pertaining to human remains, nor to protect information pertain-
(continued...)

## EXEMPTION 6

more common "reverse" FOIA cases that are based upon a business submitter's claim that information falls within Exemption 4, cases which ordinarily are triggered by the "submitter notice" requirements of Executive Order 12,600.[86] (See the further discussion of this under "Reverse" FOIA, below.) Despite this similarity, though, there is no requirement that an agency notify record subjects of the intent to disclose personal information about them or that it "track down an individual about whom another has requested information merely to obtain the former's permission to comply with the request."[87]

### Factoring in the Public Interest

Once it has been determined that a personal privacy interest is threatened by a requested disclosure, the second step in the balancing process comes into play; this stage of the analysis requires an assessment of the public interest in disclosure.[88] The burden of establishing that disclosure would serve the public interest is on the requester.[89] In its Reporters Committee decision, the Supreme Court has limited the concept of public interest under the FOIA to the "core purpose" for which Congress enacted it: To "shed[] light on an agency's performance of its statutory duties."[90] Information that does not directly reveal the operations or activities of the federal government,[91] the Su-

---

[85](...continued)
ing to large groups in which individuals are not identifiable).

[86] 3 C.F.R. 235 (1988), reprinted in 5 U.S.C. § 552 note (1994), and in FOIA Update, Vol. VIII, No. 2, at 2-3.

[87] Blakey v. Department of Justice, 549 F. Supp. 362, 365 (D.D.C. 1982) (Exemption 7(C)), aff'd in part & vacated in part, 720 F.2d 215 (D.C. Cir. 1983). But cf. War Babes v. Wilson, 770 F. Supp. 1, 4-5 (D.D.C. 1990) (allowing agency 60 days to meet burden of establishing privacy interest by obtaining affidavits from World War II servicemembers who object to release of their addresses to British citizens seeking to locate their natural fathers).

[88] See FOIA Update, Vol. X, No. 2, at 7.

[89] See Carter v. United States Dep't of Commerce, 830 F.2d 388, 391 nn.8 & 13 (D.C. Cir. 1987).

[90] 489 U.S. 749, 773 (1989); see also O'Kane v. United States Customs Serv., 169 F.3d 1308, 1310 (11th Cir. 1999) (affirming that Electronic Freedom of Information Act Amendments of 1996, Pub. L. No. 104-231, 110 Stat. 3048, do not overrule Reporters Committee definition of public interest) (per curiam); Lissner v. United States Customs Serv., No. 98-7438, slip op. at 11-15 (C.D. Cal. June 15, 1999) (same) (appeal pending). But cf. Voinche v. FBI, 940 F. Supp. 323, 330 n.4 (D.D.C. 1996) (dictum) (speculating, based upon mere newspaper report of legislative action, that Electronic FOIA amendments would "effectively overrule" Reporters Committee), aff'd on other grounds per curiam, No. 96-5304, 1997 U.S. App. LEXIS 19089 (D.C. Cir. June 19, 1997).

[91] See Landano v. United States Dep't of Justice, 956 F.2d 422, 430 (3d Cir.) (There is "no FOIA-recognized public interest in discovering wrongdoing by a state agency.") (Exemption 7(C)), cert. denied on Exemption 7(C) issue, 506
(continued...)

# EXEMPTION 6

preme Court repeatedly has stressed, "falls outside the ambit of the public interest that the FOIA was enacted to serve."[92] If an asserted public interest is found to qualify under this standard, it then must be accorded some measure of value so that it can be weighed against the threat to privacy.[93]

Even prior to Reporters Committee the law was clear that disclosure must benefit the public overall and not just the requester himself. For example, a number of courts determined that a request made for purely commercial purposes does not further a public interest.[94] The Court of Appeals for the Ninth Circuit alone had adopted a position that specifically factored into the

---

[91] (...continued)
U.S. 868 (1992), and rev'd & remanded on other grounds, 508 U.S. 165 (1993); Lissner, No. 98-7438, slip op. at 9-11 (C.D. Cal. June 15, 1999) (concluding that conduct of state and local employees "fall[s] outside FOIA's federal ambit, and, accordingly, their conduct does not constitute a public interest which FOIA recognizes") (Exemption 7(C)) (appeal pending); see also FOIA Update, Vol. XII, No. 2, at 6 (advising that "government" should mean federal government); cf. Dollinger v. United States Postal Serv., No. 95-CV-6174T, slip op. at 3-4 (W.D.N.Y. Aug. 24, 1995) (finding "that the term 'government' as used in § 552(a)(4)(A)(iii) [fee waiver provision] of the statute refers to the federal government").

[92] 489 U.S. at 775; see Bibles v. Oregon Natural Desert Ass'n, 519 U.S. 355, 355-56 (1997); DOD v. FLRA, 510 U.S. 487, 497 (1994); see also, e.g., Gallant v. NLRB, No. 92-873, slip op. at 8-10 (D.D.C. Nov. 6, 1992) (concluding that disclosure of names of individuals to whom NLRB member sent letters in attempt to secure reappointment would not add to understanding of NLRB's performance of its duties), aff'd, 23 F.3d 168 (D.C. Cir. 1994); Andrews v. United States Dep't of Justice, 769 F. Supp. 314, 316-17 (E.D. Mo. 1991) (finding that although release of individual's address, telephone number, and place of employment might serve general public interest in satisfaction of monetary judgments, "it does not implicate a public interest cognizable under the FOIA"); see also FOIA Update, Vol. XVIII, No. 1, at 1; FOIA Update, Vol. X, No. 2, at 4, 6.

[93] See, e.g., Department of the Air Force v. Rose, 425 U.S. 352, 372 (1976); Ripskis v. HUD, 746 F.2d 1, 3 (D.C. Cir. 1981); Fund for Constitutional Gov't v. National Archives & Records Serv., 656 F.2d 856, 862 (D.C. Cir. 1981).

[94] See, e.g., Multnomah County Med. Soc'y v. Scott, 825 F.2d 1410, 1413 (9th Cir. 1987) (commercial solicitation of Medicare recipients); Minnis v. USDA, 737 F.2d 784, 786-87 (9th Cir. 1984) (applicants for rafting permits requested by commercial establishment located on river); Wine Hobby USA, Inc. v. IRS, 502 F.2d 133, 137 (3d Cir. 1974) (individuals licensed to produce wine at home requested by distributor of amateur wine-making equipment); see also Aronson v. HUD, 822 F.2d 182, 185-86 (1st Cir. 1987) (Plaintiff's "commercial motivations are irrelevant for determining the public interest served by disclosure; they do, however, suggest one of the ways in which private interests could be harmed by disclosure and a reason why individuals would wish to keep the information confidential.").

**EXEMPTION 6**

balancing process the requester's personal interest in disclosure.[95]

In Reporters Committee, the Supreme Court approved the majority view that the requester's personal interest is irrelevant. First, as the Court emphasized, the requester's identity can have "no bearing on the merits of his or her FOIA request."[96] In so declaring, the Court ruled unequivocally that agencies should treat all requesters alike in making FOIA disclosure decisions; the only exception to this, the Court specifically noted, is that of course an agency should not withhold from a requester any information that implicates only that requester's own interest.[97] Furthermore, the "public interest" balancing required under the privacy exemptions should not include consideration of the requester's "particular purpose" in making the request.[98] Instead, the Court has instructed, the proper approach to the balancing process is to focus on "the nature of the requested document" and to consider "its relationship to" the public interest generally.[99] This approach thus does not permit attention to the special circumstances of any particular FOIA requester.[100] Rather, it necessarily involves a more general "public interest" assessment based upon the contents and context of the records sought and their connection to any "public interest" that would be served by disclosure. In making such assessments, agencies should look to the possible effects of disclosure to the public in general.[101]

Accordingly, a request made for the purpose of obtaining "impeachment evidence, such as that required to be produced pursuant to Brady v. Mary-

---

[95] See, e.g., Multnomah County Med. Soc'y, 825 F.2d at 1413; Minnis, 737 F.2d at 786; Van Bourg, Allen, Weinberg & Roger v. NLRB, 728 F.2d 1270, 1273 (9th Cir. 1984), vacated, 756 F.2d 692 (9th Cir.), reinstated, 762 F.2d 831 (9th Cir. 1985); Church of Scientology v. United States Dep't of the Army, 611 F.2d 738, 747 (9th Cir. 1979).

[96] 489 U.S. at 771; see also DOD v. FLRA, 510 U.S. at 496-501; FOIA Update, Vol. X, No. 2, at 5-6.

[97] 489 U.S. at 771; see FOIA Update, Vol. X, No. 2, at 5; see also, e.g., Frets v. Department of Transp., No. 88-404-W-9, 1989 WL 222608, at **5-6 (W.D. Mo. Dec. 14, 1989) (withholding names of third parties mentioned in plaintiffs' own statements).

[98] 489 U.S. at 772; see also DOD v. FLRA, 510 U.S. at 496-501.

[99] 489 U.S. at 772.

[100] See id. at 771-72 & n.20; see also Schiffer v. FBI, 78 F.3d 1405, 1410-11 (9th Cir. 1996) (noting that individual interest in obtaining information about oneself does not constitute public interest); Schwarz v. United States Dep't of State, No. 97-1342, slip op. at 1-5 (D.D.C. Mar. 20, 1998) (protecting address of individual despite incorrigibly prolific FOIA plaintiff's claim that she sought imagined "missing" husband's address so that she might "testify on his behalf and win his release from prison"), aff'd per curiam, 172 F.3d 921 (D.C. Cir.) (unpublished table decision), cert. denied, 525 U.S. 1025 (1998), reh'g denied, 525 U.S. 1096 (1999).

[101] See FOIA Update, Vol. X, No. 2, at 5-6.

# EXEMPTION 6

land"[102] does not further the public interest;[103] nor does a request made in order to obtain or supplement discovery in a private lawsuit serve the public interest.[104] In fact, one court has observed that if the requester truly had a great need for the records for purposes of litigation, he or she should seek them in that forum, where it would be possible to provide them under an appropriate protective order.[105]

One purpose that the FOIA was designed for is to "check against corruption and to hold the governors accountable to the governed."[106] Indeed, information that would inform the public of violations of the public trust has a strong public interest and is accorded great weight in the balancing process. As a general rule, proven wrongdoing of a serious and intentional nature by a high-level government official is of sufficient public interest to outweigh the

---

[102] 373 U.S. 83 (1963).

[103] Curry v. DEA, No. 97-1359, slip op. at 5 (D.D.C. Mar. 30, 1998); see Neely v. FBI, 208 F.3d 461, 464 (4th Cir. 2000) (stating that "courts have sensibly refused to recognize, for purposes of FOIA, a public interest in nothing more than the fairness of a criminal defendant's own trial"); Martin v. United States Dep't of Justice, No. 96-2866, slip op. at 10 (D.D.C. Dec. 15, 1999) (noting that "courts have consistently found Brady violations to be outside the scope of the FOIA"); Billington v. Department of Justice, 11 F. Supp. 2d 45, 63 (D.D.C. 1998) (noting that "requests for Brady material are 'outside the proper role of FOIA'" (quoting Johnson v. Department of Justice, 758 F. Supp. 2, 5 (D.D.C. 1991))); Isley v. Executive Office for United States Attorneys, No. 96-0123, slip op. at 6-7 (D.D.C. Feb. 25, 1998) ("A request for Brady material is beyond the scope of the FOIA.") (Exemption 7(C)), aff'd, 203 F.3d 52 (D.C. Cir. 1999) (unpublished table decision).

[104] See Brown v. FBI, 658 F.2d 71, 75 (2d Cir. 1981) (private litigation); Cappabianca v. Commissioner, United States Customs Serv., 847 F. Supp. 1558, 1564 (M.D. Fla. 1994) (job-related causes of action); Harry v. Department of the Army, No. 92-1654, slip op. at 7-8 (D.D.C. Sept. 10, 1993) (to appeal negative officer efficiency report); NTEU v. United States Dep't of the Treasury, 3 Gov't Disclosure Serv. (P-H) ¶ 83,224, at 83,948 (D.D.C. June 17, 1983) (grievance proceeding); FOIA Update, Vol. III, No. 4, at 6.

[105] Gilbey v. Department of the Interior, No. 89-0801, 1990 WL 174889, at *2 (D.D.C. Oct. 22, 1990); see also Billington, 11 F. Supp. 2d at 64 (noting that proper forum for challenging alleged illegal search is in district court where case was prosecuted); Bongiorno v. Reno, No. 95-72143, 1996 U.S. Dist. LEXIS 4796, at *11 (E.D. Mich. Mar. 19, 1996) (observing that proper place for noncustodial parent to seek information about his child is "state court that has jurisdiction over the parties, not a FOIA request or the federal court system").

[106] Multnomah County Med. Soc'y, 825 F.2d at 1415 (quoting NLRB v. Robbins Tire & Rubber Co., 437 U.S. 214, 242 (1978)); see also Arieff v. United States Dep't of the Navy, 712 F.2d 1462, 1468 (D.C. Cir. 1983); Washington Post Co. v. HHS, 690 F.2d 252, 264 (D.C. Cir. 1982); National Ass'n of Atomic Veterans, Inc. v. Director, Defense Nuclear Agency, 583 F. Supp. 1483, 1487 (D.D.C. 1984).

**EXEMPTION 6**

privacy interest of the official.[107]

By contrast, less serious misconduct by low-level agency employees generally is not considered of sufficient public interest to outweigh the privacy interest of the employee.[108] Nor is there likely to be strong public interest in

---

[107] See, e.g., Cochran v. United States, 770 F.2d 949, 956-57 (11th Cir. 1985) (nonjudicial punishment findings and discipline imposed on Army major general for misuse of government personnel and facilities) (Privacy Act "wrongful disclosure" suit); Stern v. FBI, 737 F.2d 84, 93-94 (D.C. Cir. 1984) (name of high-level FBI official censured for deliberate and knowing misrepresentation) (Exemption 7(C)); Columbia Packing Co. v. USDA, 563 F.2d 495, 499 (1st Cir. 1977) (federal employees found guilty of accepting bribes); Lurie v. Department of the Army, 970 F. Supp. 19, 39-40 (D.D.C. 1997) (ordering disclosure of information concerning "mid- to high-level" Army medical researcher whose apparent misrepresentation and misconduct contributed to appropriation of $20,000,000 for particular form of AIDS research), appeal voluntarily dismissed, No. 97-5248 (D.C. Cir. Oct. 22, 1997); Sullivan v. VA, 617 F. Supp. 258, 260-61 (D.D.C. 1985) (reprimand of senior official for misuse of government vehicle and failure to report accident) (Privacy Act "wrongful disclosure" suit/Exemption 7(C)); Congressional News Syndicate v. United States Dep't of Justice, 438 F. Supp. 538, 544 (D.D.C. 1977) (misconduct by White House staffers); cf. Castaneda v. United States, 757 F.2d 1010, 1012 (9th Cir.) (ordering disclosure of identity of USDA investigator when court found his reports "were inconsistent and may have been unreliable" and his motives and truthfulness were "in doubt") (Exemption 7(C)), amended upon denial of panel reh'g, 773 F.2d 251, 251 (9th Cir. 1985); Ferri v. Bell, 645 F.2d 1213, 1218 (3d Cir. 1981) (finding attempt to expose alleged deal between prosecutor and witness to be in public interest) (Exemption 7(C)), vacated & reinstated in part on reh'g, 671 F.2d 769 (3d Cir. 1982).

[108] See, e.g., Rose, 425 U.S. at 381 (protecting names of cadets found to have violated Academy honor code); Hoyos v. United States, No. 98-4178, slip op. at 3 (11th Cir. Feb. 1, 1999) (finding "little public interest in access to [identities of individuals fired from the VA], especially when the reasons for removal--the information that truly bears upon the agency's conduct, which is the focus of FOIA's concern--were readily made available"), cert. denied, 120 S. Ct. 582 (1999); Beck v. Department of Justice, 997 F.2d 1489, 1493 (D.C. Cir. 1993) ("The identity of one or two individual relatively low-level government wrongdoers, released in isolation, does not provide information about the agency's own conduct."); Stern, 737 F.2d at 94 (protecting names of mid-level employees censured for negligence); Chamberlain v. Kurtz, 589 F.2d 827, 842 (5th Cir. 1979) (protecting names of disciplined IRS agents); Butler v. United States Dep't of Justice, No. 86-2255, 1994 WL 55621, at *10 (D.D.C. Feb. 3, 1994) (protecting identity of FBI agent who received "mild admonishment" for conduct that "was not particularly egregious"), appeal dismissed, No. 94-5078 (D.C. Cir. Sept. 8, 1994); Cotton v. Adams, 798 F. Supp. 22, 26-27 (D.D.C. 1992) (finding that release of Inspector General reports on conduct of low-level Smithsonian Institution employees would not allow public to evaluate Smithsonian's performance of mission); Heller v. United States Marshals Serv., 655 F. Supp. 1088, 1091 (D.D.C. 1987) (protecting names of agency personnel found to have committed "only minor, if any, wrongdoing") (Ex-
(continued...)

**EXEMPTION 6**

the names of censured employees when the case has not "occurred against the backdrop of a well-publicized scandal" that has resulted in "widespread knowledge" that certain employees were disciplined.[109] And any general public interest in mere allegations of wrongdoing does not outweigh an individual's privacy interest in unwarranted association with such allegations.[110] Even when allegations of misconduct are known, the accused individual ordinarily has an overriding privacy interest in not having the details of the matter disclosed.[111]

As an exception to this general rule, it is the policy of the Department of Justice to disclose the results of its Office of Professional Responsibility (OPR) investigations of its attorneys more broadly. The Department has determined that because of the special role of its attorneys in litigation and investigations there is a heightened public interest in their activities, comparable to the heightened interest in the activities of high-level officials, particularly in the context of the strong public interest in the effectiveness of the OPR misconduct-investigation process.[112] Accordingly, upon completion of an OPR inves-

---

[108](...continued)
emption 7(C)).

[109] Beck, 997 F.2d at 1493-94; see Chin v. United States Dep't of the Air Force, No. 97-2176, slip op. at 3 (W.D. La. June 24, 1999) (finding significant privacy interest in records that "document[] personal and intimate incidents of misconduct [that have] not previously been a part of the public domain") (appeal pending).

[110] See, e.g., McCutchen v. HHS, 30 F.3d 183, 187-89 (D.C. Cir. 1994) (protecting identities of scientists found not to have engaged in alleged scientific misconduct) (Exemption 7(C)); Hunt v. FBI, 972 F.2d 286, 288-90 (9th Cir. 1992) (protecting investigation of named FBI agent cleared of charges of misconduct) (Exemption 7(C)); Dunkelberger v. Department of Justice, 906 F.2d 779, 781-82 (D.C. Cir. 1990) (same) (Exemption 7(C)); Carter, 830 F.2d at 391 (protecting identities of attorneys subject to disciplinary proceedings that were later dismissed). But see Dobronski v. FCC, 17 F.3d 275, 278-80 (9th Cir. 1994) (atypically ordering release of employee's sick leave slips despite fact that allegations of abuse of leave time were based upon unsubstantiated tips); Providence Journal Co. v. United States Dep't of the Army, 981 F.2d 552, 569 (1st Cir. 1992) (ordering disclosure of identities of high-ranking officers of Rhode Island National Guard accused of criminal wrongdoing even though allegations were mostly "unsubstantiated").

[111] See Mueller v. United States Dep't of the Air Force, 63 F. Supp. 2d 738, 743 (E.D. Va. 1999) (declaring that even given existence of publicity, "individuals have a strong interest in not being associated with alleged wrongful activity, particularly where, as here, the subject of the investigation is ultimately exonerated") (Exemptions 6 and 7(C)); see also Chin, No. 97-2176, slip op. at 5 (W.D. La. June 24, 1999) (finding that fact "that some of the events are known to certain members of the public . . . is insufficient to place this record for dissemination into the public domain").

[112] See FOIA Update, Vol. XV, No. 2, at 2 (discussing Deputy Attorney Gen-
(continued...)

# EXEMPTION 6

tigation, the Department's policy is to disclose the final disposition when (1) there is a finding of intentional or knowing professional misconduct in the course of an investigation or litigation and the public interest outweighs the attorney's privacy interest and any law enforcement interests; (2) there are allegations of serious professional misconduct where there has been a demonstration of public interest in the disposition, including matters in which there has been a public referral by a court or bar association, and the public interest outweighs the attorney's privacy interest and any law enforcement interests; or (3) the attorney requests disclosure and law enforcement interests would not be compromised.[113]

Prior to Reporters Committee, some courts held that the public interest in disclosure may be embodied in other federal statutes.[114] In light of Reporters Committee and National Association of Retired Federal Employees v. Horner [hereinafter NARFE],[115] the District of Columbia, First, Second, Sixth, Seventh, Tenth, and Eleventh Circuit Courts of Appeals flatly rejected this approach, refusing to order disclosure of the home addresses of government employees on the explicit basis that the public interest in disclosure evidenced in the Federal Service Labor-Management Relations Act [hereinafter FSLMRA] cannot be factored into the balance under the FOIA.[116] On the other hand, the Third, Fifth, and Ninth Circuit Courts of Appeals reached the opposite conclusion and ordered disclosure of the home addresses of bargaining unit employ-

---

[112](...continued) eral Memorandum (Dec. 13, 1993) that established policy).

[113] See Deputy Attorney General Memorandum at 1-2.

[114] See, e.g., International Bhd. of Elec. Workers Local No. 5 v. HUD, 852 F.2d 87, 90 (3d Cir. 1988) (wage rates payable by federal contractors regulated by Davis-Bacon Act); USDA v. FLRA, 836 F.2d 1139, 1143 (8th Cir.) (names and addresses of federal employees under federal labor relations statute), cert. granted & remanded, 488 U.S. 1025 (1988), vacated, 876 F.2d 50 (8th Cir. 1989); Common Cause v. National Archives & Records Serv., 628 F.2d 179, 183-85 (D.C. Cir. 1980) (political campaign activities under Federal Corrupt Practices Act) (Exemption 7(C)); Washington Post, 690 F.2d at 265 (public disclosure of financial statements required by Ethics in Government Act); see also Marzen v. HHS, 825 F.2d 1148, 1154 (7th Cir. 1987) (finding nondisclosure proper upon consideration of state statute mandating same).

[115] 879 F.2d 873 (D.C. Cir. 1989).

[116] D.C. Circuit: FLRA v. United States Dep't of the Treasury, 884 F.2d 1446, 1453 (D.C. Cir. 1989); First Circuit: FLRA v. United States Dep't of the Navy, 941 F.2d 49, 56-57 (1st Cir. 1991); Second Circuit: FLRA v. VA, 958 F.2d 503, 511-12 (2d Cir. 1992); Sixth Circuit: FLRA v. Department of the Navy, 963 F.2d 124, 125 (6th Cir. 1992); Seventh Circuit: FLRA v. United States Dep't of the Navy, 975 F.2d 348, 354-55 (7th Cir. 1992); Tenth Circuit: FLRA v. DOD, 984 F.2d 370, 375 (10th Cir. 1993); Eleventh Circuit: FLRA v. DOD, 977 F.2d 545, 548 (11th Cir. 1992). See also Reed v. NLRB, 927 F.2d 1249, 1251 (D.C. Cir. 1991) (concluding that disclosure of "Excelsior" list [names and addresses of employees eligible to vote in union representation elections] would not reveal anything about NLRB's operations).

# EXEMPTION 6

ees to unions that requested them under the FSLMRA.[117] These circuit courts all declared that the Supreme Court had not considered specifically whether the public policy favoring collective bargaining embodied in the FSLMRA could be considered in balancing under the FOIA; consequently, none of these courts found an inconsistency between its holding and the teachings of Reporters Committee.[118]

Because of this split in the circuits, the Supreme Court granted certiorari in the Fifth Circuit case and finally resolved this issue in 1994.[119] The Court decisively reiterated the principles laid down in Reporters Committee and said the fact that it was looking at Exemption 6 rather than Exemption 7(C) in this case was "of little import"; the two exemptions differ in the "magnitude of the public interest that is required," not in the "identification of the relevant public interest."[120] The Court concluded that "because all FOIA requestors have an equal, and equally qualified, right to information, the fact that [FOIA requesters] are seeking to vindicate the policies behind the Labor Statute is irrelevant to the FOIA analysis."[121] The only relevant public interest under the FOIA remains, as set forth in Reporters Committee, "'the citizens' right to be informed about what their government is up to.'"[122]

On a related question concerning another federal statute--the Davis-Bacon Act,[123] which requires that contractors on federal projects pay to their laborers no less than the wages prevailing for comparable work in their geographical area--the D.C. and Second Circuits were the first post-Reporters Committee courts of appeals to confront this issue, and the Third and Tenth Circuits subsequently addressed it as well. These four courts have firmly held that although there may be a minimal public interest in facilitating the monitoring of compliance with federal labor statutes, disclosure of personal information that reveals nothing "directly about the character of a government agency or official" bears only an "attenuated . . . relationship to governmental

---

[117] Third Circuit: FLRA v. United States Dep't of the Navy, 966 F.2d 747, 758-59 (3d Cir. 1992) (en banc) (alternative holding); Fifth Circuit: FLRA v. DOD, 975 F.2d 1105, 1113-15 (5th Cir.), rev'd, 510 U.S. 487 (1994); Ninth Circuit: FLRA v. United States Dep't of the Navy, 958 F.2d 1490, 1497 (9th Cir. 1992), reh'g granted & opinion withdrawn, No. 90-70511 (Apr. 18, 1994); see also FLRA v. Department of Commerce, 954 F.2d 994, 997 (4th Cir. 1992), appeal dismissed per stipulation, No. 90-1852 (4th Cir. Apr. 6, 1995).

[118] FLRA v. United States Dep't of the Navy, 966 F.2d at 757-59; FLRA v. United States Dep't of the Navy, 958 F.2d at 1496-97.

[119] DOD v. FLRA, 510 U.S. 487 (1994).

[120] Id. at 496-97 & n.6.

[121] Id. at 499.

[122] Id. at 497 (quoting Reporters Comm., 489 U.S. at 773).

[123] 40 U.S.C. § 276a (1994).

**EXEMPTION 6**

activity."[124] Accordingly, it has been held that such an "attenuated public interest in disclosure does not outweigh the construction workers' significant privacy interest in [their names and addresses]."[125]

Overturning the decisions of two lower courts,[126] the Ninth Circuit took a slightly different approach to reach the same result.[127] The Ninth Circuit found a public interest in monitoring the agency's "diligence in enforcing Davis-Bacon," but found the weight to be given that interest weakened when the public benefit is derived neither directly from the release of the information itself nor from mere tabulation of data or further research but rather from personal contact with the individuals whose privacy is at issue.[128]

Even though public oversight of government operations is the essence of public interest under the FOIA, one who claims such a purpose must support his claim by more than mere allegation; he must show that the information in question is "of sufficient importance to warrant such" oversight,[129] and

---

[124] Hopkins v. HUD, 929 F.2d 81, 88 (2d Cir. 1991); see Sheet Metal Workers Int'l Ass'n, Local No. 19 v. VA, 135 F.3d 891, 903-05 (3d Cir. 1998); Sheet Metal Workers Int'l Ass'n, Local No. 9 v. United States Air Force, 63 F.3d 994, 997-98 (10th Cir. 1995); Painting & Drywall Work Preservation Fund, Inc. v. HUD, 936 F.2d 1300, 1303 (D.C. Cir. 1991).

[125] Painting & Drywall, 936 F.2d at 1303; see Sheet Metal Workers, 63 F.3d at 997-98; Hopkins, 929 F.2d at 88.

[126] Painting Indus. Mkt. Recovery Fund v. United States Dep't of the Air Force, 751 F. Supp. 1410, 1417 (D. Haw.), reconsideration denied, 756 F. Supp. 452 (D. Haw. 1990); Seattle Bldg. & Constr. Trades Council v. HUD, No. C89-1346C, slip op. at 10-11 (W.D. Wash. Oct. 30, 1990).

[127] Painting Indus. Mkt. Recovery Fund v. United States Dep't of the Air Force, 26 F.3d 1479, 1484-86 (9th Cir. 1994).

[128] Id. at 1485; see also Sheet Metal Workers, 63 F.3d at 997-98.

[129] Miller v. Bell, 661 F.2d 623, 630 (7th Cir. 1981); see also Accuracy in Media, Inc. v. National Park Serv., 194 F.3d 120, 124 (D.C. Cir. 1999) (discounting inconsistencies in multiple agency reports from complex crime scene as "hardly so shocking as to suggest illegality or deliberate government falsification") (Exemption 7(C)), cert. denied, 68 U.S.L.W. 3711 (U.S. May 15, 2000) (No. 99-1578); Schiffer, 78 F.3d at 1410 (rejecting public interest argument absent evidence suggesting wrongdoing by FBI); Computer Prof'ls for Soc. Responsibility v. United States Secret Serv., 72 F.3d 897, 904-05 (D.C. Cir. 1996) ("[T]he public interest is insubstantial unless the requester puts forward compelling evidence that the agency denying the FOIA request is engaged in illegal activity and shows that the information sought is necessary in order to confirm or refute that evidence.") (Exemption 7(C)); Wichlacz v. United States Dep't of Interior, 938 F. Supp. 325, 333 (E.D. Va. 1996) (observing that plaintiff "has set forth no evidence to buttress his bald allegations" of cover-up in investigation of death of White House Deputy Counsel Vincent Foster, a theory substantially undercut by then-ongoing Office of Independent Counsel investigation), aff'd, 114 F.3d 1178 (4th Cir. 1997) (unpublished table deci-

(continued...)

**EXEMPTION 6**

he must show how the public interest would be served by disclosure in the particular case.[130] Assertions of "public interest" should be scrutinized carefully to ensure that they legitimately warrant the overriding of important privacy interests.[131] As stated by the Second Circuit in Hopkins v. HUD, "[t]he simple invocation of a legitimate public interest . . . cannot itself justify the release of personal information. Rather, a court must first ascertain whether that interest would be served by disclosure."[132] The Second Circuit in Hopkins acknowledged a legitimate public interest in monitoring HUD's enforcement of prevailing wage laws, but found that disclosure of the names and addresses of workers employed on HUD-assisted public housing projects would shed no light on the agency's performance of that duty.[133] Thus, in Minnis v. USDA,

---

[129](...continued)
sion); Allard v. HHS, No. 4:90-CV-156, slip op. at 10-11 (W.D. Mich. Feb. 14, 1992) (finding that "conclusory allegations" of plaintiff--a prisoner with violent tendencies--concerning ex-wife's misuse of children's social security benefits do not establish public interest), aff'd, 972 F.2d 346 (6th Cir. 1992) (unpublished table decision).

[130] See Halloran v. VA, 874 F.2d 315, 323 (5th Cir. 1989).

[131] See FOIA Update, Vol. III, No. 4, at 6.

[132] 929 F.2d at 88 (citing Halloran, 874 F.2d at 323).

[133] Id.; see also Abraham & Rose, P.L.C. v. United States, 138 F.3d 1075, 1083 (6th Cir. 1998) (finding that information about individual taxpayers does not serve possible public interest in "how the IRS exercises its power over the collection of taxes"); Idaho v. United States Forest Serv., No. 97-0230-S, slip op. at 6 (D. Idaho Dec. 9, 1997) (determining that while disclosure of names and cities of residence of Forest Service land permit holders will show whether permits are being granted properly, disclosure of home addresses will provide no "additional insight into agency activities"); Save Our Springs Alliance v. Babbitt, No. A-97-CA-259, slip op. at 7-8 (W.D. Tex. Nov. 19, 1997) (finding that "context of the letters" shows nature of correspondents who commented on issue before agency; release of home addresses and telephone numbers would add nothing to understanding of agency's process); Stabasefski v. United States, 919 F. Supp. 1570, 1575 (M.D. Ga. 1996) (finding that public interest is served by release of redacted vouchers showing amounts of Hurricane Andrew subsistence payment to FAA employees; disclosure of names of employees would shed no additional light on agency activities); Gannett Satellite Info. Network, Inc. v. United States Dep't of Educ., 1990 WL 251480, at *6 (D.D.C. Dec. 21, 1990) ("If in fact a student has defaulted, [his] name, address, and social security number would reveal nothing about the Department's attempts to collect on those defaulted loans. Nor would [they] reveal anything about the potential misuse of public funds."). But see Judicial Watch of Fla., Inc. v. United States Dep't of Justice, No. 97-2869, slip op. at 16-17 (D.D.C. Feb. 22, 2000) (allowing deletion of home addresses and telephone numbers, but ordering release of identities of individuals who wrote to Attorney General about campaign finance or Independent Counsel issues) (motion for reconsideration pending); Oregon Natural Desert Ass'n v. United States Dep't of the Interior, 24 F. Supp. 2d 1088, 1093 (D. Or. (continued...)

**EXEMPTION 6**

while the Ninth Circuit recognized a valid public interest in questioning the fairness of an agency lottery system that awarded permits to raft down the Rogue River, it found, upon careful analysis, that the release of the names and addresses of the applicants would in no way further that interest.[134] Similarly, in Heights Community Congress v. VA,[135] the Sixth Circuit found that the release of names and home addresses would result only in the "involuntary personal involvement" of innocent purchasers rather than appreciably furthering a concededly valid public interest in determining whether anyone had engaged in "racial steering." Several courts, moreover, have observed that the minimal amount of information of interest to the public revealed by a single incident or investigation does not shed enough light on an agency's conduct to overcome the subject's privacy interest in his records.[136]

---

[133](...continued)
1998) (finding that public interest in knowing how agency is enforcing land management laws served by release of names of cattle owners who violated federal grazing laws); Maples v. USDA, No. F 97-5663, slip op. at 14 (E.D. Cal. Jan. 13, 1998) (finding that release of names and addresses of permit holders for use of federal lands would show public how permit process works and eliminate "suspicions of favoritism in giving out permits").

[134] 737 F.2d at 787; see Times Picayune Publ'g Corp. v. United States Dep't of Justice, 37 F. Supp. 2d 472, at 480-81 (E.D. La. 1999) (concluding that release of mug shot would not inform members of public about "activities of their government") (Exemption 7(C)); Baltimore Sun Co. v. United States Customs Serv., No. 97-1991, slip op. at 7 (D. Md. Nov. 21, 1997) (finding that photograph of individual who pled guilty to trafficking in child pornography was not "sufficiently probative of the fairness of [his] sentence that its disclosure [would] inform[] the public of 'what the government is up to'") (Exemption 7(C)); New York Times Co. v. NASA, 782 F. Supp. 628, 632-33 (D.D.C. 1991) (finding that release of audiotape of Challenger astronauts' voices just prior to explosion would not serve "undeniable interest in learning about NASA's conduct before, during and after the Challenger disaster"). But see Detroit Free Press, Inc. v. Department of Justice, 73 F.3d 93, 97-98 (6th Cir. 1996) (finding that release of mug shots of indicted individuals during ongoing criminal proceeding could reveal "error in detaining the wrong person for an offense" or "circumstances surrounding an arrest and initial incarceration"); Rosenfeld v. United States Dep't of Justice, 57 F.3d 803, 811-12 (9th Cir. 1995) (concluding that disclosure of identities of individuals investigated would reveal whether "FBI abused its law enforcement mandate by overzealously investigating a political protest movement to which some members of the government may then have objected") (Exemption 7(C)).

[135] 732 F.2d 526, 530 (6th Cir. 1984).

[136] See Hunt, 972 F.2d at 289 (observing that disclosure of single internal investigation file "will not shed any light on whether all such FBI investigations are comprehensive or whether sexual misconduct by agents is common"); Mueller, 63 F. Supp. 2d at 745 ("the interest of the public in the personnel file of one Air Force prosecutor is attenuated because information concerning a single isolated investigation reveals relatively little about the conduct of the Air Force as an agency") (Exemptions 6 and 7(C)); Chin, No. 97-
(continued...)

**EXEMPTION 6**

Such holdings are entirely consistent with the Supreme Court's determination in Reporters Committee that the "rap sheet" of a defense contractor, if such existed, would reveal nothing directly about the behavior of the Congressman with whom the contractor allegedly had an improper relationship, nor would it reveal anything about the conduct of the DOD.[137] The information must clearly reveal official government activities; it is not enough that the information would permit speculative inferences about the conduct of an agency or a government official,[138] or that it might aid the requester in lobby

---

[136] (...continued)
2176, slip op. at 5 (W.D. La. June 24, 1999) (finding only "marginal benefit to the public interest" in release of facts of single case, particularly "where alternative means exist--such as statistical samples or generalized accounts--to satisfy the public interest").

[137] 489 U.S. at 774; see also NARFE, 879 F.2d at 879 (finding that names and home addresses of federal annuitants reveal nothing directly about workings of government); Halloran, 874 F.2d at 323 ("[M]erely stating that the interest exists in the abstract is not enough; rather, the court should have analyzed how that interest would be served by compelling disclosure."); Kimberlin v. Department of the Treasury, 774 F.2d 204, 208 (7th Cir. 1985) ("The record fails to reflect any benefit which would accrue to the public from disclosure and [the requester's] self-serving assertions of government wrongdoing and coverup do not rise to the level of justifying disclosure.") (Exemption 7(C)); Johnson v. United States Dep't of Justice, 739 F.2d 1514, 1519 (10th Cir. 1984) (finding that because allegations of improper use of law enforcement authority were not at all supported in requested records, disclosure of FBI special agent names would not serve public interest) (Exemption 7(C)); Stern, 737 F.2d at 92 (finding that certain specified public interests "would not be satiated in any way" by disclosure) (Exemption 7(C)); Miller, 661 F.2d at 630 (noting that plaintiff's broad assertions of government cover-up were unfounded as investigation was of consequence to plaintiff only and therefore did not "warrant probe of FBI efficiency") (Exemption 7(C)); Nation Magazine v. Department of State, No. 92-2303, slip op. at 20-24 & n.15 (D.D.C. Aug. 18, 1995) ("[T]he public interest in knowing more about [presidential candidate H. Ross] Perot's dealings with the government is also not the type of public interest protected by the FOIA."). But see Nation Magazine v. United States Customs Serv., 71 F.3d 885, 895 (D.C. Cir. 1995) (finding that agency's response to presidential candidate H. Ross Perot's offer to assist in drug interdiction would serve public interest in agency's plans regarding "'privatization of government functions'").

[138] See Reporters Comm., 489 U.S. at 774, 766 n.18; see also Robbins v. HHS, No. 1:95-cv-3258, slip op. at 8-9 (N.D. Ga. Aug. 12, 1996) (ruling that possibility that release of names and addresses of rejected social security disability claimants could ultimately reveal agency's wrongful denial is "too attenuated to outweigh the significant invasion of privacy"), aff'd per curiam, No. 96-9000 (11th Cir. July 8, 1997); Gannett, No. 90-1392, slip op. at 12 (D.D.C. Dec. 21, 1990) (finding that names, addresses, and social security numbers of student loan defaulters would reveal nothing directly about Department of Education's administration of student loan program). But see Avondale Indus. v. NLRB, 90 F.3d 955, 961-62 (5th Cir. 1996) (declaring that
(continued...)

## EXEMPTION 6

ing efforts that would result in passage of laws and thus benefit the public in that respect.[139]

The most significant recent development concerning this issue occurred in United States Department of State v. Ray,[140] when the Supreme Court recognized a legitimate public interest in whether the State Department was adequately monitoring Haiti's promise not to prosecute Haitians who were returned to their country after failed attempts to enter the United States, but the Court determined that this public interest had been "adequately served" by release of redacted summaries of the agency's interviews with the returnees and that "[t]he addition of the redacted identifying information would not shed any additional light on the Government's conduct of its obligation."[141] Although the plaintiff claimed that disclosure of the identities of the unsuccessful emigrants would allow him to reinterview them and elicit further information concerning their treatment, the Court found "nothing in the record to suggest that a second set of interviews with the already-interviewed returnees would produce any relevant information . . . . Mere speculation about hypothetical public benefits cannot outweigh a demonstrably significant invasion of privacy."[142]

The Supreme Court expressly declined in Ray to decide whether a public interest that stems not from the documents themselves but rather from a "derivative use" to which the documents could be put could ever be weighed in the balancing process against a privacy interest.[143] More recently, however, several lower courts have faced the "derivative use" issue and have ordered

---

[138](...continued) disclosure of marked unredacted voting lists in union representation election would give plaintiff information it needs to determine whether NLRB conducted election tainted with fraud and corruption); International Diatomite Producers Ass'n v. United States Soc. Sec. Admin., No. C-92-1634, 1993 WL 137286, at *5 (N.D. Cal. Apr. 28, 1993) (finding that release of vital status information concerning diatomite industry workers serves "public interest in evaluating whether public agencies (OSHA, [Mine Safety and Health Administration], and EPA) carry out their statutory duties to protect the public from the potential health hazards from crystalline silica exposure"), appeal dismissed, No. 93-16723 (9th Cir. Nov. 1, 1993).

[139] See NARFE, 879 F.2d at 875; see also FOIA Update, Vol. X, No. 2, at 6.

[140] 502 U.S. 164 (1991).

[141] Id. at 178; see also Public Citizen, Inc. v. RTC, No. 92-0010, slip op. at 8-9 (D.D.C. Mar. 19, 1993) (adjudging public interest in agency's compliance with Affordable Housing Disposition Program served by release of information with identities of bidders and purchasers redacted). But see Rosenfeld, 57 F.3d at 811-12 (concluding that disclosure of names of investigative subjects would serve public interest in knowing whether FBI "overzealously" investigated political protest group by allowing comparison of investigative subjects to group's leadership roster) (Exemption 7(C)).

[142] 502 U.S. at 178-79.

[143] Id.

**EXEMPTION 6**

the release of names and home addresses of private individuals in certain contexts despite the fact that the public benefit to be derived from release of the information depended upon the requesters' use of the lists to question those individuals concerning the government's diligence in performing its duties. They have found a "derivative use" public interest in a list of individuals who sold land to the Fish and Wildlife Service, which could be used to contact the individuals to determine how the agency acquires property throughout the United States;[144] a list of Haitian nationals returned to Haiti, which could be used for follow-up interviews with the Haitians to learn "whether the INS is fulfilling its duties not to turn away Haitians who may have valid claims for political asylum";[145] a list of citizens who reported wolf sightings, which could be used to monitor the Fish and Wildlife Service's enforcement of the Endangered Species Act;[146] the names of agents involved in the management and supervision of the FBI's 1972 investigation of John Lennon, which could be used to help determine whether the investigation was politically motivated;[147] and the name and address of an individual who wrote a letter complaining about an immigration assistance company, which could be used to determine whether the INS acted upon the complaint.[148]

The one appellate court to consider explicitly whether a public interest that relies upon a "derivative use" is cognizable under the FOIA is the Ninth Circuit. In Painting Industry Market Recovery Fund v. Department of the Air Force, it considered whether names and addresses on certified payroll records should be released to a union so that it could monitor the agency's diligence in enforcing the Davis-Bacon Act.[149] Squarely confronting the issue of a "derivative use" analysis of public interest, the Ninth Circuit reasoned that if the "'derivative' public benefits are merely those which require some tabulation of data released under FOIA, or perhaps some further research on the part of the requester," the fact that the use is a "derivative" one should not detract from the strength of the public benefit involved.[150] When, however, "the additional step requires direct contact with the employees whose payroll records are be-

---

[144] Thott v. United States Dep't of the Interior, No. 93-0177-B, slip op. at 5-6 (D. Me. Apr. 14, 1994).

[145] Ray v. United States Dep't of Justice, 852 F. Supp. 1558, 1564-65 (S.D. Fla. 1994) (distinguishing United States Dep't of State v. Ray, 502 U.S. 164, on basis that "in the instant case . . . the public interest is not adequately served by release of the redacted logs [and] this Court cannot say that interviewing the returnees would not produce any information concerning our government's conduct during the interdiction process").

[146] Urbigkit v. United States Dep't of the Interior, No. 93-CV-0232-J, slip op. at 13 (D. Wyo. May 31, 1994).

[147] Weiner v. FBI, No. 83-1720, slip op. at 5-7 (C.D. Cal. Dec. 6, 1995) (Exemptions 6 and 7(C)).

[148] Cardona v. INS, No. 93-3912, 1995 WL 68747, at *3 (N.D. Ill. Feb. 15, 1995).

[149] 26 F.3d at 1484-85.

[150] Id.

## EXEMPTION 6

ing sought, [a]ny additional public benefit the requesters might realize through those contacts is inextricably intertwined with the invasions of privacy that those contacts will work," and thus the balance weighs more heavily on the privacy side of the equation.[151]

Finally, if alternative, less intrusive means are available to obtain information that would serve the public interest, there is less need to require disclosure of information that would cause a substantial invasion of an individual's privacy. Accordingly, "[w]hile [this is] certainly not a per se defense to a FOIA request," it is entirely appropriate, when assessing the public interest side of the balancing equation, to consider "the extent to which there are alternative sources of information available that could serve the public interest in disclosure."[152] If there are alternative sources, the D.C. Circuit has firmly

---

[151] Id.; see also Horsehead Indus. v. EPA, No. 94-1299, slip op. at 6 (D.D.C. Mar. 13, 1997) (acknowledging that disclosure of identities of homeowners who volunteered to participate in Superfund study might "provide a glimpse into EPA's activities" but finding that "this interest pales in comparison to the potential harm to the privacy" of study participants, based in part upon "reports of trespassers taking environmental samples").

[152] DOD v. FLRA, 964 F.2d 26, 29-30 (D.C. Cir. 1992); see Painting Indus., 26 F.3d at 1485 (union may "pass out fliers" or "post signs or advertisements soliciting information from workers about possible violations of the Davis-Bacon Act"); FLRA v. United States Dep't of Commerce, 962 F.2d 1055, 1060 n.2 (D.C. Cir. 1992) (union may "distribute questionnaires or conduct confidential face-to-face interviews" to obtain rating information about employees); Painting & Drywall, 936 F.2d at 1303 (contact at workplace is alternative to disclosing home addresses of employees); Multnomah County Med. Soc'y, 825 F.2d at 1416 (medical society can have members send literature to their patients as alternative to disclosure of identities of all Medicare beneficiaries); Chin, No. 97-2176, slip op. at 4-5 (W.D. La. June 24, 1999) (releasing "statistical data and/or general accounts of incidents" would be alternative to releasing investigative records of named individual to show whether government policies were "administered in an arbitrary manner"); Cowles Publ'g Co. v. United States, No. 90-349, slip op. at 8-9 (E.D. Wash. Dec. 20, 1990) (advertisements soliciting injured persons and their physicians, or direct contact with physicians, in region are viable alternatives to agency's releasing identities of persons injured by radiation exposure); Hemenway v. Hughes, 601 F. Supp. 1002, 1007 (D.D.C. 1985) (personal contact with individuals whose names and work addresses were released to plaintiff is alternative to agency's releasing personal information he seeks); cf. Heat & Frost Insulators & Asbestos Workers, Local 16 v. United States Dep't of the Air Force, No. S92-2173, slip op. at 3-4 (E.D. Cal. Oct. 4, 1993) (no alternative to union's request for payroll records--with names, addresses, and social security numbers redacted--would allow union to monitor agency's collection of records in compliance with federal regulations); Cotton, 798 F. Supp. at 27 n.9 (suggesting that request for all inspector general reports, from which identifying information could be redacted, would better serve public interest in overseeing discharge of inspector general duties than does request for only two specific investigative reports involving known individuals).

**EXEMPTION 6**

ruled, the public interest in disclosure should be "discounted" accordingly.[153]

### The Balancing Process

Once both the privacy interest at stake and the public interest in disclosure have been ascertained, the two competing interests must be weighed against one another.[154] In other words, it must be determined which is the greater result of disclosure: the harm to personal privacy or the benefit to the public.[155] In balancing these interests, "the 'clearly unwarranted' language of Exemption 6 weights the scales in favor of disclosure."[156] If the public benefit is weaker than the threat to privacy, the latter will prevail, and the information should be withheld.[157] The threat to privacy need not be obvious; it need only outweigh the public interest.[158]

Although "the presumption in favor of disclosure is as strong [under Exemption 6] as can be found anywhere in the Act,"[159] the courts have most vigorously protected the personal, intimate details of an individual's life--consistently protecting personal information that, if disclosed, is likely to cause the individual involved personal distress or embarrassment. Courts regularly uphold the nondisclosure of information concerning marital status, legitimacy of children, welfare payments, family fights and reputation,[160] medical condition,[161] date of birth,[162] religious affiliation,[163] citizenship data,[164] social secu-

---

[153] DOD v. FLRA, 964 F.2d at 29-30.

[154] See Department of the Air Force v. Rose, 425 U.S. 352, 372 (1976).

[155] See Ripskis v. HUD, 746 F.2d 1, 3 (D.C. Cir. 1984); see FOIA Update, Vol. X, No. 2, at 7.

[156] Ripskis, 746 F.2d at 3.

[157] See FOIA Update, Vol. X, No. 2, at 6 (emphasizing possible applicability of Privacy Act's disclosure prohibitions, particularly in light of Reporters Committee).

[158] See Public Citizen Health Research Group v. United States Dep't of Labor, 591 F.2d 808, 809 (D.C. Cir. 1978).

[159] Washington Post Co. v. HHS, 690 F.2d 252, 261 (D.C. Cir. 1982).

[160] See, e.g., Rural Hous. Alliance v. USDA, 498 F.2d 73, 77 (D.C. Cir. 1974).

[161] See, e.g., McDonnell v. United States, 4 F.3d 1227, 1254 (3d Cir. 1993) ("living individual has a strong privacy interest in withholding his medical records"); Rural Hous. Alliance, 498 F.2d at 77; Sousa v. United States Dep't of Justice, No. 95-375, 1997 U.S. Dist. LEXIS 9010, at *22 (D.D.C. June 18, 1997) (withholding co-defendant's medical records); Isley v. Executive Office for United States Attorneys, No. 96-0123, slip op. at 5 (D.D.C. Mar. 27, 1997) (protecting medical records of third party), aff'd on other grounds, 203 F.3d 52 (D.C. Cir. 1999) (unpublished table decision); Robbins v. HHS, No. 1:95-cv-3258, slip op. at 8-9 (N.D. Ga. Aug. 12, 1996) (upholding nondisclosure of names, addresses, and claim denial letters of rejected social security disability

(continued...)

# EXEMPTION 6

rity numbers,[165] criminal history records (commonly referred to as "rap sheets"),[166] incarceration of United States citizens in foreign prisons,[167] sexual inclinations or associations,[168] and financial status.[169] Even "favorable information," such as details of an employee's outstanding performance evaluation, can be protected on the basis that it "may well embarrass an individual

---

[161](...continued) claimants), aff'd per curiam, No. 96-9000 (11th Cir. July 8, 1997); Hunt v. United States Marine Corps, 935 F. Supp. 46, 54 (D.D.C. 1996) (observing that although public may have interest in a political candidate's fitness for office, disclosure of Oliver North's medical records would not shed light on conduct of Marine Corps). But cf. Dobronski v. FCC, 17 F.3d 275, 278-79 (9th Cir. 1994) (ruling that government employee's "nominal" privacy interest in sick leave records, that do not state reason for taking sick leave, required to yield to public interest in learning about possible abuse of sick leave in a particular case).

[162] See, e.g., Judicial Watch, Inc. v. United States Dep't of Commerce, 83 F. Supp. 2d 105, 112 (D.D.C. 1999), appeal voluntarily dismissed, No. 99-5054 (D.C. Cir. Sept. 10, 1999); Centracchio v. FBI, No. 92-357, slip op. at 15 (D.D.C. Mar. 16, 1993).

[163] See, e.g., Church of Scientology v. United States Dep't of the Army, 611 F.2d 738, 747 (9th Cir. 1979).

[164] See, e.g., Hemenway v. Hughes, 601 F. Supp. 1002, 1006 (D.D.C. 1985) ("Nationals from some countries face persistent discrimination . . . [and] are potential targets for terrorist attacks."); cf. Judicial Watch, 83 F. Supp. 2d at 112 (visa and passport data).

[165] See, e.g., Norwood v. FAA, 993 F.2d 570, 575 (6th Cir. 1993); Kuffel v. United States Bureau of Prisons, 882 F. Supp. 1116, 1122 (D.D.C. 1995) (Exemption 7(C)); Rice v. Department of Transp., No. 91-3306, slip op. at 1 (D.D.C. Nov. 17, 1992); Fidelity Nat'l Title Ins. Co. v. HHS, No. 91-5484, slip op. at 6-7 (C.D. Cal. Feb. 13, 1992).

[166] See, e.g., United States Dep't of Justice v. Reporters Comm. for Freedom of the Press, 489 U.S. 749, 780 (1989).

[167] See Harbolt v. Department of State, 616 F.2d 772, 774 (5th Cir. 1980).

[168] See, e.g., Siminoski v. FBI, No. 83-6499, slip op. at 28 (C.D. Cal. Jan. 16, 1990).

[169] See, e.g., Beard v. Espy, No. 94-16748, 1995 U.S. App. LEXIS 38269, at *3 (9th Cir. Dec. 11, 1995); Hill v. USDA, 77 F. Supp. 2d 6, 8-9 (D.D.C. 1999), summary affirmance granted, No. 99-5365, 2000 WL 520724, at *1 (D.C. Cir. Mar. 7, 2000); Green v. United States, 8 F. Supp. 2d 983, 998 (W.D. Mich. 1998), appeal dismissed, No. 98-1568 (6th Cir. Aug. 11, 1998); Stabasefski v. United States, 919 F. Supp. 1570, 1575 (M.D. Ga. 1996); Biase v. Office of Thrift Supervision, No. 93-2521, slip op. at 8-10 (D.N.J. Dec. 10, 1993); Public Citizen, Inc. v. RTC, No. 92-0010, slip op. at 6-10 (D.D.C. Mar. 19, 1993).

# EXEMPTION 6

or incite jealousy" among co-workers.[170] Moreover, release of such information "reveals by omission the identities of employees who did not receive high ratings, creating an invasion of their privacy."[171]

A subject that has generated extensive litigation and that warrants special discussion is requests for compilations of names and home addresses of individuals. Traditionally, prior to the Reporters Committee decision, the courts' analyses in "mailing list" cases turned on the requester's purpose, or the "use" to which the requested information was intended to be put.[172] The Supreme Court in Reporters Committee, however, firmly repudiated any analysis based on the identity, circumstances, or intended purpose of the particular FOIA requester at hand.[173] Rather, it said, the analysis must turn on the nature of the document and its relationship to the basic purpose of the FOIA.[174] Following Reporters Committee, the Court of Appeals for the District of Columbia Circuit found that those cases relying on the stated "beneficial" purpose of the requester were grounded on the now-disapproved proposition that "Exemption 6 carries with it an implicit limitation that the information, once disclosed, [may] be used only by the requesting party and for the public

---

[170] Ripskis, 746 F.2d at 3; see HHS v. FLRA, No. 92-1012, 1992 WL 390891, at *1 (D.C. Cir. Dec. 10, 1992); FLRA v. United States Dep't of Commerce, 962 F.2d 1055, 1059-61 (D.C. Cir. 1992); Peralta v. United States Attorney's Office, 69 F. Supp. 2d. 21, 33 (D.D.C. 1999) (letters of commendation for work on investigation of plaintiff).

[171] FLRA v. United States Dep't of Commerce, 962 F.2d at 1059.

[172] See, e.g., Aronson v. HUD, 822 F.2d 182, 185-87 (1st Cir. 1987) (holding that public interest in "the disbursement of funds the government owes its citizens" outweighs the privacy interest of such citizens to be free from others' attempts "to secure a share of that sum" when the government's efforts at disbursal are inadequate); Van Bourg, Allen, Weinberg & Roger v. NLRB, 728 F.2d 1270, 1273 (9th Cir. 1984) (identifying strong public interest in determining whether election fairly conducted), vacated, 756 F.2d 692 (9th Cir.), reinstated, 762 F.2d 831 (9th Cir. 1985); Getman v. NLRB, 450 F.2d, 670, 675-76 (D.C. Cir. 1971) (holding public interest need for study of union elections sufficient to warrant release to professor); National Ass'n of Atomic Veterans, Inc. v. Director, Defense Nuclear Agency, 583 F. Supp. 1483, 1487-88 (D.D.C. 1984) (ordering disclosure of names and addresses of veterans involved in atomic testing because of public interest in increasing their knowledge of benefits and possible future health testing); Disabled Officer's Ass'n v. Rumsfeld, 428 F. Supp. 454, 458 (D.D.C. 1977) (holding nonprofit organization serving needs of retired military officers entitled to names and addresses of such personnel), aff'd, 574 F.2d 636 (D.C. Cir. 1979) (unpublished table decision).

[173] 489 U.S. at 771-72; see also Bibles v. Oregon Natural Desert Ass'n, 519 U.S. 355, 355-56 (1997) (summarily rejecting argument that there is public interest in knowing to whom government is sending information so that those persons can receive information from other sources).

[174] 489 U.S. at 772; see also FOIA Update, Vol. X, No. 2, at 5-6 (advising that old "use" test has been overruled and should no longer be followed).

# EXEMPTION 6

interest purpose upon which the balancing was based."[175]

Because agencies may neither distinguish between requesters nor limit the use to which disclosed information is put, an analysis of the consequences of disclosure of a mailing list cannot turn on the identity or purpose of the requester.[176] Thus, it was found to be irrelevant by the Supreme Court in Bibles v. Oregon Natural Desert Ass'n that the requester's purpose was to use the Bureau of Land Management mailing list to send information reflecting another viewpoint to people who had received newsletters reflecting the government's viewpoint.[177] In NARFE, it was found to be irrelevant that the requester's purpose was to use the list of federal retirees to aid in its lobbying efforts on behalf of those retirees.[178] Although stopping short of creating a nondisclosure category encompassing all mailing lists, the D.C. Circuit in NARFE did hold that mailing lists consisting of names and home addresses of federal annuitants are categorically withholdable under Exemption 6.[179] (See the discus-

---

[175] National Ass'n of Retired Fed. Employees v. Horner, 879 F.2d 873, 875 (D.C. Cir. 1989) [hereinafter NARFE]; see also Professional Programs Group v. Department of Commerce, 29 F.3d 1349, 1353-55 (9th Cir. 1994) (withholding names and addresses of persons registered to take patent bar examination); Gannett Satellite Info. Network, Inc. v. United States Dep't of Educ., No. 90-1392, 1990 WL 251480, at **6-7 (D.D.C. Dec. 21, 1990) (denying access to names, social security numbers, and addresses of individuals who have defaulted on government-backed student loans); Schoettle v. Kemp, 733 F. Supp. 1395, 1397-98 (D. Haw. 1990) (relying upon both Reporters Committee's observation that "public interest" is not equivalent to "interesting or socially beneficial in some broad sense" and HUD's improved methods of tracing people, to withhold identities of mortgagors eligible for distributions of money); cf. Schiffer v. FBI, 78 F.3d 1405, 1411 (9th Cir. 1996) (ruling that FOIA does not authorize limited access to only one individual based upon that individual's personal knowledge of information contained in records). But see Aronson v. HUD, No. 88-1524, slip op. at 1 (1st Cir. Apr. 6, 1989) (affirming award of attorney fees to plaintiff on basis that disclosure of list of mortgagors to whom HUD owes money sheds light on agency's performance of its duty to reimburse those mortgagors).

[176] See NARFE, 879 F.2d at 875.

[177] 519 U.S. at 355-56; see also FOIA Update, Vol. XVIII, No. 1, at 1.

[178] 879 F.2d at 879; see also Robbins, No. 1:95-cv-3258, slip op. at 8-9 (N.D. Ga. Aug. 12, 1996) (rejecting plaintiff's claim of intent to use names and addresses of rejected social security disability claimants to represent them and "thereby 'promote the effective uniform administration of the disability program'" and ultimately reveal agency's wrongful denials as "too attenuated" to outweigh significant invasion of privacy (quoting plaintiff's papers)); Center for Auto Safety v. National Highway Traffic Safety Admin., 809 F. Supp. 148, 150 (D.D.C. 1993) (finding that requester's function as "significant consumer rights advocate" does not imply right to "take over the functions of NHTSA").

[179] NARFE, 879 F.2d at 879; see also Retired Officers Ass'n v. Department of the Navy, 744 F. Supp. 1, 2-3 (D.D.C. May 14, 1990) (holding names and

(continued...)

**EXEMPTION 6**

sion of "derivative use" public benefit under Exemption 6, Factoring in the Public Interest, above.)

Although the Supreme Court twice has specifically considered the issue and, without dissent, held that compilations of names and home addresses of private citizens are protectible under Exemption 6,[180] several lower courts nonetheless subsequently have ordered the disclosure of such lists. Some of these courts have found little or no privacy interest in the names and addresses.[181] Other courts have ordered the release of such personal information on the rationale that the names and addresses themselves would reveal (or lead to other information that would reveal) how the agency conducted some aspect of its business.[182] One court, in a particularly unusual decision, ordered

---

[179](...continued) home addresses of retired military officers exempt); cf. Reed v. NLRB, 927 F.2d 1249, 1251-52 (D.C. Cir. 1991) (categorically protecting "Excelsior" list (names and addresses of employees eligible to vote in union representation elections)).

[180] Bibles v. Oregon Natural Desert Ass'n, 519 U.S. at 355-56 (mailing list of recipients of Bureau of Land Management publication); DOD v. FLRA, 510 U.S. 487, 494-502 (1994) (names and home addresses of federal employees in union bargaining units); cf. United States Dep't of State v. Ray, 502 U.S. 164, 173-79 (1991) (withholding from interview summaries names and addresses of Haitian refugees interviewed by State Department about treatment upon return to Haiti).

[181] See Avondale Indus. v. NLRB, 90 F.3d 955, 961 (5th Cir. 1996) (finding that names and addresses of voters in union election already were disclosed in voluminous public record); Alliance for the Wild Rockies v. Department of the Interior, 53 F. Supp. 32, 36-37 (D.D.C. 1999) (concluding that commenters to proposed rulemaking could have little expectation of privacy when rulemaking notice stated that complete file would be publicly available), remanded for further action in accordance with settlement, No. 99-5292 (D.C. Cir. Apr. 19, 2000); Washington Post Co. v. USDA, 943 F. Supp. 31, 34-36 (D.D.C. Oct. 18, 1996) (finding minimal privacy interest in home addresses at which farmers receiving subsidies under cotton price support program operate their businesses), appeal voluntarily dismissed, No. 96-5373 (D.C. Cir. May 19, 1997); Ackerson & Bishop Chartered v. USDA, No. 92-1068, slip op. at 1 (D.D.C. July 15, 1992) (finding no privacy interest in names of commercial mushroom growers operating under own names).

[182] See Oregon Natural Desert Ass'n v. United States Dep't of the Interior, 24 F. Supp. 2d 1088, 1093 (D. Or. 1998) (names of cattle owners who violated federal grazing laws found to reveal "how government is enforcing and punishing violations of land management laws"); Maples v. USDA, No. 97-5663, slip op. at 14 (E.D. Cal. Jan. 13, 1998) (names and addresses of permit holders for use of federal lands "would provide the public with an understanding of how the permit process works"); Urbigkit v. United States Dep't of the Interior, No. 93-CV-0232-J, slip op. at 13 (D. Wyo. May 31, 1994) (list of citizens who reported wolf sightings found to show agency activities "with respect to the duties imposed upon it by the Endangered Species Act"); Ray v. United
(continued...)

## EXEMPTION 6

disclosure of the names and cities of residence of individuals granted permits to use Forest Service lands to "aid in determining whether improper influence is used to obtain permits or whether permits are being granted to those with a past history of environmental abuses," but affirmed the withholding of street addresses because there was "no showing that knowledge of the street addresses will provide additional insight into agency activities that would not be revealed with disclosure of names and cities of residence alone."[183]

In another unusual decision, the D.C. Circuit remanded a case to the District Court to determine whether some of the names of individual depositors with unclaimed funds at banks for which the FDIC is now the receiver should be released to a professional money finder.[184] Introducing a new element into the balancing test for this particular type of information, the D.C. Circuit held that the standard test "is inapposite here, i.e., where the individuals whom the government seeks to protect have a clear interest in the release of the requested information."[185] As guidance to the District Court charged with applying this novel approach, the Circuit Court ordered, first, that "release of names associated with unclaimed deposits should not be matched with the amount owed to that individual" and, second, that "on remand, the District Court must determine the dollar amount below which an individual's privacy interest should be deemed to outweigh his or her interest in discovering his or her money, such that the names of depositors with lesser amounts may be redacted."[186]

Other courts, more in line with the teachings of the Supreme Court, have protected compilations of names and addresses. For example, when the request clearly is for the purpose of soliciting business or for other commer-

---

[182](...continued) States Dep't of Justice, 852 F. Supp. 1558, 1564-65 (S.D. Fla. 1994) (names and addresses of interdicted Haitians might reveal "information concerning our government's conduct during the interdiction process"); Thott v. United States Dep't of the Interior, No. 93-0177-B, slip op. at 5-6 (D. Me. Apr. 14, 1994) (list of individuals who sold land to Fish and Wildlife Service found to inform the public "about the methods used by FWS in acquiring property throughout the United States").

[183] Idaho v. United States Forest Serv., No. 97-0230-S, slip op. at 6 (D. Idaho Dec. 9, 1997); see Judicial Watch of Fla., Inc. v. United States Dep't of Justice, No. 97-2869, slip op. at 16-17 (D.D.C. Feb. 22, 2000) (allowing withholding of home addresses and telephone numbers of individuals who wrote to Attorney General about campaign finance or Independent Counsel issues, but concluding that in the event any individuals were elected officials their identities might possibly reveal information to the public "which could suggest that their Justice Department had been steered by political pressure rather than by relevant facts and law") (motion for reconsideration pending).

[184] Lepelletier v. FDIC, 164 F.3d 37, 48-49 (D.C. Cir. 1999).

[185] Id. at 48.

[186] Id.

# EXEMPTION 6

cial purposes, most courts readily have found mailing lists to be protectible.[187] Even when there is no apparent commercial interest at stake, other courts have found the possible public interest too attenuated to overcome the clear privacy interest an individual has in his name and home address.[188] Yet other courts have protected mailing lists, emphasizing the increased privacy interest inherent in a list that reveals sensitive information beyond the mere names and addresses of the individuals found on the list.[189] And when a requester seeks the address of a named individual for a purely private purpose, courts have found the privacy interest to be at its zenith and the public interest to be at its nadir.[190]

---

[187] See, e.g., Professional Programs, 29 F.3d at 1353-55 (withholding names and addresses of persons registered to take patent bar examination from business offering patent bar exam preparation courses to lawyers); Robbins, No. 1:95-cv-3258, slip op. at 8-9 (N.D. Ga. Aug. 12, 1996) (withholding names and addresses of rejected social security disability claimants from attorney hoping to solicit business); Schoettle, 733 F. Supp. at 1397-98 (declining to order release of identities of mortgagors eligible for distributions of money).

[188] See Reed, 927 F.2d at 1252 (protecting names and addresses of employees eligible to vote in union representation elections); Dayton Newspapers, Inc. v. Department of the Air Force, 35 F. Supp. 2d 1033, 1035 (S.D. Ohio 1998) (redacting "claimants' names, social security numbers, home addresses, home/work telephone numbers and places of employment" from militarywide medical tort-claims database); Horsehead Indus. v. EPA, No. 94-1299, slip op. at 6 (D.D.C. Mar. 13, 1997) (finding that possible "glimpse into EPA's activities" that would accrue from disclosure of identities of homeowners who volunteered to participate in Superfund study "pales in comparison to the potential harm to the privacy" of study participants); Stabasefski, 919 F. Supp. at 1575 (determining that disclosure of names of FAA employees who received Hurricane Andrew subsistence payments would shed no brighter light on agency activities than vouchers that were released showing amounts of payments); Gannett Satellite, No. 90-1392, 1990 WL 251480, at **6-7 (D.D.C. Dec. 21, 1990) (concluding that names, social security numbers, and addresses of individuals who defaulted on government-backed student loans do not themselves directly reveal anything about student loan programs).

[189] See Ray, 502 U.S. at 176 (observing that disclosure of list of Haitian refugees interviewed by State Department about their treatment upon return to Haiti "would publicly identify the interviewees as people who cooperated with a State Department investigation"); Campaign for Family Farms v. Glickman, 200 F.3d 1180, 1187-88 (8th Cir. 2000) (protecting list of pork producers who signed petition that declared their position on referendum that was sought by petition) ("reverse" FOIA suit); NARFE, 879 F.2d at 876 (characterizing list at issue as revealing that each individual on it "is retired or disabled (or the survivor of such a person) and receives a monthly annuity check from the federal Government"); Minnis v. USDA, 737 F.2d 784, 787 (9th Cir. 1984) ("Disclosure would reveal not only the applicants' names and addresses, but also their personal interests in water sports and the out-of-doors.").

[190] See, e.g., Schwarz v. Department of State, No. 97-1342, slip op. at 5 (D.D.C. Mar. 20, 1998) (stating, despite plaintiff's claim that she needed the
(continued...)

## EXEMPTION 6

Another area that merits particular discussion is the applicability of Exemption 6 to requests for information about civilian and military federal employees. Generally, civilian employees' names, present and past position titles, grades, salaries, and duty stations are releasable as no viable privacy interest exists in such data.[191] The Justice Department recommends the release of additional items, particularly those relating to professional qualifications for federal employment.[192] By regulation, the Department of the Army discloses the name, rank, date of rank, gross salary, duty assignments, office telephone number, source of commission, promotion sequence number, awards and decorations, educational level, and duty status of most of its military personnel.[193] And as a matter of policy, the entire Department of Defense now discloses the names and duty addresses, including electronic mail addresses, of most of its servicemembers.[194]

By recent statutory enactment as well as by regulation, certain military personnel throughout the Department of Defense are properly afforded

---

[190](...continued) address of a third party to assist her, that the "merits of an agency's FOIA determinations do not rest on the identity of the requester or the purpose for which the information is intended to be used"), aff'd per curiam, 172 F.3d 921 (D.C. Cir.) (unpublished table decision), cert. denied, 525 U.S. 1025 (1998), reh'g denied, 525 U.S. 1096 (1999); Bongiorno v. Reno, No. 95-72143, 1996 U.S. Dist. LEXIS 4796, at **10-11 (E.D. Mich. Mar. 19, 1996) (noting that the requester sought personal information concerning his adopted daughter "for his own purposes, as understandable as they may be, and not to shine a public light into the recesses of the federal bureaucracy"); Andrews v. United States Dep't of Justice, 769 F. Supp. 314, 316-17 (E.D. Mo. 1991) (declining to release individual's address, telephone number, and place of employment to requester seeking it for purpose of satisfying monetary judgment).

[191] See 5 C.F.R. § 293.311 (2000); see also FOIA Update, Vol. VII, No. 3, at 3.

[192] See FOIA Update, Vol. III, No. 4, at 3; see also Core v. United States Postal Serv., 730 F.2d 946, 948 (4th Cir. 1984) (qualifications of successful federal applicants); Samble v. United States Dep't of Commerce, No. 1:92-225, slip op. at 11 (S.D. Ga. Sept. 22, 1994) (far-reaching decision requiring disclosure of successful job applicant's "undergraduate grades; private sector performance awards; foreign language abilities; and his answers to questions concerning prior firings, etc., convictions, delinquencies on federal debt, and pending charges against him"); Associated Gen. Contractors, Inc. v. EPA, 488 F. Supp. 861, 863 (D. Nev. 1980) (education, former employment, academic achievements, and employee qualifications).

[193] Army Reg. 340-21, ¶ 3-3a(1), 5 July 1985; see also Army Reg. 25-55, ¶ 3-200, No. 6(b), 14 May 1997 (providing for withholding of names and duty addresses of military personnel assigned to units that are "sensitive, routinely deployable or stationed in foreign territories").

[194] See Memorandum from Department of Defense Directorate for Freedom of Information and Security Review 1 (Oct. 26, 1999) (applying same delineation for electronic mail addresses, on privacy-protection grounds).

**EXEMPTION 6**

greater privacy protection than other servicemembers and nonmilitary employees.[195] Even prior to enactment of such special statutory protection, courts had found that because of the threat of terrorism, military servicemembers stationed outside the United States have a greater expectation of privacy.[196] Courts have, however, ordered the release of names of military personnel stationed in the United States.[197] Additionally, certain other federal employees such as law enforcement personnel and Internal Revenue Service employees possess, by virtue of the nature of their work, protectible privacy interests in their identities and work addresses.[198] (See the further discus-

---

[195] See 10 U.S.C.A. § 130b (West Supp. 2000); Department of Defense Freedom of Information Act Program Regulations, 32 C.F.R. § 286.12(f)(2)(ii) (1999) ("Names and duty addresses (postal and/or e-mail) . . . for personnel assigned to units that are sensitive, routinely deployable, or stationed in foreign territories are withholdable under [Exemption 6].").

[196] See Jernigan v. Department of the Air Force, No. 97-35930, 1998 WL 658662, at *1 (9th Cir. Sept. 17, 1998) (agreeing with Air Force that "'[i]dentifying [its] personnel overseas increases the threat of terrorism and the likelihood that they will be targeted for attack'"); Hudson v. Department of the Army, No. 86-1114, 1987 WL 46755, at **3-4 (D.D.C. Jan. 29, 1987) (finding threat of terrorism creates privacy interest in names, ranks, and addresses of Army personnel stationed in Europe, Middle East, and Africa), aff'd, 926 F.2d 1215 (D.C. Cir. 1991) (unpublished table decision); Falzone v. Department of the Navy, No. 85-3862, 1988 WL 128474, at **1-2 (D.D.C. Nov. 21, 1986) (finding same with respect to names and addresses of naval officers serving overseas or in classified, sensitive, or readily deployable positions).

[197] See Hopkins v. Department of the Navy, No. 84-1868, 1985 WL 17673, at *2 (D.D.C. Feb. 5, 1985) (ordering disclosure of "names, ranks and official duty stations of servicemen stationed at Quantico" to life insurance salesman); Jafari v. Department of the Navy, 3 Gov't Disclosure Serv. (P-H) ¶ 83,250, at 84,014 (E.D. Va. May 11, 1983) (finding no privacy interest in "duty status" or attendance records of reserve military personnel) (Privacy Act "wrongful disclosure" suit), aff'd on other grounds, 728 F.2d 247 (4th Cir. 1984).

[198] See New England Apple Council v. Donovan, 725 F.2d 139, 142-44 (1st Cir. 1984) (protecting identities of nonsupervisory Inspector General investigators who participated in grand jury investigation of requester) (Exemption 7(C)); Lesar v. United States Dep't of Justice, 636 F.2d 472, 487-88 (D.C. Cir. 1980) (protecting identities of FBI agents) (Exemption 7(C)); Pons v. United States Customs Serv., No. 93-2094, 1998 U.S. Dist. LEXIS 6084, at **13-14 (D.D.C. Apr. 27, 1998) (protecting identities of lower- and mid-level agency employees who worked on asset forfeiture documents); Lampkin v. IRS, No. 1:96-138, 1997 U.S. Dist. LEXIS 2702, at **5-6 (W.D.N.C. Feb. 24, 1997) (protecting identities of IRS employees who, by nature of employment, are subject to harassment and annoyance) (Exemption 7(C)); Lawyers Comm. for Human Rights v. INS, 721 F. Supp. 552, 565, 569 (S.D.N.Y. 1989) (permitting withholding of identities of FBI agents and support staff, who "have a particularly strong interest in maintaining their privacy in the present action due to the divided public opinion and heightened interest in [this] case") (Exemptions 6

(continued...)

**EXEMPTION 6**

sions of these issues under Exemption 2, "Low 2": Trivial Matters, above, and Exemption 7(C), below.)

Purely personal details pertaining to government employees are protectible under Exemption 6.[199] Indeed, courts generally have recognized the sensitivity of information contained in personnel-related files and have accorded protection to the personal details of a federal employee's service.[200] In

---

[198](...continued)
and 7(C)); see also FOIA Update, Vol. VII, No. 3, at 3-4.

[199] See, e.g., American Fed'n of Gov't Employees v. United States, 712 F.2d 931, 932-33 (4th Cir. 1983) (employees' home addresses); Barvick v. Cisneros, 941 F. Supp. 1015, 1020-21 (D. Kan. 1996) (personal information such as home addresses and telephone numbers, social security numbers, dates of birth, insurance and retirement information, reasons for leaving prior employment, and performance appraisals); Plain Dealer Publ'g Co. v. United States Dep't of Labor, 471 F. Supp. 1023, 1028-30 (D.D.C. 1979) (medical, personnel, and related documents of employees filing claims under Federal Employees Compensation Act); Information Acquisition Corp. v. Department of Justice, 444 F. Supp. 458, 463-64 (D.D.C. 1978) ("core" personal information such as marital status and college grades). But see Washington Post, 690 F.2d at 258-65 (holding personal financial information required for appointment as HHS scientific consultant not exempt when balanced against need for oversight of awarding of government grants); Husek v. IRS, No. 90-CV-923, 1991 U.S. Dist. LEXIS 20971, at *1 (N.D.N.Y. Aug. 16, 1991) (holding citizenship, date of birth, educational background, and veteran's preference of federal employees not exempt), aff'd, 956 F.2d 1161 (2d Cir. 1992) (unpublished table decision).

[200] See, e.g., Ripskis, 746 F.2d at 3-4 (names and identifying data contained on evaluation forms of HUD employees who received outstanding performance ratings); Rothman v. USDA, No. 94-8151, slip op. at 6 (C.D. Cal. June 17, 1996) (settlement agreement related to charge of employment discrimination that "could conceivably lead to embarrassment or friction with fellow employees or supervisors"); Resendez v. Runyon, No. 94-434F, slip op. at 6-7 (W.D. Tex. Aug. 11, 1995) (names of applicants for supervisory training who have not yet been accepted or rejected); McLeod v. United States Coast Guard, No. 94-1924, slip op. at 8-10 (D.D.C. July 25, 1995) (Coast Guard officer's evaluation report), summary affirmance granted, No. 96-5071, 1997 U.S. App. LEXIS 6000 (D.C. Cir. Feb. 10, 1997); Putnam v. United States Dep't of Justice, 873 F. Supp. 705, 712-13 (D.D.C. 1995) (names of FBI employees mentioned in "circumstances outside of their official duties," such as attending training classes and as job applicants); Ferri v. United States Dep't of Justice, 573 F. Supp. 852, 862-63 (W.D. Pa. 1983) (FBI background investigation of Assistant United States Attorney); Rosenfeld v. HHS, 3 Gov't Disclosure Serv. (P-H) ¶ 83,082, at 83,617 (D.D.C. Jan. 31, 1983) (names of those on proposed reduction-in-force list), aff'd on other grounds, No. 83-1341 (D.C. Cir. Nov. 11, 1983); Dubin v. Department of the Treasury, 555 F. Supp. 408, 412 (N.D. Ga. 1981) (studies of supervisors' performance and recommendations for performance awards), aff'd, 697 F.2d 1093 (11th Cir. 1983) (unpublished table decision); Metropolitan Life Ins. Co. v. Usery, 426 F. Supp. 150, 167-69 (D.D.C.
(continued...)

**EXEMPTION 6**

addition, the identities of persons who apply but are not selected for federal government employment may be protected.[201] Even suggestions submitted to an Employee Suggestion Program may be withheld to protect employees with whom the suggestions are identifiable from the embarrassment that might occur from disclosure.[202]

Similarly, the courts customarily have extended protection to the identities of mid- and low-level federal employees accused of misconduct, as well as to the details and results of any internal investigations into such allegations of impropriety.[203] The D.C. Circuit has reaffirmed this position in Dunkelberger

---

[200](...continued)
1976) (job performance evaluations, reasons for termination, and affirmative action program reports), aff'd on other grounds sub nom. National Org. for Women v. Social Sec. Admin., 736 F.2d 727 (D.C. Cir. 1984); cf. Professional Review Org., Inc. v. HHS, 607 F. Supp. 423, 427 (D.D.C. 1985) (resume data of proposed staff of government contract bidder).

[201] See Core, 730 F.2d at 948-49 (protecting identities and qualifications of unsuccessful applicants for federal employment); Judicial Watch, Inc. v. Commission on U.S.-Pac. Trade & Inv. Policy, No. 97-0099, slip op. at 23-26 (D.D.C. Sept. 30, 1999) (protecting identities of individuals considered for but not appointed to Commission); Rothman, No. 94-8151, slip op. at 8-9 (C.D. Cal. June 17, 1996) ("Disclosure of information in the applications of persons who failed to get a job may 'embarrass or harm' them."); Barvick, 941 F. Supp. at 1021-22 (protecting all information about unsuccessful federal job applicants because any information about members of "select group" that applies for such jobs could identify them); Voinche v. FBI, 940 F. Supp. 323, 329-30 (D.D.C. 1996) (protecting identities of possible candidates for Supreme Court vacancies), aff'd per curiam, No. 96-5304, 1997 U.S. App. LEXIS 19089 (D.C. Cir. June 19, 1997); Putnam, 873 F. Supp. at 712-13 (protecting identities of FBI personnel who were job candidates); Holland v. CIA, No. 91-1233, 1992 WL 233820, at **13-15 (D.D.C. Aug. 31, 1992) (protecting identity of person not selected as CIA General Counsel); Commodity News Serv. v. Farm Credit Admin., No. 88-3146, 1989 U.S. Dist. LEXIS 8848, at **7-8 (D.D.C. July 31, 1989) (protecting identity of person not selected as receiver of failed bank).

[202] See Matthews v. United States Postal Serv., No. 92-1208-CV-W-8, slip op. at 5 (W.D. Mo. Apr. 15, 1994).

[203] See, e.g., Stern v. FBI, 737 F.2d 84, 94 (D.C. Cir. 1984) (protecting identities of mid-level employees censured for negligence, but requiring disclosure of identity of high-level employee found guilty of serious, intentional misconduct) (Exemption 7(C)); Chamberlain v. Kurtz, 589 F.2d 827, 841-42 (5th Cir. 1979) (names of disciplined IRS agents); Mueller v. United States Dep't of the Air Force, 63 F. Supp. 2d 738, 743-45 (E.D. Va. 1999) (unsubstantiated allegations of prosecutorial misconduct) (Exemptions 6 and 7(C)); Chin v. United States Dep't of the Air Force, No. 97-2176, slip op. at 3-5 (W.D. La. June 24, 1999) (investigations of fraternization) (appeal pending); Lurie v. Department of the Army, 970 F. Supp. 19, 40 (D.D.C. 1997) (identities of HIV researchers who played minor role in possible scientific misconduct), appeal voluntarily dismissed, No. 97-5248 (D.C. Cir. Oct. 22, 1997); McLeod v. Pena, No. 94-
(continued...)

# EXEMPTION 6

v. Department of Justice.[204] It made very clear in Dunkelberger that, even post-Reporters Committee, the D.C. Circuit's decision in Stern v. FBI remains solid guidance for the balancing of the privacy interests of federal employees accused of wrongdoing against the public interest in shedding light on agency activities.[205]

In the early 1980s, a peculiar line of cases began to develop within the

---

[203](...continued) 1924, slip op. at 4-6 (D.D.C. Feb. 9, 1996) (investigation of Coast Guard officer for alleged use of government resources for personal religious activities) (Exemption 7(C)), summary affirmance granted sub nom. McLeod v. United States Coast Guard, No. 96-5071, 1997 U.S. App. LEXIS 6000 (D.C. Cir. Feb. 10, 1997); Cotton v. Adams, 798 F. Supp. 22, 25-28 (D.D.C. 1992) (report of Inspector General's investigation of low-level employees of Smithsonian Institution museum shops); Schonberger v. National Transp. Safety Bd., 508 F. Supp. 941, 944-45 (D.D.C. 1981) (results of complaint by employee against supervisor), aff'd, 672 F.2d 896 (D.C. Cir. 1981) (unpublished table decision); Iglesias v. CIA, 525 F. Supp. 547, 561 (D.D.C. 1981) (agency attorney's response to Office of Professional Responsibility misconduct allegations); see also McCutchen v. HHS, 30 F.3d 183, 187-89 (D.C. Cir. 1994) (protecting identities of both federally and privately employed scientists investigated for possible scientific misconduct) (Exemption 7(C)); cf. Heller v. United States Marshals Serv., 655 F. Supp. 1088, 1091 (D.D.C. 1987) ("extremely strong interest" in protecting privacy of individual who cooperated with internal investigation of possible criminal activity by fellow employees). But see Gannett River States Publ'g Corp. v. Bureau of the Nat'l Guard, No. J91-455, 1992 WL 175235, at **5-6 (S.D. Miss. Mar. 2, 1992) (given previous disclosure of investigative report of helocasting accident, disclosure of actual discipline received would result in "insignificant burden" on soldiers' privacy interests).

[204] 906 F.2d 779, 782 (D.C. Cir. 1990) (upholding FBI's refusal to confirm or deny existence of letters of reprimand or suspension for alleged misconduct by undercover agent) (Exemption 7(C)).

[205] Id. at 781; see also Ford v. West, No. 97-1342, 1998 WL 317561, at **2-3 (10th Cir. June 12, 1998) (protecting information about discipline of coworker and finding that redacted information would not inform public about agency's response to racial harassment claim); Kimberlin v. Department of Justice, 139 F.3d 944, 949 (D.C. Cir.) (withholding information about investigation of staff-level attorney for allegations of unauthorized disclosure of information to media), cert. denied, 525 U.S. 891 (1998); Beck v. Department of Justice, 997 F.2d 1489, 1494 (D.C. Cir. 1993) (upholding agency's refusal to either confirm or deny existence of records concerning alleged wrongdoing of named DEA agents); Hunt v. FBI, 972 F.2d 286, 288-90 (9th Cir. 1992) (protecting contents of investigative file of nonsupervisory FBI agent accused of unsubstantiated misconduct) (Exemption 7(C)); Early v. Office of Prof'l Responsibility, No. 95-0254, slip op. at 2-3 (D.D.C. Apr. 30, 1996) (upholding Office of Professional Responsibility's refusal to confirm or deny existence of complaints or investigations concerning performance of professional duties of one United States district court judge and two Assistant United States Attorneys) (Exemption 7(C)), summary affirmance granted, No. 96-5136, 1997 WL 195523 (D.C. Cir. Mar. 31, 1997).

# EXEMPTION 6

D.C. Circuit regarding the professional or business conduct of an individual. Specifically, the courts began to require the disclosure of information concerning an individual's business dealings with the federal government; indeed, even embarrassing information, if related to an individual's professional life, was subject to disclosure.[206] Similarly, the Court of Appeals for the Sixth Circuit has suggested that the disclosure of a document prepared by a government employee during the course of his employment "will not constitute a clearly unwarranted invasion of personal privacy simply because it would invite a negative reaction or cause embarrassment in the sense that a position is thought by others to be wrong or inadequate."[207]

Although in five later cases the D.C. Circuit reached firm nondisclosure decisions, with no discussion of this consideration at all,[208] it has now clarified that any such lack of privacy an individual has in his business dealings applies

---

[206] See, e.g., Sims v. CIA, 642 F.2d 562, 574 (D.C. Cir. 1980) (names of persons who conducted scientific and behavioral research under contracts with or funded by CIA); Board of Trade v. Commodity Futures Trading Comm'n, 627 F.2d 392, 399-400 (D.C. Cir. 1980) (identities of trade sources who supplied information to CFTC); Cohen v. EPA, 575 F. Supp. 425, 430 (D.D.C. 1983) (names of suspected EPA "Superfund" violators) (Exemption 7(C)); Stern v. SBA, 516 F. Supp. 145, 149 (D.D.C. 1980) (names of agency personnel accused of discriminatory practices).

[207] Schell v. HHS, 843 F.2d 933, 939 (6th Cir. 1988); see also Kurzon v. HHS, 649 F.2d 65, 69 (1st Cir. 1981) (disclosure of names and addresses of unsuccessful grant applicants to National Cancer Institute); Lawyers Comm. for Human Rights, 721 F. Supp. at 569 ("disclosure [of names of State Department's officers and staff members involved in highly publicized case] merely establishes State [Department] employees' professional relationships or associates these employees with agency business") (Exemptions 6 and 7(C)).

[208] Beck, 997 F.2d at 1492 (finding that when no evidence of wrongdoing exists, there is "no public interest to be balanced against the two [DEA] agents' obvious interest in the continued confidentiality of their personnel records"); Dunkelberger, 906 F.2d at 781-82 (recognizing that FBI agent has privacy interest in protecting his employment records against public disclosure); Carter v. United States Dep't of Commerce, 830 F.2d 388, 391-92 (D.C. Cir. 1987) (withholding identities of private-sector attorneys subject to Patent and Trademark Office disciplinary investigations); Stern, 737 F.2d at 91 (recognizing that federal employees have privacy interest in information about their employment); Ripskis, 746 F.2d at 3-4 (identifying "substantial privacy interests" in performance appraisals of federal employees); see also Hill, 77 F. Supp. 2d at 7-8 (shielding business information related to Farmers Home Administration loans to individuals); Professional Review Org., 607 F. Supp. at 427 (finding protectible privacy interests in resumes of professional staff of successful government contract applicant sought by unsuccessful bidder); Hemenway, 601 F. Supp. at 1006 (protecting citizenship information on journalists accredited to attend press briefings). But see Washington Post Co. v. United States Dep't of Justice, 863 F.2d 96, 100-01 (D.C. Cir. 1988) (declining to shield information relating to business judgments and decisions made during development of pharmaceutical under Exemption 7(C)).

## EXEMPTION 6

only to purely "'business judgments and relationships.'"[209] An individual has a very strong interest, however, in allegations of wrongdoing or in the fact that he or she was a target of a law enforcement investigation, even when the alleged wrongdoing occurred in the course of the individual's professional activities.[210] Moreover, under Reporters Committee, an individual doing business with the federal government certainly may have some protectible privacy interest, and such dealings with the government do not alone necessarily implicate a public interest that furthers the purpose of the FOIA.[211]

In applying Exemption 6, it must be remembered that all reasonably segregable, nonexempt portions of requested records must be released.[212]

---

[209] McCutchen, 30 F.3d at 187-88 (quoting Washington Post, 863 F.2d at 100). But see Campaign for Family Farms, 200 F.3d at 1187-89 (finding privacy interest in pork producers' signatures on petition that declared signers' intended voting positions on controversial pork-production issue).

[210] See McCutchen, 30 F.3d at 187-88.

[211] See 489 U.S. at 774 (ruling that information concerning a defense contractor, if such exists, would reveal nothing directly about the behavior of the Congressman with whom he allegedly dealt or about the conduct of the Department of Defense in awarding contracts to his company); accord Halloran v. VA, 874 F.2d 315, 324 (5th Cir. 1989) (finding that public interest in learning about VA's relationship with its contractor is served by release of documents with redactions of identities of company employees suspected of fraud). But cf. Oregon Natural Desert Ass'n, 24 F. Supp. 2d at 1093 (holding privacy interests of cattle owners who violated federal grazing laws outweighed by public interest in knowing how government enforces land-management laws); Commodity News Serv., 1989 U.S. Dist. LEXIS 8848, at *5 (declining to protect personal resume of appointed receiver of failed bank under Exemption 6).

[212] See 5 U.S.C. § 552(b) (1994 & Supp. IV 1998) (sentence immediately following exemptions); see, e.g., Trans-Pac. Policing Agreement v. United States Customs Serv., 177 F.3d 1022, 1026-29 (D.C. Cir. 1999) (imposing upon district court "an affirmative duty to consider the segregability issue sua sponte" even if not raised by requester) (Exemption 4); Kimberlin, 139 F.3d at 949-50 (declining to affirm withholding of entire file pertaining to Office of Professional Responsibility investigation of Assistant United States Attorney without "more specification of the types of material in the file" and specific findings on segregability by district court); Patterson v. IRS, 56 F.3d 832, 838-40 (7th Cir. 1995) (refusing to permit agency to withhold entire document under Exemption 6 if only "portions" are exempt); Krikorian v. Department of State, 984 F.2d 461, 466-67 (D.C. Cir. 1993) ("'The "segregability" requirement applies to all documents and all exemptions in the FOIA.'" (quoting Center for Auto Safety v. EPA, 731 F.2d 16, 21 (D.C. Cir. 1984))) (Exemptions 1, 3, and 5); Judicial Watch, 83 F. Supp. 2d at 109 ("[D]istrict courts are required to consider segregability issues even when the parties have not specifically raised such claims."); Hronek v. DEA, 16 F. Supp. 2d 1260, 1270, 1278 (D. Or. 1998) ("Blanket explanations . . . do not meet FOIA's [segregability] requirements and do not permit the court to make the necessary findings . . . . The govern-
(continued...)

**EXEMPTION 6**

(See the discussions of this issue under Procedural Requirements, "Reasonably Segregable" Obligation, above, and Litigation Considerations, "Reasonably Segregable" Requirements, below.) For example, in Department of the Air Force v. Rose, the Supreme Court ordered the release of case summaries of disciplinary proceedings, provided that personal identifying information was deleted.[213] Likewise, circuit courts of appeals have upheld the nondisclosure of the names and identifying information of employee-witnesses when disclosure would link each witness to a particular previously disclosed statement,[214] have ordered the disclosure of computerized lists of numbers and types of drugs routinely ordered by the congressional pharmacy after deletion of any item identifiable to a specific individual,[215] and have ordered the disclosure of documents concerning disciplined IRS employees, provided that all names and other identifying information were deleted.[216]

Nevertheless, in some situations the deletion of personal identifying information may not be adequate to provide necessary privacy protection. It is significant in this regard that in Department of the Air Force v. Rose, the Su-

---

[212](...continued)
ment fails to indicate why the privacy interests at stake could not be protected simply by redacting particular identifying information."); see also FOIA Update, Vol. XIV, No. 3, at 11-12 ("OIP Guidance: The 'Reasonable Segregation' Obligation").

[213] 425 U.S. at 380-81; see also FOIA Update, Vol. VII, No. 1, at 6; cf. Ripskis, 746 F.2d at 4 (agency voluntarily released outstanding performance rating forms with identifying information deleted); Church of Scientology v. IRS, 816 F. Supp. 1138, 1160 (W.D. Tex. 1993) (ordering agency to protect employees' privacy in handwriting by typing records at requester's expense).

[214] See L&C Marine Transp., Ltd. v. United States, 740 F.2d 919, 923 (11th Cir. 1984) (Exemption 7(C)); cf. Ray, 502 U.S. at 175-76 (concluding that de minimis privacy invasion from release of personal information about unidentified person becomes significant when information is linked to particular individual).

[215] See Arieff v. United States Dep't of the Navy, 712 F.2d 1462, 1468-69 (D.C. Cir. 1983); cf. Dayton Newspapers, 35 F. Supp. 2d at 1035 (ordering release of militarywide medical tort-claims database with "claimants' names, social security numbers, home addresses, home/work telephone numbers and places of employment" redacted), reh'g denied in pertinent part, No. C-97-78, slip op. at 13-14 (S.D. Ohio Mar. 26, 1999); Minntech Corp. v. HHS, No. 92-2720, slip op. at 5 (D.D.C. Nov. 17, 1993) (ordering release of FDA studies concerning mortality rates and use of kidney dialyzers with names, addresses, places of birth, and last four digits of social security numbers deleted); Frets v. Department of Transp., No. 88-404-W-9, 1989 WL 222608, at *5 (W.D. Mo. Dec. 14, 1989) (ordering disclosure of urinalysis reports of air traffic controllers with identities deleted).

[216] See Chamberlain v. Kurtz, 589 F.2d at 841-42; cf. Senate of P.R. v. Department of Justice, No. 84-1829, 1993 U.S. Dist. LEXIS 12162, at **31-32 (D.D.C. Aug. 24, 1993) (ordering release of information concerning cooperating inmate after redaction of identifying details).

# EXEMPTION 6

preme Court specifically admonished that if it were determined on remand that the deletions of personal references were not sufficient to safeguard privacy, the summaries of disciplinary hearings should not be released.[217]

Despite the admonition of the Supreme Court in Rose, though, two courts in 1993 permitted redaction only of information that directly identifies the individuals to whom it pertains. In ordering the disclosure of information pertaining to air traffic controllers who were reinstated in their jobs shortly after their 1982 strike, the Sixth Circuit, in Norwood v. FAA, held that only items that "by themselves" would identify the individual--names, present and pre-removal locations, and social security numbers--could be withheld.[218] It later modified its opinion to state that, although there might be instances in which an agency could justify the withholding of "information other than 'those items which "by themselves" would identify the individuals,'" the FAA in this case had "made no such particularized effort, relying generally on the claim that 'fragments of information' might be able to be pieced together into an identifiable set of circumstances."[219]

Similarly, the District Court for the Northern District of California ordered the disclosure of application packages for candidates for an Air Force graduate degree program with the redaction of only the applicants' names, addresses, and social security numbers.[220] Although the packets regularly contained detailed descriptions of the applicants' education, careers, projects, and achievements, the court concluded that it could not "discern how there is anything more than a 'mere possibility' that [the requester] or others will be able to discern to which particular applicant each redacted application corresponds."[221] And more recently, the District Court for the Southern District of Ohio found "much too speculative" the Air Force's argument that disclosure of medical malpractice settlement figures could permit researchers to "comb local news articles, possibly discovering the identity of claimants and interfering with their privacy rights."[222] That court concluded that "[t]he mere possibility that factual information might be pieced together to supply the 'missing link,' and lead to personal identification, does not exempt such information

---

[217] 425 U.S. at 381.

[218] 993 F.2d 570, 575 (6th Cir. 1993), modified, No. 92-5820 (6th Cir. July 9, 1993), reh'g denied (6th Cir. Aug. 12, 1993).

[219] Norwood v. FAA, No. 92-5820, slip op. at 1 (6th Cir. July 9, 1993).

[220] Manos v. United States Dep't of the Air Force, No. C-92-3986, slip op. at 2-5 (N.D. Cal. Mar. 24, 1993), reconsideration denied (N.D. Cal. Apr. 9, 1993).

[221] Id. at 3; cf. Heat & Frost Insulators & Asbestos Workers, Local 16 v. United States Dep't of the Air Force, No. S92-2177, slip op. at 2-4 (E.D. Cal. Oct. 4, 1993) (ordering release of certified payroll records--with names, addresses, social security numbers, race, and gender deleted--even though number of characteristics revealed and small number of workers would make it likely that knowledgeable person could identify workers).

[222] Dayton Newspapers, Inc. v. Department of the Air Force, No. C-3-97-78, slip op. at 13-14 (S.D. Ohio Mar. 26, 1999).

**EXEMPTION 6**

from disclosure" under Exemption 6.[223]

    The majority of courts, however, take a broader view of the redaction process. For example, to protect those persons who were the subjects of disciplinary actions that were later dismissed, the D.C. Circuit has upheld the nondisclosure of public information contained in such disciplinary files when the redaction of personal information would not be adequate to protect the privacy of the subjects because the requester could easily obtain and compare unredacted copies of the documents from public sources.[224] The key consideration should be whether the information in question can be disclosed without foreseeably harming the privacy interests of the individual involved.[225] When the information in question concerns a small group of individuals who are known to each other and easily identifiable from the details contained in the information, redaction might not adequately protect privacy interests.[226] A

---

[223] Id. at 14.

[224] Carter, 830 F.2d at 391; see also, e.g., Marzen v. HHS, 825 F.2d 1148, 1152 (7th Cir. 1987) (concluding that redaction of "identifying characteristics" would not protect privacy of deceased infant's family because others could ascertain identity and "would learn the intimate details connected with the family's ordeal"); Ligorner v. Reno, 2 F. Supp. 2d 400, 405 (S.D.N.Y. 1998) (finding that redaction of complaint letter to Office of Professional Responsibility would be inadequate to protect identities of individual accused of misconduct and of accuser, because "public could deduce the identities of the individuals whose names appear in the document from its context").

[225] Accord Attorney General's Memorandum for Heads of Departments and Agencies regarding the Freedom of Information Act (Oct. 4, 1993), reprinted in FOIA Update, Vol. XIV, No. 3, at 4-5 (establishing "foreseeable harm" standard governing use of FOIA exemptions); see also Attorney General's Follow-Up Memorandum for Heads of Departments and Agencies regarding the Freedom of Information Act (Sept. 3, 1999), reprinted in FOIA Update, Vol. XIX, No. 4, at 3-5 (reiterating commitment to openness-in-government policy and "foreseeable harm" standard); FOIA Update, Vol. XV, No. 2, at 3.

[226] See, e.g., Alirez v. NLRB, 676 F.2d 423, 428 (10th Cir. 1982) (finding that mere deletion of names and other identifying data concerning small group of co-workers inadequate to protect them from embarrassment or reprisals because requester could still possibly identify individuals) (Exemption 7(C)); Whitehouse v. United States Dep't of Labor, 997 F. Supp. 172, 175 (D. Mass. 1998) (discerning no practical way to redact "personal and unique" medical evaluation reports to prevent identification by knowledgeable reader); Rothman, No. 94-8151, slip op. at 8-9 (C.D. Cal. June 17, 1996) (protecting information in employment applications that pertains to knowledge, skills, and abilities of unsuccessful applicants, because "field of candidates for this particular position (canine officer) is specialized and is limited to about 40 persons who work in same agency and may know each other personally"); McLeod, No. 94-1924, slip op. at 6 (D.D.C. Feb. 9, 1996) (concluding that redaction of investigative memoranda and witness statements would not protect privacy when "community of possible witnesses and investigators is very small"--8 officers and 20 enlisted personnel) (Exemption 7(C)); Barvick, 941

(continued...)

**EXEMPTION 6**

determination of what constitutes identifying information requires both an objective analysis and an analysis "from the vantage point of those familiar with the mentioned individuals."[227] Of course, when a FOIA request is by its very terms limited to privacy-sensitive information pertaining to an identified or identifiable individual, redaction is not possible.[228]

When a request is focused on records concerning an identifiable individual and the records are of a particularly sensitive nature, it may be necessary to go a step further than withholding in full without segregation: It may be necessary to follow special "Glomarization" procedures to protect the "targeted" individual's privacy. (See the discussion of the use and origin of the "Glomar" response under Exemption 1, In Camera Submissions, above.) If a request is formulated in such a way that even acknowledgment of the existence of responsive records would cause harm, then the subject's privacy can be protected only by refusing to confirm or deny that responsive records exist.

---

[226](...continued)
F. Supp. at 1021-22 (protecting all information about unsuccessful federal job applicants because any information about members of "select group" that applies for such job could identify them); Ortiz v. HHS, 874 F. Supp. 570, 573-75 (S.D.N.Y.) (finding that factors such as typestyle, grammar, syntax, language usage, writing style, and mention of facts "that would reasonably be known only by a few persons" could lead to identification of author if anonymous letter were released) (Exemptions 7(C) and 7(D)), aff'd on Exemption 7(D) grounds, 70 F.3d 729 (2d Cir. 1995); Harry v. Department of the Army, No. 92-1654, slip op. at 9 (D.D.C. Sept. 13, 1993) (concluding that redaction of ROTC personnel records impossible because "intimate character" of ROTC corps at requester's university would make records recognizable to him); Frets, No. 88-404-W-9, 1989 WL 222608, at *4 (W.D. Mo. Dec. 14, 1989) (determining that disclosure of handwritten statements would identify those who came forward with information concerning drug use by air traffic controllers even if names redacted); cf. Schulte v. VA, No. 86-6251, slip op. at 11 (S.D. Fla. Feb. 2, 1996) (finding that disclosure of mortality data for cardiac surgery programs compiled by VA as part of medical quality assurance program would identify head cardiac surgeon at VA facilities with only one attending head surgeon) (Exemption 3 (38 U.S.C. § 5705 (1994))).

[227] Cappabianca v. Commissioner, United States Customs Serv., 847 F. Supp. 1558, 1565 (M.D. Fla. 1994).

[228] See, e.g., Hunt, 972 F.2d at 288 (holding that "public availability" of accused FBI agent's name does not defeat privacy protection and "would make redactions of [the agent's name in] the file a pointless exercise"); Mueller, 63 F. Supp. 2d at 744 (noting that when requested documents relate to specific individual, "deleting [her] name from the disclosed documents, when it is known that she was the subject of the investigation, would be pointless"); Chin, No. 97-2176, slip op. at 5 (W.D. La. June 24, 1999) (observing that deletion of identifying information "fails to protect the identity of [the individual] who is named in the FOIA request"); Cotton, 798 F. Supp. at 27 (determining that releasing any portion of documents would "abrogate the privacy interests" when request is for documents pertaining to two named individuals); Schonberger, 508 F. Supp. at 945 (stating that no segregation was possible when request was for one employee's file).

**EXEMPTION 6**

This special procedure is a widely accepted method of protecting, for example, even the mere mention of a person in law enforcement records.[229] (For a more detailed explanation of such privacy "Glomarization," see the discussion under Exemption 7(C), below.)

This procedure is equally applicable to protect an individual's privacy interest in sensitive non-law enforcement records.[230] For example, many agencies maintain an Employee Assistance Program for their employees, operating it on a confidential basis in which privacy is assured. An agency would release neither a list of the employees who participate in such a program nor any other information concerning the program without redacting the names of participants. Logically, then, in responding to a request for any employee assistance counseling records pertaining to a named employee, the agency could protect the privacy of that individual only by refusing to confirm or deny the existence of responsive records.

Similarly, the "Glomarization" approach would be appropriate in responding to a request targeting such matters as a particular citizen's welfare records or the disciplinary records of an employee accused of relatively minor misconduct.[231] Generally, this approach is proper whenever mere acknowledgment of the existence of records would be tantamount to disclosing an actual record the disclosure of which "would constitute a clearly unwarranted invasion of personal privacy."[232] It must be remembered, however, that this response is effective only so long as it is given consistently for a distinct cate-

---

[229] See, e.g., Dunkelberger, 906 F.2d at 782; Antonelli v. FBI, 721 F.2d 615, 617-19 (7th Cir. 1983); see also FOIA Update, Vol. VII, No. 1, at 3.

[230] See FOIA Update, Vol. VII, No. 2, at 2.

[231] See Beck, 997 F.2d at 1493 (refusing to confirm or deny existence of disciplinary records pertaining to named DEA agents) (Exemptions 6 and 7(C)); Dunkelberger, 906 F.2d at 782 (refusing to confirm or deny existence of letter of reprimand or suspension of FBI agent) (Exemption 7(C)); Early, No. 95-0254, slip op. at 2-3 (D.D.C. Apr. 30, 1996) (upholding Office of Professional Responsibility's refusal to confirm or deny existence of complaints or investigations concerning performance of professional duties of one United States district court judge and two Assistant United States Attorneys) (Exemption 7(C)); Cotton, 798 F. Supp. at 26 n.8 (suggesting that "the better course would have been for the Government to refuse to confirm or deny the existence of responsive materials"); Ray v. United States Dep't of Justice, 778 F. Supp. 1212, 1213-15 (S.D. Fla. 1991) (upholding INS's refusal to confirm or deny existence of investigative records concerning INS officer) (Exemptions 6 and 7(C)). But see also Kimberlin, 139 F.3d at 946-47 (regarding "Glomar" response as certainly inapplicable once subject publicly acknowledges investigation).

[232] See FOIA Update, Vol. VII, No. 2, at 2; see also Ray v. United States Dep't of Justice, 558 F. Supp. 226, 228 (D.D.C. 1982) (dicta) (upholding agency's refusal to confirm or deny existence of records pertaining to plaintiff's former attorney), aff'd, 720 F.2d 216 (D.C. Cir. 1983) (unpublished table decision).

# EXEMPTION 7

gory of requests.[233] If it were to become known that an agency gave a "Glomar" response only when records do exist and gave a "no records" response otherwise, then the purpose of this special approach would be defeated.[234]

## EXEMPTION 7

Exemption 7 of the FOIA, as amended, protects from disclosure "records or information compiled for law enforcement purposes, but only to the extent that the production of such law enforcement records or information (A) could reasonably be expected to interfere with enforcement proceedings, (B) would deprive a person of a right to a fair trial or an impartial adjudication, (C) could reasonably be expected to constitute an unwarranted invasion of personal privacy, (D) could reasonably be expected to disclose the identity of a confidential source, including a State, local, or foreign agency or authority or any private institution which furnished information on a confidential basis, and, in the case of a record or information compiled by a criminal law enforcement authority in the course of a criminal investigation, or by an agency conducting a lawful national security intelligence investigation, information furnished by a confidential source, (E) would disclose techniques and procedures for law enforcement investigations or prosecutions, or would disclose guidelines for law enforcement investigations or prosecutions if such disclosure could reasonably be expected to risk circumvention of the law, or (F) could reasonably be expected to endanger the life or physical safety of any individual."[1]

The threshold requirement for Exemption 7 has been modified by Congress twice since the enactment of the FOIA. In its original form, this exemption simply permitted the withholding of "investigatory files compiled for law enforcement purposes except to the extent available by law to a party other than an agency."[2] As such, it was consistently construed to exempt all material contained in an investigatory file, regardless of the status of the underlying investigation or the nature of the documents requested.[3] In 1974, Congress rejected the application of a "blanket" exemption for investigatory files and narrowed the scope of Exemption 7 by requiring that withholding be justified by one of six specified types of harm.[4] Under this revised Exemption 7 structure, an analysis of whether a record was protected by this exemption involved two steps: First, the record had to qualify as an "investigatory record compiled for law enforcement purposes"; second, its disclosure had to be found to threaten one of the enumerated harms of Exemption 7's six sub-

---

[233] See FOIA Update, Vol. VII, No. 1, at 3.

[234] See id.

[1] 5 U.S.C. § 552(b)(7) (1994 & Supp. IV 1998).

[2] Pub. L. No. 90-23, 81 Stat. 54, 55 (1967) (subsequently amended).

[3] See, e.g., Weisberg v. United States Dep't of Justice, 489 F.2d 1195, 1198-1202 (D.C. Cir. 1973).

[4] Pub. L. No. 93-502, 88 Stat. 1561, 1563 (1974) (subsequently amended).

**EXEMPTION 7**

parts.[5]

Congress amended Exemption 7 again in 1986, retaining its basic structure as established by the 1974 FOIA amendments, but significantly broadening the protection given to law enforcement records virtually throughout the exemption and its subparts.[6] The Freedom of Information Reform Act of 1986, often referred to as the 1986 FOIA amendments, modified the threshold requirement of Exemption 7 in several distinct respects; it deleted the word "investigatory" and added the words "or information," such that Exemption 7 protections are now potentially available to all "records or information compiled for law enforcement purposes."[7] And, except for Exemption 7(B) and part of Exemption 7(E), it altered the requirement that an agency demonstrate that disclosure "would" cause the harm each subsection seeks to prevent, to the lesser standard that disclosure "could reasonably be expected to" cause the specified harm.[8]

Exemption 7's expansion to cover "information" compiled for law enforcement purposes extended protection to compilations of information as they are preserved in particular records and also to information within the record itself, so long as that information was compiled for law enforcement purposes.[9] It plainly was designed "to ensure that sensitive law enforcement information is protected under Exemption 7 regardless of the particular format or record in which [it] is maintained."[10] It was intended to avoid use of any mechanical process for determining the purpose for which a physical record was created and to instead establish a focus on the purpose for which in-

---

[5] See FBI v. Abramson, 456 U.S. 615, 622 (1982).

[6] Freedom of Information Reform Act of 1986, Pub. L. No. 99-570, § 1802, 100 Stat. 3207, 3207-48; see United States Dep't of Justice v. Reporters Comm. for Freedom of the Press, 489 U.S. 749, 756 n.9 (1989) (recognizing that the shift from "would constitute" standard to "could reasonably be expected to constitute" standard "represents a congressional effort to ease considerably a Federal law enforcement agency's burden in invoking [Exemption 7]"); Hopkinson v. Shillinger, 866 F.2d 1185, 1222 n.27 (10th Cir. 1989) ("The 1986 amendment[s] broadened the scope of exemption 7's threshold requirement . . . ."); Washington Post Co. v. United States Dep't of Justice, No. 84-3581, 1987 U.S. Dist. LEXIS 14936, at *26 (D.D.C. Sept. 25, 1987) (magistrate's recommendation) (holding that record created by nongovernmental entity independent of Department's investigation but later compiled for that investigation satisfied threshold of Exemption 7 as "broadened" by 1986 FOIA amendments and noting that an "[a]gency's burden of proof in this threshold test has been lightened considerably"), adopted (D.D.C. Dec. 15, 1987), rev'd in part on other grounds & remanded, 863 F.2d 96 (D.C. Cir. 1988).

[7] § 1802, 100 Stat. at 3207-48.

[8] Id.; see Attorney General's Memorandum on the 1986 Amendments to the Freedom of Information Act 9-13 (Dec. 1987) [hereinafter Attorney General's 1986 Amendments Memorandum].

[9] Attorney General's 1986 Amendments Memorandum at 5.

[10] S. Rep. No. 98-221, at 23 (1983).

## EXEMPTION 7

formation contained in a record has been generated.[11] In making their determinations of threshold Exemption 7 applicability, agencies should focus on the content and compilation purpose of each item of information involved, regardless of the overall character of the record in which it happens to be maintained.[12]

This amendment shifted the focus of Exemption 7 from a "record" to an item of "information," building upon the approach to Exemption 7's threshold that was employed by the Supreme Court in FBI v. Abramson,[13] in which the Court pragmatically focused on the "kind of information" contained in the law enforcement records before it. The amendment essentially codified prior judicial determinations that an item of information originally compiled by an agency for a law enforcement purpose does not lose Exemption 7 protection merely because it is maintained in or recompiled into a non-law enforcement record.[14] This properly places "emphasis on the contents, and not the physical format of documents."[15]

---

[11] See id.

[12] See id.; Abramson, 456 U.S. at 630-32; see also Center to Prevent Handgun Violence v. United States Dep't of the Treasury, 981 F. Supp. 20, 22-23 (D.D.C. 1997) (finding that because reports of gun sales are "starting points for investigations of illegal gun trafficking," such reports are "clearly law enforcement records"); cf. Avondale Indus. v. NLRB, No. 94-30729, 1996 WL 420194, at *7 (5th Cir. July 25, 1996) (finding no evidence in record or in case law that union "voting lists were, in any way, compiled for a law enforcement purpose"); Reed v. NLRB, 927 F.2d 1249, 1252 (D.C. Cir. 1991) (expressing skepticism of government's alternative argument that lists of eligible voters in union representative election were compiled for law enforcement purposes).

[13] 456 U.S. at 626.

[14] See id. at 631-32 ("We hold that information initially contained in a record made for law enforcement purposes continues to meet the threshold requirements of Exemption 7 where that recorded information is reproduced or summarized in a new document for a non-law-enforcement purpose."); Lesar v. United States Dep't of Justice, 636 F.2d 472, 487 (D.C. Cir. 1980) (holding that documents from review of previous FBI surveillance meet threshold); see also Assassination Archives & Research Ctr. v. CIA, 903 F. Supp. 131, 132-33 (D.D.C. 1995) (finding that information from criminal investigations recompiled into administrative file to assist FBI in responding to Senate committee hearings "certainly satisfies" threshold requirement), dismissed without prejudice, No. 94-0655 (D.D.C. May 31, 1996); Exner, 902 F. Supp. at 242 n.3 (protecting law enforcement document even if copy is maintained in non-law enforcement file). But cf. Rosenfeld v. United States Dep't of Justice, 57 F.3d 803, 811 (9th Cir. 1995) (affirming district court's refusal to apply Abramson principle to documents originally compiled for law enforcement purposes but "channelized" into non-law enforcement files when principle raised as defense for first time in motion for reconsideration).

[15] Center for Nat'l Sec. Studies v. CIA, 577 F. Supp. 584, 590 (D.D.C. 1983) (applying Abramson to hold duplicate copy of congressional record main-
(continued...)

**EXEMPTION 7**

The scope of Exemption 7 was further expanded by the 1986 FOIA amendments, which removed the requirement that records or information be "investigatory" in character in order to qualify for Exemption 7 protection.[16] Under the former formulations, agencies and courts considering Exemption 7 issues often found themselves struggling with the "investigatory" requirement, which held the potential for disqualifying sensitive law enforcement information from Exemption 7 protection. Courts construing this statutory term generally interpreted it as requiring that the records in question result from specifically focused law enforcement inquiries as opposed to more routine monitoring or oversight of government programs.[17]

The distinction between "investigatory" and "noninvestigatory" law enforcement records, however, was not always so clear.[18] Moreover, the "investigatory" requirement per se was frequently blurred together with the "law enforcement purposes" aspect of the exemption, so that it sometimes became difficult to distinguish between the two.[19] Law enforcement manuals contain-

---

[15](...continued) tained in agency files is not an "agency record"); see, e.g., Weinstein v. HHS, 977 F. Supp. 41, 45 (D.D.C. 1997) (applying Abramson to protect sensitive information under Exemption 5); Exner v. United States Dep't of Justice, 902 F. Supp. 240, 242 & n.3 (D.D.C. 1995) (explaining that documents compiled in course of FBI investigation into "underworld/criminal activities" involving federal antiracketeering statutes "clearly constitute records or information compiled for law enforcement purposes" even if "a copy of the documents might also be found in a non-law enforcement file"), appeal dismissed, No. 95-5411, 1997 WL 68352 (D.C. Cir. Jan. 15, 1997); ISC Group v. DOD, No. 88-631, 1989 WL 168858, at *5 (D.D.C. May 22, 1989) (failing to protect investigatory report prepared by private company expressly for agency criminal investigation pursuant to Exemption 7 "would elevate form over substance and frustrate the purpose of the exemption"); cf. In re Sealed Case, 856 F.2d 268, 271 (D.C. Cir. 1988) (explaining that law enforcement privilege protects testimony about contents of files which would themselves be protected, because public interest in safeguarding ongoing investigations is identical in both situations).

[16] See Attorney General's 1986 Amendments Memorandum at 6.

[17] Compare, e.g., Sears, Roebuck & Co. v. GSA, 509 F.2d 527, 529-30 (D.C. Cir. 1974) (deciding that records submitted for mere monitoring of employment discrimination are not "investigatory"), with Center for Nat'l Policy Review on Race & Urban Issues v. Weinberger, 502 F.2d 370, 373 (D.C. Cir. 1974) (ruling that records of agency review of public schools suspected of discriminatory practices are "investigatory").

[18] Compare, e.g., Gregory v. FDIC, 470 F. Supp. 1329, 1334 (D.D.C. 1979) (finding that bank examination report "typifies routine oversight" and thus is not "investigatory"), rev'd on other grounds, 631 F.2d 896 (D.C. Cir. 1980), with Copus v. Rougeau, 504 F. Supp. 534, 538 (D.D.C. 1980) (holding that compliance review forecast report is "clearly" investigative record).

[19] See, e.g., Rural Hous. Alliance v. USDA, 498 F.2d 73, 81 & n.47 (D.C. Cir. (continued...)

# EXEMPTION 7

ing sensitive information about specific procedures and guidelines followed by an agency were held not to qualify as "investigatory records" because they had not originated in connection with any specific investigation, even though they clearly had been compiled for law enforcement purposes.[20]

The 1986 FOIA amendments put an end to such troublesome distinctions and broadened the potential sweep of the exemption's coverage.[21] The protections of Exemption 7's six subparts were made available to all records or information compiled for "law enforcement purposes."[22] Even records generated pursuant to routine agency activities that previously could not be regarded as "investigatory" now qualify for Exemption 7 protection when those activities involve a law enforcement purpose. This includes records generated for general law enforcement purposes that do not necessarily relate to specific investigations. Records such as law enforcement manuals, for example, which previously were found unqualified for Exemption 7 protection only because they were not "investigatory" in character,[23] now should readily satisfy the exemption's threshold requirement.[24] The sole issue remaining is the application of the phrase "law enforcement purposes" in the context of the amended Exemption 7.

Few cases have addressed the parameters of this less demanding threshold standard under the 1986 FOIA amendments, so it is useful to examine the cases interpreting the identical "law enforcement purposes" language under the prior version of this exemption, as all law enforcement records found qualified for exemption protection under the pre-1986 language of Ex-

---

[19](...continued) 1974).

[20] See Sladek v. Bensinger, 605 F.2d 899, 903 (5th Cir. 1979) (holding Exemption 7 inapplicable to DEA manual that "was not compiled in the course of a specific investigation"); Cox v. United States Dep't of Justice, 576 F.2d 1302, 1310 (8th Cir. 1978) (same).

[21] See Attorney General's 1986 Amendments Memorandum at 7.

[22] Id.

[23] See, e.g., Sladek, 605 F.2d at 903; Cox, 576 F.2d at 1310.

[24] See Attorney General's 1986 Amendments Memorandum at 7; see, e.g., PHE, Inc. v. Department of Justice, 983 F.2d 248, 249, 251 (D.C. Cir. 1993) (holding portions of FBI's Manual of Investigative Operations and Guidelines properly withheld pursuant to Exemption 7(E)); Center for Nat'l Sec. Studies v. INS, No. 87-2068, 1990 WL 236133, at *6 (D.D.C. Dec. 19, 1990) (reiterating that documents which relate to INS's law enforcement procedures meet threshold requirement as "purpose in preparing these documents relat[es] to legitimate concerns that federal immigration laws have been or may be violated"). But see Cowsen-El v. United States Dep't of Justice, 826 F. Supp. 532, 533 (D.D.C. 1992) (explaining that threshold not met by Bureau of Prisons' guidelines covering how prison officials should count and inspect prisoners).

# EXEMPTION 7

emption 7 undoubtedly remain so.[25] The "law" to be enforced within the meaning of the term "law enforcement purposes" includes both civil and criminal statutes,[26] as well as those statutes authorizing administrative (i.e., regu-

---

[25] See Rural Hous. Alliance, 498 F.2d at 80-82 (finding that threshold of Exemption 7 met if investigation focuses directly on specific illegal acts which could result in civil or criminal penalties); Southam News v. INS, 674 F. Supp. 881, 887 (D.D.C. 1987) (finding that, based upon pre-1986 language, INS Lookout Book used to assist in exclusion of inadmissible aliens satisfies threshold requirement); U.S. News & World Report v. Department of the Treasury, No. 84-2303, 1986 U.S. Dist. LEXIS 27634, at *5 (D.D.C. Mar. 26, 1986) (reasoning that records pertaining to acquisition of two armored limousines for President meet threshold test where activities involved investigation of how best to safeguard President); Nader v. ICC, No. 82-1037, slip op. at 10-11 (D.D.C. Nov. 23, 1983) (deciding that disbarment proceeding meets Exemption 7 threshold because it is "quasi-criminal" in nature).

[26] See, e.g., Detroit Free Press, Inc. v. Department of Justice, 73 F.3d 93, 96 (6th Cir. 1996) (ruling that United States Marshals Service's mug shots of federal indictees were compiled for law enforcement purposes); Beard v. Espy, No. 94-16748, 1995 U.S. App. LEXIS 38269, at *2 (9th Cir. Dec. 11, 1995) (protecting complaint letter and notes compiled during criminal investigation involving USDA loans); Ortiz v. HHS, 70 F.3d 729, 730 (2d Cir. 1995) (holding that unsigned, unsolicited letter used to launch criminal investigation by Social Security Administration meets threshold for law enforcement purposes, although no charges filed against target); Koch v. United States Postal Serv., No. 93-1487, 1993 U.S. LEXIS 26130, at *1 (8th Cir. Oct. 8, 1993) (determining that report initiated by allegation that postal service employee threatened to bring grenade to work was compiled for law enforcement purposes); Rural Hous. Alliance, 498 F.2d at 81 & n.46 (holding that "character of the statute violated would rarely make a material distinction, because the law enforcement purposes . . . include both civil and criminal purposes"); Williams v. IRS, 479 F.2d 317, 318 (3d Cir. 1973) (affirming that data compiled in connection with audit of individual's income tax liability was compiled for law enforcement purposes); Goldstein v. Office of Indep. Counsel, No. 87-2028, 1999 WL 570862, at **8-9 (D.D.C. July 29, 1999) (magistrate's recommendation) (determining that the investigation of Lyndon LaRouche for possible criminal violations was for a legitimate law enforcement purpose even if the investigation "went nowhere"); Abraham & Rose, P.L.C. v. United States, 36 F. Supp. 2d 955, 956 (E.D. Mich. 1998) (affirming that records compiled by IRS to collect outstanding tax debts satisfy Exemption 7 threshold); Ligorner v. Reno, 2 F. Supp. 2d 400, 404 (S.D.N.Y. 1998) (holding that letter used during Office of Professional Responsibility investigation into allegations of misconduct by Department of Justice attorneys was compiled for law enforcement purposes); Rosenglick v. IRS, No. 97-747-18A, 1998 WL 773629, at *6 (M.D. Fla. Mar. 10, 1998) (holding that records compiled by IRS during its "ongoing criminal investigation [for] tax years 1990 through 1996" satisfy threshold); Lewis v. United States Postal Serv., No. 96-3467, slip op. at 1 (D. Md. Apr. 30, 1997) (noting that whether complaint that triggered investigation was solicited or not, the "records were clearly compiled for law enforcement"); Solar Sources v. United States, No. 96-0772, slip op. at 5 (S.D. Ind. Mar. 10, 1997) (holding that criminal antitrust investigation of explosives industry was "indisputably"

(continued...)

**EXEMPTION 7**

latory) proceedings.[27] In addition to federal law enforcement, Exemption 7

---

[26](...continued)
compiled for law enforcement purposes), aff'd, 142 F.3d 1033 (7th Cir. 1998); Hoffman v. Brown, No. 1:96-53, slip op. at 4 (W.D.N.C. Nov. 26, 1996) (finding that information compiled by Veterans Administration Police canvassing plaintiff's neighbors regarding "alleged criminal activity of plaintiff at home" meets threshold), aff'd, 145 F.3d 1324 (4th Cir. 1998) (unpublished table decision); Mafvadia v. Caplinger, No. 95-3542, 1996 WL 592742, at *2 (E.D. La. Oct. 11, 1996) (finding that both civil and criminal investigations of possible violations of immigration laws satisfy threshold); Cappabianca v. Commissioner, United States Customs Serv., 847 F. Supp. 1558, 1565 (M.D. Fla. 1994) (stating that records of internal investigation focusing specifically on alleged acts that could result in civil or criminal sanctions were compiled for law enforcement purposes); Stone v. Defense Investigative Serv., 816 F. Supp. 782, 787 (D.D.C. 1993) (protecting foreign counterintelligence investigation and investigation into possible violation of Interstate Transportation of Stolen Property Act), appeal dismissed for failure to prosecute, No. 93-5178 (D.C. Cir. Mar. 11, 1994); Buffalo Evening News, Inc. v. United States Border Patrol, 791 F. Supp. 386, 394 (W.D.N.Y. 1992) (reasoning that USBP form meets threshold because it is generated in investigations of violations of federal immigration law). But see Allnutt v. United States Dep't of Justice, No. Y98-1722, 2000 U.S. Dist. LEXIS 4060, at *12 (D. Md. Mar. 6, 2000) (magistrate's recommendation) (holding that bankruptcy proceeding is not law enforcement matter and records compiled for it do not meet threshold of Exemption 7).

[27] See, e.g., Center for Nat'l Policy Review, 502 F.2d at 373 (holding that administrative determination has "salient characteristics of 'law enforcement' contemplated" by Exemption 7 threshold requirement); McErlean v. Department of Justice, No. 97-7831, 1999 WL 791680, at *8 (S.D.N.Y. Sept. 30, 1999) (stating that "it is well-settled that documents compiled by the INS in connection with the administrative proceedings authorized by the Immigration and Naturalization Act are documents compiled for 'law enforcement purposes'"); General Elec. Co. v. EPA, 18 F. Supp. 2d 138, 143-44 (D. Mass. 1998) (reasoning that EPA decision to classify a site as contaminated "is not an enforcement action at all but rather ordinary informal rulemaking," which would ordinarily not meet Exemption 7 threshold, though in this case it did because "it is entirely reasonable for the agency to anticipate that enforcement proceedings are in the offing"); Johnson v. DEA, No. 97-2231, 1998 U.S. Dist. LEXIS 9802, at *9 (D.D.C. June 25, 1998) (reiterating that "law being enforced may be . . . regulatory"); Straughter v. HHS, No. 94-0567, slip op. at 4 (S.D. W. Va. Mar. 31, 1995) (magistrate's recommendation) (finding threshold met by records compiled by HHS's Office of Civil Rights in course of investigation of handicap discrimination as violation of Rehabilitation Act), adopted (S.D. W. Va. Apr. 17, 1995); Kay v. FCC, 867 F. Supp. 11, 16-18 (D.D.C. 1994) (explaining that FCC's statutory authority to revoke licenses or deny license applications is qualifying law enforcement purpose); Aircraft Gear Corp. v. NLRB, No. 92-C-6023, slip op. at 10 (N.D. Ill. Mar. 14, 1994) (stating that documents created in connection with NLRB unfair labor practices cases and union representation case meet threshold); Ehringhaus v. FTC, 525 F. Supp. 21, 22-23 (D.D.C. 1980) (deciding that documents prepared as part of FTC investigation
(continued...)

**EXEMPTION 7**

applies to records compiled to enforce state law,[28] as well as foreign law.[29] However, if the agency lacks the authority to pursue a particular law enforcement matter, Exemption 7 protection may not be afforded.[30]

---

[27](...continued)
into advertising practices of cigarette manufacturers meet threshold).

[28] See Hopkinson, 866 F.2d at 1222 n.27 (holding that Exemption 7 applies "to FBI laboratory tests conducted at the request of local law enforcement authorities"); Franklin v. DEA, No. 97-1225, slip op. at 7 (S.D. Fla. June 26, 1998) (stating that documents compiled for "federal or state" law enforcement purposes meet threshold); Code v. FBI, No. 95-1892, 1997 WL 150070, at *5 (D.D.C. Mar. 26, 1997) (finding that documents compiled in connection with FBI's efforts to assist local police in homicide investigations meet threshold); Butler, 888 F. Supp. at 180, 182 (finding that Air Force personnel background report--requested by local law enforcement agency for its investigation into murder--was compiled for law enforcement purposes); Kuffel v. Bureau of Prisons, 882 F. Supp. 1116, 1124 (D.D.C. 1995) (ruling that information from state law enforcement agency investigating various state crimes qualifies); Wojtczak v. United States Dep't of Justice, 548 F. Supp. 143, 146-48 (E.D. Pa. 1982) ("This Court must therefore interpret the statute as written and concludes that Exemption 7 applies to all law enforcement records, federal, state, or local, that lie within the possession of the federal government"); see also Shaw v. FBI, 749 F.2d 58, 64 (D.C. Cir. 1984) (explaining that authorized federal investigation into commission of state crime constitutes valid criminal law enforcement investigation, which qualifies confidential source-provided information for protection under second half of Exemption 7(D)); Rojem v. United States Dep't of Justice, 775 F. Supp. 6, 10 (D.D.C. 1991) (determining that material provided to FBI by state law enforcement agency for assistance in that state agency's criminal investigation is "compiled for law enforcement purposes"), appeal dismissed for failure to timely file, No. 92-5088 (D.C. Cir. Nov. 4, 1992).

[29] See, e.g., Bevis v. Department of State, 801 F.2d 1386, 1388 (D.C. Cir. 1986) (no distinction between foreign and domestic enforcement purposes in language of statute); cf. Schwarz v. United States Dep't of Justice, No. 95-2162, slip op. at 6 (D.D.C. May 31, 1996) (information compiled by INTERPOL at behest of foreign government), summary affirmance granted, No. 96-5183 (D.C. Cir. Oct. 23, 1996); Donovan v. FBI, 579 F. Supp. 1111, 1119-20 (S.D.N.Y. 1983) (FBI investigation undertaken and laboratory tests performed in support of foreign government's efforts to identify and prosecute perpetrators of crimes), vacated on other grounds on motion for reconsideration, 579 F. Supp. 1124 (S.D.N.Y.), appeal dismissed as moot, 751 F.2d 368 (2d Cir. 1984); see also FOIA Update, Vol. V, No. 2, at 6-7.

[30] See, e.g., Rosenfeld, 57 F.3d at 808-09 (finding no law enforcement purpose when "documents all support a conclusion that . . . any asserted purpose for compiling these documents was pretextual"); Weissman v. CIA, 565 F.2d 692, 696 (D.C. Cir. 1977) (ruling that CIA's "full background check within the United States of a citizen who never had any relationship with the CIA is not authorized and the law enforcement exemption is accordingly unavailable"); Miscavige v. IRS, No. 91-3721, slip op. at 2, 5 (C.D. Cal. Dec. 9, 1992) (finding
(continued...)

## EXEMPTION 7

Additionally, "[b]ackground security investigations by governmental units which have authority to conduct such functions"[31] have been held by most courts to meet the threshold tests under the succeeding formulations of Exemption 7.[32] Personnel investigations of government employees also are compiled for law enforcement purposes if they focus on "specific and potentially unlawful activity by particular employees" of a civil or criminal nature.[33]

---

[30](...continued)
no law enforcement purpose for post-1986 documents because IRS investigation concluded in 1985); cf. Kuzma v. IRS, 775 F.2d 66, 69 (2d Cir. 1985) (declaring that unauthorized or illegal investigative tactics may not be shielded from public by use of FOIA exemptions). But cf. Pratt v. Webster, 673 F.2d 408, 423 (D.C. Cir. 1982) ("Exemption 7 refers to purposes rather than methods"; questionable methods do not defeat exemption's coverage when law enforcement is primary purpose); Hrones v. CIA, 685 F.2d 13, 19 (1st Cir. 1982) (legality of agency's actions in national security investigation falls outside scope of judicial review in FOIA action).

[31] S. Conf. Rep. No. 93-1200, at 12 (1974), reprinted in 1974 U.S.C.C.A.N. 6267, 6291.

[32] See, e.g., Mittleman v. OPM, 76 F.3d 1240, 1241-43 (D.C. Cir. 1996) (OPM background investigation); Rosenfeld, 57 F.3d at 809 ("FBI government appointment investigations"); Melius v. National Indian Gaming Comm'n, No. 92-2210, 1999 U.S. Dist. LEXIS 17537, at **6, 15 (D.D.C. Nov. 3, 1999) ("suitability investigations" for gaming contracts); Assassination Archives, 903 F. Supp. at 132 (FBI "background investigations"); Bostic v. FBI, No. 1:94 CV 71, slip op. at 2, 11 (W.D. Mich. Dec. 16, 1994) (FBI pre-employment investigation); Doe v. United States Dep't of Justice, 790 F. Supp. 17, 20-21 (D.D.C. 1992) (background investigation of individual conditionally offered employment as attorney); Miller v. United States, 630 F. Supp. 347, 349 (E.D.N.Y. 1986) (USIA background security investigation of federal job applicant); Koch v. Department of Justice, 376 F. Supp. 313, 315 (D.D.C. 1974) (background investigations fall within Exemption 7 because they involve determinations as to whether applicants engaged in criminal conduct which would disqualify them for federal employment); see also FOIA Update, Vol. VI, No. 4, at 6.

[33] Stern v. FBI, 737 F.2d 84, 89 (D.C. Cir. 1984); see also Ford v. West, No. 97-1342, 1998 U.S. App. LEXIS 12640, at **2, 6 (10th Cir. June 12, 1998) (finding that investigation into alleged racial harassment meets threshold); Kimberlin v. Department of Justice, 139 F.3d 944, 947-48 (D.C. Cir.) (concluding that investigation "conducted in response to and focused upon a specific, potentially illegal release of information by a particular, identified official" satisfies threshold), cert. denied, 525 U.S. 891 (1998); Strang v. Arms Control & Disarmament Agency, 864 F.2d 859, 862 (D.C. Cir. 1989) (characterizing agency investigation into employee violation of national security laws as law enforcement); Jackson v. Federal Bureau of Prisons, No. 87-5186, slip op. at 4 (D.C. Cir. Jan. 5, 1988) (finding that prison investigation into allegation that prison official improperly disclosed inmate's personal file does not satisfy threshold without showing that investigation focused on law violation rather than internal personnel matters); Mueller v. Department of the Air

(continued...)

**EXEMPTION 7**

By contrast, "an agency's general monitoring of its own employees to ensure compliance with the agency's statutory mandate and regulations" does not satisfy Exemption 7's threshold requirement.[34]

---

[33](...continued)
Force, 1999 U.S. Dist. LEXIS 14331, at *7 (E.D. Va. Sept. 16, 1999) (holding that investigation into prosecutorial misconduct was for law enforcement purposes because "'an agency investigation of its own employees is for law enforcement purposes . . . if it focuses directly on specifically alleged illegal acts, illegal acts of a particular identified official, [and] acts which could, if proved, result in civil or criminal sanctions'" (quoting Stern, 737 F.2d at 89)); Hayes, 1998 U.S. Dist. LEXIS 14120, at **11-12 (explaining that records of "internal agency investigations are considered to be compiled for 'law enforcement purposes' when the investigations focus on specifically alleged acts, which, if proved, could amount to violations of civil or criminal law"); Ligorner, 2 F. Supp. 2d at 402-04 (finding threshold satisfied by investigation into allegations of misconduct by Justice Department attorneys); Lurie v. Department of the Army, 970 F. Supp. 19, 36 (D.D.C. 1997) (explaining that threshold met because investigation focused directly on specifically alleged illegal acts of identified officials (citing Rural Hous. Alliance, 498 F.2d at 81)), appeal voluntarily dismissed, No. 97-5248 (D.C. Cir. Oct. 22, 1997); Linn v. United States Dep't of Justice, No. 92-1406, slip op. at 46 (D.D.C. Aug. 22, 1995) ("[D]ocuments compiled for purposes of internal discipline of employees are not compiled for law enforcement purposes . . . , [b]ut such internal monitoring of employees may be 'for law enforcement purposes' if the focus of the investigation concerns acts that could result in civil or criminal sanctions." (quoting Stern, 737 F.2d at 89)), appeal voluntarily dismissed, No. 97-5122 (D.C. Cir. July 14, 1997); Housley v. United States Dep't of the Treasury, 697 F. Supp. 3, 5 (D.D.C. 1988) (reiterating that investigation concerning misconduct by special agent which, if proved, could have resulted in federal civil or criminal sanctions qualifies as law enforcement); cf. In re Dep't of Investigation of N.Y., 856 F.2d 481, 485 (2d Cir. 1988) (explaining that law enforcement privilege applies in discovery context when investigation served "dual purposes of evaluating conduct in office and enforcing the criminal law").

[34] Stern, 737 F.2d at 89 (dictum) (reminding that "it is necessary to distinguish between those investigations conducted 'for a law enforcement purpose' and those in which an agency, acting as the employer, simply supervises its own employees"); see also Patterson v. IRS, 56 F.3d 832, 837-38 (7th Cir. 1995) (holding that "general citation to entire body of statutes contained in United States Code under the heading 'Equal Employment Opportunity statutes'" does not establish law enforcement purpose; agency must "distinguish between internal investigations conducted for law enforcement purposes and general agency monitoring"); Rural Hous. Alliance, 498 F.2d at 81 (distinguishing between agency oversight of performance of employees and investigations focusing on specific illegal acts of employees); Varville v. Rubin, No. 3:96CV00629, 1998 WL 681438, at *14 (D. Conn. Aug. 18, 1998) (explaining that threshold not met by report discussing possible ethical violations and prohibited personnel practices because inquiry "more closely resembles an employer supervising its employees than an investigation for law enforcement purposes"); Lurie, 970 F. Supp. at 36 ("The general internal monitoring by an agency of its own employees is not shielded from public scrutiny under Ex-
(continued...)

**EXEMPTION 7**

In determining whether a document was "compiled for law enforcement purposes" under Exemption 7, the courts have generally distinguished between agencies with both law enforcement and administrative functions and those whose principal function is criminal law enforcement.[35] An agency whose functions are "mixed" usually has to show that the records at issue involved the enforcement of a statute or regulation within its authority.[36] Courts have additionally required that the records be compiled for "adjudicative or enforcement purposes."[37]

---

[34](...continued)
emption 7, because 'protection of all such internal monitoring under Exemption 7 would devastate FOIA.'" (quoting Stern, 737 F.2d at 89)); Fine v. United States Dep't of Energy, 823 F. Supp. 888, 907-08 (D.N.M. 1993) (ruling that threshold met by agency with both administrative and law enforcement functions when documents compiled during investigation of specific allegations and not as part of routine oversight); Cotton v. Adams, 798 F. Supp. 22, 25 (D.D.C. 1992) (holding agency's internal investigation of its own employees satisfies threshold only if it focuses directly on illegal acts which could result in criminal or civil sanctions); Greenpeace USA, Inc. v. EPA, 735 F. Supp. 13, 15 (D.D.C. 1990) (threshold not met for internal investigation into whether employee complied with agency conflict-of-interest regulations). But cf. Nagel v. HEW, 725 F.2d 1438, 1441 (D.C. Cir. 1984) (holding that the "employer's determination whether a federal employee is performing his job adequately constitutes an authorized law enforcement activity" within meaning of subsection (e)(7) of the Privacy Act of 1974, 5 U.S.C. § 552a (1994 & Supp. IV 1998)).

[35] See Attorney General's 1986 Amendments Memorandum at 7.

[36] See Lewis v. IRS, 823 F.2d 375, 379 (9th Cir. 1987) (holding threshold met when IRS "had a purpose falling within its sphere of enforcement authority in compiling particular documents"); Birch v. United States Postal Serv., 803 F.2d 1206, 1210-11 (D.C. Cir. 1986) (explaining that threshold was met because enforcement of laws regarding use of mails falls within statutory authority of Postal Service); Church of Scientology v. United States Dep't of the Army, 611 F.2d 738, 748 (9th Cir. 1979) (remanding to Naval Investigative Service for it to show that investigation involved enforcement of statute or regulation within its authority); Irons v. Bell, 596 F.2d 468, 473 (1st Cir. 1979) (determining that mixed-function agency must demonstrate purpose falling within its sphere of enforcement authority); see also Church of Scientology Int'l v. IRS, 995 F.2d 916, 919 (9th Cir. 1993) ("This court has clearly held that the IRS has the 'requisite law enforcement mandate'" through its enforcement provisions of the federal tax code (quoting Lewis, 823 F.2d at 379)); Philadelphia Newspapers, Inc. v. HHS, 69 F. Supp. 2d 63, 67 (D.D.C. 1999) (holding that investigative records created in response to specific allegations of Medicare fraud by physicians at a teaching hospital were compiled for law enforcement purposes) (appeal pending); Coulter v. Reno, No. 98-35170, 1998 WL 658835, at *1 (9th Cir. Sept. 17, 1998) (holding threshold met by records of Navy criminal investigation into allegations of lewd and lascivious conduct by Navy personnel).

[37] Rural Hous. Alliance, 498 F.2d at 81; see Pacific Energy Inst. v. IRS, No.
(continued...)

# EXEMPTION 7

The Supreme Court in 1990 resolved a conflict in lower court decisions[38] by decisively holding that information not initially obtained or generated for law enforcement purposes may still qualify under Exemption 7 if it is subsequently compiled for a valid law enforcement purpose at any time prior to "when the Government invokes the Exemption."[39] Rejecting the distinction

---

[37](...continued)
94-36172, 1996 WL 14244, at *1 (9th Cir. Jan. 16, 1996) (accepting that investigations involving enforcement of Internal Revenue Code satisfy threshold); Becker v. IRS, 34 F.3d 398, 407 (7th Cir. 1994) (holding that IRS has "law enforcement purpose in investigating potential illegal tax protester activity"); Church of Scientology, 995 F.2d at 919 (finding that IRS Exempt Organizations Division "performs law enforcement function by enforcing provisions of the federal tax code"); Means v. Segal, No. 97-1301, slip op. at 12 (D.D.C. Mar. 18, 1998) (magistrate's recommendation) (holding that Federal Labor Relations Authority is charged with statutory responsibility to conduct investigations related to unfair labor practices and records related to this duty meet threshold), adopted (D.D.C. Apr. 15, 1998); aff'd on other grounds, No. 98-5170 (D.C. Cir. Oct. 6, 1998); cf. Reed, 927 F.2d at 1252 (noting "skepticism" of government's alternative argument regarding application of Exemption 7(C)'s threshold to lists of names and addresses of eligible voters in union representative election compiled for NLRB compliance purposes).

[38] Compare Crowell & Moring v. DOD, 703 F. Supp. 1004, 1009-10 (D.D.C. 1989) (holding that solicitation and contract bids may be protected), and Gould Inc. v. GSA, 688 F. Supp. 688, 691 (D.D.C. 1988) (finding that routine audit reports may be protected), with John Doe Corp. v. John Doe Agency, 850 F.2d 105, 109 (2d Cir. 1988) (ruling that routine audit reports are not protectable), rev'd & remanded, 493 U.S. 146 (1989), and Hatcher v. United States Postal Serv., 556 F. Supp. 331, 335 (D.D.C. 1982) (holding that routine contract negotiation and oversight material is not protectible).

[39] John Doe Agency v. John Doe Corp., 493 U.S. 146, 153 (1989); see also KTVY-TV v. United States, 919 F.2d 1465, 1469 (10th Cir. 1990) (per curiam) (applying John Doe Agency to hold that information regarding personnel interview conducted before investigation commenced and later recompiled for law enforcement purposes satisfied Exemption 7 threshold); Kansi v. United States Dep't of Justice, 11 F. Supp. 2d 42, 44 (D.D.C. 1998) (explaining that once documents become assembled for law enforcement purposes, "all [such] documents qualify for protection under Exemption 7 regardless of their original source"); Hayes v. United States Dep't of Labor, No. 96-1149, 1998 U.S. Dist. LEXIS 14120, at *12 (S.D. Ala. June 10, 1998) (magistrate's recommendation) ("Records that are incorporated into investigatory files also qualify . . . even though those records may not have been created originally for law enforcement purposes."), adopted (S.D. Ala. Aug. 10, 1998); Perdue Farms, Inc. v. NLRB, No. 2:96-27, 1997 U.S. Dist. LEXIS 14579, at *37 (E.D.N.C. Aug. 5, 1997) (magistrate's recommendation) (stating that language of statute "contains no requirement that compilation be effected at specific time" (citing John Doe Agency, 493 U.S. at 153)), adopted (E.D.N.C. Jan. 20, 1998); Butler v. Department of the Air Force, 888 F. Supp. 174, 179-80, 182 (D.D.C. 1995) (Air Force personnel background report--requested by local law enforcement agency for its investigation into murder--held compiled for law enforcement

(continued...)

**EXEMPTION 7**

between documents originally compiled or obtained for law enforcement purposes and those later assembled for such purposes, the Court held that the term "compiled" must be accorded its ordinary meaning--which includes "materials collected and assembled from various sources or other documents"-- and it found that the plain meaning of the statute contains "no requirement that the compilation be effected at a specific time."[40]

In the case of criminal law enforcement agencies, the courts have accorded the government varying degrees of special deference when considering whether their records meet the threshold requirement of Exemption 7.[41] Indeed, the First, Second, Sixth, and Eighth Circuit Courts of Appeals have adopted a per se rule that qualifies all "investigative" records of criminal law enforcement agencies for protection under Exemption 7.[42] Other courts,

---

[39](...continued) purposes), aff'd per curiam, No. 96-5111 (D.C. Cir. May 6, 1997).

[40] John Doe Agency, 493 U.S. at 153.

[41] Compare, e.g., Pratt, 673 F.2d at 418 (declaring that "a court can accept less exacting proof from [a law enforcement agency]"), with Kuehnert v. FBI, 620 F.2d 662, 667 (8th Cir. 1980) (holding that "Exemption 7 extends to all investigative files of a criminal law enforcement agency").

[42] See First Circuit: Curran v. Department of Justice, 813 F.2d 473, 475 (1st Cir. 1987) (holding that investigatory records of law enforcement agencies are "inherently" compiled for law enforcement purposes); Irons, 596 F.2d at 474-76 (holding that "investigatory records of law enforcement agencies are inherently records compiled for 'law enforcement purposes' within the meaning of Exemption 7"); Second Circuit: Halpern v. FBI, 181 F.3d 279, 296 (2d Cir. 1999) (applying rule that when records are compiled in course of law enforcement investigation, purpose of investigation is not subject of review by court); Ferguson v. FBI, 957 F.2d 1059, 1070 (2d Cir. 1992) (finding that there is "no room for [a] district court's inquiry into whether the FBI's asserted law enforcement purpose was legitimate"); Williams v. FBI, 730 F.2d 882, 884-85 (2d Cir. 1984) (ruling that records of a law enforcement agency are given "absolute protection" even if "records were compiled in the course of an unwise, meritless or even illegal investigation"); Sixth Circuit: Detroit Free Press, 73 F.3d at 96 (holding that mug shots created for law enforcement purpose, applying per se rule adopted previously in Jones v. FBI, 41 F.3d 238, 246 (6th Cir. 1994) (adopting per se rule, FBI is "archetypical" federal law enforcement agency; "concern about overbroad withholding should therefore be addressed by proper scrutiny of the claimed exemptions themselves and not by use of a blunt instrument at the threshold")); Eighth Circuit: Miller v. USDA, 13 F.3d 260, 263 (8th Cir. 1993) (tardiness in working on case does not eliminate law enforcement purpose); Kuehnert, 620 F.2d at 666 (FBI need not show law enforcement purpose of particular investigation as precondition to invoking Exemption 7); see also Arenberg v. DEA, 849 F.2d 579, 581 (11th Cir. 1988) (suggesting that courts should be "hesitant" to reexamine law enforcement agency's decision to investigate if there is plausible basis for agency's decision); Binion v. United States Dep't of Justice, 695 F.2d 1189, 1193-94 (9th Cir. 1983) (holding that "a fortiori" approach is appropriate when FBI pardon

(continued...)

**EXEMPTION 7**

while according significant deference to criminal law enforcement agencies, have held that an agency must demonstrate some specific nexus between the records and a proper law enforcement purpose.[43]

The existing standard for review of criminal records in the Court of Appeals for the District of Columbia Circuit is somewhat more stringent than the

---

[42](...continued)
investigation was "clearly legitimate").

[43] See, e.g., Davin v. United States Dep't of Justice, 60 F.3d 1043, 1056 (3d Cir. 1995) (applying "adaptation" of two-pronged rational nexus test and holding FBI's "simple recitation of statutes, orders and public laws" insufficient; agency must describe nexus between "each document" and particular investigation), on remand, No. 92-1122, slip op. at 11-13 (W.D. Pa. Apr. 9, 1998) (finding that government demonstrated connection between target and "potential violation of law or security risk" for each investigation), aff'd, 176 F.3d 471, 471 (3d Cir. 1999) (unpublished table decision); Kern v. FBI, No. 94-0208, slip op. at 9 (C.D. Cal. Sept. 14, 1998) (rejecting FBI's Vaughn Index as inadequate because it did not demonstrate nexus between duty to investigate espionage and documents sought); Franklin, No. 97-1225, slip op. at 7-8 (S.D. Fla. June 26, 1998) (reiterating need for "nexus between the records and the enforcement of federal or state law"); Grine v. Coombs, No. 95-342, 1997 U.S. Dist. LEXIS 19578, at **14-18 (W.D. Pa. Oct. 10, 1997) (holding that "proper test is the 'rational nexus' test" and determining that investigatory reports triggered by complaints of dumping hazardous waste satisfy test); Crompton v. DEA, No. 95-8771, slip op. at 12-13 (C.D. Cal. Mar. 25, 1997) (stating that agencies with "clear law enforcement mandate such as the DEA need only establish a 'rational nexus' between enforcement of a federal law and the document for which a law enforcement exemption is claimed"; holding that there is such nexus between DEA's "law enforcement duties to manage the national narcotics intelligence system" and information withheld); Marriott Employees' Fed. Credit Union v. National Credit Union Admin., No. 96-478-A, slip op. at 5-7 (E.D. Va. Dec. 24, 1996) (finding that documents compiled by NCUA pursuant to administration of Federal Credit Union Act satisfy standard); Blanton v. United States Dep't of Justice, No. 93-2398, slip op. at 5-8 (W.D. Tenn. July 14, 1994) (finding that information concerning validity of plaintiff's counsel's purported license to practice law does not meet threshold because law licenses are a matter of public record; government failed to prove records were "compiled for a law enforcement purpose"); Rosenfeld v. United States Dep't of Justice, 761 F. Supp. 1440, 1445-48 (N.D. Cal. 1991) (explaining that FBI investigation of Free Speech Movement "was begun in good faith and with a plausible basis," but ceased to have "colorable claim [of rationality] as the evidence accumulated" and became "a case of routine monitoring . . . for intelligence purposes"; date at which FBI's initial law enforcement-related suspicions were "demonstrably unfounded" was "cut-off point for the scope of a law enforcement purpose" under Exemption 7), aff'd in pertinent part, rev'd in part & remanded, 57 F.3d 803 (9th Cir. 1995); Friedman v. FBI, 605 F. Supp. 306, 321 (N.D. Ga. 1984) (finding that FBI was "'gathering information with the good faith belief that the subject may violate or has violated federal law' rather than 'merely monitoring the subject for purposes unrelated to enforcement of federal law'" (quoting Lamont v. Department of Justice, 475 F. Supp. 761, 770 (S.D.N.Y. 1979))).

## EXEMPTION 7

per se rule discussed above. The D.C. Circuit held in Pratt v. Webster that records generated as part of a counterintelligence program of questionable legality which was part of an otherwise clearly authorized law enforcement investigation met the threshold requirement for Exemption 7 and rejected the per se approach.[44] Instead, it adopted a two-part test for determining whether the threshold for Exemption 7 has been met: (1) whether the agency's investigatory activities that give rise to the documents sought are related to the enforcement of federal laws or to the maintenance of national security; and (2) whether the nexus between the investigation and one of the agency's law enforcement duties is based on information sufficient to support at least a colorable claim of rationality.[45]

---

[44] 673 F.2d at 416 n.17.

[45] Id. at 420-21; see, e.g., Campbell v. United States Dep't of Justice, 164 F.3d 20, 32 (D.C. Cir. 1998) (requiring nexus between agency activities and law enforcement duties, finds that most FBI files of 1960s investigations of James Baldwin, believed to be associated with subversive organizations, meet threshold but elaborating that law enforcement agency may not simply rely on file names to satisfy threshold); Summers v. United States Dep't of Justice, 140 F.3d 1077, 1083 (D.C. Cir. 1998) (to show nexus, FBI must link names redacted from former FBI Director J. Edgar Hoover's telephone logs to law enforcement activities); Quiñon v. FBI, 86 F.3d 1222, 1228-29 (D.C. Cir. 1996) (reiterating that agency's basis for connection between object of investigation and asserted law enforcement duty cannot be pretextual or wholly unbelievable and remanding because FBI's affidavits found insufficient to show that Pratt nexus test satisfied when only specific fact cited is filing of motion; "filing of a non-fraudulent pleading cannot, taken alone, form the basis for a legitimate obstruction of justice investigation"); Computer Prof'ls for Soc. Responsibility v. United States Secret Serv., 72 F.3d 897, 902, 904 (D.C. Cir. 1996) (investigation into allegations of telecommunications fraud satisfies threshold, as do documents pertaining to police breakup of public meeting of computer hackers club); King v. United States Dep't of Justice, 830 F.2d 210, 229 (D.C. Cir. 1987) (supporting the Pratt two-prong test by stating that agency must identify particular individual/incident as object of its investigation and specify connection between individual/incident and possible security risk or violation of federal law and that agency must then demonstrate that relationship is based on information sufficient to support colorable claim of rationality); Founding Church of Scientology v. Smith, 721 F.2d 828, 829 n.1 (D.C. Cir. 1983) (holding that "Pratt is the law of this circuit insofar as it interprets the threshold requirement of exemption 7."); Keenan v. Department of Justice, No. 94-1909, slip op. at 12-15 (D.D.C. Mar. 2, 1997) (reiterating Pratt and finding agency's use of "ambiguous phrase 'of investigatory interest'" does not "demonstrate a nexus between the investigation and one of the FBI's law enforcement duties"), renewed motion for summary judgment denied on other grounds (D.D.C. Dec. 16, 1997); Wichlacz v. United States Dep't of Interior, 938 F. Supp. 325, 330 (E.D. Va. 1996) (observing that "investigative activities giving rise to the compilation of the records must be related to the enforcement of federal law, and there must be a rational connection between the investigative activities and the agency's law enforcement duties"), aff'd, 114 F.3d 1178 (4th Cir. 1997) (unpublished table decision); Western Journalism Ctr. v. Office of the Indep. Counsel, 926 F. Supp. 189, 191 (D.D.C. 1996) (holding that (continued...)

**EXEMPTION 7**

Since the removal of the word "investigatory" from the threshold requirement of Exemption 7 in 1986, the D.C. Circuit has had few opportunities to reconsider the Pratt test, a portion of which expressly requires a nexus between requested records and an investigation.[46] In Keys v. United States Department of Justice, however, the D.C. Circuit modified the language of the Pratt test to reflect those amendments and to require that an agency demonstrate the existence of a nexus "between [its] activity" (rather than its investigation) "and its law enforcement duties."[47] Although not specifically relying

---

[45](...continued)
documents generated by FBI's and Park Police's criminal investigations of "all aspects of the [Deputy White House Counsel Vincent] Foster death" and made part of Independent Counsel's overall investigation satisfy Pratt test), summary affirmance granted, No. 96-5178, 1997 WL 195516 (D.C. Cir. Mar. 11, 1997); Exner, 902 F. Supp. at 242-43 (finding that investigatory activities were based on legitimate concern that federal laws were being violated and that activities connected rationally to target).

[46] See, e.g., King, 830 F.2d at 229 n.141 (dictum) (holding that 1986 FOIA amendments did not "qualif[y] the authority of Pratt" test).

[47] 830 F.2d 337, 340 (D.C. Cir. 1987); see also Rochon v. Department of Justice, No. 88-5075, slip op. at 3 (D.C. Cir. Sept. 14, 1988) (holding that agency must demonstrate nexus between its compilation of records and its law enforcement duties); Hall v. United States Dep't of Justice, 63 F. Supp. 2d 14, 16 (D.D.C. 1999) (holding that Davin "is not persuasive authority" because "Third Circuit standard is more permissive" than established D.C. Circuit standard (referring to Campbell, 164 F.3d at 32)); Code, 1997 WL 150070, at **4-5 (reiterating requirement for nexus between activities and law enforcement duties); Wickline v. FBI, No. 92-1189, 1994 WL 549756, at *2 (D.D.C. Sept. 30, 1994) (finding requirement for "nexus between the agency's activity and its law enforcement duties" met when FBI compiled requested information through its investigation of series of murders involving organized crime); Abdullah v. FBI, No. 92-0356, slip op. at 3 (D.D.C. Aug. 10, 1992) (holding that "law enforcement agencies such as the FBI must show that the records at issue are related to the enforcement of federal laws and that the law enforcement activity was within the law enforcement duty of that agency."); Beck v. United States Dep't of Justice, No. 87-3356, slip op. at 26-27 (D.D.C. Nov. 7, 1989) ("[D]efendants must merely establish that the nexus between the agency's activity and its law enforcement duty" is based on a "colorable claim of rationality."). But see Simon v. Department of Justice, 980 F.2d 782, 783 (D.C. Cir. 1992) (stating that agency must demonstrate nexus between investigation and one of its law enforcement duties (citing Pratt, 673 F.2d at 420-21)); Reiter v. DEA, No. 96-0378, 1997 WL 470108, at *3 (D.D.C. Aug. 13, 1997) (describing how nexus "requires an agency to establish a connection between the individual under investigation and a possible violation of a federal law"), summary affirmance granted, No. 97-5246 (D.C. Cir. Mar. 3, 1998); Keenan, No. 94-1909, slip op. at 12-15 (D.D.C. Mar. 2, 1997) (explaining that nexus not established because it was "unclear as to whether an investigation was conducted at all"); Assassination Archives & Research Ctr. v. United States Dep't of Justice, No. 92-2193, 1993 WL 763547, at **6-7 (D.D.C. Apr. 29, 1993) (declaring that government must establish that investigation
(continued...)

## EXEMPTION 7

on the amended statutory language, the D.C. Circuit in Keys held that records compiled solely because the subject had a known affiliation with organizations that were strongly suspected of harboring Communists met the Exemption 7 threshold.[48] As no appellate decision has yet employed the modified Pratt test adopted by Keys, the impact of this change in the threshold is not yet fully realized.

Even under the test enunciated in Pratt,[49] significant deference has been accorded criminal law enforcement agencies.[50] Nevertheless, the D.C. Circuit has indicated in Pratt and elsewhere that if an investigation is shown to have been in fact conducted for an improper purpose, Exemption 7 may not be applicable to the records of that investigation.[51]

---

[47](...continued) related to enforcement of federal law raises colorable claim rationally related to one or more of agency's law enforcement duties).

[48] 830 F.2d at 341-42.

[49] 673 F.2d at 421 (A court should be "hesitant to second-guess a law enforcement agency's decision to investigate if there is a plausible basis" for its decision.).

[50] See, e.g., Rosenfeld, 57 F.3d at 808 (Pratt's rational nexus test requires "degree of deference to a law enforcement agency's decision to investigate"); King, 830 F.2d at 230-32 (subject's close association with "individuals and organizations . . . of investigative interest to the FBI" and consequent investigation of subject during the McCarthy era for possible violation of national security laws meets threshold in the absence of evidence supporting the existence of an improper purpose); Simon v. United States Dep't of Justice, 752 F. Supp. 14, 18 (D.D.C. 1990) (Given the subject's prior pacifist activities, it was not "irrational or implausible for [FBI]--operating in the climate existing during the early 1950's--[to conduct] what appears to have been a brief criminal investigation into the possibility that the plaintiff harbored Communist affiliations."), aff'd on other grounds, 980 F.2d 782 (D.C. Cir. 1992). But see Summers, 140 F.3d at 1082, 1084 (suggesting that deference to agency may be overcome when records, such as J. Edgar Hoover's "official and confidential" (O&C) files, were "not readily available to field agents" and "contain[ed] scandalous material on public figures to be used for political blackmail"), on remand, No. 87-3168, slip op. at 3 & n.4 (D.D.C. Apr. 19, 2000) (finding, after in camera review of four thousand pages of the O&C files, that the FBI "ha[d] adequately established" that Exemption 7's "threshold requirement" was met).

[51] See Pratt, 673 F.2d at 420-21 (reiterating that Exemption 7 is not intended to "include investigatory activities wholly unrelated to law enforcement agencies' legislated functions of preventing risks to the national security and violations of the criminal laws and of apprehending those who do violate the laws"); see also Quiñon, 86 F.3d at 1228-29 (explaining that agency's connection between object of investigation and asserted law enforcement duty cannot be pretextual or wholly unbelievable and holding FBI affidavits insufficient to demonstrate legitimate basis for obstruction of justice charge; "cryptic
(continued...)

# EXEMPTION 7(A)

Courts have yet to fully test the boundaries of Exemption 7's threshold after the broadening of the 1986 FOIA amendments. Under them, all federal agencies should consider which records of a noninvestigatory character may qualify for protection because they relate sufficiently to a law enforcement mission assigned to the agency.[52] Agencies may now be able to apply Exemption 7 protection, for example, to law enforcement manuals, program oversight reports, and other similar documents because of their relationship to the agency's law enforcement mission.[53] The full effects of these amendments will be realized only upon the case-by-case identification of particular items of noninvestigatory law enforcement information the disclosure of which could cause one of the "foreseeable harms" specified in Exemption 7's six subparts.[54]

## EXEMPTION 7(A)

The first subpart of Exemption 7, Exemption 7(A), authorizes the withholding of "records or information compiled for law enforcement purposes, but only to the extent that production of such law enforcement records or information . . . could reasonably be expected to interfere with enforcement proceedings."[1] The Freedom of Information Reform Act of 1986 lessened the showing of harm required from a demonstration that release "would interfere with" to "could reasonably be expected to interfere with" enforcement proceedings.[2] The courts have recognized repeatedly that the change in the lan-

---

[51](...continued) allusion to 'certain events' is especially problematic" when events "may be nothing more sinister than . . . criticisms"); Shaw, 749 F.2d at 63 (stating that "mere existence of a plausible criminal investigatory reason to investigate would not protect the files of an inquiry explicitly conducted . . . for purposes of harassment"); Lesar, 636 F.2d at 487 (questioning whether records that were generated after investigation "wrongly strayed beyond its original law enforcement scope" would meet threshold test for Exemption 7).

[52] See PHE, 983 F.2d at 249, 251, 253 (holding portions of FBI's Manual of Investigative Operations and Guidelines properly withheld pursuant to Exemption 7(E)).

[53] See Attorney General's 1986 Amendments Memorandum at 8-9.

[54] Accord Attorney General's Memorandum for Heads of Departments and Agencies regarding the Freedom of Information Act (Oct. 4, 1993), reprinted in FOIA Update, Vol. XIV, No. 3, at 4-5 (establishing "foreseeable harm" standard governing use of FOIA exemptions); Attorney General's Follow-Up Memorandum for Heads of Departments and Agencies regarding the Freedom of Information Act (Sept. 3, 1999), reprinted in FOIA Update, Vol. XIX, No. 4, at 3-5 (reiterating same).

[1] 5 U.S.C. § 552(b)(7)(A) (1994 & Supp. IV 1998).

[2] Pub. L. No. 99-570, § 1802, 100 Stat. 3207, 3207-48; see Attorney General's Memorandum on the 1986 Amendments to the Freedom of Information Act 10 (Dec. 1987) [hereinafter Attorney General's 1986 Amendments Memorandum].

## EXEMPTION 7(A)

guage for this exemption effectively broadens its protection.[3]

Determining the applicability of this Exemption 7 subsection thus requires a two-step analysis focusing on (1) whether a law enforcement proceeding is pending or prospective and (2) whether release of information about it could reasonably be expected to cause some articulable harm.[4] The courts

---

[3] See Manna v. United States Dep't of Justice, 51 F.3d 1158, 1164 n.5 (3d Cir. 1995) (stating that Congress amended statute to "relax significantly the standard for demonstrating interference"); Alyeska Pipeline Serv. v. EPA, 856 F.2d 309, 311 n.18 (D.C. Cir. 1988) (treating improper reliance of lower court on pre-amendment version of Exemption 7(A) as irrelevant as it simply "required EPA to meet a higher standard than FOIA now demands"); Wright v. OSHA, 822 F.2d 642, 647 (7th Cir. 1987) (explaining that amended language creates broad protection); Curran v. Department of Justice, 813 F.2d 473, 474 n.1 (1st Cir. 1987) ("[T]he drift of the changes is to ease--rather than to increase--the government's burden in respect to Exemption 7(A)."); Gould Inc. v. GSA, 688 F. Supp. 689, 703 n.33 (D.D.C. 1988) (The "1986 amendments relaxed the standard of demonstrating interference with enforcement proceedings."); see also Spannaus v. United States Dep't of Justice, 813 F.2d 1285, 1288 (4th Cir. 1987) (explaining that "agency's showing under the amended statute, which in part replaces 'would' with 'could reasonably be expected to,' is to be measured by a standard of reasonableness, which takes into account the 'lack of certainty in attempting to predict harm'" (quoting S. Rep. No. 98-221, 98th Cong., 1st Sess. 24 (1983)); cf. John Doe Agency v. John Doe Corp., 493 U.S. 146, 157 (1989) (taking "practical approach" when confronted with interpretation of FOIA and applying "workable balance" between interests of public in greater access and needs of government to protect certain kinds of information); United States Dep't of Justice v. Reporters Comm. for Freedom of the Press, 489 U.S. 749, 777-78 n.22 (1989) (declaring that Congress intended identical modification of language of Exemption 7(C) to provide greater "flexibility in responding to FOIA requests for law enforcement records" and replaced "a focus on the effect of a particular disclosure" with a "standard of reasonableness" which supports "categorical" approach to documents of similar character); Allen v. DOD, 658 F. Supp. 15, 23 (D.D.C. 1986) (parallel change of language of Exemption 7(C) created "broader protection" than available under former language).

[4] See, e.g., NLRB v. Robbins Tire & Rubber Co., 437 U.S. 214, 224 (1978) (holding that government must show how records "would interfere with a pending enforcement proceeding"); Manna, 51 F.3d at 1164 ("To fit within Exemption 7(A), the government must show that (1) a law enforcement proceeding is pending or prospective and (2) release of the information could reasonably be expected to cause some articulable harm."); Campbell v. HHS, 682 F.2d 256, 259 (D.C. Cir. 1982) (stating that agency must demonstrate interference with pending enforcement proceeding); Scheer v. United States Dep't of Justice, 35 F. Supp. 2d 9, 13 (D.D.C. 1999) (stating that agency "must first prove" existence of law enforcement proceeding and "must next prove" harm) (appeal pending); Franklin v. United States Dep't of Justice, No. 97-1225, slip op. at 7 (S.D. Fla. June 15, 1998) (magistrate's recommendation) (two-part test), adopted (S.D. Fla. June 26, 1998), aff'd, 189 F.3d 485 (11th Cir. 1999) (unpublished table decision); Hamilton v. Weise, No. 95-1161, 1997

(continued...)

# EXEMPTION 7(A)

have held that the mere pendency of enforcement proceedings is an inadequate basis for the invocation of Exemption 7(A); the government must also establish that some distinct harm could reasonably be expected to result if the record or information requested were disclosed.[5] For example, the Court of Appeals for the District of Columbia Circuit has held that the fact that a judge in a criminal trial specifically delayed disclosure of certain documents until

---

[4](...continued)
U.S. Dist. LEXIS 18900, at *25 (M.D. Fla. Oct. 1, 1997) (same); Butler v. Department of the Air Force, 888 F. Supp. 174, 183 (D.D.C. 1995) (same), aff'd per curiam, No. 96-5111 (D.C. Cir. May 6, 1997); accord Attorney General's Follow-Up Memorandum for Heads of Departments and Agencies regarding the Freedom of Information Act (Sept. 3, 1999) [hereinafter Attorney General Reno's Follow-Up FOIA Memorandum], reprinted in FOIA Update, Vol. XIX, No. 4, at 3-5 (reiterating that objective of maximum responsible disclosure of government information is best served when agencies apply "foreseeable harm" standard); Attorney General's Memorandum for Heads of Departments and Agencies regarding the Freedom of Information Act (Oct. 4, 1993) [hereinafter Attorney General Reno's FOIA Memorandum], reprinted in FOIA Update, Vol. XIV, No. 3, at 4-5 (establishing "foreseeable harm" standard governing use of FOIA exemptions); see also FOIA Update, Vol. XV, No. 2, at 3 (observing that harm element is "already built into" Exemption 7(A)).

[5] See, e.g., Neill v. Department of Justice, No. 93-5292, 1994 WL 88219, at *1 (D.C. Cir. Mar. 9, 1994) (explaining that conclusory affidavit lacked specificity of description necessary to ensure meaningful review of agency's Exemption 7(A) claims); Miller v. USDA, 13 F.3d 260, 263 (8th Cir. 1993) (holding that government must make specific showing of why disclosure of documents could reasonably be expected to interfere with enforcement proceedings); Crooker v. ATF, 789 F.2d 64, 65-67 (D.C. Cir. 1986) (finding that agency failed to demonstrate that disclosure would interfere with enforcement proceedings); Grasso v. IRS, 785 F.2d 70, 77 (3d Cir. 1986) (stating that "government must show, by more than conclusory statement, how the particular kinds of investigatory records requested would interfere with a pending enforcement proceeding"); Scheer, 35 F. Supp. 2d at 13-14 (finding that agency's assertion that disclosure to requester would harm its investigation "is belied" by agency's full disclosure to target of investigation; therefore, agency "has not met its burden of offering clear proof that disclosure . . . would have interfered with a law enforcement proceeding within the meaning of FOIA [E]xemption 7(A)"); Jefferson v. Reno, No. 96-1284, 1997 U.S. Dist. LEXIS 3064, at *10 (D.D.C. Mar. 17, 1997) (ruling that neither agency's declaration nor its checklist "describes how the release of any or all responsive documents could reasonably be expected to interfere with these enforcement proceedings"); American Civil Liberties Union Found. v. United States Dep't of Justice, 833 F. Supp. 399, 407 (S.D.N.Y. 1993) (explaining that possibility of interference was not so evident when investigations referred to closed or "generalized class" of cases; accordingly, government must provide sufficient information for court to decide whether disclosure will actually threaten similar, ongoing enforcement proceedings); Abdullah v. FBI, No. 92-356, slip op. at 4-5 (D.D.C. Aug. 10, 1992) (emphasizing that no "wholesale" withholding is allowed); see also Accuracy in Media v. FBI, No. 97-2107, slip op. at 5 (D.D.C. Mar. 31, 1999) (noting that agency's declaration "states in detail the problems that would arise should such information be released").

**EXEMPTION 7(A)**

the end of the trial is alone insufficient to establish interference with that ongoing proceeding.[6]

It is beyond question that Exemption 7(A) is temporal in nature and is not intended to "endlessly protect material simply because it [is] in an investigatory file."[7] Thus, as a general rule, Exemption 7(A) may be invoked so long as the law enforcement proceeding involved remains pending,[8] or so long as an enforcement proceeding is fairly regarded as prospective[9] or as preventa-

---

[6] North v. Walsh, 881 F.2d 1088, 1100 (D.C. Cir. 1989) (stating that standard is "whether disclosure can reasonably be expected to interfere in a palpable, particular way" with enforcement proceedings).

[7] Robbins Tire, 437 U.S. at 230; see Solar Sources, Inc. v. United States, 142 F.3d 1033, 1037 (7th Cir. 1998) (stating that "Exemption 7(A) does not permit the Government to withhold all information merely because that information was compiled for law enforcement purposes"); Dickerson v. Department of Justice, 992 F.2d 1426, 1431 (6th Cir. 1993) (reiterating that when investigation is over and purpose of it has expired, information should be disclosed); Hamilton, 1997 U.S. Dist. LEXIS 18900, at **25-26 (declaring that Exemption 7(A) was enacted "mainly to overrule judicial decisions that prohibited disclosure of investigatory files in 'closed' cases"); cf. Kay v. FCC, 976 F. Supp. 23, 37-38 (D.D.C. 1997) (explaining that agency "may continue to invoke Exemption 7(A) to withhold the requested documents until . . . [proceeding] comes to a conclusion"), aff'd, 172 F.3d 919 (D.C. Cir. 1998) (unpublished table decision).

[8] See, e.g., Seegull Mfg. Co. v. NLRB, 741 F.2d 882, 886-87 (6th Cir. 1984) (finding that NLRB administrative practice of continuing to assert Exemption 7(A) for six-month "buffer period" after termination of proceedings "arbitrary and capricious"); Barney v. IRS, 618 F.2d 1268, 1273-74 (8th Cir. 1980) (explaining that once enforcement proceedings are "either concluded or abandoned, exemption 7(A) will no longer apply"); Western Journalism Ctr. v. Office of the Indep. Counsel, 926 F. Supp. 189, 192 (D.D.C. 1996) ("By definition until his or her work is completed, an Independent Counsel's activities are ongoing . . . and once the task is completed . . . all the records . . . are required to be turned over to the Archivist and at that time would be subject to FOIA requests."), aff'd, No. 96-5178, 1997 WL 195516 (D.C. Cir. Mar. 11, 1997); Linn v. United States Dep't of Justice, No. 92-1406, 1995 WL 417810, at *25 (D.D.C. June 6, 1995) (ruling that Exemption 7(A) is not applicable when there is "no evidence before the Court that any investigation exists"), appeal voluntarily dismissed, No. 97-5122 (D.C. Cir. July 14, 1997); Kilroy v. NLRB, 633 F. Supp. 136, 142, 143 (S.D. Ohio 1985) (holding that Exemption 7(A) "applies only when a law enforcement proceeding is pending"), aff'd, 823 F.2d 553 (6th Cir. 1987) (unpublished table decision); Antonsen v. United States Dep't of Justice, No. K-82-008, slip op. at 9-10 (D. Alaska Mar. 20, 1984) ("It is difficult to conceive how the disclosure of these materials could have interfered with any enforcement proceedings" after a criminal defendant had been tried and convicted.).

[9] See, e.g., Manna, 51 F.3d at 1165 (ruling that when "prospective criminal or civil (or both) proceedings are contemplated," information is protected

(continued...)

# EXEMPTION 7(A)

tive.[10]

Although Exemption 7(A) is temporal in nature, it nevertheless remains viable throughout the duration of long-term investigations.[11] For example, in 1993 it was held applicable to the FBI's continuing investigation into the 1975

---

[9](...continued)
from disclosure); Scheer, 35 F. Supp. 2d at 13 (discussing necessity of "concrete prospective law enforcement proceeding"); General Elec. Co. v. EPA, 18 F. Supp. 2d 138, 144 (D. Mass. 1998) (explaining that "it is entirely reasonable for the [a]gency to anticipate that enforcement proceedings are in the offing"); Kay, 976 F. Supp. at 38 ("Moreover, if the proceeding is not pending, an agency may continue to invoke Exemption 7(A) so long as the proceeding is regarded as prospective."); Foster v. United States Dep't of Justice, 933 F. Supp. 687, 692 (E.D. Mich. 1996) (holding that disclosure "could impede ongoing government investigation (and prospective prosecution)"); Cudzich v. INS, 886 F. Supp. 101, 106 (D.D.C. 1995) (stating that "where disclosure of information would cause impermissible harm to a concrete prospective law enforcement proceeding, such a situation is also within the protective scope of Exemption 7(A)"); Richman v. United States Dep't of Justice, No. 90-C-19, slip op. at 13 (W.D. Wis. Feb. 2, 1994) (finding that files pertaining to "pending and prospective" criminal enforcement proceedings are protected); Southam News v. INS, 674 F. Supp. 881, 887 (D.D.C. 1987) (recognizing that Service Lookout Book, containing "names of violators, alleged violators and suspected violators," is protected as proceedings clearly are at least prospective against each violator); Marzen v. HHS, 632 F. Supp. 785, 805 (N.D. Ill. 1985) (concluding that Exemption 7(A) prohibits disclosure of law enforcement records when release "would interfere with enforcement proceedings, pending, contemplated, or in the future."), aff'd, 825 F.2d 1148 (7th Cir. 1987); Ehringhaus v. FTC, 525 F. Supp. 21, 22-23 (D.D.C. 1980) (stating that Exemption 7(A) applies when enforcement proceeding is "in prospect").

[10] See, e.g., Moorefield v. United States Secret Serv., 611 F.2d 1021, 1026 (5th Cir. 1980) (holding that material pertaining to "Secret Service investigations carried out pursuant to the Service's protective function"--to prevent harm to protectees--is eligible for Exemption 7(A) protection).

[11] See Antonelli v. United States Parole Comm'n, No. 93-0109, slip op. at 3-4 (D.D.C. Feb. 23, 1996) (reiterating that courts repeatedly find "lengthy, delayed or even dormant investigations" covered by Exemption 7(A) and holding that release of eight-year-old investigative file "would interfere with possible proceedings"); Butler v. United States Dep't of Justice, No. 86-2255, 1994 WL 55621, at *24 (D.D.C. Feb. 3, 1994) (stating that agency "leads" were not stale simply because several years old while indictee remains at large), appeal dismissed voluntarily, No. 94-5078 (D.C. Cir. Sept. 8, 1994); Africa Fund v. Mosbacher, No. 92-289, 1993 WL 183736, at *4 (S.D.N.Y. May 26, 1993) (finding that documents that would interfere with lengthy or delayed investigation fall within protective ambit of Exemption 7(A)); see also Davoudlarian v. Department of Justice, No. 93-1787, 1994 WL 423845, at **2-3 (4th Cir. Aug. 15, 1994) (holding that records of open investigation of 1983 murder remained protectible).

## EXEMPTION 7(A)

disappearance of Jimmy Hoffa.[12] Even when an investigation is dormant, Exemption 7(A) has been held to be applicable because of the possibility that the investigation could lead to a "prospective law enforcement proceeding."[13] The "prospective" proceeding, however, must be a concrete possibility, rather than a mere hypothetical one.[14]

Further, even after an enforcement proceeding is closed, courts have ruled that the continued use of Exemption 7(A) may be proper in certain instances. One such instance involves "related" proceedings, i.e., those instances in which information from a closed law enforcement proceeding will be used again in other pending or prospective law enforcement proceedings--for example, when charges are pending against additional defendants[15] or

---

[12] Dickerson, 992 F.2d at 1432 (affirming district court's conclusion that FBI's investigation into 1975 disappearance of Jimmy Hoffa remained ongoing and therefore was still "prospective" law enforcement proceeding).

[13] See, e.g., National Pub. Radio v. Bell, 431 F. Supp. 509, 514-15 (D.D.C. 1977) (explaining that although investigation into death of nuclear-industry worker Karen Silkwood is "dormant," it "will hopefully lead to a 'prospective law enforcement proceeding'" and that disclosure "presents the very real possibility of a criminal learning in alarming detail of the government's investigation of his crime before the government has had the opportunity to bring him to justice"); see also FOIA Update, Vol. V, No. 2, at 6.

[14] See American Civil Liberties Union Found., 833 F. Supp. at 407 (finding that possibility of interference not so evident for investigative documents related to generalized categories of cases; agency must show that disclosure would actually threaten similar, ongoing enforcement proceedings); Badran v. United States Dep't of Justice, 652 F. Supp. 1437, 1440 (N.D. Ill. 1987) (relying on pre-amendment language, court held that mere possibility that person mentioned in file might some day violate law was insufficient to invoke Exemption 7(A)); National Pub. Radio, 431 F. Supp. at 514 (holding that "dormant" investigation "is nonetheless an 'active' one," which justifies Exemption 7(A) applicability); see also 120 Cong. Rec. S9329 (daily ed. May 30, 1974) (statement of Sen. Hart).

[15] See Solar Sources, 142 F.3d at 1040 (explaining that although government has "closed" cases against certain defendants by obtaining plea agreements and convictions, withholding is proper because information "compiled against them is part of the information" in ongoing cases against other targets); New England Med. Ctr. Hosp. v. NLRB, 548 F.2d 377, 385-86 (1st Cir. 1976) (finding Exemption 7(A) applicable when "closed file is essentially contemporary with, and closely related to, the pending open case" against another defendant; applicability of exemption does not hinge on "open" or "closed" label agency places on file); Cucci v. DEA, 871 F. Supp. 508, 512 (D.D.C. 1994) (finding protection proper when information pertains to "multiple intermingled investigations and not just the terminated investigation" of subject); Engelking v. DEA, No. 91-0165, slip op. at 6 (D.D.C. Nov. 30, 1992) (reasoning that information in inmate's closed file was properly withheld because fugitive discussed in requester's file is still at large; explaining that records from closed file can relate to law enforcement efforts which are still active or in

(continued...)

**EXEMPTION 7(A)**

when additional charges are pending against the original defendant.[16]

Another circumstance in which the continued use of Exemption 7(A) has been held proper involves post-conviction motions, i.e., those instances in which the requester has filed a motion for a new trial or has otherwise appealed the court's action.[17] The extent of protection in such a circumstance, however, varies; some courts have limited Exemption 7(A) protection to only the material not used at the first trial,[18] while other courts in some cases have ex-

---

[15](...continued)
prospect), summary affirmance granted in pertinent part, vacated in part & remanded, No. 93-5091, 1993 LEXIS 33824 (D.C. Cir. Oct. 6, 1993); Warmack v. Huff, No. 88-H-1191-E, slip op. at 22-23 (N.D. Ala. May 16, 1990) (finding that Exemption 7(A) applicable to documents in multi-defendant case involving four untried fugitives), aff'd, 949 F.2d 1162 (11th Cir. 1991) (unpublished table decision); Freedberg v. Department of the Navy, 581 F. Supp. 3, 4 (D.D.C. 1982 ) (holding that Exemption 7(A) remained applicable when two murders convicted but two other remained at large). But see Linn, 1995 WL 417810, at *9 (explaining that statement that "some unspecified investigation against a fugitive, or perhaps more than one fugitive, was ongoing . . . without any explanation of how release" of information would interfere with "efforts to apprehend this (or these) fugitive (or fugitives) is patently insufficient to justify the withholding of information").

[16] See Franklin v. United States Dep't of Justice, No. 98-5339, slip op. at 3 (11th Cir. July 13, 1999) (holding that "disclosure could have reasonably been expected to interfere with [defendant's] federal appeal and state criminal trial"); Cudzich, 886 F. Supp. at 106-07 (holding that while INS investigation is complete, parts of file "containing information pertaining to pending investigations of other law enforcement agencies" are properly withheld); Kuffel v. United States Bureau of Prisons, 882 F. Supp. 1116, 1126 (D.D.C. 1995) (ruling that Exemption 7(A) remains applicable when inmate has criminal prosecutions pending in other cases); Dickie v. Department of the Treasury, No. 86-649, slip op. at 8 (D.D.C. Mar. 31, 1987) (holding that release of documents from closed federal prosecution could jeopardize state criminal proceedings).

[17] See, e.g., Kansi v. United States Dep't of Justice, 11 F. Supp. 2d 42, 45 (D.D.C. 1998) (explaining that "potential for interference . . . that drives the 7(A) exemption . . . exists at least until plaintiff's conviction is final"; thus, plaintiff's pending motion for new trial is "a pending law enforcement proceeding for purposes of FOIA").

[18] See August v. FBI, No. 98-5340, slip op. at 1-2 (D.C. Cir. Mar. 2, 1999) (remanding on court's own motion for agency to supplement record to show whether "justification [for withholding] encompasses information that was released during the original enforcement proceeding"); Pons v. United States Customs Serv., No. 93-2094, slip op. at 10 (D.D.C. Apr. 23, 1998) (ruling that disclosure of information not used in plaintiff's prior trials could "interfere with another enforcement proceeding"); Hemsley v. United States Dep't of Justice, No. 90-2413, slip op. at 10 (D.D.C. Sept. 24, 1992) (holding that Exemption 7(A) protection applied when "only pending criminal proceeding" is appeal of denial of new trial motion; "[k]nowledge of potential witnesses and
(continued...)

## EXEMPTION 7(A)

tended Exemption 7(A) protection to all of the information compiled during all of the law enforcement proceedings.[19]

Similarly, Exemption 7(A) also may be invoked when an investigation has been terminated but an agency retains oversight or some other continuing enforcement-related responsibility.[20] For example, Exemption 7(A) has been found to have been invoked properly to protect impounded ballots because their disclosure could "interfere with the authority of the NLRB" to conduct and process future collective bargaining representation elections.[21] If, however, there is no such ongoing agency oversight or continuing enforcement-related responsibility, courts do not permit an agency to continue the use of

---

[18](...continued) documentary evidence that were not used during the first trial" could "genuinely harm government's case"); cf. Senate of P.R. v. United States Dep't of Justice, 823 F.2d 574, 578 (D.C. Cir. 1987) (relying on language of statute prior to 1986 amendments to remand case for additional explanation of why no segregable portions of documents could be released without interference to related proceedings); Narducci v. FBI, No. 93-0327, slip op. at 3-4 (D.D.C. Sept. 22, 1995) (explaining that Exemption 7(A) remains applicable "in light of retrial, not yet scheduled, of several defendants," when agency had "adequately identified" how disclosure would interfere with retrial; agency must release all "public source documents").

[19] See Keen v. Executive Office for United States Attorneys, No. 96-1049, slip op. at 6-8 (D.D.C. July 14, 1999) (magistrate's recommendation) (finding use of Exemption 7(A) proper to withhold entire criminal file while motion to "redetermine" sentence is pending), adopted (D.D.C. Mar. 28, 2000); Kansi, 11 F. Supp. 2d at 45 (holding that Exemption 7(A) protection "exists at least until plaintiff's conviction is final"); Burke v. DEA, No. 96-1739, slip op. at 5 (D.D.C. Mar. 31, 1998) (ruling that protection of records "compiled for . . . prosecution of plaintiff in a previous criminal trial" is proper in light of plaintiff's post-conviction appeal because "disclosure of these records could harm the government's prosecution of the plaintiff's appeal"); Crooker v. ATF, No. 83-1646, slip op. at 1-2 (D.D.C. Apr. 30, 1984) (finding "no question that Exemption 7(A) is controlling" while motion to withdraw guilty plea still is pending).

[20] See, e.g., Alaska Pulp Corp. v. NLRB, No. 90-1510D, slip op. at 2 (W.D. Wash. Nov. 4, 1991) (stating that Exemption 7(A) remains applicable when corporation found liable for unfair labor practices, but parties remain embroiled in controversy as to compliance); Erb v. United States Dep't of Justice, 572 F. Supp. 954, 956 (W.D. Mich. 1983) (finding withholding proper when investigation "concluded 'for the time being'" and then subsequently reopened); ABC Home Health Servs. v. HHS, 548 F. Supp. 555, 556, 559 (N.D. Ga. 1982) (holding documents protected when "final settlement" was subject to reevaluation for at least three years); Timken, 531 F. Supp. at 199-200 (finding protection proper when final determination could be challenged or appealed); Zeller v. United States, 467 F. Supp. 487, 501 (S.D.N.Y. 1979) (finding that records compiled to determine whether party is complying with consent decree were protectible).

[21] Injex Indus. v. NLRB, 699 F. Supp. 1417, 1419-20 (N.D. Cal. 1986).

# EXEMPTION 7(A)

Exemption 7(A) to protect information.[22]

The "law enforcement proceedings" to which Exemption 7(A) may be applicable have been interpreted broadly. Such proceedings have been held to include not only criminal actions,[23] but civil actions[24] and regulatory proceedings[25] as well. They include "cases in which the agency has the initiative in

---

[22] See, e.g., Philadelphia Newspapers, Inc. v. HHS, 69 F. Supp. 2d 63, 66-67 (D.D.C. 1999) (finding that release of audit statistics and details of settlement from closed investigation of one hospital would not interfere with possible future settlements with other institutions when none were being investigated); Center for Auto Safety v. Department of Justice, 576 F. Supp. 739, 751-55 (D.D.C. 1983) (rejecting agency's argument that "disclosures which make consent decree negotiations more difficult" qualify as "interference" with law enforcement proceedings because "release at this time of the documents at issue will occur after the termination of any proceeding to which the documents are relevant"); see also Van Bourg, Allen, Weinberg & Roger v. NLRB, 751 F.2d 982, 985 (9th Cir. 1985) (stating that documents from unfair labor practice are not protected by Exemption 7(A) when no claim is pending or contemplated); Poss v. NLRB, 565 F.2d 654, 656-58 (10th Cir. 1977) (same); cf. Linn, 1995 WL 417810, at *9 (finding that unspecified possible investigation against unknown number of fugitives "is patently insufficient to justify the withholding of information"); Badran, 652 F. Supp. at 1440 (calling agency's position "bewildering and indefensible" when it argued that Exemption 7(A) was proper because it "could use [the information] against a person who might some day violate immigration laws").

[23] See, e.g., Manna, 51 F.3d at 1165 (finding that criminal law enforcement proceedings involving La Cosa Nostra and its "long, sordid and bloody history of racketeer domination and exploitation" meets threshold); Del Viscovo v. FBI, 903 F. Supp. 1, 3 (D.D.C. 1995) (explaining that ongoing criminal investigation of organized crime activities including narcotics, gambling, stolen property, and loan sharking satisfies threshold), summary affirmance granted, No. 95-5388 (D.C. Cir. Jan. 24, 1997); Gould, 688 F. Supp. at 703 (ruling that post-award audit reports pertaining to ongoing criminal investigation into pricing discounts qualify); National Pub. Radio, 431 F. Supp. at 510, 513-15 (reasoning that documents relating to nuclear-safety whistleblower's plutonium contamination, given "possibility of obstruction of justice," fall "within the protective scope of Exemption 7(A)").

[24] See, e.g., Manna, 51 F.3d at 1165 (disclosure would interfere with contemplated civil proceedings); Bender v. Inspector Gen. NASA, No. 90-2059, slip op. at 1-2, 8 (N.D. Ohio May 24, 1990) (information relating to "official reprimand" reasonably expected to interfere with government's proceeding to recover damages "currently pending" before same court).

[25] See, e.g., Johnson v. DEA, No. 97-2231, 1998 U.S. Dist. LEXIS 9802, at *9 (D.D.C. June 25, 1998) (reiterating that "law being enforced may be . . . regulatory"); Rosenglick v. IRS, No. 97-747-18A, 1998 U.S. Dist. LEXIS 3920, at *6 (M.D. Fla. Mar. 10, 1998) (confirming that phrase "law enforcement purposes" includes "civil, criminal, and administrative statutes and regulations such as those promulgated and enforced by the IRS"); Farm Fresh, Inc. v.
(continued...)

# EXEMPTION 7(A)

bringing an enforcement action and those . . . in which it must be prepared to respond to a third party's challenge."[26] Enforcement proceedings in state courts[27] and foreign courts[28] also qualify for Exemption 7(A) protection.

It is well established that in order to satisfy the "law enforcement proceedings" requirement of Exemption 7(A), an agency must be able to point to a specific pending or contemplated law enforcement proceeding that could be harmed by disclosure.[29] By comparison, while some courts have extended the attorney work-product privilege of Exemption 5 to instances of "foreseeable litigation, even if no specific claim is contemplated,"[30] courts have not likewise

---

[25](...continued)
NLRB, No. 91-603-N, slip op. at 1, 7-9 (E.D. Va. Nov. 15, 1991) (holding that NLRB's unfair labor practice action constitutes law enforcement proceedings); Alaska Pulp, No. 90-1510D, slip op. at 2, 5 (W.D. Wash. Nov. 4, 1991) (explaining that after finding of unfair labor practice, compliance investigation to determine back pay awards constitutes enforcement proceedings); Concrete Constr. Co. v. United States Dep't of Labor, No. 2-89-649, slip op. at 2-6 (S.D. Ohio Oct. 26, 1990) (ruling that Department of Labor's regulation and inspection of construction sites constitute enforcement proceedings); Injex, 699 F. Supp. at 1419 (finding that NLRB's responsibility to process collective bargaining representation elections constitutes law enforcement proceedings); Fedders Corp. v. FTC, 494 F. Supp. 325, 327-28 (S.D.N.Y.) (concluding that FTC investigation into allegations of unfair advertising and offering of equipment warranties constitutes law enforcement proceedings), aff'd, 646 F.2d 560 (2d Cir. 1980) (unpublished table decision).

[26] Mapother v. Department of Justice, 3 F.3d 1533, 1540 (D.C. Cir. 1993).

[27] See, e.g., Shaw v. FBI, 749 F.2d 58, 64 (D.C. Cir. 1984) (holding that "an authorized federal investigation into the commission of state crime [the JFK assassination] qualifies"); Butler, 888 F. Supp. at 182-82 (release could jeopardize pending state criminal proceeding); Dickie, No. 86-649, slip op. at 8 (D.D.C. Mar. 31, 1987) (same).

[28] See, e.g., Bevis v. Department of State, 801 F.2d 1386, 1388 (D.C. Cir. 1986) (stating that "language of the statute makes no distinction between foreign and domestic enforcement purposes") (citing Shaw, 749 F.2d at 64)).

[29] See Mapother, 3 F.3d at 1542 ("We believe that a categorical approach is appropriate in determining the likelihood of enforcement proceedings in cases where an alien is excluded from entry into the United States because of his alleged participation in Nazi persecutions on genocide. Otherwise, we must exercise our faculties as mind-readers."); National Sec. Archive v. FBI, 759 F. Supp. 872, 883 (D.D.C. 1991) (FBI's justification that disclosure would interfere with its overall counterintelligence program "must be rejected" as too general to be type of proceeding cognizable under Exemption 7(A); FBI permitted to demonstrate whether there existed any specific pending or contemplated law enforcement proceedings).

[30] Schiller v. NLRB, 964 F.2d 1205, 1208 (D.C. Cir. 1992); see also, e.g., Delaney, Migdail & Young, Chartered v. IRS, 826 F.2d 124, 127 (D.C. Cir. 1987) (extending attorney work-product privilege to documents prepared
(continued...)

# EXEMPTION 7(A)

extended the protection of Exemption 7(A).[31] As one court has observed, "[i]f an agency could withhold information whenever it could imagine circumstances where the information might have some bearing on some hypothetical enforcement proceeding, the FOIA would be meaningless."[32] Rather, it is the existence of a pending or prospective law enforcement proceeding against other investigative targets that permits the continued use of Exemption 7(A) when law enforcement proceedings against the first target are "closed."[33] Thus, information cannot properly be protected just because a law enforcement agency asserts, without a firm basis, that release would interfere with future actions.[34]

With respect to the showing of harm to law enforcement proceedings required to invoke Exemption 7(A), the Supreme Court in Robbins Tire rejected the position that "interference" must always be established on a document-by-document basis, and held that a determination of the exemption's applicability may be made "generically," based on the categorical types of records involved.[35] Indeed, the Supreme Court in Reporters Committee emphatically affirmed the vitality of its Robbins Tire approach and further extended it

---

[30](...continued)
when identity of prospective litigation opponent not yet known).

[31] See Philadelphia Newspapers, 69 F. Supp. at 66-67 (rejecting agency's argument that disclosure of audit statistics would interfere with possible future action because "investigation is over"); Center for Auto Safety, 576 F. Supp. at 751-55 (stating that modification of consent decree from closed proceeding not protected when not being used in on going proceeding; rejecting agency's argument that disclosure would make future negotiations more difficult); see also Van Bourg, Allen, Weinberg & Roger, 751 F.2d at 985 (finding that Exemption 7(A) does not apply to documents from closed proceeding when no other claim is pending or contemplated); Poss, 565 F.2d at 656-58 (same); Linn, 1995 WL 417810, at *25 (ruling that Exemption 7(A) is not applicable when no investigation exists); Badran, 652 F. Supp. at 1440 (rejecting agency's attempt to equate "might some day" with "pending").

[32] Badran, 652 F. Supp. at 1440.

[33] See, e.g., Solar Sources, 142 F.3d at 1040 (finding use of Exemption 7(A) proper in closed case when there is ongoing case against other targets); New England Med. Ctr. Hosp., 548 F.2d at 385-86 (stating that protection of closed file is proper when it relates to pending open case); Concrete Constr., No. 2-89-649, slip op. at 3-5 (S.D. Ohio Oct. 26, 1990) (approving use of Exemption 7(A) when release of program plans would permit prospective targets to gauge "potential of being investigated").

[34] See, e.g., Center for Auto Safety, 576 F. Supp. at 751-55 (holding that records concerning modification of consent decree from closed proceeding are not protectible when "not being used in an on-going proceeding"; disclosure would not interfere with future settlements); see also Van Bourg, Allen, Weinberg & Roger, 751 F.2d at 985 (stating that documents from unfair labor practice are not protected by Exemption 7(A) when no claim is pending or contemplated); Poss, 565 F.2d at 656-58 (same).

[35] 437 U.S. at 236.

## EXEMPTION 7(A)

to include situations arising under other FOIA exemptions in which records can be entitled to protection on a "categorical" basis.[36] Thus, almost all courts have accepted affidavits in Exemption 7(A) cases that specify the distinct, generic categories of documents at issue and the harm that would result from their release, rather than requiring extensive, detailed itemizations of each document.[37]

Specific guidance has been provided by the Courts of Appeals for the First, Fourth, and D.C. Circuits as to what constitutes an adequate "generic category" in an Exemption 7(A) affidavit.[38] The general principle uniting their

---

[36] Reporters Comm., 489 U.S. at 776-80 (Exemption 7(C)).

[37] See, e.g., Lynch v. Department of the Treasury, No. 98-56368, 2000 WL 123236, at *2 (9th Cir. Jan. 28, 2000) (explaining that "government need not 'make a specific factual showing with respect to each withheld document'" (quoting Lewis v. IRS, 823 F.2d 375, 380 (9th.Cir. 1987)), petition for cert. filed, 68 U.S.L.W. 3686 (U.S. Apr. 21, 2000) (No. 99-1697); Solar Sources, 142 F.3d at 1038 (reiterating that government "may justify its withholdings by reference to generic categories of documents, rather than document-by-document"); In re Dep't of Justice, 999 F.2d 1302, 1308 (8th Cir. 1993) (en banc) ("Supreme Court has consistently interpreted Exemption 7 of the FOIA (specifically so far subsections 7(A), 7(C), and 7(D))" to permit government to proceed on "categorical basis" and to not require document-by-document Vaughn Index), on remand sub nom. Crancer v. United States Dep't of Justice, No. 89-234, slip op. at 6 (E.D. Mo. Oct. 4, 1994) (magistrate's recommendation) (approving FBI's "generic" affidavit as sufficient and denying plaintiff's requests for methodology of document review and accounting of time spent reviewing documents), adopted (E.D. Mo. Nov. 7, 1994); Dickerson, 992 F.2d at 1431 (stating that it is "often feasible for courts to make 'generic determinations' about interference"); Wright, 822 F.2d at 646 (explaining that "a detailed listing is generally not required under Exemption 7(A)"); Spannaus, 813 F.2d at 1288 (stating that Supreme Court accepts generic determinations); Curran, 813 F.2d at 475 (holding that generic determinations permitted); Bevis, 801 F.2d at 1389 (finding that agency may take "generic approach, grouping documents into relevant categories"); Crooker, 789 F.2d at 67 ("Because generic determinations are permitted, the government need not justify its withholdings document-by-document; it may instead do so category-of-document by category-of-document."); Campbell, 682 F.2d at 265 ("government may focus upon categories of records"); American Civil Liberties Union Found., 833 F. Supp. at 407 (An agency "must supply sufficient facts about the alleged interference . . . . This does not, however, necessarily require an individualized showing for each document."); see also FOIA Update, Vol. V, No. 2, at 3-4 ("FOIA Counselor: The 'Generic' Aspect of Exemption 7(A)").

[38] See Spannaus, 813 F.2d at 1287, 1289 (stating that "details regarding initial allegations giving rise to this investigation; notification of [FBI Headquarters] of the allegations and ensuing investigation; interviews with witnesses and subjects; investigative reports furnished to the prosecuting attorneys," and similar categories are all sufficient); Curran, 813 F.2d at 476 (same); Bevis, 801 F.2d at 1390 (explaining that "identities of possible witnesses and informants, reports on the location and viability of potential evidence, and

(continued...)

**EXEMPTION 7(A)**

decisions is that affidavits must provide at least a general, "functional" description of the types of documents at issue sufficient to indicate the type of interference threatening the law enforcement proceeding.[39] It should be noted, however, that both the First and the Fourth Circuits have approved a "miscellaneous" category of "other sundry items of information."[40] Although

---

[38](...continued)
polygraph reports" are sufficient; categories "identified only as 'teletypes,' 'airtels,' or 'letters'" are insufficient); see also Cucci, 871 F. Supp. at 511-12 (holding that "evidentiary matters category"--described as "witness statements, information exchanged between the FBI and local law enforcement agencies, physical evidence, evidence obtained pursuant to search warrants and documents related to the case's documentary and physical evidence" is sufficient); cf. Solar Sources, 142 F.3d at 1036-39 (explaining that agency's six broad categories and eight subcategories "may have provided a sufficient factual basis" for judicial review, but cautioning that "we might give some weight to appellants' argument [that categories did not provide functional descriptions] had the district court not conducted a thorough in camera review").

[39] See, e.g., Curran, 813 F.2d at 475 ("Withal, a tightrope must be walked: categories must be distinct enough to allow meaningful judicial review, yet not so distinct as prematurely to let the cat out of the investigative bag."); Crooker, 789 F.2d at 67 ("The hallmark of an acceptable Robbins category is thus that it is functional; it allows the court to trace a rational link between the nature of the document and the alleged likely interference."); Voinche v. FBI, 46 F. Supp. 2d 26, 31 (D.D.C. 1999) (explaining that generic approach is appropriate, but that agency must demonstrate how each category of documents, if disclosed, could reasonably be expected to interfere with law enforcement proceedings); Hoffman v. United States Dep't of Justice, No. 98-1733, slip op. at 15, 18 (W.D. Okla. Dec. 15, 1999) (explaining that while Supreme Court has approved categorical approach, responsive documents must be grouped into "categories that can be linked to cogent reasons for nondisclosure"); Kitchen v. DEA, No. 93-2035, slip op. at 12-13 (D.D.C. Oct. 11, 1995) (approving categorical descriptions when court can trace rational link between nature of document and likely interference); cf. Institute for Justice & Human Rights v. Executive Office of the United States Attorney, No. 96-1469, 1998 U.S. Dist. LEXIS 3709, at **14-15 (N.D. Cal. Mar. 18, 1998) (explaining that four categories--confidential informant, agency reports, co-defendant extradition documents, and attorney work-product--are too general to be functional and ordering government to "recast" categories to show how documents in "new categories would interfere with the pending proceedings"); Putnam v. United States Dep't of Justice, 873 F. Supp. 705, 714 (D.D.C. 1995) (stating that agency "administrative inquiry file" is "patently inadequate" description); SafeCard Servs. v. SEC, No. 84-3073, slip op. at 6 n.3 (D.D.C. May 19, 1988) (holding that agency "file" is not sufficient generic category to justify withholding), aff'd in part, rev'd in part on other grounds & remanded, 926 F.2d 1197 (D.C. Cir. 1991); Pruitt Elec. Co. v. United States Dep't of Labor, 587 F. Supp. 893, 895-96 (N.D. Tex. 1984) (explaining that disclosure of reference material consulted by investigator that might aid an unspecified target in unspecified manner found not to cause interference).

[40] Spannaus, 813 F.2d at 1287, 1289; Curran, 813 F.2d at 476 (wide range of
(continued...)

## EXEMPTION 7(A)

the D.C. Circuit has not yet specifically addressed an affidavit containing such a category, a recent decision of the District Court for the District of Columbia held that documents categorized as "Other Agency Records," and described in agency affidavits as "material evidence that was the basis for the conviction," were described "sufficient[ly] to allow the court to determine that the files were properly withheld."[41]

The functional test set forth by the D.C. Circuit does not require a detailed showing that release of the records is likely to interfere with the law enforcement proceedings; it is sufficient for the agency to make a generalized showing that release of these particular kinds of documents would generally interfere with enforcement proceedings.[42] Making this showing has become easier under the current language of the statute.[43]

However, it is important to note that the D.C. Circuit in Bevis v. Department of State, held that even though an agency "need not justify its withholding on a document-by-document basis in court, [it] must itself review each document to determine the category in which it properly belongs."[44] Indeed,

---

[40](...continued)
records made some generality "understandable--and probably essential").

[41] Keen, No. 96-1049, slip op. at 10 (D.D.C. July 14, 1999).

[42] See Kay, 976 F. Supp. at 39 (stating that agency "need not establish that witness intimidation is certain to occur, only that it is a possibility"); Wichlacz v. United States Dep't of Interior, 938 F. Supp. 325, 331 (E.D. Va. 1996) (holding that "particularized showing of interference is not required; rather, the government may justify nondisclosure in a generic fashion"), aff'd, 114 F.3d 1178 (4th Cir. 1997) (unpublished table decision); Pully v. IRS, 939 F. Supp. 429, 436 (E.D. Va. 1996) ("All that is required is an objective showing that interference could reasonably occur as the result of the documents' disclosure."); Gould, 688 F. Supp. at 703-04 n.34 (describing functional test as steering "middle ground" between detail required by Vaughn Index and blanket withholding); Alyeska Pipeline Serv. v. EPA, No. 86-2176, 1987 WL 17081, at **2-3 (D.D.C. Sept. 9, 1987) (explaining that government need not "show that intimidation will certainly result," but that it must "show that the possibility of witness intimidation exists"), aff'd, 856 F.2d 309 (D.C. Cir. 1988).

[43] See Manna, 51 F.3d at 1164 n.5 ("Congress amended this exemption to relax significantly the standard for demonstrating interference with enforcement proceedings."); Gould, 688 F. Supp. at 703 n.33 (explaining that 1986 FOIA amendments "relaxed the standard of demonstrating interference with enforcement proceedings").

[44] 801 F.2d at 1389; see also Crooker, 789 F.2d at 67 (explaining that while government can justify its withholding category-by-category, government cannot justify its withholdings file-by-file); accord In re Dep't of Justice, 999 F.2d at 1309 (The "government may meet its burden by . . . conducting a document-by-document review to assign documents to proper categories."); Institute for Justice, 1998 U.S. LEXIS 3709, at **16-17 (determining that declarations "do not establish that each document was reviewed"); Kay, 976 F.
(continued...)

**EXEMPTION 7(A)**

when an agency elects to use the "generic" approach, the court held that the agency "has a three-fold task. First, it must define its categories functionally. Second, it must conduct a document-by-document review in order to assign the documents to the proper category. Finally, it must explain to the court how the release of each category would interfere with enforcement proceedings."[45] (For a further discussion, see Litigation Considerations, "Vaughn Index," below.) These requirements are entirely compatible with the "foreseeable harm" standard established by Attorney General Reno's FOIA Memorandum of October 4, 1993.[46]

The courts have long accepted that Congress intended that Exemption 7(A) apply "whenever the government's case in court would be harmed by the premature release of evidence or information,"[47] or when disclosure would

---

[44](...continued)
Supp. at 35 (explaining that "agency must conduct a document-by-document review in order to assign each document to a proper category" (citing Bevis, 801 F.2d at 1389-90)); Jefferson, 1997 U.S. Dist. LEXIS 3064, at *10 n.1 (stating that "it would appear from a review of their declaration that Defendants may have never conducted a document-by-document review of responsive material," and denying government's motion for summary judgment pending further submission); Hillcrest Equities, Inc. v. United States Dep't of Justice, No. CA3-85-2351-R, slip op. at 7 (N.D. Tex. Jan. 26, 1987) (declaring that government must review each document to determine category in which it belongs).

[45] Bevis, 801 F.2d at 1389-90; see also Voinche, 46 F. Supp. 2d at 31 (threefold task); Kay, 976 F. Supp. at 35 (same); Jefferson, 1997 U.S. Dist. LEXIS 3064, at *12 (same); Maccaferri Gabions, Inc. v. United States Dep't of Justice, No. 95-2576, slip op. at 11-13 (D. Md. Mar. 26, 1996) (same), appeal voluntarily dismissed, No. 96-1513 (4th Cir. Sept. 19, 1996); Cudzich, 886 F. Supp. at 106 (same); Bruscino v. Federal Bureau of Prisons, No. 94-1955, 1995 WL 44406, at *7 (D.D.C. May 12, 1995) (same); Cucci, 871 F. Supp. at 511 (same).

[46] Attorney General Reno's FOIA Memorandum, reprinted in FOIA Update, Vol. XIV, No. 3, at 4-5; see also Attorney General Reno's Follow-Up FOIA Memorandum, reprinted in FOIA Update, Vol. XIX, No. 4, at 3-5; FOIA Update, Vol. XVIII, No. 2, at 1; FOIA Update, Vol. XV, No. 2, at 3.

[47] Robbins Tire, 437 U.S. at 232; see, e.g., Mapother, 3 F.3d at 1543 (holding that release of prosecutor's index of all documents he deems relevant would provide "critical insights into [government's] legal thinking and strategy"); Rosenberg v. Freeh, No. 97-0476, slip op. at 1, 9 (D.D.C. May 13, 1998) (stating that release of code name would be "premature and damaging"); Rosenglick, 1998 U.S. Dist. LEXIS 3920, at **7-8 (explaining that "courts have liberally interpreted the term interference" and holding that "[s]uch an interpretation makes sense" because early access could "aid a wrongdoer in secreting or tampering with evidence [as well as reveal] nature, scope, strategy and direction of the investigation"); Palmer Communications v. United States Dep't of Justice, No. 96-M-777, slip op. at 4 (D. Colo. Oct. 30, 1996) (finding that release would harm "court's ability to control the use of discov-
(continued...)

**EXEMPTION 7(A)**

impede any necessary investigation prior to the enforcement proceeding.[48] In

---

[47](...continued)
ery materials . . . [resulting in] an unacceptable interference with a law enforcement proceeding"); Durham v. United States Postal Serv., No. 91-2234, 1992 WL 700246, at *1 (D.D.C. Nov. 25, 1992) (deciding that release of investigative memoranda, witness files, and electronic surveillance material would substantially interfere with pending homicide investigation by impeding government's ability to prosecute its strongest case), aff'd, No. 92-5511 (D.C. Cir. July 27, 1993); cf. Cecola v. FBI, No. 94 C 4866, 1995 WL 143548, at *2 (N.D. Ill. Mar. 30, 1995) (disallowing deposition of agency affiant when it might alert plaintiff to government's investigative strategy). But see LeMaine v. IRS, No. 89-2914, 1991 U.S. Dist. LEXIS 18651, at *13 (D. Mass. Dec. 10, 1991) (finding that agency failed to demonstrate that release would "seriously impair any ongoing effort to collect taxes or penalties . . . or to pursue criminal charges").

[48] See, e.g., Lynch, 2000 WL 123236, at *2 (stating that agency declarations "made clear" that release of records could harm "efforts at corroborating witness statements . . . alert potential suspects . . . [and] interfere with surveillance"); Solar Sources, 142 F.3d at 1039 (stating that disclosure could interfere by revealing "scope and nature" of investigation); Dickerson, 992 F.2d at 1429 (holding that public disclosure of information in Hoffa kidnapping file could reasonably be expected to interfere with enforcement proceedings); Kay, 976 F. Supp. at 38-39 (holding that agency "specifically established that release" would permit requester to gain insight into FCC's evidence against him, to discern narrow focus of the investigation, to assist in circumventing the investigation, and to create witness intimidation, court finds disclosure would "reveal the scope, direction and nature" of investigation); Pully, 939 F. Supp. at 436 (explaining that requester's promise not to interfere with investigation is of "no consequence" because government "need not take into account the individual's propensity or desire to interfere"; objective showing that disclosure could lead to interference found sufficient); Western Journalism, 926 F. Supp. at 192 (noting that disclosure could "contaminate the investigative process"); Butler, 888 F. Supp. at 182-83 (finding that disclosure would interfere with pending investigations by local police department of requester for stalking and murder); Kay v. FCC, 867 F. Supp. 11, 19 (D.D.C. 1994) (holding that documents, including letters to FCC from informants, would reveal scope of investigation and strength of case against plaintiff; disclosure of documents, "even redacted to exclude proper names," could lead to retaliatory action and intimidation of witnesses); Vosburgh v. IRS, No. 93-1493, 1994 WL 564699, at **2-3 (D. Or. July 5, 1994) (stating that disclosure of "DMV" record, memoranda of interview, police report, and portions of search warrants could interfere with IRS's investigation by revealing nature, scope, and direction of investigation, evidence obtained, government's strategies, and by providing requester with opportunity to create defenses and tamper with evidence); International Collision Specialists, Inc. v. IRS, No. 93-2500, 1994 WL 395310, at **2, 4 (D.N.J. Mar. 2, 1994) (ruling that disclosure could reasonably be expected to interfere with enforcement proceedings by enabling requester "to determine nature, source, direction, and limits" of IRS investigation and to "fabricate defenses and tamper with evidence"); Church of Scientology Int'l v. IRS, 845 F. Supp. 714, 721 (C.D. Cal. 1993) (finding that
(continued...)

## EXEMPTION 7(A)

Robbins Tire, the Supreme Court found that the NLRB had established interference with its unfair labor practice enforcement proceeding by showing that release of its witness statements would create a great potential for witness intimidation and could deter their cooperation.[49] Other courts have ruled that interference has been established when, for example, the disclosure of infor-

---

[48] (...continued)
disclosure likely to interfere with IRS's ability to investigate requester pursuant to Church Audit Procedures Act, 26 U.S.C. § 7611 (1994)); Church of Scientology v. IRS, 816 F. Supp. 1138, 1157 (W.D. Tex. 1993) (stating that disclosure could reasonably be expected to interfere with enforcement proceedings, subject IRS employees to harassment or reprisal, and reveal direction and scope of IRS investigation); National Pub. Radio, 431 F. Supp. at 514-15 (explaining that disclosure would impair agency's continued, long-term investigation into suspicious death of nuclear-safety whistleblower); cf. Wrenn v. Kemp, No. 91-5383, 1992 WL 381060, at *1 (D.C. Cir. Dec. 2, 1992) (holding that agency failed to explain its reasons for withholding and failed to demonstrate how disclosure could reasonably be expected to interfere with its ongoing enforcement investigation).

[49] 437 U.S. at 239; see also Solar Sources, 142 F.3d at 1039 (stating that disclosure could result in "chilling and intimidation of witnesses"); Judicial Watch, Inc. v. United States Dep't of Justice, No. 97-2869, slip op. at 19 (D.D.C. Feb. 22, 2000) (reiterating that prematurely disclosing documents related to witnesses could result in witness tampering or intimidation and could discourage continued cooperation); Anderson v. United States Dep't of Treasury, No. 98-1112, slip op. at 7-8 (W.D. Tenn. Mar. 24, 1999) (finding that disclosure allows "possibility of witness intimidation" and interference with proceedings); Accuracy in Media, Inc. v. National Park Serv., No. 97-2109, 1998 U.S. Dist. LEXIS 18373, at *26 (D.D.C. Nov. 13, 1998) (acknowledging that "disclosure of witnesses' statements and reports acquired by law enforcement personnel may impede the [Office of Independent Counsel's] investigation"), aff'd on other grounds, 194 F.3d 120 (D.C. Cir. 1999), cert. denied, 68 U.S.L.W. 3771 (U.S. May 15, 2000) (No. 99-1578); Kansi, 1998 WL 413578, at **1-2 (holding that disclosure provides "potential for interference with witnesses and highly sensitive evidence"); Anderson v. United States Postal Serv., No. 98-1661, 1998 WL 306207, at *2 (E.D. Pa. June 9, 1998) (explaining that release "would expose actual or prospective witnesses to undue influence or retaliation"); Rosenglick, 1998 U.S. Dist. LEXIS 3920, at **7-8 (reasoning that disclosure "could aid a wrongdoer in secreting or tampering with evidence or witnesses"); Wichlacz, 938 F. Supp. at 331 (finding Independent Counsel "justified in concluding that there are substantial risks of witnesses intimidation or harassment [and] reduced witness cooperation" in investigation which remains active and ongoing); Holbrook, 914 F. Supp. 314, 316 (S.D. Iowa 1996) (releasing information might permit targets of pending investigation to "tamper with or intimidate potential witnesses"); cf. Franklin, No. 98-5339, slip op. at 2, 3 (11th Cir. July 13, 1999) (ruling that "district court correctly determined" that disclosure of statements made by eight government witnesses who testified at criminal trial "could have reasonably been expected to interfere with ... appeal and state criminal trial").

**EXEMPTION 7(A)**

mation could prevent the government from obtaining data in the future.[50] Indeed, the D.C. Circuit in Alyeska Pipeline Service Co. v. EPA ruled that disclosure of documents pertaining to a corporation under investigation that might identify which of that corporation's employees had provided those documents to a private party (who in turn had provided them to EPA) would "thereby subject them to potential reprisals and deter them from providing further information to [the] EPA."[51]

The exemption has been held to be properly invoked when release would hinder an agency's ability to control or shape investigations,[52] would

---

[50] See, e.g., Kay, 976 F. Supp. at 38, 39 (finding potential for "witness intimidation and discourage[ment of] future witness cooperation" in ongoing investigation of alleged violation of FCC's rules); Wichlacz, 938 F. Supp. at 331 (reducing cooperation of potential witnesses when they learn of disclosure, thus interfering with ongoing investigation); Dow Jones & Co. v. United States Dep't of Justice, 880 F. Supp. 145, 150 (S.D.N.Y. 1995) (Disclosing "statements by interviewees . . . might affect the testimony or statements of other witnesses and could severely hamper the Independent Counsel's ability to elicit untainted testimony."), vacated on other grounds, 907 F. Supp. 79 (S.D.N.Y. 1995); Kay, 867 F. Supp. at 19 (explaining that witness "intimidation would likely dissuade informants from cooperating with the investigation as it proceeds"); Manna, 815 F. Supp. at 808 (disclosing FBI reports could result in chilling effect on potential witnesses), aff'd, 51 F.3d at 1165 (finding "equally persuasive the district court's concern for persons who have assisted or will assist law enforcement personnel"); Crowell & Moring v. DOD, 703 F. Supp. 1004, 1011 (D.D.C. 1989) (holding that disclosure of identities of witnesses would impair grand jury's ability to obtain cooperation and would impede government's preparation of its case); Gould, 688 F. Supp. at 703 (disclosing information would have chilling effect on sources who are employees of requester); Nishnic v. United States Dep't of Justice, 671 F. Supp. 776, 794 (D.D.C. 1987) (disclosing identity of foreign source would end its ability to provide information in unrelated ongoing law enforcement activities); Timken, 531 F. Supp. at 199-200 (Disclosure of investigation records would interfere with the agency's ability "in the future to obtain this kind of information.").

[51] 856 F.2d at 311. But cf. Clyde v. United States Dep't of Labor, No. 85-139, slip op. at 6 (D. Ariz. July 3, 1986) (describing possible reluctance of contractors to enter into voluntary conciliations with government if substance of negotiations released does not constitute open law enforcement proceeding when specific conciliation process has ended); Cohen v. EPA, 575 F. Supp. 425, 428-29 (D.D.C. 1983) (holding Exemption 7(A) inapplicable to protect letters sent to entities suspected of unlawfully releasing hazardous substances where such disclosure not shown to deter parties from cooperating with voluntary cleanup programs).

[52] See, e.g., Swan v. SEC, 96 F.3d 498, 500 (D.C. Cir. 1996) (holding that release "could reveal much about the focus and scope" of investigation); J.P. Stevens & Co. v. Perry, 710 F.2d 136, 143 (4th Cir. 1983) (finding that premature disclosure would "hinder [agency's] ability to shape and control investigations"); Youngblood v. Commissioner, No. 2:99-cv-9253, 2000 U.S. Dist.
(continued...)

# EXEMPTION 7(A)

enable targets of investigations to elude detection[53] or to suppress or fabricate evidence,[54] or would prematurely reveal evidence or strategy in the government's case.[55] Additionally, information that would reveal investigative

---

[52](...continued)
LEXIS 5083, at *36 (C.D. Cal. Mar. 6, 2000) (holding that disclosure "could reveal the nature, scope, direction and limits" of the investigation); Kay, 976 F. Supp. at 38-39 (discussing how release would reveal scope, direction, and nature of investigation).

[53] See, e.g., Moorefield, 611 F.2d at 1026 (explaining that disclosures of information would enable targets "to elude the scrutiny of the [Secret] Service").

[54] See, e.g., Solar Sources, 142 F.3d at 1039 (stating that disclosure "could result in destruction of evidence"); Alyeska Pipeline, 856 F.2d at 312 (ruling that disclosure could allow for destruction or alteration of evidence, fabrication of alibis, and identification of witnesses); Accuracy in Media, Inc. v. United States Secret Serv., No. 97-2108, 1998 WL 185496, at *4 (D.D.C. Apr. 16, 1998) (explaining that release could permit witnesses to modify, tailor, or fabricate testimony); Cujas v. IRS, No. 1:97-00741, U.S. Dist. LEXIS 6466, at *14 (M.D.N.C. Apr. 15, 1998) (finding that release of information would "alert" plaintiff to scope and direction of case and provide "opportunity to dispose" of assets), aff'd, 162 F.3d 1154 (4th Cir. 1998) (unpublished table decision); Rosenglick, 1998 U.S. Dist. LEXIS 3920, at *7 (reiterating that disclosure "could aid wrongdoer in secreting or tampering with evidence"); Maccaferri, No. 95-2576, slip op. at 14 (D. Md. Mar. 26, 1996) (determining that disclosure of information could provide plaintiff with opportunity to alter or destroy evidence); Holbrook, 914 F. Supp. at 316 (releasing information could allow targets to construct defenses); Nishnic, 671 F. Supp. at 794 (releasing information might allow subjects to suppress or fabricate evidence); see also Manna v. United States Dep't of Justice, No. 92-1840, slip op. at 11 n.3 (D.N.J. Aug. 25, 1993) (finding that possible suppression of evidence manifest when copy of search warrant was left on body of gangland-style murder victim), aff'd, 51 F.3d 1158, 1162, 1164-65 (3d Cir. 1995).

[55] See, e.g., Solar Sources, 142 F.3d at 1039 (determining that disclosure could result in "revelation of the scope and nature of the Government's investigation"); Mapother, 3 F.3d at 1543 (holding that release of prosecutor's index of all documents he deems relevant would afford a "virtual roadmap through the [government's] evidence . . . which would provide critical insights into its legal thinking and strategy"); Hambarian v. Commissioner, No. 99-9000, 2000 U.S. Dist. LEXIS 6217, at *7 (C.D. Cal. Feb. 16, 2000) (explaining that disclosure would reveal agency's theories and analysis of evidence); McErlean v. United States Dep't of Justice, No. 97-7831, 1999 WL 791680, at *8 (S.D.N.Y. Sept. 30, 1999) (finding that release of memoranda would reveal substance of information gathered and thus interfere with enforcement proceedings); Anderson, No. 98-1112, slip op. at 7 (W.D. Tenn. Mar. 24, 1999) (reasoning that disclosure of "checkspread" (agency's compilation of checks written by requester) "could very well jeopardize the proceedings by more fully revealing the scope and nature" of the government's case); Anderson, 1998 WL 306207, at *2 (stating that release of requested information "would disclose the focus" of government's investigation); Maccaferri, No. 95-2576,
(continued...)

## EXEMPTION 7(A)

trends, emphasis, and targeting schemes has been determined to be eligible for protection under Exemption 7(A) in those instances when disclosure would provide targets with the ability to perform a "cost/benefit analysis" of compliance with agency regulations.[56] Still other courts have indicated that any premature disclosure, by and of itself, can constitute interference with an enforcement proceeding.[57] In contrast, the D.C. Circuit has held that the mere fact that defendants in related ongoing criminal proceedings might obtain documents through the FOIA that were ruled unavailable "through discovery, or at least before [they] could obtain them through discovery," is insufficient alone to "constitute interference with a law enforcement proceeding."[58]

---

[55](...continued) slip op. at 14 (D. Md. Mar. 26, 1996) (releasing information would give "premature insight into the Government's strategy and strength of its position"); Cecola, 1995 WL 143548, at *3 (finding that release of information in ongoing criminal investigation might alert plaintiff to government's investigative strategy); Africa Fund, 1993 WL 183736, at *4 (explaining that disclosure "risks alerting targets to the existence and nature" of investigation); Manna, 815 F. Supp. at 808 (holding that disclosure would obstruct justice by revealing agency's strategy and extent of its knowledge); Raytheon Co. v. Department of the Navy, 731 F. Supp. 1097, 1101 (D.D.C. 1989) (holding that information "could be particularly valuable to [target] in the event of settlement negotiations"); Ehringhaus, 525 F. Supp. at 22-23 (stating that disclosure would reveal focus, "important aspects of the planned strategy of [FTC] attorneys, [and] the strengths and weaknesses of the government's case").

[56] Concrete Constr., No. 2-89-649, slip op. at 3-5 (S.D. Ohio Oct. 26, 1990) (holding that disclosure of past fiscal year's Field Operation Program Plans, containing projections for inspections and areas of concentration, would be "obviously a detriment to the enforcement objectives of the Department of Labor" because disclosure "takes away the guessing" about the potential of being investigated); see also Farmworkers Legal Servs. v. United States Dep't of Labor, 639 F. Supp. 1368, 1374 (E.D.N.C. 1986) (approving use of Exemptions 7(A) and 7(E) for information pertaining to agency's "targeting scheme," disclosure of which "would 'reveal the amount of investigative resources targeted and allocated'" for inspections).

[57] See Robbins Tire, 437 U.S. at 224-25, 234-37 (concluding disclosure of "witness statements in pending unfair labor practice proceedings" would generally interfere with enforcement proceedings); Lewis v. IRS, 823 F.2d at 380 (agreeing with "reasoning of the Eight Circuit" that "'government is not required to make a specific factual showing [of harm] with respect to each withheld document'" (quoting Barney, 618 F.2d at 1273)); Barney, 618 F.2d at 1273 (stating that disclosure "prior to the institution of civil or criminal tax enforcement proceedings, would necessarily interfere with such proceedings"); Steinberg v. IRS, 463 F. Supp. 1272, 1273 (S.D. Fla. 1979) (explaining that "premature disclosure of [requested] records could seriously hamper the ongoing investigations and prejudice the government's prospective case").

[58] North, 881 F.2d at 1097; cf. Senate of P.R., 823 F.2d at 589 (finding that trial court's failure to describe harm from release of undescribed documents developed for closed law enforcement investigation but allegedly relevant to

(continued...)

# EXEMPTION 7(A)

Furthermore, Exemption 7(A) ordinarily will not afford protection when the target of the investigation has possession of or submitted the information in question.[59] Nevertheless, it is increasingly clear that courts will protect such material if an agency can demonstrate that its "selectivity of recording" information provided by the target would suggest the nature and scope of the investigation,[60] or if it can articulate with specificity how each category of documents, if disclosed, would cause interference.[61] Indeed, in a case in which two clients requested statements that their attorney made to the SEC and argued that the "information their attorney conveyed to the [agency] must be treated as coming from them," it was held that the "harm in releasing this information flows mainly from the fact that it reflects the [agency] staff's selec-

---

[58](...continued) open criminal law enforcement proceeding did not permit upholding Exemption 7(A) applicability).

[59] See, e.g., Wright, 822 F.2d at 646 (observing that disclosure of information provided by plaintiff would not provide plaintiff "with any information that it does not already have"); Grasso, 785 F.2d at 77 (holding that IRS has not shown how disclosure of plaintiff's "own statement would interfere with enforcement proceedings"); Campbell, 682 F.2d at 262 (distinguishing between records generated by government and those "submitted to the government by such targets" and holding that government must "show in the latter case precisely how disclosure would [impede] . . . investigation"); Ginsberg v. IRS, No. 96-2265-CIV-T-26E, 1997 WL 882913, at *3 (M.D. Fla. Dec. 23, 1997) (reiterating that "where the documents requested are those of the [requester] rather than the documents of a third party . . . 'it is unlikely that their disclosure could reveal . . . anything [the requester] does not know already'" (quoting Grasso, 785 F.2d at 77)); see also Oncology Servs. Corp. v. NRC, No. 93-0939, slip op. at 17 (W.D. Pa. Feb. 7, 1994) (finding that agency may not categorically withhold transcribed interviews, conducted in presence of requester's attorney, for these interviewed individuals who consented to release of their own transcripts).

[60] See Swan, 96 F.3d at 500-01 (explaining that harm in disclosing information "flows mainly from the fact that it reflects the [SEC] staff's selective recording . . . and thereby reveals the scope and focus of the investigation"); Willard v. IRS, 776 F.2d 100, 103 (4th Cir. 1985) (concluding that "selectivity in recording" those portions of interviews that agents considered relevant "would certainly provide clues . . . of the nature and scope of the investigation"); see also Gould, 688 F. Supp. at 704 n.37 (reiterating that "disclosure of which records were selected by investigators from the universe of available materials for copying or compiling would reveal the nature, scope and focus of the government's investigation").

[61] See Linsteadt v. IRS, 729 F.2d 998, 1004 & n.10, 1005 (5th Cir. 1984) (stating that release would frustrate the investigation by revealing reliance government placed upon particular evidence and by aiding targets in tampering with evidence); Campbell, 682 F.2d at 265 (remanding for district court to show how each "category of documents, if disclosed, would interfere with the investigation"); cf. Alyeska Pipeline, 856 F.2d at 314 (mere assertions that requester knows scope of investigation not sufficient to present genuine issue of material fact that would preclude summary judgment).

## EXEMPTION 7(A)

tive recording . . . and thereby reveals the scope and focus of the investigation."[62]

Because Exemption 7(A) is temporal in nature, it usually has been recognized that once Exemption 7(A) applicability ceases with a change in underlying circumstances an agency then may invoke other applicable exemptions; therefore, agencies generally need not determine what other, underlying exemptions are appropriate until the underlying investigation reaches a point at which the documents no longer merit Exemption 7(A) protection.[63] Furthermore, it also has been held that an agency is not expected to monitor the investigation after completion of the FOIA administrative process and to process the documents once the investigation is closed.[64]

---

[62] Swan, 96 F.3d at 500-01.

[63] See Computer Prof'ls for Soc. Responsibility v. United States Secret Serv., 72 F.3d 897, 906-07 (D.C. Cir. 1996) (permitting agency on remand to apply exemptions other than Exemption 7(A) for records of investigation which was terminated during litigation); Dickerson, 992 F.2d at 1430 n.4 (explaining that "when exemption (7)(A) has become inapplicable," records may still be protected under other exemptions); Senate of P.R., 823 F.2d at 589 (finding that "district court did not abuse its discretion in permitting the DOJ to press additional FOIA exemptions after its original, all-encompassing (7)(A) exemption claim became moot"); Chilivis v. SEC, 673 F.2d 1205, 1208 (11th Cir. 1982) (holding government not barred from invoking other exemptions after reliance on Exemption 7(A) rendered untenable by conclusion of underlying law enforcement proceeding); Western Journalism, 926 F. Supp. at 192 (explaining that once Independent Counsel's task is completed, documents are "turned over to the Archivist and at that time would be subject to FOIA requests"); Curcio v. FBI, No. 89-0941, slip op. at 4-6 (D.D.C. Mar. 24, 1995) (permitting agency to invoke new exemptions when Exemption 7(A) is no longer applicable, agency has "made a clear showing of what the changed circumstances are and how they justify permitting the agency to raise new claims of exemption" and has "proffered a legitimate reason why it did not previously argue all applicable exemptions"); cf. Miller Auto Sales, Inc. v. Casellas, No. 97-0032, slip op. at 3 (W.D. Va. Jan. 6, 1998) (remanding to give agency "opportunity to make a new FOIA determination at the administrative level now that enforcement proceedings have ended").

[64] See Church of Scientology, 816 F. Supp. at 1157 (An "agency is not required to monitor the investigation and release the documents once the investigation is closed and there is no reasonable possibility of future proceedings."); see also Tellier v. Executive Office for United States Attorneys, No. 96-5323, 1997 WL 362497, at *1 (D.C. Cir. May 15, 1997) (per curiam) (finding law enforcement proceeding pending at time of request, affirms withholding of documents because "'[t]o require an agency to adjust or modify its FOIA responses on post-response occurrences could create an endless cycle of . . . reprocessing'" (quoting Bonner v. United States Dep't of State, 928 F.2d 1148, 1152 (D.C. Cir. 1991))); Gomez v. United States Attorney, No. 93-2530, 1996 U.S. Dist. LEXIS 6439, at *2 (D.D.C. May 13, 1996) (Exemption 7(A) claimed properly at receipt of request; when circumstances change, plaintiff is "free to file a new FOIA request"), appeal voluntarily dismissed, No. 96-5185 (D.C.

(continued...)

# EXEMPTION 7(A)

Under Exemption 7(A), though, a question can arise regarding the effect of "changed circumstances" and the appropriate time for an agency to determine the continued applicability of Exemption 7(A) and for courts to "evaluate the correctness of an agency's FOIA decision."[65] Although some case law indicates otherwise,[66] the sounder and certainly safer course is for an agency to take into account "changed circumstances"--i.e., any change in the status of the law enforcement proceedings occurring after the time of a FOIA request-- and to reprocess requested records whenever Exemption 7(A) ceases to apply during the pendency of a case, without waiving any underlying exemption protections.[67] Indeed, one court recently noted that ignoring changed circum-

---

[64](...continued)
Cir. May 12, 1997); cf. Lesar v. United States Dep't of Justice, 636 F.2d 472, 480 (D.C. Cir. 1980) (finding that FOIA processing would be delayed by remanding whenever new classification schemes are established); FOIA Update, Vol. XVI, No. 2, at 3, 12 (same).

[65] See Institute for Justice, 1998 U.S. Dist. LEXIS 3709, at **10-12.

[66] See Lynch, 2000 WL 123236, at *3 (stating that judicial review is to be made as of time agency decided to withhold documents); Keen, No. 96-1049, slip op. at 6-7 (D.D.C. July 14, 1999) (maintaining that court review is limited to time at which agency made determination); Local 32B-32J, Serv. Employees Int'l Union v. GSA, No. 97-8509, 1998 WL 726000, at *8 (S.D.N.Y. Oct. 15, 1998) (stating that judicial review of agency's decision must be made in light of status of enforcement proceedings at time at which agency responded); see also Tellier, 1997 WL 362497, at *1 (finding law enforcement proceeding pending at time of request and affirming withholding of documents because "'[t]o require an agency to adjust or modify its FOIA responses on post-response occurrences could create an endless cycle of . . . reprocessing'" (quoting Bonner, 928 F.2d at 1152 )); Gomez, 1996 U.S. Dist. LEXIS 6439, at *2 (finding that Exemption 7(A) applied as of receipt of request).

[67] See Jefferson, No. 96-1284, slip op. at 5 (D.D.C. Aug. 12, 1997) (stating that it would be "inefficient" to limit court review to status of enforcement proceeding at time of initial agency determination); see also Computer Prof'ls, 72 F.3d at 906-07 (on issue not briefed by either party, ordering agency to process records of recently terminated investigation to which agency initially had applied Exemption 7(A)); Senate of P.R., 823 F.2d at 589 (explaining that agency should employ additional FOIA exemptions after termination of criminal trial made Exemption 7(A) moot); Chilivis, 673 F.2d at 1205, 1209-10 (noting that agency processed documents after conclusion of investigation); Institute for Justice, 1998 U.S. LEXIS 3709, at **10-12 (explaining that government should be required to justify its withholdings based on present circumstances); Miller Auto Sales, No. 97-0032, slip op. at 2 (W.D. Va. Jan. 6, 1998) (finding that "changed factual circumstances render exemption 7(A) inapplicable" and that agency must "make a new FOIA determination"); Curcio, No. 89-0941, slip op. at 4-6 (D.D.C. Mar. 24, 1995) (stating that "changed circumstances" made Exemption 7(A) inapplicable, thus permitting agency to invoke other exemptions). But see Scheer v. United States Dep't of Justice, No. 98-1613, slip op. at 7 (D.D.C. July 24, 1999) (barring agency from raising other exemptions after granting plaintiff's cross-motion for summary judg-
(continued...)

# EXEMPTION 7(B)

stances is a "largely academic exercise that is both inefficient and contrary to the goals of the [FOIA]."[68] Even if an agency were not to consider changed circumstances, it would nevertheless have to reprocess documents considering other applicable exemptions whenever original FOIA requests are resubmitted or new FOIA requests are made.[69] (See the further discussion under Litigation Considerations, Waiver of Exemptions in Litigation, below.)

As a final Exemption 7(A)-related matter, agencies should be aware of the "(c)(1) exclusion,"[70] which was enacted by the FOIA Reform Act in 1986.[71] This special record exclusion applies to situations in which the very fact of a criminal investigation's existence is as yet unknown to the investigation's subject, and disclosure of the existence of the investigation (which would be revealed by any acknowledgment of the existence of responsive records) could reasonably be expected to interfere with enforcement proceedings.[72] In such circumstances, an agency may treat the records as not subject to the requirements of the FOIA. (See the discussion of the operation of subsection (c)(1) under Exclusions, below.)

## EXEMPTION 7(B)

Exemption 7(B) of the FOIA, which is aimed at preventing prejudicial pretrial publicity that could impair a court proceeding, protects "records or information compiled for law enforcement purposes [the disclosure of which] would deprive a person of a right to a fair trial or an impartial adjudication."[1] Despite the possible constitutional significance of its function, in practice this exemption is rarely invoked. In the situation in which it would most logically be employed--i.e., an ongoing law enforcement proceeding--an agency's application of Exemption 7(A) to protect its institutional law enforcement interests invariably would serve to protect the interests of the defendants to the prosecution as well. Even in the non-law enforcement realm, the circumstances that call for singular reliance upon Exemption 7(B) occur only rarely.

Consequently, Exemption 7(B) has been featured prominently in only one FOIA case to date, Washington Post Co. v. United States Department of

---

[67](...continued)
ment on inapplicability of Exemption 7(A)) (appeal pending).

[68] Jefferson, No. 96-1284, slip op. at 5 (D.D.C. Aug. 12, 1997).

[69] See, e.g., Lynch, 2000 WL 123126, at *3 (stating that plaintiff's "recourse is to resubmit" original FOIA request); Gomez, 1996 U.S. Dist. LEXIS 6439, at **2-3 (explaining that requester is "free to file a new FOIA request" and noting that "government has notified [requester] that it has begun processing").

[70] 5 U.S.C. § 552(c)(1).

[71] Pub. L. No. 99-570, § 1802, 100 Stat. at 3207-49.

[72] See Attorney General's 1986 Amendments Memorandum at 18-22.

[1] 5 U.S.C. § 552(b)(7)(B) (1994 & Supp. IV 1998).

# EXEMPTION 7(C)

Justice.[2] At issue there was whether public disclosure of a pharmaceutical company's internal self-evaluative report, submitted to the Justice Department in connection with a grand jury investigation, would jeopardize the company's ability to receive a fair and impartial civil adjudication of several personal injury cases pending against it.[3] In remanding the case for further consideration, the Court of Appeals for the District of Columbia Circuit articulated a two-part standard to be employed in determining Exemption 7(B)'s applicability: "(1) that a trial or adjudication is pending or truly imminent; and (2) that it is more probable than not that disclosure of the material sought would seriously interfere with the fairness of those proceedings."[4] Although the D.C. Circuit in Washington Post offered a single example of proper Exemption 7(B) applicability--i.e., when "disclosure through FOIA would furnish access to a document not available under the discovery rules and thus would confer an unfair advantage on one of the parties"--it did not limit the scope of the exemption to privileged documents only.[5]

## EXEMPTION 7(C)

Exemption 7(C) provides protection for personal information in law enforcement records. This exemption is the law enforcement counterpart to Exemption 6, providing protection for law enforcement information the disclosure of which "could reasonably be expected to constitute an unwarranted invasion of personal privacy."[1] Despite their similarities in language, though, the sweep of the two exemptions can be significantly different. (See the discussion of Exemption 6, above.)

Whereas Exemption 6 routinely requires an identification and balancing of the relevant privacy and public interests, Exemption 7(C) can be even more "categorized" in its application. Indeed, the Court of Appeals for the

---

[2] 863 F.2d 96, 101-02 (D.C. Cir. 1988); see also Alexander & Alexander Servs. v. SEC, No. 92-1112, 1993 WL 439799, at **10-11 (D.D.C. Oct. 19, 1993) (citing Washington Post to find that company "failed to meet its burden of showing how release of particular documents would deprive it of the right to a fair trial") (reverse FOIA suit), appeal dismissed, No. 93-5398 (D.C. Cir. Jan. 4, 1996).

[3] Washington Post, 863 F.2d at 99; see also Palmer Communications v. United States Dep't of Justice, No. 96-M-777, slip op. at 4 (D. Colo. Oct. 30, 1996) ("[T]he unavoidable conclusion is that granting the requested relief would harm this court's ability to control the use of discovery materials in the criminal case. That is an unacceptable interference with a law enforcement proceeding as defined by Exemption 7(A). Moreover, disclosure of the material sought under these circumstances would seriously interfere with the fairness of the procedures as defined by Exemption 7(B).").

[4] 863 F.2d at 102.

[5] Id.

[1] 5 U.S.C. § 552(b)(7)(C) (1994 & Supp. IV 1998).

**EXEMPTION 7(C)**

District of Columbia Circuit held in SafeCard Services v. SEC[2] that, based upon the traditional recognition of the strong privacy interests inherent in law enforcement records and the logical ramifications of United States Department of Justice v. Reporters Committee for Freedom of the Press,[3] the "categorical withholding" of information that identifies third parties in law enforcement records will ordinarily be appropriate under Exemption 7(C).[4] (See

---

[2] 926 F.2d 1197 (D.C. Cir. 1991).

[3] 489 U.S. 749 (1989); see also FOIA Update, Vol. X, No. 2, at 3-7 (discussing mechanics of privacy-protection decisionmaking process employed under Exemptions 6 and 7(C)).

[4] 926 F.2d at 1206; see, e.g., Fiduccia v. United States Dep't of Justice, 185 F.3d 1035, 1047-48 (9th Cir. 1999) (categorically protecting records concerning FBI searches of house of two named individuals); Nation Magazine v. United States Customs Serv., 71 F.3d 885, 896 (D.C. Cir. 1995) (restating that those portions of records in investigatory files which would reveal subjects, witnesses, and informants in law enforcement investigations are categorically exempt (citing SafeCard)); Juda v. United States Customs Serv., No. 98-0533, 1999 U.S. Dist. LEXIS 12536, at *19 (D.D.C. Aug. 2, 1999) (allowing categorical withholding of law enforcement records identifying third parties) (appeal pending); Coolman v. IRS, No. 98-6149, 1999 WL 675319, at *5 (W.D. Mo. July 12, 1999) (finding categorical withholding of third-party information in law enforcement records to be proper), summary affirmance granted, 1999 WL 1419039 (8th Cir. 1999); Center to Prevent Handgun Violence v. United States Dep't of the Treasury, 981 F. Supp. 20, 23 (D.D.C. 1997) (reiterating that "categorical exclusion from release of names in law enforcement reports applies only to subjects, witnesses, or informants in law enforcement investigations"); McNamera v. United States Dep't of Justice, 974 F. Supp. 946, 957-60 (W.D. Tex. 1997) (allowing categorical withholding of information concerning criminal investigation of private citizens); Tanks v. Huff, No. 95-568, 1996 U.S. Dist. LEXIS 7266, at **12-13 (D.D.C. May 28, 1996) (holding that absent compelling evidence of agency wrongdoing, criminal histories and other personal information about informants are categorically exempt), appeal voluntarily dismissed, No. 96-5180 (D.C. Cir. Aug. 13, 1996); Straughter v. HHS, No. 94-0567, slip op. at 5 (S.D. W. Va. Mar. 31, 1995) (magistrate's recommendation) (affording per se protection under Exemption 7(C) for witnesses and third parties when requester has identified no public interest), adopted (S.D. W. Va. Apr. 17, 1995); Grove v. Department of Justice, 802 F. Supp. 506, 511 (D.D.C. 1992) (holding that information concerning criminal investigations of private citizens categorically exempt); cf. Alexander & Alexander Servs. v. SEC, No. 92-1112, 1993 WL 439799, at *10 (D.D.C. Oct. 19, 1993) (requiring categorical withholding of personal information, even when records concern only professional activity of subjects, when no compelling evidence of illegal agency activity exists) (reverse FOIA case), appeal dismissed, No. 93-5398 (D.C. Cir. Jan. 4, 1996). But see Kimberlin v. United States Dep't of Justice, 139 F.3d 944, 948 (D.C. Cir.) (eschewing categorical rule of nondisclosure for Office of Professional Responsibility files and suggesting case-by-case balancing test involving consideration of "rank of public official involved and the seriousness of misconduct alleged"), cert. denied, 525 U.S. 891 (1998); Davin v. United States Dep't of Justice, 60 F.3d 1043, 1060

(continued...)

# EXEMPTION 7(C)

the discussion of the Supreme Court's Reporters Committee decision under Exemption 6, The Reporters Committee Decision, above.)

At the outset, certain distinctions between Exemption 6 and Exemption 7(C) are apparent. In contrast with Exemption 6, Exemption 7(C)'s language establishes a lesser burden of proof to justify withholding in two distinct respects. It is well established that the omission of the word "clearly" from the language of Exemption 7(C) eases the burden of the agency and stems from the recognition that law enforcement records are inherently more invasive of privacy than "personnel and medical files and similar files."[5] Indeed, the "'strong interest' of individuals, whether they be suspects, witnesses, or investigators, 'in not being associated unwarrantedly with alleged criminal activity'" has been repeatedly recognized.[6]

---

[4](...continued)
(3d Cir. 1995) (ruling that "government must conduct a document by document fact-specific balancing").

[5] See Congressional News Syndicate v. United States Dep't of Justice, 438 F. Supp. 538, 541 (D.D.C. 1977) ("[A]n individual whose name surfaces in connection with an investigation may, without more, become the subject of rumor and innuendo."); see also, e.g., Iglesias v. CIA, 525 F. Supp. 547, 562 (D.D.C. 1981).

[6] Fitzgibbon v. CIA, 911 F.2d 755, 767 (D.C. Cir. 1990) (quoting Stern v. FBI, 737 F.2d 84, 91-92 (D.C. Cir. 1984)); see also Quiñon v. FBI, 86 F.3d 1222, 1230 (D.C. Cir. 1996) (ruling that "'[p]ersons involved in FBI investigations--even if they are not the subject of the investigation--"have a substantial interest in seeing that their participation remains secret"'" (quoting Fitzgibbon, 911 F.2d at 767, quoting, in turn, King v. United States Dep't of Justice, 830 F.2d 210, 233 (D.C. Cir. 1987))); Schiffer v. FBI, 78 F.3d 1405, 1410 (9th Cir. 1996) (stating persons named in FBI files have "strong interest in 'not being associated unwarrantedly with alleged criminal activity'" (quoting Fitzgibbon, 911 F.2d at 767)); Computer Prof'ls for Soc. Responsibility v. United States Secret Serv., 72 F.3d 897, 904 (D.C. Cir. 1996) (finding release of names of individuals, including nonsuspects, who attended public meeting that attracted attention of law enforcement officials would impinge upon their privacy); Hunt v. FBI, 972 F.2d 286, 288 (9th Cir. 1992) (finding association of FBI "agent's name with allegations of sexual and professional misconduct could cause the agent great personal and professional embarrassment"); Dunkelberger v. Department of Justice, 906 F.2d 779, 781 (D.C. Cir. 1990) (refusing to confirm or deny existence of letter of reprimand or suspension of named FBI agent); Franklin v. United States Dep't of Justice, No. 97-1225, slip op. at 10 (S.D. Fla. June 15, 1998) (magistrate's recommendation) (stating law enforcement officers, suspects, witnesses, innocent third parties, and individuals named in investigative files have substantial privacy interests in nondisclosure (citing Wichlacz v. United States Dep't of Interior, 938 F. Supp. 325, 330 (E.D. Va. 1996))), adopted (S.D. Fla. June 26, 1998), aff'd per curiam, 189 F.3d 485 (11th Cir. 1999); Tanks, 1996 U.S. Dist. LEXIS 7266, at *9 (holding that "Exemption 7(C) does not 'require a balance tilted emphatically in favor of disclosure,' but rather 'recognizes the stigma potentially associated with law enforcement investigations and affords broader privacy rights to suspects, wit-

(continued...)

# EXEMPTION 7(C)

Additionally, the Freedom of Information Reform Act of 1986 further broadened the protection afforded by Exemption 7(C) by lowering the risk-of-harm standard from "would" to "could reasonably be expected to."[7] This amendment to the Act eased the standard for evaluating a threatened privacy invasion through disclosure of law enforcement records.[8] One court, in interpreting the amended language, pointedly observed that it affords the agency "greater latitude in protecting privacy interests" in the law enforcement context.[9] Such information "is now evaluated by the agency under a more elastic standard; exemption 7(C) is now more comprehensive."[10]

Under the balancing test that traditionally has been applied to both Exemption 6 and Exemption 7(C), the agency must first identify and evaluate

---

[6](...continued) nesses, and investigators'" (quoting Bast v. Department of Justice, 665 F.2d 1251, 1254 (D.C. Cir. 1981))); Straughter, No. 94-0567, slip op. at 5 (S.D. W. Va. Mar. 31, 1995) (holding privacy of witnesses and third parties not outweighed by public interest absent proof of misconduct); Buros v. HHS, No. 93-571, slip op. at 10 (W.D. Wis. Oct. 26, 1994) (refusing to confirm or deny existence of criminal investigatory records concerning county official, even though subject's alleged mishandling of funds already known to public; "confirming . . . federal criminal investigation brushes the subject with an independent and indelible taint of wrongdoing"). But see Detroit Free Press, Inc. v. Department of Justice, 73 F.3d 93, 98 (6th Cir. 1996) (finding that disclosure of mug shots of indicted individuals who had already appeared in court and had their names divulged did not constitute unwarranted invasion of privacy); Davin v. United States Dep't of Justice, No. 92-1122, slip op. at 9 (W.D. Pa. Apr. 9, 1998) (concluding individuals' privacy interests diluted due to more than 20 years having passed since investigation conducted), aff'd, 176 F.3d 471 (3d Cir. 1999) (unpublished table decision).

[7] Pub. L. No. 99-570, § 1802, 100 Stat. 3207, 3207-48; see Attorney General's Memorandum on the 1986 Amendments to the Freedom of Information Act 9-12 (Dec. 1987) [hereinafter Attorney General's 1986 Amendments Memorandum].

[8] See Reporters Comm., 489 U.S. at 756 n.9; Stone v. FBI, 727 F. Supp. 662, 665 (D.D.C. 1990) (stating that 1986 FOIA amendments have "eased the burden of an agency claiming that exemption"), aff'd, No. 90-5065 (D.C. Cir. Sept. 14, 1990).

[9] Washington Post Co. v. United States Dep't of Justice, No. 84-3581, 1987 U.S. Dist. LEXIS 14936, at *32 (D.D.C. Sept. 25, 1987) (magistrate's recommendation), adopted (D.D.C. Dec. 15, 1987), rev'd on other grounds & remanded, 863 F.2d 96 (D.C. Cir. 1988).

[10] Id.; see also Keys v. United States Dep't of Justice, 830 F.2d 337, 346 (D.C. Cir. 1987) (finding "government need not 'prove to a certainty that release will lead to an unwarranted invasion of personal privacy,'" at least after 1986 FOIA amendments (quoting Reporters Comm., 816 F.2d 730, 738 (D.C. Cir. 1987))); Nishnic v. Department of Justice, 671 F. Supp. 776, 788 (D.D.C. 1987) (holding phrase "could reasonably be expected to" to be more easily satisfied standard than "likely to materialize").

# EXEMPTION 7(C)

the privacy interests, if any, implicated in the requested records.[11] But in the case of records related to investigations by criminal law enforcement agencies, the case law has long recognized, either expressly or implicitly, that "'the mention of an individual's name in a law enforcement file will engender comment and speculation and carries a stigmatizing connotation.'"[12] Accordingly, Ex-

---

[11] See Straughter, No. 94-0567, slip op. at 5 (S.D. W. Va. Mar. 31, 1995) (deciding agency must first identify and evaluate specific privacy interest implicated); Albuquerque Publ'g Co. v. United States Dep't of Justice, 726 F. Supp. 851, 855 (D.D.C. 1989) ("Our preliminary inquiry is whether a personal privacy interest is involved."); FOIA Update, Vol. X, No. 2, at 7.

[12] Fitzgibbon, 911 F.2d at 767 (quoting Branch v. FBI, 658 F. Supp. 204, 209 (D.D.C. 1987)); see also Massey v. FBI, 3 F.3d 620, 624 (2d Cir. 1993) (same); Miller v. Bell, 661 F.2d 623, 631-32 (7th Cir. 1981) ("real potential for harassment"); Lesar v. United States Dep't of Justice, 636 F.2d 472, 488 (D.C. Cir. 1980) ("'It is difficult if not impossible, to anticipate all respects in which disclosure might damage reputation or lead to personal embarrassment and discomfort.'" (quoting Lesar v. United States Dep't of Justice, 455 F. Supp. 921, 925 (D.D.C. 1978))); Maroscia v. Levi, 569 F.2d 1000, 1002 (7th Cir. 1977) (protecting references to third parties "to minimize the public exposure or possible harassment"); Times Picayune Publ'g Corp. v. United States Dep't of Justice, 37 F. Supp. 2d 472, 477 (E.D. La. 1999) (maintaining that a "mug shot's stigmatizing effect can last well beyond the actual criminal proceeding"); Abraham & Rose, P.L.C. v. United States, 36 F. Supp. 2d 955, 957 (E.D. Mich. 1998) (noting that filing of tax lien against individual could cause "comment, speculation and stigma"); Ligorner v. Reno, 2 F. Supp. 2d 400, 405 (S.D.N.Y. 1998) (protecting names in file to avoid retaliation, discrimination, and encourage whistleblowers to come forward in future); Thompson v. United States Dep't of Justice, No. 96-1118, slip op. at 24 (D. Kan. July 14, 1998) (finding that release of third-party names could invite harassment, embarrassment, or annoyance); Anderson v. United States Postal Serv., 7 F. Supp. 2d 583, 586 (E.D. Pa. 1998) (disclosing identities of interviewees and witnesses may result in embarrassment and harassment); Cujas v. IRS, No. 1:97-00741, 1998 U.S. Dist. LEXIS 6466, at *9 (M.D.N.C. Apr. 15, 1998) (finding that "third parties named in these law enforcement records have a very strong privacy interest in avoiding the stigma and embarrassment resulting from their identification as a person that is or was under investigation), summary affirmance granted, No. 98-1641, 1998 WL 539686 (4th Cir. Aug. 25, 1998); Hamilton v. Weise, No. 95-1161, 1997 U.S. Dist. LEXIS 18900, at *20 (M.D. Fla. Oct. 1, 1997) (protecting third-party names to avoid harassment, embarrassment, and unwanted public attention); McNamera, 974 F. Supp. at 958 (rejecting argument that individual already investigated by one agency cannot be stigmatized by acknowledgment of investigation by another agency); Southam News v. INS, 674 F. Supp. 881, 887 (D.D.C. 1987) (finding disclosure of identities of individuals excludable from U.S. "would result in derogatory inferences about and possible embarrassment to those individuals"); cf. Cerveny v. CIA, 445 F. Supp. 772, 776 (D. Colo. 1978) (finding mere mention of individual's name as subject of CIA file could be damaging to his or her reputation) (Exemption 6). But see Blanton v. United States Dep't of Justice, No. 93-2398, 1994 U.S. Dist. LEXIS 21444, at **8-12 (W.D. Tenn. July 14, 1993) (holding no privacy interest in mere mention of defense attorney's name in

(continued...)

**EXEMPTION 7(C)**

emption 7(C) has been regularly applied to withhold references to persons who are not targets of investigations and who were merely mentioned in law enforcement files,[13] as well as to persons of "investigatory interest" to a criminal law enforcement agency;[14] indeed, the Supreme Court in Reporters Com-

---

[12](...continued)
criminal file or in validity of law license when attorney represented requester at criminal trial) (Exemptions 6 and 7(C)).

[13] See SafeCard, 926 F.2d at 1206 (protecting names of third parties); Neely v. FBI, 208 F.3d 461, 464 (4th Cir. 2000) (withholding names of third parties mentioned or interviewed in course of investigation); Isley v. Executive Office for United States Attorneys, No. 98-5098, 1999 WL 1021934, at *4 (D.C. Cir. Oct. 21, 1999) (protecting names of third parties); Halpern v. FBI, 181 F.3d 279, 297 (2d Cir. 1999) (protecting identities of third parties); Johnston v. United States Dep't of Justice, No. 97-2173, 1998 U.S. App. LEXIS 18557, at *2 (8th Cir. Aug. 10, 1998) (same); Gabel v. IRS, 134 F.3d 377, 377 (9th Cir. 1998) (protecting third-party names in Department of Motor Vehicles computer printout included in plaintiff's IRS file); Computer Prof'ls, 72 F.3d at 904 (finding that release of names of any individuals who attended public meeting that attracted attention of law enforcement officials would impinge upon their privacy); Murphy v. IRS, 79 F. Supp. 2d 1180, 1185 (D. Haw. 1999) (protecting identities of third parties); Franklin, No. 97-1225, slip op. at 13 (S.D. Fla. June 15, 1998) (magistrate's recommendation) (protecting names, addresses, and other information that would identify individuals associated with plaintiff), adopted (S.D. Fla. June 26, 1998); Crump v. EEOC, No. 97-0275, slip op. at 6 (M.D. Tenn. May 30, 1997) (magistrate's recommendation) (protecting personal information of third parties who filed charges with EEOC), adopted (M.D. Tenn. June 18, 1997); Feshbach v. SEC, 5 F. Supp. 2d 774, 785 (N.D. Cal. 1997) (withholding identities of third parties against whom SEC did not take action); Ajluni v. FBI, 947 F. Supp. 599, 604-05 (N.D.N.Y. 1996) (protecting identities of third parties merely mentioned in FBI files); Perrone v. FBI, 908 F. Supp. 24, 26-27 (D.D.C. 1995) (holding that release of names of persons mentioned in law enforcement files could lead to "stigmatizing public attention and even harassment").

[14] See, e.g., Neely, 208 F.3d at 464 (withholding names and identifying information of third-party suspects); Halpern, 181 F.3d at 297 (finding strong privacy interest in material that suggests person has at one time been subject to criminal investigation); O'Kane v. United States Customs Serv., 169 F.3d 1308, 1309 (11th Cir. 1999) (protecting home addresses of individuals whose possessions were seized by government); Spirko v. United States Postal Serv., 147 F.3d 992, 998-99 (D.C. Cir. 1998) (protecting suspects' palm- and fingerprints, their interviews and discussions with law enforcement officers, and photographs of former suspects and their criminal histories); Computer Prof'ls, 72 F.3d at 904 (holding potential suspects would have their privacy impinged if names disclosed); Massey, 3 F.3d at 624 (finding third parties' privacy interests in nondisclosure "potentially greater" than those of law enforcement officers); McDonnell v. United States, 4 F.3d 1227, 1255 (3d Cir. 1993) (finding suspects have "obvious privacy interest in not having their identities revealed"); Maynard v. CIA, 986 F.2d 547, 566 (1st Cir. 1993) (reiterating "potential for harassment, reprisal or embarrassment" if names of in-
(continued...)

**EXEMPTION 7(C)**

mittee placed strong emphasis on such protection.[15] Hence, the small minority of older federal district court decisions that failed to appreciate the strong privacy interests inherent in the association of an individual with a law enforcement investigation should no longer be regarded as authoritative.[16]

The identities of federal, state, and local law enforcement personnel referenced in investigatory files are also routinely withheld, usually for reasons similar to those described quite aptly by the Court of Appeals for the Fourth Circuit:

One who serves his state or nation as a career public servant is not

---

[14](...continued)
dividuals investigated by FBI disclosed); Davis v. United States Dep't of Justice, 968 F.2d 1276, 1281 (D.C. Cir. 1992) (deciding that "embarrassment and reputational harm" would result from disclosure of taped conversations of individuals with boss of New Orleans organized crime family); Silets v. United States Dep't of Justice, 945 F.2d 227, 230 (7th Cir. 1991) (en banc) (protecting associates of Jimmy Hoffa who were subjects of electronic surveillance); Antonelli v. FBI, 721 F.2d 615, 618 (7th Cir. 1983) ("revealing that a third party has been the subject of FBI investigations is likely to constitute an invasion of [personal privacy]"); Fund for Constitutional Gov't v. National Archives & Records Serv., 656 F.2d 856, 861-66 (D.C. Cir. 1981) (withholding identities of those investigated but not charged unless "exceptional interests militate in favor of disclosure"); Philadelphia Newspapers, Inc. v. HHS, 69 F. Supp. 2d 63, 68 (D.D.C. 1999) (protecting names of doctors "investigated for--but not charged with--Medicare fraud"); Thompson, No. 96-1118, slip op. at 24 (D. Kan. July 14, 1998) (withholding names of complainant, information provided by third-party subject, and names of individuals interviewed); Perdue Farms, Inc. v. NLRB, No. 2:96-27, slip op. at 10 (E.D.N.C. Jan. 20, 1998) (protecting information pertaining to, and names of, individuals involved in ongoing criminal investigation); Tawalbeh v. United States Dep't of the Air Force, No. 96-6241, slip op. at 7 (C.D. Cal. Aug. 8, 1997) (protecting names of third parties who were potential targets of criminal investigation); Marriott Employees' Fed. Credit Union v. National Credit Union Admin., No. 96-478-A, slip op. at 8 (E.D. Va. Dec. 24, 1996) (protecting identities of individuals cooperating with credit union investigation); Buros, No. 93-571, slip op. at 10 (W.D. Wis. Oct. 26, 1994) (finding that even though subject's alleged mishandling of funds already known to public, confirming federal criminal investigation "brushes the subject with an independent and indelible taint of wrongdoing"). But see Detroit Free Press, 73 F.3d at 98 (finding no unwarranted invasion of privacy in disclosure of mug shots of indicted individuals who had already appeared in court and had their names divulged); Rosenfeld v. United States Dep't of Justice, 57 F.3d 803, 811-12 (9th Cir. 1995) (making exceptional finding of public interest in disclosure of names of subjects of investigatory interest).

[15] 489 U.S. at 779.

[16] See, e.g., Silets v. FBI, 591 F. Supp. 490, 498 (N.D. Ill. 1984); Cunningham v. FBI, 540 F. Supp. 1, 2 (N.D. Ohio 1981), rev'd & remanded with order to vacate, No. 84-3367 (6th Cir. May 9, 1985); Lamont v. Department of Justice, 475 F. Supp. 761, 778 (S.D.N.Y. 1979).

# EXEMPTION 7(C)

thereby stripped of every vestige of personal privacy, even with respect to the discharge of his official duties. Public identification of any of these individuals could conceivably subject them to harassment and annoyance in the conduct of their official duties and in their private lives.[17]

---

[17] Nix v. United States, 572 F.2d 998, 1006 (4th Cir. 1978); see FOIA Update, Vol. V, No. 2, at 5; see, e.g., Neely, 208 F.3d at 464 (withholding FBI agents' names); Isley, 1999 WL 1021934, at *4 (upholding nondisclosure of "names and other personal information of special agents . . . [and] local law enforcement officials"); Fiduccia, 185 F.3d at 1045 (withholding DEA and INS agents' names); Halpern, 181 F.3d at 296 (protecting identities of nonfederal law enforcement officers); Johnston, 1998 U.S. App. LEXIS 18557, at *2 (protecting names of DEA agents and personnel and local law enforcement personnel); Manna v. United States Dep't of Justice, 51 F.3d 1158, 1166 (3d Cir. 1995) (finding law enforcement officers have substantial privacy interest in nondisclosure of names, particularly when requester held high position in La Cosa Nostra); Jones v. FBI, 41 F.3d 238, 246 (6th Cir. 1994) (protecting names of FBI agents and federal, state, and local law enforcement personnel); Becker v. IRS, 34 F.3d 398, 405 n.23 (7th Cir. 1994) (protecting initials, names, and phone numbers of IRS employees); Massey, 3 F.3d at 624 (finding disclosure of names of FBI agents and other law enforcement personnel "could subject them to embarrassment and harassment"); Church of Scientology Int'l v. IRS, 995 F.2d 916, 920-21 (9th Cir. 1993) (deciding privacy interest exists in handwriting of IRS agents in official documents); Maynard, 986 F.2d at 566 (protecting names and initials of low-level FBI agents and support personnel); Hale v. United States Dep't of Justice, 973 F.2d 894, 902 (10th Cir. 1992) (finding FBI employees have substantial privacy interest in concealing their identities), cert. granted, vacated & remanded on other grounds, 509 U.S. 918 (1993); In re Wade, 969 F.2d 241, 246 (7th Cir. 1992) (identifying risk of "annoyance and harassment" of FBI agent); Davis, 968 F.2d at 1281 (holding that "undercover agents" have protectible privacy interests); New England Apple Council v. Donovan, 725 F.2d 139, 142-44 (1st Cir. 1984) (inspector general investigator has "interest in retaining the capability to perform his tasks effectively by avoiding untoward annoyance or harassment"); Miller, 661 F.2d at 630 ("It is not necessary that harassment rise to the level of endangering physical safety before the protections of 7(C) can be invoked."); Lesar, 636 F.2d at 487-88 (annoyance or harassment); Galpine v. FBI, No. 99-1032, slip op. at 11 (E.D.N.Y. Apr. 28, 2000) (withholding names of probation officers); May v. IRS, 85 F. Supp. 2d 939, 946 (W.D. Mo. 1999) (protecting agents' social security numbers); McCall v. United States Marshals Serv., 36 F. Supp. 2d 3, 6 (D.D.C. 1999) (withholding names of deputy marshals who transported requester in courthouse); Ortiz v. United States Dep't of Justice, No. 97-140, slip op. at 5 (M.D. La. Aug. 25, 1998) (magistrate's recommendation) (protecting names and identifying information pertaining to local and foreign law enforcement officers), adopted (M.D. La. Oct. 1, 1998); Coleman v. FBI, 13 F. Supp. 2d 75, 79-80 (D.D.C. 1998) (protecting names of FBI agents and support personnel and commercial, state, and other federal employees who voluntarily assisted in investigation); Thompson, No. 96-1118, slip op. at 24 (D. Kan. July 14, 1998) (withholding name and room number of third-party Department of Justice employee who provided information and/or advice in course of investigation); Hamilton, 1997 U.S. Dist. LEXIS 18900, at *17

(continued...)

# EXEMPTION 7(C)

It should be noted that prior to the Reporters Committee and SafeCard decisions, courts ordinarily held that because Exemption 7(C) involves a balancing of the private and public interests on a case-by-case basis, there existed no "blanket exemption for the names of all [law enforcement] personnel in all documents."[18] Nonetheless, absent proven, significant misconduct on the parts of investigators, the overwhelming majority of courts have held the identities of law enforcement personnel exempt from disclosure pursuant to Exemption 7(C).[19] Those few decisions ordering disclosure of the names of

---

[17](...continued)
(withholding names of customs officers); Lampkin v. IRS, No. 96-138, 1997 U.S. Dist. LEXIS 2702, at **5-6 (W.D.N.C. Feb. 24, 1997) (protecting names of lower-level IRS employees because "'tax protesters' have used the federal courts to file vexatious suits against public servants" such as "bogus liens filed against their property"); Braslavsky v. FBI, No. 92-C-3027, 1994 U.S. Dist. LEXIS 7357, at *8 (N.D. Ill. June 3, 1994) (protecting names and initials of lower-level FBI agents and support personnel because employee conducting routine background investigation may be concurrently involved in more serious matters), aff'd, No. 94-2609, 1995 U.S. App. LEXIS 14413 (7th Cir. June 8, 1995); Church of Scientology v. IRS, 816 F. Supp. 1138, 1160 (W.D. Tex. 1993) (finding disclosure of identifying information and handwriting could subject IRS employees to "harassment and annoyance"); see also Sosa v. FBI, No. 93-1126, slip op. at 8 (D.D.C. Apr. 9, 1998) (protecting murdered law enforcement officer's autopsy reports). But see Hardy v. FBI, No. 95-883, slip op. at 21, 28 (D. Ariz. July 29, 1997) (ordering release of names of ATF supervisory agents involved in raid at Waco); Williams, No. 91-1054, slip op. at 5 (D.D.C. Apr. 18, 1997) (ordering release of names of arresting officers and officers who participated in search and seizure); Butler v. United States Dep't of Justice, No. 86-2255, 1994 WL 55621, at **5-6 (D.D.C. Feb. 3, 1994) (ordering release of names of supervisory FBI personnel involved in requester's case), appeal voluntarily dismissed, No. 94-5078 (D.C. Cir. Sept. 8, 1994).

[18] Lesar, 636 F.2d at 487; see, e.g., Stern, 737 F.2d at 94 (ordering release of name of high-level FBI agent-in-charge who directly participated in intentional wrongdoing; protecting names of two mid-level agents whose negligence incidentally furthered cover-up).

[19] See, e.g., Manna, 51 F.3d at 1166 (finding unfounded complaints of government misconduct insufficient to outweigh law enforcement officers' substantial privacy interests); Hale, 973 F.2d at 901 (holding unsubstantiated allegations of government wrongdoing do not justify disclosing law enforcement personnel names); Davis, 968 F.2d at 1281 ("undercover agents"); Wade, 969 F.2d at 246 (FBI agent); Patterson v. FBI, 893 F.2d 595, 601 (3d Cir. 1990) (FBI personnel); Doherty v. United States Dep't of Justice, 775 F.2d 49, 52 (2d Cir. 1985) ("Identities of FBI agents, of FBI non-agent personnel [and] of employees of the Immigration and Naturalization Service are embraced by exemption (b)(7)(C)."); Johnson, 739 F.2d at 1519 (deciding that FBI agents' identities are properly protectible absent evidence in record of impropriety); Manchester v. DEA, 823 F. Supp. 1259, 1271 (E.D. Pa. 1993) (withholding agents' names despite plaintiff's sweeping allegations of governmental misconduct); Ray v. United States Dep't of Justice, 778 F. Supp. 1212, 1215 (S.D. Fla. 1991) (affirming government may neither confirm nor deny exist-

(continued...)

## EXEMPTION 7(C)

government investigators--other than when proven misconduct has been involved either predate Reporters Committee[20] or find an unusually significant public interest in disclosure.[21]

The history of one case in the District Court for the District of Columbia illustrates the impact of the Reporters Committee decision in this area of law. In Southam News,[22] the district court initially held that the identities of FBI clerical personnel who performed administrative tasks with respect to requested records could not be withheld under Exemption 7(C). Even then, this position was inconsistent with other, contemporaneous decisions.[23] Following the Supreme Court's decision in Reporters Committee, the government sought reconsideration of the Southam News decision. Agreeing that revelation of identities and activities of low-level agency personnel ordinarily will shed no light on government operations, as required by Reporters Committee, the district court reversed its earlier disclosure order and held the names to be properly protected.[24] Significantly, the court also recognized that "the only imaginable contribution that this information could make would be to enable the public to seek out individuals who had been tangentially involved in inves-

---

[19](...continued) ence of records concerning results of INS investigation of alleged misconduct of employee); Heller, 655 F. Supp. at 1090-91 (protecting identities of federal marshals when there was "virtually no wrongdoing" on their parts).

[20] See, e.g., Castaneda v. United States, 757 F.2d 1010, 1012 (9th Cir.) (treating USDA investigator's privacy interest as "not great," based upon novel reasoning that his "name would be discoverable in any civil case brought [against the agency]"), amended upon denial of panel reh'g, 773 F.2d 251 (9th Cir. 1985); Iglesias, 525 F. Supp. at 563 (disclosing names of government employees involved in conducting investigation); Canadian Javelin, Ltd. v. SEC, 501 F. Supp. 898, 904 (D.D.C. 1980) (releasing names of SEC investigators).

[21] See Hardy, No. 95-883, slip op. at 21 (D. Ariz. July 29, 1997) (releasing identities of supervisory ATF agents and other agents publicly associated with Waco incident, finding that public's interest in Waco raid "is greater than in the normal case where release of agent names affords no insight into an agency's conduct or operations"); Butler, 1994 WL 55621, at *13 (releasing identities of supervisory FBI personnel upon finding of "significant" public interest in protecting requester's due process rights); cf. Weiner v. FBI, No. 83-1720, slip op. at 7 (C.D. Cal. Dec. 6, 1995) (finding public interest in release of names and addresses of agents involved in management and supervision of FBI investigation of music legend John Lennon) (applying FOIA in civil discovery context).

[22] 674 F. Supp. at 888.

[23] See, e.g., Doherty, 775 F.2d at 52 (protecting identities of FBI agents and nonagent personnel); Kirk v. United States Dep't of Justice, 704 F. Supp. 288, 292 (D.D.C. 1989) ("Just like FBI agents, administrative and clerical personnel could be subject to harassment, questioning, and publicity, and the Court concludes that the FBI did not need to separate the groups of employees for purposes of explaining why disclosure of their identities was opposed.").

[24] Southam News v. INS, No. 85-2721, slip op. at 3 (D.D.C. Aug. 30, 1989).

## EXEMPTION 7(C)

tigations and to question them for unauthorized access to information as to what the investigation entailed and what other FBI personnel were involved."[25] More recently, after undertaking a post-Reporters Committee analysis, the same district court strongly reaffirmed that identities of both FBI clerical personnel and low-level special agents are properly withheld as a routine matter under Exemption 7(C), even when they take part in a highly publicized investigation.[26]

---

[25] Id.; see also Isley, 1999 WL 1021934, at *4 (recognizing that "investigators have a substantial privacy interest against harassment"); Halpern, 181 F.3d at 296 (concluding that disclosure of names of law enforcement personnel could subject them to "harassment in the conduct of their official duties"); Manna, 51 F.3d at 1166 (holding law enforcement officers involved in La Cosa Nostra investigation have substantial privacy interest in nondisclosure of their names); Hambarian v. IRS, No. 99-9000, 2000 U.S. Dist. LEXIS 6317, at *10 (C.D. Cal. Feb. 15, 2000) (protecting names and identification numbers of IRS employees "who participated in the investigation of" the requester); Ortiz, No. 97-140, slip op. at 7 (M.D. La. Aug. 25, 1998) (magistrate's recommendation) (finding that disclosure of names of FBI personnel could subject them to "harassment and annoyance"), adopted (M.D. La. Oct. 1, 1998); Smith, 977 F. Supp. at 499 (finding disclosure of law enforcement officers' names "might seriously prejudice their effectiveness in conduct of investigations"); Harvey v. United States Dep't of Justice, No. 96-0509, 1997 WL 669640, at *3 (D.D.C. Oct. 23, 1997) (recognizing that release of names of DEA support personnel could target them for "'harassing inquiries for unauthorized access' to information"); Putnam v. United States Dep't of Justice, 880 F. Supp. 40, 42 (D.D.C. 1995) ("identities of federal, state and local law enforcement personnel, or other individuals assisting in criminal investigations, would not shed light on the government's conduct with respect to any closed or ongoing investigation"); Simon v. United States Dep't of Justice, 752 F. Supp. 14, 19 (D.D.C. 1990) (protecting identities of FBI agents and other government personnel involved in processing FOIA request), aff'd, 980 F.2d 782 (D.C. Cir. 1992).

[26] Stone, 727 F. Supp. at 663 n.1 (protecting identities of FBI special agents and clerical employees who participated in investigation of assassination of Robert F. Kennedy); see also Hoffman v. Brown, No. 97-1145, 1998 WL 279575 (4th Cir. May 19, 1998) (per curiam) (withholding portions of transcript of unauthorized audiotaped conversations of Veterans Administration Medical Center employees made during IG investigation); Wichlacz, 938 F. Supp. at 334 (E.D. Va. 1996) (protecting names of Park Police officers who investigated suicide of Deputy White House Counsel Vincent Foster, as well as psychiatrists who were listed on paper found in Foster's wallet, because disclosure would cause "onslaught of media attention" and could cause camera crews to "besiege" their workplaces and homes), aff'd per curiam, 114 F.3d 1178 (4th Cir. 1997) (unpublished table decision); Exner v. United States Dep't of Justice, 902 F. Supp. 240, 243-45 (D.D.C. 1995) (protecting identities of deceased former FBI special agent and his two sons, one of whom FBI may have observed "in criminally suspect behavior" at requester's apartment, which requester claimed had been searched for political reasons involving her alleged relationship with President Kennedy), appeal dismissed, No. 95-5411, 1997 WL 68352 (D.C. Cir. Jan. 15, 1997); cf. Armstrong v. Executive Office of

(continued...)

## EXEMPTION 7(C)

Traditionally, it had been held that Exemption 7(C) could not be invoked to shield the fact that a third party has been investigated once the agency has publicly confirmed the existence of such an investigation, because there is little or no privacy interest in such public-record information.[27] However, in Reporters Committee, the Supreme Court found that substantial privacy interests can exist in personal information such as is contained in "rap sheets," even though the information has been made available to the general public at some place and point in time. Applying a "practical obscurity" standard,[28] the Court observed that if such items of information actually "were 'freely available,' there would be no reason to invoke the FOIA to obtain access to [them]."[29] (See Exemption 7(D), below, for a discussion of the status of

---

[26](...continued)
the President, 97 F.3d 575, 581-82 (D.C. Cir. 1996) (finding that agency had not adequately defended categorical rule for withholding identities of low-level FBI agents (Exemption 6)).

[27] See, e.g., Rizzo v. United States Dep't of Justice, No. 84-2080, slip op. at 5-6 (D.D.C. Feb. 28, 1985) (finding facts elicited at public trial are matters of public knowledge); Tennessean Newspapers, Inc. v. Levi, 403 F. Supp. 1318, 1320-21 (M.D. Tenn. 1975) (ordering identities of individuals recently arrested or indicted disclosed); see also Akron Standard Div. of Eagle-Picher Indus. v. Donovan, 780 F.2d 568, 572 (6th Cir. 1986) (deciding information relating to job performance that "had been fully explored in public proceedings" not exempt); Blanton v. United States Dep't of Justice, 63 F. Supp. 2d 35, 47 (D.D.C. 1999) (ordering disclosure of informants' identities after they extensively publicized their status as informants). But see Kimberlin v. Department of the Treasury, 774 F.2d 204, 209 (7th Cir. 1985) (holding Exemption 7(C) applicable to third party's driver's license and passport "which were introduced into evidence" in federal criminal trial); Mueller v. United States Dep't of the Air Force, 63 F. Supp. 2d 738, 743 (E.D. Va. 1999) (agreeing that "[e]ven when allegations of misconduct are known, the accused party still has a privacy interest in 'avoiding disclosure of the details of the investigation'" (quoting Kimberlin, 139 F.3d at 949)); Lissner v. United States Customs Serv., No. 98-7438, slip op. at 20 (C.D. Cal. June 15, 1999) (concluding that fact that "certain information is public does not limit [an individual's] privacy interest") (appeal pending).

[28] 489 U.S. at 762-63, 780.

[29] Id. at 764; see Fiduccia, 185 F.3d at 1047 (protecting FBI records reflecting information that is also available in "various courthouses"); Abraham & Rose, P.L.C. v. United States, 138 F.3d 1075, 1083 (6th Cir. 1998) (stating that clear privacy interest exists with respect to names, addresses, and other identifying information, even if already available in publicly recorded filings; remanding for findings of applicability of exemptions (citing DOD v. FLRA, 510 U.S. 487, 500 (1994) (Exemption 6)); Times Picayune, 37 F. Supp. 2d at 478 (holding that a "person's status as a 'public figure' does not eviscerate" his or her privacy interests); Billington v. United States Dep't of Justice, 11 F. Supp. 2d 45, 61 (D.D.C. 1998) (finding that "agency is not compelled to release information just because it may have been disclosed previously"); Greenberg v. United States Dep't of Treasury, No. 87-898, 1998 U.S. Dist. LEXIS 9803, at
(continued...)

**EXEMPTION 7(C)**

open-court testimony under that exemption.)

All courts of appeals to have addressed the issue have found protectible privacy interests in conjunction with or in lieu of protection under Exemption 7(D)--in the identities of individuals who provide information to law enforcement agencies.[30] Consequently, the names of witnesses, their home and busi-

---

[29](...continued)
*55 (D.D.C. July 1, 1998) (finding third party's privacy interest not extinguished because public may be aware he was target of investigation); Baltimore Sun Co. v. United States Customs Serv., No. 97-1991, slip op. at 4 (D. Md. Nov. 12, 1997) (holding that inclusion of poor copy of defendant's photograph in publicly available court record did not eliminate privacy interest in photo altogether); Willis v. FBI, No. 96-1455, slip op. at 8 (D.D.C. Aug. 6, 1997) (magistrate's recommendation) (deciding that individual retains undiminished privacy interest even if identity previously has been disclosed), adopted (D.D.C. Feb. 14, 1998), aff'd in part & remanded in part, No. 98-5071, 1999 WL 236891 (D.C. Cir. Mar. 19, 1999); Lewis v. United States Postal Serv., No. 96-3467, slip op. at 2 (D. Md. Apr. 30, 1997) (holding that fact that complainant's name is already known, whether disclosed by investigating agency or otherwise, is irrelevant; declaring that "limited oral disclosure" does not constitute waiver of exemption).

[30] See, e.g., Hoffman, 1998 WL 279575 (protecting "private citizen identifiers" in VA investigative report); Beard v. Espy, No. 94-16748, 1995 U.S. App. LEXIS 38269, at *2 (9th Cir. Dec. 11, 1995) (protecting complaint letter); Manna, 51 F.3d at 1166 (holding interviewees and witnesses involved in criminal investigation have substantial privacy interest in nondisclosure of their names, particularly when requester held high position in La Cosa Nostra); McDonnell, 4 F.3d at 1256 (protecting identities of witnesses and third parties involved in criminal investigation of maritime disaster); Massey, 3 F.3d at 624 (disclosing names of cooperating witnesses and third parties, including cooperating law enforcement officials, could subject them to "embarrassment and harassment"); KTVY-TV v. United States, 919 F.2d 1465, 1469 (10th Cir. 1990) (per curiam) (withholding interviewees' names as "necessary to avoid harassment and embarrassment"); Cleary v. FBI, 811 F.2d 421, 424 (8th Cir. 1987) (deciding disclosure would subject "sources to unnecessary questioning concerning the investigation [and] to subpoenas issued by private litigants in civil suits incidentally related to the investigation"); Cuccaro v. Secretary of Labor, 770 F.2d 355, 359 (3d Cir. 1985) ("privacy interest of . . . witnesses who participated in OSHA's investigation outweighs public interest in disclosure"); L&C Marine Transp., Ltd. v. United States, 740 F.2d 919, 923 (11th Cir. 1984) (disclosing identities of employee-witnesses in OSHA investigation could cause "problems at their jobs and with their livelihoods"); New England Apple, 725 F.2d at 144-45 ("Disclosure could have a significant, adverse effect on this individual's private or professional life."); Kiraly v. FBI, 728 F.2d 273, 279 (6th Cir. 1984) (finding that, in absence of public benefit in disclosure, informant's personal privacy interests do not lapse at death); Holy Spirit Ass'n v. FBI, 683 F.2d 562, 564-65 (D.C. Cir. 1982) (concurring opinion) (citing "risk of harassment" and fear of reprisals); Alirez v. NLRB, 676 F.2d 423, 427 (10th Cir. 1982) (holding disclosure would result in "embarrassment or reprisals"); Lesar, 636 F.2d at 488 ("'Those cooperating with law enforcement should not

(continued...)

**EXEMPTION 7(C)**

ness addresses, and their telephone numbers have been held properly protectible under Exemption 7(C).[31] Additionally, Exemption 7(C) protection has

---

[30](...continued)
now pay the price of full disclosure of personal details.'" (quoting Lesar, 455 F. Supp. at 925)); Scherer v. Kelley, 584 F.2d 170, 176 (7th Cir. 1978) (finding need to protect informants' identities "cannot be questioned"); cf. Grand Cent. Partnership v. Cuomo, 166 F.3d 473, 486 (2d Cir. 1999) (finding that HUD failed to prove that disclosure of documents would identify individuals).

[31] See Isley, 1999 WL 1021934, at *4 (protecting identities of witnesses); Coulter v. Reno, No. 98-35170, 1998 WL 658835, at *1 (9th Cir. Sept. 17, 1998) (protecting names of witnesses and of requester's accusers); Spirko, 147 F.3d at 998 (protecting notes and phone messages concerning witnesses); Computer Prof'ls, 72 F.3d at 904 (protecting names of witnesses); Manna, 51 F.3d at 1166 (deciding witnesses in La Cosa Nostra case have "substantial" privacy interest in nondisclosure of their names); L&C Marine, 740 F.2d at 922 ("employee-witnesses . . . have a substantial privacy interest"); Antonelli v. Sullivan, 732 F.2d 560, 562 (7th Cir. 1984) ("[The requester] has mentioned no legitimate need for the witnesses' phone numbers and we can well imagine the invasions of privacy that would result should he obtain them."); May, 85 F. Supp. 2d at 946 (protecting personal information about witnesses); Anderson v. United States Dep't of Justice, No. 95-1880, 1999 U.S. Dist. LEXIS 5048, at *12 (D.D.C. Apr. 12, 1999) (protecting names of potential and actual witnesses); Telegraph Publ'g Co. v. United States Dep't of Justice, No. 95-521, slip op. at 13 (D.N.H. Aug. 31, 1998) (protecting identities of witnesses); Cujas, 1998 U.S. Dist. LEXIS 6466, at *9 (holding that witnesses in IRS investigation have strong privacy interests in nondisclosure); Foster v. United States Dep't of Justice, 933 F. Supp. 687, 692 (E.D. Mich. 1996) (protecting prospective witnesses); Crooker v. Tax Div. of the United States Dep't of Justice, No. 94-30129, 1995 WL 783236, at *18 (D. Mass. Nov. 17, 1995) (magistrate's recommendation) (holding names of witnesses and individuals who cooperated with government protected to prevent "undue embarrassment and harassment"), adopted (D. Mass. Dec. 15, 1995), aff'd per curiam, 94 F.3d 640 (1st Cir. 1996) (unpublished table decision); Cappabianca v. Commissioner, United States Customs Serv., 847 F. Supp. 1558, 1566 (M.D. Fla. 1994) (witnesses, investigators, and other subjects of investigation have "substantial privacy interests"); Taylor v. Office of Special Counsel, No. 91-N-734, slip op. at 10 (D. Colo. Mar. 22, 1993) (releasing documents would subject witnesses to a reasonable likelihood of harassment and embarrassment); Farese v. United States Dep't of Justice, 683 F. Supp. 273, 275 (D.D.C. 1987) (protecting names and number of family members of participants in Witness Security Program, as well as funds authorized to each, because disclosure "would pose a possible danger to the persons named" or "might subject those persons to harassment"); see also Kilroy v. NLRB, 633 F. Supp. 136, 145 (S.D. Ohio 1985) (protecting names and telephone numbers of persons who provided affidavits), aff'd, 823 F.2d 553 (6th Cir. 1987) (unpublished table decision); cf. Brown v. FBI, 658 F.2d 71, 75-76 (2d Cir. 1981) (protecting information concerning witness who testified against requester) (Exemption 6); Fritz v. IRS, 862 F. Supp. 234, 236 (W.D. Wis. 1994) (protecting name and address of person who purchased requester's seized car). But see Lipman v. United States, No. 3:97-667, slip op. at 3 (M.D. Pa. June 3, 1998) (releasing names of wit-

(continued...)

# EXEMPTION 7(C)

been afforded to the identities of informants,[32] even when it was shown that "the information provided to law enforcement authorities was knowingly

---

[31](...continued)
nesses who testified at trial based upon assumption defendant had already received information under Jencks v. United States, 353 U.S. 657 (1957)), appeal voluntarily dismissed, No. 98-7489 (3d Cir. Feb. 23, 1999).

[32] See Fiduccia, 185 F.3d at 1044 (withholding names of informants); Quiñon, 86 F.3d at 1227, 1231 (protecting informants' identities in absence of agency misconduct); Schiffer, 78 F.3d at 1410 (protecting names of persons who provided information to FBI); Computer Prof'ls, 72 F.3d at 904-05 (protecting names of informants, including name of company that reported crime to police, because disclosure might permit identification of corporate officer who reported crime); Manna, 51 F.3d at 1162 (safeguarding names of informants in La Cosa Nostra case); Jones, 41 F.3d at 246 (protecting informants' identities); McCutchen v. HHS, 30 F.3d 183, 189 (D.C. Cir. 1994) (protecting names of individuals alleging scientific misconduct); Koch v. United States Postal Serv., No. 93-1487, 1993 U.S. App. LEXIS 26130, at *2 (8th Cir. Oct. 8, 1993) ("The informant's interest in maintaining confidentiality is considerable [because] the informant risked embarrassment, harassment, and emotional and physical retaliation."); Nadler v. United States Dep't of Justice, 955 F.2d 1479, 1490 (11th Cir. 1992) ("Disclosure of the identities of the FBI's sources will disclose a great deal about those sources but in this case will disclose virtually nothing about the conduct of the government."); Unger v. IRS, No. 99-698, 2000 U.S. Dist. LEXIS 5260, at *12 (N.D. Ohio Mar. 28, 2000) (protecting "identities of private citizens who provided information to law enforcement officials"); Petterson v. IRS, No. 98-6020, slip op. at 8 (W.D. Mo. Apr. 22, 1999) (protecting informant's personal data); Pfannenstiel v. FBI, No. 98-0386, slip op. at 7 (D.N.M. Feb. 18, 1999) (withholding identities of confidential informants); Schlabach v. IRS, No. 98-0075, 1998 U.S. Dist. LEXIS 19579, at *2 (E.D. Wash. Nov. 10, 1998) (withholding personal information obtained from private citizens during investigation); Local 32B-32J, Serv. Employees Int'l Union v. GSA, No. 97-8509, 1998 WL 726000, at *9 (S.D.N.Y. Oct. 15, 1998) (finding that disclosure of names of individuals who provided information during investigation may subject them to threats of reprisal); Billington, 11 F. Supp. 2d at 63 (finding that witnesses' privacy interests outweigh public interest, even when witnesses appeared in court or participated in media interview): Thompson, No. 96-1118, slip op. at 24 (D. Kan. July 14, 1998) (protecting names and identifying information about individuals who provided or could provide information concerning investigation); Hayes v. United States Dep't of Labor, No. 96-1149, slip op. at 16 (S.D. Ala. June 10, 1998) (magistrate's recommendation) (withholding identity of confidential source), adopted (S.D. Ala. Aug. 10, 1998); Rosenberg, No. 97-0476, slip op. at 10 (D.D.C. May 13, 1998) (protecting names of individuals who cooperated and actively participated in investigation, as well as of "individuals who provided assistance to the operation because of their occupation or use of their property"); Steinberg v. United States Dep't of Justice, 179 F.R.D. 357, 363 (D.D.C. 1998) (withholding informants' names, alias names, and portions of interview regarding terrorist activities); see also Wrenn v. Vanderbilt Univ. Hosp., No. 3:91-1005, slip op. at 14-15 (M.D. Tenn. June 10, 1993) (protecting identity of person alleging discrimination), aff'd, 16 F.3d 1224 (6th Cir. 1994) (unpublished table decision).

**EXEMPTION 7(C)**

false."[33]

Although on occasion a pre-Reporters Committee decision found that an individual's testimony at trial precluded Exemption 7(C) protection,[34] under the Reporters Committee "practical obscurity" standard trial testimony should not ordinarily diminish Exemption 7(C) protection.[35] Plainly, if a person who actually testifies retains a substantial privacy interest, the privacy of someone who is identified only as a potential witness likewise should be pre-

---

[33] Gabrielli v. United States Dep't of Justice, 594 F. Supp. 309, 313 (N.D.N.Y. 1984); see also Block v. FBI, No. 83-813, slip op. at 11 (D.D.C. Nov. 19, 1984) ("[The requester's] personal interest in knowing who wrote letters concerning him . . . is not sufficient to demonstrate a public interest.") (Exemption 6).

[34] Compare Myers, No. 85-1746, 1986 U.S. Dist. LEXIS 20058, at **4-7 (D.D.C. Sept. 22, 1986) ("no privacy interest exists" as to names of law enforcement personnel who testified at requester's trial), with Prows v. United States Dep't of Justice, No. 87-1657, 1989 WL 39288, at *3 (D.D.C. Apr. 13, 1989) ("[T]he protection of Exemption 7(C) is not waived by the act of testifying at trial."), summary affirmance granted, No. 89-5185 (D.C. Cir. Feb. 26, 1990).

[35] See Jones, 41 F.3d at 247 (holding fact that law enforcement employee chose to testify or was required to testify or otherwise come forward in other settings does not amount to waiver of personal privacy); Burge, 934 F.2d at 579 (affirming refusal, under Exemption 7(C), to confirm or deny existence of information in FBI files regarding individuals who testified at plaintiff's murder trial); Galpine, No. 99-1032, slip op. at 12 (E.D.N.Y. Apr. 28, 2000) (reiterating that Exemption 7(C) protects "identities of individual's who testified at [requester's] criminal trial"); Rivera v. FBI, No. 98-0649, slip op. at 5 (D.D.C. Aug. 31, 1999) ("Individuals who testify at trial do not waive their privacy interest[s] beyond the scope of the trial record."); Canning v. United States Dep't of the Treasury, No. 94-2704, slip op. at 6 (D.D.C. May 7, 1998) (finding that being witness in criminal trial or being mentioned once in public document concerning investigation does not extinguish privacy interest); Robinson v. DEA, No. 97-1578, slip op. at 9 (D.D.C. Apr. 2, 1998) (stating that "[t]he disclosure during a trial of otherwise exempt information does not make the information public for all purposes"); Baltimore Sun, No. 97-1991, slip op. at 5 (D. Md. Nov. 21, 1997) (reasoning that request for original photograph of defendant because court's copy was unreproducible is evidence that "substance of photograph had not been fully disclosed to the public," so defendant retained privacy interest in preventing further dissemination); Tanks, 1996 U.S. Dist. LEXIS 7266, at *10 (holding that requester's knowledge of identities of informants who testified against him does not diminish their privacy interests); see also Isley, 1999 WL 1021934, at *4 (stating that testimony at trial does not place all documents relating thereto in public domain). But see Linn v. United States Dep't of Justice, No. 92-1406, 1997 U.S. Dist. LEXIS 9321, at *17 (D.D.C. May 29, 1997) (finding no justification for withholding identities of witnesses who testified against requester at trial) (Exemptions 7(C) and 7(F)), appeal voluntarily dismissed, No. 97-5122 (D.C. Cir. July 14, 1997).

**EXEMPTION 7(C)**

served.[36]

Moreover, courts have repeatedly recognized that the passage of time will not ordinarily diminish the applicability of Exemption 7(C).[37] This may be especially true in instances in which the information was obtained through questionable law enforcement investigations.[38] In fact, the "practical obscu-

---

[36] See Rosenglick v. IRS, No. 97-747-18A, 1998 U.S. Dist. LEXIS 3920, at *9 (M.D. Fla. Mar. 10, 1998); Watson v. United States Dep't of Justice, 799 F. Supp. 193, 196 (D.D.C. 1992); Harvey v. United States Dep't of Justice, 747 F. Supp. 29, 35 (D.D.C. 1990).

[37] See, e.g., Halpern, 181 F.3d at 297 ("Confidentiality interests cannot be waived through . . . the passage of time."); McDonnell, 4 F.3d at 1256 (deciding that passage of 49 years does not negate individual's privacy interest); Maynard, 986 F.2d at 566 n.21 (finding effect of passage of time upon individual's privacy interests to be "simply irrelevant"); Fitzgibbon, 911 F.2d at 768 (concluding that passage of more than 30 years irrelevant when records reveal nothing about government activities); Keys, 830 F.2d at 348 (holding that passage of 40 years did not "dilute the privacy interest as to tip the balance the other way"); King, 830 F.2d at 234 (rejecting argument that passage of time diminished privacy interests at stake in records more than 35 years old); Diamond v. FBI, 707 F.2d 75, 77 (2d Cir. 1983) ("the danger of disclosure may apply to old documents"); Franklin, No. 97-1225, slip op. at 12 (S.D. Fla. June 15, 1998) (magistrate's recommendation) (rejecting argument that passage of time vitiates individual's privacy interest in nondisclosure), adopted (S.D. Fla. June 26, 1998); Johnson v. DEA, 1998 U.S. Dist. LEXIS 9802, at *8 (finding that "the privacy of third parties mentioned in the context of law enforcement files is closely guarded, despite the passage of time"), summary affirmance denied in pertinent part & remanded, 1999 U.S. App. LEXIS 7332 (D.C. Cir. Mar. 2, 1999); Stone, 727 F. Supp. at 664 (explaining that FBI agents who participated in investigation over 20 years ago, even one as well known as RFK assassination, "have earned the right to be 'left alone' unless an important public interest outweighs that right"); see also Exner, 902 F. Supp. at 244 n.7 (holding that fact that incidents in question "occurred more than thirty years ago may, but does not necessarily, diminish the privacy interest"); Branch, 658 F. Supp. at 209 (The "privacy interests of the persons mentioned in the investigatory files do not necessarily diminish with the passage of time."); cf. Oglesby v. United States Dep't of the Army, 79 F.3d 1172, 1183 (D.C. Cir. 1996) (ruling that "mere passage of time is not a per se bar to reliance on [E]xemption 1"). But see Davin, 60 F.3d at 1058 (finding that for some individuals, privacy interest may become diluted by passage of over 60 years, though under certain circumstances potential for embarrassment and harassment may endure); Outlaw v. United States Dep't of the Army, 815 F. Supp. 505, 506 (D.D.C. Mar. 25, 1993) (ordering release of 25-year-old photographs of murder victim with no known surviving next of kin); Silets, 591 F. Supp. at 498 ("[W]here documents are exceptionally old, it is likely that their age has diminished the privacy interests at stake.").

[38] See, e.g., Dunaway v. Webster, 519 F. Supp. 1059, 1079 (N.D. Cal. 1981) ("[The target of a McCarthy era investigation] may . . . deserve greater protection, because the connection to such an investigation might prove particularly
(continued...)

## EXEMPTION 7(C)

rity" concept expressly recognizes that the passage of time may actually increase the privacy interest at stake when disclosure would revive information that was once public knowledge but has long since faded from memory.[39]

An individual's Exemption 7(C) privacy interest likewise is not extinguished merely because a requester might on his own be able to "piece together" the identities of third parties whose names have been deleted.[40] Nor do persons mentioned in law enforcement records lose all their rights to privacy merely because their names have been disclosed.[41] Similarly, "[t]he fact

---

[38](...continued) embarrassing or damaging.").

[39] See Reporters Comm., 489 U.S. at 767 ("[O]ur cases have also recognized the privacy interest inherent in the nondisclosure of certain information even when the information may at one time have been public."); Rose v. Department of the Air Force, 495 F.2d 261, 267 (2d Cir. 1974) ("[A] person's privacy may be as effectively infringed by reviving dormant memories as by imparting new information.") (Exemption 6), aff'd, 425 U.S. 352 (1976); see also Assassination Archives & Research Ctr. v. CIA, 903 F. Supp. 131, 133 (D.D.C. 1995) (finding that passage of 30 or 40 years "may actually increase privacy interests, and that even a modest privacy interest will suffice" to protect identities).

[40] Weisberg v. United States Dep't of Justice, 745 F.2d 1476, 1491 (D.C. Cir. 1984); see also Ford v. West, No. 97-1342, 1998 WL 317561, at *3 (10th Cir. June 12, 1998) (holding fact that requester obtained some information through other channels does not change privacy protection under FOIA and no waiver of third parties' privacy interests due to "inadequate redactions"); L&C Marine, 740 F.2d at 922 ("An individual does not lose his privacy interest under 7(C) because his identity . . . may be discovered through other means."); Billington v. Department of Justice, 69 F. Supp. 2d 128, 137 (D.D.C. 1999) (deciding that disclosure of unredacted records due to administrative error did not "diminish the magnitude of the privacy interests of the individuals" involved) (appeal pending); Cujas, 1998 U.S. Dist. LEXIS 6466, at *9 (reiterating that fact that information available elsewhere does not diminish third-party privacy interests in such law enforcement records); Smith, 977 F. Supp. at 500 (finding fact that plaintiff "can guess" names withheld does not waive privacy interest); Master v. FBI, 926 F. Supp. 193, 198-99 (D.D.C. 1996) (protecting subjects of investigative interest even though plaintiffs allegedly know their names), summary affirmance granted, 124 F.3d 1309 (D.C. Cir. 1997) (unpublished table decision); Larson v. Executive Office for United States Attorneys, No. 85-2575, 1988 WL 285732, at *3 n.6 (fact that requester "might know the names of some agents and witnesses who testified against him [as he alleges] does not justify release of documents that may or may not contain similar information.").

[41] See, e.g., Fiduccia, 185 F.3d at 1047 (concluding that privacy interests are not lost by reason of earlier publicity); Halpern, 181 F.3d at 297 ("Confidentiality interests cannot be waived through prior public disclosure. . . ."); Kimberlin, 139 F.3d at 949 (finding that even after subject's public acknowledgment of charges and sanction against him, he retained privacy interest in nondisclosure of "'details of investigation, of his misconduct, and of his punish-

(continued...)

# EXEMPTION 7(C)

that one document does disclose some names . . . does not mean that the privacy rights of these or others are waived; it has been held that [requesters] do not have the right to learn more about the activities and statements of persons merely because they are mentioned once in a public document about the investigation."[42]

Under the traditional Exemption 7(C) analysis, once a privacy interest has been identified and its magnitude has been assessed, it is balanced against the magnitude of any recognized public interest that would be served by dis-

---

[41] (...continued)
ment,'" and in "preventing speculative press reports of his misconduct from receiving authoritative confirmation from official source" (citing Bast v. United States Dep't of Justice, 665 F.2d 1251, 1255 (D.C. Cir. 1981))); Schiffer, 78 F.3d at 1410-11 (deciding fact that much of information in requested documents was made public during related civil suit does not reduce privacy interest); Jones, 41 F.3d at 247 (holding fact that law enforcement employee chose to testify or was required to testify or otherwise come forward in other settings does not amount to waiver of personal privacy); Hunt, 972 F.2d at 288 ("public availability" of accused FBI agent's name does not defeat privacy protection and "would make redaction of [the agent's name in] the file a pointless exercise"); Fitzgibbon, 911 F.2d at 768 (concluding fact that CIA or FBI may have released information about individual elsewhere does not diminish the individual's "substantial privacy interests"); Bast, 665 F.2d at 1255 (finding that "previous publicity amounting to journalistic speculation cannot vitiate the FOIA privacy exemption"); McGhghy v. DEA, No. C 97-0185, slip op. at 11 (N.D. Iowa May 29, 1998), (holding that "mere fact that individuals named in withheld documents may have previously waived their confidentiality interests, either voluntarily or involuntarily, does not mandate disclosure of withheld documents"), aff'd per curiam, No. 98-2989, 1999 U.S. App. LEXIS 16709 (8th Cir. July 13, 1999); Steinberg v. United States Dep't of Justice, No. 93-2409, slip op. at 11 (D.D.C. July 14, 1997) ("Even widespread knowledge about a person's business dealings cannot serve to diminish his or her privacy interests in matters that are truly personal."); Thomas v. Office of United States Attorney, 928 F. Supp. 245, 250 & n.8 (E.D.N.Y. 1996) (holding that despite public disclosure of some information about attorney's connection with crime family, he still retains privacy interests in preventing further disclosure), appeal dismissed, No. 93-CV-3128 (2d Cir. Oct. 29, 1996); Crooker, 1995 WL 783236, at *18 (holding that despite fact that requester may have learned identities of third parties through criminal discovery, Exemption 7(C) protection remains). But see Detroit Free Press, 73 F.3d at 98 (finding no unwarranted invasion of privacy in disclosure of mug shots of indicted individuals who had already appeared in court and had their names divulged); Steinberg v. United States Dep't of Justice, 179 F.R.D. 366, 371 (D.D.C. 1998) (holding content of sources' interviews must be disclosed once agency disclosed their identities); cf. Grove v. CIA, 752 F. Supp. 28, 32 (D.D.C. 1990) (ordering FBI to further explain Exemption 7(C) withholdings in light of highly publicized nature of investigation and fact that CIA and Secret Service released other records pertaining to same individuals).

[42] Kirk, 704 F. Supp. at 292.

## EXEMPTION 7(C)

closure.[43] And under Reporters Committee, the standard of public interest to consider is one specifically limited to the FOIA's "core purpose" of "shed[ding] light on an agency's performance of its statutory duties."[44] Accordingly, for example, the courts have consistently refused to recognize any public interest, as defined by Reporters Committee, in disclosure of information to assist a convict in challenging his conviction.[45] Indeed, a FOIA requester's pri-

---

[43] See Schiffer, 78 F.3d at 1410 (explaining once agency shows that privacy interest exists, court must balance it against public's interest in disclosure); Computer Prof'ls, 72 F.3d at 904 (finding after privacy interest found, court must identify public interest to be served by disclosure); Massey, 3 F.3d at 624-25 (holding once agency establishes that privacy interest exists, that interest must be balanced against value of information in furthering FOIA's disclosure objectives); Church of Scientology, 995 F.2d at 921 (remanding case because district court failed to determine whether public interest in disclosure outweighed privacy concerns); Grine v. Coombs, No. 95-342, 1997 U.S. Dist. LEXIS 19578, at *19 (W.D. Pa. Oct. 10, 1997) (requiring balancing of privacy interest and extent to which it is invaded against public benefit that would result from disclosure); Thomas, 928 F. Supp. at 250 (observing that since personal privacy interest in information is implicated, court must inquire whether any countervailing factors exist that would warrant invasion of that interest); Globe Newspaper Co. v. FBI, No. 91-13257, 1992 WL 396327, at *4 (D. Mass. Dec. 29, 1992) (finding public interest in disclosing amount of money government paid to officially confirmed informant guilty of criminal wrongdoing outweighs informant's de minimis privacy interest); Church of Scientology, 816 F. Supp. at 1160 (concluding while employees have privacy interest in their handwriting, that interest does not outweigh public interest in disclosure of information contained in documents not otherwise exempt); see also FOIA Update, Vol. X, No. 2, at 7.

[44] 489 U.S. at 773.

[45] See, e.g., Neely, 208 F.3d at 464 (ruling that requester's wish to establish his own innocence does not create FOIA-recognized public interest); Hale, 973 F.2d at 901 (finding no FOIA-recognized public interest in death-row inmate's allegation of unfair trial); Landano v. United States Dep't of Justice, 956 F.2d 422, 430 (3d Cir. 1991) (concluding no public interest in disclosure of identities of individuals involved in murder investigation because such release would not shed light on how FBI fulfills its responsibilities), cert. denied on Exemption 7(C) grounds, 506 U.S. 868 (1992), rev'd & remanded on other grounds, 508 U.S. 165 (1993); Burge, 934 F.2d at 580 ("requester's need, however significant, does not warrant disclosure"); Galpine, No. 99-1032, slip op. at 13 (E.D.N.Y. Apr. 28, 2000) (restating that requests for exculpatory evidence are "'outside the proper role of FOIA'" (quoting Colon, 1998 WL 695631, at *5)); Martin v. United States Dep't of Justice, No. 96-2866, slip op. at 10 (D.D.C. Dec. 15, 1999) (acknowledging that "courts have consistently found Brady violations to be outside the scope of FOIA"); Hazel v. Department of Justice, No. 95-1992, slip op. at 8 (D.D.C. July 2, 1998) (reiterating that collateral attack on conviction "'reveals little or nothing about an agency's own conduct'" (quoting Reporters Comm., 489 U.S. at 773)); Fedrick v. United States Dep't of Justice, 984 F. Supp. 659, 664 (W.D.N.Y. 1997) (magistrate's recommendation) (finding that requester's personal interest in seeking infor-

(continued...)

# EXEMPTION 7(C)

vate need for information in connection with litigation plays no part whatsoever in determining whether disclosure is warranted.[46]

---

[45](...continued)
mation for use in collateral challenge to his conviction does not raise "FOIA-recognized interest"), adopted (W.D.N.Y. Oct. 28, 1997), aff'd sub nom. Fedrick v. Huff, 165 F.3d 13 (2d Cir. 1998); Trupei, 1998 WL 8986, at *3 (concluding that request for Brady v. Maryland, 373 U.S. 83 (1963), material is not within role of FOIA); Curry v. DEA, No. 97-1359, slip op. at 5 (D.D.C. Mar. 30, 1998) (affirming denial of request for witness-impeachment evidence as part of FOIA response); Smith, 977 F. Supp. at 499 (holding that requester's personal interest in obtaining exculpatory statements does not give him greater rights under FOIA); Thomas, 928 F. Supp. at 251 (holding that prisoner's personal interest in information to challenge his conviction "does not raise a FOIA-recognized interest that should be weighed against the subject's privacy interests"); Durham v. United States Postal Serv., No. 91-2234, 1992 WL 700246, at *2 (D.D.C. Nov. 25, 1992) (holding "Glomar" response appropriate even though plaintiff argued that information would prove his innocence), summary affirmance granted, No. 92-5511 (D.C. Cir. July 27, 1993); Johnson, 758 F. Supp. at 5 ("Resort to Brady v. Maryland as grounds for waiving confidentiality [under Exemptions 7(C) and 7(D)] is . . . outside the proper role of the FOIA. Exceptions cannot be made because of the subject matter or [death-row status] of the requester."). But see Lipman, No. 3:97-667, slip op. at 4 (M.D. Pa. June 3, 1998) (making exceptional finding of public interest in plaintiff's quest to discover whether government withheld Brady material).

[46] See Massey, 3 F.3d at 625 ("[The] mere possibility that information may aid an individual in the pursuit of litigation does not give rise to a public interest."); Joslin v. United States Dep't of Labor, No. 88-1999, slip op. at 8 (10th Cir. Oct. 20, 1989) (finding no public interest in release of documents sought for use in private tort litigation); Exner, 902 F. Supp. at 244 & n.8 (explaining requester's interest in pursuing legal remedies against person who entered her apartment does not pertain to workings of government); Bruscino, No. 94-1955, 1995 WL 444406, at *9 (D.D.C. May 12, 1995) (concluding no public interest in release of information concerning other inmates sought for use in private litigation); Andrews v. United States Dep't of Justice, 769 F. Supp. 314, 317 (E.D. Mo. 1991) (deciding no public interest in satisfaction of private judgments); Wagner v. FBI, No. 90-1314, 1991 U.S. Dist. LEXIS 7506, at *8 (D.D.C. June 4, 1991) ("purpose of the FOIA is not to support the needs or purposes of the individual requester"; finding that public interest "is that of the public at large in investigating the actions of government agencies, not plaintiff's interest"), summary affirmance granted, No. 91-5220 (D.C. Cir. Aug. 3, 1992). But see Sousa v. United States Dep't of Justice, No. 95-375, 1996 U.S. Dist. LEXIS 18627, at *26 (D.D.C. Dec. 9, 1996) (recognizing that "[t]here certainly is at least some amount of public interest in overturning incorrect convictions," though finding that public interest insufficient to outweigh "significant" privacy interests of individuals mentioned); Butler, No. 86-2255, 1994 WL 55621, at **5-6 (D.D.C. Feb. 3, 1994) (ordering identities of supervisory FBI personnel disclosed because of "significant" public interest in protecting requester's due process rights in his attempt to vacate sentence); Outlaw, 815 F. Supp. at 506 (releasing 25-year-old photographs of murder victim partly in recognition of "obvious public interest in the disclosure as a
(continued...)

# EXEMPTION 7(C)

Unsubstantiated allegations of official misconduct have been held insufficient to establish a public interest in disclosure.[47] It also has been held that

---

[46](...continued)
check on the administration of justice").

[47] See, e.g., Spirko, 147 F.3d at 999 (finding no public interest in names and information pertaining to suspects and law enforcement officers absent any evidence of alleged misconduct by agency); Enzinna v. United States Dep't of Justice, No. 97-5078, 1997 WL 404327, at *1 (D.C. Cir. June 30, 1997) (finding that without evidence that Assistant United States Attorney made misrepresentation at trial, public interest in disclosure is insubstantial); Quiñon, 86 F.3d at 1231 (holding that in absence of evidence FBI engaged in wrongdoing, public interest is "insubstantial"); Schiffer, 78 F.3d at 1410 (finding "little to no" public interest in disclosure when requester made unsubstantiated claim that FBI's decision to investigate him had been affected by "undue influence"); McCutchen, 30 F.3d at 189 (finding "negligible" public interest in disclosure of identities of agency scientists who did not engage in scientific misconduct); Beck v. Department of Justice, 997 F.2d 1489, 1492-94 (D.C. Cir. 1993) (holding that agency properly "Glomarized" request for records concerning alleged wrongdoing by two named employees; no public interest absent any evidence of wrongdoing or widespread publicity of investigation); KTVY-TV, 919 F.2d at 1470 (allegations of "possible neglect"); Ligorner, 2 F. Supp. 2d at 405 (when considering privacy interests of person accused of misconduct, public interest is "de minimis"); Greenberg v. United States Dep't of Treasury, 10 F. Supp. 2d 3, 25 (D.D.C. 1998) (rejecting plaintiffs' "post-hoc rationalization of public interest" in FBI investigation because they had not even suggested FBI wrongdoing during investigation); Exner, 902 F. Supp. at 244-45 & n.9 (finding allegation of FBI cover-up of "extremely sensitive political operation" provides "minimal at best" public interest); Triestman v. United States Dep't of Justice, 878 F. Supp. 667, 673 (S.D.N.Y. 1995) (finding no substantial public interest in disclosure when request seeks information concerning possible investigations of wrongdoing by named DEA agents); Buros, No. 93-571, slip op. at 10 (W.D. Wis. Oct. 26, 1994) (holding even though subject's potential mishandling of funds already known to public, "confirming . . . federal criminal investigation brushes the subject with an independent and indelible taint of wrongdoing"); Williams v. McCausland, No. 90-7563, 1994 WL 18510, at *12 (S.D.N.Y. Jan. 18, 1994) (protecting identities of government employees accused of improper conduct) (Exemptions 6 and 7(C)); Manchester, 823 F. Supp. at 1271 (sweeping allegations of governmental misconduct). But see Dobronski v. FCC, 17 F.3d 275, 278 (9th Cir. 1994) (atypically finding public interest in disclosure of sick leave records so that requester might be able to substantiate "tip" that agency official had improperly taken sick leave) (Exemption 6); Providence Journal Co. v. United States Dep't of the Army, 981 F.2d 552, 567-69 (1st Cir. 1992) (making aberrational finding of public interest in disclosure of unsubstantiated allegations against two senior officials); McLaughlin v. Sessions, No. 92-0454, 1993 U.S. Dist. LEXIS 13817, at *18 (D.D.C. Sept. 22, 1993) (reasoning that because request seeks information to determine whether FBI investigation was improperly terminated, requester's interest in scope and course of investigation constitutes recognized public interest which must be balanced against privacy interests of named individuals); cf. Weiner, No. 83-1720, slip op. at 2, 7 (C.D. Cal. Dec. 6, 1995) (ordering
(continued...)

## EXEMPTION 7(C)

no public interest exists in federal records that might reveal alleged misconduct by state officials;[48] such an attenuated interest "falls outside the ambit of the public interest the FOIA was enacted to serve."[49] Moreover, it should be remembered that any special expertise claimed by the requester is irrelevant in assessing any public interest in disclosure.[50]

It also is important to remember that a requester must do more than identify a public interest that qualifies for consideration under Reporters Committee: The requester must demonstrate that the public interest in disclosure is sufficiently compelling to, on balance, outweigh legitimate privacy interests.[51] Of course, "[w]here the requester fails to assert a public interest

---

[47](...continued)
disclosure of names and addresses of FBI agents involved in management and supervision of investigation of John Lennon; release would "provide meaningful way to open agency action to the light of public scrutiny" when it allegedly used unlawful activities) (applying FOIA standards in civil discovery context).

[48] See Landano, 956 F.2d at 430 (stating that there is "no FOIA-recognized public interest in discovering wrongdoing by a state agency"); Lissner, No. 98-7438, slip op. at 11 (C.D. Cal. June 15, 1999) (finding that state or local employees "fall outside FOIA's federal ambit, and, accordingly, their conduct does not constitute a public interest which FOIA recognizes"); Thomas, 928 F. Supp. at 251 (recognizing that FOIA cannot serve as basis for requests about conduct of state agency).

[49] Reporters Comm., 489 U.S. at 775; see also FOIA Update, Vol. XII, No. 2, at 6 (explaining that "government activities" in Reporter's Committee standard means activities of federal government).

[50] See Ford, 1998 WL 317561, at *3 (holding that plaintiff's prior EEO successes against agency do not establish public interest in disclosure of third-party names in this investigation); Massey, 3 F.3d at 625 (finding that the identity of the requesting party and the use that that party plans to make of the requested information have "no bearing on the assessment of the public interest served by disclosure"); Stone, 727 F. Supp. at 668 n.4 (stating that court looks to public interest served by release of information, "not to the highly specialized interests of those individuals who understandably have a greater personal stake in gaining access to that information"). But cf. Manna, 51 F.3d at 1166 (deciding that although court does not usually consider requester's identity, fact that requester held high position in La Cosa Nostra is certainly material to protection of individual privacy).

[51] See Senate of P.R. v. United States Dep't of Justice, 823 F.2d 574, 588 (D.C. Cir. 1987) (holding general interest of legislature in "getting to the bottom" of highly controversial investigation not sufficient to overcome "substantial privacy interests"); Schrecker v. United States Dep't of Justice, 74 F. Supp. 2d 26, 34 (D.D.C. 1999) (finding requester's "own personal curiosity" about names of third parties and agents insufficient to outweigh privacy interests); Times Picayune, 37 F. Supp. 2d at 482 (describing public interest in public figure's mug shot as "purely speculative" and therefore outweighed by privacy interest); Ajluni, 947 F. Supp. at 605 ("In the absence of any strong counter-
(continued...)

## EXEMPTION 7(C)

purpose for disclosure, even a less than substantial invasion of another's privacy is unwarranted."[52] In the wake of Reporters Committee, the public interest standard ordinarily will not be satisfied when FOIA requesters seek law enforcement information pertaining to living persons.[53]

---

[51](...continued)
vailing public interest in disclosure, the privacy interests of the individuals who are the subjects of the redacted material must prevail."); Fitzgibbon v. United States Secret Serv., 747 F. Supp. 51, 59 (D.D.C 1990) (holding public interest in alleged plot in United States by agents of now deposed dictatorship insufficient to overcome "strong privacy interests"); Stone, 727 F. Supp. at 667-68 n.4 ("[N]ew information considered significant by zealous students of the RFK assassination investigation would be nothing more than minutia of little or no value in terms of the public interest."); see also Center to Prevent Handgun Violence, 981 F. Supp. at 23-24 (finding "minuscule privacy interest" in identifying sellers in multiple-sales gun reports in comparison to public interest in scrutinizing ATF's performance of its duty to enforce gun control laws and to curtail illegal interstate gun trafficking); Steinberg, 1998 WL 384084, at *3 (finding significant public interest in criminal investigation of alleged counterterrorist activities, which outweighs privacy interests of informants known to plaintiff).

[52] King v. United States Dep't of Justice, 586 F. Supp. 286, 294 (D.D.C. 1983), aff'd, 830 F.2d 210 (D.C. Cir. 1987); see also Beck, 997 F.2d at 1494 (observing that request implicates no public interest at all, court "'need not linger over the balance; something . . . outweighs nothing every time'" (quoting National Ass'n of Retired Fed. Employees v. Horner, 879 F.2d 873, 879 (D.C. Cir. 1989)) (Exemptions 6 and 7(C)); Fitzgibbon, 911 F.2d at 768 (same); FOIA Update, Vol. X, No. 2, at 7.

[53] See, e.g., Abraham & Rose, 138 F.3d at 1083 (stating that public may have interest in learning how IRS exercises its power over collection of taxes but this does not mean that identity or other personal information concerning taxpayers will shed light on agency's performance); Spirko, 147 F.3d at 999 (recognizing strong privacy interests of suspects and law enforcement officers when requested documents neither confirm nor refute plaintiff's allegations of government misconduct); Quiñon, 86 F.3d at 1231 (finding insufficient public interest in disclosing individuals mentioned in FBI files when no evidence of wrongdoing; even if individuals had engaged in wrongdoing, such misconduct would have to shed light on agency's action); Schiffer, 78 F.3d at 1410 (recognizing "little to no" public interest in disclosure of persons in FBI file, including some who provided information to FBI, when no evidence of FBI wrongdoing); Schwarz v. INTERPOL, No. 94-4111, 1995 U.S. App. LEXIS 3987, at *7 (10th Cir. Feb. 28, 1995) (ruling that disclosure of any possible information about whereabouts of requester's "alleged husband" is not in public interest); Maynard, 986 F.2d at 566 (disclosing information concerning low-level FBI employees and third parties not in public interest); Fitzgibbon, 911 F.2d at 768 ("[T]here is no reasonably conceivable way in which the release of one individual's name . . . would allow citizens to know 'what their government is up to.'" (quoting Reporters Comm., 489 U.S. at 1481)); Greenberg, 10 F. Supp. 2d at 29 (holding that privacy interests of individuals mentioned in FBI surveillance tapes and transcripts obtained in arms-for-hostages investigation

(continued...)

# EXEMPTION 7(C)

In Reporters Committee, the Supreme Court also emphasized the desirability of establishing "categorical balancing" under Exemption 7(C) as a means of achieving "workable rules" for processing FOIA requests.[54] In so doing, it recognized that entire categories of cases can properly receive uniform disposition "without regard to individual circumstances; the standard virtues of bright-line rules are thus present, and the difficulties attendant to ad hoc adjudication may be avoided."[55] This approach, in conjunction with other elements of Reporters Committee and traditional Exemption 7(C) principles, subsequently led the D.C. Circuit to largely eliminate the need for case-by-case balancing in favor of "categorical" withholding of individuals' identities in law enforcement records.[56]

In SafeCard, the plaintiff sought information pertaining to an SEC investigation of manipulation of SafeCard stock, including "names and addresses of third parties mentioned in witness interviews, of customers listed in stock transaction records obtained from investment companies, and of persons in correspondence with the SEC."[57] Reiterating the fundamentally inherent privacy interest of individuals mentioned in any way in law enforcement

---

[53](...continued) clearly outweigh any public interest in disclosure); McNamera, 974 F. Supp. at 958-61 (finding, where no evidence of agency wrongdoing, no public interest in disclosure of information concerning criminal investigations of private citizens); Stone, 727 F. Supp. at 666-67 (disclosing identities of low-level FBI agents who participated in RFK assassination investigation not in public interest); see also KTVY-TV, 919 F.2d at 1470 (disclosing identities of witnesses and third parties would not further plaintiff's unsupported theory that post office shootings could have been prevented by postal authorities); Halloran v. VA, 874 F.2d 315, 323 (5th Cir. 1989) ("[M]erely stating that the interest exists in the abstract is not enough; rather, the court should have analyzed how that interest would be served by compelling disclosure."); FOIA Update, Vol. X, No. 2, at 6; cf. Nation Magazine, 71 F.3d at 895 (finding "in some, perhaps many," instances when third party seeks information on named individual in law enforcement files, public interest will be "negligible"; but when individual had publicly offered to help agency, disclosure of records concerning that fact might be in public interest by reflecting "agency activity" in how it responded to offer of assistance). But cf. Accuracy in Media, Inc. v. National Park Serv., 194 F.3d 120, 123 (D.C. Cir. 1999), cert. denied, 68 U.S.L.W. 3711 (U.S. May 15, 2000) (No. 99-1578) (protecting autopsy and death-scene photographs arising out of investigation of Deputy White House Counsel Vincent Foster's suicide; rejecting plaintiff's categorical argument that "FOIA's protection of personal privacy ends upon the death of the individual depicted"); Campbell v. United States Dep't of Justice, 164 F.3d 20, 32 (D.C. Cir. 1998) (suggesting that person's privacy interests may survive death).

[54] 489 U.S. at 776-80.

[55] Id. at 780.

[56] SafeCard, 926 F.2d at 1206.

[57] Id. at 1205.

## EXEMPTION 7(C)

files,[58] the D.C. Circuit found that the plaintiff's asserted public interest--providing the public "with insight into the SEC's conduct with respect to SafeCard"--was "not just less substantial [but] insubstantial."[59] Based upon the Supreme Court's endorsement of categorical rules in Reporters Committee, it then further determined that the identities of individuals who appear in law enforcement files would virtually never be "very probative of an agency's behavior or performance."[60] It observed that such information would serve a "significant" public interest only if "there is compelling evidence that the agency . . . is engaged in illegal activity."[61] Consequently, the D.C. Circuit held

---

[58] Id. (recognizing privacy interests of suspects, witnesses, and investigators).

[59] Id.

[60] Id.

[61] Id. at 1206; see also Quiñon, 86 F.3d at 1231 (finding insufficient public interest in revealing individuals mentioned in FBI files absent evidence of wrongdoing; even if individuals had engaged in wrongdoing, such misconduct would have to shed light on agency's action); McCutchen, 30 F.3d at 188 ("Mere desire to review how an agency is doing its job, coupled with allegations that it is not, does not create a public interest sufficient to override the privacy interests protected by Exemption 7(C)."); Davis, 968 F.2d at 1282 ("[W]hen . . . governmental misconduct is alleged as the justification for disclosure, the public interest is 'insubstantial' unless the requester puts forward 'compelling evidence that the agency denying the FOIA request is engaged in illegal activity' and shows that the information sought 'is necessary in order to confirm or refute that evidence.'" (quoting SafeCard, 926 F.2d at 1205-06)); Goldstein v. Office of Indep. Counsel, No. 87-2028, 1999 WL 570862, at *9 (D.D.C. July 29, 1999) (magistrate's recommendation) (finding "significant public interest" in documents relating to FBI's terrorism investigations but concluding that withholding of third-party names is proper absent compelling evidence of illegal activity by FBI); Chasse v. United States Dep't of Justice, No. 98-207, slip op. at 11 (D. Vt. Jan. 12, 1999) (magistrate's recommendation) (deciding that Exemption 7(C) does not apply to information regarding job-related activities of high-level INS officials alleged to have deceived members of congressional task force), adopted (D. Vt. Feb. 9, 1999), aff'd, No. 99-6059 (2d Cir. Apr. 6, 2000); McGhghy, No. C 97-0185, slip op. at 10 (N.D. Iowa May 29, 1998) (holding that there is "no compelling public interest rationale" for disclosing the names of law enforcement officers, private individuals, investigative details, or suspects' names from DEA files); cf. Nation Magazine, 71 F.3d at 895-96 (finding when individual had publicly offered to help agency, disclosure of records concerning that fact might be in public interest by reflecting "agency activity" in how it responded to offer of assistance); Dunkelberger, 906 F.2d at 782 (finding some cognizable public interest in "FBI agent's alleged participation in a scheme to entrap a public official and in the manner in which the agent was disciplined"); Oregon Natural Desert Ass'n v. United States Dep't of the Interior, 24 F. Supp. 2d 1088, 1093-94 (D. Or. 1998) (finding that public interest in knowing how government enforces and punishes violations of land-management laws outweighs privacy interests of cattle trespassers who admitted violations) (Exemptions 6 and 7(C)). But see
(continued...)

## EXEMPTION 7(C)

that "unless access to the names and addresses of private individuals appearing in files within the ambit of Exemption 7(C) is necessary in order to confirm or refute compelling evidence that the agency is engaged in illegal activity, such information is [categorically] exempt from disclosure."[62] Nevertheless, agencies should be sure to redact their law enforcement records so that only identifying information is withheld under Exemption 7(C).[63] (See the further discussion of privacy redaction under Exemption 6, above.)

Protecting the privacy interests of individuals who are the targets of FOIA requests and are named in investigatory records requires special procedures. Most agencies with criminal law enforcement responsibilities follow the approach of the FBI, which is generally to respond to FOIA requests for records concerning other individuals by refusing to confirm or deny whether such records exist. Such a response is necessary because, as previously discussed, members of the public may draw adverse inferences from the mere

---

[61](...continued)
Detroit Free Press, 73 F.3d at 98 (finding, despite no evidence of government wrongdoing, public interest in disclosure of mug shots of indicted individuals who had already appeared in court and had their names divulged); Rosenfeld, 57 F.3d at 811-12 (making exceptional finding of public interest in disclosure of names of subjects of investigatory interest because disclosure would serve public interest by shedding light on FBI actions and showing whether and to what extent FBI "abused its law enforcement mandate by overzealously investigating a political protest movement"); Providence Journal, 981 F.2d at 567-69 (making exceptional finding of public interest in disclosure of unsubstantiated allegations); Bennett v. DEA, 55 F. Supp. 2d 36, 41 (D.D.C. 1999) (ordering release of informant's rap sheet after finding "very compelling" evidence of "extensive government misconduct" in handling informant); Davin, No. 92-1122, slip op. at 9 (W.D. Pa. Apr. 9, 1998) (ordering disclosure of names and addresses of individuals in records of FBI investigation of Workers Alliance of America conducted between 1938 and 1964).

[62] SafeCard, 926 F.2d at 1206; see also Neely, 208 F.3d at 464 (adopting SafeCard approach).

[63] See, e.g., Church of Scientology Int'l v. United States Dep't of Justice, 30 F.3d 224, 230-31 (1st Cir. 1994) (deciding agency's Vaughn index must explain why documents entirely withheld under Exemption 7(C) could not have been released with identifying information redacted); Prows v. United States Dep't of Justice, No. 90-2561, 1996 WL 228463, at *3 (D.D.C. Apr. 25, 1996) (concluding that rather than withholding documents in full, agency simply can delete identifying information about third-party individuals to eliminate stigma of being associated with law enforcement investigation); Kitchen v. FBI, No. 93-2382, slip op. at 10-11 (D.D.C. Mar. 18, 1996) (same), complaint dismissed for failure to prosecute (D.D.C. Apr. 16, 1997); accord Attorney General's Memorandum for Heads of Departments and Agencies regarding the Freedom of Information Act (Oct. 4, 1993) [hereinafter Attorney General Reno's FOIA Memorandum], reprinted in FOIA Update, Vol. XIV, No. 3, at 4-5 (articulating FOIA policy of "maximum responsible disclosure"); Attorney General's Follow-Up Memorandum for Heads of Departments and Agencies regarding the Freedom of Information Act (Sept. 3, 1999), reprinted in FOIA Update, Vol. XIX, No. 4, at 3-5 (reiterating importance of policy).

## EXEMPTION 7(C)

fact that an individual is mentioned in the files of a criminal law enforcement agency.[64] Except when the third-party subject is deceased or provides a written waiver of his privacy rights, law enforcement agencies ordinarily "Glomarize" such third-party requests--refusing either to confirm or deny the existence of responsive records--in order to protect the privacy of those who are in fact the subject of or mentioned in investigatory files.[65]

---

[64] See Ray, 778 F. Supp. at 1215; FOIA Update, Vol. X, No. 3, at 5; FOIA Update, Vol. VII, No. 1, at 3-4 ("OIP Guidance: Privacy 'Glomarization'"); FOIA Update, Vol. III, No. 4, at 2; see also Enzinna, 1997 WL 404327, at *2 (finding government's "Glomar" response appropriate because acknowledging existence of responsive documents would associate witnesses with criminal investigation); Massey, 3 F.3d at 624 ("individuals have substantial privacy interests in information that either confirms or suggests that they have been subject to criminal investigations or proceedings"); Antonelli, 721 F.2d at 617 ("even acknowledging that certain records are kept would jeopardize the privacy interests that the FOIA exemptions are intended to protect"); Burke v. United States Dep't of Justice, No. 96-1739, 1999 WL 1032814, at *5 (D.D.C. Sept. 30, 1999) (permitting agency to "simply 'Glomarize'" as to portion of request that seeks investigatory records); Greenberg, 10 F. Supp. 2d at 24 (holding "Glomar" response appropriate when existence of records would link named individuals with taking of American hostages in Iran and disclosure would not shed light on agency's performance); McNamera, 974 F. Supp. at 957-60 (allowing FBI and INTERPOL to refuse to confirm or deny whether they have criminal investigatory files on private individuals who have "great privacy interest" in not being associated with stigma of criminal investigation); Tanks, 1996 U.S. Dist. LEXIS 7266, at **12-13 (permitting FBI to refuse to confirm or deny existence of any law enforcement records, unrelated to requester's case, concerning informants who testified against requester); Latshaw v. FBI, No. 93-571, slip op. at 1 (W.D. Pa. Feb. 21, 1994) (deciding that FBI may refuse to confirm or deny existence of any law enforcement records on third party), aff'd, 40 F.3d 1240 (3d Cir. 1994) (unpublished table decision).

[65] See, e.g., Reporters Comm., 489 U.S. at 775 (upholding FBI's refusal to confirm or deny that it maintained "rap sheets" on named individual); Schwarz, 1995 U.S. App. LEXIS 3987, at *7 (holding "Glomar" response proper for third-party request for file of requester's "alleged husband" when no public interest shown); Antonelli, 721 F.2d at 617 (deciding that "Glomar" response is appropriate for third-party requests when requester has identified no public interest in disclosure); McNamera, 974 F. Supp. at 954 (deciding that "Glomar" response concerning possible criminal investigatory files on private individuals is appropriate where records would be categorically exempt); Early v. Office of Prof'l Responsibility, No. 95-0254, slip op. at 3 (D.D.C. Apr. 30, 1996) (concluding that "Glomar" response concerning possible complaints against or investigations of judge and three named federal employees was proper absent any public interest in disclosure), summary affirmance granted, No. 96-5136, 1997 WL 195523 (D.C. Cir. Mar. 31, 1997); Durham, No. 91-2234, 1992 WL 700246, at *2 (D.D.C. Nov. 25, 1992) (finding "Glomar" response concerning possible subject of murder investigation warranted); see also FOIA Update, Vol. X, No. 3, at 5; FOIA Update, Vol. VII, No. 1, at 3-4.

**EXEMPTION 7(C)**

In employing privacy "Glomarization," however, agencies must be careful to use it only to the extent that it is warranted by the terms of the particular FOIA request at hand.[66] For a request that involves more than just a law enforcement file, the agency must take a "bifurcated" approach to it, distinguishing between the exceptionally sensitive law enforcement part of the request and any part that is not so sensitive as to require "Glomarization."[67] In so doing, agencies apply the following general rules: (1) FOIA requests that merely seek law enforcement records pertaining to a named individual, without any elaboration, can be given a standard "Glomarization" response; (2) any request that is specifically and exclusively directed to an agency's non-law enforcement files (e.g., one aimed at personnel files only) should receive purely conventional treatment, without "Glomarization"; and (3) FOIA requests that do more than simply seek law enforcement records on a named individual (e.g., ones that encompass personnel or possible administrative files as well) must be bifurcated for conventional as well as "Glomarization" treat-

---

[66] See Nation Magazine, 71 F.3d at 894-96 (holding categorical "Glomar" response concerning law enforcement files on individual inappropriate when individual had publicly offered to help agency; records discussing reported offers of assistance to agency by former presidential candidate H. Ross Perot "may implicate a less substantial privacy interest than any records associating Perot with criminal activity," so conventional processing required for such records); see also FOIA Update, Vol. XVII, No. 2, at 3-4 ("OIP Guidance: The Bifurcation Requirement for Privacy 'Glomarization'").

[67] See, e.g., Nation Magazine, 71 F.3d at 894-96 (deciding that "Glomar" response is appropriate only as to existence of records associating former presidential candidate H. Ross Perot with criminal activity), on remand, 937 F. Supp. 39, 45 (D.D.C. 1996) (finding that "Glomar" response as to whether Perot was subject, witness, or informant in law enforcement investigation appropriate after agency searched law enforcement files for records concerning Perot's efforts to assist agency), further proceedings, No. 94-00808, slip op. at 9-11 (D.D.C. Feb. 14, 1997) (ordering agency to file in camera declaration with court explaining whether it ever assigned informant code to named individual and results of any search performed using that code; agency not required to state on record whether individual was ever assigned code number), further proceedings, No. 94-00808, slip op. at 9-10 (D.D.C. May 21, 1997) (accepting agency's in camera declaration that search of its records using code number assigned to named individual uncovered no responsive documents); Burke, 1999 WL 1032814, at *5 (finding no need to bifurcate request that "specifically and exclusively" sought investigative records on third parties); Tanks, 1996 U.S. Dist. LEXIS 7266, at *4 (upholding privacy "Glomarization" after agency bifurcated between aspects of request); Nation Magazine v. Department of State, No. 92-2303, slip op. at 23-24 (D.D.C. Aug. 18, 1995) (requiring FBI to search for any "noninvestigative" files on Perot); Grove, 802 F. Supp. at 510-11 (finding agency conducted search for administrative records sought but "Glomarized" part of request concerning investigatory records); accord Reporters Comm., 489 U.S. at 757 (involving "Glomarization" bifurcation along "public interest" lines); Gardels v. CIA, 510 F. Supp. 977, 979 (D.D.C. 1981), aff'd, 689 F.2d 1100, 1102-03 (D.C. Cir. 1982) (employing "Glomarization" bifurcation in national security context).

## EXEMPTION 7(C)

ment.[68]

Prior to Reporters Committee, before an agency could give a "Glomarization" response, it was required to check the requested records, if any existed, for any official acknowledgment of the investigation (e.g., as a result of prosecution) or for any overriding public interest in disclosure that would render "Glomarization" inapplicable. However, in Reporters Committee, the Supreme Court eliminated the need to consider whether there has been a prior acknowledgment when it expressly "recognized the privacy interest inherent in the nondisclosure of certain information even when the information may have been at one time public."[69] Further, as the very fact of an arrest and conviction of a person, as reflected in his FBI "rap sheet," creates a cognizable privacy interest, any underlying investigative file, containing a far more detailed account of the subject's activities, gives rise to an even greater privacy interest.[70]

At the litigation stage, the agency must demonstrate to the court, either through a Vaughn affidavit or an in camera submission, that its refusal to confirm or deny the existence of responsive records is appropriate.[71] Although this "refusal to confirm or deny" approach is now widely accepted in the case

---

[68] Accord FOIA Update, Vol. XVII, No. 2, at 3-4; see, e.g., Nation Magazine, 937 F. Supp. at 45 (finding that "Glomar" response as to whether H. Ross Perot was subject, witness, or informant in law enforcement investigation appropriate after agency searched law enforcement files for less sensitive law enforcement records); Tanks, 1996 U.S. Dist. LEXIS 7266, at *4 (finding that agency properly bifurcated between aspects of request); Grove, 802 F. Supp. at 510-14 (allowing Navy to bifurcate between "administrative documents" and those held by its investigative component, Naval Investigative Service).

[69] 489 U.S. at 767.

[70] See FOIA Update, Vol. X, No. 3, at 5 (stating that under Reporters Committee, Exemption 7(C) "Glomarization" can be undertaken without review of any responsive records, in response to third-party requests for routine law enforcement records pertaining to living private citizens who have not given consent to disclosure); see also FOIA Update, Vol. XII, No. 2, at 6 (warning agencies not to notify requesters of identities of other agencies to which record referrals are made, in any exceptional case in which doing so would reveal sensitive abstract fact about existence of records).

[71] See Ely v. FBI, 781 F.2d 1487, 1492 n.4 (11th Cir. 1986) ("the government must first offer evidence, either publicly or in camera to show that there is a legitimate claim"); McNamera, 974 F. Supp. at 957-58 (finding agencies' affidavits sufficient to support "Glomar" response); Nation Magazine, No. 94-00808, slip op. at 9-11 (D.D.C. Feb. 14, 1997) (ordering agency to file in camera declaration with court explaining whether it ever assigned informant code to named individual and results of any search performed using that code); Grove, 752 F. Supp. at 30 (requiring agency to conduct search to properly justify use of "Glomar" response in litigation).

**EXEMPTION 7(C)**

law,[72] several cases have illustrated the procedural difficulties involved in defending a "Glomar" response when the requester's "speculation" as to the contents of the records (if any exist) raises a qualifying public interest.[73]

The significantly lessened certainty of harm now required under Exemption 7(C) and the approval of "categorical" withholding of privacy-related law enforcement information in most instances should permit agencies to afford full protection to personal privacy interests in law enforcement files whenever it can reasonably be foreseen that those interests are threatened by

---

[72] See, e.g., Reporters Comm., 489 U.S. at 757 (request for any "rap sheet" on individual defense contractor); Schwarz, 1995 U.S. App. LEXIS 3987, at *7 (request for file on "alleged husband"); Beck, 997 F.2d at 1493-94 (request for records concerning alleged wrongdoing by two named DEA agents); Dunkelberger, 906 F.2d at 780, 782 (request for information that could verify alleged misconduct by an undercover FBI agent); Freeman v. United States Dep't of Justice, No. 86-1073, slip op. at 2 (4th Cir. Dec. 29, 1986) (request for alleged FBI informant file of Teamsters president); Strassman v. United States Dep't of Justice, 792 F.2d 1267, 1268 (4th Cir. 1986) (request for records allegedly indicating whether governor of West Virginia threatened to invoke Fifth Amendment); Antonelli, 721 F.2d at 616-19 (request seeking files on eight third parties); Greenberg, 10 F. Supp. 2d at 10 (request for information relating to involvement of named individuals in "October Surprise" allegations); Early, No. 95-0254, slip. op. at 3 (D.D.C. Apr. 30, 1996) (request for complaints against or investigations of judge and three named federal employees); Triestman, 878 F. Supp. at 669 (request by prisoner seeking records of investigations of misconduct by named DEA agents); Durham, No. 91-2234, 1992 WL 700246, at *1 (D.D.C. Nov. 25, 1992) (request by prisoner seeking file on possible suspect in murder investigation); Ray, 778 F. Supp. at 1215 (request for any records reflecting results of INS investigation of alleged employee misconduct); Knight Publ'g Co. v. United States Dep't of Justice, No. 84-510, slip op. at 1-2 (W.D.N.C. Mar. 28, 1985) (request by newspaper seeking any DEA investigatory file on governor, lieutenant governor, or attorney general of North Carolina); Ray v. United States Dep't of Justice, 558 F. Supp. 226, 228-29 (D.D.C. 1982) (request by convicted killer of Dr. Martin Luther King, Jr., seeking any file on requester's former attorney or Congressman Louis Stokes), aff'd, 720 F.2d 216 (D.C. Cir. 1983) (unpublished table decision); Blakey v. Department of Justice, 549 F. Supp. 362, 365-66 (D.D.C. 1982) (request by professor seeking any records relating to a minor figure in investigation of assassination of President Kennedy who was indexed under topics other than Kennedy assassination), aff'd in part & vacated in part, 720 F.2d 215 (D.C. Cir. 1983) (unpublished table decision).

[73] See Shaw v. FBI, 604 F. Supp. 342, 344-45 (D.D.C. 1985) (seeking any investigatory files on individuals whom requester believed participated in assassination of President Kennedy); Flynn v. United States Dep't of Justice, No. 83-2282, slip op. at 1-3 (D.D.C. Feb. 18, 1984) (alleging documents reflect judicial bias), summary judgment for agency granted (D.D.C. Apr. 6, 1984); see also Knight Publ'g, No. 84-510, slip op. at 2 (W.D.N.C. Mar. 28, 1985) (unsealing of in camera affidavit on motion to compel).

# EXEMPTION 7(D)

a contemplated FOIA disclosure.[74]

## EXEMPTION 7(D)

Exemption 7(D) provides protection for "records or information compiled for law enforcement purposes [which] could reasonably be expected to disclose the identity of a confidential source, including a State, local, or foreign agency or authority or any private institution which furnished information on a confidential basis, and, in the case of a record or information compiled by a criminal law enforcement authority in the course of a criminal investigation or by an agency conducting a lawful national security intelligence investigation, information furnished by a confidential source."[1]

It has long been recognized that Exemption 7(D) affords the most comprehensive protection of all of the FOIA's law enforcement exemptions. Indeed, both Congress and the courts have clearly manifested their appreciation that a "robust" Exemption 7(D)[2] is important to ensure that "confidential sources are not lost through retaliation against the sources for past disclosure or because of the sources' fear of future disclosure."[3]

---

[74] See Attorney General's 1986 Amendments Memorandum at 9-12; see also Stone, 727 F. Supp. at 665 (discussing breadth of Exemption 7(C) protection after 1986 FOIA amendments); accord Attorney General Reno's FOIA Memorandum, reprinted in FOIA Update, Vol. XIV, No. 3, at 4-5 (establishing "foreseeable harm" standard governing use of FOIA exemptions); see also FOIA Update, Vol. XV, No. 2, at 3.

[1] 5 U.S.C. § 552(b)(7)(D) (1994 & Supp. IV 1998).

[2] See Brant Constr. Co. v. EPA, 778 F.2d 1258, 1262 (7th Cir. 1985).

[3] Id.; see, e.g., Ortiz v. HHS, 70 F.3d 729, 732 (2d Cir. 1995) (stating that "Exemption 7(D) is meant to . . . protect confidential sources from retaliation that may result from the disclosure of their participation in law enforcement activities"); McDonnell v. United States, 4 F.3d 1227, 1258 (3d Cir. 1993) (finding that "goal of Exemption 7(D) [is] to protect the ability of law enforcement agencies to obtain the cooperation of persons having relevant information and who expect a degree of confidentiality in return for their cooperation"); Providence Journal Co. v. United States Dep't of the Army, 981 F.2d 552, 563 (1st Cir. 1992) (explaining that Exemption 7(D) is intended to avert "drying-up" of sources); Nadler v. United States Dep't of Justice, 955 F.2d 1479, 1486 (11th Cir. 1992) (observing that "fear of exposure would chill the public's willingness to cooperate with the FBI . . . [and] would deter future cooperation" (citing Irons v. FBI, 880 F.2d 1446, 1450-51 (1st Cir. 1989))); Shaw v. FBI, 749 F.2d 58, 61 (D.C. Cir. 1984) (holding that purpose of Exemption 7(D) is "to prevent the FOIA from causing the 'drying up' of sources of information in criminal investigations"); Inducto Therm Corp. v. OSHA, No. 5:95cv157, slip op. at 10 (E.D. Tex. Oct. 31, 1996) (magistrate's recommendation) ("Exemption 7(D) was not designed to solely protect the source, but rather to protect law enforcement agencies in their efforts to find future sources."), adopted (E.D. Tex. Dec. 5, 1996).

# EXEMPTION 7(D)

Sources' identities are protected wherever they have provided information under either an express promise of confidentiality[4] or "under circumstances from which such an assurance could be reasonably inferred."[5] As the Supreme Court in 1993 made clear in United States Department of Justice v. Landano,[6] not all sources furnishing information in the course of criminal investigations are entitled to a "presumption" of confidentiality.[7] Instead, the Supreme Court ruled that source confidentiality must be determined on a case-by-case basis,[8] particularly noting that such a presumption should not be applied automatically to cooperating law enforcement agencies.[9]

The term "source" is meant to include a wide variety of individuals and institutions. The legislative history of the 1974 amendments to the FOIA indicates that the term "confidential source" was chosen by design to encompass a broader group than would have been included had the word "informer" been used.[10] This was reinforced in the Freedom of Information Reform Act of 1986,[11] which added to the statute specific categories of individuals and institutions to be included in the term "source."[12]

By its own terms, however, this statutory enumeration is not exhaustive. Indeed, courts have interpreted the term "source" to include a wide variety of individuals and institutions that are not necessarily specified on the face of

---

[4] See Rosenfeld v. United States Dep't of Justice, 57 F.3d 803, 814 (9th Cir. 1995) ("[A]n express promise of confidentiality is 'virtually unassailable' [and is] easy to prove: 'The FBI need only establish the informant was told his name would be held in confidence.'" (quoting Wiener v. FBI, 943 F.2d 972, 986 (9th Cir. 1991))); Jones v. FBI, 41 F.3d 238, 248 (6th Cir. 1994) (stating that "sources who spoke with express assurances of confidentiality are always 'confidential' for FOIA purposes"); McDonnell, 4 F.3d at 1258 (holding that "identity of and information provided by [persons given express assurances of confidentiality] are exempt from disclosure under the express language of Exemption 7(D)"); Buhovecky v. Department of Justice, 700 F. Supp. 566, 571 (D.D.C. 1988) (ruling that "there is clear authority to withhold the names of those sources to whom confidentiality was expressly granted").

[5] S. Conf. Rep. No. 93-1200, at 13.

[6] 508 U.S. 165 (1993).

[7] Id. at 175.

[8] Id. at 179-80.

[9] Id. at 176; see also FOIA Update, Vol. XIV, No. 3, at 10.

[10] See S. Conf. Rep. No. 93-1200, at 13 (1974), reprinted in 1974 U.S.C.C.A.N. 6285, 6291.

[11] Freedom of Information Reform Act of 1986, Pub. L. No. 99-570, § 1802, 100 Stat. 3207, 3207-48.

[12] Id.

## EXEMPTION 7(D)

the statute--such as crime victims,[13] citizens providing unsolicited allegations of misconduct,[14] citizens responding to inquiries from law enforcement agencies,[15] private employees responding to OSHA investigators about the circumstances of an industrial accident,[16] employees providing information about their employers,[17] prisoners,[18] mental healthcare facilities,[19] medical personnel,[20] commercial or financial institutions,[21] state and local law enforcement

---

[13] See, e.g., Coleman v. FBI, No. 89-2773, slip op. at 21 (D.D.C. Dec. 10, 1991), summary affirmance granted, 1992 WL 373976 (D.C. Cir. Dec. 4, 1992); Gula v. Meese, 699 F. Supp. 956, 960 (D.D.C. 1988).

[14] See, e.g., Brant Constr., 778 F.2d at 1263; Pope v. United States, 599 F.2d 1383, 1386-87 (5th Cir. 1979); Almy v. Department of Justice, No. 90-0362, 1995 WL 476255, at **12-13 (N.D. Ind. Apr. 13, 1995), aff'd, 114 F.3d 1191 (7th Cir. 1997) (unpublished table decision); Mobil Oil Corp. v. FTC, No. 74-Civ-311, slip op. at 3 (S.D.N.Y. Dec. 7, 1978).

[15] See, e.g., Providence Journal, 981 F.2d at 565; Miller v. Bell, 661 F.2d 623, 627-28 (7th Cir. 1981); Kowalczyk v. O'Brien, No. 94-1333, slip op. at 2 (D.D.C. Jan. 30, 1996); Steinberg v. United States Dep't of Justice, No. 93-2409, slip op. at 23 (D.D.C. Oct. 31, 1995); Kitchen v. DEA, No. 93-2035, slip op. at 14 (D.D.C. Oct. 11, 1995), appeal dismissed for failure to prosecute, No. 95-5380 (D.C. Cir. Dec. 11, 1996); Augarten v. DEA, No. 93-2192, 1995 WL 350797, at *2 (D.D.C. May 22, 1995); Anderson v. DEA, No. 92-0225, slip op. at 10 (W.D. Pa. May 18, 1994) (magistrate's recommendation), adopted (W.D. Pa. June 27, 1994), appeal dismissed, No. 94-3387 (3d Cir. Sept. 12, 1994); Almy, 1995 WL 476255, at **21, 23.

[16] See, e.g., L&C Marine Transp., Ltd. v. United States, 740 F.2d 919, 924-25 (11th Cir. 1984).

[17] See, e.g., United Techs. Corp. v. NLRB, 777 F.2d 90, 94 (2d Cir. 1985); Government Accountability Project v. NRC, No. 86-3201, slip op. at 9-10 (D.D.C. June 30, 1993).

[18] See, e.g., Johnson v. Federal Bureau of Prisons, No. 90-H-645, 1990 U.S. Dist. LEXIS 18358, at *9 (N.D. Ala. Nov. 1, 1990).

[19] See, e.g., Sanders v. United States Dep't of Justice, No. 91-2263, 1992 WL 97785, at **4-5 (D. Kan. Apr. 21, 1992).

[20] See, e.g., Putnam v. United States Dep't of Justice, 873 F. Supp. 705, 716 (D.D.C. 1995).

[21] See, e.g., Davin v. United States Dep't of Justice, No. 98-3343, slip op. at 9 (3d Cir. Jan. 27, 1999); Williams v. FBI, 69 F.3d 1155, 1158 (D.C. Cir. 1995); Jones, 41 F.3d at 248; Kowalczyk, No. 94-1333, slip op. at 2 (D.D.C. Jan. 30, 1996); Biase v. Office of Thrift Supervision, No. 93-2521, slip op. at 11 (D.N.J. Dec. 10, 1993); Coleman, No. 89-2773, slip op. at 22 (D.D.C. Dec. 10, 1991); McCoy v. Moschella, No. 89-2155, 1991 WL 212208, at *1 (D.D.C. Sept. 30, 1991); Founding Church of Scientology v. Levi, 579 F. Supp. 1060, 1063 (D.D.C. 1982), aff'd, 721 F.2d 828 (D.C. Cir. 1983); Biberman v. FBI, 528 F. Supp. 1140, 1143 (S.D.N.Y. 1982); Dunaway v. Webster, 519 F. Supp. 1059,

(continued...)

# EXEMPTION 7(D)

agencies,[22] and foreign law enforcement agencies.[23] By contrast, neither federal law enforcement agencies nor federal employees acting in their official capacities should receive any "confidential source" protection.[24]

The same underlying considerations that mandate that a broad spectrum of individuals and institutions be encompassed by the term "source" also require that the adjective "confidential" be given a similarly broad construction: It signifies that the "source furnished information with the understanding that the . . . [agency] would not divulge the communication except to the extent the . . . [agency] thought necessary for law enforcement purposes."[25]

Most significantly, "the question is not whether the requested document is of the type that the agency usually treats as confidential, but whether the particular source spoke with an understanding that the communication would

---

[21](...continued)
1082 (N.D. Cal. 1981); cf. Hunsberger v. United States Dep't of Justice, No. 92-2587, slip op. at 6-7 (D.D.C. July 22, 1997) (upholding confidential source protection for employee of financial institution).

[22] See, e.g., Williams, 69 F.3d at 1160 (local law enforcement agency); Jones, 41 F.3d at 248 (law enforcement agencies); Bell v. FBI, No. 93-1485, 1993 U.S. App. LEXIS 27235, at *5 (6th Cir. Oct. 18, 1993) (local law enforcement agencies and their officers); Ferguson v. FBI, 957 F.2d 1059, 1068 (2d Cir. 1992) (local police department); Hopkinson v. Shillinger, 866 F.2d 1185, 1222 & n.27 (10th Cir. 1989) (state law enforcement agencies); Parton v. United States Dep't of Justice, 727 F.2d 774, 775-77 (8th Cir. 1984) (state prison officials interviewed in connection with civil rights investigation); Lesar v. United States Dep't of Justice, 636 F.2d 472, 489-91 (D.C. Cir. 1980) (local police departments); Peralta v. United States Dep't of Justice, 69 F. Supp. 2d 21, 35 (D.D.C. 1999) (state and local authorities); Almy, 1995 WL 476255, at *13 (state and local law enforcement agencies); Anderson, No. 92-0225, slip op. at 11 (W.D. Pa. May 18, 1994) (other law enforcement authorities).

[23] See, e.g., Shaw, 749 F.2d at 62 (foreign law enforcement agencies); Weisberg v. United States Dep't of Justice, 745 F.2d 1476, 1491-92 (D.C. Cir. 1984) (same); Founding Church of Scientology v. Regan, 670 F.2d 1158, 1161-62 (D.C. Cir. 1981) (foreign INTERPOL national bureaus); Billington v. Department of Justice, 69 F. Supp. 2d 128, 138 (D.D.C. 1999) (foreign government entities) (appeal pending); Schwarz v. United States Dep't of Justice, No. 95-2162, slip op. at 7-8 (D.D.C. May 31, 1996) (foreign INTERPOL national bureaus), summary affirmance granted, No. 96-5183 (D.C. Cir. Oct. 23, 1996); Badalamenti v. Department of State, 899 F. Supp. 542, 549 (D. Kan. 1995) (foreign law enforcement officials); Linn v. United States Dep't of Justice, No. 92-1406, 1995 WL 417810, at **11, 22, 32 (D.D.C. June 6, 1995) (foreign law enforcement agencies, including foreign INTERPOL national bureaus).

[24] See Retail Credit Co. v. FTC, No. 75-0895, 1976 WL 1206, at *4 n. 3 (D.D.C. 1976); see also FOIA Update, Vol. V, No. 3, at 7.

[25] Landano, 508 U.S. at 174.

# EXEMPTION 7(D)

remain confidential."[26] And because the applicability of this exemption hinges on the circumstances under which the information is provided, and not on the harm resulting from disclosure (in contrast to Exemptions 6 and 7(C)), no balancing test is applied under the case law of Exemption 7(D).[27]

Courts have uniformly recognized that express promises of confidentiality deserve protection under Exemption 7(D),[28] but they usually require affi-

---

[26] Id. at 172; see Ortiz, 70 F.3d at 733; McDonnell, 4 F.3d at 1258 (holding that "content based test [is] not appropriate in evaluating a document for Exemption 7(D) status[;] rather the proper focus of the inquiry is on the source of the information"); Providence Journal, 981 F.2d at 563 (explaining that "confidentiality depends not on [document's] contents but on the terms and circumstances under which" agency acquired information); Ferguson, 957 F.2d at 1069 (maintaining that key to withholding under Exemption 7(D) is document content and not circumstances under which information obtained); Weisberg, 745 F.2d at 1492 (stating that availability of Exemption 7(D) depends not upon factual contents of document sought, but upon whether source was confidential); Shaw, 749 F.2d at 61 (same); Lesar, 636 F.2d at 492 (noting that applicability of Exemption 7(D) does not depend on factual content of document); Gordon v. Thornberg, 790 F. Supp. 374, 377 (D.R.I. 1992) (defining "confidential" as "provided in confidence or trust; neither the information nor the source need be 'secret'").

[27] See, e.g., Jones, 41 F.3d at 247 (clarifying that Exemption 7(D) "does not involve a balancing of public and private interests; if the source was confidential, the exemption may be claimed regardless of the public interest in disclosure"); McDonnell, 4 F.3d at 1257 (stating that Exemption "7(D) does not entail a balancing of public and private interests"); Nadler, 955 F.2d at 1487 n.8 (holding that "[o]nce a source has been found to be confidential, Exemption 7(D) does not require the Government to justify its decision to withhold information against the competing claim that the public interest weighs in favor of disclosure."); Parker v. Department of Justice, 934 F.2d 375, 380 (D.C. Cir. 1991) (stating that "judiciary is not to balance interests under Exemption 7(D)"); Schmerler v. FBI, 900 F.2d 333, 336 (D.C. Cir. 1990) (declaring that "statute admits no such balancing"); Irons v. FBI, 811 F.2d 681, 685 (1st Cir. 1987) (stating that "the judiciary is not permitted to undertake a balancing of conflicting interests, but is required to uphold a claimed 7(D) exemption so long as the statutory criteria are met"); Katz v. FBI, No. 87-3712, slip op. at 9 (5th Cir. Mar. 30, 1988) (noting that "unlike [with] the privacy exemption, no balancing of interests is allowed once material qualifies for the confidential source exemption"); Brant Constr., 778 F.2d at 1262-63 (observing that "Congress has struck the balance in favor of nondisclosure"); Cuccaro v. Secretary of Labor, 770 F.2d 355, 360 (3d Cir. 1985) (noting that "Exemption 7(D) provides that [information provided by] confidential sources may be withheld and the court is not required to engage in the balancing test of Exemption 7(C)"); Sands v. Murphy, 633 F.2d 968, 971 (1st Cir. 1980) (stating that "a judicial balancing test is not appropriate in applying Exemption 7(D)").

[28] See, e.g., Williams, 69 F.3d at 1159 (finding information provided under express assurances of confidentiality to be exempt from disclosure); Jones, 41 F.3d at 248 ("[o]n the basis of [court's] in camera review," express confidenti-
(continued...)

**EXEMPTION 7(D)**

davits demonstrating the firm existence of such an express promise,[29]

---

[28](...continued)
ality justified); KTVY-TV v. United States, 919 F.2d 1465, 1470 (10th Cir. 1990) (upholding express assurances of confidentiality given interviewees who provided information regarding postal employee who shot and killed fellow workers); Birch v. United States Postal Serv., 803 F.2d 1206, 1212 (D.C. Cir. 1986) (withholding found proper when "informant requested and received express assurances of confidentiality prior to assisting the investigation"); Pfannenstiel v. Director of the Fed. Bureau of Investigation, No. 98-0386, slip op. at 7 (D.N.M. Feb. 18, 1999) (finding withholding proper when FBI "entered express verbal agreements . . . by promising [sources] that their identities would be kept confidential"); Colon v. Executive Office for United States Attorneys, No. 98-0180, 1998 WL 695631, at *5 (D.D.C. Sept. 29, 1998) (ruling that information provided by informant referred to as "CI" may be withheld pursuant to express promise of confidentiality); Franklin v. United States Dep't of Justice, No. 97-1225, slip op. at 13-15 (S.D. Fla. June 15, 1998) (magistrate's recommendation) (withholding of "identities and information provided by coded and noncoded sources based upon express promises of confidentiality" was proper), adopted (S.D. Fla. June 26, 1998), aff'd, 189 F.3d 485 (11th Cir. 1999) (unpublished table decision); Fedrick v. United States Dep't of Justice, 984 F. Supp. 659, 665 (W.D.N.Y. 1997) (magistrate's recommendation) (withholding upheld when express promises of confidentiality were given to informants "in accordance with DEA policy and procedure"), adopted (W.D.N.Y. Oct. 28, 1997), aff'd sub nom. Fedrick v. Huff, 165 F.3d 13 (2d Cir. 1998) (unpublished table decision); Jimenez v. FBI, 938 F. Supp. 21, 30 (D.D.C. 1996) (withholding ruled proper when source who "provided information about possible suppliers or illegal drugs" was expressly promised confidentiality by DEA); Mittleman v. OPM, No. 92-0158, slip op. at 2 & n.2 (D.D.C. Jan. 18, 1995) (withholding proper when sources given express promise of confidentiality during OPM's background investigation), aff'd on other grounds per curiam, 76 F.3d 1240 (D.C. Cir. 1996); Cappabianca v. Commissioner, United States Customs Serv., 847 F. Supp. 1558, 1566 (M.D. Fla. 1994) (explaining that "application of Landano to a case where a witness [to an internal investigation] gave full cooperation only after receiving an express assurance of confidentiality . . . clearly leads to the conclusion that the witness is a confidential source"); Simon v. United States Dep't of Justice, 752 F. Supp. 14, 21 (D.D.C. 1991) (withholding proper when "source explicitly requested that his identity be kept confidential"), aff'd, 980 F.2d 782 (D.C. Cir. 1992).

[29] See, e.g., Neely v. FBI, 208 F.3d 461, 466 (4th Cir. 2000) (remanding with instructions that if the "district court finds that the [withheld] documents . . . do in fact, as the FBI claims, bear evidence 'on their face' of 'express promises of confidentiality,' . . . then the FBI would most likely be entitled to withhold such documents"); Halpern v. FBI, 181 F.3d 279, 299 (2d Cir. 1999) (finding insufficient agency's "bare assertions that express assurances were given to the sources in question, and that the information received was treated in a confidential manner during and subsequent to its receipt"); Davin, No. 98-3343, slip op. at 8 (3d Cir. Jan. 27, 1999) (finding express confidentiality established when "source is referred to as a 'confidential informant,' coupled with the FBI Manuals' policy that confidential informants should be given express assurances of confidentiality"); Campbell v. United States Dep't of Jus-
(continued...)

# EXEMPTION 7(D)

sometimes even with regard to "symbol-numbered" sources.[30] Indeed, courts

---

[29](...continued)
tice, 164 F.3d 20, 34-35 (D.C. Cir. 1998) (remanding case to district court because agency's affidavit "simply asserts that various sources received express assurances of confidentiality without providing any basis for the declarant's knowledge of this alleged fact"); King v. United States Dep't of Justice, 830 F.2d 210, 235 (D.C. Cir. 1987) (finding express confidentiality when agency showed "documents marked 'confidential informant' at the time of their compilation"); Guccione v. National Indian Gaming Comm'n, No. 98-CV-164, 1999 U.S. Dist. LEXIS 15475, at *8 (S.D. Cal. Aug. 4, 1999) (declaring that express confidentiality exists when agency declaration "provides sufficient context and explanation of the [withheld] documents' contents"); Goldstein v. Office of Indep. Counsel, No. 87-2028, 1999 WL 570862, at *13 (D.D.C. July 29, 1999) (magistrate's recommendation) (warning agency "that the generic, 'cookie-cutter,' one size fits all declaration . . . which speaks generally of policies and procedures but does not specifically indicate when, where, and by whom each confidential source was in fact expressly promised confidentiality, will not do"); Voinche v. FBI, 46 F. Supp. 2d 26, 34 (D.D.C. 1999) (rejecting agency's "general arguments for protecting confidential informants as well as [its] unsupported assertion . . . that the FBI made an express promise of confidentiality to the informant"); Hronek v. DEA, 16 F. Supp. 2d 1260, 1275 (D. Or. 1998) (ordering supplemental affidavit because agency failed to sufficiently "discuss the [express] grant of confidentiality"); Rosenberg v. Freeh, No. 97-0476, slip op. at 13 (D.D.C. May 13, 1998) (ruling that agency demonstrated express confidentiality when "protect identity" was written next to informant's name); Steinberg v. United States Dep't of Justice, No. 93-2409, slip op. at 14 (D.D.C. July 14, 1997) (ordering supplemental affidavit when agency's generalized statement concerning maintenance of future cooperation of sources found insufficient to demonstrate express assurances of confidentiality).

[30] See, e.g., Davin v. United States Dep't of Justice, 60 F.3d 1043, 1062 (3d Cir. 1995) (stating that "government . . . must produce evidence of its alleged policy and practice of giving all symbol numbered informants or code name sources express assurances of confidentiality, evidence that the policy was in force throughout the [time] spanned by the documents . . . and evidence that the policy was applied to each of the separate investigations and in each case in which a document or portion has been withheld"), aff'd on appeal after remand, 176 F.3d 471 (3d Cir. 1999) (unpublished table decision); Rosenfeld, 57 F.3d at 81 (determining that FBI affidavits do not demonstrate that symbol-numbered sources were given express promises of confidentiality). But see, e.g., Manna v. United States Dep't of Justice, 51 F.3d 1158, 1167 (3d Cir. 1995) (finding that express confidentiality exists as to sources "assigned numbers" who provided information regarding organized crime); McDonnell, 4 F.3d at 1258 (reasoning that "source was considered so sensitive that he or she was assigned a symbol source number and was never referred to by name in the file [leading to the] conclusion that [the information is] exempt from disclosure under the express language of Exemption 7(D)"); Green v. DEA, No. 98-0728, slip op. at 10 (D.D.C. Sept. 30, 1999) (finding sufficient agency's attestation that written policy in effect at time sources supplied information required that individuals who became informants be issued "cooperating individual"

(continued...)

**EXEMPTION 7(D)**

have held that the identities of persons providing statements in response to routinely given "unsolicited assurances of confidentiality" are protectible under Exemption 7(D) as well.[31]

In contrast to the situation involving express confidentiality, a particularly difficult issue under Exemption 7(D) involves the circumstances under which an expectation of confidentiality can be inferred. Over the years, a number of courts of appeals employed a "presumption" of confidentiality in criminal cases, particularly those involving the FBI.[32] Historically, these

---

[30](...continued)
codes and be given express assurances of confidentiality), aff'd in pertinent part & remanded in part, No. 99-5356, 2000 WL 271988 (D.C. Cir. Feb. 17, 2000); Johnson v. DEA, No. 97-2231, 1998 U.S. Dist. LEXIS 9802, at *14 (D.D.C. June 25, 1998) (holding sufficient agency attestation that coded informants "have a continuing cooperative association with [the] DEA" and "are assured confidentiality in their identities and the information they provide"), remanded, No. 98-5468, 1999 U.S. Dist. LEXIS 7332, at *2 (D.C. Cir. 1999) (remanding to district court because "affidavit's conclusory and generalized allegations do not give appellant a realistic opportunity to challenge the agency's exemption claims"); Wickline v. FBI, No. 92-1189, 1994 WL 549756, at *4 (D.D.C. Sept. 30, 1994) (holding sufficient agency attestation that "permanent source's ongoing relationship with the FBI involves an 'express assurance' that his or her identity will not be disclosed either directly or indirectly").

[31] See, e.g., Davin, No. 98-3343, slip op. at 8 (3d Cir. Jan. 27, 1999) (relying on "FBI Manuals of Rules and Regulations [to] establish that there was a practice and policy during the relevant time period of assigning code names or source symbol numbers to sources given express grants of confidentiality"); Brant Constr., 778 F.2d at 1263; L&C Marine, 740 F.2d at 924 n.5; Pope, 599 F.2d at 1386-87; Borton, Inc. v. OSHA, 566 F. Supp. 1420, 1422 (E.D. La. 1983) (magistrate's recommendation published as "appendix"); see also Church of Scientology Int'l v. United States Dep't of Justice, 30 F.3d 224, 239 (1st Cir. 1994) (ruling that "investigator's policy of affording confidentiality in interviews is an adequate basis upon which the government may consider the information provided . . . confidential"); Providence Journal, 981 F.2d at 555, 565 (finding express promises of confidentiality for 24 individuals based upon inspector general regulation); Badalamenti, 899 F. Supp. at 549 (withholding proper when agency attests that expectation of confidentiality for information about criminal activity documented by governing body of INTERPOL by resolutions); Kuffel v. United States Bureau of Prisons, 882 F. Supp. 1116, 1125 (D.D.C. 1995) (discussing how "ongoing understanding" between local law enforcement agencies and FBI that information shared about criminal investigation conducted by local agency would remain confidential alone could support conclusion that explicit grant of confidentiality existed).

[32] D.C. Circuit: Parker, 934 F.2d at 378; Dow Jones & Co. v. Department of Justice, 917 F.2d 571, 576 (D.C. Cir. 1990); Schmerler, 900 F.2d at 337; Second Circuit: Donovan v. FBI, 806 F.2d 55, 61 (2d Cir. 1986); Diamond v. FBI, 707 F.2d 75, 78 (2d Cir. 1983); Sixth Circuit: Ingle v. Department of Justice, 698 F.2d 259, 269 (6th Cir. 1983); Seventh Circuit: Kimberlin v. Department of the Treasury, 774 F.2d 204, 208 (7th Cir. 1985); Miller, 661 F.2d at 627;
(continued...)

## EXEMPTION 7(D)

courts applied a "categorical" approach to this aspect of Exemption 7(D), of the type generally approved by the Supreme Court in United States Department of Justice v. Reporters Committee for Freedom of the Press,[33] thereby eliminating the burdensome task for criminal law enforcement agencies of proving implied confidentiality on a case-by-case basis. In its 1993 decision in Landano, however, the Supreme Court effectively reversed all of these cases on this point of evidentiary presumption.[34]

At issue in Landano was "whether the Government is entitled to a presumption that all sources supplying information to the Federal Bureau of Investigation . . . in the course of a criminal investigation are confidential sources."[35] In deciding Landano, the Supreme Court first made it clear that its decision affects only implied assurances of confidentiality[36] and that a source need not have an expectation of "total secrecy" in order to be deemed a confidential source.[37] However, the Court found that it was not Congress's intent to provide for a "universal" presumption or broad categorical withholding under Exemption 7(D);[38] rather, it declared, a "more particularized approach" is

---

[32](...continued) Eighth Circuit: Parton, 727 F.2d at 776; Tenth Circuit: KTVY-TV, 919 F.2d at 1470; Hopkinson, 866 F.2d at 1222-23; Eleventh Circuit: Nadler, 955 F.2d at 1486 & n.7. But see Third Circuit: Lame v. United States Dep't of Justice, 654 F.2d 917, 928 (3d Cir. 1981) (requiring "detailed explanations relating to each alleged confidential source" so that court can determine whether Exemption 7(D) withholding appropriate as to "each source"); Ninth Circuit: Wiener, 943 F.2d at 986 (observing that "a claim that confidentiality was impliedly granted . . . requires the court to engage in a highly contextual, fact-based inquiry").

[33] 489 U.S. 749 (1989).

[34] See 508 U.S. at 179-80.

[35] Id. at 167.

[36] See id. at 172 (acknowledging that "precise question before us . . . is how the Government can meet its burden of showing that a source provided information on an implied assurance of confidentiality"); see Rosenfeld, 57 F.3d at 814 (stating that "Landano did not affect the application of Exemption 7(D) to sources and information covered by an express assurance of confidentiality").

[37] Landano, 508 U.S. at 174 (observing that "an exemption so limited that it covered only sources who reasonably could expect total anonymity would be, as a practical matter, no exemption at all"); see Cappabianca, 847 F. Supp. at 1566 (stating that "[t]he Landano Court noted that 'confidential' does not necessarily mean completely secret, but that a statement may still be made in confidence when the speaker knows it will be shared with limited others"); Butler v. United States Dep't of Justice, No. 86-2255, 1994 WL 55621, at *6 (D.D.C. Feb. 3, 1994) (holding that "source need not be promised total secrecy . . . for material to be covered by [Exemption 7(D)]"), appeal voluntarily dismissed, No. 94-5078 (D.C. Cir. Sept. 8, 1994).

[38] Landano, 508 U.S. at 174-78; see Rosenfeld, 57 F.3d at 814 (reiterating (continued...)

**EXEMPTION 7(D)**

required.[39] Under this refined approach, agencies seeking to invoke Exemption 7(D) must prove expectations of confidentiality based upon the "circumstances" of each case.[40]

Such specific showings of confidentiality, the Supreme Court indicated, can be made on a "generic" basis,[41] when "certain circumstances characteristi-

---

[38](...continued)
that "presumption of confidentiality [no longer] attaches from the mere fact of an FBI investigation. . . . [Instead,] the confidentiality determination turns on the circumstances under which the subject provided the requested information."); Jones, 41 F.3d at 247 (observing that "[Supreme] Court unanimously held that the government is not entitled to a presumption that all sources supplying information to the FBI in the course of a criminal investigation are confidential within the meaning of Exemption 7(D)"); Lesar v. United States Dep't of Justice, No. 92-2216, slip op. at 10 (D.D.C. Oct. 18, 1993) (stating that "Supreme Court recently rejected the presumption that all FBI sources should be deemed confidential").

[39] Landano, 508 U.S. at 179-80; see Quiñon v. FBI, 86 F.3d 1222, 1231 (D.C. Cir. 1996) (restating that "[Supreme] Court rejected . . . a broad presumption of confidentiality in favor of a 'particularized approach' that looks to 'factors such as the nature of the crime that was investigated and the source's relation to it' in order to determine whether a promise of confidentiality may be inferred" (quoting Landano, 508 U.S. at 179-80)); Steinberg v. United States Dep't of Justice, 23 F.3d 548, 549 (D.C. Cir. 1994) (stating that Landano requires government to make "more particularized showing" of confidentiality"); Spirko v. United States Postal Serv., No. 96-0458, slip op. at 7 (D.D.C. Feb. 25, 1997) (stating that "government must make a 'particularized' showing as to each source of information"), aff'd on other grounds, 147 F.3d 992 (D.C. Cir. 1998); LeGrand v. FBI, No. 94-0300, slip op. at 10 (S.D.N.Y. July 10, 1995) (magistrate's recommendation) (applying Landano and stating that "a particularized showing that the information was provided in confidence must be made"), adopted (S.D.N.Y. Nov. 29, 1995); cf. Computer Prof'ls for Soc. Responsibility v. United States Secret Serv., 72 F.3d 897, 906 (D.C. Cir. 1996) (holding that "the manner in which an agency 'routinely' handles information is not sufficient to establish an implied assurance of confidentiality").

[40] Landano, 508 U.S. at 180; see Hale v. United States Dep't of Justice, 99 F.3d 1025, 1030 (10th Cir. 1996) (explaining that inferences of confidentiality "should be evaluated on a case-by-case basis"); see also FOIA Update, Vol. XIV, No. 3, at 10. But see Ortiz v. United States Dep't of Justice, No. 97-140-A-3, slip op. at 9 (M.D. La. Aug. 25, 1998) (magistrate's recommendation) (relying on pre-Landano cases for proposition that assurance of confidentiality, either express or implied, can be assumed when individual gives information to criminal law enforcement official unless circumstances indicate otherwise), adopted (M.D. La. Oct. 1, 1998), aff'd, 194 F.3d 1309 (5th Cir. 1999) (unpublished table decision).

[41] Landano, 508 U.S. at 179.

## EXEMPTION 7(D)

cally support an inference of confidentiality."[42] Throughout Landano, the Court stressed two "factors" to be applied in deciding whether implicit confidentiality exists: "the nature of the crime . . . and the source's relation to it."[43] It also pointed to five lower court rulings in which courts highlighted the potential for harm to the witnesses involved, as examples of decisions in which courts have correctly applied these two factors.[44]

A majority of the courts that have addressed this issue thus far under the Landano rule have recognized the nature of the crime and the source's

---

[42] Id. at 177; see Billington v. Department of Justice, 11 F. Supp. 2d 45, 67 (D.D.C. 1998) (concluding that investigation of violent organization involved "exactly the type of serious offenses which would warrant" an inference of implied confidentiality) (appeal pending); Coleman v. FBI, 13 F. Supp. 2d 75, 81-82 (D.D.C. 1998) ("Where there is an ongoing relationship between an informant and the Bureau and their communication occurs via secret rendezvous, it is reasonable to infer confidentiality."); Greenberg v. United States Dep't of Treasury, 10 F. Supp. 2d 3, 19 (D.D.C. 1998) (ruling that implied assurance can be inferred when source advised agency he received threat to life); Steinberg v. United States Dep't of Justice, 179 F.R.D. 357, 365 (D.D.C. Apr. 28, 1998) (finding "generic circumstances" met when source would speak to FBI only through an intermediary); Isley v. Executive Office for United States Attorneys, No. 96-0123, slip op. at 8 (D.D.C. Mar. 27, 1997) (finding agency presented sufficient evidence pertaining to murder investigation to support "generic circumstances" of implied confidentiality), aff'd in pertinent part & remanded in part, 203 F.3d 52 (D.C. Cir. 1999) (unpublished table decision); Butler v. Department of the Treasury, No. 95-1931, 1997 U.S. Dist. LEXIS 802, at *10 (D.D.C. Jan. 14, 1997) (emphasizing that monitoring of conversation in prison setting between cooperating sources and plaintiff "is precisely the situation contemplated by the 'generic' circumstances of confidentiality" in Landano); see also McNamera v. United States Dep't of Justice, 974 F. Supp. 946, 963 (W.D. Tex. 1997) (ruling that major narcotics conspiracy case involved circumstances that characteristically support inference of confidentiality); Steinberg, No. 93-2409, slip op. at 15 (D.D.C. July 14, 1997) (finding it reasonable to infer confidentiality under circumstances of case involving foreign source, drug trafficking, and possible assassination).

[43] Landano, 508 U.S. at 179.

[44] Id. at 179-80 (citing Keys v. United States Dep't of Justice, 830 F.2d 337, 345-46 (D.C. Cir. 1987) (believing that individuals providing information regarding possible Communist sympathies, criminal activity, and murder by foreign operatives would have worried about retaliation); Donovan, 806 F.2d at 60-61 (ruling that individuals providing information about four American churchwomen murdered in El Salvador may likely face fear of disclosure); Parton, 727 F.2d at 776-77 (reasoning that prison officials providing information regarding alleged attack on inmate faced "high probability of reprisal"); Nix v. United States, 572 F.2d 998, 1003-04 (4th Cir. 1978) (finding implicit confidentiality when guards and prison inmates providing information about guards who allegedly beat another inmate face risk of reprisal); Miller, 661 F.2d at 628 (determining that individuals providing information about self-proclaimed litigious subject seeking to enlist them in "anti-government crusades" faced "strong potential for harassment")).

# EXEMPTION 7(D)

relation to it as the primary factors in determining whether implied confidentiality exists.[45] These courts have uniformly recognized that a key consideration is of course the potential for retaliation against the source,[46] and they

---

[45] See Grand Cent. Partnership v. Cuomo, 166 F.3d 473, 486-87 (2d Cir. 1999); Hale, 99 F.3d 1030; Quiñon, 86 F.3d at 1231; Ortiz, 70 F.3d at 733; Williams, 69 F.3d at 1159; Davin, 60 F.3d at 1063; Rosenfeld, 57 F.3d at 814; Jones, 41 F.3d at 247-48; Steinberg, 23 F.3d at 549; Koch v. United States Postal Serv., No. 93-1487, 1993 U.S. App. LEXIS 26130, at **3-4 (8th Cir. Oct. 8, 1993); McDonnell, 4 F.3d at 1260; Massey v. FBI, 3 F.3d 620, 623 (2d Cir. 1993); Peralta, 69 F. Supp. 2d at 34; Gansterer v. United States Dep't of Justice, No. 95-1614, slip op. at 16 (C.D. Cal. July 6, 1998) (magistrate's recommendation), adopted (C.D. Cal. Aug. 24, 1998); Valera v. DEA, No. 92-0575, slip op. at 5 (M.D. Fla. Sept. 20, 1994) (magistrate's recommendation), adopted (M.D. Fla. Oct. 19, 1994); Manna v. United States Dep't of Justice, 832 F. Supp. 866, 876-77 (D.N.J. 1993), aff'd, 51 F.3d 1158 (3d Cir. 1995); Manchester v. DEA, 823 F. Supp. 1259, 1262 (E.D. Pa. 1993), aff'd, 40 F.3d 1240 (3d Cir. 1994) (unpublished table decision).

[46] See, e.g., Hale, 99 F.3d at 1031 (recognizing that nature of crime supports inference of confidentiality when "discrete aspects" of it "make it particularly likely" for source to fear reprisal); Williams, 69 F.3d at 1159 (finding withholding justified based on "risk of retaliation, harassment and bodily harm"); Koch, 1993 U.S. App. LEXIS 26130, at **3-4 (finding withholding proper as to whistleblower who reported another employee's threat to bring grenade in to work because of "nature of alleged threat" and possibility of retaliation); Coleman, 13 F. Supp. 2d at 82 (recognizing potential for "third party retaliation" even when imprisoned murderer, rapist, and kidnapper has "slim likelihood" of freedom); Gansterer, No. 95-1614, slip op. at 21 (C.D. Cal. July 6, 1998) (recognizing that criminals engaged in drug trafficking are often "heavily armed, making violent retaliation a very real fear for those who provide information to the government"); Hazel v. Department of Justice, No. 95-01992, slip op. at 11 (D.D.C. July 2, 1998) (identifying risk of reprisal in "close-quarter context of prison" for sources who provided information about "cold-blooded murder" of inmate); McQueen v. United States, 179 F.R.D. 522, 531 (S.D. Tex. May 6, 1998) (considering requester's ability to harm informants in upholding Exemption 7(D) protection); Campbell v. United States Dep't of Justice, No. 89-3016, 1996 WL 554511, at *9 (D.D.C. Sept. 19, 1996) (approving consideration of sources' fears of retribution), subsequent decision, No. 89-3016, slip op. at 6 (D.D.C. Aug. 6, 1997), rev'd & remanded on other grounds, 164 F.3d 20, 34-35 (D.C. Cir. 1998); Butler, 1997 U.S. Dist. LEXIS 802, at *10 (recognizing danger of cooperating with prison or law enforcement officials); Jimenez, 938 F. Supp. at 29 (finding withholding of name and identifying information of source proper when plaintiff had previously harassed and threatened government informants); Gomez v. United States Attorney, No. 93-2530, slip op. at 13 (D.D.C. Apr. 1, 1996) (finding withholding justified because drug trafficking is of a "serious and potentially violent nature"); Kitchen v. FBI, No. 93-2382, slip op. at 12 (D.D.C. Mar. 18, 1996) (Exemption 7(D) protection warranted because of threat of personal harassment or physical danger in investigation of illegal drug activities); Wickline v. FBI, 923 F. Supp. 1, 3 (D.D.C. 1996) (finding withholding proper based on violent nature of crime when requester had been convicted of multiple dismember-
(continued...)

**EXEMPTION 7(D)**

have recognized that the "danger of retaliation encompasses more than the source's physical safety."[47]

In post-Landano cases, courts have found implied confidentiality in situations involving investigations of organized crime,[48] murder,[49] drug traf-

---

[46](...continued)
ment murders); Perrone v. FBI, 908 F. Supp. 24, 27 (D.D.C. 1995) (withholding proper when those interviewed face fear of retribution or harm based on fact of their cooperation with FBI); Linn v. United States Dep't of Justice, No. 92-1406, 1995 WL 631847, at *34 (D.D.C. Aug. 22, 1995) (finding withholding proper when "persons associated with the investigation and prosecution were subject to threats of harm when their cooperation was divulged"); Landano v. United States Dep't of Justice, 873 F. Supp. 884, 888 (D.N.J. 1994) (stating that "the violent nature of the crime, the potential involvement of the motorcycle gang, and the broad publication of the murder persuade the court that an implied assurance of confidentiality is warranted"); Putnam, 873 F. Supp. at 716 (fearing retribution, FBI properly withheld "names and information provided by relatives and close associates of the victim and the plaintiff" when former FBI agent pled guilty to first degree manslaughter of an informant); Valera, No. 92-0575, slip op. at 5 (M.D. Fla. Sept. 20, 1994) (determining that information regarding individual convicted of racketeering/drug trafficking would "pose a threat of violence to . . . sources if those sources were revealed"); see also Germosen v. Cox, No. 98CIV1294, 1999 WL 1021559, at *17 (S.D.N.Y. Nov. 9, 1999) (observing that requester sought names of confidential informants "for the specific purpose of inflicting the precise harm that Exemption 7(D) seeks to prevent--harassment of the confidential source") (appeal pending).

[47] Ortiz, 70 F.3d at 733 (citing Irons, 880 F.2d at 1451); see Grand Cent. Partnership, 166 F.3d at 487 (recognizing that retaliation "may constitute work place harassment, demotions, job transfers or loss of employment"); Schrecker v. United States Dep't of Justice, 74 F. Supp. 2d 26, 35 (D.D.C. 1999) (finding implied confidentiality in case involving passport fraud and contempt of Congress when disclosure of source's identity "would likely subject him to potential reprisal from others") (appeal pending); see also United Techs., 777 F.2d at 94 (concluding that "[a]n employee-informant's fear of employer retaliation can give rise to a justified expectation of confidentiality").

[48] See, e.g., Pray v. FBI, No. 95-0380, 1998 WL 440843, at **4-5 (S.D.N.Y. Aug. 3, 1998) (racketeering investigation); Wickline, 923 F. Supp. at 3 (organized crime case); Del Viscovo v. FBI, 903 F. Supp. 1, 3 (D.D.C. 1995) (major racketeering investigation), summary affirmance granted, No. 95-5388 (D.C. Cir. Jan. 24, 1997); Cudzich v. INS, 886 F. Supp. 101, 107 (D.D.C. 1995) (suspected alien smuggling ring); Landano, 873 F. Supp. at 888 (possible motorcycle gang-related violence); Anderson, No. 92-0225, slip op. at 11 (W.D. Pa. May 18, 1994) (gang-related shootings); Manna, 832 F. Supp. at 876 (organized crime activity).

[49] See, e.g., Burke v. United States Dep't of Justice, No. 96-1739, 1999 WL 1032814, at *8 (D.D.C. Sept. 30, 1999); Green, No. 98-0728, slip op. at 10-11
(continued...)

**EXEMPTION 7(D)**

ficking,[50] extortion,[51] illegal possession of firearms,[52] domestic terrorism,[53] national security,[54] loan sharking and gambling,[55] armed bank robbery,[56] brib-

---

[49](...continued)
(D.D.C. Sept. 30, 1999); Russell v. Barr, No. 92-2546, slip op. at 11 (D.D.C. Aug. 28, 1998); Coleman, 13 F. Supp. 2d at 82; Isley, No. 96-0123, slip op. at 8 (D.D.C. Mar. 27, 1997); Wickline, 923 F. Supp. at 3; Eagle Horse v. FBI, No. 92-2357, slip op. at 1, 5 (D.D.C. July 28, 1995); LeGrand, No. 94-0300, slip op. at 12 (S.D.N.Y. July 10, 1995); Proctor v. United States Dep't of Justice, No. 88-3340, slip op. at 1 (D.D.C. Aug. 8, 1994); Linn, 1995 WL 417810, at *11; Putnam, 873 F. Supp. at 716; Landano, 873 F. Supp. at 888.

[50] See, e.g., Bell, 1993 U.S. App. LEXIS 27235, at *5; Jefferson v. O'Brien, No. 96-1365, slip op. at 10 (D.D.C. Feb. 22, 2000); Mays v. DEA, No. 98-2496, slip op. at 4-5 (D.D.C. Sept. 14, 1999) (appeal pending); Gansterer, No. 95-1614, slip op. at 16, 21 (C.D. Cal. July 6, 1998); Robinson v. DEA, No. 97-1578, slip op. at 11 (D.D.C. Apr. 2, 1998); Trupei v. Huff, No. 96-2850, 1998 WL 8986, at *4 (D.D.C. Jan. 7, 1998); McNamera, 974 F. Supp. at 963; Jimenez, 938 F. Supp. at 29; Gomez, No. 93-2530, slip op. at 12-13 (D.D.C. Apr. 1, 1996); Kitchen, No. 93-2382, slip op. at 12 (D.D.C. Mar. 18, 1996); Perrone, 908 F. Supp. at 27; Kitchen, No. 93-2035, slip op. at 7, 16 (D.D.C. Oct. 11, 1995); Del Viscovo, 903 F. Supp. at 3; Badalamenti, 899 F. Supp. at 549; Linn, 1995 WL 417810, at *11; Valera, No. 92-0575, slip op. at 5, (M.D. Fla. Sept. 20, 1994); Kennedy v. DEA, No. 92-2731, 1994 U.S. Dist. LEXIS 2275, at *2 (D.D.C. Feb. 28, 1994).

[51] See, e.g., Perrone, 908 F. Supp. at 27; Del Viscovo, 903 F. Supp. at 3.

[52] See Perrone, 908 F. Supp. at 27.

[53] See, e.g., Blanton v. United States Dep't of Justice, 63 F. Supp. 2d 35, 49 (D.D.C. 1999) (finding implied confidentiality for sources who assisted in investigation of bombing of African-American church "during a time of great unrest in the South") (motion for partial reconsideration pending); Ajluni v. FBI, 947 F. Supp. 599, 602, 606 (N.D.N.Y. 1996); Steinberg, No. 93-2409, slip op. at 24 (D.D.C. Oct. 31, 1995).

[54] See Campbell, 1996 WL 554511, at *9 (finding implied confidential relationship "given the customary trust" that exists for relaying information between nonfederal and foreign law enforcement agencies and FBI).

[55] See Del Viscovo, 903 F. Supp. at 3.

[56] See Anderson v. United States Dep't of Justice, No. 95-1880, 1999 U.S. Dist. LEXIS 5048, at *9 n.8 (D.D.C. Apr. 12, 1999) (finding Exemption 7(D) properly applied when witnesses to armed bank robbery provided information during police line-up).

## EXEMPTION 7(D)

ery,[57] interstate transportation of stolen property,[58] and passport fraud and contempt of Congress.[59] Courts have also found that a possibility for retaliation existed for paid informants,[60] for anonymous sources,[61] and for symbol-numbered sources.[62]

Moreover, implied confidentiality has been found where former members of targeted organizations disclosed self-incriminating information,[63] where sources provided information as a result of plea-bargains,[64] where sources were interviewed during an unfair labor practice investigation,[65] and where an employee provided information about an employer.[66] Recently, the Court of Appeals for the Second Circuit found implied confidentiality for sources who furnished information in connection with a civil law enforcement investigation of a company that was alleged to have harassed homeless persons.[67]

---

[57] See Melius v. National Indian Gaming Comm'n, No. 98-2210, 1999 U.S. Dist. LEXIS 17537, at **17-18 (D.D.C. Nov. 3, 1999) (holding that criminal investigation involving allegations of bribery suggests an implied promise of confidentiality).

[58] See Del Viscovo, 903 F. Supp. at 3.

[59] See Schrecker, 74 F. Supp. at 35 (upbraiding requester for "cavalier suggestion" that "passport fraud and contempt of Congress are not serious enough crimes to warrant . . . implied confidentiality").

[60] See, e.g., Jones, 41 F.3d at 248; Anderson, No. 92-0225, slip op. at 11 (W.D. Pa. May 18, 1994); Lesar, No. 92-2216, slip op. at 11 (D.D.C. Oct. 18, 1993).

[61] See, e.g., Ortiz, 70 F.3d at 733; Hamilton v. Weise, No. 95-1161, 1997 U.S. Dist. LEXIS 18900, at *28 (M.D. Fla. Oct. 1, 1997).

[62] See, e.g., Tamayo v. United States Dep't of Justice, 932 F. Supp. 342, 345 (D.D.C. 1996), summary affirmance granted, 1997 U.S. App. LEXIS 16367 (D.C. Cir. May 22, 1997); Jones, 41 F.3d at 248; Putnam, 873 F. Supp. at 716.

[63] See Campbell, 1996 WL 554511, at *9.

[64] See Engelking v. DEA, No. 91-0165, 1997 U.S. Dist. LEXIS 1881, at *6 (D.D.C. Feb. 21, 1997) (finding implied confidentiality and observing that plea bargains frequently are only way to obtain information about other suspected criminals).

[65] See Means v. Segal, No. 97-1301, slip op. at 14-15 (D.D.C. Mar. 18, 1998) (magistrate's recommendation) (finding withholding consistent with written policy of Federal Labor Relations Authority), adopted (D.D.C. Apr. 14, 1998), aff'd per curiam on other grounds, No. 98-5170 (D.C. Cir. Oct. 6, 1998), cert. denied, 525 U.S. 1183 (1999).

[66] See, e.g., Government Accountability Project, No. 86-3201, slip op. at 9-10 (D.D.C. June 30, 1993).

[67] Grand Cent. Partnership, 166 F.3d at 487-88 (stating that "[t]hough the (continued...)

# EXEMPTION 7(D)

Some courts, however, have found agency attestations as to the circumstances surrounding a claim of implied confidentiality to be insufficient, holding that a more "specific" showing as to the nature of the crime and the source's relation to it is required under Landano.[68] For example, the Court of Appeals for the First Circuit has held that "[i]t is not enough . . . for the government simply to state blandly that the source's relationship to the crime permits an inference of confidentiality. Rather, the government has an obligation to spell out that relationship . . . [without] compromising the very interests it is seeking to protect."[69]

---

[67](...continued) HUD investigation was civil in nature, the allegations of misconduct contained in the sources' documents are 'serious and damaging' and led to the imposition of civil sanctions" and reasoning that "[i]f the identities of the sources . . . were disclosed, they would face an objectively real and substantial risk of retaliation, reprisal or harassment").

[68] See, e.g., Neely, 208 F.3d at 467 (remanding with observation that "district court would be well within its discretion to require the FBI . . . to fully shoulder its responsibility--which to date it has not done--to provide specific justifications" for claim of implied confidentiality); Hale, 99 F.3d at 1033 (finding that government's claim of implied confidentiality lacked particularized justification); Crompton v. United States Air Force, No. 98-0479, slip op. at 2-3 (D.D.C. Sept. 3, 1999) (finding that agency declaration and redacted document attached to it "neither show nor permit the inference" that source cooperated with an implied assurance of confidentiality) (appeal pending); Hall v. United States Dep't of Justice, 26 F. Supp. 2d 78, 81 (D.D.C. 1998) (finding that "FBI's generalized assertion of crimes relating to Communist Party activities is not enough to support . . . 'reasonable assumption'" that sources expected confidentiality); Kern v. FBI, No. 94-0208, slip op. at 11-12 (C.D. Cal. Sept. 14, 1998) (stating that agency's justification for the application of Exemption 7(D) is "vague and fails to sufficiently describe the circumstances from which an inference of implied confidentiality could be made") (appeal pending); Rosenberg, No. 97-0476, slip op. at 13 (D.D.C. May 13, 1998) (finding agency's claim of implied confidentiality "too general to pass muster under the case law"); Linn, 1995 WL 417810, at **15-16, 32 (determining that agency failed to link document's use to particular documents, to specify nature of material withheld and to explain why withheld information could not be segregated); Senate of P.R. v. United States Dep't of Justice, No. 84-1829, 1993 U.S. Dist. LEXIS 12162, at **35-36 (D.D.C. Aug. 24, 1993) (charging that government "has not carried its burden [under Landano] of justifying its nondisclosure of the documents, and the documents must be released"); see also Computer Prof'ls, 72 F.3d at 906 (holding that agency offered no evidence that fear of retaliation was "sufficiently widespread" to justify inference of confidentiality for sources of information and information they provided); Ajluni v. FBI, No. 94-CV-325, slip op. at 13 (N.D.N.Y. July 13, 1996) (finding agency's statements "unacceptably conclusory" when circumstances surrounding its receipt of information not described), summary judgment granted, 947 F. Supp. 599, 606 (N.D.N.Y. 1996) (holding, after in camera review, that information was provided under implied assurance of confidentiality).

[69] Scientology Int'l, 30 F.2d at 234.

## EXEMPTION 7(D)

Therefore, law enforcement agencies seeking to invoke Exemption 7(D) for "implied confidentiality" sources must specifically address both factors in order to meet Landano's higher evidentiary standard on a case-by-case basis,[70] which in practice should result in greater disclosure in many instances.[71] The Supreme Court specifically stated that when "institutional" sources--such as local law enforcement agencies and private commercial enterprises--are involved, greater disclosure should occur, because these sources typically provide a "wide variety of information" under circumstances that do not necessarily warrant confidentiality.[72] Accordingly, federal agencies now have the burden of determining and proving through the use of detailed affidavits in litigation that cooperating law enforcement agencies have provided information under either an express[73] or an implied promise of confidentiality.[74]

---

[70] 508 U.S. at 180; see also Hale, 99 F.3d at 1030.

[71] See FOIA Update, Vol. XV, No. 2, at 3 (emphasizing stringency of revised disclosure requirements).

[72] 508 U.S. at 176; see, e.g., Hale, 99 F.3d at 1033 (finding that agency did not adequately justify withholding information provided by commercial and financial institutions); Linn, 1995 WL 417810, at *32 (noting that agency disclosed "much of the information it previously withheld . . . in light of Landano," but ordering disclosure of institutional source document, "particularly in light of the fact that this document obviously originated from the Louisiana state authorities, and the application of Exemption 7(D) depends on the source of the information rather than its contents"); see also FOIA Update, Vol. XIV, No. 3, at 10 (emphasizing applicability of Landano standards to "institutional" sources as primary examples of potential for greater disclosure).

[73] See, e.g., Linn, 1995 WL 417810, at *32 (ruling that agency's conclusory attestation that "'policy of confidentiality . . . between [local and federal] law enforcement justifies nondisclosure' . . . [is] insufficient to justify withholding").

[74] See, e.g., Davin, No. 98-3343, slip op. at 9 (3d Cir. Jan. 27, 1999) (upholding finding of implied assurances of confidentiality for state or local bureaus or agencies and financial institution "accustomed to maintaining confidential files, and as to which a policy of routinely granting confidentiality was cited"); Savage v. FBI, No. C2-90-797, slip op. at 15 (S.D. Ohio Mar. 8, 1996) (finding implied confidentiality when agency attested that local law enforcement authorities suggested they might "revisit the extent of their cooperation with the FBI if confidentiality is not maintained") aff'd, 124 F.3d 199 (6th Cir. 1997) (unpublished table decision); Beard v. Department of Justice, 917 F. Supp. 61, 63 (D.D.C. 1996) (finding implied confidentiality when agency attested that "[t]he FBI requested permission from the [local law enforcement agency] to release the information [and t]he request was denied"); Putnam, 873 F. Supp. at 717 (finding implied confidentiality when agency attests that "documents provided by [state police] are not accessible to the public absent authorization from the state law enforcement agency"); Cucci v. DEA, 871 F. Supp. 508, 513 (D.D.C. 1994) (finding implied confidentiality when agency attests that document stamped "not to be distributed outside your agency" and response by state police representative that state police "provide . . . law

(continued...)

# EXEMPTION 7(D)

In the past, there existed a conflict in the case law as to the availability of Exemption 7(D) protection for sources who were advised that they might be called to testify if a trial eventually were to take place.[75] However, in <u>Landano</u>, the Supreme Court resolved this conflict by holding that "[a] source should be deemed confidential if the source furnished information with the understanding that the [agency] would not divulge the communication except to the extent . . . thought necessary for law enforcement purposes."[76] (It should be noted that the effect of a source's <u>actual testimony</u> upon continued Exemption 7(D) protection presents a distinctly different issue,[77] which is addressed below together with other issues regarding waiver of this exemption.)

The first clause of Exemption 7(D), with respect to any civil or criminal law enforcement records, focuses upon the identity of a confidential source, rather than the information furnished by the source. The 1974 legislative history of Exemption 7(D), though, plainly evidences Congress's intention to absolutely and comprehensively protect the identity of anyone who provided information to a government agency in confidence.[78] Thus, this exemption's first clause protects "both the identity of the informer and information which might reasonably be found to lead to disclosure of such identity."[79] Consequently, the courts have readily recognized that the first clause of Exemption 7(D) safeguards not only such obviously identifying information as an informant's name and address,[80] but also all information which would "tend to re-

---

[74](...continued) enforcement records to other agencies based upon an express understanding of confidentiality"); <u>see also</u> <u>FOIA Update</u>, Vol. XIV, No. 3, at 10 (advising agencies that they should pay particular attention under <u>Landano</u> to "institutional sources").

[75] <u>Compare</u> <u>Van Bourg, Allen, Weinberg & Roger v. NLRB</u>, 751 F.2d 982, 986 (9th Cir. 1985) (no confidentiality recognized), <u>and</u> <u>Poss v. NLRB</u>, 565 F.2d 654, 658 (10th Cir. 1977) (same), <u>with</u> <u>Irons</u>, 811 F.2d at 687 (confidentiality recognized), <u>Schmerler</u>, 900 F.2d at 339 (same), <u>and</u> <u>United Techs.</u>, 777 F.2d at 95 (same).

[76] 508 U.S. at 174 (clarifying that "'confidential,' as used in Exemption 7(D), refers to a degree of confidentiality less than total secrecy").

[77] <u>See</u> <u>Parker</u>, 934 F.2d at 381 (distinguishing cases in which source actually testifies from cases "consider[ing] whether a source, knowing he is likely to testify at the time he furnishes information to [an] agency, is, or remains after testimony, a 'confidential source'").

[78] <u>See</u> S. Conf. Rep. No. 93-1200, at 13.

[79] 120 Cong. Rec. 17033 (1974) (statement of Sen. Hart).

[80] <u>See, e.g.</u>, <u>Cuccaro</u>, 770 F.2d at 359-60; <u>Crooker v. IRS</u>, No. 94-0755, 1995 U.S. Dist. LEXIS 7031, at *17 (D.D.C. Apr. 27, 1995) (protecting names and addresses); <u>Ferreira v. DEA</u>, 874 F. Supp. 15, 16 (D.D.C. 1995) (protecting names); <u>Cleveland & Vicinity Dist. Council v. United States Dep't of Labor</u>, No. 1:87-2384, slip op. at 12-14 (N.D. Ohio Apr. 22, 1992) (magistrate's recommendation) (protecting names and addresses), <u>adopted</u> (N.D. Ohio May 11, (continued...)

# EXEMPTION 7(D)

veal" the source's identity.[81]

Accordingly, protection for source-identifying information extends well beyond material that is merely a substitute for the source's name. To prevent indirect identification of a source, even the name of a third party who is not a confidential source--but who acted as an intermediary for the source in his

---

[80](...continued)
1992).

[81] See Pollard v. FBI, 705 F.2d 1151, 1155 (9th Cir. 1983); Ajluni, 947 F. Supp. at 606 (finding information properly withheld where disclosure could result in narrowing sources "to a limited group of individuals"); Mavadia v. Caplinger, No. 95-3542, 1996 WL 592742, at *3 (E.D. La. Oct. 11, 1996) (ordering protection for information that would identify informants); Kitchen, No. 93-2382, slip op. at 13 (D.D.C. Mar. 18, 1996) (ruling that "Exemption 7(D) protects more than the names of confidential sources; it protects information . . . that might identify such sources"); see, e.g., Billington, 69 F. Supp. 2d at 138 (finding that "FBI is well within its rights to withhold [the city of origin of various teletypes] where revealing the city would reveal the identity of the source" and protecting identities of foreign agencies that requested law enforcement information where disclosure would "reveal that they have also agreed to provide such information in return" and would therefore "betray these foreign entities' status as confidential sources"); Lodi v. IRS, No. 96-2095, slip op. at 4-5 (E.D. Cal. Apr. 14, 1998) (finding entire pages of material properly withheld because release would disclose identity of confidential source); Spirko v. United States Postal Serv., No. 96-0458, slip op. at 2 (D.D.C. Apr. 11, 1997) (ruling that agency properly withheld location where certain event took place and specific information imparted by informant because release would allow a "knowledgeable person to deduce informant's identity"), aff'd on other grounds, 147 F.3d 992 (D.C. Cir. 1998); Crooker, 1995 U.S. Dist. LEXIS 7031, at *17 (determining that IRS properly "deleted . . . telephone numbers, recent activities, and other information tending to reveal the identity of confidential informants"); Putnam, 873 F. Supp. at 716 (finding "coded identification numbers, file numbers and information that could be used to identify sources" properly withheld); Ferreira, 874 F. Supp. at 16 (holding that DEA properly withheld identifying information); Church of Scientology v. IRS, 816 F. Supp. 1138, 1161 (W.D. Tex. 1993) (ruling that "agency may withhold any portion of the document that would reveal the identity of the confidential source"); Doe v. United States Dep't of Justice, 790 F. Supp. 17, 21 (D.D.C. 1992) (stating that where source is well known to investigated applicant, agency must protect "even the most oblique indications of identity"); Soto v. DEA, No. 90-1816, slip op. at 6 (D.D.C. Apr. 13, 1992) (finding that "dates, locations, and circumstances by which someone familiar with the criminal enterprise could deduce the informant's identity" need to be protected); see also Accuracy in Media v. FBI, No. 97-2107, slip op. at 5 (D.D.C. Mar. 31, 1999) (reasoning that if informant symbol numbers "were routinely released, over time an informant may be identified by revealing the informant's connections with dates, times, places, events, or names connected with certain cases").

**EXEMPTION 7(D)**

dealings with the agency--can be withheld.[82] And when circumstances warrant, a law enforcement agency may employ a "Glomar" response–refusing to confirm or deny the very existence of records about a particular individual--if a more specific response to a narrowly targeted request would reflect that he, she, or it acted as a confidential source.[83]

Even greater source-identification protection is provided by the "(c)(2) exclusion,"[84] which permits a criminal law enforcement agency to entirely exclude records from the FOIA under specified circumstances when necessary to avoid divulging the existence of a source relationship. (See the discussion of this provision under Exclusions, below.) Additionally, information provided by a source may be withheld under this first clause of Exemption 7(D) wherever disclosure of that information would permit the "linking" of a source to specific source-provided material.[85]

The second clause of Exemption 7(D) broadly protects all information furnished to law enforcement authorities by confidential sources in the course of criminal or lawful national security intelligence investigations.[86] Thus, the statutory requirement of an "investigation," while not a component of Exemption 7's threshold language, is "a predicate of exemption under the second

---

[82] See Birch, 803 F.2d at 1212; United Techs., 777 F.2d at 95.

[83] See Benavides v. DEA, 769 F. Supp. 380, 381-82 (D.D.C. 1990), rev'd & remanded on procedural grounds, 968 F.2d 1243 (D.C. Cir.), modified, 976 F.2d 751 (D.C. Cir. 1992).

[84] 5 U.S.C. § 552(c)(2).

[85] See L&C Marine, 740 F.2d at 923-25; see, e.g., Stone v. Defense Investigative Serv., 816 F. Supp. 782, 788 (D.D.C. 1993) (protecting "information so singular that to release it would likely identify the individual"); Barrett v. OSHA, No. C2-90-147, slip op. at 13 (S.D. Ohio Oct. 18, 1990) (protecting statements obtained from witnesses regarding single incident involving only three or four persons).

[86] See Shaw, 749 F.2d at 63-65 (articulating standard for determining if law enforcement undertaking satisfies "criminal investigation" threshold); see also Pray v. Department of Justice, No. 95-5383, 1996 WL 734142, at *1 (D.C. Cir. Nov. 20, 1996) (per curiam) (upholding agency's use of Exemption 7(D) for source information); Ferguson, 957 F.2d at 1069 (finding FBI's withholding of publicly circulated material provided to it by confidential source proper); Reiter v. DEA, No. 96-0378, 1997 WL 470108, at *6 (D.D.C. Aug. 13, 1997) (holding all source-supplied information protectible when source is confidential), summary affirmance granted, No. 97-5246, 1998 WL 202247 (D.C. Cir. Mar. 3, 1998); Kuffel, 882 F. Supp. at 1126 ("qualifying criminal investigation" exists when "FBI gather[s] information on criminals who violated specific state crimes for the purpose of using the information as possible leads in investigations of robberies and burglaries that could be in violation of federal law"); Meeropol v. Smith, No. 75-1121, slip op. at 76-78 (D.D.C. Feb. 29, 1984) (protecting information obtained during intelligence investigations), aff'd in part & remanded in part sub nom. Meeropol v. Meese, 790 F.2d 942 (D.C. Cir. 1986).

## EXEMPTION 7(D)

clause of paragraph (D)."[87] For the purposes of this clause, criminal law enforcement authorities include federal agency inspectors general.[88]

In an interesting elaboration on the definition of a "criminal investigation," courts have recognized that information originally compiled by local law enforcement authorities in conjunction with a nonfederal criminal investigation fully retains its criminal investigatory character when subsequently obtained by federal authorities,[89] even if received solely for use in a federal civil enforcement proceeding.[90] In addition, protection for source-provided information has been extended to information supplied to federal officials by state or local enforcement authorities seeking assistance in pursuing a nonfederal investigation.[91]

Under the case law, the confidential source information that falls within the broad coverage of this second clause of Exemption 7(D) need not necessarily be source-identifying.[92] Thus, under the second clause of Exemption

---

[87] Keys, 830 F.2d at 343.

[88] See Ortiz, 70 F.3d at 732 (ruling that Exemption 7(D) properly applied when "HHS's Office of Inspector General . . . use[d anonymous] letter to launch a criminal investigation"); Providence Journal, 981 F.2d at 563 n.13 (deeming inspectors general same as criminal law enforcement authorities); Brant Constr., 778 F.2d at 1265 (recognizing "substantial similarities between the activities of the FBI and the OIGs").

[89] See Harvey v. United States Dep't of Justice, 747 F. Supp. 29, 38 (D.D.C. 1990).

[90] See Cleveland, No. 1:87-2384, slip op. at 12 n.3 (N.D. Ohio Apr. 22, 1992) (holding that Exemption 7(D) "clearly applies to information obtained from confidential sources in all investigations, both civil and criminal"); Dayo v. INS, No. C-2-83-1422, slip op. at 5-6 (S.D. Ohio Dec. 31, 1985).

[91] See, e.g., Hopkinson, 866 F.2d at 1222 (protecting state law enforcement agency's request for FBI laboratory evaluation of evidence submitted by state agency and results of FBI's analysis); Gordon, 790 F. Supp. at 377-78 (emphasizing that "when a state law enforcement agency sends material to an FBI lab for testing, confidentiality is 'inherently implicit'" and that "all information from another agency must be protected to provide the confidence necessary to law enforcement cooperation"); Rojem v. United States Dep't of Justice, 775 F. Supp. 6, 12 (D.D.C. 1991) (finding that disclosure of criminal files provided to FBI by state authorities "would unduly discourage" states from enlisting FBI's assistance), appeal dismissed for failure to timely file, No. 92-5088 (D.C. Cir. Nov. 4, 1992); Payne v. United States Dep't of Justice, 722 F. Supp. 229, 231 (E.D. Pa. 1989) (stating that "requirement is met . . . [when] the documents sought are FBI laboratory and fingerprint examinations of evidence collected by local law enforcement agencies"), aff'd, 904 F.2d 695 (3d Cir. 1990) (unpublished table decision).

[92] See, e.g., Parker, 934 F.2d at 375; Shaw, 749 F.2d at 61-62; Radowich v. United States Attorney, Dist. of Md., 658 F.2d 957, 964 (4th Cir. 1981); Duffin v. Carlson, 636 F.2d 709, 712 (D.C. Cir. 1980); Simon, 752 F. Supp. at 22; see

(continued...)

# EXEMPTION 7(D)

7(D), courts have permitted the withholding of confidential information even after the source's identity has been officially divulged or acknowledged,[93] or when the requester knows the source's identity.[94] Similarly, information provided by an anonymous source is eligible for protection.[95] Moreover, even when source-provided information has been revealed and the identities of

---

[92](...continued) also FOIA Update, Vol. XIV, No. 3, at 10 (pointing out breadth of this coverage, together with corresponding potential for discretionary disclosure). See generally FOIA Update, Vol. XV, No. 2, at 3 (discussing application of "foreseeable harm" standard to Exemption 7(D)).

[93] See, e.g., Neely, 208 F.3d at 466 (holding that district court erred to extent it denied withholding based on belief that Exemption 7(D) cannot be claimed to protect identities of confidential sources whose identities previously have been disclosed); Ferguson, 957 F.2d at 1068 (holding that subsequent disclosure of source's identity or some of information provided by source does not require "full disclosure of information provided by such a source"); Shafmaster Fishing Co. v. United States, 814 F. Supp. 182, 185 (D.N.H. 1993) (ruling that source's identity or information provided need not be "secret" to justify withholding); Church of Scientology, 816 F. Supp. at 1161 (declaring it "irrelevant that the identity of the confidential source is known"); see also Cleary v. FBI, 811 F.2d 421, 423 (8th Cir. 1987); Shaw, 749 F.2d at 62; Radowich, 658 F.2d at 964; Lesar, 636 F.2d at 491.

[94] See, e.g., Jones, 41 F.3d at 249 (explaining that Exemption 7(D) "focuses on the source's intent, not the world's knowledge"); Radowich, 658 F.2d at 960 (declaring that Exemption 7(D) applies even when "identities of confidential sources ... [are] known"); see also L&C Marine, 740 F.2d at 923, 925 (noting that fact that employee-witnesses could be matched to their statements does not diminish Exemption 7(D) protection); Keeney v. FBI, 630 F.2d 114, 119 n.2 (2d Cir. 1980) (ruling that Exemption 7(D) applies to "local law enforcement agencies [that] have now been identified"); Ortiz, No. 97-140-A-3, slip op. at 10 (M.D. La. Aug. 25, 1998) (stating that "[i]t is irrelevant that the identity of the confidential source is known"); Crooker, 1995 U.S. Dist. LEXIS 7031, at *15 (stating that "an agency may withhold confidential information even if the requester or the public know[s] the source's identity"); Wickline, 1994 WL 549756, at *4 n.8 (reiterating that "confidentiality is not waived or revoked when a [requester] already knows the protected names"); Shafmaster Fishing Co., 814 F. Supp. at 185 (stating that source's identity need not be secret to justify withholding information under Exemption 7(D)); Sanders, 1992 WL 97785, at *4 (holding that fact that requester knows identity of source does not eviscerate Exemption 7(D) protection).

[95] See Ortiz, 70 F.3d at 735 (reasoning that extending confidentiality to anonymous hotline communications "reflects a common sense judgment" given the importance of encouraging public cooperation in combatting fraud); Providence Journal, 981 F.2d at 565-67 (extending confidentiality to unsolicited anonymous letters regarding investigation against officers in Rhode Island Army National Guard); Hamilton, 1997 U.S. Dist. LEXIS 18900, at *28 (finding it "reasonable to assume" that anonymous caller expected confidentiality); Mitchell v. Ralston, No. 81-4478, slip op. at 2 (S.D. Ill. Oct. 14, 1982) (ruling that anonymity of source does not negate confidentiality).

## EXEMPTION 7(D)

some of the confidential sources have been independently divulged, Exemption 7(D) can protect against the matching of witnesses' names with the specific information that they supplied.[96]

Because the phrase "confidential information furnished only by the confidential source" sometimes caused confusion in the past, the 1986 FOIA amendments unequivocally clarified the congressional intent by deleting the word "confidential" as a modifier of "information" and omitting the word "only" from this formulation.[97] Even prior to that legislative change, courts regularly employed this portion of Exemption 7(D) to protect all information provided by a confidential source, both because such withholdings were anticipated by the language and legislative history of the statute,[98] and in recognition of the fact that disclosure of any of this material would jeopardize the system of confidentiality that ensures a free flow of information from sources to investigatory agencies.[99] Now, however, courts need look no further than the

---

[96] See Spannaus v. United States Dep't of Justice, No. 92-0372, slip op. at 16 (D.D.C. June 20, 1995) (determining that any "plaintiff asserting a claim of prior disclosure must designate specific information in the public domain that duplicates what is being withheld"), summary affirmance granted in part, vacated in other part & remanded, No. 95-5267, 1996 WL 523814 (D.C. Cir. Aug. 16, 1996); Kirk v. United States Dep't of Justice, 704 F. Supp. 288, 293 (D.D.C. 1989); see also L&C Marine, 740 F.2d at 925 (ruling that names of employee-witnesses in OSHA accident investigation were properly withheld "even if use of civil discovery procedures might provide plaintiffs-appellees with information sufficient to match the workers with their statements").

[97] See Freedom of Information Reform Act of 1986, Pub. L. No. 99-570, § 1802, 100 Stat. 3207, 3207-48; see also FOIA Update, Vol. VII, No. 4, at 3-6 (setting out statute in its amended form, interlineated to show exact changes made).

[98] See Irons, 880 F.2d at 1450-51.

[99] See id. at 1449; see also, e.g., Ortiz, 70 F.3d at 732 (reiterating that "Exemption 7(D) is meant to . . . 'encourage cooperation with law enforcement agencies by enabling the agencies to keep their informants' identities confidential'" (quoting United Techs., 777 F.2d at 94)); Kennedy, 1994 U.S. Dist. LEXIS 2275, at **14-15 (stating that release of information would "jeopardize [agency's] ability to conduct future law enforcement operations premised upon promises of confidentiality"); Duffin, 636 F.2d at 712-13 (reiterating Congress's belief that disclosure of confidential information would discourage cooperation from sources); Biase, No. 93-2521, slip op. at 11 n.14 (D.N.J. Dec. 10, 1993) (stating that the "goal of Exemption 7(D) [is] to protect the ability of law enforcement agencies to obtain the cooperation of persons having relevant information"); Church of Scientology, 816 F. Supp. at 1161 (explaining that Exemption 7(D) was enacted "to ensure that the FOIA did not impair federal law enforcement agencies' ability to gather information"); Dayton Newspapers, Inc. v. FBI, No. C-3-85-815, slip op. at 13 (S.D. Ohio Feb. 9, 1993) (noting that "purpose of Exemption 7(D) is to ensure that the FOIA did not impair the ability of federal law enforcement agencies to gather information, thus to ensure that information continued to flow to those agencies"); Shaf-
(continued...)

# EXEMPTION 7(D)

Act's literal language to see that all source-provided information is covered in criminal and national security investigations.[100]

Once courts determine the existence of confidentiality under Exemption 7(D), they are reluctant to find a subsequent waiver of the exemption's protections.[101] This restraint stems both from the potentially adverse repercussions that may result from additional disclosures and from a recognition that any "judicial effort[] to create a 'waiver' exception" to exemption 7(D)'s language runs afoul of the statute's intent to provide "workable rules."[102] It therefore has been observed that a waiver of Exemption 7(D)'s protections should be recognized only upon "'absolutely solid evidence showing that the source of an FBI interview in a law enforcement investigation has manifested complete disregard for confidentiality.'"[103]

Thus, even authorized or official disclosure of some information provided by a confidential source does not open the door to disclosure of any of the other information the source has provided.[104] In this vein, it is well estab-

---

[99] (...continued)
master Fishing, 814 F. Supp. at 185 (stating that object of Exemption 7(D) "'not simply to protect the source, but also to protect the flow of information to the law enforcement agency'" (quoting Irons, 880 F.2d at 1449)).

[100] See, e.g., Irons, 880 F.2d at 1448.

[101] See, e.g., Reiter, 1997 WL 470108, at *6 ("[O]nce an informant's confidentiality has been established, almost nothing can eviscerate Exemption 7(D) protection.").

[102] Parker, 934 F.2d at 380; see also Neely, 208 F.3d at 466 (observing that "the statute by its terms does not provide for . . . waiver"); Irons, 880 F.2d at 1455-56 (citing Reporters Comm., 489 U.S. at 779).

[103] Parker, 934 F.2d at 378 (quoting Dow Jones & Co. v. Department of Justice, 908 F.2d 1006, 1011 (D.C. Cir.), superseded, 917 F.2d 571 (D.C. Cir. 1990)); see, e.g., Billington, 69 F. Supp. 2d at 139 (concluding that plaintiff's allegation that source was "unafraid," even if true, does not constitute "absolutely solid evidence" that source "manifested complete disregard for confidentiality"); Billington, 11 F. Supp. 2d at 69 (finding that alleged source did not exhibit "complete disregard for confidentiality" by giving newspaper interview); Freeman v. United States Dep't of Justice, No. 92-0557, 1993 WL 260694, at **3-4 (D.D.C. June 28, 1993) (ruling that "fact that federal, state, and local authorities were publicly cooperating in the . . . investigation, or that certain individuals publicly acknowledged that they were 'working closely' with the investigation . . . does not 'manifest complete disregard for confidentiality'"), vacated in other part on denial of reconsideration, No. 92-0557, 1994 WL 35871 (D.D.C. Jan. 26, 1994).

[104] See Shaw, 749 F.2d at 62 (holding that "[d]isclosure of one piece of information received from a particular party--and even the disclosure of that party as its source--does not prevent that party from being a 'confidential source' for other purposes"); Brant Constr., 778 F.2d at 1265 n.8 (ruling that "subsequent disclosure of the information, either partially or completely, does
(continued...)

# EXEMPTION 7(D)

lished that source-identifying and source-provided information remains protected even when some of it has been the subject of testimony in open court.[105]

---

[104](...continued)
not affect its exempt status under 7(D)"); Johnson v. Department of Justice, 758 F. Supp. 2, 5 (D.D.C. 1991) (stating that fact that someone made public statement concerning incident "does not constitute a waiver of the Bureau's confidential file [because a] . . . press account may be erroneous or false or, more likely, incomplete").

[105] See, e.g., Neely, 208 F.3d at 466 (recognizing that source can "remain a 'confidential source' . . . even if the source's communication with [the agency] is subsequently disclosed at trial"); Jones, 41 F.3d at 249 (holding that Exemption 7(D) "provides for nondisclosure of all sources who provided information with an understanding of confidentiality, not for protection of only those sources whose identity remains a secret at the time of future FOIA litigation [because they do not testify]"); Davis v. United States Dep't of Justice, 968 F.2d 1276, 1281 (D.C. Cir. 1992) (concluding that informant's testimony in open court did not "'waive the [government's] right to invoke Exemption 7(D)'" (quoting Parker, 934 F.2d at 379-80)); Ferguson, 957 F.2d at 1068 (affirming that local law enforcement officer does not lose status as confidential source by testifying in court); Parker, 934 F.2d at 379-81 (stating that "government agency is not required to disclose the identity of a confidential source or information conveyed to the agency in confidence in a criminal investigation notwithstanding the possibility that the informant may have testified at a public trial"); Irons, 880 F.2d at 1454 (recognizing that "[t]here is no reason grounded in fairness for requiring a source who disclosed information during testimony to reveal, against his will (or to have the FBI reveal for him), information that he did not disclose in public"); Kimberlin, 774 F.2d at 209 (determining that "disclosure [prior to or at trial] of information given in confidence does not render non-confidential any of the information originally provided"); Scherer v. Kelley, 584 F.2d 170, 176 n.7 (7th Cir. 1978); Jefferson, No. 96-1365, slip op. at 10-11 (D.D.C. Feb. 22, 2000) (stating that "disclosure at trial that an individual spoke with FBI agents is insufficient under the FOIA to require the FBI to disclose all references to such witnesses"); Coleman, 13 F. Supp. 2d at 82 (opining that "witnesses do not check their confidentiality at the courtroom door"); Smith v. ATF, 977 F. Supp. 496, 501 (D.D.C. 1997) (ruling that "mere fact that a confidential informant has testified at trial does not waive Exemption 7(D) protection"); Reiter, 1997 WL 470108, at *7 (finding continued protection for "publicly identified" informants and information supplied by informants); Foster v. United States Dep't of Justice, 933 F. Supp. 687, 693 (E.D. Mich. 1996) (finding Exemption 7(D) "not waived even if the source has testified in court or the information provided by the source has otherwise been made public"); Guerrero v. DEA, No. 93-2006, slip op. at 10 (D. Ariz. Feb. 21, 1996) (ruling that "full disclosure of information provided by a confidential informant is not required simply because the confidential source testified in court"); Plazas-Martinez v. DEA, 891 F. Supp. 1, 4 (D.D.C. 1995) (explaining that Exemption 7(D) applies to information given by informant who was confidential "even if the informant later testifies at trial"); Crooker, 1995 U.S. Dist. LEXIS 7031, at *15 (holding that "even if a confidential source testifies in court against the requester" source does not lose his confidentiality); Wickline, 1994 WL 549756, at *4 n.8 (clarifying that confi-
(continued...)

# EXEMPTION 7(D)

Moreover, in order to demonstrate a waiver by disclosure through authorized channels, the requester must demonstrate both that "'the exact information given to the [law enforcement authority] has already become public, and the fact that the informant gave the same information to the [law enforcement authority] is also public.'"[106] Consequently, one court has found that the government is not required even to "confirm or deny that persons who testify at trial are also confidential informants."[107]

The lengths to which it is proper to go when necessary to safeguard informant identification through informant-provided information are illustrated by one decision holding that letters shown to a suspect for the purpose of prompting a confession were properly denied to the suspect under the FOIA--even though the suspect was the very author of the letters (which, in turn, had been provided to authorities by a third party).[108] Similarly, the release of informant-related material to a party aligned with an agency in an administrative proceeding in no way diminishes the government's ability to invoke Exemption 7(D) in response to a subsequent request by a nonallied party.[109] Logically, this principle should be extended to encompass parties aligned with the government in actual litigation as well.

---

[105](...continued) dentiality not waived when source testified in public trial and stating that "FBI simply must disclose the 'exact information' about which the source testified"); Proctor, No. 88-3340, slip op. at 1 (D.D.C. Aug. 8, 1994) (withholding proper when "individuals ... testified or were listed as possible witnesses"); Johnson, 1990 U.S. Dist. LEXIS 18358, at **8-9 (rejecting waiver notwithstanding fact that individuals were called as plaintiff's witnesses at prison disciplinary hearing and testified in plaintiff's presence); cf. Sanderson v. IRS, No. 98-2369, 1999 WL 35290, at *3 (E.D. La. Jan. 25, 1999) (concluding that source's deposition testimony in civil action did not act as "wholesale waiver" of information provided to agency).

[106] Parker, 934 F.2d at 378; Dow Jones, 917 F.2d at 577; see also Davis, 968 F.2d at 1280 (holding that government entitled to withhold tapes obtained through informant's assistance "unless it is specifically shown that those tapes, or portions of them, were played during the informant's testimony"); Sanderson, No. 98-2369, 1999 WL 35290, at **3-4 (ordering disclosure of "exact information to which [source] testified in her deposition"); cf. Hale v. United States Dep't of Justice, No. 89-1175, slip op. at 6 (W.D. Okla. Jan. 17, 1995) (stating that "individuals who testified in court could not be expected to have their identities or the topic of their testimony withheld"), rev'd in part on other grounds, 99 F.3d 1025 (10th Cir. 1996).

[107] Schmerler, 900 F.2d at 339 (reasoning that testimony by source does not automatically waive confidentiality because source may be able "to camouflage his true role notwithstanding his court appearance" (quoting Irons, 811 F.2d at 687)); see also Parker, 934 F.2d at 381.

[108] See Gula, 699 F. Supp. at 960.

[109] See United Techs., 777 F.2d at 95-96; see also FOIA Update, Vol. IV, No. 2, at 6.

# EXEMPTION 7(D)

Nor is the protection of Exemption 7(D) forfeited by "court-ordered and court-supervised" disclosure to an opponent in civil discovery.[110] Although it had previously been held that when the government fails to object in any way to such discovery and then consciously and deliberately puts confidential source information into the public record a waiver of the exemption will be found to have occurred,[111] more recent Exemption 7(D) decisions have undermined such a conclusion.[112] As noted above, however, "if the exact information given to the [law enforcement agency] has already become public, and the fact that the informant gave the same information to the [agency] is also public, there would be no grounds to withhold."[113]

Obviously, if no waiver of Exemption 7(D) results from authorized release of relevant information, "[t]he per se limitation on disclosure under 7(D) does not disappear if the identity of the confidential source becomes known through other means."[114] It should be observed that in the unusual situation in which an agency elects to publicly disclose source-identifying or source-provided information as necessary in furtherance of an important agency function, it "has no duty to seek the witness's permission to waive his confidential status under the Act."[115] Conversely, because Exemption 7(D) "mainly seeks to protect law enforcement agencies in their efforts to find future sources,"[116] acts of "'waiver' by 'sources' will not automatically prove sufficient

---

[110] Donohue v. United States Dep't of Justice, No. 84-3451, 1987 U.S. Dist. LEXIS 15185, at *14 (D.D.C. Dec. 23, 1987).

[111] See Nishnic v. United States Dep't of Justice, 671 F. Supp. 776, 812 (D.D.C. 1987).

[112] See Glick v. Department of Justice, No. 89-3279, 1991 WL 118263, at *4 (D.D.C. June 20, 1991) (finding that disclosure "pursuant to discovery in another case . . . does not waive the confidentiality of the information or those who provided it"); see also Parker, 934 F.2d at 380 (observing that judicial efforts to create "waiver" exception run "contrary to statute's intent to provide workable rules" (quoting Irons, 811 F.2d at 1455-56)).

[113] Dow Jones, 917 F.2d at 577.

[114] L&C Marine, 740 F.2d at 925 (citing Radowich, 658 F.2d at 960); see, e.g., Lesar, 636 F.2d at 491 (finding that no waiver of confidentiality occurs when confidential information finds its way into public domain); Keeney, 630 F.2d at 119 n.2 (declaring that Exemption 7(D) continues to protect confidential sources even after their identification).

[115] Borton, 566 F. Supp. at 1422; see, e.g., Doe, 790 F. Supp. at 21-22 (declaring that "the FBI is not required to try to persuade people to change their minds" and that any such requirement "would undermine the Bureau's effectiveness").

[116] Irons, 880 F.2d at 1453; see, e.g., Koch v. United States Postal Serv., No. 92-0233, slip op. at 12 (W.D. Mo. Dec. 17, 1992) (stating that individuals would be less likely to come forward with information in future investigations if informant's identity were disclosed), aff'd, 7 F.3d 1042 (8th Cir. 1993) (unpublished table decision).

## EXEMPTION 7(D)

to release the [source-provided] information."[117] (See the discussion of this point under Discretionary Disclosure and Waiver, below.)

Under the case law, Exemption 7(D)'s protection for sources and the information they have provided also is in no way diminished by the fact that an investigation has been closed.[118] Indeed, because of the vital role that Exemption 7(D) plays in promoting effective law enforcement, courts have consistently recognized that its protections cannot be lost through the mere passage of time.[119] Additionally, unlike with Exemption 7(C), the safeguards of

---

[117] Irons, 880 F.2d at 1452; see, e.g., Guerrero, No. 93-2006, slip op. at 10 (D. Ariz. Feb. 21, 1996) (holding that "full disclosure of information provided by confidential informant . . . not required simply because" informant made "public statements"); Spurlock v. FBI, No. 91-5602, slip op. at 2 (C.D. Cal. Nov. 29, 1993) (concluding that "fact that [source] had any sense of braggadocio in his telling the world he had talked to the FBI cannot vitiate the protections of the exemption and the nature of his statements to the FBI as confidential"), rev'd on other grounds, 69 F.3d 1010 (9th Cir. 1995). But see Providence Journal, 981 F.2d at 567 n.16 (holding that express waiver of confidentiality by source vitiates Exemption 7(D) protection); Blanton, 63 F. Supp. 2d at 49 (ruling that sources "have waived any assurance of confidentiality, express or implied, by writing books about their experiences as confidential FBI informants").

[118] See Ortiz, 70 F.3d at 733 (ruling that "the status of the investigation is . . . immaterial to the application of the exemption"); KTVY-TV, 919 F.2d at 1470-71; Akron Standard Div. of Eagle-Picher Indus. v. Donovan, 780 F.2d 568, 573 (6th Cir. 1986); Ortiz, No. 97-140-A-3, slip op. at 10 (E.D. La. Aug. 25, 1998) (stating that "information and/or identity of the individual remains confidential subject to Exemption 7(D) after the investigation is concluded"); Foster, 933 F. Supp. at 693 (observing that Exemption 7(D) "may be claimed even when an investigation generating records containing information concerning a confidential source has been closed"); Almy, 1995 WL 476255, at *13 (stating that Exemption 7(D)'s protection "not diminished" by fact that investigation has been closed); Church of Scientology, 816 F. Supp. at 1161 (holding that source identity and information provided "remains confidential . . . after the investigation is concluded"); Soto, No. 90-1816, slip op. at 7 (D.D.C. Apr. 13, 1992) (ruling that "[i]t is of no consequence that these sources provided information relating to a criminal investigation which has since been completed"); Gale v. FBI, 141 F.R.D. 94, 98 (N.D. Ill. 1992) (protecting statements made even "while no investigation is pending" under Exemption 7(D)).

[119] See, e.g., Halpern, 181 F.3d at 300 (declaring that "it makes no difference in our analysis whether now, in hindsight, the objective need for confidentiality has diminished; what counts is whether then, at the time the source communicated with the FBI, the source understood that confidentiality would attach"); Schmerler, 900 F.2d at 336 (indicating that Exemption 7(D) "contains no sunset provision"); Keys, 830 F.2d at 346 (stating that "'Congress has not established a time limitation for exemption (7)(D) and it would be both impractical and inappropriate for the Court to do so.'" (quoting Keys v. Department of Justice, No. 85-2588, slip op. at 9 (D.D.C. May 12, 1986))); King, 830 F.2d at 212-13, 236 (protecting interviews conducted in 1941 and 1952); Irons, (continued...)

**EXEMPTION 7(D)**

Exemption 7(D) remain wholly undiminished by the death of the source.[120]

It should be remembered, though, that in implementation of the statements of FOIA policy issued by President Clinton[121] and Attorney General Janet Reno[122] in 1993, the Department of Justice adopted an Exemption 7(D) policy that encourages the discretionary disclosure of information furnished by confidential sources whenever possible under the FOIA.[123] This policy ac-

---

[119](...continued)
811 F.2d at 689 (applying Exemption 7(D) protection to information regarding 1948-1956 Smith Act trials); Brant Constr., 778 F.2d at 1265 n.8 (emphasizing that "policy of 7(D) [is] to protect future sources of information" and that passage of time "does not alter status" of source-provided information); Diamond, 707 F.2d at 76-77 (protecting McCarthy-era documents); Fitzgibbon v. United States Secret Service, 747 F. Supp. 51, 60 (D.D.C. 1990) (protecting information regarding alleged 1961 plot against President Kennedy by Trujillo regime in Dominican Republic); Abrams v. FBI, 511 F. Supp. 758, 762-63 (N.D. Ill. 1981) (protecting 27-year-old documents).

[120] See, e.g., McDonnell, 4 F.3d at 1258 (holding that issue of whether source is "deceased does not extend to the information withheld pursuant to Exemption 7(D)"); Schmerler, 900 F.2d at 336 ("that the sources may have died is of no moment to the analysis"); Kiraly v. FBI, 728 F.2d 273, 279 (6th Cir. 1984) (finding information provided by deceased source who also testified at trial properly withheld); Cohen v. Smith, No. 81-5365, slip op. at 4 (9th Cir. Mar. 25, 1983); Blanton, 63 F. Supp. 2d at 49 (ruling that "alleged fact of [sources'] deaths does not bear on whether they received assurances of confidentiality while they were alive and whether those assurances, if any, survive their deaths"); Schrecker v. United States Dep't of Justice, 14 F. Supp. 2d 111, 118 (D.D.C. 1998) (finding identity of informant withholdable "regardless of whether he/she is alive"); see also FOIA Update, Vol. IV, No. 3, at 5; cf. Swidler & Berlin v. United States, 524 U.S. 399, 407 (1998) (recognizing that "posthumous disclosure of [attorney-client] communications may be as feared as disclosure during the client's lifetime") (non-FOIA case); Allen v. DOD, 658 F. Supp. 15, 20 (D.D.C. 1986) (protecting deceased intelligence sources under Exemption 1).

[121] President's Memorandum for Heads of Departments and Agencies regarding the Freedom of Information Act, 29 Weekly Comp. Pres. Doc. 1999 (Oct. 4, 1993), reprinted in FOIA Update, Vol. XIV, No. 3, at 3.

[122] Attorney General's Memorandum for Heads of Departments and Agencies regarding the Freedom of Information Act (Oct. 4, 1993), reprinted in FOIA Update, Vol. XIV, No. 3, at 4-5; see also Attorney General's Follow-Up Memorandum for Heads of Departments and Agencies regarding the Freedom of Information Act (Sept. 3, 1999) [hereinafter Attorney General Reno's Follow-Up FOIA Memorandum], reprinted in FOIA Update, Vol. XIX, No. 4, at 3-5.

[123] See FOIA Update, Vol. XIV, No. 3, at 10 ("Justice Changes Policy on Exemption 7(D) Disclosure") (encouraging agencies not to employ breadth of protection technically available for all source-furnished information under
(continued...)

## EXEMPTION 7(D)

commodates the use of a "foreseeable harm" analysis[124] and promotes the withholding of information only to the extent necessary to prevent actual source identification.[125] To this end, agencies should undertake a "more particularized approach" to this broad exemption in order to ensure that its underlying harm rationale is truly applicable in each instance in which it is employed.[126]

Perhaps because Exemption 7(D) has been traditionally afforded such a broad construction by the courts, few court decisions since the passage of the 1986 FOIA amendments have hinged on its specific revisions. It is evident, however, that the 1986 FOIA amendments' relaxation of Exemption 7(D)'s harm standard, in conjunction with other revisions, is designed to ensure that the utmost protections possible will continue to be afforded to confidential sources.[127] All federal agencies maintaining law enforcement information should apply Exemption 7(D) where necessary to provide adequate source protection,[128] but at the same time apply the "foreseeable harm" standard[129]

---

[123](...continued)
Exemption 7(D)'s second clause).

[124] See FOIA Update, Vol. XIV, No. 3, at 1-2; see also FOIA Update, Vol. XVIII, No. 2, at 1 (describing Attorney General's reiteration of importance of "foreseeable harm" standard to federal agencies in order to promote further discretionary disclosure in agency decisionmaking).

[125] See id.; see also FOIA Update, Vol. XV, No. 2, at 3 (distinguishing between two clauses of Exemption 7(D) in implementation of "foreseeable harm" standard); FOIA Update, Vol. XV, No. 4, at 7 (citing examples of discretionary disclosure of Exemption 7(D) information upon application of "foreseeable harm" standard); cf. Meeropol v. Reno, No. 75-1121, slip op. at 5 (D.D.C. Mar. 26, 1998) (finding agency's withholding of entire pages too sweeping "when the information that might actually lead to identification of the source is contained in a single phrase, or a word or two").

[126] See FOIA Update, Vol. XIV, No. 3, at 10 (setting forth higher standards for determining both confidentiality and disclosure harm under current policy and recent Supreme Court case law); see also FOIA Update, Vol. XV, No. 4, at 7; FOIA Update, Vol. XV, No. 2, at 3.

[127] See Attorney General's 1986 Amendments Memorandum at 13.

[128] See Sluby v. United States Dep't of Justice, No. 86-1503, 1987 WL 10509, at **2-3 (D.D.C. Apr. 30, 1987) ("'robust' reading of [E]xemption 7(D) is supported by . . . Congressional events"); Randle v. Commissioner, 866 F. Supp. 1080, 1085 (N.D. Ill. 1994) (although most exemptions construed narrowly, confidential source exemption applied "'robustly'"); accord Irons, 811 F.2d at 687-89 (post-amendment decision extending Exemption 7(D) protection to sources who received only conditional assurances of confidentiality).

[129] See Attorney General Reno's Follow-Up FOIA Memorandum, reprinted in FOIA Update, Vol. XIX, No. 4, at 3-5 (emphasizing that application of "foreseeable harm" standard requires agencies to "consider whether they can make a discretionary disclosure of a requested record or portion of a record
(continued...)

# EXEMPTION 7(E)

and make discretionary disclosures of information falling within the exemption's broad coverage whenever it is possible to do so without harm to the confidential source involved.[130]

## EXEMPTION 7(E)

Exemption 7(E) affords protection to all law enforcement information that "would disclose techniques and procedures for law enforcement investigations or prosecutions, or would disclose guidelines for law enforcement investigations or prosecutions if such disclosure could reasonably be expected to risk circumvention of the law."[1] This exemption contains two distinct protective clauses.

The first clause of Exemption 7(E) permits the withholding of "records or information compiled for law enforcement purposes . . . [that] would disclose techniques and procedures for law enforcement investigations or prosecutions."[2] This clause is phrased in such a way so as to not require a showing of any particular determination of harm--or risk of circumvention of law--that would be caused by disclosure of the records or information within its coverage.[3] Rather, it is designed to provide "categorical" protection of the information so described.[4]

---

[129](...continued)
even though it falls within one of the Act's exemptions").

[130] See FOIA Update, Vol. XV, No. 2, at 3; FOIA Update, XIV, No. 3, at 10; see also FOIA Update, Vol. XV, No. 4, at 7 (citing examples of discretionary disclosure of Exemption 7(D) information upon application of "foreseeable harm" standard).

[1] 5 U.S.C. § 552(b)(7)(E) (1994 & Supp. IV 1998).

[2] Id.

[3] See, e.g., Coleman v. FBI, No. 89-2773, slip op. at 25 (D.D.C. Dec. 10, 1991), summary affirmance granted, No. 92-5040, 1992 WL 373976 (D.C. Cir. Dec. 4, 1992); see also Burke v. United States Dep't of Justice, No. 96-1739, 1999 WL 1032814, at *8 (D.D.C. Sept. 30, 1999) (noting that Exemption 7(E) "does not require the FBI to show that disclosure of [FBI Form FD-515] ratings [of effectiveness of investigative techniques] would cause any particular harm"). But see Davin v. United States Dep't of Justice, 60 F.3d 1043, 1064 (3d Cir. 1995) (abberational decision requiring agency to submit "evidence that specific documents it has withheld contain secret information about techniques for recruiting informants [the disclosure of which] would risk circumvention of the law").

[4] See Attorney General's Memorandum on the 1986 Amendments to the Freedom of Information Act 16 n.27 (Dec. 1987) [hereinafter Attorney General's 1986 Amendments Memorandum]; see, e.g., Summers v. United States Dep't of Justice, No. 87-3168, slip op. at 11, 12, 15 (D.D.C. Apr. 19, 2000) (finding technical information about FBI's telephone surveillance to be protected by Exemption 7(E), in language implying categorical protection), on
(continued...)

## EXEMPTION 7(E)

Notwithstanding the broad scope of Exemption 7(E)'s protection, in order for the exemption to apply the technique or procedure at issue must not be well known to the public.[5] Accordingly, techniques such as "wiretapping,"[6] "mail covers" and the "use of post office boxes,"[7] "'security flashes' or the tagging of fingerprints,"[8] pretext telephone calls,[9] and "planting transponders on

---

[4](...continued)
remand from 140 F.3d 1077 (D.C. Cir. 1998); Rivera v. FBI, No. 98-0649, slip op. at 9-10 (D.D.C. Aug. 31, 1999) (upholding categorical protection for bank security measures); American Civil Liberties Union Found. v. United States Dep't of Justice, 833 F. Supp. 399, 407 (S.D. N.Y. 1993) (The first clause of Exemption 7(E) does not "necessarily require an individualized showing for each document."); Fisher v. United States Dep't of Justice, 772 F. Supp. 7, 12 n.9 (D.D.C. 1991), aff'd, 968 F.2d 92 (1992) (unpublished table decision); see also FOIA Update, Vol. XV, No. 2, at 3 (distinguishing between Exemption 7(E)'s two clauses); cf. Canning v. United States Dep't of the Treasury, No. 94-2704, slip op. at 11 (D.D.C. May 7, 1998) (directing Secret Service to provide further explanation that information constitutes "techniques and procedures").

[5] See Attorney General's 1986 Amendments Memorandum at 16 n.27 (citing S. Rep. No. 98-221, at 25 (1983) (citing, in turn, H.R. Rep. No. 93-180, at 12 (1974), reprinted in 1974 U.S.C.C.A.N. 6267)); see also Campbell v. United States Dep't of Justice, No. 89-cv-3016, slip op. at 6 (D.D.C. Aug. 6, 1997) (declaring that Exemption 7(E) applies to "obscure or secret techniques"), rev'd & remanded on other grounds, 164 F.3d 20 (D.C. Cir. 1998); Albuquerque Publ'g Co. v. United States Dep't of Justice, 726 F. Supp. 851, 858 (D. Ariz. 1989) (stating that agencies "should avoid burdening the Court with techniques commonly described in movies, popular novels, stories or magazines or television"); cf. Don Ray Drive-A-Way Co. v. Skinner, 785 F. Supp. 198, 200 (D.D.C. 1992) (finding that computer algorithm used by Department of Transportation to determine safety rating of motor carriers "does not simply involve investigative techniques or procedures" because "it has same status as regulations or agency law" and "is regularly followed in all ratings").

[6] Public Employees for Envtl. Responsibility v. EPA, 978 F. Supp. 955, 963 (D. Colo. 1997), appeal voluntarily dismissed, No. 97-1384 (10th Cir. Nov. 25, 1997).

[7] Dunaway v. Webster, 519 F. Supp. 1059, 1082-83 (N.D. Cal. 1981).

[8] Ferguson v. Kelley, 448 F. Supp. 919, 926 (N.D. Ill. 1977), reconsideration granted & denied in part, 455 F. Supp. 324 (N.D. Ill. 1978).

[9] Rosenfeld v. United States Dep't of Justice, 57 F.3d 803, 815 (9th Cir. 1995); see also Struth v. FBI, 673 F. Supp. 949, 970 (E.D. Wis. 1987) (dismissing pretext as merely "garden variety ruse or misrepresentation"). But see Nolan v. United States Dep't of Justice, No. 89-A-2035, 1991 WL 36547, at *8 (D. Colo. Mar. 18, 1991) (concluding that disclosure of information surrounding pretext phone call may harm ongoing investigations), aff'd on other grounds, 973 F.2d 843 (10th Cir. 1992).

## EXEMPTION 7(E)

aircraft suspected of smuggling"[10] have been denied protection under Exemption 7(E) when courts have found them to be generally known to the public.

In some cases, however, even commonly known procedures have been protected from disclosure when "'the circumstances of their usefulness . . . may not be widely known,'"[11] or "their use in concert with other elements of an investigation and in their totality directed toward a specific investigative goal constitute a 'technique' which merits protection."[12] Increasingly, moreover,

---

[10] Hamilton v. Weise, No. 95-1161, 1997 U.S. Dist. LEXIS 18900, at *30 (M.D. Fla. Oct. 1, 1997).

[11] Wickline v. FBI, No. 92-1189, 1994 WL 549756, at *5 (D.D.C. Sept. 30, 1994) (quoting Parker v. United States Dep't of Justice, No. 88-0760, slip op. at 8 (D.D.C. Feb. 28, 1990), aff'd in pertinent part, No. 90-5070 (D.C. Cir. June 28, 1990)); see, e.g., Coleman v. FBI, 13 F. Supp. 2d 75, 83 (D.D.C. 1998) (protecting "manner and circumstances," but not the identities, of various techniques that are "generally known to the public"); Del Viscovo v. FBI, 903 F. Supp. 1, 3 (D.D.C. 1995) (declaring withholding of FBI accomplishment report (containing information on use and effectiveness of investigative techniques) to be "well established" and "proper"), summary affirmance granted, No. 95-5388 (D.C. Cir. Jan. 24, 1997); Buffalo Evening News, Inc. v. United States Border Patrol, 791 F. Supp. 386, 392 n.5, 393 n.6 (W.D.N.Y. 1992) (accepting that Exemption 7(E) correctly protects fact of whether alien's name is listed in INS Lookout Book); Wagner v. FBI, No. 90-1314, 1991 U.S. Dist. LEXIS 7506, at *6 (D.D.C. June 4, 1991) (finding that exemption protects detailed surveillance and undercover investigative methods and techniques), summary affirmance granted, No. 91-5220 (D.C. Cir. Aug. 3, 1992); see also Biase v. Office of Thrift Supervision, No. 93-2521, slip op. at 12 (D.N.J. Dec. 16, 1993) (upholding protection of "investigative techniques and procedures that are either not commonly known to the public, or if publicly known, their disclosure could lessen their effectiveness"). But see Goldstein v. Office of Indep. Counsel, No. 87-2028, 1998 WL 570862, at *14 (D.D.C. July 29, 1998) (finding portions of two documents improperly withheld because they do not contain "a secret or an exceptional investigative technique," nor would their disclosure risk circumvention of law, and treating age of documents (10 and 16 years old) as factor in ruling); Campbell, No. 89-cv-3016, slip op. at 7 (D.D.C. Aug. 6, 1997) (refusing to approve nondisclosure of particular circumstances surrounding use of "basic" techniques).

[12] PHE, Inc. v. United States Dep't of Justice, No. 90-1461, slip op. at 7 (D.D.C. Jan. 31, 1991), aff'd in pertinent part, rev'd in part & remanded, 983 F.2d 248 (D.C. Cir. 1993); see, e.g., Hassan v. FBI, No. 91-2189, 1992 U.S. Dist. LEXIS 22655, at *12 (D.D.C. July 13, 1992) (protecting common techniques used with uncommon technique to achieve unique investigative goal), summary affirmance granted, No. 92-5318 (D.C. Cir. Mar. 17, 1993); Beck v. United States Dep't of the Treasury, No. 88-493, slip op. at 26 (D.D.C. Nov. 8, 1989) (approving nondisclosure of certain documents, including map, because disclosure would reveal surveillance technique used by Customs Service, as well as why certain individuals were contacted with regard to investigations), aff'd, 946 F.2d 1563 (D.C. Cir. 1992) (unpublished table decision). But see Campbell v. United States Dep't of Justice, No. 89-cv-3016, 1996 WL 554511,

(continued...)

**EXEMPTION 7(E)**

courts have justified withholding a wide variety of commonly known procedures--for example, polygraph examinations[13]--on the basis that disclosure of their details could reduce or nullify their effectiveness.[14]

---

(...continued)
at *10 (D.D.C. Sept. 19, 1996) (requiring in camera review to determine whether circumstances surrounding particular type of pretext telephone call, coupled with basic procedure itself, form unique investigative technique warranting protection), subsequent decision, No. 89-cv-3016, slip op. at 7 (D.D.C. Aug. 6, 1997) (finding, after in camera review, rationale for protection of some techniques "inadequate").

[13] See, e.g., Hale v. United States Dep't of Justice, 973 F.2d 894, 902-03 (10th Cir. 1992) (concluding that disclosure of "polygraph matters" could lessen effectiveness), cert. granted, vacated & remanded on other grounds, 509 U.S. 918 (1993); McDaniel v. United States Dep't of Justice, No. 99-1935, slip op. at 5-6 (D.D.C. May 8, 2000) (determining that FBI properly withheld polygraph information "to preserve the effectiveness of polygraph examinations as a law enforcement technique"); Blanton v. United States Dep't of Justice, 63 F. Supp. 2d 35, 49-50 (D.D.C. 1999) (finding that disclosing certain polygraph information--e.g., "sequence of questions"--would allow individuals to employ countermeasures); Coleman, 13 F. Supp. 2d at 83 (holding that disclosure of behavioral science analysis and details of polygraph examination would frustrate enforcement of law); Perrone v. FBI, 908 F. Supp. 24, 28 (D.D.C. 1995) (finding that release of precise polygraph questions and their sequence would allow circumvention of examination).

[14] See, e.g., Hale, 973 F.2d at 902-03 (concluding that disclosure of use of security devices and their modus operandi could lessen their effectiveness); Bowen v. FDA, 925 F.2d 1225, 1228 (9th Cir. 1991) (deciding that release of specifics of cyanide-tracing techniques would present serious threat to future product-tampering investigations); Burke, No. 96-1739, 1999 WL 1032814, at *8 (D.D.C. Sept. 30, 1999) (finding FBI redaction of Form FD-515 ratings necessary to prevent criminals from developing countermeasures against FBI techniques); Peralta v. United States Attorney's Office, No. 94-760, slip op. at 10 (D.D.C. May 17, 1999) (upholding redaction of FBI Forms FD-515, as well as information that would identify radio channels used during surveillance and transmitter numbers used to monitor conversations, in order "to prevent potential harm to future law enforcement activities"); Rosenberg v. Freeh, No. 97-0476, slip op. at 17 (D.D.C. May 13, 1998) (protecting "information on the use of false identities for undercover special agents" because disclosure "'could significantly reduce future effectiveness of this investigative technique'"); Pons v. United States Customs Serv., No. 93-2094, 1998 U.S. Dist. LEXIS 6084, at *18 (D.D.C. Apr. 23, 1998) (protecting "cooperative arrangements between Customs and other law enforcement agencies" to keep them effective); Burke v. DEA, No. 96-1739, slip op. at 9 (D.D.C. Mar. 30, 1998) (upholding Postal Service refusal to disclose detailed description of surveillance techniques); Steinberg v. United States Dep't of Justice, No. 93-2409, slip op. at 15-16 (D.D.C. July 14, 1997) (approving nondisclosure of precise details of telephone and travel surveillance despite fact that criminals know such techniques are used); Code v. FBI, No. 95-1892, 1997 WL 150070, at *8 (D.D.C. Mar. 26, 1997) (recognizing that disclosure of criminal personality

(continued...)

## EXEMPTION 7(E)

Recent case law generally continues a trend apparent in older cases[15] of allowing agencies to describe the general nature of the technique while withholding the full details.[16] Often, however, it is not possible to describe secret

---

[14](...continued)
profiles could assist criminals in evading detection); Butler v. Department of the Treasury, No. 95-1931, 1997 WL 138720, at *4 (D.D.C. Jan. 14, 1997) (deciding that disclosing methods of monitoring or type of equipment used could enable future targets to avoid surveillance); Pray v. Department of Justice, 902 F. Supp. 1, 4 (D.D.C. 1995) (concluding that release of information about particular investigative techniques and their effectiveness in FBI accomplishment report could enable criminals to employ countermeasures to neutralize their effectiveness), summary affirmance granted in pertinent part, 1996 WL 734142 (D.C. Cir. Nov. 20, 1996); Fisher, 772 F. Supp. at 12 (finding that disclosure could alert subjects of investigation about FBI techniques); see also FOIA Update, Vol. V, No. 2, at 5; cf. Billington v. United States Dep't of Justice, 69 F. Supp. 2d 128, 140 (D.D.C. 1999) (granting summary judgment to FBI where "plaintiff . . . offer[ed] no more than an unsubstantiated guess that a 'photo album' or common technique [was ] withheld"). But cf. Linn v. United States Dep't of Justice, No. 92-1406, 1995 WL 417810, at *26 (D.D.C. June 5, 1995) (rejecting invocation of Exemption 7(E) because no justification provided to show how release of commonly known technique could interfere with future law enforcement efforts).

[15] See, e.g., Cohen v. Smith, No. 81-5365, slip op. at 8 (9th Cir. Mar. 25, 1983) (protecting details of telephone interviews); Destileria Serralles, Inc. v. Department of the Treasury, No. 85-837, slip op. at 15 (D.P.R. Sept. 22, 1988) (finding properly withheld technique for examining records of alcoholic beverage retailers "to determine whether discounts offered by a wholesale liquor dealer were used as a subterfuge for the giving of a thing of value to the retailer"); Laroque v. United States Dep't of Justice, No. 86-2677, 1988 WL 75942, at *3 (D.D.C. July 12, 1988) (protecting "reason codes" and "source codes" in State Department "lookout notices"); U.S. News & World Report v. Department of the Treasury, No. 84-2303, 1986 U.S. Dist. LEXIS 27634, at *8 (D.D.C. Mar. 26, 1986) (protecting Secret Service's contract specifications for President's armored limousine); LeClair v. United States Secret Serv., No. 82-2162, slip op. at 5 (D. Mass. Feb. 23, 1983) (upholding nondisclosure of Administrative Profile used to evaluate individuals in connection with protective services); Windels, Marx, Davies & Ives v. Department of Commerce, 576 F. Supp. 405, 413-14 (D.D.C. 1983) (alternative holding) (shielding computer program used to detect anti-dumping law violations); Hayward v. United States Dep't of Justice, 2 Gov't Disclosure Serv. (P-H) ¶ 81,231, at 81,646 (D.D.C. July 14, 1981) (protecting methods and techniques used by U.S. Marshals Service to relocate protected witnesses); Malloy v. United States Dep't of Justice, 457 F. Supp. 543, 545 (D.D.C. 1978) (protecting details concerning "bait money" and "bank security devices"); Ott v. Levi, 419 F. Supp. 750, 752 (E.D. Mo. 1976) (protecting laboratory techniques used in arson investigation).

[16] See, e.g., Bowen, 925 F.2d at 1228 (ruling that release of specifics of cyanide-tracing techniques would present serious threat to future product-tampering investigations); Peyton v. Reno, No. 98-1457, 2000 U.S. Dist. LEXIS
(continued...)

**EXEMPTION 7(E)**

law enforcement techniques, even in general terms, without disclosing the very information sought to be withheld.[17] A court's in camera review of the documents at issue may be required to substantiate such nondisclosure claims.[18]

Prior to the Freedom of Information Reform Act of 1986,[19] Exemption 7(E) protected law enforcement techniques and procedures only when they could be regarded as "investigatory" or "investigative" in character,[20] but this limitation was removed by those FOIA amendments. Exemption 7(E), as amended, simply covers "techniques and procedures for law enforcement investigations or prosecutions."[21] As such, it authorizes the withholding of information consisting of, or reflecting, a law enforcement "technique" or a law enforcement "procedure," wherever it is used "for law enforcement investiga-

---

[16](...continued) 873, at *3 (D.D.C. Jan. 6, 2000) (protecting Discriminant Function Scores used to select tax returns for evaluation); Klunzinger v. IRS, 27 F. Supp. 2d 1015, 1027-28 (W.D. Mich. 1998) (upholding protection of documents which, if disclosed, would "reveal confidential information regarding when the IRS would undertake compliance activity"); Becker v. IRS, No. 91-C-1203, 1992 WL 67849, at *6 (N.D. Ill. Mar. 27, 1992) (protecting techniques used by IRS to identify and investigate tax protestors), aff'd, 34 F.3d 398 (7th Cir. 1994).

[17] See, e.g., Juda v. United States Customs Serv., No. 98-0533, 1999 U.S. Dist. LEXIS 12536, at **22-23 (D.D.C. Aug. 3, 1999) (finding affidavits sufficient to justify claim that "in this case it is impossible to describe secret . . . techniques without disclosing the information that USCS is trying to withhold") (appeal pending); Butler, 1997 WL 137720, at *4 (observing that "[i]t is sometimes impossible" to describe secret law enforcement techniques without disclosing information sought to be withheld); Soto v. DEA, No. 90-1816, slip op. at 7 (D.D.C. Apr. 13, 1992) (concluding that detailed description of technique pertaining to detection of drug traffickers would effectively disclose it).

[18] See, e.g., Jones v. FBI, 41 F.3d 238, 249 (6th Cir. 1994) (concluding, upon in camera review, investigative techniques properly withheld); Public Employees for Envtl. Responsibility, 978 F. Supp. at 961 (concluding, upon in camera review, that certain documents must be released while others may be withheld); Campbell, 1996 WL 554511, at *10; Linn, 1995 WL 417810, at *12; Rojem v. United States Dep't of Justice, 775 F. Supp. 6, 12 (D.D.C. 1991) (ordering in camera inspection), subsequent decision, No. 90-3021 (D.D.C. Oct. 31, 1991) (upholding Exemption 7(E) upon in camera inspection), appeal dismissed for failure to timely file, No. 92-5088 (D.C. Cir. Nov. 4, 1992); cf. Smith v. ATF, 997 F. Supp. 496, 501 (D.D.C. 1997) (requiring in camera declaration to address "why the release of the information deleted . . . would compromise law enforcement").

[19] Pub. L. No. 99-570, § 1802, 100 Stat. 3207, 3207-48, 3207-49.

[20] Pub. L. No. 93-502, 88 Stat. 1561, 1563 (1974).

[21] 5 U.S.C. § 552(b)(7)(E).

## EXEMPTION 7(E)

tions or prosecutions" generally.[22] Law enforcement manuals, including those that pertain to the "prosecutions" stage of the law enforcement process, accordingly meet the requirements for withholding under Exemption 7(E) to the extent that they consist of, or reflect, law enforcement techniques and procedures that are confidential.[23]

Agencies should be mindful, however, that Exemption 7(E) is characteristically an exemption that protects, in the words of Attorney General Reno's

---

[22] Id.; see Attorney General's 1986 Amendments Memorandum at 15; see also Nowak v. IRS, No. 98-56656, 2000 WL 60067, at *1 (9th Cir. Jan. 18, 2000) (affirming district court conclusion "that the redacted information, if disclosed, 'would significantly hamper the defendant's tax collection and law enforcement functions, and facilitate taxpayer circumvention of federal Internal Revenue laws'"); Unger v. District Disclosure Office IRS, No. 99-698, 2000 U.S. Dist. LEXIS 5260, at *5 (N.D. Ohio Mar. 28, 2000) (finding that IRS properly withheld references to "specific dollar tolerance" used as "threshold in determining whether to prosecute"); Tax Analysts v. IRS, No. 94-923, slip op. at 5-9 (D.D.C. Nov. 3, 1999) (distinguishing protection of one Field Service Advice [FSA] memorandum concerning "procedure for ascertaining taxpayer's last known address" from required release of portions of a different FSA consisting of "guidelines for evaluating the litigating hazards in employee reclassification cases" and "settlement criteria [in this type of case]," based on court's finding regarding latter of "no danger of taxpayers evading Defendant's lawsuits solely through knowledge derived from the redactions in [it]"); Guerrero v. DEA, No. 93-2006, slip op. at 14-15 (D. Ariz. Feb. 22, 1996) (holding that Exemption 7(E) properly protects portions of DEA Agents Manual concerning undercover operations, confidential informant codes, surveillance devices, and enforcement and security procedures); Hammes v. United States Customs Serv., No. 94 Civ. 4868, 1994 WL 693717, at *1 (S.D.N.Y. Dec. 9, 1994) (protecting Customs Service criteria used to determine which passengers to stop and examine). But see Feshbach v. SEC, 5 F. Supp. 2d 774, 786 & n.11 (N.D. Cal. 1997) (finding agency reasons for withholding SEC's checklists and internal database to be conclusory and insufficient); Cowsen-El v. United States Dep't of Justice, 826 F. Supp. 532, 533-34 (D.D.C. 1992) (finding Bureau of Prisons program statement to be internal policy document wholly unrelated to investigations or prosecutions).

[23] See Attorney General's 1986 Amendments Memorandum at 16; see, e.g., Guerrero, No. 93-2006, slip op. at 14-15 (D. Ariz. Feb. 22, 1996) (approving nondisclosure of portions of DEA Agents Manual); Church of Scientology Int'l v. IRS, 845 F. Supp. 714, 723 (C.D. Cal. 1993) (concluding that parts of IRS Law Enforcement Manual concerning "procedures for handling applications for tax exemption and examinations of Scientology entities" and memorandum regarding application of such procedures properly withheld); Williston Basin Interstate Pipeline Co. v. Federal Energy Regulatory Comm'n, No. 88-592, 1989 WL 44655, at *2 (D.D.C. Apr. 17, 1989) (finding portions of regulatory audit describing significance of each page in audit report, investigatory technique utilized, and auditor's conclusions to constitute "the functional equivalent of a manual of investigative techniques").

# EXEMPTION 7(E)

FOIA Memorandum of October 4, 1993, "only a governmental interest."[24] As Attorney General Reno's FOIA Memorandum points out, such information is particularly well suited for discretionary disclosure when such disclosure can be made without "foreseeable harm."[25] The very broad, nonharm-based nature of Exemption 7(E)'s first clause leaves much room for discretionary disclosure upon application of the "foreseeable harm" standard.[26] (See the discussion of discretionary disclosure under Discretionary Disclosure and Waiver, below.)

The second clause of Exemption 7(E) protects "guidelines for law enforcement investigations or prosecutions if [their] disclosure could reasonably be expected to risk circumvention of the law."[27] As such, it has a distinct harm standard built into it--not unlike the "anti-circumvention," "high 2" aspect of Exemption 2.[28] (See the discussion under Exemption 2, "High 2": Risk of Circumvention, above.) This distinct protection is intended to ensure proper protection for the type of law enforcement guideline information found ineligible to be withheld in the en banc decision of the Court of Appeals for the District of Columbia Circuit in Jordan v. Department of Justice,[29] a case involving guidelines for prosecutions. It reflects a dual concern with the need to remove any lingering effect of that decision, while at the same time ensuring that agencies do not unnecessarily maintain "secret law" on the standards used to regulate behavior.[30]

---

[24] Attorney General's Memorandum for Heads of Departments and Agencies regarding the Freedom of Information Act (Oct. 4, 1993) [hereinafter Attorney General Reno's FOIA Memorandum], reprinted in FOIA Update, Vol. XIV, No. 3, at 4.

[25] Id. (establishing "foreseeable harm" standard governing use of FOIA exemptions); see also Attorney General's Follow-Up Memorandum for Heads of Departments and Agencies regarding the Freedom of Information Act (Sept. 3, 1999) [hereinafter Attorney General Reno's Follow-Up FOIA Memorandum], reprinted in FOIA Update, Vol. XIX, No. 4, at 3-5 (reiterating importance of "foreseeable harm" standard to federal agencies in order to promote further discretionary disclosure in agency decisionmaking).

[26] See FOIA Update, Vol. XV, No. 2, at 3 (distinguishing between two clauses of Exemption 7(E)).

[27] 5 U.S.C. § 552(b)(7)(E).

[28] See Berg v. Commodity Futures Trading Comm'n, No. 93 C 6741, slip op. at 11 n.2 (N.D. Ill. June 23, 1994) (magistrate's recommendation) ("[I]t would appear that exemption (b)(7)(E) is essentially a codification of the 'high 2' exemption."), accepted & dismissed per stipulation (N.D. Ill. July 26, 1994); see also FOIA Update, Vol. XV, No. 2, at 3.

[29] 591 F.2d 753, 771 (D.C. Cir. 1978) (en banc).

[30] See S. Rep. No. 98-221, at 25 (1983); see Attorney General's 1986 Amendments Memorandum at 16-17; see also Don Ray Drive-A-Way, 785 F. Supp. at 200 & n.1 (finding disclosure of safety ratings system necessary to permit regulated entities to know what agency considers to be most serious

(continued...)

**EXEMPTION 7(E)**

Accordingly, this clause of Exemption 7(E) is available to protect any "law enforcement guideline" information of the type involved in Jordan, whether it pertains to the prosecution or basic investigative stage of a law enforcement matter, whenever[31] it is determined that its disclosure "could reasonably be expected to risk circumvention of the law."[32] In choosing this particular harm formulation, Congress employed the more relaxed harm standard now used widely throughout Exemption 7 and obviously "was guided by the 'circumvention of the law' standard that the D.C. Circuit established in its

---

[30](...continued) safety breaches).

[31] See Buckner v. IRS, 25 F. Supp. 2d 893, 899 (N.D. Ind. 1998) (noting that "the age of the [DIF] scores is of no consequence" in upholding protection of Discriminant Function Scores used to evaluate tax returns).

[32] See, e.g., PHE, 983 F.2d at 251 (holding "release of FBI guidelines as to what sources of information are available to its agents might encourage violators to tamper with those sources of information and thus inhibit investigative efforts"); Wishart v. Commissioner, No. 97-20614, 1998 WL 667638, at *17 (N.D. Cal. Aug. 6, 1998) (protecting Discriminant Function Scores to avoid possibility that "taxpayers could manipulate" return information to avoid IRS audits), aff'd, 199 F.3d (9th Cir. 1999) (unpublished table decision); Voinche v. FBI, 940 F. Supp. 323, 331 (D.D.C. 1996) (alternative holding) (upholding nondisclosure of Criminal Intelligence Digest used to assist and guide FBI personnel), aff'd per curiam, No. 96-5304, 1997 U.S. App. LEXIS 19089 (D.C. Cir. June 19, 1997); Jimenez v. FBI, 938 F. Supp. 21, 27 (D.D.C. 1996) (approving invocation of Exemption 7(E) to protect gang-validation criteria used by Bureau of Prisons to determine whether individual is gang member); Foster v. United States Dep't of Justice, 933 F. Supp. 687, 693 (E.D. Mich. 1996) (holding that release of techniques and guidelines used in undercover operations would diminish their effectiveness); Pully v. IRS, 939 F. Supp. 429, 437 (E.D. Va. 1996) (finding that release of discriminant function scores would enable taxpayers to "flag" IRS computers); Berg, No. 93 C 6742, slip op. at 11-12 (N.D. Ill. June 23, 1994) (concluding that release of guidelines concerning use of consumer complaints and correspondence in investigations could risk circumvention of law); Silber v. United States Dep't of Justice, No. 91-876, transcript at 25 (D.D.C. Aug. 13, 1992) (bench order) (ruling that disclosure of monograph on fraud litigation "would present the specter of circumvention of the law"); Small v. IRS, 820 F. Supp. 163, 165-66 (D.N.J. 1992) (protecting Discriminant Function Scores and IRS tolerance and audit guidelines because disclosure would allow taxpayers to devise circumvention strategies); Center for Nat'l Sec. Studies v. INS, No. 87-2068, slip op. at 14 (D.D.C. Dec. 19, 1990) (protecting final contingency plan in event of attack on United States, guidelines for response to terrorist attacks, and contingency plans for immigration emergencies). But see Church of Scientology v. IRS, 816 F. Supp. 1138, 1162 (W.D. Tex. 1993) (holding that IRS did not establish how release of records "regarding harassment of Service employees" written during investigation "could reasonably be expected to circumvent the law"), appeal dismissed per stipulation, No. 93-8431 (5th Cir. Oct. 21, 1993).

## EXEMPTION 7(E)

en banc decision"[33] in Crooker v. ATF.[34] However, in applying this clause of Exemption 7(E) to law enforcement manuals, agencies should be careful to focus on only the portions of those guidelines that specifically correlate to foreseeable harm to law enforcement efforts[35] and to meet their obligations to disclose all reasonably segregable, nonexempt information.[36] (See the further discussions of this point under Procedural Requirements, "Reasonably Segregable" Obligation, above, and Litigation Considerations, "Reasonably Segregable" Requirements, below.)

Law enforcement agencies therefore may avail themselves of the distinct protections provided in Exemption 7(E)'s two clauses. Their "noninvestigatory" law enforcement records, to the extent that they can be fairly regarded as reflecting techniques or procedures, are entitled to categorical protection under Exemption 7(E)'s first clause--subject, of course, to administrative application of the "foreseeable harm" standard.[37] In addition, law enforcement guidelines that satisfy the broad "could reasonably be expected to risk circumvention of law" standard can be protected under Exemption 7(E)'s second clause.[38] (See the discussion of Exemption 2's overlapping "anti-circumvention" protection under Exemption 2, "High 2": Risk of Circumvention, above.)

---

[33] S. Rep. No. 98-221, at 25 (1983); see Attorney General's 1986 Amendments Memorandum at 17.

[34] 670 F.2d 1051 (D.C. Cir. 1981).

[35] See, e.g., PHE, 983 F.2d at 252 (finding that National Obscenity Enforcement Unit failed to submit affidavit containing "precise descriptions of the nature of the redacted material and providing reasons why releasing each withheld section would create a risk of circumvention of the law"); Linn, 1995 WL 417810, at *32 (affirming nondisclosure of one page from Drug Agent's Guide to Forfeiture of Assets on basis that agency explained harm); see also Attorney General Reno's FOIA Memorandum, reprinted in FOIA Update, Vol. XIV, No. 3, at 4-5; FOIA Update, Vol. XV, No. 2, at 3.

[36] See PHE, 983 F.2d at 252 (finding that agency must "clearly indicate why disclosable material could not be segregated from exempted material"); see, e.g., Wightman v. ATF, 755 F.2d 979, 982-83 (1st Cir. 1985) (remanding for determination of segregability) (Exemption 2); Schreibman v. United States Dep't of Commerce, 785 F. Supp. 164, 166 (D.D.C. 1991) requiring agency to segregate and release portions of documents that merely identify computer systems rather than contain security plans, which remain protected as vulnerability assessments) (Exemption 2); see also FOIA Update, Vol. XIV, No. 3, at 11-12 ("OIP Guidance: The 'Reasonable Segregation' Obligation").

[37] See Attorney General Reno's FOIA Memorandum, reprinted in FOIA Update, Vol. XIV, No. 3, at 4-5; see also Attorney General Reno's Follow-Up FOIA Memorandum, reprinted in FOIA Update, Vol. XIX, No. 4, at 3-5; FOIA Update, Vol. XV, No. 2, at 3.

[38] See Attorney General's 1986 Amendments Memorandum at 17 & n.31.

# EXEMPTION 7(F)

## EXEMPTION 7(F)

Exemption 7(F) permits the withholding of information necessary to protect the physical safety of a wide range of individuals. This exemption provides protection to "any individual" when disclosure of information about him "could reasonably be expected to endanger [his] life or physical safety."[1]

Prior to the 1986 FOIA amendments,[2] Exemption 7(F) protected records that "would . . . endanger the life or physical safety of law enforcement personnel,"[3] and had been invoked to protect both federal and local law enforcement officers.[4] Cases decided after the 1986 FOIA amendments continue this strong protection for law enforcement agents.[5]

---

[1] 5 U.S.C. § 552(b)(7)(F) (1994 & Supp. IV 1998).

[2] Pub. L. No. 99-570, § 1802, 100 Stat. 3207, 3207-48 to 3207-49 (1986).

[3] Pub. L. No. 93-502, 88 Stat. 1561, 1563 (1974) (subsequently amended).

[4] See, e.g., Maroscia v. Levi, 569 F.2d 1000, 1002 (7th Cir. 1977) (FBI special agents and "other law enforcement personnel"); Barham v. Secret Serv., No. 82-2130, slip op. at 5 (W.D. Tenn. Sept. 13, 1982) (Secret Service agents); Docal v. Bennsinger, 543 F. Supp. 38, 48 (M.D. Pa. 1981) (DEA special agents, supervisory special agents, and local law enforcement officers); Nunez v. DEA, 497 F. Supp. 209, 212 (S.D.N.Y. 1980) (DEA special agents); Ray v. Turner, 468 F. Supp. 730, 735 (D.D.C. 1979) (U.S. Customs Service agent).

[5] See, e.g., Johnston v. United States Dep't of Justice, No. 97-2173, 1998 U.S. App. LEXIS 18557, at *2 (8th Cir. Aug. 10, 1998) (protecting names of DEA agents); Green v. DEA, No. 98-0728, slip op. at 11-12 (D.D.C. Sept. 30, 1999) (protecting names of agents and other law enforcement personnel), summary affirmance granted in pertinent part, No. 99-5356 (D.C. Cir. Feb. 17, 2000); Bennett v. DEA, 55 F. Supp. 2d 36, 41 (D.D.C. 1999) (protecting DEA agents' names); Hronek v. DEA, 16 F. Supp. 2d 1260, 1275 (D. Or. 1998) (protecting names and identities of DEA agents, supervisory agents, and other law enforcement officers); Hazel v. Department of Justice, No. 95-01992, slip op. at 13 (D.D.C. July 2, 1998) (protecting correctional officers' names); Johnson v. DEA, No. 97-2231, 1998 U.S. Dist. LEXIS 9802, at *14 (D.D.C. June 25, 1998) (protecting DEA agents' names because disclosure could have detrimental effect on operations), aff'd in pertinent part, 1999 U.S. App. LEXIS 7332 (D.C. Cir. Mar. 2, 1999); Franklin v. United States Dep't of Justice, No. 97-1225, slip op. at 15 (S.D. Fla. June 15, 1998) (magistrate's recommendation) ("It is in the public interest not to disclose the identity of [DEA] Special Agents so that they may continue to effectively pursue undercover and investigative assignments."), adopted (S.D. Fla. June 26, 1998), aff'd per curiam, 189 F.3d 485 (11th Cir. 1999); McGhghy v. DEA, No. C 97-0185, slip op. at 12 (N.D. Iowa May 29, 1998) (finding that DEA "established a clear nexus between disclosure and harm to agents and officers"), aff'd per curiam, No. 98-2989 (8th Cir. July 19, 1999); Fedrick v. United States Dep't of Justice, 984 F. Supp. 659, 665 (W.D.N.Y. 1997) (magistrate's recommendation) (protecting names of DEA agents, supervisory agents, and other law enforcement personnel), adopted (W.D.N.Y. Oct. 28, 1997), aff'd sub nom. Fedrick v. Huff, 165

(continued...)

**EXEMPTION 7(F)**

Under the amended language of Exemption 7(F), courts have applied the broader coverage now offered by the exemption, holding that it can afford protection of the "names and identifying information of . . . federal employees, and third persons who may be unknown" to the requester in connection with particular law enforcement matters.[6] Withholding of such information can be

---

[5](...continued)
F.3d 13 (2d Cir. 1998); Jimenez v. FBI, 938 F. Supp. 21, 30-31 (D.D.C. 1996) (holding that disclosure of names of DEA special agents, supervisors, and local law enforcement officer could result in "physical attacks, threats, or harassment"; disclosure of DEA's investigative personnel would endanger lives of its agents and have "detrimental effect" on its operations); Badalamenti v. United States Dep't of State, 899 F. Supp. 542, 550 (D. Kan. 1995) (protecting names of law enforcement personnel); Augarten v. DEA, No. 93-2192, 1995 WL 350797, at *3 (D.D.C. May 22, 1995) (protecting "law enforcement officers and DEA agents who are particularly likely to be in contact with violent suspects"); Almy v. Department of Justice, No. 90-362, slip op. at 26 (N.D. Ind. Apr. 13, 1995) (protecting names of DEA agents, supervisory agents, and other law enforcement personnel), aff'd, 114 F.3d 1191 (7th Cir. 1997) (unpublished table decision); Manchester v. DEA, 823 F. Supp. 1259, 1273 (E.D. Pa. 1993) (protecting names and identities of DEA special agents, supervisory special agents, and other law enforcement officers); see also Housley v. DEA, No. 92-16946, 1994 U.S. App. LEXIS 11232, at *4 (9th Cir. May 4, 1994) (finding Exemption 7(F) properly used to protect "physical safety"). But see Public Employees for Envtl. Responsibility v. EPA, 978 F. Supp. 955, 964 (D. Colo. 1997) (finding no risk to agency investigators in disclosing EPA Inspector General guidelines).

[6] Luther v. IRS, No. 5-86-130, slip op. at 6 (D. Minn. Aug. 13, 1987); see also Johnston, 1998 U.S. App. LEXIS 18557, at *2 (protecting names of DEA personnel, local law enforcement personnel, and third parties); Russell v. Barr, No. 92-2546, slip op. at 11-12 (D.D.C. Aug. 28, 1998) (protecting identities of individuals who cooperated in investigation and prosecution involving spousal murder when agency demonstrated requester's reputation for violent behavior); Pray v. FBI, No. 95-0380, 1998 WL 440843, at *3 (S.D.N.Y. Aug. 3, 1998) (protecting names of sources); Isley v. Executive Office for United States Attorneys, No. 96-0123, slip op. at 8-9 (D.D.C. Mar. 27, 1997) (upholding agency's nondisclosure of identifying information about individuals who provided information during murder investigation when reasonable likelihood that disclosure would threaten their lives), appeal dismissed, No. 97-5105 (D.C. Cir. Sept. 8, 1997); Anderson v. United States Marshals Serv., 943 F. Supp. 37, 40 (D.D.C. 1996) (protecting identity of individual who required separation from requester when disclosure could endanger his safety); Jimenez, 938 F. Supp. at 30-31 (protecting names and identifying information furnished by confidential sources, as well as names of law enforcement personnel); Foster v. United States Dep't of Justice, 933 F. Supp. 687, 693 (E.D. Mich. 1996) (protecting identities of confidential informants when, because of nature of investigation concerning plaintiff, informants' lives or safety would be endangered); Bruscino v. Federal Bureau of Prisons, No. 94-1955, 1995 WL 444406, at *11 (D.D.C. May 12, 1995) (protecting investigatory information obtained from sources whose lives would be endangered by disclosure, especially in view of "rough justice" to be rendered upon informants should identi-
(continued...)

## EXEMPTION 7(F)

necessary to protect such persons from possible harm by a requester who has threatened them in the past.[7] Accordingly, one court also has held that the very expansive language of "any individual" encompasses protection of the identities of informants who have been threatened with harm.[8]

Significantly, Exemption 7(F) protection has been held to remain applicable even after a law enforcement officer subsequently retired.[9] Moreover, it has been held that Exemption 7(F) can be employed to protect the identities of individuals who testified at the requester's criminal trial.[10] And one court

---

[6](...continued)
ties be disclosed), summary affirmance granted in pertinent part, vacated & remanded in part, No. 95-5213, 1996 WL 393101 (D.C. Cir. June 24, 1996); Sanders v. United States Dep't of Justice, No. 91-2263, 1992 WL 97785, at *4 (D. Kan. Apr. 21, 1992) (finding that disclosing identities of medical personnel who prepared requester's mental health records would endanger their safety, in view of requester's mental difficulties). But see Trupei v. Huff, No. 96-2850, 1998 WL 8986, at *4 (D.D.C. Jan. 7, 1998) (finding government's concern for safety of individuals whose identities are unknown to requester to be "conclusory," warranting only Exemption 7(C) protection); Linn v. United States Dep't of Justice, No. 92-1406, 1995 WL 631847, at *9 (D.D.C. Aug. 22, 1995) (finding that agency "has not established even a minimal nexus" between withheld information and harm to persons discussed in file).

[7] See, e.g., Burke v. United States Dep't of Justice, No. 96-1739, 1999 WL 1032814, at *9 (D.D.C. Sept. 30, 1999) (finding that disclosing identities of "agents, other agencies' personnel and sources could expose [them] to violent retaliation," given requester's violent history); Anderson v. United States Dep't of Justice, No. 95-1888, 1999 U.S. Dist. LEXIS 4731, at **10-11 (D.D.C. Mar. 31, 1999) (finding that releasing witnesses' names could subject them to harassment and threats, given requester's history of carrying firearms); Crooker v. IRS, No. 94-0755, 1995 WL 430605, at *5 (D.D.C. Apr. 27, 1995) (protecting confidential informants when requester has history of harassing, intimidating, and abusing witnesses); Manna v. United States Dep't of Justice, 815 F. Supp. 798, 810 (D.N.J. 1993) (finding that releasing FBI reports would endanger life or physical safety of associates of requester in organized crime case), aff'd on other grounds, 51 F.3d 1158 (3d Cir. 1995); Author Servs. v. IRS, No. 90-2187, slip op. at 7 (C.D. Cal. Nov. 14, 1991) (withholding identities of third parties and handwriting and identities of IRS employees in view of previous conflict and hostility between parties).

[8] Housley v. FBI, No. 87-3231, 1988 WL 30751, at *3 (D.D.C. Mar. 24, 1988) (protecting identities of informants).

[9] See Moody v. DEA, 592 F. Supp. 556, 559 (D.D.C. 1984).

[10] See Linn v. United States Dep't of Justice, No. 92-1406, 1997 U.S. Dist. LEXIS 9321, at *17 (D.D.C. May 29, 1997) (protecting witnesses who testified) (Exemptions 7(C) and 7(F)), appeal voluntarily dismissed, No. 97-5122 (D.C. Cir. July 14, 1997); Beck v. United States Dep't of Justice, No. 88-3433, 1991 U.S. Dist. LEXIS 1179, at **10-11 (D.D.C. July 24, 1991) (finding that exemption was not necessarily waived when information revealed at public trial);
(continued...)

## EXEMPTION 7(F)

approved a rather novel, but certainly appropriate, application of this exemption to a description in an FBI laboratory report of a homemade machine gun because its disclosure would create the real possibility that law enforcement officers would have to face "individuals armed with homemade devices constructed from the expertise of other law enforcement people."[11]

Although Exemption 7(F)'s coverage is in large part duplicative of that afforded by Exemption 7(C), it is potentially broader in that no balancing is required for withholding under Exemption 7(F).[12] It is difficult to imagine any circumstance, though, in which the public's interest in disclosure could outweigh the personal safety of any individual.[13] Moreover, Exemption 7(F) has proven to be of great utility to law enforcement agencies, given the lessened "could reasonably be expected" harm standard now in effect.[14] Agencies can reasonably infer from this modification Congress's approval to withhold information whenever there is a reasonable likelihood of its disclosure risking

---

[10](...continued)
Prows v. United States Dep't of Justice, No. 87-1657, 1989 WL 39288, at *2 (D.D.C. Apr. 13, 1989) (finding, similar to under Exemption 7(C), DEA agents' identities protectible even though they testified at trial), aff'd, No. 89-5185 (D.C. Cir. Feb. 26, 1990). But see Myers v. United States Dep't of Justice, No. 85-1746, 1986 U.S. Dist. LEXIS 20058, at *6 (D.D.C. Sept. 22, 1986) (declining to protect law enforcement personnel who testified (Exemptions 7(C) and 7(F)).

[11] LaRouche v. Webster, No. 75-6010, 1984 WL 1061, at *8 (S.D.N.Y. Oct. 23, 1984); see also Pfeffer v. Director, Bureau of Prisons, No. 89-899, 1984 WL 1061, at *11 (D.D.C. Apr. 18, 1990) (holding that information about smuggling weapons into prisons could reasonably be expected to endanger physical safety of "some individual" and therefore was properly withheld).

[12] See FOIA Update, Vol. V, No. 2, at 5.

[13] See Colon v. Executive Office for United States Attorneys, No. 98-0180, 1998 WL 695631, at *6 (D.D.C. Sept. 29, 1998) (reiterating that it is not in public interest to disclose identities of law enforcement officers); Franklin, No. 97-1225, slip op. at 15 (S.D. Fla. June 15, 1998) (magistrate's recommendation) (finding that "it is in the public interest" to protect names of DEA agents), adopted (S.D. Fla. June 26, 1998).

[14] See, e.g., Spirko v. United States Postal Serv., 147 F.3d 992, 994 (D.C. Cir. 1998) (protecting handwritten notes of suspects); Colon, 1998 WL 695631, at *6 (finding withholding of names and identities of DEA agents, supervisory agents, and law enforcement officers proper); Fedrick, 984 F. Supp. at 665 (finding that DEA properly withheld names of agents and other law enforcement personnel); Johnson, 1998 U.S. Dist. LEXIS 9802, at *4 (protecting agents' names and identities); McGhghy, No. C 97-0185, slip op. at 12 (N.D. Iowa May 29, 1998) (finding names of agents and other law enforcement personnel properly withheld); Crompton, No. 95-8771, slip op. at 16 (C.D. Cal. Mar. 26, 1997) (finding withholding of agents' names, signatures, and identifying information proper).

**EXEMPTION 8**

physical harm to someone.[15]

## EXEMPTION 8

Exemption 8 of the FOIA protects matters that are "contained in or related to examination, operating, or condition reports prepared by, on behalf of, or for the use of an agency responsible for the regulation or supervision of financial institutions."[1]

This exemption received little judicial attention during the first dozen years of the FOIA's operation. The only significant decision during that period was M.A. Schapiro & Co. v. SEC, in which the District Court for the District of Columbia held that national securities exchanges and broker-dealers are not "financial institutions" within the meaning of the exemption.[2] Fourteen years later, after passage of the Government in the Sunshine Act[3]--the legislative history of which broadly defines the term "financial institutions" --that same court disavowed its early narrow interpretation of the term and held that stock exchanges qualify as "financial institutions" under Exemption 8.[4] As a result, subsequent attempts by FOIA requesters to have courts rely on the ruling in M.A. Schapiro have been unsuccessful.[5]

Instead, courts interpreting Exemption 8 have largely declined to restrict the "particularly broad, all-inclusive" scope of the exemption.[6] They

---

[15] See Attorney General's Memorandum on the 1986 Amendments to the Freedom of Information Act 18 & n.34 (Dec. 1987); see also, e.g., Dickie v. Department of the Treasury, No. 86-649, slip op. at 13 (D.D.C. Mar. 31, 1987) (upholding application of Exemption 7(F) as amended based upon agency judgment of "very strong likelihood" of harm); accord Attorney General's Memorandum for Heads of Departments and Agencies regarding the Freedom of Information Act (Oct. 4, 1993), reprinted in FOIA Update, Vol. XIV, No. 3, at 4-5 (establishing "foreseeable harm" standard governing use of FOIA exemptions); see also FOIA Update, Vol. XV, No. 2, at 3.

[1] 5 U.S.C. § 552(b)(8) (1994 & Supp. IV 1998).

[2] 339 F. Supp. 467, 470 (D.D.C. 1972).

[3] 5 U.S.C. § 552b (1994 & Supp. IV 1998).

[4] Mermelstein v. SEC, 629 F. Supp. 672, 673-75 (D.D.C. 1986).

[5] See Feshbach v. SEC, 5 F. Supp. 2d 774, 781 (N.D. Cal. 1997) (rejecting argument that court should follow M.A. Schapiro definition of term "financial institutions" because "the same district court [had] noted [in Mermelstein] that [M.A. Schapiro] was no longer good law"); Berliner, Zisser, Walter & Gallegos v. SEC, 962 F. Supp. 1348, 1351 n.5 (D. Colo. 1997) (likewise rejecting cramped reading of term "financial institutions" because court in Mermelstein had noted that "subsequent passage of the Sunshine Act" rendered decision in M.A. Schapiro "no longer good law").

[6] Consumers Union of United States, Inc. v. Office of the Comptroller of the
(continued...)

# EXEMPTION 8

have reasoned that "if Congress has intentionally and unambiguously crafted a particularly broad, all-inclusive definition, it is not [the courts'] function, even in the FOIA context, to subvert that effort."[7] As one court stated: "Exemption 8 was intended by Congress--and has been interpreted by courts--to be very broadly construed."[8]

The Court of Appeals for the District of Columbia Circuit has gone so far as to state that in Exemption 8 Congress has provided "absolute protection regardless of the circumstances underlying the regulatory agency's receipt or preparation of examination, operating or condition reports."[9] Similarly, in a major Exemption 8 decision, the D.C. Circuit broadly construed the term "financial institutions" and held that it is not limited to "depository" institutions.[10] More recently, the District Court for the District of Colorado relied upon that D.C. Circuit decision when ruling that an "investment advisor company" is a "financial institution" under Exemption 8, observing that "investment advisors, as a matter of common practice, are fiduciaries of their clients who direct, and in reality make, important investment decisions."[11] The District Court for the Northern District of California, "following the logic" of these earlier cases, broadly held "that the term 'financial institutions' encompasses brokers and dealers of securities or commodities as well as self-regulatory organizations, such as the [National Association of Securities Dealers]."[12]

In examining the sparse legislative history of Exemption 8, courts have

---

[6](...continued)
Currency, No. 86-1841, slip op. at 2 (D.D.C. Mar. 11, 1988); see also McCullough v. FDIC, 1 Gov't Disclosure Serv. (P-H) ¶ 80,194, at 80,494 (D.D.C. July 28, 1980).

[7] Consumers Union of United States, Inc. v. Heimann, 589 F.2d 531, 533 (D.C. Cir. 1978); see also Sharp v. FDIC, 2 Gov't Disclosure Serv. (P-H) ¶ 81,107, at 81,270 (D.D.C. Jan. 28, 1981); McCullough, 1 Gov't Disclosure Serv. (P-H) at 80,494.

[8] Pentagon Fed. Credit Union v. National Credit Union Admin., No. 95-1476, slip op. at 8 (E.D. Va. June 7, 1996).

[9] Gregory v. FDIC, 631 F.2d 896, 898 (D.C. Cir. 1980); see also Clarkson v. Greenspan, No. 97-2035, slip op. at 14-15 (D.D.C. June 30, 1998) (extending Exemption 8 protection to records of examinations conducted by Federal Reserve Banks for Board of Governors of Federal Reserve System), summary affirmance granted, No. 98-5349, 1999 WL 229017 (D.C. Cir. Mar. 2, 1999).

[10] Public Citizen v. Farm Credit Admin., 938 F.2d 290, 293-94 (D.C. Cir. 1991) (holding that National Consumer Cooperative Bank (NCCB) is "financial institution" for purposes of Exemption 8; exemption protects audit reports prepared by Farm Credit Administration (FCA) for submission to Congress regarding NCCB, although FCA does not regulate or supervise NCCB).

[11] Berliner, 962 F. Supp. at 1352 (relying on "legislative history of the Sunshine Act" in absence of "unambiguous definition of financial institutions provided in [the] FOIA's text or legislative history").

[12] Feshbach, 5 F. Supp. 2d at 781.

-449-

## EXEMPTION 8

discerned two major purposes underlying it: (1) "to protect the security of financial institutions by withholding from the public reports that contain frank evaluations of a bank's stability," and (2) "to promote cooperation and communication between employees and examiners."[13] Accordingly, different types of documents have been held to fall within the broad confines of Exemption 8.

First and foremost, the authority of federal agencies to withhold bank examination reports prepared by federal bank examiners has not been questioned.[14] Further, matters that are "related to" such reports--that is, documents that "represent the foundation of the examination process, the findings of such an examination, or its follow-up"--have also been held exempt from disclosure.[15] Likewise, Exemption 8 has been employed to withhold portions of documents--such as internal memoranda and policy statements--that con-

---

[13] Atkinson v. FDIC, 1 Gov't Disclosure Serv. (P-H) ¶ 80,034, at 80,102 (D.D.C. Feb. 13, 1980); see Berliner, 962 F. Supp. at 1353 (delineating Exemption 8's "dual purposes" as "protecting the integrity of financial institutions and facilitating cooperation between [agencies] and the entities regulated by [them]"); see also Consumers Union, 589 F.2d at 534 (identifying primary reasons for adoption of Exemption 8 as protecting disclosure of examination, operation, and condition reports--which, if disclosed, might undermine public confidence in financial institutions--and safeguarding relationship between supervisory agencies and banks); Feinberg v. Hibernia Corp., No. 90-4245, 1993 WL 8620, at *4 (E.D. La. Jan. 6, 1993) (noting Exemption 8's dual purpose of protecting operation and condition reports containing frank evaluations of investigated banks, and protecting relationship between financial institutions and supervisory government agencies); Fagot v. FDIC, 584 F. Supp. 1168, 1173 (D.P.R. 1984) (recognizing purposes of Exemption 8 in protecting information containing frank evaluations which might undermine public confidence and relationship between financial institutions and supervisory agencies), aff'd in pertinent part & rev'd in part, 760 F.2d 252 (1st Cir. 1985) (unpublished table decision).

[14] See Sharp, 2 Gov't Disclosure Serv. (P-H) at 81,270; Atkinson, 1 Gov't Disclosure Serv. (P-H) at 80,102; see also Clarkson, No. 97-2035, slip op. at 14-15 (D.D.C. June 30, 1998) (holding that Board of Governors of Federal Reserve System may withhold records of examinations prepared by Federal Reserve Banks).

[15] Atkinson, 1 Gov't Disclosure Serv. (P-H) at 80,102; see, e.g., Parsons v. Freedom of Info. Act Officer, Office of Consumer Affairs SEC, No. 96-4128, 1997 WL 461320, at *1 (6th Cir. Aug. 12, 1997) (summarily holding that "all communication[s] between" SEC and National Association of Securities Dealers (NASD), including "any SEC audits" of NASD, "were exempt from disclosure"); Biase v. Office of Thrift Supervision, No. 93-2521, slip op. at 12 (D.N.J. Dec. 16, 1993); Teichgraeber v. Board of Governors, Fed. Reserve Sys., No. 87-2505, 1989 WL 32183, at *1 (D. Kan. Mar. 20, 1989); Consumers Union, No. 86-1841, slip op. at 2-3 (D.D.C. Mar. 11, 1988); Folger v. Conover, No. 82-4, slip op. at 6-8 (E.D. Ky. Oct. 25, 1983); Sharp, 2 Gov't Disclosure Serv. (P-H) at 81,271.

# EXEMPTION 8

tain specific information about named financial institutions.[16]

Bank examination reports and related documents prepared by state regulatory agencies have been found protectible under Exemption 8 on more than one ground. The purposes of the exemption are plainly served by withholding such material because of the "interconnected" purposes and operations of federal and state banking authorities.[17] In one case, a state agency report, transferred to a federal agency strictly for its confidential use and thus still within the control of the state agency, was held as a threshold matter not even to be an "agency record" under the FOIA subject to disclosure.[18] In general, "all records, regardless of the source, of a bank's financial condition and operations [that are] in the possession of a federal agency 'responsible for the regulation or supervision of financial institutions,' are exempt."[19]

Indeed, even records pertaining to banks that are no longer in operation can be withheld under Exemption 8 in order to serve the policy of promoting "frank cooperation" between bank and agency officials.[20] The exemption protects even bank examination reports and related memoranda relating to insol-

---

[16] Wachtel v. Office of Thrift Supervision, No. 3-90-833, slip op. at 19-20, 23, 26-28, 30, 33 (M.D. Tenn. Nov. 20, 1990) (protecting portions of documents containing information about two named financial institutions--specifically, names of institutions, names of officers and agents, any references to their geographic locations, and specific information about their financial conditions).

[17] Atkinson, 1 Gov't Disclosure Serv. (P-H) at 80,102.

[18] McCullough, 1 Gov't Disclosure Serv. (P-H) at 80,495.

[19] Id. (quoting legislative history); see also Snoddy v. Hawke, No. 99-1636, slip op. at 2 (D. Colo. Dec. 20, 1999) (holding that electronic mail, notes, and correspondence pertaining to matters discussed by employees of Citibank and Office of Comptroller of Currency were properly withheld as "matters prepared by or for the [regulating] agency . . . [and pertaining to] examination, operating or condition reports"), appeal dismissed, No. 00-1039 (10th Cir. Mar. 13, 2000); Clarkson, No. 97-2035, slip op. at 15 (D.D.C. June 30, 1998) (finding that records of examinations conducted by Federal Reserve Banks for Board of Governors of Federal Reserve System were properly withheld because the "examinations were done by or for the agency responsible for regulating Reserve Banks").

[20] Gregory, 631 F.2d at 899; accord Berliner, 962 F. Supp. at 1353 (upholding applicability of Exemption 8 to documents relating to company that had "been defunct for at least four years" and declining to adopt argument that passage of time abated "need for confidentiality"). But cf. In re Sunrise Sec. Litig., 109 B.R. 658, 664-67 (E.D. Pa. 1990) (holding that Federal Home Loan Bank of Atlanta could not rely upon regulation implementing Exemption 8 as independent evidentiary "bank examination privilege," and even under more general "official information privilege," finding that there exists no absolute protection for internal working papers and other documents generated in government's examination of failed bank) (non-FOIA case).

# EXEMPTION 8

vency proceedings.[21] Documents relating to cease-and-desist orders that issue after a bank examination as the result of a closed administrative hearing are also properly exempt.[22] Also, reports examining bank compliance with consumer laws and regulations have been held to "fall squarely within the exemption."[23]

Moreover, in keeping with the expansive construction of Exemption 8, courts have generally not required agencies to segregate and disclose portions of documents unrelated to the financial state of the institution. As one court has observed, "an entire examination report, not just that related to the 'condition of the bank' may be properly withheld."[24] Although some courts have declined to extend the protection of Exemption 8 to "purely factual material,"[25] the District Court for the Eastern District of Virginia recently permitted its withholding, reasoning that "facts cannot be considered in isolation " and instead "must be considered with respect to the overall context of the documents in which they are contained."[26]

---

[21] See, e.g., Tripati v. United States Dep't of Justice, No. 87-3301, 1990 U.S. Dist. LEXIS 6249, at **2-3 (D.D.C. May 18, 1990).

[22] See, e.g., Atkinson, 1 Gov't Disclosure Serv. (P-H) at 80,103.

[23] Id.; see also Snoddy, No. 99-1636, slip op. at 2 (D. Colo. Dec. 20, 1999) (holding that e-mail, notes, and other correspondence pertaining to whether Citibank violated regulation fell within purview of Exemption 8); Consumers Union, No. 86-1841, slip op. at 2-3 (D.D.C. Mar. 11, 1988) (finding that reports fall within Exemption 8 "because they analyze and summarize information concerning consumer complaints"); cf. Consumers Union, 589 F.2d at 534-35 (concluding that Truth in Lending Act, 15 U.S.C. § 1601 (1994 & Supp. IV 1998), does not narrow Exemption 8's broad language).

[24] Atkinson, 1 Gov't Disclosure Serv. (P-H) at 80,103. But see Fagot v. FDIC, No. 84-1523, slip op. at 5-6 (1st Cir. Mar. 27, 1985) (finding that portion of document which does not relate to bank report or examination cannot be withheld); see also FOIA Update, Vol. XIV, No. 3, at 11-12 ("OIP Guidance: The 'Reasonable Segregation' Obligation").

[25] Pentagon Fed., No. 95-1476, slip op. at 9 (E.D. Va. June 7, 1996) (declining to extend Exemption 8 protection to "purely factual material"); Lee v. FDIC, 923 F. Supp. 451, 459 (S.D.N.Y. 1996) (likewise denying protection for information found to be "primarily factual"), dismissed, No. 1:95 CV 7963 (S.D.N.Y. Sept. 15, 1997); cf. Schreiber v. Society for Sav. Bancorp, Inc., 11 F.3d 217, 220 (D.C. Cir. 1993) (declaring, in context of discovery, that "bank examination privilege protects only agency opinions and recommendations from disclosure; purely factual information falls outside the privilege") (non-FOIA case); In re Subpoena, 967 F.2d 630, 634 (D.C. Cir. 1992) ("The bank examination privilege, like the deliberative process privilege, shields from discovery only agency opinions or recommendations; it does not protect purely factual material.") (non-FOIA case).

[26] Marriott Employees' Fed. Credit Union v. National Credit Union Admin., No. 96-478-A, slip op. at 9 (E.D. Va. Dec. 24, 1996) (protecting facts because "disclosure of this information would undermine the spirit of cooperation be-

(continued...)

# EXEMPTION 8

It should be noted, however, that a provision of the Federal Deposit Insurance Corporation Improvement Act of 1991 explicitly limits Exemption 8's applicability with respect to specific reports prepared pursuant to it.[27] That statute requires federal banking agency inspectors general to conduct a review and to make a written report when a deposit insurance fund incurs a material loss with respect to an insured depository institution.[28] The statute further provides that, with the exception of information that would reveal the identity of any customer of the institution, the federal banking agency "shall disclose the report upon request under [the FOIA] without excising . . . any information about the insured depository institution under [Exemption 8]."[29]

Additionally, agencies should apply the governmentwide policy of government openness[30] and the "foreseeable harm " standard set forth in Attorney General Reno's FOIA Memorandum of October 4, 1993,[31] to information covered by Exemption 8.[32] Given the breadth of this exemption, and its purely institutional nature, the application of the "foreseeable harm" standard holds potential for increased agency disclosure as a matter of administrative discretion--particularly regarding factual portions of bank examination reports and related documents.[33]

---

[26](...continued) tween banks and regulating agencies that Exemption 8 attempts to foster").

[27] 12 U.S.C. § 1831o(k) (1994 & Supp. II 1996).

[28] Id. § 1831o(k)(1).

[29] Id. § 1831o(k)(4).

[30] See President's Memorandum for Heads of Departments and Agencies regarding the Freedom of Information Act, 29 Weekly Comp. Pres. Doc. 1999 (Oct. 4, 1993), reprinted in FOIA Update, Vol. XIV, No. 3, at 3.

[31] Attorney General's Memorandum for Heads of Departments and Agencies regarding the Freedom of Information Act (Oct. 4, 1993), reprinted in FOIA Update, Vol. XIV, No. 3, at 4-5; see also Attorney General's Follow-Up Memorandum for Heads of Departments and Agencies regarding the Freedom of Information Act (Sept. 3, 1999), reprinted in FOIA Update, Vol. XIX, No. 4, at 3-5 (reiterating importance of "foreseeable harm" standard to federal agencies in order to promote further discretionary disclosure in agency decisionmaking).

[32] See FOIA Update, Vol. XV, No. 2, at 3 (noting applicability of "foreseeable harm" standard to Exemption 8); see also Gregory, 631 F.2d at 899 & n.4 (noting agency regulation providing for discretionary disclosure of Exemption 8 information).

[33] See FOIA Update, Vol. XV, No. 2, at 3.

# EXEMPTION 9

## EXEMPTION 9

Exemption 9 of the FOIA covers "geological and geophysical information and data, including maps, concerning wells."[1] While this exemption is very rarely invoked or interpreted,[2] one court has held that it applies only to "well information of a technical or scientific nature."[3] Only two other decisions have mentioned Exemption 9; however, neither case discussed its scope or application.[4]

## EXCLUSIONS

In amending the Freedom of Information Act in 1986, Congress created a novel mechanism for protecting certain especially sensitive law enforcement matters, under subsection (c) of the Act.[1] These three special protection provisions, referred to as record "exclusions," expressly authorize federal law enforcement agencies, for especially sensitive records under certain specified circumstances, to "treat the records as not subject to the requirements of [the FOIA]."[2] The procedures required to properly employ these special record exclusions are by no means straightforward and must be implemented with the utmost care.[3] Any agency considering employing an exclusion or having a question as to their implementation should first consult with the Office of Information and Privacy, at (202) 514-3642.[4]

---

[1] 5 U.S.C. § 552(b)(9) (1994 & Supp. IV 1998).

[2] See National Broad. Co. v. SBA, 836 F. Supp. 121, 124 n.2 (S.D.N.Y. 1993) (merely noting that document withheld under Exemption 4 "also contains geographic or geological information which is exempted from disclosure pursuant to FOIA Exemption 9 ").

[3] Black Hills Alliance v. United States Forest Serv., 603 F. Supp. 117, 122 (D.S.D. 1984) (withholding number, locations, and depths of proposed uranium exploration drill holes).

[4] See Superior Oil Co. v. Federal Energy Regulatory Comm'n, 563 F.2d 191, 203-04 & n.20 (5th Cir. 1977) (non-FOIA case); Pennzoil Co. v. Federal Power Comm'n, 534 F.2d 627, 629-30 & n.2 (5th Cir. 1976) (non-FOIA case). See generally Ecee, Inc. v. Federal Energy Regulatory Comm'n, 645 F.2d 339, 348-49 (5th Cir. 1981) (holding that requirement that producers of natural gas submit confidential geological information was valid) (non-FOIA case).

[1] See Attorney General's Memorandum on the 1986 Amendments to the Freedom of Information Act 18-30 (Dec. 1987) [hereinafter Attorney General's 1986 Amendments Memorandum].

[2] 5 U.S.C. § 552(c)(1), (c)(2), (c)(3) (1994 & Supp. IV 1998); see Tanks v. Huff, No. 95-568, 1996 WL 293531, at *5 (D.D.C. May 28, 1996), appeal dismissed, No. 96-5180 (D.C. Cir. Aug. 13, 1996).

[3] See Attorney General's 1986 Amendments Memorandum at 27 n.48.

[4] See id.

# EXCLUSIONS

At the outset, it is important to recognize the somewhat subtle, but very significant, distinction between the result of employing a record exclusion and the concept that is colloquially known as "Glomarization."[5] That latter term refers to the situation in which an agency expressly refuses to confirm or deny the existence of records responsive to a request.[6] (A more detailed discussion of "Glomarization" can be found under Exemption 1, In Camera Submissions, above, and also under Exemption 7(C), above.) The application of one of the three record exclusions, on the other hand, results in a response to the FOIA requester stating that no records responsive to his FOIA request exist.[7] While "Glomarization" remains adequate to provide necessary protection in certain situations, these special record exclusions should prove invaluable in addressing the exceptionally sensitive situations in which even "Glomarization" is inadequate to the task.

### The (c)(1) Exclusion

The first of these novel provisions, known as the "(c)(1) exclusion," provides as follows:

> Whenever a request is made which involves access to records described in subsection (b)(7)(A) and (A) the investigation or proceeding involves a possible violation of criminal law; and (B) there is reason to believe that (i) the subject of the investigation or proceeding is not aware of its pendency, and (ii) disclosure of the existence of the records could reasonably be expected to interfere with enforcement proceedings, the agency may, during only such time as that circumstance continues, treat the records as not subject to the requirements of this section.[8]

In most cases, the protection of Exemption 7(A) is sufficient to guard against any impairment of law enforcement investigations or proceedings through the FOIA. To avail itself of Exemption 7(A), however, an agency must routinely specify that it is doing so--first administratively and then, if sued, in court--even when it is invoking the exemption to withhold all responsive records in their entireties. Thus, in specific situations in which the very fact of an investigation's existence is yet unknown to the investigation's subject, invok-

---

[5] See id. at 26 & n.47; see also Benavides v. DEA, 968 F.2d 1243, 1246-48 (D.C. Cir.) (initially confusing exclusion mechanism with "Glomarization"), modified, 976 F.2d 751, 753 (D.C. Cir. 1992); Valencia Lucena v. DEA, No. 99-0633, slip op. at 8 (D.D.C. Feb. 8, 2000) (recognizing that Benavides "was subsequently clarified") (appeal pending).

[6] See, e.g., Gardels v. CIA, 689 F.2d 1100, 1103 (D.C. Cir. 1982); Phillippi v. CIA, 546 F.2d 1009, 1013 (D.C. Cir. 1976).

[7] See Attorney General's 1986 Amendments Memorandum at 18 (cited in Tanks, 1996 WL 293531, at *5); see also Steinberg v. United States Dep't of Justice, No. 93-2409, 1997 WL 349997, at *1 (D.D.C. June 18, 1997) ("[T]he government need not even acknowledge the existence of excluded information.").

[8] 5 U.S.C. § 552(c)(1) (1994 & Supp. IV 1998).

## EXCLUSIONS

ing Exemption 7(A) in response to a FOIA request for pertinent records permits an investigation's subject to be "tipped off" to its existence. By the same token, any person (or entity) engaged in criminal activities could use a carefully worded FOIA request to try to determine whether he, she, or it is under federal investigation. An agency response that does not invoke Exemption 7(A) to withhold law enforcement files tells such a requester that his activities have thus far escaped detection.

The (c)(1) exclusion authorizes federal law enforcement agencies, under specified circumstances, to shield the very existence of records of ongoing investigations or proceedings by excluding them entirely from the FOIA's reach.[9] To qualify for such exclusion from the FOIA, the records in question must be those which would otherwise be withheld in their entireties under Exemption 7(A). Further, they must relate to an "investigation or proceeding [that] involves a possible violation of criminal law."[10] Hence, any records pertaining to a purely civil law enforcement matter cannot be excluded from the FOIA under this provision, although they may qualify for ordinary Exemption 7(A) withholding. However, the statutory requirement that there be only a "possible violation of criminal law," by its very terms, admits a wide range of investigatory files maintained by more than just criminal law enforcement agencies.[11]

Next, the statute imposes two closely related requirements which go to the very heart of the particular harm addressed through this record exclusion. An agency determining whether it can employ (c)(1) protection must consider whether it has "reason to believe" that the investigation's subject is not aware of its pendency and that, most fundamentally, the agency's disclosure of the very existence of the records in question "could reasonably be expected to interfere with enforcement proceedings."[12]

Obviously, where all investigatory subjects are already aware of an investigation's pendency, the "tip off" harm sought to be prevented through this record exclusion is not of concern. Accordingly, the language of this exclusion expressly obliges agencies contemplating its use to consider the level of awareness already possessed by the investigative subjects involved. It is appropriate that agencies do so, as the statutory language provides, according to a good-faith, "reason to believe" standard--which very much comports with the "could reasonably be expected to" standard utilized both elsewhere in this

---

[9] See Attorney General's Memorandum on the 1986 Amendments to the Freedom of Information Act 18-22 (Dec. 1987) [hereinafter Attorney General's 1986 Amendments Memorandum].

[10] 5 U.S.C. § 552(c)(1)(A).

[11] See Attorney General's 1986 Amendments Memorandum at 20 & n.37 (files of agencies that are not primarily engaged in criminal law enforcement activities may be eligible for protection if they contain information about potential criminal violations that are pursued with the possibility of referral to Department of Justice for further prosecution).

[12] 5 U.S.C. § 552(c)(1)(B).

# EXCLUSIONS

exclusion and in the amended language of Exemption 7(A).[13]

This "reason to believe" standard for considering a subject's present awareness should afford agencies all necessary latitude in making such determinations. As the exclusion is phrased, this requirement is satisfied so long as an agency determines that it affirmatively has a "reason to believe" that such awareness does not in fact exist. While it is always possible that an agency might possess somewhat conflicting or even contradictory indications on such a point, unless an agency can resolve that a subject is aware of an investigation, it should not risk impairing the investigation through a telling FOIA disclosure.[14] Moreover, agencies are not obligated to accept any bald assertions by investigative subjects that they "know" of ongoing investigations against them; such assertions might well constitute no more than sheer speculation. Because such a ploy, if accepted, could defeat the exclusion's clear statutory purpose, agencies should rely upon their own objective indicia of subject awareness and consequent harm.[15]

In the great majority of cases, invoking Exemption 7(A) will protect the interests of law enforcement agencies in responding to FOIA requests for active law enforcement files. The (c)(1) exclusion should be employed only in the exceptional case in which an agency reaches the judgment that, given its belief of the subject's unawareness of the investigation, the mere invocation of Exemption 7(A) could reasonably be expected to cause harm--a judgment that should be reached distinctly and thoughtfully.[16]

Finally, the clear language of this exclusion specifically restricts its applicability to "during only such time" as the above required circumstances continue to exist. This limitation comports with the extraordinary nature of the protection afforded by the exclusion, as well as with the basic temporal nature of Exemption 7(A) underlying it. It means, of course, that an agency that has employed the exclusion in a particular case is obligated to cease doing so once the circumstances warranting it cease to exist.

Once a law enforcement matter reaches a stage at which all subjects are aware of its pendency, or at which the agency otherwise determines that the public disclosure of that pendency no longer could lead to harm, the exclusion should be regarded as no longer applicable. If the FOIA request which triggered the agency's use of the exclusion remains pending either administra-

---

[13] See Attorney General's 1986 Amendments Memorandum at 21.

[14] See id.

[15] See id. at n.38.

[16] See id. at 21; accord Attorney General's Memorandum for Heads of Departments and Agencies regarding the Freedom of Information Act (Oct. 4, 1993), reprinted in FOIA Update, Vol. XIV, No. 3, at 4-5 (establishing "foreseeable harm" standard, based upon all "reasonably expected consequences" involved); see also Attorney General's Follow-Up Memorandum for Heads of Departments and Agencies regarding the Freedom of Information Act (Sept. 3, 1999), reprinted in FOIA Update, Vol. XIX, No. 4, at 3-5 (reiterating importance of "foreseeable harm" standard).

## EXCLUSIONS

tively or in court at such time, the excluded records should be identified as responsive to that request and processed in the ordinary manner.[17] However, an agency is under no legal obligation to spontaneously reopen a closed FOIA request, even though records were excluded during its entire pendency: By operation of law, the records simply were not subject to the FOIA during the pendency of the request.[18]

Where all of these requirements are met, and an agency reaches the judgment that it is necessary and appropriate that the (c)(1) exclusion be employed in connection with a request, the records in question will be treated, as far as the FOIA requester is concerned, as if they did not exist.[19] Where it is the case that the excluded records are just part of the totality of records responsive to a FOIA request, the request will be handled as a seemingly routine one, with the other responsive records processed as if they were the only responsive records in existence. Where the only records responsive to a request fall within the exclusion, the requester will lawfully be advised that no records responsive to his FOIA request exist.[20]

In order to maintain the integrity of an exclusion, each agency that employs it must ensure that its FOIA responses are consistent throughout. Therefore, all agencies that could possibly employ at least one of the three record exclusions should ensure that their FOIA communications are consistently phrased so that a requester cannot ever discern the existence of any excluded records, or of any matter underlying them, through the agency's response to his FOIA request.

### The (c)(2) Exclusion

The second exclusion applies to a narrower situation, involving the threatened identification of confidential informants in criminal proceedings.[21] The "(c)(2) exclusion" provides as follows:

> Whenever informant records maintained by a criminal law enforcement agency under an informant's name or personal identifier are requested by a third party according to the informant's name or personal identifier, the agency may treat the records as not subject to the requirements of [the FOIA] unless the inform-

---

[17] See Attorney General's 1986 Amendments Memorandum at 22.

[18] See id. at 22 n.39.

[19] See id. at 22.

[20] See id.

[21] See Attorney General's Memorandum on the 1986 Amendments to the Freedom of Information Act 22-24 (Dec. 1987) [hereinafter Attorney General's 1986 Amendments Memorandum]; see also Tanks v. Huff, No. 95-568, 1996 WL 293531, at *5 (D.D.C. May 28, 1996), appeal dismissed, No. 96-5180 (D.C. Cir. Aug. 13, 1996).

# EXCLUSIONS

ant's status as an informant has been officially confirmed.[22]

This exclusion contemplates the situation in which a sophisticated requester could try to identify an informant by forcing a law enforcement agency into a position in which it otherwise would have no lawful choice but to tellingly invoke Exemption 7(D) in response to a request which encompasses informant records maintained on a named person.[23] In the ordinary situation, Exemption 7(D), as amended, should adequately allow a law enforcement agency to withhold all items of information necessary to prevent the identification of any of its confidential sources.[24]

But as with Exemption 7(A), invoking Exemption 7(D) in response to a FOIA request tells the requester that somewhere within the records encompassed by his particular request there is reference to at least one confidential source. Again, under ordinary circumstances the disclosure of this fact poses no direct threat. But under certain extraordinary circumstances, this disclosure could result in devastating harms to the source and to the system of confidentiality existing between sources and criminal law enforcement agencies.

The scenario in which the exclusion is most likely to be employed is one in which the ringleaders of a criminal enterprise suspect that they have been infiltrated by a source and therefore force all participants in the criminal venture either to directly request that any law enforcement files on them be disclosed to the organization or to execute privacy waivers authorizing disclosure of their files in response to a request from the organization. Absent the (c)(2) exclusion, a law enforcement agency could effectively be forced to disclose information to the subject organization (i.e., through the very invocation of Exemption 7(D)) indicating that the named individual is a confidential source.[25]

The (c)(2) exclusion is principally intended to address this unusual, but dangerous situation, by permitting an agency to escape the necessity of giving a response that would be tantamount to identifying a named party as a law enforcement source.[26] Any criminal law enforcement agency is authorized to

---

[22] 5 U.S.C. § 552(c)(2) (1994 & Supp. IV 1998).

[23] See Attorney General's 1986 Amendments Memorandum at 23.

[24] See, e.g., Keys v. United States Dep't of Justice, 830 F.2d 337, 345-46 (D.C. Cir. 1987); see also United States Dep't of Justice v. Landano, 508 U.S. 165, 179-81 (1993) (Although "the Government is not entitled to a presumption that a source is confidential within the meaning of Exemption 7(D) whenever the source provides information to the FBI in the course of a criminal investigation," it should "often" be able to identify circumstances supporting an inference of confidentiality.); FOIA Update, Vol. XIV, No. 3, at 10.

[25] See Attorney General's 1986 Amendments Memorandum at 23; Tanks, No. 95-568, 1996 WL 293531, at ** 5-6.

[26] See Attorney General's 1986 Amendments Memorandum at 23-24; Tanks, 1996 WL 293531, at *6 (stating that "[t]he (c)(2) exclusion is princi-
(continued...)

# EXCLUSIONS

treat such requested records, within the extraordinary context of such a FOIA request, as beyond the FOIA's reach. As with the (c)(1) exclusion, the agency would have "no obligation to acknowledge the existence of such records in response to such request."[27]

By its terms, the exclusion simply becomes inapplicable once the individual's status as a source has been officially confirmed.[28] But by merely confirming a source's status as such, a law enforcement agency does not thereby obligate itself to confirm the existence of any specific records regarding that source.[29] Thus, the (c)(2) exclusion cannot be read to automatically require disclosure of source-related information once a source has been officially acknowledged,[30] so long as such information may properly be protected under a FOIA exemption.[31]

A criminal law enforcement agency forced to employ this exclusion

---

[26](...continued) pally intended to permit an agency to avoid giving a response that would identify a named party as a source" (citing Attorney General's 1986 Amendments Memorandum at 23)).

[27] S. Rep. No. 98-221, at 25 (1983).

[28] See 5 U.S.C. § 552(c)(2); Valencia Lucena v. DEA, No. 99-0633, slip op. at 8 (D.D.C. Feb. 8, 2000) (concluding that "[subs]ection (c)(2) is irrelevant to the resolution of this action" because the subject's status as an informant was "officially confirmed at [the requester's] criminal trial") (appeal pending); Tanks, 1996 WL 293531, at *5 (holding that "given the fact that the status of [the subjects] as government informants in Plaintiff's case is confirmed, the (c)(2) exclusion simply has no bearing on the instant case").

[29] See Valencia Lucena, No. 99-0633, slip op. at 8 (D.D.C. Feb. 8, 2000) (rejecting plaintiff's argument that "when FOIA [subs]ection (c)(2) does not apply, the agency must confirm the existence of responsive records"); Tanks, 1996 WL 293531, at **5-6 (same).

[30] See Benavides v. DEA, 968 F.2d 1243, 1248 (D.C. Cir.) ("There is no evidence that Congress intended subsection (c)(2) to repeal or supersede the other enumerated FOIA exemptions or to require disclosure whenever the informant's status has been officially confirmed."), modified on other grounds, 976 F.2d 751, 753 (D.C. Cir. 1992); cf. Valencia Lucena, No. 99-0633, slip op. at 8-9 (D.D.C. Feb. 8, 2000) (holding that once subsection (c)(2) was rendered inapplicable by official confirmation of source's status as such, FBI appropriately relied on Exemptions 6 and 7(C) to refuse to confirm or deny existence of any responsive records).

[31] See Benavides, 968 F.2d at 1248 ("The legislative history suggests, in fact, that Congress intended to permit the DEA to withhold documents under 7(C) and 7(D), even if the agency must, under subsection (c)(2), acknowledge their existence."); Tanks, 1996 WL 293531, at *6 ("Accepting the status of [two named individuals] as government informants, the FBI explained why disclosure of any information in its files unrelated to the Plaintiff and his prosecution would constitute an unwarranted invasion of personal privacy pursuant to Exemption 7(C), 5 U.S.C. § 552(b)(7)(C).").

# EXCLUSIONS

should do so in the same fashion as it would employ the (c)(1) exclusion discussed above.[32] It is imperative that all information which ordinarily would be disclosed to a first-party requester, other than information which would reflect that an individual is a confidential source, be disclosed. If, for example, the Federal Bureau of Investigation were to respond to a request for records pertaining to an individual having a known record of federal prosecutions by replying that "there exist no records responsive to your FOIA request," the interested criminal organization would surely recognize that its request had been afforded extraordinary treatment and would draw its conclusions accordingly. Therefore, the (c)(2) exclusion must be employed in a manner entirely consistent with its source-protection objective.

### The (c)(3) Exclusion

The third of these special record exclusions pertains only to certain law enforcement records that are maintained by the FBI.[33] The "(c)(3) exclusion" provides as follows:

> Whenever a request is made which involves access to records maintained by the Federal Bureau of Investigation pertaining to foreign intelligence or counterintelligence, or international terrorism, and the existence of the records is classified information as provided in [Exemption 1], the Bureau may, as long as the existence of the records remains classified information, treat the records as not subject to the requirements of [the FOIA].[34]

This exclusion recognizes the exceptional sensitivity of the FBI's activities in the areas of foreign intelligence, counterintelligence, and the battle against international terrorism, as well as the fact that the classified files of these activities can be particularly vulnerable to targeted FOIA requests. Sometimes, within the context of a particular FOIA request, the very fact that the FBI does or does not hold any records on a specified person or subject can itself be a sensitive fact, properly classified in accordance with the applicable executive order on the protection of national security information[35] and protectible under FOIA Exemption 1.[36] Once again, however, the mere invocation of Exemption 1 to withhold such information can provide information to the requester which would have an extremely adverse effect on the government's interests. In some possible contexts, the furnishing of an actual "no records"

---

[32] See Attorney General's 1986 Amendments Memorandum at 24.

[33] See Attorney General's Memorandum on the 1986 Amendments to the Freedom of Information Act 24-27 (Dec. 1987) [hereinafter Attorney General's 1986 Amendments Memorandum].

[34] 5 U.S.C. § 552(c)(3) (1994 & Supp. IV 1998).

[35] See Exec. Order No. 12,958, 3 C.F.R. 333 (1996), reprinted in 50 U.S.C. § 435 note (Supp. II 1996), and reprinted in abridged form in FOIA Update, Vol. XVI, No. 2, at 5-10.

[36] See 5 U.S.C. § 552(b)(1); see also Attorney General's 1986 Amendments Memorandum at 25.

## EXCLUSIONS

response, even in response to a seemingly innocuous "first-party" request, could compromise sensitive activities.[37]

Congress took cognizance of this through the (c)(3) exclusion, in which it authorizes the FBI to protect itself against such harm in connection with any of its records pertaining to these three, especially sensitive, areas. To do so, the FBI must of course reach the judgment, in the context of a particular request, that the very existence or nonexistence of responsive records is itself a classified fact and that it need employ this record exclusion to prevent its disclosure.[38] By the terms of this provision, the excluded records may be treated as such so long as their existence, within the context of the request, "remains classified information."[39]

Additionally, it should be noted that while the statute refers to records maintained by the FBI, exceptional circumstances could possibly arise in which it would be appropriate for another component of the Department of Justice or another federal agency to invoke this exclusion.[40] Such a situation could occur where information in records of another component or agency is derived from FBI records which fully qualify for (c)(3) exclusion protection. In such extraordinary circumstances, the agency processing the derivative information should consult with the FBI regarding the possible joint invocation of the exclusion in order to avoid a potentially damaging inconsistent response.[41]

### Procedural Considerations

Several procedural considerations regarding the implementation and operation of these special record exclusions should be noted. First, it should be self-evident that the decision to employ an exclusion in response to a particular request must not be reflected on anything made available to the requester. When an agency reaches the judgment that it is necessary to employ an exclusion, it should do so as a specific official determination that is reviewed carefully by appropriate supervisory agency officials.[42] The particular records covered by an exclusion action should be concretely and carefully identified and segregated from any responsive records that are to be processed ac-

---

[37] See Attorney General's 1986 Amendments Memorandum at 25.

[38] See id.

[39] 5 U.S.C. § 552(c)(3); see also FOIA Update, Vol. XVI, No. 2, at 1-2, 11 (noting that executive order places emphasis on limited classification and automatic declassification).

[40] See Attorney General's 1986 Amendments Memorandum at 25 n.45.

[41] See id.

[42] See Attorney General's Memorandum on the 1986 Amendments to the Freedom of Information Act 27 (Dec. 1987) [hereinafter Attorney General's 1986 Amendments Memorandum].

-462-

# EXCLUSIONS

cording to ordinary procedures.[43]

It must be remembered that providing a "no records" response as part of an exclusion strategy does not insulate the agency from either administrative or judicial review of the agency's action. The recipient of a "no records" response may challenge it because he believes that the agency has failed to conduct a sufficiently detailed search to uncover the requested records.[44] Alternately, any requester, mindful of the exclusion mechanism and seeking information of a nature which could possibly trigger an exclusion action, could seek review in an effort to pursue his suspicions and to have a court determine whether an exclusion, if in fact used, was employed appropriately.

Moreover, because the very objective of the exclusions is to preclude the requester from learning that there exist such responsive records, all administrative appeals and court cases involving a "no records" response must receive extremely careful attention. If one procedure is employed in adjudicating appeals or litigating cases in which there are genuinely no responsive records, and any different course is followed where an exclusion is in fact being used, sophisticated requesters could quickly learn to distinguish between the two and defeat an exclusion's very purpose.[45]

Consequently, agencies should prepare in advance a uniform procedure to handle administrative appeals and court challenges which seek review of the possibility that an exclusion was employed in a given case. In responding to administrative appeals from "no record" responses,[46] agencies should accept any clear request for review of the possible use of an exclusion and specifically address it in evaluating and responding to the appeal.[47]

In the exceptional case in which an exclusion was in fact invoked, the appellate review authority should examine the correctness of that action and come to a judgment as to the exclusion's continued applicability as of that time.[48] In the event that an exclusion is found to have been improperly employed or to be no longer applicable, the appeal should be remanded for prompt processing of all formerly excluded records, with the requester ad-

---

[43] See id.

[44] See id. at 29; see also Oglesby v. United States Dep't of the Army, 920 F.2d 57, 67 (D.C. Cir. 1990).

[45] See Attorney General's 1986 Amendments Memorandum at 29.

[46] See FOIA Update, Vol. XII, No. 2, at 5 ("OIP Guidance: Procedural Rules Under the D.C. Circuit's Oglesby Decision") (agencies obligated to advise any requester who receives "no record" response of its procedures for filing administrative appeal) (superseding FOIA Update, Vol. V, No. 3, at 2).

[47] See Attorney General's 1986 Amendments Memorandum at 29 (superseded in part by FOIA Update, Vol. XII, No. 2, at 5).

[48] See id. at 28.

# EXCLUSIONS

vised accordingly.[49] When it is determined either that an exclusion was properly employed or that, as in the overwhelming bulk of cases, no exclusion was used, the result of the administrative appeal should be, by all appearances, the same: The requester should be specifically advised that this aspect of his appeal was reviewed and found to be without merit.[50]

Such administrative appeal responses, of course, necessarily must be stated in such a way that does not indicate whether an exclusion was in fact invoked.[51] Moreover, in order to preserve the exclusion mechanism's effectiveness, requesters who inquire in any way whether an exclusion has been used should routinely be advised that it is the agency's standard policy to refuse to confirm or deny that an exclusion was employed in any particular case.[52]

Exclusion issues in court actions must be handled with similarly careful and thoughtful preparation. First, it need be recognized that any judicial review of a suspected exclusion determination must of course be conducted ex parte, based upon an in camera court filing submitted directly to the judge.[53] Second, it is essential to the integrity of the exclusion mechanism that requesters not be able to determine whether an exclusion was employed at all in a given case based upon how any case is handled in court. Thus, it is critical that the in camera defenses of exclusion issues raised in FOIA cases occur not merely in those cases in which an exclusion actually was employed and is in fact being defended.[54]

Accordingly, it is the government's standard litigation policy in the defense of FOIA lawsuits that, whenever a FOIA plaintiff raises a distinct claim regarding the suspected use of an exclusion, the government will routinely submit an in camera declaration addressing that claim, one way or the other.[55] When an exclusion was in fact employed, the correctness of that action will be justified to the court. When an exclusion was not in fact employed, the in camera declaration will state simply that it is being submitted to the court so

---

[49] See id.

[50] See id. at 28-29.

[51] See id. at 29.

[52] See id. at 29 & n.52.

[53] See id. at 29; see also Steinberg v. United States Dep't of Justice, No. 93-2409, 1997 WL 349997, at *1 (D.D.C. June 18, 1997) (approving use of agency in camera declaration when plaintiff "alleged that certain requested information may have been excluded pursuant to [sub]section 552(c)").

[54] See Attorney General's 1986 Amendments Memorandum at 29.

[55] See id. at 30; see also, e.g., Steinberg, 1997 WL 349997, at *1 ("[T]he government is permitted to file an in camera declaration, which explains either that no exclusion was invoked or that the exclusion was invoked appropriately."); Steinberg v. United States Dep't of Justice, No. 91-2740, 1993 WL 524528, at *2 (D.D.C. Dec. 2, 1993) (agency "volunteered an in camera submission related to the allegation of covert reliance on § 552(c)").

## DISCRETIONARY DISCLOSURE AND WAIVER

as to mask whether or not an exclusion is being employed, thus preserving the integrity of the exclusion process overall.[56] In either case, the government will of course urge the court to issue a public decision which does not indicate whether it is or is not an actual exclusion case. Such a public decision, like an administrative appeal determination of an exclusion-related request for review, should specify only that a full review of the claim was had and that, if an exclusion was in fact employed, it was, and remains, amply justified.[57]

## DISCRETIONARY DISCLOSURE AND WAIVER

The Freedom of Information Act is an information disclosure statute which, through its exemption structure, strikes a balance between information disclosure and nondisclosure,[1] with an emphasis on the "fullest responsible disclosure."[2] Inasmuch as the FOIA's exemptions are discretionary, not mandatory,[3] agencies are free to make "discretionary disclosures" of exempt information, as a matter of sound policy, whenever they are not otherwise prohibited from doing so.[4]

---

[56] See Attorney General's 1986 Amendments Memorandum at 30.

[57] See id.; see also, e.g., Steinberg, 1997 WL 349997, at *1 (where plaintiff alleged possible use of exclusion, "without confirming or denying the existence of any exclusion, the Court finds and concludes [after review of in camera declaration] that if an exclusion was invoked, it was and remains amply justified"); Beauman v. FBI, No. CV-92-7603, slip op. at 2 (C.D. Cal. Apr. 12, 1993) ("'In response to the plaintiff's claim of the (c)(1) exclusion being utilized in this action, . . . [w]ithout confirming or denying that any such exclusion was actually invoked by the defendant, the Court finds and concludes [after review of an in camera declaration] that if an exclusion was in fact employed, it was, and remains, amply justified.'" (adopting agency's proposed conclusion of law)).

[1] See John Doe Agency v. John Doe Corp., 493 U.S. 146, 153 (1989).

[2] S. Rep. No. 89-813, at 3 (1965); see also Attorney General's Memorandum on the 1986 Amendments to the Freedom of Information Act 30 (Dec. 1987) [hereinafter Attorney General's 1986 Amendments Memorandum]; FOIA Update, Vol. IX, No. 3, at 14.

[3] See Chrysler Corp. v. Brown, 441 U.S. 281, 293 (1979); Bartholdi Cable Co. v. FCC, 114 F.3d 274, 282 (D.C. Cir. 1997) ("FOIA's exemptions simply permit, but do not require, an agency to withhold exempted information").

[4] See CNA Fin. Corp. v. Donovan, 830 F.2d 1132, 1334 n.1 (D.C. Cir. 1987) (An agency's FOIA disclosure decision can "be grounded either in its view that none of the FOIA exemptions applies, and thus that disclosure is mandatory, or in its belief that release is justified in the exercise of its discretion, even though the data fall within one or more of the statutory exemptions."); see also Chenkin v. Department of the Army, No. 94-7109, slip op. at 1 (3d Cir. June 7, 1995) (discretionary disclosure of documents during appellate litigation process renders case moot as to those documents); FOIA Update, Vol. VI, No. 3, at 3 ("[A]gencies generally have discretion under the Freedom of Infor-
(continued...)

## DISCRETIONARY DISCLOSURE AND WAIVER

The statements of FOIA policy issued by President Clinton and Attorney General Janet Reno on October 4, 1993,[5] together set forth a strong policy of openness in government, in which the making of discretionary FOIA disclosures plays a prominent part.[6] President Clinton's FOIA Memorandum emphasizes that "the more the American people know about their government, the better they will be governed."[7] In turn, Attorney General Reno's FOIA Memorandum establishes a "foreseeable harm" standard governing the use of FOIA exemptions, regardless of whether the information in question "might technically or arguably fall within an exemption."[8] As an essential corollary to that, and based upon the principle that information "ought not to be withheld from a FOIA requester unless it need be," Attorney General Reno's FOIA Memorandum states:

> Accordingly, I strongly encourage [all] FOIA officers to make "discretionary disclosures" whenever possible under the Act. Such disclosures are possible under a number of FOIA exemptions, especially when only a governmental interest would be affected.[9]

When agencies make discretionary disclosures of exempt information "as a matter of good public policy" under Attorney General Reno's FOIA Memorandum,[10] they should not be held to have "waived" their ability to invoke applicable FOIA exemptions for similar or related information in the future. In other situations, however, various types of agency conduct and circumstances can reasonably be held to result in exemption waiver.

---

[4](...continued) mation Act to decide whether to invoke applicable FOIA exemptions."); cf. FOIA Update, Vol. XIII, No. 2, at 5-6 (discussing exercise of agency discretion in processing of requests for information maintained in electronic form).

[5] President's Memorandum for Heads of Departments and Agencies regarding the Freedom of Information Act, 29 Weekly Comp. Pres. Doc. 1999 (Oct. 4, 1993) [hereinafter President Clinton's FOIA Memorandum], reprinted in FOIA Update, Vol. XIV, No. 3, at 3; Attorney General's Memorandum for Heads of Departments and Agencies regarding the Freedom of Information Act (Oct. 4, 1993) [hereinafter Attorney General Reno's FOIA Memorandum], reprinted in FOIA Update, Vol. XIV, No. 3, at 4-5.

[6] See FOIA Update, Vol. XIV, No. 3, at 1.

[7] President Clinton's FOIA Memorandum, reprinted in FOIA Update, Vol. XIV, No. 3, at 3.

[8] Attorney General Reno's FOIA Memorandum, reprinted in FOIA Update, Vol. XIV, No. 3, at 4-5.

[9] Id.

[10] See id.; see also Attorney General's Follow-Up Memorandum for Heads of Departments and Agencies regarding the Freedom of Information Act (Sept. 3, 1999) [hereinafter Attorney General Reno's Follow-Up FOIA Memorandum], reprinted in FOIA Update, Vol. XIX, No. 4, at 3-5 (reiterating importance of "foreseeable harm" standard to federal agencies in order to promote further discretionary disclosure in agency decisionmaking).

# DISCRETIONARY DISCLOSURE AND WAIVER

## Discretionary Disclosure

As a general rule, an agency's ability to make a discretionary disclosure of exempt information in accordance with Attorney General Reno's FOIA Memorandum[11] will vary according to the nature of the FOIA exemption and the underlying interests involved. First, while the FOIA does not itself prohibit the disclosure of any information,[12] an agency's ability to make a discretionary disclosure of information covered by a FOIA exemption can hinge on whether there exists any legal barrier to disclosure of that information. Some of the FOIA's exemptions--such as Exemption 2,[13] and Exemption 5,[14] for example--protect a type of information that is not subject to any such disclosure prohibition. Other FOIA exemptions--most notably Exemption 3[15]--directly correspond to, and serve to accommodate, distinct prohibitions on information disclosure that operate independently of the FOIA. Agencies are constrained from making a discretionary FOIA disclosure of the types of information covered by the following FOIA exemptions:

Exemption 1 of the FOIA protects from disclosure national security information concerning the national defense or foreign policy, provided that it has been properly classified in accordance with both the substantive and procedural requirements of an existing executive order.[16] As a rule, an agency official holding classification authority determines whether information requires classification and then that determination is implemented under the FOIA through the invocation of Exemption 1.[17] Thus, if information is in fact properly classified, and therefore is exempt from disclosure under Exemption 1, it is not appropriate for discretionary FOIA disclosure. (See the discussion of Exemption 1, above.)

Exemption 3 of the FOIA explicitly accommodates the nondisclosure provisions that are contained in a variety of other federal statutes. Some of these statutory nondisclosure provisions, such as those pertaining to grand

---

[11] Attorney General's Memorandum for Heads of Departments and Agencies regarding the Freedom of Information Act (Oct. 4, 1993) [hereinafter Attorney General Reno's FOIA Memorandum], reprinted in FOIA Update, Vol. XIV, No. 3, at 4-5.

[12] See 5 U.S.C. § 552(d) (1994 & Supp. IV 1998).

[13] Id. § 552(b)(2).

[14] Id. § 552(b)(5).

[15] Id. § 552(b)(3).

[16] Id. § 552(b)(1) (implementing Exec. Order No. 12,958, 3 C.F.R. 333 (1996), reprinted in 50 U.S.C. § 435 note (Supp. II 1996), and reprinted in abridged form in FOIA Update, Vol. XVI, No. 2, at 5-10).

[17] See generally FOIA Update, Vol. VI, No. 1, at 1-2.

## DISCRETIONARY DISCLOSURE AND WAIVER

jury information[18] and census data,[19] categorically prevent disclosure harm and establish absolute prohibitions on agency disclosure; others leave agencies with some discretion as to whether to disclose certain information, but such administrative discretion generally is exercised independently of the FOIA.[20] (See the discussion of Exemption 3, above.) Therefore, agencies ordinarily do not make discretionary disclosure under the FOIA of information that falls within the scope of Exemption 3.[21]

Exemption 4 of the FOIA protects "trade secrets and commercial or financial information obtained from a person [that is] privileged or confidential."[22] For the most part, Exemption 4 protects information implicating private commercial interests that would not ordinarily be the subject of discretionary FOIA disclosure. (See the discussions of Exemption 4, above, and "Reverse" FOIA, below.) Even more significantly, a specific criminal statute, the Trade Secrets Act,[23] prohibits the unauthorized disclosure of most (if not all) of the information falling within Exemption 4; its practical effect is to constrain an agency's ability to make a discretionary disclosure of Exemption 4 information,[24] absent an agency regulation (based upon a federal statute) that expressly authorizes disclosure.[25] (See the discussion of this point under "Reverse" FOIA, below.)

Exemptions 6 and 7(C) of the FOIA protect personal privacy interests,

---

[18] See Fed. R. Crim. P. 6(e) (enacted as statute in 1977).

[19] See 13 U.S.C. §§ 8(b), 9(a) (1994).

[20] See, e.g., Aronson v. IRS, 973 F.2d 962, 966 (1st Cir. 1992).

[21] See, e.g., Association of Retired R.R. Workers v. Railroad Retirement Bd., 830 F.2d 331, 335 (D.C. Cir. 1987) (FOIA jurisdiction does not extend to exercise of agency disclosure discretion within Exemption 3 statute); see also FOIA Update, Vol. XV, No. 4, at 7 (describing firm limitation imposed on disclosure of "tax return information" under 26 U.S.C. § 6103). But see Palmer v. Derwinski, No. 91-197, slip op. at 3-4 (E.D. Ky. June 10, 1992) (exceptional FOIA case in which court ordered Veterans Administration to disclose existence of certain medical records pursuant to discretionary terms of 38 U.S.C. § 7332(b) (1994)); see also, e.g., Craig v. United States, 131 F.3d 99, 101-07 (2d Cir. 1997) (articulating factors according to which courts make discretionary disclosure determinations for grand jury information) (non-FOIA case).

[22] 5 U.S.C. § 552(b)(4).

[23] 18 U.S.C. § 1905 (1994 & Supp. IV 1998).

[24] See CNA Fin. Corp. v. Donovan, 830 F.2d 1132, 1144 (D.C. Cir. 1987); see also FOIA Update, Vol. VI, No. 3, at 3 ("OIP Guidance: Discretionary Disclosure and Exemption 4").

[25] See Chrysler v. Brown, 441 U.S. 281, 295-96 (1979); see, e.g., St. Mary's Hosp., Inc. v. Harris, 604 F.2d 407, 409-10 (5th Cir. 1979).

## DISCRETIONARY DISCLOSURE AND WAIVER

in non-law enforcement records[26] and law enforcement records,[27] respectively. As with private commercial information covered by Exemption 4, the personal information protected by Exemptions 6 and 7(C) is not the type of information ordinarily considered appropriate for discretionary FOIA disclosure; with these exemptions, a balancing of public interest considerations is built into the determination of whether the information is exempt in the first place. (See the discussions of this issue under Exemption 6, above, and Exemption 7(C), above.)

Moreover, the personal information covered by Exemptions 6 and 7(C) in many cases falls within the protective coverage of the Privacy Act of 1974,[28] which mandates that any such information concerning U.S. citizens and permanent-resident aliens that is maintained in a "system of records"[29] not be disclosed unless that disclosure is permitted under one of the specific exceptions to the Privacy Act's general disclosure prohibition.[30] Inasmuch as the FOIA-disclosure exception in the Privacy Act permits only those disclosures that are "required" under the FOIA,[31] the making of discretionary FOIA disclosures of personal information is fundamentally incompatible with the Privacy Act and, in many instances, is prohibited by it.[32]

With the exception of information that is subject to the disclosure prohibitions accommodated by the above FOIA exemptions, agencies may make discretionary disclosures of any information that is exempt under the FOIA. As Attorney General Reno's FOIA Memorandum points out, such disclosures are most appropriate when the interest protected by the exemption in question is "only a governmental interest" of the agency (rather than the private interest of an individual or commercial entity)--one that the agency may choose to forego as an exercise of sound administrative discretion in furtherance of the objectives of government openness and "maximum responsible disclosure" under the Act.[33] While it does not create any justiciable rights for

---

[26] 5 U.S.C. § 552(b)(6).

[27] Id. § 552(b)(7)(C).

[28] Id. § 552a (1994 & Supp. IV 1998).

[29] Id. § 552a(a)(5).

[30] Id. § 552a(b).

[31] Id. § 552a(b)(2).

[32] See DOD v. FLRA, 964 F.2d 26, 30-31 n.6 (D.C. Cir. 1992) (discussing Privacy Act's limitations on discretionary FOIA disclosure); see also FOIA Update, Vol. V, No. 3, at 2 (discussing interplay between FOIA and Privacy Act); cf. Crumpton v. United States, 843 F. Supp. 751, 756 (D.D.C. 1994) (holding that disclosure under FOIA of personal information not subject to Privacy Act creates no liability under Federal Tort Claims Act (FTCA), given applicability of FTCA's discretionary function exception), aff'd on other grounds sub nom. Crumpton v. Stone, 59 F.3d 1400 (D.C. Cir. 1995).

[33] Attorney General Reno's FOIA Memorandum, reprinted in FOIA Update,
(continued...)

## DISCRETIONARY DISCLOSURE AND WAIVER

requesters in FOIA litigation,[34] the "foreseeable harm" standard established by Attorney General Reno's FOIA Memorandum serves to promote such disclosures whenever possible.[35]

A prime example is the type of administrative information that can fall within the "low 2" aspect of Exemption 2, which was uniquely designed to shield agencies from sheer administrative burden rather than from any substantive disclosure harm. (See the discussion of Exemption 2, above.) In many instances, especially when the information in question is a portion of a document page not otherwise exempt in its entirety, such information is more efficiently released than withheld.[36] As a practical matter, moreover, nearly all "low 2" information should be appropriate for discretionary disclosure upon application of the "foreseeable harm" standard of Attorney General Reno's FOIA Memorandum.[37]

By far, the most common examples of information appropriate for discretionary FOIA disclosure can be found under Exemption 5, which incorporates discovery privileges that almost always protect only the institutional interests of the agency possessing the information. (See the discussion of Exemption 5, above.) Information that might otherwise be withheld under the

---

[33](...continued)
Vol. XIV, No. 3, at 4-5.

[34] Id.; see, e.g., Spannaus v. United States Dep't of Justice, 942 F.2d 656, 658 (D.D.C. 1996) (refusing to review agency "foreseeable harm" determination as possible abuse of administrative discretion); Greenberg v. United States Dep't of Treasury, 10 F. Supp. 2d 3, 17 (D.D.C. 1998) (refusing to order re-review of documents based on Attorney General Reno's FOIA Memorandum, as "defendants claim, and plaintiffs do not appear to dispute, that the memorandum created no rights in individual litigants"). But see Tax Analysts v. IRS, No. 94-923, 1999 U.S. Dist. LEXIS 14950, at *20 (D.D.C. Sept. 2, 1999) (mistakenly relying on the "presumption of disclosure" and "forseeable harm standard" set forth in Attorney General Reno's FOIA Memorandum as a basis for ordering disclosure, and opining that disclosure was warranted because the "IRS candidly admitt[ed] that it erred on the side of confidentiality, rather than disclosure . . . [in a manner which is] speculative, attenuated, and directly contrary to the Attorney General's presumption of disclosure, [and is] unsupported by any foreseeable harm").

[35] Attorney General Reno's FOIA Memorandum, reprinted in FOIA Update, Vol. XIV, No. 3, at 4-5; see also Attorney General's Follow-Up Memorandum for Heads of Departments and Agencies regarding the Freedom of Information Act (Sept. 3, 1999) [hereinafter Attorney General Reno's Follow-Up FOIA Memorandum], reprinted in FOIA Update, Vol. XIX, No. 4, at 3-5; FOIA Update, Vol. XVIII, No. 2, at 1; FOIA Update, Vol. XV, No. 2, at 3.

[36] See FOIA Update, Vol. V, No. 1, at 11-12 ("FOIA Counselor: The Unique Protection of Exemption 2") (advising agencies not to invoke exemption heedlessly).

[37] See also FOIA Update, Vol. XV, No. 2, at 3 (distinguishing between "low 2" and "high 2" aspects of Exemption 2).

## DISCRETIONARY DISCLOSURE AND WAIVER

deliberative process privilege to protect the deliberative process in general can be disclosed when to do so would cause no "foreseeable harm" to any particular process of agency deliberation.[38] A range of factors--including the particular circumstances of the decisionmaking process involved, as well as the passage of time--can compel the conclusion that such information should be disclosed as a matter of administrative discretion.[39] (For a detailed discussion of this, see Exemption 5, Applying the "Foreseeable Harm" Standard, above.)

Many litigation-related records that otherwise might routinely be withheld under Exemption 5's attorney work-product privilege can be disclosed on the same basis.[40] This privilege broadly covers practically all information prepared in connection with litigation, without any temporal limitation whatsoever. (See the discussion of Exemption 5, Attorney Work-Product Privilege, above.) Consequently, it holds an exceptionally large potential for the making of discretionary disclosures after the conclusion of litigation--and even during the course of litigation--upon consideration of certain basic elements of harm.[41] This is likewise possible for information covered by the attorney-client privilege of Exemption 5.[42] (See Exemption 5, Applying the "Foreseeable Harm" Standard, above, for a detailed discussion of all three major privileges of Exemption 5 in this regard.)

The potential held by other FOIA exemptions for discretionary disclosure upon application of the "foreseeable harm" standard necessarily varies from exemption to exemption. Overall, the greatest potential for making such disclosures should be found, as Attorney General Reno's FOIA Memorandum indicates, in the FOIA exemptions (or parts of exemptions) designed to protect "governmental interests."[43] Exemption 7(E),[44] for example, affords very broad coverage of "law enforcement techniques" in its first clause, and therefore holds much potential for discretionary disclosure.[45] (See the discussion of Exemption 7(E), above.)

---

[38] See, e.g., FOIA Update, Vol. XV, No. 2, at 1 (describing discretionary disclosure of entire document found properly withheld in Mapother v. Department of Justice, 3 F.3d 1533 (D.C. Cir. 1993)).

[39] See FOIA Update, Vol. XV, No. 2, at 3-5; see, e.g., FOIA Update, Vol XV, No. 4, at 7; see also FOIA Update, Vol. XIV, No. 3, at 2.

[40] See, e.g., FOIA Update, Vol. VI, No. 3, at 5 (encouraging consideration of discretionary disclosure of attorney work-product information when possible to do so without causing harm to litigation process).

[41] See FOIA Update, Vol. XV, No. 2, at 5-6.

[42] See id. at 6.

[43] Attorney General Reno's FOIA Memorandum, reprinted in FOIA Update, Vol. XIV, No. 3, at 4-5.

[44] 5 U.S.C. § 552(b)(7)(E).

[45] See FOIA Update, Vol. XV, No. 2, at 3 (distinguishing between Exemption 7(E)'s two clauses).

## DISCRETIONARY DISCLOSURE AND WAIVER

Similarly, the second clause of Exemption 7(D)[46] broadly covers all information furnished by confidential sources in criminal investigations, regardless of its source-identification utility; the Department of Justice has specifically changed its policy for the treatment of such information to encourage its discretionary disclosure whenever that is possible without foreseeable source identification and harm.[47] (See the discussion of Exemption 7(D), above.) The broad coverage of bank examination reports and related records that is afforded by Exemption 8[48] holds strong potential for discretionary disclosure as well. (See the discussion of Exemption 8, above.) By contrast, other exemptions are more narrowly rooted with harm standards that do not hold such discretionary disclosure potential.[49]

In this regard, it also should be remembered that the FOIA requires agencies to focus on individual portions of records in connection with the applicability of all exemptions of the Act and to disclose all individual, "reasonably segregable" record portions that are not covered by an exemption.[50] (See the discussions of this issue under Procedural Requirements, "Reasonably Segregable" Obligation, above, and Litigation Considerations, "Reasonably Segregable" Requirements, below.) This focus is essential to meeting the Act's

---

[46] 5 U.S.C. § 552(b)(7)(D).

[47] See FOIA Update, Vol. XIV, No. 3, at 10; see also FOIA Update, Vol. XV, No. 4, at 7 (describing such discretionary disclosure through process of Justice Department litigation review).

[48] 5 U.S.C. § 552(b)(8).

[49] See FOIA Update, Vol. XV, No. 2, at 3.

[50] 5 U.S.C. § 552(b) (sentence immediately following exemptions); see also, e.g., Trans-Pac. Policing Agreement v. United States Customs Serv., 177 F.3d 1022, 1028 (D.C. Cir. 1999) (holding that district courts have affirmative duty to consider issue of segregability sua sponte even if issue has not been specifically raised by plaintiff); Kimberlin v. United States Dep't of Justice, 139 F.3d 944, 946, 949-51 (D.C. Cir.) (holding that district court erred in approving agency's withholding of entire documents without making specific finding on segregability), cert. denied, 525 U.S. 891 (1998); PHE, Inc. v. Department of Justice, 983 F.2d 248, 252 (D.C. Cir. 1993) (both agency and court must determine whether any nonexempt information can be segregated from exempt information and released); Hronek v. DEA, 16 F. Supp. 2d 1260, 1270 (D. Or. 1998) (making extensive finding on segregability and stating that "[b]lanket explanations . . . do not meet FOIA's requirements and do not permit the court to make the necessary findings"); Steinberg v. United States Dep't of Justice, 179 F.R.D. 357, 364 (D.D.C. 1998) (requiring agency to submit documents for in camera review of segregability where "substantial segments of material--several consecutive paragraphs or pages" were withheld "based on assurances that the entirety of each redaction would identify a third-party [sic] with a privacy interest"); Brooks v. IRS, No. CV-F-96-6284, 1997 U.S. Dist. LEXIS 21075, at *4 (E.D. Cal. Nov. 17, 1997) ("The court may not simply approve the withholding of an entire document without entering a finding on segregability.").

## DISCRETIONARY DISCLOSURE AND WAIVER

primary objective of "maximum responsible disclosure."[51] As Attorney General Reno's FOIA Memorandum emphasizes,[52] the satisfaction of this important statutory requirement can involve an onerous delineation process, one that readily lends itself to the making of discretionary disclosures, particularly at the margins of FOIA exemption applicability.[53]

Furthermore, as Attorney General Reno's FOIA Memorandum additionally points out,[54] making a discretionary disclosure under the FOIA can significantly lessen an agency's burden at all levels of the administrative process, and it also eliminates the possibility that the information in question will become the subject of protracted litigation--thus serving an additional public interest in the conservation of increasingly scarce agency resources.[55]

As Attorney General Reno's FOIA Memorandum also notes, when an agency considers making a discretionary disclosure of exempt information under the FOIA, it should be able to do so free of any concern that in exercising its administrative discretion with respect to particular information it is impairing its ability to invoke applicable FOIA exemptions for any arguably similar information in the future.[56]

Indeed, in the leading judicial precedent on this point, Mobil Oil Corp. v. EPA,[57] a FOIA requester argued that by making a discretionary disclosure of certain records that could have been withheld under Exemption 5, the agency had waived its right to invoke that exemption for a group of "related" records.[58] In rejecting such a waiver argument, however, the Court of Appeals for the Ninth Circuit surveyed the law of waiver under the FOIA and found "no case . . . in which the release of certain documents waived the exemption as to other documents. On the contrary, [courts] generally have found that the re-

---

[51] FOIA Update, Vol. XIV, No. 3, at 11-12 ("OIP Guidance: The 'Reasonable Segregation' Obligation") (quoting Attorney General Reno's FOIA Memorandum, reprinted in FOIA Update, Vol. XIV, No. 3, at 4-5).

[52] See id.

[53] See, e.g., Army Times Publ'g Co. v. Department of the Air Force, 998 F.2d 1067, 1071 (D.C. Cir. 1993) (emphasizing significance of segregation requirement in connection with deliberative process privilege under Exemption 5); Wightman v. ATF, 755 F.2d 979, 983 (1st Cir. 1985) ("detailed process of segregation" held not unreasonable for request involving 36 pages).

[54] Attorney General Reno's FOIA Memorandum, reprinted in FOIA Update, Vol. XIV, No. 3, at 4-5.

[55] See FOIA Update, Vol. XV, No. 4, at 7 (listing examples of discretionary disclosure and resulting disposition of FOIA litigation cases through process of Justice Department litigation review).

[56] Attorney General Reno's FOIA Memorandum, reprinted in FOIA Update, Vol. XIV, No. 3, at 4-5.

[57] 879 F.2d 698 (9th Cir. 1989).

[58] Id. at 700.

## DISCRETIONARY DISCLOSURE AND WAIVER

lease of certain documents waives FOIA exemptions only for those documents released."[59]

Such a general rule of nonwaiver through discretionary disclosure is supported by sound policy considerations, as the Ninth Circuit in Mobil Oil discussed at some length:

> Implying such a waiver could tend to inhibit agencies from making any disclosures other than those explicitly required by law because voluntary release of documents exempt from disclosure requirements would expose other documents [of a related nature] to risk of disclosure. An agency would have an incentive to refuse to release all exempt documents if it wished to retain an exemption for any documents . . . . [R]eadily finding waiver of confidentiality for exempt documents would tend to thwart the [FOIA's] underlying statutory purpose, which is to implement a policy of broad disclosure of government records.[60]

In fact, this rule was presaged by the Court of Appeals for the District of Columbia Circuit many years ago, when it observed:

> Surely this is an important consideration. The FOIA should not be construed so as to put the federal bureaucracy in a defensive or hostile position with respect to the Act's spirit of open government and liberal disclosure of information.[61]

As another court more recently phrased it: "A contrary rule would create an

---

[59] Id. at 701; see Salisbury v. United States, 690 F.2d 966, 971 (D.C. Cir. 1982) ("[D]isclosure of a similar type of information in a different case does not mean that the agency must make its disclosure in every case."); Stein v. Department of Justice, 662 F.2d 1245, 1259 (7th Cir. 1981) (exercise of discretion should waive no right to withhold records of "similar nature"); Schiller v. NLRB, No. 87-1176, slip op. at 7 (D.D.C. July 10, 1990) ("Discretionary release of a document pertains to that document alone, regardless of whether similar documents exist."), rev'd on other grounds, 964 F.2d 1205 (D.C. Cir. 1992); see also, e.g., United States Student Ass'n v. CIA, 620 F. Supp. 565, 571 (D.D.C. 1985) (no waiver through prior disclosure except as to "duplicate" information); Dow, Lohnes & Albertson v. Presidential Comm'n on Broad. to Cuba, 624 F. Supp. 572, 578 (D.D.C. 1984) (same); cf. Silber v. United States Dep't of Justice, No. 91-876, transcript at 18 (D.D.C. Aug. 13, 1992) (bench order) (no waiver would be found even if it were to be established that other comparable documents had been disclosed).

[60] 879 F.2d at 701; see also Army Times, 998 F.2d at 1068 (articulating general principle of no waiver of exemption simply because agency released "information similar to that requested" in past); Halkin v. Helms, 598 F.2d 1, 9 (D.C. Cir. 1978) ("The government is not estopped from concluding in one case that disclosure is permissible while in another case it is not.").

[61] Nationwide Bldg. Maintenance, Inc. v. Sampson, 559 F.2d 704, 712 n.34 (D.C. Cir. 1977).

## DISCRETIONARY DISCLOSURE AND WAIVER

incentive against voluntary disclosure of information."[62]

By the same token, moreover, when discretionary disclosures are made by agencies in accordance with Attorney General Reno's FOIA Memorandum, courts should find that they do not constitute a basis for awarding attorneys fees under the Act.[63] Agencies ought to feel free to make discretionary disclo-

---

[62] Mehl v. EPA, 797 F. Supp. 43, 47 (D.D.C. 1992); see also Military Audit Project v. Casey, 656 F.2d 724, 754 (D.C. Cir. 1981) (agency should not be penalized for declassifying and releasing documents during litigation; otherwise, there would be "a disincentive for an agency to reappraise its position and, when appropriate, release documents previously withheld"); Greenberg, 10 F. Supp. 2d at 23-24 ("Penalizing agencies by holding that they waive their exhaustion defense if they make a discretionary document release after the time for an administrative appeal had expired would not advance the underlying purpose of the FOIA--the broadest possible responsible disclosure of government documents."); Shewchun v. INS, No. 95-1920, slip op. at 8 (D.D.C. Dec. 10, 1995) (to find agency bad faith after agency conducted new search and released more information "would create a disincentive for agencies to conduct reviews of their initial searches"), summary affirmance granted, No. 97-5044 (D.C. Cir. June 5, 1997); Berg v. United States Dep't of Energy, No. 94-0488, slip op. at 8 (D.D.C. Nov. 7, 1994) (release of information after initial search does not prove inadequacy of search; to hold otherwise would end "laudable agency practice of updating and reconsidering the release of information after the completion of the initial FOIA search"); Gilmore v. NSA, No. 92-3646, 1993 U.S. Dist. LEXIS 22027, at *29 (N.D. Cal. May 3, 1993) (following Military Audit and declining to penalize agency), aff'd on other grounds, 76 F.3d 386 (9th Cir. 1995) (unpublished table decision); Stone v. FBI, 727 F. Supp. 662, 666 (D.D.C. 1990) (agencies should be free to make "voluntary" disclosures without concern that they "could come back to haunt" them in other cases); cf. Public Citizen v. Department of State, 11 F.3d 198, 203 (D.C. Cir. 1993) (agency should not be required to disclose "related materials" where "to do so would give the Government a strong disincentive ever to provide its citizenry with briefings of any kind on sensitive topics"). But see Billington v. United States Dep't of Justice, 11 F. Supp. 2d 45, 59 (D.D.C. 1998) (citing Bonner v. Department of State, 928 F.2d 1148, 1151 (D.C. Cir. 1991), for proposition that "[w]hile a full release of documents previously withheld does not demonstrate bad faith, doubt may be cast on the agency's original exemption claim when the information in question is found releasable within two years" and that a district court in such a case must accordingly "examine closely the initial exemption claims") (appeal pending).

[63] See Lovell v. Alderete, 630 F.2d 428, 432 & n.4 (5th Cir. 1980) (alternative holding) ("[The] Government's compliance with [plaintiff's] request was not caused mainly by the institution of the suit, but rather was also affected by a change in the United States Attorney General's [May 5, 1977] guidelines concerning disclosure of exempted materials."); Lissner v. United States Customs Serv., No. 98-7438, slip op. at 7 (C.D. Cal. Aug. 19, 1999) (refusing to award attorney fees because such an award would punish the agency "for its disclosure of information it believed was exempt [and would] . . . lead to the undesirable result that agencies would simply entrench themselves in their original positions, for fear that releasing subsequent documents would subject them to
(continued...)

## DISCRETIONARY DISCLOSURE AND WAIVER

sures of exempt information, at any stage of the FOIA administrative or litigative process, without concern for such consequences either.[64] While agencies are strongly encouraged to make such disclosures at the outset of the administrative process,[65] one court has had occasion to express this principle in broad terms:

> Were the courts to construe disclosure of a document as an agency's concession of wrongful withholding, . . . agencies would be forced to either never disclose a document once withheld or risk being assessed fees. This result would frustrate the policy of encouraging disclosure that prompted enactment of the FOIA and its amendments. . . . Penalizing an agency for disclosure at any stage of the proceedings is simply not in the spirit of the FOIA.[66]

Agencies should be mindful, though, that these principles apply to true discretionary disclosures made under the FOIA--which should be made available to anyone--as distinguished from any "selective" disclosure made more narrowly outside the context of the FOIA.[67] Such non-FOIA disclosures can

---

[63](...continued)
attorney fees liability") (appeal pending); cf. Bubar v. FBI, 3 Gov't Disclosure Serv. (P-H) ¶ 83,218, at 89,930-31 (D.D.C. June 13, 1983) (no attorney fees found appropriate when disclosure was caused by administrative reprocessing of request "pursuant to newly-adopted procedures"). But see O'Neill, Lysaght & Sun v. DEA, 951 F. Supp. 1413, 1423 (C.D. Cal. 1996) ("That the suit was pending at the time of the new directives is the reason the request was eligible for reevaluation."); cf. McDonnell v. United States, 870 F. Supp. 576, 583-84 (D.N.J. 1994) (causation found when plaintiff challenged government's long-standing withholding practice and entirely separate case contemporaneously proceeding through judicial system ultimately resulted in Supreme Court modification of government's stance and yielded additional disclosures to plaintiff).

[64] See Nationwide, 559 F.2d at 712 n.34 ("Certainly where the government can show that information disclosed . . . was nonetheless exempt from the FOIA a plaintiff should not be awarded attorney fees."); see also FOIA Update, Vol. XV, No. 4, at 7 (listing examples of discretionary disclosures in FOIA litigation); cf. Public Law Educ. Inst. v. United States Dep't of Justice, 744 F.2d 181, 183-84 (D.C. Cir. 1984) (no attorney fees awarded when agency disclosed requested records discretionarily in related proceeding).

[65] See FOIA Update, Vol. XIV, No. 3, at 1-2; see also Attorney General Reno's Follow-Up FOIA Memorandum, reprinted in FOIA Update, Vol. XIX, No. 4, at 3-5 (emphasizing importance of discretionary disclosure in agency decisionmaking).

[66] American Commercial Barge Lines v. NLRB, 758 F.2d 1109, 1112 (6th Cir. 1985).

[67] See, e.g., North Dakota ex rel. Olson v. Andrus, 581 F.2d 177, 182 (8th Cir. 1978) (finding waiver when agency made "selective" disclosure to one interested party only); Committee to Bridge the Gap v. Department of Energy, No.
(continued...)

-476-

## DISCRETIONARY DISCLOSURE AND WAIVER

lead to more difficult waiver questions.

### Waiver

Sometimes, when a FOIA exemption is being invoked, a further inquiry must be undertaken: a determination of whether, through some prior disclosure or an express authorization, the applicability of the exemption has been waived. Resolution of this inquiry requires a careful analysis of the specific nature of, and circumstances surrounding, the prior disclosure involved.[68]

First and foremost, if the prior disclosure does not "match" the exempt information in question, the difference between the two might itself be a sufficient basis for reaching the conclusion that no waiver has occurred.[69] Further

---

[67](...continued)
90-3568, transcript at 5 (C.D. Cal. Oct. 11, 1991) (bench order) (waiver found when agency gave preferential treatment to interested party; such action is "offensive" to FOIA and "fosters precisely the distrust of government the FOIA was intended to obviate"), aff'd on other grounds, 10 F.3d 808 (9th Cir. 1993) (unpublished table decision).

[68] See FOIA Update, Vol. IV, No. 2, at 6; see also Mobil Oil Corp. v. EPA, 879 F.2d 698, 700 (9th Cir. 1989) ("The inquiry into whether a specific disclosure constitutes a waiver is fact specific."); Carson v. United States Dep't of Justice, 631 F.2d 1008, 1016 n.30 (D.C. Cir. 1980) ("[T]he extent to which prior agency disclosure may constitute a waiver of the FOIA exemptions must depend both on the circumstances of prior disclosure and on the particular exemptions claimed.").

[69] See, e.g., Nowak v. IRS, No. 98-56656, 2000 WL 60067, at *2 (9th Cir. Jan. 21, 2000) (determining that in order for FOIA plaintiff to establish waiver of FOIA exemption, he must be able to establish that information in his possession originated from same documents as those released in prior disclosure); Davis v. United States Dep't of Justice, 968 F.2d 1276, 1280 (D.C. Cir. 1992) (finding no waiver as plaintiff failed to demonstrate that "exact portions" of records sought are in public domain); Afshar v. Department of State, 702 F.2d 1125, 1132 (D.C. Cir. 1983) (finding that "withheld information is in some material respect different" from that which requester claimed had been released previously); Students Against Genocide (SAGE) v. Department of State, 50 F. Supp. 2d 20, 25 (D.D.C. 1999) (magistrate's recommendation) (finding no waiver absent showing that specific information in question is in public domain), adopted, No. 96-667 (D.D.C. July 22, 1999) (appeal pending); Pease v. United States Dep't of Interior, No. 1:99CV113, slip op. at 7 (D. Vt. Sept. 11, 1999) (disclosing similar records prior to enactment of Exemption 3 statute does not result in waiver of current records covered by that statute); Heeney v. FDA, No. 97-5461, slip op. at 19 (C.D. Cal. Mar. 16, 1999) (holding that mere fact that withheld documents may contain information previously released is insufficient because context in which documents were previously released may differ from context in which documents are currently being withheld); Kay v. FCC, 867 F. Supp. 11, 20-21 (D.D.C. 1994) (inadvertent disclosure of some informants' names does not waive Exemption 7(A) protection for information about other informants); see also, e.g., Fitzgibbon v. CIA, 911
(continued...)

## DISCRETIONARY DISCLOSURE AND WAIVER

more, general or limited public discussion of a subject does not usually lead to waiver with respect to specific information or records.[70] Similarly, it has been

---

[69](...continued)
F.2d 755, 766 (D.C. Cir. 1990) (no waiver when withheld information "pertain[s] to a time period later than the date of the publicly documented information"); Freeman v. United States Dep't of Justice, No. 92-0557, slip op. at 9 (D.D.C. June 28, 1993) (no waiver when requester failed to show that information available to public duplicates that being withheld); Hunt v. FBI, No. C-92-1390, slip op. at 15-16 (N.D. Cal. Sept. 16, 1992) (agency not required to disclose documents when "similar" ones were previously released; none of released documents were "as specific as" or "matched" requested documents). But see Cottone v. Reno, 193 F.3d 550, 555-56 (D.C. Cir. 1999) (citing Davis and finding waiver where plaintiff had identified specific tapes in public domain); Committee to Bridge the Gap v. Department of Energy, No. 90-3568, transcript at 2-5 (C.D. Cal. Oct. 11, 1991) (bench order) (distinguishing Mobil Oil and finding deliberative process privilege waived for draft order by prior voluntary disclosure of earlier draft order to interested party; agency ordered to release earlier draft order and all subsequent revisions), aff'd on other grounds, 10 F.3d 808 (9th Cir. 1993) (unpublished table decision).

[70] See, e.g., Kimberlin v. Department of Justice, 139 F.3d 944, 949 (D.C. Cir.) (holding that public acknowledgment of investigation and "vague reference to its conclusion" does not waive use of Exemption 7(C) to protect "details of the investigation"), cert. denied, 525 U.S. 891 (1998); Public Citizen v. Department of State, 11 F.3d 198, 201 (D.C. Cir. 1993) (finding that an "agency official does not waive FOIA exemption 1 by publicly discussing the general subject matter of documents which are otherwise properly exempt from disclosure"); Billington v. United States Dep't of Justice, 11 F. Supp. 2d 45, 55 (D.D.C. 1999) (finding no waiver where requester failed to show that "exact activities" claimed to be in public domain "have been disclosed in these documents") (appeal pending); Rothschild v. Department of Energy, 6 F. Supp. 2d 38, 40-41 (D.D.C. 1998) (finding no waiver where requester failed to specify how public discussion of particular economic theory revealed agency deliberative process with respect to long-term, wide-ranging study); Steinberg v. United States Dep't of Justice, 179 F.R.D. 357, 361 (D.D.C. 1998) (finding no waiver where requester did not produce evidence that specific withheld material is public, even though general subject matter appeared to be in public domain); Marriott Employees' Fed. Credit Union v. National Credit Union Admin., No. 96-478-A, slip op. at 4 (E.D. Va. Dec. 24, 1996) (finding no waiver because "[a]lthough the existence and general subject of the investigations is known to the public, there is no evidence in the record indicating that specific information concerning these investigations has been shared with unauthorized parties"); Dow Jones & Co. v. United States Dep't of Justice, 880 F. Supp. 145, 151 (S.D.N.Y. 1995) (agency's "limited, general and cursory discussions" of investigative subject matter during press conference held not to waive Exemption 7(A)), vacated on other grounds, 907 F. Supp. 79 (S.D.N.Y. 1995); Blazar v. OMB, No. 92-2719, slip op. at 11-12 (D.D.C. Apr. 15, 1994) (following Public Citizen and finding no waiver of Exemptions 1 and 3 when published autobiography refers to information sought but provides no more than general outline of it). But see Washington Post Co. v. United States Dep't of the Air Force, 617 F. Supp. 602, 605 (D.D.C. 1985) (disclosure of document's conclu-
(continued...)

## DISCRETIONARY DISCLOSURE AND WAIVER

held that "[t]he fact that [a FOIA requester] can guess which names have been deleted from the released documents does not act as a waiver to disclosure."[71]

Although courts are generally sympathetic to the necessities of effective agency functioning when confronted with an issue of waiver,[72] courts do look harshly upon prior disclosures that result in unfairness.[73] In one case for ex-

---

[70](...continued)
sions waived privilege for body of document).

[71] Valencia-Lucena v. DEA, No. 99-0633, slip op. at 7 (D.D.C. Feb. 8, 2000) (citing Weisberg v. United States Department of Justice, 745 F.2d 1476, 1491 (D.C. Cir. 1984)).

[72] See, e.g., Neely v. FBI, 208 F.3d 461, 466 (4th Cir. 2000) ("[P]ublic availability [does not] effect a waiver of the government's right" to invoke Exemption 7(D).); Isley v. Executive Office for United States Attorneys, No. 98-5098, 1999 WL 1021934, at *4 (D.C. Cir. Oct. 21, 1999) (finding that witnesses' testimony at trial does not waive the "government's right to withhold specific information about matters as to which [the witnesses have] testified" at trial); Schiffer v. FBI, 78 F.3d 1405, 1410-11 (9th Cir. 1996) (finding no waiver of FBI's right to invoke Exemption 7(C) for information made public during related civil action); Massey v. FBI, 3 F.3d 620, 624 (2d Cir. 1993) (individuals held not to waive "strong privacy interests in government documents containing information about them even where the information may have been public at one time"); Irons v. FBI, 880 F.2d 1446, 1456-57 (1st Cir. 1989) (en banc) (public testimony by confidential source does not waive FBI's right to withhold information pursuant to Exemption 7(D)); Cooper v. Department of the Navy, 558 F.2d 274, 278 (5th Cir. 1977) (prior disclosure of aircraft accident investigation report to aircraft manufacturer held not to constitute waiver); SAGE, 50 F. Supp. 2d at 24 (reiterating that sharing of classified information with foreign government does not result in waiver); McGilvra v. National Transp. Safety Bd., 840 F. Supp. 100, 102 (D. Colo. 1993) (citing Cooper and finding that release of cockpit voice recorder tapes to parties in accident investigation is not "public" disclosure under FOIA); Van Atta v. Defense Intelligence Agency, No. 87-1508, 1988 WL 73856, at *2 (D.D.C. July 6, 1988) (disclosure to foreign government does not constitute waiver); Medera Community Hosp. v. United States, No. 86-542, slip op. at 6-9 (E.D. Cal. June 28, 1988) (no waiver where memoranda interpreting agency's regulations sent to state auditor involved in enforcement proceeding); Erb v. United States Dep't of Justice, 572 F. Supp. 954, 956 (W.D. Mich. 1983) (nondisclosure under Exemption 7(A) upheld after "limited disclosure" of FBI criminal investigative report to defense attorney and state prosecutor); cf. Gilmore v. NSA, No. 92-3646, 1993 U.S. Dist. LEXIS 22027, at *23 (N.D. Cal. May 3, 1993) (fact that material was once in public domain does not prove its subsequent classification is invalid).

[73] See, e.g., North Dakota ex rel. Olson v. Andrus, 581 F.2d 177, 182 (8th Cir. 1978) ("selective disclosure" of record to one party in litigation deemed "offensive" to FOIA and held to prevent agency's subsequent invocation of Exemption 5 against other party to litigation); Committee to Bridge the Gap, No. 90-3568, transcript at 3-5 (C.D. Cal. Oct. 11, 1991) (bench order) (deliberative
(continued...)

## DISCRETIONARY DISCLOSURE AND WAIVER

ample, Hopkins v. Department of the Navy,[74] a commercial life insurance company sought access to records reflecting the name, rank, and duty locations of servicemen stationed at Quantico Marine Corps Base. The district court, while not technically applying the doctrine of waiver, rejected the agency's privacy arguments on the grounds that officers' reassignment stations were routinely published in the Navy Times and that the Department of Defense had disclosed the names and addresses of 1.4 million service members to a political campaign committee.[75]

An agency's failure to heed its own regulations regarding circulation of internal agency documents has been found sufficient to warrant a finding of waiver.[76] Similarly, an agency's regulation requiring disclosure of the information,[77] an agency's carelessness in permitting access to certain information,[78] and an agency's mistaken disclosure of the contents of a document[79] have all resulted in waiver.[80]

---

[73](...continued) process privilege waived for draft order by prior voluntary disclosure of earlier draft order to interested party; selective disclosure is "offensive" to FOIA); Northwest Envtl. Defense Ctr. v. United States Forest Serv., No. 91-125, slip op. at 12 (D. Or. Aug. 23, 1991) (magistrate's recommendation) (deliberative process privilege waived as to portion of agency report discussed with "interested" third party), adopted (D. Or. Feb. 12, 1992).

[74] No. 84-1868, 1985 WL 17673, at *1 (D.D.C. Feb. 5, 1985).

[75] Id. at *3; see also In re Subpoena Duces Tecum, 738 F.2d 1367, 1371-74 (D.C. Cir. 1984) (voluntary disclosure by private party of information to one agency waived attorney work-product and attorney-client privileges when same information was sought by second agency) (non-FOIA case).

[76] Shermco Indus. v. Secretary of the Air Force, 613 F.2d 1314, 1320 (5th Cir. 1980).

[77] See Johnson v. HHS, No. 88-243-5, slip op. at 10-11 (E.D.N.C. Feb. 7, 1989); cf. Missouri ex rel. Shorr v. United States Army Corps of Eng'rs, 147 F.3d 708, 710-11 (8th Cir. 1998) (addressing Council on Environmental Quality regulation (40 C.F.R. § 1506.6(f) (1997)) that mandates categorical disclosure of inter-agency comments pertaining to environmental impact statements, but finding it inapplicable because of intra-agency character of document).

[78] See, e.g., Cooper v. Department of the Navy, 594 F.2d 484, 488 (5th Cir. 1978).

[79] See, e.g., Dresser Indus. Valve Operations, Inc. v. EEOC, 2 Gov't Disclosure Serv. (P-H) ¶ 82,197, at 82,575 (W.D. La. Jan. 19, 1982).

[80] See also Gannett River States Publ'g Corp. v. Bureau of the Nat'l Guard, No. J91-0455-L, 1992 WL 175235, at *6 (S.D. Miss. Mar. 2, 1992) (finding privacy interests in withholding identities of soldiers disciplined for causing accident to be de minimis because agency previously released much identifying information); Powell v. United States, 584 F. Supp. 1508, 1520-21 (N.D. Cal.
(continued...)

## DISCRETIONARY DISCLOSURE AND WAIVER

On the other hand, waiver is not necessarily found when an agency makes an entirely mistaken disclosure,[81] or when an agency official mistakenly promises to make a disclosure.[82] And it has been firmly held that the mere fact that a confidential source testifies at a trial does not waive Exemption 7(D) protection for any source-provided information not actually re-

---

[80] (...continued)
1984) (suggesting that attorney work-product privilege may be waived when agency made earlier release of such information which "reflect[ed] positively" on agency, and later may have withheld work-product information on same matter which did not reflect so "positively" on agency).

[81] See Ford v. West, No. 97-1342, 1998 U.S. App. LEXIS 12640, at **8-9 (10th Cir. June 12, 1998) (rejecting claim that defendant's inadvertent release of names constituted waiver: "[D]efendant's inadequate redactions do not operate to waive the personal privacy interests of the individuals discussed in the investigative file."); Billington, 11 F. Supp. 2d at 66 (finding no waiver of Exemption 7(D) protection in case involving more than 40,000 documents where agency mistakenly released one withheld document to previous requester, and observing: "One document in such an enormous document request is merely a needle in a haystack. That one FBI agent may have redacted a document differently than another, or that the same FBI agent did not redact a document in precisely the same manner in different years, did not constitute bad faith."); Martin Marietta Corp. v. Dalton, 974 F. Supp. 37, 40 (D.D.C. 1997) (finding no waiver under Exemption 4 where prior release of data in contract had been made); Public Citizen Health Research Group v. FDA, 953 F. Supp. 400, 404-06 (D.D.C. 1996) (holding no waiver where material accidentally released and information not disseminated by requester); Nation Magazine v. Department of State, 805 F. Supp. 68, 73 (D.D.C. 1992) (dicta) ("[N]o rule of administrative law requires an agency to extend erroneous treatment of one party to other parties, 'thereby turning an isolated error into a uniform misapplication of the law.'" (quoting Sacred Heart Med. Ctr. v. Sullivan, 958 F.2d 537, 548 n.24 (3d Cir. 1992))); Astley v. Lawson, No. 89-2806, 1991 WL 7162, at *8 (D.D.C. Jan. 11, 1991) (inadvertent placement of documents into public record held not to waive exemption when it was remedied immediately upon agency's awareness of mistake); cf. Kay, 867 F. Supp. at 23-24 (inadvertent disclosure of documents caused entirely by clerical error has no effect on remaining material at issue); Fleet Nat'l Bank v. Tonneson & Co., 150 F.R.D. 10, 16 (D. Mass. 1993) (inadvertent production of one volume of three-volume report did not constitute waiver of attorney work-product privilege as to that volume, nor as to remaining two volumes of report) (non-FOIA case); Myers v. Williams, No. 92-1609, 1993 U.S. Dist. LEXIS 5304, at **5-7 (D. Or. Apr. 21, 1993) (preliminary injunction granted prohibiting FOIA requester from disclosing original and all copies of erroneously disclosed document containing trade secrets) (non-FOIA case).

[82] See Anderson v. United States Dep't of Treasury, No. 98-1112, slip op. at 9 (W.D. Tenn. Mar. 24, 1999) (finding that the mere promise of an IRS agent to disclose a document to a FOIA requester at a later date, even if the document was previously disclosed to the requester during a face-to-face meeting, did not constitute waiver; "[n]othing in [the] FOIA . . . make[s] such a statement binding and irrevocable").

## DISCRETIONARY DISCLOSURE AND WAIVER

vealed in public.[83] Nor does public congressional testimony waive Exemption 1 protection when the context of the information publicized is different and

---

[83] See Neely, 208 F.3d at 466 (concluding that government does not waive its right to protect confidential sources and information furnished by those sources even where their identities have previously been disclosed); Isley, 1999 WL 1021934, at *4 (finding that the fact that a witness testifies "only bars the government from withholding the [witnesses'] testimony itself"); Irons, 880 F.2d at 1454; Housley v. DEA, No. 92-16946, 1994 U.S. App. LEXIS 11232, at **4-5 (9th Cir. May 4, 1994) (fact that some information may have been disclosed at criminal trial does not result in waiver as to other information); see also Davoudlarian v. Department of Justice, No. 93-1787, 1994 WL 423845, at *3 (4th Cir. Aug. 15, 1994) (per curiam) (requester must demonstrate that specific witness statements were disclosed at civil trial in order to show waiver); Jefferson v. O'Brien, No. 96-1365, slip op. at 9-11 (D.D.C. Feb. 22, 2000) (finding that third parties and confidential informants do not waive their privacy interests by testifying at trial); Sanderson v. IRS, No. 98-2369, 1999 WL 35290, at *3 (E.D. La. Jan. 25, 1999) (holding that "deposition testimony [does] not act as a wholesale waiver of . . . [Exemption 7(D) protection]"); Coleman v. FBI, 13 F. Supp. 2d 75, 80 (D.D.C. 1998) (finding that "an individual who testifies at trial does not waive this privacy interest beyond the scope of the trial[;] . . . [to] hold otherwise would discourage essential witness testimony"); Jones v. FBI, No. C77-1001, slip op. at 13-14 (N.D. Ohio Aug. 12, 1992) (identities of confidential informants and third parties are not waived even if they have testified in court and are publicly known), aff'd, 41 F.3d 238, 249 (6th Cir. 1994) (Exemption 7(D) "focuses on the source's intent, not the world's knowledge . . . . [H]old[ing] otherwise would discourage sources from cooperating with the FBI because of fear of revelation via FOIA."); LaRouche v. United States Dep't of Justice, No. 90-2753, 1993 WL 388601, at *7 (D.D.C. June 24, 1993) (agency must review requested file and disclose those portions which were revealed at trial); Church of Scientology Int'l v. FBI, No. 91-10850-Y, slip op. at 4-5 (D. Mass. Nov. 23, 1992) (privacy protection waived for information about individuals who publicly testified at trial and who have been identified); cf. Billington, 11 F. Supp. 2d at 68-69 (finding no waiver because "[i]nformation withheld under Exemption 7(D) applies to information given by an informant who was confidential at the time, even if the informant later testifies at trial"); Reiter v. DEA, No. 96-0378, 1997 WL 470108, at *6 (D.D.C. Aug. 13, 1997) ("An agency may . . . continue to invoke Exemption 7(D) in the event that the requester learns of the source's identity and the information supplied by him through the source's open court testimony."), aff'd, No. 97-5246, 1998 WL 202247 (D.C. Cir. Apr. 27, 1998); Williams v. FBI, 822 F. Supp. 808, 814 n.3 (D.D.C. 1993) (public testimony by confidential sources does not waive exemption); Spannaus v. United States Dep't of Justice, No. 85-1015, slip op. at 25-26 (D. Mass. Nov. 12, 1992) (neither testimony at trial nor actual trial itself waives protection for documents prepared in anticipation of litigation); Wechsler v. United States Consumer Prod. Safety Comm'n, No. 92-402, slip op. at 4 (S.D. Fla. Oct. 19, 1992) (magistrate's recommendation) (fact that confidential source and/or confidential information may subsequently be disclosed does not affect exemption), adopted sub nom. United States v. United States Consumer Prod. Safety Comm'n (S.D. Fla. Dec. 1, 1992).

## DISCRETIONARY DISCLOSURE AND WAIVER

only some of the information is revealed.[84] Furthermore, disclosure in a congressional report does not waive Exemption 1 applicability if the agency itself has never publicly acknowledged the information.[85]

In one case it was held that the oral disclosure of only the conclusion reached in a predecisional document "does not, without more, waive the [deliberative process] privilege."[86] In another, an agency disclosure to a small group of nongovernmental personnel, with no copies permitted, was held not to inhibit agency decisionmaking, so the deliberative process privilege was not waived.[87] Nonetheless, an oral disclosure may be treated as not so different from a written one, risking a waiver result.[88]

---

[84] See Fitzgibbon, 911 F.2d at 765 (prior disclosure does not waive "information pertaining to a time period later than the date of the publicly documented information"); Public Citizen, 11 F.3d at 201 (finding no waiver when agency official publicly discussed general subject matter of documents); see also Afshar, 702 F.2d at 1131-32 (finding no waiver when withheld information is in some respect materially different); Billington, 11 F. Supp. 2d at 55 (finding no waiver although "FBI may have released similar types of information" previously, reasoning that aggregation of previously released information with currently withheld material "might assist a hostile analyst's attempt to piece together classified information"); cf. Heeney, No. 97-5461, slip op. at 19 (C.D. Cal. Mar. 16, 1999) (finding no waiver where documents at issue contained information that was previously released in different context).

[85] See Earth Pledge Found. v. CIA, 988 F. Supp. 623, 627 (S.D.N.Y. 1996), aff'd, 128 F.3d 788 (2d Cir. 1997); see also Frugone v. CIA, 169 F.3d 772, 774 (D.C. Cir. 1999) (finding that a disclosure made by an employee from an agency other than the one from which the information is sought is not official and thus does not constitute waiver); Salisbury v. United States, 690 F.2d 966, 971 (D.C. Cir. 1982) (holding that information in Senate report "cannot be equated with disclosure by the agency itself"); Military Audit Project v. Casey, 656 F.2d 724, 744 (D.C. Cir. 1981) (finding that publication of Senate report does not constitute official release of agency information); SAGE, 50 F. Supp. 2d at 25 (affirming principle that only agency that is original source of information in question can waive applicability of FOIA exemption).

[86] Morrison v. United States Dep't of Justice, No. 87-3394, 1988 WL 47662, at *1 (D.D.C. Apr. 29, 1988).

[87] Dow, Lohnes & Albertson v. Presidential Comm'n on Broad. to Cuba, 624 F. Supp. 572, 577-78 (D.D.C. 1984); see also Brinderson Constructors, Inc. v. Army Corps of Eng'rs, No. 85-0905, 1986 WL 293230, at *5 (D.D.C. June 11, 1986) (requester's participation in agency enterprise did not entitle requester to all related documents).

[88] See Catchpole v. Department of Transp., No. 97-8058, slip op. at 5-7 (11th Cir. Feb. 25, 1998) (remanding to determine if official read memorandum to requester over telephone, thereby waiving privilege); Myles-Pirzada v. Department of the Army, No. 91-1080, slip op. at 6 (D.D.C. Nov. 20, 1992) (finding privilege waived when agency official read report to requester over telephone); Shell Oil Co. v. IRS, 772 F. Supp. 202, 211 (D. Del. 1991) (finding
(continued...)

## DISCRETIONARY DISCLOSURE AND WAIVER

As is suggested above, if an agency is able to establish that it acted in furtherance of a legitimate governmental purpose and under circumstances of confidentiality in making a disclosure, its later claim of exemption will likely prevail.[89] Of course, circulation of a document within the agency does not waive an exemption,[90] nor does disclosure among agencies,[91] or to advisory committees (even those including members of the public).[92] Similarly, in deference to the common agency practice of disclosing specifically requested information to a congressional committee,[93] to the General Accounting Office

---

[88](...continued) waiver when agency employee read aloud entire draft document at public meeting: "Where an authorized disclosure is voluntarily made to a non-federal party, the government waives any claim that the information is exempt from disclosure under the deliberative process privilege.").

[89] See FOIA Update, Vol. IV, No. 2, at 6; see, e.g., Rashid v. HHS, No. 98-0898, slip op. at 7 (D.D.C. Mar. 2, 2000) (disclosure of memorandum to expert witnesses in anticipation of their testimony at trial); McGilvra, 840 F. Supp. at 102 (release of cockpit voice recorder tapes to parties in accident investigation); Badhwar v. United States Dep't of the Air Force, 629 F. Supp. 478, 481 (D.D.C. 1986) (disclosure to outside person held necessary to assemble report in first place), aff'd in part & remanded in part on other grounds, 829 F.2d 182 (D.C. Cir. 1987); see also FOIA Update, Vol. V, No. 1, at 4.

[90] See, e.g., Direct Response Consulting Serv. v. IRS, No. 94-1156, 1995 WL 623282, at *5 (D.D.C. Aug. 21, 1995) (attorney-client privilege not waived when documents sent to other divisions within agency); Chemcentral/Grand Rapids Corp. v. EPA, No. 91-C-4380, 1992 WL 281322, at *7 (N.D. Ill. Oct. 5, 1992) (no waiver of attorney-client privilege when documents in question were circulated to only those employees who needed to review legal advice contained in them); Lasker-Goldman Corp. v. GSA, 2 Gov't Disclosure Serv. (P-H) ¶ 81,125, at 81,322 (D.D.C. Feb. 27, 1981) (no waiver when document was circulated to management officials within agency).

[91] See, e.g., Chilivis v. SEC, 673 F.2d 1205, 1211-12 (11th Cir. 1982) (agency does not automatically waive exemption by releasing documents to other agencies); Silber v. United States Dep't of Justice, No. 91-876, transcript at 10-18 (D.D.C. Aug. 13, 1992) (bench order) (distribution of manual to other agencies does not constitute waiver). But cf. Lacefield v. United States, No. 92-N-1680, 1993 WL 268392, at *6 (D. Colo. Mar. 10, 1993) (attorney-client privilege waived with respect to letter from City of Denver attorney to Colorado Department of Safety because letter was circulated to IRS).

[92] See, e.g., Aviation Consumer Action Project v. Washburn, 535 F.2d 101, 107-08 (D.C. Cir. 1976).

[93] See, e.g., Florida House of Representatives v. United States Dep't of Commerce, 961 F.2d 941, 946 (11th Cir. 1992) (holding no waiver of exemption due to court-ordered disclosure, involuntary disclosure to Congress, or disclosure of related information); Aspin v. DOD, 491 F.2d 24, 26 (D.C. Cir. 1973); Rockwell v. United States Dep't of Justice, No. 98-761, slip op. at 10 (D.D.C. Mar. 24, 1999) (finding no waiver for documents provided to Congress with express agreement that they would not be made public) (appeal pending); see also

(continued...)

## DISCRETIONARY DISCLOSURE AND WAIVER

(an arm of Congress),[94] to state or local law enforcement officials,[95] or to state attorneys general,[96] such disclosures do not waive FOIA exemption protection.[97]

Indeed, when an agency has been compelled to disclose a document under limited and controlled conditions, such as under a protective order in an administrative proceeding, its authority to withhold the document thereafter is not diminished.[98] This applies as well to disclosures made in the criminal discovery context.[99]

---

[93](...continued)
Eagle-Picher Indus. v. United States, 11 Ct. Cl. 452, 460-61 (1987) (work-product privilege not waived in nonspecific congressional testimony "if potentially thousands of documents need be reviewed to determine if the gist or a significant part of documents were revealed") (non-FOIA case); FOIA Update, Vol. V, No. 1, at 3-4 ("OIP Guidance: Congressional Access Under FOIA") (analyzing and cabining Murphy v. Department of the Army, 613 F.2d 1151 (D.C. Cir. 1979)).

[94] See, e.g., Shermco, 613 F.2d at 1320-21.

[95] See, e.g., General Elec. Co. v. EPA, 18 F. Supp. 2d 138, 143 (D. Mass. 1998) (finding that because EPA is obligated to consult with state agencies in formulating federal policy, disclosures made pursuant to that obligation do not constitute waiver of applicability of FOIA exemption); Kansi v. United States Dep't of Justice, 11 F. Supp. 2d 42, 44-45 (D.D.C. 1998) (stating that even if plaintiff had adduced evidence that information was actually disclosed to local prosecutor, such disclosure would not have waived Exemption 7(A) protection); Erb, 572 F. Supp. at 956 (holding that disclosure of FBI report to local prosecutor did not cause waiver of Exemption 7(A)).

[96] See Interco, Inc. v. FTC, 490 F. Supp. 39, 44 (D.D.C. 1979).

[97] See FOIA Update, Vol. IV, No. 2, at 6.

[98] See, e.g., Lead Indus. Ass'n v. OSHA, 610 F.2d 70, 79 n.13 (2d Cir. 1979); see also Allnet Communication Servs. v. FCC, 800 F. Supp. 984, 989 (D.D.C. 1992) (no waiver where information disclosed under "strict confidentiality"), aff'd, No. 92-5351 (D.C. Cir. May 27, 1994); Silverberg v. HHS, No. 89-2743, 1991 WL 633740, at *3 (D.D.C. June 14, 1991) (fact that individual who is subject of drug test by particular laboratory has right of access to its performance and testing information does not render such information publicly available), appeal dismissed per stipulation, No. 91-5255 (D.C. Cir. Sept. 2, 1993).

[99] See, e.g., Cottone, 193 F.3d at 556 (limiting finding of waiver to specific wiretapped recordings played in open court and refusing to extend finding of waiver to wiretapped recordings provided to plaintiff's counsel as Brady material); Ferguson v. FBI, 957 F.2d 1059, 1068 (2d Cir. 1992) (fact that local police department released records pursuant to New York Freedom of Information Law and one of its officers testified at length in court held not to waive police department's status as confidential source under Exemption 7(D)); Parker v. Department of Justice, 934 F.2d 375, 379 (D.C. Cir. 1991) (nondisclosure under Exemption 7(D) upheld even though confidential informant
(continued...)

## DISCRETIONARY DISCLOSURE AND WAIVER

The one circumstance in which an agency's failure to treat information in a responsible, appropriate fashion should not result in waiver is when the failure is not fairly attributable to the agency--i.e., when an agency employee has made an unauthorized disclosure, a "leak" of information. Recognizing that a finding of waiver in such circumstances would only lead to "exacerbation of the harm created by the leaks,"[100] the courts have consistently refused to penalize agencies by ruling that a waiver has occurred due to such conduct.[101]

---

[99](...continued) may have testified at requester's trial); National Ass'n of Criminal Defense Lawyers v. United States Dep't of Justice, No. 97-372, slip op. at 8-10 (D.D.C. July 22, 1998) (limited disclosure of draft report to defendants pursuant to criminal discovery rules does not waive Exemption 5 protection); Willis v. FBI, No. 96-1455, slip op. at 2-6 (D.D.C. Feb. 14, 1998) ("The mere fact that at one time the Plaintiff's counsel may have had a right of access to portions of the transcript for a limited purpose hardly suffices to show that all of the requested transcripts now are a part of the public domain."), aff'd in part & remanded in part on other grounds, 194 F.3d 175 (D.C. Cir. 1999) (unpublished table decision); Fisher v. United States Dep't of Justice, 772 F. Supp. 7, 12 (D.D.C. 1991) (even if some of withheld information has appeared in print, nondisclosure is proper because disclosure from official source would confirm unofficial information and thereby cause harm to third parties); Beck v. United States Dep't of Justice, No. 88-3433, slip op. at 2 (D.D.C. July 24, 1991) ("Exemption 7(C) is not necessarily waived where an individual has testified at trial."), summary affirmance granted in pertinent part & denied in part, No. 91-5292 (D.C. Cir. Nov. 19, 1992); Glick v. Department of Justice, No. 89-3279, 1991 WL 118263, at *4 (D.D.C. June 20, 1991) (fact that agency discloses information in one context does not waive confidentiality of information or of those who provide it); Crooker v. ATF, No. 85-615, slip op. at 4-5 (D.D.C. Aug. 2, 1985) (nondisclosure under Exemption 7(A) upheld even though requester reviewed document in prior parole hearing), rev'd on other grounds, 789 F.2d 64 (D.C. Cir. 1986); Erb, 572 F. Supp. at 956 (nondisclosure to third party upheld under Exemption 7(A) even though document provided to defendant through criminal discovery); Krohn v. Department of Justice, 3 Gov't Disclosure Serv. (P-H) ¶ 83,120, at 83,724 (D.D.C. Sept. 7, 1979) (nondisclosure under Exemption 7(D) upheld even though requester previously reviewed documents as criminal defendant); cf. Johnston v. United States Dep't of Justice, No. 97-2173, 1998 U.S. App. LEXIS 18557, at **3-4 (8th Cir. July 6, 1998) ("'[T]he fact that an agent decided or was required to testify . . . does not give plaintiff a right under FOIA to documents revealing the fact and nature of [agent's] employment.'" (quoting Jones v. FBI, 41 F.3d 238, 246-47 (6th Cir. 1994))). But see Kronberg v. United States Dep't of Justice, 875 F. Supp. 861, 867 (D.D.C. 1995) (waiver of exemption found when agency had previously released same documents during requester's criminal trial).

[100] Murphy, 490 F. Supp. at 1142.

[101] See, e.g., Simmons v. United States Dep't of Justice, 796 F.2d 709, 712 (4th Cir. 1986) (unauthorized disclosure does not constitute waiver); Medina-Hincapie v. Department of State, 700 F.2d 737, 742 n.20 (D.C. Cir. 1983) (official's ultra vires release does not constitute waiver); Trans-Pac. Policing

(continued...)

## DISCRETIONARY DISCLOSURE AND WAIVER

On the other hand, "official" disclosures--i.e., direct acknowledgments by authoritative government officials--may well waive an otherwise applicable FOIA exemption.[102] In this context, one decision held that information that

---

[101](...continued)
Agreement v. United States Customs Serv., No. 97-2188, 1998 U.S. Dist. LEXIS 7800, at *13 (D.D.C. May 14, 1998) (finding no waiver from "isolated and unauthorized" disclosures that were not "in accordance with [agency] regulations or directions"), rev'd & remanded on other grounds, 177 F.3d 1022 (D.C. Cir. 1999); Harper v. Department of Justice, No. 92-462, slip op. at 19 (D. Or. Aug. 9, 1993) ("alleged, unauthorized, unofficial, partial disclosure" in private publication does not waive Exemption 1), aff'd in part, rev'd in part & remanded on other grounds sub nom. Harper v. DOD, 60 F.3d 833 (9th Cir. 1995) (unpublished table decision); LaRouche, 1993 WL 388601, at *7 (fact that some aspects of grand jury proceeding were leaked to press has "no bearing" on FOIA litigation); RTC v. Dean, 813 F. Supp. 1426, 1429-30 (D. Ariz. 1993) (no waiver of attorney-client privilege when agency took precautions to secure confidentiality of document, but inexplicable leak nonetheless occurred) (non-FOIA case); Silber, No. 91-876, transcript at 18 (D.D.C. Aug. 13, 1992) (bench order) (unauthorized publication of parts of document does not constitute any waiver); Washington Post Co. v. DOD, No. 84-2949, 1987 U.S. Dist. LEXIS 16108, at *25 n.9 (D.D.C. Feb. 25, 1987) ("unprincipled disclosure" by Members of Congress who had signed statements of confidentiality "cannot be the basis to compel disclosure" by agency); Laborers' Int'l Union v. United States Dep't of Justice, 578 F. Supp. 52, 58 n.3 (D.D.C. 1983), aff'd, 772 F.2d 919 (D.C. Cir. 1984); Safeway Stores, Inc. v. FTC, 428 F. Supp. 346, 347-48 (D.D.C. 1977) (finding no waiver where congressional committee leaked report to press); cf. Hunt v. CIA, 981 F.2d 1116, 1120 (9th Cir. 1992) (agency not required to confirm or deny accuracy of information released by other government agencies regarding its interest in certain individuals); Rush v. Department of State, 748 F. Supp. 1548, 1556 (S.D. Fla. 1990) (finding that author of agency documents, who had since left government service, did not have authority to waive Exemption 5 protection). But cf. In re Engram, No. 91-1722, 1992 WL 233820, at *7 (4th Cir. June 2, 1992) (per curiam) (permitting discovery as to circumstances of suspected leak).

[102] See Abbotts v. NRC, 766 F.2d 604, 607 (D.C. Cir. 1985) (holding agency's official "level of threat nuclear facility should guard against" is not waived by prior public estimates of appropriate level by congressional and other agency reports); Melendez-Colon v. United States Dep't of the Navy, 56 F. Supp. 2d 142, 145 (D.P.R. 1999) (finding in civil discovery dispute that because Navy previously disclosed document in question pursuant to FOIA, that prior disclosure waived Navy's privilege claim); Kimberlin v. United States Dep't of Justice, 921 F. Supp. 833, 835-36 (D.D.C. 1996) (holding exemption waived when material was released pursuant to "valid, albeit misunderstood, authorization"), aff'd in part & remanded in part, 139 F.3d 944 (D.C. Cir.), cert. denied, 525 U.S. 891 (1998); Quinn v. HHS, 838 F. Supp. 70, 75 (W.D.N.Y. 1993) (attorney work-product privilege waived where "substantially identical" information was previously released to requester); Myles-Pirzada, No. 91-1080, slip op. at 6 (D.D.C. Nov. 20, 1992) (privilege waived when agency official read report to requester over telephone); Schlesinger v. CIA, 591 F. Supp. 60, 66 (D.D.C. 1984); see also Krikorian v. Department of State,

(continued...)

## DISCRETIONARY DISCLOSURE AND WAIVER

was the subject of an "off-the-record" disclosure to the press cannot be protected under Exemption 1.[103] Similarly, an individual's express disclosure authorization with respect to his own interests implicated in requested records can also result in a waiver.[104]

---

[102](...continued)
984 F.2d 461, 467-68 (D.C. Cir. 1993) (court on remand must determine whether redacted portions of document has been "officially acknowledged"); United States Student Ass'n, 620 F. Supp. at 571 (waiver found for prior disclosure of "duplicate" information); cf. Isley, 1999 WL 1021934, at *4 (finding no waiver where plaintiff failed to demonstrate that documents at issue were a part of permanent public record); Afshar, 702 F.2d at 1133 (books by former agency officials do not constitute "an official and documented disclosure"); SAGE, 50 F. Supp. 2d at 25 (holding that agency does not waive applicability of FOIA exemption unless there has been official disclosure of information sought); Rockwell, No. 98-761, slip op. at 12 (D.D.C. Mar. 24, 1999) (finding no waiver of Exemption 5 where prior disclosure did not contain any of privileged communications); Heeney, No. 97-5461, slip op. at 19 (C.D. Cal. Mar. 18, 1999) (reiterating that any waiver by prior release is limited to those items previously disclosed); Armstrong v. Executive Office of the President, No. 89-142, slip op. at 16-17 (D.D.C. July 28, 1995) (book by former agency official containing information "substantially different" from documents sought is not official disclosure); Hunt, No. C-92-1390, slip op. at 16-18 (N.D. Cal. Sept. 16, 1992) (alleged nongovernmental disclosure of contents of requested documents does not constitute "official" acknowledgment); Holland v. CIA, No. 91-1233, slip op. at 13-14 (D.D.C. Aug. 31, 1992) (applying Afshar and finding that requester has not demonstrated that specific information in public domain has been "officially acknowledged").

[103] Lawyers Comm. for Human Rights v. INS, 721 F. Supp. 552, 569 (S.D.N.Y. 1989), motion for reargument denied, No. 87-Civ-1115, slip op. at 1-3 (S.D.N.Y. May 23, 1990). But cf. Grand Cent. Partnership v. Cuomo, 166 F.3d 473, 484 (2d Cir. 1999) (refusing to extend Exemption 5 protection to "[a] letter [which] appear[ed] to report matters that were aired at a public hearing").

[104] See, e.g., Providence Journal Co. v. United States Dep't of the Army, 981 F.2d 552, 567 (1st Cir. 1992) (source statements not entitled to Exemption 7(D) protection when individuals expressly waived confidentiality); Blanton v. United States Dep't of Justice, 63 F. Supp. 2d 35, 47 (D.D.C. 1999) (finding that FBI confidential sources waive their privacy interests where they extensively publicize their status as confidential sources); Key Bank of Me., Inc. v. SBA, No. 91-362, 1992 U.S. Dist. LEXIS 22180, at **25-26 (D. Me. Dec. 31, 1992) (given that subject of documents has specifically waived any privacy interest she might have in requested information, agency has not demonstrated that release of information would harm any privacy interest) (Exemption 6). But cf. Campaign for Family Farms v. Glickman, 200 F.3d 1180, 1188 (8th Cir. 1999) (finding that although parties who signed the petition in question did so with knowledge that subsequent signatories would be able to view their names, they did not waive their privacy interests under FOIA) ("reverse" FOIA suit); Kimberlin, 139 F.2d at 949 (holding that fact that employee publicly acknowledged that he had been investigated and disciplined by Office of

(continued...)

# DISCRETIONARY DISCLOSURE AND WAIVER

Finally, it should be noted that an agency should not be required to demonstrate in a FOIA case that it has positively determined that not a single disclosure of any withheld information has occurred.[105] Indeed, the burden is on the plaintiff to show that the information sought is public.[106] As the Court

---

[104](...continued) Professional Responsibility did not "waive all his interest in keeping the contents of the OPR file confidential"); Church of Scientology Int'l v. IRS, 995 F.2d 916, 921 (9th Cir. 1993) (IRS agents' purported waivers of privacy interests held insufficient to compel disclosure).

[105] See Williams v. United States Dep't of Justice, 556 F. Supp. 63, 66 (D.D.C. 1982) (court refused, in FOIA action brought by former senator convicted in Abscam investigation, to impose upon agency duty to search for possibility that privacy interests "may have been partially breached in the course of many-faceted proceedings occurring in different courts over a period of prior years," for to do so "would defeat the exemption in its entirety or at least lead to extended delay and uncertainty"); cf. McGehee v. Casey, 718 F.2d 1137, 1141 n.9 (D.C. Cir. 1983) (in non-FOIA case involving CIA's prepublication review, agency "cannot reasonably bear the burden of conducting an exhaustive search to prove that a given piece of information is not published anywhere" else).

[106] See, e.g., Cottone, 193 F.3d at 555 (holding that requester has burden of demonstrating "precisely which tapes . . . were played" in open court and that because trial transcript clearly indicated precise date and time of particular conversations in question, plaintiff had discharged his burden of production by pointing to those specific tapes); Isley, 1999 WL 1021934, at *4 (holding that party may gain access to information on waiver basis only if it can point to specific information identical to information which is currently being withheld); Nowak, 2000 WL 60067, at *2 (holding that "[i]n order to establish a waiver, the [plaintiff must be able to demonstrate that the previous disclosure was] authorized and voluntary"); Davoudlarian, 1994 WL 423845, at *3 (requester has burden of demonstrating that specific information was disclosed at trial); Public Citizen, 11 F.3d at 201 (applying Afshar and holding "plaintiffs cannot simply show that similar information has been released, but must establish that a specific fact already has been placed in the public domain"); Davis, 968 F.2d at 1279-82 ("party who asserts [that] material [is] publicly available carries the burden of production on that issue . . . because the task of proving the negative--that the information has not been revealed--might require the government to undertake an exhaustive, potentially limitless search"; when neither requester nor agency knows exactly which portions of wiretap tapes were played in open court, requester has burden of proving actual disclosure to establish waiver); SAGE, 50 F. Supp. 2d at 24 (holding that the burden is on the plaintiff to demonstrate that "the exact information sought is already in the public domain"); Scott v. CIA, No. 95-0686, 1996 WL 93640, at *6 (D.D.C. Mar. 1, 1996) (requiring requester to compile list of any public source material believed to mirror withheld information); Freeman, 1993 WL 260694, at **3-4 (finding that requester failed to demonstrate that agencies have shown "complete disregard for confidentiality" and had not shown that information available to public duplicated that being withheld); Pfeiffer v. CIA, 721 F. Supp. 337, 342 (D.D.C. 1989) (plaintiff must do more

(continued...)

## FEES AND FEE WAIVERS

of Appeals for the District of Columbia Circuit pointedly observed: "It is far more efficient, and obviously fairer, to place the burden of production on the party who claims that the information is publicly available."[107] Upon fulfillment of the plaintiff's burden of production, "it is up to the government, if it so chooses, to rebut the plaintiff's proof [and demonstrate] that the specific ... [records] identified" are not publicly available."[108]

(The related issue of whether an agency waives its ability to invoke an exemption in litigation by not raising it at an early stage of the proceedings is discussed under Litigation Considerations, Waiver of Exemptions in Litigation, below.)

## FEES AND FEE WAIVERS

Prior to the passage of the Freedom of Information Reform Act of 1986,[1] the FOIA authorized agencies to assess reasonable charges only for document search and duplication, and any assessable fees were to be waived or reduced if disclosure of the requested information was found to be generally in the "public interest."[2] The FOIA Reform Act brought significant changes to the way in which fees are now assessed under the FOIA. A new fee structure was established, including a new provision authorizing agencies to assess "review" charges when processing records in response to a commercial-use request.[3] Specific fee limitations and restrictions were set on the assessment of certain

---

[106](...continued) than simply identify "information that happens to find its way into a published account" to meet this burden); Dow, Lohnes & Albertson, 624 F. Supp. at 578 ("Unless plaintiff can demonstrate that specific information in the public domain appears to duplicate that being withheld, it has failed to bear its burden of showing prior disclosure."); United States Student Ass'n, 620 F. Supp. at 571 (plaintiff's generalized assertion rejected as unsupported by factual submission). But see Dean, 813 F. Supp. at 1429 ("[A] party seeking to invoke the attorney-client privilege has the burden of affirmatively demonstrating non-waiver.") (non-FOIA case); Washington Post v. DOD, 766 F. Supp. 1, 12-13 (D.D.C. 1991) (agency has ultimate burden of proof when comparing publicly disclosed information with information being withheld, determining whether information is identical and, if not, determining whether release of slightly different information would harm national security).

[107] Occidental Petroleum Corp. v. SEC, 873 F.2d 325, 342 (D.C. Cir. 1989) (reverse FOIA suit).

[108] Cottone, 193 F.3d at 556.

[1] Pub. L. No. 99-570, §§ 1801-04, 100 Stat. 3207.

[2] Pub. L. No. 93-502, §§ 1-3, 88 Stat. 1561-64 (1974) (codified as amended at 5 U.S.C. § 552(a)(4)(A) (1994 & Supp. IV 1998)).

[3] § 1803, 100 Stat. at 3207-49.

## FEES AND FEE WAIVERS

fees both in general as well as for certain categories of requesters.[4] Additionally, this FOIA amendment replaced the statutory fee waiver provision with a revised standard.[5] These revised fee and fee waiver provisions were made effective as of mid-1987, but required implementing agency regulations to become fully effective.[6]

Under the FOIA Reform Act, the Office of Management and Budget was charged with the responsibility of promulgating, pursuant to notice and receipt of public comment, a "uniform schedule of fees" for individual agencies to follow when promulgating their FOIA fee regulations.[7] On March 27, 1987, OMB issued its Uniform Freedom of Information Act Fee Schedule and Guidelines [hereinafter OMB Fee Guidelines].[8] As mandated by the 1986 FOIA amendments, agencies are obligated to conform their fee schedules to these guidelines.[9]

The FOIA Reform Act also required agencies to promulgate specific "procedures and guidelines for determining when such fees should be waived or reduced."[10] The Department of Justice, in accordance with its statutory responsibility to encourage agency compliance with the FOIA,[11] developed new governmentwide policy guidance on the waiver of FOIA fees, to replace its previously issued guidance implementing the predecessor statutory fee waiver standard.[12] In April 1987, to assist federal agencies in addressing fee waivers in their revised FOIA fee regulations, the Department of Justice issued its New FOIA Fee Waiver Policy Guidance to the heads of all federal departments and agencies, which remains in effect.[13] While the Electronic Freedom of In-

---

[4] Id. at 3207-50.

[5] Id.

[6] Id. § 1804(b), 100 Stat. at 3207-50; see also FOIA Update, Vol. VIII, No. 1, at 2 (advising agencies that until implementing regulations were in place, they "should give FOIA requesters the full benefits of both . . . old and new" statutory provisions).

[7] Pub. L. No. 99-570, § 1803, 100 Stat. at 3207-49; see Media Access Project v. FCC, 883 F.2d 1063, 1069 (D.C. Cir. 1989) (finding OMB expressly mandated to establish fee schedule and guidelines for statutory fee categories).

[8] 52 Fed. Reg. 10,011 (1987).

[9] See 5 U.S.C. § 552(a)(4)(A)(i) (1994 & Supp. IV 1998).

[10] Pub. L. No. 99-570, § 1803, 100 Stat. at 3207-49.

[11] See 5 U.S.C. § 552(e); see also FOIA Update, Vol. XIX, No. 3, at 6; FOIA Update, Vol. XIV, No. 3, at 8.

[12] See FOIA Update, Vol. VIII, No. 1, at 1-2; FOIA Update, Vol. VII, No. 3, at 3; FOIA Update, Vol. IV, No. 1, at 3-4.

[13] See FOIA Update, Vol. VIII, No. 1, at 3-10; Attorney General's Memorandum on the 1986 Amendments to the Freedom of Information Act 41-50 (Dec. 1987); see also, e.g., Department of Justice FOIA Regulations, 28 C.F.R.

(continued...)

## FEES AND FEE WAIVERS

formation Act Amendments of 1996[14] made no direct changes to either the fee or fee waiver provisions of the FOIA,[15] several of those amendments can have an effect on fee matters.[16]

### Fees

As amended by the Freedom of Information Reform Act of 1986, the FOIA provides for three levels of fees that may be assessed in response to FOIA requests according to categories of FOIA requesters. These categorical provisions contain limitations on the assessment of fees, with the level of fees to be charged depending upon the identity of the requester and the intended use of the information sought.[17] The following discussion summarizes these fee provisions. The OMB Fee Guidelines, which provide general principles for how agencies should set fee schedules and make fee determinations, discuss these provisions in greater, authoritative detail.[18] Anyone with a FOIA fee (as opposed to fee waiver) question should consult these guidelines in conjunction with the appropriate agency's FOIA regulations for the records at issue. Agency personnel should attempt to resolve such fee questions by consulting first with their FOIA officers. Whenever fee questions cannot be resolved that way, agency FOIA officers should direct them to OMB's Office of Information and Regulatory Affairs, Information Policy and Technology Branch, at (202) 395-3785.

The first level of fees includes charges for "document search, duplication and review, when records are requested for commercial use."[19] The OMB Fee Guidelines define the term "commercial use" as "a use or purpose that furthers the commercial, trade or profit interests of the requester or the per-

---

[13](...continued)
§ 16.11 (1999) (example of fee regulation).

[14] Pub. L. No. 104-231, 110 Stat. 3048 (codified as amended at 5 U.S.C. § 552 (1994 & Supp. IV 1998)).

[15] See 5 U.S.C. § 552(a)(4)(A).

[16] See, e.g., 5 U.S.C. § 552(a)(3)(B) (providing for information to be disclosed in requester's choice of form or format if "readily reproducible" by agency).

[17] See 5 U.S.C. § 552(a)(4)(A)(ii) (1994 & Supp. IV 1998); see also FOIA Update, Vol. VIII, No. 1, at 4.

[18] See OMB Fee Guidelines, 52 Fed. Reg. 10,011 (1987).

[19] 5 U.S.C. § 552(a)(4)(A)(ii)(I); see Avondale Indus. v. NLRB, No. 96-1227, slip op. at 14 n.4 (E.D. La. Mar. 20, 1998) (noting that case law is "sparse" as to what constitutes "commercial use"). See generally Los Angeles Police Dep't v. United Reporting Publ'g Corp., 120 S. Ct. 483 (1999) (upholding state statute which denied commercial publishers access to arrest records but which permitted journalists access to same records; tangentially raising questions as to how to define "commercial user" and "journalist" in electronic age) (non-FOIA case).

## FEES AND FEE WAIVERS

son on whose behalf the request is being made,"[20] which can include furthering those interests through litigation.[21] Designation of a requester as a "commercial-use requester," therefore, will turn on the use to which the requested information would be put, rather than on the identity of the requester.[22] Agencies are encouraged to seek additional information or clarification from the requester when the intended use is not clear from the request itself.[23]

Charges for document "search" include all the time spent looking for responsive material, including page-by-page or line-by-line identification of material within documents.[24] Additionally, agencies may charge for search time even if they fail to locate any records responsive to the request or even if the records located are subsequently determined to be exempt from disclosure.[25] Searches for responsive records should be done in the "most efficient

---

[20] OMB Fee Guidelines, 52 Fed. Reg. at 10,017-18; see Avondale, No. 96-1227, slip op. at 14 (E.D. La. Mar. 20, 1998) (embracing OMB's definition of "commercial use").

[21] See Rozet v. HUD, 59 F. Supp. 2d 55, 57 (D.D.C. 1999) (finding commercial interest where requester sought documents to defend his corporations in civil fraud action). But see McClellan Ecological Seepage Situation v. Carlucci, 835 F.2d 1282, 1285 (9th Cir. 1987) (finding no commercial interest in records sought in furtherance of requesters' tort claim); Muffoletto v. Sessions, 760 F. Supp. 268, 277-78 (E.D.N.Y. 1991) (finding no commercial interest when records were sought to defend against state court action to recover debts).

[22] See OMB Fee Guidelines, 52 Fed. Reg. at 10,018; see also Comer v. IRS, No. 97-CV-76329, 1999 U.S. Dist. LEXIS 16268, at *12 (E.D. Mich. Sept. 30, 1999) (reiterating that requester's motives in seeking records relevant to "commercial user" determination); Hospital & Physician Publ'g v. DOD, No. 98-CV-4117, slip op. at 8 (S.D. Ill. June 22, 1999) (stating that requester's past commercial use of such records is not relevant to present case) (appeal pending); S.A. Ludsin & Co. v. SBA, No. 96 CV 5972, 1998 WL 355394, at *2 (E.D.N.Y. Apr. 2, 1998) (finding requester who sought documents to enhance prospect of securing government contract to be commercial requester); Avondale, No. 96-1227, slip op. at 14 (E.D. La. Mar. 20 1998) (finding company's intent to use requested documents to contest union election results to be commercial use); cf. Rozet, 59 F. Supp. 2d at 57 (discounting plaintiff's assertion that information was not of commercial interest where timing and content of requests in connection with other non-FOIA litigation conclusively demonstrated otherwise).

[23] See OMB Fee Guidelines, 52 Fed. Reg. at 10,018.

[24] See id. at 10,017.

[25] See id. at 10,019; see also Guzzino v. FBI, No. 95-1780, 1997 WL 22886, at *4 (D.D.C. Jan. 10, 1997) (upholding agency's assessment of search fees to conduct search for potentially responsive records within files of individuals "with names similar to" requester's when no files identifiable to requester existed), appeal dismissed for lack of prosecution, No. 97-5083 (D.C. Cir. Dec. 8, 1997); Linn v. United States Dep't of Justice, No. 92-1406, 1995 WL 417810, at *13 (D.D.C. June 6, 1995) (holding no entitlement to refund of search fees

(continued...)

## FEES AND FEE WAIVERS

and least expensive manner."[26] As now defined by the Electronic Freedom of Information Act Amendments of 1996,[27] the term "search" means locating records or information either "manually or by automated means"[28] and requires agencies to expend "reasonable efforts" in electronic searches, if requested to do so by requesters willing to pay for that search activity.[29]

The "review" costs which may be charged to commercial-use requesters consist of the "direct costs incurred during the initial examination of a document for the purposes of determining whether [it] must be disclosed [under the FOIA]."[30] Review time thus includes processing the documents for disclosure, i.e., doing all that is necessary to prepare them for release; but it does not include time spent resolving general legal or policy issues regarding the applicability of particular exemptions or reviewing on appeal exemptions already applied.[31]

Under the 1986 FOIA amendments, "duplication" charges represent the reasonable "direct costs" of making copies of documents.[32] Copies can take various forms, including paper copies, microforms, or machine-readable doc-

---

[25](...continued) when search unproductive); cf. Stabasefski v. United States, 919 F. Supp. 1570, 1573 (M.D. Ga. 1996) (holding no entitlement to reimbursement of copying fees when agency redacts portion of requested material).

[26] OMB Fee Guidelines, 52 Fed. Reg. at 10,017; accord President's Memorandum for Heads of Departments and Agencies regarding the Freedom of Information Act, 29 Weekly Comp. Pres. Doc. 1999 (Oct. 4, 1993), reprinted in FOIA Update, Vol. XIV, No. 3, at 3 ("Federal departments and agencies should handle requests for information in a customer-friendly manner.").

[27] Pub. L. No. 104-231, 110 Stat. 3048.

[28] 5 U.S.C. § 552(a)(3)(D).

[29] Id. at § 552(a)(3)(C); see also FOIA Update, Vol. XVIII, No. 1, at 6; Department of Justice FOIA Regulations, 28 C.F.R. § 16.11(b)(8) (1999); OMB Fee Guidelines, 52 Fed. Reg. at 10,018, 10,019 (agencies should charge "the actual direct cost of providing [computer searches]"; for certain requester categories, cost equivalent of two hours of manual search provided without charge).

[30] 5 U.S.C. § 552(a)(4)(A)(iv).

[31] See OMB Fee Guidelines, 52 Fed. Reg. at 10,017, 10,018; see also OSHA Data/C.I.H., Inc. v. United States Dep't of Labor, No. 98-283, slip op. at 10-11 (D.N.J. June 11, 1998) (granting defendant agency's motion for stay and holding that expense of providing submitter notice pursuant to Exemption 4 is appropriately borne by commercial use requester as "review" cost) (appeal pending).

[32] 5 U.S.C. § 552(a)(4)(A)(iv); see OMB Fee Guidelines, 52 Fed. Reg. at 10,018.

## FEES AND FEE WAIVERS

umentation.[33] As further required by the Electronic FOIA amendments, which were enacted a decade later, agencies must honor a requester's choice of form or format if the record is "readily reproducible" in that form or format with "reasonable efforts" by the agency.[34] For copies prepared by computer, such as printouts, agencies should charge the actual costs of production of the printout.[35] Agencies should consult with their technical support staff for assistance in determining their actual costs associated with producing copies of various types of media.[36] In this regard, it is standard practice that duplication charges are assessed only for those copies that are released, not for any responsive record withheld in its entirety.[37] (For further discussions of agency responsibilities when searching for or producing responsive records under the Electronic FOIA amendments, see Procedural Requirements, Searching for Records, above, and Procedural Requirements, Responding to FOIA Requests, above.)

The second level of fees limits charges to document duplication costs only, "when records are not sought for commercial use and the request is made by an educational or noncommercial scientific institution, whose purpose is scholarly or scientific research; or a representative of the news media."[38] FOIA requesters falling into one or more of these three subcategories of requesters under the 1986 FOIA amendments enjoy a complete "exemption" from the assessment of search and review fees. Their requests, like those made by any FOIA requester, still must "reasonably describe" the records sought in order to not impose upon an agency "'an unreasonably burdensome search.'"[39] (For a further discussion of this requirement, see Procedural Requirements, Proper FOIA Requests, above.)

The OMB Fee Guidelines define "educational institution" to include various categories of schools, as well as institutions of higher learning and voca-

---

[33] See OMB Fee Guidelines, 52 Fed. Reg. at 10,017.

[34] 5 U.S.C. § 552(a)(3)(B); see FOIA Update, Vol. XVIII, No. 1, at 5-6 (advising agencies on new format disclosure obligations); FOIA Update, Vol. XVII, No. 4, at 2 (same); see also FOIA Update, Vol. XIX, No. 1, at 6 (encouraging agencies to consider providing records in multiple forms as matter of administrative discretion if requested to do so).

[35] See OMB Fee Guidelines, 52 Fed. Reg. at 10,018; see also 28 C.F.R. § 16.11(c)(2); FOIA Update, Vol. XI, No. 3, at 4 & n.25.

[36] See OMB Fee Guidelines at 10,017-18 (advising agencies to "charge the actual cost, including computer operator time, of production of [a computer] tape or printout").

[37] See generally OMB Fee Guidelines, 52 Fed. Reg. at 10,017-19.

[38] 5 U.S.C. § 552(a)(4)(A)(ii)(II).

[39] AFGE v. United States Dep't of Commerce, 907 F.2d 203, 209 (D.C. Cir. 1990) (quoting Goland v. CIA, 607 F.2d 339, 353 (D.C. Cir. 1978)).

tional education.[40] This definition is limited, however, by the requirement that the educational institution be one "which operates a program or programs of scholarly research."[41] The definition of a "noncommercial scientific institution" refers to a "noncommercial" institution "operated solely for the purpose of conducting scientific research the results of which are not intended to promote any particular product or industry."[42]

The definition of a "representative of the news media" refers to any person actively gathering information of current interest to the public for an organization that is organized and operated to publish or broadcast news to the general public.[43] The Court of Appeals for the District of Columbia Circuit has elaborated upon this definition, holding that "a representative of the news media is, in essence, a person or entity that gathers information of potential interest to a segment of the public, uses its editorial skills to turn the raw materials into a distinct work, and distributes that work to an audience."[44] Such a definition, the D.C. Circuit made clear, excludes "'private librar[ies]' or 'private repositories'" of government records, or middlemen such as "'information vendors [or] data brokers,'" who request records for use by others.[45] This fee category, however, may include freelance journalists, when they can demonstrate a solid basis for expecting the information disclosed to be published by a news organization.[46] A request from a representative of the news media that supports a news-dissemination function "shall not be considered to be a request that is for a commercial use."[47] The first case to construe this subcategory of requesters held that even a foreign news service may qualify as a representative of the news media.[48]

The third level of fees, which applies to all requesters who do not fall within either of the preceding two fee levels, consists of reasonable charges for

---

[40] See OMB Fee Guidelines, 52 Fed. Reg. at 10,018.

[41] See id.; see also National Sec. Archive v. DOD, 880 F.2d 1381, 1383-85 (D.C. Cir. 1989) (approving implementation of this standard in DOD regulation).

[42] OMB Fee Guidelines, 52 Fed. Reg. at 10,018.

[43] Id.

[44] National Sec. Archive, 880 F.2d at 1387.

[45] Id.

[46] See OMB Fee Guidelines, 52 Fed. Reg. at 10,018. But see Hospital & Physician Publ'g, No. 98-CV-4117, slip op. at 6 (S.D. Ill. June 22, 1999) (in fact-specific case, ordering defendant to apply news media status to plaintiff for purposes of assessing fees even though plaintiff has not gathered news in past nor does so now, but has expressed intention to "begin gathering news for dissemination . . . to news media via free news releases").

[47] See OMB Fee Guidelines, 52 Fed. Reg. at 10,019; accord FOIA Update, Vol. VIII, No. 1, at 10; see also National Sec. Archive, 880 F.2d at 1387-88.

[48] Southam News v. INS, 674 F. Supp. 881, 892 (D.D.C. 1987).

## FEES AND FEE WAIVERS

document search and duplication,[49] as was provided for in the former statutory FOIA fee provision.

When any FOIA request is submitted by someone on behalf of another person--for example, by an attorney on behalf of a client--it is nevertheless the underlying requester's identity and intended use that determines the level of fees.[50] When such information is not readily apparent from the request itself, agencies should seek clarification from the requester before assigning a requester to a specific requester category.[51] Agencies also should be alert to the fact that a requester's category can change over time.[52]

Additionally, all categories of requesters may be charged the actual "direct costs" involved when an agency complies with a request for "special services," such as certifying records as true copies or mailing records by express mail.[53] In this regard, agencies should strive to use the most efficient and least costly means of complying with a request.[54] This may include the use of contractor services, as long as an agency does not relinquish responsibilities it alone must perform, such as making fee waiver determinations.[55]

The fee structure also includes restrictions both on the assessment of certain fees and on the authority of agencies to ask for an advance payment of a fee.[56] No FOIA fee may be charged by an agency if the government's cost of collecting and processing the fee is likely to equal or exceed the amount of the fee itself.[57] In addition, except with respect to commercial-use requesters, agencies must provide the first 100 pages of duplication, as well as the first

---

[49] 5 U.S.C. § 552(a)(4)(A)(ii)(III).

[50] See OMB Fee Guidelines, 52 Fed. Reg at 10,013, 10,017-18.

[51] See id. at 10,013, 10,018; cf. Long v. ATF, 964 F. Supp. 494, 498, 499 (D.D.C. 1997) (upholding agency's determination that "it did not 'find it necessary'" to make requester category determination when full fee waiver granted; rejecting plaintiff's request for declaratory judgment as to requester category when no fee at issue, and finding question not ripe as to future requests).

[52] See National Sec. Archive, 880 F.2d at 1388 (stating that court's determination of requester's news media status is "not chiselled in granite"); Long, 964 F. Supp. at 498 (indicating that "an entity's status can change").

[53] OMB Fee Guidelines, 52 Fed. Reg. at 10,018; see, e.g., 28 C.F.R. § 16.11(f) (Department of Justice fee regulation).

[54] See OMB Fee Guidelines, 52 Fed. Reg. at 10,018; cf. FOIA Update, Vol. XVI, No. 1, at 1-2 (stressing importance of cost-efficiency to overall process of FOIA administration).

[55] See OMB Fee Guidelines, 52 Fed. Reg. at 10,018; see also FOIA Update, Vol. IV, No. 1, at 2 (citing applicable Comptroller General decisions).

[56] See 5 U.S.C. § 552(a)(4)(A)(iv)-(v).

[57] Id. § 552(a)(4)(A)(iv)(I); see also OMB Fee Guidelines, 52 Fed. Reg. at 10,018.

## FEES AND FEE WAIVERS

two hours of search time, without cost to the requester.[58] These two provisions work together so that, except with respect to commercial-use requesters, agencies should not begin to assess fees until after they provide this amount of free search and duplication; the assessable fee for any requester then must be greater than the agency's cost to collect and process it in order for the fee actually to be charged.[59]

Agencies also may not require a requester to make an advance payment, i.e., payment before work is begun or continued on a request, unless the agency first estimates that the assessable fee is likely to exceed $250, or unless the requester has previously failed to pay a properly assessed fee in a timely manner (i.e., within thirty days of the billing date).[60] This statutory restriction does not prevent agencies from requiring payment before records which have been processed are released.[61] Additionally, when an agency reasonably be-

---

[58] 5 U.S.C. § 552(a)(4)(A)(iv)(II); see also OMB Fee Guidelines, 52 Fed. Reg. at 10,018-19.

[59] 5 U.S.C. § 552(a)(4)(A)(iv)(I); see also OMB Fee Guidelines, 52 Fed. Reg. at 10,018.

[60] 5 U.S.C. § 552(a)(4)(A)(v); see also OMB Fee Guidelines, 52 Fed. Reg. at 10,020; O'Meara v. IRS, No. 97-3383, 1998 WL 123984, at **1-2 (7th Cir. Mar. 17, 1998) (upholding agency's demand for advance payment when fees exceeded $800); Comer, 1999 U.S. Dist. LEXIS 16268, at *13 (authorizing agency "to not respond to any further FOIA requests by plaintiff" until current debt is paid and "to require plaintiff to pay in advance any fees likely to be incurred as a result of processing" further requests); Bauer v. United States, No. 96-1165, 1998 U.S Dist. LEXIS 3813, at *6 (D.D.C. Mar. 20, 1998) (recognizing that when requester fails to remit prior FOIA fee, agency may require requester to pay amount owed, interest on that amount, and advance payment of fees for new request); Wade v. IRS, No. 96-1855, slip op. at 1-2 (D.D.C. Aug. 21, 1997) (ordering plaintiff to make advance payment "in the manner required by the [agency]" when fees exceeded $250); Rothman v. Daschle, No. 96-5898, 1997 U.S. Dist. LEXIS 13009, at *2 (E.D. Pa. Aug. 20, 1997) (upholding agency's request for advance payment when fees exceeded $250); Mason v. Bell, No. 78-719-A, slip op. at 1 (E.D. Va. May 16, 1979) (finding dismissal of FOIA case proper when plaintiffs failed to pay fees to other federal agencies for prior requests). But cf. Ruotolo v. Department of Justice, 53 F.3d 4, 9-10 (2d Cir. 1995) (suggesting that agency should have processed request up to amount offered by requesters rather than state that estimated cost "would greatly exceed" $250 without providing an amount to be paid or offering assistance in reformulating request).

[61] See Strout v. United States Parole Comm'n, 40 F.3d 136, 139 (6th Cir. 1994) (finding that agency regulation requiring payment before release of processed records does not conflict with statutory prohibition against advance payment); Taylor v. United States Dep't of the Treasury, No. A-96-CA-933, 1996 U.S. Dist. LEXIS 19909, at *5 (W.D. Tex. Dec. 17, 1996) (same); Trueblood v. United States Dep't of the Treasury, 943 F. Supp. 64, 68 (D.D.C. 1996) (stating that agency may require payment before sending processed records); Putnam v. United States Dep't of Justice, 880 F. Supp. 40, 42

(continued...)

## FEES AND FEE WAIVERS

lieves that a requester is attempting to break a request into a series of requests for the purpose of avoiding the assessment of fees, the agency may aggregate those requests and charge accordingly.[62] The OMB Fee Guidelines should be consulted for additional guidance on aggregating requests.[63]

The FOIA also provides that FOIA fees are superseded by "fees chargeable under a statute specifically providing for setting the level of fees for particular types of records."[64] Thus, when documents responsive to a FOIA request are maintained for distribution by an agency according to a statutorily based fee schedule, requesters should obtain the documents from that source and pay the applicable fees in accordance with the fee schedule of that other statute.[65] This may at times result in the assessment of fees that are higher than those that would otherwise be chargeable under the FOIA,[66] but it ensures that such fees are properly borne by the requester and not by the gen-

---

[61](...continued) (D.D.C. 1995) (allowing agency to require payment of current and outstanding fees before releasing records); Crooker v. ATF, 882 F. Supp. 1158, 1162 (D. Mass. 1995) (finding no obligation to provide records until current and past due fees paid); see also, e.g., 28 C.F.R. § 16.11(i)(1) ("Payment owed for work already completed (i.e., a prepayment before copies are sent to the requester) is not an advance payment.").

[62] See OMB Fee Guidelines, 52 Fed. Reg. at 10,019; see also Atkin v. EEOC, No. 91-2508, slip op. at 20-21 (D.N.J. Dec. 4, 1992) (finding agency's decision to aggregate requests proper; reasonable for agency to believe 13 requests relating to same subject matter submitted within three-month period were made by requester to evade payment of fees), appeal dismissed for failure to timely prosecute sub nom. Atkin v. Kemp, No. 93-5548 (3d Cir. Dec. 6, 1993).

[63] OMB Fee Guidelines, 52 Fed. Reg. at 10,019-20.

[64] 5 U.S.C. § 552(a)(4)(A)(vi); see, e.g., Oglesby v. United States Dep't of the Army, 79 F.3d 1172, 1177 (D.C. Cir. 1996) (stating that NARA statute fits within exception of FOIA subsection (a)(4)(A)(vi)); see also National Technical Information Act, 15 U.S.C. §§ 1151-57 (1994) (providing for dissemination of technological, scientific, and engineering information to business and industry); OMB Fee Guidelines, 52 Fed. Reg. at 10,017, 10,018.

[65] See OMB Fee Guidelines, 52 Fed. Reg. at 10,012-13, 10,017-18 (implementing 5 U.S.C. § 552(a)(4)(A)(vi)); id. at 10,017 (contemplating "statutory-based fee schedule programs . . . such as the NTIS [National Technical Information Service]"); Wade v. Department of Commerce, No. 96-0717, slip op. at 5-6 (D.D.C. Mar. 26, 1998) (concluding that fee was "properly charged by NTIS" under its fee schedule); cf. SDC Dev. Corp. v. Mathews, 542 F.2d 1116, 1120 (9th Cir. 1976) (in decision predating 1986 FOIA amendments and turning on issue of "agency records," holding that records for which charges were specifically authorized by another statute were not required to be made available under FOIA).

[66] See, e.g., Wade, No. 96-0717, slip op. at 2, 6 (D.D.C. Mar. 26, 1998) (approving assessment of $1300 fee pursuant to NTIS's superseding fee statute and noting agency's return of requester's $210 check for anticipated FOIA fees).

## FEES AND FEE WAIVERS

eral public.[67] Given the increasing availability of low-cost and free government information through the Internet and other electronic sources, it remains to be seen whether those agencies with such statutorily based fee schedules--and which do not receive appropriated funds to support their record-distribution services, but are required by law to be self-sustaining--will continue to be viable sources of government information.[68] The superseding of FOIA fees by the fee provisions of another statute raises a related question as to whether an agency with a statutorily based fee schedule for particular types of records is subject to the FOIA's fee waiver provision; although this question has been raised, it has not yet been reached by an appellate court.[69]

The FOIA requires that requesters follow the agency's published rules for making FOIA requests, including those pertaining to the payment of authorized fees.[70] Requesters have been found not to have exhausted their administrative remedies when fee requirements have not been met.[71] A re-

---

[67] See OMB Fee Guidelines, 52 Fed. Reg. at 10,017.

[68] See, e.g., Press Release of Secretary William M. Daley, Department of Commerce (Aug. 12, 1999) (announcing proposal to close National Technical Information Service (NTIS), Department of Commerce's scientific and technical clearinghouse, because "the core function of NTIS, providing government information for a fee, is no longer needed in this day of advanced electronic technology") (available at the Department of Commerce's site on the World Wide Web (www.doc.gov)).

[69] Compare Oglesby, 79 F.3d at 1178 (refusing to rule on district court's finding that NARA's fee provision is exempt from FOIA's fee waiver requirement, because appellant failed to raise argument in timely manner), and Oglesby v. United States Dep't of the Army, 920 F.2d 57, 70 n.17 (D.C. Cir. 1990) (declining to reach fee waiver issue because plaintiff failed to exhaust administrative remedies), with St. Hilaire v. Department of Justice, No. 91-0078, slip op. at 4-5 (D.D.C. Sept. 10, 1991) (avoiding fee waiver issue because requested records made publicly available), summary judgment granted (D.D.C. Mar. 18, 1992), aff'd per curiam, No. 92-5153 (D.C. Cir. Apr. 28, 1994).

[70] 5 U.S.C. § 552(a)(3)(B); 28 C.F.R. § 16.11(e); see also Irons v. FBI, 571 F. Supp. 1241, 1243 (D. Mass. 1983); cf. Oglesby, 920 F.2d at 66; O'Meara, 1998 WL 123984, at *1 ("Congress intended people making FOIA requests to bear the costs of processing such requests" unless they qualify for fee waiver).

[71] See, e.g., Trenerry v. IRS, No. 95-5150, 1996 WL 88459, at *2 (10th Cir. Mar. 1, 1996) (explaining exhaustion includes payment of FOIA fees); Oglesby, 920 F.2d at 66 & n.11, 71 ("Exhaustion does not occur until fees are paid or an appeal is taken from the refusal to waive fees."); Grecco v. Department of Justice, No. 97-0419, slip op. at 4 (D.D.C. Apr. 1, 1999) (finding no exhaustion where plaintiff neither paid assessed fee nor asked for fee waiver); Smith v. IRS, No. 2:94-CV-989, slip op. at 2 (D. Utah Mar. 24, 1999) (concluding that no exhaustion existed where requester failed to pay fees); Loomis v. United States Dep't of Energy, No. 96-CV-149, slip op. at 9-10 (N.D.N.Y. Mar. 9, 1999) (stating that exhaustion occurred where plaintiff agreed to pay initial estimate for identified records which agency subsequently found covered only

(continued...)

## FEES AND FEE WAIVERS

quester's obligation to comply with the agency's fee requirements does not cease after litigation has been initiated under the FOIA.[72] (For a further discussion of the exhaustion requirement, including "fee" exhaustion, see Litigation Considerations, Exhaustion of Administrative Remedies, below.) Furthermore, the Act contains no provision for reimbursement of fees if the requester is dissatisfied with the agency's response.[73]

Because the FOIA Reform Act was silent with respect to the standard and scope of judicial review of FOIA fee issues, including a requester's fee category,[74] the standard should remain the same as that under the predecessor statutory fee provision--i.e., agency action should be upheld unless it is found to be "arbitrary or capricious," in accordance with the Administrative Procedure Act.[75] Perhaps due to this lack of statutory clarity, the appropriate stand-

---

[71](...continued)
portion of fees), appeal dismissed for lack of juris., 199 F.3d 1322 (2d Cir. 1999) (unpublished table cite); Stanley v. DOD, No. 93-CV-4247 (S.D. Ill. July 28, 1998) (stating that agency's failure to inform plaintiff of right to administratively appeal its fee estimate amounted to constructive exhaustion where agency's regulations allowed appeal of such estimates); Center to Prevent Handgun Violence v. Department of the Treasury, 981 F. Supp. 20, 23 (D.D.C. 1997) (finding that requester failed to exhaust administrative remedies regarding fee status); Kuchta v. Harris, No. 92-1121, slip op. at 5-9 (D. Md. Mar. 25, 1993) (recognizing that failure to pay fees stops administrative process and precludes exhaustion); cf. Tinsley v. Commissioner, No. 3:96-1769-P, 1998 WL 59481, at *4 (N.D. Tex. Feb. 9, 1998) (finding that because plaintiff failed to appeal fee waiver denial, exhaustion was not achieved). But cf. Payne v. Minihan, No. 97-0266, slip op. at 34 n.17 (D.N.M. Apr. 30, 1998) (holding, in fact-specific case, plaintiff not required to exhaust by appealing fee waiver denial when requester's right to sue already perfected on different issue) (appeal pending).

[72] See Pollack v. Department of Justice, 49 F.3d 115, 119-20 (4th Cir. 1995) (providing that commencement of FOIA action does not relieve requester of obligation to pay for documents); Goulding v. IRS, No. 97 C 5628, 1998 WL 325202, at *9 (N.D. Ill. June 8, 1998) (finding plaintiff's constructive exhaustion did not relieve his obligation to pay authorized fees), summary judgment granted, No. 97 C 5628 (N.D. Ill. July 30, 1998) (restating that plaintiff's failure to comply with fee requirements is fatal to claim against government); Trueblood, 943 F. Supp. at 68 (stating even if request for payment not made until after litigation commences, that fact does not relieve requester of obligation to pay reasonably assessed fees).

[73] See Stabasefski, 919 F. Supp. at 1573 (stating that FOIA does not provide for reimbursement of fees when agency redacts portions of records that are released).

[74] See 5 U.S.C. § 552(a)(4)(A)(vii) (establishing revised de novo/administrative record standard and scope of review for fee waiver issues).

[75] 5 U.S.C. §§ 701-06 (1994); see Trenerry v. IRS, No. 90-C-444-B, 1993 WL 56534, at *6 (N.D. Okla. Oct. 28, 1993) (finding assessed fees reasonable, in
(continued...)

# FEES AND FEE WAIVERS

ard of review has yet to be clearly established.[76] In 1989, in an important case brought in the D.C. Circuit,[77] the government argued that the defendant agency's interpretation of the 1986 fee amendments to the FOIA, reflected by the agency's implementing regulations, was owed great deference under the rule established by the Supreme Court in Chevron USA, Inc. v. National Resources Defense Council.[78] The D.C. Circuit avoided addressing the judicial review issue, however, by finding that with reference to the underlying fee issue, "the statute, read in light of the legislative history . . . [was] clear."[79] Thus, over a decade later, the extent of judicial deference given to agency fee regulations based upon the OMB Fee Guidelines, remains unclear.[80]

## Fee Waivers

The FOIA, as strengthened by the 1974 FOIA amendments,[81] authorized waiver of fees when it was determined that such action was "in the public interest because furnishing the information can be considered as primarily benefitting the general public."[82] As the Court of Appeals for the District of Columbia Circuit had emphasized, this provision "was enacted to ensure that the public would benefit from any expenditure of public funds for the disclosure

---

[75](...continued) accordance with agency regulations, and not arbitrary and capricious); cf. Long, 964 F. Supp. at 497 (finding plaintiff's allegation that assessment of fees was arbitrary and capricious was mooted by subsequent grant of fee waiver); Knowles v. United States Coast Guard, No. 96-1018, 1997 WL 151397, at *13 (S.D.N.Y. Mar. 31, 1997) (rejecting requester's claim of excessive fee where agency subsequently reduced it).

[76] Compare Rozet, 59 F. Supp. 2d at 56 (emphasizing that although denial of fee waiver requests are reviewed de novo, "the appropriate standard of review for an agency determination of fee status under FOIA . . . has not been decided in this Circuit"), with Hospital & Physician Publ'g, No. 98-CV-4117, slip op. at 5 (S.D. Ill. June 22, 1999) (stating in single sentence that court review of fee category is de novo citing to statutory provision for de novo review of fee waivers).

[77] See National Sec. Archive, 880 F.2d at 1383.

[78] 467 U.S. 837, 844 (1984) (emphasizing that where agency's statutory interpretation "fills a gap or defines a term in a way that is reasonable in light of the legislature's revealed design, [the court] give[s that] judgment 'controlling weight'") (non-FOIA case).

[79] National Sec. Archive, 880 F.2d at 1383.

[80] Compare Media Access Project v. FCC, 883 F.2d 1063, 1071 (D.C. Cir. 1989) (agency's interpretation of its own fee regulations "must be given at least some deference"), with National Sec. Archive, 880 F.2d at 1383 (question of deference owed to agency's fee regulations not resolved).

[81] Pub. L. No. 93-502, §§ 1-3, 88 Stat. 1561-64 (1974) (subsequently amended).

[82] Id.

## FEES AND FEE WAIVERS

of public records."[83] In January 1983, the Department of Justice issued fee waiver guidelines that set forth specific criteria, developed in numerous court decisions, for federal agencies to apply in determining whether the public interest warranted a waiver or reduction of fees.[84]

The current fee waiver standard, which was established by the Freedom of Information Reform Act of 1986,[85] more specifically defines the term "public interest" by providing that fees should be waived or reduced "if disclosure of the information is in the public interest because it is likely to contribute significantly to public understanding of the operations or activities of the government and is not primarily in the commercial interest of the requester."[86] In accordance with this provision, the Department of Justice issued revised fee waiver policy guidance on April 2, 1987--which superseded its 1983 substantive fee waiver guidance, as well as that issued in November 1986 (concerning institutions and record repositories)--and it advised agencies of six analytical factors to be considered in applying this statutory fee waiver standard.[87] These six factors were applied and implicitly approved by the Court of Appeals for the Ninth Circuit in McClellan Ecological Seepage Situation v. Carlucci.[88]

The statutory fee waiver standard as amended in 1986 contains two basic requirements--the public interest requirement and the requirement that the requester's commercial interest in the disclosure, if any, must be less than the public interest in it.[89] Both of these requirements must be satisfied by the requester before properly assessable fees are waived or reduced under the statutory standard.[90] Requests for a waiver or reduction of fees must be con-

---

[83] Ely v. United States Postal Serv., 753 F.2d 163, 165 (D.C. Cir. 1985).

[84] See FOIA Update, Vol. IV, No. 1, at 3-4.

[85] Pub. L. No. 99-570, § 1803, 100 Stat. 3207, 3207-50 (codified as amended at 5 U.S.C. § 552(a)(4)(A)(iii) (1994 & Supp. IV 1998)).

[86] Id.

[87] See FOIA Update, Vol. VIII, No. 1, at 3-10; see also id. at 10 (specifying that previous "procedural" guidance on fee waiver issues remains in effect); FOIA Update, Vol. IV, No. 1, at 4.

[88] 835 F.2d 1282, 1286 (9th Cir. 1987); see also, e.g., Pederson v. RTC, 847 F. Supp. 851, 855 (D. Colo. 1994); Sloman v. United States Dep't of Justice, 832 F. Supp. 63, 68 (S.D.N.Y. 1993).

[89] 5 U.S.C. § 552(a)(4)(A)(iii) (1994 & Supp. IV 1998); see also Department of Justice FOIA Regulations, 28 C.F.R. § 16.11(k) (1999).

[90] See FOIA Update, Vol. VIII, No. 1, at 4; see also Slater v. Executive Office for United States Attorneys, No. 98-1663, 1999 U.S. Dist. LEXIS 8399, at *13 (D.D.C. May 2, 1999) (reiterating that it is plaintiff's burden to establish that statutory standard is met); Klamath Water Users Protective Ass'n v. United States Dep't of the Interior, No. 96-3077, slip op. at 47 (D. Or. June 19, 1997) (magistrate's recommendation) (observing that burden is on requester to
(continued...)

## FEES AND FEE WAIVERS

sidered on a case-by-case basis and should address both of these requirements in sufficient detail for the agency to make an informed decision as to whether it can appropriately waive or reduce the fees in question.[91] As with disclosures made under the FOIA, agencies analyzing fee waiver requests are not bound by previous administrative decisions.[92]

In order to determine whether the first fee waiver requirement has been met--i.e., that disclosure of the requested information is in the public interest because it is likely to contribute significantly to public understanding of government operations or activities[93]--agencies should consider the following

---

[90](...continued) show eligibility for fee waiver), adopted (D. Or. Oct. 16, 1997), rev'd on other grounds, 189 F.3d 1034 (9th Cir. 1999), petition for cert. filed, No. 99-1871 (U.S. May 22, 2000); S.A. Ludsin & Co. v. SBA, No. 96 Civ. 2146, 1997 U.S. Dist. LEXIS 8617, at **10-11 (S.D.N.Y. June 19, 1997) (noting that fee waiver provision contains two requirements and that requester carries burden of proof on both), summary affirmance granted, 162 F.3d 1148 (2d Cir.) (unpublished table decision), cert. denied, 525 U.S. 828 (1998); Anderson v. DEA, No. 93-253, slip op. at 4 (W.D. Pa. May 11, 1995) (magistrate's recommendation) (stating that burden is on requester to establish fee waiver standard met), adopted (W.D. Pa. June 21, 1995); Sloman, 832 F. Supp. at 67 (acknowledging two-pronged statutory test used to determine when fees should be waived).

[91] See FOIA Update, Vol. VIII, No. 1, at 6; National Sec. Archive v. DOD, 880 F.2d 1381, 1383 (D.C. Cir. 1989) (dictum) (noting fee waiver decisions made on "case-by-case" basis); National Wildlife Fed'n v. Hamilton, No. 95-017-BU, slip op. at 2 (D. Mont. July 15, 1996) (same); Martorano v. FBI, No. 89-1345, 1991 WL 212521, at *4 (D.D.C. Sept. 30, 1991) (finding requester not entitled to documents when he neither provided agency with information necessary to justify fee waiver nor agreed to pay fees); see also McClellan, 835 F.2d at 1285 (stating that conclusory statements will not support fee waiver request); cf. Judicial Watch, Inc. v. United States Dep't of Justice, No. 97-2089, slip op. at 14 (D.D.C. July 14, 1998) (finding, in case at hand, that it was "wholly irrelevant" that requester received fee waivers in other cases).

[92] See Dollinger v. United States Postal Serv., No. 95-CV-6174T, slip op. at 7-8 (W.D.N.Y. Aug. 24, 1995) (concluding that agency not bound by previous decision on fee waiver for similar request from same requester).

[93] See, e.g., S.A. Ludsin & Co. v. SBA, No. 97-7884, 1998 WL 642416, at *1 (2d Cir. Mar. 26, 1998) (reiterating that first requirement not met when requester "merely paraphrased" fee waiver provision), cert. denied, 525 U.S. 828 (1998) (No. 97-2085); Oglesby v. United States Dep't of the Army, 920 F.2d 57, 66 n.11 (D.C. Cir. 1990) (conclusory statements insufficient to make public interest showing); S.A. Ludsin & Co. v. SBA, No. 96-5972, 1998 WL 355394, at *2 (E.D.N.Y. Apr. 2, 1998) (observing that mere recitation of statute does not satisfy requester's burden); Trueblood v. United States Dep't of the Treasury, 943 F. Supp. 64, 69 (D.D.C. Oct. 30, 1996) (rejecting contention that public interest requirement met by identifying personal benefit to requester); National Wildlife Fed'n, No. 95-017-BU, slip op. at 3 (D. Mont. July

(continued...)

# FEES AND FEE WAIVERS

four factors in sequence:

1. First, the subject matter of the requested records, in the context of the request, must specifically concern identifiable "operations or activities of the government."[94] As the D.C. Circuit specifically indicated in applying the predecessor fee waiver standard, "the links between furnishing the requested information and benefiting the general public" should not be "tenuous."[95] Although in most cases records possessed by a federal agency will meet this threshold, the records must be sought for their informative value with respect to specifically identified government operations or activities;[96] a request for access to records for their intrinsic informational content alone would not sat-

---

[93](...continued)
15, 1996) (reiterating that requester bears burden of demonstrating that requested information is in public interest); Sloman, 832 F. Supp. at 68 (finding public interest requirement not met by merely quoting statutory standard); cf. S.A. Ludsin, 1998 WL 642416, at *1 (noting that requester's claim that disclosure to it would "create[] revenue for the federal government" does not demonstrate that disclosure "is in the public interest" for fee waiver purposes); Sierra Club Legal Defense Fund v. Bibles, No. 93-35383, slip op. at 3-4 (9th Cir. Aug. 29, 1994) (reasoning that disclosure to group that is "in the public interest" not same as saying disclosure without fees is likely to contribute to public understanding; status as public interest law firm does not automatically entitle it to fee waiver at taxpayer expense); NTEU v. Griffin, 811 F.2d 644, 647 (D.C. Cir. 1987) (observing under previous standard that requester seeking fee waiver bears burden of identifying "public interest" involved). But cf. Judicial Watch of Florida, Inc. v. United States Dep't of Justice, No. 97-2869, slip op. at 4-5 (D.D.C. Aug. 25, 1998) (despite fact that disclosed information "not necessarily all new," finding public interest served "by exposing government actions through litigation").

[94] 5 U.S.C. § 552(a)(4)(A)(iii); see Dollinger, No. 95-CV-6174T, slip op. at 4 (W.D.N.Y. Aug. 24, 1995) (concluding that "government" as used in fee waiver standard refers to federal government).

[95] NTEU, 811 F.2d at 648.

[96] See, e.g., Van Fripp v. Parks, No. 97-0159, slip op. at 10 (D.D.C. Mar. 16, 2000) (characterizing request as a "fishing expedition that does not relate to defined operations or activities of the [agency]"); S.A. Ludsin, 1997 U.S. Dist. LEXIS 8617, at *14 (holding that disclosure of appraisals of government property do not "in any readily apparent way" contribute to public's understanding of operations or activities of government); Atkin v. EEOC, No. 91-2508, slip op. at 27-28 (D.N.J. Dec. 4, 1992) (finding requested list of agency attorneys and their bar affiliations "clearly does not concern identifiable government activities or operations"), appeal dismissed for failure to timely prosecute sub nom. Atkin v. Kemp, No. 93-5548 (3d Cir. 1993); Nance v. United States Postal Serv., No. 91-1183, 1992 WL 23655, at *2 (D.D.C. Jan. 24, 1992) (reiterating that disclosure of illegally cashed money orders will not contribute significantly to public understanding of operations of government).

## FEES AND FEE WAIVERS

isfy this threshold consideration.[97]

2. Second, in order for the disclosure to be "likely to contribute" to an understanding of specific government operations or activities, the disclosable portions of the requested information must be meaningfully informative in relation to the subject matter of the request.[98] Requests for information that is already in the public domain, either in a duplicative or a substantially identical form, may not warrant a fee waiver because the disclosure would not be likely to contribute to an understanding of government operations or activities when nothing new would be added to the public's understanding.[99] Un-

---

[97] See FOIA Update, Vol. VIII, No. 1, at 6.

[98] See id.; Carney v. United States Dep't of Justice, 19 F.3d 807, 814 (2d Cir. 1994) (stating relevant to consider subject matter of fee waiver request); Larson v. CIA, 843 F.2d 1481, 1483 (D.C. Cir. 1988) (noting character of information proper factor to consider); see also Gray v. USDA, No. 91-1383, slip op. at 3 (D.D.C. Nov. 25, 1991) (explaining that no showing that minute amount of relevant information that may be found among masses of irrelevant material will enlighten public understanding of agency's operations); Conklin v. United States, 654 F. Supp. 1104, 1106 (D. Colo. 1987) (finding mere allegations of agency "oppression" did not justify fee waiver under predecessor fee waiver standard); AFGE v. United States Dep't of Commerce, 632 F. Supp. 1272, 1278 (D.D.C. 1986) (stating union's allegations of malfeasance too ephemeral to warrant waiver of search fees without further evidence that informative material will be found), aff'd on other grounds, 907 F.2d 203 (D.C. Cir. 1990).

[99] See Sierra Club Legal Defense Fund, No. 93-35383, slip op. at 4 (9th Cir. Aug. 29, 1994) (determining that plaintiff failed to explain "how its work would add anything to 'public understanding'" where requested material already widely disseminated and publicized); Carney, 19 F.3d at 815 (observing that "where records are readily available from other sources . . . further disclosure by the agency will not significantly contribute to public understanding"); McClellan, 835 F.2d at 1286 (recognizing new information has more potential to contribute to public understanding); Sloman, 832 F. Supp. at 68 (stating public's understanding would not be enhanced to a significant extent where material was previously released to other writers and "more important[ly]" available in agency's public reading room "where public has access and has used the information extensively"); Durham v. United States Dep't of Justice, 829 F. Supp. 428, 434-35 (D.D.C. 1993) (denying fee waiver for 2340 pages of public court records), appeal dismissed for failure to timely file, No. 93-5354 (D.C. Cir. Nov. 29, 1994); Harrison v. United States Nat'l Archives, No. 93-0448, slip op. at 1-2 (D.D.C. May 21, 1993) (upholding agency denial of fee waiver request on voluminous amount of JFK assassination records already released under FOIA and available through NARA); FOIA Update, Vol. VIII, No. 1, at 7; cf. Tax Analysts v. United States Dep't of Justice, 965 F.2d 1092, 1094-96 (D.C. Cir. 1992) (finding that news organization not entitled to attorney fees because, inter alia, requested information was already in public domain). But see Campbell v. United States Dep't of Justice, 164 F.3d 20, 35 (D.C. Cir. 1998) (remanding case for reconsideration of grant of partial fee waiver, but "declin[ing] to hold that the FBI cannot charge . . . any copying fees"; finding agency's fee waiver analysis "flawed" with regard to summaries

(continued...)

**FEES AND FEE WAIVERS**

der existing case law, however, there is no clear consensus yet as to what "is and what is not" considered information in the public domain.[100] As a further consideration, agency records that are created through a public process may not warrant a fee waiver.

    3. Third, the disclosure must contribute to the understanding of the public at large, as opposed to the individual understanding of the requester or a narrow segment of interested persons.[101] In the past, courts have generally

---

[99] (...continued)
of public domain information, information that was repetitious but not asserted to be duplicative, and nonsubstantive administrative information); Judicial Watch, No. 97-2869, slip op. at 4 (D.D.C. Aug. 25, 1998) (while accepting that information sought by requester was "not necessarily all new," nevertheless concluding that it had "high potential" for contributing to public understanding); Sinito v. United States Dep't of Justice, No. 87-814, slip op. at 4-5 (D.D.C. Feb. 13, 1991) (stating that although documents did not appear to add to information already disclosed in media, they were likely to contribute to public's understanding of government activities).

[100] Schrecker v. Department of Justice, 970 F. Supp. 49, 50 (D.D.C. 1997). Compare Conner v. CIA, No. 84-3625, slip op. at 2 (D.D.C. Jan. 31, 1986) (upholding denial of fee waiver for records available in agency's public reading room), appeal dismissed for lack of prosecution, No. 86-5221 (D.C. Cir. Jan. 23, 1987), and Blakey v. Department of Justice, 549 F. Supp. 362, 364-65 (D.D.C. 1982) (applying same principle under previous statutory fee waiver standard), aff'd, 720 F.2d 215 (D.C. Cir. 1983) (unpublished table decision), with Friends of the Coast Fork v. United States Dep't of the Interior, 110 F.3d 53, 55 (9th Cir. 1997) (holding that availability in agency's public reading room alone does not justify denial of fee waiver), Carney, 19 F.3d at 815 (finding that mere fact records released to others does not mean same information is readily available to public), Judicial Watch, No. 97-2869, slip op. at 4 (D.D.C. Aug 25, 1998) (same), and Fitzgibbon v. Agency for Int'l Dev., 724 F. Supp. 1048, 1051 & n.10 (D.D.C. 1989) (stating that agencies failed to demonstrate "public's understanding" of publicly available information in public reading rooms and reports to Congress).

[101] See Carney, 19 F.3d at 814 (observing that relevant inquiry is "whether requester will disseminate the disclosed records to a reasonably broad audience of persons interested in the subject"); Wagner v. United States Dep't of Justice, No. 86-5477, slip op. at 2 (D.C. Cir. Mar. 24, 1987) (reiterating that general public must benefit from release); Cox v. O'Brien, No. 86-1639, slip op. at 2 (D.D.C. Dec. 16, 1986) (finding fee waiver denial proper when prisoners, not general public, would be beneficiaries of information pertaining to wholesalers for prison commissary); Crooker v. Department of the Army, 577 F. Supp. 1220, 1223 (D.D.C. 1984) (rejecting fee waiver under previous standard for information of interest to "a small segment of the scientific community," which would not "benefit the public at large"), appeal dismissed as frivolous, No. 84-5089 (D.C. Cir. June 22, 1984); see also NTEU, 811 F.2d at 648 (rejecting "union's suggestion that its size insures that any benefit to it amounts to a public benefit"); Fazzini v. United States Dep't of Justice, No. 90 C 3303, 1991 WL 74649, at *5 (N.D. Ill. May 2, 1991) (requester cannot estab-
(continued...)

## FEES AND FEE WAIVERS

not defined the "public-at-large" to include the prison population.[102] More recently, courts have considered prisoners as the "public" within the meaning of the FOIA,[103] though the issue has not yet been conclusively decided. Further, whether the "public-at-large" encompasses only the population of the United States has not been clearly resolved by the courts either. Only one case has directly raised this issue, one in which it was held that disclosure to a foreign news syndicate that publishes only in Canada satisfies the requirement that it contribute to "public understanding."[104]

As the proper focus must be on the benefit to be derived by the public, any personal benefit to be derived by the requester, or the requester's particular financial situation, are not factors entitling him or her to a fee waiver.[105]

---

[101](...continued) lish public benefit merely by alleging he has "corresponded" with members of media and intends to share requested information with them), summary affirmance granted, No. 91-2219 (7th Cir. July 26, 1991).

[102] See, e.g., Wagner, No. 86-5477, slip op. at 2 (D.C. Cir. Mar. 24, 1987) (stating that general public must benefit from release); Cox, No. 86-1639, slip op. at 2 (D.D.C. Dec. 16, 1986) (upholding denial of fee waiver where prisoners, not general public, would be beneficiaries of release).

[103] See Van Fripp, No. 97-0159, slip op. at 8 (D.D.C. Mar. 16, 2000) (construing term "public" to include those who are incarcerated); Linn v. United States Dep't of Justice, No. 92-1406, 1995 WL 631847, at *14 (D.D.C. Aug. 22, 1995) (rejecting agency's position that dissemination to prison population is not to public-at-large; statute makes no distinction between incarcerated and nonincarcerated public).

[104] Southam News v. INS, 674 F. Supp. 881, 892-93 (D.D.C. 1987). But cf. NLRB v. Robbins Tire & Rubber Co., 437 U.S. 214, 242 (1978) (observing that basic purpose of FOIA is "to hold the governors accountable to the governed").

[105] See, e.g., McClain v. United States Dep't of Justice, 13 F.3d 220, 220-21 (7th Cir. 1993) (stating that fee waiver inappropriate when requester sought to serve private interest rather than "public understanding of operations or activities of the government"); Allnutt v. United States Dep't of Justice, No. Y98-1722, 2000 U.S. Dist. LEXIS 4060, at **18-19 & n.9 (D. Md. Mar. 6, 2000) (observing that notwithstanding plaintiff's passionate statement, plaintiff failed to establish that public would benefit from release of records pertaining to his own bankruptcy case); Nance, 1992 WL 23655, at *2 n.2 (D.D.C. Jan. 24, 1992) (holding that fee waiver inappropriate when only purpose for seeking records is collateral attack on criminal conviction); Crooker, 577 F. Supp. at 1223-24 (finding that prison inmate's intent to write book about brother's connection with dangerous toxin not considered benefit to public). But see Johnson v. United States Dep't of Justice, No. 89-2842, slip op. at 3 (D.D.C. May 2, 1990) (stressing that death-row prisoner seeking previously unreleased and possibly exculpatory information entitled to partial fee waiver because potential "miscarriage of justice . . . is a matter of great public interest"), summary judgment granted, 758 F. Supp. 2, 5 (D.D.C. 1991) (holding, ultimately,

(continued...)

## FEES AND FEE WAIVERS

Indeed, it is well settled that indigence alone, without a showing of a public benefit, is insufficient to warrant a fee waiver.[106]

Additionally, agencies should evaluate the identity and qualifications of the requester--e.g., expertise in the subject area of the request and ability and intention to disseminate the information to the public--in order to determine whether the public would benefit from disclosure to that requester.[107] Special

---

[105](...continued)
that FBI not required to review records or to forego FOIA exemption for possibly exculpatory information); see also Pederson, 847 F. Supp. at 856 (concluding that requester's personal interest in disclosure of requested information did not undercut fee waiver request when requester established existence of concurrent public interest); cf. Harper v. DOD, No. 93-35876, 1995 WL 392032, at *2 (9th Cir. July 3, 1995) (explaining prisoner presented no evidence that requested technical reports might contain exculpatory material which would entitle him to consideration for fee waiver).

[106] See, e.g., Wagner, No. 86-5477, slip op. at 2 (D.C. Cir. Mar. 24, 1987) (stating "indigency does not ipso facto require a fee waiver"); Ely, 753 F.2d at 165 ("Congress rejected a fee waiver provision for indigents."); Durham, 829 F. Supp. at 435 n.10 (finding indigence alone does not constitute adequate grounds for fee waiver); Rodriguez-Estrada v. United States, No. 92-2360, slip op. at 2 (D.D.C. Apr. 16, 1993) (explaining no entitlement to fee waiver on basis of in forma pauperis status under 28 U.S.C. § 1915 (1994 & Supp. II 1996)); Crooker, 577 F. Supp. at 1224 (holding indigence alone does not automatically entitle requester to fee waiver); see also S. Conf. Rep. No. 93-1200, at 8 (1974), reprinted in 1974 U.S.C.C.A.N. 6285, 6287 (specific fee waiver provision for indigents eliminated; "such matters are properly the subject for individual agency determination in regulations").

[107] See, e.g., McClain, 13 F.3d at 221 (stating fee waiver must be assessed in light of identity and objectives of requester); Larson, 843 F.2d at 1483 & n.5 (holding inability to disseminate information alone is sufficient basis for denying fee waiver request; requester cannot rely on tenuous link to newspaper); Van Fripp, No. 97-0159, slip op. at 11-12 (D.D.C. Mar. 16, 2000) (finding that "it is plaintiff's burden to disseminate the requested information to the public and not, merely, to make it available"); Slater, 1999 U.S. Dist. LEXIS 8399, at *14 (stating that plaintiff bears burden of establishing capacity to disseminate requested information); Judicial Watch, No. 97-2089, slip op. at 13 (D.D.C. July 14, 1998) (finding failure to establish intent and ability to convey information to public fatal to requester's fee waiver request); Anderson, No. 93-253, slip op. at 4 (W.D. Pa. May 11, 1995) (finding requester's inability to disseminate fatal to fee waiver); Larson v. CIA, 644 F. Supp. 15, 19 n.3 (D.D.C. 1987) (stating that "even if" appropriately before court, it would reject letter from newspaper to requester indicating interest in "anything you get" on subject of request "as evidence of [requester's] ability to disseminate" because "such a rule would enable requesters to avoid fees simply by asserting an intention to give released documents to a newspaper"), aff'd, 843 F.2d 1481 (D.C. Cir. 1988); cf. Wilson v. CIA, No. 91-0087, slip op. at 2 (D.D.C. Nov. 5, 1991) (noting plaintiff's failure to demonstrate intent and ability to disseminate information no impediment to filing revised and perfected request). But
(continued...)

## FEES AND FEE WAIVERS

ized knowledge may be required to extract, synthesize, and effectively convey the information to the public and requesters vary in their ability to do so.[108] Although established representatives of the news media, as defined in the OMB Fee Guidelines,[109] should readily be able to meet this aspect of the statutory requirement by showing their connection to a ready means of effective dissemination,[110] other requesters should be required to describe with greater substantiation their expertise in the subject area and their ability and intention to disseminate the information.[111]

Some decisions under the former fee waiver standard suggested that journalists should presumptively be granted fee waivers.[112] The Department

---

[107](...continued)
cf. Linn v. United States Dep't of Justice, No. 92-1406, 1997 WL 577586, at *6 (D.D.C. May 29, 1997) (granting fee waiver when agency failed to challenge requester's "claimed ability to disseminate" and when administrative record gave court no reason to doubt requester's representations concerning same), appeal voluntarily dismissed, No. 97-5122 (D.C. Cir. July 14, 1997).

[108] See McClellan, 835 F.2d at 1286 (observing that fee waiver request gave no indication of requesters' ability to understand and process information nor whether they intended to actually disseminate it); Klamath Water Users Protective Ass'n, No. 96-3077, slip op. at 47 (D. Or. June 19, 1997) (stating that requester provided insufficient information to establish its ability to understand, make use of, and disseminate requested information); S.A. Ludsin, 1997 U.S. Dist. LEXIS 8617, at *16 (finding requester's intention to make raw appraisal data available on computer network, without analysis, to be insufficient to meet public interest requirement); see also FOIA Update, Vol. VIII, No. 1, at 7.

[109] 52 Fed. Reg. 10,011, 10,018 (1987); cf. National Sec. Archive, 880 F.2d at 1387 (elaborating on OMB definition of news media representative to include requester organization).

[110] See FOIA Update, Vol. VIII, No. 1, at 8 & n.5.

[111] See id.; see also, e.g., Oglesby, 920 F.2d at 66 n.11 (explaining that requester's assertion that he was writer and had disseminated in past, coupled with bare statement of public interest, was insufficient to meet statutory standard); McClellan, 835 F.2d at 1286-87 (stating agency may request additional information; 23 questions not burdensome); Burriss v. CIA, 524 F. Supp. 448, 449 (M.D. Tenn. 1981) (holding that denial of plaintiff's fee waiver request "based upon mere representation that he is a researcher who plans to write a book" was not abuse of discretion). But see Carney, 19 F.3d at 815 (noting that while requester had only tentative book publication plans, "fact that he is working on a related dissertation is sufficient evidence . . . that his book will be completed").

[112] See NTEU, 811 F.2d at 649; Goldberg v. United States Dep't of State, No. 85-1496, slip op. at 3-4 (D.D.C. Apr. 29, 1986), modified (D.D.C. July 25, 1986); Badhwar v. United States Dep't of the Air Force, 615 F. Supp. 698, 708 (D.D.C. 1985); Rosenfeld v. United States Dep't of Justice, No. C-85-2247, slip op. at 4-5 (N.D. Cal. Oct. 29, 1985), motion for reconsideration denied (N.D.

(continued...)

# FEES AND FEE WAIVERS

of Justice encourages agencies to give special weight to journalistic credentials under this factor,[113] though the statute provides no specific presumption that journalistic status alone is to be dispositive under the fee waiver standard overall and such a presumption would run counter to the 1986 amendments that set forth a special fee category for representatives of the news media.[114] (For a discussion of news media requesters in the context of attorney fee awards under the FOIA, see Tax Analysts v. United States Department of Justice[115] and Litigation Considerations, Attorney Fees and Litigation Costs, below.)

Further, the requirement that a requester demonstrate a contribution to the understanding of the public at large is not satisfied simply because a fee waiver request is made by a library or other record repository, or by a requester who intends merely to disseminate the information to such an institution.[116] Requests that make no showing of how the information would be disseminated, other than through passively making it available to anyone who might seek access to it, do not meet the burden of demonstrating with particularity that the information will be communicated to the public.[117] These requests,

---

[112](...continued)
Cal. Mar. 25, 1986).

[113] See FOIA Update, Vol. VIII, No. 1, at 8; accord FOIA Update, Vol. IV, No. 4, at 14.

[114] 5 U.S.C. § 552(a)(4)(A)(ii)(II); OMB Fee Guidelines, 52 Fed. Reg. at 10,019; see also McClain, 13 F.3d at 221 (dictum) (concluding that status as newspaper or nonprofit institution does not lead to automatic waiver of fee); cf. Sierra Club Legal Defense Fund, No. 93-35383, slip op. at 4 (9th Cir. Aug. 29, 1994) (explaining that status as public interest law firm does not entitle requester to fee waiver); National Sec. Archive, 880 F.2d at 1383 (dictum) (observing that fee waiver decisions are to be made on "case-by-case" basis); McClellan, 835 F.2d at 1284 (stating legislative history makes plain that "public interest" groups must satisfy statutory test); Judicial Watch, No. 97-2089, slip op. at 13 (D.D.C. July 14, 1998) (emphasizing that requester's mere status as public interest group does not entitle it to fee waiver); National Wildlife Fed'n, No. 95-017-BU, slip op. at 3-4 (D. Mont. July 15, 1996) (finding that public interest groups must satisfy statutory test; requester not entitled to fee waiver solely because of status as large conservation organization).

[115] 965 F.2d at 1095-96 (holding that litigant's status as news organization does not render award of attorney fees automatic).

[116] See FOIA Update, Vol. VIII, No. 1, at 8.

[117] See, e.g., Van Fripp, No. 97-0159, slip op. at 12 (D.D.C. Mar. 16, 2000) (emphasizing that placement in library amounts to, "at best, a passive method of distribution" that does not establish entitlement to fee waiver); Klamath Water Users Protective Ass'n, No. 96-3077, slip op. at 47 (D. Or. June 19, 1997) (finding placement in library insufficient in itself to establish entitlement to fee waiver); cf. S.A. Ludsin, 1997 U.S. Dist. LEXIS 8617, at *16 (indicating that requester, who intended merely to make raw appraisal data available in electronic form, failed to explain how disclosure would provide expla-
(continued...)

## FEES AND FEE WAIVERS

like those of other requesters, should be analyzed to identify a particular person who actually will use the requested information in scholarly or other analytic work and then disseminate it to the general public.[118]

4. Lastly, the disclosure must contribute "significantly" to public understanding of government operations or activities. To warrant a waiver or reduction of fees, the public's understanding of the subject matter in question, as compared to the level of public understanding existing prior to the disclosure, must be likely to be enhanced by the disclosure to a significant extent.[119] Such a determination must be an objective one; agencies are not permitted to make separate value judgments as to whether any information that would in fact contribute significantly to public understanding of government operations or activities is "important" enough to be made public.[120]

Once an agency determines that the "public interest" requirement for a fee waiver has been met, the statutory standard's second requirement calls for the agency to determine whether "disclosure of the information . . . is not primarily in the commercial interest of the requester."[121] In order to decide whether this requirement has been satisfied, agencies should consider the following two factors in sequence:

1. First, an agency must determine as a threshold matter whether the

---

[117](...continued) nation to public about government activities); see also FOIA Update, Vol. VIII, No. 1, at 8.

[118] See FOIA Update, Vol. VIII, No. 1, at 8.

[119] See Sierra Club Legal Defense Fund, No. 93-35383, slip op. at 4 (9th Cir. Aug. 29, 1994) (concluding requester failed to explain how disclosure to it "would add anything to 'public understanding' in light of vast amount of material already disseminated and publicized"); Carney, 19 F.3d at 815 (observing when requested records readily available from other sources, further disclosure will not significantly contribute to public understanding); D.C. Technical Assistance Org. v. HUD, 85 F. Supp. 2d 46, 49 (D.D.C. 2000) (noting that while plaintiff demonstrated ability to disseminate information, it failed to establish that disclosure would contribute significantly to public's understanding of government activities or operations); Dollinger, No. 95-CV-6174T, slip op. at 5-6 (W.D.N.Y. Aug. 24, 1995) (finding that routine, generic information "lacks substantial informative value" and would not significantly contribute to public understanding); Sloman, 832 F. Supp. at 68 (stating information previously released to other writers and "more important[ly]" available in agency's reading room will not contribute significantly to public understanding of operations of government). But see Pederson, 847 F. Supp. at 855 (finding that despite requesters' failure to specifically assert such significance, widespread media attention referenced in appeal letter sufficient to demonstrate information's significant contribution to public understanding).

[120] See Ettlinger v. FBI, 596 F. Supp. 867, 875 (D. Mass. 1984); see also FOIA Update, Vol. VIII, No. 1, at 8.

[121] 5 U.S.C. § 552(a)(4)(A)(iii).

## FEES AND FEE WAIVERS

request involves any commercial interest of the requester which would be furthered by the disclosure.[122] A "commercial interest" is one that furthers a commercial, trade, or profit interest as those terms are commonly understood.[123] Information sought in furtherance of a tort claim for compensation or retribution for the requester is not considered to involve a "commercial interest."[124] However, not only profit-making corporations but also individuals or other organizations may have a commercial interest to be furthered by the disclosure, depending upon the circumstances involved.[125] Agencies may properly consider the requester's identity and the circumstances surrounding the request and draw reasonable inferences regarding the existence of a commercial interest.[126]

When a commercial interest is found to exist and that interest would be furthered by the requested disclosure, an agency must assess the magnitude of such interest in order subsequently to compare it to the "public interest" in disclosure.[127] In assessing the magnitude of the commercial interest, the agency should reasonably consider the extent to which the FOIA disclosure will serve the requester's identified commercial interest.[128]

2. Then an agency must balance the requester's commercial interest against the identified public interest in disclosure and determine which interest is "primary." A fee waiver or reduction must be granted when the public interest in disclosure is greater in magnitude than the requester's commercial

---

[122] See FOIA Update, Vol. VIII, No. 1, at 9.

[123] See id.; OMB Fee Guidelines, 52 Fed. Reg. at 10,017-18; cf. American Airlines, Inc. v. National Mediation Bd., 588 F.2d 863, 870 (2d Cir. 1978) (defining "commercial" in Exemption 4 as meaning anything "pertaining or relating to or dealing with commerce").

[124] See McClellan, 835 F.2d at 1285; cf. Detroit Free Press, Inc. v. Department of Justice, 73 F.3d 93, 98 (6th Cir. 1996) (stating, in context of attorney fees, that "'news interests should not be considered commercial interests'" when examining commercial benefit to requester (quoting Fenster v. Brown, 617 F.2d 740, 742 n.4 (D.C. Cir. 1979))).

[125] See OMB Guidelines, 52 Fed. Reg. at 10,013; FOIA Update, Vol. VIII, No. 1, at 9; see also Judicial Watch, No. 97-2869, slip op. at 5 (D.D.C. Aug. 25, 1998) (stating that nonprofit status "does not determine the character of the information"); cf. Critical Mass Energy Project v. NRC, 830 F.2d 278, 281 (D.C. Cir. 1987) (recognizing that entity's "non-profit status is not determinative" of commercial status) (Exemption 4 case).

[126] See FOIA Update, Vol. VIII, No. 1, at 9; cf. Tax Analysts, 965 F.2d at 1096 (clarifying that in context of attorney fees, status of requester as news organization does not "render[] irrelevant the news organization's other interests in the information").

[127] See FOIA Update, Vol. VIII, No. 1, at 9.

[128] See id.

## FEES AND FEE WAIVERS

interest.[129] Or, as one court phrased it when considering the balance to be struck under the predecessor fee waiver standard: "[In simple terms, the public should not foot the bill unless it will be the primary beneficiary of the [disclosure]."[130]

Although news gathering organizations ordinarily have a commercial interest in obtaining information, agencies may generally presume that when a news media requester has satisfied the "public interest" standard, that will be the primary interest served.[131] On the other hand, disclosure to private repositories of government records or data brokers may not be presumed to primarily serve the public interest; rather, requests on behalf of such entities can more readily be considered as primarily in their commercial interest, depending upon the nature of the records and their relation to the exact circumstances of the enterprise.[132]

When agencies analyze fee waiver requests by considering these six factors, they can rest assured that they have carried out their statutory obligation to determine whether a waiver is in the public interest.[133] When an agency has relied on factors unrelated to the public benefit standard to deny a fee waiver request, however, courts have found an abuse of discretion.[134] Additionally,

---

[129] See id.

[130] Burriss, 524 F. Supp. at 449.

[131] See FOIA Update, Vol. VIII, No. 1, at 10; see also National Sec. Archive, 880 F.2d at 1388 (requests from news media entities, in furtherance of their newsgathering function, are not for "commercial use").

[132] See FOIA Update, Vol. VIII, No. 1, at 10; see also National Sec. Archive, 880 F.2d at 1387-88.

[133] See FOIA Update, Vol. VIII, No. 1, at 10; cf. Oregon Natural Desert Ass'n v. United States Dep't of the Interior, 24 F. Supp. 2d 1088, 1095 (D. Or. 1998) (finding that fee waiver denial must fail when agency did not fully follow its multifactor regulation); Friends of the Coast Fork, 110 F.3d at 55 (emphasizing that where agency's regulations provide for multifactor test, inappropriate to rely solely on single factor).

[134] See, e.g., Goldberg, No. 85-1496, slip op. at 3-5 (D.D.C. Apr. 29, 1986) (holding that agency policy of granting waiver of search fees but not for duplication fees "both irrational and in violation of the statute"); Idaho Wildlife Fed'n v. United States Forest Serv., 3 Gov't Disclosure Serv. (P-H) ¶ 83,271, at 84,056 (D.D.C. July 21, 1983) (emphasizing that reliance on regulation that proscribes granting of fee waiver when records are sought for litigation is abuse of discretion because regulation is overbroad in that it ignores "public interest" in certain litigation); Diamond v. FBI, 548 F. Supp. 1158, 1160 (S.D.N.Y. 1982) (maintaining that agency may not decline to waive fees based merely upon perceived obligation to collect them); Common Cause v. IRS, 1 Gov't Disclosure Serv. (P-H) ¶ 79,188, at 79,351 (D.D.C. Nov. 8, 1979) (explaining IRS cannot deny requests for waiver of search fees simply on ground that search would be burdensome), aff'd, 646 F.2d 656 (D.C. Cir. 1981) (unpublished table decision); Eudey v. CIA, 478 F. Supp. 1175, 1177 (D.D.C. 1979)

(continued...)

# FEES AND FEE WAIVERS

when only some of the requested records satisfy the statutory test, a waiver should be granted for those records.[135]

An analysis of the foregoing factors routinely requires an agency to first assess the nature of the information likely to be released in response to an access request, because the statutory standard speaks to whether "disclosure" of the responsive information will significantly contribute to public understanding.[136] This assessment necessarily focuses on the information that would be disclosed,[137] which in turn logically requires an estimation of the applicability of any relevant FOIA exemption(s). Yet the extent to which an agency must establish at the fee waiver determination stage the precise contours of its anticipated withholdings was raised in Project on Military Procurement v. Department of the Navy,[138] when the district court seemed to suggest that an agency must defend the contemplated application of FOIA exemptions in the fee waiver context with an index pursuant to the requirements of Vaughn v. Rosen.[139]

Such a requirement not only was unprecedented, it is also unworkable--as it would compel an agency to actually process responsive records at the threshold fee waiver determination stage in order to compile the Vaughn Index; it would turn the normal, longstanding procedure for responding to FOIA/fee waiver requests on its head. Until a fee waiver determination has been made and (if a full fee waiver is not granted) the requester has agreed to pay all the assessable fees, the request is not yet ripe for processing because there has been no compliance with the fee requirements of the FOIA.[140] Be-

---

[134](...continued)
(stating agency may not consider quantity of documents to be released).

[135] See 28 C.F.R. § 16.11(k)(4) ("Where only some of the records to be released satisfy the requirements for a waiver of fees, a waiver shall be granted for those records."); cf. Samuel Gruber Educ. Project v. United States Dep't of Justice, 24 F. Supp. 2d 1, 2 (D.D.C. 1998) (upholding, without discussion, 70% fee waiver granted by agency). But see Schrecker, 970 F. Supp. at 50-51 (granting full fee waiver despite agency's determination that portion of requested information already was in public domain); cf. Campbell, 164 F.3d at 35 (finding fault with analysis used by agency to award partial fee waiver; remanding case for reconsideration but declining to hold that agency may not charge any fee).

[136] 5 U.S.C. § 552(a)(4)(A)(iii); see also, e.g., 28 C.F.R. 16.11(k)(2).

[137] Van Fripp, No. 97-159, slip op. at 10 (D.D.C. Mar. 16, 2000) (stating that "reviewing agencies and courts should consider . . . whether the disclosable portions of requested information are meaningfully informative in relation to the subject matter requested" (citing agency's fee waiver regulation)).

[138] 710 F. Supp. 362, 366-68 (D.D.C. 1989).

[139] 484 F.2d 820, 826-28 (D.C. Cir. 1973).

[140] See 5 U.S.C. § 552(a)(3); Pollack v. Department of Justice, 49 F.3d 115, 120 (4th Cir. 1995) (finding when requester refused to commit to pay fees,
(continued...)

## FEES AND FEE WAIVERS

cause the decision on this issue in Project on Military Procurement would yield impracticable results, it should not be followed. Agencies should retain the general discretion, though, to consider the cost-effectiveness of their investment of administrative resources in their fee waiver determinations[141] and should not impose any "unnecessary bureaucratic hurdles" in this area of FOIA administration.[142]

The FOIA does not specifically provide for administrative appeals of denials of requests for fee waivers. Nevertheless, many agencies, either by regulation or by practice, have appropriately considered appeals of such actions.[143] The Courts of Appeals for the Fifth and D.C. Circuits have made it clear, moreover, that administrative appeal exhaustion is required for any ad-

---

[140](...continued)
agency "had the authority to cease processing [his] request"); Vennes v. IRS, No. 89-5136, slip op. at 2-3 (8th Cir. Oct. 13, 1989) (explaining agency under no obligation to produce material until either requester agrees to pay fee or fee waiver approved); Irons v. FBI, 571 F. Supp. 1241, 1243 (D. Mass. 1983) (upholding regulation requiring payment of fees or waiver of fees before FOIA request is deemed to have been received); see also FOIA Update, Vol. XIX, No. 3, at 2 (advising agencies how to count requests closed for nonpayment of fees, for purposes of annual FOIA reports); cf. Johnston v. United States, No. 93-CV-5605, 1997 U.S. Dist. LEXIS 597, at *4 (E.D. Pa. Jan. 27, 1997) (upholding agency's decision to make availability of records contingent upon agreement to pay estimated fees); Nance, 1992 WL 23655, at *2 (reiterating that when fee waiver inappropriate and fees exceed $250, agency may refuse to begin search until requester makes advance payment). But see Carney, 19 F.3d at 815 (finding it not proper to deny fee waiver request on basis that records may have been exempt; fee waiver "should be evaluated on face of request"); see also Wilson v. CIA, No. 89-3356, slip op. at 3-4 (D.D.C. Mar. 25, 1991) (stating agency may not deny fee waiver request based upon "likelihood" that information will be withheld).

[141] See Rodriguez v. United States Postal Serv., No. 90-1886, slip op. at 3 n.1 (D.D.C. Oct. 2, 1991) (suggesting agency "consider" waiving de minimis fee despite requester's failure to comply with exhaustion requirement); FOIA Update, Vol. XVI, No. 1, at 1-2 (emphasizing cost-effective approaches to information disclosure).

[142] President's Memorandum for Heads of Departments and Agencies regarding the Freedom of Information Act, 29 Weekly Comp. Pres. Doc. 1999 (Oct. 4, 1993), reprinted in FOIA Update, Vol. XIV, No. 3, at 3; see also Attorney General's Memorandum for Heads of Departments and Agencies regarding the Freedom of Information Act (Oct. 4, 1993), reprinted in FOIA Update, Vol. XIV, No. 3, at 4-5.

[143] See, e.g., 28 C.F.R. § 16.9(a) ("If you are dissatisfied with [the agency's] response to your request, you may appeal an adverse determination denying your request"); see also, e.g., id. at § 16.6(c) (including in its listing of adverse determinations "a denial of a request for a fee waiver").

# FEES AND FEE WAIVERS

verse determination, including fee waiver denials.[144]

Prior to the 1986 FOIA amendments, the discretionary nature of the FOIA's fee waiver provision led the majority of courts to conclude that the proper standard for judicial review of an agency denial of a fee waiver is whether that decision was arbitrary and capricious,[145] in accordance with the Administrative Procedure Act.[146] This meant that a court could not "replace its own judgment for that of [an agency] without first concluding that the [agency's] decision was completely unreasonable and unfair."[147]

This standard was changed, however, when a specific judicial review provision was included in the FOIA,[148] which now provides for the review of agency fee waiver denials according to a de novo standard.[149] Yet this provision also explicitly provides that the scope of judicial review remains limited to the administrative record established before the agency,[150] and thus it is

---

[144] See Voinche v. United States Dep't of the Air Force, 983 F.2d 667, 669 (5th Cir. 1993) (emphasizing that requester seeking fee waiver under FOIA must exhaust administrative remedies before seeking judicial review); Oglesby, 920 F.2d at 66 & n.11, 71 ("Exhaustion does not occur until fees are paid or an appeal is taken from the refusal to waive fees."); see also AFGE, 907 F.2d at 209 (declining consideration of fee waiver request when not pursued during agency administrative proceeding); 28 C.F.R. § 16.9(c) (Department of Justice regulation providing for administrative appeal exhaustion before court review); cf. Campbell v. Unknown Power Superintendent of Flathead Irrigation & Power Project, No. 91-35104, slip op. at 3 (9th Cir. Apr. 22, 1992) (explaining exhaustion requirement not imposed when agency ignored fee waiver request).

[145] See NTEU, 811 F.2d at 647 (agency's denial of fee waiver will be upheld unless finding is arbitrary or capricious); Eudey, 478 F. Supp. at 1176; see also Ely, 753 F.2d at 165; Ettlinger, 596 F. Supp. at 871; cf. Walker v. IRS, No. 86-0073, 1986 WL 12049, at *2 (M.D. Pa. June 16, 1986) (noting that FOIA gives agency broad discretion to waive fees). But see Rizzo v. Tyler, 438 F. Supp. 895, 899 (S.D.N.Y. 1977) (observing that agency fee waiver denials were reviewed de novo).

[146] 5 U.S.C. §§ 701-06 (1994).

[147] Crooker, 577 F. Supp. at 1224.

[148] 5 U.S.C. § 552(a)(4)(A)(vii).

[149] See Campbell, 164 F.3d at 35 (stating that judicial review for action regarding wavier of fees is de novo); Schrecker, 970 F. Supp. at 50 (same).

[150] 5 U.S.C. § 552(a)(4)(A)(vii); see also, e.g., Campbell, 164 F.3d at 35 (observing that scope of review is limited to administrative record before agency); Friends of the Coast Fork, 110 F.3d at 55 (stating that court's consideration of fee waiver must be limited to administrative record before agency); Carney, 19 F.3d at 814 (same); AFGE, 907 F.2d at 209 (same); Anderson, No. 93-253, slip op. at 2 (W.D. Pa. May 11, 1995) (same; stating that new material not reviewed by agency cannot be given any weight); Linn, 1995 WL 631847, at *13
(continued...)

## FEES AND FEE WAIVERS

crucial that the agency's fee waiver denial letter create a comprehensive administrative record of <u>all</u> the reasons for the denial.[151]

A requester wishing to challenge an agency's denial of a fee waiver may seek judicial review of the agency's decision.[152] In this regard, agencies should also be aware that a challenge to an agency's fee waiver policy is not automatically rendered moot when the agency reverses itself and grants the specific fee waiver request; courts may still entertain challenges when they concern the legality of the standards used and not the belated grant of a fee waiver.[153]

Because the FOIA's current fee waiver provision still has received relatively limited interpretation by the courts,[154] it remains to be seen how novel issues of interpretation regarding its "public interest" standard will be adjudicated. For additional guidance on any particular fee waiver issue, agency

---

[150](...continued)
(same); Pederson, 847 F. Supp. at 854 (same).

[151] See, e.g., Friends of the Coast Fork, 110 F.3d at 55 (reiterating that agency's letter "must be reasonably calculated to put the requester on notice" as to reasons for fee waiver denial); NTEU, 811 F.2d at 648 (court may consider only information before the agency at time of decision); Larson, 843 F.2d at 1483 (information not part of administrative record may not be considered by district court when reviewing agency fee waiver denial); S.A. Ludsin, 1997 U.S. Dist. LEXIS 8617, at *16 (stating that court cannot consider reasons not provided by agency); Fitzgibbon, 724 F. Supp. at 1051 n.10 (finding government's "post hoc rationales" offered in response to lawsuit untimely); see also FOIA Update, Vol. VIII, No. 1, at 10; FOIA Update, Vol. VI, No. 1, at 6.

[152] See 5 U.S.C. § 552(a)(4)(B); see also, e.g., 28 C.F.R. § 16.9(b) (requiring agency to inform requester of right to judicial review of agency's adverse determination); id. at § 16.6(c) (adverse determinations include "a denial of a fee waiver request"); cf. Klein v. United States Patent & Trademark Office, No. 97-5285, 1998 U.S. App. LEXIS 4720, at *2 (D.C. Cir. Feb. 9, 1998) (holding that review of fee waiver denial may not be sought in appellate court in first instance); Kansi v. United States Dep't of Justice, 11 F. Supp. 2d 42, 43 (D.D.C. 1998) (refusing to consider fee waiver request when issue not raised in complaint and not adequately substantiated before agency).

[153] See Better Gov't Ass'n v. Department of State, 780 F.2d 86, 91-92 (D.C. Cir. 1986) (concluding that arguments concerning facial validity of fee waiver guidelines not moot when agency intends to apply same standards to future requests); Public Citizen v. OSHA, No. 86-705, slip op. at 2-3 (D.D.C. Aug. 5, 1987) (same); cf. Long v. ATF, 964 F. Supp. 464, 497-98 (D.D.C. 1997) (holding, in context of requester category, no "independent right" to such determination once fee waiver granted; status of requester found moot); Project on Military Procurement, 710 F. Supp. at 368 (finding no need to determine requester category where plaintiff entitled to fee waiver).

[154] See Anderson, No. 93-253, slip op. at 3 (W.D. Pa. May 11, 1995) (noting scant precedent applying statutory fee waiver standard); Hoffman, No. 90-0459, slip op. at 3 (D.D.C. Oct. 23, 1991) (observing that relatively little precedent exists that construes revised fee waiver standard).

# LITIGATION CONSIDERATIONS

FOIA officers may contact OIP's FOIA Counselor service, at (202) 514-3642.

## LITIGATION CONSIDERATIONS

A Freedom of Information Act lawsuit involves unique procedural and substantive concerns that even the experienced litigator might at first find bewildering. As one appellate court has frankly acknowledged: "Freedom of Information Act cases are peculiarly difficult."[1] To provide a general overview of FOIA litigation considerations, this discussion will follow a rough chronology of a typical FOIA lawsuit, from the threshold question of whether jurisdictional prerequisites have been met to the assessment of costs on appeal. It is important to bear in mind that, in accordance with the Attorney General's FOIA Memorandum of October 4, 1993, and as reinforced in the Attorney General's Follow-Up FOIA Memorandum of September 3, 1999, the Department of Justice "defend[s] the assertion of a FOIA exemption only in those cases where an agency reasonably foresees that disclosure would be harmful to an interest protected by that exemption."[2]

### Jurisdiction and Venue

The United States district courts are vested with exclusive jurisdiction over FOIA cases by section (a)(4)(B) of the Act, which provides in pertinent part:

> On complaint, the district court of the United States in the district in which the complainant resides, or has his principal place of business, or in which the agency records are situated, or in the District of Columbia, has jurisdiction to enjoin the agency from withholding agency records and to order the production of

---

[1] Miscavige v. IRS, 2 F.3d 366, 367 (11th Cir. 1993); see also Summers v. Department of Justice, 140 F.3d 1077, 1080 (D.C. Cir. 1998) (noting "peculiar nature of the FOIA").

[2] Attorney General's Memorandum for Heads of Departments and Agencies regarding the Freedom of Information Act (Oct. 4, 1993) [hereinafter Attorney General Reno's FOIA Memorandum], reprinted in FOIA Update, Vol. XIV, No. 3, at 4-5; see President's Memorandum for Heads of Departments and Agencies regarding the Freedom of Information Act, 29 Weekly Comp. Pres. Doc. 1999 (Oct. 4, 1993), reprinted in FOIA Update, Vol. XIV, No. 3, at 3 (explicitly referencing "litigation guidance issued by the Attorney General"); see also Attorney General's Follow-Up Memorandum for Heads of Departments and Agencies regarding the Freedom of Information Act (Sept. 3, 1999) [hereinafter Attorney General Reno's Follow-Up Memorandum], reprinted in FOIA Update, Vol. XIX, No. 4, at 3-5; (reiterating importance of "foreseeable harm" standard to federal agencies in order to promote further discretionary disclosure in agency decisionmaking); FOIA Update, Vol. XV, No. 4, at 7 (listing examples of discretionary disclosure and resulting disposition of litigation cases through process of Justice Department litigation review); FOIA Update, Vol. XV, No. 2, at 1 (summarizing Attorney General's speech on annual Freedom of Information Day).

**LITIGATION CONSIDERATIONS**

any agency records improperly withheld from the complainant.[3]

This provision has been held to govern judicial review under all three of the FOIA's access provisions.[4] Consequently, this language limits relief under the FOIA to disclosure of records to a particular requester;[5] it does not authorize a court to order publication of information, even information required to be published under subsection (a)(1) of the FOIA.[6] Nor does it appear to empower a court to order that agency records be made available for public inspection and copying in an agency reading room under subsection (a)(2).[7]

---

[3] 5 U.S.C. § 552(a)(4)(B) (1994 & Supp. IV 1998); see also Rogers v. United States, 15 Ct. Cl. 692, 698 (1988) (holding that there is no FOIA jurisdiction in Court of Claims).

[4] See Kennecott Utah Copper Corp. v. United States Dep't of the Interior, 88 F.3d 1191, 1202 (D.C. Cir. 1996) ("The 'judicial review provisions apply to requests for information under subsections (a)(1) and (a)(2) of section 552 as well as under subsection (a)(3).'" (quoting American Mail Line v. Gulick, 411 F.2d 696, 701 (D.C. Cir. 1969))).

[5] See Kennecott, 88 F.3d at 1202-03 (holding that remedial provision of FOIA limits relief to ordering disclosure of documents); see also Green v. NARA, 992 F. Supp. 811, 817 (E.D. Va. 1998) (concluding that unless agency records have been improperly withheld, "'a district court lacks jurisdiction to devise remedies to force an agency to comply with FOIA's disclosure requirements'" (quoting United States Dep't of Justice v. Tax Analysts, 492 U.S. 136, 142 (1989))). But cf. Pennsylvania Dep't of Pub. Welfare v. United States, No. 99-175, 1999 WL 1051963, at *2 (W.D. Pa. Oct. 12, 1999) (suggesting that "[Administrative Procedure Act] review is available to enforce provisions of the FOIA for which the FOIA provides no express remedy"); Public Citizen v. Lew, No. 97-2891, slip op. at 4 (D.D.C. July 14, 1998) (refusing to dismiss claim alleging noncompliance with FOIA requirement to publish descriptions of "major information systems" compiled under Paperwork Reduction Act, 44 U.S.C. §§ 3501-20 (1994 & Supp. III 1997), because, even in the absence of an express judicial review provision in the FOIA, the Administrative Procedure Act, 5 U.S.C. § 704 (1994), provides a "strong presumption that Congress intend[ed] judicial review of administrative action").

[6] See Kennecott, 88 F.3d at 1203 ("We think it significant, however, that § 552(a)(4)(B) is aimed at relieving the injury suffered by the individual complainant, not by the general public. It allows district courts to order 'the production of any agency records improperly withheld from the complainant,' not agency records withheld from the public." (quoting 5 U.S.C. § 552(a)(4)(B) (emphasis added by court))).

[7] See id.; see also Tax Analysts v. IRS, 117 F.3d 607, 610 (D.C. Cir. 1997) (treating as "conceded for the purposes of this case only" that sole remedy under section 552(a)(4)(B) is order directing agency to produce records to complaining party). But see Stanley v. DOD, No. 98-4116, slip op. at 5 (S.D. Ill. June 22, 1999) (going so far as to suggest that jurisdictional clause of FOIA is "meaningless" unless court can enjoin agency from withholding records that are required to be made available in reading room) (appeal pending); Tax An-
(continued...)

## LITIGATION CONSIDERATIONS

This statutory language, as the Supreme Court ruled in <u>Kissinger v. Reporters Committee for Freedom of the Press</u>, makes federal jurisdiction

> dependent upon a showing that an agency has (1) "improperly"; (2) "withheld"; (3) "agency records." Judicial authority to devise remedies and enjoin agencies can only be invoked, under the jurisdiction grant conferred by § 552, if the agency has contravened all three components of this obligation.[8]

Some courts have given the Supreme Court's language a literal reading, taking this statement to mean that a plaintiff who does not allege any improper withholding of agency records fails to state a claim for which a court has subject matter jurisdiction under Federal Rule of Civil Procedure 12(b)(1).[9] However, in affirming a district court holding that a particular White House office is not an "agency" for FOIA purposes, the Court of Appeals for the District of Columbia Circuit concluded that the district court had incorrectly dismissed that action for lack of subject matter jurisdiction.[10] Rather, the D.C.

---

[7](...continued)
alysts v. IRS, No. 94-923, 1998 WL 419755, at **4-6 (D.D.C. May 1, 1998) (ordering disclosure of exceptionally large volume of records upon remand and also ordering uniquely fashioned remedy that, in accordance with 5 U.S.C. § 552(a)(2)(D), such FOIA-processed records be placed in reading room on weekly basis as they are processed), <u>appeal voluntarily dismissed</u>, No. 98-5252 (D.C. Cir. Aug. 11, 1998).

[8] 445 U.S. 136, 150 (1980).

[9] <u>See, e.g.</u>, <u>Martin v. United States Dep't of Justice</u>, No. 96-2866, slip op. at 4 (D.D.C. Dec. 15, 1999) (dismissing portion of complaint for lack of subject matter jurisdiction where no FOIA request was made (and thus no records could have been improperly withheld)); <u>Shafmaster Fishing Co. v. United States</u>, 814 F. Supp. 182, 184 (D.N.H. 1993) ("The court thus lacks subject matter jurisdiction if the information was properly withheld under FOIA exemptions."); <u>National Fed'n of Fed. Employees v. United States</u>, No. 87-2284, slip op. at 39 (D.D.C. May 27, 1988) (The FOIA "authorizes this Court only to 'enjoin the agency from withholding agency records and to order the production of any agency records improperly withheld.'" (quoting 5 U.S.C. § 552(a)(4)(B))); <u>see also</u> <u>Unigard Ins. Co. v. Department of the Treasury</u>, 997 F. Supp. 1339, 1341 (S.D. Cal. 1997) ("The court presumes a lack of jurisdiction until the party asserting [it] proves otherwise."). <u>But see</u> <u>Payne Enters. v. United States</u>, 837 F.2d 486, 490-92 (D.C. Cir. 1988) (finding repeated, unacceptably long agency delays in providing nonexempt information sufficient to create jurisdiction); <u>Public Citizen v. Office of the United States Trade Representative</u>, 804 F. Supp. 385, 387 (D.D.C. 1992) (deciding that court has jurisdiction to consider "agency's policy to withhold temporarily, on a regular basis, certain types of documents").

[10] <u>Sweetland v. Walters</u>, 60 F.3d 852, 855 (D.C. Cir. 1995) (citing both <u>Haddon v. Walters</u>, 43 F.3d 1488, 1490 (D.C. Cir. 1995) (Title VII case), and <u>Kleiman v. Department of Energy</u>, 956 F.2d 335, 339 (D.C. Cir. 1992) (Privacy Act case)); <u>see also</u> <u>Griffith v. IRS</u>, No. 95-20526, 1995 WL 853038 at *1 (N.D....
(continued...)

## LITIGATION CONSIDERATIONS

Circuit ruled that dismissal should have been grounded solely on a failure to state a claim upon which relief could be granted, pursuant to Federal Rule of Civil Procedure 12(b)(6).[11] Were Kissinger to be applied otherwise, all FOIA cases resolved in favor of the government would ultimately be dismissed for lack of subject matter jurisdiction, which clearly has not been the case in practice.[12] (See the discussion under Litigation Considerations, Summary Judgment, below.)

In a companion case to Kissinger, the Supreme Court elaborated upon the definition of "agency records," explaining that "an agency must first either create or obtain a record as a prerequisite to its becoming an 'agency record' within the meaning of the FOIA."[13] Subsequently, in United States Department of Justice v. Tax Analysts, the Supreme Court further refined the "agency record" definition by requiring that a record be in the agency's possession for official purposes at the time of the FOIA request.[14] The Electronic Free-

---

[10](...continued)
Cal. Dec. 14, 1995) (reasoning that whether responsive agency records exist "is a factual question, not a jurisdictional question").

[11] Sweetland, 60 F.3d at 855 (concluding that "district court has jurisdiction over substantive claims arising under laws of [the] United States" (citing Haddon, 43 F.3d at 1490)); Williams v. Reno, No. 95-5155, 1996 WL 460093, at *2 (D.C. Cir. Aug. 7, 1996) ("[T]he district court has subject matter jurisdiction over FOIA claims."); Mace v. EEOC, 37 F. Supp. 2d 1144, 1146 (E.D. Mo.) (concluding that court had jurisdiction to hear plaintiff's complaint but, because agency properly withheld record, holding that court lacked further jurisdiction to grant relief), aff'd, 197 F.3d 329 (8th Cir. 1999); see also Hart v. FBI, No. 95-2110, 1996 WL 403016, at *3 n.11 (7th Cir. July 16, 1996) (although plaintiff's "los[s] on the merits does not retroactively revoke a district court's jurisdiction," district court's grant of summary judgment to government deprived it of further jurisdiction to act); Prado v. Ilchert, No. 95-1497, 1997 WL 383239, at *3 (N.D. Cal. June 10, 1997) (dismissing, for failure to state claim upon which relief can be granted under FOIA, when agency to whom request was made lacked responsive records); cf. Kennecott, 88 F.3d at 1202 (dismissing, for lack of jurisdiction, claim seeking court-ordered publication of information, when court concluded that no such remedy exists under FOIA).

[12] See Torres v. CIA, 39 F. Supp. 2d 960, 962 n.3 (N.D. Ill. 1999) (suggesting that government's summary judgment motion predicated on lack of jurisdiction was "an imprecise use of the notion of 'jurisdiction' . . . [and if] CIA's position were sound, no court could ever decide a FOIA case in favor of a governmental defendant on the merits, for it would lose jurisdiction as soon as it found that no documents responsive to a plaintiff's FOIA request had been improperly withheld").

[13] Forsham v. Harris, 445 U.S. 169, 182 (1980), overruled in part by Omnibus Consolidated and Emergency Supplemental Appropriations Act for Fiscal Year 1999, Pub. L. No. 105-277, 112 Stat. 2681 (1998) (making certain research data generated by private federal grantees subject to FOIA requests).

[14] 492 U.S. 136, 145 (1989); see also Morris v. Commissioner, No. F-97-
(continued...)

## LITIGATION CONSIDERATIONS

dom of Information Act Amendments of 1996[15] for the first time defined the term "record" to include "any information that would be an agency record subject to the [FOIA] when maintained by an agency in any format, including an electronic format."[16] This definition thus seems to broadly encompass within the concept of "agency record" the information maintained by agencies in electronic form.[17] Of course, the FOIA provides no jurisdiction over records other than those of a federal agency.[18] (For further discussions of the terms "agency" and "agency records," see Procedural Requirements, Entities Subject to the FOIA, above, and Procedural Requirements, Agency Records, above.)

Whether an agency has "improperly" withheld records usually turns on the application of one or more exemptions applied to the documents at is-

---

[14] (...continued)
5031, 1997 U.S. Dist. LEXIS 21030, at *4 (E.D. Cal. Nov. 19, 1997) (finding that request for determination of tax status "was not a request for a document in existence" and thus not "a valid FOIA request"). But see OMB Circular A-110, "Uniform Administrative Requirements for Grants and Agreements with Institutions of Higher Education, Hospitals, and Other Non-Profit Organizations," 64 Fed. Reg. 54,926 (1999) (requiring agencies to respond to FOIA requests for certain grantee research data by first obtaining that data from grantee, in implementation of Omnibus Consolidated and Emergency Supplemental Appropriations Act for Fiscal Year 1999).

[15] Pub. L. No. 104-231, 110 Stat. 3048.

[16] 5 U.S.C. § 552(f)(2).

[17] See FOIA Update, Vol. XVII, No. 4, at 2.

[18] See, e.g., McDonnell v. Clinton, No. 97-5179, 1997 WL 812536, at *1 (D.C. Cir. Dec. 29, 1997) (dismissing FOIA complaint brought solely against the President); Ortez v. Washington County, 88 F.3d 804, 811 (9th Cir. 1996) (dismissing FOIA claims against county and county officials); Ferguson v. Alabama Criminal Justice Info. Ctr., 962 F. Supp. 1446, 1447 (M.D. Ala. Apr. 23, 1997) ("5 U.S.C. §§ 552 and 552a, however, do not apply to state agencies."); Anderson v. Federal Pub. Defender, No. 95-1485, slip op. at 1 (D.D.C. Mar. 28, 1996) (The "Federal Public Defender is not an agency subject to the requirements of the Freedom of Information Act."); Mamarella v. County of Westchester, 898 F. Supp. 236, 237-38 (S.D.N.Y. 1995) (disallowing FOIA claim against state or local agencies or against individuals). See generally Price v. County of San Diego, 165 F.R.D. 614, 620 (S.D. Cal. 1996) (emphasizing that the FOIA applies only "to authorities of the Government of the United States").

## LITIGATION CONSIDERATIONS

sue.[19] Of course, if the agency can establish that no responsive records exist,[20] or that all responsive records have been released to the requester,[21] the agen-

---

[19] See Tax Analysts, 492 U.S. at 151 (generalizing that "agency records which do not fall within one of the exemptions are improperly withheld"); Abraham & Rose, P.L.C. v. United States, 138 F.2d 1075, 1078 (6th Cir. 1998) (indicating that agency denying FOIA request bears burden of establishing that requested information falls within exemption and remanding case for consideration of appropriate exemptions).

[20] See, e.g., Jones v. FBI, 41 F.3d 238, 249 (6th Cir. 1994) (finding no remedy for records destroyed prior to FOIA request); Cal-Almond, Inc. v. USDA, 960 F.2d 105, 108-09 (9th Cir. 1992) (adjudging that absent improper conduct by government, FOIA does not require recreation of destroyed records); Ray v. United States Dep't of Justice, 908 F.2d 1549, 1558-59 (11th Cir. 1990) (ruling that search that produced information about 384 out of 582 interviews was "diligent"), rev'd on other grounds sub nom. United States Dep't of State v. Ray, 502 U.S. 164 (1991); Kuffel v. United States Bureau of Prisons, 882 F. Supp. 1116, 1120 (D.D.C. 1995) (dismissing complaint because no records were located after "good faith, reasonable search"); Bartlett v. United States Dep't of Justice, 867 F. Supp. 314, 316 (E.D. Pa. 1994) (dismissing case for lack of jurisdiction after finding that "plaintiff's request seeks presently nonexistent material[;] therefore [it] does not seek a record within the meaning of the FOIA"); Folstad v. Board of Governors of the Fed. Reserve Sys., No. 1:99-124, 1999 U.S. Dist. LEXIS 17852, at *5 (W.D. Mich. Nov. 16, 1999) (declaring that the FOIA "does not impose a retention obligation" on an agency and that "[e]ven if the agency failed to keep documents that it should have kept, that failure would create neither responsibility under FOIA to reconstruct those documents nor liability for the lapse"). But see Cal-Almond, Inc. v. USDA, No. 89-574, slip op. at 2-3 (E.D. Cal. Mar. 12, 1993) (ruling that when agency returned requested records to submitter four days after denying requester's administrative appeal, in violation of its own records-retention requirements, and court determined such records were required to be disclosed, agency must seek return of records from submitter for disclosure to requester), appeal dismissed per stipulation, No. 93-16727 (9th Cir. Oct. 26, 1994); see also FOIA Update, Vol. XII, No. 2, at 5 (advising agencies to afford administrative appeal rights to FOIA requesters in "no record" situations (citing Oglesby v. United States Dep't of the Army, 920 F.2d 57, 67 (D.C. Cir. 1990))); cf. Urban v. United States, 72 F.3d 94, 95 (8th Cir. 1995) (district court erred by dismissing complaint prior to service on grounds no records existed; case remanded for submission of evidence as to existence of responsive records).

[21] See, e.g., Sorrells v. United States, No. 97-5586, 1998 WL 58080, at *1 (6th Cir. Feb. 6, 1998) (finding no improper withholding when agency does not have document with "full, legible signature"); Green, 992 F. Supp. at 818 (in response to "imaginative[] if unpersuasive[]" argument, deciding no improper withholding for records to which access discontinued because of scheduled disposal under Disposal of Records Act, 44 U.S.C. § 3301 (1994)); Regional Management Corp. v. Legal Servs. Corp., 10 F. Supp. 2d 565, 573-74 (D.S.C. 1998) (concluding that "no case or controversy exists" because agency produced all requested documents); Gabel v. Commissioner, No. 94-16245, 1995 WL 267203, at *2 (9th Cir. May 5, 1995) (finding no improper withhold-

(continued...)

## LITIGATION CONSIDERATIONS

cy's refusal to produce them should not be deemed an "improper" withholding and summary judgment should be granted.[22]

Similarly, an agency has not improperly withheld records when it is prohibited from disclosing them by a preexisting court order.[23] While the validity of such a preexisting court order does not depend upon whether it is based upon FOIA exemptions,[24] it is the agency's burden to demonstrate that the order was intended to operate as an injunction against the agency, rather than as a mere court seal.[25] Moreover, in a decision involving state records, but which may be no less applicable to federal records, the Court of Appeals for the Third Circuit held that a district court must consider the impact on public

---

[21](...continued)
ing because "it was uncontested" that agency provided complete response to request).

[22] See Folstad, 1999 U.S. Dist. LEXIS 17852, at **1, 7 (granting summary judgment over plaintiff's objection that agency should have retrieved requested documents from private institution that maintained copies); Morris, 1997 U.S. Dist. LEXIS 21030, at *4 (granting judgment to agency because request did not seek document in existence); D'Angelica v. IRS, No. S-94-1998, 1996 U.S. Dist. LEXIS 6681, at *3 (E.D. Cal. Apr. 25, 1996) (granting summary judgment when requested records either did not exist or were fully disclosed).

[23] See, e.g., GTE Sylvania, Inc. v. Consumers Union, 445 U.S. 375, 384-86 (1980); Freeman v. United States Dep't of Justice, 723 F. Supp. 1115, 1120 (D. Md. 1988); Legal Times, Inc. v. FDIC, 1 Gov't Disclosure Serv. (P-H) ¶ 80,234, at 80,585 (D.D.C. Sept. 2, 1980); see also FOIA Update, Vol. IV, No. 3, at 5. But see also FOIA Update, Vol. XIII, No. 3, at 5 (advising that "protective orders" issued by agency administrative law judges do not qualify as court orders).

[24] See Wagar v. United States Dep't of Justice, 846 F.2d 1040, 1047 (6th Cir. 1988).

[25] See, e.g., Morgan v. United States Dep't of Justice, 923 F.2d 195, 197-99 (D.C. Cir. 1991); Armstrong v. Executive Office of the President, 830 F. Supp. 19, 23 (D.D.C. 1993) ("[I]t is also clear that the Protective Order was not intended to act as a limitation on the Government's ability to determine the final disposition of these classified materials."); Senate of P.R. v. United States Dep't of Justice, No. 84-1829, 1993 U.S. Dist. LEXIS, at **18-19 (D.D.C. Aug. 24, 1993) (finding that agency declaration failed to satisfy Morgan test and requiring more detailed explanation of intended effect of sealing order); McDonnell Douglas Corp. v. NASA, No. 91-3134, slip op. at 1-2 (D.D.C. July 12, 1993) ("While this court's sealing Order temporarily precluded release, that order was not intended to operate as the functional equivalent of an injunction prohibiting release. It was only approved by the court for the purposes of expediting this litigation and protecting information . . . until this lawsuit was resolved."); see also Lykins v. United States Dep't of Justice, 725 F.2d 1455, 1460-61 & n.7 (D.C. Cir. 1984) (determining that federal district court policy--"now enshrined in an order [that was] not issued as part of a concrete case or controversy before [that] court"--does not constitute type of "court order" contemplated in GTE Sylvania).

## LITIGATION CONSIDERATIONS

access statutes, such as the FOIA, before imposing a confidentiality order.[26] The Third Circuit noted that a court could avoid potential conflicts over disclosure by expressly limiting the scope of court-mandated confidentiality to information that would not otherwise be disclosed under the FOIA.[27]

Once a court determines that information has been properly withheld pursuant to a FOIA exemption, absent some other statute mandating disclosure, the court has no inherent, equitable power to order disclosure.[28] By the same token, however, it is not at all clear that a court has inherent, equitable power to refuse to order disclosure of nonexempt information.[29]

It is well settled, though, that it is not appropriate for a court to order

---

[26] Pansy v. Borough of Stroudsburg, 23 F.3d 772, 791 (3d Cir. 1994) ("[W]here it is likely that information is accessible under a relevant freedom of information law, a strong presumption exists against granting or maintaining an order of confidentiality whose scope would prevent disclosure of that information pursuant to the relevant freedom of information law."); accord Attorney General Reno's FOIA Memorandum, reprinted in FOIA Update, Vol. XIV, No. 3, at 4-5 (articulating general "presumption of disclosure"); see also Final Settlement Agreements and Consent Decrees, 64 Fed. Reg. 59,122 (1999) (to be codified at 28 C.F.R. § 50.23) (setting forth Department of Justice's general policy against entering into final settlement agreements or consent decrees that are subject to confidentiality provisions).

[27] Pansy, 23 F.3d at 791; cf. 5 U.S.C. § 552a(b)(2) (1994 & Supp. IV 1998) (comparable provision of Privacy Act of 1974).

[28] See Spurlock v. FBI, 69 F.3d 1010, 1016-18 (9th Cir. 1995) (concluding that when court finds records exempt under FOIA, it has no "inherent" authority to order disclosure of agency information just because it might conflict with depositions or other public statements of informant).

[29] See Abraham & Rose, 138 F.3d at 1077 ("Basing a denial of a FOIA request on a factor unrelated to any of the[] nine exemptions clearly contravenes [the FOIA]."); Maricopa Audubon Soc'y v. United States Forest Serv., 108 F.3d 1082, 1087 (9th Cir. 1997) ("We conclude that a district court lacks inherent power, equitable or otherwise, to exempt materials that FOIA itself does not exempt."); Weber Aircraft Corp. v. United States, 688 F.2d 638, 645 (9th Cir. 1982) ("The careful balancing of interests which Congress attempted to achieve in the FOIA would be upset if courts could exercise their general equity powers to authorize nondisclosure of material not covered by a specific exemption."), rev'd on other grounds, 465 U.S. 792 (1984)). But see Halperin v. United States Dep't of State, 565 F.2d 699, 706 (D.C. Cir. 1977) ("The power of a court to refuse to order the release of information that does not qualify for one of the nine statutory exemptions exists, if at all, only in "exceptional circumstances." (citing Soucie v. David, 448 F.2d 1067, 1077 (D.C. Cir. 1971))); see also Patriarca v. FBI, No. 85-707, slip op. at 1 (D.R.I. Nov. 13, 1985) (order preliminarily enjoining defendants from making release of nonexempt records), motion to dismiss denied, 639 F. Supp. 1193 (D.R.I. 1986); cf. Renegotiation Bd. v. Bannercraft Clothing Co., 415 U.S. 1, 20 (1973) (suggesting, in dicta, that the FOIA does not "limit the inherent powers of an equity court"); Campos v. INS, 32 F. Supp. 2d 1337, 1345-46 (S.D. Fla. 1998) (same).

## LITIGATION CONSIDERATIONS

FOIA disclosure of information to a FOIA requester with a special restriction, either explicit or implicit, that the requester not further disseminate the information received. This step has been taken by some courts in a misguided effort to minimize damage from disclosure of records that, in fact, should be found exempt, but where the requester had established a particular need for or interest in the information.[30] Because the Supreme Court has clearly instructed that neither "the identity of the requesting party" nor "the particular purpose for which the document is being requested" can have any bearing on the release of information under the FOIA,[31] appellate courts generally find this practice improper and should overturn any such restrictive (or selective) disclosure order.[32]

The venue provision of the FOIA, quoted above, provides requesters with a broad choice of forums in which to bring suit.[33] Of course, when a requester sues in a jurisdiction other than the District of Columbia, he is obliged to allege the nexus giving rise to proper venue in that jurisdiction.[34] Largely

---

[30] See, e.g., Schiffer v. FBI, 78 F.3d 1405, 1408 (9th Cir. 1996) (describing erroneous district court order to plaintiff not to "provide copies of the documents [or] disclose their contents to any other person or company"); cf. Caplan v. ATF, 587 F.2d 544, 545-46 (2d Cir. 1978) (describing district court order denying disclosure of manual despite fact that no exemptions applied, but affirming ruling on basis of Exemption 2).

[31] United States Dep't of Justice v. Reporters Comm. for Freedom of the Press, 489 U.S. 749, 771-72 (1989); see also FOIA Update, Vol. X, No. 2, at 3-4.

[32] See, e.g., Schiffer, 78 F.3d at 1411 (overruling district court's order limiting access to persons other than plaintiff "is not authorized by FOIA"); Spurlock, 69 F.3d at 1016 (finding that district court erred when, after determining that requested material was exempt, it nevertheless ordered disclosure of any "falsified statements" made to FBI about requester); cf. Maricopa, 108 F.3d at 1088-89 (rejecting, as irrelevant, plaintiff's offer to agree not to further disclose requested information: "FOIA does not permit selective disclosure of information only to certain parties . . . . [O]nce the information is disclosed to [this requester], it must also be made available to all members of the public who request it.").

[33] See 5 U.S.C. § 552(a)(4)(B) (providing for venue in any of four locations).

[34] See Cosio v. INS, No. 97-5380, slip op. at 3 (C.D. Cal. Dec. 29, 1997) (finding venue improper for plaintiffs who do not reside or have their principal places of business in judicial district and who do not allege that their records were maintained there); Schwarz v. IRS, 998 F. Supp. 201, 203 (N.D.N.Y. 1998) (finding venue improper where agency maintains regional office unless substantial part of activity complained of also occurred there), appeal dismissed for lack of merit, No. 98-6065 (2d Cir. July 30, 1998), cert. denied, 525 U.S. 1031 (1998), reh'g denied, 525 U.S. 1096 (1999); Handlery Hotels, Inc. v. United States Consumer Prod. Safety Comm'n, No. 97-1100, slip op. at 3 (S.D. Cal. Dec. 5, 1997) (finding venue improper where based on location of plaintiff's counsel); Keen v. FBI, No. 97-2657, 1997 U.S. Dist.

(continued...)

## LITIGATION CONSIDERATIONS

due to the statutory designation of the District of Columbia as an appropriate forum for any FOIA action,[35] the District Court for the District of Columbia and Court of Appeals for the District of Columbia Circuit have, over the years, decided a great many of the leading cases under the FOIA.[36]

Indeed, the District Court for the District of Columbia has been held to be the sole appropriate forum for cases in which the requester resides and works outside the United States and the records requested are located in the District of Columbia.[37] It is not yet settled, however, whether this provision affords "personal jurisdiction" in that judicial district for FOIA suits brought against the Tennessee Valley Authority, a wholly owned federal corporation outside the court's normal extraterritorial service of process.[38] It should also be noted that, unlike under other federal venue provisions, aliens are treated the same as citizens for FOIA venue purposes.[39]

The judicial doctrine of forum non conveniens, as codified in 28 U.S.C. § 1404(a),[40] can permit the transfer of a FOIA case to a different judicial district.[41] The courts have invoked this doctrine to transfer FOIA cases under a variety of circumstances.[42] Similarly, when the requested records are the sub-

---

[34](...continued) LEXIS, at *2 (N.D. Cal. Oct. 17, 1997) (finding venue improper where pro se plaintiff housed temporarily); see also Morrell v. United States Dep't of Justice, No. 96-4356, 1996 WL 732499, at *1 (N.D. Cal. Dec. 16, 1996) (transferring pro se action improperly filed in Northern District of California to Eastern District of California, where plaintiff resided).

[35] See, e.g., FOIA Update, Vol. XI, No. 2, at 2 (citing "universal venue" provision of FOIA, 5 U.S.C. § 552(a)(4)(B)).

[36] See, e.g., Matlack, Inc. v. EPA, 868 F. Supp. 627, 630 (D. Del. 1994) ("The United States Court of Appeals for the District of Columbia Circuit has long been on the leading edge of interpreting the parameters of what a federal agency must disclose and may withhold consistent with the terms of FOIA."); see also FOIA Update, Vol. VI, No. 3, at 1-2 (describing FOIA litigation process within D.C. Circuit).

[37] See Akutowicz v. United States, 859 F.2d 1122, 1126 (2d Cir. 1988).

[38] Compare Jones v. NRC, 654 F. Supp. 130, 132 (D.D.C. 1987) (no), with Murphy v. TVA, 559 F. Supp. 58, 59 (D.D.C. 1983) (yes).

[39] See Arevalo-Franco v. INS, 889 F.2d 589, 590-91 (5th Cir. 1989) (ruling that resident alien may bring FOIA suit in district where he in fact resides).

[40] (1994 & Supp. IV 1998).

[41] See generally Ross v. Reno, No. 95-CV-1088, 1996 WL 612457, at **3-4 (E.D.N.Y. Aug. 13, 1996) (discussing factors in favor of and in opposition to transfer of case to neighboring jurisdiction).

[42] See, e.g., Cecola v. FBI, No. 94 C 4866, 1995 WL 645620, at *3 (N.D. Ill. Nov. 1, 1995) (transferring remainder of case to district where remaining rec-
(continued...)

## LITIGATION CONSIDERATIONS

ject of pending FOIA litigation in another judicial district, the related doctrine of "federal comity" can permit a court to defer to the jurisdiction of the other court, in order to avoid unnecessarily burdening the federal judiciary and delivering conflicting FOIA judgments.[43]

On rare occasions, FOIA plaintiffs have attempted to expedite judicial consideration of their suits by seeking a preliminary injunction to "enjoin" the agency from continuing to withhold the requested records.[44] When such ex-

---

[42](...continued)
ords and government's declarant are located, where plaintiff operates business, and where activities described in requested records presumably took place); Southmountain Coal Co. v. Mine Safety & Health Admin., No. 94-0110, slip op. at 2-3 (D.D.C. Mar. 10, 1994) (justifying transfer of suit to district where corporate requester resides and has principal place of business and where criminal case on which request is based is pending, on grounds that "a single court [handling] both FOIA and criminal discovery would obviate the possibility of contradictory rulings, and would prevent the use of FOIA as a mere substitute for criminal discovery"); Bauer v. United States, No. Civ. 91-374A, slip op. at 3 (W.D.N.Y. Feb. 3, 1992) (finding venue improper where pro se suit filed; action transferred to jurisdiction where records located); Housley v. United States Dep't of Justice, No. 89-436, slip op. at 3-4 (D.D.C. Nov. 13, 1989) (transferring case to district where criminal proceeding against plaintiff was held and where evidence obtained by government's electronic surveillance allegedly was improperly withheld); cf. Environmental Crimes Project v. EPA, 928 F. Supp. 1, 1-2 (D.D.C. 1995) (finding that "[t]he interest of justice clearly favors transfer of this case," but absent "precise" information as to location of records sought, declining to order transfer in view of "substantial weight due to plaintiff's choice of forum"). But see In re Scott, 709 F.2d 717, 721-22 (D.C. Cir. 1983) (issuing writ of mandamus and remanding case when district court sua sponte transferred case, without determination of whether venue was proper in other forum, merely in effort to reduce burden of "very large number of in forma pauperis cases").

[43] See, e.g., Hunsberger v. United States Dep't of Justice, No. 93-1945, slip op. at 1 (D.D.C. Mar. 16, 1994) (concluding that lack of responsiveness of court in which similar action was previously filed is "inadequate" ground to maintain independent action in second court); Atkin v. EEOC, No. 92-1061, slip op. at 2 (D.D.C. July 7, 1992); Beck v. United States Dep't of Justice, No. 88-3433, 1991 U.S. Dist. LEXIS 11179, at **15-16 (D.D.C. Jan. 31, 1991), summary affirmance granted in pertinent part & denied in part, No. 91-5292 (D.C. Cir. Nov. 19, 1992), aff'd on remaining issues, 997 F.2d 1489 (D.C. Cir. 1993); see also Environmental Crimes Project, 928 F. Supp. at 2 (denying government's transfer motion, but ordering stay of proceedings pending resolution of numerous discovery disputes in related cases in other jurisdiction); FOIA Update, Vol. VI, No. 3, at 6 ("[G]iving a litigant more than one opportunity in court is a 'luxury that cannot be afforded.'" (quoting C. Wright, Law of Federal Courts 678 (4th ed. 1983))).

[44] See United States Dep't of Commerce v. Assembly of Cal., 501 U.S. 1272 (1991) (staying preliminary injunction); Aronson v. HUD, 869 F.2d 646, 648 (1st Cir. 1989) (denying preliminary injunction); Beta Steel Corp. v. NLRB,
(continued...)

## LITIGATION CONSIDERATIONS

traordinary relief is sought, the court does not adjudicate the parties' substantive claims, but rather weighs: (1) whether the plaintiff is likely to prevail upon the merits; (2) whether the plaintiff will be irreparably harmed absent relief; (3) whether the defendant will be substantially harmed by the issuance of injunctive relief; and (4) whether the public interest will be benefitted by such relief.[45]

In a FOIA case, the granting of such an injunction would invariably force the government to disclose the very information that is the subject of the litigation prematurely, without affording it any opportunity to fully and fairly litigate its position on the merits; such an injunction would moot the government's claims before they could ever be adjudicated and would effectively destroy any possibility of appellate review.[46] Consequently, the government would presumptively sustain irreparable harm in any instance in which a preliminary injunction were issued in a FOIA case.[47]

Moreover, because a court can exercise FOIA jurisdiction only after it has first determined that there has been an improper withholding, there exists a substantial question as to whether the statute even empowers a court to issue a preliminary injunction.[48] These considerations lead to the conclusion

---

[44](...continued)
No. 2:97 CV 358, 1997 WL 836525, at *2 (N.D. Ind. Oct. 22, 1997) (denying preliminary injunction); see also Cullinane v. Arnold, No. 97-779, 1998 U.S. Dist. LEXIS 5575, at *4 (C.D. Cal. Mar. 24, 1998) (denying writ of mandamus because FOIA provides adequate remedy).

[45] See Nation Magazine v. United States Dep't of State, 805 F. Supp. 68, 72 (D.D.C. 1992); Ray v. Reno, No. 94-1384, slip op. at 3 (D.D.C. Oct. 24, 1995), appeal dismissed for lack of prosecution, No. 96-5005 (D.C. Cir. Dec. 26, 1996); Hunt v. United States Marine Corps, No. 94-2317, slip op. at 2 (D.D.C. Oct. 28, 1994); Assassination Archives & Research Ctr. v. CIA, No. 88-2600, 1988 U.S. Dist. LEXIS 18606, at *1 (D.D.C. Sept. 29, 1988); see also Mayo v. United States Gov't Printing Office, 839 F. Supp. 697, 700 (N.D. Cal. 1992) (finding fact that FOIA expressly authorizes injunctive relief does not divest district court of obligation to "exercise its sound discretion," relying on traditional legal standards, in granting such relief (citing Weinberger v. Romero Barcelo, 456 U.S. 305, 312 (1982))), aff'd, 9 F.3d 1450 (9th Cir. 1993).

[46] See Aronson, 869 F.2d at 648 ("To issue the preliminary injunction discloses the names, permanently injuring the interest HUD seeks to protect ...."); see also Hunt, No. 94-2317, slip op. at 5 (D.D.C. Oct. 28, 1994) (denying temporary restraining order, in part on basis of strong "public interest in an 'orderly, fair and efficient administration of the FOIA'").

[47] See generally FOIA Update, Vol. XII, No. 3, at 1-2 (discussing comparable situation of "unstayed" disclosure orders).

[48] See Kissinger, 455 U.S. at 150 (absent improper withholding, FOIA confers no "[j]udicial authority to devise remedies and enjoin agencies"); Sears, 421 U.S. 132, 147-48 (1975) (once it is determined that withheld information falls within one of FOIA's exemptions, FOIA "'does not apply' to such docu-

## LITIGATION CONSIDERATIONS

that the extraordinary mechanism of preliminary injunctive relief should be unavailable in FOIA cases, although expedited processing may be appropriate.[49] (See the discussion of expedited processing under Litigation Considerations, "Open America" Stays of Proceedings, below.)

As a final jurisdictional point, it should be remembered that a FOIA plaintiff, like any other, must file suit before expiration of the applicable statute of limitations. In Spannaus v. Department of Justice, the D.C. Circuit applied the general federal statute of limitations, which is found at 28 U.S.C. § 2401(a),[50] to FOIA actions.[51] Section 2401(a) states, in pertinent part, that "every action commenced against the United States shall be barred unless the complaint is filed within six years after the right of action first accrues." In Spannaus it was held that the FOIA cause of action accrued--and, therefore, the statute of limitations began to run--once the plaintiff had "constructively" exhausted his administrative remedies (see the discussion of Exhaustion of Administrative Remedies, below) and not when all administrative appeals had been finally adjudicated.[52] In accordance with the Spannaus decision, the National Archives and Records Administration propounded General Records Schedule 14,[53] which sets the record-retention period at six years for all correspondence and supporting documentation relating to denied FOIA requests.[54]

---

[48](...continued) ments").

[49] See Perdue Farms, Inc. v. NLRB, 927 F. Supp. 897, 906 (E.D.N.C. 1996) (granting injunction mandating processing of month-old FOIA request pertaining to challenged union election "immediately and with all deliberate speed").

[50] (1994).

[51] 824 F.2d 52, 55-56 (D.C. Cir. 1987); see also, e.g., McClain v. United States Dep't of Justice, No. 97 C 0385, 1999 WL 759505, at *4 (N.D. Ill. Sept. 1, 1999) (dismissing complaint after calculating that cause of action was filed three years after statute of limitations expired); Madden v. Runyon, 899 F. Supp. 217, 226 (E.D. Pa. 1995) (finding that even assuming plaintiff exhausted his administrative remedies, statute of limitations would have expired four years prior to commencement of suit).

[52] 824 F.2d at 57-59; see Peck v. CIA, 787 F. Supp. 63, 65-66 (S.D.N.Y. 1992) (once constructive exhaustion period has run, statute of limitations is not tolled while request for information is pending before agency).

[53] National Archives & Records Admin., General Records Schedule, Schedule 14 (1998).

[54] Id.; see also Attorney General's Memorandum on the 1986 Amendments to the Freedom of Information Act 28 n.51 (Dec. 1987) (advising that agencies should be sure to maintain any "excluded" records for purposes of possible further review (citing FOIA Update, Vol. V, No. 4, at 4 (advising same regarding "personal" records))); FOIA Update, Vol. XVIII, No. 1, at 5-6 (advising that provision of Electronic FOIA amendments, 5 U.S.C. § 552(a)(3)(B), does not require agencies to alter their records-disposition or records-maintenance
(continued...)

**LITIGATION CONSIDERATIONS**

### Pleadings

The agency's time to answer a FOIA complaint is thirty days from the date of service of process,[55] not the usual sixty days that are permitted by Federal Rule of Civil Procedure 12(a). While courts are no longer required to automatically accord expedited treatment to FOIA lawsuits, they may still, in their discretion, expedite any such case "if good cause therefor is shown."[56]

FOIA lawsuits are adjudicated according to standards and procedures that are quite atypical within the field of administrative law. Not only is the usual "substantial evidence" standard of review of agency action replaced in the FOIA by a de novo review standard, but the defendant agency bears the burden of justifying its decision to withhold any information.[57] When Exemption 1 is invoked, however, most courts have applied a somewhat lesser standard of review for classified documents to avoid compromising national security. (See the discussion under Exemption 1, Standard of Review, above.) Regarding FOIA issues other than those involving the propriety of agency withholding of records, one circuit court has applied the de novo standard of review in a lawsuit dealing with an alleged violation of subsection (a)(1) of the FOIA.[58]

---

[54](...continued) practices); cf. Cal-Almond, No. 89-574, slip op. at 2-3 (E.D. Cal. Mar. 12, 1993) (requiring agency to seek return of records for disclosure to requester after agency erroneously gave them back to submitter in violation of its own records-retention requirements, and court determined such records were required to be disclosed).

[55] See 5 U.S.C. § 552(a)(4)(C) (1994 & Supp. IV 1998).

[56] 28 U.S.C. § 1657 (1994 & Supp. IV 1998) (repealing former 5 U.S.C. § 552(a)(4)(D) (1982)); see also Freedom Communications, Inc. v. FDIC, 157 F.R.D. 485, 487 (C.D. Cal. 1994) ("The Court offers its assurance to all concerned that it will continue to handle all matters in this action in an expeditious manner. However, we do not see the value in issuing an order that does no more than reiterate policies already announced by statute and the court itself."); FOIA Update, Vol. VI, No. 2, at 6.

[57] See 5 U.S.C. § 552(a)(4)(B); see also Halpern v. FBI, 181 F.3d 279, 288 (2d Cir. 1999) (observing that de novo standard of review comports with congressional intent); Summers v. Department of Justice, 140 F.3d 1077, 1080 (D.C. Cir. 1998); Church of Scientology Int'l v. United States Dep't of Justice, 30 F.3d 224, 228 (1st Cir. 1994); Alyeska Pipeline Serv. v. EPA, 856 F.2d 309, 315 (D.C. Cir. 1988); cf. Trenerry v. United States Dep't of the Treasury, No. 92-5053, 1993 WL 26813, at *5 (10th Cir. Feb. 5, 1993) (recognizing that although district court used phrase "arbitrary and capricious" in discussing scope of review, its decision should be upheld if "reviewing the entire order clearly reveals that the court performed a de novo review and correctly placed the burden on IRS").

[58] 5 U.S.C. § 552(a)(1); see Mada-Luna v. Fitzpatrick, 813 F.2d 1006, 1011 (9th Cir. 1987).

## LITIGATION CONSIDERATIONS

A major exception to the de novo standard of review is "reverse" FOIA lawsuits, in which courts apply the more deferential "arbitrary and capricious" standard under the Administrative Procedure Act.[59] (See the discussion of this point under "Reverse" FOIA, Standard of Review, below.) Although judicial review of fee waiver denials was undertaken according to the "arbitrary and capricious" standard prior to the 1986 FOIA amendments, the statute now mandates that courts determine fee waiver issues under the de novo standard of review, but that they limit their scope of review to the record before the agency.[60] (For a further discussion of fee waiver review standards, see Fees and Fee Waivers, above.)

There is a sound general rule that only federal departments and agencies are proper party defendants in FOIA litigation. This rule is derived from the plain language of the Act, which vests the district courts with jurisdiction to enjoin "the agency" from withholding records.[61] The great majority of courts have held that the head of an agency or other agency officials or employees that are sued in their official capacities are not proper party defendants under the FOIA.[62] A minority of courts, however, disagree with this position.[63] It also has been observed that "the United States," as such, is not a

---

[59] 5 U.S.C. §§ 701-06 (1994).

[60] 5 U.S.C. § 552(a)(4)(A)(vii).

[61] 5 U.S.C. § 552(a)(4)(B) (emphasis added). But see Peralta v. United States Attorney's Office, 136 F.3d 169, 172 (D.C. Cir. 1998) (dictum) (suggesting, despite both statutory language and agency structure, that "the FBI is subject to the FOIA in its own name").

[62] See, e.g., Thompson v. Walbran, 990 F.2d 403, 405 (8th Cir. 1993); Petrus v. Bowen, 833 F.2d 581, 582 (5th Cir. 1987); Parola v. IRS, No. 98-CV-7179, 1999 WL 1215557, at *6 (E.D.N.Y. Dec. 15, 1999) (appeal pending); Eison v. Kallstrom, 75 F. Supp. 2d 113, 114 (S.D.N.Y. 1999); Lissner v. United States Customs Serv., No. 98-7438-ABC, slip op. at 7-8 (C.D. Cal. June 17, 1999) (appeal pending); Pyne v. Commissioner, No. 98-00253, 1999 U.S. Dist. LEXIS 1059, at *3 (D. Haw. Jan. 6, 1999); Ballard v. IRS, No. 4:97-CV-071, slip op. at 1 (N.D. Tex. Oct. 21, 1998); Gilbert v. Social Sec. Admin., No. 93-C-1055, slip op. at 11-12 (E.D. Wis. Dec. 28, 1994) (citing Brown-Bey v. United States, 720 F.2d 467, 469 (7th Cir. 1983) (Privacy Act case); Stone v. Defense Investigative Serv., 816 F. Supp. 782, 785 (D.D.C. 1993), appeal dismissed for failure to prosecute, No. 93-5170 (D.C. Cir. Mar. 11, 1994); Friedman v. FBI, 605 F. Supp. 314, 317 (N.D. Ga. 1984); Providence Journal Co. v. FBI, 460 F. Supp. 778, 782-83 & n.2 (D.R.I. 1978), rev'd on other grounds, 602 F.2d 1010 (1st Cir. 1979); see also Payne v. Minihan, No. 97-0266SC, slip op. at 14-15 (D.N.M. Apr. 30, 1998) (agreeing with majority view that agency personnel not proper parties to FOIA suit, but nevertheless declining to dismiss action because agency did "not challenge" suit on basis of improper party and was "on notice" of suit) (appeal pending).

[63] See, e.g., Henry v. FBI, No. 90-1987, slip op. at 5-6 (W.D. La. Oct. 7, 1991); Diamond v. FBI, 532 F. Supp. 216, 219-20 (S.D.N.Y. 1981), aff'd on other grounds, 707 F.2d 75 (2d Cir. 1983); Hamlin v. Kelley, 433 F. Supp. 180,

(continued...)

## LITIGATION CONSIDERATIONS

proper party defendant in a FOIA case.[64] Similarly, there is a sound general rule that only the person who has actually submitted a FOIA request at the administrative level can be the proper party plaintiff in any subsequent court action based on that request.[65]

It is clear that an agency in possession of records originating with another agency cannot refuse to process those records merely by advising the requester to seek them directly from the other agency.[66] In litigation, the defendant agency ordinarily will include, in its court submissions, affidavits from the originating agency to address any contested withholdings in its records.[67] (For a further discussion of agency referral practices, see Procedural

---

[63](...continued)
181 (N.D. Ill. 1977).

[64] See Sanders v. United States, No. 96-5372, 1997 WL 529073, at *1 (D.C. Cir. July 3, 1997) (dismissing complaint because United States is not agency subject to FOIA); Maginn v. United States, No. 92-313, 1995 WL 355241, at *4 (W.D. Pa. May 29, 1992) (same (citing Western Life Ins. Co. v. United States, 512 F. Supp. 454, 463 (N.D. Tex. 1980))).

[65] See Maxxam, Inc. v. FDIC, No. 98-0989, slip op. at 5-6 (D.D.C. Jan. 29, 1999) (finding that only plaintiff's attorney was real party in interest when FOIA request was made in attorney's own name, not plaintiff's name); Payne, No. 97-0266SC, slip op. at 12-14 (D.N.M. Apr. 30, 1998) (dismissing plaintiff who sued as "concerned citizen" because "[i]t is the filing of his requests and their actual or constructive denials which distinguishes the harm suffered by [the actual requester] from the harm incurred by . . . [the concerned citizen]"); Wade v. Department of Commerce, No. 96-0717, slip op. at 4 (D.D.C. Mar. 26, 1998) (finding failure to exhaust administrative remedies because plaintiff was not "'the person making'" the FOIA request (quoting 5 U.S.C. § 552(a)(6)(A)(i))); Unigard Ins. Co. v. Department of the Treasury, 997 F. Supp. 1339, 1342 (S.D. Cal. 1997) ("A person whose name does not appear on the request for disclosure lacks standing to sue under FOIA, even if his interest was asserted in the request." (citing United States v. McDonnell, 4 F.3d 1227, 1237 (3d Cir. 1993))); cf. Burka v. HHS, 142 F.3d 1286, 1290-91 (D.C. Cir. 1998) (refusing to award attorney fees to plaintiff who claimed he was suing for unnamed party, because of "dangers inherent in recognizing an 'undisclosed' client as the real plaintiff").

[66] See, e.g., In re Wade, 969 F.2d 241, 247-48 (7th Cir. 1992) (explaining that agency cannot avoid request or withhold documents merely by referring requester to agency where documents originated); Ostrer v. United States Dep't of Justice, No. 85-506, slip op. at 7-8 (D.D.C. Feb. 7, 1986), amended, slip op. at 2-3 (D.D.C. Apr. 9, 1986); see also FOIA Update, Vol. XV, No. 3, at 6.

[67] See, e.g., Williams v. FBI, No. 92-5176, slip op. at 2 (D.C. Cir. May 7, 1993); Oglesby v. United States Dep't of the Army, 920 F.2d 57, 69 & n.15 (D.C. Cir. 1990); Fitzgibbon v. CIA, 911 F.2d 755, 757 (D.C. Cir. 1990); Greenberg v. United States Dep't of Treasury, 10 F. Supp. 2d 3, 11, 18 (D.D.C. 1998) (requiring agency or component that referred documents to justify nondis-
(continued...)

## LITIGATION CONSIDERATIONS

Requirements, Referrals and Consultations, above.)

Lastly, there is the fact that although Rule 15(a) of the Federal Rules of Civil Procedure counsels that leave to amend complaints "shall be freely given when justice so requires,"[68] the decision to grant such leave is entrusted to the sound discretion of the district court.[69] Courts have recognized limitations on a plaintiff's ability to amend a FOIA complaint, even when the plaintiff is proceeding pro se.[70] In particular, courts have rejected attempts to amend complaints due to the plaintiff's undue delay,[71] when the plaintiff's complaint, as amended, would still fail to state a justiciable claim,[72] when the plaintiff sought to dramatically alter the scope and nature of the FOIA litigation,[73] or

---

[67](...continued) closure); Jan-Xin Zang v. FBI, 756 F. Supp. 705, 706-07 & n.1 (W.D.N.Y. 1991); see also FOIA Update, Vol. XII, No. 3, at 3-4 ("OIP Guidance: Referral and Consultation Procedures"); FOIA Update, Vol. XIV, No. 3, at 6-8; cf. Peralta, 136 F.2d at 175 (remanding for consideration of whether referral procedures could result in "improper withholding" of referred documents).

[68] See Foman v. Davis, 371 U.S. 178, 182 (1962) (non-FOIA case); Katzman v. Sessions, 156 F.R.D. 35, 38 (E.D.N.Y. 1994) (holding that to defeat a motion to supplement pleadings, "the nonmovant must demonstrate either bad faith on the part of the moving party, the futility of the claims asserted within the application, or undue prejudice to the nonmovant") (non-FOIA case).

[69] See, e.g., Mississippi Ass'n of Coops. v. Farmers Home Admin., 139 F.R.D. 542, 543 (D.D.C. 1991).

[70] See Trenerry v. IRS, No. 90-C-444, 1993 WL 565354, at *3 (N.D. Okla. Oct. 28, 1993); Szymanski v. DEA, No. 93-1314, 1993 WL 433592, at **1-3 (D.D.C. Oct. 5, 1993); Slade, No. 93-177-2, slip op. at 1-2 (E.D. Va. Mar. 17, 1993). But see Eison, 75 F. Supp. 2d at 116 n.2 (recognizing that plaintiffs proceeding pro se are given "considerable latitude to correct superficial pleading errors").

[71] See Friedman v. FBI, 605 F. Supp. 306, 314-15 (N.D. Ga. 1984) (amendment denied when sought six years into litigation without sufficient cause); see also Becker v. IRS, 1992 WL 67849, at *3 (N.D. Ill. Mar. 27, 1992) ("Any attempt by the [plaintiffs] to expand the nature of the search at this late date must be rejected.").

[72] See, e.g., Rzeslawski v. United States Dep't of Justice, No. 97-1156, slip op. at 7 (D.D.C. Mar. 16, 1999) (disallowing amendment to add defendants because administrative remedies were not exhausted); Slade, No. 93-177-2, slip op. at 1-2 (E.D. Va. Mar. 17, 1993) (denying amendment when "there has been no showing that plaintiff has exhausted or even attempted to exhaust his administrative remedies"); Lanter v. Department of Justice, No. 93-34, slip op. at 1-2 (W.D. Okla. Aug. 30, 1993) (noting that plaintiffs' amended complaint does "not show exhaustion of their administrative remedies, or other exception to the exhaustion requirements"), aff'd on other grounds, 19 F.3d 33 (10th Cir. 1994) (unpublished table decision).

[73] See, e.g., Szymanski, 1993 WL 433592, at *2 ("This Court will not permit
(continued...)

**LITIGATION CONSIDERATIONS**

when the plaintiff sought to add an unreasonable number of claims.[74]

### Exhaustion of Administrative Remedies

Under the FOIA, administrative remedies must be exhausted prior to judicial review.[75] Indeed, when a FOIA plaintiff attempts to obtain judicial review without first properly undertaking full and timely administrative exhaustion, the lawsuit is subject to ready dismissal,[76] although the courts are

---

[73](...continued)
a F.O.I.A. complaint, properly filed, to become the narrow edge of a wedge which forces open the court house door to unrelated claims against unrelated parties."); Mississippi Ass'n, 139 F.R.D. at 544 ("Where, however, the complaint, as amended, would radically alter the scope and nature of the case and bears no more than a tangential relationship to the original action, leave to amend should be denied."); see also Trenerry, No. 90-C-444, slip op. at 5 (N.D. Okla. Oct. 28, 1993) ("Plaintiff's motion to amend the pleadings is untimely, seeks to add a new unrelated cause of action and appears on its face to be frivolous.").

[74] Allnutt v. United States Trustee, No. 97-02414, slip op. at 8 (D.D.C. July 31, 1999) (allowing amendment to add six FOIA claims, but noting that further attempts to amend would be disallowed to prevent plaintiff from advancing "a never-ending case by perpetually amending his complaint to add the latest FOIA request"), appeal dismissed for lack of juris., No. 99-5410 (D.C. Cir. Feb. 2, 2000).

[75] See, e.g., Pollack v. Department of Justice, 49 F.3d 115, 118 (4th Cir. 1995) ("[A] requester may generally seek judicial review of his FOIA request only after he has exhausted all administrative remedies."); Taylor v. Appleton, 30 F.3d 1365, 1367 (11th Cir. 1994) ("The FOIA clearly requires a party to exhaust all administrative remedies before seeking redress in the federal courts."); McDonnell v. United States, 4 F.3d 1227, 1240, 1241 (3d Cir. 1993) (same (citing Oglesby v. United States Dep't of the Army, 920 F.2d 57, 61 (D.C. Cir. 1990))); Tuchinsky v. Selective Serv. Sys., 418 F.2d 155, 158 (7th Cir. 1969) (concluding that exhaustion not satisfied by "leapfrogging over any substantive step in the administrative process"); McClain v. United States Dep't of Justice, No. 97 C 0385, 1999 WL 759505, at *2 (N.D. Ill. Sept. 1, 1999) ("To state a FOIA claim, a plaintiff must also assert that he has exhausted his administrative remedies."); Greenberg v. United States Dep't of Treasury, No. 87-898, 1998 U.S. Dist. LEXIS 9803, at *46 (D.D.C. July 1, 1998) (finding exhaustion "particularly important" in FOIA cases because of court's need to "'acquire access to reams of paper, make intensive review of that material, and reach document-specific conclusions'" (quoting Summers v. Department of Justice, 140 F.3d 1077, 1080 (D.C. Cir. 1998))); Chaklos v. Reich, No. 95-1763, slip op. at 5 (W.D. Pa. Feb. 20, 1998) ("It is well established that the filing of an administrative appeal is a prerequisite to the commencement of [a FOIA] action in district court."), aff'd, 101 F.3d 689 (unpublished table decision).

[76] See, e.g., Lumarse, Inc. v. HHS, No. 98-55880, 1999 WL 644355, at *5 (9th Cir. 1999) (affirming dismissal of FOIA claim where no administrative appeal was taken); Teplitsky v. Department of Justice, No. 96-36208, 1997
(continued...)

## LITIGATION CONSIDERATIONS

somewhat divided as to whether such dismissal is properly grounded on lack of subject matter jurisdiction,[77] or failure to state a claim upon which relief can be granted.[78] Furthermore, a plaintiff cannot evade proper FOIA administrative procedures by attempting to file his FOIA request as part of a judicial proceeding,[79] or in the course of administratively appealing a previously filed

---

[76](...continued)
WL 665705, at *1 (9th Cir. Oct. 20, 1997); Dettman v. United States Dep't of Justice, 802 F.2d 1472, 1477 (D.C. Cir. 1986); Brumley v. United States Dep't of Labor, 767 F.2d 444, 445 (8th Cir. 1985); Stebbins v. Nationwide Mut. Ins. Co., 757 F.2d 364, 366 (D.C. Cir. 1985) (per curiam) ("Exhaustion of [administrative] remedies is required under the Freedom of Information Act before a party can seek judicial review."); Penners v. Commissioner, No. S-97-1327, 1997 U.S. Dist. LEXIS 21869, at *10 (E.D. Cal. Dec. 30, 1997) (finding no jurisdiction when no attempt to appeal agency decision was made); Center to Prevent Handgun Violence v. United States Dep't of the Treasury, 981 F. Supp. 20, 23 (D.D.C. 1997) ("Strict enforcement of the exhaustion doctrine is favored in FOIA cases."), appeal dismissed, No. 97-5357 (D.C. Cir. Feb. 26, 1997).

[77] See, e.g., McDonnell, 4 F.3d at 1240 & n.9 (affirming dismissal for lack of subject matter jurisdiction because plaintiff failed to exhaust administrative remedies); Hymen v. MSPB, 799 F.2d 1421, 1423 (9th Cir. 1986) (same); Colon v. Executive Office for United States Attorneys, No. 98-0180, 1998 WL 695631, at *2 (D.D.C. Sept. 29, 1998) (concluding that court lacked subject matter jurisdiction because plaintiff failed to file administrative appeal of agency action); Maples v. USDA, No. 97-5663, slip op. at 6 (E.D. Cal. Jan. 15, 1998) ("When a complaint contains an unexhausted request in its prayer for relief, the court must dismiss this portion for lack of subject matter jurisdiction."); Rabin v. United States Dep't of State, 980 F. Supp. 116, 119 (E.D.N.Y. 1997) (suggesting that defense of failure to exhaust is most properly raised in Rule 12(b)(1) dismissal motion); Thomas v. Office of the United States Attorney, 171 F.R.D. 53, 55 (E.D.N.Y. 1997) ("Failure to properly exhaust . . . precludes a federal court of subject matter jurisdiction over a requester's claims."); Jones v. Shalala, 887 F. Supp. 210, 214 (S.D. Iowa 1995).

[78] See Taylor, 30 F.3d at 1367 n.3 (claim "should have been dismissed pursuant to Rule 12(b)(6) for failure to state a claim upon which relief can be granted"); Scherer v. Balkema, 840 F.2d 437, 443 (7th Cir. 1988); see also Payne v. Minihan, No. 97-0266SC, slip op. at 24 (D.N.M. Apr. 30, 1998) (deciding that exhaustion of administrative remedies is "prudential concern" based on failure to state claim upon which relief can be granted) (appeal pending); cf. Sweetland v. Walters, 60 F.3d 852, 855 (D.C. Cir. 1995) (inappropriate for district court to find lack of jurisdiction because federal defendant not an agency for FOIA purposes; dismissal for failure "to state a claim upon which relief could be granted" proper).

[79] See Gillin v. IRS, 980 F.2d 819, 822-23 (1st Cir. 1992) (per curiam) (when "flawed" request was predicated upon a misunderstanding with agency but, within one week after submission, information provided by agency should have prompted requester to revise his request, requester cannot salvage request by clarification in litigation); Hillman v. Commissioner, No. 1:97-cv-760, 1998 U.S. Dist. LEXIS 12431, at *15 (W.D. Mich. July 10, 1998) (rejecting
(continued...)

## LITIGATION CONSIDERATIONS

FOIA request.[80] However, when a plaintiff in litigation produces proper evidence that a request was made, his claim should not be dismissed solely because the defendant agency cannot locate the request in its files.[81] (For a further discussion of the proper submission of requests, see Procedural Requirements, Proper FOIA Requests, above.)

The FOIA permits requesters to treat an agency's failure to comply with its specific time limits as full, or "constructive," exhaustion of administrative

---

[79](...continued)
plaintiff's attempt to have discovery demand treated as access request because "a governmental agency is not required to respond to interrogatories disguised as a FOIA request"); Smith v. Reno, No. C-93-1316, 1996 U.S. Dist. LEXIS 5594, at *8 n.3 (N.D. Cal. Apr. 23, 1996) ("A request for documents in a complaint does not constitute a proper discovery request, much less a proper FOIA request."), aff'd sub nom. Smith v. City of Berkeley, 133 F.3d 929 (9th Cir. 1998) (unpublished table decision); Juda v. United States Dep't of Justice, No. 94-1521, slip op. at 4, 6 (D.D.C. Mar. 28, 1996) (plaintiff cannot interpose new request through vehicle of "motion for leave to pursue discovery"); Pray v. Department of Justice, 902 F. Supp. 1, 2-3 (D.D.C. 1995) (disallowing request to FBI field office "made only in response to the government's motion for summary judgment"), aff'd in part & remanded in part on other grounds, No. 95-5383, 1996 WL 734142, at *1 (D.C. Cir. Nov. 20, 1996); Pollack v. United States Dep't of Justice, No. 89-2569, 1993 WL 293692, at *4 (D. Md. July 23, 1993) (court lacks subject matter jurisdiction when request not submitted until after litigation filed), aff'd on other grounds, 49 F.3d 115 (4th Cir. 1995); Muhammad v. United States Bureau of Prisons, 789 F. Supp. 449, 450-51 (D.D.C. 1992) (requester cannot submit request to court with litigation filings); see also Kowalczyk v. Department of Justice, 73 F.3d 386, 388 (D.C. Cir. 1996) ("Requiring an additional search each time the agency receives a letter that clarifies a prior request could extend indefinitely the delay in processing new requests."); cf. Payne, No. 97-0266, slip op. at 12 (D.N.M. Apr. 30, 1998) ("The FOIA creates a cause of action only for persons who have followed its procedures."); Moore v. Aspin, 916 F. Supp. 32, 36 (D.D.C. 1996) ("Sending an appeal to a different agency does not initiate a proper FOIA request for that agency to conduct a search."); Epps, 801 F. Supp. at 790 (finding that although United States Attorney's Office realized that information that requester sought from FBI included certain United States Attorney's Office material, it was under no obligation to independently search its own files for responsive information absent direct request).

[80] See Thomas, 171 F.R.D. at 55.

[81] See Hammie v. Social Sec. Admin., 765 F. Supp. 1224, 1226 (E.D. Pa. 1991) (in considering government's dismissal motion, court is required to accept plaintiff's averments that he submitted requests); see also Linn v. United States Dep't of Justice, No. 92-1406, 1995 WL 631847, at **15-16 (D.D.C. Aug. 22, 1995) (when plaintiff introduces copy of appeal letter and attests that it was sent, case should not be dismissed for failure to exhaust administrative remedies).

## LITIGATION CONSIDERATIONS

remedies.[82] Thus, when an agency does not respond to a perfected request within the twenty-day (excepting Saturdays, Sundays, and legal public holidays) statutory time limit set forth in the Act,[83] the requester is deemed to have exhausted his administrative remedies and can seek immediate judicial review, even though the requester has not filed an administrative appeal.[84] Indisputably, though, an agency's failure to comply with the statutory deadline neither requires nor empowers a court to ignore the agency's right to invoke applicable statutory exemptions and summarily order disclosure of any or all information sought.[85]

The special right to immediate judicial review that arises from the lack of a timely response lapses if an agency responds to a request at any time before the suit is filed; in that situation, the requester must administratively appeal a denial and wait at least twenty working days for the agency to adjudicate that appeal--as is required by 5 U.S.C. § 552(a)(6)(A)(ii)--before commencing litigation. This latter point was made by the Court of Appeals for the District of Columbia Circuit in Oglesby v. United States Department of the Army, which held that "an administrative appeal is mandatory if the agency cures its failure to respond within the statutory period by responding to the

---

[82] See 5 U.S.C. § 552(a)(6)(C) (1994 & Supp. IV 1998); see also FOIA Update, Vol. XVII, No. 4, at 2 (describing Electronic FOIA amendments' modification of Act's basic time limit from 10 to 20 working days).

[83] 5 U.S.C. § 552(a)(6)(A)(i).

[84] See, e.g., Pollack, 49 F.3d at 118-19 ("Under FOIA's statutory scheme, when an agency fails to comply in a timely fashion with a proper FOIA request, it may not insist on the exhaustion of administrative remedies unless the agency responds to the request before suit is filed."); Campbell v. Unknown Power Superintendent of the Flathead Irrigation & Power Project, No. 91-35104, 1992 WL 84315, at *1 (9th Cir. Apr. 22, 1992) (noting that exhaustion is deemed to have occurred if agency fails to respond to request within statutory time limit); Gabel v. IRS, No. 97-1653, 1998 U.S. Dist. LEXIS 12467, at *10 (N.D. Cal. June 25, 1998) (deciding that plaintiff who did not receive timely response "was entitled to file his complaint without further pursuing an administrative appeal or seeking further explanation"); Anderson v. United States Postal Serv., No. 98-1661, 1998 WL 306207, at *2 (E.D. Pa. June 9, 1998) (finding that "vague positive response" from agency received after statutory time limit allows plaintiff to claim "constructive" exhaustion); see also FOIA Update, Vol. IV, No. 1, at 6.

[85] See Barvick v. Cisneros, 941 F. Supp. 1015, 1019-20 (D. Kan. 1996) ("This court is persuaded that an agency's failure to respond within ten days does not automatically entitle a FOIA requester to summary judgment."); M.K. v. United States Dep't of Justice, No. 96 CIV. 1307, 1996 WL 509724, at *3 (S.D.N.Y. Sept. 9, 1996) ("[T]he government's failure to respond to M.K.'s request within the statutory . . . time limit does not give M.K. the right to obtain the requested documents; it merely amounts to an exhaustion of administrative remedies and allows M.K. to bring this lawsuit.").

## LITIGATION CONSIDERATIONS

FOIA request before suit is filed."[86] Thus, under Oglesby, if a FOIA requester waits beyond the twenty-day period for the agency's initial response and then, in fact, receives that response before suing the agency, the requester must exhaust his administrative appeal rights before litigating the matter.[87] If an agency makes an adverse determination after the requester has filed suit, however, the requester need not first administratively appeal that determination before pressing forward with the court action.[88]

Regardless of whether the agency's response is timely, the requester's exhaustion obligation may be excused if the agency's response fails to supply notice of the right to file an administrative appeal, as required by 5 U.S.C. § 552(a)(6)(A)(i).[89] However, so long as such notice is given, there is no particular formula or set of "magic words" that the agency must employ in giving it.[90] (For a further discussion of administrative notification requirements, see

---

[86] 920 F.2d at 63.

[87] Id. at 63-64; see, e.g., Almy v. Department of Justice, No. 96-1207, 1997 WL 267884, at **2-3 (7th Cir. May 7, 1997) (requester's failure to appeal agencies' "no records" responses constitutes a "failure to exhaust his administrative remedies"); Taylor, 30 F.3d at 1369 ("We therefore join the District of Columbia Circuit and the Third Circuit on this issue."); McDonnell, 4 F.3d at 1240 (applying Oglesby); Samuel v. United States Dep't of Justice, No. 93-0348, slip op. at 3-4 (D. Idaho Feb. 3, 1995) (same); Sloman v. United States Dep't of Justice, 832 F. Supp. 63, 66-67 (S.D.N.Y. 1993) (same); see also FOIA Update, Vol. XII, No. 2, at 3-5 ("OIP Guidance: Procedural Rules Under the D.C. Circuit's Oglesby Decision").

[88] See Pollack, 49 F.3d at 119 ("[I]t was error for the district court to conclude that it was somehow deprived of jurisdiction because [the requester] failed to file administrative appeals . . . during the litigation."); Crooker v. Tax Div. of the United States Dep't of Justice, No. 94-30129, 1995 WL 783236, at *8 (D. Mass. Nov. 17, 1995) (magistrate's recommendation) ("Plaintiff's complaint, in seeking the 'disclos[ure of] agency records being improperly withheld' remained alive to test the adequacy of the disclosures, once made."), adopted (D. Mass. Dec. 15, 1995), aff'd on other grounds per curiam, No. 96-1094 (1st Cir. Aug. 20, 1996). But see Voinche v. FBI, 999 F.2d 962, 963-64 (5th Cir. 1993) (holding that in action based on agency's failure to comply with FOIA's time limits for responses, disclosures made only after litigation commenced rendered action moot).

[89] See Ruotolo v. Department of Justice, 53 F.3d 4, 9 (2d Cir. 1995); Oglesby, 920 F.2d at 65; Lamb v. IRS, 871 F. Supp. 301, 303 (E.D. Mich. 1994); see also FOIA Update, Vol. VI, No. 4, at 6.

[90] See Kay v. FCC, 884 F. Supp. 1, 2-3 (D.D.C. 1995) (letter which "gave the Plaintiff notice of his right to secure further agency review of the adverse determination, of the manner in which he could exercise that right, of the time limits for filing such request, and of the regulatory provisions containing general procedures pertaining to review applications" held to "more than adequately fulfill[] the purposes behind the notice provision"); see also Jones, No. 94-2294, slip op. at 5 (D. Md. Jan. 18, 1995) (requester not relieved of appeal

(continued...)

## LITIGATION CONSIDERATIONS

Procedural Requirements, Responding to FOIA Requests, above.) Furthermore, Oglesby counsels that a requester must file an administrative appeal within the time limit specified in an agency's FOIA regulations or else face dismissal for failure to exhaust administrative remedies.[91]

An agency response that merely acknowledges receipt of a request does not constitute a "determination" under the FOIA in that it neither denies records nor grants the right to appeal the agency's determination.[92] Significantly, though, the twenty-day time period does not run until the request is received by the appropriate office in the agency, as set forth in the agency's regulations.[93] In fact, when an agency has regulations requiring that requests be

---

[90](...continued) obligation simply because agency response included statement that requester would be notified if missing records were later located; response letter also advised that it constituted "final action" of agency component and notified plaintiff of right to administratively appeal).

[91] See Oglesby, 920 F.2d at 65 n.9 (citing regulations of agencies involved); see, e.g., Voinche v. CIA, No. 96-1708, slip op. at 3 (W.D. La. Nov. 25, 1996) (plaintiff's filing of administrative appeal 11 months after agency's response justifies dismissal notwithstanding delay of almost four years by agency in responding to request), appeal dismissed as frivolous, 119 F.3d 3 (5th Cir. 1997) (unpublished table decision); Jones, No. 94-2294, slip op. at 6 (D. Md. Jan. 18, 1995) (summary judgment awarded to government when time limit prescribed by agency regulations for administrative appeal had expired); Kay, 884 F. Supp. at 3 ("[B]ecause the time period within which the plaintiff might have filed his administrative appeal has long since expired, the case shall be dismissed with prejudice."); Lanter v. Department of Justice, No. 93-0034, slip op. at 2 (W.D. Okla. July 30, 1993) (court compelled to dismiss FOIA claim when plaintiff's administrative appeal from agency's response not filed in timely manner), aff'd, 19 F.3d 33 (10th Cir. 1994) (unpublished table decision); see also FOIA Update, Vol. XII, No. 2, at 4-5. But cf. Kennedy v. United States Dep't of Justice, No. 93-0209, slip op. at 2-3 (D.D.C. July 12, 1993) (when requester's affidavit attests to mailing of timely administrative appeal but agency affidavit denies receipt, court may permit requester additional time to submit another appeal and agency additional time to respond; "nothing in the FOIA statute or regulations requires the Plaintiff to do more than mail his administrative appeal in a timely fashion").

[92] See Martinez v. FBI, 3 Gov't Disclosure Serv. (P-H) ¶ 83,005, at 83,435 (D.D.C. Dec. 1, 1982); FOIA Update, Vol. XIII, No. 3, at 5; see also Brumley, 767 F.2d at 445; cf. Dickstein v. IRS, 635 F. Supp. 1004, 1006 (D. Alaska 1986) (letter referring requester to alternative "procedures which involved less red tape and bureaucratic hassle" not deemed to be denial).

[93] See Brumley, 767 F.2d at 445; Judicial Watch, Inc. v. United States Dep't of Justice, No. 97-2089, slip op. at 9-11 (D.D.C. July 14, 1998) (dismissing complaint filed "prior to the existence of any statutory obligation" because FOIA offices had not even received request that was improperly addressed prior to suit being filed); Kessler v. United States, 899 F. Supp. 644, 645 (D.D.C. 1995) (because plaintiff submitted request to IRS Headquarters, not
(continued...)

**LITIGATION CONSIDERATIONS**

made to specific offices for specific records,[94] a request will not be deemed received--and no search for responsive records need be performed--if the requester does not follow those regulations.[95] (For a further discussion of time limits, see Procedural Requirements, Time Limits, above.) Additionally, even when a requester has "constructively" exhausted his administrative remedies by the agency's failure to respond determinatively to the request within the statutory time limits, the requester is not entitled to a Vaughn Index during the administrative process.[96]

Regardless of whether the agency has met or exceeded its twenty-day

---

[93](...continued) district office where he resided, "it is as if he had made no request at all on which the IRS could render a determination"); Agunbiade, 1995 WL 351058, at *6 ("In failing to direct his requests, in accordance with agency-specific rules, to the appropriate parties and agencies from which he sought information, [the requester] ignored the most fundamental dictates of FOIA."). But cf. National Ass'n of Criminal Defense Lawyers v. United States Dep't of Justice, No. 97-372, slip op. at 13 (D.D.C. June 26, 1998) (while acknowledging that complaint was amended to add request for which "the administrative process had [not] run its course," nevertheless awarding interim attorney fees based upon notion that lawsuit, not preexisting administrative process, resulted in release of records in question), interlocutory appeal dismissed for lack of juris., 182 F.3d 981 (D.C. Cir. 1999).

[94] See, e.g., Department of Justice FOIA Regulations, 28 C.F.R. § 16.3 (1999).

[95] See Church of Scientology v. IRS, 792 F.2d 146, 150 (D.C. Cir. 1986); Leytman v. New York Stock Exch., No. 95 CV 902, 1995 WL 761843, at *2 (E.D.N.Y. Dec. 6, 1995); Hahn v. IRS, No. 3-89-3254-D, 1990 U.S. Dist. LEXIS 11594, at **2-3 (N.D. Tex. Aug. 24, 1990); see also Nash v. United States Dep't of Justice, 992 F. Supp. 447, 449 (D.D.C. 1998) (rejecting plaintiff's argument that location of one agency component's records in second component's files necessitates separate search of first component's files, in absence of proper FOIA request to first component), summary affirmance granted, No. 98-5096 (D.C. Cir. July 20, 1998); Rogers v. United States Nat'l Reconnaissance Office, No. 94-B-2934, slip op. at 5 (N.D. Ala. Sept. 13, 1995) (dismissal of Air Force appropriate when request is made to Department of Defense: "It is the plaintiff's burden to make his FOIA request to the agency component which he believes possesses responsive material. Plaintiff has provided no basis to shift that burden to the agency."). But cf. Lehrfeld v. Richardson, 132 F.3d 1463, 1466 (D.C. Cir. 1998) (assuming that proper FOIA request was made, rather than deciding "whether reference to a Vaughn index in a request for information suffices to put the agency on notice that the request is being made pursuant to the FOIA").

[96] See, e.g., Schaake v. IRS, No. 91-958, 1992 U.S. Dist. LEXIS 9418, at *11 (S.D. Ill. June 3, 1992); SafeCard Servs. v. SEC, No. 84-3073, slip op. at 3-5 (D.D.C. Apr. 21, 1986); see also FOIA Update, Vol. VII, No. 3, at 6; cf. Judicial Watch, Inc. v. Clinton, 880 F. Supp. 1, 11 (D.D.C. 1995) (holding that there is no right to Vaughn Index when agency responds within 10 working days), aff'd on other grounds, 76 F.3d 1232 (D.C. Cir. 1996).

## LITIGATION CONSIDERATIONS

time limit for the processing of initial responses to a request, its twenty-day time limit for the processing of administrative appeals, or its ten-day extension of either time limit,[97] requesters have been deemed not to have constructively exhausted administrative remedies when they have failed to comply with necessary requirements of the FOIA's administrative process--for example, when they have failed to provide required proof of identity[98] in first-party requests[99] or disclosure authorization by third parties;[100] failed to "reasonably describe" the records sought;[101] failed to comply with fee requirements;[102]

---

[97] See 5 U.S.C. § 552(a)(6)(A), (a)(6)(B).

[98] See Summers v. United States Dep't of Justice, 999 F.2d 570, 572-73 (D.C. Cir. 1993) (holding that authorization for release of records need not be notarized, but can be attested to under penalty of perjury pursuant to 28 U.S.C. § 1746 (1994)); Davis v. United States Attorney, Dist. of Md., No. 92-3233, slip op. at 2-3 (D. Md. July 5, 1994) (dismissing suit without prejudice when plaintiff failed to provide identification by notarized consent, attestation under 28 U.S.C. § 1746, or alternative form of identification in conformity with agency regulations).

[99] See, e.g., Lilienthal v. Parks, 574 F. Supp. 14, 17-18 (E.D. Ark. 1983).

[100] See Pusa v. FBI, No. 99-04603, slip op. at 5 (C.D. Cal. Aug. 5, 1999) (dismissing case because plaintiff did not comply with agency regulations concerning third-party requests); Harvey v. United States Dep't of Justice, No. CV 92-176, slip op. at 17-18 (D.C. Mont. Jan. 9, 1996) (declining to grant motion for production of third-party records because plaintiff failed to submit authorization at the administrative level), aff'd on other grounds, 116 F.3d 484 (9th Cir. June 3, 1997) (unpublished table decision ); Freedom Magazine v. IRS, No. 91-4536, 1992 U.S. Dist. LEXIS, at **10-13 (C.D. Cal. Nov. 13, 1992) (finding that court lacked jurisdiction when, prior to filing suit, plaintiff failed to provide waivers for third-party records as required by IRS regulations). But see Martin v. United States Dep't of Justice, No. 96-2866, slip op. at 7-8 (D.D.C. Dec. 15, 1999) (ruling that agency was not justified in refusing to process third-party request in absence of privacy waiver because agency's regulation on privacy waivers was permissive, not mandatory, but nevertheless dismissing complaint because all records would be subject to Exemption 7(C) protection in any event); Tanoue v. IRS, 904 F. Supp. 1161, 1165 (D. Haw. 1995) (finding exhaustion despite plaintiff's failure to provide third-party waiver for IRS "return information" because agency ignored request in mistaken belief that no action was necessary inasmuch as information was unreleasable without consent in any case); LaRouche v. United States Dep't of Justice, No. 90-2753, 1993 WL 388601, at *7 (D.D.C. June 25, 1993) (although third-party waivers were not submitted during administrative process, "they present solely legal issues which can properly be resolved by [the] Court").

[101] See, e.g., Gillin, 980 F.2d at 822-23 (when defective request was predicated upon misunderstanding with agency, but within one week after submission, information provided by agency should have prompted requester to revise his request, request does not "reasonably describe" records actually sought); Marks v. United States Dep't of Justice, 578 F.2d 261, 263 (9th Cir. 1978); see also Voinche v. United States Dep't of the Air Force, 983 F.2d 667,

(continued...)

## LITIGATION CONSIDERATIONS

failed to pay authorized fees incurred in a prior request before making new requests;[103] failed to present for review at the administrative appeal level any objection to earlier processing practices;[104] failed to administratively request a waiver of fees;[105] or failed to challenge a fee waiver denial at the administrative appeal stage.[106]

---

[101](...continued)
669 n.5 (5th Cir. 1993) (administrative remedies on fee waiver request not exhausted when requester failed to amend request to achieve specificity required by agency regulations).

[102] See, e.g., Pollack, 49 F.3d at 119-20 (rejecting plaintiff's novel argument that untimeliness of agency response required it to provide documents free of charge); Center to Prevent Handgun Violence, 981 F. Supp. at 23 (rejecting requester's "equitable tolling" argument; requester's agreement to accept sampling of documents for free does not excuse noncompliance with exhaustion requirement in subsequent fee waiver suit covering all records); Trueblood v. United States Dep't of the Treasury, 943 F. Supp. 64, 68 (D.D.C. 1996) ("Regardless of whether the plaintiff 'filed' suit before or after receiving a request for payment, the plaintiff has an obligation to pay for the reasonable copying and search fees assessed by the defendant."); Kuchta v. Harris, No. 92-1121, 1993 WL 87750, at **3-4 (D. Md. Mar. 25, 1993) (failure to either pay fees or request fee waiver halts administrative process and precludes exhaustion); Centracchio v. FBI, No. 92-0357, slip op. at 5 (D.D.C. Mar. 16, 1993) ("Plaintiff's failure to pay the deposit or request a waiver is fatal to his claim and requires dismissal . . . ."); Atkin v. EEOC, No. 91-2508, slip op. at 21-22 (D.N.J. Dec. 4, 1992) ("[E]xhaustion does not occur where the requester has failed to pay the assessed fees, even though the agency failed to timely process a request."), appeal dismissed for failure to prosecute, No. 93-5548 (3d Cir. Dec. 6, 1993); see also Atkin v. EEOC, No. 92-5522, slip op. at 5 n.3 (D.N.J. Jan. 24, 1994) (subject matter jurisdiction determined as of date complaint filed; fact that plaintiff paid fees after suit instituted does not confer jurisdiction).

[103] See, e.g., Trenerry v. IRS, No. 95-5150, 1996 WL 88459, at *1 (10th Cir. Mar. 1, 1996); Crooker, 577 F. Supp. at 1219-20; Mahler v. Department of Justice, 2 Gov't Disclosure Serv. (P-H) ¶ 82,032, at 82,262 (D.D.C. Sept. 29, 1981).

[104] See, e.g., Halpern v. FBI, 181 F.3d 279, 289 (2d Cir. 1999) (approving FBI practice of seeking clarification of requester's interest in "cross-references" and dismissing portion of suit challenging failure to process those records when plaintiff did not dispute agency action until after suit was filed); Dettman, 802 F.2d at 1477 (same).

[105] See, e.g., Trenerry, 1996 WL 88459, at *2; Voinche, 983 F.2d at 669.

[106] See, e.g., Tinsley v. Commissioner, No. 3:96-1769-P, 1998 WL 59481, at *4 (N.D. Tex. Feb. 9, 1998); Crooker v. CIA, No. 86-3055, 1988 WL 50724, at *1 (D.D.C. May 10, 1988).

# LITIGATION CONSIDERATIONS

## "Open America" Stays of Proceedings

Even when a requester has constructively exhausted administrative remedies, due to an agency's failure to comply with the FOIA's time deadlines, and then files a suit in court, the Act provides that the court may retain jurisdiction and allow the agency additional time to complete its processing of the request--ordinarily through issuance of a stay of the court proceedings--if it can be shown that "exceptional circumstances exist and that the agency is exercising due diligence in responding to the request."[107] This provision of the FOIA provides an important "safety valve" for agencies that have been, and continue to be, overwhelmed by increasing numbers of FOIA requests.[108]

The leading case construing this FOIA provision is Open America v. Watergate Special Prosecution Force.[109] In Open America, the Court of Appeals for the District of Columbia Circuit held that "exceptional circumstances" may exist when an agency can show that it "is deluged with a volume of requests for information vastly in excess of that anticipated by Congress [and] when the existing resources are inadequate to deal with the volume of such requests within the time limits of subsection (6)(A)."[110]

The Electronic Freedom of Information Act Amendments of 1996 tightened the standard for obtaining a stay of proceedings by redefining the term "exceptional circumstances" so as to exclude any "delay that results from a predictable agency workload of requests . . . unless the agency demonstrates reasonable progress in reducing its backlog of pending requests."[111] The intent of this provision was to raise the hurdle for agencies seeking a stay of proceedings based only on the existence of a FOIA backlog.[112] The amendments mitigated the impact of this modification somewhat, though, by including a com-

---

[107] 5 U.S.C. § 552(a)(6)(C)(i) (1994 & Supp. IV 1998).

[108] See Manna v. United States Dep't of Justice, No. 93-81, 1994 WL 808070, at *10 (D.N.J. Apr. 13, 1994) (noting "huge number of FOIA requests that have overwhelmed [agency's] human and related resources"); Cohen v. FBI, 831 F. Supp. 850, 854 (S.D. Fla. 1993) (explaining that court "cannot focus on theoretical goals alone, and completely ignore the reality that these agencies cannot possibly respond to the overwhelming number of requests received within the time constraints imposed by FOIA").

[109] 547 F.2d 605 (D.C. Cir. 1976).

[110] Id. at 616.

[111] Electronic Freedom of Information Act Amendments of 1996, Pub. L. No. 104-231, § 7(c), 110 Stat. 3048 (codified as amended at 5 U.S.C. § 552(a)(6)(C)(ii)); see also FOIA Update, Vol. XVIII, No. 3, at 3-7 (advising agencies regarding reporting of backlog-related information in annual FOIA reports, beginning with annual reports for Fiscal Year 1998).

[112] See H.R. Rep. No. 104-795, at 18-19 (1996); see also Eltayib v. United States Coast Guard, No. 99-1033, slip op. at 3 (D.D.C. Nov. 11, 1999) (explaining intent of Electronic FOIA amendments' modification of FOIA's "exceptional circumstances" provision); see also FOIA Update, Vol. XVII, No. 4, at 10.

## LITIGATION CONSIDERATIONS

panion provision that specifies that a requester's "refusal . . . to reasonably modify the scope of a request or arrange for an alternative time frame for processing . . . shall be considered as a factor in determining whether exceptional circumstances exist."[113]

In <u>Open America</u>, the D.C. Circuit ruled that the "due diligence" requirement in the FOIA may be satisfied by an agency's good faith processing of all requests on a "first-in/first-out" basis and that a requester's right to have his request processed out of turn requires a particularized showing of "exceptional need or urgency."[114] In so ruling, the D.C. Circuit rejected the notion that the mere filing of a lawsuit was a basis for such expedited treatment.[115] The Electronic FOIA amendments modified this approach by explicitly allowing agencies to establish "multitrack" processing for requests, based on the amount of time and/or work involved in a particular request.[116] They nevertheless preserved the principle that, within such multiple tracks, requests should still be handled on a first-in, first-out basis in order for an agency to be found to be exercising "due diligence."[117]

When the requirements of the statute and <u>Open America</u> are met, an agency can move for a stay of judicial proceedings to obtain any additional time necessary to complete the administrative processing of the request.[118]

---

[113] 5 U.S.C. § 552(a)(6)(C)(iii); <u>see also</u> H.R. Rep. No. 104-795, at 24-25.

[114] <u>See</u> <u>Open Am.</u>, 547 F.2d at 616.

[115] <u>Id.</u> at 615; <u>see also</u> <u>Fiduccia v. United States Dep't of Justice</u>, 185 F.3d 1035, 1040-41 (9th Cir. 1999) (refusing to approve automatic preference for FOIA requesters who file suit, because it "would generate many pointless and burdensome lawsuits"); <u>Cohen</u>, 831 F. Supp. at 854 ("[L]ittle progress would result from allowing FOIA requesters to move to the head of the line by filing a lawsuit. This would do nothing to eliminate the FOIA backlog; it would merely add to the judiciary's backlog."). <u>But see</u> <u>Exner v. FBI</u>, 542 F.2d 1121, 1123 (9th Cir. 1976) (adopting approach of concurring opinion in <u>Open America</u> and holding that filing of suit can move requester "up the line").

[116] Electronic Freedom of Information Act Amendments of 1996, Pub. L. No. 104-231, § 7(a)(D)(i), 110 Stat. 3048 (codified at 5 U.S.C. § 552(a)(6)(D)(i)).

[117] <u>Id.</u> § 7(a)(D)(ii) (codified at 5 U.S.C. § 552(a)(6)(D)(iii)).

[118] <u>See, e.g.</u>, <u>Judicial Watch, Inc. v. United States Dep't of State</u>, No. 99-1130, slip op. at 2 (D.D.C. Feb. 17, 2000) (approving 10-month stay because "unanticipated workload, the inadequate resources of the agency, and the complexity of many of the requests" constitute exceptional circumstances) (appeal pending); <u>Emerson v. CIA</u>, No. 99-0274, 1999 U.S. Dist. LEXIS 19511, at \*\*3-4 (D.D.C. Dec. 16, 1999) (granting two-year stay because of "extraordinary circumstances" and multiple agency efforts to alleviate FOIA backlog); <u>Summers v. CIA</u>, No. 98-1682, slip op. at 4 (D.D.C. July 26, 1999) (finding that FBI's FOIA procedures are "fair and expeditious" and that exceptional circumstances exists, warranting six-month stay of proceedings); <u>Judicial Watch, Inc. v. United States Dep't of Justice</u>, No. 97-2869, slip op. at 6-8

(continued...)

## LITIGATION CONSIDERATIONS

This includes the time required to consult with other agencies whose information is included in the responsive records, particularly when such review by the originating agency is mandatory,[119] as well as the time necessary to complete any administrative appeal process.[120]

When there is a large volume of responsive documents that have not been processed, a court may grant a stay of proceedings that provides for interim or "timed" releases and/or interim status reports on agency processing efforts.[121] In addition, an "Open America" stay should, when necessary, include the time required for preparation of a Vaughn Index.[122] While the Open America decision itself does not address the additional time needed by an agency to justify nondisclosure of any withheld records once they are processed, courts have, as a practical matter, tended to merge the record-processing and affidavit-preparation stages of a case when issuing stays of proceedings under Open America.[123]

---

[118](...continued)
(D.D.C. Aug. 25, 1998) (finding that agency exercised due diligence when both parties agreed that exceptional circumstances existed and requester failed to show exceptional need for records); Narducci v. FBI, No. 98-0130, slip op. at 1 (D.D.C. July 17, 1998) (ordering 34-month stay because of "deluge[]" of requests coupled with "reasonable progress" in reducing backlog). See generally FOIA Update, Vol. XIII, No. 2, at 8-10; FOIA Update, Vol. XI, No. 1, at 1-2. But see Los Alamos Study Group v. Department of Energy, No. 99-201, slip op. at 4-5 (D.N.M. Oct. 26, 1999) (declining to approve stay of proceedings predicated on agency's need to review sensitive materials because such review "is part of the predictable agency workload of requests").

[119] See, e.g., Gilmore v. United States Dep't of State, No. C 95-1098, slip op. at 25-26, 29 (N.D. Cal. Feb. 9, 1996) ("[A]gency receiving requests for information classified by another agency 'shall refer copies . . . to the originating agency for processing.'" (quoting Exec. Order No. 12,958 § 3.7(b), 3 C.F.R. 333 (1996), reprinted in 50 U.S.C. § 435 note (Supp. II 1996), and reprinted in abridged form in FOIA Update, Vol. XVI, No. 2, at 5-10)).

[120] See, e.g., Steinberg v. United States Dep't of Justice, No. 93-2348, 1994 WL 86603, at *1 (D.D.C. 1994).

[121] See, e.g., Raulerson v. Reno, No. 95-2053, slip op. at 1 (D.D.C. Sept. 11, 1998) (approving 30-month stay to process over 19,000 pages, but ordering four interim status reports); Samuel Gruber Educ. Project v. United States Dep't of Justice, No. 90-1912, slip op at 6 (D.D.C. Feb. 8, 1991) (granting nearly two-year stay, but requiring six-month progress reports); Hinton v. FBI, 527 F. Supp. 223, 223-25 (E.D. Pa. 1981) (staying proceedings, but ordering interim releases at 90-day intervals).

[122] See FOIA Update, Vol. IX, No. 4, at 5.

[123] See, e.g., Lisee, 741 F. Supp. at 989-90 ("Open America" stay granted for both processing records and preparing Vaughn Index); Ettlinger v. FBI, 596 F. Supp. 867, 878-79 (D. Mass. 1984) (same); Shaw v. Department of State, 1 Gov't Disclosure Serv. (P-H) ¶ 80,250, at 80,630 (D.D.C. July 31, 1980) (same).

## LITIGATION CONSIDERATIONS

Since enactment of the Electronic FOIA amendments, agencies have had continued success in demonstrating "exceptional circumstances" and the concomitant "due diligence" required to obtain a stay of proceedings because of their backlog-reduction efforts.[124] At the same time, though, some courts have taken increasing scrutiny of agency claims that long processing delays are warranted.[125]

Of course, once an "Open America" stay has been granted, "[i]t would make no sense to require the government to produce a Vaughn Index before the government has processed [the] FOIA request."[126] Nor can a requester

---

[124] See, e.g., Emerson, 1999 U.S. Dist. LEXIS 19511, at **3-4 (allowing agency two-year stay); Reed v. United States Dep't of Justice, No. 97-2150, slip op. at 2 (D. Ariz. Nov. 10, 1998) (staying proceedings for 18 months); Narducci, No. 98-0130, slip op. at 1 (D.D.C. July 17, 1998) (granting nearly three-year stay). See generally FOIA Update, Vol. XIX, No. 4, at 7 (describing FBI effort to reduce backlog through use of negotiation team); FOIA Update, No. XIX, No. 3, at 5-6 (describing Department of Justice efforts at backlog reduction). But see Eltayib v. United States Coast Guard, No. 99-1033, slip op. at 4 (D.D.C. Nov. 11, 1999) (denying stay and taking agency to task for failing to take any measures to comport with statutory requirements for showing reasonable progress).

[125] See Fiduccia, 185 F.3d at 1040 (overturning stay of proceedings allowed by district court because delay was only "ordinary and expected"); Beneville v. United States Dep't of Justice, No. 98-6137, slip op. at 8 (D. Or. Dec. 17, 1998) (declining to approve full stay of proceedings requested by FBI for Unabomber files); Grecco v. Department of Justice, No. 97-0419, slip op. at 2 (D.D.C. Aug. 24, 1998) (granting two-year rather than four-year stay that was requested by FBI); see also Peralta v. FBI, No. 94-760, slip op. at 2 (D.D.C. June 6, 1997) (reducing Open America stay by four months because of enactment of Electronic FOIA amendments and requiring that agency justify additional time needed for processing on basis of new statutory standard), vacated & remanded on other grounds, 136 F.3d 169 (D.C. Cir. 1998); cf. Jimenez v. FBI, 938 F. Supp. 21, 31-32 (D.D.C. 1996) (pre-Electronic FOIA amendment decision granting stay totaling approximately five years from date of request in view of FBI's "two track system and the large volume of documents expected to be responsive to plaintiff's request"); Cecola v. FBI, No. 94 C 4866, 1995 U.S. Dist. LEXIS 13253, at **6-8 (N.D. Ill. Sept. 8, 1995) (pre-Electronic FOIA amendment decision dismissing plaintiff's action without prejudice and allowing FBI more than six years from date of request to process documents); Fox v. United States Dep't of Justice, No. 94-4622, 1004 WL 923072, at *3 (C.D. Cal. Dec. 14, 1994) (pre-Electronic FOIA amendment decision granting stay until 1999 for request submitted to FBI in July 1993; agency required to file status report approximately one year after decision), appeal dismissed, No. 94-56788 (9th Cir. Feb. 21, 1995). But cf. Gilmore v. United States Dep't of Energy, 4 F. Supp. 2d 912, 925 (N.D. Cal. 1998) ("Where a pattern and practice of late responses is alleged . . . a normal, predictable workload cannot constitute 'exceptional circumstances.'"), dismissed per stipulation, No. 95-0285 (N.D. Cal. Apr. 3, 2000).

[126] Edmond v. United States Attorney, 959 F. Supp. 1, 5 (D.D.C. 1997); see
(continued...)

## LITIGATION CONSIDERATIONS

effectively circumvent an "Open America" stay by the simple expedient of filing a new complaint based on the same request.[127]

An "Open America" stay may be denied when the requester can show an "exceptional need or urgency" for having his request processed out of turn.[128] Traditionally, such a showing was made if the requester's life or personal safety, or substantial due process rights, would be jeopardized by the failure to process a request immediately.[129] The Department of Justice, as a matter of administrative policy, also expedited FOIA requests when there was "widespread and exceptional media interest" in information which "involve[d] pos-

---

[126](...continued)
Cohen, 831 F. Supp. at 854.

[127] See Hunsberger v. United States Dep't of Justice, No. 94-0168, 1994 U.S. Dist. LEXIS, at **1-2 (D.D.C. May 3, 1994), summary affirmance granted, No. 94-5234 (D.C. Cir. Apr. 10, 1995).

[128] See Open Am., 547 F.2d at 616; see also Aguilera v. FBI, 941 F. Supp. 144, 149-52 (D.D.C. 1996) (initially finding that FBI satisfied "exceptional circumstances-due diligence test" warranting 87-month delay, but granting expedited access due to exigent circumstances), appeal dismissed, No. 98-5035 (D.C. Cir. Mar. 18, 1998).

[129] See, e.g., Neely v. FBI, No. 97-0786, slip op. at 9 (W.D. Va. July 27, 1998) (granting expedited processing of FOIA request where plaintiff has pending motion for new criminal trial based on alleged false trial testimony and needs documents for proof), vacated & remanded on other grounds, 208 F.3d 461 (4th Cir. 2000); Ferguson v. FBI, 722 F. Supp. 1137, 1141-44 (S.D.N.Y. 1989) (need for documents, not otherwise available, in post-conviction challenge and upcoming criminal trial); Cleaver v. Kelley, 427 F. Supp. 80, 81 (D.D.C. 1976) (plaintiff facing multiple criminal charges carrying possible death penalty in state court); see also FOIA Update, Vol. IV, No. 3, at 3 ("OIP Guidance: When to Expedite FOIA Requests"); cf. Kitchen v. FBI, No. 94-5159, 1995 WL 311615, at *1 (D.C. Cir. Apr. 27, 1995) (per curiam) (requester has not shown sufficiently serious harm to warrant interlocutory appeal when deportation hearing not yet scheduled (citing Ray, 770 F. Supp. at 1550-51)); Billington v. United States Dep't of Justice, No. 92-462, slip op. at 3-5 (D.D.C. July 27, 1992) (expedited treatment denied despite pendency of prosecutions, when requester had not shown any likelihood that files contain "materially exculpatory information"). Compare Freeman v. United States Dep't of Justice, No. 92-557, slip op. at 6 (D.D.C. Oct. 2, 1992) (expedited processing granted when scope of request limited, "Jencks Act" type material unavailable in state prosecution, and information useful to plaintiff's criminal defense might have been contained in requested documents), with Freeman v. United States Dep't of Justice, No. 92-557, 1993 WL 260694, at *5 (D.D.C. June 28, 1993) (denying further expedited treatment when processing "would require a hand search of approximately 50,000 pages, taking approximately 120 days"). But see Gilmore v. FBI, No. 93-2117, slip op. at 1, 3 (N.D. Cal. July 26, 1994) (expediting request despite showing of due diligence and exceptional circumstances, based upon perfunctory finding that "[p]laintiff has sufficiently shown that the information he seeks will become less valuable if the FBI processes his request on a first-in, first-out basis").

## LITIGATION CONSIDERATIONS

sible questions about the government's integrity which affect public confidence."[130] In all such instances, however, the burden of demonstrating "a genuine need and reason for urgency in gaining access to Government records" fell upon the requester.[131]

The Electronic FOIA amendments generally codified these requirements. Under them, agencies must have regulations providing for the granting of expedited treatment in cases of "compelling need" or "in other cases determined by the agency."[132] "Compelling need" is defined by law to encompass a situation in which withholding of the requested records "could reasonably be expected to pose an imminent threat to the life or physical safety of an individual."[133] Additionally, the Electronic FOIA amendments specify that expedited processing will be granted when there exists, "with respect to a request made by a person primarily engaged in disseminating information, urgency to inform the public concerning actual or alleged Federal Government activity."[134]

Absent truly exceptional circumstances, though, courts have generally declined to order expedited processing when records are "needed" for post-judgment attacks on criminal convictions,[135] or for use in other civil litiga-

---

[130] FOIA Update, Vol. XV, No. 2, at 2 (encouraging other federal agencies to adopt similar policies); see also Department of Justice FOIA Regulations, 28 C.F.R. § 16.5(d)(iv) (1999) (continuing such policy).

[131] Open Am., 547 F.2d at 615-16; see Edmond, 959 F. Supp. at 3; Ohaegbu v. FBI, 936 F. Supp. 8-9 (D.D.C. 1996), appeal dismissed for lack of prosecution, No. 96-5261 (D.C. Cir. Nov. 22, 1996); Lisee v. CIA, 741 F. Supp. 988, 989 (D.D.C. 1990).

[132] 5 U.S.C. § 552(a)(6)(E)(i); see FOIA Update, Vol. XVII, No. 4, at 10.

[133] 5 U.S.C. § 552(a)(6)(E)(v)(I).

[134] Id. § 552(a)(6)(E)(v)(II); see also 28 C.F.R. § 16.5(d) (1999) (specifying procedures for expedited processing, including when there is "[a]n urgency to inform the public about an actual or alleged federal government activity, if made by a person primarily engaged in disseminating information").

[135] See, e.g., Edmond, 959 F. Supp. at 4; Schweihs v. FBI, 933 F. Supp. 719, 723 (N.D. Ill. 1996) (denying expedited processing of records related to plaintiff's conviction, despite plaintiff's claims of ill health); Russell v. Barr, No. 92-2546, slip op. at 2 (D.D.C. Mar. 5, 1993) (holding "[p]laintiff's claim that the requested information may 'minister [his] defense in the civil proceeding and motion for a new trial' in his criminal proceeding" inadequate to justify expedition); Thompson v. FBI, No. 90-3020, slip op. at 3 (D.D.C. July 8, 1991); Shilling v. ATF, No. 90-1422, slip op. at 3 (D.D.C. Dec. 3, 1990). But see Aguilera, 941 F. Supp. at 152-53 (ordering expedited processing for request not scheduled for completion for nearly 90 months because "[p]laintiff has demonstrated that he faces grave punishment, his reason to believe the documents may assist in his defense has been corroborated by objective proof, his request is limited in scope, and the criminal discovery process is unavailable").

## LITIGATION CONSIDERATIONS

tion.[136] In addition, it has been held firmly that publishing deadlines are not sufficient grounds for expedited processing.[137] Employing an extremely unusual tactic, one plaintiff sought, in lieu of seeking expedited processing of his FOIA request, to have a federal court stay his state habeas corpus proceedings pending a response to his FOIA request.[138] Rejecting such a novel stay application, the court found that it was constrained by the constitutional doctrine of Younger v. Harris[139] from interfering in the state court proceedings.[140] (For a further discussion of expedited processing, see Procedural Requirements, Time Limits, above.)

### Adequacy of Search

In many suits under the FOIA, the defendant agency will face challenges not only to its reliance on particular exemptions, but also to the nature and extent of its search for responsive documents. (For a discussion of administrative considerations in conducting searches, see Procedural Requirements, Searching for Records, above.) To prevail in a FOIA action, the agency must prove that "'each document that falls within the class requested either has been produced, is unidentifiable, or is wholly exempt from the Act's inspection requirements.'"[141] Thus, the agency is under a duty to conduct a "reason-

---

[136] See, e.g., Price v. CIA, No. 90-1507, slip op. at 2 (4th Cir. Oct. 2, 1990); Rogers v. United States Nat'l Reconnaissance Office, No. 94-B-2934, slip op. at 17 (N.D. Ala. Sept. 13, 1995) ("Courts have consistently rejected claims of urgency based on private litigation concerns."); Fox, No. 94-4622, slip op. at 10-11 (C.D. Cal. Dec. 14, 1994); Cohen, 831 F. Supp. at 854; cf. Armstrong v. Bush, 807 F. Supp. 816, 819 (D.D.C. 1992) (priority accorded to additional FOIA requests added to those already subject of litigation, when responsive records might otherwise be destroyed).

[137] See, e.g., Freeman v. United States Dep't of Justice, 822 F. Supp. 1064, 1067 (S.D.N.Y. 1993) ("Plaintiff's desire to inform the public [through publication and submission to a Congressional committee], while commendable, does not constitute an exceptional need. Since almost every request can be linked to such a desire, granting expedited treatment for that purpose would allow the exception to swallow the rule."); Nation Magazine v. United States Dep't of State, 805 F. Supp. 68, 73 (D.D.C. 1992) ("[T]here are numerous reasons why this Court should not broaden the definition of 'exceptional need or urgency' to include FOIA requests concerning Presidential candidates pending weeks before an election."); Lisee, 741 F. Supp. at 989; Summers v. United States Dep't of Justice, 733 F. Supp. 443, 444 (D.D.C. 1990), appeal dismissed on procedural grounds, 925 F.2d 450 (D.C. Cir. 1991).

[138] See Sosa v. FBI, No. 93-1126, slip op. at 1 (D.D.C. Nov. 4, 1993).

[139] 401 U.S. 37 (1971).

[140] See Sosa, No. 93-1126, slip op. at 1 (D.D.C. Nov. 4, 1993).

[141] May v. IRS, 85 F. Supp. 2d 939, 944 (W.D. Mo. 1999) (quoting Miller v. United States Dep't of State, 779 F.2d 1378, 1383 (8th Cir. 1985) (quoting, in turn, National Cable Television Ass'n v. FCC, 479 F.2d 183, 186 (D.C. Cir. 1973)).

## LITIGATION CONSIDERATIONS

able" search for responsive records.[142]

The adequacy of a search is necessarily "dependent upon the circumstances of the case."[143] The agency "must show that it made a good faith effort to conduct a search for the requested records, using methods which can be reasonably expected to produce the information requested."[144] The fundamental question is not "'whether there might exist any other documents possibly responsive to the request, but rather whether the search for those documents was adequate.'"[145] In other words, "the search need only be reasonable;

---

[142] See, e.g., Patterson v. IRS, 56 F.3d 832, 841 (7th Cir. 1995); Citizens Comm'n on Human Rights v. FDA, 45 F.3d 1325, 1328 (9th Cir. 1995); Oglesby v. United States Dep't of the Army, 920 F.2d 57, 68 (D.C. Cir. 1990); Weisberg v. United States Dep't of Justice, 705 F.2d 1344, 1352 (D.C. Cir. 1983).

[143] Truitt v. Department of State, 897 F.2d 540, 542 (D.C. Cir. 1990); see Maynard v. CIA, 986 F.2d 547, 559 (1st Cir. 1993) ("depends upon the facts of each case"); Kronberg v. United States Dep't of Justice, 875 F. Supp. 861, 869 (D.D.C. 1995) (same).

[144] Oglesby, 920 F.2d at 68; see Maynard, 986 F.2d at 559; SafeCard Servs. v. SEC, 926 F.2d 1197, 1201 (D.C. Cir. 1991); see also Keenan v. United States Dep't of Justice, No. 94-1909, slip op. at 6 (D.D.C. Apr. 25, 1996) ("A search for all documents referring to an 'FBI representative' is an unreasonably burdensome search and the CIA is therefore not obligated to undertake it."); Crompton v. Criminal Div., No. CV 95-8176, slip op. at 10 (C.D. Cal. Apr. 1, 1996) (search adequate when "Criminal Division would search for documents relevant to the plaintiff for its own uses in the same manner that it attempted to locate any documents responsive to the plaintiff's FOIA request"); Spannaus v. United States Dep't of Justice, No. 92-372, slip op. at 5 (D.D.C. June 20, 1995) (unreasonable to require search through files of agency employees who had no significant involvement with, nor maintained separate files on, subject of request), summary affirmance granted in relevant part & remanded in part, No. 95-5267 (D.C. Cir. Aug. 16, 1996); Kubany v. Board of Governors, Fed. Reserve Sys., No. 93-1428, slip op. at 8-9 (D.D.C. July 19, 1994) ("The FOIA does not require an agency to undertake the openended, broadbased, and ill-defined searches requested by the plaintiff."); Spannaus v. CIA, 841 F. Supp. 14, 18 (D.D.C. 1993) ("FOIA does not require . . . a burdensome tape-by-tape listening search" of hundreds of 90-minute audiotapes).

[145] Steinberg v. United States Dep't of Justice, 23 F.3d 548, 551 (D.C. Cir. 1994) (quoting Weisberg v. United States Dep't of Justice, 745 F.2d 1476, 1485 (D.C. Cir. 1984)); see Citizens Comm'n, 45 F.3d at 1328 (same); see also Nation Magazine v. United States Customs Serv., 71 F.3d 885, 892 n.7 (D.C. Cir. 1995) ("there is no requirement that an agency [locate] all responsive documents"); Ethyl Corp. v. EPA, 25 F.3d 1241, 1246 (4th Cir. 1994) ("In judging the adequacy of an agency search for documents the relevant question is not whether every single potentially responsive document has been unearthed."); In re Wade, 969 F.2d 241, 249 n.11 (7th Cir. 1992); Meeropol v. Meese, 790 F.2d 942, 952-53 (D.C. Cir. 1986) ("[A] search is not unreasonable simply because it fails to produce all relevant material; no search of this [large] size . . . will be free from error."); Miller, 779 F.2d at 1385 ("[P]laintiff alleges that the
(continued...)

## LITIGATION CONSIDERATIONS

it does not have to be exhaustive."[146] A reasonable search, though, may require a search of records that an agency has stored at a federal records center, because such records are deemed "'to be maintained by the agency which deposited [them].'"[147]

While the initial burden certainly rests with the agency to demonstrate the adequacy of the search,[148] once that obligation is satisfied, the agency's position can be rebutted "only by showing that the agency's search was not made in good faith."[149] Consequently, a requester's "'[m]ere speculation that

---

[145](...continued) search was insufficient because the Department did not do all that it could; we agree . . . however, that it did all the Act required."); Freeman v. United States Dep't of Justice, No. 90-2754, slip op. at 3 (D.D.C. Oct. 16, 1991) ("The FOIA does not require that the government go fishing in the ocean for fresh water fish."); Fitzgibbon v. United States Secret Serv., 747 F. Supp. 51, 54 (D.D.C. 1990) (paucity of documents produced held to be "of no legal consequence" when search is shown to be reasonable); cf. Raulerson v. Reno, No. 96-120, slip op. at 5 (D.D.C. Feb. 26, 1999) (suggesting that agency's failure to locate complaints filed by plaintiff, the existence of which agency did not dispute, "casts substantial doubt" on adequacy of agency's search), summary affirmance granted, No. 99-5300 (D.C. Cir. Nov. 23, 1999), cert. denied, 68 U.S.L.W. 3685 (U.S. May 1, 2000) (No. 99-8595).

[146] Miller, 779 F.2d at 1383 (citing Shaw v. United States Dep't of State, 559 F. Supp. 1053, 1057 (D.D.C. 1983)); see also Citizens Against UFO Secrecy, Inc. v. DOD, No. 99-0108, slip op. at 8 (D. Ariz. Mar. 30, 2000) (declaring that "[a] fruitless search result is immaterial if Defendant can establish that it conducted a search reasonably calculated to uncover all relevant documents"); Rothschild v. Department of Energy, 6 F. Supp. 2d 38, 40 (D.D.C. 1998) (explaining that "[p]erfection . . . is not the standard" for judging an agency's search); Boggs v. United States, 987 F. Supp. 11, 20 (D.D.C. 1997) (noting that role of court is to determine reasonableness of search, "not whether the fruits of the search met plaintiff's aspirations").

[147] Valencia-Lucena v. United States Coast Guard, 180 F.3d 321, 327 (D.C. Cir. 1999) (quoting regulations of National Archives and Records Administration codified at 36 C.F.R. § 1228.162 (1998)).

[148] See Patterson, 56 F.3d at 840; Maynard, 986 F.2d at 560; Miller, 779 F.2d at 1378; Weisberg, 705 F.2d at 1351; see also Williams v. United States Attorney's Office, No. 96-1367, slip op. at 5 (D.D.C. Sept. 21, 1999) (explaining that to prove adequacy of search, agency's affidavit should describe "where and how it looked for responsive records" and "what it was looking for"); Bennett v. DEA, 55 F. Supp. 2d 36, 40 (D.D.C. 1999) (pointing out that affidavit must provide details of scope of search; "simply stating that 'any and all records' were searched is insufficient").

[149] Maynard, 986 F.2d at 560 (citing Miller, 779 F.2d at 1383); see, e.g., Carney v. United States Dep't of Justice, 19 F.3d 807, 812 (2d Cir. 1994); Weisberg, 705 F.2d at 1351-52; Triestman v. United States Dep't of Justice, 878 F. Supp. 667, 672 (S.D.N.Y. 1995); U.S. News, No. 84-2303, slip op. at 3 (D.D.C.
(continued...)

## LITIGATION CONSIDERATIONS

as yet uncovered documents may exist does not undermine the finding that the agency conducted a reasonable search for them.'"[150] Even when a request-

---

[149](...continued)
Oct. 29, 1985) ("Plaintiff's burden of proof on the issue of agency bad faith is heavy indeed."); see also Wright v. IRS, No. S-95-0483, 1995 U.S. Dist. LEXIS 16118, at *3 (E.D. Cal. Oct. 17, 1995) ("Although the decoding information provided plaintiff is far from helpful and of doubtful accuracy, the IRS has represented that this information is all that it has. The court has no reason to question that representation, and therefore cannot order further disclosure."); cf. Harvey v. United States Dep't of Justice, No. 92-176, slip op. at 10 (D. Mont. Jan. 9, 1996) ("The purported bad faith of government agents in separate criminal proceedings is irrelevant to [the] question of the adequate, good faith search for documents responsive to a FOIA request."), aff'd on other grounds, 116 F.3d 484 (9th Cir. 1997) (unpublished table decision).

[150] Steinberg, 23 F.3d at 552 (quoting SafeCard, 926 F.2d at 1201); see Kucernak v. FBI, No. 96-17143, 1997 WL 697377, at *1 (9th Cir. Nov. 4, 1997) ("Mere allegations that the government is shielding or destroying documents does [sic] not undermine the adequacy . . . of the search."), cert. denied, 523 U.S. 1051 (1998); Oglesby, 920 F.2d at 67 n.13 ("[H]ypothetical assertions are insufficient to raise a material question of fact with respect to the adequacy of the agency's search."); Hightower v. FBI, No. 98-2817, slip op. at 7 (D.D.C. Mar. 20, 2000) (noting that "[plaintiff's speculation that additional or different documents may exist" is not sufficient to rebut presumption of reasonable search because "[i]t is the method of search that determines whether it was reasonable, rather than the results"); Chamberlain v. United States Dep't of Justice, 957 F. Supp. 292, 294 (D.D.C. 1997) ("It is well established that '[a]gency affidavits enjoy a presumption of good faith that withstand[s] purely speculative claims about the existence and discoverability of other documents.'" (quoting Albuquerque Publ'g Co. v. United States Dep't of Justice, 726 F. Supp. 851, 860 (D.D.C. 1989)); Spannaus, No. 92-372, slip op. at 6 (D.D.C. June 20, 1995) (plaintiff's unsubstantiated assertion that documents released by other agencies must also be maintained in files of United States Attorney's Office held insufficient to overcome "detailed affidavits describing the numerous searches undertaken to locate documents responsive to plaintiff's request"); Judicial Watch, Inc. v. Clinton, 880 F. Supp. 1, 10 (D.D.C. 1995) ("Nor can plaintiff rely on unsupported inferences that other documents must have been created."), aff'd on other grounds, 76 F.3d 1232 (D.C. Cir. 1996); Okon v. IRS, No. 91-660, slip op. at 8-9 (D.N.M. Jan. 12, 1995) ("Ms. Okon has articulated intelligent and logical reasons why she believes other documents responsive to her FOIA request may exist. That fact notwithstanding, I cannot say the search undertaken was not reasonably calculated to uncover all responsive documents."); Bay Area Lawyers Alliance for Nuclear Arms Control v. Department of State, 818 F. Supp. 1291, 1295 (N.D. Cal. 1992) ("Plaintiff's incredulity at the fact that no responsive documents were uncovered . . . does not constitute evidence of unreasonableness or bad faith."). But see Meyer v. Federal Bureau of Prisons, 940 F. Supp. 9, 14 (D.D.C. 1996) (reference to responsive pages in agency memorandum, coupled with equivocal statement in declaration that it "appears" responsive pages do not exist, requires further clarification by agency); Katzman v. Freeh, 926 F. Supp. 316, 320 (E.D.N.Y. 1996) (because additional documents were

(continued...)

## LITIGATION CONSIDERATIONS

ed document indisputably exists or once existed, summary judgment will not be defeated by an unsuccessful search for the document, so long as the search was diligent.[151] Indeed, "[n]othing in the law requires the agency to document the fate of documents it cannot find."[152] And when an agency does subsequently locate additional documents, or documents initially believed to have been lost or destroyed, courts have accepted this as evidence of the agency's

---

[150](...continued)
referenced in released documents, summary judgment was withheld "until defendant releases these documents or demonstrates that they either are exempt from disclosure or cannot be located").

[151] See Nation Magazine, 71 F.3d at 892 n.7 ("Of course, failure to turn up [a specified] document does not alone render the search inadequate."); Citizens Comm'n, 45 F.3d at 1328 (adequacy of search not undermined by inability to locate 137 out of 1000 volumes of responsive material, absent evidence of bad faith, and when affidavit contained detailed, nonconclusory account of search); Maynard, 986 F.2d at 564 ("'The fact that a document once existed does not mean that it now exists; nor does the fact that an agency created a document necessarily imply that the agency has retained it.'" (quoting Miller, 779 F.2d at 1385)); Coalition on Political Assassinations v. DOD, No. 99-0594, slip op. at 7 (D.D.C. Mar. 29, 2000) (noting that even if agency once possessed responsive records, agency's unsuccessful search was nevertheless thorough and well-explained and thus agency "fulfilled its obligation under the FOIA"); Kay v. FCC, 976 F. Supp. 23, 33 (D.D.C. 1997) (explaining that search not inadequate simply because plaintiff received in discovery documents not produced in response to FOIA request; discovery "may differ from FOIA disclosure procedures"), aff'd, 172 F.3d 919 (D.C. Cir. 1998) (unpublished table decision); Antonelli v. United States Parole Comm'n, No. 93-0109, slip op. at 2 (D.D.C. Feb. 23, 1996) ("While it is undisputed that [plaintiff] provided the U.S. Marshals Service with a copy of the document he now seeks, the fact that the USMS cannot find it is not evidence of an insufficient search."); Shewchun v. INS, No. 95-1920, slip op. at 7 (D.D.C. Dec. 10, 1995) ("Nor does plaintiff's identification of undisclosed documents that he has obtained through other sources render the search unreasonable."), summary affirmance granted, No. 97-5044 (D.C. Cir. June 5, 1997). But cf. Kronberg, 875 F. Supp. at 870-71 (requiring government to provide additional explanation for absence of documentation required by statute and agency regulations to be created, when plaintiff presented evidence that other files, reasonably expected to contain responsive records, were not identified as having been searched).

[152] Roberts v. United States Dep't of Justice, No. 92-1707, 1995 WL 356320, at *2 (D.D.C. Jan. 28, 1993); see Miller, 779 F.2d at 1385 ("Thus, the Department is not required by the Act to account for documents which the requester has in some way identified if it has made a diligent search for those documents in places in which they might be expected to be found."). But see Valencia-Lucena, 180 F.3d at 328 (suggesting that unless it would be "fruitless" to do so, agency is required to seek out employee responsible for record "when all other sources fail to provide leads to the missing record," and when "there is a close nexus . . . between the person and the particular record").

## LITIGATION CONSIDERATIONS

good-faith efforts.[153]

Although an agency's search may be found insufficient if the court concludes that it interpreted the scope of the request too narrowly,[154] the Court of Appeals for the District of Columbia Circuit has expressly held that an agency "is not obligated to look beyond the four corners of the request for leads to the location of responsive documents."[155] Nor is an agency required to undertake a new search based on a subsequent clarification of a request, after the requester has examined the documents released.[156] The D.C. Circuit has observ-

---

[153] See Maynard, 986 F.2d at 565 ("Rather than bad faith, we think that the forthright disclosure by the INS that it had located the misplaced file suggests good faith on the part of the agency."); Meeropol, 790 F.2d at 953; Goland, 607 F.2d at 370 (revelation one week following decision by court of appeals that agency had discovered numerous, potentially responsive, additional documents several months earlier, found insufficient to undermine validity of agency's prior search); Torres v. CIA, 39 F. Supp. 2d 960, 963 (N.D. Ill. 1999) (refusing to allow dispute about adequacy of search even though "a couple of pieces of paper--having no better than marginal relevance"--were uncovered during additional searches); Klunzinger v. IRS, 27 F. Supp. 2d 1015, 1024 (W.D. Mich. 1998) (concluding that continued release of responsive documents attests to agency's good faith in providing complete response); Gilmore v. NSA, No. 92-3646, 1993 U.S. Dist. LEXIS 7694, at *27 (N.D. Cal. Apr. 30, 1993) (acceptance of plaintiff's "'perverse theory that a forthcoming agency is less to be trusted in its allegations than an unyielding agency'" would "'work mischief in the future by creating a disincentive for the agency to reappraise its position'" (quoting Military Audit Project v. Casey, 656 F.2d 724, 754 (D.C. Cir. 1981))), aff'd, 76 F.3d 386 (9th Cir. 1995) (unpublished table decision).

[154] See, e.g., Nation Magazine, 71 F.3d at 889-91 (finding that agency improperly limited scope of request to records indexed under subject's name when request also sought information "pertaining to" subject and concluding that related subject-matter files should have been searched also); Horsehead Indus. v. EPA, No. 94-1299, slip op. at 4-5 (D.D.C. Jan. 3, 1997) (holding that agency may not "artificially narrow a request's plain meaning" in order to delay or deny disclosure (citing Hemenway v. Hughes, 601 F. Supp. 1002, 1005 (D.D.C. 1985))); see also FOIA Update, Vol. XVI, No. 3, at 3-5 ("OIP Guidance: Determining the Scope of a FOIA Request").

[155] Kowalczyk v. Department of Justice, 73 F.3d 386, 389 (D.C. Cir. 1996); see also Western Ctr. for Journalism v. IRS, No. 99-906, 2000 U.S. Dist. LEXIS 5073, at **23-24 (D.D.C. Mar. 31, 2000) (concluding that diligent search was shown when, even though not required to do so, agency searched for records beyond scope of request) (motion for reconsideration pending).

[156] See id. at 388; Schwarz v. FBI, No. 2:97-CV-86C, slip op. at 2 (D. Utah Feb. 26, 1998) (finding "no duty to continue searching" for documents identified in supplementary requests), aff'd, 161 F.3d 18 (10th Cir. 1998) (unpublished table decision), petition for cert. denied for failure to pay filing fee, 526 U.S. 122 (1999); see also McQueen v. United States, 179 F.R.D. 522, 525 n.5 (S.D. Tex 1998) ("FOIA contains no provision which obligates an agency to update FOIA disclosures." (citing United States Dep't of Justice v. Tax Ana-

(continued...)

## LITIGATION CONSIDERATIONS

ed that "[r]equiring an additional search each time the agency receives a letter that clarifies a prior request could extend indefinitely the delay in processing new requests"[157] and that "if the requester discovers leads in the documents he receives from the agency, he may pursue those leads through a second FOIA request."[158] Moreover, in extraordinarily onerous cases, an agency may not be compelled to undertake a requested search that is of such enormous magnitude as to make it "unreasonably burdensome."[159]

As a general principle, therefore, "[t]here is no requirement that an agency search every record system."[160] As a corollary, though, an agency "'cannot limit its search to only one record system if there are others that are likely to turn up the information requested.'"[161] Stated another way, "if an agency has reason to know that certain places may contain responsive documents, it is obligated under FOIA to search [those places] barring an undue burden."[162] Accordingly, the FBI's search of its record indices has been deemed "reasonable" when it has searched through "main files" (when the subject of the request was the subject of the file) and "cross" or "see references" (when the subject of the request was merely mentioned in a file in

---

[156](...continued)
lysts, 492 U.S. 136, 139-40 (1989))).

[157] Kowalczyk, 73 F.3d at 388.

[158] Id. at 389; see Nash v. United States Dep't of Justice, 992 F. Supp. 447, 449 (D.D.C.) ("The fact that some EOUSA information was located in BOP files when the BOP conducted its search for records maintained by the BOP does not require the EOUSA to conduct a separate search of its own files, absent receipt of a FOIA request submitted to the EOUSA."), summary affirmance granted, No. 98-5096 (D.C. Cir. July 20, 1998). But see Kefalos v. IRS, No. 2-97-117, 1998 U.S. Dist. LEXIS 5974, at *25 (S.D. Ohio Apr. 3, 1998) (refusing to grant summary judgment because affidavit inadequate in face of allegation by plaintiff that documents released reference existence of other documents), subsequent opinion granting summary judgment to agency, No. 2-97-117, 1998 U.S. Dist. LEXIS 10432 (S.D. Ohio May 19, 1998).

[159] Nation Magazine, 71 F.3d at 891-92 (rejecting demand that agency search "through 23 years of unindexed files for records pertaining" to subject, while remanding for focus on narrower search for dated memorandum in files indexed chronologically).

[160] Oglesby, 920 F.2d at 68 (citing cases); see Chamberlain, 957 F. Supp. at 294; Moore v. Aspin, 916 F. Supp. 32, 35 (D.D.C. 1996).

[161] Campbell v. United States Dep't of Justice, 164 F.3d 20, 28 (D.C. Cir. 1998) (quoting Oglesby, 920 F.2d at 68); see Comer v. IRS, No. 97-76329, 1999 U.S. Dist. LEXIS 16268, at *2 (E.D. Mich. Sept. 30, 1999) (questioning agency's search because it failed to justify why it would not be feasible to search specific places that plaintiff requested to be searched).

[162] Valencia-Lucena, 180 F.3d at 327.

## LITIGATION CONSIDERATIONS

which another individual or organization was the subject).[163] Similar indices searches by other agencies, either manually or by computer, have also been approved as adequate.[164] But when the documents located as a result of a narrow search suggest other fruitful areas to search, an agency should explore those areas because "the court evaluates the reasonableness of an agency's

---

[163] See Blanton v. United States Dep't of Justice, 63 F. Supp. 2d 35, 41 (D.D.C. 1999) (finding no requirement to search informant files for references to individual when such references would be "flagged" by agency's cross-reference search about that individual) (motion for partial reconsideration pending); Leebove v. United States Dep't of Justice, No. 96-72463, 1998 U.S. Dist. LEXIS 12364, at *13 (E.D. Mich. July 13, 1998) ("[H]aving searched both its main and cross-reference indices, the FBI has met its burden that its search was reasonable."); Master v. FBI, 926 F. Supp. 193, 196-97 (D.D.C. 1996), summary affirmance granted, 124 F.3d 1309 (D.C. Cir. 1997) (unpublished table decision); Beauman v. FBI, No. 92-7603, slip op. at 9 (C.D. Cal. Apr. 28, 1993); Lawyers Comm. for Human Rights v. INS, 721 F. Supp. 552, 567 n.12 (S.D.N.Y. 1989); Freeman v. United States Dep't of Justice, No. 85-0958A, slip op. at 6 (E.D. Va. Mar. 12, 1986), aff'd, 808 F.2d 834 (4th Cir. 1986) (unpublished table decision); Friedman v. FBI, 605 F. Supp. 306, 311 (N.D. Ga. 1981); see also Kowalczyk, 73 F.3d at 389. But see Summers v. United States Dep't of Justice, No. 89-3300, slip op. at 6 (D.D.C. June 13, 1995) (despite retrieval of over 30,000 responsive pages, FBI Central Records System indices search for documents pertaining to former FBI Director J. Edgar Hoover's telephone logs and appointment calendars held inadequate when agency declaration did "not explain the search terms used, the type of search performed and [did] not aver 'that all files likely to contain responsive materials . . . were searched'").

[164] See, e.g., Church of Scientology Int'l v. United States Dep't of Justice, 30 F.3d 224, 230 (1st Cir. 1994) (United States Attorney's Office search of computerized record system sufficient); Maynard, 986 F.2d at 562 (concluding that Treasury Department properly limited its search to its automated Treasury Enforcement Communications System (TECS)); Murphy v. IRS, 79 F. Supp. 2d 1180, 1185 (D. Haw. 1999) (noting that because technical advice memoranda would all be logged into Technical Management Information System, search of that database was adequate); Jimenez v. FBI, 938 F. Supp. 21, 26 (D.D.C. 1996) (finding adequate ATF search of "its 'primary law enforcement computer records system, which indexes all ATF law enforcement records, including those located in regional offices'"); Jacoby v. HUD, No. 95-893, slip op. at 3 (D.D.C. July 28, 1995) ("The database [HUD] searched was appropriate to the request."); Manna v. United States Dep't of Justice, 832 F. Supp. 866, 875 (D.N.J. 1993) (finding that DEA indices search was adequate and noting that "district courts have sanctioned the use of general indices maintained on computer systems or even index cards to locate responsive documents as a reasonable search technique"); Manna v. United States Dep't of Justice, 815 F. Supp. 798, 817-18 (D.N.J. 1993) (suggesting that indices search by United States Attorney's Office were adequate), aff'd on other grounds, 51 F.3d 1158 (3d Cir. 1995). But see Steinberg v. United States Dep't of the Treasury, No. 93-2348, slip op. at 8 (D.D.C. Sept. 18, 1995) (declaring that search solely of TECS was inadequate when "it is reasonable to conclude that additional systems exist," that TECS does not include these record systems, and that it would not be unduly burdensome to search other systems).

## LITIGATION CONSIDERATIONS

search based on what the agency knew at [the search's] conclusion rather than what the agency speculated at its inception."[165]

Agencies that maintain field offices in various locations are not ordinarily obligated to search offices other than those to which the request has been directed.[166] Similarly, "[b]ecause the scope of a search is limited by a plaintiff's FOIA request, there is no general requirement that an agency search second-

---

[165] Campbell, 164 F.3d at 28; see Truitt, 897 F.2d at 545-46 (admonishing agency to "admit and correct error when error is revealed" and conduct additional searches if requester suggests other areas in which to look). But cf. Hall v. United States Dep't of Justice, 63 F. Supp. 2d 14, 18 (D.D.C. 1999) (inviting plaintiff to make another FOIA request for records the existence of which were only "suggested" by documents already released).

[166] See, e.g., Kowalczyk, 73 F.3d at 389 (stating that when "the requester clearly states that he wants all agency records . . . regardless of their location, but fails to direct the agency's attention to any particular office other than the one receiving the request, then the agency need pursue only a lead . . . that is both clear and certain."); Church of Scientology v. IRS, 792 F.2d 146, 150 (D.C. Cir. 1986) (finding that when agency regulations require requests be made to specific offices for specific records, there is no need to search additional offices when those regulations are not followed); Marks v. United States Dep't of Justice, 578 F.2d 261, 263 (9th Cir. 1978) (finding no duty to search FBI field offices when requester directed request only to FBI Headquarters and did not specify which field offices he wanted searched); Sacco v. FBI, No. 98-1247, slip op. at 5-6 (D.D.C. Nov. 30, 1999) (finding inadequate FBI search that failed to encompass field offices when plaintiff specifically mentioned field office investigations of himself); Church of Scientology Int'l v. IRS, No. 90-2567, slip op. at 5-6 (C.D. Cal. Aug. 2, 1991) (ruling that IRS is under no obligation to search offices other than those specified in request); cf. Domingues v. FBI, No. 98-74612, slip op. at 7 (E.D. Mich. June 23, 1999) (magistrate's recommendation) (alternative holding) (suggesting that request to agency headquarters that does not ask for field office search does not "reasonably describe" field office records, so headquarters search is all that is required), adopted (E.D. Mich. July 29, 1999); AFGE v. United States Dep't of Commerce, 632 F. Supp. 1272, 1278 (D.D.C. 1986) (holding that agency's refusal to perform canvass of 356 bureau offices for multitude of files was justified), aff'd, 907 F.2d 203 (D.C. Cir. 1990). But see Krikorian v. United States Dep't of State, 984 F.2d 461, 468-69 (D.C. Cir. 1993) (remanding so district court could explain why it was unnecessary for agency to search 11 regional security offices identified in article that formed basis for plaintiff's request); Kitchen v. FBI, No. 93-2382, slip op. at 5 (D.D.C. Mar. 18, 1996) (requiring FBI to justify lack of search of field offices when plaintiff's request to FBI Headquarters specified particular field offices to be searched, even though FBI notified requester of address of those offices and instructed him to request records directly from field offices), dismissed for lack of prosecution (D.D.C. Apr. 16, 1997); Harvey, No. CV 92-176, slip op. at 11-12 (D. Mont. Jan. 9, 1996) (counseling that plaintiff's reference to file prepared by FBI Special Agent in Wyoming "should have alerted the FBI to the need to search beyond the agency's Central Records system").

## LITIGATION CONSIDERATIONS

ary references or variant spellings."[167]

Of course, when a requester has set limitations on the scope of his request, either at the administrative stage[168] or in the course of litigation,[169] he cannot subsequently challenge the adequacy of the search on the ground that the agency limited its search accordingly. Moreover, the D.C. Circuit has held that when the subject of a request is implicated in several separate matters, but information is sought regarding only one of them, an agency is not automatically obligated to extend the search to other files or documents referenced in material retrieved in response to the initial search, so long as that search was complete and reasonable.[170]

Similarly, with respect to the processing of "cross" or "see references," only those portions of the file which pertain directly to the subject of the request are considered within the scope of the request.[171] As one court has phrased it: "To require the government to release an entire document where

---

[167] Maynard, 986 F.2d at 560; Russell v. Barr, No. 92-2546, 1998 U.S. Dist. LEXIS 14515, at **6-7 (D.D.C. Aug. 28, 1998) (ruling that agency was not required to search for records under requester's wife's maiden name when requester provided only her married name); cf. Lowe v. FBI, No. 96-512, slip op. at 2-3 (E.D. Okla. July 31, 1998) (finding no improper withholding of records when plaintiff failed to provide agency with additional information requested in order to conduct a more thorough search); Spannaus, No. 92-372, slip op. at 6-7 (D.D.C. June 20, 1995) (holding that agency was not required to search files of individual known to be connected with bankruptcy proceedings when request sought records on proceedings, not on individual). But see Canning v. United States Dep't of Justice, No. 92-0463, slip op. at 21-22 (D.D.C. Nov. 3, 1994) (when records on subject of request filed under two different names and agency is aware of the dual filing, agency obligated to search under both names, especially after requester brought second name to agency's attention).

[168] See Nation Magazine v. Department of State, No. 92-2303, slip op. at 13-15 (D.D.C. Aug. 18, 1995) (search that was limited to single DEA field office based on information supplied in request held "particularly appropriate here due to the fact that DEA must manually search its noninvestigative records").

[169] See id. at 15-16 (holding that plaintiff was bound to scope of request as narrowed in litigation).

[170] Steinberg, 23 F.3d at 552 (concluding that "[otherwise] an agency . . . might be forced to examine virtually every document in its files, following an interminable trail of cross-referenced documents like a chain letter winding its way through the mail"); see also Canning v. United States Dep't of Justice, 848 F. Supp. 1037, 1050 (D.D.C. 1994) (adequacy of search not undermined by fact that requester has received additional documents mentioning subject through separate request, when such documents are "tagged" to name of subject's associate). See generally Campbell, 164 F.3d at 28 ("[T]he proper inquiry is whether the requesting party has established a sufficient predicate to justify searching for a particular type of record.").

[171] See Posner v. Department of Justice, 2 Gov't Disclosure Serv. (P-H) ¶ 82,229, at 82,650 (D.D.C. Mar. 9, 1982).

## LITIGATION CONSIDERATIONS

plaintiff's name is only mentioned a few times would be to impose on the government a burdensome and time consuming task."[172] With respect to a document in the requester's file that pertained entirely to a third party, one court has held that "[g]iven the lack of any relation between these pages and [the requester], as well as the minimal information that would remain after redaction, [the agency's] decision not to release these documents was not erroneous."[173]

To prove the adequacy of its search, as in sustaining its claims of exemption, an agency may rely upon affidavits (see the discussion of Vaughn Indexes, below), provided that they are "relatively detailed, nonconclusory, and submitted in good faith."[174] Such affidavits must show "that the search method was reasonably calculated to uncover all relevant documents" and must "identify the terms searched or explain how the search was conducted."[175] It is not necessary that the agency employee who actually performed the search supply an affidavit describing the search; rather, the affidavit of an official responsible for supervising or coordinating the search efforts should be sufficient to fulfill the personal knowledge requirement of Rule 56(e) of the

---

[172] Dettman v. United States Dep't of Justice, No. 82-1108, slip op. at 5-6 (D.D.C. Mar. 21, 1985); see also Osborne v. United States Dep't of Justice, No. 84-1910, slip op. at 2-3 (D.D.C. Feb. 28, 1985) (holding sufficient DEA search of relevant records systems and case files regarding requester); Dunaway v. Webster, 519 F. Supp. 1059, 1083 (N.D. Cal. 1981).

[173] Greenspun v. IRS, No. 84-3426, slip op. at 4 (D.D.C. Sept. 30, 1985).

[174] Pollack v. Bureau of Prisons, 879 F.2d 406, 409 (8th Cir. 1989); see Miller, 779 F.2d at 1383; Weisberg, 705 F.2d at 1351; Perry v. Block, 684 F.2d 121, 127 (D.C. Cir. 1982) ("[A]ffidavits that explain in reasonable detail the scope and method of the search conducted by the agency will suffice to demonstrate compliance with the obligations imposed by the FOIA."); Goland, 607 F.2d at 352; Triestman, 878 F. Supp. at 672 ("[A]ffidavits attesting to the thoroughness of an agency search of its records and its results are presumptively valid."); Grove v. United States Dep't of Justice, 802 F. Supp. 506, 518 (D.D.C. 1992); see also FOIA Update, Vol. IV, No. 1, at 6.

[175] Oglesby, 920 F.2d at 68 (declaring that although agency was not required to search "every" record system, "[a]t the very least, [it] was required to explain in its affidavit that no other record system was likely to produce responsive documents"); see Maynard, 986 F.2d at 559 ("The affidavit should additionally 'describe at least generally the structure of the agency's file system which makes further search difficult.'" (quoting Church of Scientology, 792 F.2d at 151)); Smith v. ATF, 977 F. Supp. 496, 502 (D.D.C. 1997) (stating that agency affidavits must establish adequacy of both search methods and scope of search); Carreras v. United States Customs Serv., No. 96-1435, slip op. at 2 (D.D.C. Feb. 25, 1997) ("The agency must denote which files were searched and reflect a systematic approach to document location in order to enable the requester to challenge the procedures utilized."), summary affirmance granted, No. 97-5174 (D.C. Cir. Dec. 23, 1997).

## LITIGATION CONSIDERATIONS

Federal Rules of Civil Procedure.[176] (For a further discussion of this "personal knowledge" requirement, see Litigation Considerations, Summary Judgment, below.)

An inadequate description of the search process, or a description which reveals an inadequate search, will necessitate denial of summary judgment.[177] Summary judgment has also been denied when staff members conducting the search received inadequate instructions as to what could be considered a "personal" record as opposed to an "agency" record.[178] If an agency's search is disputed, a grant of summary judgment to the agency may be reversed and remanded when the district court fails to expressly hold that a disputed search

---

[176] See, e.g., Carney, 19 F.3d at 814 ("There is no basis in either the statute or the relevant caselaw to require that an agency effectively establish by a series of sworn affidavits a 'chain of custody' over its search process. The format of the proof submitted by defendant--declarations of supervisory employees, signed under penalty of perjury--is sufficient for purposes of both the statute and [Rule 56(e)]."); Maynard, 986 F.2d at 560 ("[A]n agency need not submit an affidavit from the employee who actually conducted the search. Instead, an agency may rely on an affidavit of an agency employee responsible for supervising the search."); SafeCard, 926 F.2d at 1202 (ruling that employee "in charge of coordinating the [agency's] search and recovery efforts [is] most appropriate person to provide a comprehensive affidavit"); see also Patterson, 56 F.3d at 841 (holding appropriate declarant's reliance on standard search form completed by his predecessor); Kay, 976 F. Supp. at 33 n.29 ("Generally, declarations accounting for searches of documents that contain hearsay are acceptable."); Spannaus v. United States Dep't of Justice, No. 85-1015, slip op. at 7 (D. Mass. July 13, 1992) (finding affidavit of agency employee sufficient when third party claimed to have knowledge of additional documents and employee contacted that individual). But see Linn v. United States Dep't of Justice, No. 92-1406, 1995 WL 631847, at *11 (D.D.C. Aug. 22, 1995) (rejecting statement by Bureau of Prisons attorney stationed in Washington, D.C. that search of prison in Texas located no records); cf. Katzman v. CIA, 903 F. Supp. 434, 438-39 (E.D.N.Y. 1995) (finding declaration from agency's FOIA coordinator inadequate when agency initially misidentified requester's attorney as subject of request, and requiring declarations from supervisors in each of agency's three major divisions attesting that search was conducted for correct subject); Mehl v. EPA, 797 F. Supp. 43, 46 (D.D.C. 1992) (ruling that agency employee with "firsthand knowledge" of relevant files was appropriate person to supervise search undertaken by contractor).

[177] See, e.g., Steinberg, 23 F.3d at 552 (finding description of search inadequate when it failed "to describe in any detail what records were searched, by whom, and through what process"); Oglesby, 920 F.2d at 68; Judicial Watch, Inc. v. United States Dep't of Commerce, 34 F. Supp. 2d 28, 46 (D.D.C. 1998) (denying unprecedented partial summary judgment motion filed by agency against itself and requiring "restrictive and rigorous" search because of "egregious" agency conduct); Law Firm of Tidwell Swaim & Assocs. v. Herrmann, No. 3:97-2097, 1998 WL 740765, at *4 (N.D. Tex. Oct. 16, 1998) (denying summary judgment because of dispute as to proper scope of agency search).

[178] See Ethyl Corp., 25 F.3d at 1247-48.

## LITIGATION CONSIDERATIONS

was adequate under the "reasonableness" standard.[179]

### Mootness and Other Grounds for Dismissal

As is generally the case in civil litigation, a FOIA lawsuit may be barred from consideration on the merits due to the operation of the doctrines of mootness or issue or claim preclusion, or because some other factor warrants dismissal.

In a FOIA lawsuit, the courts can grant a requester relief only when an agency has improperly withheld agency records.[180] Therefore, if, during litigation, it is determined that all documents found responsive to the underlying FOIA request have been released in full to the requester, the suit should be dismissed on mootness grounds as there is no justiciable case or controversy.[181]

In Payne Enterprises v. United States, however, the Court of Appeals for the District of Columbia Circuit held that when records are routinely withheld at the initial processing level, but consistently released after an administrative appeal, and when this situation results in continuing injury to the requester, a lawsuit challenging that practice is ripe for adjudication and is not subject to

---

[179] See Krikorian, 984 F.2d at 468 (requiring express findings by district court on adequacy of search issue).

[180] See 5 U.S.C. § 552(a)(4)(B) (1994 & Supp. IV 1998); see also Kissinger v. Reporters Comm. for Freedom of the Press, 445 U.S. 136, 150 (1980).

[181] See Anderson v. HHS, 3 F.3d 1383, 1384 (10th Cir. 1993) (citing Carter v. VA, 780 F.2d 1479, 1481 (9th Cir. 1986), and DeBold v. Stimson, 735 F.2d 1037, 1040 (7th Cir. 1984)); Tijerina v. Walters, 821 F.2d 789, 799 (D.C. Cir. 1987) ("'[H]owever fitful or delayed the release of information, . . . if we are convinced appellees have, however belatedly, released all nonexempt material, we have no further judicial function to perform under the FOIA.'" (quoting Perry v. Block, 684 F.2d 121, 125 (D.C. Cir. 1982))); Parks v. Department of Educ., No. 99-1052, 1999 U.S. Dist. LEXIS 600, at *6 (D. Or. Jan. 26, 2000) ("Mootness occurs when the requested documents are produced."); Kruger v. IRS, No. 99-347, 1999 U.S. Dist. LEXIS 15520, at *3 (D. Nev. Aug. 19, 1999) (same); see also, e.g., Constangy, Brooks & Smith v. NLRB, 851 F.2d 839, 842 (6th Cir. 1988) (full disclosure of records pursuant to court order moots appeal); cf. Long v. ATF, 964 F. Supp. 494, 497-98 (D.D.C. 1997) (holding that agency's grant of fee waiver renders moot issue of requester's status for purposes of assessing fees on that request). But cf. Anderson v. HHS, 907 F.2d 936, 941 (10th Cir. 1990) (declaring that although plaintiff had already obtained all responsive documents in private civil litigation, albeit subject to protective order, plaintiff's FOIA litigation to obtain documents free from any such restriction remained viable); Looney v. Walters-Tucker, 20 F. Supp. 2d 70, 72 (D.D.C. 1998) (refusing to dismiss action where agency's claim that no responsive records existed was unsupported by affidavit or declaration and was contradicted by plaintiff's evidence).

## LITIGATION CONSIDERATIONS

dismissal on the basis of mootness.[182] The defendant agency's "voluntary cessation" of that practice in Payne did not moot the case when the plaintiff challenged the agency's policy as an unlawful, continuing wrong.[183] Although Payne has been used as the springboard for a number of suits by plaintiffs contending that individual agencies have engaged in a "pattern and practice" of ignoring their obligations under the FOIA, in most of these cases they have not found a sympathetic reception to their complaints.[184]

---

[182] 837 F.2d 486, 488-93 (D.C. Cir. 1988); see also Gilmore v. United States Dep't of Energy, 4 F. Supp. 2d 912, 924 (N.D. Cal. 1998) (finding "independent cause of action" for agency's failure to respond within statutory time limits, despite correctness of agency's disclosure determination), dismissed per stipulation, No. 95-0285 (N.D. Cal. Apr. 3, 2000). But see OSHA Data/C.I.H., Inc. v. United States Dep't of Labor, No. 98-283, 1999 U.S. Dist. LEXIS 10503, at **27-29 (D.N.J. May 11, 1999) (refusing to permit claim to go forward when no proof existed that agency would routinely refuse to release data for period of time); Regional Management Corp. v. Legal Servs. Corp., 10 F. Supp. 2d 565, 573 (D.S.C. 1998) (refusing to permit further consideration of moot claim as there was no evidence of continuing injury to requester from "isolated event"), aff'd, 186 F.3d 457 (4th Cir. 1999).

[183] Id. at 491; see also, e.g., Hercules, Inc. v. Marsh, 839 F.2d 1027, 1028 (4th Cir. 1988) (threat of disclosure of agency telephone directory not mooted by release because new request for subsequent directory pending; agency action thus "capable of repetition yet evading review") (reverse FOIA suit); Better Gov't Ass'n v. Department of State, 780 F.2d 86, 90-91 (D.C. Cir. 1986) (although challenge to fee waiver standards as applied held moot, challenge to facial validity of standards held ripe and not moot); Public Citizen v. Office of the United States Trade Representative, 804 F. Supp. 385, 387 (D.D.C. 1992) (despite disclosure of specific records requested, court retains jurisdiction when plaintiff challenges "agency's policy to withhold temporarily, on a regular basis, certain types of documents"). But see Atkins v. Department of Justice, No. 90-5095, slip op. at 1 (D.C. Cir. Sept. 18, 1991) ("The question whether DEA complied with the [FOIA's] time limitation in responding to [plaintiff's] request is moot because DEA has now responded to this request."); cf. Long, 964 F. Supp. at 498 (rejecting, as not yet ripe, plaintiff's request for determination of status for fee categorization when agency granted request for fee waiver and no new fee dispute remained pending).

[184] See, e.g., Regional Management Corp. v. Legal Servs. Corp., 186 F.3d 457, 464-65 (4th Cir. 1999) (refusing to consider challenge to alleged policy of nondisclosure of documents relating to ongoing investigations because claim was not "ripe"); Gilmore v. NSA, No. 94-16165, 1995 WL 792079, at *1 (9th Cir. Dec. 11, 1995) (refusing to grant injunction for alleged "systemic agency abuse" in responding to FOIA requests where system of handling requests was "reasonable" and records were "diverse and complex," requiring "painstaking review"); Swan View Coalition v. USDA, 39 F. Supp. 2d 42, 47 (D.D.C. 1999) (refusing to grant declaratory relief where agency's failure to timely respond was "an aberration"); cf. Eison v. Kallstrom, 75 F. Supp. 2d 113, 114, 117 (S.D.N.Y. 1999) (allowing plaintiff to amend original complaint in order to allege improper withholding of records, where original complaint had asked for injunction against "pattern and practice" of delayed agency responses,

(continued...)

## LITIGATION CONSIDERATIONS

Of course, a claim for attorney fees or costs survives dismissal of a FOIA action for mootness.[185] When agencies belatedly and without explanation release requested records in the midst of a FOIA lawsuit, courts frown upon efforts to avoid, on mootness grounds, the payment of attorney fees.[186] (See the discussion under Litigation Considerations, Attorney Fees and Litigation Costs, below.)

Dismissal of a FOIA lawsuit can be appropriate also when the plaintiff fails to prosecute the suit.[187] Dismissal likewise may be appropriate when (1) records are publicly available under a separate statutory scheme upon pay-

---

[184](...continued) which court deemed "now moot"). But see Gilmore v. United States Dep't of Energy, 33 F. Supp. 2d 1184, 1189 (N.D. Cal. 1998) (allowing discovery on "pattern and practice" claim of agency delay in processing FOIA requests), dismissed per stipulation, No. 95-0285 (N.D. Cal. Apr. 3, 2000).

[185] See Anderson, 3 F.3d at 1385 ("'We think it indisputable that a claim for attorney's fees is not part of the merits of the action to which the fees pertain.'" (quoting Budinich v. Becton Dickinson & Co., 486 U.S. 196, 200 (1988))); Carter, 780 F.2d at 1481-82; Seegull Mfg. Co. v. NLRB, 741 F.2d 882, 884-86 (6th Cir. 1984); DeBold, 735 F.2d at 1040; Webb v. HHS, 696 F.2d 101, 107-08 (D.C. Cir. 1982).

[186] See, e.g., Phoenix Newspapers, Inc. v. FBI, No. 86-1199, slip op. at 4-5 (D. Ariz. Dec. 12, 1987) (ruling that government should not be able to foreclose recovery of attorney fees whenever it chooses to moot an action by releasing records after having denied disclosure at administrative level); Harrison Bros. Meat Packing Co. v. USDA, 640 F. Supp. 402, 405-06 (M.D. Pa. 1986) (finding it "ludicrous" for government to "suddenly and inexplicably" release records and assert mootness to avoid paying fees after having denied disclosure at administrative level).

[187] See, e.g., Antonelli v. Executive Office for United States Attorneys, No. 92-2416, slip op. at 2 (7th Cir. June 6, 1994) (affirming district court's dismissal of complaint when, seven months after plaintiff's complaint was found defective for lack of specificity, plaintiff had failed to amend); Nuzzo v. FBI, No. 95-1708, 1996 U.S. Dist. LEXIS 15594, at **8-10 (D.D.C. Oct. 8, 1996) (after appropriate warning, dismissing action against several defendants because of plaintiff's failure to respond to motions for summary judgment); Ahmed v. Reno, No. 94-2438, slip op. at 2 (D.D.C. Nov. 15, 1995) (dismissing case "seven months since the Court first warned plaintiff that he must prosecute this case or face dismissal" and four months following filing of defendants' motion for summary judgment); Messino v. IRS, No. 95-15, slip op. at 1 (D.D.C. Sept. 15, 1995) (case dismissed when plaintiff failed to respond to order requiring proposal of deadline for dispositive motions); Fritchey v. United States, No. 93-1613, 1994 U.S. Dist. LEXIS 16401, at *5 (D.D.C. Oct. 11, 1994) (plaintiff's failure to respond to government's dispositive motions, after notice from court of consequences of not responding, held to be grounds for dismissal with prejudice); Valona v. DEA, No. 93-1256, slip op. at 1 (D.D.C. May 12, 1994) (plaintiff's failure to comply with court's orders merits dismissal).

## LITIGATION CONSIDERATIONS

ment of fees;[188] (2) a complete factual record has yet to be presented to the agency;[189] (3) there is a change in the factual circumstances underlying the lawsuit;[190] or (4) the agency is processing responsive records.[191] However, it has been held that a FOIA claim may survive the death of the plaintiff and, under some circumstances, may be continued by a properly substituted party.[192]

A FOIA lawsuit may be precluded by the doctrine of res judicata (claim preclusion) when it is brought by a plaintiff against the same agency for the

---

[188] See Kleinerman v. Patent & Trademark Office, No. 82-295, 1983 WL 658, at *1 (D. Mass. Apr. 25, 1983) (dismissing FOIA action because Patent and Trademark Act gave plaintiff independent right of access provided he paid for records).

[189] See, e.g., Rodrequez v. United States Postal Serv., No. 90-1886, 1991 WL 212202, at *2 (D.D.C. Oct. 2, 1991) (absent submission of further information enabling identification of plaintiff's records from among those of 36 persons with same name, case not yet ripe); National Sec. Archive v. United States Dep't of Commerce, No. 87-1581, slip op. at 6 (D.D.C. Nov. 25, 1987) (fee waiver case).

[190] See, e.g., Miller Auto Sales v. Casellas, No. 97-0032-H, slip op. at 3 (W.D. Va. Jan. 9, 1998) (dismissing case in which agency invoked Exemption 7(A) to protect documents concerning enforcement proceedings that subsequently terminated, so that agency could "have the opportunity to make a new FOIA determination at the administrative level"); cf. Lynch v. Department of the Treasury, No. 98-56368, 2000 WL 123236, at *3 (9th Cir. Jan. 28, 2000) (granting agency summary judgment and declaring that if plaintiff believes that law enforcement proceedings warranting applicability of Exemption 7(A) no longer are pending, "his recourse is to resubmit a[] FOIA request for the records at this time"), petition for cert. filed, 68 U.S.L.W. 3686 (U.S. Apr. 21, 2000) (No. 99-1697). But see Scheer v. United States Dep't of Justice, No. 98-1613, slip op. at 4-5 (D.D.C. July 26, 1999) (refusing to permit agency to invoke other exemptions when Exemption 7(A) claim was found to be invalid) (appeal pending).

[191] See, e.g., Voinche v. FBI, 999 F.2d 962, 963 (5th Cir. 1993) (because sole issue in action is "tardiness" of agency response, district court litigation rendered moot by agency's disclosure determination); Larson v. Executive Office for United States Attorneys, No. 85-6226, slip op. at 4-5 (D.C. Cir. Apr. 6, 1988) (appeal of district court denial of relief to plaintiff for defendant's processing delays mooted upon completion of processing).

[192] See Sinito v. United States Dep't of Justice, 176 F.3d 512, 515-16 (D.C. Cir. 1999) (finding that FOIA cause of action survives death of original requester, but restricting substitution of parties to successor or representative of deceased, pursuant to Fed. R. Civ. P. 25); D'Aleo v. Department of the Navy, No. 89-2347, 1991 U.S. Dist. LEXIS, at **2-4 (D.D.C. Mar. 27, 1991) (appointing as plaintiff deceased plaintiff's sister, who was executrix of his estate). But cf. Hayles v. United States Dep't of Justice, No. H-79-1599, slip op. at 3 (S.D. Tex. Nov. 2, 1982) (dismissing case upon death of plaintiff when no timely motion for substitution filed).

## LITIGATION CONSIDERATIONS

same documents the withholding of which previously has been adjudicated.[193] However, a subsequent claim for records is not precluded by res judicata when the litigation of an earlier, non-FOIA case involving the same records did not permit raising a FOIA claim.[194] In addition, res judicata is not applicable where there has been a change in the factual circumstances or legal principles applicable to the lawsuit.[195]

---

[193] See Schwarz v. National Inst. of Corrections, No. 98-1230, 1998 WL 694510, at *1 (10th Cir. Oct. 15, 1998) (affirming dismissal of case because plaintiff's argument that defendant was not party to earlier action was found to be without factual basis), petition for cert. denied for failure to pay filing fee, 526 U.S. 122 (1999); Wrenn v. Shalala, No. 94-5198, 1995 WL 225234, at *1 (D.C. Cir. Mar. 8, 1995) (affirming dismissal of requests that were subject of plaintiff's previous litigation, but reversing dismissal on "claims that were not and could not have been litigated in that prior action"); Fazzini v. United States Dep't of Justice, No. 92-5043, 1992 U.S. App. LEXIS, at **1-2 (D.C. Cir. Oct. 14, 1992) (per curiam); NTEU v. IRS, 765 F.2d 1174, 1177 (D.C. Cir. 1985); Hanner v. Stone, No. 92-CV-72719, slip op. at 3-7 (E.D. Mich. Oct. 26, 1992), aff'd, 1 F.3d 1240 (6th Cir. 1993) (unpublished table decision); see also Schwartz v. United States Dep't of Justice, No. 95-2162, slip op. at 2-3 (D.D.C. May 31, 1996), summary affirmance granted, No. 96-5183 (D.C. Cir. Oct. 23, 1996); Greyshock v. United States Coast Guard, No. 94-563, slip op. at 2-3 (D. Haw. Jan. 25, 1996) ("All of the claims brought in the instant actions were undeniably claims which either were or could have been brought in this first action in the District Court for the District of Columbia. For that reason alone, plaintiff is precluded from any further pursuit of these claims in this or any other court."), aff'd in part, rev'd in part on other grounds, 107 F.3d 16 (9th Cir. 1997) (unpublished table decision); Heckman v. Olive, No. CV-88-2981, 1992 WL 3290249, at *5 (E.D.N.Y. Dec. 9, 1992), aff'd, 9 F.3d 1537 (2d Cir. 1993) (unpublished table decision); FOIA Update, Vol. VI, No. 3, at 6 ("FOIA Counselor: 'Preclusion' Doctrines Under the FOIA"). Compare Hanner v. Stone, No. 92-2565, 1992 WL 361382, at *1 (6th Cir. Aug. 6, 1993) (holding that under doctrine of res judicata, "a final judgment on the merits of an action precludes the parties or their privies from relitigating issues that were or could have been raised in a prior action") (emphasis added), with Hanner v. Stone, No. 92-1579, 1992 WL 361382, at *1 (6th Cir. Dec. 8, 1992) (determining that present claim was not precluded under doctrine of res judicata when appellate court had previously adjudicated claim that was similar, but involved different issue).

[194] See North v. Walsh, 881 F.2d 1088, 1093-95 (D.C. Cir. 1989) (deciding that claim for records under FOIA was not barred by prior discovery prohibition for same records in criminal case in which FOIA claim could not have been interposed).

[195] See, e.g., Graphic Communications Int'l Union, Local 554 v. Salem-Gravure, 843 F.2d 1490, 1493 (D.C. Cir. 1988) (non-FOIA case); Croskey v. United States Office of Special Counsel, No. 96-5114, 1997 WL 702364, at *3 (D.C. Cir. Oct. 17, 1997) (finding res judicata inapplicable because document was not in existence when earlier litigation brought); Wolfe v. Froehlke, 358 F. Supp. 1318, 1219 (D.D.C. 1973) (stating that lawsuit was not barred where national security status had changed), aff'd, 510 F.2d 654 (D.C. Cir. 1974); see

(continued...)

## LITIGATION CONSIDERATIONS

Litigation also may be foreclosed by the applicability of the doctrine of collateral estoppel (issue preclusion), which precludes relitigation of an issue previously litigated by one party to the action.[196] As with the doctrine of res judicata, collateral estoppel is not applicable to a subsequent lawsuit if there is an intervening material change in the law or factual predicate.[197]

### "Vaughn Index"

A distinguishing feature of FOIA litigation is that the defendant agency bears the burden of sustaining its action of withholding records.[198] The most commonly used device for meeting this burden of proof is the "Vaughn Index," fashioned by the Court of Appeals for the District of Columbia Circuit

---

[195](...continued) also FOIA Update, Vol. VI, No. 3, at 6.

[196] See Yamaha Corp. of Am. v. United States, 961 F.2d 245, 254 (D.C. Cir. 1992) (non-FOIA case); Church of Scientology v. United States Dep't of the Army, 611 F.2d 738, 750-51 (9th Cir. 1980) (declaring that complete identity of plaintiff and document at issue precludes relitigation); MCI Telecomms. Corp. v. GSA, No. 89-0746, slip op. at 5-7 (D.D.C. Feb. 27, 1995) (same); Williams v. Executive Office for United States Attorneys, No. 89-3071, slip op. at 3-4 (D.D.C. Mar. 19, 1991) (same); see also FOIA Update, Vol. VI, No. 3, at 6; cf. Cotton v. Heyman, 63 F.3d 1115, 1118 nn.1-2 (D.C. Cir. 1995) (holding that doctrine of direct estoppel, which precludes relitigating issue finally decided in "separate proceeding" within same suit, prevented Smithsonian Institution from challenging district court determination that it is subject to FOIA on appeal from award of attorney fees; however, "Smithsonian is free to relitigate the issue against another party in a separate proceeding"). But see North, 881 F.2d at 1093-95 (finding issue preclusion inapplicable when exemption issues raised in FOIA action differ from relevancy issues raised in prior action for discovery access to same records); Ely v. FBI, No. 83-876-T-15, slip op. at 4 (M.D. Fla. July 13, 1988) (stating that collateral estoppel was not appropriate when plaintiff did not have "full and fair opportunity to litigate" defendant's claim of privilege); Robertson v. DOD, 402 F. Supp. 1342, 1347 (D.D.C. 1973) (concluding that private citizen's interest in subsequent FOIA action was not protected by government in prior reverse FOIA suit over same documents because interests not congruent).

[197] See, e.g., Croskey, 1997 WL 702364, at *5 (concluding that access to investigator's notes and impressions of witnesses adjudicated in prior proceeding was "sufficiently different" from witness statements themselves to bar application of collateral estoppel); Minnis v. USDA, 737 F.2d 784, 786 n.1 (9th Cir. 1984).

[198] See 5 U.S.C. § 552(a)(4)(B) (1994 & Supp. IV 1998); see also O'Harvey v. Office of Workers' Compensation Programs, No. 96-35015, 1997 U.S. App. LEXIS 1363, at **3-4 (9th Cir. Jan. 21, 1997) (vacating grant of summary judgment for government when "the Department failed to submit an affidavit or offer any oral testimony" to sustain its burden of proof on FOIA issues).

## LITIGATION CONSIDERATIONS

more than two decades ago in a case entitled Vaughn v. Rosen.[199]

The Vaughn Index came into prominence mainly as a result of the 1974 amendments to the FOIA, with the addition of the "reasonably segregable" provision to subsection (b).[200] This requirement that agencies segregate and release disclosable information from that which is exempt grew out of congressional concern in 1974 over the agencies' sweeping application of exemptions up to that time.[201] Particularly in cases involving large numbers of documents, the requirement that courts conduct a de novo review of each portion of a record at issue effectively transferred the burden from agencies to the courts themselves. Moreover, reliance on in camera examination had the effect of weakening the adversarial process somewhat, as it afforded a plaintiff and his counsel no real input on the merits of a case.[202]

The Vaughn decision addressed these concerns by requiring agencies to prepare an itemized index, correlating each withheld document (or portion) with a specific FOIA exemption and the relevant part of the agency's nondisclosure justification.[203] Such an index makes the trial court's job more manageable and enhances appellate review by ensuring that a full public record is available upon which to base an appellate decision.[204] It also helps "create balance between the parties."[205] If a court finds that an index is not sufficient-

---

[199] 484 F.2d 820 (D.C. Cir. 1973); see, e.g., Canning v. United States Dep't of Justice, 848 F. Supp. 1037, 1042 (D.D.C. 1994) ("Agencies are typically permitted to meet [their] heavy burden by 'filing affidavits describing the material withheld and the manner in which it falls within the exemption claimed.'" (quoting King v. United States Dep't of Justice, 830 F.2d 210, 217 (D.C. Cir. 1987))).

[200] 5 U.S.C. § 552(b) (sentence immediately following exemptions).

[201] See generally H.R. Rep. No. 93-876, at 7 (1974), reprinted in 1974 U.S.C.C.A.N. 6267, 6292.

[202] See King, 830 F.2d at 218; Vaughn, 484 F.2d at 826; Cucci v. DEA, 871 F. Supp. 508, 514 (D.D.C. 1994) ("An adequate Vaughn index facilitates the trial court's duty of ruling on the applicability of certain invoked FOIA exemptions, gives the requester as much information as possible that he may use to present his case to the trial court and thus enables the adversary system to operate.").

[203] See Vaughn, 484 F.2d at 827; accord King, 830 F.2d at 217.

[204] See King, 830 F.2d at 219; Vaughn, 484 F.2d at 824-25; see also Ingle v. Department of Justice, 698 F.2d 259, 263-64 (6th Cir. 1983); cf. Antonelli v. Sullivan, 732 F.2d 560, 562 (7th Cir. 1984) (no index required when small number of documents at issue and affidavit contains sufficient detail); NTEU v. United States Customs Serv., 602 F. Supp. 469, 473 (D.D.C. 1984) (fact that only one exemption is involved "nullif[ies] the need to formulate the type of itemization and correlation system required by the Court of Appeals in Vaughn"), aff'd, 802 F.2d 525 (D.C. Cir. 1986).

[205] Long v. United States Dep't of Justice, 10 F. Supp. 205, 209 (N.D.N.Y.
(continued...)

## LITIGATION CONSIDERATIONS

ly detailed, it may require one that is more detailed.[206] However, "[a]ffidavits submitted by an agency are 'accorded a presumption of good faith.'"[207] In certain circumstances a Vaughn affidavit, which by itself would be inadequate to support withholding, may be supplemented by in camera review of withheld material.[208] (See the discussion under Litigation Considerations, In Camera

---

[205](...continued)
1998); see, e.g., King, 830 F.2d at 218 (describing one purpose of Vaughn Index as "afford[ing] the FOIA requester a meaningful opportunity to contest" withholding); see also Kern v. FBI, No. 94-0208, slip op at 5 (C.D. Cal. Sept. 14, 1998) (opining that one purpose of Vaughn Index is "to afford the requester an opportunity to intelligently advocate release of the withheld documents"); cf. Fiduccia v. United States Dep't of Justice, 185 F.3d 1035, 1042 (9th Cir. 1999) (pointing out that Vaughn Index is not required where it is unnecessary to be particularly concerned about adversarial balance); Brooks v. IRS, No. F-96-6284, 1997 U.S. Dist. LEXIS, at **6-7 (E.D. Cal. Nov. 17, 1997) (Vaughn Index not always needed).

[206] See Davin v. United States Dep't of Justice, 60 F.3d 1043, 1065 (3d Cir. 1995); Church of Scientology Int'l v. United States Dep't of Justice, 30 F.3d 224, 230-40 (1st Cir. 1994); Wiener v. FBI, 943 F.2d 972, 979 (9th Cir. 1991); Founding Church of Scientology v. Bell, 603 F.2d 945, 949 (D.C. Cir. 1979) (seemingly establishing additional requirement that Vaughn Index be contained in no more than one document per case); Coleman v. FBI, 972 F. Supp. 5, 9 (D.D.C. 1997) (rejecting narratives on "deleted page sheets" that apply to multiple documents and requiring agency to redo index to "inform the court as to the contents of individual documents and the applicability of the various Exemptions"); see also Bryce v. Overseas Private Inv. Corp., No. 96-595, slip op. at 10 (W.D. Tex. Sept. 28, 1998) ("An agency may submit a revised index at any time prior to the summary judgment hearing." (citing Coastal States Gas Corp. v. Department of Energy, 644 F.2d 969, 971, 981 (3d Cir. 1981))).

[207] Carney v. United States Dep't of Justice, 19 F.3d 807, 812 (2d Cir. 1994) (quoting SafeCard Servs. v. SEC, 926 F.2d 1197, 1200 (D.C. Cir. 1991)); see Jones v. FBI, 41 F.3d 238, 242 (6th Cir. 1994); Cohen v. FBI, No. 93-1701, slip op. at 4 (D.D.C. Oct. 11, 1994) ("[M]inor contradictions in defendants' affidavits do not evince intentional misrepresentation on their part."). But see Church of Scientology, 30 F.3d at 233 (explaining that a good-faith presumption is applicable only "when the agency has provided a reasonably detailed explanation for its withholdings . . . court may not without good reason second-guess an agency's explanation, but it also cannot discharge its de novo review obligation unless that explanation is sufficiently specific").

[208] See, e.g., Fiduccia, 185 F.3d at 1042-43 (suggesting, notwithstanding Wiener, 943 F.2d at 979, that in camera inspection could by itself be sufficient); Maynard v. CIA, 986 F.2d 547, 557 (1st Cir. 1993) ("Where, as here, the agency, for good reason, does not furnish publicly the kind of detail required for a satisfactory Vaughn index, a district court may review the documents in camera."); Simon v. United States Dep't of Justice, 980 F.2d 782, 784 (D.C. Cir. 1992) (holding that despite inadequacy of Vaughn Index, in camera review--"although admittedly imperfect . . . is the best way to assure both that the agency is entitled to the exemption it claims and that the confidential
(continued...)

## LITIGATION CONSIDERATIONS

Inspection, below.)

The Vaughn Index has evolved into an extremely effective tool with which to resolve FOIA cases, developing various permutations to fit particular circumstances. Courts have routinely observed that "[t]here is no set formula for a Vaughn index; . . . it is the function, not the form, which is important."[209] In fact, "[a]ll that is required, and the least that is required, is that the requester and the trial judge be able to derive from the index a clear explanation of why each document or portion of a document withheld is putatively exempt from disclosure."[210] Indeed, a document specifically denominated as a "Vaughn Index" is not essential, so long as the nature of the withheld information is adequately attested to by the agency.[211]

---

[208] (...continued) source is protected"); King, 830 F.2d at 225; see also National Wildlife Fed'n v. United States Forest Serv., 861 F.2d 1114, 1116 (9th Cir. 1988) ("[W]here a trial court properly reviewed contested documents in camera, an adequate factual basis for the decision exists."). But see Wiener, 943 F.2d at 979 ("In camera review of the withheld documents by the [district] court is not an acceptable substitute for an adequate Vaughn index.").

[209] Jones, 41 F.3d at 242; see Fiduccia, 185 F.3d at 1044 ("Any form . . . may be adequate or inadequate, depending on the circumstances."); Church of Scientology, 30 F.3d at 231; Hinton v. Department of Justice, 844 F.2d 126, 129 (3d Cir. 1988); Gallant v. NLRB, 26 F.3d 168, 172-73 (D.C. Cir. 1994); Vaughn v. United States, 936 F.2d 862, 867 (6th Cir. 1991) ("A court's primary focus must be on the substance, rather than the form, of the information supplied by the government to justify withholding requested information."); Keys v. United States Dep't of Justice, 830 F.2d 337, 349 (D.C. Cir. 1987).

[210] Jones, 41 F.3d at 242 (holding that Vaughn Index is adequate so long as it "'enables the court to make a reasoned independent assessment of the claim[s] of exemption'" (quoting Vaughn, 936 F.2d at 866-67)); Hinton, 844 F.2d at 129; Manna v. United States Dep't of Justice, 832 F. Supp. 866, 873 (D.N.J. 1993).

[211] See, e.g., Wishart v. Commissioner, No. 98-17248, 1999 WL 985142, at *1 (9th Cir. Oct. 27, 1999) (suggesting that Vaughn Index is unnecessary if declarations are detailed enough); Miscavige v. IRS, 2 F.3d 366, 368 (11th Cir. 1993) (deciding that separate document expressly designated as "Vaughn Index" is unnecessary when agency "declarations are highly detailed, focus on the individual documents, and provide a factual base for withholding each document at issue"); Minier v. CIA, 88 F.3d 796, 804 (9th Cir. 1996) ("[W]hen a FOIA requester has sufficient information to present a full legal argument, there is no need for a Vaughn index."); Brown v. FBI, 658 F.2d 71, 74 (2d Cir. 1981) ("Thus, when the facts in plaintiff's possession are sufficient to allow an effective presentation of its case, an itemized and indexed justification of the specificity contemplated by Vaughn may be unnecessary."); Goulding v. IRS, No. 97 C 5728, 1998 WL 325202, at *7 (N.D. Ill. June 8, 1998) ("A Vaughn index is not necessary in every case, so long as the function it serves is sufficiently performed by the agency's affidavits or declarations."); Ferri v. United States Dep't of Justice, 573 F. Supp. 852, 856-57 (W.D. Pa. 1983) (holding that

(continued...)

## LITIGATION CONSIDERATIONS

The hallmark of an adequate "Vaughn Index" is that it provides "'a relatively detailed justification, specifically identifying the reasons why a particular exemption is relevant and correlat[es] those claims with the particular part of a withheld document to which they apply.'"[212] Of course, "[t]he degree of specificity of itemization, justification, and correlation required in a particular case will ... depend on the nature of the document at issue and the particular exemption asserted."[213] A crucial part of the Vaughn Index is that it should expressly indicate for each document that any reasonably segregable information has been disclosed.[214] Indeed, the Court of Appeals for the District of Columbia Circuit has repeatedly held that it is reversible error for a district court not to make a finding of segregability.[215] In its most recent pronouncement on this issue, the D.C. Circuit ruled that even if the segregability issue has not

---

[211](...continued)
6000 pages of unindexed grand jury testimony were sufficiently described).

[212] Animal Legal Defense Fund v. Department of the Air Force, 44 F. Supp. 2d 295, 300 (D.D.C. 1999) (quoting King, 830 F.2d at 224).

[213] Information Acquisition Corp. v. Department of Justice, 444 F. Supp. 458, 462 (D.D.C. 1978); see, e.g., Citizens Comm'n on Human Rights v. FDA, 45 F.3d 1325, 1328 (9th Cir. 1995) (finding adequate, for responsive records consisting of 1000 volumes of 300 to 400 pages each, agency's volume-by-volume summary when Vaughn Indexes "specifically describe the documents' contents and give specific reasons for withholding them"); Davis v. United States Dep't of Justice, 968 F.2d 1276, 1282 n.4 (D.C. Cir. 1992) (opining that precise matching of exemptions with specific withheld items "may well be unnecessary" when all government's generic claims have merit); Vaughn, 936 F.2d at 868 (approving category-of-document approach when over 1000 pages were withheld under Exemptions 3, 5, 7(A), 7(C), 7(D), and 7(E)); NTEU v. United States Customs Serv., 602 F. Supp. 469, 472-73 (D.D.C. 1984) (no index required for 44 employee-evaluation forms withheld under Exemption 2); Agee v. CIA, 517 F. Supp. 1335, 1337-38 (D.D.C. 1981) (accepting index listing 15 categories when more specific index would compromise national security). But see King, 830 F.2d at 224 (requiring more complete Vaughn Index to support Exemption 1 withholding of especially old records).

[214] See, e.g., Isley v. Executive Office for United States Attorneys, No. 98-5098, 1999 WL 1021934, at *7 (D.C. Cir. Oct. 21, 1999) ("The segregability requirement applies to all documents and all exemptions in the FOIA."); Krikorian v. Department of State, 984 F.2d 461, 467 (D.C. Cir. 1993) (remanding for segregability determination for "each of the withheld documents").

[215] See Kimberlin v. Department of Justice, 139 F.3d 944, 950 (D.C. Cir. (in remanding case for segregability determination, stating that it is reversible error for district court to fail to make segregability finding), cert. denied, 525 U.S. 891 (1998); Schiller v. NLRB, 964 F.2d 1205, 1210 (D.C. Cir. 1992) (same); see also Voinche v. FBI, 46 F. Supp. 2d 26, 33 (D.D.C. 1999) (refusing to grant summary judgment because agency's blanket segregability statement was inadequate); Animal Legal Defense Fund, 44 F. Supp. at 299 (chastising agency for failing to discharge "its duty under § 552(b)"); see also FOIA Update, Vol. XIV, No. 3, at 11-12 ("OIP Guidance: The 'Reasonable Segregation' Obligation").

## LITIGATION CONSIDERATIONS

first been raised by the parties, the district court has "an affirmative duty" to consider the matter "sua sponte."[216] (For further discussions of this issue, see Procedural Requirements, "Reasonably Segregable" Obligation, above, and Litigation Considerations, "Reasonably Segregable" Requirements, below.) Questions regarding segregability also may be resolved through in camera inspection of documents by the district court, when necessary.[217] (For a further discussion of in camera inspection, see Litigation Considerations, In Camera Inspection, below.)

When voluminous records are at issue, courts have sanctioned the use of Vaughn Indexes based upon representative samplings of the withheld documents.[218] This special procedure "allows the court and the parties to reduce a voluminous FOIA exemption case to a manageable number of items" for the

---

[216] Trans-Pac. Policing Agreement v. United States Customs Serv., 177 F.3d 1022, 1028 (D.C. Cir. 1999).

[217] See Solar Sources, Inc. v. United States, 142 F.3d 1033, 1039 (7th Cir. 1998) (finding that in camera review, coupled with sworn agency declaration, "provided the district court with a sufficient factual basis to determine that the documents were properly withheld"); Becker v. IRS, 34 F.3d 398, 406 (7th Cir. 1994) (finding remand unnecessary as judge "did not simply rely on IRS affidavits describing the documents, but conducted an in camera review" (citing Hopkins v. HUD, 929 F.2d 81, 85 (2d Cir. 1991) (holding that absence of district court's findings on segregability warrants "remand with instructions to the district court to examine the inspector reports in camera"))).

[218] See, e.g., Neely v. FBI, 208 F.3d 461, 467 (4th Cir. 2000) (suggesting that, on remand, district court "resort to the well-established practice . . . of randomly sampling the documents in question"); Solar Sources, 142 F.3d at 1038-39 (approving use of sample of 6000 pages out of 5 million); Jones, 41 F.3d at 242 (approving sample comprising two percent of total number of documents at issue); Meeropol v. Meese, 790 F.2d 942, 956-57 (D.C. Cir. 1986) (allowing sampling of every 100th document when approximately 20,000 documents were at issue); Weisberg v. United States Dep't of Justice, 745 F.2d 1476, 1490 (D.C. Cir. 1984) (approving index of sampling of withheld documents, when over 60,000 pages at issue, even though no example of certain exemptions provided); Jefferson v. O'Brien, No. 96-1365, slip op. at 5 (D.D.C. Feb. 22, 2000) (approving sample index of approximately four percent of responsive records); see also Washington Post v. DOD, 766 F. Supp. 1, 15-16 (D.D.C. 1991) (deciding that with more than 14,000 pages of responsive material involved, agency should produce detailed Vaughn Index for sample of files, such sample to be determined by parties or court); cf. Kronisch v. United States, No. 83 CIV. 2458, 1995 WL 303625, at **1, 13 n.1 (S.D.N.Y. May 18, 1995) (holding sampling of 50 documents selected by plaintiff, out of universe of approximately 30,000 pages, to be appropriate basis for resolution of discovery dispute). But see Martinson v. Violent Drug Traffickers Project, No. 95-2161, 1996 U.S. Dist. LEXIS 11658, at *25 (D.D.C. Aug. 7, 1996) ("This Court does not believe that 173 pages of located documents is even close to being 'voluminous.'"); SafeCard Servs. v. SEC, No. 84-3073, slip op. at 7-9 (D.D.C. May 19, 1988) (concluding that burden of indexing relatively small number of requested documents--approximately 200--was insufficient to justify sampling).

## LITIGATION CONSIDERATIONS

Vaughn Index and, "[i]f the sample is well-chosen, a court can, with some confidence, 'extrapolate its conclusions from the representative sample to the larger group of withheld materials.'"[219] Once a representative sampling of the withheld documents is agreed to, however, the agency's subsequent release of some of those documents may destroy the representativeness of the sample and thereby raise questions about the propriety of withholding other responsive, non-sample, documents.[220] In recognition of this danger, the D.C. Circuit has held that an agency "must justify its initial withholdings and is not relieved of that burden by a later turnover of sample documents," and that "the district court must determine whether the released documents were properly redacted [when] initially reviewed."[221]

Many agencies use "coded" Vaughn indexes--which break certain FOIA exemptions into several categories, explain the particular nondisclosure rationales for each category, and then correlate the exemption and category to the particular documents at issue.[222] Courts have generally accepted the use of such "coded" indexes when "[e]ach deletion was correlated specifically and unambiguously to the corresponding exemption . . . [which] was adequately explained by functional categories . . . [so as to] place[] each document into its historical and investigative perspective."[223] Innovative formats for "coded"

---

[219] Bonner v. United States Dep't of State, 928 F.2d 1148, 1151 (D.C. Cir. 1991) (quoting Fensterwald v. CIA, 443 F. Supp. 667, 669 (D.D.C. 1977)).

[220] See Bonner, 928 F.2d at 1153-54; Schrecker v. United States Dep't of Justice, 14 F. Supp. 2d 111, 117 (D.D.C. 1998) (ordering reprocessing of all documents because of problems with representative sampling).

[221] Bonner, 928 F.2d at 1154; see also Davin, 60 F.3d at 1053 (plaintiff's agreement to sampling does not relieve government of obligation to disclose reasonably segregable, nonexempt material in all responsive documents, including those not part of sample).

[222] See, e.g., Jones, 41 F.3d at 242-43 (noting that coded indices "have become accepted practice"); Maynard, 986 F.2d at 559 & n.13 (noting use by FBI and explaining format).

[223] Keys, 830 F.2d at 349-50; see, e.g., Maynard, 986 F.2d at 559 n.13 (1993); Canning, 848 F. Supp. at 1043; Steinberg v. United States Dep't of Justice, 801 F. Supp. 800, 803 (D.D.C. 1992), aff'd in pertinent part & remanded in part, 23 F.3d 548 (D.C. Cir. 1994); Pray v. FBI, No. 95 Civ. 0380, 1998 WL 44083, at *2 (S.D.N.Y. Aug. 3, 1998) (finding coded Vaughn Index "adequate"); Albuquerque Publ'g Co. v. United States Dep't of Justice, 726 F. Supp. 851, 859 (D.D.C. 1989); Branch v. FBI, 658 F. Supp. 204, 206-07 (D.D.C. 1987); United States Student Ass'n v. CIA, 620 F. Supp. 565, 568 (D.D.C. 1985); cf. Fiduccia, 185 F.3d at 1043-44 (observing that "[t]he form of disclosure is not critical" and that "redacted documents [can be] an entirely satisfactory (perhaps superior) alternative to a Vaughn index or affidavit performing this function"); Davin, 60 F.3d at 1051 ("While the use of the categorical method does not per se render a Vaughn index inadequate, an agency using justification codes must also include specific factual information concerning the documents withheld and correlate the claimed exemptions to the with-

(continued...)

## LITIGATION CONSIDERATIONS

affidavits have been found acceptable, so long as they enhance the ultimate goal of overall "descriptive accuracy" of the affidavit.[224]

The D.C. Circuit has gone so far as to hold that the district court judge's review of only the expurgated documents--an integral part of the "coded" affidavit--was sufficient in a situation in which the applicable exemption was obvious from the face of the documents.[225] However, this approach has been found inadequate when the coded categories are too "far ranging" and more detailed subcategories could be provided.[226] Indeed, when numerous pages of records are withheld in full, a "coded" affidavit that does not specifically correlate multiple exemption claims to particular portions of the pages withheld has been found to be impermissibly conclusory.[227]

---

[223](...continued) held documents."), on remand, No. 92-1122, slip op. at 6 (W.D. Pa. Apr. 9, 1998) (approving revised coded Vaughn Index), aff'd, 176 F.3d 471 (3d Cir. 1999) (unpublished table decision). But see Wiener, 943 F.2d at 978-79 (rejecting coded affidavits on belief that such categorical descriptions fail to give requester sufficient opportunity to contest withholdings); Samuel Gruber Educ. Project v. United States Dep't of Justice, 24 F. Supp. 2d 1, 8 (D.D.C. Feb. 20, 1998) (magistrate's recommendation) (erroneously speaking of "near universal condemnation" of coded indexes), adopted with modifications, No. 90-1912 (D.D.C. Mar. 17, 1998).

[224] See National Sec. Archive v. Office of the Indep. Counsel, No. 89-2308, slip op. at 6-7 (D.D.C. Aug. 28, 1992) (when information was withheld by multiple agencies under various exemptions, "alphabetical classification" found properly employed to facilitate coordination of withholding justifications); see also King, 830 F.2d at 225; Canning, 848 F. Supp. at 1043.

[225] Delaney, Migdail & Young, Chartered v. IRS, 826 F.2d 124, 128 (D.C. Cir. 1987); see Whittle v. Moschella, 756 F. Supp. 589, 595 (D.D.C. 1991) ("For two large redactions, the contents are not readily apparent, but since the information there redacted was provided by confidential sources, it is entirely protected from disclosure."); see also King, 830 F.2d at 221 ("Utilization of reproductions of the material released to supply contextual information about material withheld is clearly permissible, but caution should be exercised in resorting to this method of description."); cf. Fiduccia, 185 F.3d at 1043 (recognizing that a Vaughn Index is "a superfluity" when the plaintiff and the court can ascertain the nature of information withheld by reviewing the redacted documents).

[226] See King, 830 F.2d at 221-22. But see Canning, 848 F. Supp. at 1044-45 (approving coded Vaughn Index for classified information and differentiating it from that filed in King).

[227] See Coleman v. FBI, No. 89-2773, 1991 WL 333709, at *4 (D.D.C. Apr. 3, 1991) (allowing "coded" affidavit for expurgated pages, but rejecting it as to pages withheld in full), summary affirmance granted, No. 92-5040, 1992 WL 373976 (D.C. Cir. Dec. 4, 1992); see also Williams v. FBI, No. 90-2299, slip op. at 11-12 (D.D.C. Aug. 6, 1991) (finding "coded" affidavit insufficiently descriptive as to documents withheld in their entireties).

## LITIGATION CONSIDERATIONS

Agencies employing "coded" indexes ordinarily attach copies of the records released in part--i.e., the "expurgated" documents--as part of their public Vaughn submission.[228] But agencies seeking to justify withholding records from first-party FOIA requesters should be mindful of the fact that the public filing of expurgated documents about the individual requester (or even detailed descriptions of them in briefs) may constitute a "disclosure" under subsection (b) of the Privacy Act of 1974.[229] Unless proceeding under seal, or with the prior written consent of the requester, an agency should strive to make such a disclosure only in accordance with one of the exceptions set forth in the Privacy Act--such as its "routine use" exception or its "court order" exception.[230]

Although an agency ordinarily must justify its withholdings on a page-by-page or document-by-document basis, under certain circumstances courts have approved withholdings of entire, but discrete, categories of records which encompass similar information.[231] Most commonly, courts have per-

---

[228] See, e.g., Maynard, 986 F.2d at 559 n.13 (explaining coded Vaughn procedure).

[229] 5 U.S.C. § 552a(b) (1994 & Supp. IV 1998); see, e.g., Krohn v. United States Dep't of Justice, No. 78-1536, slip op. at 2-7 (D.D.C. Mar. 19, 1984), vacated in part on other grounds (D.D.C. Nov. 29, 1984); Citizens Bureau of Investigation v. FBI, No. C78-80, slip op. at 3 (N.D. Ohio Dec. 12, 1979); see also Laningham v. United States Navy, No. 83-3238, slip op. at 2-3 (D.D.C. Sept. 25, 1984), summary judgment granted (D.D.C. Jan. 7, 1985), aff'd per curiam, 813 F.2d 1236 (D.C. Cir. 1987).

[230] 5 U.S.C. § 552a(b)(3), (11); see also, e.g., 63 Fed. Reg. 8665, 8666 (1998) (listing routine use applicable to records in Justice Department's Civil Division Case File System); 63 Fed. Reg. 8666, 8667-68 (1998) (listing routine uses applicable to records in United States Attorneys' Offices' Civil Case Files); cf. Blazy v. Tenet, 979 F. Supp. 10, 27 (D.D.C. 1997) (agreeing to uncontested order to seal Privacy Act-protected documents released pursuant to routine use, while chiding plaintiff that "[h]aving obtained three volumes of released documents through this litigation, [he] somewhat ironically complains that the government improperly filed these documents with the Court in violation of his privacy rights"), summary affirmance granted, No. 97-5330 (D.C. Cir. May 12, 1998).

[231] See NLRB v. Robbins Tire & Rubber Co., 437 U.S. 214, 223-24 (1978) (stating that language of Exemption 7(A) "appears to contemplate that certain generic determinations may be made"); Crooker v. ATF, 789 F.2d 64, 66-67 (D.C. Cir. 1986) (distinguishing between unacceptable "blanket" exemptions and permissible generic determinations); Pully v. IRS, 939 F. Supp. 429, 433-38 (E.D. Va. 1996) (accepting categorization of 5624 documents into 26 separate categories protected under several exemptions); see also United States Dep't of Justice v. Landano, 508 U.S. 165, 179 (1993) ("There may well be other generic circumstances in which an implied assurance of confidentiality fairly can be inferred."); United States Dep't of Justice v. Reporters Comm. for Freedom of the Press, 489 U.S. 749, 776 (1989) ("categorical decisions may be appropriate and individual circumstances disregarded when a case fits into a

(continued...)

## LITIGATION CONSIDERATIONS

mitted the withholding of records under Exemption 7(A) on a category-by-category or "generic" basis.[232] While the outermost contours of what constitutes an acceptable "generic" Exemption 7(A) Vaughn presentations are sometimes unclear,[233] it appears well established that if the agency has (1) de-

---

[231](...continued) genus in which the balance characteristically tips in one direction"); cf. Coleman v. FBI, 972 F. Supp. 5, 8 (D.D.C. 1997) ("For an agency to break from the norm of a document-by-document index, the agency must at least argue that a 'categorical' index is warranted.").

[232] See, e.g., Robbins Tire, 417 U.S. at 218-23 (endorsing government's position "that a particularized, case-by-case showing is neither required nor practical, and that witness statements in pending unfair labor practice proceedings are exempt as a matter of law from disclosure [under Exemption 7(A)] while the hearing is pending"); Solar Sources, 142 F.3d at 1040 (reiterating that detailed Vaughn Index is not generally required in Exemption 7(A) cases); In re Department of Justice, 999 F.2d 1302, 1309 (8th Cir. 1993) (en banc); Dickerson v. Department of Justice, 992 F.2d 1426, 1428, 1433-34 (6th Cir. 1993) (approving FBI justification of Exemption 7(A) for documents pertaining to disappearance of Jimmy Hoffa on "category-of-document" basis by supplying "a general description of the contents of the investigatory files, categorizing the records by source or function"); Lewis, 823 F.2d at 389 ("The IRS need only make a general showing that disclosure of its investigatory records would interfere with its enforcement proceedings."); Bevis v. Department of State, 801 F.2d 1386, 1389 (D.C. Cir. 1986); Western Journalism Ctr. v. Office of the Indep. Counsel, 926 F. Supp. 189, 192 (D.D.C. 1996) ("The Independent Counsel's declaration certainly satisfies Exemption 7(A) and the Independent Counsel 'need not proceed on a document-by-document basis, detailing to the court the interference that would result from the disclosure of each of them.'" (quoting Bevis, 801 F.2d at 1389)), summary affirmance granted, No. 96-5178, 1997 WL 195516, at *1 (D.C. Cir. Mar. 11, 1997) ("[A]ppellee was not required to describe the records retrieved in response to appellants' request, or the harm their disclosure might cause, on a document-by-document basis, as appellee's description of the information contained in the three categories it devised is sufficient to permit the court to determine whether the information retrieved is exempt from disclosure."); May v. IRS, No. 90-1123-CV-W-2, 1991 U.S. Dist. LEXIS 18906, at *7 (W.D. Mo. Dec. 9, 1991) ("Because the plaintiff's requests basically encompass all documents relating to his pending investigation, the documents in question fit into a genus that does not warrant a document-by-document review."); see also Citizens Comm'n, 45 F.3d at 1328 (for responsive records consisting of 1000 volumes of 300 to 400 pages each, volume-by-volume summary held adequate when Vaughn Indexes "specifically describe the documents' contents and give specific reasons for withholding them"); FOIA Update, Vol. V, No. 2, at 3-4. But see Institute for Justice & Human Rights v. Executive Office of the United States Attorney, No. C 96-1469, 1998 U.S. Dist. LEXIS 3709, at **18-19 (N.D. Cal. Mar. 18, 1998) (refusing to permit agency to justify Exemption 7(A) withholdings by category when it had already submitted Vaughn Indexes justifying withholdings on document-by-document basis).

[233] Compare Curran v. Department of Justice, 813 F.2d 473, 476 (1st Cir.
(continued...)

-577-

**LITIGATION CONSIDERATIONS**

fined its Exemption 7(A) categories functionally, (2) conducted a document-by-document review in order to assign documents to the proper category, and (3) explained how the release of each category of information would interfere with the enforcement proceedings, the description will be found sufficient.[234] (See the discussion of Vaughn Indexes under Exemption 7(A), above.) Moreover, when "a claimed FOIA exemption consists of a generic [exemption], dependent upon the category of records rather than the subject matter which each individual record contains [so that] resort to a Vaughn index is futile,"[235] such generic descriptions can also satisfy an agency's Vaughn obligation with regard to other exemptions as well.[236]

---

[233](...continued)
1987) (approving category entitled "other sundry items of information" because "[a]bsent a 'miscellaneous' category of this sort, the FBI would, especially in the case of one-of-a-kind records, have to resort to just the sort of precise description which would itself compromise the exemption"), and May, No. 90-1123, slip op. at 6-7 (W.D. Mo. Dec. 9, 1991) (approving categories of "intra-agency memoranda" and "work sheets"), with Bevis, 801 F.2d at 1390 ("categories identified only as 'teletypes,' or 'airtels,' or 'letters'" held inadequate).

[234] See In re Department of Justice, 999 F.2d at 1309 (citing Bevis, 801 F.2d at 1389-90); Manna v. United States Dep't of Justice, 815 F. Supp. 798, 806 (D.N.J. 1993); see also Dickerson, 992 F.2d at 1433 (enumerating categories of information withheld); Curran, 813 F.2d at 476 (same); May, No. 90-1123, slip op. at 6-7 (W.D. Mo. Dec. 9, 1991) (same); Docal v. Bennsinger, 543 F. Supp. 38, 44 n.12 (M.D. Pa. 1981) (enumerating categories of "interference"); cf. Curran, 813 F.2d at 476 (stating that FBI affidavit met Bevis test and therefore finding it unnecessary to determine whether Bevis test is too demanding).

[235] Church of Scientology v. IRS, 792 F.2d 146, 152 (D.C. Cir. 1986).

[236] See Reporters Comm., 489 U.S. at 779-80 (authorizing "categorical" protection of information under Exemption 7(C)); Gallant, 26 F.3d at 173 (categorical withholding of names under Exemption 6 approved); Church of Scientology, 792 F.2d at 152 (generic exemption under IRS Exemption 3 statute, 26 U.S.C. § 6103 (1994), appropriate if "affidavit sufficiently detailed to establish that the document or group of documents in question actually falls into the exempted category"); Antonelli v. FBI, 721 F.2d 615, 617-19 (7th Cir. 1983) (no index required in third-party request for records when agency categorically neither confirmed nor denied existence of records on particular individuals absent showing of public interest in disclosure); Brown, 658 F.2d at 74 (protecting personal information under Exemption 6); Pully, 939 F. Supp. at 433-38 (accepting categorical descriptions for documents protected under Exemptions 3 (in conjunction with 21 U.S.C. § 6103(a) (1994)), 5 (attorney-client privilege), 7(A), 7(C), and 7(E) when 5624 documents arranged into 26 categories); Helmsley v. United States Dep't of Justice, No. 90-2413, slip op. at 3-13 (D.D.C. Sept. 24, 1992) (categorical descriptions accepted for withholdings under Exemptions 3 (in conjunction with Rule 6(e) of Federal Rules of Criminal Procedure and 26 U.S.C. § 6103 (1994)), 5, 7(A), 7(C), and 7(D)); MCI Telecomms. Corp. v. GSA, No. 89-0746, 1992 WL 71394, at **3-4 (D.D.C. (continued...)

## LITIGATION CONSIDERATIONS

In a broad range of contexts, most courts have refused to require agencies to file public Vaughn Indexes that are so detailed as to reveal sensitive information the withholding of which is the very issue in the litigation.[237] Therefore, in camera affidavits are frequently utilized in Exemption 1 cases when a public description of responsive documents would compromise national security.[238] (For a further discussion of this point, see Litigation Consid-

---

[236](...continued)
Mar. 25, 1992) (Exemption 5 withholdings); May, No. 90-1123, slip op. at 9 (W.D. Mo. Dec. 9, 1991) (withholdings protected under both Exemption 7(A) and Exemption 3 (in conjunction with 26 U.S.C. § 6103)); NTEU v. United States Customs Serv., 602 F. Supp. 469, 472-73 (D.D.C. 1984) (no index required for 44 employee-evaluation forms withheld under Exemption 2); see also Church of Scientology, 30 F.3d at 234 ("[A] categorical approach to nondisclosure is permissible only when the government can establish that, in every case, a particular type of information may be withheld regardless of the specific surrounding circumstances."); FOIA Update, Vol. X, No. 2, at 6. But see McNamera v. United States Dep't of Justice, 949 F. Supp. 478, 483 (W.D. Tex. 1996) (rejecting apparent categorical indices for criminal files on third parties that were withheld under Exemptions 6 and 7(C) because "there is no way for the court to tell whether some, a portion of some, or all the documents being withheld fall within any of the exemptions claimed").

[237] See, e.g., Landano, 508 U.S. at 180 ("To the extent that the Government's proof may compromise legitimate interests, of course, the Government still can attempt to meet its burden with in camera affidavits."); Maricopa Audubon Soc'y v. United States Forest Serv., 108 F.3d 1089, 1093 (9th Cir. 1997) ("Indeed we doubt that the agency could have introduced further proof without revealing the actual contents of the withheld materials."); Oglesby, 79 F.3d at 1176 ("The description and explanation the agency offers should reveal as much detail as possible as to the nature of the document without actually disclosing information that deserves protection."); Patterson, 56 F.3d at 837 ("[W]e do not wish to force the government to disclose so much information about the investigation or the particular documents that an exemption loses its intended effect."); Maynard, 986 F.2d at 557 (emphasizing that although public declaration "lacked specifics, a more detailed affidavit could have revealed the very intelligence sources or methods that the CIA wished to keep secret"); Lewis, 823 F.2d at 380 ("[A] Vaughn index of the documents here would defeat the purpose of Exemption 7(A). It would aid [the requester] in discovering the exact nature of the documents supporting the government's case against him earlier than he otherwise would or should."); Curran, 813 F.2d at 476 (agency should not be forced "to resort to just the sort of precise description which would itself compromise the exemption"); Church of Scientology v. United States Dep't of the Army, 611 F.2d 738, 742 (9th Cir. 1980) (recognizing that "the government need not specify its objections in such detail as to compromise the secrecy of the information"). But see Wiener, 943 F.2d at 977-87.

[238] See, e.g., Doyle v. FBI, 722 F.2d 554, 556 (9th Cir. 1983) (approving use of in camera affidavits in certain cases involving national security exemption); Public Educ. Ctr., Inc. v. DOD, 905 F. Supp. 19, 22 (D.D.C. 1995) (granting summary judgment on basis of in camera affidavit and noting that "there are

(continued...)

## LITIGATION CONSIDERATIONS

erations, In Camera Inspection, below.) This same important principle also has been applied to other FOIA exemptions--for example, in Exemption 5 cases,[239] in Exemption 7(A) cases,[240] and in Exemption 7(D) cases.[241] However, in all cases in which explanations for withholding are presented in camera, the agency is obliged to ensure that it has first set forth on the public record an explanation that is as complete as possible without compromising the sensitive information.[242]

With regard to the timing of the creation of a Vaughn Index, it is well settled that a requester is not entitled to receive one during the administrative

---

[238](...continued)
occasions when extensive public justification would threaten to reveal the very information for which a FOIA exemption is claimed"); Springmann v. United States Dep't of State, No. 93-1238, slip op. at 2-3 (D.D.C. Feb. 24, 2000) (granting renewed motion for summary judgment after reviewing in camera affidavit); Keys v. United States Dep't of Justice, No. 85-2588, slip op. at 3 (D.D.C. May 12, 1986) (noting "the inherent problems that necessarily arise whenever a FOIA affiant is confronted with the need to be circumspect" due to national security concerns), aff'd on other grounds, 830 F.2d at 337; see also CIA v. Sims, 471 U.S. 159, 179 (1985) (recognizing that "the mere explanation of why information must be withheld can convey [harmful] information").

[239] See, e.g., Ethyl Corp. v. EPA, 25 F.3d 1241, 1250 (4th Cir. 1994) ("If the district court is satisfied that the EPA cannot describe documents in more detail without breaching a properly asserted confidentiality, then the court is still left with the mechanism provided by the statute--to conduct an in camera review of the documents."); Wolfe v. HHS, 839 F.2d 768, 771 n.3 (D.C. Cir. 1988) (en banc) ("Where the index itself would reveal significant aspects of the deliberative process, this court has not hesitated to limit consideration of the Vaughn index to in camera inspection.").

[240] See, e.g., Alyeska Pipeline Serv. v. EPA, No. 86-2176, slip op. at 8 (D.D.C. Sept. 9, 1987) ("[R]equiring a Vaughn index in this matter will result in exactly the kind of harm to defendant's law enforcement proceedings which it is trying to avoid under exemption 7(A)."), aff'd on other grounds, 856 F.2d 309 (D.C. Cir. 1988); Dickerson v. Department of Justice, No. 90-60045, slip op. at 4-5 (E.D. Mich. July 31, 1991), aff'd, 992 F.2d 1426 (6th Cir. 1993).

[241] See, e.g., Landano, 508 U.S. at 180 (ruling that government can meet its burden with in camera affidavits in order to avoid identification of sources in Exemption 7(D) withholdings); Church of Scientology, 30 F.3d at 240 n.23 (same); Keys, 830 F.2d at 349 (announcing that there is no requirement to produce Vaughn Index in "degree of detail that would reveal precisely the information that the agency claims it is entitled to withhold"); Doe v. United States Dep't of Justice, 790 F. Supp. 17, 21 (D.D.C. 1992) ("[A] meaningful description beyond that provided by the Vaughn code utilized in this case would probably lead to disclosure of the identity of sources.").

[242] See Armstrong v. Executive Office of the President, 97 F.3d 575, 580-81 (D.C. Cir. 1996) (citing Lykins v. United States Dep't of Justice, 725 F.2d 1455, 1465 (D.C. Cir. 1984)); Philippi v. CIA, 546 F.2d 1009, 1013 (D.C. Cir. 1976).

## LITIGATION CONSIDERATIONS

process.[243] Furthermore, courts generally do not require the submission of a Vaughn Index prior to the time at which a dispositive motion is filed; this standard practice is based upon the need to maintain an orderly and efficient adjudicative process in FOIA cases, and upon the practical reality that some form of affidavit, declaration, or index virtually always accompanies the defendant agency's motion for summary judgment.[244] Efforts to compel the preparation of Vaughn Indexes prior to the filing of an agency's dispositive motion are typically denied as premature.[245]

---

[243] See, e.g., Edmond v. United States Attorney, 959 F. Supp. 1, 5 (D.D.C. 1997) (rejecting, as premature, request for Vaughn Index when agency had not processed plaintiff's request); cf. Judicial Watch, 880 F. Supp. at 11. Schaake v. IRS, No. 91-958, slip op. at 7-8 (S.D. Ill. June 3, 1992); SafeCard, No. 84-3073, slip op. at 3-5 (D.D.C. May 19, 1988); see also FOIA Update, Vol. VII, No. 3, at 6.

[244] See, e.g., Tannehill v. Department of the Air Force, No. 87-1335, slip op. at 1 (D.D.C. Aug. 20, 1987) (noting that standard practice is to await filing of agency's dispositive motion before deciding whether additional indexes will be necessary); British Airports Auth. v. CAB, 2 Gov't Disclosure Serv. (P-H) ¶ 81,234, at 81,654 (D.D.C. June 25, 1981) (explaining that "standard practice which has developed is for the Court to commit the parties to a schedule for briefing summary judgment motions," with "defendant typically fil[ing] first and simultaneously with or in advance of filing submit[ting] supporting affidavits and indices").

[245] See, e.g., Miscavige, 2 F.3d at 369 ("The plaintiff's early attempt in litigation of this kind to obtain a Vaughn Index . . . is inappropriate until the government has first had a chance to provide the court with the information necessary to make a decision on the applicable exemptions."); Pyne v. Commissioner, No. 98-00253, 1999 U.S. Dist. LEXIS 1059, at *8 (D. Haw. Jan. 6, 1999) (denying motion to compel submission of Vaughn Index as "premature" when agency had not yet refused to release records or provided supporting affidavit for nondisclosure); Stimac v. United States Dep't of Justice, 620 F. Supp. 212, 213 (D.D.C. 1985) (denying as premature motion to compel Vaughn Index denied on ground that "filing of a dispositive motion, along with detailed affidavits, may obviate the need for indexing the withheld documents"); see also Cohen v. FBI, 831 F. Supp. 850, 855 (S.D. Fla. 1993) (confirming that Vaughn Index is not required when "Open America" stay is granted "because no documents have been withheld on the grounds that they are exempt from disclosure"); Government Accountability Project v. NRC, No. 87-2053, slip op. at 1 (D.D.C. Aug. 13, 1987) ("[U]ntil defendant files an answer this Court is unable to determine precisely what will be contested and whether a Vaughn Index is appropriate and proper."). But see Rosenfeld v. United States Dep't of Justice, No. C-90-3576, slip op. at 18-19 (N.D. Cal. Feb. 18, 1992) (maintaining that there is no "indication that the provision of material justifying claimed exemptions should be delayed until a dispositive motion has been filed by the government"); Providence Journal Co. v. United States Dep't of the Army, 769 F. Supp. 67, 69 (D.R.I. 1991) (finding contention that Vaughn Index must await dispositive motion to be "insufficient and sterile" when agency "has not even indicated when it plans to file such a motion").

# LITIGATION CONSIDERATIONS

## "Reasonably Segregable" Requirements

The FOIA requires that "[a]ny reasonably segregable portion of a record shall be provided to any person requesting such a record after deletion of the portions which are exempt."[246] Added as part of the 1974 FOIA amendments,[247] this important provision was designed to narrow the focus of the application of exemptions from documents to specific segments of information within them.[248]

With increasing emphasis, the United States Court of Appeals for the District of Columbia Circuit has led the way in ensuring that this statutory mandate is honored by requiring specific findings on segregability.[249] Summary judgment may be denied to an agency if its declarations do not adequately demonstrate that all reasonably segregable, nonexempt information has been disclosed.[250] (For a further discussion of summary judgment requirements, see Litigation Considerations, Summary Judgment, above.) Indeed, a district court decision may be reversed entirely on procedural

---

[246] 5 U.S.C. § 552(b) (1994 & Supp. IV 1998) (sentence immediately following exemptions).

[247] Pub. L. No. 93-502, 88 Stat. 1561.

[248] See Schiller v. NLRB, 964 F.2d 1205, 1209 (D.C. Cir. 1992) ("'The focus in the FOIA is information not documents and an agency cannot justify withholding an entire document simply by showing that it contains some exempt material.'" (quoting Mead Data Cent., Inc. v. United States Dep't of the Air Force, 566 F.2d 242, 368 (D.C. Cir. 1977))); see also Attorney General's Memorandum on the 1974 Amendments to the Freedom of Information Act 14 (Feb. 1975); FOIA Update, Vol. XIV, No. 3, at 11-12 ("OIP Guidance: The 'Reasonable Segregation' Obligation").

[249] See, e.g., Trans-Pac. Policing Agreement v. United States Customs Serv., 177 F.3d 1022, 1028 (D.C. Cir. 1999) (holding that district court had an affirmative duty to consider segregability issue sua sponte); Kimberlin v. Department of Justice, 139 F.3d 944, 950 (D.C. Cir.) (remanding, despite in camera review, because "'[i]t is error for the district court simply to approve withholding . . . without entering a finding on segregability.'" (quoting Schiller, 964 F.2d at 1209-10)), cert. denied, 525 U.S. 89 (1998); see also Wiener v. FBI, 943 F.2d 972, 988 (9th Cir. 1991). But cf. Becker v. IRS, 34 F.3d 398, 406 (7th Cir. 1994) (finding remand unnecessary because judge "did not simply rely on IRS affidavits describing the documents, but conducted an in camera review"); Solar Sources, Inc. v. United States, 142 F.3d 1033, 1039 (7th Cir. 1998) ("[C]ourts should not order segregation when such a process would be significantly unwieldy.").

[250] See, e.g., Animal Legal Defense Fund, Inc. v. Department of the Air Force, 44 F. Supp. 2d 295, 301 (D.D.C. 1999) (denying government's motion for summary judgment, in part, because declaration was insufficient on segregability issue); Carlton v. Department of the Interior, No. 97-2105, slip op. at 12 (D.D.C. Sept. 3, 1998) (finding agency declaration to be insufficient because it provided only "general statement that the withheld documents do not contain segregable portions").

## LITIGATION CONSIDERATIONS

grounds--even if it is correct in all substantive exemption respects--if it fails to make segregability findings.[251]

Traditionally, the district court's segregability obligation arose upon a plaintiff's specific complaint or argument about the defendant agency's compliance with that statutory requirement.[252] In Trans-Pacific Policing Agreement v. United States Customs Service,[253] however, the D.C. Circuit recently treated this obligation as a sua sponte requirement for the court--i.e., one to be met even if neither party has raised the issue.[254] To meet this requirement, agency declarations must address the issue of document segregability "with reasonable specificity."[255] This means that, even in the absence of a specific challenge by a FOIA plaintiff, an agency declaration likely will be found insufficient if it attempts to "justify withholding of an entire document simply because it contains some exempt material."[256] Further, conclusory language in agency declarations that do not provide a specific basis for segregability find-

---

[251] See, e.g., Isley v. Executive Office for United States Attorneys, No. 98-5098, 1999 WL 1021934, at *7 (D.C. Cir. Oct. 21, 1999) (remanding case for segregability finding); Summers v. Department of Justice, 140 F.3d 1077, 1081 (D.C. Cir. 1998) (finding that district court abused its discretion by not making "'specific findings of segregability regarding each of the . . . documents withheld . . . .'" (quoting Krikorian v. Department of State, 984 F.2d 461, 467 (D.C. Cir. 1993))); Kimberlin, 139 F.3d at 950 ("[W]e must remand this case to the district court to determine whether any of the withheld documents contains material that can be segregated and disclosed . . . ."); PHE, Inc. v. NLRB, 964 F.2d 1205, 1210 (D.C. Cir. 1992); Wiener, 943 F.2d at 988 (holding that "district court erred by failing to make specific findings on the issue of segregability" and remanding for "specific finding that no information contained in each document or substantial portion of a document withheld is segregable").

[252] See, e.g., Summers, 140 F.3d at 1081; Judicial Watch v. HHS, 27 F. Supp. 2d 240, 246-47 & n.2 (D.D.C. 1998).

[253] 177 F.3d 1022 (D.C. Cir. 1999).

[254] Id. at 1027 (indicating that district court had duty to consider reasonable segregability even though requester never sought segregability finding); see Isley, 1999 WL 1021934, at *7 (explaining that district court erred in failing to make a segregability finding even though neither party raised issue at trial); Schrecker v. United States Dep't of Justice, 74 F. Supp. 2d 26, 29 (D.D.C. 1999) ("[D]istrict courts are required to consider segregability issues even when the parties have not specifically raised such claims.").

[255] Animal Legal Defense Fund, 44 F. Supp. 2d at 301 (citing Armstrong v. Executive Office of the President, 97 F.3d 575, 578 (D.C. Cir. 1996)); Judicial Watch, 27 F. Supp. 2d at 246 ("If a court is to make specific findings of segregability without conducting in camera review in every FOIA case, the government simply must provide more specific information in its Vaughn affidavits.").

[256] Mead Data, 566 F.2d at 260; see Kimberlin, 139 F.3d at 950.

**LITIGATION CONSIDERATIONS**

ings by district courts may be found inadequate.[257]

Ultimately, the duty to deal with "reasonably segregable," nonexempt portions of records begins at the administrative level and, indeed, an agency's careful action at this level may forestall problems later on. (For a discussion of document segregation at the administrative level, see Procedural Requirements, "Reasonably Segregable" Obligation, above.) This is so because "regardless of whether a particular FOIA request proceeds to litigation, the obligation nonetheless is the same--it 'applies to all documents and all exemptions in the FOIA.'"[258]

## In Camera Inspection

In camera examination of documents is specifically authorized in the statutory language of the FOIA,[259] but whether to employ this tool for review is a matter firmly committed to the "'broad discretion of the trial court judge.'"[260] A district court typically uses in camera inspection in exceptional

---

[257] Animal Legal Defense Fund, 44 F. Supp 2d at 301 (holding that conclusory statement regarding segregability is "patently insufficient"); Bay Area Lawyers Alliance for Nuclear Arms Control v. Department of State, 818 F. Supp. 1291, 1300 (N.D. Cal. 1992) (finding that "boilerplate" statement that "no segregation of non-exempt, meaningful information can be made for disclosure" is "entirely insufficient"); see also Patterson v. IRS, 56 F.3d 832, 839 (7th Cir. 1995) ("[B]ecause the [agency declaration] lumps all of the withheld information together in justifying nondisclosure, the district court could not have independently evaluated whether exempt information alone was being withheld or deleted in each instance.").

[258] FOIA Update, Vol. XIV, No. 3, at 12 (quoting Center for Auto Safety v. EPA, 731 F.2d 16, 21 (D.C. Cir. 1984)).

[259] See 5 U.S.C. § 552(a)(4)(B) (1994 & Supp. IV 1998); see also S. Conf. Rep. No. 93-1200, at 9 (1974), reprinted in 1974 U.S.C.C.A.N. 6267, 6287.

[260] Spirko v. United States Postal Serv., 147 F.3d 992, 996 (D.C. Cir. 1998) (quoting Lam Lek Chong v. DEA, 929 F.2d 729, 735 (D.C. Cir. 1991) (quoting, in turn, Carter v. United States Dep't of Commerce, 830 F.2d 388, 392 (D.C. Cir. 1987))); accord Quiñon v. FBI, 86 F.3d 1222, 1227 (D.C. Cir. 1996); see, e.g., NLRB v. Robbins Tire & Rubber Co., 437 U.S. 214, 224 (1978) ("The in camera review provision is discretionary by its terms . . . ."); Halpern v. FBI, 181 F.3d 279, 295 (2d Cir. 1999) (noting that in camera "review would have been appropriate," but leaving this to "the trial court's discretion on remand"); Jernigan v. Department of the Air Force, No. 97-35930, 1998 WL 658662, at *1 n.3 (9th Cir. Sept. 14, 1998) ("Section 552(a)(4)(B) empowers, but does not require, a district court to examine the contents of agency records in camera . . . ."); Parsons v. Freedom of Info. Act Officer, No. 96-4128, 1997 WL 461320, at *1 (6th Cir. Aug. 12, 1997) (explaining that district court has discretion to conduct in camera inspection, but that it is neither "favored nor necessary" so long as adequate factual basis for decision exists); Armstrong v. Executive Office of the President, 97 F.3d 575, 579 (D.C. Cir. 1996) (finding that district court did not abuse its discretion when it undertook in

(continued...)

# LITIGATION CONSIDERATIONS

rather than routine cases,[261] primarily because it "circumvents the adversarial process."[262]

When agencies meet their burden of proof by means of sufficiently detailed affidavits, in camera review is unnecessary and inappropriate.[263] When

---

[260](...continued) camera review of one document, but not of another (similarly characterized) document); Miscavige v. IRS, 2 F.3d 366, 368 (11th Cir. 1993) (holding that in camera review "is discretionary and not required, absent an abuse of discretion"); Ingle v. Department of Justice, 698 F.2d 259, 267 (6th Cir. 1983) (listing four factors courts should consider before exercising discretion to review records in camera); Pons v. United States Customs Serv., No. 93-2094, 1998 U.S. Dist. LEXIS 6084, at *4 (D.D.C. Apr. 23, 1998) ("The ultimate criterion is whether the district judge believes that in camera inspection is necessary to make a responsible de novo determination on the agency's compliance with the FOIA statute.").

[261] See, e.g., Robbins Tire, 437 U.S. at 224 (explaining that in camera review provision "is designed to be invoked when the issue before the District Court could not be otherwise resolved"); Wishart v. Commissioner, No. 98-17248, 1999 WL 985142, at *1 (9th Cir. Oct. 27, 1999) (noting that in camera review is "not required"); PHE, Inc. v. United States Dep't of Justice, 983 F.2d 248, 252-53 (D.C. Cir. 1993) (observing that in camera review is generally disfavored, but permissible on remand arising from inadequate affidavit); Lykins v. United States Dep't of Justice, 725 F.2d 1455, 1463 (D.C. Cir. 1984) (explaining that in camera examination is not substitute for government's obligation to provide detailed indexes and justifications); Ingle, 698 F.2d at 264 ("'In camera inspection requires effort and resources and therefore a court should not resort to it routinely on the theory that "it can't hurt."'" (quoting Ray v. Turner, 587 F.2d 1187, 1195 (D.C. Cir. 1978))); Animal Legal Defense Fund, Inc. v. Department of the Air Force, 44 F. Supp. 2d 295, 304 (D.D.C. 1999) ("'[I]n camera review should not be resorted to as a matter of course....'" (quoting Quiñon, 86 F.3d at 1228)); Tax Analysts v. IRS, No. 94-923, 1999 U.S. Dist. LEXIS 19514, at **12-13 (D.D.C. Nov. 3, 1999) (noting presumption against in camera review, but finding it necessary because parties disagreed about nature of redacted material).

[262] Jones v. FBI, 41 F.3d 238, 243 (6th Cir. 1994) (citing Vaughn v. United States, 936 F.2d 862, 866 (6th Cir. 1991)); see McNamera v. United States Dep't of Justice, 974 F. Supp. 946, 955 (W.D. Tex. 1997) (suggesting that Vaughn Index is preferable to in camera inspection because "it keeps in tact [sic] our system of adversarial dispute resolution").

[263] See, e.g., Nowak v. United States, No. 98-56656, 2000 WL 60067, at *2 (9th Cir. Jan. 21, 2000) (finding in camera review unnecessary where affidavits were sufficiently detailed); Young v. CIA, 972 F.2d 536, 538 (4th Cir. 1992) (rejecting in camera inspection when affidavits and Vaughn Indexes were sufficiently specific); Silets v. United States Dep't of Justice, 945 F.2d 227, 229-32 (7th Cir. 1991) (en banc) (same); Vaughn v. United States, 936 F.2d 862, 869 (6th Cir. 1991) (finding in camera review "neither favored nor necessary where other evidence provides adequate detail and justification");
(continued...)

## LITIGATION CONSIDERATIONS

agency affidavits are insufficiently detailed to permit meaningful review of exemption claims, however, or when an agency's claims of exemption are too vague or sweeping, in camera inspection may be ordered.[264] Additionally, when there is actual evidence of bad faith on the part of the agency, in camera review may be "particularly appropriate."[265] Moreover, even with the submission of adequately detailed affidavits--and in the absence of any bad faith in

---

[263] (...continued) Local 3, Int'l Bhd. of Elec. Workers v. NLRB, 845 F.2d 1177, 1180 (2d Cir. 1988) (rejecting in camera review because "detailed affidavit was sufficient"); Brinton v. Department of State, 636 F.2d 600, 606 (D.C. Cir. 1980); Germosen v. Cox, No. 98 Civ. 1294, 1999 WL 1021559, at *19 (S.D.N.Y. Nov. 9, 1999) (appeal pending); Guccione v. National Indian Gaming Comm'n, No. 98-CV-164 BTM, 1999 U.S. Dist. LEXIS 15475, at *3 (S.D. Cal. Aug. 5, 1999) ("[I]n camera review is a last resort, to be used only when the propriety of the withholding cannot otherwise be determined."); Ligorner v. Reno, 2 F. Supp. 2d 400, 405 (S.D.N.Y. 1998) ("In camera review is only necessary when the evidence presented by the government is insufficient on its face to establish that non-disclosure is required, or when there is some evidence of agency bad faith."); Cappabianca v. Commissioner, United States Customs Serv., 847 F. Supp. 1558, 1562 (M.D. Fla. 1994).

[264] See, e.g., Halpern, 181 F.3d at 295 (observing that "[in camera] review would have been appropriate" because agency affidavit was conclusory, but noting that "such action is one best left to the trial court's discretion"); Spirko, 147 F.3d at 997 ("If the agency fails to provide a sufficiently detailed explanation to enable the district court to make a de novo determination of the agency's claims of exemption, the district court then has several options, including inspecting the documents in camera."); Quiñon, 86 F.3d at 1229 ("[W]here an agency's affidavits merely state in conclusory terms that documents are exempt from disclosure, an in camera review is necessary."); In re Department of Justice, 999 F.2d 1302, 1310 (8th Cir. 1993) (en banc) ("If the [Vaughn Index] categories remain too general, the district court may also examine the disputed documents in camera to make a first hand determination."); King v. United States Dep't of Justice, 830 F.2d 210, 225 (D.C. Cir. 1987). But cf. J.P. Stevens & Co. v. Perry, 710 F.2d 136, 142 (4th Cir. 1983) (holding that district court erred in conducting in camera inspection because Exemption 7(A) Vaughn affidavit was sufficient to show "interference" on category-by-category basis).

[265] Quiñon, 86 F.3d at 1228; see, e.g., Jones, 41 F.3d at 242-43 (reviewing, at request of both parties, documents compiled as part of FBI's widely criticized COINTELPRO operations during 1960s and 1970s because of "evidence of bad faith or illegality with regard to the underlying activities which generated the documents at issue"); cf. Ford v. West, No. 97-1342, 1998 WL 317561, at *3 (10th Cir. June 12, 1998) ("'[M]ere allegations of bad faith' should not 'undermine the sufficiency of agency submissions.'" (quoting Minier v. CIA, 88 F.3d 796, 803 (9th Cir. 1996))); Silets, 945 F.2d at 231 (finding mere assertion, as opposed to actual evidence, of bad faith on part of agency insufficient to warrant court's in camera review); Rugiero v. United States Dep't of Justice, 35 F. Supp. 2d 977, 982-83 (E.D. Mich. 1998) (explaining that "substantial showing" of bad faith is required to justify in camera review); Pons, 1998 U.S. Dist. LEXIS 6084, at *7 (same).

## LITIGATION CONSIDERATIONS

the agency's FOIA processing--in camera inspection has been undertaken based upon "evidence of bad faith or illegality with regard to the underlying activities which generated the documents at issue."[266] The Court of Appeals for the Sixth Circuit has reasoned that in camera review is appropriate in such a case in order to reassure the plaintiff and the public that justice has been served.[267]

Several other considerations may support the use of in camera inspection in a variety of different circumstances. For example, if the number of records involved is relatively small, in camera review may save both the court and the parties time and resources.[268] In this regard, in camera review of a

---

[266] Jones, 41 F.3d at 242-43 (reviewing documents compiled as part of FBI's widely criticized COINTELPRO operations during 1960s and 1970s); see Lissner v. United States Customs Serv., No. 98-7438-ABC, slip op. at 1 (C.D. Cal. June 17, 1999) (undertaking in camera review to determine whether there is evidence of agency "misconduct or illegal activity, and, if so, whether that activity justifies disclosure when weighed against . . . privacy interests") (appeal pending); see also Summers v. Department of Justice, 140 F.3d 1077, 1085 (D.C. Cir. 1998) (Silberman, J., concurring) (urging in camera review of the "Official and Confidential" files of former FBI Director J. Edgar Hoover "to fully understand the enormous public interest in these materials"). But see Accuracy in Media, Inc. v. National Park Serv., 194 F.3d 120, 124 (D.C. Cir. 1999) (holding that alleged "evidentiary discrepancies" noted in published materials concerning highly publicized suicide of former Deputy White House Counsel Vincent Foster was not evidence of bad faith warranting in camera review of death-scene and autopsy photographs), cert. denied, 68 U.S.L.W. 3711 (U.S. May 15, 2000) (No. 99-1578).

[267] See Jones, 41 F.3d at 242-43.

[268] See Quiñon, 86 F.3d at 1228 (suggesting that number of documents is "another . . . factor to be considered" when determining whether in camera review is appropriate); Maynard v. CIA, 986 F.2d 547, 558 (1st Cir. 1993); Carter, 830 F.2d at 393; Currie v. IRS, 704 F.2d 523, 531 (11th Cir. 1983); Tax Analysts, 1999 U.S. Dist. LEXIS 19514, at *14 (noting, as factor justifying in camera review, minimal burden on court where only one sentence is to be reviewed); Local 32B-32J, Service Employees Int'l Union, AFL-CIO v. GSA, No. 97 Civ. 8509, 1998 WL 726000, at *11 (S.D.N.Y. Oct. 15, 1998) (observing that in camera review is "ordered most often in cases in which only a small number of documents are to be examined"); Steinberg v. United States Dep't of Justice, 179 F.R.D. 357, 364 (D.D.C. Apr. 28, 1998) (ordering in camera inspection of seven documents "[i]n the interests of efficiency"); see also Klunzinger v. IRS, 27 F. Supp. 2d 1015, 1028 (W.D. Mich. 1998) ("The withheld documents in this case are far too numerous to be considered the proper subject of an in camera inspection."); Agee v. CIA, 517 F. Supp. 1335, 1336 (D.D.C. 1981) (utilizing selective in camera review); cf. Young, 972 F.2d at 549 (rejecting per se rule which would require in camera review "whenever the examination could be completed quickly"); Animal Legal Defense Fund, 44 F. Supp. 2d at 304 (rejecting in camera review, but requiring agency to "submit a more detailed affidavit" in order to conserve judicial resources); Smith v. ATF, 977 F. Supp. 496, 503 (D.D.C. 1997) (finding that "judicial economy is best served"

(continued...)

## LITIGATION CONSIDERATIONS

small sample of a larger set of documents may be warranted.[269] When a discrepancy exists between representations in an agency's affidavit and other information that the agency has publicly disclosed about the withheld records, in camera inspection may be an appropriate method to resolve that discrepancy.[270] Similarly, in camera inspection may be ordered in cases in which the plaintiff alleges that the government has waived its right to claim an exemption.[271] On the other hand, it has been held that in camera review is not a procedure to be employed as a means of determining whether a requester should be charged duplication fees.[272]

If a court undertakes in camera inspection, it necessarily establishes an adequate factual basis for determining the applicability of the claimed exemptions.[273] This should be true regardless of the adequacy of an agency's affidavit.[274]

---

[268](...continued)
by allowing correction of deficient affidavits rather than by in camera review of two documents).

[269] See, e.g., Wilson v. CIA, No. 89-3356, slip op. at 5-6 (D.D.C. Oct. 15, 1991) (ordering 50-document sample of approximately 1000 pages withheld in whole or in part, selected equally by parties, for in camera examination); Wilson v. Department of Justice, No. 87-2415, slip op. at 4 (D.D.C. June 17, 1991) (requiring sample of eight of approximately 80 withheld documents, to be selected equally by each side, for detailed in camera description). But cf. Lame v. United States Dep't of Justice, 654 F.2d 917, 927 (3d Cir. 1981) (holding in camera sampling of criminal law enforcement documents insufficient).

[270] See Mehl v. EPA, 797 F. Supp. 43, 46 (D.D.C. 1992) (conducting in camera inspection because affidavits contradicted published report).

[271] See Public Citizen v. United States Dep't of State, 787 F. Supp. 12, 13 (D.D.C. 1992), aff'd, 11 F.3d 198 (D.C. Cir. 1993) (finding exemptions properly invoked after reviewing records in camera).

[272] See Larson v. United States Dep't of Justice, No. 85-2991, slip op. at 2 (D.D.C. Sept. 30, 1986).

[273] See National Wildlife Fed'n v. United States Forest Serv., 861 F.2d 1114, 1116 (9th Cir. 1988) ("[W]here a trial court properly reviewed contested documents in camera, an adequate factual basis for the decision exists."); see also City of Va. Beach v. United States Dep't of Commerce, 995 F.2d 1247, 1252 n.12 (4th Cir. 1993) ("By conducting in camera review, the district court established an adequate basis for its decision.").

[274] See, e.g., Church of Scientology, Inc. v. United States Dep't of the Army, 611 F.2d 738, 743 (9th Cir. 1979) (holding that despite "conclusory" affidavits, after in camera inspection trial court had "adequate factual basis" for its decision); see also Fiduccia v. United States Dep't of Justice, 185 F.3d 1035, 1042-43 (9th Cir. 1999) (suggesting, notwithstanding Wiener v. FBI, 943 F.2d 972, 979 (9th Cir. 1991), that in camera inspection could by itself be sufficient); Spirko, 147 F.3d at 997 (ruling that in camera inspection is one alternative for district court when agency fails sufficiently to detail exemption claims). But
(continued...)

## LITIGATION CONSIDERATIONS

In camera review often is employed in cases involving national security, where detailed public affidavits may be impracticable.[275] (For a further discussion of in camera review of classified materials, see Exemption 1, In Camera Submissions, above.) Even in national security cases, however, it has been observed that "a district court exercises a wise discretion when it limits the number of documents it reviews in camera."[276] Sometimes in these cases, in addition to in camera inspection, an agency will employ in camera declarations to explain the basis for its withholdings.[277] Such a step, though, should be taken only when clearly necessary.[278]

Indeed, it has been held that a district court may properly review in camera declarations only if it publicly explains its rationale for so doing and ensures that the agency has provided as complete a public explanation as possible without jeopardizing the sensitive, exempt information.[279] Additionally, in limited circumstances, in camera, ex parte oral testimony may be permitted because providing a more informative public description of the documents would risk revealing the very information that the agency states is exempt from disclosure under the FOIA.[280] When in camera testimony is taken, it

---

[274](...continued)
see Wiener, 943 F.2d at 979 ("In camera review of the withheld documents by the court is not an acceptable substitute for an adequate Vaughn index.").

[275] See, e.g., Public Citizen v. Department of State, 11 F.3d 198, 200-01 (D.C. Cir. 1993) (tacitly approving use of in camera inspection to determine whether Exemption 1 protection waived); Weberman v. NSA, 668 F.2d 676, 678 (2d Cir. 1982) (finding in camera inspection of classified affidavit appropriate when "[d]isclosure of the details . . . might result in serious consequences to the nation's security"); Schlesinger v. CIA, 591 F. Supp. 60, 67-68 (D.D.C. 1984) (undertaking in camera review in Exemption 1 case to determine whether classification and agency justifications for withholding were proper when more elaborate public affidavit would compromise national security).

[276] Armstrong, 97 F.3d at 580 ("First, [limited in camera review] makes it less likely that sensitive information will be disclosed. Second, if there is an unauthorized disclosure, having reduced the number of people with access to the information makes it easier to pinpoint the source of the leak.").

[277] See, e.g., Maynard, 986 F.2d at 557 (noting that in camera declarations filed); Hunt v. CIA, 981 F.2d 1116, 1118 (9th Cir. 1992) (same); Springmann v. United States Dep't of State, No. 93-1238, slip op. at 2-3 (D.D.C. Feb. 24, 2000) (granting renewed motion for summary judgment after reviewing in camera affidavit).

[278] See Armstrong, 97 F.3d at 580-81 ("[T]he use of in camera affidavits has generally been disfavored.").

[279] See id. (holding that district court "must both make its reasons for [relying on an in camera declaration] clear and make as much as possible of the in camera submission available to the opposing party" (citing Lykins, 725 F.2d at 1465)); see also Phillippi v. CIA, 546 F.2d 1009, 1013 (D.C. Cir. 1976).

[280] See, e.g., Stein v. Department of Justice, 662 F.2d 1245, 1255 (7th Cir. (continued...)

**LITIGATION CONSIDERATIONS**

should be transcribed and maintained under seal.[281] Regardless of whether the court inspects documents or receives testimony in camera, however, counsel for the plaintiff ordinarily is not entitled to participate in these in camera proceedings.[282]

Summary Judgment

Summary judgment is the procedural vehicle by which nearly all FOIA cases are resolved.[283] Motions for summary judgment are governed by Rule 56 of the Federal Rules of Civil Procedure, which provides, in part, that the "judgment sought shall be rendered forthwith if the pleadings, depositions, answers to interrogatories, and admissions on file, together with the affida-

---

[280](...continued)
1981); Agee, 517 F. Supp. at 1338; see also Arieff v. United States Dep't of the Navy, 712 F.2d 1462, 1469-71 (D.C. Cir. 1983); North Am. Man/Boy Love Ass'n v. FBI, 3 Gov't Disclosure Serv. (P-H) ¶ 83,094, at 83,639 (S.D.N.Y. July 9, 1982), aff'd, 718 F.2d 1086 (2d Cir. 1983) (unpublished table decision).

[281] See Pollard v. FBI, 705 F.2d 1151, 1154 (9th Cir. 1983); Physicians for Soc. Responsibility v. United States Dep't of Justice, No. 85-0169, slip op. at 3-4 (D.D.C. Aug. 23, 1985); cf. Martin v. United States Dep't of Justice, No. 85-3091, slip op. at 3 (3d Cir. July 2, 1986) (ordering nonexempt portion of in camera transcript disclosed).

[282] See Solar Sources, Inc. v. United States, 142 F.3d 1033, 1040 (7th Cir. 1998) ("[T]he general rule is that counsel are not entitled to participate in in camera FOIA proceedings."); Arieff, 712 F.2d at 1470-71 & n.2 (prohibiting participation by plaintiff's counsel even when information withheld was personal privacy information); Pollard, 705 F.2d at 1154 (finding no reversible error when court not only reviewed affidavit and documents in camera, but also received authenticating testimony ex parte); Salisbury v. United States, 690 F.2d 966, 973 n.3 (D.C. Cir. 1982); Weberman, 668 F.2d at 678; cf. Ellsberg v. Mitchell, 709 F.2d 51, 61 (D.C. Cir. 1983) (holding that plaintiff's counsel is not permitted to participate in in camera review of documents arguably covered by state secrets privilege) (non-FOIA case). But cf. Lederle Labs. v. HHS, No. 88-249, slip op. at 2-3 (D.D.C. May 2, 1988) (issuing restrictive protective order in Exemption 4 case permitting counsel for requester to review contested business information).

[283] See Sanderson v. IRS, No. 98-2369, 1999 WL 35290, at *2 (E.D. La. Jan. 25, 1999) ("'Summary judgment is the usual means for resolving FOIA cases.'" (quoting Struth v. FBI, 673 F. Supp. 949, 953 (E.D. Wis. 1987))), dismissed (E.D. La. June 11, 1999); Public Employees for Envtl. Responsibility v. EPA, 978 F. Supp. 955, 959 (D. Colo. 1997) ("FOIA claims are typically resolved on summary judgment . . . ."), appeal voluntarily dismissed, No. 97-1384 (10th Cir. Nov. 25, 1997); Cappabianca v. Commissioner, United States Customs Serv., 847 F. Supp. 1558, 1561 (M.D. Fla. 1994) ("[O]nce documents in issue are properly identified, FOIA cases should be handled on motions for summary judgment." (citing Miscavige v. IRS, 2 F.3d 366, 368 (11th Cir. 1993))); Manna v. United States Dep't of Justice, 832 F. Supp. 866, 870 (D.N.J. 1993) ("Summary judgment is typically used to adjudicate FOIA cases.").

## LITIGATION CONSIDERATIONS

vits, if any, show that there is no genuine issue as to any material fact."[284] So long as there are no material facts at issue and no facts "susceptible to divergent inferences bearing upon an issue critical to disposition of the case," summary judgment is appropriate.[285] Of course, an agency's failure to respond to a FOIA request in a timely manner does not, by itself, justify an award of summary judgment to the requester.[286]

The Court of Appeals for the District of Columbia Circuit has held that "a motion for summary judgment adequately underpinned is not defeated simply by bare opinion or an unaided claim that a factual controversy persists."[287] For example, summary judgment will not be defeated by unsupport-

---

[284] Fed. R. Civ. P. 56(c).

[285] Alyeska Pipeline Serv. v. EPA, 856 F.2d 309, 314 (D.C. Cir. 1988); see, e.g., Plazas-Martinez v. DEA, 891 F. Supp. 1, 3 (D.D.C. 1995) ("Plaintiff's submission does create a dispute on an issue of fact; it is not a material issue, however."); Kuffel v. United States Bureau of Prisons, 882 F. Supp. 1116, 1122 (D.D.C. 1995) (holding that plaintiff's disagreement with application of exemptions does not constitute a dispute as to material facts precluding summary judgment "because he does not put forth any facts to prove that they were wrongfully applied"); Patterson v. IRS, No. 90-1941, slip op. at 3 (S.D. Ind. Nov. 3, 1992) ("[T]he disputed fact must be outcome determinative."), aff'd in part, rev'd & remanded in part on other grounds, 56 F.3d 841 (7th Cir. 1995).

[286] See Iacoe v. IRS, No. 98-C-0466, 1999 U.S. Dist. LEXIS 12809, at *13 (E.D. Wis. July 23, 1999) ("The effect of the agency's failure to meet the time limit is merely to permit the requester to bring an action in district court . . . ."); Barvick v. Cisneros, 941 F. Supp. 1015, 1019-20 (D. Kan. 1996) ("This court is persuaded that an agency's failure to respond within [the statutory time limits] does not automatically entitle a FOIA requester to summary judgment.").

[287] Alyeska Pipeline, 856 F.2d at 314; see Mace v. EEOC, 197 F.3d 329, 330 (8th Cir. 1999) ("[S]peculative claims about [the] existence of other documents cannot rebut [the] presumption of good faith afforded [to] agency affidavits." (citing SafeCard Servs. v. SEC, 926 F.2d 1197, 1200 (D.C. Cir. 1991))); Germosen v. Cox, No. 98 Civ. 1294, 1999 WL 1021559, at **18-19 (S.D.N.Y. Nov. 9, 1999) (ruling that plaintiff cannot defeat summary judgment by speculating that further evidence will develop to support his allegations) (appeal pending); Iacoe, 1999 U.S. Dist. LEXIS 12809, at *12 ("Plaintiff's speculations about a cover-up are insufficient to overcome the presumption of good faith to which the agency's declaration is entitled."); Judicial Watch, Inc. v. HHS, 27 F. Supp. 2d 240, 243-44 (D.D.C. 1998) (explaining that plaintiff's "bare suspicion" will not call into question adequacy of agency's search); Gale v. FBI, 141 F.R.D. 94, 96 (N.D. Ill. 1992) (holding that plaintiff's "own self-serving statements [alone] are insufficient to create a genuine issue of material fact barring summary judgment"); Lawyers Alliance for Nuclear Arms Control v. Department of Energy, No. 88-CV-7635, slip op. at 3-5 (E.D. Pa. Dec. 17, 1991) (finding plaintiff's reliance on "inadmissible hearsay" statements insufficient to preclude summary judgment when rebutted by government's "highly persua-

(continued...)

## LITIGATION CONSIDERATIONS

ed claims that an agency is withholding information that already is in the public domain.[288] Nor will summary judgment necessarily be precluded by discrepancies in the agency's page counts, particularly when the agency has processed a voluminous number of pages, so long as the agency has supplied a "well-detailed and clear" explanation for the differences.[289] Moreover, even a pro se plaintiff will be found to have conceded the government's factual assertions if he fails to contest them, once it is clear that he understands his responsibility to do so.[290]

In a FOIA case, the agency has the burden of justifying nondisclosure,[291]

---

[287](...continued)
sive" sworn statements); see also Marks v. United States, 578 F.2d 261, 263 (9th Cir. 1978) ("Conclusory allegations unsupported by factual data will not create a triable issue of fact."); Ashton v. VA, No. 94-3793, slip op. at 4 (E.D.N.Y. Nov. 24, 1998) (holding that "conclusory statements" that government is withholding information will not defeat summary judgment), aff'd, 198 F.3d 233 (2d Cir. 1999) (unpublished table decision). But cf. Washington Post Co. v. HHS, 865 F.2d 320, 325-26 (D.C. Cir. 1989) (observing that summary judgment is inappropriate, in Exemption 4 case, when affidavits conflicted on "critical factual issue" of whether government's information-gathering ability would be impaired by disclosure); Washington Post Co. v. United States Dep't of State, 840 F.2d 26, 29 (D.C. Cir. 1988) (holding summary judgment to be inappropriate "when litigants quarrel over key factual premises"), vacated & remanded on petition for reh'g en banc, 898 F.2d 793 (D.C. Cir. 1989).

[288] See Steinberg v. United States Dep't of Justice, 179 F.R.D. 357, 360 (D.D.C. Apr. 28, 1998) (finding summary judgment not defeated "with pure conjecture about the possible content of withheld information, raising 'some metaphysical doubt as to the material facts.'" (quoting Matsushita Elec. Indus. Co. v. Zenith Radio Corp., 475 U.S. 574, 586 (1986))).

[289] Master v. FBI, 926 F. Supp. 193, 197-98 (D.D.C. 1996), summary affirmance granted, 124 F.3d 1309 (D.C. Cir. 1997) (unpublished table decision).

[290] See Davis v. CIA, No. 4:CV-99-838, slip op. at 4-5 (M.D. Pa. Nov. 18, 1999); Knight v. FDA, No. 95-4097, 1997 WL 109971, at *1 (D. Kan. Feb. 11, 1997); Nuzzo v. FBI, No. 95-cv-1708, 1996 U.S. Dist. LEXIS 15594, at **8-9 (D.D.C. Oct. 8, 1996); Butler v. Department of the Air Force, 888 F. Supp. 174, 178-79 (D.D.C. 1995), aff'd per curiam, No. 96-5111 (D.C. Cir. May 6, 1997); see also Hart v. FBI, No. 94 C 6010, slip op. at 4 (N.D. Ill. Apr. 6, 1995) (holding that "plaintiff has not asserted any facts which convince this Court that the FBI has any records which relate to him or has failed to conduct an adequate search"), aff'd, 1996 U.S. App. LEXIS 17684, at **8-9 (7th Cir. July 16, 1996); cf. Ruotolo v. IRS, 28 F.3d 6, 8-9 (2d Cir. 1994) (finding that although plaintiffs were generally aware of summary judgment rules, district court should have specifically notified them of consequences of not complying with litigation deadlines before dismissing case).

[291] See 5 U.S.C. § 552(a)(4)(B) (1994 & Supp. IV 1998); see, e.g., United States Dep't of Justice v. Reporters Comm. for Freedom of the Press, 489 U.S.
(continued...)

## LITIGATION CONSIDERATIONS

and it must sustain its burden by submitting detailed affidavits[292] that identify the documents at issue and explain why they fall under the claimed exemptions.[293] (A federal statute specifically permits unsworn declarations (i.e., without notarizations) to be utilized in all cases in which affidavits otherwise would be required.[294]) The widespread use of Vaughn Indexes, of course, means that affidavits, in the form of Vaughn Indexes, will nearly always be submitted in FOIA lawsuits, notwithstanding Rule 56's language making affidavits optional in general.

As one court has put it, "[s]ummary judgment is available to the defendant in a FOIA case when the agency proves that it has fully discharged its obligations under the FOIA, after the underlying facts and the inferences to be drawn from them are construed in the light most favorable to the FOIA requester."[295] Summary judgment may be granted solely on the basis of agency affidavits if they are clear, specific, and reasonably detailed, if they describe the withheld information in a factual and nonconclusory manner, and if there is no contradictory evidence on the record or evidence of agency bad faith.[296]

---

[291](...continued) 749, 755 (1989); Wishart v. Commissioner, No. 98-17248, 1999 WL 985142, at *1 (9th Cir. June 25, 1999); Coastal States Gas Corp. v. Department of Energy, 617 F.2d 854, 868 (D.C. Cir. 1980).

[292] See, e.g., O'Harvey v. Office of Workers' Compensation Programs, No. 96-33015, 1997 WL 31589, at *1 (9th Cir. Jan. 21, 1997) (holding that when district court relied on agency's denial letter "[w]ithout an affidavit or oral testimony, [it] lacked a factual basis to make its decision").

[293] See Summers v. Department of Justice, 140 F.3d 1077, 1080 (D.C. Cir. 1998); King v. United States Dep't of Justice, 830 F.2d 210, 217 (D.C. Cir. 1987); Vaughn v. Rosen, 484 F.2d 820, 826-28 (D.C. Cir. 1973).

[294] 28 U.S.C. § 1746 (1994); see Summers v. United States Dep't of Justice, 999 F.2d 570, 572-73 (D.C. Cir. 1993).

[295] Miller v. United States Dep't of State, 779 F.2d 1378, 1382 (8th Cir. 1985).

[296] See, e.g., Hayden v. NSA, 608 F.2d 1381, 1387 (D.C. Cir. 1979); Barvick, 914 F. Supp. at 1018; Hemenway v. Hughes, 601 F. Supp. 1002, 1004 (D.D.C. 1985) (recognizing that in FOIA cases, summary judgment does not hinge on existence of genuine issue of material fact, but rather on basis of agency affidavits if they are reasonably specific, demonstrate logical use of exemptions, and are not controverted by evidence in record or by bad faith) (applying standard developed in national security context to Exemption 6); see also In re Wade, 969 F.2d 241, 246 (7th Cir. 1992) ("Without evidence of bad faith, the veracity of the government's submissions regarding reasons for withholding the documents should not be questioned."); Pease v. United States Dep't of Interior, No. 1:99CV113, slip op. at 7 (D. Vt. Sept. 11, 1999) (holding that plaintiff's "hearsay assertion is insufficient to rebut presumption of good faith otherwise accorded agency affidavits"); cf. Niagara Mohawk Power Corp. v. United States Dep't of Energy, 169 F.3d 16, 18 (D.C. Cir. 1999) (finding agency affidavits conclusory and denying summary judgment despite plaintiff's fail-
(continued...)

## LITIGATION CONSIDERATIONS

If all of these requisites are met, such affidavits are usually accorded substantial weight by the courts.[297]

However, in a controversial two-to-one panel opinion, the D.C. Circuit indicated that, at least in the Exemption 4 context, it would give great weight to the rebuttal evidence of the requester and therefore require particular specificity in the affidavit of a company that submitted information to the FDA that both the agency and the company argued was protectible pursuant to Exemption 4.[298] In the event of a trial on a contested issue of fact, it will be decided by a judge alone because a FOIA requester is "not entitled to a jury trial."[299]

In certain circumstances, opinions or conclusions may be asserted in agency affidavits, especially in cases in which disclosure would compromise national security.[300] On the other hand, "[c]ourts have consistently held that a

---

[296](...continued)
ure to controvert agency assertions by remaining silent); Kamman v. IRS, 56 F.3d 46, 49 (9th Cir. 1995) (finding agency failed to satisfy burden of proof and awarding summary judgment to plaintiff when agency affidavits "are nothing more than 'conclusory and generalized allegations'"); Voinche v. FBI, 46 F. Supp. 2d 26, 30 (D.D.C. 1999) (denying summary judgment when agency provided conclusory affidavit to support invocation of Exemption 7(A)); Demma v. United States Dep't of Justice, No. 93 C 7296, 1995 WL 360731, at *3 (N.D. Ill. June 15, 1995) (denying summary judgment when affidavits addressed only one subject of plaintiff's multiple-subject request), appeal voluntarily dismissed, No. 96-1231 (7th Cir. June 12, 1996).

[297] See, e.g., Gardels v. CIA, 689 F.2d 1100, 1104 (D.C. Cir. 1982); Taylor v. Department of the Army, 684 F.2d 99, 106-07 (D.C. Cir. 1982); Judicial Watch, Inc. v. Clinton, 880 F. Supp. 1, 10 (D.D.C. 1995), aff'd on other grounds, 76 F.3d 1232 (D.C. Cir. 1996).

[298] Greenberg v. FDA, 803 F.2d 1213, 1217-18 (D.C. Cir. 1986) (finding that plaintiff "introduced evidence that placed material issues of fact in dispute"); see also Washington Post, 865 F.2d at 325-26 (holding that "competing experts' affidavits as to the effect of disclosure" constitute "genuinely controverted factual issue" under Exemption 4); Public Citizen Health Research Group v. FDA, 953 F. Supp. 400, 403 (D.D.C. 1996) (same); MCI Telecomms. Corp. v. GSA, No. 89-746, 1992 WL 71394, at *6 (D.D.C. Mar. 25, 1992) (holding that "fact-intensive question" under Exemption 4 as to whether disclosure will cause submitter competitive harm precludes summary judgment).

[299] Clarkson v. IRS, No. 8:88-3036, slip op. at 8 (D.S.C. May 10, 1990); see also Spurlock v. FBI, 69 F.3d 1010, 1013 (9th Cir. 1995) (noting district court "bench trial" on issue of propriety of exemption claims); Public Citizen, 953 F. Supp. at 403 (denying summary judgment in face of conflicting affidavits and ordering bench trial on issue of whether disclosure would cause substantial competitive harm to submitter).

[300] See Gardels, 689 F.2d at 1106 (recognizing that there is "necessarily a region for forecasts in which informed judgment as to potential harm should

(continued...)

## LITIGATION CONSIDERATIONS

requester's opinion disputing the risk created by disclosure is not sufficient to preclude summary judgment for the agency when the agency possessing the relevant expertise has provided sufficiently detailed affidavits."[301]

Rule 56(e) of the Federal Rules of Civil Procedure provides that the affidavit must be based upon the personal knowledge of the affiant, must demonstrate the affiant's competency to testify as to matters stated, and must set forth only facts that would be admissible in evidence.[302] "Gratuitous recitations of the affiant's own interpretation of the law," however, are inappropriate.[303]

The affidavit or declaration of an agency official who is knowledgeable about the way in which information is processed satisfies the personal knowledge requirement.[304] Similarly, in instances in which an agency's search is

---

[300] (...continued)
be respected"); Halperin v. CIA, 629 F.2d 144, 149 (D.C. Cir. 1980) (declaring that "courts must take into account . . . that any affidavit of threatened harm to national security will always be speculative"); Hoch v. CIA, 593 F. Supp. 675, 683-84 (D.D.C. 1984), aff'd, 807 F.2d 1227 (D.C. Cir. 1990) (unpublished table decision); see also Moore v. FBI, No. 83-1541, slip op. at 2 (D.D.C. Aug. 30, 1984) (finding "particular incident" sufficiently identified given national security nature of documents), aff'd, 762 F.2d 138 (D.C. Cir. 1985) (unpublished table decision).

[301] Struth v. FBI, 673 F. Supp. 949, 954 (E.D. Wis. 1987); see, e.g., Goldberg v. United States Dep't of State, 818 F.2d 71, 78-79 (D.C. Cir. 1987) (Exemption 1); Spannaus v. United States Dep't of Justice, 813 F.2d 1285, 1289 (4th Cir. 1987) (Exemption 7(A)); Curran v. Department of Justice, 813 F.2d 473, 477 (1st Cir. 1987) (Exemption 7(A)); Gardels, 689 F.2d at 1106 n.5 (Exemptions 1 and 3); Windels, Marx, Davis & Ives v. Department of Commerce, 576 F. Supp. 405, 410-11 (D.D.C. 1983) (Exemptions 2 and 7(E)); see also Lindsey v. NSC, No. 84-3897, slip op. at 3 (D.D.C. July 12, 1985) (holding that plaintiff cannot defeat summary judgment by saying that he will raise genuine issue "at a time of his own choosing").

[302] Fed. R. Civ. P. 56(e).

[303] Alamo Aircraft Supply, Inc. v. Weinberger, No. 85-1291, slip op. at 3 (D.D.C. Feb. 21, 1986).

[304] See, e.g., Spannaus, 813 F.2d at 1289 (holding that declarant's attestation "to his personal knowledge of the procedures used in handling [the] request and his familiarity with the documents in question" is sufficient); Hoffman v. United States Dep't of Justice, No. 98-1733, slip op. at 7 (W.D. Okla. Apr. 16, 1999) (finding personal knowledge requirement met when declarant was "aware of what was done by virtue of information provided to him in his official capacity"); Cucci v. DEA, 871 F. Supp. 508, 513 (D.D.C. 1994) (finding that declarant "had the requisite personal knowledge based on her examination of the records and her discussion with a representative of the [state police]" to attest that information was provided with express understanding of confidentiality); Laborers' Int'l Union v. United States Dep't of Justice, 578 F.
(continued...)

## LITIGATION CONSIDERATIONS

questioned, an affidavit of an agency employee responsible for coordinating the search efforts satisfies the personal knowledge requirement.[305] Likewise, in justifying the withholding of classified information under Exemption 1, the affiant is required only to possess document-classification authority for the records in question, not personal knowledge of the particular substantive area that is the subject of the request.[306] However, affiants must establish that they

---

[304](...continued)
Supp. 52, 55-56 (D.D.C. 1983) (finding affiant competent when observations were based on review of investigative report and upon general familiarity with nature of investigations similar to that documented in requested report), aff'd, 772 F.2d 919 (D.C. Cir. 1984); see also Avondale Indus. v. NLRB, No. 96-1227, slip op. at 8 (E.D. La. Mar. 23, 1998) (holding that there is no requirement that author of records prepare Vaughn Index); Coleman v. FBI, No. 89-2773, slip op. at 8-9 (D.D.C. Dec. 10, 1991) ("The law does not require the affiant preparing a Vaughn Index to be personally familiar with more than the procedures used in processing the particular request."), summary affirmance granted, No. 92-5040 (D.C. Cir. Dec. 4, 1992); cf. FOIA Update, Vol. XIX, No. 3, at 2 (advising that agency FOIA officers are authorized to review grand jury materials for purposes of FOIA administration, notwithstanding strict secrecy requirements of Rule 6(e) of Federal Rules of Criminal Procedure (citing Canning v. Department of Justice, No. 92-0463, slip op. at 4-5 (D.D.C. June 26, 1995))).

[305] See, e.g., Carney v. United States Dep't of Justice, 19 F.3d 807, 814 (2d Cir. 1994), aff'g in pertinent part, rev'g & remanding in part, No. 92-CV-6204, slip op. at 12 (W.D.N.Y. Apr. 27, 1993) ("There is no basis in either the statute or the relevant caselaw to require that an agency effectively establish by a series of sworn affidavits a 'chain of custody' over its search process. The format of the proof submitted by defendant--declarations of supervisory employees, signed under penalty of perjury--is sufficient for purposes of both the statute and Fed.R.Civ.P. 56."); Maynard v. CIA, 986 F.2d 547, 560 (1st Cir. 1993) ("[A]n agency need not submit an affidavit from the employee who actually conducted the search. Instead, an agency may rely on an affidavit of an agency employee responsible for supervising the search."); SafeCard, 926 F.2d at 1202 (finding that employee "in charge of coordinating the [agency's] search and recovery efforts [is the] most appropriate person to provide a comprehensive affidavit"); Inner City Press/Community on the Move v. Board of Governors of the Fed. Reserve Sys., No. 98 Civ. 4608, 1998 WL 690371, at *4 (S.D.N.Y. Sept. 30, 1998) ("[I]t is even routine to accept affidavits from agency officials who have supervised but not personally conducted a FOIA search."), aff'd, 182 F.3d 900 (2d Cir. 1999) (unpublished table decision); see also Horsehead Indus. v. EPA, No. 94-1299, slip op. at 9 (D.D.C. Oct. 1, 1996) (declaring that agency cannot meet its burden by filing declaration from someone with no responsibility for activities at issue or for files that may contain responsive documents).

[306] See Holland v. CIA, No. 91-1233, slip op. at 15-16 (D.D.C. Aug. 31, 1992); McTigue v. United States Dep't of Justice, No. 84-3583, slip op. at 8-9 (D.D.C. Dec. 3, 1985), aff'd, 808 F.2d 137 (D.C. Cir. 1987).

## LITIGATION CONSIDERATIONS

are personally familiar with all of the withheld records,[307] and should not be selected merely because they occupy particular positions in the agency.[308]

### Discovery

Discovery is greatly restricted in FOIA actions.[309] It is generally limited to the scope of an agency's search,[310] its indexing and classification procedures, and similar factual matters.[311] Permissible discovery concerning such

---

[307] See Kamman, 56 F.3d at 49 (rejecting affidavit which revealed that signer "did not even review the actual documents at issue" and which attested only "that the documents are in a file that is marked with the name of a taxpayer other than [plaintiff]"); Sellar v. FBI, No. 84-1611, slip op. at 3 (D.D.C. July 22, 1988).

[308] See Timken Co. v. United States Customs Serv., 3 Gov't Disclosure Serv. (P-H) ¶ 83,234, at 83,975 n.9 (D.D.C. June 24, 1983) (rejecting attestations of affiant who merely sampled documents that staff had reviewed for him).

[309] See Public Citizen Health Research Group v. FDA, 997 F. Supp. 56, 72 (D.D.C. 1998) ("Discovery is to be sparingly granted in FOIA actions."), aff'd in part, rev'd in part & remanded, 185 F.3d 898 (D.C. Cir. 1999); Katzman v. Freeh, 926 F. Supp. 316, 319 (E.D.N.Y. 1996) ("[D]iscovery in a FOIA action is extremely limited . . . ."); Center for Nat'l Sec. Studies v. Office of Indep. Counsel, No. 91-1691, slip op. at 3 (D.D.C. Mar. 2, 1993) ("In the context of FOIA cases, discovery is generally inappropriate.").

[310] See Ruotolo v. Department of Justice, 53 F.3d 4, 11 (2d Cir. 1995) (holding that discovery on scope of burden that search would entail should have been granted); Weisberg v. United States Dep't of Justice, 627 F.2d 365, 371 (D.C. Cir. 1980) (finding discovery appropriate to inquire into adequacy of document search); Exxon Corp. v. FTC, 384 F. Supp. 755, 760 (D.D.C. 1974) (limiting discovery to issue of adequacy of search for identifiable records).

[311] See Public Citizen, 997 F. Supp. at 72 (holding that discovery is limited to "investigating the scope of the agency search for responsive documents, the agency's indexing procedures, and the like"); Katzman, 926 F. Supp. at 319-20; Church of Scientology v. IRS, 137 F.R.D. 201, 202 (D. Mass. 1991); Murphy v. FBI, 490 F. Supp. 1134, 1136 (D.D.C. 1980); see also Washington Post Co. v. United States Dep't of Justice, No. 84-3581, slip op. at 1-2 (D.D.C. Aug. 2, 1990) (permitting discovery, in Exemption 7(B) case, on issue of whether it is more probable than not that disclosure would seriously interfere with fairness of pending or "truly imminent" trial or adjudication); Silverberg v. HHS, No. 89-2743, slip op. at 2-3 (D.D.C. June 26, 1990) (permitting discovery, in Exemption 4 case, of responses by private drug-testing laboratories to agency's inquiry concerning whether their "performance test results" are customarily released to public); ABC v. USIA, 599 F. Supp. 765, 768-70 (D.D.C. 1984) (ordering agency head to submit to deposition on issue of whether transcripts of tape-recorded telephone calls constitute "personal records" or "agency records"); cf. United States v. Owens, 54 F.3d 271, 277 (6th Cir. 1995) (allowing discovery on issue of ownership of joint state/federal task force records in action by United States to enjoin state court disclosure order under state public

(continued...)

## LITIGATION CONSIDERATIONS

factual issues properly should take place, if at all, only after the government moves for summary judgment and submits its supporting affidavits and memorandum of law.[312]

Discovery also may be appropriate when the plaintiff can raise sufficient question as to the agency's good faith in processing or in its search.[313] Even

---

[311](...continued)
records law). But see Local 3, Int'l Bhd. of Elec. Workers v. NLRB, 845 F.2d 1177, 1179 (2d Cir. 1988) (holding that discovery is permitted to determine whether complete disclosure was made and whether exemptions properly applied); Pennsylvania Dep't of Pub. Welfare v. United States, No. 99-175, 1999 WL 1951963, at *3 (W.D. Pa. Oct. 12, 1999) (allowing limited discovery "regarding the authenticity and completeness of the material produced by HHS, as well as the methodology used to compile it," because plaintiff "'does not know the contents of the information sought and is, therefore, helpless to contradict the government's description of the information or assist the trial judge'" (quoting Davin v. United States Dep't of Justice, 60 F.3d 1043, 1049 (3d Cir. 1995))).

[312] See, e.g., Miscavige v. IRS, 2 F.3d 366, 369 (11th Cir. 1993) ("The plaintiff's early attempt in litigation of this kind . . . to take discovery depositions is inappropriate until the government has first had a chance to provide the court with the information necessary to make a decision on the applicable exemptions."); Farese v. United States Dep't of Justice, No. 86-5528, slip op. at 6 (D.C. Cir. Aug. 12, 1987) (affirming denial of discovery filed prior to affidavits because discovery "sought to short-circuit the agencies' review of the voluminous amount of documentation requested"); Simmons v. United States Dep't of Justice, 796 F.2d 709, 711-12 (4th Cir. 1986); Military Audit Project v. Casey, 656 F.2d 724, 750 (D.C. Cir. 1981); Founding Church of Scientology v. United States Marshals Serv., 516 F. Supp. 151, 156 (D.D.C. 1980) (barring discovery until defendant had opportunity to submit second Vaughn affidavit). But see Center for Nat'l Sec. Studies v. INS, No. 87-2068, slip op. at 2 (D.D.C. July 27, 1988) (permitting discovery on issue of due diligence even prior to filing of government's affidavits).

[313] See, e.g., Carney v. United States Dep't of Justice, 19 F.3d 807, 812 (2d Cir. 1994) ("In order to justify discovery once the agency has satisfied its burden, the plaintiff must make a showing of bad faith on the part of the agency sufficient to impugn the agency's affidavits or declarations, or provide some tangible evidence that an exemption claimed by the agency should not apply or summary judgment is otherwise inappropriate.") (citations omitted); Gilmore v. United States Dep't of Energy, 33 F. Supp. 2d 1184, 1190 (N.D. Cal. 1998) (permitting discovery when plaintiff claimed existence of pattern and practice of unreasonable delay in responding to FOIA requests, but limiting discovery to agency's "policies and practices for responding to FOIA requests, and the resources allocated to ensure its compliance the FOIA time limitations"); Judicial Watch, Inc. v. Department of Commerce, 34 F. Supp. 2d 28, 46 (D.D.C. 1998) (allowing discovery "under the rigorous supervision of a Magistrate Judge" concerning alleged illegal destruction and removal of records subsequent to plaintiff's FOIA request), partial summary judgment granted, 83 F. Supp. 2d 105 (D.D.C. 1999); Long v. United States Dep't of Jus-
(continued...)

## LITIGATION CONSIDERATIONS

so, however, the plaintiff must adequately explain "why, at that point in time, it cannot present by affidavit facts needed to defeat the [agency's] motion [for summary judgment]."[314] In any event, determinations of whether discovery should be permitted--and, if so, the type and extent of such discovery--are always vested in the sound discretion of the district court.[315]

---

[313](...continued)
tice, 10 F. Supp. 2d 205, 210 (N.D.N.Y. 1998) (finding discovery appropriate to test adequacy of search); Hawthorn Management Servs. v. HUD, No. 3:96CV2435, 1997 WL 821767, at *3 (D. Conn. Dec. 18, 1997) (permitting discovery because affiant's failure to disclose all pertinent information concerning bidding process in initial declaration amounted to "bad faith"); Armstrong v. Bush, 139 F.R.D. 547, 553 (D.D.C. 1991) (allowing discovery to test government's claim that request for electronically stored records "would place an unreasonable burden on the agency"); Van Strum v. EPA, 680 F. Supp. 349, 350-51 (D. Or. 1987) (finding discovery appropriate where documents received by anonymous source raised "valid concerns" of affiant's credibility and good faith of search); Shurberg Broad. v. FCC, 617 F. Supp. 825, 832 (D.D.C. 1985) (permitting discovery after receiving Vaughn affidavit and determining that there was genuine issue as to thoroughness of agency's search); cf. Accuracy in Media, Inc. v. National Park Serv., 194 F.3d 120, 124 (D.C. Cir. 1999) (upholding denial of discovery based on "speculative criticism" of agency's search), cert. denied, 68 U.S.L.W. 3711 (U.S. May 15, 2000) (No. 99-1578); Grand Cent. Partnership, Inc. v. Cuomo, 166 F.3d 473, 489 (2d Cir. 1999) (finding discovery unwarranted based on plaintiff's "speculation that there must be more documents" and that agency acted in "bad faith" by not producing them); Jones v. FBI, 41 F.3d 238, 249 (6th Cir. 1994) (finding discovery unwarranted when court convinced that agency "has acted in good faith and has properly withheld responsive material"; declaring fact that agency destroyed documents prior to receipt of FOIA request was not evidence of lack of "good faith").

[314] Code v. FBI, No. 95-1892, 1997 WL 150070, at *8 (D.D.C. Mar. 26, 1997) (citing Strang v. United States Arms Control & Disarmament Agency, 864 F.2d 859, 861 (D.C. Cir. 1989)); accord Fed. R. Civ. P. 56(f); see Nation Magazine v. United States Customs Serv., No. 94-00808, slip op. at 9 (D.D.C. May 21, 1997) (denying discovery on adequacy of search because plaintiff's affidavit failed to raise genuine issue of material fact).

[315] See Grand Cent. Partnership, 166 F.3d at 488 (noting that district court has "'broad discretion to manage the scope of discovery'" (quoting SafeCard Servs. v. SEC, 926 F.2d 1197, 1200 (D.C. Cir. 1991))); Becker v. IRS, 34 F.3d 398, 406 (7th Cir. 1994); Maynard v. CIA, 986 F.2d 547, 567 (1st Cir. 1993); Gillin v. IRS, 980 F.2d 819, 823 (1st Cir. 1992) (per curiam); Nolan v. United States Dep't of Justice, 973 F.2d 843, 849 (10th Cir. 1992); North Carolina Network for Animals, Inc. v. USDA, No. 90-1443, 1991 WL 10757, at *4 (4th Cir. Feb. 5, 1991) ("The district court should exercise its discretion to limit discovery in this as in all FOIA cases, and may enter summary judgment on the basis of agency affidavits when they are sufficient to resolve issues . . . ."); Petrus v. Brown, 833 F.2d 581, 583 (5th Cir. 1987) ("A trial court has broad discretion and inherent power to stay discovery until preliminary questions that may dispose of the case are determined."); Meeropol v. Meese, 790 F.2d 942,
(continued...)

## LITIGATION CONSIDERATIONS

A FOIA plaintiff should not in any case be permitted to extend his discovery efforts into the agency's thought processes for claiming particular exemptions.[316] Moreover, discovery should not be permitted when a plaintiff seeks thereby to obtain the contents of withheld documents--the issue that lies at the very heart of a FOIA case.[317]

Discovery also should not be permitted when the plaintiff is plainly using the FOIA lawsuit as a means of questioning investigatory action taken by the agency or the underlying reasons for undertaking such investigations.[318] Courts will refuse to "allow [a] plaintiff to use this limited discovery opportunity as a fishing expedition [for] investigating matters related to separate lawsuits."[319]

---

[315](...continued)
960-61 (D.C. Cir. 1986); see also Anderson v. HHS, 80 F.3d 1500, 1507 (10th Cir. 1996) (holding that district court did not abuse its discretion in denying plaintiff discovery on attorney fees issue).

[316] See Ajluni v. FBI, 947 F. Supp. 599, 608 (N.D.N.Y. 1996); Pearson v. ATF, No. 85-3079, slip op. at 1-2 (D.D.C. Sept. 22, 1986); Murphy, 490 F. Supp. at 1136 (citing United States v. Morgan, 313 U.S. 409, 422 (1941) (non-FOIA case).

[317] See, e.g., Local 3, 845 F.2d at 1179 (finding plaintiff not entitled to discovery that would be tantamount to disclosure of contents of exempt documents); Pollard v. FBI, 705 F.2d 1151, 1154 (9th Cir. 1983) (affirming denial of discovery when directed to substance of withheld documents at issue); Public Citizen, 997 F. Supp. at 73 (same); Katzman, 926 F. Supp. at 319 (same); Moore v. FBI, No. 83-1541, slip op. at 6 (D.D.C. Mar. 9, 1984) (denying discovery requests that "would have to go to the substance of the classified materials" at issue and noting that "[t]his is precisely the case when the court can and should exercise its discretion to deny that discovery"), aff'd, 762 F.2d 138 (D.C. Cir. 1985) (unpublished table decision); Laborers' Int'l Union v. United States Dep't of Justice, 578 F. Supp. 52, 56 (D.D.C. 1983) (sustaining objections to interrogatories when answers would "serve to confirm or deny the authenticity of the document held by plaintiff"), aff'd, 772 F.2d 919 (D.C. Cir. 1984).

[318] See RNR Enters. v. SEC, 122 F.3d 93, 98 (2d Cir. 1997) (finding no abuse of discretion in district court denial of discovery propounded for "investigative purposes"); Cecola v. FBI, No. 94 C 4866, 1995 WL 143548, at *3 (N.D. Ill. Mar. 31, 1995) (disallowing deposition concerning factual basis for assertion of Exemption 7(A), as "there is concern that the subject of the investigation not be alerted to the government's investigative strategy"); Williams v. FBI, No. 90-2299, slip op. at 7-8 (D.D.C. Aug. 6, 1991); see also Frydman v. Department of Justice, No. 78-4257, slip op. at 3-4 (D. Kan. Jan. 3, 1990) (denying discovery concerning electronic surveillance investigative practices).

[319] Tannehill v. Department of the Air Force, No. 87-1335, slip op. at 4 (D.D.C. Nov. 12, 1987) (limiting discovery to determination of FOIA issues, not to underlying personnel decision); see also Immanuel v. Secretary of Treasury, No. 94-884, 1995 WL 464141, at *1 (D. Md. Apr. 4, 1995) (rejecting
(continued...)

## LITIGATION CONSIDERATIONS

Discovery should be denied altogether if the court is satisfied from the agency's affidavits that no factual dispute remains,[320] and when the affidavits are "relatively detailed" and submitted in good faith.[321] Consequently, discovery should routinely be denied when the plaintiff's "efforts are made with [nothing] more than a 'bare hope of falling upon something that might impugn the affidavits'" submitted by the defendant agency.[322] In any event, "'curtailment of discovery' is particularly appropriate where the court makes

---

[319] (...continued) discovery that would constitute "a fishing expedition into all the possible funds held by the Department of Treasury which may fall within the terms of [plaintiff's] broad FOIA request. Such an expedition is certainly not going to come at the government's expense when it is evident that [plaintiff] seeks this information only for his own commercial use."), aff'd on other grounds, No. 95-1953, 1996 WL 157732 (4th Cir. Apr. 5, 1996).

[320] See Goland v. CIA, 607 F.2d 339, 352 (D.C. Cir. 1978), vacated in part & reh'g denied, 607 F.2d 367 (D.C. Cir. 1979); see also Becker, 34 F.3d at 406 (finding that district court did not err by granting summary judgment to government without addressing plaintiff's motion for discovery; judge "must have been satisfied that discovery was unnecessary when she concluded that the IRS's search was reasonable and ruled in favor of the IRS on summary judgment").

[321] See SafeCard, 926 F.2d at 1200-02 (affirming decision to deny discovery as to adequacy of search on ground that agency's affidavits were sufficiently detailed); Military Audit Project, 656 F.2d at 751 (affirming trial court's refusal to permit discovery when plaintiffs had failed to raise "substantial questions concerning the substantive content of the [defendants'] affidavits"); Pease v. United States Dep't of Interior, No. 1:99CV113, slip op. at 6 (D. Vt. Sept. 11, 1999) ("'[D]iscovery relating to the agency's search and the exemptions it claims for withholding records generally is unnecessary if the agency's submissions are adequate on their face.'" (quoting Carney, 19 F.3d at 812)); Hunt v. United States Marine Corps, 935 F. Supp. 46, 50 (D.D.C. 1996) (denying discovery because "defendants have met their burden of showing that they made a good faith effort to conduct a search for the requested records, using methods reasonably expected to produce the desired information"); Spannaus v. United States Dep't of Justice, No. 85-1015, slip op. at 7 (D. Mass. July 13, 1992) (denying discovery because "[p]laintiff has not offered any evidence to rebut the presumption of good faith that is accorded to [defendant's affidavit detailing its search]"); cf. Animal Legal Defense Fund, Inc. v. Department of the Air Force, 44 F. Supp. 2d 295, 304 (D.D.C. 1999) (finding agency affidavit insufficient but ordering more detailed affidavit and Vaughn Index rather than permitting discovery); Long, 10 F. Supp. 2d at 210 (allowing discovery because agency affidavit was found to be insufficient).

[322] Public Citizen, 997 F. Supp. at 73 (quoting Founding Church of Scientology v. NSA, 610 F.2d 824, 836-37 n.101 (D.C. Cir. 1979)); see Military Audit Project, 656 F.2d at 751-52; Kay v. FCC, 976 F. Supp. 23, 34 n.35 (D.D.C. 1997) (concluding that because plaintiff failed to submit "concrete evidence of bad faith," discovery actually sought only to discredit agency declaration), aff'd, 172 F.3d 919 (D.C. Cir. 1998) (unpublished table decision).

## LITIGATION CONSIDERATIONS

an in camera inspection."[323] Finally, there is the fact that in appropriate cases, the government can conduct discovery against the requester,[324] but there is no jurisdiction under the FOIA to permit either party to take discovery against a private citizen.[325]

### Waiver of Exemptions in Litigation

The FOIA directs district courts to review agency actions de novo.[326] Thus, an agency is not barred from invoking a particular exemption in litigation merely because that exemption was not cited in responding to the request at the administrative level.[327]

---

[323] Ajluni v. FBI, 947 F. Supp. 599, 608 (N.D.N.Y. 1996) (quoting Katzman, 926 F. Supp. at 320); see Mehl v. EPA, 797 F. Supp. 43, 46 (D.D.C. 1992) (employing in camera review, rather than discovery, to resolve inconsistency between representations in Vaughn Index and agency's prior public statements); Laborers' Int'l, 772 F.2d at 921.

[324] See, e.g., In re Engram, No. 91-1722, slip op. at 6-7 (4th Cir. June 2, 1992) (per curiam) (permitting discovery regarding how plaintiff obtained defendant's document as relevant to issue of waiver under Exemption 5); Weisberg v. United States Dep't of Justice, 749 F.2d 864, 868 (D.C. Cir. 1984) (ruling that agency "should be able to use the discovery rules in FOIA suits like any other litigant"); McSheffrey v. Executive Office for United States Attorneys, No. 98-0650, slip op. at 3 (D.D.C. Sept. 8, 1999) (recognizing that by conducting discovery against plaintiff, government could have confirmed receipt of agency's response to FOIA request) (appeal pending).

[325] See Kurz-Kasch, Inc. v. DOD, 113 F.R.D. 147, 148 (S.D. Ohio 1986); see also In re Shackelford, No. 93-25, slip op. at 1 (D.D.C. Feb. 19. 1993) ("[P]laintiff's effort to depose two former FBI agents, now retired, concerning the purpose and conduct of the investigation of John Lennon over 20 years ago, is beyond the scope of allowable discovery in a [FOIA] action."); Forest Guardians v. United States Forest Serv., No. 99-615, slip op. at 4 (D.N.M. Mar. 29, 2000) (disallowing discovery by submitters against FOIA requesters, who received redacted submitted material, when discovery was sought for purpose of determining whether requesters made further disclosures).

[326] 5 U.S.C. § 552(a)(4)(B) (1994 & Supp. IV 1998).

[327] See, e.g., Young v. CIA, 972 F.2d 536, 538-39 (4th Cir. 1992); Juda v. United States Customs Serv., No. 98-0533, 1999 U.S. Dist. LEXIS 12536, at *9 n.1 (D.D.C. Aug. 2, 1999) (noting that "[d]efendant may assert new exemptions at the federal district court level") (appeal pending); Frito-Lay v. EEOC, 964 F. Supp. 236, 239 (W.D. Ky. 1997) ("[A]n agency's failure to raise an exemption at any level of the administrative process does not constitute a waiver of that defense."); Farmworkers Legal Servs. v. United States Dep't of Labor, 639 F. Supp. 1368, 1370-71 (E.D.N.C. 1986); Illinois Inst. for Continuing Legal Educ. v. United States Dep't of Labor, 545 F. Supp. 1229, 1236 (N.D. Ill. 1982); Dubin v. Department of the Treasury, 555 F. Supp. 408, 412 (N.D. Ga. 1981), aff'd, 697 F.2d 1093 (11th Cir. 1983) (unpublished table decision); see also Conoco Inc. v. United States Dep't of Justice, 521 F. Supp. 1301, 1306 (D. Del.

(continued...)

## LITIGATION CONSIDERATIONS

Failure to raise an exemption in a timely fashion in litigation at the district court level, however, may result in a waiver. Although an agency should not be required to plead its exemptions in its answer,[328] it has been held that "'agencies [may] not make new exemption claims to a district court after the judge has ruled in the other party's favor,' nor may they 'wait until appeal to raise additional claims of exemption or additional rationales for the same claim.'"[329] Thus, an agency's failure to preserve its exemption claims can lead

---

[327] (...continued)
1981) (holding that agency is not barred from asserting work-product claim under Exemption 5 merely because it had not acceded to plaintiff's demand for Vaughn Index at administrative level), aff'd in part, rev'd in part & remanded, 687 F.2d 724 (3d Cir. 1982). But cf. AT&T Info. Sys. v. GSA, 810 F.2d 1233, 1236 (D.C. Cir. 1987) (holding that in reverse FOIA context--when standard of review is "arbitrary [and] capricious" standard based upon "whole" administrative record--agency may not at litigation stage initially offer its reasons for refusal to withhold material); Gilday v. United States Dep't of Justice, No. 85-292, slip op. at 5 (D.D.C. July 22, 1985) (ruling that agency rationale asserted in litigation over denial of fee waiver cannot correct shortcomings of administrative record).

[328] See, e.g., Frito-Lay, 964 F. Supp. at 239 ("According to the Sixth Circuit, there is no waiver of an affirmative defense not pleaded in the responsive pleading, as long as the opposing party has had sufficient notice of, and an opportunity to rebut the defense."); Johnson v. Federal Bureau of Prisons, No. 90-H-645-E, slip op. at 4-5 (N.D. Ala. Nov. 1, 1990); Farmworkers Legal Servs., 639 F. Supp. at 1371; Berry v. Department of Justice, 612 F. Supp. 45, 47 (D. Ariz. 1985); see also AFGE v. United States Dep't of Commerce, 907 F.2d 203, 206-07 (D.C. Cir. 1990). But see Ray v. United States Dep't of Justice, 908 F.2d 1549, 1557 (11th Cir. 1990) (suggesting that all exemptions must be raised by defendant agency "'in a responsive pleading'" (quoting Chilivis v. SEC, 673 F.2d 1205, 1208 (11th Cir. 1982))), rev'd on other grounds sub nom. United States Dep't of State v. Ray, 502 U.S. 164 (1991); Maccaferri Gabions, Inc. v. United States Dep't of Justice, No. 95-2576, slip op. at 4-6 (D. Md. Mar. 26, 1996) (holding that government's withholding pursuant to FOIA exemption constitutes affirmative defense which must be set forth in answer, but finding that government's reference to exemption in its answer and requester's knowledge of basis for withholding cured any pleading defect), appeal voluntarily dismissed, No. 96-1513 (4th Cir. Sept. 19, 1996); cf. Kansi v. United States Dep't of Justice, 11 F. Supp. 2d 42, 43 (D.D.C. 1998) (finding that entitlement to litigate fee waiver claim by not raising issue in his complaint).

[329] Senate of P.R. v. United States Dep't of Justice, 823 F.2d 574, 580 (D.C. Cir. 1987) (quoting Holy Spirit Ass'n v. CIA, 636 F.2d 838, 846 (D.C. Cir. 1980)). But see Williams v. FBI, No. 91-1054, 1997 WL 198109, at *2 (D.D.C. Apr. 16, 1997) (distinguishing rule in case where exemption raised first in motion for reconsideration because "policy militating against piecemeal litigation is less weighty where the district court proceedings are not yet completed") (appeal pending); Judicial Watch of Florida, Inc. v. United States Dep't of Justice, No. 97-2869, slip op. at 6 & n.4 (D.D.C. Jan. 22, 2000) (explaining that agency may not raise exemption for first time in brief replying to plaintiff's response to motion for summary judgment, but may raise it in future motion
(continued...)

## LITIGATION CONSIDERATIONS

to serious waiver consequences as FOIA litigation progresses, not only during the initial district court proceedings,[330] but also at the appellate level,[331] and even following a remand.[332]

---

[329](...continued)
for summary judgment, thereby affording plaintiff opportunity to respond) (motion for reconsideration pending); cf. Steinberg v. United States Dep't of Justice, No. 93-2409, slip op. at 10 (D.D.C. July 14, 1997) (offering agency option of either further justifying withholding documents in full under Exemption 7(C) or invoking another exemption, such as Exemption 7(D)).

[330] See, e.g., Rosenfeld v. United States Dep't of Justice, 57 F.3d 803, 811 (9th Cir. 1995) (holding new exemption claims waived when raised for first time after district court ruled against government on its motion for summary judgment); Ray, 908 F.2d at 1551 (same); Scheer v. United States Dep't of Justice, No. 98-1613, slip op. at 4-5 (D.D.C. July 24, 1999) (denying motion for reconsideration to present new exemption claims, in part, because defendant did not show "why, through the exercise of due diligence, it could not have presented this evidence before judgment was rendered") (appeal pending); Miller v. Sessions, No. 77-C-3331, slip op. at 2 (N.D. Ill. May 2, 1988) (holding "misunderstanding" on part of government counsel of court's order to submit additional affidavits insufficient to overcome waiver and denying motion for reconsideration); Powell v. United States Dep't of Justice, No. C-82-326, slip op. at 4 (N.D. Cal. June 14, 1985) (holding that government may not raise Exemption 7(D) for documents declassified during pendency of case when only Exemption 1 raised at outset).

[331] See, e.g., Jordan v. United States Dep't of Justice, 591 F.2d 753, 779-80 (D.C. Cir. 1978) (en banc) (refusing to consider government's Exemption 7 claim first raised in a "supplemental memorandum" filed one month prior to appellate oral argument).

[332] See, e.g., Fendler v. Parole Comm'n, 774 F.2d 975, 978 (9th Cir. 1985) (barring government from raising Exemption 5 on remand to protect presentence report because it was raised for first time on appeal); Ryan v. Department of Justice, 617 F.2d 781, 792 & n.38a (D.C. Cir. 1980) (holding government barred from invoking Exemption 6 on remand because it was raised for first time on appeal); cf. Benavides v. United States Bureau of Prisons, 995 F.2d 269, 273 (D.C. Cir. 1993) ("[T]he government is not entitled to raise defenses to requests for information seriatim until it finds a theory that the court will accept, but must bring all its defenses at once before the district court.") (Privacy Act access case). Compare Washington Post Co. v. HHS, 795 F.2d 205, 208-09 (D.C. Cir. 1986) (finding that "privilege" prong of Exemption 4 may not be raised for first time on remand--even though "confidential" prong was previously raised--absent sufficient extenuating circumstances), and Washington Post Co. v. HHS, 865 F.2d 320, 327 (D.C. Cir. 1989) (prohibiting agency from raising new aspect of previously raised prong of Exemption 4), with Lame v. United States Dep't of Justice, 767 F.2d 66, 71 n.7 (3d Cir. 1985) (permitting new exemptions to be raised on remand, as compared to raising new exemptions on appeal). But see Morgan v. United States Dep't of Justice, 923 F.3d 195, 199 n.5 (D.C. Cir. 1991) (remanding for district court to determine whether sealing order actually prohibits disclosure under FOIA,

(continued...)

## LITIGATION CONSIDERATIONS

The effect of these holdings is somewhat mitigated by the Court of Appeals for the District of Columbia Circuit's observation in Jordan v. United States Department of Justice that if the government "through pure mistake" failed to invoke the proper exemption in the district court and the information involved was of a very sensitive nature and was "highly likely" to be protected by an exemption, then the appellate court would have discretion under 28 U.S.C. § 2106[333] to remand the case for such further proceedings "as may be just under the circumstances."[334]

Sometimes, changes in factual circumstances may dictate that an agency revise its exemption position--for example, when an agency's invocation of Exemption 7(A) becomes moot due to subsequent factual developments in an underlying investigation,[335] or when an intervening declassification decision

---

[332](...continued) but noting that government can invoke other exemptions "if the court determines that the seal does not prohibit disclosure").

[333] (1994 & Supp. IV 1998); see Trans-Pac. Policing Agreement v. United States Customs Serv., 177 F.3d 1022, 1027 (D.C. Cir. 1999) (describing court's remedial power under 28 U.S.C. § 2106 as "very broad").

[334] Jordan, 591 F.2d at 780; see Schanen v. United States Dep't of Justice, 798 F.2d 348, 349-50 (9th Cir. 1986) (ruling that although government's Rule 60(b) motion based on procedural errors was properly denied, government may withhold identities of informers and DEA agents due to possibility of imminent harm to those individuals; holding government subject to attorney fees, however); see also Oklahoma Publ'g Co. v. HUD, No. 87-1935-P, slip op. at 4 (W.D. Okla. June 17, 1988) (holding that because Exemption 6 found applicable to material originally ordered disclosed, exemption not waived--to protect subject--but imposing sanctions on defendant and counsel); Washington Post Co. v. DOD, No. 84-2402, slip op. at 5 (D.D.C. Apr. 11, 1988) (permitting agency to raise new Exemption 1 claim for records previously found not protected by Exemption 5, when disclosure "could compromise the nation's foreign relations or national security" (citing Jordan, 591 F.2d at 780)); see also Ryan, 617 F.2d at 792 (following Jordan, rejecting exemption not raised at district court level because no "extraordinary circumstances" warrant relief under 28 U.S.C. § 2106).

[335] See, e.g., Chilivis v. SEC, 673 F.2d 1205, 1208 (11th Cir. 1982) (deciding that government is not barred from invoking other exemptions after reliance on Exemption 7(A) rendered untenable by conclusion of underlying law enforcement proceeding); Donovan v. FBI, 625 F. Supp. 808, 809 (S.D.N.Y. 1986) (same); see also Senate of P.R., 823 F.2d at 581 (making no "broad pronouncement" on whether conclusion of law enforcement proceedings used to justify Exemption 7(A) claim will always be sufficient factual change but finding, based upon showing of good faith by agency, that trial judge did not abuse discretion in allowing agency to advance other exemptions); Miller Auto Sales v. Casellas, No. 97-0032-H, slip op. at 3 (W.D. Va. Jan. 9, 1998) (rejecting waiver argument and remanding case to agency to make new administrative determination upon conclusion of enforcement proceedings); Curcio v. FBI, No. 89-0941, slip op. at 4-5 (D.D.C. Mar. 24, 1995) (explaining
(continued...)

## LITIGATION CONSIDERATIONS

renders Exemption 1 applicable.[336] (See the discussion of the former point under Exemption 7(A), above.) Similarly, an agency should be able to belatedly assert new defenses if there is "an interim development in applicable legal doctrine."[337]

In the district court, exemption claims should, of course, be substantiated by adequate Vaughn submissions. (See the discussion under Litigation Considerations, "Vaughn Index," above.) Failure to submit an adequate

---

[335] (...continued)
that, in determining whether FBI can assert new exemptions in litigation based on termination of Exemption 7(A), court considers: "(1) whether the FBI has made a clear showing of what the changed circumstances are and how they justify permitting the agency to raise new claims of exemption, and (2) whether the FBI has now proffered a legitimate reason why it did not previously argue all applicable exemptions"); see also Church of Scientology v. IRS, 816 F. Supp. 1138, 1157 (W.D. Tex. 1993) ("If the investigation is open . . . at the time of the request, the documents are exempt. Furthermore, the agency is not required to monitor the investigation and release the documents once the investigation is closed and there is no reasonable possibility of future proceedings." (citing Bonner v. United States Dep't of State, 928 F.2d 1148, 1152 (D.C. Cir. 1991))). But see Scheer, No. 98-1613, slip op. at 7 (barring agency from raising other exemptions after granting plaintiff's cross-motion for summary judgment on propriety of Exemption 7(A), but noting that "generally in FOIA cases if the government's motion for summary judgment [based on Exemption 7(A)] fails, it will be permitted to file an answer raising new exemptions" (citing Chilivis, 673 F.2d at 1208)) (appeal pending); cf. Washington Post, 795 F.2d at 208 (rationalizing that fact that court recommended in previous decision that HHS raise new argument could not be considered "extraordinary circumstance" justifying actually raising argument on remand).

[336] See, e.g., Council for a Livable World v. United States Dep't of State, No. 96-1807, slip op. at 7 (D.D.C. Nov. 23, 1998) (holding that "interim confidential classification of the documents . . . represents an interim change in the factual context of this case").

[337] Jordan, 591 F.2d at 780; see also Cotner v. United States Parole Comm'n, 747 F.2d 1016, 1018-19 (5th Cir. 1984) (recognizing that new exemptions may be asserted when remand due to "fundamental" change in government's position "not calculated to gain any tactical advantage in this particular case"); Carson v. United States Dep't of Justice, 631 F.2d 1008, 1015 n.29 (D.C. Cir. 1980) (declining to preclude consideration of particular FOIA exemptions on remand when, in holding that presentence report was agency record of Parole Commission for purposes of FOIA, court was "embark[ing] upon previously uncharted territory"); Council for a Livable World, No. 96-1807, slip op. at 6 (D.D.C. Nov. 23, 1998) ("[T]he interim developments standard is 'properly invoked when the government failed to raise an exemption in reliance on a case holding it inapplicable, and the case thereafter is the subject of legislative, Supreme Court, en banc, or appellate reversal.'" (quoting Lykins v. Rose, 608 F. Supp. 693, 695-96 (D.D.C. 1984))). But see Lykins, 608 F. Supp. at 695 (holding that "interim developments" justification for new exemptions does not include losses in instant case or rejection of alternative defense).

## LITIGATION CONSIDERATIONS

Vaughn affidavit, however, should not result in a waiver of exemptions and justify the granting of summary judgment against an agency.[338] The most prudent practice for agency defendants, though, generally is to ensure that their initial Vaughn affidavits contain detailed justifications of every exemption that they plan to invoke on the basis of all known facts.[339] By the same token, courts have held that they ordinarily will not consider issues raised for the first time on appeal by FOIA plaintiffs.[340]

---

[338] See Coastal States Gas Corp. v. Department of Energy, 644 F.2d 969, 982 (3d Cir. 1981) (finding it abuse of discretion to refuse to consider revised index and instead award "partial judgment" to plaintiff, even though corrected index was submitted one day before oral argument on plaintiff's "partial judgment" motion); cf. Wilkinson v. FBI, No. 80-1048, slip op. at 3 (C.D. Cal. June 17, 1987) (providing government 30 days to further justify exemptions but, after reviewing subsequent declarations, finding same faults with new declarations as with original ones and ordering in camera review). But see Carroll v. IRS, No. 82-3524, slip op. at 28 (D.D.C. Jan. 31, 1986) (holding affidavits insufficient and affording agencies no further opportunities to reassert their claims because "[a]fter years of litigation, the suit must be resolved").

[339] See Coastal States, 644 F.2d at 981 (suggesting that agencies might be restricted to one Vaughn affidavit); see also ABC v. USIA, 599 F. Supp. 765, 768 (D.D.C. 1984) (denying government's request to first litigate "agency record" issue and to raise other exemptions only if threshold defense fails).

[340] See, e.g., In re Wathey, No. 98-1589, 1999 WL 151417 (D.C. Cir. 1999) (denying writ of mandamus and explaining that "[c]hallenges to . . . handling of petitioner's FOIA request must be brought in the district court in the first instance"); Greyshock v. United States Coast Guard, No. 96-15266, 1997 WL 51514, at *3 (9th Cir. Feb. 5, 1997) (declining to consider challenge to separate FOIA request not "mentioned in the complaint or any other pleading before the district court"); McCutchen v. HHS, 30 F.3d 183, 186-87 (D.C. Cir. 1994) (refusing to consider correctness of agency's interpretation of FOIA request when raised for first time on appeal); Curran v. Department of Justice, 813 F.2d 473, 477 (1st Cir. 1987) (deciding that in camera inspection of records will not be considered when raised for first time on appeal); Wightman v. ATF, 755 F.2d 979, 983 (1st Cir. 1985) (deciding that appointment of counsel will not be considered when raised for first time on appeal); Kimberlin v. United States Dep't of the Treasury, 774 F.2d 204, 207 (7th Cir. 1985) (permitting issue of deletions taken pursuant to FOIA exemptions raised for first time on appeal). But see Trans-Pac. Policing Agreement v. United States Customs Serv., 177 F.3d 1022, 1027 (D.C. Cir. 1999) (allowing segregability issue to be raised for first time on appeal, in new exception to general rule); Carter v. United States Dep't of Commerce, 830 F.2d 388, 390 n.8 (D.C. Cir. 1987) (sua sponte considering new theories of public interest in its Exemption 6 balancing that were not raised by plaintiff at district court); Farese v. United States Dep't of Justice, No. 86-5528, slip op. at 9-10 (D.C. Cir. Aug. 12, 1987) (finding plaintiff not estopped from challenging use of specific exemptions at appellate stage when he argued at trial court level merely that agency had failed to meet its burden of establishing documents exempt).

# LITIGATION CONSIDERATIONS

## Attorney Fees and Litigation Costs

The FOIA is one of more than a hundred different federal statutes that contain a "fee-shifting" provision permitting the trial court to award reasonable attorney fees and litigation costs if a plaintiff has "substantially prevailed."[341] The FOIA's attorney fees provision limits an award to fees and costs incurred in litigating a FOIA case; accordingly, fees and other costs may not be awarded for services rendered at the administrative level.[342]

The FOIA's attorney fees provision, added as subsection (a)(4)(E) of the Act as part of the 1974 FOIA amendments, requires courts to engage in a two-step substantive inquiry: (1) Is the plaintiff eligible for an award of fees and/or costs? (2) If so, is the plaintiff entitled to the award?[343] Even if a plaintiff meets both of these tests, the award of fees and costs is entirely within the discretion of the court.[344]

---

[341] 5 U.S.C. § 552(a)(4)(E) (1994 & Supp. IV 1998).

[342] See Nichols v. Pierce, 740 F.2d 1249, 1252-54 (D.C. Cir. 1984) (refusing to award fees under FOIA for plaintiff's success under Administrative Procedure Act in forcing agency to issue regulations, despite plaintiff's claim of victory under FOIA's subsection (a)(1)); Northwest Coalition for Alternatives to Pesticides v. Browner, 965 F. Supp. 59, 65 (D.D.C. 1997); Associated Gen. Contractors v. EPA, 488 F. Supp. 861, 864 (D. Nev. 1980); cf. Kennedy v. Andrus, 459 F. Supp. 240, 244 (D.D.C. 1978) (rejecting attorney fees claim for services rendered at administrative level under Privacy Act of 1974, 5 U.S.C. § 552a (1994 & Supp. IV 1998)), aff'd, 612 F.2d 586 (D.C. Cir. 1980) (unpublished table decision).

[343] 5 U.S.C. § 552(a)(4)(E); see, e.g., Tax Analysts v. United States Dep't of Justice, 965 F.2d 1092, 1093 (D.C. Cir. 1992); Church of Scientology v. United States Postal Serv., 700 F.2d 486, 489 (9th Cir. 1983); see also Wheeler v. IRS, 37 F. Supp. 2d 407, 411 n.1 (W.D. Pa. 1998) ("The test for whether the court should award a FOIA plaintiff litigation costs is the same as the test for whether attorney fees should be awarded.").

[344] See, e.g., Anderson v. HHS, 80 F.3d 1500, 1504 (10th Cir. 1996) ("Assessment of attorney's fees in an FOIA case is discretionary with the district court."); Detroit Free Press, Inc. v. Department of Justice, 73 F.3d 93, 98 (6th Cir. 1996) ("We review the court's determination [to grant fees] for an abuse of discretion."); Young v. Director, CIA, No. 92-2561, 1993 WL 305970, at *2 (4th Cir. 1993) (noting that court has discretion to deny fees even if eligibility threshold is met); Maynard v. CIA, 986 F.2d 547, 567 (1st Cir. 1993) (holding that decision whether to award attorney fees "will be reversed only for an abuse of . . . discretion"); Tax Analysts, 965 F.2d at 1094 ("sifting of those [fee] criteria over the facts of a case is a matter of district court discretion"); Bangor Hydro-Electric Co. v. Department of the Interior, 903 F. Supp. 160, 170 (D. Me. 1995) ("Awards of litigation costs and attorney fees under FOIA are left to the sound discretion of the trial court.").

## LITIGATION CONSIDERATIONS

The Supreme Court's decision in Kay v. Ehrler[345] clearly establishes that subsection (a)(4)(E) does not authorize the award of fees to a pro se nonattorney plaintiff, because "the word 'attorney,' when used in the context of a fee-shifting statute, does not encompass a layperson proceeding on his own behalf."[346] In order to be eligible for attorney fees, therefore, a FOIA plaintiff must have a representational relationship with an attorney.[347] Furthermore, nearly all courts have read Kay to preclude an award of attorney fees to a pro se plaintiff who is also an attorney.[348] Because the fee-shifting provision of the FOIA was intended "'to encourage potential claimants to seek legal advice before commencing litigation,'"[349] and because a pro se attorney does not, by definition, seek out the "'detached and objective perspective necessary'" to litigate his FOIA case,[350] courts have suggested that he should not be eligible for an award of the fees that otherwise would have had to be paid to counsel.[351] This is particularly so because "[a]n award of attorney's fees was intended to relieve plaintiffs of the burden of legal costs, not reward successful

---

[345] 499 U.S. 432 (1991).

[346] Benavides v. Bureau of Prisons, 993 F.2d 257, 259 (D.C. Cir. 1993) (explaining Kay decision).

[347] See Kooritzky v. Herman, 178 F.3d 1315, 1323 (D.C. Cir. 1999) (holding that for all similarly worded fee-shifting statutes, "the term 'attorney' contemplates an agency relationship between a litigant and an independent lawyer"), cert. denied, 120 S. Ct. 1160 (2000); Blazy v. Tenet, 194 F.3d 90, 94 (D.C. Cir. 1999) (concluding that attorney need not file formal appearance in order for litigant to claim fees for consultations, as long as attorney-client relationship existed) (Privacy Act case); cf. Anderson v. United States Dep't of the Treasury, 648 F.2d 1, 3 (D.C. Cir. 1979) (indicating that when an organization litigates through in-house counsel, any payable attorney fees should not "exceed[] the expenses incurred by [that party] in terms of [in-house counsel] salaries and other out-of-pocked expenses").

[348] See, e.g., Burka v. HHS, 142 F.3d 1286, 1290 (D.C. Cir. 1998); Ray v. United States Dep't of Justice, 87 F.3d 1250, 1252 (11th Cir. 1996); Manos v. Department of the Air Force, 829 F. Supp. 1191, 1193 (N.D. Cal. 1993); Whalen v. IRS, No. 92C 4841, 1993 WL 532506, at *11 (N.D. Ill. Dec. 20, 1993). But see Texas v. ICC, 935 F.2d 728, 731 (5th Cir. 1991) (arguing that "lawyers who represent themselves in FOIA actions may recover under the fee-shifting provision"); Cazalas v. United States Dep't of Justice, 709 F.2d 1051, 1055-57 (5th Cir. 1983) (pre-Kay decision, granting fee award to pro se attorney); cf. Barrett v. United States Dep't of Justice, No. 3:95-264, slip op. at 5 (S.D. Miss. Mar. 17, 1997) (declining to decide whether Fifth Circuit would overrule Cazalas in light of the Kay decision because alternative ground exists for deciding fee issue), aff'd, No. 97-60223 (5th Cir. Nov. 20, 1997).

[349] Kay, 499 U.S. at 434 n.4 (quoting Falcone v. IRS, 714 F.2d 646, 647 (6th Cir. 1983)).

[350] Id.

[351] See Kay, 499 U.S. at 438 ("The statutory policy of furthering the successful prosecution of meritorious claims is better served by a rule that creates an incentive to retain counsel . . . .").

## LITIGATION CONSIDERATIONS

claimants or penalize the government."[352]

Claims of a pro se attorney that his or her status is merely "technical" because he or she represents an undisclosed client are looked upon with disfavor. In rejecting such a claim, the Court of Appeals for the District of Columbia Circuit has declared that "status as both attorney and litigant may be a 'technicality,' but it is a legally meaningful one and not to be ignored."[353] Finding that the pro se attorney "controlled the legal strategy and presentation" of the case, the D.C. Circuit similarly denied fees for the services of that pro se attorney's lawyer-colleagues who worked under his direction, "because there was no attorney-client relationship between them."[354] Of course, if an attorney actually retains outside counsel to represent him or her, those fees may be compensable.[355]

Unlike attorney fees, the costs of litigating a FOIA suit can be reasonably incurred by, and awarded to, even a pro se litigant who is not an attorney.[356] In fact, FOIA costs may be awarded independently of those provided for in 28 U.S.C. § 1920[357]--which is a "general provision permitting the Court to tax as costs certain enumerated items."[358] "Costs" in a FOIA case have accordingly been interpreted to include photocopying, postage, typing, transcription, parking, and transportation expenses, in addition to routine filing costs and marshals' fees paid at the trial level,[359] as well as the fees paid to a

---

[352] Burka, 142 F.3d at 1289-90. But cf. Jefferson v. Reno, No. 96-1284, slip op. at 7 (D.D.C. Mar. 29, 2000) (awarding attorney fees based on court's belief in its "inherent authority to impose monetary sanctions to maintain control of the litigation")

[353] Burka, 142 F.3d at 1291.

[354] Id.

[355] See, e.g., Ray v. United States Dep't of Justice, 856 F. Supp. 1576, 1582 (S.D. Fla. 1994), aff'd, 87 F.3d 1250 (11th Cir. 1996); Whalen, 1993 WL 532506, at *11.

[356] See Carter, 780 F.2d at 1481-82; DeBold, 735 F.2d at 1043; Clarkson, 678 F.2d at 1371; Crooker, 632 F.2d at 921-22; Malone v. Freeh, No. 97-3043, slip op. at 3 (D.D.C. July 12, 1999) (awarding pro se plaintiff $200 for costs); Wheeler, 37 F. Supp. 2d at 411; Hamilton v. Weise, No. 95-1161-ORL-22, 1997 U.S. Dist. LEXIS 18900, at *33 (M.D. Fla. Oct. 1, 1997).

[357] (1994).

[358] Four Corners Action Coalition v. United States Dep't of the Interior, No. 92-Z-2106, slip op. at 4 (D. Colo. Jan. 4, 1994); see Gregory v. FDIC, 631 F.2d 896, 900 n.8 (D.C. Cir. 1980) ("The fixing of costs, if any, is handled routinely under 28 U.S.C. § 1920."); see also Ray, 856 F. Supp. at 1585 (granting costs under 28 U.S.C. § 1920 for expert witness fees relating to issue on which plaintiff did not substantially prevail, but limiting them to $40-per-day amount provided as costs by 28 U.S.C. § 1821(b) (1994)).

[359] See Kuzma v. IRS, 821 F.2d 930, 931-34 (2d Cir. 1987); see also Tax Ana-
(continued...)

## LITIGATION CONSIDERATIONS

special master appointed by the court to review documents on its behalf.[360] However, a plaintiff cannot seek to have work done by an attorney compensated under the guise of "costs."[361]

Any plaintiff, including a State or a corporation, that engages the services of an attorney is eligible to claim attorney fees and costs.[362] By the same token, if it prevails, even a defendant agency may recover its costs pursuant to Rule 54(d) of the Federal Rules of Civil Procedure, although such recoveries are uncommon.[363]

To be eligible for a fee award, the plaintiff must "substantially prevail" within the meaning of subsection (a)(4)(E). The determination of whether the plaintiff has substantially prevailed is "largely a question of causation."[364] Though a court order compelling disclosure is not a condition precedent to an award of fees, the plaintiff must prove that prosecution of the suit was reasonably necessary to obtain the requested records and that a causal nexus existed

---

[359](...continued) lysts v. IRS, No. 94-923, 1999 WL 744169, at *1 (D.D.C. Mar. 16, 1998) (refusing to limit costs under FOIA only to those provided by 28 U.S.C. § 1920); Four Corners Action Coalition, No. 92-Z-2106, slip op. at 4 (D. Colo. Jan. 4, 1994) (same).

[360] See Washington Post v. DOD, 789 F. Supp. 423, 424 (D.D.C. 1992) (apportioning special master's fees equally between plaintiff and government).

[361] See Anderson, 80 F.3d at 1508 (suggesting that work done by attorneys is not "properly a cost item").

[362] See, e.g., Texas, 935 F.2d at 733 ("[T]he goal of encouraging litigation of meritorious FOIA claims is doubtlessly furthered by reimbursing the legal fees of all complainants who substantially prevail and who meet the traditional criteria--even those complainants, such as corporations or states, who could finance their own lawsuit."); Assembly of Cal. v. United States Dep't of Commerce, No. Civ-S-91-990, 1993 WL 188328, at *6 (E.D. Cal. May 28, 1993) ("Although the Assembly may have more resources than some private citizens, this does not mean the Assembly is any less restricted with respect to allocating its resources.").

[363] See, e.g., Donohue v. United States Dep't of Justice, No. 84-3451, slip op. at 1-2 (D.D.C. Mar. 7, 1988) (granting government's bill of costs for reimbursement of reporter, witness, and deposition expenses); Medoff v. CIA, No. 78-733, Order at 1 (D.N.J. Mar. 13, 1979) (awarding government, as prevailing party, its litigation costs in full amount of $93 in accordance with statutory authorization contained in 28 U.S.C. § 1920); see also Baez v. United States Dep't of Justice, 684 F.2d 999, 1005-06 (D.C. Cir. 1982) (en banc) (assessing against unsuccessful plaintiff all costs of appeal).

[364] Weisberg v. United States Dep't of Justice, 745 F.2d 1476, 1496 (D.C. Cir. 1984); Church of Scientology v. Harris, 653 F.2d 584, 587 (D.C. Cir. 1981).

## LITIGATION CONSIDERATIONS

between the suit and the agency's disclosure of the records.[365] The mere filing of the lawsuit and the subsequent release of records does not necessarily mean that the plaintiff substantially prevailed.[366] Indeed, eligibility for a fee award may be lacking when the plaintiff could reasonably have obtained the same information through other means,[367] when the release resulted from events independent of the lawsuit,[368] or when it was due to routine, though

---

[365] See, e.g., Maynard, 986 F.2d at 568; Cox, 601 F.2d at 6 (citing Vermont Low Income Advocacy Council, Inc. v. Usery, 546 F.2d 509, 513 (2d Cir. 1976)); Cuneo, 553 F.2d at 1366; cf. Transit Performance Eng'g v. Department of Transp., No. 92-722, 1992 U.S. Dist. LEXIS 9153, at *5 (D.D.C. June 26, 1992) (finding no causation when "undisputed evidence [showed] that the officials who decided to release the documents were not even aware that a lawsuit had been filed until after the requested documents were released").

[366] See Maynard, 986 F.2d at 568 (holding production of documents by two agencies after suit filed "not determinative" as to causation); Weisberg, 745 F.2d at 1496; Feshbach v. SEC, 5 F. Supp. 2d 788, 792 (N.D. Cal. 1998) (concluding that agency's discovery of 11 boxes of responsive records after Vaughn Index was filed was not "sufficient" to find that plaintiff substantially prevailed); Frye v. EPA, No. 90-3041, 1992 WL 237370, at *4 (D.D.C. Aug. 31, 1992) ("[W]hile plaintiff's lawsuit appears to have served as a catalyst for EPA's eventual disclosures, it is not at all clear that it was the cause" of EPA's voluntary disclosure.); see also Gray v. USDA, No. 91-1383, slip op. at 3 (D.D.C. Mar. 27, 1992) (castigating plaintiff for "tactics" he employed and refusing to award attorney fees, even though agency granted fee waiver after court case was filed, because there was no indication that agency action resulted from litigation). But see Stigall v. IRS, No. S-97-1283, slip op. at 4-5 (E.D. Cal. Feb. 20, 1998) (awarding fees because "attempts to comply with plaintiff's request were apparently undertaken only after the filing of this action"); Ajluni v. FBI, 947 F. Supp. 599, 609 (N.D.N.Y. 1996) ("Given the FBI's foot-dragging approach in responding to plaintiff's requests, and the additional and significant material released only after the Magistrate Judge ordered the FBI to produce a Vaughn Index, plaintiff has shown that this lawsuit was reasonably necessary, and that a sufficient causal connection existed between the initiation of the lawsuit and the FBI's release of a substantial number of documents.").

[367] See, e.g., Murty v. OPM, 707 F.2d 815, 816 (4th Cir. 1983) (pointing out that simply making "telephone call of inquiry as to what had happened to his request . . . would have produced the same result as the law suit"); Mendez-Suarez v. Veles, 698 F. Supp. 905, 907 (N.D. Ga. 1988) (denying fees when "the pendency of the discovery requests conclusively demonstrates that the information sought was available through means other than the filing of a FOIA claim"); see also Nicolau v. United States Dep't of Justice, 699 F. Supp. 1063, 1066 (S.D.N.Y. 1988) (refusing to award fees when "no reason to believe that the suit was necessary . . . [i]ndeed, it is not even clear that . . . the [agency was] aware of the suit at the time the documents were turned over").

[368] See, e.g., Ostrer v. FBI, No. 83-0328, slip op. at 12 (D.C. Cir. Jan. 19, 1988) (finding no causation when release of records was due to change in factual circumstances during course of litigation); Pyramid Lake Paiute Tribe of

(continued...)

## LITIGATION CONSIDERATIONS

delayed, administrative processing.[369] Of course, if a requester uncondition-

---

[368](...continued)
Indians v. United States Dep't of Justice, 750 F.2d 117, 119-21 (D.C. Cir. 1984) (finding no connection between senator's release of document to plaintiffs and institution of FOIA suit against agency for same record); Public Law Educ. Inst. v. United States Dep't of Justice, 744 F.2d 181, 183-84 (D.C. Cir. 1984) (concluding that no causation shown when government exercised its discretion to release requested document in unrelated, non-FOIA suit); Chilivis v. SEC, 673 F.2d 1205, 1212 (11th Cir. 1982) (determining that disclosure resulted from termination of investigation and consequent expiration of Exemption 7(A) protection); Nash v. United States Dep't of Justice, 992 F. Supp. 447, 449 (D.D.C. 1998) (denying fees because submission of Privacy Act waiver, not lawsuit, led to release of records), summary affirmance granted, No. 98-5096, 1998 WL 545424 (D.C. Cir. July 20, 1998); Abernethy v. IRS, 909 F. Supp. 1562, 1569 (N.D. Ga. 1995) (finding no causation when records were disclosed only after they had already been provided to plaintiff through discovery in unrelated civil actions), aff'd, No. 95-9489 (11th Cir. Feb. 13, 1997). But cf. McDonnell v. United States, 870 F. Supp. 576, 583-84 (D.N.J. 1994) (concluding that causation shown when plaintiff challenged government's longstanding withholding practice and entirely separate case contemporaneously proceeding through judicial system ultimately resulted in Supreme Court modification of government's stance and yielded additional disclosures to plaintiff).

[369] See, e.g., Van Strum v. EPA, No. 91-35404, slip op. at 5 (9th Cir. Aug. 17, 1992) (finding no causation when, in litigation, agency disclosed 18,000 pages within two months after narrowing of request); Weisberg v. United States Dep't of Justice, 848 F.2d 1265, 1268-71 (D.C. Cir. 1988) (finding no causation when majority of records were released as result of administrative processing and not suits); Church of Scientology, 700 F.2d at 491 (deciding that plaintiff does not substantially prevail when "an unavoidable delay accompanied by due diligence in the administrative process, rather than the threat of an adverse court order, was the actual reason for the agency's failure to respond to a request"); Bricker v. FBI, 54 F. Supp. 2d 1, 4 (D.D.C. 1999) ("[C]ourts should require some showing of improper conduct or purpose before awarding fees and costs against an agency on the basis of delay alone."), motion for reconsideration denied, 63 F. Supp. 2d 57 (D.D.C. 1999); Kuffel v. United States Bureau of Prisons, 882 F. Supp. 1116, 1127 (D.D.C. 1995) ("[R]elease of records was due to routine administrative processing that was done in good faith and with due diligence."); Arevalo-Franco v. INS, 772 F. Supp. 959, 961 (W.D. Tex. 1991) (holding that requesters "generally" have not substantially prevailed when they "know that administrative problems are causing the delay . . . and file lawsuits anyway"). But see City of Detroit v. United States Dep't of State, No. 93-CV-72310, slip op. at 2-3 (E.D. Mich. Mar. 24, 1995) (finding that requester substantially prevailed when litigation resulted in release of documents at least six months earlier than anticipated); Northwest Coalition for Alternatives to Pesticides v. Reilly, No. 90-707, 1992 WL 122718, at *2 (D.D.C. May 26, 1992) (rejecting government's claim that disclosure was made in course of "administrative processing" when agency failed to respond to plaintiff's letters of administrative appeal); Church of Scientology v. IRS, 769 F. Supp. 328, 330 (C.D. Cal. 1991) (finding plaintiff eligible, notwith-
(continued...)

## LITIGATION CONSIDERATIONS

ally waives his right to fees as part of a settlement, he cannot go back on his agreement.[370]

Federal agencies are strongly urged to make discretionary disclosures of exempt information whenever possible as a matter of FOIA policy.[371] When such a discretionary disclosure is made, a court should find that it resulted not from the institution of litigation, but rather from a discretionary, policy-governed motivation.[372] Indeed, the Court of Appeals for the Sixth Circuit has

---

[369](...continued) standing agency appeal backlog, when government denied documents initially, had yet to respond to administrative appeal, and released documents only following order to produce Vaughn Index); Muffoletto v. Sessions, 760 F. Supp. 268, 274 (E.D.N.Y. 1991) (noting that lawsuit provided "impetus" for FBI to act, "even if simply to negotiate . . . in a more expeditious manner").

[370] See National Senior Citizens Law Ctr. v. Social Sec. Admin., 849 F.2d 401, 402-03 (9th Cir. 1988); Krikorian v. Department of State, No. 95-5216, slip op. at 1 (D.C. Cir. Feb. 6, 1996) (rejecting "appellant's proposed extrinsic evidence that the Stipulation of Dismissal was intended to condition dismissal on the payment of attorney's fees"). But see Fitzgibbon v. Agency for Int'l Dev., No. 87-1548, slip op. at 2-3 (D.D.C. Mar. 26, 1992) (finding that in FOIA context, stipulation in which plaintiff renounces any claim for "costs or fees" precludes claims for court costs only and does not waive plaintiff's right to seek attorney's fees).

[371] See Attorney General's Memorandum for Heads of Departments and Agencies regarding the Freedom of Information Act (Oct. 4, 1993), reprinted in FOIA Update, Vol. XIV, No. 3, at 4-5 ("strongly encourag[ing]" FOIA personnel to make discretionary disclosures); see also Attorney General's Follow-Up Memorandum to Heads of Departments and Agencies regarding the Freedom of Information Act (Sept. 3, 1999), reprinted in FOIA Update, Vol. XIX, No. 4, at 3-5 (reiterating importance of "foreseeable harm" standard to federal agencies in order to promote further discretionary disclosure in agency decisionmaking); President's Memorandum for Heads of Departments and Agencies regarding the Freedom of Information Act, 29 Weekly Comp. Pres. Doc. 1999 (Oct. 4, 1993), reprinted in FOIA Update, Vol. XIV, No. 3, at 3 (establishing policy of greater "[o]penness in government").

[372] See, e.g., Lovell v. Alderete, 630 F.2d 428, 432 & n.4 (5th Cir. 1980) (alternative holding) ("[The] Government's compliance with [plaintiff's] request was not caused mainly by the institution of the suit, but rather was also affected by a change in the United States Attorney General's [May 5, 1977] guidelines concerning disclosure of exempted materials."); Nationwide Bldg. Maintenance, Inc. v. Sampson, 559 F.2d 704, 712 n.34 (D.C. Cir. 1977) (announcing that when delay in disclosure was due to agency's consideration of appropriateness of discretionary disclosure, "FOIA should not be construed so as to put the federal bureaucracy in a defensive or hostile position with respect to the Act's spirit of open government and liberal disclosure of information"). But see O'Neill, Lysaght & Sun v. DEA, 951 F. Supp. 1413, 1423 (C.D. Cal. 1996) (finding that, despite the issuance of new processing directives by the Attorney General, "but for the pendency of" the lawsuit, agency would not

(continued...)

## LITIGATION CONSIDERATIONS

perceptively identified the dangers of assessing fees where the agency disclosure is truly voluntary:[373]

> Were the courts to construe disclosure of a document as an agency's concession of wrongful withholding, as did the District Court here, agencies would be forced to either never disclose a document once withheld or risk being assessed fees. This result would frustrate the policy of encouraging disclosure that prompted enactment of the FOIA and its amendments. . . . Penalizing an agency for disclosure at any stage of the proceedings is simply not in the spirit of the FOIA.[374]

In reviewing attorney fees claims in connection with discretionary disclosure, courts may find it appropriate to examine whether the information so disclosed would, in fact, have been found exempt--a practice courts have routinely undertaken in the past when agencies have argued that changed circumstances and not the institution of litigation caused the disclosure.[375] Of course, courts might view discretionary disclosures in litigation with some degree of skepticism--which only underscores the importance of fully evaluating records for discretionary action at the administrative level.[376]

---

[372](...continued) have reevaluated and disclosed withheld documents).

[373] American Commercial Barge Lines v. NLRB, 758 F.2d 1109, 1112 (6th Cir. 1985) ("It clearly would not be inconsistent with the FOIA for an agency to initially withhold an exempt document and later disclose it after determining that disclosure was in the public interest even though the document was exempt. Disclosure therefore does not establish that the agency considers a document non-exempt.").

[374] Id.

[375] See, e.g., Chesapeake Bay Found., v. USDA, 11 F.3d 211, 216 (D.C. Cir. 1993) (directing that when, following disclosure in litigation, "the Government continues to insist that it had a valid basis for withholding requested documents, the District Court must determine whether the Government's position is legally correct in assessing a claim for fees under FOIA"); Anderson v. HHS, 3 F.3d 1383, 1385 (10th Cir. 1993) (concluding that when agency's disclosure moots FOIA action, "the court may (and must) refer to the merits of the underlying FOIA action in determining whether [plaintiff] is entitled to fees" (citing Aviation Data Serv. v. FAA, 687 F.2d 1319, 1322-24 (10th Cir. 1982))); Lovell, 630 F.2d at 430-34; Nationwide Bldg., 559 F.2d at 712 n.34 ("Certainly where the government can show that information disclosed after initial resistance was nonetheless exempt from the FOIA a plaintiff should not be awarded attorney fees . . . .").

[376] See Seegull Mfg. Co. v. NLRB, 741 F.2d 882, 885 (6th Cir. 1984) (rejecting assertion of voluntary disclosure for documents previously claimed absolutely privileged, made six months after close of enforcement proceeding and after suit had been filed); O'Neill, 951 F. Supp. at 1423 (rejecting "discretionary" disclosure claim by agency when it "had contested the disclosure of these
(continued...)

## LITIGATION CONSIDERATIONS

A requester also may be deemed not to have substantially prevailed where the records disclosed were "not significant in terms of the overall FOIA request."[377] On the other hand, in some instances, a plaintiff might be deemed to have substantially prevailed even if no records are released. For example, if the lawsuit results in a fee waiver,[378] in a new search locating additional records,[379] in expedited processing,[380] or in a significant change in the agency's FOIA policies or practices,[381] the plaintiff might be deemed eligible for a fee

---

[376](...continued) documents up to the point where it was evident that it would be ordered to disclose"); Ajluni, 947 F. Supp. at 610 (rejecting agency's assertion that supplemental disclosure resulted, in part, from liberalized disclosure policies when release was made only after agency was ordered to produce Vaughn Index and its assertions were "nowhere supported, illustrated or indexed with reference to the released materials"); accord FOIA Update, Vol. XIV, No. 3, at 1, 4 (emphasizing importance of making discretionary disclosures at administrative level).

[377] Union of Concerned Scientists v. NRC, 824 F.2d 1219, 1226 (D.C. Cir. 1987) (stating that the "sheer volume of [a] release is not determinative," but remanding case for the trial court to "explain why it believes the release of eleven pages [out of the 1500 pages at issue] is of such substance and quality as to make [plaintiff] eligible for an attorney's fee award"); see Pacific Energy Inst. v. IRS, No. 94-36172, 1996 WL 14244, at *1 (9th Cir. Jan. 16, 1996) (ruling that plaintiff did not "substantially prevail" because it "obtained only five of 80 documents it sought, and none that was particularly noteworthy"); Maynard, 986 F.2d at 568 (pointing out that court-ordered "disclosure of a single name was of minimal importance when compared with plaintiff's overall FOIA request"); Weisberg, 848 F.2d at 1270-71 (refusing to disturb district court ruling that documents released as result of litigation were "essentially duplicative" of information already made public); Torres v. CIA, 39 F. Supp. 2d 906, 964 (N.D. Ill. 1999) (finding that "delivery . . . of a couple of pages of not really meaningful material" does not entitle plaintiff to attorney fees). But see GMRI, Inc. v. EEOC, 149 F.3d 449, 451-52 (6th Cir. 1998) (finding that plaintiff substantially prevailed upon receipt of one document that agency had argued was not responsive, because document was the only record relating to misplaced or lost file); Church of Scientology, 653 F.2d at 589 (contending that there was "no reason in law or logic to discount significance of" 108 envelopes and transmittal slips).

[378] See, e.g., Wilson v. United States Dep't of Justice, No. 87-2415, slip op. at 2 (D.D.C. Sept. 12, 1989), appeal dismissed, No. 89-5206 (D.C. Cir. Mar. 9, 1990); Ettlinger v. FBI, 596 F. Supp. 867, 879-82 (D. Mass. 1984).

[379] See National Pizza Co. v. INS, No. 94-2972, slip op. at 1-2 (W.D. Tenn. Aug. 29, 1995) (inexplicably granting commercial requester 20% of fees claimed).

[380] See Exner v. FBI, 443 F. Supp. 1349, 1353 (S.D. Cal. 1978) (basing fee award on plaintiff's success in obtaining court-ordered expedited processing), aff'd, 612 F.2d 1202 (9th Cir. 1980).

[381] See, e.g., Crooker v. United States Parole Comm'n, 776 F.2d 366, 367 (1st (continued...)

## LITIGATION CONSIDERATIONS

award. Of course, the benefit to the plaintiff must result from a favorable action taken by the agency that involves one of its obligations under the FOIA.[382]

Even if a plaintiff satisfies the eligibility test, a court still must exercise its equitable discretion in separately determining whether that plaintiff is entitled to an award.[383] This discretion is ordinarily guided by four traditional criteria that derive from the FOIA's legislative history.[384] These factors are: (1) the public benefit derived from the case; (2) the commercial benefit to the complainant; (3) the nature of the complainant's interest in the records sought; and (4) whether the government's withholding had a reasonable basis in law.[385] These four entitlement factors, of course, have nothing to do with determining an appropriate fee amount; therefore, they cannot be considered in that entirely separate analysis.[386]

While any FOIA disclosure hypothetically benefits the public by generally increasing public knowledge about the government, this "broadly defined

---

[381] (...continued) Cir. 1985) (ruling that suit ultimately resulted in disclosure of records by causing Solicitor General to abandon prior position that presentence reports were not "agency records" subject to FOIA); Halperin v. Department of State, 565 F.2d 699, 706 n.11 (D.C. Cir. 1977) (noting that suit caused agency to revise its manner of recording "off-the-record" briefings, even though litigation caused no records to be disclosed); Washington Post, 789 F. Supp. at 425 (concluding that plaintiff "substantially prevailed" where government produced several key documents and undertook "to reexamine 2000 more that had been previously withheld"). But cf. Hendricks v. United States Dep't of Justice, No. 92-5621, slip op. at 2 (E.D. Pa. July 29, 1993) (finding that, in absence of agency bad faith, plaintiff did not "substantially prevail" where filing suit clarified that records agency previously "withheld" did not in fact exist).

[382] See Wrenn v. Department of the Treasury, 866 F. Supp. 525, 526-27 (N.D. Ala. 1994) (rejecting plaintiff's "novel claim" that he had satisfied "substantially prevailed" criteria because IRS withdrew its claim of unpaid taxes following its FOIA response acknowledging that no records existed to document its grounds for that claim).

[383] See Young, No. 92-2561, slip op. at 4 (4th Cir. Aug. 10, 1993) ("Even if a plaintiff substantially prevails, however, a district court may nevertheless, in its discretion, deny the fees."); Texas, 935 F.2d at 733 ("The district court did not specify which of the criteria [plaintiff] failed to satisfy. But so long as the record supports the court's exercise of discretion, the decision will stand.").

[384] See S. Rep. No. 93-854, at 19 (1974); cf. Cotton v. Heyman, 63 F.3d 1115, 1123 (declining to review remaining factors after finding no public benefit from release and recognizing reasonableness of agency's position).

[385] See Detroit Free Press, 73 F.3d at 98; Cotton, 63 F.3d at 1117; Tax Analysts, 965 F.2d at 1093; Church of Scientology, 700 F.2d at 492; Fenster v. Brown, 617 F.2d 740, 742-45 (D.C. Cir. 1979); Cuneo, 553 F.2d at 1364-66. But see Burka, 142 F.3d at 1293 (Randolph, J., concurring) ("Although we have applied these criteria in the past, they deserve another look.").

[386] See Long v. IRS, 932 F.2d 1309, 1315-16 (9th Cir. 1991).

## LITIGATION CONSIDERATIONS

benefit" is not what Congress had in mind when it provided for awards of attorney fees.[387] Rather, the "public benefit" factor ""'speaks for an award [of attorney fees] when the complainant's victory is likely to add to the fund of information that citizens may use in making vital political choices.""'[388] Such a determination necessarily entails an evaluation of the nature of the specific information disclosed.[389] Thus, it has been held that "[m]inimal, incidental and speculative public benefit will not suffice" to satisfy the requirements of subsection (a)(4)(E),[390] and that it is similarly unavailing to show simply that the prosecution of the suit has compelled an agency to improve the efficiency of its FOIA processing.[391]

Similarly, it has been held by the D.C. Circuit that "public benefit" should not be grounded solely on "the potential release of present and future information" resulting from the legal precedent set by the case in which fees are sought.[392] As the D.C. Circuit perceptively noted in one case: "Such an inherently speculative observation is . . . inconsistent with the structure of FOIA

---

[387] Cotton, 63 F.3d at 1120 (citing Fenster, 617 F.2d at 744).

[388] Cotton, 63 F.3d at 1120 (quoting Fenster, 617 F.2d at 744 (quoting, in turn, Blue v. Bureau of Prisons, 570 F.2d 529, 534 (5th Cir. 1978))).

[389] See Cotton, 63 F.3d at 1120.

[390] Aviation Data, 687 F.2d at 1323; see Ellis v. United States, 941 F. Supp. 1068, 1078 (D. Utah 1996) ("[T]he successful FOIA plaintiff always achieves some degree of public benefit by bringing the government into compliance with FOIA and by the benefit assumed to flow from public disclosure of government information."); Bangor Hydro-Elec., 903 F. Supp. at 171 (same); Texas, 935 F.2d at 733-34 (suggesting that there is "little public benefit" in disclosure of documents that fail to reflect agency wrongdoing: "Texas went fishing for bass and landed an old shoe. Under the circumstances, we decline to require the federal government to pay the cost of tackle."). But see Williams v. FBI, 17 F. Supp. 2d 6, 9 (D.D.C. 1997) (awarding fees to encourage "service on the Civil Pro Bono Counsel panel"), appeal voluntarily dismissed, No. 98-5249 (D.C. Cir. Oct. 7, 1998); Landano v. United States Dep't of Justice, 873 F. Supp. 884, 892 (D.N.J. 1994) ("Here, the public clearly benefits from this disclosure since it has an interest in the fair and just administration of the criminal justice system as [applied to the plaintiff].").

[391] See Solone v. IRS, 830 F. Supp. 1141, 1143 (N.D. Ill. 1993) ("While the public would benefit from the court's imprimatur to the IRS to comply voluntarily with the provisions of the FOIA, this is not the type of benefit that FOIA attorneys' fees were intended to generate."); Muffoletto, 760 F. Supp. at 277 (maintaining that public benefit in compelling FBI to act more expeditiously is insufficient).

[392] Cotton, 63 F.3d at 1120; see Chesapeake Bay Found. v. USDA, 108 F.3d 375, 377 (D.C. Cir. 1997) ("Nor is the establishment of a legal right to information a public benefit for the purpose of awarding attorneys' fees." (citing Cotton, 63 F.3d at 1120)); see also Bangor Hydro-Elec., 903 F. Supp. at 170 (rejecting argument that public benefitted by precedent which would "allow other utilities to easily acquire similar documents for the benefit of those utilities ratepayers").

## LITIGATION CONSIDERATIONS

itself."[393] However, this view has not always been applied.[394] On the other hand, "the degree of dissemination and likely public impact that might be expected from a particular disclosure" is a highly pertinent consideration.[395] When the information released is already in the public domain, of course, this factor does not weigh in favor of a fee award.[396]

The second factor--the commercial benefit to the plaintiff--requires an examination of whether the plaintiff had an adequate private commercial incentive to litigate its FOIA demand even in the absence of an award of attorney fees.[397] The third factor--the nature of the plaintiff's interest in the rec-

---

[393] Cotton, 63 F.3d at 1120.

[394] See Church of Scientology, 700 F.2d at 493 (determining that appellate ruling that specific statutory provision does not qualify under Exemption 3 "in our view, benefits the public"); Aronson, 866 F.2d at 3 (suggesting that public interest is served by disclosure to "private tracer" of information concerning mortgagors who were owed "distributive share" refunds); Landano, 873 F. Supp. at 892 ("[T]he public benefits from the Supreme Court's guidelines which permit much easier access to government-held information.").

[395] Blue, 570 F.2d at 533; Church of Scientology, 769 F. Supp. at 331 (recognizing public interest in "the apparently improper designation of a religion as a 'tax shelter' project"); see Polynesian Cultural Ctr. v. NLRB, 600 F.2d 1327, 1330 (9th Cir. 1979) (per curiam) (denying fees when "disclosure was unlikely to result in widespread dissemination, or substantial public benefit"); Frydman v. Department of Justice, 852 F. Supp. 1497, 1503 (D. Kan. 1994) (deciding that requester's suggestion that he might write book was "too speculative to warrant much weight"), aff'd, 57 F.3d 1080 (10th Cir. 1995) (unpublished table decision).

[396] See, e.g., Tax Analysts, 965 F.2d at 1094 (affirming district court's finding that more prompt reporting by Tax Analysts of additional 25% of publicly available district court tax decisions was "less than overwhelming" contribution to public interest); Laughlin v. Commissioner, No. 99-1566, slip op. at 7 (S.D. Cal. Mar. 23, 2000) (declining to award fees for disclosure of document that is "readily accessible commercially"); Petroleum Info. Corp. v. United States Dep't of the Interior, No. 89-3173, slip op. at 5-6 (D.D.C. Nov. 16, 1993) (holding that public benefit is only "slight" where litigation resulted in disclosure of information in electronic form that was previously publicly available in printed form).

[397] See, e.g., Fenster, 617 F.2d at 742-44 (affirming denial of fees to law firm that obtained disclosure of government auditor's manual used in reviewing contracts of the type entered into by firm's clients); Chamberlain v. Kurtz, 589 F.2d 827, 842-43 (5th Cir. 1979) (concluding that plaintiff who faced $1.8 million deficiency claim for back taxes and penalties "needed no additional incentive" to bring FOIA suit against IRS for documents relevant to his defense); Horsehead Indus., 999 F. Supp. 59, 69 (D.D.C. 1998) (finding that requester would have brought suit regardless of availability of fees); Viacom Int'l v. EPA, No. 95-2243, 1996 U.S. Dist. LEXIS, at *6 (E.D. Pa. Aug. 30, 1996) (dismissing as "divorced from reality" corporation's contention that its
(continued...)

# LITIGATION CONSIDERATIONS

ords--often is evaluated in tandem with the second factor and militates against awarding fees in cases where the plaintiff had an adequate personal incentive to seek judicial relief.[398] To disqualify a fee applicant under the second and third factors, "a motive need not be strictly commercial; any private interest will do."[399]

---

[397](...continued)
"'knowing the extent of its potential liability will not promote any commercial interests'"); Frye, No. 90-3041, 1992 WL 237370, at *4 (denying fees where "plaintiff does not effectively dispute that the prime beneficiaries of the information requested will be commercial entities with commercial interests that either are, or might become, his clients"); Hill Tower, Inc. v. Department of the Navy, 718 F. Supp. 568, 572 (N.D. Tex. 1989) (ruling that plaintiff who had filed tort claims against government arising from aircraft crash "had a strong commercial interest in seeking [related] information [as] it was [its] antenna that was damaged by the crash"). But see Aronson, 866 F.2d at 3 (finding that "potential for commercial personal gain did not negate the public interest served" by private tracer's lawsuit since "failure of HUD to comply reasonably with its reimbursement duty would probably only be disclosed by someone with a specific interest in ferreting out unpaid recipients").

[398] See, e.g., Polynesian Cultural Ctr., 600 F.2d at 1330 (ruling that attorney fees award should not "'merely subsidize a matter of private concern' at taxpayer expense" (quoting Blue, 570 F.2d at 533-34)); Viacom, 1996 U.S. Dist. LEXIS, at *4 ("[W]e harbor strong doubts that Viacom entered into this proceeding to foster the public interest in disclosure. Its motivation, as evinced by its conduct of this litigation, was to assert its own interests as a potentially responsible party to the clean up operation."); Abernethy, 909 F. Supp. at 1569 (suggesting that when plaintiff sought records of investigation of which he was target to challenge his removal from management position, "[p]laintiff's strong personal motivation for filing this lawsuit outweighs any public interest which may result from disclosure"); Frydman, 852 F. Supp. at 1504 ("Although plaintiff's interest in the information in this case is not pecuniary, it is strictly personal."); Solone, 830 F. Supp. at 1143 (where plaintiffs sought information to help challenge IRS income calculations; plaintiffs' "private self-interest motive . . . is sufficient to insure the vindication of their rights under FOIA"). See generally Church of Scientology, 700 F.2d at 494 (noting that it is "logical to read the two criteria together where a private plaintiff has pursued a private interest"). But see Crooker, 776 F.2d at 368 (finding third factor to favor plaintiff where "interest was neither commercial nor frivolous, [but] to ensure that the Parole Commission relied on accurate information in making decisions affecting his liberty"); Williams, 17 F. Supp. 2d at 9 (awarding fees "[e]ven if [the requester's] own interest in the records is personal," in order to "serve the larger public purpose of encouraging" representation by pro bono counsel).

[399] Tax Analysts, 965 F.2d at 1095 ("'[P]laintiff was not motivated simply by altruistic instincts, but rather by its desire for efficient, easy access to [tax] decisions.'" (quoting Tax Analysts v. United States Dep't of Justice, 759 F. Supp. 28, 31 (D.D.C. 1991))); see Bangor Hydro-Elec., 903 F. Supp. at 171 (rejecting public utility's argument that it incurred no commercial benefit because under "'traditional regulatory principles'" utility would be obliged to

(continued...)

## LITIGATION CONSIDERATIONS

Sometimes a plaintiff's motives may change over the course of the litigation, leading a court to bifurcate the fee award on the basis of such shifting interests.[400] The use of the FOIA as a substitute for discovery has routinely been found to constitute a private, noncompensable interest.[401] However, "news interests should not be considered commercial interests."[402]

The fourth factor--the reasonableness of the agency's withholding--counsels against a fee award when the agency had a reasonable basis in law for concluding that the information in issue was exempt. If an agency's position is correct as a matter of law, this factor should be dispositive.[403] If an

---

[399](...continued)
pass any commercial gain on to its ratepayers); Mosser Constr. Co. v. United States Dep't of Labor, No. 93CV7525, slip op. at 4 (N.D. Ohio Mar. 29, 1994) (explaining that factor weighs against not-for-profit organization whose actions are motivated by commercially related concerns on behalf of its members). But see Assembly of Cal., 1993 WL 188328, at *5 (refusing to preclude fees where state legislature sought information to challenge federal census count, even though benefits could accrue to state because "plaintiffs did not stand to personally benefit but acted as public servants").

[400] See, e.g. Anderson, 80 F.3d at 1504-05 (affirming district court's denial of fees for first phase of litigation--when plaintiff's primary motive was to obtain records for state court action, while approving them for second phase--when plaintiff's primary interest in records was public dissemination).

[401] See, e.g., Ellis, 941 F. Supp. at 1079 (compiling cases); Muffoletto, 760 F. Supp. at 275 (rejecting plaintiff's entitlement to fees on grounds that "[t]he plaintiff's sole motivation in seeking the requested information was for discovery purposes, namely, to assist him in the defense of a private civil action"); Republic of New Afrika, 645 F. Supp. 117, 121 (D.D.C. 1986) (stating that purely personal motives of plaintiff--to exonerate its members of criminal charges and to circumvent civil discovery--dictated against award of fees), aff'd sub nom. Provisional Gov't of the Republic of New Afrika v. ABC, 821 F.2d 821 (D.C. Cir. 1987) (unpublished table decision); Simon v. United States, 587 F. Supp. 1029, 1033 (D.D.C. 1984) (articulating that use of FOIA as substitute for civil discovery "is not proper and this court will not encourage it by awarding fees").

[402] S. Rep. No. 93-854, at 19 (1974), quoted in Fenster, 617 F.2d at 742 n.4; accord FOIA Update, Vol. VIII, No. 1, at 10 ("New Fee Waiver Policy Guidance").

[403] See Chesapeake Bay Found., 11 F.3d at 216 ("If the Government was right in claiming that the [records] were exempt from disclosure under FOIA, then no fees are recoverable."); Cotton, 63 F.3d at 1117 ("[T]here can be no doubt that a party is not entitled to fees if the government's legal basis for withholding requested records is correct."); Polynesian Cultural Ctr., 600 F.2d at 1330 (denying fees, despite court-ordered disclosure, because "[t]he Board's claim of exemption was not only reasonable, but correct," based upon subsequent Supreme Court decision); Horsehead Indus., 999 F. Supp. at 64 (ruling that "fees will not be awarded" when agency's withholding "is correct
(continued...)

## LITIGATION CONSIDERATIONS

agency had only a "colorable basis in law" for withholding information, then this factor should be weighed with other relevant considerations to determine entitlement.[404] In general, an agency's legal basis for withholding is "reasonable" if pertinent authority exists to support the claimed exemption.[405] Even in the absence of supporting authority, withholding may also be "reasonable" where no precedent directly contradicts the agency's position.[406]

In an illustrative example, the D.C. Circuit has upheld a district court's finding of reasonableness in a case in which when there was "no clear precedent on the issue,"[407] even though the district court's decision in favor of the agency's withholding was reversed unanimously by the court of appeals, which decision, in turn, was affirmed by a near-unanimous decision of the

---

[403](...continued)
as a matter of law"); see also Wheeler, 37 F. Supp. 2d at 413 (finding that reasons for government's refusal to disclose records "may even be dispositive"). But see Williams, 17 F. Supp. 2d at 8 (stating that "'courts must be careful not to give any particular factor dispositive weight'" (quoting Nationwide Bldg., 559 F.2d at 714)).

[404] Tax Analysts, 965 F.2d at 1097 (quoting Cuneo, 553 F.2d at 1365-66)); Education/Instruccion, Inc. v. HUD, 649 F.2d 4, 8 (1st Cir. 1981) (government's withholding must "have 'a colorable basis in law' and not appear designed 'merely to avoid embarrassment or to frustrate the requester'" (quoting S. Rep. No. 93-854, at 19)); LaSalle Extension Univ. v. FTC, 627 F.2d 481, 484-86 (D.C. Cir. 1980); Fenster, 617 F.2d at 744; Ellis, 941 F. Supp. at 1080 (government need show only "reasonable or colorable basis for the withholding" and that it has not engaged in recalcitrant or obdurate behavior); Solone, 830 F. Supp. at 1143 (government acted reasonably when agency had "at least a colorable basis in law for its decision to withhold" and there are no allegations of harassment of requester or avoidance of embarrassment by agency).

[405] See Adams, 673 F. Supp. at 1259-60; see also American Commercial Barge Lines, 758 F.2d at 1112-14; Republic of New Afrika, 645 F. Supp. at 122. But see United Ass'n of Journeymen & Apprentices, Local 598 v. Department of the Army, 841 F.2d 1459, 1462-64 (9th Cir. 1988) (withholding held unreasonable where agency relied on one case that was "clearly distinguishable" and where "strong contrary authority [was] cited by the [plaintiff]"); Northwest Coalition, 965 F. Supp. at 64 (finding that EPA decision "to rely solely on manufacturers' claims of confidentiality, rather than conduct more extensive questioning of the manufacturers' claims or make its own inquiry . . . was essentially a decision not to commit resources to questioning claims of confidentiality but instead to confront issues as they arise in litigation--and to pay attorneys' fees if EPA loses").

[406] See Frydman, 852 F. Supp. at 1504 ("Although the government did not offer case authority to support its position regarding the [records], we believe the government's position had a colorable basis. There is little, if any, case authority which directly holds contrary to the government's position.").

[407] Tax Analysts, 965 F.2d at 1096-97.

## LITIGATION CONSIDERATIONS

Supreme Court.[408] Likewise, the mere fact that an agency foregoes an appeal on the merits of a case and complies with a district court disclosure order does not foreclose it from asserting the reasonableness of its original position in opposing a subsequent fee claim.[409] When the delay in releasing records, rather than the agency's substantive claim of exemption, is challenged, that delay does not favor a fee award so long as the agency has not engaged in "obdurate behavior or bad faith."[410]

Typically, FOIA plaintiffs most often seek attorney fees at the conclusion of a case. Even when the underlying action has been decided, a petition for attorney fees "survive[s] independently under the court's equitable jurisdiction."[411] The fact that an attorney fees petition is pending, moreover, does not preclude appellate review of the district court's decision on the merits.[412]

---

[408] Tax Analysts v. Department of Justice, 492 U.S. 136 (1989).

[409] See Cotton, 63 F.3d at 1119.

[410] Ellis, 941 F. Supp. at 1080 (noting that agency was "in frequent contact with plaintiffs' counsel" and that "[d]ue to the scope of plaintiffs' request, some delay was inherent"); see Horsehead Indus. 999 F. Supp. at 66 (finding narrow reading of request not "bad faith"); Republic of New Afrika, 645 F. Supp. at 122; Smith v. United States, No. 95-1950, 1996 WL 696452, at *7 (E.D. La. Dec. 4, 1996) (finding that "[t]he government did not act with due diligence, and has offered no reason to find that the delay was 'unavoidable[,]'" but holding in favor of government on this factor as "[t]he evidence in this case is that the Coast Guard's noncompliance was due to administrative ineptitude rather than any unwillingness to comply with [plaintiff's] FOIA request"), aff'd, No. 97-30184 (5th Cir. Sept. 12, 1997); Frye, No. 90-3041, 1992 WL 237370, at *3 (explaining that although agency failed to adequately explain plaintiff's more than two-year wait for final response (such delay previously having been found "unreasonable" by court), agency's voluntary disclosure of documents two days before Vaughn Index deadline did not warrant finding of "obdurate" behavior absent affirmative evidence of bad faith). But see Miller v. United States Dep't of State, 779 F.2d 1378, 1390 (8th Cir. 1985) ("While these reasons [for delay] are plausible, and we do not find them to be evidence of bad faith . . . they are practical explanations, not reasonable legal bases."); Claudio v. Social Sec. Admin., No. H-98-1911, slip op. at 20 (S.D. Tex. May 24, 2000) (despite finding all four factors unmet, nevertheless awarding fees because of "the Government's action in not delivering the majority of the documents until after suit was filed and in failing to provide a Vaughn Index until after ordered to do so by the Court") (motion for reconsideration pending); United Merchants & Mfrs. v. Meese, No. 87-3367, slip op. at 3 (D.D.C. Aug. 10, 1988) (declaring it unnecessary for plaintiff to show "that defendant was obdurate in order to prevail" where there was "no reasonable basis for defendant to have failed to process plaintiff's [FOIA request] for nearly a year").

[411] Carter v. VA, 780 F.2d 1479, 1481 (9th Cir. 1986); see Anderson, 3 F.3d at 1385 ("[T]he fee issue is ancillary to the merits of the controversy.").

[412] See McDonnell v. United States, 4 F.3d 1227, 1236 (3d Cir. 1993) ("Even if a motion for attorney's fees is still pending in the district court, that motion
(continued...)

## LITIGATION CONSIDERATIONS

Some FOIA plaintiffs, however, have sought "interim" attorney fees before the conclusion of a case, but this relief has been termed "inefficient"[413] and "piecemeal."[414] Although it is clearer at the end of a FOIA case whether a plaintiff has "substantially prevailed," sometimes a plaintiff can point to a threshold determination concerning eligibility to receive records that sufficiently supports eligibility to an interim award.[415] Of course, a plaintiff still must prove entitlement to an interim award.[416] If interim fees are approved, payment of the fees need not await final judgment in the action.[417] If an agency wishes to appeal an interim award, however, it must wait for a final court decision on the underlying merits of the case.[418]

If a court decides to make a fee award--either interim or otherwise--its next task is to determine an appropriate fee amount, based upon attorney time shown to have been reasonably expended. Fee claims should be supported by well-documented, contemporaneous billing records;[419] while some

---

[412](...continued) does not constitute a bar to our exercise of jurisdiction under § 1291." (citing Budinich v. Becton Dickinson & Co., 486 U.S. 196, 198-202 (1988))).

[413] Biberman v. FBI, 496 F. Supp. 263, 265 (S.D.N.Y. 1980) (noting "inefficiency" of interim fee award). See generally Allen v. FBI, 716 F. Supp. 667, 669-72 (D.D.C. 1989) (recognizing that although court may order payment of interim fees, it should be done only "in limited circumstances").

[414] Hydron Lab., Inc. v. EPA, 560 F. Supp. 718, 722 (D.R.I. 1983) (refusing to deal "piecemeal" with questions concerning entitlement to attorney fees).

[415] See Washington Post v. DOD, 789 F. Supp. 423, 424-26 (D.D.C. 1992) (awarding interim fees for special master whose work established plaintiff's right to receive certain records); Allen v. DOD, 713 F. Supp. 7, 12-13 (D.D.C. 1989) (awarding interim fees, but only "for work leading toward the threshold release of non-exempt documents").

[416] See National Ass'n of Criminal Defense Lawyers v. United States Dep't of Justice, No. 97-372, slip op. at 2 (D.D.C. June 26, 1998) (awarding interim fees based on court's conclusion that, inter alia, even brief litigation had "imposed concrete hardship on Plaintiff's counsel"), interlocutory appeal dismissed for lack of juris., 182 F.3d 981 (D.C. Cir. 1999); Allen v. FBI, 716 F. Supp. at 671 (suggesting that interim fee awards should be made only in unusual case of protracted litigation and financial hardship); Powell v. United States Dep't of Justice, 569 F. Supp. 1192, 1200 (N.D. Cal. 1983) (listing four factors to be considered in court's discretion for award of interim fees).

[417] See Rosenfeld v. United States, 859 F.2d 717, 727 (9th Cir. 1988); Washington Post, 789 F. Supp. at 425.

[418] See National Ass'n of Criminal Defense Lawyers v. United States Dep't of Justice, 182 F.3d 981, 986 (D.C. Cir. 1999) (concluding that prior to conclusion of case in district court, appellate court has no jurisdiction to review attorney fees award).

[419] See Blazy, 194 F.3d at 92 (rejecting otherwise valid claim for attorney
(continued...)

## LITIGATION CONSIDERATIONS

courts will consider reconstructed records, the amount ultimately awarded may be reduced accordingly.[420]

The starting point in setting a fee award is to multiply the number of hours reasonably expended by a reasonable hourly rate--a calculation that yields the "lodestar."[421] Not all hours expended in litigating a case will be deemed to have been "reasonably" expended. For example, courts have directed attorneys to subtract hours spent litigating claims upon which the party seeking the fee ultimately did not prevail.[422] In such cases, a distinction has been made between a loss on a legal theory where "the issue was all part and parcel of one [ultimately successful] matter,"[423] and a rejected claim that is "truly fractionable" from the successful claim.[424] In some cases when the

---

[419](...continued) fees "for want of substantiation"); Ajluni v. FBI, No. 94-CV-325, 1997 WL 196047, at *2 (N.D.N.Y. Apr. 14, 1997) ("Moreover, '[t]he rule in this Circuit prohibits the submission of reconstructed records, where no contemporaneous records have been kept.'" (quoting Lenihan v. City of New York, 640 F. Supp. 822, 824 (S.D.N.Y. 1986))). See generally National Ass'n of Concerned Veterans v. Secretary of Defense, 675 F.2d 1319, 1327 (D.C. Cir. 1982) (per curiam) ("Attorneys who anticipate making a fee application must maintain contemporaneous, complete and standardized time records which accurately reflect the work done by each attorney.").

[420] See Anderson, 80 F.3d at 1506 ("Reconstructed records generally do not accurately reflect the actual time spent; and we have directed district courts to scrutinize such records and adjust the hours if appropriate.").

[421] See Hensley v. Eckerhart, 461 U.S. 424, 433 (1982) (civil rights case); Copeland v. Marshall, 641 F.2d 880, 891 (D.C. Cir. 1980) (en banc) (Title VII case). See generally Lindy Bros. Builders, Inc. v. American Radiator & Standard Sanitary Corp., 487 F.2d 161, 168 (3d Cir. 1973) (describing the product of a reasonable hourly rate and hours actually worked as "the lodestar of the court's fee determination").

[422] See, e.g., Hensley, 461 U.S. at 434-40; Anderson, 80 F.3d at 1506; Copeland, 641 F.2d at 891-92; Ajluni, 947 F. Supp. at 611 (limiting fees to those incurred up to point at which "the last of the additional documents were released"); McDonnell, 870 F. Supp. at 589.

[423] Copeland, 641 F.2d at 892 n.18; see National Ass'n of Concerned Veterans, 675 F.2d at 1327 n.13; National Ass'n of Atomic Veterans v. Director, Defense Nuclear Agency, No. 81-2662, slip op. at 7 (D.D.C. July 15, 1987) (deciding that because plaintiff "clearly prevailed" on its only claim for relief, it is "entitled to recover fees for time expended on the few motions upon which it did not prevail").

[424] See, e.g., Weisberg v. Webster, No. 78-322, slip op. at 3 (D.D.C. June 13, 1985); Newport Aeronautical Sales v. Department of the Navy, No. 84-0120, slip op. at 10-11 (D.D.C. Apr. 17, 1985); see also Weisberg, 745 F.2d at 1499 (declining to award fees for issues on which plaintiff did "not ultimately prevail" and for "non-productive time"); Steenland v. CIA, 555 F. Supp. 907, 911 (W.D.N.Y. 1983) (declaring that award for work performed after release of

(continued...)

## LITIGATION CONSIDERATIONS

plaintiff's numerous claims are so intertwined that the court can discern "no principled basis for eliminating specific hours from the fee award," courts have employed a "general reduction method," allowing only a percentage of fees commensurate with the estimated degree to which that plaintiff had prevailed.[425]

Additionally, prevailing plaintiffs' counsel are obligated to exercise sound billing judgment. This means that "[c]ounsel for the prevailing party should make a good-faith effort to exclude from a fee request hours that are excessive, redundant, or otherwise unnecessary."[426] Furthermore, the D.C. Circuit has admonished that "[s]ome expense items, though perhaps not unreasonable between a first class law firm and a solvent client, are not supported by indicia of reasonableness sufficient to allow us justly to tax the same against the United States."[427] Although "contests over fees should not be per-

---

[424](...continued)
records, where all claims of exemptions subsequently upheld, "would assess a penalty against defendants which is clearly unwarranted"); Agee v. CIA, No. 79-2788, slip op. at 1 (D.D.C. Nov. 3, 1982) ("[P]laintiff is not entitled to fees covering work where he did not substantially prevail."); Dubin v. Department of the Treasury, 555 F. Supp. 408, 413 (N.D. Ga. 1981) (holding that fees awarded "should not include fees for plaintiffs' counsel for their efforts after the release of documents by the Government . . . since they failed to prevail on their claims at trial"), aff'd, 697 F.2d 1093 (11th Cir. 1983) (unpublished table decision); cf. Anderson, 80 F.3d at 1504 (affirming district court's denial of fees for portion of lawsuit during which plaintiff's primary motivation was her personal interest, while allowing fees for remainder of suit when public interest was paramount motivation). But see Badhwar v. United States Dep't of the Air Force, No. 84-154, slip op. at 3 (D.D.C. Dec. 11, 1986) ("[D]efendants' attempts to decrease [fees] on the grounds that the plaintiffs did not prevail as to all issues raised . . . are not persuasive. [The FOIA] requires only that the plaintiff should have 'substantially prevailed.'").

[425] See, e.g., Kempker-Cloyd v. United States Dep't of Justice, No. 5:97-253, slip op. at 14 (W.D. Mich. Apr. 2, 1999) (magistrate's recommendation) (dividing claimed amount of attorney fees in half because "[s]egregating litigation efforts spent on intertwined issues . . . is impracticable, if not impossible"), adopted (W.D. Mich. Aug. 17, 1999); McDonnell, 870 F. Supp. at 589 (reducing plaintiff's requested award by 60% because the amount of relief denied was greater than that awarded").

[426] Hensley, 461 U.S. at 434, quoted in Assembly of Cal., No. Civ-S-91-990, 1993 WL 188328, at *11 (E.D. Cal. May 28, 1993); see City of Detroit, No. 93-CV-72310, slip op. at 3-4 (E.D. Mich. Mar. 24, 1995) (reducing requested fees by 60% because city employed eight attorneys when two would have sufficed, utilized two principal litigators when one would have sufficed, and generated nearly half of all fees sought in connection with its fees petition).

[427] In re North (Schultz Fee Application), 8 F.3d 847, 852 (D.C. Cir. 1993) (non-FOIA case).

## LITIGATION CONSIDERATIONS

mitted to evolve into exhaustive trial-type proceedings,"[428] when attorney fees are awarded, the hours expended by counsel for the plaintiff pursuing the fee award also are ordinarily compensable.[429]

To determine a reasonable hourly rate--which has been defined "as that prevailing in the community for similar work"[430]--courts will accept affidavits from local attorneys to support hourly rate claims, but they should be couched in terms of specific market rates for particular types of litigation and they must be well documented.[431] The pertinent legal market, for purposes of calculating legal fees, is the jurisdiction in which the district court sits.[432] Within the D.C. Circuit, the rate standard most often employed is an updated version of the "Laffey Matrix," based on the eponymous court case.[433]

The lodestar calculation is strongly presumed to yield the reasonable fee. Indeed, the Supreme Court has clarified that such enhancements are not available under statutes authorizing an award of attorney fees to a "prevailing or substantially prevailing party," such as the FOIA.[434] Moreover, FOIA fee awards may not be increased to provide plaintiffs' attorneys "interest" to com-

---

[428] National Ass'n of Concerned Veterans, 675 F.2d at 1324.

[429] See Copeland, 641 F.2d at 896; see also National Veterans Legal Servs. Program v. VA, No. 96-1740, slip op. at 4 (D.D.C. Apr. 13, 1999) (approving award of "fees-on-fees"); Assembly of Cal., No. S91-990, 1993 WL 188328, at *16 (E.D. Cal. May 28, 1993); Katz v. Webster, No. 82-1092, slip op. at 4-5 (S.D.N.Y. Feb. 1, 1990).

[430] National Ass'n of Concerned Veterans, 675 F.2d at 1323.

[431] See id.; cf. Confederated Tribes v. Babbitt, No. 96-197, slip op at 3 (D. Or. Sept. 30, 1997) (rejecting area market rate because attorneys in fact contracted for substantially lower rate with client).

[432] Northwest Coalition, 965 F. Supp. at 65.

[433] Laffey v. Northwest Airlines, 746 F.2d 4, 24-25 (D.C. Cir. 1984), overruled in part on other grounds by Save Our Cumberland Mountains, Inc. v. Hodel, 857 F.2d 1516, 1524 (D.C. Cir. 1988) (en banc); see, e.g., Covington v. District of Columbia, 57 F.3d 1101, 1109 (D.C. Cir. 1995) (noting circuit court approval of use of Laffey Matrix) (non-FOIA cases).

[434] City of Burlington v. Dague, 505 U.S. 557, 562 (prohibiting contingency enhancement in environmental fee-shifting statutes and noting that case law "construing what is a 'reasonable' fee applies uniformly to all [federal fee-shifting statutes]"); see Ray v. United States Dep't of Justice, 856 F. Supp. 1576, 1583 (S.D. Fla. 1994) (noting that "Dague calls into question the applicability of an enhancement for contingency cases," but declining to decide whether decision also forbids fee enhancement for "exceptional" cases by holding that this FOIA case result was not exceptional), aff'd, 87 F.3d 1250 (11th Cir. 1996); Assembly of Cal., 1993 WL 188328, at *14 (refusing to approve upward adjustment in lodestar).

## LITIGATION CONSIDERATIONS

pensate for delays in their receipt of payments for legal services rendered.[435] Also, if a case has been in litigation for a prolonged period of time, "[a]ttorneys' fees awarded against the United States must be based on the prevailing market rates at the time the services were performed, rather than rates current at the time of the award."[436]

Lastly, in ruling on a petition for attorney fees and costs, a district court should provide a concise but clear explanation of its reasons for any award encompassing eligibility, entitlement, and the rationale for its calculations.[437] Upon appeal, such rulings are reviewed for abuse of discretion.[438]

### Sanctions

The FOIA does not authorize any award of monetary damages to a requester,[439] either for an agency's unjustified refusal to release requested records,[440] or for allegedly improper disclosure of information.[441] The Act does,

---

[435] See Library of Congress v. Shaw, 478 U.S. 310, 314 (1986) ("In the absence of express congressional consent to the award of interest separate from a general waiver of immunity to suit, the United States is immune from an interest award."); Weisberg, 848 F.2d at 1272.

[436] Northwest Coalition, 965 F. Supp. at 66 ("Contrary to plaintiffs' assertions, it is not proper to adjust historic rates to take inflation into account." (citing Library of Congress, 478 U.S. at 322)).

[437] Hensley, 461 U.S. at 437; Union of Concerned Scientists, 824 F.2d at 1228.

[438] See Weisberg, 848 F.2d at 1272 (citing Copeland, 641 F.2d at 901).

[439] See Butler v. Nelson, No. 96-48, 1997 WL 580331, at *3 (D. Mont. May 16, 1997) ("Section 552 of Title 5 includes a comprehensive and defined list of remedies available; the conspicuous absence of a provision allowing an action for money damages convinces the court that Plaintiff may not seek damages under the FOIA."); Stabasefski v. United States, 919 F. Supp. 1570, 1573 (M.D. Ga. 1996) ("[T]he remedial measures available under the Freedom of Information Act are limited to injunctive relief, costs, and attorney's fees." (citing 5 U.S.C. § 552(a)(4)(B), (E) (1994))). See generally O'Meara v. IRS, No. 97-3383, 1998 WL 123984, at *1 (7th Cir. Mar. 12, 1998) ("FOIA . . . does not authorize sanctions as a remedy for failure to disclose documents. Instead, courts are limited to ordering the production of agency records, and assessing reasonable attorney fees and litigation costs against the United States.").

[440] See Schwartz v. United States Patent & Trademark Office, No. 95-5349, 1996 U.S. App. LEXIS 4609, at **2-3 (D.C. Cir. Feb. 22, 1996); Thompson v. Walbran, 990 F.2d 403, 405 (8th Cir. 1993); Wren v. Harris, 675 F.2d 1144, 1147 (10th Cir. 1982); Gilbert v. Social Sec. Admin., No. 93-C-1055, slip op. at 10 (E.D. Wis. Dec. 28, 1994); Bologna v. Department of the Treasury, No. 93-1495, slip op. at 8-9 (D.N.J. Mar. 29, 1994); Duffy v. United States, No. 87-C-10826, slip op. at 31-32 (N.D. Ill. May 29, 1991); Daniels v. St. Louis Veterans Admin. Reg'l Office, 561 F. Supp. 250, 251 (E.D. Mo. 1983); Diamond v. FBI, 532 F. Supp. 216, 233 (S.D.N.Y. 1981), aff'd on other grounds, 707 F.2d 75 (2d

(continued...)

## LITIGATION CONSIDERATIONS

however, provide that, in certain narrowly prescribed circumstances, agency employees who arbitrarily or capriciously withhold information may be subject to disciplinary action. Specifically, subsection (a)(4)(F) of the FOIA, as amended, provides:

> Whenever the court orders the production of any agency records improperly withheld from the complainant and assesses against the United States reasonable attorney fees and other litigation costs, and the court additionally issues a written finding that the circumstances surrounding the withholding raise questions whether agency personnel acted arbitrarily or capriciously with respect to the withholding, the [United States Office of] Special Counsel shall promptly initiate a proceeding to determine whether disciplinary action is warranted against the officer or employee who was primarily responsible for the withholding.[442]

Thus, there are three distinct jurisdictional prerequisites to the initiation of a Special Counsel investigation under the FOIA: (1) the court must order the production of agency records found to be improperly withheld; (2) it must award attorney fees and litigation costs; and (3) it must issue a specific "written finding" of suspected arbitrary or capricious conduct.[443] In one case,

---

[440](...continued)
Cir. 1983).

[441] See Crumpton v. Stone, 59 F.3d 1400, 1406 (D.C. Cir. 1995) (holding that agency decision to disclose information under FOIA constitutes "a discretionary function exempt from suit under the [Federal Tort Claims Act]"); Sterling v. United States, 798 F. Supp. 47, 48 & n.2 (D.D.C. 1992) (ruling that neither FOIA nor Administrative Procedure Act, 5 U.S.C. §§ 701-06 (1994 & Supp. IV 1998), authorizes award of monetary damages for alleged improper disclosure), summary affirmance granted, No. 93-5264 (D.C. Cir. Mar. 11, 1994).

[442] 5 U.S.C. § 552(a)(4)(F) (1994 & Supp. IV 1998); see 5 U.S.C. § 1211 (establishing "Office of Special Counsel" independent of Merit Systems Protection Board); see also President's Memorandum for Heads of Departments and Agencies regarding the Freedom of Information Act, 29 Weekly Comp. Pres. Doc. 1999 (Oct. 4, 1993), reprinted in FOIA Update, Vol. XIV, No. 3, at 3 (emphasizing that "unnecessary bureaucratic hurdles [have] no place in [FOIA's] implementation").

[443] See, e.g., Kempker-Cloyd v. United States Dep't of Justice, No. 5:97-253, 1999 U.S. Dist. LEXIS 4813, at *23 (W.D. Mich. Mar. 12, 1999) (finding that even though agency's action was "incomplete and untimely" and "not in good faith," there was no evidence of arbitrary or capricious behavior), motion for fees & costs granted, slip op. at 14 (W.D. Mich. Apr. 2, 1999) (magistrate's recommendations), adopted (W.D. Mich. Aug. 17, 1999); Judicial Watch, Inc. v. United States Dep't of Commerce, 34 F. Supp. 2d 28, 43 n.9 (D.D.C.) (finding "merit in the view that the district court should be more willing to refer disciplinary matters to the Office of Special Counsel when agencies act arbitrarily and capriciously," but declining to consider appropriateness of referral until

(continued...)

## LITIGATION CONSIDERATIONS

Miller v. Webster, the court found that the circumstances surrounding the withholding of small portions of three documents did "suggest that the agency decision was arbitrary and capricious."[444] Despite having ordered disclosure of this information and awarding attorney fees, the court refused to refer the "alleged violation" to the Merit Systems Protection Board, citing the common law maxim of "de minimis non curat lex" (the law takes no notice of trifling matters).[445] Nevertheless, agency FOIA personnel should not overlook the importance and viability of this sanction provision.[446]

Additionally, a provision of the Whistleblower Protection Act of 1989 authorizes the Office of Special Counsel to investigate certain allegations concerning arbitrary or capricious withholding of information requested under the FOIA.[447] A significant distinction between this provision and subsection (a)(4)(F) of the FOIA is that the former does not require a judicial finding--indeed, no lawsuit need even be filed to invoke this other sanction procedure.[448]

Further, as in all civil cases, courts may exercise their discretion to im-

---

[443](...continued)
conclusion of litigation), further discovery ordered, 34 F. Supp. 2d 47 (D.D.C. 1998), partial summary judgment granted, 83 F. Supp. 2d 105 (D.D.C. 1999); Gabel v. IRS, No. 97-1653, 1998 U.S. Dist. LEXIS 12467, at **17-18 (N.D. Cal. June 25, 1998) (declining to issue "sanctions" finding when all requested records had been produced and thus no records improperly were withheld); Emery v. Laise, 421 F. Supp. 91, 93 (D.D.C. 1976) (same), aff'd sub nom. Emery v. Reinhardt, 566 F.2d 797 (D.C. Cir. 1977); see also Wilder v. IRS, 601 F. Supp. 241, 243 (M.D. Ala. 1984) (concluding that disclosure was delayed, but refusing to impose sanctions because all requested information was released); Idaho Wildlife Fed'n v. Forest Serv., 3 Gov't Disclosure Serv. (P-H) ¶ 83,271, at 84,058 (D.D.C. July 21, 1983) (finding sanctions inappropriate when agency records were not improperly withheld); Norwood v. FAA, No. 83-2315, slip op. at 20 (W.D. Tenn. Dec. 11, 1991) (finding that when court denies fees on ground that plaintiff is pro se, "the issuance of written findings pursuant to 5 U.S.C. § 552(a)(4)(F) would be inappropriate since both prerequisites have not been met"), aff'd in part & rev'd in part on other grounds, 993 F.2d 570 (6th Cir. 1993). But see Ray v. United States Dep't of Justice, 716 F. Supp. 1449, 1451-52 (S.D. Fla. 1989) ("court order" requirement held satisfied even though no record found to be improperly withheld).

[444] No. 77-C-3331, slip op. at 4 (N.D. Ill. Oct. 27, 1983), summary judgment granted (N.D. Ill. Feb. 29, 1984).

[445] Id. at 4.

[446] See FOIA Update, Vol. IV, No. 3, at 5.

[447] 5 U.S.C. § 1216(a)(3) (1994 & Supp. IV 1998).

[448] See H.R. Rep. No. 95-1717, at 137 (1978), reprinted in 1978 U.S.C.C.A.N. 2723, 2870 ("[T]his provision is not intended to require that an administrative or court decision be rendered concerning withholding of information before the Special Counsel may investigate allegations of such a prohibited practice.").

## LITIGATION CONSIDERATIONS

pose sanctions on FOIA litigants and government counsel who have violated court rules or shown disrespect for the judicial process.[449] One court has even referred an Assistant United States Attorney who handled a FOIA requester's criminal case to the Department of Justice's Office of Professional Responsibility following a finding that he prematurely "destroyed records responsive to [the] FOIA request while [the FOIA] litigation was pending."[450] In general, claims of "bad faith" actions by a government agency ordinarily are considered in administrative proceedings or in judicial decisions on whether to grant attorney fees.[451]

In determining whether to impose sanctions on plaintiffs, district courts

---

[449] See, e.g., Voinche v. CIA, No. 96-31270, slip op. at 2 (5th Cir. June 18, 1997) (cautioning plaintiff that "future frivolous appeals will invite the imposition of sanctions"); Jefferson v. Reno, No. 96-1284, slip op. at 11-12 (D.D.C. Mar. 29, 2000) (assessing $10,000 fine against agency for violating court order requiring that "destroyed" records be reconstructed and sent to both plaintiff and his attorney); Nash v. United States Dep't of Justice, 992 F. Supp. 447, 450 (D.D.C. 1998) (alternative holding) (dismissing suit as sanction for "continuing violation" of Rule 11 by plaintiff's counsel), summary affirmance granted, No. 98-5096 (D.C. Cir. July 20, 1998); Hill v. Department of the Air Force, No. 85-1485, slip op. at 7 (D.N.M. Sept. 4, 1987) (ordering documents processed at no further cost to plaintiff because of unreasonable delay in processing FOIA request), aff'd on other grounds, 844 F.2d 1407 (10th Cir. 1988); see also Van Bourg, Allen, Weinberg & Roger v. NLRB, 762 F.2d 831, 833 (9th Cir. 1985) (warning that sanctions will be imposed if plaintiff's counsel again "fails to inform us about material facts or procrastinates in obeying our orders"); Salman v. Secretary of the Treasury, No. CV-N-96-296, slip op. at 4-7 (D. Nev. Jan. 2, 1997) (ordering plaintiff to show cause why he should not be sanctioned under Rule 11 of Federal Rules of Civil Procedure, after having warned him against filing frivolous lawsuits); cf. Center for Nat'l Sec. Studies v. INS, No. 87-2068, slip op. at 2 (D.D.C. July 27, 1988) (ordering discovery against government for failure to comply with previous estimates of processing time and to explain discrepancies in time estimates).

[450] Jefferson, No. 96-1284, slip op. at 10 (D.D.C. Mar. 29, 2000) (taking action based upon facts learned through depositions).

[451] See, e.g., Schanen v. United States Dep't of Justice, 798 F.2d 348, 350 (9th Cir. 1986) (upholding exemption claims, but ordering government to pay plaintiff's attorney fees and costs due to government counsel's failure to competently defend claims); Jefferson, No. 96-1284, slip op. at 7 (D.D.C. Mar. 29, 2000) (assessing attorney fees and costs associated with reconstruction of records, following violation of court order that had required that records be reconstructed and sent to both plaintiff and his attorney); Ellis v. United States, 941 F. Supp. 1068, 1081 (D. Utah 1996); Oklahoma Publ'g Co. v. HUD, No. 87-1935-P, slip op. at 7 (W.D. Okla. June 17, 1988) (attorney fees assessed against government when counsel failed to comply with scheduling and disclosure orders). But see Jefferson, No. 96-1284, slip op. at 6, 11-12 (D.D.C. Mar. 29, 2000) (assessing, in addition to attorney fees and costs, $10,000 fine against agency for "purpose of deterring future violations" of such court orders; also threatening to impose sanctions if agency component were ever found to employ Exemption 7(A) in unsupported "blanket" fashion again).

## LITIGATION CONSIDERATIONS

ordinarily review the number and content of court filings and their effect on the courts as indicia of frivolousness or harassment.[452] For example, as a sanction under Rule 11 of the Federal Rules of Civil Procedure, a frequent FOIA requester who filed nearly fifty FOIA lawsuits over eight years and who routinely failed to oppose motions to dismiss, was ordered to show cause in any subsequent lawsuit why the principle of res judicata did not bar the intended suit.[453] As a general rule, however, "mere litigiousness alone does not support the issuance of an injunction" against filing further lawsuits.[454]

---

[452] See, e.g., Schwarz v. NSA, 119 S. Ct. 1109, 1109 (1999) (barring plaintiff from further filings, citing 35 frivolous petitions for certiorari); Schwarz v. CIA, No. 99-4016, 1999 WL 330237, at *1 (10th Cir. May 26, 1999) (admonishing plaintiff for "frivolousness" in light of "recurring pattern of similarly unsuccessful FOIA actions" and warning that "future frivolous filings . . . will result in sanctions"); Hoyos v. VA, No. 98-4178, slip op. at 4 (11th Cir. Feb. 1, 1999) (affirming district court's order barring plaintiff from future filings without court's permission, and noting that plaintiff "has frivolously sued just about everyone even remotely associated with the VA . . . and has burdened the district court with over 130 motions and notices, many of them duplicative"), cert. denied, 120 S. Ct. 582 (1999); Goldgar v. Office of Admin., 26 F.3d 32, 35-36 & n.3 (5th Cir. 1994) (warning plaintiff that subsequent filing or appeal of FOIA lawsuits without jurisdictional basis may result in assessment of costs, attorney's fees and proper sanctions or that plaintiff may be required to "obtain judicial preapproval of all future filings"); In re Powell, 851 F.2d 427, 431-34 (D.C. Cir. 1988) (per curiam) (explaining that pre-filing injunction may be appropriate where actions are so "frivolous and harassing" as to impede the "orderly and expeditious administration of justice"); Urban v. United Nations, 768 F.2d 1497, 1500 (D.C. Cir. 1985) (enjoining plaintiff from further filings to "protect the integrity of the courts and the orderly administration of justice"); In re Green, 669 F.2d 779, 786-87 (D.C. Cir. 1981) (barring plaintiff from submitting further filings without first certifying that claims are new and were never before raised, citing "the frustration experienced by the district court here as well as by other district courts deluged with . . . parade of pleadings, petitions, and other papers"); Peck v. Merletti, 64 F. Supp. 2d 599, 603 (E.D. Va. 1999) (noting plaintiff's "continued pursuit of nonexistent information . . . and the drain on valuable judicial and law enforcement resources," requiring that plaintiff's future filings comply with "Federal Rule of Civil Procedure 8 in regards to 'a short and plain statement of the claim'" (quoting Fed. R. Civ. P. 8(a)(2))); Wrenn v. Gallegos, No. 92-3358, slip op. at 1-2 (D.D.C. May 26, 1994) (barring plaintiff's future filings absent prior leave of court because plaintiff "has been adjudicated a vexatious litigant in several other forums and remains so in this court").

[453] See Crooker v. United States Marshals Serv., 641 F. Supp. 1141, 1143 (D.D.C. 1986); see also Crooker v. ATF, No. 96-01790, slip op. at 1-2 (D.D.C. Nov. 22, 1996) (dismissing complaint for failure to comply with requirements of Crooker v. United States Marshals Serv.).

[454] In re Powell, 851 F.2d at 434; cf. Zemansky v. EPA, 767 F.2d 569, 573-74 (9th Cir. 1995) (holding that district court exceeded its authority by requiring frequent requester, whose requests included "questions, commentary, narrative" and other extraneous material, to make future requests in "'separate doc-
(continued...)

## LITIGATION CONSIDERATIONS

Lastly, it should be noted that in the case of a litigant who is incarcerated, a special federal statute--the Prison Litigation Reform Act of 1995[455]--now provides that an action in forma pauperis cannot be filed by any such prisoner who, on three or more prior occasions while incarcerated, "brought an action or appeal in a court of the United States that was dismissed on the grounds that it is frivolous, malicious, or fails to state a claim upon which relief may be granted."[456] Although this statute applies only to suits that have been brought in federal court, it applies both to federal prisoners and to state prisoners alike.[457]

### Considerations on Appeal

An exceptionally large percentage of FOIA cases are decided by means of summary judgment.[458] Nevertheless, not all orders granting judgment to a party on a FOIA issue are immediately appealable.[459] The grant of an Open

---

[454] (...continued)
ument which is clearly defined as an FOIA request' and not 'intertwined with non-FOIA matters'"). But see Hunsberger v. United States Dep't of Energy, No. 96-0455, slip op. at 2 (D.D.C. Mar. 14, 1996) (enjoining plaintiff from filing any further civil actions without first obtaining leave of court because "[p]laintiff's numerous actions have demanded countless hours from this Court").

[455] 28 U.S.C. § 1915A (1994 & Supp. IV 1998).

[456] Id. § 1915A(b)(1); see, e.g., Wiggins v. Huff, No. C 98-1072, 1998 WL 226300, at *1 (N.D. Cal. Apr. 28, 1998) (denying request, from prisoner who had three or more prior dismissals, to proceed in forma pauperis and dismissing FOIA action without prejudice to refiling it with payment of filing fee).

[457] See Wiggins, 1998 W.L. 226300, at *11 (dismissing state prisoner's FOIA suit against federal agency); Willis v. FBI, No. 2:96-cv-276, slip op. at 1-2 (W.D. Mich. Oct. 21, 1996) (ordering warden of state prison to "place a hold on plaintiff's prisoner account" to provide for payment of filing fee).

[458] See, e.g., Public Employees for Envtl. Responsibility v. EPA, 978 F. Supp. 955, 959 (D. Colo. 1997) (explaining that "FOIA claims are typically resolved on summary judgment" (citing KTVY-TV v. United States, 919 F.2d 1465, 1468 (10th Cir. 1990))); Cappabianca v. United States Customs Serv., 847 F. Supp. 1558, 1561 (M.D. Fla. 1994) ("[O]nce documents in issue are properly identified, FOIA cases should be handled on motions for summary judgment." (citing Miscavige v. IRS, 2 F.3d 366, 368 (11th Cir. 1993))).

[459] See, e.g., Loomis v. United States Dep't of Energy, No. 99-6084, 1999 WL 1012451, at *1 (2d Cir. Oct. 14, 1999) (holding that partial grant of summary judgment is not final order); Church of Scientology Int'l v. IRS, 995 F.2d 916, 921 (9th Cir. 1993) (ruling that document is "not exempt," without accompanying disclosure order, held nonappealable); Ferguson v. FBI, 957 F.2d 1059, 1063-64 (2d Cir. 1992) (noting that while "partial disclosure orders in FOIA cases are appealable," fact that district court may have erred in deciding question of law does not vest jurisdiction in appellate court when no disclosure order has yet been entered and, consequently, no irreparable harm would

(continued...)

## LITIGATION CONSIDERATIONS

America stay of proceedings, for example, is not an appealable final decision.[460] Similarly, it has been held that an "interim" award of attorney fees is not appealable until the conclusion of the district court proceedings in the case.[461]

Once a case is properly on appeal, though, the government must obtain a stay of any trial court disclosure order if disclosure is required by a date certain or when the order provides for disclosure "forthwith." The government's motion for such a stay should be granted as a matter of course as denial would destroy the status quo and would cause irreparable harm to the government appellant by mooting the issue on appeal. In comparison, granting such a stay causes relatively minimal harm to the appellee.[462]

---

[459](...continued) result); Center for Nat'l Sec. Studies v. CIA, 711 F.2d 409, 413-14 (D.C. Cir. 1983) (finding no appellate jurisdiction to review court order granting summary judgment to defendant on only one of twelve counts in complaint because order did not affect "predominantly all" merits of case and plaintiffs did not establish that denial of relief under 28 U.S.C. § 1292(a)(1) (1994) would cause them irreparable injury); Hinton v. FBI, 844 F.2d 126, 129-33 (3d Cir. 1988) (declining to review district court order that a Vaughn Index be filed); In re Motion to Compel filed by Steele, 799 F.2d 461, 464-65 (9th Cir. 1986); cf. John Doe Corp. v. John Doe Agency, 850 F.2d 105, 107-08 (2d Cir. 1988) (finding district court order denying motion for disclosure of documents, preparation of Vaughn Index, and answers to interrogatories appealable and reversing on merits), rev'd on other grounds, 493 U.S. 146 (1989); Irons v. FBI, 811 F.2d 681, 683 (1st Cir. 1987) (allowing government to appeal motion for partial summary judgment for plaintiff, stating that appellate jurisdiction vests at time order requiring government to disclose records is issued).

[460] See Summers v. United States Dep't of Justice, 925 F.2d 450, 453 (D.C. Cir. 1991).

[461] See National Ass'n of Criminal Defense Lawyers v. United States Dep't of Justice, 182 F.3d 981, 984-85 (D.C. Cir. 1999) (finding that award of "interim" attorney fees is appealable neither as final judgment nor as collateral order).

[462] See, e.g., Assembly of Cal. v. United States Dep't of Commerce, No. S-91-990, slip op. at 3 (E.D. Cal. Aug. 20, 1991) (granting preliminary injunction and refusing to stay disclosure), stay denied, No. 91-16266 (9th Cir. Aug. 30, 1991), stay granted, 501 U.S. 1272 (1991); Rosenfeld v. United States Dep't of Justice, 501 U.S. 1227 (1991) (granting full stay pending appeal); John Doe Agency v. John Doe Corp., 488 U.S. 1306, 1307 (Marshall, Circuit Justice 1989) (granting stay based upon "balance of the equities"); see also Providence Journal Co. v. FBI, 595 F.2d 889, 890 (1st Cir. 1979); Antonelli v. FBI, 553 F. Supp. 19, 25 (N.D. Ill. 1982). But see Manos v. United States Dep't of the Air Force, No. 93-15672, slip op. at 2 (9th Cir. Apr. 28, 1993) (denying stay of district court disclosure order when government "failed to demonstrate . . . any possibility of success on the merits of its appeal," despite appellate court's recognition that such denial would render appeal moot); Powell v. United States Dep't of Justice, No. C-82-326, slip op. at 5 (N.D. Cal. June 14, 1985) (denying stay of decision ordering release of, inter alia, classified information,

(continued...)

## LITIGATION CONSIDERATIONS

The legal standard governing the scope of appellate review of FOIA decisions can best be described as "unsettled." The more recent trend in the law, led by the Courts of Appeals for the District of Columbia,[463] Second,[464] Sixth,[465] and Tenth Circuits,[466] is to regard cases in which the district court awarded

---

[462](...continued)
because of governmental delay and "obfuscation"), stay denied, No. 85-1918 (9th Cir. July 18, 1985), stay denied, No. A-84 (Rehnquist, Circuit Justice July 31, 1985) (undocketed order); see also Armstrong v. Executive Office of the President, No. 89-142, slip op. at 2-6 (D.D.C. Feb. 27, 1995) (denying stay of determination that National Security Council is an "agency" under FOIA). See generally FOIA Update, Vol. XII, No. 4, at 1-2.

[463] See Isley v. Executive Office for the United States Attorneys, No. 98-5098, 1999 WL 1021934, at *3 (D.C. Cir. 1999) ("This court reviews orders granting summary judgment de novo."); Summers v. Department of Justice, 140 F.3d 1077, 1079 (D.C. Cir. 1998) ("[I]t is well-understood law that '[w]e review orders granting summary judgment de novo.'" (quoting Gallant v. NLRB, 26 F.3d 168, 171 (D.C. Cir. 1994))); Kimberlin v. Department of Justice, 139 F.3d 944, 947 (D.C. Cir.) ("We review de novo the district court's grant of summary judgment, applying the same standards that governed the district court's decision."), cert. denied, 525 U.S. 89 (1998); see also Petroleum Info. Corp. v. United States Dep't of the Interior, 976 F.2d 1429, 1433 & n.3 (D.C. Cir. 1992) ("This circuit applies in FOIA cases the same standard of appellate review applicable generally to summary judgments." (explicitly contrasting Ninth Circuit's "clearly erroneous" standard and citing Washington Post Co. v. HHS, 865 F.2d 320, 325-26 & n.8 (D.C. Cir. 1989))).

[464] See Halpern v. FBI, 181 F.3d 279, 287 (2d Cir. 1999) (applying de novo standard in FOIA cases "to determine whether there are genuine issues of material fact requiring trial").

[465] See Sorrells v. United States, No. 97-5586, 1998 WL 58080, at *1 (6th Cir. Feb. 6, 1998) (deciding appeal "[u]pon de novo review"); Abraham & Rose, P.L.C. v. United States, 138 F.3d 1075, 1077 (6th Cir. 1997) (holding that grant of summary judgment is reviewed de novo on appeal); cf. Vonderheide v. IRS, No. 98-4277, 1999 WL 1000875, at *1 (6th Cir. 1999) ("Where an appeal concerns a factual attack on subject matter jurisdiction, this court reviews the factual findings of the district court for clear error and the legal conclusions de novo.").

[466] See Sheet Metal Workers Int'l Ass'n v. United States Air Force, 63 F.3d 994, 997 (10th Cir. 1995) ("[O]ur court reviews de novo any legal determinations made by the district court, once we have assured ourselves that the district court had 'had an adequate factual basis upon which to base its decision.'" (quoting Anderson v. HHS, 907 F.2d 936, 942 (10th Cir. 1990))); Hale v. United States Dep't of Justice, 973 F.2d 894, 897 (10th Cir. 1992) ("[W]e decline the government's invitation to adopt a clearly erroneous standard."), cert. granted, vacated & remanded on other grounds, 509 U.S. 918 (1993); KTVY-TV v. United States, 919 F.2d 1465, 1468 (10th Cir. 1990) (per curiam); Anderson, 907 F.2d at 942 ("[W]e must review de novo the district court's legal conclusions that the requested materials are covered by the relevant

(continued...)

## LITIGATION CONSIDERATIONS

summary judgment as involving exclusively questions of law and to apply a purely de novo review standard. This is entirely consistent with the nearly universal practice of adjudicating FOIA cases on the basis of summary judgment motions--which, in theory, can be utilized only in the absence of any material, factual disputes.[467]

By contrast, the Court of Appeals for the Third Circuit undertakes de novo review of any questions of law, but limits review of factual issues to the two-pronged deferential standard.[468] This is likewise the current position of the Courts of Appeals for the Fourth Circuit,[469] the Fifth Circuit,[470] and the Seventh Circuit.[471] While earlier decisions of the Court of Appeals for the

---

[466](...continued)
FOIA exemptions.").

[467] See New England Apple Council v. Donovan, 725 F.2d 139, 141 n.2 (1st Cir. 1984) ("Rule 56(c) bars the district court from resolving any disputed factual issues at the summary judgment stage. Assuming the absence of genuine issues of material fact, the issue on appeal from a grant of summary judgment concerns whether the movant was entitled to judgment as a matter of law." (citing 10 Charles A. Wright et al., Federal Practice and Procedure § 2716 (1983))).

[468] See, e.g., Davin v. United States Dep't of Justice, No. 98-3343, slip op. at 4-5 (3d Cir. Jan. 27, 1999); Sheet Metal Workers Int'l Ass'n v. VA, 135 F.3d 891, 896 & n.3 (3d Cir. 1998).

[469] See Ethyl Corp. v. EPA, 25 F.3d 1241, 1246 (4th Cir. 1994) ("Although any factual conclusions that place a document within a stated exemption of FOIA are reviewed under a clearly erroneous standard, 'the question of whether a document fits within one of FOIA's prescribed exemptions is one of law, upon which the district court is entitled to no deference.'" (quoting City of Va. Beach v. Department of Commerce, 995 F.2d 1247, 1252 n.12 (4th Cir. 1993))). But see also Bowers v. United States Dep't of Justice, 930 F.2d 350, 353 (4th Cir. 1991) (quoting two-pronged deferential standard but further specifying that findings of fact not entitled to "clearly erroneous" deference); Spannaus v. United States Dep't of Justice, 813 F.2d 1285, 1288 & n.4 (4th Cir. 1987) (same).

[470] Compare Calhoun v. Lyng, 864 F.2d 34, 36 (5th Cir. 1988) (two-pronged, deferential standard of review), with Avondale Indus. v. NLRB, 90 F.3d 955, 958 (5th Cir. 1996) (finding de novo review appropriate when parties' dispute focuses "'not upon the unique facts of [the] case, but upon categorical rules,'" a question of law to which district court is not entitled to deference (quoting Halloran v. VA, 874 F.2d 315, 320 (5th Cir. 1989))).

[471] See Solar Sources, Inc. v. United States, 142 F.3d 1033, 1038 (7th Cir. 1998) ("We review a district court's determination on summary judgment . . . by determining whether the district court had an adequate factual basis to make its decision and, if so, whether its decision was clearly erroneous."); Becker v. IRS, 34 F.3d 398, 402 (7th Cir. 1994) (explaining that whether withheld material fits within established standards of exemption reviewed is under two-pronged, deferential test); Wright v. OSHA, 822 F.2d 642, 645 (7th

(continued...)

## LITIGATION CONSIDERATIONS

Eleventh Circuit explicitly identified the two-pronged, deferential standard of review for factual issues,[472] in its most recent pronouncements on this issue, it, too, has adopted the de novo standard.[473]

The state of the law in the Courts of Appeals for the First and Ninth Circuits cannot be conclusively ascertained and perhaps best illustrates the confusion that has frequently surrounded this issue. In an early case, the First Circuit alluded to an "abuse of discretion" standard,[474] but subsequently eschewed any deference to the district court's decision.[475] Then, in two 1987 decisions issued less than five months apart, it appeared to articulate opposite standards.[476] Its most recent application of a de novo standard of review was limited to review of the district court's determination of whether the government supplied an adequate Vaughn Index.[477] This issue, however, logically falls within the category of whether the district court had an adequate factual basis for its determination, a question which is subject to de novo review even

---

[471] (...continued) Cir. 1987) (same). But see also Kaganove v. EPA, 856 F.2d 884, 886 (7th Cir. 1988) (concluding that questions of law are reviewed de novo).

[472] See, e.g., Miscavige v. IRS, 2 F.3d 366, 367 (11th Cir. 1993); Currie v. IRS, 704 F.2d 523, 528 (11th Cir. 1983); Chilivis v. SEC, 673 F.2d 1205, 1210 (11th Cir. 1982).

[473] See Catchpole v. Department of Transp., No. 97-8058, slip op. at 2 (11th Cir. Feb. 25, 1998) (applying de novo standard of review to FOIA case (citing Hale v. Tallapoosa County, 50 F.3d 1579, 1581 (11th Cir. 1995), and McGuire Oil Co. v. Mapco, Inc., 958 F.2d 1552, 1557 (11th Cir. 1992)) (non-FOIA cases)).

[474] Columbia Packing Co. v. USDA, 562 F.2d 495, 500 (1st Cir. 1977) ("We are also satisfied that the court did not abuse its discretion [in its balancing under Exemption 6].").

[475] See New England Apple Council v. Donovan, 725 F.2d 139, 141 n.2 (1st Cir. 1984) ("Appellees incorrectly state that this court may reverse the district court only if its conclusions are 'clearly erroneous.' In summary judgment there can be no review of factual issues, because Rule 56(c) bars the district court from resolving any disputed factual issues at the summary judgment stage.").

[476] Compare Aronson v. HUD, 822 F.2d 182, 188 (1st Cir. 1987) ("In reviewing a district court's grant of summary judgment, we apply the same standard as the district court."), with Irons, 811 F.2d at 684 ("where the conclusions of the trial court depend on its . . . choice of which competing inferences to draw from undisputed basic facts, appellate courts should defer to such fact-intensive findings, absent clear error"; however, questions of pure legal interpretation reviewed de novo).

[477] See Church of Scientology Int'l v. United States Dep't of Justice, 30 F.3d 224, 231 (1st Cir. 1994).

## LITIGATION CONSIDERATIONS

in those circuits employing the more deferential, two-pronged test.[478]

A similar situation prevails in the Ninth Circuit. In a line of earlier cases, the Ninth Circuit routinely employed a pure, two-pronged deferential standard.[479] More recently, however, this appellate court appears to have changed course and to have decided that whether an exemption has been properly applied involves a legal determination, one subject to de novo review.[480] In sum, the case law on this point simply cannot be reconciled among the various circuits, and conflicting decisions are not uncommon even within the same circuit.

In contrast, it is well settled that a trial court decision refusing to allow

---

[478] See, e.g., Davin v. United States Dep't of Justice, 60 F.3d 1043, 1048-49 (3d Cir. 1995) (explaining that review of adequacy of factual basis for district court's decision "is de novo and requires us to examine the affidavits below"); Wiener v. FBI, 943 F.2d 972, 978 (9th Cir. 1991) ("Whether the government's public affidavits constituted an adequate Vaughn index is a question of law reviewed de novo.").

[479] See Painting Indus. v. Air Force, 26 F.3d 1479, 1482 (9th Cir. 1994) ("We determine whether the district court had an adequate factual basis on which to make its decision and, if so, review for clear error the district court's finding that the documents were exempt."); Assembly of Cal. v. United States Dep't of Commerce, 968 F.2d 916, 919 (9th Cir. 1992) ("In reviewing a district court's judgment under the FOIA, we 'must determine whether the district judge had an adequate factual basis for his or her decision' and, if so, we 'must determine whether the decision below was clearly erroneous.'" (quoting Church of Scientology, 611 F.2d at 742)); National Wildlife Fed'n v. United States Forest Serv., 861 F.2d 1114, 1116 (9th Cir. 1988); Lewis v. IRS, 823 F.2d 275, 377-78 (9th Cir. 1987) ("First, we determine whether the district court had an adequate factual basis on which to make its decision. If the district court had such an adequate basis, we review the district court's finding that the documents were exempt for clear error.").

[480] See Klamath Water Users Protective Ass'n v. United States Dep't of the Interior, 189 F.3d 1034, 1036 (9th Cir. 1999) ("We first determine whether the district court had an adequate factual basis upon which to base its decision. If so, we review the district court's conclusion of an exemption's applicability de novo."), petition for cert. filed, No. 99-1871 (U.S. May 22, 2000); Frazee v. United States Forest Serv., 97 F.3d 367, 370 (9th Cir. 1996) (describing "special standard" of review of factual issues; if adequate factual basis supports district court's ruling, appellate court overturns only if ruling "is clearly erroneous"); Minier v. CIA, 88 F.3d 796, 800 (9th Cir. 1996) ("We must first determine whether the district court had an adequate factual basis upon which to base its decision. If so, the district's conclusion of an exemption's applicability is reviewed de novo."); Schiffer v. FBI, 78 F.3d 1405, 1409 (9th Cir. 1996) ("[W]hile we review the underlying facts supporting the district court's decision for clear error, we review de novo its conclusion [regarding the applicability of specific exemptions].").

## LITIGATION CONSIDERATIONS

discovery will be reversed only if the court abused its discretion.[481] Similarly, a "reverse" FOIA case--which is brought under the Administrative Procedure Act[482]--is reviewed only with reference to whether the agency acted in a manner that was "arbitrary, capricious, an abuse of discretion, or otherwise not in accordance with law," based upon the "whole [administrative] record."[483] (For a further discussion of this point, see "Reverse" FOIA, below.)

It is noteworthy that in a routine FOIA case where the merits and law of the case are so clear as to justify summary disposition, summary affirmance or reversal may be appropriate.[484] An otherwise routine case, however, could be remanded if the district court fails to make a segregability finding--even if the district court's decision is in all other respects entirely correct.[485] (For a further discussion of this point, see Litigation Considerations, "Reasonably Segregable" Requirements, above.) Other procedures are available for discharging the appellate court's functions in unusual procedural circumstances.[486]

Lastly, Rule 39(a) of the Federal Rules of Appellate Procedure is applied to award costs to the government when it is successful in a FOIA appeal; the

---

[481] See Anderson v. HHS, 80 F.3d 1500, 1507 (10th Cir. 1996) (holding that district court decision to deny further discovery on attorney fees issue "was not an abuse of discretion"); Church of Scientology v. IRS, 991 F.2d 560, 562 (9th Cir. 1993), vacated in part on other grounds & remanded, No. 91-15730 (9th Cir. July 14, 1994); Meeropol v. Meese, 790 F.2d 942, 960 (D.C. Cir. 1986); Northrop Corp. v. McDonnell Douglas Corp., 751 F.2d 395, 399 (D.C. Cir. 1988).

[482] 5 U.S.C. §§ 701-06 (1994).

[483] AT&T Info. Sys. v. GSA, 810 F.2d 1233, 1236 (D.C. Cir. 1987) (citing Chrysler Corp. v. Brown, 441 U.S. 281, 318 (1979)); accord Reliance Elec. Co. v. Consumer Prod. Safety Comm'n, 924 F.2d 274, 277 (D.C. Cir. 1991); cf. Campaign for Family Farms v. Glickman, 200 F.3d 1180, 1187 n.6 (8th Cir. 2000) (explaining that review ordinarily is based upon administrative record, but noting that de novo review could be appropriate if it is shown that agency's "factfinding procedures in ["reverse"] FOIA cases are inadequate").

[484] See, e.g., Taxpayers Watchdog, Inc. v. Stanley, 819 F.2d 294, 297 (D.C. Cir. 1987) (per curiam); Walker v. Washington, 627 F.2d 541, 545 (D.C. Cir. 1980) (per curiam).

[485] See Trans-Pac. Policing Agreement v. United States Customs Serv., 177 F.3d 1022, 1028 (D.C. Cir. 1999) ("[T]he District Court had an affirmative duty to consider the segregability issue sua sponte."); see also, e.g., Kimberlin, 139 F.3d at 949-50.

[486] See, e.g., Constangy, Brooks & Smith v. NLRB, 851 F.2d 839, 842 (6th Cir. 1988) (determining that it is inappropriate to vacate district court order, after fully complied with, when attorney fees issue pending; proper procedure is to dismiss appeal); Larson v. Executive Office for United States Attorneys, No. 85-6226, slip op. at 4 (D.C. Cir. Apr. 6, 1988) (concluding that when only issue on appeal is mooted, initial lower court order should be vacated without prejudice and case remanded).

## "REVERSE" FOIA

D.C. Circuit has held that this rule's presumption favoring such awards of costs is fully applicable in FOIA cases.[487]

## "REVERSE" FOIA

A "reverse" FOIA action is one in which the "submitter of information--usually a corporation or other business entity" that has supplied an agency with "data on its policies, operations or products--seeks to prevent the agency that collected the information from revealing it to a third party [usually] in response to the latter's FOIA request."[1] The agency's decision to release the information will ordinarily "be grounded either in its view that none of the FOIA exemptions applies, and thus that disclosure is mandatory, or in its belief that release is justified in the exercise of its discretion, even though the information falls within one or more of the statutory exemptions."[2] Typically, the submitter contends that the requested information falls within Exemption

---

[487] See Baez v. United States Dep't of Justice, 684 F.2d 999, 1005-07 (D.C. Cir. 1982) (en banc).

[1] CNA Fin. Corp. v. Donovan, 830 F.2d 1132, 1133 n.1 (D.C. Cir. 1987); see Cortez III Serv. Corp. v. NASA, 921 F. Supp. 8, 11 (D.D.C. 1996) (in reverse FOIA actions "courts have jurisdiction to hear complaints brought by parties claiming that an agency decision to release information adversely affects them"), appeal voluntarily dismissed, No. 96-5163 (D.C. Cir. July 3, 1996); see also Bartholdi Cable Co. v. FCC, 114 F.3d 274, 279 (D.C. Cir. 1997) (submitter challenged agency order requiring it to publicly disclose information, which was issued in context of federal licensing requirements and was not connected to any FOIA request); McDonnell Douglas Corp. v. Widnall, No. 94-0091, slip op. at 13 (D.D.C. Apr. 11, 1994) (submitter challenged agency release decision that was based upon disclosure obligation imposed by Federal Acquisition Regulation (FAR), rather than by FOIA request), and McDonnell Douglas Corp. v. Widnall, No. 92-2211, slip op. at 8 (D.D.C. Apr. 11, 1994) (same), cases consolidated on appeal & remanded for further development of the record, 57 F.3d 1162, 1167 (D.C. Cir. 1995).

[2] CNA, 830 F.2d at 1134 n.1; see Alexander & Alexander Servs. v. SEC, No. 92-1112, 1993 WL 439799, at **9, 11-12 (D.D.C. Oct. 19, 1993) (agency determined that Exemptions 4, 7(B), and 7(C) did not apply to certain requested information and "chose not to invoke" Exemption 5 for certain other requested information), appeal dismissed, No. 93-5398 (D.C. Cir. Jan. 4, 1996). See generally Attorney General's Memorandum for Heads of Departments and Agencies regarding the Freedom of Information Act (Oct. 4, 1993), reprinted in FOIA Update, Vol. XIV, No. 3, at 4-5 (establishing "foreseeable harm" standard governing use of exemptions); Attorney General's Follow-Up Memorandum for Heads of Departments and Agencies regarding the Freedom of Information Act (Sept. 3, 1999), reprinted in FOIA Update, Vol. XIX, No. 4, at 3-5 (reiterating importance of "foreseeable harm" standard to federal agencies in order to promote further discretionary disclosure in agency decisionmaking); FOIA Update, Vol. XV, No. 2, at 3.

# "REVERSE" FOIA

4 of the FOIA,[3] but submitters have also challenged the contemplated disclosure of information that they contended was exempt under other FOIA exemptions as well.[4] (See the further discussion of this under Exemption 6, Privacy Considerations, above.)

In a reverse FOIA suit "the party seeking to prevent a disclosure the government itself is otherwise willing to make" assumes the "burden of justifying nondisclosure."[5] Moreover, a challenge to an agency's disclosure decision is reviewed in light of the "basic policy" of the FOIA to "'open agency action to the light of public scrutiny'" and in accordance with the "narrow con-

---

[3] 5 U.S.C. § 552(b)(4) (1994 & Supp. IV 1998).

[4] See, e.g., Campaign for Family Farms v. Glickman, 200 F.3d 1180, 1182 (8th Cir. 2000) (agreeing with submitter that Exemption 6 should have been invoked and ordering permanent injunction requiring agency to withhold requested information); Bartholdi, 114 F.3d at 282 (denying submitter's request for injunction based on claim that agency's balancing of interests under Exemption 6 was "arbitrary or capricious" and holding that "even were [the submitter] correct that its submissions fall within Exemption 6, the [agency] is not required to withhold the information from public disclosure" because the "FOIA's exemptions simply permit, but do not require, an agency to withhold exempted information"); Na Iwi O Na Kupuna v. Dalton, 894 F. Supp. 1397, 1411-13 (D. Haw. 1995) (denying plaintiff's request to enjoin release of information that plaintiff contended was exempt pursuant to Exemptions 3 and 6); Church Universal & Triumphant, Inc. v. United States, No. 95-0163, slip op. at 2, 3 & n.3 (D.D.C. Feb. 8, 1995) (rejecting submitter's argument "that the documents in question are 'return information' that is protected from disclosure under" Exemption 3, but sua sponte asking agency "to consider whether any of the materials proposed for disclosure are protected by" Exemption 6); Alexander, 1993 WL 439799, at **10-12 (agreeing with submitter that Exemption 7(C) should have been invoked and ordering agency to withhold additional information; finding that submitter failed to "timely provide additional substantiation" to justify its claim that Exemption 7(B) applied; and finding that deliberative process privilege of Exemption 5 "belongs to the governmental agency to invoke or not," and noting "absence of any record support" that agency, "as a general matter, arbitrarily declined to invoke that privilege").

[5] Martin Marietta Corp. v. Dalton, 974 F. Supp. 37, 40 n.4 (D.D.C. 1997); accord Frazee v. United States Forest Serv., 97 F.3d 367, 371 (9th Cir. 1996) ("party seeking to withhold information under Exemption 4 has the burden of proving that the information is protected from disclosure"); Occidental Petroleum Corp. v. SEC, 873 F.2d 325, 342 (D.C. Cir. 1989) (explaining that "statutory policy favoring disclosure requires that the opponent of disclosure" bear burden of persuasion); TRIFID Corp. v. National Imagery & Mapping Agency, 10 F. Supp. 2d 1087, 1097 (E.D. Mo. 1998) (same); cf. Kansas Gas & Elec. Co. v. NRC, No. 87-2748, slip op. at 4 (D.D.C. July 2, 1993) (holding that submitter's "unsuccessful earlier attempt" to suppress disclosure in state court "effectively restrains it" from raising same arguments again in reverse FOIA action).

## "REVERSE" FOIA

struction" afforded to the FOIA's exemptions.[6] If the underlying FOIA request is subsequently withdrawn, the basis for the court's jurisdiction will dissipate and the case will be dismissed as moot.[7]

The landmark case in the reverse FOIA area is Chrysler Corp. v. Brown, in which the Supreme Court held that jurisdiction for a reverse FOIA action cannot be based on the FOIA itself "because Congress did not design the FOIA exemptions to be mandatory bars to disclosure" and, as a result, the FOIA "does not afford" a submitter "any right to enjoin agency disclosure."[8] Moreover, the Supreme Court held that jurisdiction cannot be based on the Trade Secrets Act[9] (a broadly worded criminal statute prohibiting the unauthorized disclosure of "practically any commercial or financial data collected by any federal employee from any source"[10]), because it is a criminal statute that does

---

[6] Martin Marietta, 974 F. Supp. at 40 (quoting United States Dep't of the Air Force v. Rose, 425 U.S. 352, 372 (1976)); see, e.g., TRIFID, 10 F. Supp. 2d at 1097 (reviewing submitter's claims in light of FOIA principle that "[i]nformation in the government's possession is presumptively disclosable unless it is clearly exempt"); Daisy Mfg. Co. v. Consumer Prod. Safety Comm'n, No. 96-5152, 1997 WL 578960, at *1 (W.D. Ark. Feb. 5, 1997) (examining submitter's claims in light of "the policy of the United States government to release records to the public except in the narrowest of exceptions" and observing that "[o]penness is a cherished aspect of our system of government"), aff'd, 133 F.3d 1081 (8th Cir. 1998).

[7] See McDonnell Douglas Corp. v. NASA, No. 95-5288, slip op. at 1 (D.C. Cir. Apr. 1, 1996) (ordering reverse FOIA case "dismissed as moot in light of the withdrawal of the [FOIA] request at issue"); General Dynamics Corp. v. Department of the Air Force, No. 92-5186, slip op. at 1 (D.C. Cir. Sept. 23, 1993) (same); Gulf Oil Corp. v. Brock, 778 F.2d 834, 838 (D.C. Cir. 1985) (same); cf. Sterling v. United States, 798 F. Supp. 47, 48 (D.D.C. 1992) (declaring that once record has been released, "there are no plausible factual grounds for a 'reverse FOIA' claim"), aff'd, No. 93-5264 (D.C. Cir. Mar. 11, 1994).

[8] 441 U.S. 281, 293-94 (1979); accord Campaign for Family Farms, 200 F.3d at 1185 ("agency has discretion to disclose information within a FOIA exemption, unless something independent of FOIA prohibits disclosure"); Bartholdi, 114 F.3d at 281 ("mere fact that information falls within a FOIA exemption does not of itself bar an agency from disclosing the information"); RSR Corp. v. Browner, 924 F. Supp. 504, 509 (S.D.N.Y. 1996) ("FOIA itself does not provide a cause of action to a party seeking to enjoin an agency's disclosure of information, even if the information requested falls within one of FOIA's exemptions"), aff'd, No. 96-6186, 1997 WL 134413 (2d Cir. Mar. 26, 1997), affirmance vacated without explanation, No. 96-6186 (2d Cir. Apr. 17, 1997); Kansas Gas, No. 87-2748, slip op. at 3 (D.D.C. July 2, 1993) ("party seeking to prevent disclosure . . . must rely on other sources of law, independent of FOIA, to justify enjoining disclosure").

[9] 18 U.S.C. § 1905 (1994 & Supp. IV 1998).

[10] CNA, 830 F.2d at 1140.

not afford a "private right of action."[11] Instead, the Court found that review of an agency's "decision to disclose" requested records[12] can be brought under the Administrative Procedure Act (APA).[13] Accordingly, reverse FOIA plaintiffs ordinarily argue that an agency's contemplated release would violate the Trade Secrets Act and thus would "not be in accordance with law" or would be "arbitrary and capricious" within the meaning of the APA.[14]

In Chrysler, the Supreme Court specifically did not address the "relative ambits" of Exemption 4 and the Trade Secrets Act, nor did it determine whether the Trade Secrets Act qualified as an Exemption 3[15] statute.[16] Almost a decade later, the Court of Appeals for the District of Columbia Circuit, after repeatedly skirting these difficult issues, "definitively" resolved them.[17] With regard to the Trade Secrets Act and Exemption 3, the D.C. Circuit held that the Trade Secrets Act does not qualify as an Exemption 3 statute under either of that exemption's subparts, particularly as it acts only as a prohibition

---

[11] Chrysler, 441 U.S. at 316-17.

[12] Id. at 318.

[13] 5 U.S.C. §§ 701-06 (1994); see, e.g., CC Distribs. v. Kinzinger, No. 94-1330, 1995 WL 405445, at *2 (D.D.C. June 28, 1995) ("neither FOIA nor the Trade Secrets Act provides a cause of action to a party who challenges an agency decision to release information . . . [but] a party may challenge the agency's decision" under APA); Comdisco, Inc. v. GSA, 864 F. Supp. 510, 513 (E.D. Va. 1994) ("sole recourse" of "party seeking to prevent an agency's disclosure of records under FOIA" is review under APA); Atlantis Submarines Haw., Inc. v. United States Coast Guard, No. 93-00986, slip op. at 5 (D. Haw. Jan. 28, 1994) (in reverse FOIA suit, "an agency's decision to disclose documents over the objection of the submitter is reviewable only under" APA) (denying motion for preliminary injunction), dismissed per stipulation (D. Haw. Apr. 11, 1994); Environmental Tech., Inc. v. EPA, 822 F. Supp. 1226, 1228 (E.D. Va. 1993).

[14] See, e.g., McDonnell Douglas Corp. v. Widnall, 57 F.3d 1162, 1164 (D.C. Cir. 1995) (Trade Secrets Act "can be relied upon in challenging agency action that violates its terms as 'contrary to law' within the meaning of" APA); Acumenics Research & Tech. v. Department of Justice, 843 F.2d 800, 804 (4th Cir. 1988); General Elec. Co. v. NRC, 750 F.2d 1394, 1398 (7th Cir. 1984); Cortez, 921 F. Supp. at 11; Lykes Bros. S.S. Co. v. Pena, No. 92-2780, slip op. at 5 (D.D.C. Sept. 2, 1993); General Dynamics Corp. v. United States Dep't of the Air Force, 822 F. Supp. 804, 806 (D.D.C. 1992), vacated as moot, No. 92-5186 (D.C. Cir. Sept. 23, 1993); McDonnell Douglas Corp. v. NASA, No. 91-3134, transcript at 6 (D.D.C. Jan. 24, 1992) (bench order), remanded, No. 92-5342 (D.C. Cir. Feb. 14, 1994); Raytheon Co. v. Department of the Navy, No. 89-2481, 1989 WL 550581, at *1 (D.D.C. Dec. 22, 1989).

[15] 5 U.S.C. § 552(b)(3).

[16] 441 U.S. at 319 n.49.

[17] CNA, 830 F.2d at 1134.

"REVERSE" FOIA

against "unauthorized" disclosures.[18] Indeed, because "agencies conceivably could control the frequency and scope of its application through regulations adopted on the strength of statutory withholding authorizations which do not themselves survive the rigors of Exemption 3," the D.C. Circuit found it inappropriate to classify the Trade Secrets Act as an Exemption 3 statute.[19] (For a further discussion of this point, see Exemption 3, Additional Considerations, above.)

In addition, the D.C. Circuit ruled that the scope of the Trade Secrets Act is not narrowly limited to that of its three predecessor statutes and that, instead, its scope is "at least co-extensive with that of Exemption 4."[20] Thus, information falling within the ambit of Exemption 4 would also fall within the scope of the Trade Secrets Act.[21] Accordingly, in the absence of a statute or properly promulgated regulation giving an agency authority to release the information--which would remove the Trade Secrets Act's disclosure prohibition[22]--a determination that requested material falls within Exemption 4 is

---

[18] Id. at 1141.

[19] Id. at 1139-40.

[20] Id. at 1151; accord Bartholdi, 114 F.3d at 281 (citing CNA and declaring: "[W]e have held that information falling within Exemption 4 of [the] FOIA also comes within the Trade Secrets Act."); Alexander, 1993 WL 439799, at *9; General Dynamics, 822 F. Supp. at 806. But see McDonnell Douglas, 57 F.3d at 1165 n.2 (D.C. Circuit panel noting in dicta that "we suppose it is possible that this statement [from CNA] is no longer accurate in light of [the court's] recently more expansive interpretation of the scope of Exemption 4" in Critical Mass Energy Project v. NRC, 975 F.2d 871, 879 (D.C. Cir. 1992) (en banc)).

[21] See, e.g., Bartholdi, 114 F.3d at 281 (when information is shown to be protected by Exemption 4, the government is generally "precluded from releasing" it due to provisions of Trade Secrets Act); McDonnell Douglas Corp. v. NASA, 895 F. Supp. 319, 322 n.4 (D.D.C. 1995) (because two provisions are "co-extensive," it is "unnecessary to perform a redundant analysis"), vacated as moot, No. 95-5288 (D.C. Cir. Apr. 1, 1996); Chemical Waste Management, Inc. v. O'Leary, No. 94-2230, 1995 WL 115894, at *6 n.1 ("analysis under either regime is identical"); Raytheon, 1989 WL 550581, at *1.

[22] See, e.g., RSR, 924 F. Supp. at 512 (Clean Water Act and "regulations promulgated under it permit disclosure" of submitter's "effluent data" and so agency's contemplated disclosure of such data is authorized by law); McDonnell Douglas, No. 94-0091, slip op. at 13 (D.D.C. Apr. 11, 1994) (FAR disclosure provision serves as legal authorization for agency to release exercised option prices and thus such prices are "not protected from disclosure by the Trade Secrets Act"); McDonnell Douglas, No. 92-2211, slip op. at 8 (D.D.C. Apr. 11, 1994) (same); FOIA Update, Vol. XVIII, No. 4, at 1 (describing post-award notice and debriefing provisions of FAR that expressly authorize public disclosure of unit prices); see also St. Mary's Hosp., Inc. v. Harris, 604 F.2d 407, 409-10 (5th Cir. 1979); Jackson v. First Fed. Sav., 709 F. Supp. 887, 890-94 (E.D. Ark. 1989); cf. McDonnell Douglas Corp. v. NASA, 180 F.3d 303, 306

(continued...)

# "REVERSE" FOIA

tantamount to a determination that the material cannot be released, because the Trade Secrets Act "prohibits" disclosure.[23] To the extent information falls outside the scope of Exemption 4, the D.C. Circuit found that there was no need to determine whether it nonetheless still fits within the outer boundaries of the Trade Secrets Act.[24] Such a ruling was unnecessary, the court found, because the FOIA itself would provide the necessary authorization to release any information not falling within one of its exemptions.[25]

## Standard of Review

In Chrysler Corp. v. Brown, the Supreme Court held that the Administrative Procedure Act's predominant scope and standard of judicial review--review on the administrative record according to an arbitrary and capricious standard--should "ordinarily" apply to reverse FOIA actions.[26] Indeed, the

---

[22](...continued)
(D.C. Cir. 1999) (repeatedly noting absence of agency reliance on "any independent legal authority to release" requested information as a basis for concluding that it was subject to Trade Secrets Act's disclosure prohibition). See generally Bartholdi, 114 F.3d at 281-82 (rejecting challenge to validity of disclosure regulation for failure to first exhaust issue before agency); South Hills Health Sys. v. Bowen, 864 F.2d 1084, 1093 (3d Cir. 1988) (rejecting challenge to validity of disclosure regulation as unripe).

[23] CNA, 830 F.2d at 1151-52; see, e.g., Pacific Architects & Eng'rs v. United States Dep't of State, 906 F.2d 1345, 1347 (9th Cir. 1990) (when release of requested information is barred by the Trade Secrets Act, agency "does not have discretion to release it"); Environmental Tech., 822 F. Supp. at 1228 (Trade Secrets Act "bars disclosure of information that falls within Exemption 4"); General Dynamics, 822 F. Supp. at 806 (Trade Secrets Act "is an independent prohibition on the disclosure of information within its scope"); see also FOIA Update, Vol. VI, No. 3, at 3 (discussing Trade Secrets Act bar to discretionary disclosure under Exemption 4).

[24] CNA, 830 F.2d at 1152 n.139.

[25] Id.; see Frazee, 97 F.3d at 373 (emphasizing that submitters gave "no reason as to why the Trade Secrets Act should, in their case, provide protection from disclosure broader than the protection provided by Exemption 4 of [the] FOIA" and finding that because requested document was "not protected from disclosure under Exemption 4," it also was "not exempt from disclosure under the Trade Secrets Act"); Alexander, 1993 WL 439799, at *9 (declaring that "if the documents are not deemed confidential pursuant to Exemption 4, they will not be protected under the Trade Secrets Act").

[26] 441 U.S. 281, 318 (1979); accord Campaign for Family Farms v. Glickman, 200 F.3d 1180, 1184 (8th Cir. 2000); Reliance Elec. Co. v. Consumer Prod. Safety Comm'n, 924 F.2d 274, 277 (D.C. Cir. 1991); General Dynamics Corp. v. United States Dep't of the Air Force, 822 F. Supp. 804, 806 (D.D.C. 1992), vacated as moot, No. 92-5186 (D.C. Cir. Sept. 23, 1993); International Computaprint Corp. v. United States Dep't of Commerce, No. 87-1848, slip op. at 12 (D.D.C. Aug. 16, 1988); Davis Corp. v. United States, No. 87-3365,
(continued...)

## "REVERSE" FOIA

Court of Appeals for the District of Columbia Circuit has strongly emphasized that judicial review in reverse FOIA cases should be based on the administrative record, with de novo review reserved for only those cases in which an agency's administrative procedures were "severely defective."[27]

The D.C. Circuit subsequently reaffirmed its position on the appropriate scope of judicial review in reverse FOIA cases, holding that the district court "behaved entirely correctly" when it rejected the argument advanced by the submitter--that it was entitled to de novo review because the agency's factfinding procedures were inadequate--and instead confined its review to an examination of the administrative record.[28] The Court of Appeals for the

---

[26](...continued)
1988 U.S. Dist. LEXIS 17611, at **5-6 (D.D.C. Jan. 19, 1988); see also McDonnell Douglas Corp. v. NASA, No. 91-3134, transcript at 6 (D.D.C. Jan. 24, 1992) (bench order) (recognizing that court has "very limited scope of review"), remanded, No. 92-5342 (D.C. Cir. Feb. 14, 1994).

[27] National Org. for Women v. Social Sec. Admin., 736 F.2d 727, 745 (D.C. Cir. 1984) (per curiam) (McGowan & Mikva, JJ., concurring in result); accord Campaign for Family Farms v. Glickman, 200 F.3d at 1186 n.6; Acumenics Research & Tech. v. United States Dep't of Justice, 843 F.2d 800, 804-05 (4th Cir. 1988); RSR Corp. v. Browner, 924 F. Supp. 504, 509 (S.D.N.Y. 1996), aff'd, No. 96-6186, 1997 WL 134413 (2d Cir. Mar. 26, 1997), affirmance vacated without explanation, No. 96-6186 (2d Cir. Apr. 17, 1997); Comdisco, Inc. v. GSA, 864 F. Supp. 510, 513 (E.D. Va. 1994); Burnside-Ott Aviation Training Ctr. v. United States, 617 F. Supp. 279, 282-84 (S.D. Fla. 1985); cf. Alcolac, Inc. v. Wagoner, 610 F. Supp. 745, 749 (W.D. Mo. 1985) (agency's decision to deny claim of confidentiality upheld as "rational"). But see Carolina Biological Supply Co. v. USDA, No. 93CV00113, slip op. at 4 & n.2 (M.D.N.C. Aug. 2, 1993) (applying de novo review after observing that standard of review issue presented close "judgment call"); Artesian Indus. v. HHS, 646 F. Supp. 1004, 1005-06 (D.D.C. 1986) (court flatly rejected position advanced by both parties that it should base its decision on agency record according to arbitrary and capricious standard).

[28] CNA Fin. Corp. v. Donovan, 830 F.2d 1132, 1162 (D.C. Cir. 1987); see, e.g., TRIFID Corp. v. National Imagery & Mapping Agency, 10 F. Supp. 2d 1087, 1092-96 (E.D. Mo. 1998) (agency's factfinding procedures found adequate when submitter "received notice of the FOIA request and was given the opportunity to object"; challenges to brevity of agency's disclosure decision, lack of administrative appeal right, as well as "procedural irregularities" concerning time period allotted for providing objections and dispute over appropriate decisionmaker, did not justify de novo review); RSR, 924 F. Supp. at 509 (agency's factfinding procedures found adequate when submitter was "promptly notified" of FOIA request and "given an opportunity to object to disclosure" and "to substantiate [those] objections" before agency decision made); Comdisco, 864 F. Supp. at 514 (agency's factfinding procedures found adequate when submitter "accorded a full and fair opportunity to state and support its position on disclosure"); see also CC Distribs. v. Kinzinger, No. 94-1330, 1995 WL 405445, at *3 (D.D.C. June 28, 1995) (review confined to record when submitter did "not actually challenge the agency's factfinding pro-
(continued...)

-646-

Ninth Circuit, similarly rejecting a submitter's challenge to an agency's factfinding procedures, has also held that judicial review in a reverse FOIA suit is properly based on the administrative record.[29]

Review on the administrative record is a "deferential standard of review [that] only requires that a court examine whether the agency's decision was 'based on a consideration of the relevant factors and whether there has been a clear error of judgment.'"[30] Because judicial review is based on the agency's administrative record, it is vitally important that agencies take care to develop a comprehensive one.[31] Indeed, the Court of Appeals for the Seventh Circuit once chastised an agency for failing to develop an adequate record in a reverse FOIA action. Although recognizing that procedures designed to determine the confidentiality of requested records need not be "as elaborate as a licensing," it found that the agency's one-line decision rejecting the submitter's position "validates congressional criticisms of the excessive casualness displayed by some agencies in resolving disputes over the application of exemption 4."[32]

---

[28](...continued) cedures," but instead challenged how agency "applied" those procedures); Chemical Waste Management, Inc. v. O'Leary, No. 94-2230, 1995 WL 115894, at *6 n.4 (D.D.C. Feb. 28, 1995) (review confined to record even when agency's factfinding itself found to be inadequate because agency's "factfinding procedures" not challenged).

[29] See Pacific Architects & Eng'rs v. United States Dep't of State, 906 F.2d 1345, 1348 (9th Cir. 1990).

[30] McDonnell Douglas Corp. v. NASA, 981 F. Supp. 12, 14 (D.D.C. 1997) (quoting Citizens to Preserve Overton Park v. Volpe, 401 U.S. 402, 416 (1971)), rev'd on other grounds, 180 F.3d 303 (D.C. Cir. 1999); accord Campaign for Family Farms, 200 F.3d at 1187 (likewise quoting Citizens to Preserve Overton Park).

[31] See Reliance, 924 F.2d at 277 (insisting that court "cannot properly perform" its reviewing function "unless the agency has explained the reasons for its decision"); see also McDonnell Douglas, 981 F. Supp. at 14 (ordering record supplemented to include "additional comments" provided by submitter as well as agency's "lengthy response" because submitter's comments, though untimely, were considered by agency); McDonnell Douglas Corp. v. NASA, 895 F. Supp. 319, 323-24 (D.D.C. 1995) (ordering record supplemented after finding that certain documents "specifically referenced" in submitter's letter to agency "were improperly omitted from the administrative record" and holding that even though those referenced documents had not been examined by agency, the letter itself was, and agency "cannot pick and choose what information in the document will be considered"), vacated as moot, No. 95-5288 (D.C. Cir. Apr. 1, 1996). Compare McDonnell Douglas, No. 91-3134, transcript at 6 (D.D.C. Jan. 24, 1992) (finding agency's action arbitrary and capricious based on insufficient agency record), with General Dynamics, 822 F. Supp. at 806 (deeming agency's action not arbitrary and capricious based upon "lengthy and thorough" administrative record).

[32] General Elec. Co. v. NRC, 750 F.2d 1394, 1403 (7th Cir. 1984) (remand-
(continued...)

## "REVERSE" FOIA

Similarly, the D.C. Circuit has remanded several reverse FOIA cases back to the agency for development of a more complete administrative record. In one, the D.C. Circuit ordered a remand so that it would have the benefit of "one considered and complete statement" of the agency's position on disclosure.[33] In another, the D.C. Circuit reversed the decision of the district court, which had permitted an inadequate record to be supplemented in court by an agency affidavit, holding that because the agency had failed at the administrative level to give a reason for its refusal to withhold certain price information, it was precluded from offering a "post-hoc rationalization" for the first time in court.[34]

Likewise, the court ordered a remand after holding that an "agency's administrative decision must stand or fall upon the reasoning advanced by the agency therein" and that an "agency cannot gain the benefit of hindsight in defending its decision" by advancing a new argument once the matter gets to litigation.[35] Thus, the D.C. Circuit has emphasized that judicial review in reverse FOIA cases must be conducted on the basis of the "administrative record compiled by the agency in advance of litigation."[36] Of course, agency affidavits that do "no more than summarize the administrative record" have been found to be permissible.[37]

In another case remanded to the agency for further proceedings due to

---

[32](...continued)
ing case for elaboration of basis for agency's decision).

[33] McDonnell Douglas Corp. v. Widnall, 57 F.3d 1162, 1167 (D.C. Cir. 1995) (inexplicably deeming case to have come to court in "unusual posture" with "confusing administrative record" stemming from "intersection" of FOIA actions and contract award announcements).

[34] AT&T Info. Sys. v. GSA, 810 F.2d 1233, 1236 (D.C. Cir. 1987).

[35] Data-Prompt, Inc. v. Cisneros, No. 94-5133, slip op. at 3 (D.C. Cir. Apr. 5, 1995).

[36] AT&T, 810 F.2d at 1236; see also TRIFID, 10 F. Supp. 2d at 1097 (refusing to consider affidavits proffered by submitter as they "were not submitted to [agency] during the administrative process"); CC Distribs., 1995 WL 405445, at *3 (same); Chemical Waste, 1995 WL 115894, at *6 n.4 (same); Alexander & Alexander Servs. v. SEC, No. 92-1112, 1993 WL 439799, at *13 n.9 (D.D.C. Oct. 19, 1993) (same), appeal dismissed, No. 93-5398 (D.C. Cir. Jan. 4, 1996); General Dynamics, 822 F. Supp. at 805 n.1 (same).

[37] Hercules, Inc. v. Marsh, 839 F.2d 1027, 1030 (4th Cir. 1988); accord McDonnell Douglas Corp. v. EEOC, 922 F. Supp. 235, 238 n.2 (E.D. Mo. 1996) (agency affidavit that "helps explain the administrative record" permitted), appeal dismissed, No. 96-2662 (8th Cir. Aug. 29, 1996); Lykes Bros. S.S. Co. v. Pena, No. 92-2780, slip op. at 16 (D.D.C. Sept. 2, 1993) (agency affidavit that "merely elaborates" on basis for agency decision and "provides a background for understanding the redactions" permitted); see also, e.g., International Computaprint, No. 87-1848, slip op. at 12 n.36 (D.D.C. Aug. 16, 1988) ("The record in this case has been supplemented with explanatory affidavits that do not alter the focus on the administrative record.").

an inadequate record, the D.C. Circuit rejected the argument proffered by the agency that a reverse FOIA plaintiff bears the burden of proving the "nonpublic availability" of information, finding that it is "far more efficient, and obviously fairer" for that burden to be placed on the party who claims that the information is public.[38] The D.C. Circuit also upheld the district court's requirement that the agency prepare a document-by-document explanation for its denial of confidential treatment.[39] Specifically, the D.C. Circuit found that the agency's burden of justifying its decision "cannot be shirked or shifted to others simply because the decision was taken in a reverse-FOIA rather than a direct FOIA context."[40] Moreover, it observed, in cases in which the public availability of information is the basis for an agency's decision to disclose, the justification of that position is "inevitably document-specific."[41] Similarly, the District Court for the District of Columbia ordered a remand in a case in which the agency "never did acknowledge," let alone "respond to," the submitter's competitive harm argument.[42]

Rather than order a remand, however, that same district court, in an earlier case, simply ruled against the agency--even going so far as to permanently enjoin it from releasing the requested information--on the basis of a record that it found insufficient under the standards of the APA.[43] Specifically, the court noted that the agency "did not rebut any of the evidence produced" by the submitter, "did not seek or place in the record any contrary evidence, and simply ha[d] determined" that the evidence offered by the submitter was "insufficient or not credible."[44] This, the court found, "is classic arbitrary and capricious action by a government agency."[45] When the agency sub-

---

[38] Occidental Petroleum Corp. v. SEC, 873 F.2d 325, 342 (D.C. Cir. 1989).

[39] Id. at 343-44.

[40] Id. at 344.

[41] Id.

[42] Chemical Waste, 1995 WL 115894, at *5.

[43] McDonnell Douglas, No. 91-3134, transcript at 5-6, 10 (D.D.C. Jan. 24, 1992).

[44] Id. at 6.

[45] Id.; see, e.g., McDonnell Douglas, 922 F. Supp. at 241-42 (declaring agency "arbitrary and capricious" because its "finding that the documents [at issue] were required [to be submitted was] not supported by substantial evidence in the agency record" and elaborating that it was "not at all clear" that agency "even made a factual finding on [that] issue" and "to the extent" that it "did consider the facts of [the] case, it viewed only the facts favorable to its predetermined position"); Cortez III Serv. Corp. v. NASA, 921 F. Supp. 8, 13 (D.D.C. 1996) (declaring agency decision "not in accordance with law" when "[n]either the administrative decision nor the sworn affidavits submitted by the [agency] support the conclusion that [the submitter] was required to provide" requested information), appeal voluntarily dismissed, No. 96-5163 (D.C. Cir. July 3, 1996). See generally Environmental Tech., Inc. v. EPA, 822 F.
(continued...)

## "REVERSE" FOIA

sequently sought an opportunity to "remedy" those "inadequacies in the record" by seeking a remand, the court declined to order one, reasoning that the agency was "not entitled to a second bite of the apple just because it made a poor decision [for,] if that were the case, administrative law would be a never ending loop from which aggrieved parties would never receive justice."[46]

This same court--when later presented with an administrative record that "differ[ed] substantially" from that earlier case and which "rebutted [the submitter's] arguments with detailed analysis" and indicated that the agency had "consulted" experienced individuals who were "intimately familiar with [the submitter's] arguments and evidence"--readily upheld the agency's disclosure decision.[47] When the submitter later sought reconsideration of the court's ruling, contending that the court improperly sustained the agency's decision on the basis of "'secret testimony from anonymous witnesses,'" the court dismissed those contentions as "inapposite and inaccurate," reasoning that "none of the issues before the court concerned the relative prestige of the experts on each party's side."[48] Rather, the court held, the "more appropriate concern [was] whether [the agency's] factual decisions [were] supported by substantial evidence" in the administrative record.[49] This decision was, nevertheless, abruptly overturned on appeal for what the court of appeals tersely characterized as the agency's "illogical application of the competitive harm test," with no mention made of the extensive evidence in the agency's administrative record.[50]

That same district court readily upheld another agency's disclosure determination that was based on an administrative record that demonstrated that the agency "specifically considered" and "understood" the arguments of the submitter and "provided reasons for rejecting them."[51] In so ruling, the court took note of the "lengthy and thorough" administrative process, during which the agency "repeatedly solicited and welcomed" the submitter's views

---

[45](...continued)
Supp. 1226, 1230 (E.D. Va. 1993) (perfunctorily granting submitter's motion for permanent injunction without even addressing adequacy of agency record).

[46] McDonnell Douglas Corp. v. NASA, 895 F. Supp. 316, 319 (D.D.C. 1995) (permanent injunction ordered to "remain[] in place"), aff'd for agency failure to timely raise argument, No. 95-5290 (D.C. Cir. Sept. 17, 1996).

[47] McDonnell Douglas, 981 F. Supp. at 16.

[48] McDonnell Douglas Corp. v. NASA, No. 96-2611, slip op. at 3 (D.D.C. May 1, 1998), rev'd on other grounds, 180 F.3d 303 (D.C. Cir. 1999).

[49] Id. at 4.

[50] McDonnell Douglas Corp. v. NASA, 180 F.3d 303, 307 (D.C. Cir. 1999) (brusquely dismissing agency's disclosure determination).

[51] General Dynamics, 822 F. Supp. at 807.

on whether a FOIA exemption applied.[52] This record demonstrated that the agency's action was not arbitrary or capricious.[53]

Similarly, when an agency provided a submitter with "numerous opportunities to substantiate its confidentiality claim," afforded it "vastly more than the amount of time authorized" by its regulations, and "explain[ed] its reasons for [initially] denying the confidentiality request," the court found that the agency had "acted appropriately by issuing its final decision denying much of the confidentiality request on the basis that it had not received further substantiation."[54] In so holding, the court specifically rejected the submitter's contention that "it should have received even more assistance" from the agency and held that the agency was "under no obligation to segregate the documents into categories or otherwise organize the documents for review."[55] The court also specifically noted that the agency's acceptance of some of the submitter's claims for confidentiality in this matter "buttresses" the conclusion that its decision was "rational."[56]

## Executive Order 12,600

Administrative practice in potential reverse FOIA situations is generally

---

[52] Id. at 806.

[53] Id. at 807; see, e.g., Atlantis Submarines Haw., Inc. v. United States Coast Guard, No. 93-00986, slip op. at 10 (D. Haw. Jan. 28, 1994) (finding that agency "appears to have fully examined the evidence and carefully followed its own procedures," that its decision to disclose "was conscientiously undertaken" and that it thus was not "arbitrary and capricious") (denying motion for preliminary injunction), dismissed per stipulation (D. Haw. Apr. 11, 1994); Source One Management, Inc. v. United States Dep't of the Interior, No. 92-Z-2101, transcript at 4 (D. Colo. Nov. 10, 1993) (bench order) (declaring that "Government has certainly been open in listening to" submitter's arguments "and has made a decision which . . . is rational and is not an abuse of discretion and is not arbitrary and capricious"); Lykes Bros., No. 92-2780, slip op. at 15 (D.D.C. Sept. 2, 1993) (noting that agency "provided considerable opportunity" for submitters to "contest the proposed disclosures, and provided sufficient reasons on the record for rejecting" submitters' arguments).

[54] Alexander, 1993 WL 439799, at **5-6; see CC Distribs., 1995 WL 405445, at *6 n.2 (ruling that agency's procedures were adequate when agency gave submitter "adequate notice" of existence of FOIA request, afforded it "numerous opportunities to explain its position," repeatedly advised it to state its objections "with particularity," and "at least, provided [submitter] with occasion to make the best case it could").

[55] Alexander, 1993 WL 439799, at **5 & 13 n.5.

[56] Id. at *13 n.6; accord Daisy Mfg. Co. v. Consumer Prod. Safety Comm'n, No. 96-5152, 1997 WL 578960, at *3 (W.D. Ark. Feb. 5, 1997) (finding it significant that record revealed that agency had been "careful in its selection of records for release, and in fact [had] denied the release of some records"), aff'd, 133 F.3d 1081 (8th Cir. 1998); Source One, No. 92-Z-2101, transcript at 4 (D. Colo. Nov. 10, 1993).

# "REVERSE" FOIA

governed by an executive order issued more than a decade ago. Executive Order 12,600 requires federal agencies to establish certain predisclosure notification procedures which will assist agencies in developing adequate administrative records.[57] The executive order recognizes that submitters of proprietary information have certain procedural rights and it therefore requires, with certain exceptions,[58] that notice be given to submitters of confidential commercial information whenever the agency "determines that it may be required to disclose" the requested data.[59]

When submitters are given notice under this procedure, they must be given a reasonable period of time within which to object to disclosure of any of the requested material.[60] As one court has emphasized, however, this consultation is "appropriate as one step in the evaluation process, [but] is not sufficient to satisfy [an agency's] FOIA obligations."[61] Consequently, an agency is "required to determine for itself whether the information in question should be disclosed."[62]

---

[57] 3 C.F.R. 235 (1988) (applicable to all executive branch departments and agencies), reprinted in 5 U.S.C. § 552 note (1994), and in FOIA Update, Vol. VIII, No. 2, at 2-3.

[58] Exec. Order No. 12,600, § 8 (listing six circumstances in which notice is not necessary, for example, when an agency determines that the requested information should be withheld, or conversely, when it is already public or its release is required by law); see also FOIA Update, Vol. XVIII, No. 4, at 1 (advising agencies that due to Federal Acquisition Regulation's express authorization to publicly release unit prices, formal submitter notification prior to release is not necessary (though agencies now are best advised as a matter of administrative discretion and courtesy to inform the submitter of an imminent disclosure)).

[59] Exec. Order No. 12,600, § 1. But cf. McDonnell Douglas Corp. v. NASA, 895 F. Supp. 319, 323 (D.D.C. 1995) (finding that agency "simply does not have the authority to require [submitter] to justify again and again why information, the disclosure of which has been enjoined by a federal court, should continue to be enjoined" and that agency must instead take steps to "have the existing injunction modified or dissolved"), vacated as moot, No. 95-5288 (D.C. Cir. Apr. 1, 1996). See generally OSHA Data/C.I.H., Inc. v. United States Dep't of Labor, No. 98-283, slip op. at 9-11 (D.N.J. June 11, 1998) (concluding that costs of notifying over 80,000 submitters are properly charged to requester seeking documents for commercial use) (appeal pending).

[60] Exec. Order No. 12,600, § 4; see McDonnell Douglas, 895 F. Supp. at 328 (submitter "not denied due process of law just because [agency] regulations do not allow cumulative opportunities to submit justifications and to refute agency decisions").

[61] Lee v. FDIC, 923 F. Supp. 451, 455 (S.D.N.Y. 1996).

[62] Id.; accord Exec. Order No. 12,600, § 5 (notification procedures specifically contemplate that agency makes ultimate determination concerning release); see also National Parks & Conservation Ass'n v. Morton, 498 F.2d 765, 767 (D.C. Cir. 1974) (in justifying nondisclosure, submitter's treatment of in-

(continued...)

If the submitter's objection is not, in fact, sustained by the agency, the submitter must be notified in writing and given a brief explanation of the agency's decision.[63] Such a notification must be provided a reasonable number of days prior to a specified disclosure date, which gives the submitter an opportunity to seek judicial relief.[64] Executive Order 12,600 mirrors in many ways the policy guidance issued by the Office of Information and Privacy in 1982,[65] and for most federal agencies it reflects what already had been existing practice.[66]

This executive order predates the decision of the Court of Appeals for the District of Columbia Circuit in Critical Mass Energy Project v. NRC,[67] and thus does not contain any procedures for notifying submitters of voluntarily provided information in order to determine if that information is "of a kind that would customarily not be released to the public by the person from whom it was obtained."[68] (For a further discussion of this "customary treatment" standard, see Exemption 4, Applying Critical Mass, above.) As a matter of sound administrative practice, however, agencies should employ procedures analogous to those set forth in Executive Order 12,600 when making determinations under this "customary treatment" standard.[69] Accordingly, if an agency is uncertain of the submitter's customary treatment of information, the submitter should be notified and given an opportunity to provide the agency with a description of its treatment--including any disclosures that are customarily made and the conditions under which such disclosures occur.[70] The agency should then make an objective determination as to whether or not the "customary treatment" standard is satisfied.[71] Of course, in the event a submitter challenges an agency's threshold determination under Critical Mass

---

[62](...continued) formation held not to be "the only relevant inquiry"; rather, agency must be satisfied that harms underlying exemption are likely to occur).

[63] Exec. Order No. 12,600, § 5; see TRIFID Corp. v. National Imagery & Mapping Agency, 10 F. Supp. 2d 1087, 1093 (E.D. Mo. 1998) (An "agency's explanation of its decision may be 'curt,'" provided that it "indicate[s] the determinative reason for the action taken.").

[64] Exec. Order No. 12,600, § 5.

[65] See FOIA Update, Vol. III, No. 3, at 3 ("OIP Guidance: Submitters' Rights").

[66] See FOIA Update, Vol. IV, No. 4, at 1 (describing agency submitter notice practice); see also FOIA Update, Vol. VIII, No. 2, at 1 (same).

[67] 975 F.2d 871 (D.C. Cir. 1992) (en banc).

[68] Id. at 879.

[69] See FOIA Update, Vol. Vol. XIV, at 6-7 ("Exemption 4 Under Critical Mass: Step-By-Step Decisionmaking"); see also id. at 3-5 ("OIP Guidance: The Critical Mass Distinction Under Exemption 4").

[70] See id. at 7.

[71] See id.

concerning whether the submission is "required" or "voluntary," the agency should be careful to include in the administrative record a full justification for its position on that issue as well.[72]

The procedures set forth in Executive Order 12,600 do not provide a submitter with a formal evidentiary hearing. This is entirely consistent with what has now become well-established law--i.e., that an agency's procedures for resolving a submitter's claim of confidentiality are not inadequate simply because they do not afford the submitter a right to an evidentiary hearing.[73] Agencies should be aware, though, that confusion and litigation can result from using undocumented conversations as a short-cut method of avoiding scrupulous adherence to these submitter-notice procedures.[74]

Similarly, procedures in the executive order do not provide for an administrative appeal of an adverse decision on a submitter's claim for confidentiality. The lack of such an appeal right has not been considered by the D.C. Circuit, but it has been addressed by the District Court for the District of Columbia, which has flatly rejected a submitter's contention that an agency's decision to disclose information "<u>must</u>" be subject to an administrative appeal.[75]

The Court of Appeals for the Fourth Circuit had an opportunity to confront this issue in <u>Acumenics Research & Technology v. Department of Jus-</u>

---

[72] See <u>McDonnell Douglas Corp. v. EEOC</u>, 922 F. Supp. 235, 241-42 (E.D. Mo. 1996) (agency's finding that submission was required "not supported by substantial evidence" and consequently agency decision found to be "contrary to the law"), <u>appeal dismissed</u>, No. 96-2662 (8th Cir. Aug. 29, 1996); <u>Cortez III Serv. Corp. v. NASA</u>, 921 F. Supp. 8, 13 (D.D.C. 1996) (agency's failure to provide "support" for its conclusion that submission was required rendered its decision "not in accordance with law"), <u>appeal voluntarily dismissed</u>, No. 96-5163 (D.C. Cir. July 3, 1996).

[73] See <u>CNA Fin. Corp. v. Donovan</u>, 830 F.2d 1132, 1159 (D.C. Cir. 1987); <u>National Org. for Women v. Social Sec. Admin.</u>, 736 F.2d 727, 746 (D.C. Cir. 1984) (per curiam) (McGowan & Mikva, JJ., concurring in result); <u>McDonnell Douglas Corp. v. NASA</u>, No. 96-2611, slip op. at 4 (D.D.C. May 1, 1998), <u>rev'd on other grounds</u>, 180 F.3d 303 (D.C. Cir. 1999).

[74] See <u>Federal Elec. Corp. v. Carlucci</u>, 687 F. Supp. 1, 5 (D.D.C. 1988) (disappointed bidder brought action seeking to have solicitation declared void after agency had released its cost data, in absence of submitter objections to release, which submitter claimed was due to "apparent misunderstanding as to what was actually going to be released"), <u>grant of summary judgment to agency aff'd</u>, 866 F.2d 1530 (D.C. Cir. 1989).

[75] <u>Lykes Bros. S.S. Co. v. Pena</u>, No. 92-2780, slip op. at 6 (D.D.C. Sept. 2, 1993); see also <u>TRIFID</u>, 10 F. Supp. 2d at 1093-94 (noting lack of appeal provision in executive order and concluding that "absence of an appeal mechanism and a formal mechanism to provide additional information [did] not render [agency's] procedures defective").

tice.[76] There, in analyzing Department of Justice regulations which do not provide for an administrative appeal, the Fourth Circuit found that the procedures provided for in the regulations--namely, notice of the request, an opportunity to submit objections to disclosure, careful consideration of those objections by the agency, and issuance of a written statement describing the reasons why any objections were not sustained--in combination with a "face-to-face meeting that, in essence, amounted to an opportunity to appeal [the agency's] tentative decision in favor of disclosure," were adequate.[77] The Fourth Circuit, however, expressly declined to render an opinion as to whether the procedures implemented by the regulations alone would have been adequate.[78]

Likewise, the Court of Appeals for the Ninth Circuit has upheld the adequacy of an agency's factfinding procedures that did not provide for an administrative appeal per se.[79] In that case, the agency's procedures provided for notice and an opportunity to object to disclosure, for consideration of the objection by the agency, for a written explanation as to why the objection was not sustained, and then for another opportunity for the submitter to provide information in support of its objection.[80] After independently reviewing the record, the Ninth Circuit found that such procedures were adequate and accordingly held that the agency's decision to disclose the information did not require review in a trial de novo.[81]

## BASIC FOIA REFERENCES

The following is a list of primary reference materials pertaining to the Freedom of Information Act, 5 U.S.C. § 552 (1994 & Supp. IV 1998). Further reference materials can be found in the extensive list of related law review articles contained in the Department of Justice's Freedom of Information Case List. Additionally, the Department's FOIA Update publication contains a current listing of the principal FOIA administrative and legal contacts at federal agencies. See FOIA Update, Vol. XX, No. 1, at i-iv. Another basic reference tool is the cumulative index to FOIA Update, covering all issues from 1979 through 1997. See FOIA Update, Vol. XVIII, No. 4, at i-ix; see also FOIA Update, Vol. XIX, No. 1, at 5 (listing primary reference materials pertaining to Electronic Freedom of Information Act Amendments of 1996, Pub. L. No. 104-231, 110 Stat. 3048).

A growing number of reference materials pertaining to the FOIA are available to the public electronically, through FOIA-related sites on the World

---

[76] 843 F.2d 800, 805 (4th Cir. 1988).

[77] Id.

[78] Id. at 805 n.4.

[79] See Pacific Architects & Eng'rs v. United States Dep't of State, 906 F.2d 1345, 1348 (9th Cir. 1990).

[80] Id.

[81] Id.

**BASIC FOIA REFERENCES**

Wide Web. The Department of Justice maintains a comprehensive FOIA Web site (www.usdoj.gov/04foia), which contains links to many of the basic reference materials listed below. The Department of Justice's FOIA Web site also contains links to the FOIA Web sites of other federal agencies, and it serves as a single electronic access point for linkage to the annual FOIA reports of all federal agencies. In order to best facilitate public access to FOIA-related materials, individual electronic addresses are included below, and the Office of Information and Privacy will add additional electronic addresses to this list as they become available. See FOIA Update, Vol. XVIII, No. 3, at 2.

### Congressional References

House of Representatives Committee on Government Operations, Clarifying and Protecting the Right of the Public to Information. H.R. Rep. No. 1497, 89th Cong., 2d Sess. (1966), 14 pages. Out of print. Available at most law libraries.

House of Representatives Committee on Government Operations, Freedom of Information Act (Compilation and Analysis of Department Regulations Implementing 5 U.S.C. § 552). Committee Print, 90th Cong., 2d Sess. (1968), 303 pages with appendices. Out of print. Available at most law libraries.

House of Representatives Committee on Government Operations and Senate Committee on the Judiciary, Freedom of Information Act and Amendments of 1974 (P.L. 93-502). Joint Committee Print, 94th Cong., 1st Sess. (1975), 571 pages. Known as the "Joint Source Book." Out of print. Available at most law libraries.

House of Representatives Committee on Government Operations, Freedom of Information Act Requests for Business Data and Reverse FOIA Lawsuits. H.R. Rep. No. 1382, 95th Cong., 2d Sess. (1978), 67 pages. Out of print. Available at most law libraries.

House of Representatives Committee on Government Operations, Subcommittee on Government Information, Justice, and Agriculture, The Freedom of Information Reform Act: Hearings on S. 774. 98th Cong., 2d Sess. (1984), 1155 pages. Available at Federal Depository Libraries.

House of Representatives Committee on Government Operations, Subcommittee on Government Information, Justice, and Agriculture, Federal Information Dissemination Policies and Practices. 101st Cong., 1st Sess. (1989), 904 pages. Available at most law libraries.

House of Representatives Committee on the Judiciary, Subcommittee on Civil and Constitutional Rights, FBI Oversight and Authorization Request for Fiscal Year 1991. Committee Print, 101st Cong., 2d Sess. (1990), 566 pages. Available at most law libraries.

House of Representatives Committee on Government Reform and Oversight, Electronic Freedom of Information Amendments of 1996. H.R. Rep. No. 795, 104th Cong., 2d Sess. (1996), 40 pages. Available at most law libraries. Also available on the World Wide Web (thomas.loc.gov/cgi-bin/cpquery/

**BASIC FOIA REFERENCES**

z?cp104:hr795.104:).

House of Representatives Committee on Government Reform and Oversight, Federal Information Policy Oversight. 104th Cong., 2d Sess. (1996), 485 pages. Available at most law libraries.

House of Representatives Committee on Government Reform, A Citizen's Guide on Using the Freedom of Information Act and the Privacy Act of 1974 to Request Government Records. H.R. Rep. No. 50, 106th Cong., 1st Sess. (1999), 33 pages and appendices. Available from the Superintendent of Documents, U.S. Government Printing Office, Washington, D.C. 20402. (Stock number: 052-071-01287-7; price: $5.00.) Also available on the World Wide Web (thomas.loc.gov/cgi-bin/cpquery/z?cp106:hr50.106:).

Senate Committee on the Judiciary, Clarifying and Protecting the Right of the Public to Information, and Other Purposes. S. Rep. No. 813, 89th Cong., 1st Sess. (1965), 10 pages. Out of print. Available at most law libraries.

Senate Committee on the Judiciary, Freedom of Information Act Source Book: Legislative Materials, Cases, Articles. S. Doc. No. 82, 93d Cong., 2d Sess. (1974), 432 pages on the Act prior to the 1974 Amendments. Out of print. Available at most law libraries.

Senate Committee on the Judiciary, Subcommittee on Criminal Laws and Procedures, The Erosion of Law Enforcement Intelligence and Its Impact on the Public Security. Committee Print, 95th Cong., 2d Sess. (1978), 179 pages. Out of print. Available at most law libraries.

Senate Committee on the Judiciary, Freedom of Information: A Compilation of State Laws. Committee Print, 95th Cong., 2d Sess. (1978), 475 pages. Out of print. Available at most law libraries.

Senate Committee on the Judiciary, Agency Implementation of the 1974 Amendments to the Freedom of Information Act. Committee Print, 95th Cong., 2d Sess. (1980), 188 pages. Out of print. Available at most law libraries.

Senate Committee on the Judiciary, Subcommittee on the Constitution, Freedom of Information Act, Vols. 1-2. Committee Print, 97th Cong., 1st Sess. (1981), 1147 pages and appendix. Available at most law libraries.

Senate Committee on the Judiciary, Subcommittee on the Constitution, Freedom of Information Reform Act Report, Together with Supplemental Views, to Accompany S. 1730. Committee Print 97-690, 97th Cong. 2d Sess. (1982), 17 pages. Available at most law libraries.

Senate Committee on the Judiciary, Subcommittee on the Constitution, Freedom of Information Reform Act Report (on S. 774). Committee Print 98-221, 98th Cong., 1st Sess. (1983), 48 pages. Available at most law libraries.

Senate Committee on the Judiciary, Subcommittee on Technology and the Law, The Freedom of Information Act. Committee Print, 100th Cong., 2d Sess. (1988), 244 pages. Out of print. Available at most law libraries.

**BASIC FOIA REFERENCES**

Senate Committee on the Judiciary, <u>Electronic Freedom of Information Improvement Act of 1994</u>. S. Rep. No. 1365, 103d Cong., 2d Sess. (1994), 28 pages. Available at most law libraries.

Senate Committee on the Judiciary, <u>Electronic Freedom of Information Improvement Act of 1995</u>. S. Rep. No. 272, 104th Cong., 2d Sess. (1996), 39 pages. Available at most law libraries. Also available on the World Wide Web (www.fas.org/irp/congress/1996_rpt/s104272.htm).

<u>Justice Department Materials</u>

<u>Attorney General's Memorandum on the Public Information Section of the Administrative Procedure Act (FOIA)</u>, June 1967, 40 pages. Out of print. Reprinted in Gov't Disclosure Serv. (Prentice-Hall), Vol. 1, ¶ 300,601.

<u>Attorney General's Memorandum on the 1974 Amendments to the Freedom of Information Act</u>, February 1975, 26 pages and appendices. Available from the Office of Information and Privacy, U.S. Department of Justice, Washington, D.C. 20530-0001.

<u>Attorney General's Memorandum on the 1986 Amendments to the Freedom of Information Act</u>, December 1987, 30 pages and appendices. Available from the Office of Information and Privacy.

Attorney General's Memorandum for Heads of Departments and Agencies regarding the Freedom of Information Act, October 4, 1993. Reprinted in <u>FOIA Update</u>, Vol. XIV, No. 3, at 4-5. Also available at the Department of Justice's FOIA site on the World Wide Web (www.usdoj.gov/04foia/931004a.htm).

Attorney General's Memorandum for Heads of Departments and Agencies regarding the Freedom of Information Act, September 3, 1999. Reprinted in <u>FOIA Update</u>, Vol. XIX, No. 4, at 3-5. Also available at the Department of Justice's FOIA site on the World Wide Web (www.usdoj.gov/ag/readingroom/990903.htm).

Department of Justice Freedom of Information Act Reference Guide (1999). Available in paper form from the Office of Information and Privacy, but primarily available at the Department of Justice's FOIA site on the World Wide Web (www.usdoj.gov/04foia/04_3.html).

<u>FOIA Update</u>, a newsletter of information and guidance for federal agencies, published three times a year by the Office of Information and Privacy, U.S. Department of Justice. Distributed without charge by OIP to all FOIA offices and other interested offices governmentwide. Available from the Superintendent of Documents, U.S. Government Printing Office, Washington, D.C. 20402. (Stock number: 727-002-00000-6. Annual subscription price: $10.00, domestic; $12.50, foreign.) Also available at the Department of Justice's FOIA site on the World Wide Web (www.usdoj.gov/oip/foi-upd.htm).

<u>Freedom of Information Case List</u>, September 1998 edition, 520 pages. A compilation of judicial decisions, both published and unpublished, addressing access issues under the Freedom of Information Act and the Privacy Act of

## BASIC FOIA REFERENCES

1974, categorized and indexed according to subject-matter topics. Also includes decisions issued under the Federal Advisory Committee Act and the Government in the Sunshine Act, as well as a list of "reverse" FOIA decisions. Published biennially as of 1994. Available from the Office of Information and Privacy, U.S. Department of Justice, Washington, D.C. 20530-0001 or from the Superintendent of Documents, U.S. Government Printing Office, Washington, D.C. 20402. Also available at the Department of Justice's FOIA site on the World Wide Web (www.usdoj.gov/04foia/04_7.html).

Department of Justice's Freedom of Information Act and Privacy Act Regulations, 28 C.F.R. Part 16 (1999), published by the Office of the Federal Register, but primarily available at the Department of Justice's FOIA site on the World Wide Web (www.usdoj.gov/04foia/04_1_1.html).

President's Memorandum for Heads of Departments and Agencies regarding the Freedom of Information Act, October 4, 1993. Published at 29 Weekly Compilation of Presidential Documents 1999 (Oct. 4, 1993). Reprinted in FOIA Update, Vol. XIV, No. 3, at 3. Also available at the Department of Justice's FOIA site on the World Wide Web (www.usdoj.gov/04foia/93_clntmem.htm).

Your Right to Federal Records (1996) (revision now scheduled by GSA for publication by September 2000), a joint publication of the General Services Administration and the Department of Justice. Available from the Consumer Information Center, Department 319E, Pueblo, CO 81009. (Publication number: 319E; price: $.50.) Also available on the World Wide Web at www.pueblo.gsa.gov/cic_text/fed_prog/foia/foia.htm and at the Department of Justice's FOIA site on the World Wide Web (www.usdoj.gov/oip/foia_rights.htm).

### Nongovernment Publications

Access Reports, a biweekly newsletter published (together with Access Reports Reference File) by Access Reports, Inc., Lynchburg, VA 24503. World Wide Web address www.accessreports.com.

Federal Information Disclosure (2d ed. 1998), James T. O'Reilly, West Group, Rochester, NY 14694. Annual supplements. World Wide Web address www.westgroup.com.

Getting and Protecting Competitive Business Information: A Business Guide to Using the Freedom of Information Act (1997), Burt A. Braverman, Frances J. Chetwynd, and Harry A. Hammitt, Management Concepts, Inc., Vienna, VA 22182. World Wide Web address www.crblaw.com.

Government Disclosure Service ("GDS"), Prentice-Hall, Englewood Cliffs, NJ 07632. A monthly summary of FOIA-related matters which included full-text publication of FOIA and Privacy Act decisions from 1980 through October 1983. (Discontinued as of October 1983.)

Guidebook to the Freedom of Information and Privacy Acts (2d ed. 1986), Justin D. Franklin and Robert F. Bouchard, West Group, Rochester, NY 14694. Annual supplements. World Wide Web address

**BASIC FOIA REFERENCES**

www.westgroup.com.

How to Use the Federal FOI Act (8th ed. 1998), Reporters Committee for Freedom of the Press, Arlington, VA 22209. World Wide Web address www.rcfp.org.

Information Law: Freedom of Information, Privacy, Open Meetings, and Other Access Laws (1985), Burt A. Braverman and Frances J. Chetwynd, Practising Law Institute, New York City, NY 10019. Two volumes. Supplement published in 1990. World Wide Web address www.crblaw.com.

Privacy Times, a newsletter that reports Privacy Act/Freedom of Information Act news, published biweekly by Privacy Times, Inc., P.O. Box 21501, Washington, D.C. 20009. World Wide Web address www.privacytimes.com.

Step-By-Step Guide to Using the Freedom of Information Act (1997), American Civil Liberties Union Foundation, Washington, D.C. 20002. World Wide Web address www.aclu.org.

Tapping Officials' Secrets: A State Open Government Compendium (3d ed. 1997), Reporters Committee for Freedom of the Press, Arlington, VA 22209. Available as a complete set or on a state-by-state basis. Complete set also available on CD-ROM. World Wide Web address www.rcfp.org.

# OVERVIEW OF THE PRIVACY ACT OF 1974

The "Overview of the Privacy Act of 1974" is a discussion of the Privacy Act's disclosure prohibition, its access and amendment provisions, and its agency recordkeeping requirements. Prepared by the Office of Information and Privacy in coordination with the Office of Management and Budget (OMB), it is updated and expanded biennially. Any inquiry about the Privacy Act's provisions should be made to individual agency Privacy Act officers in conjunction with use of this "Overview." Particularly important Privacy Act policy/litigation questions, or questions concerning the OMB Guidelines, may be directed to the Office of the Chief Counselor for Privacy, OMB, at (202) 395-1095.

## TABLE OF CONTENTS

| | Page |
|---|---|
| INTRODUCTION | 663 |
| LEGISLATIVE HISTORY | 663 |
| ROLE OF THE PRIVACY PROTECTION STUDY COMMISSION | 663 |
| ROLE OF THE OFFICE OF MANAGEMENT AND BUDGET | 663 |
| COMPUTER MATCHING | 664 |
| POLICY OBJECTIVES | 665 |
| DEFINITIONS | 665 |
|     A. Agency | 665 |
|     B. Individual | 669 |
|     C. Maintain | 671 |
|     D. Record | 672 |
|     E. System of Records | 678 |
|         1. Disclosure: Subsection (b) | 681 |
|         2. Access and Amendment: Subsections (d)(1) and (d)(2) | 686 |
|         3. Other Aspects | 687 |
| CONDITIONS OF DISCLOSURE TO THIRD PARTIES | 689 |
|     A. The "No Disclosure Without Consent" Rule | 689 |
|     B. Twelve Exceptions to the "No Disclosure Without Consent" Rule | 696 |
|         1. 5 U.S.C. § 552a(b)(1) ("need to know" within agency) | 696 |
|         2. 5 U.S.C. § 552a(b)(2) (required FOIA disclosure) | 700 |
|         3. 5 U.S.C. § 552a(b)(3) (routine uses) | 703 |
|         4. 5 U.S.C. § 552a(b)(4) (Bureau of the Census) | 713 |
|         5. 5 U.S.C. § 552a(b)(5) (statistical research) | 713 |
|         6. 5 U.S.C. § 552a(b)(6) (National Archives) | 713 |
|         7. 5 U.S.C. § 552a(b)(7) (law enforcement request) | 714 |
|         8. 5 U.S.C. § 552a(b)(8) (health or safety of an individual) | 714 |
|         9. 5 U.S.C. § 552a(b)(9) (Congress) | 715 |
|         10. 5 U.S.C. § 552a(b)(10) (General Accounting Office) | 715 |
|         11. 5 U.S.C. § 552a(b)(11) (court order) | 715 |
|         12. 5 U.S.C. § 552a(b)(12) (Debt Collection Act) | 722 |

|  | Page |
|---|---|
| ACCOUNTING OF CERTAIN DISCLOSURES | 723 |
| INDIVIDUAL'S RIGHT OF ACCESS | 724 |
| INDIVIDUAL'S RIGHT OF AMENDMENT | 732 |
| AGENCY REQUIREMENTS | 733 |
|     A. 5 U.S.C. § 552a(e)(1) | 733 |
|     B. 5 U.S.C. § 552a(e)(2) | 734 |
|     C. 5 U.S.C. § 552a(e)(3) | 736 |
|     D. 5 U.S.C. § 552a(e)(4) | 738 |
|     E. 5 U.S.C. § 552a(e)(5) | 739 |
|     F. 5 U.S.C. § 552a(e)(6) | 747 |
|     G. 5 U.S.C. § 552a(e)(7) | 747 |
|     H. 5 U.S.C. § 552a(e)(8) | 753 |
|     I. 5 U.S.C. § 552a(e)(9) | 753 |
|     J. 5 U.S.C. § 552a(e)(10) | 754 |
|     K. 5 U.S.C. § 552a(e)(11) | 754 |
| AGENCY RULES | 754 |
|     A. 5 U.S.C. § 552a(f)(1) | 754 |
|     B. 5 U.S.C. § 552a(f)(2) | 754 |
|     C. 5 U.S.C. § 552a(f)(3) | 755 |
|     D. 5 U.S.C. § 552a(f)(4) | 757 |
|     E. 5 U.S.C. § 552a(f)(5) | 757 |
| CIVIL REMEDIES | 757 |
|     A. Amendment Lawsuits | 759 |
|     B. Access Lawsuits | 766 |
|     C. Accuracy Lawsuits for Damages | 769 |
|     D. Other Damages Lawsuits | 777 |
|     E. Intentional/Willful Standard and Actual Damages in Accuracy and Other Damages Lawsuits | 779 |
|     F. Principles Applicable to All Privacy Act Civil Actions | 789 |
|         1. Attorney Fees and Costs | 789 |
|         2. Jurisdiction and Venue | 792 |
|         3. Statute of Limitations | 793 |
|         4. Jury Trial | 801 |
| CRIMINAL PENALTIES | 801 |
| TEN EXEMPTIONS | 802 |
|     A. One Special Exemption--5 U.S.C. § 552a(d)(5) | 802 |
|     B. Two General Exemptions--5 U.S.C. § 552a(j)(1) and (j)(2) | 804 |
|     C. Seven Specific Exemptions--5 U.S.C. § 552a(k) | 810 |
|         1. 5 U.S.C. § 552a(k)(1) | 810 |
|         2. 5 U.S.C. § 552a(k)(2) | 810 |
|         3. 5 U.S.C. § 552a(k)(3) | 816 |
|         4. 5 U.S.C. § 552a(k)(4) | 816 |
|         5. 5 U.S.C. § 552a(k)(5) | 816 |
|         6. 5 U.S.C. § 552a(k)(6) | 819 |
|         7. 5 U.S.C. § 552a(k)(7) | 820 |
| SOCIAL SECURITY NUMBER USAGE | 820 |
| GOVERNMENT CONTRACTORS | 823 |
| MAILING LISTS | 824 |
| MISCELLANEOUS PROVISIONS | 824 |

## INTRODUCTION

The Privacy Act of 1974, 5 U.S.C. § 552a (1994 & Supp. IV 1998), which became effective on September 27, 1975, can generally be characterized as an omnibus "code of fair information practices" which attempts to regulate the collection, maintenance, use, and dissemination of personal information by federal government agencies. However, the Act's imprecise language, limited legislative history, and somewhat outdated regulatory guidelines have rendered it a difficult statute to decipher and apply. Moreover, even after twenty years of administrative and judicial analysis, numerous Privacy Act issues remain unresolved or unexplored. Adding to these interpretational difficulties is the fact that many of the most significant Privacy Act cases are unpublished district court decisions. A particular effort has been made in this "Overview" to clarify the existing state of Privacy Act law while at the same time highlighting those controversial, unsettled areas where further litigation and case law development can be expected.

## LEGISLATIVE HISTORY

The entire legislative history of the Privacy Act is contained in a convenient, one-volume compilation. See House Comm. on Gov't Operations and Senate Comm. on Gov't Operations, 94th Cong., 2d Sess., Legislative History of the Privacy Act of 1974--S. 3418 (Public Law 93-579) Source Book on Privacy (1976) [hereinafter Source Book]. The Act was passed in great haste during the final week of the Ninety-Third Congress. No conference committee was convened to reconcile differences in the bills passed by the House and Senate. Instead, staffs of the respective committees--led by Senators Ervin and Percy, and Congressmen Moorhead and Erlenborn--prepared a final version of the bill that was ultimately enacted. The original reports are thus of limited utility in interpreting the final statute, while the more reliable legislative history consists of a brief analysis of the compromise amendments--entitled "Analysis of House and Senate Compromise Amendments to the Federal Privacy Act"--prepared by the staffs of the counterpart Senate and House committees and submitted in both the House and Senate in lieu of a conference report. See 120 Cong. Rec. 40,405-09, 40,881-83 (1974), reprinted in Source Book at 858-68, 987-94.

## ROLE OF THE PRIVACY PROTECTION STUDY COMMISSION

Section 5 of the original Privacy Act established the "U.S. Privacy Protection Study Commission" to evaluate the statute and to issue a report containing recommendations for its improvement. The Commission issued its final report and ceased operation in 1977. See U.S. Privacy Protection Study Commission, Personal Privacy in an Information Society (1977) [hereinafter Privacy Commission Report].

## ROLE OF THE OFFICE OF MANAGEMENT AND BUDGET

Subsection (v) of the Privacy Act requires the Office of Management and Budget (OMB) to: (1) prescribe guidelines and regulations for the use of federal agencies in implementing the Act, see 5 U.S.C. § 552a(v)(1); and (2) provide continuing assistance to and oversight of the implementation of the Act by agencies, see 5 U.S.C. § 552a(v)(2).

The vast majority of OMB's Privacy Act Guidelines [hereinafter OMB Guidelines] are published at 40 Fed. Reg. 28,948-78 (1975). However, these original guidelines have been supplemented in particular subject areas over the years. See 40 Fed. Reg. 56,741-43 (1975) (system of records definition, routine use and intra-agency disclosures, consent and congressional inquiries, accounting of disclosures, amendment appeals, rights of parents and legal guardians, relationship to Freedom of Information Act (FOIA)); 48 Fed. Reg. 15,556-60 (1983) (relationship to Debt Collection Act); 52 Fed. Reg. 12,990-93 (1987) ("call detail" programs); 54 Fed. Reg. 25818-29 (1989) (computer matching); 56 Fed. Reg. 18,599-601 (proposed Apr. 23, 1991) (computer matching); 61 Fed. Reg. 6428, 6435-39 (1996) ("Federal Agency Responsibilities for Maintaining Records About Individuals").

As a general rule, the OMB Guidelines are entitled to the deference usually accorded the interpretations of the agency that has been charged with the administration of a statute. See Quinn v. Stone, 978 F.2d 126, 133 (3d Cir. 1992); Baker v. Department of the Navy, 814 F.2d 1381, 1383 (9th Cir. 1987); Perry v. FBI, 759 F.2d 1271, 1276 n.7 (7th Cir. 1985) (citing Bartel v. FAA, 725 F.2d 1403, 1408 n.9 (D.C. Cir. 1984); Albright v. United States, 631 F.2d 915, 919 n.5 (D.C. Cir. 1980)), rev'd en banc on other grounds, 781 F.2d 1294 (7th Cir. 1986); Smiertka v. United States Dep't of the Treasury, 604 F.2d 698, 703 n.12 (D.C. Cir. 1979); Rogers v. United States Dep't of Labor, 607 F. Supp. 697, 700 n.2 (N.D. Cal. 1985); Sanchez v. United States, 3 Gov't Disclosure Serv. (P-H) ¶ 83,116, at 83,709 (S.D. Tex. Sept. 10, 1982); Golliher v. United States Postal Serv., 3 Gov't Disclosure Serv. (P-H) ¶ 83,114, at 83,703 (N.D. Ohio June 10, 1982); Greene v. VA, No. C-76-461-S, slip op. at 6-7 (M.D.N.C. July 3, 1978); Daniels v. FCC, No. 77-5011, slip op. at 8-9 (D.S.D. Mar. 15, 1978); see also Martin v. Office of Special Counsel, 819 F.2d 1181, 1188 (D.C. Cir. 1987) (OMB interpretation is "worthy of our attention and solicitude"). However, a few courts have rejected particular aspects of the OMB Guidelines as inconsistent with the statute. See Kassel v. VA, No. 87-217-S, slip op. at 24-25 (D.N.H. Mar. 30, 1992) (subsection (e)(3)); Saunders v. Schweiker, 508 F. Supp. 305, 309 (W.D.N.Y. 1981) (same); Metadure Corp. v. United States, 490 F. Supp. 1368, 1373-74 (S.D.N.Y. 1980) (subsection (a)(2)); Florida Med. Ass'n v. HEW, 479 F. Supp. 1291, 1307-11 (M.D. Fla. 1979) (same); Zeller v. United States, 467 F. Supp. 487, 497-99 (E.D.N.Y. 1979) (same).

On May 14, 1998, President Clinton called upon all federal agencies to take further privacy-protection steps within the next year. Memorandum on Privacy and Personal Information in Federal Records, 34 Weekly Comp. Pres. Doc. 870 (May 14, 1998), available in Westlaw, 1998 WL 241263 (May 14, 1998). Specifically, the President directed each agency to designate a senior official with responsibility for privacy policy, to apply the Principles for Providing and Using Personal Information that were developed through the Information Infrastructure Task Force under the auspices of the Department of Commerce in 1995, and to conduct a series of reviews of agency record systems in order to ensure compliance with Privacy Act requirements. Id. The agencies reported the results of their reviews to OMB, where they are to be summarized. Id. The memorandum also provided that OMB will issue further guidance on the making of "routine use" disclosures under the Act. Id.

Questions concerning the Act should first be directed to agency Privacy Act officers. However, important policy/litigation questions, or questions concerning the OMB Guidelines, may be directed to the Office of the Chief Counselor for Privacy, OMB, at (202) 395-1095.

**COMPUTER MATCHING**

The Computer Matching and Privacy Protection Act of 1988 (Pub. L. No. 100-503) amended the Privacy Act to add several new

provisions.  See 5 U.S.C. § 552a(a)(8)-(13), (e)(12), (o), (p),
(q), (r), (u) (1994 & Supp. IV 1998).  These provisions add
procedural requirements for agencies to follow when engaging in
computer-matching activities; provide matching subjects with
opportunities to receive notice and to refute adverse information before having a benefit denied or terminated; and require
that agencies engaged in matching activities establish Data
Protection Boards to oversee those activities.  These provisions became effective on December 31, 1989.  OMB's guidelines
on computer matching should be consulted in this area.  See 54
Fed. Reg. 25,818-29 (1989).

Subsequently, Congress enacted the Computer Matching and Privacy Protection Amendments of 1990 (Pub. L. No. 101-508), which
further clarify the due process provisions found in subsection
(p).  OMB's proposed guidelines on these amendments appear at
56 Fed. Reg. 18,599-601 (proposed Apr. 23, 1991).

The highly complex and specialized provisions of the Computer
Matching and Privacy Protection Act of 1988 and the Computer
Matching and Privacy Protection Amendments of 1990 are not
further addressed herein.  For guidance on these provisions,
agencies should consult the OMB Guidelines cited above.

## POLICY OBJECTIVES

Broadly stated, the purpose of the Privacy Act is to balance
the government's need to maintain information about individuals
with the rights of individuals to be protected against unwarranted invasions of their privacy stemming from federal agencies' collection, maintenance, use, and disclosure of personal
information about them.  The historical context of the Act is
important to an understanding of its remedial purposes:  In
1974, Congress was concerned with curbing the illegal surveillance and investigation of individuals by federal agencies that
had been exposed during the Watergate scandal; it was also
concerned with potential abuses presented by the government's
increasing use of computers to store and retrieve personal data
by means of a universal identifier--such as an individual's
social security number.  The Act focuses on four basic policy
objectives:

(1)   To restrict disclosure of personally identifiable records
      maintained by agencies.

(2)   To grant individuals increased rights of access to agency
      records maintained on themselves.

(3)   To grant individuals the right to seek amendment of agency
      records maintained on themselves upon a showing that the
      records are not accurate, relevant, timely or complete.

(4)   To establish a code of "fair information practices" which
      requires agencies to comply with statutory norms for col-
      lection, maintenance, and dissemination of records.

## DEFINITIONS

### A.  Agency

"any Executive department, military department, Government
corporation, Government controlled corporation, or other
establishment in the executive branch of the [federal]
Government (including the Executive Office of the President), or any independent regulatory agency."  5 U.S.C.
§ 552a(1) (incorporating 5 U.S.C. § 552(f) (1994 & Supp. II
1996), which in turn incorporates 5 U.S.C. § 551(1)
(1994)).

PRIVACY ACT OVERVIEW

comment -- The Privacy Act--like the Freedom of Information Act, 5 U.S.C. § 552--applies only to a federal "agency." See OMB Guidelines, 40 Fed. Reg. 28,948, 28,950-51 (1975); 120 Cong. Rec. 40,408 (1974), reprinted in Source Book at 866; see also, e.g., NLRB v. United States Postal Serv., 841 F.2d 141, 144 n.3 (6th Cir. 1988) (Postal Service is an "agency" because it is an "independent establishment of the executive branch"); Ehm v. National R.R. Passenger Corp., 732 F.2d 1250, 1252-55 (5th Cir. 1984) (Amtrak held not to constitute a "Government-controlled corporation"). But cf. Alexander v. FBI, 971 F. Supp. 603, 606-07 (D.D.C. 1997) (although recognizing that definition of "agency" under Privacy Act is same as in FOIA and that courts have interpreted that definition under FOIA to exclude the President's immediate personal staff and units within Executive Office of the President whose sole function is to advise and assist the President, nevertheless rejecting such limitation with regard to "agency" as used in Privacy Act due to different purposes that two statutes serve), petition for permission to appeal from interlocutory order denied, No. 97-8059 (D.C. Cir. Oct. 10, 1997), subsequent related decision, No. 96-2123, 2000 WL 329249 (D.D.C. Mar. 29, 2000), mandamus denied per curiam sub nom. In re Executive Office of the President, No. 00-5134, 2000 WL 656113, at *4 (D.C. Cir. May 26, 2000) (stating that the White House "remains free to adhere to the position that the Privacy Act does not cover members of the White House Office"); Shannon v. General Elec. Co., 812 F. Supp. 308, 313, 315 n.5 (N.D.N.Y. 1993) ("no dispute" that GE falls within definition of "agency" subject to requirements of Privacy Act where pursuant to contract it operated Department of Energy-owned lab under supervision, control, and oversight of Department and where by terms of contract GE agreed to comply with Privacy Act).

Thus, state and local government agencies are not covered by the Privacy Act, see Ortez v. Washington County, Or., 88 F.3d 804, 811 (9th Cir. 1996); Brown v. Kelly, No. 93-5222, 1994 WL 36144, at *1 (D.C. Cir. Jan. 27, 1994) (per curiam); Monk v. Teeter, No. 89-16333, 1992 WL 1681, at *2 (9th Cir. Jan. 8, 1992); Davidson v. Georgia, 622 F.2d 895, 896 (5th Cir. 1980); Markun v. Hillsborough County Dep't of Corrections, No. 97-208, 1999 WL 813949, at *1 (D.N.H. Sept. 17, 1999); Ferguson v. Alabama Criminal Justice Info. Ctr., 962 F. Supp. 1446, 1446-47 (M.D. Ala. 1997); Williams v. District of Columbia, No. 95CV0936, 1996 WL 422328, at **2-3 (D.D.C. July 19, 1996); Martinson v. Violent Drug Traffickers Project, No. 95-2161, 1996 WL 411590, at **1-2 (D.D.C. July 11, 1996), summary affirmance granted, No. 96-5262 (D.C. Cir. Sept. 22, 1997); Mamarella v. County of Westchester, 898 F. Supp. 236, 237-38 (S.D.N.Y. 1995); Reno v. United States, No. 4:94CV243, 1995 U.S. Dist. LEXIS 12834, at *6 (W.D.N.C. Aug. 14, 1995) (state national guard); Connolly v. Beckett, 863 F. Supp. 1379, 1383-84 (D. Colo. 1994); MR by RR v. Lincolnwood Bd. of Educ., Dist. 74, 843 F. Supp. 1236, 1239-40 (N.D. Ill. 1994), aff'd sub nom. Rheinstrom v. Lincolnwood Bd. of Educ., Dist. 74, No. 94-1357, 1995 U.S. App. LEXIS 10781 (7th Cir. May 10, 1995); Malewich v. United States Postal Serv., No. 91-4871, slip op. at 19 (D.N.J. Apr. 8, 1993), aff'd, 27 F.3d 557 (3d Cir. 1994) (unpublished table decision); Shields v. Shetler, 682 F. Supp. 1172, 1176 (D. Colo. 1988); Ryans v. New Jersey Comm'n, 542 F. Supp. 841, 852 (D.N.J. 1982), nor does federal funding or regulation convert such entities into covered agencies, see St. Michaels Convalescent Hosp. v. California, 643 F.2d 1369, 1373 (9th Cir. 1981); Adelman v. Discover Card Servs., 915 F. Supp. 1163, 1166 (D. Utah 1996).

Similarly, private entities are not subject to the Act, see, e.g., Sutton v. Providence St. Joseph Med. Ctr., 192 F.3d 826, 844 (9th Cir. 1999); Mitchell v. G.E. American Spacenet, No. 96-2624, 1997 WL 226369, at *1 (4th Cir. May 7, 1997); Gilbreath v. Guadalupe Hosp. Found., 5 F.3d 785, 791 (5th Cir. 1993); Locke v. MedLab/Gen. Chem., No. 99-2137, 2000 WL 127111 (E.D. Pa. Feb. 3, 2000); Davis v. Boston Edison Co., No. 83-1114-2, 1985 U.S. Dist. LEXIS 23275 (D. Mass. Jan. 21, 1985); Friedlander v. United States Postal Serv., No. 84-773, slip op. at 5-6 (D.D.C. Oct. 16, 1984); Marshall v. Park Place Hosp., 3 Gov't Disclosure Serv. (P-H) ¶ 83,088, at 83,057 (D.D.C. Feb. 25, 1983); see also Bybee v. Pirtle, No. 96-5077, 1996 WL 596458, at *1 (6th Cir. Oct. 16, 1996) (appellant did not state claim under Privacy Act because Act does not apply to conduct of individuals who refused to hire him due to his failure to furnish his social security number or fill out W-4 forms for income tax purposes); Steadman v. Rocky Mountain News, No. 95-1102, 1995 U.S. App. LEXIS 34986, at *4 (10th Cir. Dec. 11, 1995) (Privacy Act claims "cannot be brought against defendant because defendant is not a governmental entity"); United States v. Mercado, No. 94-3976, 1995 U.S. App. LEXIS 2054, at **3-4 (6th Cir. Jan. 31, 1995) (appellant's retained defense counsel not an "agency"), nor does federal funding or regulation render such entities subject to the Act, see Unt v. Aerospace Corp., 765 F.2d 1440, 1448 (9th Cir. 1985); United States v. Haynes, 620 F. Supp. 474, 478-79 (M.D. Tenn. 1985); Dennie v. University of Pittsburgh Sch. of Med., 589 F. Supp. 348, 351-52 (D.V.I. 1984), aff'd, 770 F.2d 1068 (3d Cir. 1985) (unpublished table decision); see also United States v. Miller, 643 F.2d 713, 715 n.1 (10th Cir. 1981) (finding that definition of "agency" does not encompass national banks); Boggs v. Southeastern Tidewater Opportunity Project, No. 2:96cv196, 1996 U.S. Dist. LEXIS 6977, at **5-9 (E.D. Va. May 22, 1996) (rejecting plaintiff's argument concerning entity's acceptance of federal funds and stating that "[i]t is well settled that the Administrative Procedures [sic] Act, 5 U.S.C. § 551 . . . applies only to Federal agencies").

Note also that federal entities outside of the executive branch, such as a grand jury, see Standley v. Department of Justice, 835 F.2d 216, 218 (9th Cir. 1987), a probation office, see

PRIVACY ACT OVERVIEW

Schwartz v. United States Dep't of Justice, No. 95-6423, 1996 WL 335757, at *1 (2d Cir. June 6, 1996), aff'g No. 94 CIV. 7476, 1995 WL 675462, at *7 (S.D.N.Y. Nov. 14, 1995); Callwood v. Department of Probation of the V.I., 982 F. Supp. 341, 343 (D.V.I. 1997); Chambers v. Division of Probation, No. 87-0163, 1987 WL 10133, at *1 (D.D.C. Apr. 8, 1987), or a federal bankruptcy court, see In re Adair, 212 B.R. 171, 173 (Bankr. N.D. Ga. 1997), are not subject to the Act. Similarly, the Smithsonian Institution, although having many "links" with the federal government, "is not an agency for Privacy Act purposes." Dong v. Smithsonian Inst., 125 F.3d 877, 879-80 (D.C. Cir. 1997), cert. denied, 524 U.S. 922 (1998).

An exception to this rule, however, is the social security number usage restrictions, contained in Section 7 of the Privacy Act, which do apply to federal, state, and local government agencies. (Section 7, originally part of the Privacy Act, Pub. L. No. 93-579, was not codified; it can be found at 5 U.S.C. § 552a note (Disclosure of Social Security Number)). This special provision is discussed below under "Social Security Number Usage."

A Privacy Act lawsuit is properly filed against an "agency" only, not against an individual, a government official, or an employee. See, e.g., Connelly v. Comptroller of the Currency, 876 F.2d 1209, 1215 (5th Cir. 1989); Petrus v. Bowen, 833 F.2d 581, 582-83 (5th Cir. 1987); Schowengerdt v. General Dynamics Corp., 823 F.2d 1328, 1340 (9th Cir. 1987); Hewitt v. Grabicki, 794 F.2d 1373, 1377 & n.2 (9th Cir. 1986); Unt, 765 F.2d at 1447; Brown-Bey v. United States, 720 F.2d 467, 469 (7th Cir. 1983); Windsor v. The Tennessean, 719 F.2d 155, 159-60 (6th Cir. 1983); Bruce v. United States, 621 F.2d 914, 916 n.2 (8th Cir. 1980); Parks v. IRS, 618 F.2d 677, 684 (10th Cir. 1980); Armstrong v. United States Bureau of Prisons, 976 F. Supp. 17, 23 (D.D.C. 1997), summary affirmance granted sub nom. Armstrong v. Federal Bureau of Prisons, No. 97-5208, 1998 WL 65543 (D.C. Cir. Jan. 30, 1998); Claasen v. Brown, No. 94-1018, 1996 WL 79490, at **3-4 (D.D.C. Feb. 16, 1996); Lloyd v. Coady, No. 94-5842, 1995 U.S. Dist. LEXIS 2490, at **3-4 (E.D. Pa. Feb. 28, 1995), upon consideration of amended complaint, 1995 U.S. Dist. LEXIS 6258, at *3 n.2 (E.D. Pa. May 9, 1995); Hill v. Blevins, No. 3-CV-92-0859, slip op. at 4-5 (M.D. Pa. Apr. 12, 1993), aff'd, 19 F.3d 643 (3d Cir. 1994) (unpublished table decision); Malewich, No. 91-4871, slip op. at 19 (D.N.J. Apr. 8, 1993); Sheptin v. United States Dep't of Justice, No. 91-2806, 1992 U.S. Dist. LEXIS 6221, at **5-6 (D.D.C. Apr. 30, 1992); Williams v. McCausland, 791 F. Supp. 992, 1000 (S.D.N.Y. 1992); Mittleman v. United States Treasury, 773 F. Supp. 442, 450 (D.D.C. 1991); Stephens v. TVA, 754 F. Supp. 579, 580 n.1 (E.D. Tenn. 1990); B.J.R.L. v. Utah, 655 F. Supp. 692, 696-97 (D. Utah 1987); Dennie, 589 F. Supp. at 351-53; Gonzalez v. Leonard, 497 F. Supp. 1058, 1075-76 (D. Conn. 1980); cf. Stewart v. FBI, No.

97-1595, 1999 U.S. Dist. LEXIS 21335, at **15-22 (D. Or. Dec. 10, 1999) (magistrate's recommendation) (actions of two Air Force officers assigned to other agencies were not attributable to Air Force; neither were their actions attributable to State Department, because although they both physically worked at embassy and ambassador had supervisory responsibility over all executive branch agency employees, neither reported to State Department or ambassador), adopted, No. 97-1595, 2000 U.S. Dist. LEXIS 2954 (D. Or. Mar. 15, 2000). Note, however, that a prosecution enforcing the Privacy Act's criminal penalties provision, 5 U.S.C. § 552a(i) (see "Criminal Penalties" discussion below), would of course properly be filed against an individual. See Stone v. Defense Investigative Serv., 816 F. Supp. 782, 785 (D.D.C. 1993) ("Under the Privacy Act, this Court has jurisdiction over individually named defendants only for unauthorized disclosure in violation of 5 U.S.C. § 552a(i)."); see also Hampton v. FBI, No. 93-0816, slip op. at 8, 10-11 (D.D.C. June 30, 1995) (citing Stone).

However, some courts have held that the head of an agency, if sued in his or her official capacity, can be a proper party defendant. See, e.g., Hampton, No. 93-0816, slip op. at 8, 10-11 (D.D.C. June 30, 1995); Jarrell v. Tisch, 656 F. Supp. 237, 238 (D.D.C. 1987); Diamond v. FBI, 532 F. Supp. 216, 219-20 (S.D.N.Y. 1981), aff'd, 707 F.2d 75 (2d Cir. 1983); Nemetz v. Department of the Treasury, 446 F. Supp. 102, 106 (N.D. Ill. 1978); Rowe v. Tennessee, 431 F. Supp. 1257, 1264 (M.D. Tenn. 1977), vacated on other grounds, 609 F.2d 259 (6th Cir. 1979). Further, leave to amend a complaint to substitute a proper party defendant ordinarily is freely granted where the agency is on notice of the claim. See, e.g., Reyes v. Supervisor of DEA, 834 F.2d 1093, 1097 (1st Cir. 1987); Petrus, 833 F.2d at 583. But cf. Doe v. Rubin, No. 95-CV-75874, 1998 U.S. Dist. LEXIS 14755, at *9 (E.D. Mich. Aug. 10, 1998) (granting summary judgment for defendant where plaintiff had named Secretary of the Treasury as defendant and had filed no motion to amend).

**B. Individual**

"a citizen of the United States or an alien lawfully admitted for permanent residence." 5 U.S.C. § 552a(a)(2).

comment -- Compare this definition with the FOIA's much broader "any person" definition (5 U.S.C. § 552(a)(3) (1994 & Supp. IV 1998)). See, e.g., Fares v. INS, No. 94-1339, 1995 WL 115809, at *4 (4th Cir. 1995) (per curiam) ("[Privacy] Act only protects citizens of the United States or aliens lawfully admitted for permanent residence."); Raven v. Panama Canal Co., 583 F.2d 169, 170-71 (5th Cir. 1978) (same as Fares, and comparing "use of the word 'individual' in the Privacy Act, as opposed to the word 'person,' as more broadly used in the FOIA"); Cudzich v. INS, 886 F. Supp. 101, 105 (D.D.C. 1995) (A plaintiff whose permanent resident status had been revoked "is not an 'individual' for the purposes of the Privacy Act. . . . Plaintiff's only potential access to the requested information is therefore under the Freedom of Information Act.").

Deceased individuals do not have any Privacy Act rights, nor do executors or next-of-kin. See OMB Guidelines, 40 Fed. Reg. 28,948, 28,951 (1975); see also Monk v. Teeter, No. 89-16333, 1992 WL 1681, at *2 (9th Cir. Jan. 8. 1992); Crumpton v. United States, 843 F. Supp. 751, 756 (D.D.C. 1994), aff'd on other grounds sub nom. Crumpton v. Stone, 59 F.3d 1400 (D.C. Cir. 1995).

Corporations and organizations also do not have any Privacy Act rights. See St. Michaels Convalescent Hosp. v. California, 643 F.2d 1369, 1373 (9th Cir. 1981); OKC v. Williams, 614 F.2d 58, 60 (5th Cir. 1980); Dresser Indus. v. United States, 596 F.2d 1231, 1237-38 (5th Cir. 1980); Cell Assocs. v. NIH, 579 F.2d 1155, 1157 (9th Cir. 1978); Stone v. Export-Import Bank of the United States, 552 F.2d 132, 137 n.7 (5th Cir. 1977); Committee in Solidarity v. Sessions, 738 F. Supp. 544, 547 (D.D.C. 1990), aff'd on other grounds, 929 F.2d 742 (D.C. Cir. 1991); United States v. Haynes, 620 F. Supp. 474, 478-79 (M.D. Tenn. 1985); Utah-Ohio Gas & Oil, Inc. v. SEC, 1 Gov't Disclosure Serv. (P-H) ¶ 80,038, at 80,114 (D. Utah Jan. 9, 1980); see also OMB Guidelines, 40 Fed. Reg. at 28,951.

The OMB Guidelines suggest that an individual has no standing under the Act to challenge agency handling of records that pertain to him solely in his "entrepreneurial" capacity. OMB Guidelines, 40 Fed. Reg. at 28,951 (quoting legislative history and stating that it "suggests that a distinction can be made between individuals acting in a personal capacity and individuals acting in an entrepreneurial capacity (e.g., as sole proprietors) and that th[e] definition [of 'individual'] (and, therefore, the Act) was intended to embrace only the former"). However, there is a split of authority concerning OMB's personal/entrepreneurial distinction as applied to an individual. Compare Shermco Indus. v. Secretary of the United States Air Force, 452 F. Supp. 306, 314-15 (N.D. Tex. 1978) (accepting distinction), rev'd & remanded on other grounds, 613 F.2d 1314 (5th Cir. 1980), and Daniels v. FCC, No. 77-5011, slip op. at 8-9 (D.S.D. Mar. 15, 1978) (same), with Henke v. Department of Commerce, No. 94-189, 1995 WL 904918, at *2 (D.D.C. May 26, 1995) (rejecting distinction), vacated & remanded on other grounds, 83 F.3d 1453 (D.C. Cir. 1996); Henke v. United States Dep't of Commerce, No. 94-0189, 1996 WL 692020, at **2-3 (D.D.C. Aug. 19, 1994) (same), aff'd on other grounds, 83 F.3d 1445 (D.C. Cir. 1996); Metadure Corp. v. United States, 490 F. Supp. 1368, 1373-74 (S.D.N.Y. 1980) (same); Florida Med. Ass'n v. HEW, 479 F. Supp. 1291, 1307-11 (M.D. Fla. 1979) (same), and Zeller v. United States, 467 F. Supp. 487, 496-99 (E.D.N.Y. 1979) (same). Cf. St. Michaels Convalescent Hosp., 643 F.2d at 1373 (stating

## PRIVACY ACT OVERVIEW

that "sole proprietorships[] are not 'individuals' and thus lack standing to raise a claim under the Privacy Act").

Privacy Act rights are <u>personal</u> to the individual who is the subject of the record and cannot be asserted derivatively by others. <u>See, e.g.</u>, <u>Parks v. IRS</u>, 618 F.2d 677, 684-85 (10th Cir. 1980) (union lacks standing to sue for damages to its members); <u>Word v. United States</u>, 604 F.2d 1127, 1129 (8th Cir. 1979) (criminal defendant lacks standing to allege Privacy Act violations regarding use at trial of medical records concerning third party); <u>Dresser Indus.</u>, 596 F.2d at 1238 (company lacks standing to litigate employees' Privacy Act claims); <u>Sirmans v. Caldera</u>, 27 F. Supp. 2d 248, 250 (D.D.C. 1998) (plaintiffs "may not object to the Army's failure to correct the records of other officers"); <u>Shulman v. Secretary of HHS</u>, No. 94 CIV. 5506, 1997 WL 68554, at **1, 3 (S.D.N.Y. Feb. 19, 1997) (plaintiff had no standing to assert any right that might have belonged to former spouse), <u>aff'd</u>, No. 96-6140 (2d Cir. Sept. 3, 1997); <u>Harbolt v. United States Dep't of Justice</u>, No. A-84-CA-280, slip op. at 2 (W.D. Tex. Apr. 29, 1985) (prisoner lacks standing to assert Privacy Act claims of other inmates regarding disclosure of their records to him); <u>Abramsky v. United States Consumer Prod. Safety Comm'n</u>, 478 F. Supp. 1040, 1041-42 (S.D.N.Y. 1979) (union president cannot compel release of records pertaining to employee's termination); <u>Attorney Gen. of the United States v. Irish N. Aid Comm.</u>, No. 77-700, 1977 U.S. Dist. LEXIS 13581, at *12 (S.D.N.Y. Oct. 7, 1977) (committee lacks standing to sue in representative capacity). But see <u>National Fed'n of Fed. Employees v. Greenberg</u>, 789 F. Supp. 430, 433 (D.D.C. 1992) (union has associational standing because members whose interests union seeks to represent would themselves have standing), <u>vacated & remanded on other grounds</u>, 983 F.2d 286 (D.C. Cir. 1993).

Note, however, that the parent of any minor, or the legal guardian of an incompetent, may act on behalf of that individual. <u>See</u> 5 U.S.C. § 552a(h); <u>see also</u> <u>Gula v. Meese</u>, 699 F. Supp. 956, 961 (D.D.C. 1988). The OMB Guidelines note that subsection (h) is "discretionary and that individuals who are minors are authorized to exercise the rights given to them by the Privacy Act or, in the alternative, their parents or those acting <u>in loco parentis</u> may exercise them in their behalf." OMB Guidelines, 40 Fed. Reg. at 28,970; <u>see also</u> OMB Guidelines, 40 Fed. Reg. 56,741, 56,742 (1975) (noting that "[t]here is no absolute right of a parent to have access to a record about a child absent a court order or consent").

**C. Maintain**

"maintain, collect, use or disseminate." 5 U.S.C. § 552a(a)(3).

comment -- This definition embraces various activities with

respect to records and has a meaning much broader than the common usage of the term. See OMB Guidelines, 40 Fed. Reg. 28,948, 28,951 (1975); see also, e.g., Albright v. United States, 631 F.2d 915, 918-20 (D.C. Cir. 1980) (analyzing scope of "maintain" in context of subsection (e)(7) challenge to record describing First Amendment-protected activity).

### D. Record

"any item, collection, or grouping of information about an individual that is maintained by an agency, including, but not limited to, his education, financial transactions, medical history, and criminal or employment history and that contains his name, or the identifying number, symbol, or other identifying particular assigned to the individual, such as a finger or voice print or a photograph." 5 U.S.C. § 552a(a)(4).

comment -- To qualify as a "record," the information must identify an individual. Compare Reuber v. United States, 829 F.2d 133, 142 (D.C. Cir. 1987) (letter reprimanding individual sent to and disclosed by agency was "record" because it clearly identified individual by name and address), with Robinson v. United States Dep't of Educ., No. 87-2554, 1988 WL 5083, at *1 (E.D. Pa. Jan. 20, 1988) (letter describing individual's administrative complaint not "record" because it did not mention his name).

The OMB Guidelines state that the term "record" means "any item of information about an individual that includes an individual identifier," OMB Guidelines, 40 Fed. Reg. 28,948, 28,951 (1975), and "'can include as little as one descriptive item about an individual,'" id. at 28,952 (quoting legislative history appearing at 120 Cong. Rec. 40,408, 40,883 (1974), reprinted in Source Book at 866, 993).

Several courts of appeals have articulated tests for determining whether an item qualifies as a "record" under the Privacy Act, resulting in three different tests for determining "record" status:

(1) Consistent with the OMB Guidelines, the Courts of Appeals for the Second and Third Circuits have broadly interpreted the term "record." See Bechhoefer v. United States Dep't of Justice Drug Enforcement Admin., 209 F.3d 57 (2d Cir. 2000); Quinn v. Stone, 978 F.2d 126 (3d Cir. 1992). The Third Circuit held that the term "record" "encompass[es] any information about an individual that is linked to that individual through an identifying particular" and is not "limited to information which taken alone directly reflects a characteristic or quality." Quinn v. Stone, 978 F.2d at 133 (out-of-date home address on roster and time card information held to be records covered by Privacy Act). The Second Circuit, after analyzing the tests established by the other courts of appeals, adopted a test "much like the Third Circuit's test." Bechhoefer, 209 F.3d at 60. The Second Circuit did so for three reasons: First, it found the Third Circuit's test to be "most consistent with the 'broad terms' . . . of the statutory definition," id.; second, it found

-672-

the Third Circuit's test to be the only one consistent with the Supreme Court's decision in DOD v. FLRA, 510 U.S. 487, 494 (1994), which held that federal civil service employees' home addresses qualified for protection under the Privacy Act, Bechhoefer, 209 F.3d at 61; and, finally, it found the Third Circuit's test to be supported by the legislative history of the Privacy Act and by the guidelines issued by OMB, id. at 61-62.  Emphasizing that "the legislative history makes plain that Congress intended 'personal information' . . . to have a broad meaning," the Second Circuit held that the term "record" "has 'a broad meaning encompassing,' at the very least, any personal information 'about an individual that is linked to that individual through an identifying particular.'"  Id. at 62 (quoting Quinn and holding that letter containing Bechhoefer's name and "several pieces of 'personal information' about him, including his address, his voice/fax telephone number, his employment, and his membership in [an association]" was record covered by Privacy Act).

Several other courts have likewise broadly interpreted the term "record."  See Doe v. Herman, No. 2:97CV00043, 1999 U.S. Dist. LEXIS 17302, at *28 (W.D. Va. Oct. 29, 1999) (magistrate's recommendation) ("social security numbers . . . constitute records as defined by the Privacy Act"); Henke v. United States Dep't of Commerce, No. 94-0189, 1996 WL 692020, at *3 (D.D.C. Aug. 19, 1994) (names of four reviewers who evaluated grant applicant's proposal are applicant's "records" under Privacy Act), aff'd on other grounds, 83 F.3d 1445 (D.C. Cir. 1996); cf. Williams v. VA, 104 F.3d 670, 673-74 (4th Cir. 1997) (quoting legislative history and finding that materials qualified as "records" because they "substantially pertain to Appellant," "contain 'information about' [him], as well as his 'name' or 'identifying number,'" and "do more than merely apply to him"); Unt v. Aerospace Corp., 765 F.2d 1440, 1449-50 (9th Cir. 1985) (Ferguson, J., dissenting) (opining that majority's narrow interpretation of term "record," (discussed below), "is illogical, contrary to the legislative intent, and defies the case laws' consistent concern with the actual effect of a record on a person's employment when assessing that record's nature or subject"); Sullivan v. United States Postal Serv., 944 F. Supp. 191, 196 (W.D.N.Y. 1996) (finding that disclosure to job applicant's employer that applicant had applied for employment with Postal Service constituted disclosure of "record" under Privacy Act; although no other information was disclosed from application, rejecting Postal Service's attempt to distinguish between disclosing fact of record's existence and disclosing information contained in record, as applicant's name was part of information contained in application and Postal Service disclosed that particular applicant by that name had applied for employment).

(2)  The Courts of Appeals for the Ninth and Eleventh Circuits have limited Privacy Act coverage by adopting a narrow construction of the term "record"--requiring that in order to qualify, the information "must reflect some quality or characteristic of the individual involved."  Boyd v.

Secretary of the Navy, 709 F.2d 684, 686 (11th Cir. 1983) (per curiam) (although stating narrow test, finding that memorandum reflecting "Boyd's failure to follow the chain of command and his relationship with management" qualified as Privacy Act record); accord Unt v. Aerospace Corp., 765 F.2d 1440, 1448-49 (9th Cir. 1985) (letter written by employee--containing allegations of mismanagement against corporation that led to his dismissal--held not his "record" because it was "about" the corporation and reflected "only indirectly on any quality or characteristic" of employee).

(3) The Court of Appeals for the District of Columbia Circuit has also adopted a narrow construction of the term by holding that in order to qualify as a "record" an item must contain "information that actually describes the individual in some way." Tobey v. NLRB, 40 F.3d 469, 471-73 (D.C. Cir. 1994). Examining the Third Circuit's statement in Quinn that information could qualify as a record "'if that piece of information were linked with an identifying particular (or was itself an identifying particular),'" the D.C. Circuit rejected the Third Circuit's interpretation "[t]o the extent that . . . [it] fails to require that information both be 'about' an individual and be linked to that individual by an identifying particular." Id. In order to qualify as a "record," the D.C. Circuit ruled that the information "must both be 'about' an individual and include his name or other identifying particular." Id. at 471. On the other hand, the D.C. Circuit rejected "as too narrow the Ninth and Eleventh Circuits' definitions" in Unt and Boyd, and stated that: "So long as the information is 'about' an individual, nothing in the Act requires that it additionally be about a 'quality or characteristic' of the individual." Tobey, 40 F.3d at 472. Ultimately, the D.C. Circuit, "[w]ithout attempting to define 'record' more specifically than [necessary] to resolve the case at bar," held that an NLRB computer system for tracking and monitoring cases did not constitute a system of records, because its files contained no information "about" individuals, despite the fact that the case information contained the initials or identifying number of the field examiner assigned to the case. Id. at 471-73. Although the court recognized that the case information could be, and apparently was, used in connection with other information to draw inferences about a field examiner's job performance, it stated that that "does not transform the [computer system] files into records about field examiners." Id. at 472-73.

Several other courts have also limited Privacy Act coverage by applying narrow constructions of the term "record." See Hassell v. Callahan, No. 97-0037-B, slip op. at 3-5 (W.D. Va. Aug. 7, 1997) (finding that public sign-up sheet that asked for name of claimant and name of his representative for disability benefits did not constitute "record"; stating that "this court is not inclined to lump the name of a person's representative within the same category as information regarding his medical or financial history"); Fisher v. NIH, 934

F. Supp. 464, 466-67, 469-72 (D.D.C. 1996) (following Tobey and finding that information in database about articles published in scientific journals that contained bibliographic information including title of article and publication, name and address of author, and summary of article and also included annotation "[scientific misconduct-- data to be reanalyzed]," provides "information 'about' the article described in each file and does not provide information 'about' [the author]," even though information "could be used to draw inferences or conclusions about [the author]"; "The fact that it is possible for a reasonable person to interpret information as describing an individual does not mean the information is about that individual for purposes of the Privacy Act."), summary affirmance granted, No. 96-5252 (D.C. Cir. Nov. 27, 1996); Wolde-Giorgis v. United States, No. 94-254, slip op. at 5-6 (D. Ariz. Dec. 9, 1994) (citing Unt with approval and holding that Postal Service claim form and information concerning estimated value of item sent through mail was "not a 'record' within the meaning of the [Privacy Act]" because it "disclosed no information about the plaintiff" and did not reflect any "'quality or characteristic' concerning the plaintiff"), aff'd, 65 F.3d 177 (9th Cir. 1995) (unpublished table decision); Ingerman v. IRS, No. 89-5396, slip op. at 6 (D.N.J. Apr. 3, 1991) ("An individual's social security number does not contain his name, identifying number or other identifying particular. . . . [A] social security number is the individual's identifying number, and therefore, it cannot qualify as a record under . . . the Privacy Act."), aff'd, 953 F.2d 1380 (3d Cir. 1992) (unpublished table decision); Nolan v. United States Dep't of Justice, No. 89-A-2035, 1991 WL 36547, at *10 (D. Colo. Mar. 18, 1991) (names of FBI agents and other personnel held not requester's "record" and therefore "outside the scope of the [Privacy Act]"), aff'd, 973 F.2d 843 (10th Cir. 1992); Doe v. United States Dep't of Justice, 790 F. Supp. 17, 22 (D.D.C. 1992) (applying Nolan and alternatively holding that "names of agents involved in the investigation are properly protected from disclosure"); Shewchun v. United States Customs Serv., No. 87-2967, 1989 WL 7351, at *1 (D.D.C. Jan. 11, 1989) (letter concerning agency's disposition of plaintiff's merchandise "lacks a sufficient informational nexus with [plaintiff] (himself, as opposed to his property) to bring it within the definition of 'record'"); Blair v. United States Forest Serv., No. A85-039, slip op. at 4-5 (D. Alaska Sept. 24, 1985) ("Plan of Operation" form completed by plaintiff held not his "record" as it "reveals nothing about his personal affairs"), appeal dismissed, No. 85-4220 (9th Cir. Apr. 1, 1986); Windsor v. A Fed. Executive Agency, 614 F. Supp. 1255, 1260-61 (M.D. Tenn. 1983) (record includes only sensitive information about individual's private affairs), aff'd, 767 F.2d 923 (6th Cir. 1985) (unpublished table decision); Cohen v. United States Dep't of Labor, 3 Gov't Disclosure Serv. (P-H) ¶ 83,157, at 83,791 (D. Mass. Mar. 21, 1983) (record includes only "personal" information); AFGE v. NASA, 482 F. Supp. 281, 282-83 (S.D. Tex. 1980) (determining that sign-in/sign-out sheet was not "record" because, standing alone, it did not reveal any "substantive information about the employees"); Houston v. United States Dep't of the Treasury, 494 F. Supp. 24, 28 (D.D.C. 1979) (same as Cohen); see also Drake v. 136th Airlift Wing, Tex. Air Nat'l Guard, No. 3:98-CV-1673D, 1998 WL 872915, at **1-2 (N.D. Tex. Nov. 30, 1998) (stating that list of names of witnesses is not record, as it "does not include personal information regarding any particular individual"), aff'd, 209 F.3d 718 (5th Cir. 2000) (unpublished table decision); Benson v. United States, No. 80-15-MC, slip op. at 4 (D. Mass. June 12, 1980) (permitting withholding of OPM investigator's name where identities of informants were properly excised under subsection (k)(5)); cf. Topuridze v. FBI, No. 86-3120, 1989 WL 11709, at *2 (D.D.C. Feb. 6, 1989) (citing Unt with approval and holding that letter written about requester, authored by third party, cannot be regarded as third party's record; it "does not follow that a document reveals some quality or characteristic of an individual simply by virtue of the individual having authored the document"), reconsideration denied sub nom. Topuridze v. USIA, 772 F. Supp. 662, 664-65 (D.D.C. 1991) (after in camera review, although reaffirming that "[i]n order to be about an individual a record must 'reflect some quality or characteristic of the individual involved,'" stating that document "may well be 'about' the author," as it discussed author's family status, employment, and fear of physical retaliation if letter were disclosed to plaintiff, and ultimately ruling that it need not reach issue of whether or not letter was "about" author and denying reconsideration on ground that letter was without dispute about subject/plaintiff and therefore must be released to him). But cf. Williams v. VA, 104 F.3d 670, 673-74 (4th Cir. 1997) (quoting legislative history and finding that materials qualified as "records" because they "substantially pertain to Appellant," "contain 'information about' [him], as well as his 'name' or 'identifying number,'" and "do more than merely apply to him").

For a further illustration of conflicting views concerning the meaning of the term "record" in the subsection (d)(1) access context, compare Voelker v. IRS, 646 F.2d 332, 334 (8th Cir. 1981), with Nolan v. United States Dep't of Justice, No. 89-A-2035, 1991 WL 36547, at *3 (D. Colo. Mar. 18, 1991), aff'd, 973 F.2d 843 (10th Cir. 1992), and DePlanche v. Califano, 549 F. Supp. 685, 693-98 (W.D. Mich. 1982). These important cases are further discussed below under "Individual's Right of Access."

One district court, in a case concerning the Privacy Act's subsection (b)(3) routine use exception, has held that a plaintiff may choose which particular "item of information" (one document) contained within a "collection or grouping of information" disclosed (a prosecutive report indicating a potential violation of law) to denominate as a "record" and challenge as wrongfully disclosed. Covert v. Harrington, 667 F. Supp. 730, 736-37 (E.D. Wash. 1987), aff'd on other grounds, 876 F.2d 751 (9th Cir. 1989). Purporting to construe the term "record" narrowly, the district court in Covert ruled that the Department of Energy's routine use--47 Fed. Reg. 14,333 (1982) (permitting disclosure of relevant records where "a record" indicates a potential violation of law)--did not permit its Inspector General to disclose personnel security questionnaires to the Justice Department for prosecution because the questionnaires themselves did not reveal a potential violation of law on their face. 667 F. Supp. at 736-37. Covert is further discussed below under "Conditions of Disclosure to Third Parties," "Agency Requirements," and "Civil Remedies."

Note also that purely private notes--such as personal memory refreshers--are generally regarded as not subject to the Privacy Act because they are not "agency records." See Johnston v. Horne, 875 F.2d 1415, 1423 (9th Cir. 1989); Bowyer v. United States Dep't of the Air Force, 804 F.2d 428, 431 (7th Cir. 1986); Boyd v. Secretary of the Navy, 709 F.2d 684, 686 (11th Cir. 1983) (per curiam); Harmer v. Perry, No. 95-4197, 1998 WL 229637, at *3 (E.D. Pa. Apr. 28, 1998), aff'd, No. 98-1532 (3d Cir. Jan. 29, 1999); Sherwin v. Department of Air Force, No. 90-34-CIV-3, slip op. at 2-7 (E.D.N.C. Apr. 15, 1992), aff'd, 37 F.3d 1495 (4th Cir. 1994) (unpublished table decision); Glass v. United States Dep't of Energy, No. 87-2205, 1988 WL 118408, at *1 (D.D.C. Oct. 29, 1988); Mahar v. National Parks Serv., No. 86-0398, slip op. at 16-17 (D.D.C. Dec. 23, 1987); Kalmin v. Department of the Navy, 605 F. Supp. 1492, 1494-95 (D.D.C. 1985); Machen v. United States Army, No. 78-582, slip op. at 4 (D.D.C. May 11, 1979); see also OMB Guidelines, 40 Fed. Reg. at 28,952 ("Uncirculated personal notes, papers and records which are retained or discarded at the author's discretion and over which the agency exercises no control or dominion (e.g., personal telephone lists) are not considered to be agency records within the meaning of the Privacy Act.").

However, in Chapman v. NASA, 682 F.2d 526, 529 (5th Cir. 1982), the Court of Appeals for the Fifth Circuit, relying on the fair recordkeeping duties imposed by subsection (e)(5), ruled that private notes may "evanesce" into records subject to the Act when they are used to make a decision on the individual's employment status well after the evaluation period for which they were compiled. See also Lawrence v. Dole, No. 83-2876, slip op. at 5-6 (D.D.C. Dec. 12, 1985) ("[a]bsent timely incorporation into the employee's file, the private notes may not be used as a basis for an adverse employment action"); Thompson v. Department of Transp. United States Coast Guard, 547 F. Supp. 274, 283-84 (S.D. Fla. 1982) (timeliness requirement of subsection (e)(5) met where private notes upon which disciplinary action is based are placed in system of records "contemporaneously with or within a reasonable time after an adverse disciplinary action is proposed"). But cf. Sherwin, No. 90-34-CIV-3, slip op. at 2-7 (E.D.N.C. Apr. 15, 1992) (distinguishing Chapman and finding that notes of telephone conversations between two of plaintiff's supervisors concerning plaintiff were not "agency 'records'" because plaintiff was

PRIVACY ACT OVERVIEW

"well aware of the general content" of notes, "essence" of notes was incorporated in agency's records, "private notes played no role" in plaintiff's discharge, and although some of notes were shared between two supervisors, "they remained personal notes at all times").

Note that publicly available information, such as newspaper clippings or press releases, can constitute a "record." See Clarkson v. IRS, 678 F.2d 1368, 1372 (11th Cir. 1982) (permitting subsection (e)(7) challenge to agency's maintenance of newsletters and press releases); Murphy v. NSA, 2 Gov't Disclosure Serv. (P-H) ¶ 81,389, at 82,036-37 (D.D.C. Sept. 29, 1981) (same as to newspaper clippings); see also OMB Guidelines, 40 Fed. Reg. 56,741, 56,742 (1975) ("[c]ollections of newspaper clippings or other published matter about an individual maintained other than in a conventional reference library would normally be a system of records"); cf. Fisher, 934 F. Supp. at 469 (discussing difference between definition of "record" for purposes of FOIA and statutory definition under Privacy Act and rejecting argument, based on FOIA case law, that "library reference materials" are not covered by Privacy Act).

One court has relied on non-Privacy Act case law concerning grand jury records to hold that a grand jury transcript, "though in possession of the U. S. Attorney, is not a record of the Justice Department within the meaning of the Privacy Act." Kotmair v. United States Dep't of Justice, No. S 94-721, slip op. at 1 (D. Md. July 12, 1994) (citing United States v. Penrod, 609 F.2d 1092, 1097 (4th Cir. 1979), for above proposition, but then confusingly not applying same theory to analysis of FOIA accessibility), aff'd, 42 F.3d 1386 (4th Cir. 1994) (unpublished table decision).

The Privacy Act--like the FOIA--does not require agencies to create records that do not exist. See DeBold v. Stimson, 735 F.2d 1037, 1041 (7th Cir. 1984); Perkins v. IRS, No. 86-CV-71551, slip op. at 4 (E.D. Mich. Dec. 16, 1986); see also, e.g., Villanueva v. Department of Justice, 782 F.2d 528, 532 (5th Cir. 1986) (rejecting argument that FBI was required to "find a way to provide a brief but intelligible explanation for its decision . . . without [revealing exempt information]"). But compare May v. Department of the Air Force, 777 F.2d 1012, 1015-17 (5th Cir. 1985) ("reasonable segregation requirement" obligates agency to create and release typewritten version of handwritten evaluation forms so as not to reveal identity of evaluator under exemption (k)(7)), with Church of Scientology W. United States v. IRS, No. CV-89-5894, slip op. at 4 (C.D. Cal. Mar. 5, 1991) (FOIA decision rejecting argument based upon May and holding that agency not required to create records).

E.  System of Records

"a group of any records under the control of any agency from which information is retrieved by the name of the individual or by some identifying number, symbol, or other

identifying particular assigned to the individual."
5 U.S.C. § 552a(a)(5).

comment -- The OMB Guidelines explain that a system of records exists if: (1) there is an "indexing or retrieval capability using identifying particulars [that is] built into the system"; and (2) the agency "does, in fact, retrieve records about individuals by reference to some personal identifier." OMB Guidelines, 40 Fed. Reg. 28,948, 28,952 (1975). The Guidelines state that the "is retrieved by" criterion "implies that the grouping of records under the control of an agency _is accessed_ by the agency by use of a personal identifier; not merely that a capability or potential for retrieval exists." Id. (emphasis added).

The Court of Appeals for the District of Columbia Circuit addressed the "system of records" definition in the context of computerized information in Henke v. United States Dep't of Commerce, 83 F.3d 1453 (D.C. Cir. 1996), and noted that "the OMB guidelines make it clear that it is not sufficient that an agency has the capability to retrieve information indexed under a person's name, but the agency must _in fact_ retrieve records in this way in order for a system of records to exist." Id. at 1460 n.12. The issue in Henke was whether or not computerized databases that contained information concerning technology grant proposals submitted by businesses constituted a "system of records" as to individuals listed as the "contact persons" for the grant applications, where the agency had acknowledged that "it could theoretically retrieve information by the name of the contact person." Id. at 1457-58. The D.C. Circuit looked to Congress's use of the words "is retrieved" in the statute's definition of a system of records and focused on whether the agency "in practice" retrieved information. Id. at 1459-61. The court held "that in determining whether an agency maintains a system of records keyed to individuals, the court should view the entirety of the situation, including the agency's function, the purpose for which the information was gathered, and the agency's actual retrieval practice and policies." Id. at 1461. Applying this test, the D.C. Circuit determined that the agency did "not maintain a system of records keyed to individuals listed in the contact person fields of its databases" because the agency's "purpose in requesting the name of a technical contact [was] essentially administrative and [was] not even necessary for the conduct of the [program's] operations," nor was there "any evidence that the names of contact persons [were] used regularly or even frequently to obtain information about those persons." Id. at 1456, 1461-62; cf. Alexander v. FBI, No. 96-2123, 2000 WL 329249, at **6-7 (D.D.C. Mar. 29, 2000) (applying Henke and finding maintenance of system of records, considering "purpose for which the information was gathered and the ordinary retrieval practices and procedures") (appeal pending); Smith v. Henderson, No. C-99-4665, 1999 WL 1029862, at *5 (N.D. Cal. Oct. 29,

1999) (applying <u>Henke</u> and finding that "locked drawer containing a file folder in which [were] kept . . . notes or various other pieces of paper relating to special circumstances hires" did not constitute a system of records because the agency "did not utilize the drawer to systematically file and retrieve information about individuals indexed by their names") (appeal pending). <u>But cf.</u> <u>Williams v. VA</u>, 104 F.3d 670, 674-77 & n.4 (4th Cir. 1997) (although remanding case for further factual development as to whether records were contained within system of records, and noting that it was "express[ing] no opinion on the <u>Henke</u> court's rationale when applied to circumstances where a plaintiff seeks to use retrieval capability to transform a group of records into a 'system of records,' as in <u>Henke</u>," nevertheless finding the "narrow <u>Henke</u> rationale . . . unconvincing" in circumstances before the court where there "appear[ed] to exist already a formal system of records," where "published characteristics of the agency's formal system of records ha[d] not kept current with advances in and typical uses of computer technology," and where record was "poorly developed" on such point).

Two district courts have also reached this result in the context of computerized information. <u>See</u> <u>Fisher v. NIH</u>, 934 F. Supp. 464, 472-73 (D.D.C. 1996) (applying <u>Henke</u> and stating: "[T]he primary practice and policy of the agency [during the time of the alleged disclosures] was to index and retrieve the investigatory files by the name of the institution in which the alleged misconduct occurred, rather than by the name of the individual scientist accused of committing the misconduct. The fact that it was possible to use plaintiff's name to identify a file containing information about the plaintiff is irrelevant."), <u>summary affirmance granted</u>, No. 96-5252 (D.C. Cir. Nov. 27, 1996); <u>Beckette v. United States Postal Serv.</u>, No. 88-802, slip op. at 19-22 (E.D. Va. July 3, 1989) (Although the plaintiff demonstrated that the agency "could retrieve . . . records by way of an individual's name or other personal identifier," that fact "does not make those records a Privacy Act system of records. The relevant inquiry is whether the records or the information they contain are [in fact] retrieved by name or other personal identifier.").

The D.C. Circuit in <u>Henke</u>, in looking to the "purpose" for which the information was gathered, also drew a distinction between information gathered for investigatory purposes and information gathered for, in that case, administrative purposes. The court stated that where information is compiled about individuals "primarily for investigatory purposes, Privacy Act concerns are at their zenith, and if there is evidence of even a few retrievals of information keyed to individuals' names, it may well be the case that the agency is maintaining a system of records." 83 F.3d at 1461; <u>see also</u> <u>Fisher</u>, 934 F. Supp. at 473 (quoting <u>Henke</u> but determining that agency's "primary practice and policy" was to retrieve investigatory files by name of institution rather than by name of individual).

Recently, the Court of Appeals for the Tenth Circuit, in Pippinger v. Rubin, finding the approach in Henke "instructive," held that, "consistent with Henke, a properly 'narrow' construction of 5 U.S.C. § 552a(a)(5)" led it to the conclusion that an Internal Revenue Service database containing an "abstraction" of information from two existing Privacy Act systems did not constitute a new system of records because it could be "accessed only by the same users, and only for the same purposes, as those published in the Federal Register for the original 'system[s] of records.'" 129 F.3d 519, 526-27 (10th Cir. 1997).

The highly technical "system of records" definition is perhaps the single most important Privacy Act concept, because (with some exceptions discussed below) it makes coverage under the Act dependent upon the method of retrieval of a record rather than its substantive content. See Baker v. Department of the Navy, 814 F.2d 1381, 1384 (9th Cir. 1987); Shannon v. General Elec. Co., 812 F. Supp. 308, 321 (N.D.N.Y. 1993); see also Crumpton v. United States, 843 F. Supp. 751, 755-56 (D.D.C. 1994) (although records disclosed to press under FOIA contained information about plaintiff, they were not retrieved by her name and therefore Privacy Act did not apply), aff'd on other grounds sub nom. Crumpton v. Stone, 59 F.3d 1400 (D.C. Cir. 1995). Indeed, a major criticism of the Privacy Act is that it can easily be circumvented by not filing records in name-retrieved formats. See Privacy Commission Report at 503-04 & n.7. A recognition of this potential for abuse has led some courts to relax the "actual retrieval" standard in particular cases (examples given below). Moreover, certain subsections of the Act (discussed below) have been construed to apply even to records not incorporated into a "system of records."

1. **Disclosure: Subsection (b)**

With varying degrees of clarity, the courts generally have ruled that a disclosure in violation of subsection (b) does not occur unless the plaintiff's record was actually retrieved by reference to his name or personal identifier. See, e.g., Barhorst v. Marsh, 765 F. Supp. 995, 999-1000 (E.D. Mo. 1991) (Privacy Act claim under subsection (b) dismissed on alternative grounds where record retrieved by job announcement number, not by individual's name; noting that "'mere potential for retrieval' by name or other identifier is insufficient to satisfy the 'system of records' requirement") (quoting Fagot v. FDIC, 584 F. Supp. 1168, 1175 (D.P.R. 1984), aff'd in part & rev'd in part, 760 F.2d 252 (1st Cir. 1985) (unpublished table decision)). But see Wall v. IRS, No. 1:88-CV-1942, 1989 U.S. Dist. LEXIS 9427, at **4-7 (N.D. Ga. July 5, 1989) (because agency official retrieved applicant's folder by name from file maintained under vacancy announcement number, records were kept within "system of records" and thus subsection (b) was applicable).

Several courts have stated that the first element a plaintiff must prove in a wrongful disclosure suit is that the information disclosed is a record within a system of records. See Quinn v. Stone, 978 F.2d 126, 131 (3d Cir. 1992); Kinchen v. United States Postal Serv., No. 90-1180, slip op. at 5 (W.D. Tenn. June 17, 1994); Hass v. United States Air Force, 848 F. Supp. 926, 932 (D. Kan. 1994); Swenson v. United States Postal Serv., No. S-87-1282, 1994 U.S. Dist. LEXIS 16524, at **14-15 (E.D. Cal. Mar. 10, 1994); see also Davis v. Runyon, No. 96-4400, 1998 WL 96558, at **4-5 (6th Cir. Feb. 23, 1998) (affirming district court's dismissal of Privacy Act wrongful disclosure claim where appellant had failed to allege any facts as to whether "'information' was a 'record' contained in a 'system of records,'" whether it was "disclos[ed] within the meaning of the Act," whether disclosure had "adverse effect," or whether disclosure was "willful or intentional"); Doe v. United States Dep't of the Interior, No. 95-1665, slip op. at 2-5 (D.D.C. Mar. 11, 1996) (alleged disclosure that plaintiff was HIV positive and had been treated for AIDS-related illnesses was not violation of Privacy Act because "[w]hile it appears to be true that some breach in confidentiality occurred . . . plaintiff cannot show that the breach stemmed from an improper disclosure of plaintiff's personnel records"); Mittleman v. United States Dep't of the Treasury, 919 F. Supp. 461, 468 (D.D.C. 1995) ("statement of general provisions of law" that was "not a disclosure of information retained in the [agency's] records on plaintiff . . . does not implicate the general nondisclosure provisions of the Privacy Act"), aff'd in part & remanded in part on other grounds, 104 F.3d 410 (D.C. Cir. 1997).

In fact, the Court of Appeals for the First Circuit has held that a complaint that fails to allege a disclosure from a "system of records" is facially deficient. Beaulieu v. IRS, 865 F.2d 1351, 1352 (1st Cir. 1989); see also Whitson v. Department of the Army, No. SA-86-CA-1173, slip op. at 8-12 (W.D. Tex. Feb. 25, 1988); Bernson v. ICC, 625 F. Supp. 10, 13 (D. Mass. 1984). But see Sterling v. United States, 798 F. Supp. 47, 49 (D.D.C. 1992) (individual "not barred from stating a claim for monetary damages [under (g)(1)(D)] merely because the record did not contain 'personal information' about him and was not retrieved through a search of indices bearing his name or other identifying characteristics"); see also Sterling v. United States, 826 F. Supp. 570, 571-72 (D.D.C. 1993) (subsequent opinion), summary affirmance granted, No. 93-5264 (D.C. Cir. Mar. 11, 1994); cf. Krieger v. Fadely, No. 99-5311, 2000 WL 489428, at **1-2 (D.C. Cir. May 5, 2000) (holding that complaint that alleged wrongful disclosure of records "subject to protection under the Privacy Act," "alleged the essential elements of [plaintiff's] claim and put the government on notice," and that "[n]othing more was required to survive a motion to dismiss for failure to state a claim"; "If his lawsuit went forward, there would come a time when [plaintiff] would have to identify the particular records [defendant] unlawfully disclosed. But that point surely was not as early as the pleading stage.").

Thus, it has frequently been held that subsection (b) is not violated when a dissemination is made on the basis of knowledge acquired independent of actual retrieval from an agency's system of records (such as a disclosure purely from memory), regardless of whether the identical information also happens to be contained in the agency's systems of records. The leading case articulating the "actual retrieval" and "independent knowledge" concepts is Savarese v. HEW, 479 F. Supp. 304, 308 (N.D. Ga. 1979), aff'd, 620 F.2d 298 (5th Cir. 1980) (unpublished table decision), in which the court ruled that for a disclosure to be covered by subsection (b), "there must have initially been a retrieval from the system of records which was at some point a source of the information." 479 F. Supp. at 308. In adopting this stringent "actual retrieval" test, the court in Savarese reasoned that a more relaxed rule could result in excessive governmental liability, or an unworkable requirement that agency employees "have a pansophic recall concerning every record within every system of records within the agency." Id.

There are numerous subsection (b) cases that follow Savarese and apply the "actual retrieval" and "independent knowledge" concepts in varying factual situations. See, e.g., Kline v. HHS, 927 F.2d 522, 524 (10th Cir. 1991); Manuel v. VA Hosp., 857 F.2d 1112, 1119-20 (6th Cir. 1988); Thomas v. United States Dep't of Energy, 719 F.2d 342, 344-46 (10th Cir. 1983); Boyd v. Secretary of the Navy, 709 F.2d 684, 687 (11th Cir. 1983) (per curiam); Doyle v. Behan, 670 F.2d 535, 538-39 & n.5 (5th Cir. 1982) (per curiam); Hanley v. United States Dep't of Justice, 623 F.2d 1138, 1139 (6th Cir. 1980) (per curiam); Fisher v. NIH, 934 F. Supp. 464, 473-74 (D.D.C. 1996) (plaintiff failed to demonstrate that individuals who disclosed information learned it from investigatory file or through direct involvement in investigation), summary affirmance granted, No. 96-5252 (D.C. Cir. Nov. 27, 1996); Balbinot v. United States, 872 F. Supp. 546, 549-51 (C.D. Ill. 1994); Coakley v. United States Dep't of Transp., No. 93-1420, 1994 U.S. Dist. LEXIS 21402, at **2-3 (D.D.C. Apr. 7, 1994); Swenson, No. S-87-1282, 1994 U.S. Dist. LEXIS 16524, at **19-22 (E.D. Cal. Mar. 10, 1994); Gibbs v. Brady, 773 F. Supp. 454, 458 (D.D.C. 1991); McGregor v. Greer, 748 F. Supp. 881, 885-86 (D.D.C. 1990); Avant v. Postal Serv., No. 88-T-173-S, slip op. at 4-5 (M.D. Ala. May 4, 1990); Howard v. Marsh, 654 F. Supp. 853, 855 (E.D. Mo. 1986); Krowitz v. USDA, 641 F. Supp. 1536, 1545 (W.D. Mich. 1986), aff'd, 826 F.2d 1063 (6th Cir. 1987) (unpublished table decision); Blanton v. United States Dep't of

Justice, No. 82-0452, slip op. at 4-5 (D.D.C. Feb. 17, 1984); Sanchez v. United States, 3 Gov't Disclosure Serv. (P-H) ¶ 83,116, at 83,708-09 (S.D. Tex. Sept. 10, 1982); Golliher v. United States Postal Serv., 3 Gov't Disclosure Serv. (P-H) ¶ 83,114, at 83,703 (N.D. Ohio June 10, 1982); Thomas v. United States Dep't of the Navy, No. C81-0654-L(A), slip op. at 2-3 (W.D. Ky. Nov. 4, 1982), aff'd, 732 F.2d 156 (6th Cir. 1984) (unpublished table decision); Olberding v. DOD, 564 F. Supp. 907, 913 (S.D. Iowa 1982), aff'd per curiam, 709 F.2d 621 (8th Cir. 1983); Balk v. United States Int'l Communications Agency, No. 81-0896, slip op. at 2-4 (D.D.C. May 7, 1982), aff'd, 704 F.2d 1293 (D.C. Cir. 1983) (unpublished table decision); Johnson v. United States Dep't of the Air Force, 526 F. Supp. 679, 681 (W.D. Okla. 1980), aff'd, 703 F.2d 583 (Fed. Cir. 1981) (unpublished table decision); Carin v. United States, 1 Gov't Disclosure Serv. (P-H) ¶ 80,193, at 80,491-92 (D.D.C. Aug. 5, 1980); Jackson v. VA, 503 F. Supp. 653, 655-57 (N.D. Ill. 1980); King v. Califano, 471 F. Supp. 180, 181 (D.D.C. 1979); Greene v. VA, No. C-76-461-S, slip op. at 6-7 (M.D.N.C. July 3, 1978); see also Stephens v. TVA, 754 F. Supp. 579, 582 (E.D. Tenn. 1990) (comparing Olberding and Jackson and noting "confusion in the law with respect to whether the Privacy Act bars the disclosure of personal information obtained indirectly as opposed to directly from a system of records"); cf. Rice v. United States, 166 F.3d 1088, 1092 n.4 (10th Cir. 1999) (in action for wrongful disclosure in violation of tax code, noting that plaintiff similarly had no Privacy Act claim for IRS's disclosure in press releases of information regarding plaintiff's criminal trial and conviction because information disclosed was procured by agency public affairs officer through review of indictment and attendance at plaintiff's trial and sentencing); Smith v. Henderson, No. C-96-4665, 1999 WL 1029862, at **6-7 (N.D. Cal. Oct. 29, 1999) (although finding no evidence of existence of written record retrieved from system of records, finding further that alleged disclosure was made from information "obtained independently of any system of records") (appeal pending); Viotti v. United States Air Force, 902 F. Supp. 1331, 1338 (D. Colo. 1995) ("Section 552a(b) contemplates a 'system of records' as being the direct or indirect source of the information disclosed" and although agency employee admitted disclosure of information to press "based on personal knowledge," plaintiff "was obligated to come forward with some evidence indicating the existence of a triable issue of fact as to the identity of the 'indirect' source" of disclosure to press), aff'd, 153 F.3d 730 (10th Cir. 1998) (unpublished table decision); Mittleman, 919 F. Supp. at 469 (although no evidence indicated that there had been disclosure of information about plaintiff, even assuming there had been, information at issue would not have been subject to restrictions of Privacy Act because "it was a belief . . . derived from conversations . . . and which was acquired independent from a system of records");

<u>Doe v. United States Dep't of the Interior</u>, No. 95-1665, slip op. at 4-5 (D.D.C. Mar. 11, 1996) (where plaintiff could "not show that the breach [in confidentiality] stemmed from an improper disclosure of [his] records," stating further that "[t]his is especially true in light of the fact that several other employees knew of, and could have told . . . of, plaintiff's illness").

However, the Court of Appeals for the District of Columbia Circuit, in <u>Bartel v. FAA</u>, 725 F.2d 1403, 1408-11 (D.C. Cir. 1984), suggested that the "actual retrieval" standard is inapplicable where a disclosure is undertaken by agency personnel who had a role in creating the record that contains the released information. This particular aspect of <u>Bartel</u> has been noted with approval by several other courts. <u>See</u> <u>Manuel</u>, 857 F.2d at 1120 & n.1; <u>Pilon v. United States Dep't of Justice</u>, 796 F. Supp. 7, 12 (D.D.C. 1992) (denying agency's motion to dismiss or alternatively for summary judgment where information "obviously stem[med] from confidential Department documents and oral statements derived therefrom"); <u>Kassel v. VA</u>, 709 F. Supp. 1194, 1201 (D.N.H. 1989); <u>Cochran v. United States</u>, No. 83-216, slip op. at 9-13 (S.D. Ga. July 2, 1984), <u>aff'd</u>, 770 F.2d 949 (11th Cir. 1985); <u>Fitzpatrick v. IRS</u>, 1 Gov't Disclosure Serv. (P-H) ¶ 80,232, at 80,580 (N.D. Ga. Aug. 22, 1980), <u>aff'd in part, vacated & remanded in part, on other grounds</u>, 665 F.2d 327 (11th Cir. 1982). But cf. <u>Abernethy v. IRS</u>, 909 F. Supp. 1562, 1570 (N.D. Ga. 1995) (holding that alleged statements made to other IRS employees that plaintiff was being investigated pertaining to allegations of EEO violations, assuming they were in fact made, did not violate the Act "because information allegedly disclosed was not actually retrieved from a system of records" even though individual alleged to have made such statements was same individual who ordered investigation), <u>aff'd per curiam</u>, No. 95-9489 (11th Cir. Feb. 13, 1997).

In particular, the Court of Appeals for the Ninth Circuit held that an Administrative Law Judge for the Department of Health and Human Services violated the Privacy Act when he stated in an opinion that one of the parties' attorneys had been placed on a Performance Improvement Plan (PIP) while he was employed at HHS--despite the fact that there was no actual retrieval by the ALJ--because, as the creator of the PIP, the ALJ had personal knowledge of the matter. <u>Wilborn v. HHS</u>, 49 F.3d 597, 600-02 (9th Cir. 1995). The Ninth Circuit noted the similarity of the facts to those of <u>Bartel</u> and held that "'independent knowledge,' gained by the creation of records, cannot be used to sidestep the Privacy Act." <u>Id.</u> at 601. Additionally, it rejected the lower court's reasoning that not only was there no retrieval, but there was no longer a record capable of being retrieved because as the result of a grievance action, all records relating to the PIP had been required to be expunged from the agency's records and in fact were expunged by the ALJ himself. <u>Id.</u> at 599-

602. The Ninth Circuit found the district court's ruling "inconsistent with the spirit of the Privacy Act," and stated that the "fact that the agency ordered expungement of all information relating to the PIP makes the ALJ's disclosure, if anything, more rather than less objectionable." Id. at 602.

### 2. Access and Amendment: Subsections (d)(1) and (d)(2)

One of Congress's underlying concerns in narrowly defining a "system of records" appears to have been efficiency--i.e., a concern that any broader definition would require elaborate cross-references among records and/or burdensome hand-searches for records. See OMB Guidelines, 40 Fed. Reg. at 28,957; see also Baker v. Department of the Navy, 814 F.2d 1381, 1385 (9th Cir. 1987); Carpenter v. IRS, 938 F. Supp. 521, 522-23 (S.D. Ind. 1996).

Consistent with OMB's guidance, numerous courts have held that, under subsection (d)(1), an individual has no Privacy Act right of access to his record if it is not indexed and retrieved by his name or personal identifier. See Williams v. VA, 104 F.3d 670, 673 (4th Cir. 1997); Manuel v. VA Hosp., 857 F.2d 1112, 1116-17 (6th Cir. 1988); Baker, 814 F.2d at 1383-84; Cuccaro v. Secretary of Labor, 770 F.2d 355, 360-61 (3d Cir. 1985); Wren v. Heckler, 744 F.2d 86, 89 (10th Cir. 1984); Bettersworth v. FDIC, No. A-97-CA-624, slip op. at 8-9 (W.D. Tex. Feb. 1, 2000) (magistrate's recommendation), adopted (W.D. Tex. Feb. 17, 2000) (appeal pending); Springmann v. United States Dep't of State, No. 93-1238, slip op. at 9 n.2 (D.D.C. Apr. 21, 1997); Fuller v. IRS, No. 96-888, 1997 WL 191034, at **3-5 (W.D. Pa. Mar. 4, 1997); Carpenter, 938 F. Supp. at 522-23; Quinn v. HHS, 838 F. Supp. 70, 76 (W.D.N.Y. 1993); Shewchun v. United States Customs Serv., No. 87-2967, 1989 WL 7351, at *2 (D.D.C. Jan. 11, 1989); Bryant v. Department of the Air Force, No. 85-4096, slip op. at 4 (D.D.C. Mar. 31, 1986); Fagot v. FDIC, 584 F. Supp. 1168, 1174-75 (D.P.R. 1984), aff'd in part & rev'd in part, 760 F.2d 252 (1st Cir. 1985) (unpublished table decision); Grachow v. United States Customs Serv., 504 F. Supp. 632, 634-36 (D.D.C. 1980); Smiertka v. United States Dep't of the Treasury, 447 F. Supp. 221, 228 (D.D.C. 1978), remanded on other grounds, 604 F.2d 698 (D.C. Cir. 1979); see also OMB Guidelines, 40 Fed. Reg. at 28,957 (giving examples).

Likewise, with regard to amendment, several courts have ruled that where an individual's record is being maintained allegedly in violation of subsection (e)(1) or (e)(5), the individual has no Privacy Act right to amend his record, under subsection (d)(2), if it is not indexed and retrieved by his name or personal identifier. See Baker, 814 F.2d at 1384-85 ("the scope of accessibility and the scope of amendment are coextensive"); Pototsky v. Department of the Navy, 717 F. Supp. 20, 22 (D. Mass. 1989) (following Baker), aff'd per curiam, 907

F.2d 142 (1st Cir. 1990) (unpublished table decision); see also Clarkson v. IRS, 678 F.2d 1368, 1377 (11th Cir. 1982) (subsections (e)(1) and (e)(5) apply only to records contained in system of records).

However, with respect to access under subsection (d)(1), and amendment under subsection (d)(2), several courts have cautioned that an agency's purposeful filing of records in a non-name retrieved format, in order to evade those provisions, will not be permitted. See, e.g., Pototsky v. Department of the Navy, No. 89-1891, slip op. at 2 (1st Cir. Apr. 3, 1990) (per curiam); Baker, 814 F.2d at 1385; Kalmin v. Department of the Navy, 605 F. Supp. 1492, 1495 n.5 (D.D.C. 1985); see also Manuel, 857 F.2d at 1120 ("The Court does not want to give a signal to federal agencies that they should evade their responsibility to place records within their 'system of records' in violation of the [Act].").

Following the rationale of the Fifth Circuit Court of Appeals in Chapman v. NASA, 682 F.2d 526, 529 (5th Cir. 1982), several courts have recognized a subsection (e)(5) duty to incorporate records into a system of records (thus making them subject to access and amendment) where such records are used by the agency in taking an adverse action against the individual. See MacDonald v. VA, No. 87-544-CIV-T-15A, slip op. at 2-5 (M.D. Fla. Feb. 8, 1988); Lawrence v. Dole, No. 83-2876, slip op. at 5-6 (D.D.C. Dec. 12, 1985); Waldrop v. United States Dep't of the Air Force, 3 Gov't Disclosure Serv. (P-H) ¶ 83,016, at 83,453 (S.D. Ill. Aug. 5, 1981); Nelson v. EEOC, No. 83-C-983, slip op. at 6-11 (E.D. Wis. Feb. 14, 1984); cf. Manuel, 857 F.2d at 1117-19 (no duty to place records within system of records where records "are not part of an official agency investigation into activities of the individual requesting the records, and where the records requested do not have an adverse effect on the individual"). But cf. Gowan v. Department of the Air Force, No. 90-94, slip op. at 7, 11, 13, 16, 30, 33 (D.N.M. Sept. 1, 1995) (although ultimately finding access claim moot, stating that "personal notes and legal research" in file "marked 'Ethics'" that was originally kept in desk of Deputy Staff Judge Advocate but that was later given to Criminal Military Justice Section and used in connection with court martial hearing were not in system of records for purposes of either Privacy Act access or accuracy lawsuit for damages), aff'd, 148 F.3d 1182, 1191 (10th Cir.) (concluding "that the word 'Ethics' was not a personal identifier" and stating that it did "not find the district court's rulings regarding those documents to be clearly erroneous"), cert. denied, 525 U.S. 1042 (1998).

### 3. Other Aspects

The "system of records" threshold requirement is not necessarily applicable to all subsections of the Act. See OMB Guidelines, 40 Fed. Reg. at 28,952 (system of records definition "limits the applicability of some of the provisions of the Act") (emphasis added). But see Privacy Commission Report at 503-04 (assuming that definition limits entire Act).

For example, in Albright v. United States, 631 F.2d 915, 918-20 (D.C. Cir. 1980), the Court of Appeals for the District of Columbia Circuit held that subsection (e)(7)--which restricts agencies from maintaining records describing how an individual exercises his First Amendment rights--applies even to records not incorporated into a system of records. Albright involved a challenge on subsection (e)(7) grounds to an agency's maintenance of a videotape--kept in a file cabinet in an envelope that was not labeled by any individual's name--of a meeting between a personnel officer and agency employees affected by the officer's job reclassification decision. Id. at 918. Relying on both the broad definition of "maintain," 5 U.S.C. § 552a(a)(3), and the "special and sensitive treatment accorded First Amendment rights," the D.C. Circuit held that the mere collection of a record regarding those rights could be a violation of subsection (e)(7), regardless of whether the record was contained in a system of records retrieved by an individual's name or personal identifier. Id. at 919-20.

Albright's broad construction of subsection (e)(7) has been adopted by several other courts. See MacPherson v. IRS, 803 F.2d 479, 481 (9th Cir. 1986); Boyd, 709 F.2d at 684; Clarkson, 678 F.2d at 1373-77; Fagot, 584 F. Supp. at 1175. Further, the Court of Appeals for the Eleventh Circuit in Clarkson, 678 F.2d at 1375-77, held that, at least with respect to alleged violations of subsection (e)(7), the Act's amendment provision (subsection (d)(2)) also can apply to a record not incorporated into a system of records. However, Judge Tjoflat's concurring opinion in Clarkson intimated that something more than a bare allegation of a subsection (e)(7) violation would be necessary in order for an agency to be obligated to search beyond its systems of records for potentially offensive materials. Id. at 1378-79.

Two district courts have gone even further. In Connelly v. Comptroller of the Currency, 673 F. Supp. 1419, 1424 (S.D. Tex. 1987), rev'd on other grounds, 876 F.2d 1209 (5th Cir. 1989), the court construed the broad "any record" language contained in 5 U.S.C. § 552a(g)(1)(C) to permit a damages action arising from an allegedly inaccurate record that was not incorporated into a system of records. But cf. Bettersworth v. FDIC, No. A-97-CA-624, slip op. at 10 (W.D. Tex. Feb. 1, 2000) (magistrate's recommendation) (recognizing holding in Connelly, but noting that both subsections (d)(1) and (g)(1)(C) contain same "system of records" language, and stating that court is "unpersuaded that Congress intended any other meaning than what has previously been applied"), adopted (W.D. Tex. Feb. 17, 2000) (appeal pending). In a subsequent opinion, the court in Connelly went on to find a

PRIVACY ACT OVERVIEW

cause of action under subsections (e)(5) and (g)(1)(C) with regard to records not in a system. Connelly v. Comptroller of the Currency, No. H-84-3783, slip op. at 3-4, 42-43 (S.D. Tex. June 3, 1991). In Reuber v. United States, No. 81-1857, slip op. at 5 (D.D.C. Oct. 27, 1982), partial summary judgment denied (D.D.C. Aug. 15, 1983), partial summary judgment granted (D.D.C. Apr. 13, 1984), subsequent decision (D.D.C. Sept. 6, 1984), aff'd, 829 F.2d 133 (D.C. Cir. 1987), the court relied on Albright for the proposition that subsections (d)(2), (e)(1)-(2), (e)(5)-(7), and (e)(10) all apply to a record not incorporated into a system of records. See also Fiorella v. HEW, 2 Gov't Disclosure Serv. (P-H) ¶ 81,363, at 81,946 n.1 (W.D. Wash. Mar. 9, 1981) (noting that subsections (e)(5) and (e)(7) "are parallel in structure and would seem to require the same statutory construction"). But see Felsen v. HHS, No. CCB-95-975, slip op. at 61-62, 65 (D. Md. Sept. 30, 1998) (granting defendants summary judgment on alternative ground that subsection (e)(2) is inapplicable to records not included in system of records); Barhorst, 765 F. Supp. at 999-1000 (dismissing on alternative grounds Privacy Act claims under subsections (b), (e)(1)-(3), (e)(5)-(6), and (e)(10) because information found not in system of records; information was retrieved by job announcement number, not by name or other identifying particular).

Albright and its progeny establish that the "system of records" limitation on the scope of the Act is not uniformly applicable to all of the statute's subsections. As is apparent from the above discussion, there is some uncertainty about which particular subsections of the statute are limited to records contained in a "system of records."

## CONDITIONS OF DISCLOSURE TO THIRD PARTIES

### A. The "No Disclosure Without Consent" Rule

"No agency shall disclose any record which is contained in a system of records by any means of communication to any person, or to another agency, except pursuant to a written request by, or with the prior written consent of, the individual to whom the record pertains [subject to 12 exceptions]." 5 U.S.C. § 552a(b).

comment -- A "disclosure" can be by any means of communication--written, oral, electronic, or mechanical. See OMB Guidelines, 40 Fed. Reg. 28,948, 28,953 (1975).

A plaintiff has the burden of demonstrating that a disclosure by the agency has occurred. See, e.g., Askew v. United States, 680 F.2d 1206, 1209-11 (8th Cir. 1982); Zerilli v. Smith, 656 F.2d 705, 715-16 (D.C. Cir. 1981); cf. Meldrum v. United States Postal Serv., No. 5:97CV1482, slip op. at 11 (N.D. Ohio Jan. 21, 1999) (finding lack of evidence that disclosure occurred where plaintiff alleged that, among other things, file had been left in unsecured file cabinet).

PRIVACY ACT OVERVIEW

It has frequently been held that a "disclosure" under the Privacy Act does not occur if the communication is to a person who is already aware of the information. See, e.g., Quinn v. Stone, 978 F.2d 126, 134 (3d Cir. 1992) (dictum); Kline v. HHS, 927 F.2d 522, 524 (10th Cir. 1991); Hollis v. United States Dep't of the Army, 856 F.2d 1541, 1545 (D.C. Cir. 1988); Reyes v. Supervisor of DEA, 834 F.2d 1093, 1096 n.1 (1st Cir. 1987); Schowengerdt v. General Dynamics Corp., 823 F.2d 1328, 1341 (9th Cir. 1987); Pellerin v. VA, 790 F.2d 1553, 1556 (11th Cir. 1986); FDIC v. Dye, 642 F.2d 833, 836 (5th Cir. 1981); Ash v. United States, 608 F.2d 178, 179 (5th Cir. 1979); Sullivan v. United States Postal Serv., 944 F. Supp. 191, 196 (W.D.N.Y. 1996); Viotti v. United States Air Force, 902 F. Supp. 1331, 1337 (D. Colo. 1995), aff'd, 153 F.3d 730 (10th Cir. 1998) (unpublished table decision); Abernethy v. IRS, 909 F. Supp. 1562, 1571 (N.D. Ga. 1995), aff'd per curiam, No. 95-9489 (11th Cir. Feb. 13, 1997); Kassel v. VA, 709 F. Supp. 1194, 1201 (D.N.H. 1989); Krowitz v. USDA, 641 F. Supp. 1536, 1545 (W.D. Mich. 1986), aff'd, 826 F.2d 1063 (6th Cir. 1987) (unpublished table decision); Golliher v. United States Postal Serv., 3 Gov't Disclosure Serv. ¶ 83,114, at 83,702 (N.D. Ohio June 10, 1982); King v. Califano, 471 F. Supp. 180, 181 (D.D.C. 1979); Harper v. United States, 423 F. Supp. 192, 197 (D.S.C. 1976); see also Hoffman v. Rubin, 193 F.3d 959, 966 (8th Cir. 1999) (no Privacy Act violation found where agency disclosed same information in letter to journalist that plaintiff himself had previously provided to journalist; plaintiff "waiv[ed], in effect, his protection under the Privacy Act"); Loma Linda Community Hosp. v. Shalala, 907 F. Supp. 1399, 1404-05 (C.D. Cal. 1995) (policy underlying Privacy Act of protecting confidential information from disclosure not implicated by release of information health care provider had already received through patients' California "Medi-Cal" cards); Owens v. MSPB, No. 3-83-0449-R, slip op. at 2-3 (N.D. Tex. Sept. 14, 1983) (mailing of agency decision affirming employee's removal to his former attorney held not a "disclosure" as "attorney was familiar with facts of [employee's] claim" and "no new information was disclosed to him"); cf. Pippinger v. Rubin, 129 F.3d 519, 532-33 (10th Cir. 1997) (finding no evidence that disclosure "could possibly have had 'an adverse effect'" on plaintiff where recipient "had been privy to every event described in [plaintiff's] records at the time the event occurred"); Jones v. Runyon, 32 F. Supp. 2d 873, 876 (N.D. W. Va. 1998) (although finding disclosure to credit reporting service valid under routine use exception, stating further that information disclosed was already in possession of recipient and that other courts had held that Privacy Act is not violated in such cases), aff'd, 173 F.3d 850 (4th Cir. 1999) (unpublished table decision).

However, the Court of Appeals for the District of Columbia Circuit clarified that this principle does not apply to all disseminations of protected records to individuals with prior knowledge of their existence or contents. Pilon v. United States Dep't of Justice, 73 F.3d 1111, 1117-24 (D.C. Cir. 1996). In Pilon, the D.C. Circuit held that the Justice Department's transmission of a Privacy Act-protected record to a former employee of the agency constituted a "disclosure" under the Privacy Act, even though the recipient had come "into contact with the [record] in the course of his duties" while an employee. Id. The court's "review of the Privacy Act's purposes, legislative history, and integrated structure convince[d it] that Congress intended the term 'disclose' to apply in virtually all instances to an agency's unauthorized transmission of a protected record, regardless of the recipient's prior familiarity with it." Id. at 1124.

In an earlier case, Hollis v. United States Dep't of the Army, 856 F.2d 1541 (D.C. Cir. 1988), the D.C. Circuit had held that the release of a summary of individual child-support payments previously deducted from plaintiff's salary and sent directly to his ex-wife, who had requested it for use in pending litigation, was not an unlawful disclosure under the Privacy Act as she, being the designated recipient of the child-support payments, already knew what had been remitted to her. Id. at 1545. In Pilon, the D.C. Circuit reconciled its opinion in Hollis by "declin[ing] to extend Hollis beyond the limited factual circumstances that gave rise to it," 73 F.3d at 1112, 1124, and holding that:

> [A]n agency's unauthorized release of a protected record does constitute a disclosure under the Privacy Act except in those rare instances, like Hollis, where the record merely reflects information that the agency has previously, and lawfully, disseminated outside the agency to the recipient, who is fully able to reconstruct its material contents.

Id. at 1124; cf. Osborne v. United States Postal Serv., No. 94-30353, slip op. at 2-4, 6-11 (N.D. Fla. May 18, 1995) (assuming without discussion that disclosure of plaintiff's injury-compensation file to retired employee who had prepared file constituted "disclosure" for purposes of Privacy Act).

A few courts, though, have extended the principle that there is no "disclosure" to rule that the release of previously published or publicly available information is not a Privacy Act "disclosure"--regardless of whether the particular persons who received the information were aware of the previous publication. See FDIC v. Dye, 642 F.2d at 836; Lee v. Dearment, No. 91-2175, 1992 WL 119855, at *2 (4th Cir. June 3, 1992); Smith v. Continental Assurance Co., No. 91-C-0963, 1991 WL 164348, at *5 (N.D. Ill. Aug. 22, 1991); Friedlander v. United States Postal Serv., No. 84-0773, slip op. at 8 (D.D.C. Oct. 16, 1984); King, 471 F. Supp. at 181. But see

Quinn, 978 F.2d at 134 (holding that release of information that is "merely readily accessible" to public "is a disclosure under 552a(b)"); Gowan v. United States Dep't of the Air Force, 148 F.3d 1182, 1193 (10th Cir.) ("adopt[ing] the Third Circuit's reasoning [in Quinn] and hold[ing] that an agency may not defend a release of Privacy Act information simply by stating that the information is a matter of public record"), cert. denied, 525 U.S. 1042 (1998); cf. Doe v. Herman, No. 2:97CV00043, 1999 U.S. Dist. LEXIS 17302, at **34-35 (W.D. Va. Oct. 29, 1999) (magistrate's recommendation) (agreeing with Quinn in dictum); Pilon v. United States Dep't of Justice, 796 F. Supp. 7, 11-12 (D.D.C. 1992) (rejecting argument that information was already public and therefore could not violate Privacy Act where agency had republished statement that was previously publicly disavowed as false by agency). The D.C. Circuit had recognized in dictum that other courts had so held, and perhaps had indicated a willingness to go that far. Hollis, 856 F.2d at 1545 (holding that disclosure did not violate Privacy Act because recipient of information was already aware of it, but stating that "[o]ther courts have echoed the sentiment that when a release consists merely of information to which the general public already has access, or which the recipient of the release already knows, the Privacy Act is not violated").

However, the D.C. Circuit's more recent holding in Pilon v. United States Dep't of Justice, 73 F.3d 1111 (D.C. Cir. 1996), discussed above, seems to foreclose such a possibility. In Pilon, the D.C. Circuit further held that even under the narrow Hollis interpretation of "disclose," the agency would not be entitled to summary judgment because it had "failed to adduce sufficient evidence that [the recipient of the record] remembered and could reconstruct the document's material contents in detail at the time he received it." 73 F.3d at 1124-26. Nevertheless, the D.C. Circuit in Pilon noted that "[t]his case does not present the question of whether an agency may . . . release a document that has already been fully aired in the public domain through the press or some other means" but that "the Privacy Act approves those disclosures that are 'required' under the [FOIA] . . . and that under various FOIA exemptions, prior publication is a factor to be considered in determining whether a document properly is to be released." Id. at 1123 n.10; see also Barry v. United States Dep't of Justice, 63 F. Supp. 2d 25, 27-28 (D.D.C. 1999) (distinguishing Pilon and finding no disclosure where agency posted Inspector General report on Internet Web site, after report had already been fully released to media by Congress and had been discussed in public congressional hearing, even though some Internet users might encounter report for first time on Web site). Furthermore, though, and consistent with the D.C. Circuit's note in Pilon, one might argue that to say that no "disclosure" occurs for previously published or public information is at least somewhat inconsistent with the Supreme Court's decision in United States Department of Justice v. Reporters Committee for Freedom of the Press, 489 U.S 749, 762-71 (1989), which held that a privacy interest can exist, under the FOIA, in publicly available--but "practically obscure"--information, such as a criminal history record. Cf. Finley v. National Endowment for the Arts, 795 F. Supp. 1457, 1468 (C.D. Cal. 1992) (alleged disclosure of publicly available information states claim for relief under Privacy Act; recognizing Reporters Committee).

The Act's legislative history indicates that a court is not a "person" or "agency" within the meaning of subsection (b), and that the Act was "not designed to interfere with access to information by the courts." 120 Cong. Rec. 36,967 (1974), reprinted in Source Book at 958-59. However, the public filing of records with a court, during the course of litigation, does constitute a subsection (b) disclosure. See Laningham v. United States Navy, No. 83-3238, slip op. at 2-3 (D.D.C. Sept. 25, 1984), summary judgment granted (D.D.C. Jan. 7, 1985), aff'd per curiam, 813 F.2d 1236 (D.C. Cir. 1987); Citizens Bureau of Investigation v. FBI, No. 78-60, slip op. at 2-3 (N.D. Ohio Dec. 14, 1979). Accordingly, any such public filing must be undertaken with written consent or in accordance with either the subsection (b)(3) routine use exception or the subsection (b)(11) court order exception, both discussed below. See generally Krohn v. United States Dep't of Justice, No. 78-1536, slip op. at 3-11 (D.D.C. Mar. 19, 1984) (finding violation of Privacy Act where agency's disclosure of records as attachments to affidavit in FOIA lawsuit "did not fall within any of the exceptions listed in Section 552a"), reconsideration granted & vacated in nonpertinent part (D.D.C. Nov. 29, 1984) (discussed below).

Often during the course of litigation, an agency will be asked to produce Privacy Act-protected information pursuant to a discovery request by an opposing party. An agency in receipt of such a request must object on the ground that the Privacy Act prohibits disclosure. Although courts have unanimously held that the Privacy Act does not create a discovery privilege, see Laxalt v. McClatchy, 809 F.2d 885, 888-90 (D.C. Cir. 1987); Weahkee v. Norton, 621 F.2d 1080, 1082 (10th Cir. 1980); Forrest v. United States, No. 95-3889, 1996 WL 171539, at *2 (E.D. Pa. Apr. 11, 1996); Ford Motor Co. v. United States, 825 F. Supp. 1081, 1083 (Ct. Int'l Trade 1993); Clavir v. United States, 84 F.R.D. 612, 614 (S.D.N.Y. 1979); cf. Baldrige v. Shapiro, 455 U.S. 345, 360-62 (1982) (Census Act confidentiality provisions constitute privilege because they "embody explicit congressional intent to preclude all disclosure"), an agency can disclose Privacy Act-protected records only as permitted by the Act. The most appropriate method of disclosure in this situation is pursuant to a (b)(11) court order. See generally Doe v. DiGenova, 779 F.2d 74 (D.C. Cir. 1985); Doe v. Stephens, 851 F.2d 1457 (D.C. Cir. 1988) (both discussed below under subsection (b)(11)); see also Boudreaux v. United States, No. 97-1592, 1999 WL 499911, at **1-2 (E.D. La. July 14, 1999) (recognizing relevancy of subsection (b)(11) to court's resolution of dispute over motion to compel responses to production of documents subject to Privacy Act, but ordering in camera review of documents so that legitimacy of agency objections may be determined "in the considered and cautious manner contemplated by the Privacy Act"). Indeed, the courts that have rejected the Privacy Act as a discovery privilege have pointed to subsection (b)(11)'s allowance for court-ordered disclosures in support of their holdings. See Laxalt, 809 F.2d at 888-89; Weahkee, 621 F.2d at 1082; Hernandez v. United States, No. 97-3367, 1998 WL 230200, at **2-3 (E.D. La. May 6, 1998); Forrest, 1996 WL 171539, at *2; Ford Motor Co., 825 F. Supp. at 1082-83; Clavir, 84 F.R.D. at 614; cf. Alford v. Todco, No. CIV-88-731E, slip op. at 4-5 (W.D.N.Y. June 12, 1990) ("Even assuming the Privacy Act supplies a statutory privilege . . . the plaintiff has waived any such privilege by placing his physical condition at issue"; ordering production of records); Tootle v. Seaboard Coast Line R.R., 468 So. 2d 237, 239 (Fla. Dist. Ct. App. 1984) (recognizing that privacy interests in that case "must give way to the function of the discovery of facts" and that subsection (b)(11) provides the mechanism for disclosure).

On the other hand, when an agency wishes to make an affirmative disclosure of information during litigation it may either rely on a routine use permitting such disclosure or seek a court order. Because the Privacy Act does not constitute a statutory privilege, agencies need not worry about breaching or waiving such a privilege when disclosing information pursuant to subsections (b)(3) or (b)(11). Cf. Mangino v. Department of the Army, No. 94-2067, 1994 WL 477260, at **5-6 (D. Kan. Aug. 24, 1994) (finding that disclosure to court was appropriate pursuant to agency routine use and stating that to extent Privacy Act created privilege, such privilege was waived by plaintiff when he placed his records at issue through litigation); Lemasters v. Thomson, No. 92 C 6158, 1993 U.S. Dist. LEXIS 7513, at **3-8 (N.D. Ill. June 3, 1993) (same finding as in Mangino, despite fact that "court ha[d] not located" applicable routine use). For further discussions of disclosures during litigation, see the discussions of subsections (b)(3) and (b)(11), below.

By its own terms, subsection (b) does not prohibit an agency from releasing to an individual his own record, contained in a system of records retrieved by his name or personal identifier, in response to his "first-party" access request under subsection (d)(1). However, as is discussed below under "Individual's Right of Access," one exception to this point could conceivably arise in the first-party access context where a record is also about another individual and is "dually retrieved." Such a position has been rejected, though, by the only court to consider it. See Topuridze v. USIA, 772 F. Supp. 662, 665-66 (D.D.C. 1991).

Additionally, although it may seem self-evident, the factual pattern in one case caused a court to explicitly hold that an agency cannot be sued for disclosures which an individual makes himself. Abernethy, 909 F. Supp. at 1571 (plaintiff had informed employees that he was being removed from his position as their supervisor and reason for his removal).

The Act does not define "written consent." Implied consent has been held to be insufficient. See Taylor v. Orr, No. 83-0389, 1983 U.S. Dist. LEXIS 20334, at *6 n.6 (D.D.C. Dec. 5, 1983) ("Implied consent is never enough" as the Act's protections "would be seriously eroded if plaintiff's written submission of [someone's] name were construed as a voluntary written consent to the disclosure of her [medical] records to him."). But see OMB Guidelines, 40 Fed. Reg. 56,741, 56,742 (1975) (consent may be implied when responding to inquiry from Member of Congress acting on basis of written request for assistance from constituent); Pellerin, 790 F.2d at 1556 (applying doctrine of "equitable estoppel" to bar individual from complaining of disclosure of his record to congressmen "when he requested their assistance in gathering such information") (distinguished in Swenson v. United States Postal Serv., 890 F.2d 1075, 1077-78 (9th Cir. 1989)); cf. Baitey v. VA, No. 8:CV89-706, slip op. at 5 (D. Neb. June 21, 1995) (concluding that "at a minimum, the phrase 'written consent' necessarily requires either (1) a medical authorization signed by [plaintiff] or (2) conduct which, coupled with the unsigned authorization, supplied the necessary written consent for the disclosure").

The scope of express consent, however, cannot be "so vague or general that it is questionable whether [the individual] knew what he was authorizing or whether the [agency] knew what documents it could lawfully release." Perry v. FBI, 759 F.2d 1271, 1276 (7th Cir. 1985), rev'd en banc on other grounds, 781 F.2d 1294 (7th Cir. 1986); see also AFGE v. United States R.R. Retirement Bd., 742 F. Supp. 450, 457 (N.D. Ill. 1990) (SF-86 "release form" held overbroad and contrary to subsection (b)); Taylor, No. 83-0389, 1983 U.S. Dist. LEXIS 20334, at *6 n.6 (D.D.C. Dec. 5, 1983) ("It is not unreasonable to require that a written consent to disclosure address the issue of such disclosure and refer specifically to the records permitted to be disclosed."); Thomas v. VA, 467 F. Supp. 458, 460 n.4 (D. Conn. 1979) (consent held adequate as it was both agency- and record-specific); cf. Doe v. Herman, No. 2:97CV00043, 1999 U.S. Dist. LEXIS 17302, at **30-31 (W.D. Va. Oct. 29, 1999) (magistrate's recommendation) (rejecting argument that when plaintiffs provided their social security numbers for purpose of determining eligibility for and amount of benefits payable, they consented to use of those numbers as identifiers on multi-captioned hearing notices sent to numerous other individuals and companies as well as to publication of numbers in compilations of opinions); Doe v. GSA, 544 F. Supp. 530, 539-41 (D. Md. 1982) (authorization which was neither record- nor entity-specific was insufficient under GSA's own internal interpretation of Privacy Act). The OMB Guidelines caution that "the consent provision was not intended to permit a blanket or open-ended consent clause, i.e., one which would permit the agency to disclose a record without limit," and that, "[a]t a minimum, the consent clause should state the general purposes for, or types of recipients[ to,] which disclosure may be made." 40 Fed. Reg. at 28,954.

In light of the D.C. Circuit's decision in Summers v. United States Dep't of Justice, 999 F.2d 570, 572-73 (D.C. Cir. 1993), agencies whose regulations require that privacy waivers be notarized to verify identity must also accept declarations in accordance with 28 U.S.C. § 1746 (1994) (i.e., an unsworn declaration subscribed to as true under penalty of perjury). See, e.g., 28 C.F.R. § 16.41(d) (1999) (Department of Justice regulation regarding verification of identity).

B. **Twelve Exceptions to the "No Disclosure Without Consent" Rule**

Note that with the exception of disclosures under subsection (b)(2) (see the discussion below), disclosures under the following exceptions are permissive, not mandatory. See OMB Guidelines, 40 Fed. Reg. at 28,953.

1. **5 U.S.C. § 552a(b)(1) ("need to know" within agency)**

    "to those officers and employees of the agency which maintains the record who have a need for the record in the performance of their duties."

    comment -- This "need to know" exception authorizes the intra-agency disclosure of a record for necessary, official purposes. See OMB Guidelines, 40 Fed. Reg. 28,948, 28,950-01 (1975); 120 Cong. Rec. 36,967 (1974), reprinted in Source Book at 958 (recognizing propriety of "need to know" disclosures between Justice Department components).

    Intra-agency disclosures for improper purposes will not be condoned. See, e.g., Parks v. IRS, 618 F.2d 677, 680-81 & n.1 (10th Cir. 1980) (publication of names of employees who did not purchase savings bonds, "for solicitation purposes," held improper); MacDonald v. VA, No. 87-544-CIV-T-15A, slip op. at 8-9 (M.D. Fla. July 28, 1989) (disclosure of counseling memorandum in "callous attempt to discredit and injure" employee held improper); Koch v. United States, No. 78-273T, slip op. at 1-2 (W.D. Wash. Dec. 30, 1982) (letter of termination posted in agency's entrance hallway held improper); Smigelsky v. United States Postal Serv., No. 79-110-RE, slip op. at 3-4 (D. Or. Oct. 1, 1982) (publication of employees'

PRIVACY ACT OVERVIEW

reasons for taking sick leave held improper); Fitzpatrick v. IRS, 1 Gov't Disclosure Serv. (P-H) ¶ 80,232, at 80,580 (N.D. Ga. Aug. 22, 1980) (disclosure of fact that employee's absence was due to "mental problems" held improper; "quelling rumors and gossip [and] satisfying curiosity is not to be equated with a need to know"), aff'd in part, vacated & remanded in part, on other grounds, 665 F.2d 327 (11th Cir. 1982).

The cases are replete with examples of proper intra-agency "need to know" disclosures. See, e.g., Hudson v. Reno, 130 F.3d 1193, 1206-07 (6th Cir. 1997) (disclosure of plaintiff's performance evaluation to individual who typed it originally, for re-typing), cert. denied, 525 U.S. 822 (1998); Pippinger v. Rubin, 129 F.3d 519, 529-31 (10th Cir. 1997) (disclosure of identity of investigation's subject by supervisor investigating allegations of employee misconduct to staff members to assist in investigation; disclosure to agency attorney charged with defending agency's actions in related MSPB proceeding against another individual); Mount v. United States Postal Serv., 79 F.3d 531, 533-34 (6th Cir. 1996) (disclosure of information in plaintiff's medical records to other employees "with responsibilities for making employment and/or disciplinary decisions regarding plaintiff"; "In light of the questions surrounding plaintiff's mental stability, each had at least an arguable need to access the information in plaintiff's medical records."); Britt v. Naval Investigative Serv., 886 F.2d 544, 549 n.2 (3d Cir. 1989) (disclosure of investigative report to commanding officer approved "since the Reserves might need to reevaluate Britt's access to sensitive information or the level of responsibility he was accorded"); Covert v. Harrington, 876 F.2d 751, 753-54 (9th Cir. 1989) (disclosure of security questionnaires to Inspector General for purpose of detecting fraud); Daly-Murphy v. Winston, 837 F.2d 348, 354-55 (9th Cir. 1988) (disclosure of letter suspending doctor's clinical privileges to participants in peer-review proceeding); Lukos v. IRS, No. 86-1100, 1987 WL 36354, at **1-2 (6th Cir. Feb. 12, 1987) (disclosure of employee's arrest record to supervisor for purpose of evaluating his conduct and to effect discipline); Howard v. Marsh, 785 F.2d 645, 647-49 (8th Cir. 1986) (disclosure of employee's personnel records to agency attorney and personnel specialist for purpose of preparing response to discrimination complaint); Hernandez v. Alexander, 671 F.2d 402, 410 (10th Cir. 1982) (disclosure of employee's EEO files to personnel advisors for purpose of determining whether personnel action should be taken against employee); Grogan v. IRS, 3 Gov't Disclosure Serv. (P-H) ¶ 82,385, at 82,977-78 (4th Cir. Mar. 22, 1982) (disclosure of questionable income tax returns prepared by professional tax preparer while he was IRS employee to IRS examiners for purpose of alerting them to possible irregularities); Beller v. Middendorf, 632 F.2d 788, 798 n.6 (9th Cir. 1980) (disclosure of record revealing serviceman's homosexuality by Naval Investigative Service to commanding officer for purpose of reporting "a ground for discharging someone under his command"); Khalfani v. Secretary, Dep't of Veterans Affairs, No. 94-CV-5720, 1999 WL 138247, at **7-8 (E.D.N.Y. Mar. 10, 1999) (disclosure of plaintiff's medical records within VA so that his supervisor could document his request for medical leave and determine level of work he could perform) (appeal pending); Blazy v. Tenet, 979 F. Supp. 10, 26 (D.D.C. 1997) (disclosure of status of plaintiff's security investigation to his supervisor and disclosure of records needed by members of Employee Review Panel responsible for assessing plaintiff's employment performance and prospects), summary affirmance granted, No. 97-5330, 1998 WL 315583 (D.C. Cir. May 12, 1998); Porter v. United States Postal Serv., No. CV595-30, slip op. at 23-24 (S.D. Ga. July 24, 1997) (disclosure of employee's medical records to supervisory personnel in order to "figure out exactly what level of duty [employee] was fit and able to perform"), aff'd, 166 F.3d 352 (11th Cir. 1998) (unpublished table decision); Jones v. Department of the Air Force, 947 F. Supp. 1507, 1515-16 (D. Colo. 1996) (Air Force investigator's review of plaintiff's medical and mental health records and publication of statements about the records in report of investigation compiled in preparation for plaintiff's court-martial, which was distributed to certain Air Force personnel); Viotti v. United States Air Force, 902 F. Supp. 1331, 1337 (D. Colo. 1995) (disclosure by general to academic department staff that he was removing acting head of department because he had lost confidence in his leadership; subsequent disclosure by new head of department to department staff of same information regarding removal of prior department head), aff'd, 153 F.3d 730 (10th Cir. 1998) (unpublished table decision); Abernethy v. IRS, 909 F. Supp. 1562, 1570-71 (N.D. Ga. 1995) ("[investigatory] panel's review of Plaintiff's performance appraisals was not a violation of the Privacy Act because the members had a need to know the contents of the appraisals"; member of panel that recommended that plaintiff be removed from management in response to EEO informal class complaint "had a need to know the contents of the [EEO] complaint file"), aff'd per curiam, No. 95-9489 (11th Cir. Feb. 13, 1997); Magee v. United States Postal Serv., 903 F. Supp. 1022, 1029 (W.D. La. 1995) (disclosure of employee's medical report following fitness-for-duty examination to Postmaster of Post Office where employee worked to determine whether employee could perform essential functions of job and to Postmaster's supervisor who was to review Postmaster's decision), aff'd, 79 F.3d 1145 (5th Cir. 1996) (unpublished table decision); McNeill v. IRS, No. 93-2204, 1995 U.S. Dist. LEXIS 2372, at *8 (D.D.C. Feb. 7, 1995) (disclosures made to Treasury Department's Equal Employment Opportunity (EEO) personnel in course of their investigation of EEO allegations initiated by plaintiff); Harry v. United States Postal Serv., 867 F. Supp. 1199, 1206 (M.D. Pa. 1994) (disclosure from one internal subdivision of Postal Service to another--the Inspection Service (Inspector General)--which was conducting an investigation); Hass v. United States Air Force, 848 F. Supp. 926, 932 (D. Kan. 1994) (disclosure of mental health evaluation to officers who ultimately made decision to revoke plaintiff's security clearance and discharge her); Lachenmyer v. Frank, No. 88-2414, slip op. at 3-4 (C.D. Ill. July 16, 1990) (disclosure of investigative report, referencing employee's admission that he had been treated for alcohol abuse, to supervisor); Williams v. Reilly, 743 F. Supp. 168, 175 (S.D.N.Y. 1990) (admission of drug use disclosed by the Naval Investigative Service to plaintiff's employer, the Defense Logistics Agency); Bengle v. Reilly, No. 88-587, 1990 U.S. Dist. LEXIS 2006, at *21 (D.D.C. Feb. 28, 1990) (disclosure to personnel consulted by employee's supervisors in order to address employee's complaints); Glass v. United States Dep't of Energy, No. 87-2205, 1988 WL 118408, at *1 (D.D.C. Oct. 29, 1988) (disclosure to "officials or counsel for the agency for use in the exercise of their responsibility for management of the agency or for defense of litigation initiated by plaintiff"); Krowitz v. USDA, 641 F. Supp. 1536, 1545-46 (W.D. Mich. 1986) (details of employee's performance status disclosed to other personnel who were assigned to assist plaintiff), aff'd, 826 F.2d 1063 (6th Cir. 1987) (unpublished table decision); Marcotte v. Secretary of Defense, 618 F. Supp. 756, 763 (D. Kan. 1985) (disclosure of "talking paper" chronicling officer's attempts to correct effectiveness ratings to Inspector General for purpose of responding to officer's challenge to "staff advisories"); Nutter v. VA, No. 84-2392, slip op. at 8-9 (D.D.C. July 9, 1985) (disclosure of record reflecting employee's impending indictment to personnel responsible for responding to public and press inquiries); Brooks v. Grinstead, 3 Gov't Disclosure Serv. (P-H) ¶ 83,054, at 83,551-53 (E.D. Pa. Dec. 12, 1982) (disclosure of employee's security file to supervisor for purpose of ascertaining employee's trustworthiness); Carin v. United States, 1 Gov't Disclosure Serv. (P-H) ¶ 80,193, at 80,492 & n.1 (D.D.C. Aug. 5, 1980) (disclosure of employee's EEO complaint to other employees during grievance process); Lydia R. v. United States Army, No. 78-069, slip op. at 3-6 (D.S.C. Feb. 28, 1979) (disclosure of derogatory information from employee's file to officer for purpose of determining appropriateness of assigning employee to particular position).

Although subsection (b)(1) permits disclosure only to "those officers and employees of the agency which maintains the record," two courts have upheld a disclosure to a contractor who serves the function of an agency employee. See Coakley v. United States Dep't of Transp., No. 93-1420, 1994 U.S. Dist. LEXIS 21402, at **3-4 (D.D.C. Apr. 7, 1994) (holding that EEO investigator who was independent contractor "must be considered an employee of DOT for Privacy Act purposes" and that disclosure of information by former Department employee to contractor, "[g]iven that the disclosure in question occurred in connection with an official agency investigation . . . must be considered an intra-agency communication under the Act"); Hulett v. Department of the Navy, No. TH 85-310-C, slip op. at 3-4 (S.D. Ind. Oct. 26, 1987) (release of medical and personnel records to contractor/psychiatrist for purpose of assisting him in performing "fitness for duty" examination), aff'd, 866 F.2d 432 (7th Cir. 1988) (unpublished table decision). Another court, however, has held to the contrary on facts nearly identical to those in Hulett. Taylor v. Orr, No. 83-0389, 1983 U.S. Dist. LEXIS 20334, at **7-10 (D.D.C. Dec. 5, 1983). See generally OMB Guidelines, 40 Fed. Reg. at 28,954 (noting that "movement of records between personnel of different agencies may in some instances be viewed as intra-agency disclosures if that movement is in connection with an inter-agency support agreement").

2. **5 U.S.C. § 552a(b)(2) (required FOIA disclosure)**

"required under section 552 of this title."

comment -- The point of this exception is that the Privacy Act never prohibits a disclosure that the Freedom of Information Act actually requires. See Greentree v. United States Customs Serv., 674 F.2d 74, 79 (D.C. Cir. 1982) (subsection (b)(2) "represents a Congressional mandate that the Privacy Act not be used as a barrier to FOIA access").

Thus, if an agency is in receipt of a FOIA request for information about an individual that is contained in a system of records and that is not properly withholdable under any FOIA exemption, then it follows that the agency is "required under Section 552 of this title" to disclose the information to the FOIA requester. This would be a permissible subsection (b)(2) disclosure. However, if a FOIA exemption--typically, Exemption 6 or Exemption 7(C)--applies to a Privacy Act-protected record, the Privacy Act prohibits an agency from making a "discretionary" FOIA release because that disclosure would not be "required" by the FOIA

within the meaning of subsection (b)(2).
See, e.g., DOD v. FLRA, 510 U.S. 487, 502
(1994); United States Dep't of the Navy v.
FLRA, 975 F.2d 348, 354-56 (7th Cir. 1992);
DOD v. FLRA, 964 F.2d 26, 30 n.6 (D.C. Cir.
1992); Andrews v. VA, 838 F.2d 418, 422-24 &
n.8 (10th Cir. 1988); Robbins v. HHS, No.
1:95-cv-3258, slip op. at 2-9 (N.D. Ga. Aug.
13, 1996), aff'd, No. 96-9000 (11th Cir.
July 8, 1997); Kassel v. VA, 709 F. Supp.
1194, 1199-1200 (D.N.H. 1989); Howard v.
Marsh, 654 F. Supp. 853, 855-56 (E.D. Mo.
1986); Florida Med. Ass'n v. HEW, 479 F.
Supp. 1291, 1305-07 (M.D. Fla. 1979); Providence Journal Co. v. FBI, 460 F. Supp. 762,
767 (D.R.I. 1978), rev'd on other grounds,
602 F.2d 1010 (1st Cir. 1979); Philadelphia
Newspapers, Inc. v. United States Dep't of
Justice, 405 F. Supp. 8, 10 (E.D. Pa. 1975);
see also OMB Guidelines, 40 Fed. Reg.
28,948, 28,954 (1975).

In United States Department of Justice v.
Reporters Committee for Freedom of the
Press, 489 U.S. 749, 762-75 (1989), the
Supreme Court significantly expanded the
breadths of FOIA Exemptions 6 and 7(C). The
Court ruled that a privacy interest may
exist in publicly available information--
such as the criminal history records (rap
sheets) there at issue--where the information is "practically obscure." Id. at 764-
71. Even more significantly, the Court held
that the identity of the FOIA requester, and
any socially useful purpose for which the
request was made, are not to be considered
in evaluating whether the "public interest"
would be served by disclosure. Id. at 771-
75. The Court determined that the magnitude
of the public interest side of the balancing
process can be assessed only by reference to
whether disclosure of the requested records
directly advances the "core purpose" of the
FOIA--to shed light on the operations and
activities of the government. Id. at 774-
75.

In light of Reporters Committee, personal
information of the sort protected by the
Privacy Act is less likely to be "required"
to be disclosed under the FOIA, within the
meaning of subsection (b)(2). Specifically,
where an agency determines that the only
"public interest" that would be furthered by
a disclosure is a nonqualifying one under
Reporters Committee (even where it believes
that disclosure would be in furtherance of
good public policy generally), it no longer
may balance in favor of disclosure under the
FOIA and therefore disclosure will be prohibited under the Privacy Act--unless authorized by another Privacy Act exception or
by written consent. See, e.g., DOD v. FLRA,
510 U.S. at 497-502 (declining to "import
the policy considerations that are made
explicit in the Labor Statute into the FOIA
Exemption 6 balancing analysis" and, following the principles of Reporters Committee,

holding that home addresses of bargaining unit employees are covered by FOIA Exemption 6 and thus that Privacy Act "prohibits their release to the unions"); Schwarz v. Interpol, No. 94-4111, 1995 U.S. App. LEXIS 3987, at **4-7 & n.2 (10th Cir. Feb. 28, 1995) (balancing under Reporters Committee and holding that individual clearly has protected privacy interest in avoiding disclosure of his whereabouts to third parties; disclosure of this information would not "contribute anything to the public's understanding of the operations or activities of the government"; and thus any information was exempt from disclosure under FOIA Exemption 7(C) and does not fall within Privacy Act exception (b)(2)); FLRA v. United States Dep't of Commerce, 962 F.2d 1055, 1059 (D.C. Cir. 1992) (Privacy Act prohibits disclosure of identities of individuals who received outstanding or commendable personnel evaluations, as such information falls within FOIA Exemption 6); Burke v. United States Dep't of Justice, No. 96-1739, 1999 WL 1032814, at **3-5 (D.D.C. Sept. 30, 1999) (stating that the "Privacy Act prohibits the FBI from disclosing information about a living third party without a written privacy waiver, unless FOIA requires disclosure," and upholding the FBI's refusal to confirm or deny the existence of investigative records related to third parties in response to a FOIA request); see also FOIA Update, Vol. X, No. 2, at 6. As a result of Reporters Committee, agencies depend more on the subsection (b)(3) routine use exception to make compatible disclosures of records that are no longer required by the FOIA to be disclosed. See, e.g., USDA v. FLRA, 876 F.2d 50, 51 (8th Cir. 1989); see also FLRA v. United States Dep't of the Treasury, 884 F.2d 1446, 1450 & n.2 (D.C. Cir. 1989).

The Court of Appeals for the District of Columbia Circuit significantly limited the utility of subsection (b)(2) in Bartel v. FAA, 725 F.2d 1402 (D.C. Cir. 1984). In Bartel, the D.C. Circuit held that subsection (b)(2) cannot be invoked unless an agency actually has a FOIA request in hand. 725 F.2d at 1411-13. The D.C. Circuit's approach in Bartel has not been taken by other courts. See Cochran v. United States, 770 F.2d 949, 957-58 & n.14 (11th Cir. 1985) (applying subsection (b)(2)--in absence of written FOIA request--because requested records would not be withholdable under any FOIA exemption); Jafari v. Department of the Navy, 728 F.2d 247, 249-50 (4th Cir. 1984) (same); see also Florida Med. Ass'n, 479 F. Supp. at 1301, 1305-07. However, because the D.C. Circuit is the jurisdiction of "universal venue" under the Privacy Act (which means that any Privacy Act lawsuit for wrongful disclosure could be filed within that judicial circuit), see 5 U.S.C. § 552a(g)(5), its holding in Bartel is of

PRIVACY ACT OVERVIEW

paramount importance. See FOIA Update, Vol. V, No. 3, at 2.

Note, though, that the Bartel decision left open the possibility that certain types of information "traditionally released by an agency to the public" might properly be disclosed even in the absence of an actual FOIA request. 725 F.2d at 1413 (dictum). Reacting to Bartel, OMB issued guidance indicating that records that have "traditionally" been considered to be in the public domain, and those that are required to be disclosed to the public--such as final opinions of agencies and press releases--can be released without waiting for an actual FOIA request. OMB Guidelines, 52 Fed. Reg. 12,990, 12,992-93 (1987) (discussing Bartel, in context of guidance on "call detail" programs, and referring to OMB Memorandum For The Senior Agency Officials For Information Resources Management (May 24, 1985) at 4-6 (unpublished)). At least one pre-Bartel case appears to support this idea. Owens v. MSPB, No. 3-83-0449-R, slip op. at 3 (N.D. Tex. Sept. 14, 1983) (release of agency's final decision is public information that "simply cannot be an unlawful disclosure under the Privacy Act"). But see Zeller v. United States, 467 F. Supp. 487, 503 (E.D.N.Y. 1979) (subsection (b)(2) inapplicable to press release as "nothing in the FOIA appears to require such information to be released in the absence of a request therefor").

3. **5 U.S.C. § 552a(b)(3) (routine uses)**

"for a routine use as defined in subsection (a)(7) of this section and described under subsection (e)(4)(D)."

Cross-references:

Subsection (e)(4)(D) requires Federal Register publication of "each routine use of the records contained in the system, including the categories of users and the purpose of such use."

Subsection (a)(7) defines the term "routine use" to mean "with respect to the disclosure of a record, the use of such record for a purpose which is compatible with the purpose for which it was collected."

comment -- The routine use exception, because of its potential breadth, is one of the most controversial provisions in the Act. See Privacy Commission Report at 517-18. The trend in recent cases is toward a narrower construction of the exception. President Clinton directed the Office of Management and Budget to issue additional guidance regarding the routine use exception in an executive memorandum on privacy issued two years ago. Memorandum on Privacy and Personal Information in Federal Records, 34 Weekly Comp. Pres. Doc. 870 (May 14, 1998), available in Westlaw, 1998 WL 241263 (May 14, 1998).

By its terms, this exception sets forth <u>two</u> requirements for a proper routine use disclosure: (1) <u>Federal Register</u> publication, thereby providing constructive notice; and (2) compatibility. See <u>Britt v. Naval Investigative Serv.</u>, 886 F.2d 544, 547-50 (3d Cir. 1989); <u>Shannon v. General Elec. Co.</u>, 812 F. Supp. 308, 316 (N.D.N.Y. 1993).

However, the Court of Appeals for the Ninth Circuit has engrafted a <u>third</u> requirement onto this exception: Actual notice of the routine use under subsection (e)(3)(C) (i.e., at the time of information collection from the individual). <u>Covert v. Harrington</u>, 876 F.2d 751, 754-56 (9th Cir. 1989) (discussed below). Subsequently, the Court of Appeals for the District of Columbia Circuit cited this aspect of <u>Covert</u> with approval and remanded a case for determination as to whether (e)(3)(C) notice was provided, stating that "[a]lthough the statute itself does not provide, in so many terms, that an agency's failure to provide employees with actual notice of its routine uses would prevent a disclosure from qualifying as a 'routine use,' that conclusion seems implicit in the structure and purpose of the Act." <u>United States Postal Serv. v. National Ass'n of Letter Carriers</u>, 9 F.3d 138, 146 (D.C. Cir. 1993).

### Federal Register Constructive Notice

The routine use exception's notice requirement "is intended to serve as a caution to agencies to think out in advance what uses [they] will make of information." 120 Cong. Rec. 40,881 (1974), <u>reprinted in</u> Source Book at 987. Indeed, it is possible for a routine use to be deemed facially invalid if it fails to satisfy subsection (e)(4)(D)--i.e., if it does not specify "the categories of users and the purpose of such use." See <u>Britt</u>, 886 F.2d at 547-48 (dictum) (suggesting that routine use (50 Fed. Reg. 22,802-03 (1985)) permitting disclosure to "federal regulatory agencies with investigative units" is overbroad as it "does not provide adequate notice to individuals as to what information concerning them will be released and the purposes of such release"); <u>cf.</u> <u>Krohn v. United States Dep't of Justice</u>, No. 78-1536, slip op. at 4-7 (D.D.C. Mar. 19, 1984) ("to qualify as a 'routine use,' the agency must . . . publish in the Federal Register . . . 'each routine use of the records contained in the system, including the categories of users and the purpose of such use'"), <u>reconsideration granted & vacated in nonpertinent part</u> (D.D.C. Nov. 29, 1984) (discussed below).

It is well settled that the "scope of [a] routine use is confined to the published definition." <u>Doe v. Naval Air Station, Pensacola, Fla.</u>, 768 F.2d 1229, 1231 (11th Cir. 1985); <u>see also</u> <u>Parks v. IRS</u>, 618 F.2d

677, 681-82 (10th Cir. 1980); Quilico v. United States Navy, No. 80-C-3568, 1983 U.S. Dist. LEXIS 14090, at **9-12 (N.D. Ill. Sept. 2, 1983); Local 2047, AFGE v. Defense Gen. Supply Ctr., 423 F. Supp. 481, 484-86 (E.D. Va. 1976), aff'd, 573 F.2d 184 (4th Cir. 1978). In other words, a particular disclosure is unauthorized if it does not fall within the clear terms of the routine use. See, e.g., Swenson v. United States Postal Serv., 890 F.2d 1075, 1078 (9th Cir. 1989) (47 Fed. Reg. 1203 (1982) held inapplicable to agency's disclosure of record referencing employee's EEO complaints to her congressmen as their inquiries were not "made at the request of" employee); Tijerina v. Walters, 821 F.2d 789, 798 (D.C. Cir. 1987) (47 Fed. Reg. 24,012 (1982) held inapplicable to VA's unsolicited letter notifying state board of bar examiners of possible fraud committed by bar applicant because no violation of state law was "reasonably imminent," and letter was not in response to "official request"); Doe v. DiGenova, 779 F.2d 74, 86 (D.C. Cir. 1985) (43 Fed. Reg. 44,743 (1978) held inapplicable to VA psychiatric report because disclosed record itself did not "indicate a potential violation of law"); Greene v. VA, No. C-76-461-S, slip op. at 3-6 (M.D.N.C. July 3, 1978) (40 Fed. Reg. 38,105 (1975) held inapplicable to VA's disclosure of medical evaluation to state licensing bureau because routine use permitted disclosure only to facilitate VA decision); see also Covert, 667 F. Supp. at 736-39 (discussed below).

Note that an agency's construction of its routine use should be entitled to deference. See Department of the Air Force, Scott Air Force Base, Ill. v. FLRA, 104 F.3d 1396, 1402 (D.C. Cir. 1997); FLRA v. United States Dep't of the Treasury, 884 F.2d 1446, 1455-56 (D.C. Cir. 1989). But see NLRB v. United States Postal Serv., 790 F. Supp. 31, 33 (D.D.C. 1992) (rejecting Postal Service's interpretation of its own routine use).

Compatibility

The precise meaning of the term "compatible" is quite uncertain and must be assessed on a case-by-case basis. According to OMB, the "compatibility" concept encompasses (1) functionally equivalent uses, and (2) other uses that are necessary and proper. OMB Guidelines, 52 Fed. Reg. 12,990, 12,993 (1987).

The leading case on "compatibility" is Britt v. Naval Investigative Serv., 886 F.2d at 547-50, in which the Court of Appeals for the Third Circuit ruled that the Naval Investigative Service's gratuitous disclosure of records, describing a then-pending criminal investigation of a Marine Corps reservist, to that individual's civilian employer (the Immigration and Naturalization Service), was not "compatible" with the "case-specific purpose for collecting" such records. Id. In holding that the employment/suitability purpose for disclosure was incompatible with the criminal law enforcement purpose for collection, the Third Circuit deemed it significant that "the [Immigration and Naturalization Service] was not conducting its own criminal investigation of the same activity or any other activity" by the subject, and that the records at issue concerned "merely a preliminary investigation with no inculpatory findings." Id. at 549-50. Employing especially broad language, the Third Circuit pointedly condemned the agency's equating of "compatibility" with mere "relevance" to the recipient entity, observing that "[t]here must be a more concrete relationship or similarity, some meaningful degree of convergence, between the disclosing agency's purpose in gathering the information and in its disclosure." Id. (citing Covert, 876 F.2d at 755 (dictum); Mazaleski v. Truesdale, 562 F.2d 701, 713 n.31 (D.C. Cir. 1977) (dictum)); accord Swenson, 890 F.2d at 1078; cf. Quinn v. Stone, 978 F.2d 126, 139 (3d Cir. 1992) (Nygaard, J., dissenting) (concluding that disclosure was authorized by routine use because disclosure was compatible with one of the purposes for collection, even if not with main purpose for collection).

More recently, the D.C. Circuit interpreted the term "compatibility" in considering a routine use providing for disclosure to labor organizations as part of the collective bargaining process. The court stated that application of the "common usage" of the word would require simply that "a proposed disclosure would not actually frustrate the purposes for which the information was gathered." United States Postal Serv. v. National Ass'n of Letter Carriers, 9 F.3d 138, 144 (D.C. Cir. 1993). The D.C. Circuit recognized the "far tighter nexus" that was required by the Third and Ninth Circuits in Britt and Swenson, and that is consistent with the legislative history, but stated:

> Whatever the merit of the decisions of prior courts that have held . . . that a finding of a substantial similarity of purpose might be appropriate in the non-labor law context in order to effectuate congressional intent, the compatibility requirement imposed by section 552a(a)(7) cannot be understood to prevent an agency from disclosing to a union information as part of the collective bargaining process.

Id. at 145. In a concurring opinion, Judge Williams agreed with the disposition of the case, but noted that he did not share the "belief that the meaning of 'compatible'

. . . may depend on the identity of the entity to which the information is being disclosed." Id. at 147 n.1 (Williams, J., concurring). Rather, seeing "no conflict between the purposes for which the information was collected and those for which it will be disclosed," he found the disclosure compatible without further inquiry. Id. at 146-47.

There are two examples of "compatible" routine uses that frequently occur in the law enforcement context. First, in the context of investigations/prosecutions, law enforcement agencies may routinely share law enforcement records with each other. See OMB Guidelines, 40 Fed. Reg. at 28,955 (proper routine use is "transfer by a law enforcement agency of protective intelligence information to the Secret Service"); see also 28 U.S.C. § 534 (1994 & Supp. III 1997) (authorizing Attorney General to exchange criminal records with "authorized officials of the Federal Government, the States, cities, and penal and other institutions"). Second, agencies may routinely disclose any records indicating a possible violation of law (regardless of the purpose for collection) to law enforcement agencies for purposes of investigation/prosecution. See OMB Guidelines, 40 Fed. Reg. at 28,953; 120 Cong. Rec. 36,967, 40,884 (1974), reprinted in Source Book at 957-58, 995 (remarks of Congressman Moorhead); see also 28 U.S.C. § 535(b) (1994) (requiring agencies of the executive branch to expeditiously report "[a]ny information, allegation, or complaint" relating to crimes involving government officers and employees to United States Attorney General). These kinds of routine uses have been criticized on the ground that they circumvent the more restrictive requirements of subsection (b)(7). See Privacy Commission Report at 517-18; see also Britt, 886 F.2d at 548 n.1 (dictum); Covert, 667 F. Supp. at 739, 742 (dictum). Yet they have never been successfully challenged on that basis. Cf. Nwangoro v. Department of the Army, 952 F. Supp. 394, 398 (N.D. Tex. 1996) (disclosure by Military Police of financial records obtained in ongoing criminal investigation to foreign customs officials likewise involved in investigation of possible infractions of foreign tax and customs laws was "permitted by the 'routine use' exception and d[id] not constitute a violation of the Privacy Act"); Little v. FBI, 793 F. Supp. 652, 655 (D. Md. 1992) (disclosure did not violate Privacy Act prohibition because it was made pursuant to routine use that allows disclosure of personnel matters to other government agencies when directly related to enforcement function of recipient agency), aff'd on other grounds, 1 F.3d 255 (4th Cir. 1993).

In Covert v. Harrington, 667 F. Supp. at 736-39, however, the district court held that a routine use permitting the Department of Energy's Inspector General to disclose to the Justice Department relevant records when "a record" indicates a potential violation of law, 47 Fed. Reg. 14,333 (1982), did not permit the disclosure of personnel security questionnaires submitted by the plaintiffs because such questionnaires did not on their face reveal potential violations of law. The court rejected the agency's argument that disclosure was proper because each questionnaire was disclosed as part of a prosecutive report that (when viewed as a whole) did reveal a potential violation of law. Id. at 736-37. Further, the court found that the Inspector General's disclosure of the questionnaires to the Justice Department (for a criminal fraud prosecution) was not compatible with the purpose for which they were originally collected by the Department of Energy (for a security-clearance eligibility determination), notwithstanding the fact that the questionnaires were subsequently acquired by the Inspector General--on an intra-agency "need to know" basis pursuant to 5 U.S.C. § 552a(b)(1)--for the purpose of a fraud investigation. Id. at 737-39.

On cross-appeals, a divided panel of the Court of Appeals for the Ninth Circuit affirmed the district court's judgment on other grounds. Covert, 876 F.2d at 754-56. The panel majority held that the Department of Energy's failure to provide actual notice of the routine use on the questionnaires at the time of original collection, under subsection (e)(3)(C), precluded the Department of Energy from later invoking that routine use under subsection (b)(3). Id. at 755-56; see also United States Postal Serv. v. National Ass'n of Letter Carriers, 9 F.3d at 146 (citing Covert with approval and remanding case for factual determination as to whether (e)(3)(C) notice was given). No other court had ever so held. See the additional discussion under subsection (e)(3), below.

In Doe v. Stephens, 851 F.2d 1457, 1465-67 (D.C. Cir. 1988), the Court of Appeals for the District of Columbia Circuit held that a VA routine use--permitting disclosure of records "in order for the VA to respond to and comply with the issuance of a federal subpoena [47 Fed. Reg. 51,841 (1982)]"--was invalid under the Administrative Procedure Act because it was inconsistent with the Privacy Act as interpreted in Doe v. DiGenova, 779 F.2d at 78-84--where the court had found that disclosures pursuant to subpoenas were not permitted by the subsection (b)(11) court order exception. In light of Doe v. Stephens, the decision in Fields v. Leuver, No. 83-0967, slip op. at 5-7 (D.D.C. Sept. 22, 1983) (upholding routine use permitting disclosure of payroll records "in response to a court subpoena"), is unreli-

PRIVACY ACT OVERVIEW

able. But cf. Osborne v. United States Postal Serv., No. 94-30353, slip op. at 6-9 (N.D. Fla. May 18, 1995) (holding on alternative ground that disclosure of plaintiff's injury-compensation file to retired employee who had prepared file and who had been subpoenaed by plaintiff and was expecting to be deposed on matters documented in file was proper pursuant to routine use that "'specifically contemplates that information may be released in response to relevant discovery and that any manner of response allowed by the rules of the forum may be employed'").

A particular area of controversy concerns whether the routine use exception can be invoked to publicly file records in court. The Act's legislative history recognizes the "compatibility" of this type of disclosure. See 120 Cong. Rec. 40,405, 40,884 (1974), reprinted in Source Book at 858, 995 (routine use appropriate where Justice Department "presents evidence [tax information from IRS] against the individual" in court); see also Schuenemeyer v. United States, No. SA-85-773, slip op. at 4 (W.D. Tex. Mar. 31, 1988) (permitting disclosure of litigant's medical records to Justice Department and U.S. Claims Court for use "in preparing the position of the USAF before the [court]").

In Krohn, No. 78-1536, slip op. at 4-7 (D.D.C. Mar. 19, 1984), however, the court invalidated an FBI routine use allowing for "dissemination [of records] during appropriate legal proceedings," finding that such a routine use was impermissibly "vague" and was "capable of being construed so broadly as to encompass all legal proceedings." In response to Krohn, OMB issued guidance to agencies in which it suggested a model routine use--employing a "relevant and necessary to the litigation" standard--to permit the public filing of protected records with a court. OMB Memorandum for the Senior Agency Officials for Information Resources Management 2-4 (May 24, 1985) (unpublished). Many agencies, including the Justice Department, have adopted "post-Krohn" routine uses designed to authorize the public filing of relevant records in court. See, e.g., 63 Fed. Reg. 8665, 8666 (1998) (routine use [number 7] applicable to records in Justice Department's "Civil Division Case File System"); 63 Fed. Reg. 8666, 8667-68 (1998) (routine uses [letters "o" and "p"] applicable to records in U.S. Attorney's Office's "Civil Case Files").

It should be noted that none of the "post-Krohn" routine uses--such as the ones cited above which employ an "arguably relevant to the litigation" standard--have yet been successfully challenged in the courts. Cf. Russell v. GSA, 935 F. Supp. 1142, 1145-46 (D. Colo. 1996) (without analyzing propriety of routine use, finding disclosure in public

-709-

PRIVACY ACT OVERVIEW

pleadings of information regarding investigation of plaintiff was permissible under routine use providing for disclosure in proceeding before court where agency is party and records are determined "to be arguably relevant to the litigation"); Osborne, No. 94-30353, slip op. at 6-9 (N.D. Fla. May 18, 1995) (holding on alternative ground that disclosure of plaintiff's injury-compensation file to retired employee who had prepared file and who had been subpoenaed by plaintiff and was expecting to be deposed on matters documented in file was proper pursuant to routine use providing for disclosures "incident to litigation" and "in a proceeding before a court" because "deposition was a proceeding before [the] Court"); Sheptin v. United States Dep't of Justice, No. 91-2806, 1992 U.S. Dist. LEXIS 6221, at **6-7 (D.D.C. Apr. 30, 1992) (no wrongful disclosure where agency routine uses permit use of presentence report during course of habeas proceeding). Such challenges may be expected, either based upon an argument that the routine use does not satisfy the "compatibility" requirement of subsection (a)(7) of the Act, cf. Britt, 886 F.2d at 547-50 (mere "relevance" to recipient entity held to be improper standard for a "compatible" routine use disclosure), or based upon an argument that the routine use effectively circumvents the more restrictive, privacy-protective requirements of subsection (b)(11), cf. Doe v. Stephens, 851 F.2d at 1465-67 (agency cannot use routine use exception to disclose records in response to subpoena where court had earlier ruled that such disclosure was improper under subsection (b)(11)).

Numerous types of information sharing between agencies and with organizations or individuals have been upheld as valid routine uses. See, e.g., Pippinger v. Rubin, 129 F.3d 519, 531-32 (10th Cir. 1997) (disclosure of plaintiff's personnel information to MSPB in deposition testimony in another individual's related MSPB proceeding, and to the other individual, his attorney, and court reporter in conjunction with MSPB proceeding); Taylor v. United States, 106 F.3d 833, 836-37 (8th Cir. 1997) (disclosure of federal taxpayer information collected for purpose of federal tax administration to state tax officials for purpose of state tax administration), aff'g Taylor v. IRS, 186 B.R. 441, 446-47, 453-54 (N.D. Iowa 1995); Mount v. United States Postal Serv., 79 F.3d 531, 534 (6th Cir. 1996) (disclosure of plaintiff's medical information to union official representing him in administrative action in which his mental health was central issue); Alphin v. FAA, No. 89-2405, 1990 WL 52830, at *1 (4th Cir. Apr. 13, 1990) (disclosure of enforcement investigation final report to subject's customers); Hastings v. Judicial Conference of the United States, 770 F.2d 1093, 1104 (D.C. Cir.

1985) (disclosure of criminal investigative records to judicial committee investigating judge); United States v. Miller, 643 F.2d 713, 715 (10th Cir. 1981) (records submitted by individual to parole officer became part of Justice Department files and Department's use in criminal investigation constitutes routine use); United States v. Collins, 596 F.2d 166, 168 (6th Cir. 1979) (HEW's disclosure of plaintiff's Medicaid cost reports to Justice Department for use in criminal case against plaintiff); Puerta v. HHS, No. EDCV 94-0148, slip op. at 7 (C.D. Cal. Jan. 5, 1999) (disclosure of grant application to qualified expert for opinion as part of application review and award process) (appeal pending); Jones v. Runyon, 32 F. Supp. 2d 873, 876 (N.D. W. Va. 1998) (disclosure to credit reporting service of information about plaintiff when requesting employment reports in course of routine investigation of possible workers' compensation fraud), aff'd, 173 F.3d 850 (4th Cir. 1999) (unpublished table decision); Blazy v. Tenet, 979 F. Supp. 10, 26 (D.D.C. 1997) (CIA's disclosure of information about employee to FBI while FBI was investigating employee's application for FBI employment), summary affirmance granted, No. 97-5330, 1998 WL 315583 (D.C. Cir. May 12, 1998); Magee v. United States Postal Serv., 903 F. Supp. 1022, 1029 (W.D. La. 1995) (disclosure of employee's medical records to clinical psychologist hired by agency to perform fitness-for-duty examination on employee), aff'd, 79 F.3d 1145 (5th Cir. 1996) (unpublished table decision); McNeill v. IRS, No. 93-2204, 1995 U.S. Dist. LEXIS 2372, at *6 (D.D.C. Feb. 7, 1995) (disclosure of IRS personnel records to prospective federal agency employer); Harry v. United States Postal Serv., 867 F. Supp. 1199, 1206-07 (M.D. Pa. 1994) (disclosure of documents regarding individual's employment history, including details of settlement agreement, in response to congressional inquiries "made at the prompting of that individual"); Lachenmyer v. Frank, No. 88-2414, slip op. at 4 (C.D. Ill. July 16, 1990) (disclosure of investigative report to persons at arbitration hearing held proper under routine use permitting disclosure of "record relating to a case or matter" in a "hearing in accordance with the procedures governing such proceeding or hearing"); Choe v. Smith, No. C-87-1764R, slip op. at 10-11 (W.D. Wash. Apr. 20, 1989) (INS's disclosure to its informant during investigation "to elicit information required by the Service to carry out its functions and statutory mandates"), aff'd, 935 F.2d 274 (9th Cir. 1991) (unpublished table decision); Brown v. FBI, No. 87-C-9982, 1988 WL 79653, at *1 (N.D. Ill. July 25, 1988) (disclosure of rap sheet to local police department); Ely v. Department of Justice, 610 F. Supp. 942, 945-46 (N.D. Ill. 1985) (disclosure to plaintiff's lawyer), aff'd, 792 F.2d 142 (7th Cir. 1986) (unpublished table decision); Kimberlin v. United States Dep't of Justice, 605 F. Supp. 79, 82-83 (N.D. Ill. 1985) (Bureau of Prisons' disclosure of prisoner's commissary account record to probation officer), aff'd, 788 F.2d 434 (7th Cir. 1986); Burley v. DEA, 443 F. Supp. 619, 623-24 (M.D. Tenn. 1977) (transmittal of DEA records to state pharmacy board); Harper v. United States, 423 F. Supp. 192, 198-99 (D.S.C. 1976) (IRS's disclosure of plaintiff's identity to other targets of investigation); see also Gowan v. United States Dep't of the Air Force, 148 F.3d 1182, 1187, 1194 (10th Cir.) (disclosure of information regarding individual to Members of Congress in response to inquiries made pursuant to individual's letters requesting assistance; stating that such disclosure is not "incompatible" and thus "would likely be protected under the routine use exception"), cert. denied, 525 U.S. 1042 (1998).

Four courts have required an agency to invoke its routine use to permit disclosure to unions of names of employees on the theory that refusal to so disclose was an unfair labor practice under the National Labor Relations Act. See NLRB v. United States Postal Serv., No. 92-2358, 1994 WL 47743, at **3-4 (4th Cir. Feb. 16, 1994); NLRB v. United States Postal Serv., 888 F.2d 1568, 1572-73 (11th Cir. 1989); NLRB v. United States Postal Serv., 841 F.2d 141, 144-45 & n.3 (6th Cir. 1988); NLRB v. United States Postal Serv., 790 F. Supp. 31, 33 (D.D.C. 1992); see also United States Postal Serv. v. National Ass'n of Letter Carriers, 9 F.3d 138, 141-46 (D.C. Cir. 1993) (holding that "if Postal Service could disclose the information under [its routine use] then it must disclose that information, because in the absence of a Privacy Act defense the arbitrator's award must be enforced," but remanding case for determination as to whether proper (e)(3)(C) notice was given before requiring invocation of routine use); FLRA v. United States Dep't of the Navy, 966 F.2d 747, 761-65 (3d Cir. 1992) (alternative holding) (en banc) (release to union of home addresses of bargaining unit employees pursuant to routine use was required under Federal Service Labor-Management Relations Act).

In addition, the Court of Appeals for the District of Columbia Circuit, in Department of the Air Force v. FLRA, granted enforcement of a Federal Labor Relations Authority decision requiring the Air Force to disclose to a union a disciplinary letter that was issued to a bargaining unit employee's supervisor. 104 F.3d 1396, 1399, 1401-02 (D.C. Cir. 1997). The court held that the Federal Management Relations Statute required disclosure of the letter, and that because the "union's request f[ell] within the Act's 'routine use' exception, the Privacy Act d[id] not bar disclosure," and the union was entitled to disclosure of the letter. Id. at 1401-02.

Apart from the FOIA (see subsection (b)(2)) and the Debt Collection Act (see subsection (b)(12)), the Privacy Act makes no provision for any nonconsensual disclosures that are provided for by other statutes. See, e.g., 42 U.S.C. § 653 (1994 & Supp. III 1997) (establishing "Parent Locator Service" and requiring agencies to comply with requests from Secretary of HHS for addresses and places of employment of absent parents "[n]otwithstanding any other provision of law"). Recognizing this difficulty, the OMB Guidelines note that "[s]uch disclosures, which are in effect congressionally mandated 'routine uses,' should still be established as 'routine uses' pursuant to subsections (e)(11) and (e)(4)(D)." OMB Guidelines, 40 Fed. Reg. at 28,954.

4. **5 U.S.C. § 552a(b)(4) (Bureau of the Census)**

"to the Bureau of the Census for purposes of planning or carrying out a census or survey or related activity pursuant to the provisions of Title 13."

comment -- For a discussion of this provision, see OMB Guidelines, 40 Fed. Reg. 28,948, 28,954 (1975).

5. **5 U.S.C. § 552a(b)(5) (statistical research)**

"to a recipient who has provided the agency with advance adequate written assurance that the record will be used solely as a statistical research or reporting record, and the record is to be transferred in a form that is not individually identifiable."

comment -- The term "statistical record" is defined in the Act as a record that is not used in making individual determinations. 5 U.S.C. § 552a(a)(6). One might question whether this exception to subsection (b) is anomalous: The information it permits to be released is arguably not a "record," see 5 U.S.C. § 552a(a)(4), or a "disclosure," see 5 U.S.C. § 552a(b), in the first place as it is not identifiable to any individual. However, the OMB Guidelines provide a plausible explanation for this unique provision: "One may infer from the legislative history and other portions of the Act that an objective of this provision is to reduce the possibility of matching and analysis of statistical records with other records to reconstruct individually identifiable records." OMB Guidelines, 40 Fed. Reg. 28,948, 28,954 (1975).

6. **5 U.S.C. § 552a(b)(6) (National Archives)**

"to the National Archives and Records Administration as a record which has sufficient historical or other value to warrant its continued preservation by the United States Government, or for evaluation by the Archivist

PRIVACY ACT OVERVIEW

of the United States or the designee of the Archivist to determine whether the record has such value."

comment -- For a discussion of this provision, see OMB Guidelines, 40 Fed. Reg. 28,948, 28,955 (1975).

7. **5 U.S.C. § 552a(b)(7) (law enforcement request)**

"to another agency or to an instrumentality of any governmental jurisdiction within or under the control of the United States for a civil or criminal law enforcement activity if the activity is authorized by law, and if the head of the agency or instrumentality has made a written request to the agency which maintains the record specifying the particular portion desired and the law enforcement activity for which the record is sought."

comment -- This provision, in addition to providing for disclosures to federal law enforcement agencies, also allows an agency, "upon receipt of a written request, [to] disclose a record to another agency or unit of State or local government for a civil or criminal law enforcement activity." OMB Guidelines, 40 Fed. Reg. 28,948, 28,955 (1975).

Note that the request must be submitted in writing and must be from the head of the agency or instrumentality. See Doe v. DiGenova, 779 F.2d 74, 85 (D.C. Cir. 1985); Doe v. Naval Air Station, 768 F.2d 1229, 1232-33 (11th Cir. 1985); see also Reyes v. Supervisor of DEA, 834 F.2d 1093, 1095 (1st Cir. 1987); United States v. Collins, 596 F.2d 166, 168 (6th Cir. 1979); SEC v. Dimensional Entertainment Corp., 518 F. Supp. 773, 775 (S.D.N.Y. 1981).

Record-requesting authority may be delegated down to lower-level agency officials when necessary, but not below the "section chief" level. See OMB Guidelines, 40 Fed. Reg. at 28,955; see also 120 Cong. Rec. 36,967 (1974), reprinted in Source Book at 958. The Department of Justice has delegated record-requesting authority to a "head of a component or a United States Attorney, or either's designee." 28 C.F.R. § 16.40(c) (1999).

8. **5 U.S.C. § 552a(b)(8) (health or safety of an individual)**

"to a person pursuant to a showing of compelling circumstances affecting the health or safety of an individual if upon such disclosure notification is transmitted to the last known address of such individual."

comment -- For cases discussing this provision, see Schwarz v. Interpol, No. 94-4111, 1995 U.S. App. LEXIS 3987, at *6 n.2 (10th Cir. Feb. 28, 1995) (unsubstantiated allegations alone do not constitute "showing of compelling circumstances"), and DePlanche v. Califano, 549 F. Supp. 685, 703-04 (W.D. Mich. 1982) (emphasizing emergency nature of exception).

PRIVACY ACT OVERVIEW

According to the OMB Guidelines, the individual about whom records are disclosed "need not necessarily be the individual whose health or safety is at peril; e.g., release of dental records on several individuals in order to identify an individual who was injured in an accident." OMB Guidelines, 40 Fed. Reg. 28,948, 28,955 (1975). This construction, while certainly sensible as a policy matter, appears to conflict with the actual wording of subsection (b)(8).

9. **5 U.S.C. § 552a(b)(9) (Congress)**

"to either House of Congress, or, to the extent of matter within its jurisdiction, any committee or subcommittee thereof, any joint committee of Congress or subcommittee of any such joint committee."

comment -- This exception does *not* authorize the disclosure of a Privacy Act-protected record to an individual Member of Congress acting on his or her own behalf or on behalf of a constituent. See OMB Guidelines, 40 Fed. Reg. 28,948, 28,955 (1975); 40 Fed. Reg. 56,741, 56,742 (1975); see also Swenson v. United States Postal Serv., 890 F.2d 1075, 1077 (9th Cir. 1989); Lee v. Dearment, No. 91-2175, 1992 WL 119855, at *2 (4th Cir. June 3, 1992); cf. FOIA Update, Vol. V, No. 1, at 3-4 (interpreting counterpart provision of FOIA).

The Court of Appeals for the Second Circuit in Devine v. United States, in holding that the unsolicited disclosure of an Inspector General letter to a congressional subcommittee chairman and member fell "squarely within the ambit of § 552a(b)(9)," rejected the appellant's argument that subsection (b)(9) should not apply if the government agency knew or should have known that the information would eventually be released to the public. 202 F.3d 547, 551-553 (2d Cir. 2000).

10. **5 U.S.C. § 552a(b)(10) (General Accounting Office)**

"to the Comptroller General, or any of his authorized representatives, in the course of the performance of the duties of the General Accounting Office."

11. **5 U.S.C. § 552a(b)(11) (court order)**

"pursuant to the order of a court of competent jurisdiction."

comment -- This exception--like the subsection (b)(3) routine use exception--has generated a great deal of uncertainty. Unfortunately, neither the Act's legislative history, see 120 Cong. Rec. 36,959 (1974), reprinted in Source Book at 936, nor the OMB Guidelines, see 40 Fed. Reg. 28,948, 28,955 (1975), shed light on its meaning.

As a general proposition, it appears that the essential point of this exception is that the Privacy Act "cannot be used to block the normal course of court proceedings, including court-ordered discovery." Clavir v. United States, 84 F.R.D. 612, 614 (S.D.N.Y. 1979); see also, e.g., Martin v. United States, 1 Cl. Ct. 775, 780-82 (Cl. Ct. 1983); Newman v. United States, No. 81-2480, slip op. at 3 (D.D.C. Sept. 13, 1982).

## What Does "Court Order" Mean?

In Doe v. DiGenova, 779 F.2d 74, 77-85 (D.C. Cir. 1985), the Court of Appeals for the District of Columbia Circuit decisively ruled that a subpoena routinely issued by a court clerk--such as a federal grand jury subpoena--is not a "court order" within the meaning of this exception because it is not "specifically approved" by a judge. Prior to Doe v. DiGenova, a split of authority existed on this point. Compare Bruce v. United States, 621 F.2d 914, 916 (8th Cir. 1980) (dictum) (subpoena not court order), and Stiles v. Atlanta Gas Light Co., 453 F. Supp. 798, 800 (N.D. Ga. 1978) (same), with Adams v. United States Lines, No. 80-0952, slip op. at 2-3 (E.D. La. Mar. 16, 1981) (subpoena is court order). Cf. Moore v. United States Postal Serv., 609 F. Supp. 681, 682 (E.D.N.Y. 1985) (subpoena is court order where required to be approved by judge under state law).

Note that an agency cannot avoid the result in Doe v. DiGenova by relying on a routine use that seeks to authorize disclosure pursuant to a subpoena. See Doe v. Stephens, 851 F.2d 1457, 1465-67 (D.C. Cir. 1988) (discussed above under routine use exception).

## What is the Standard for Issuance of a Court Order?

Unlike similar provisions in other federal confidentiality statutes, see, e.g., 42 U.S.C. § 290dd-2 (1994) (listing "good cause" factors to be weighed by court in evaluating applications for orders permitting disclosure of records pertaining to substance abuse), subsection (b)(11) contains no standard governing the issuance of an order authorizing the disclosure of otherwise protected Privacy Act information. However, several courts have addressed the issue with varying degrees of clarity. It has been held, for example, that because the Privacy Act does not itself create a qualified discovery "privilege," a showing of "need" is not a prerequisite to initiating discovery of protected records. See Laxalt v. McClatchy, 809 F.2d 885, 888-90 (D.C. Cir. 1987); see also Weahkee v. Norton, 621 F.2d 1080, 1082 (10th Cir. 1980) (noting that objection to discovery of protected records "does not state a claim of privilege"); Bosaw v. NTEU, 887 F. Supp. 1199, 1215-17 (S.D. Ind. 1995) (citing Laxalt with approval, although ultimately determining that court did not have jurisdiction to rule on merits of case); Ford Motor Co. v. United States, 825 F. Supp. 1081, 1083 (Ct. Int'l Trade 1993) ("[T]he Privacy Act does not establish a qualified discovery privilege that requires a party seeking disclosure under 5 U.S.C. § 552a(b)(11) to prove that its need for the information outweighs the privacy interest of the individual to whom the information relates."); Clavir v. United States, 84 F.R.D. at 614 ("it has never been suggested that the Privacy Act was intended to serve as a limiting amendment to . . . the Federal Rules of Civil Procedure"); cf. Baldrige v. Shapiro, 455 U.S. 345, 360-62 (1981) (Census Act held to constitute statutorily created discovery "privilege" because it precludes all disclosure of raw census data despite need demonstrated by litigant).

Rather, Laxalt v. McClatchy establishes that the only test for discovery of Privacy Act-protected records is "relevance" under Rule 26(b)(1) of the Federal Rules of Civil Procedure. 809 F.2d at 888-90; see also, e.g., Hernandez v. United States, No. 97-3367, 1998 WL 230200, at **2-3 (E.D. La. May 6, 1998); Forrest v. United States, No. 95-3889, 1996 WL 171539, at *2 (E.D. Pa. Apr. 11, 1996); Bosaw, 887 F. Supp. at 1216-17 (citing Laxalt with approval, although ultimately determining that court did not have jurisdiction to rule on merits of case); Ford Motor Co., 825 F. Supp. at 1083-84; Mary Imogene Bassett Hosp. v. Sullivan, 136 F.R.D. 42, 49 (N.D.N.Y. 1991); O'Neill v. Engels, 125 F.R.D. 518, 520 (S.D. Fla. 1989); Murray v. United States, No. 84-2364, slip op. at 1-3 (D. Kan. Feb. 21, 1988); Broderick v. Shad, 117 F.R.D. 306, 312 (D.D.C. 1987); Smith v. Regan, No. 81-1401, slip op. at 1-2 (D.D.C. Jan. 9, 1984); In re Grand Jury Subpoenas Issued to United States Postal Serv., 535 F. Supp. 31, 33 (E.D. Tenn. 1981); Christy v. United States, 68 F.R.D. 375, 378 (N.D. Tex. 1975). But see Perry v. State Farm Fire & Cas. Co., 734 F.2d 1441, 1447 (11th Cir. 1984) (requests for court orders "should be evaluated by balancing the need for the disclosure against the potential harm to the subject of the disclosure"); Newman, No. 81-2480, slip op. at 3 (D.D.C. Sept. 13, 1982) (evaluating "legitimacy" of discovery requests and "need" for records as factors governing issuance of court order).

However, it is important to note that a protective order limiting discovery under Rule 26(c) of the Federal Rules of Civil Procedure (based, if appropriate, upon a court's careful in camera inspection) is a proper procedural device for protecting particularly sensitive Privacy Act-protected records when subsection (b)(11) court orders are sought. See Laxalt, 809 F.2d at 889-90; see also, e.g., Boudreaux v. United States,

No. 97-1592, 1999 WL 499911, at **1-2 (E.D. La. July 14, 1999) (recognizing relevancy of subsection (b)(11) to court's resolution of dispute over motion to compel responses to production of documents subject to Privacy Act, but ordering in camera review of documents so that legitimacy of agency objections may be determined "in the considered and cautious manner contemplated by the Privacy Act"); Gary v. United States, No. 3:97-cv-658, 1998 U.S. Dist. LEXIS 16722, at **10-11 (E.D. Tenn. Sept. 4, 1998) (finding that while third party's personnel file may contain relevant information, disclosure of that file must be made pursuant to protective order); Bustillo v. Hawk, No. 97-WM-445, 1998 WL 299980, at **4-6 (D. Colo. May 28, 1998) (ordering defendant to provide United States Marshals Service with addresses of individually named defendants for service of process on behalf of inmate and ordering that addresses be safeguarded by Marshals Service); Hernandez, No. 97-3367, 1998 WL 230200, at **2-3 (E.D. La. May 6, 1998) (granting motion to compel agency to produce individual's personnel file "which is likely to contain information 'relevant to the subject matter involved in the pending action,'" but accommodating "legitimate privacy and confidentiality concerns" with protective order); Wright v. United States, No. 95-0274, 1996 WL 525324 (D.D.C. Sept. 10, 1996) (order "pursuant to the Privacy Act and Rule 26 of the Federal Rules of Civil Procedure" establishing procedures to be followed by parties "[i]n order to permit the parties to use information relevant to th[e] case without undermining the legislative purposes underlying the Privacy Act"); Bosaw, 887 F. Supp. at 1216-17 (citing Laxalt with approval, although ultimately determining that court did not have jurisdiction to rule on merits of case); PHE, Inc. v. Department of Justice, No. 90-0693, slip op. at 13 & accompanying order (D.D.C. Nov. 14, 1991); Mary Imogene Bassett Hosp. v. Sullivan, 136 F.R.D. at 49; Avirgan v. Hull, Misc. No. 88-0112, slip op. at 1-3 (Bankr. D.D.C. May 2, 1988); Baron & Assocs. v. United States Dep't of the Army, No. 84-2021, slip op. at 2-4 (D.D.C. Apr. 1, 1985); Granton v. HHS, No. 83-C-3538, 1984 U.S. Dist. LEXIS 19113, at **2-3 (N.D. Ill. Feb. 27, 1984); White House Vigil for the ERA Comm. v. Watt, No. 83-1243, slip op. at 1-3 (D.D.C. Oct. 14, 1983); LaBuguen v. Bolger, No. 82-C-6803, 1983 U.S. Dist. LEXIS 13559 (N.D. Ill. Sept. 21, 1983) (order); Clymer v. Grzegorek, 515 F. Supp. 938, 942 (E.D. Va. 1981); cf. Forrest, 1996 WL 171539, at **2-3 (parties ordered to "explore the possibility of entering into a voluntary confidentiality agreement regarding protecting the privacy interests of those individuals affected by disclosure"); Loma Linda Community Hosp. v. Shalala, 907 F. Supp. 1399, 1405 (C.D. Cal. 1995) ("Even if release of the data . . . had unexpectedly included information not already known to [the recipient], a confidentiality order could have been imposed to protect the privacy interests in issue."); Williams v. McCausland, No. 90 Civ. 7563, 1992 WL 309826, at *3 (S.D.N.Y. Oct. 15, 1992) (parties directed to agree on and execute appropriate protective stipulation for information sought in discovery that, under Privacy Act's subsection (b)(2) standard, would not be required to be disclosed under FOIA).

In some instances, it may even be appropriate for a court to entirely deny discovery. See, e.g., Farnsworth v. Proctor & Gamble Co., 758 F.2d 1545, 1546-48 (11th Cir. 1985); Oslund v. United States, 125 F.R.D. 110, 114-15 (D. Minn. 1989); cf. Barnett v. Dillon, 890 F. Supp. 83, 88 (N.D.N.Y. 1995) (declining to order disclosure of FBI investigative records protected by Privacy Act to arrestees despite their assertion that records were essential to proper prosecution and presentment of claims in their civil rights lawsuit).

In Redland Soccer Club, Inc. v. Department of the Army of the United States, No. 1:CV-90-1072, slip op. 1-3 & accompanying order (M.D. Pa. Jan. 14, 1991), aff'd, rev'd & remanded on other grounds, 55 F.3d 827 (3d Cir. 1995), the court, recognizing the "defendants' initial reluctance to respond to plaintiffs' [discovery] requests without a specific order of court [as] a reasonable precaution in light of the terms of the Privacy Act," solved the dilemma by ordering that the Army respond to "all properly framed discovery requests in th[e] proceeding" and that such responses were to "be deemed made pursuant to an order of court." Id.

Must an Agency Obtain a Court Order to Publicly File Protected Records with the Court?

As noted above, the Act's legislative history indicates that a court is not a "person" or "agency" within the meaning of subsection (b), and that the Act was "not designed to interfere with access to information by the courts." 120 Cong. Rec. 36,967 (1974), reprinted in Source Book at 958-59.

However, the nonconsensual public filing of protected records with a court, during the course of litigation, does constitute a subsection (b) disclosure. See Laningham v. United States Navy, No. 83-3238, slip op. at 2-3 (D.D.C. Sept. 25, 1984), summary judgment granted (D.D.C. Jan. 7, 1985), aff'd per curiam, 813 F.2d 1236 (D.C. Cir. 1987); Citizens Bureau of Investigation v. FBI, No. 78-60, slip op. at 3 (N.D. Ohio Dec. 14, 1979). Thus, such public filing is proper only if it is undertaken pursuant to: (1) the subsection (b)(3) routine use exception (previously discussed), or (2) the subsection (b)(11) court order exception. See generally Krohn v. United States Dep't of Justice, No. 78-1536, slip op. at 3-11 (D.D.C. Mar. 19, 1984) (finding violation of Privacy Act where agency's disclosure of records as attachments to affidavit in FOIA lawsuit "did not fall within any of the exceptions listed in Section 552a"), reconsideration granted & vacated in nonpertinent part (D.D.C. Nov. 29, 1984).

Where the routine use exception is unavailable, an agency should obtain a subsection (b)(11) court order permitting such public filing. Cf. Doe v. DiGenova, 779 F.2d at 85 n.20 ("This is not to say that a prosecutor, a defendant, or a civil litigant, cannot submit an in camera ex parte application for a [subsection (b)(11)] court order."). However, in light of Laningham, No. 83-3238, slip op. at 2-3 (D.D.C. Sept. 25, 1984), agencies should take care to apprise the court of the Privacy Act-related basis for seeking the order. In Laningham, the district court ruled that the government's nonconsensual disclosure of plaintiff's "disability evaluation" records to the United States Claims Court was improper--even though such records were filed only after the agency's motion for leave to file "out of time" was granted. Id. The court held that subsection (b)(11) applies only when "for compelling reasons, the court specifically orders that a document be disclosed," and it rejected the agency's argument that the exception applies whenever records happen to be filed with leave of court. Id. at 4.

One unique solution to the problem of filing Privacy Act-protected records in court is illustrated by In re A Motion for a Standing Order, 1 Vet. App. 555, 558-59 (Ct. Vet. App. 1990), in which the Court of Veterans Appeals issued a "standing order" permitting the Secretary of Veterans Affairs to routinely file relevant records from a veteran's case file with that court.

What Does "Competent Jurisdiction" Mean?

One of the few Privacy Act decisions to even mention this oft-overlooked requirement is Laxalt v. McClatchy, 809 F.2d at 890-91. In that case, the Court of Appeals for the District of Columbia Circuit appeared to equate the term "competent jurisdiction" with personal jurisdiction, noting that the requests for discovery of the nonparty agency's records "were within the jurisdiction of the District Court for the District of Columbia" as "[n]either party contends that the District Court lacked personal jurisdiction over the FBI's custodian of records." Id.

Of course, where an agency is a proper party in a federal case, the district court's personal jurisdiction over the agency presumably exists and thus court-ordered discovery of the agency's records is clearly proper under subsection (b)(11).

However, where a party seeks discovery of a nonparty agency's records--pursuant to a subpoena duces tecum issued under Rule 45 of the Federal Rules of Civil Procedure--<u>Laxalt</u> suggests that the district court issuing the discovery order must have personal jurisdiction over the nonparty agency in order to be regarded as a court of "competent jurisdiction" within the meaning of subsection (b)(11). <u>See</u> 809 F.2d at 890-91; <u>cf.</u> <u>Mason v. South Bend Community Sch. Corp.</u>, 990 F. Supp. 1096, 1097-99 (N.D. Ind. 1997) (determining that Social Security Administration's regulations "generally do not authorize the release of . . . records upon order of a court, even a federal court, in the absence of a special circumstance as defined by the statutes and regulations" and thus finding SSA not to be in contempt of court for failure to comply with prior order compelling SSA, a nonparty, to produce documents). <u>But cf.</u> <u>Lohrenz v. Donnelly</u>, 187 F.R.D. 1, 8-9 (D.D.C. 1999) (finding that requisite showing of good cause had been made by nonparty agency and providing for entry of protective order with no discussion of jurisdiction over nonparty agency). The issue of whether personal jurisdiction exists in this kind of situation is not always a clear-cut one--particularly where the nonparty agency's records are kept at a place beyond the territorial jurisdiction of the district court that issued the discovery order. Indeed, this very issue was apparently raised but not decided in <u>Laxalt</u>, 809 F.2d at 890-91 (finding it unnecessary to decide whether federal district court in Nevada would have had jurisdiction to order discovery of FBI records located in District of Columbia).

The existence of "competent jurisdiction" is likewise questionable whenever a state court orders the disclosure of a nonparty federal agency's records--because ordinarily the doctrine of "sovereign immunity" will preclude state court jurisdiction over a federal agency or official. <u>See, e.g.</u>, <u>Bosaw</u>, 887 F. Supp. at 1210-17 (state court lacked jurisdiction to order federal officers to produce documents because government did not explicitly waive its sovereign immunity and, because federal court's jurisdiction in this case was derivative of state court's jurisdiction, federal court was likewise barred from ordering officers to produce documents); <u>Boron Oil Co. v. Downie</u>, 873 F.2d 67, 70-71 (4th Cir. 1989) (state court subpoena held to constitute "action" against United States and thus sovereign immunity applied even though EPA was not party in suit); <u>Sharon Lease Oil Co. v. Federal Energy Regulatory Comm'n</u>, 691 F. Supp. 381, 383-85 (D.D.C. 1988) (state court subpoena quashed as state court lacked jurisdiction to compel nonparty federal official to testify or produce documents absent waiver of sovereign immunity); see also Moore v. Armour Pharm. Co., 129 F.R.D. 551, 555 (N.D. Ga. 1990) (citing additional cases on point); cf. Louisiana v. Sparks, 978 F.2d 226, 235 n.15 (5th Cir. 1992) (noting that "[t]here is no indication that [(b)(11)] evinces congressional intent to broadly waive the sovereign immunity of [federal] agencies . . . when ordered to comply with state court subpoenas").

In Moore v. United States Postal Serv., 609 F. Supp. 681, 682 (E.D.N.Y. 1985), the court assumed without explanation that a state court subpoena, required by state law to be approved by a judge, constituted a proper subsection (b)(11) court order; the issue of "competent jurisdiction" was not addressed. Cf. Henson v. Brown, No. 95-213, slip op. at 4-5 (D. Md. June 23, 1995) (although not disputed by parties, stating that judge's signature elevated subpoena to court order within meaning of subsection (b)(11) in context of determining whether defendant complied with order).

At least one state court has ruled that it has "competent jurisdiction" to issue a subsection (b)(11) court order permitting the disclosure of a Privacy Act-protected record. Tootle v. Seaboard Coast Line R.R., 468 So. 2d 237, 239 (Fla. Dist. Ct. App. 1984); cf. Saulter v. Municipal Court for the Oakland-Piedmont Judicial Dist., 142 Cal. App. 3d 266, 275 (Cal. Ct. App. 1977) (suggesting that state court can order state prosecutor to subpoena federal records for purpose of disclosing them to criminal defendant in discovery).

Agencies that construe state court orders as providing authority to disclose under subsection (b)(11) should be aware that compliance with such an order might be taken by a court as acquiescence to the court's jurisdiction, notwithstanding applicable principles of sovereign immunity.

12. **5 U.S.C. § 552a(b)(12) (Debt Collection Act)**

"to a consumer reporting agency in accordance with section 3711(e) of Title 31."

comment -- This disclosure exception was added to the original eleven exceptions by the Debt Collection Act of 1982. It authorizes agencies to disclose bad-debt information to credit bureaus. Before doing so, however, agencies must complete a series of due process steps designed to validate the debt and to offer the individual an opportunity to repay it. See OMB Guidelines, 48 Fed. Reg. 15,556-60 (1983).

## ACCOUNTING OF CERTAIN DISCLOSURES

(1) Each agency, with respect to each system of records under its control, must keep a record of the date, nature, and purpose of each disclosure of a record to any person or to another agency under subsection (b) and the name and address of the person or agency to whom the disclosure is made. See 5 U.S.C. § 552a(c)(1). An accounting need not be kept of intra-agency disclosures (5 U.S.C. § 552a(b)(1)) or FOIA disclosures (5 U.S.C. § 552a(b)(2)). See 5 U.S.C. § 552a(c)(1).

(2) This accounting of disclosures must be kept for five years or the life of the record, whichever is longer, after the disclosure for which the accounting is made. See 5 U.S.C. § 552a(c)(2).

(3) Except for disclosures made under subsection (b)(7), an individual is entitled, upon request, to get access to this accounting of disclosures of his record. See 5 U.S.C. § 552a(c)(3).

(4) An agency must inform any person or other agency about any correction or notation of dispute made by the agency in accordance with subsection (d) of any record that has been disclosed to the person or agency if an accounting of the disclosure was made. See 5 U.S.C. § 552a(c)(4).

comment -- The language of subsection (c)(1) explicitly excepts both intra-agency "need to know" disclosures and FOIA disclosures from its coverage. See, e.g., Quinn v. United States Navy, No. 94-56067, 1995 WL 341513, at *1 (9th Cir. June 8, 1995) (only disclosure of records was within Navy and thus was exempt from accounting requirements); Clarkson v. IRS, 811 F.2d 1396, 1397-98 (11th Cir. 1987) (per curiam) (IRS's internal disclosure of records to its criminal investigation units does not require accounting).

It is important to recognize that subsection (c)(3) grants individuals a right of access similar to the access right provided by subsection (d)(1). See Standley v. Department of Justice, 835 F.2d 216, 219 (9th Cir. 1987) (plaintiff entitled to gain access to list, compiled by U.S. Attorney, of persons in IRS to whom disclosures of grand jury materials about plaintiff were made); Ray v. United States Dep't of Justice, 558 F. Supp. 226, 228 (D.D.C. 1982) (addresses of private persons who requested plaintiff's records required to be released to plaintiff notwithstanding that "concern about possible harrassment [sic] of these individuals may be legitimate"), aff'd, 720 F.2d 216 (D.C. Cir. 1983) (unpublished table decision); cf. Quinn, 1995 WL 341513, at *1 (no records to disclose in response to request for accounting because there were no disclosures that required accounting).

Of course, it should not be overlooked that certain Privacy Act exemptions--5 U.S.C. § 552a(j) and (k)--are potentially available to shield an "accounting of disclosures" record from release to the subject thereof under subsection (c)(3). See Standley, 835 F.2d at 219 (remanding case for consideration of whether exemptions are applicable); Mittleman v. United States Dep't of the

PRIVACY ACT OVERVIEW

Treasury, 919 F. Supp. 461, 469 (D.D.C. 1995) (finding that "application of exemption (k)(2) . . . is valid" and that Department of the Treasury Inspector General's "General Allegations and Investigative Records System" is exempt "because, inter alia, application of the accounting-of-disclosures provision . . . would alert the subject to the existence of an investigation, possibly resulting in hindrance of an investigation"), aff'd in part & remanded in part on other grounds, 104 F.3d 410 (D.C. Cir. 1997); Bagley v. FBI, No. 88-4075, slip op. at 2-4 (N.D. Iowa Aug. 28, 1989) (applying subsection (j)(2)); see also Hart v. FBI, No. 94 C 6010, 1995 U.S. Dist. LEXIS 4542, at *6 n.1 (N.D. Ill. Apr. 7, 1995) (noting exemption of FBI's Criminal Justice Information Services Division Records System), aff'd, 91 F.3d 146 (7th Cir. 1996) (unpublished table decision).

For a further discussion of this provision, see OMB Guidelines, 40 Fed. Reg. 28,948, 28,955-56 (1975).

## INDIVIDUAL'S RIGHT OF ACCESS

"Each agency that maintains a system of records shall--upon request by any individual to gain access to his record or to any information pertaining to him which is contained in the system, permit him and upon his request, a person of his own choosing to accompany him, to review the record and have a copy made of all or any portion thereof in a form comprehensible to him, except that the agency may require the individual to furnish a written statement authorizing discussion of that individual's record in the accompanying person's presence." 5 U.S.C. § 552a(d)(1).

comment -- The Privacy Act provides individuals with a means of access similar to that of the Freedom of Information Act. The statutes do overlap, but not entirely. See generally Greentree v. United States Customs Serv., 674 F.2d 74, 76-80 (D.C. Cir. 1982). The FOIA is entirely an access statute; it permits "any person" to seek access to any "agency record" that is not subject to any of its nine exemptions or its three exclusions. By comparison, the Privacy Act permits only an "individual" to seek access to only his own "record," and only if that record is maintained by the agency within a "system of records"-- i.e., is retrieved by that individual requester's name or personal identifier--subject to ten Privacy Act exemptions (see the discussion of Privacy Act exemptions, below). Thus, the primary difference between the FOIA and the access provision of the Privacy Act is in the scope of information requestable under each statute.

An individual's access request for his own record maintained in a system of records should be processed under both the Privacy Act and the FOIA, regardless of the statute(s) cited. See H.R. Rep. No. 98-726, pt. 2, at 16-17 (1984), reprinted in 1984 U.S.C.C.A.N. 3741, 3790-91 (regarding amendment of Privacy Act in 1984 to include subsection (t)(2) and stating: "Agencies that had made it a practice to treat a request made under either [the Privacy Act or the FOIA] as if the request had been made under both laws should continue to do so."); FOIA Update, Vol. VII, No. 1, at 6; see also Blazy v. Tenet, 979

F. Supp. 10, 16 (D.D.C. 1997) (quoting subsection (t)(2) and stating that "[d]ocument requests therefore must be analyzed under both Acts"), summary affirmance granted, No. 97-5330, 1998 WL 315583 (D.C. Cir. May 12, 1998); Harvey v. United States Dep't of Justice, No. 92-176-BLG, slip op. at 8 (D. Mont. Jan. 9, 1996) ("Even though information may be withheld under the [Privacy Act], the inquiry does not end. The agency must also process requests under the FOIA, since the agency may not rely upon an exemption under the [Privacy Act] to justify nondisclosure of records that would otherwise be accessible under the FOIA. 5 U.S.C. § 552a(t)(2)."), aff'd, 116 F.3d 484 (9th Cir. 1997) (unpublished table decision); cf. Wren v. Harris, 675 F.2d 1144, 1146 & n.5 (10th Cir. 1982) (per curiam) (construing pro se complaint to seek information under either Privacy Act or FOIA even though only FOIA was referenced by name); Hunsberger v. United States Dep't of Justice, No. 92-2587, slip op. at 2 n.2 (D.D.C. July 22, 1997) (system from which documents at issue were retrieved was exempt pursuant to Privacy Act exemption (j)(2), "[c]onsequently, the records were processed for release under the FOIA"); Kitchen v. FBI, No. 93-2382, slip op. at 7 (D.D.C. Mar. 18, 1996) (although all requested documents were exempt under Privacy Act, they "were also processed under FOIA in the interest of full disclosure"); Kitchen v. DEA, No. 93-2035, slip op. at 9 (D.D.C. Oct. 12, 1995) (same), appeal dismissed for failure to prosecute, No. 95-5380 (D.C. Cir. Dec. 11, 1996); Freeman v. United States Dep't of Justice (FBI), 822 F. Supp. 1064, 1066 (S.D.N.Y. 1993) (implicitly accepting agency's rationale that "because documents releasable pursuant to FOIA may not be withheld as exempt under the Privacy Act," it is proper for agency not to distinguish between FOIA and Privacy Act requests when assigning numbers to establish order of processing, and quoting Report of House Committee on Government Operations, H.R. Rep. No. 726, which was cited by agency as "mandat[ing]" such practice); Pearson v. DEA, No. 84-2740, slip op. at 2 (D.D.C. Jan. 31, 1986) (same as Wren).

It should be noted that the Privacy Act--like the FOIA--does not require agencies to create records that do not exist. See DeBold v. Stimson, 735 F.2d 1037, 1041 (7th Cir. 1984); Perkins v. IRS, No. 86-CV-71551, slip op. at 4 (E.D. Mich. Dec. 16, 1986); see also, e.g., Villanueva v. Department of Justice, 782 F.2d 528, 532 (5th Cir. 1986) (rejecting argument that FBI was required to "find a way to provide a brief but intelligible explanation for its decision . . . without [revealing exempt information]"). But compare May v. Department of the Air Force, 777 F.2d 1012, 1015-17 (5th Cir. 1985) ("reasonable segregation requirement" obligates agency to create and release typewritten version of handwritten evaluation forms so as not to reveal identity of evaluator under exemption (k)(7)), with Church of Scientology W. United States v. IRS, No. CV-89-5894, slip op. at 4 (C.D. Cal. Mar. 5, 1991) (FOIA decision rejecting argument based upon May and holding that agency not required to create records).

For a discussion of the unique procedures involved in processing first-party requests for medical records, see the discussion below under 5 U.S.C. § 552a(f)(3).

## FOIA/PRIVACY ACT INTERFACE EXAMPLE: ACCESS

Suppose John Q. Citizen writes to Agency: "Please send to me all records that you have on me."

For purposes of this example, assume that the only responsive records are contained in a system of records retrieved by Mr. Citizen's own name or personal identifier. Thus, both the Privacy Act and the FOIA potentially apply to the records.

(1) IF NO PRIVACY ACT EXEMPTION APPLIES

　　Result: Mr. Citizen should receive access to his Privacy Act records where Agency can invoke no Privacy Act exemption.

The Agency cannot rely upon a FOIA exemption alone to deny Mr. Citizen access to any of his records under the Privacy Act. See 5 U.S.C. § 552a(t)(1); see also Martin v. Office of Special Counsel, 819 F.2d 1181, 1184 (D.C. Cir. 1987) ("If a FOIA exemption covers the documents, but a Privacy Act exemption does not, the documents must be released under the Privacy Act.") (emphasis added); Hoffman v. Brown, No. 1:96cv53-C, slip op. at 4 (W.D.N.C. Nov. 26, 1996) (agreeing with plaintiff that "no provision of the Privacy Act allows the government to withhold or redact records concerning [his] own personnel records" and ordering production of e-mail and other correspondence regarding plaintiff's employment), aff'd, 145 F.3d 1324 (4th Cir. 1998) (unpublished table decision); Viotti v. United States Air Force, 902 F. Supp. 1331, 1336-37 (D. Colo. 1995) ("If the records are accessible under the Privacy Act, the exemptions from disclosure in the FOIA are inapplicable."), aff'd, 153 F.3d 730 (10th Cir. 1998) (unpublished table decision); Savada v. DOD, 755 F. Supp. 6, 9 (D.D.C. 1991) (citing Martin for proposition that "[i]f an individual is entitled to a document under FOIA and the Privacy Act, to withhold this document an agency must prove that the document is exempt from release under both statutes"); cf. Stone v. Defense Investigative Serv., 816 F. Supp. 782, 788 (D.D.C. 1993) ("[T]he Court must determine separately [from the FOIA] whether plaintiff is entitled to any of the withheld information under the Privacy Act."); Rojem v. United States Dep't of Justice, 775 F. Supp. 6, 13 (D.D.C. 1991) ("[T]here are instances in which the FOIA denies access and the Privacy Act compels release."), appeal dismissed for failure to timely file, No. 92-5088 (D.C. Cir. Nov. 4, 1992); Ray v. United States Dep't of Justice, 558 F. Supp. 226, 228 (D.D.C. 1982) (requester entitled, under subsection (c)(3), to addresses of private persons who requested information about him as "defendant is unable to cite a specific [Privacy Act] exemption that justifies non-disclosure of this information"), aff'd, 720 F.2d 216 (D.C. Cir. 1983) (unpublished table decision).

PRIVACY ACT OVERVIEW

In other words, a requester is entitled to the combined total of what both statutes provide. See Clarkson v. IRS, 678 F.2d 1368, 1376 (11th Cir. 1982); Wren v. Harris, 675 F.2d 1144, 1147 (10th Cir. 1982) (per curiam); Searcy v. Social Sec. Admin., No. 91-C-26 J, slip op. at 7-8 (D. Utah June 25, 1991) (magistrate's recommendation), adopted (D. Utah Sept. 19, 1991), aff'd, No. 91-4181 (10th Cir. Mar. 2, 1992); Whittle v. Moschella, 756 F. Supp. 589, 595 (D.D.C. 1991); Fagot v. FDIC, 584 F. Supp. 1168, 1173-74 (D.P.R. 1984), aff'd in part & rev'd in part, 760 F.2d 252 (1st Cir. 1985) (unpublished table decision); see also 120 Cong. Rec. 40,406 (1974), reprinted in Source Book at 861. For access purposes, the two statutes work completely independently of one another.

(2) IF A PRIVACY ACT EXEMPTION APPLIES

   Result: Where a Privacy Act exemption applies, Mr. Citizen is not entitled to obtain access to his records under the Privacy Act.

   But he may still be able to obtain access to his records (or portions thereof) under the FOIA. See 5 U.S.C. § 552a(t)(2) (Privacy Act exemption(s) cannot defeat FOIA access); Martin, 819 F.2d at 1184 ("[I]f a Privacy Act exemption but not a FOIA exemption applies, the documents must be released under FOIA.") (emphasis added); Savada, 755 F. Supp. at 9 (citing Martin and holding that agency must prove that document is exempt from release under both FOIA and Privacy Act); see also Shapiro v. DEA, 762 F.2d 611, 612 (7th Cir. 1985); Grove v. CIA, 752 F. Supp. 28, 30 (D.D.C. 1990); Simon v. United States Dep't of Justice, 752 F. Supp. 14, 22 (D.D.C. 1990), aff'd, 980 F.2d 782 (D.C. Cir. 1992); Miller v. United States, 630 F. Supp. 347, 348-49 (E.D.N.Y. 1986); Nunez v. DEA, 497 F. Supp. 209, 211 (S.D.N.Y. 1980). The outcome will depend upon FOIA exemption applicability. See generally FOIA Update, Vol. XV, No. 2, at 3-6 (encouraging discretionary disclosure whenever possible despite FOIA exemption applicability); FOIA Update, Vol. XIX, No. 4, at 3-5 (same).

(3) IF NO PRIVACY ACT EXEMPTION AND NO FOIA EXEMPTION APPLIES

   Result: The information should be disclosed.

(4) IF BOTH PRIVACY ACT AND FOIA EXEMPTIONS APPLY

   Result: The record may be withheld. But remember: When an individual requests access to his own record (a first-party request) maintained in a system of records, an agency must be able to invoke properly both a Privacy Act exemption and a FOIA exemption in order to withhold that record.

      Rule: ALL PRIVACY ACT ACCESS REQUESTS SHOULD ALSO BE TREATED AS FOIA REQUESTS

      Note also that Mr. Citizen's first-party request--because it is a FOIA request as well--additionally obligates Agency to search for any records on him that are not maintained in a Privacy Act system of records. With respect to those records, only the FOIA's exemptions are relevant; the Privacy Act's access provision and exemptions are <u>entirely inapplicable</u> to any records not maintained in a system of records.

comment -- A particularly troubling and unsettled problem under the Privacy Act arises where a file indexed and retrieved by the requester's name or personal identifier contains information pertaining to a third party that, if released, would invade that third party's privacy.

As a preliminary matter, it should be noted that this problem arises only when a requester seeks access to his record contained in a non-law enforcement system of records--typically a personnel or background security investigative system--inasmuch as agencies are generally permitted to exempt the entirety of their criminal and civil law enforcement systems of records from the subsection (d)(1) access provision pursuant to 5 U.S.C. § 552a(j)(2) and (k)(2).

The problem stems from the fact that unlike under the FOIA, <u>see</u> 5 U.S.C. § 552(b)(6), (7)(C), the Privacy Act (ironically) does <u>not</u> contain any exemption that protects a third party's privacy. <u>Cf.</u> 5 U.S.C. § 552a(k)(5) (protecting only confidential source-identifying information in background security investigative systems). The Privacy Act's access provision simply permits an individual to gain access to "his record or to any information pertaining to him" that is contained in a system of records indexed and retrieved by his name or personal identifier. 5 U.S.C. § 552a(d)(1).

The leading case in this area is <u>Voelker v. IRS</u>, 646 F.2d 332, 333-35 (8th Cir. 1981). In <u>Voelker</u>, the Court of Appeals for the Eighth Circuit held that where the requested information--contained in a system of records indexed and retrieved by the requester's name--is "about" that requester within the meaning of subsection (a)(4)'s definition of a "record," <u>all</u> such information is subject to the subsection (d)(1) access provision. <u>Id.</u> at 334. In construing subsection (d)(1), the Eighth Circuit noted that there is "no justification for requiring that information in a requesting individual's record meet some separate 'pertaining to' standard before disclosure is authorized [and i]n any event, it defies logic to say that information properly contained in a person's record does not pertain to that person, even if it may also pertain to another individual." <u>Id.</u> Relying on the importance of the access provision to the enforcement of other provisions of the Privacy Act, and the lack of any provision in the exemption portion of the statute to protect a third party's privacy, the Eighth Circuit rejected the government's argument that subsection (b) prohibited disclosure to the requester of the information about a third party. <u>Id.</u> at 334-35. A careful reading of <u>Voelker</u> reveals that the Eighth Circuit appeared to equate the term "record" with "file" for subsection (d)(1) access purposes.

The District Court for the District of Columbia agreed with, and applied the reasoning of, Voelker in Henke v. United States Dep't of Commerce, No. 94-0189, 1996 WL 692020, at *4 (D.D.C. Aug. 19, 1994), aff'd on other grounds, 83 F.3d 1445 (D.C. Cir. 1996). In Henke, the government argued that information pertaining to third parties was exempt from disclosure because the same information was also contained in a system of records as to the third parties, and that disclosure of the information would violate subsection (b). Relying on Voelker, the court rejected the government's argument that information contained in one individual's records is exempt from the disclosure requirements of the Privacy Act simply because the same information is also contained in another individual's records, and it further stated that it would "not create an exemption to the Privacy Act that [C]ongress did not see fit to include itself." Id. On two earlier occasions, the D.C. District Court had held that subsection (b) could protect third-party information in a requester's file. See Savada v. DOD, 755 F. Supp. 6, 10 (D.D.C. 1991) (names of DIA security officials involved in investigation of plaintiff); Anderson v. United States Dep't of the Treasury, No. 76-1404, slip op. at 11-13 (D.D.C. July 19, 1977) (name of complainant). However, the rationale of these decisions is not entirely clear, and neither opinion was even mentioned in the more recent Henke opinion.

The result in Voelker also finds some tangential support in two other decisions--Wren v. Harris, 675 F.2d 1144, 1147 (10th Cir. 1982) (per curiam), and Ray v. United States Dep't of Justice, 558 F. Supp. 226, 228 (D.D.C. 1982), aff'd, 720 F.2d 216 (D.C. Cir. 1983) (unpublished table decision). In Wren, the Court of Appeals for the Tenth Circuit reversed a district court's judgment that FOIA Exemption 6 protected certain third-party information requested under the Privacy Act. 675 F.2d at 1147. In so ruling, the Tenth Circuit stated that "[o]n remand, should the district court find that the documents requested by Mr. Wren consist of 'his record' or 'any information pertaining to him,' and that they are 'records' contained in a 'system of records,' § 552a(a)(4), (5), (d)(1), then the court must grant him access to those documents as provided in § 552a(d)(1), unless the court finds that they are exempt from disclosure under [Privacy Act exemptions]," and it further observed that "the [district] court's reliance on [FOIA Exemption 6] to withhold the documents would be improper if the court determines that the [Privacy Act] permits disclosure." Id. In Ray, the court ruled that the requester was entitled to access, under subsection (c)(3), to the addresses of private persons who had requested information about him because no Privacy Act exemption justified withholding such information, notwithstanding that the agency's "concern about possible harrassment [sic] of these individuals may be legitimate." 558 F. Supp. at 228.

Voelker's rationale was purportedly distinguished (but in actuality was rejected) in DePlanche v. Califano, 549 F. Supp. 685, 693-98 (W.D. Mich. 1982), a case involving a father's request for access to a social security benefits file indexed and retrieved by his social security number which contained the address of his two minor children. In denying the father access to the children's address, the court reasoned that such third-party information, although contained in the father's file, was not "about" the father, and therefore by definition was not his "record" within the meaning of subsection (a)(4), nor was it information "pertaining" to him within the meaning of the subsection (d)(1) access provision. Id. at 694-96. In distinguishing Voelker, the court relied upon an array of facts suggesting that the father might harass or harm his children if their location were to be disclosed. Id. at 693, 696-98.

Other courts, too, have made findings that certain items of information, although contained in a file or document retrieved by an individual's name, did not qualify as Privacy Act records "about" that individual. See Nolan v. United States Dep't of Justice, No. 89-A-2035, 1991 WL 36547, at *10 (D. Colo. Mar. 18, 1991) (names of FBI agents and other personnel held not requester's "record" and therefore "outside the scope of the [Privacy Act]"), aff'd, 973 F.2d 843 (10th Cir. 1992); Haddon v. Freeh, 31 F. Supp. 2d 16, 22 (D.D.C. 1998) (applying Nolan and Doe, infra, to hold that identities and telephone extensions of FBI agents and personnel were not "about" plaintiff and thus were properly withheld); Springmann v. United States Dep't of State, No. 93-1238, slip op. at 8 & n.1 (D.D.C. Apr. 21, 1997) (citing Nolan and holding that name of foreign official who provided information to State Department and names of foreign service officers (other than plaintiff) who were denied tenure were "not accessible to plaintiff under the Privacy Act because the identities of these individuals d[id] not constitute information 'about' plaintiff, and therefore [we]re not 'records' with respect to plaintiff under the Privacy Act"); Hunsberger v. CIA, No. 92-2186, slip op. at 3-4 (D.D.C. Apr. 5, 1995) (citing Nolan and holding that names of employees of private insurance company used by Director of Central Intelligence and Director's unique professional liability insurance certificate number maintained in litigation file created as result of plaintiff's prior suit against CIA Director were not "about" plaintiff and therefore were not "record[s]" within meaning of Privacy Act); Doe v. United States Dep't of Justice, 790 F. Supp. 17, 22 (D.D.C. 1992) (citing Nolan and alternatively holding that "names of agents involved in the investigation are properly protected from disclosure"); cf. Allard v. HHS, No. 4:90-CV-156, slip op. at 9-11 (W.D. Mich. Feb. 14, 1992) (citing DePlanche with approval and arriving at same result, but conducting analysis solely under FOIA Exemption 6), aff'd, 972 F.2d 346 (6th Cir. 1992) (unpublished table decision).

The District Court for the District of Columbia was confronted with a more complex version of this issue in Topuridze v. USIA, 772 F. Supp. 662 (D.D.C. 1991), reconsidering Topuridze v. FBI, No. 86-3120, 1989 WL 11709 (D.D.C. Feb. 6, 1989), when the subject of a letter requested access to it and the agencies withheld it to protect the author's privacy interests. In Topuridze, the issue of access to third party information in a requester's file was further complicated by the fact that the information

was "retrievable" by both the requester's identifier
and the third party's identifier, Topuridze v. FBI,
No. 86-3120, 1989 WL 11709, at *1 (D.D.C. Feb. 6,
1989)--the record was subject to "dual retrieval."
In apparent contradiction to the subsection (d)(1)
access provision, subsection (b) prohibits the
nonconsensual disclosure of an individual's record
contained in a system of records indexed and retrieved by his name or personal identifier to any
third party. See 5 U.S.C. § 552a(b). Because the
letter was both the requester's and the third party's Privacy Act record, the government argued that
subsection (b), though technically not an "exemption," nevertheless restricts first-party access
under subsection (d)(1) where the record is about
both the requester and the third-party author, and
is located in a system of records that is "retrievable" by both their names. See Topuridze v. FBI,
No. 86-3120, 1989 WL 11709, at *1 (D.D.C. Feb. 6,
1989); Topuridze v. USIA, 772 F. Supp. at 665-66.
Although the court had previously ruled that the
document was not about the author, see Topuridze v.
FBI, No. 86-3120, 1989 WL 11709, at **2-3 (D.D.C.
Feb. 6, 1989), on reconsideration it ruled that it
need not reach that issue, finding that "[b]ecause
the document is without dispute about the [request-
er], it must be released to him in any event." 772
F. Supp. at 665. On reconsideration, the court
embraced Voelker and rejected the government's argument that subsection (b) created a "dual record
exemption" to Privacy Act access. Id. at 665-66.

Although Topuridze has provided some further guidance, the difficult issue of an individual's right
to access third party information retrieved by his
name can be resolved only with careful consideration
given to the following points:

(1)  If the third-party information in the request-
     er's file is truly not "about" him or her,
     could have no possible adverse effect on the
     requester, and is not retrieved by the third
     party's name or personal identifier, a plausi-
     ble argument might be made (as in DePlanche,
     Nolan, and Doe) for withholding such informa-
     tion on the ground that it does not constitute
     an accessible "record" within the meaning of
     subsections (d)(1) and (a)(4).

(2)  If third-party information in the requester's
     file is also "about" the requester--i.e., a
     "dual record"--subsections (d)(1) and (a)(4)
     seem to require release to the requester, for
     the reasons set forth in Voelker. See 646 F.2d
     at 333-35. The Act's definition of an accessi-
     ble "record" does not contain any "exclusivity"
     requirement. See Unt v. Aerospace Corp., 765
     F.2d 1440, 1450 (9th Cir. 1985) (Ferguson, J.,
     dissenting). However, where release could lead
     to harassment or harm to the third party, as
     was the case in DePlanche, see 594 F. Supp. at
     693, 696-98, a strong argument for withholding
     (one that, essentially, is an equitable one)
     may be possible. Yet, it is significant that
     the court in Topuridze concluded that the rec-
     ord at issue in that case must be released
     despite the credible argument that doing so
     could endanger the author; the court seemed to

be no less concerned that such an argument "could be freely invoked by authors of even the most unfounded, defamatory and damaging records." See Topuridze v. USIA, 772 F. Supp. at 666. Furthermore, in light of the court's rejection of the government's more compelling "dual retrieval" argument in Topuridze, it would seem even less likely that the court would permit the withholding of third-party information that was not "dually retrieved," as was the case in DePlanche. Therefore, where DePlanche-type facts are present, agencies should consider use of in camera submissions to justify withholding such third-party information. See, e.g., Patton v. FBI, 626 F. Supp. 445, 447-48 (M.D. Pa. 1985), aff'd, 782 F.2d 1030 (3d Cir. 1986) (unpublished table decision).

(3) If the third-party information in the requester's file is also "about" the requester--i.e., a "dual record"--and the file is also indexed and retrieved by the third party's name or personal identifier--i.e., "dually retrieved," the Topuridze decision suggests that the information should be released to both parties. 772 F. Supp. at 665-66. The court in Topuridze specifically rejected the argument that subsection (b) prohibits disclosure to the requester absent consent of the third party, and it recognized that such a rule would operate to restrict "dual records" from disclosure to anyone other than the agency itself. Id.

A requester need not state his reason for seeking access to records under the Privacy Act, but an agency should verify the identity of the requester in order to avoid violating subsection (b). See OMB Guidelines, 40 Fed. Reg. 28,948, 28,957-58 (1975); see also 5 U.S.C. § 552a(i)(1) (criminal penalties for disclosure of information to parties not entitled to receive it); 5 U.S.C. § 552a(i)(3) (criminal penalties for obtaining records about an individual under false pretenses); cf., e.g., 28 C.F.R. § 16.41(d) (1999) (Department of Justice regulation regarding verification of identity).

Also, note that subsection (d)(1), like the FOIA, "carries no prospective obligation to turn over new documents that come into existence after the date of the request." Crichton v. Community Servs. Admin., 567 F. Supp. 322, 325 (S.D.N.Y. 1983).

**INDIVIDUAL'S RIGHT OF AMENDMENT**

(1) An individual can request amendment of his own record. 5 U.S.C. § 552a(d)(2).

(2) Ten "working" days after receipt of an amendment request, an agency must acknowledge it in writing and promptly either:

    (a) correct any information which the individual asserts is not accurate, relevant, timely, or complete; or

    (b) inform the individual of its refusal to amend in accordance with the request, the reason for refusal, and the procedures for administrative appeal. 5 U.S.C. § 552a(d)(2).

PRIVACY ACT OVERVIEW

(3) The agency must permit an individual who disagrees with its refusal to amend his record to request review of such refusal, and not later than 30 "working" days from the date the individual requests such review, the agency must complete it. If the reviewing official also refuses to amend in accordance with the request, the individual must be permitted to file with the agency a concise statement setting forth the reasons for disagreement with the agency. 5 U.S.C. § 552a(d)(3). The individual's statement of disagreement must be included with any subsequent disclosure of the record. 5 U.S.C. § 552a(d)(4). In addition, where the agency has made prior disclosures of the record and an accounting of those disclosures was made, the agency must inform the prior recipients of the record of any correction or notation of dispute that concerns the disclosed record. 5 U.S.C. § 552a(c)(4).

   comment -- For a discussion of subsections (d)(2)-(4), see OMB Guidelines, 40 Fed. Reg. 28,948, 28,958-60 (1975). For a discussion of amendment lawsuits, see the section entitled "Civil Remedies," below.

**AGENCY REQUIREMENTS**

Each agency that maintains a system of records shall--

**A. 5 U.S.C. § 552a(e)(1)**

   "maintain in its records only such information about an individual as is relevant and necessary to accomplish a purpose of the agency required to be accomplished by statute or by executive order of the President."

   comment -- This subsection is not violated so long as the maintenance of the information at issue is relevant and necessary to accomplish a legal purpose of the agency. See, e.g., Reuber v. United States, 829 F.2d 133, 139-40 (D.C. Cir. 1987); National Fed'n of Fed. Employees v. Greenberg, 789 F. Supp. 430, 433-34 (D.D.C. 1992), vacated & remanded on other grounds, 983 F.2d 286 (D.C. Cir. 1993); Beckette v. United States Postal Serv., No. 88-802, slip op. at 9-10 (E.D. Va. July 3, 1989); NTEU v. IRS, 601 F.. Supp. 1268, 1271 (D.D.C. 1985); Chocallo v. Bureau of Hearings & Appeals, 548 F. Supp. 1349, 1368 (E.D. Pa.), aff'd, 716 F.2d 889 (3d Cir. 1983) (unpublished table decision); see also Felsen v. HHS, No. CCB-95-975, slip op. at 59-61 (D. Md. Sept. 30, 1998) (subsection (e)(1) "refers to the types of information maintained and whether they are germane to the agency's statutory mission," and "does not incorporate [an] accuracy standard"); Jones v. United States Dep't of the Treasury, No. 82-2420, slip op. at 2 (D.D.C. Oct. 18, 1983) (ruling that maintenance of record concerning unsubstantiated allegation that BATF Special Agent committed crime was "relevant and necessary"), aff'd, 744 F.2d 878 (D.C. Cir. 1984) (unpublished table decision); OMB Guidelines, 40 Fed. Reg. 28,948, 28,960-61 (1975); 120 Cong. Rec. 40,407 (1974), reprinted in Source Book at 863; cf. AFGE v. HUD, 118 F.3d 786, 794 (D.C. Cir. 1997) (holding agency use of release form on employment suitability questionnaire constitutional in light of Privacy Act's subsection (e)(1) requirement and "relying on the limitation that the release form authorizes the government to obtain only relevant information used to verify representations made by the employee"); Barlow v. VA, No. 92-16744, 1993 WL 355099, at *1 (9th Cir. Sept. 13, 1993) (VA's request for appellant's medical records did not violate Privacy Act because VA is authorized to request such information and it is "relevant and necessary" to appellant's claim for benefits; citing subsection (e)(1)).

B.  5 U.S.C. § 552a(e)(2)

"collect information to the greatest extent practicable directly from the subject individual when the information may result in adverse determinations about an individual's rights, benefits, and privileges under Federal programs."

comment -- The leading cases under this provision are Waters v. Thornburgh, 888 F.2d 870 (D.C. Cir. 1989), and Brune v. IRS, 861 F.2d 1284 (D.C. Cir. 1988). Waters involved a Justice Department employee whose supervisor became aware of information that raised suspicions concerning the employee's unauthorized use of administrative leave. 888 F.2d at 871-72. Without first approaching the employee for clarification, the supervisor sought and received from a state board of law examiners verification of the employee's attendance at a bar examination. Id. at 872. In finding a violation of subsection (e)(2) on these facts, the Court of Appeals for the District of Columbia Circuit ruled that "[i]n the context of an investigation that is seeking objective, unalterable information, reasonable questions about a subject's credibility cannot relieve an agency from its responsibility to collect that information first from the subject." Id. at 873 (emphasis added); accord Dong v. Smithsonian Inst., 943 F. Supp. 69, 72-73 (D.D.C. 1996) ("concern over Plaintiff's possible reaction to an unpleasant rumor" did not warrant Institution's "fail[ure] to elicit information regarding alleged unauthorized trip directly from her"), rev'd on grounds of statutory inapplicability, 125 F.3d 877 (D.C. Cir. 1997) (ruling that "Smithsonian is not an agency for Privacy Act purposes"), cert. denied, 524 U.S. 922 (1998). The D.C. Circuit in Waters distinguished its earlier decision in Brune, which had permitted an IRS supervisor to contact taxpayers to check on an agent's visits to them without first interviewing the agent, based upon the "special nature of the investigation in that case--possible false statements by an IRS agent" and the concomitant risk that the agent, if contacted first, could coerce the taxpayers to falsify or secret evidence. Waters, 888 F.2d at 874.

Consistent with Brune, two other decisions have upheld the IRS's practice of contacting taxpayers prior to confronting agents who were under internal investigations. See Alexander v. IRS, No. 86-0414, 1987 WL 13958, at **6-7 (D.D.C. June 30, 1987); Merola v. Department of the Treasury, No. 83-3323, slip op. at 5-9 (D.D.C. Oct. 24, 1986).

PRIVACY ACT OVERVIEW

In addition, the Court of Appeals for the Sixth Circuit relied on Brune and the OMB Guidelines, referenced below, to hold that subsection (e)(2) had not been violated by an investigator looking into charges of misconduct by an Assistant United States Attorney who had interviewed others before interviewing her. Hudson v. Reno, 130 F.3d 1193, 1205 (6th Cir. 1997), cert. denied, 525 U.S. 822 (1998). Given that the district court had found that the attorney "was suspected of making false statements and she was allegedly intimidating and threatening people and otherwise dividing the U.S. Attorney's office," the Sixth Circuit held that "[a]ll of these practical considerations demonstrate that [the investigator] did not violate the Privacy Act when he interviewed others before interviewing [her]." 130 F.3d at 1205; see also Jacobs v. Reno, No. 3:97-CV-2698-D, 1999 U.S. Dist. LEXIS 3104, at **19-22, 29-35 (N.D. Tex. Mar. 11, 1999) (finding no subsection (e)(2) violation in agency's "extensive, multifaceted investigation of an entire district office" where plaintiff was "both a charging party in several complaints and an accused in several others," as it "was not always practical" for agency to interview plaintiff first, given nature of allegations against him), subsequent decision, 1999 WL 493056, at *1 (N.D. Tex. July 9, 1999) (denying motion for relief from March 11, 1999 order because "newly-discovered evidence" would not have produced different result), aff'd, 208 F.3d 1006 (5th Cir. 2000) (unpublished table decision).

The Court of Appeals for the Eighth Circuit recently examined the issue of whether a "collection" subject to the requirements of subsection (e)(2) occurs when an agency reviews its own files to obtain information. Darst v. Social Sec. Admin., 172 F.3d 1065 (8th Cir. 1999). The Eighth Circuit held that because the "situation merely involved a review of the agency's files," the agency "did not contact third party sources to gather information," and because "the indications of impropriety were apparent from the face of the documents and the sequence of events" reflected in the file, there was "no need to interview Darst about the sequence of events," and thus no violation of subsection (e)(2). Id. at 1068. The Eighth Circuit further stated that, "[a]s the district court noted, the Privacy Act does not require that the information be collected directly from the individual in all circumstances," and that "[h]ere the information in the [agency] file obviated the need to interview Darst or third persons." Id.; see also Brune v. IRS, 861 F.2d 1284, 1287 (D.C. Cir. 1988) (stating that "investigations of false statement charges, by their nature, involve a suspect who has already given the government his version of the facts").

For other decisions concerning this provision, see Olivares v. NASA, No. 95-2343, 1996 WL 690065, at **2-3 (4th Cir. Dec. 3, 1996), aff'g per curiam 882 F. Supp. 1545 (D. Md. 1995); Hubbard v. United States Envtl. Protection Agency, Adm'r, 809 F.2d 1, 11 n.8 (D.C. Cir.), va-

-735-

cated in nonpertinent part & reh'g en banc
granted (due to conflict in circuit), 809 F.2d 1
(D.C. Cir. 1986), resolved on reh'g en banc sub
nom. Spagnola v. Mathis, 859 F.2d 223 (D.C. Cir.
1988); Jones v. Runyon, 32 F. Supp. 2d 873, 876
(N.D. W. Va. 1998), aff'd, 173 F.3d 850 (4th
Cir. 1999) (unpublished table decision); Magee
v. United States Postal Serv., 903 F. Supp.
1022, 1028-29 (W.D. La. 1995), aff'd, 79 F.3d
1145 (5th Cir. 1996) (unpublished table decision); and Kassel v. VA, 709 F. Supp. 1194, 1203
(D.N.H. 1989). Cf. Felsen v. HHS, No. CCB-95-
975, slip op. at 62-65 (D. Md. Sept. 30, 1998)
(granting defendants summary judgment on alternative ground on subsection (e)(2) claim due to
"lack of a 'practicable' need to collect information directly from the plaintiffs"); Beckette
v. United States Postal Serv., No. 88-802, slip
op. at 10 (E.D. Va. July 3, 1989) (subsection
(e)(2) requirements satisfied where information
contained in records was derived from other
records containing information collected directly from individual).

The OMB Guidelines suggest several factors to be
evaluated in determining whether it is impractical to contact the subject first. OMB Guidelines, 40 Fed. Reg. 28,948, 28,961 (1975); see
also 120 Cong. Rec. 40,407 (1974), reprinted in
Source Book at 863.

C.  5 U.S.C. § 552a(e)(3)

"inform each individual whom it asks to supply information,
on the form which it uses to collect the information or on
a separate form that can be retained by the individual--(A)
the authority (whether granted by statute, or by executive
order of the President) which authorizes the solicitation
of the information and whether disclosure of such information is mandatory or voluntary; (B) the principal purpose
or purposes for which the information is intended to be
used; (C) the routine uses which may be made of the information as published pursuant to paragraph (4)(D) of this
subsection; and (D) the effects on him, if any, of not
providing all or any part of the requested information."

comment -- The OMB Guidelines note that "[i]mplicit in this
subsection is the notion of informed consent
since an individual should be provided with
sufficient information about the request for
information to make an informed decision on
whether or not to respond." OMB Guidelines, 40
Fed. Reg. 28,948, 28,961 (1975). The OMB Guidelines also note that subsection (e)(3) is applicable to both written and oral (i.e., interview)
solicitations of personal information. Id.

There is some authority for the proposition that
subsection (e)(3) is inapplicable when an agency
solicits information about an individual from a
third party. See Truxal v. Casey, 2 Gov't Disclosure Serv. (P-H) ¶ 81,391, at 82,043 (S.D.
Ohio Apr. 3, 1981); see also Gardner v. United
States, No. 96-1467, 1999 U.S. Dist. LEXIS 2195,
at *19 (D.D.C. Jan. 29, 1999) (noting that although it is correct that Privacy Act mandates
actual notice of routine uses, "information in
the instant case was not gathered from Plain-

tiff, but from third parties"), summary affirmance granted on other grounds, No. 99-5089, 1999 WL 728359 (D.C. Cir. Aug. 4, 1999); McTaggart v. United States, 570 F. Supp. 547, 550 (E.D. Mich. 1983) (individual lacks standing to complain of insufficient Privacy Act notice to third party). The OMB Guidelines support this view, but suggest that "agencies should, where feasible, inform third-party sources of the purposes for which information they are asked to provide will be used." OMB Guidelines, 40 Fed. Reg. at 28,961. The practice of not providing notice to third parties was condemned by the Privacy Protection Study Commission, see Privacy Commission Report at 514, and, indeed, several courts have disagreed with Truxal and the OMB Guidelines on this point. See Usher v. Secretary of HHS, 721 F.2d 854, 856 (1st Cir. 1983) (costs awarded to plaintiff due to agency "intransigence" in refusing to provide information specified in subsection (e)(3) to third party); Kassel v. VA, No. 87-217-S, slip op. at 24-25 (D.N.H. Mar. 30, 1992) (in light of "the express language of §(e)(3) and the Privacy Act's overall purposes . . . §(e)(3) applies to information supplied by third-parties"); Saunders v. Schweiker, 508 F. Supp. 305, 309 (W.D.N.Y. 1981) (plain language of subsection (e)(3) "does not in any way distinguish between first-party and third-party contacts").

In Covert v. Harrington, 876 F.2d 751, 755-56 (9th Cir. 1989), a divided panel of the Court of Appeals for the Ninth Circuit held that an agency component's failure to provide actual notice of a routine use under subsection (e)(3)(C), at the time information is submitted, precludes a separate component of the agency (an Inspector General) from later invoking the routine use as a basis for disclosing such information. See also United States Postal Serv. v. National Ass'n of Letter Carriers, 9 F.3d 138, 146 (D.C. Cir. 1993) (citing Covert with approval and remanding case for factual determination as to whether (e)(3)(C) notice was given). But see OMB Guidelines at 28,961-62 ("It was not the intent of [subsection (e)(3)] to create a right the nonobservance of which would preclude the use of the information or void an action taken on the basis of that information.").

It has been held that "[n]othing in the Privacy Act requires agencies to employ the exact language of the statute to give effective notice." United States v. Wilber, 696 F.2d 79, 80 (8th Cir. 1982); see also Field v. Brown, 610 F.2d 981, 986-88 (D.C. Cir. 1979); Glasgold v. Secretary of HHS, 558 F. Supp. 129, 149-51 (E.D.N.Y. 1982). Thus, for example, subsection (e)(3)(D) does not require an agency to provide notice of the specific criminal penalty which may be imposed for failure to provide information. See, e.g., United States v. Bressler, 772 F.2d 287, 292-93 (7th Cir. 1985); United States v. Bell, 734 F.2d 1315, 1318 (8th Cir. 1984) (per curiam); United States v. Annunziato, 643 F.2d 676, 678 (9th Cir. 1981); United States v. Rickman, 638 F.2d 182, 183 (10th Cir. 1980); United

PRIVACY ACT OVERVIEW

States v. Gillotti, 822 F. Supp. 984, 988 (W.D.N.Y. 1993); see also United States v. Bishop, No. 90-4077, 1991 WL 213755, at *4 (6th Cir. Oct. 23, 1991) (citing Bressler and holding that IRS form 1040 instruction booklet informing taxpayers of obligation to file return or statement with IRS is sufficient notice under Privacy Act); Beller v. Middendorf, 632 F.2d 788, 798-99 n.6 (9th Cir. 1980); Field, 610 F.2d at 987 (requirements of Privacy Act satisfied where Privacy Act statement provided that failure to provide information would result in "notification to the Department of Justice" for appropriate action).

### D. 5 U.S.C. § 552a(e)(4)

"[subject to notice and comment], publish in the Federal Register upon establishment or revision a notice of the existence and character of the system of records, which notice shall include--(A) the name and location of the system; (B) the categories of individuals on whom records are maintained in the system; (C) the categories of records maintained in the system; (D) each routine use of the records contained in the system, including the categories of users and the purpose of such use; (E) the policies and practices of the agency regarding storage, retrievability, access controls, retention, and disposal of the records; (F) the title and business address of the agency official who is responsible for the system of records; (G) the agency procedures whereby an individual can be notified at his request if the system of records contains a record pertaining to him; (H) the agency procedures whereby an individual can be notified at his request how he can gain access to any record pertaining to him contained in the system of records, and how he can contest its contents; and (I) the categories of sources of records in the system."

comment -- For a discussion of this provision, see OMB Guidelines, 40 Fed. Reg. 28,948, 28,962-64 (1975). Although Privacy Act system notices are spread throughout the Federal Register, the Office of the Federal Register publishes a biennial compilation of all such system notices. See 5 U.S.C. § 552a(f). This "Privacy Act Compilation," is available on the Government Printing Office's World Wide Web site, which can be accessed at http://www.access.gpo.gov/su_docs.

Recently, the Court of Appeals for the Tenth Circuit, in Pippinger v. Rubin, addressed whether the Internal Revenue Service had complied with several of the requirements of subsection (e)(4) with regard to a computer database known as the "Automated Labor Employee Relations Tracking System" (ALERTS). 129 F.3d 519, 524-28 (10th Cir. 1997). The database was used by the IRS to record all disciplinary action proposed or taken against any IRS employee and contained a limited subset of information from two existing Privacy Act systems that the IRS had properly noticed in the Federal Register. Id. at 524-25. Of particular note, the Tenth Circuit found that ALERTS, being an "abstraction of certain individual records" from other systems of records, did not constitute a new system of records requiring Federal Register publication, because it could be accessed only by the same users and only for the same purposes as those published in the Federal Register for the original systems of records. Id. at 526-27.

E. 5 U.S.C. § 552a(e)(5)

"maintain all records which are used by the agency in making any determination about any individual with such accuracy, relevance, timeliness, and completeness as is reasonably necessary to assure fairness to the individual in the determination."

comment -- This provision (along with subsections (e)(1) and (e)(7)) sets forth the standard to which records must conform in the context of an amendment lawsuit, as well as in the context of an accuracy lawsuit for damages. See 5 U.S.C. § 552a(g)(1)(A); 5 U.S.C. § 552a(g)(1)(C). As the Court of Appeals for the District of Columbia Circuit has held, "whether the nature of the relief sought is injunctive or monetary, the standard against which the accuracy of the record is measured remains constant [and] that standard is found in 5 U.S.C. § 552a(e)(5) and reiterated in 5 U.S.C. § 552a(g)(1)(C)." Doe v. United States, 821 F.2d 694, 697 n.8 (D.C. Cir. 1987) (en banc).

In theory, a violation of this provision (or any other part of the Act) could also give rise to a damages action under 5 U.S.C. § 552a(g)(1)(D). Cf. Perry v. FBI, 759 F.2d 1271, 1275 (7th Cir. 1985), rev'd en banc on other grounds, 781 F.2d 1294 (7th Cir. 1986). However, the Court of Appeals for the District of Columbia Circuit has held that "a plaintiff seeking damages for noncompliance with the standard set out in subsection (e)(5) must sue under subsection (g)(1)(C) and not subsection (g)(1)(D)." Deters v. United States Parole Comm'n, 85 F.3d 655, 660-61 & n.5 (D.C. Cir. 1996) (noting that although court had suggested in Dickson v. OPM, 828 F.2d 32, 39 (D.C. Cir. 1987), "that subsection (g)(1)(D) could cover a violation of subsection (e)(5), the holding in that case is limited to the scope of subsection (g)(1)(C)").

Perfect records are not required by subsection (e)(5); instead, "reasonableness" is the standard. See Johnston v. Horne, 875 F.2d 1415, 1421 (9th Cir. 1989); DeBold v. Stimson, 735 F.2d 1037, 1041 (7th Cir. 1984); Edison v. Department of the Army, 672 F.2d 840, 843 (11th Cir. 1982); Vymetalik v. FBI, No. 82-3495, slip op. at 3-5 (D.D.C. Jan. 30, 1987); Marcotte v. Secretary of Defense, 618 F. Supp. 756, 762 (D. Kan. 1985); Smiertka v. United States Dep't of the Treasury, 447 F. Supp. 221, 225-26 & n.35 (D.D.C. 1978), remanded on other grounds, 604 F.2d 698 (D.C. Cir. 1979); see also, e.g., Halus v. United States Dep't of the Army, No. 87-4133, 1990 WL 121507, at *11 (E.D. Pa. Aug. 15, 1990) (erroneous information held not subject to amendment if it is merely a "picayune" and immaterial error); Jones v. United States Dep't of the Treasury, No. 82-2420, slip op. at 2-3 (D.D.C. Oct. 18, 1983) (ruling it reasonable for agency--without conducting its own investigation--to maintain

PRIVACY ACT OVERVIEW

record concerning unsubstantiated allegation of sexual misconduct by BATF agent conveyed to it by state and local authorities), aff'd, 744 F.2d 878 (D.C. Cir. 1984) (unpublished table decision); cf. Sullivan v. Federal Bureau of Prisons, No. 94-5218, 1995 WL 66711, at *1 (D.C. Cir. Jan. 17, 1995) (even if (e)(5) claim were not time-barred, "Parole Commission met the requirements of the Act by providing [plaintiff] with a parole revocation hearing at which he was represented by counsel and given the opportunity to refute the validity of his continued confinement"); Pons v. United States Dep't of the Treasury, No. 94-2250, 1998 U.S. Dist. LEXIS 5809, at **11-15 (D.D.C. Apr. 21, 1998) (entering judgment in favor of agency where agency presented "substantial evidence to suggest that [it] acted in the reasonable belief that there were no grounds to amend plaintiff's records"; plaintiff failed to identify any records that contained alleged false statements and even if file did contain those statements, plaintiff never presented any evidence from which to conclude that statements were false); Smith v. United States Bureau of Prisons, No. 94-1798, 1996 WL 43556, at **3-4 (D.D.C. Jan. 31, 1996) (finding that plaintiff's record was not inaccurate with respect to his pre-commitment status in light of Bureau of Prisons' "full authority to promulgate rules governing the treatment and classification of prisoners" and "broad discretionary power," and because there was "no evidence that the BOP's interpretation of its own regulations was an abuse of discretion or discriminatorily administered," "BOP officials reconsidered their decision at least once," and "the determination of which plaintiff complains ha[d] been resolved in his favor"); Hampton v. FBI, No. 93-0816, slip op. at 3-6, 13-17 (D.D.C. June 30, 1995) (although not mentioning (e)(5), finding that FBI "acted lawfully under the Privacy Act in the maintenance of the plaintiff's arrest record" when FBI refused to expunge challenged entries of arrests that did not result in conviction absent authorization by local law enforcement agencies that had originally submitted the information); Buxton v. United States Parole Comm'n, 844 F. Supp. 642, 644 (D. Or. 1994) (subsection (e)(5) fairness standard satisfied where Parole Commission complied with statutory procedures regarding parole hearings even though it did not investigate or correct alleged inaccuracies in presentence report).

Erroneous facts--as well as opinions, evaluations, and subjective judgments based entirely on erroneous facts--can be amended. See, e.g., Hewitt v. Grabicki, 794 F.2d 1373, 1378 (9th Cir. 1986); Douglas v. Farmers Home Admin., 778 F. Supp. 584, 585 (D.D.C. 1991); Rodgers v. Department of the Army, 676 F. Supp. 858, 860-61 (N.D. Ill. 1988); Ertell v. Department of the Army, 626 F. Supp. 903, 910-12 (C.D. Ill. 1986); R.R. v. Department of the Army, 482 F. Supp. 770, 773-74 (D.D.C. 1980); Murphy v. NSA, 2 Gov't Disclosure Serv. (P-H) ¶ 81,389, at 82,036 (D.D.C. Sept. 29, 1981); Trinidad v. United States Civil Serv. Comm'n, 2 Gov't Disclosure

-740-

Serv. (P-H) ¶ 81,322, at 81,870-71 (N.D. Ill. Apr. 7, 1980); <u>Turner v. Department of the Army</u>, 447 F. Supp. 1207, 1213 (D.D.C. 1978), <u>aff'd</u>, 593 F.2d 1372 (D.C. Cir. 1979). As the Court of Appeals for the Seventh Circuit has noted, "[t]he Privacy Act merely requires an agency to attempt to keep accurate records, and provides a remedy to a claimant who demonstrates that facts underlying judgments contained in his records have been discredited." <u>DeBold</u>, 735 F.2d at 1040-41.

In addition, one court has held that where records contain disputed hearsay and reports from informants and unnamed parties, "the records are maintained with adequate fairness if they accurately reflect the nature of the evidence" (i.e., indicate that the information is a hearsay report from an unnamed informant). <u>Graham v. Hawk</u>, 857 F. Supp. 38, 40 (W.D. Tenn. 1994), <u>aff'd</u>, 59 F.3d 170 (6th Cir. 1995) (unpublished table decision); <u>cf.</u> <u>Hass v. United States Air Force</u>, 848 F. Supp. 926, 931 (D. Kan. 1994) (although acknowledging possibility that agency relied upon incorrect information in making determination about plaintiff, finding no Privacy Act violation because no evidence was suggested that information was <u>recorded</u> inaccurately).

As a general rule, courts are reluctant to disturb judgmental matters in an individual's record when such judgments are based on a number of factors or when the factual predicates for a judgment or evaluation are diverse. As the D.C. Circuit has ruled, where a subjective evaluation is "based on a multitude of factors" and "there are various ways of characterizing some of the underlying [factual] events," it is proper to retain and rely on the record. <u>White v. OPM</u>, 787 F.2d 660, 662 (D.C. Cir. 1986); <u>see also</u> <u>Webb v. Magaw</u>, 880 F. Supp. 20, 25 (D.D.C. 1995) (records were not based on demonstrably false premise, but rather on subjective evaluation "'based on a multitude of factors'" (quoting <u>White</u>, 787 F.2d at 662)); <u>Bernson v. ICC</u>, 625 F. Supp. 10, 13 (D. Mass. 1984) (court cannot order amendment of opinions "to reflect the plaintiffs' version of the facts"); <u>cf.</u> <u>Phillips v. Widnall</u>, No. 96-2099, 1997 WL 176394, at **2-3 (10th Cir. Apr. 14, 1997) (although not mentioning subsection (e)(5), holding that appellant was not entitled to court-ordered amendment, nor award of damages, concerning record in her medical files that contained "physician's notation to the effect that [appellant] was probably dependent upon a prescription medication," as such notation "reflected the physician's medical conclusion, which he based upon a number of objective factors and [appellant's] own complaints of neck and low back pain," and "Privacy Act does not permit a court to alter documents that accurately reflect an agency decision, no matter how contestable the conclusion may be").

Many courts have held that <u>pure</u> opinions and judgments are not subject to amendment. <u>See, e.g.</u>, <u>Reinbold v. Evers</u>, 187 F.3d 348, 361 (4th

Cir. 1999); Hewitt, 794 F.2d at 1378-79; Blevins v. Plummer, 613 F.2d 767, 768 (9th Cir. 1980) (per curiam); Fields v. NRC, No. 98-1714, slip op. at 5-7 (D.D.C. May 12, 1999); Blazy v. Tenet, 979 F. Supp. 10, 20-21 (D.D.C. 1997), summary affirmance granted, No. 97-5330, 1998 WL 315583 (D.C. Cir. May 12, 1998); Gowan v. Department of the Air Force, No. 90-94, slip op. at 28-30 (D.N.M. Sept. 1, 1995), aff'd, 148 F.3d 1182 (10th Cir.), cert. denied, 525 U.S. 1042 (1998); Webb, 880 F. Supp. at 25; Linneman v. FBI, No. 89-505, slip op. at 14 (D.D.C. July 13, 1992); Nolan v. United States Dep't of Justice, No. 89-A-2035, 1991 WL 134803, at *3 (D. Colo. July 17, 1991), appeal dismissed in pertinent part on procedural grounds, 973 F.2d 843 (10th Cir. 1992); Frobish v. United States Army, 766 F. Supp. 919, 926-27 (D. Kan. 1991); Daigneau v. United States, No. 88-54-D, slip op. at 3-4 (D.N.H. July 8, 1988); Brumley v. United States Dep't of Labor, No. LR-C-87-437, slip op. at 4 (E.D. Ark. June 15, 1988), aff'd, 881 F.2d 1081 (8th Cir. 1989) (unpublished table decision); Tannehill v. United States Dep't of the Air Force, No. 87-M-1395, slip op. at 2 (D. Colo. May 23, 1988); Rogers v. United States Dep't of Labor, 607 F. Supp. 697, 699-700 (N.D. Cal. 1985); Fagot v. FDIC, 584 F. Supp. 1168, 1176 (D.P.R. 1984), aff'd in part & rev'd in part, 760 F.2d 252 (1st Cir. 1985) (unpublished table decision); DeSha v. Secretary of the Navy, 3 Gov't Disclosure Serv. (P-H) ¶ 82,496, at 82,251 (C.D. Cal. Feb. 26, 1982), aff'd, 780 F.2d 1025 (9th Cir. 1985) (unpublished table decision); Lee v. United States Dep't of Labor, 2 Gov't Disclosure Serv. (P-H) ¶ 81,335, at 81,891 (D. Va. Apr. 17, 1980); Hacopian v. Marshall, 2 Gov't Disclosure Serv. (P-H) ¶ 81,312, at 81,856 (C.D. Cal. Apr. 16, 1980); Castle v. United States Civil Serv. Comm'n, No. 77-1544, slip op. at 5 (D.D.C. Jan. 23, 1979); Rowe v. Department of the Air Force, No. 3-77-220, slip op. at 5 (E.D. Tenn. Mar. 20, 1978); cf. Turner, 447 F. Supp. at 1212-13 (where negative rating had been expunged, court declined to add its opinion about quality of plaintiff's service).

In determining what steps an agency must take in order to satisfy the accuracy standard of subsection (e)(5), the Court of Appeals for the District of Columbia Circuit has looked to whether the information at issue is capable of being verified. In Doe v. United States, 821 F.2d at 697-701, the D.C. Circuit, sitting en banc, in a seven-to-four decision, held that the inclusion in a job applicant's record of both the applicant's and agency interviewer's conflicting versions of an interview (in which only they were present) satisfies subsection (e)(5)'s requirement of maintaining reasonably accurate records. The D.C. Circuit, in rejecting the argument that the agency and reviewing court must themselves make a credibility determination of which version of the interview to believe, ruled that subsections (e)(5) and (g)(1)(C) "establish as the record-keeper's polestar, 'fairness' to the individual about whom information is gathered," and that "the 'fairness'

**PRIVACY ACT OVERVIEW**

criterion does not demand a credibility determination in the <u>atypical</u> circumstances of this case." <u>Id.</u> at 699 (emphasis added); <u>see also</u> <u>Harris v USDA</u>, No. 96-5783, 1997 WL 528498, at \*\*2-3 (6th Cir. Aug. 26, 1997) (agency "reasonably excluded" information from plaintiff's record where there was "substantial evidence that the [information] was unreliable," and in absence of "verifiable information which contradicted its investigators' records," agency "reasonably kept and relied on the information gathered by its investigators when it terminated plaintiff"); <u>Graham</u>, 857 F. Supp. at 40 (agency under no obligation to resolve whether hearsay contained in report is true, so long as information characterized as hearsay); <u>Doe v. FBI</u>, No. 91-1252, slip op. at 6-7 (D.N.J. Feb. 27, 1992) (following <u>Doe v. United States</u>, 821 F.2d at 699, and holding that FBI fulfilled its obligations under Privacy Act by including plaintiff's objections to statements contained in FBI polygrapher's memorandum and by verifying to extent possible that polygraph properly conducted).

Subsequently, the D.C. Circuit held that in a "typical" case, where the records at issue are "not ambivalent" and the facts described therein are "susceptible of proof," the agency and reviewing court must determine accuracy as to each filed item of information. <u>Strang v. United States Arms Control & Disarmament Agency</u>, 864 F.2d 859, 866 (D.C. Cir. 1989). In order to "assure fairness" and render the record "complete" under subsection (e)(5), an agency may even be required to include contrary or qualifying information. See <u>Strang v. United States Arms Control & Disarmament Agency</u>, 920 F.2d 30, 32 (D.C. Cir. 1990); <u>Kassel v. VA</u>, 709 F. Supp. 1194, 1204-05 (D.N.H. 1989).

More recently, the D.C. Circuit adhered to its holding in <u>Strang</u> and held:

> As long as the information contained in an agency's files is capable of being verified, then, under sections (e)(5) and (g)(1)(C) of the Act, the agency must take reasonable steps to maintain the accuracy of the information to assure fairness to the individual. If the agency wilfully or intentionally fails to maintain its records in that way and, as a result, it makes a determination adverse to an individual, then it will be liable to that person for money damages. . . . [T]he agency did not satisfy the requirements of the Privacy Act simply by noting in [the individual's] files that he disputed some of the information the files contained.

<u>Sellers v. Bureau of Prisons</u>, 959 F.2d 307, 312 (D.C. Cir. 1992). (It is worth noting that <u>Sellers</u> was solely a subsection (e)(5)/(g)(1)(C) case; the system of records at issue was exempt from subsection (d).) <u>See also</u> <u>Griffin v. United States Parole Comm'n</u>, No. 97-5084, 1997 U.S.

-743-

App. LEXIS 22401, at **3-5 (D.C. Cir. July 16, 1997) (citing Doe and Deters and finding itself presented with "typical" case in which information was capable of verification, and therefore vacating district court opinion that had characterized case as "atypical"), vacating & remanding No. 96-0342, 1997 U.S. Dist. LEXIS 2846 (D.D.C. Mar. 11, 1997); Deters, 85 F.3d at 658-59 (quoting Sellers and Doe, and although finding itself presented with "an atypical case because the 'truth' . . . is not readily ascertainable . . . assum[ing] without concluding that the Commission failed to maintain Deters's records with sufficient accuracy" because Commission had "not argued that this was an atypical case"); Blazy, 979 F. Supp. at 20-21 (citing Sellers and Doe and finding that alleged inaccuracies were either nonexistent, corrected, or "unverifiable opinions of supervisors, other employees and/or informants"); Bayless v. United States Parole Comm'n, No. 94CV0686, 1996 WL 525325, at *5 (D.D.C. Sept. 11, 1996) (citing Sellers and Doe and finding itself presented with an "atypical" case because "truth concerning plaintiff[']s culpability in the conspiracy and the weight of drugs attributed to him involves credibility determinations of trial witnesses and government informants and, therefore, is not 'clearly provable'"); Webb, 880 F. Supp. at 25 (finding that record at issue contained "justified statements of opinion, not fact" and "[c]onsequently, they were not 'capable of being verified' as false and cannot be considered inaccurate statements" (quoting Sellers, 959 F.2d at 312, and citing Doe, 821 F.2d at 699)); Thomas v. United States Parole Comm'n, No. 94-0174, 1994 WL 487139, at **4-6 (D.D.C. Sept. 7, 1994) (discussing Doe, Strang, and Sellers, but finding that Parole Commission "verified the external 'verifiable' facts"; further holding that plaintiff should not be allowed to use Privacy Act "to collaterally attack the contents of his presentence report," as he "originally had the opportunity to challenge the accuracy . . . before the judge who sentenced him"); Linneman, No. 89-505, slip op. at 11-22 (D.D.C. July 13, 1992) (applying Sellers and Doe to variety of items of which plaintiff sought amendment).

The D.C. Circuit has noted that where "an agency has no subsection (d) duty to amend, upon request, it is not clear what residual duty subsection (e)(5) imposes when an individual challenges the accuracy of a record." Deters, 85 F.3d at 658 n.2. It went on to question whether subsection (e)(5) would still require an agency to amend or expunge upon the individual's request, or whether the agency merely must "address the accuracy of the records at some point before using it to make a determination of consequence to the individual." Id. Although stating that the Sellers opinion was "not entirely clear on this point," the D.C. Circuit reasoned that "the language of subsection (e)(5) . . . suggests the latter course," id. (citing OMB Guidelines, 40 Fed. Reg. 28,948, 28,964 (1975)), and went on to state that subsection (e)(5) suggests that an agency has "no duty to act on an [individual's] challenge and verify his record until the agency uses the record in making a determination affecting his rights, benefits, entitlements or opportunities," 85 F.3d at 660; see also Bayless, 1996 WL 525325, at *6 n.19 (quoting Deters and determining that agency "fulfilled its requisite duty by 'addressing' plaintiff's allegations prior to rendering a parole determination").

The Court of Appeals for the Ninth Circuit has held that an agency can comply with subsection (e)(5) by simply including a complainant's rebuttal statement with an allegedly inaccurate record. Fendler v. United States Bureau of Prisons, 846 F.2d 550, 554 (9th Cir. 1988) (subsections (e)(5) and (g)(1)(C) lawsuit); see also Graham, 857 F. Supp. at 40 (citing Fendler and holding that where individual disputes accuracy of information that agency has characterized as hearsay, agency satisfies (e)(5) by permitting individual to place rebuttal in file); cf. Harris, No. 96-5783, 1997 WL 528498, at *2 (6th Cir. Aug. 26, 1997) (although holding that exclusion of information from appellant's record due to unreliability of information was reasonable, finding it "notabl[e]" that appellant had not contested district court's finding that agency "did not prevent him from adding to the file his disagreement with the [agency] investigators' conclusions"). Fendler thus appears to conflict with both Doe and Strang, as well as with the D.C. Circuit's earlier decision in Vymetalik v. FBI, 785 F.2d 1090, 1098 n.12 (D.C. Cir. 1986) (noting that subsection (d)(2) "guarantees an individual the right to demand that his or her records be amended if inaccurate" and that mere inclusion of rebuttal statement was not "intended to be [the] exclusive [remedy]").

In Chapman v. NASA, 682 F.2d 526, 528-30 (5th Cir. 1982), the Court of Appeals for the Fifth Circuit recognized a "timely incorporation" duty under subsection (e)(5). It ruled that a supervisor's personal notes "evanesced" into Privacy Act records when they were used by the agency to effect an adverse disciplinary action, and that such records must be placed into the employee's file "at the time of the next evaluation or report on the employee's work status or performance." Id. at 529. In reversing the district court's ruling that such notes were not records within a system of records, the Fifth Circuit noted that such incorporation ensures fairness by allowing employees a meaningful opportunity to make refutatory notations, and avoids an "ambush" approach to maintaining records. Id.; see also Thompson v. Department of Transp. United States Coast Guard, 547 F. Supp. 274, 283-84 (S.D. Fla. 1982) (explaining Chapman). Chapman's "timely incorporation" doctrine has been followed in several other cases. See, e.g., MacDonald v. VA, No. 87-544-CIV-T-15A, slip op. at 2-5 (M.D. Fla. Feb. 8, 1988) (counseling memorandum used in preparation of proficiency report "became" part of VA system of records); Lawrence v. Dole, No. 83-2876, slip op. at 5-6

(D.D.C. Dec. 12, 1985) (notes not incorporated in timely manner cannot be used as basis for adverse employment action); Waldrop v. United States Dep't of the Air Force, 3 Gov't Disclosure Serv. (P-H) ¶ 83,016, at 83,453 (S.D. Ill. Aug. 5, 1981) (certain of records at issue became Privacy Act records; others were merely "memory joggers"); Nelson v. EEOC, No. 83-C-983, slip op. at 6-11 (E.D. Wis. Feb. 14, 1984) (memorandum was used in making determination about an individual and therefore must be included in system of records and made available to individual); cf. Hudson v. Reno, 103 F.3d 1193, 1205-06 & n.9 (6th Cir. 1997) (distinguishing facts in Chapman and holding that supervisor's "notes about [p]laintiff's misconduct which were kept in a locked drawer and labeled the 'First Assistant's' files do not fall within th[e system of records] definition," as they "were not used to make any determination with respect to [p]laintiff"), cert. denied, 525 U.S. 822 (1998); Manuel v. VA Hosp., 857 F.2d 1112, 1117-19 (6th Cir. 1988) (no duty to place records within system of records where records "are not part of an official agency investigation into activities of the individual requesting the records, and where the records requested do not have an adverse effect on the individual"); Magee v. United States, 903 F. Supp. 1022, 1029-30 (W.D. La. 1995) (plaintiff's file kept in supervisor's desk, separate from other employee files, because of plaintiff's concerns about access to it and with plaintiff's acquiescence did "not fall within the proscriptions of maintaining a 'secret file' under the Act"), aff'd, 79 F.3d 1145 (5th Cir. 1996) (unpublished table decision).

Also note that subsection (e)(5)'s "timeliness" requirement does not require that agency records contain only information that is "hot off the presses." White, 787 F.2d at 663 (rejecting argument that use of year-old evaluation violates Act, as it "would be an unwarranted intrusion on the agency's freedom to shape employment application procedures"); see also Beckette v. United States Postal Serv., No. 88-802, slip op. at 12-14 (E.D. Va. July 3, 1989) (stating that "[a]ll of the record maintenance requirements of subsection 552a(e)(5), including timeliness, concern fairness," and finding that as to records regarding "restricted sick leave," "[w]iping the . . . slate clean after an employee has remained off the listing for only six months is not required to assure fairness to the individual"; also finding that maintenance of those records for six months after restricted sick leave had been rescinded "did not violate the relevancy requirement of subsection 552a(e)(5)").

For a further discussion of subsection (e)(5), see OMB Guidelines, 40 Fed. Reg. 28,948, 28,964-65 (1975).

**PRIVACY ACT OVERVIEW**

**F. 5 U.S.C. § 552a(e)(6)**

"prior to disseminating any record about an individual to any person other than an agency, unless the dissemination is made pursuant to subsection (b)(2) of this section [FOIA], make reasonable efforts to assure that such records are accurate, complete, timely, and relevant for agency purposes."

comment -- This provision requires a reasonable effort by the agency to review records prior to their dissemination. See NTEU v. IRS, 601 F. Supp. 1268, 1272 (D.D.C. 1985); see also Stewart v. FBI, No. 97-1595, slip op. at 4 (D. Or. Mar. 12, 1999) (provision violated where agency failed to establish that it conducted reasonable efforts to ensure the accuracy of information "'of a factual nature'" that was "'capable of being verified'"); Gang v. Civil Serv. Comm'n, No. 76-1263, slip op. at 2-5 (D.D.C. May 10, 1977) (provision violated where agency failed to review personnel file to determine relevance and timeliness of dated material concerning political activities before disseminating it to Library of Congress).

The District Court for the District of Columbia has held that an agency was not liable under subsection (e)(6) for damages for the dissemination of information that plaintiff had claimed was inaccurate but that the court determined consisted of statements of opinion and subjective evaluation that were not subject to amendment. Webb v. Magaw, 880 F. Supp. 20, 25 (D.D.C. 1995). The District Court for the Southern District of California has also considered a claim under subsection (e)(6), and in doing so took into account the requirements of causation and intentional and willful wrongdoing in Privacy Act damages actions, discussed below. Guccione v. National Indian Gaming Comm'n, No. 98-CV-164, 1999 U.S. Dist. LEXIS 15475, at **14-19 (S.D. Cal. Aug. 5, 1999). The court found that an administrative hearing concerning inconsistencies in plaintiff's employment application "smacked generally of reprimand even though no talismanic phrases akin to reprimand were used," and that therefore "there was no 'intentional' or 'willful' misconduct in the [agency's] use of the term reprimand," nor was there sufficient causation where the recipients of the information also had reviewed the transcript of the administrative hearing and could draw their own conclusions. Id. at **16-19.

By its terms, this provision does not apply to mandatory FOIA disclosures. See Smith v. United States, 817 F.2d 86, 87 (10th Cir. 1987); Kassel v. VA, 709 F. Supp. 1194, 1205 & n.5 (D.N.H. 1989); see also OMB Guidelines, 40 Fed. Reg. 28,948, 28,965 (1975).

**G. 5 U.S.C. § 552a(e)(7)**

"maintain no record describing how any individual exercises rights guaranteed by the First Amendment unless expressly authorized by statute or by the individual about whom the

## PRIVACY ACT OVERVIEW

record is maintained or unless pertinent to and within the scope of an authorized law enforcement activity."

comment -- The OMB Guidelines advise agencies in determining whether a particular activity constitutes exercise of a right guaranteed by the First Amendment to "apply the broadest reasonable interpretation." 40 Fed. Reg. 28,948, 28,965 (1975); see also 120 Cong. Rec. 40,406 (1974), reprinted in Source Book at 860. As noted above, Albright v. United States, 631 F.2d 915, 918-20 (D.C. Cir. 1980), establishes that the record at issue need not be within a system of records to violate subsection (e)(7); see also MacPherson v. IRS, 803 F.2d 479, 481 (9th Cir. 1986); Boyd v. Secretary of the Navy, 709 F.2d 684, 687 (11th Cir. 1983) (per curiam); Clarkson v. IRS, 678 F.2d 1368, 1373-77 (11th Cir. 1982). See also discussion under "System of Records" definition, above.

However, the record at issue "must implicate an individual's First Amendment rights." Boyd, 709 F.2d at 684; accord Banks v. Garrett, 901 F.2d 1084, 1089 (Fed. Cir. 1990); see also Reuber v. United States, 829 F.2d 133, 142-43 (D.C. Cir. 1987) (noting threshold requirement that record itself must describe First Amendment-protected activity); Pototsky v. Department of the Navy, 717 F. Supp. 20, 22 (D. Mass. 1989) (same), aff'd, 907 F.2d 142 (1st Cir. 1990) (unpublished table decision). Thus, subsection (e)(7) is not triggered in the first place unless the record describes First Amendment-protected activity. See, e.g., England v. Commissioner, 798 F.2d 350, 352-53 (9th Cir. 1986) (record identifying individual as having "tax protester" status does not describe how individual exercises First Amendment rights); Weeden v. Frank, No. 1:91CV0016, slip op. at 7-8 (N.D. Ohio Apr. 10, 1992) (to read subsection (e)(7) as requiring privacy waiver for agency to even file plaintiff's request for religious accommodation is "a broad and unreasonable interpretation of subsection (e)(7)"; however, agency would need to obtain waiver to collect information to verify plaintiff's exercise of religious beliefs), aff'd, 16 F.3d 1223 (6th Cir. 1994) (unpublished table decision); Cloud v. Heckler, 3 Gov't Disclosure Serv. (P-H) ¶ 83,230, at 83,962 (W.D. Ark. Apr. 21, 1983) (maintenance of employee's letters criticizing agency--written while on duty--does not violate subsection (e)(7) because "[p]oor judgment is not protected by the First Amendment").

Assuming that the challenged record itself describes activity protected by the First Amendment, subsection (e)(7) is violated unless maintenance of the record is:

(1) expressly authorized by statute, see, e.g., Abernethy v. IRS, 909 F. Supp. 1562, 1570 (N.D. Ga. 1995) (IRS "authorized by statute" to maintain copies of documents relevant to processing of plaintiff's requests under FOIA and Privacy Act, which both "provide implied authorization to federal agencies to maintain copies for their

own records of the documents which are released to requesters under those Acts"), aff'd per curiam, No. 95-9489 (11th Cir. Feb. 13, 1997); Hass v. United States Air Force, 848 F. Supp. 926, 930-31 (D. Kan. 1994) (agency's maintenance of FOIA and PA requests "cannot logically violate the Privacy Act"); Attorney Gen. of the United States v. Irish N. Aid Comm., No. 77-708, 1977 U.S. Dist. LEXIS 13581, at *14 (S.D.N.Y. Oct. 7, 1977) (Foreign Agents Registration Act); OMB Guidelines, 40 Fed. Reg. at 28,965 (Immigration and Nationality Act); cf. Abernethy, 909 F. Supp. at 1570 (maintenance of documents in congressional communications files "does not violate the Privacy Act" because IRS "must respond to Congressional inquiries" and maintenance was necessary to carry out that responsibility (citing Internal Revenue Manual 1(15)29, Chapter 500, Congressional Communications)); Gang v. United States Civil Serv. Comm'n, No. 76-1263, slip op. at 5-7 & n.5 (D.D.C. May 10, 1977) (recognizing that 5 U.S.C. § 7311, which prohibits individual from holding position with federal government if he advocates--or is member of organization that he knows advocates--overthrow of government, may be read together with subsection (e)(7) as permitting maintenance of files relating to membership in such groups, but ruling that "it cannot fairly be read to permit wholesale maintenance of all materials relating to political beliefs, association, and religion"; nor does 5 U.S.C. § 3301, which authorizes President to ascertain fitness of federal applicants for employment as to character, provide authorization for maintenance of such information); or

(2) expressly authorized by the individual about whom the record is maintained, see Abernethy, 909 F. Supp. at 1570 ("Plaintiff authorized the maintenance of the documents at issue by submitting copies to various components of the Defendant IRS."); OMB Guidelines, 40 Fed. Reg. at 28,965 ("volunteered" information is properly maintained); see also Radford v. Social Sec. Admin., No. 81-4099, slip op. at 4-5 (D. Kan. July 11, 1985) (plaintiff's publication of contents of offending record does not constitute "express authorization"); Murphy v. NSA, 2 Gov't Disclosure Serv. (P-H) ¶ 81,389, at 82,036 (D.D.C. Sept. 29, 1981) (consent to maintain may be withdrawn); cf. Weeden v. Frank, No. 93-3681, 1994 WL 47137, at *2 (6th Cir. Feb. 16, 1994) (Postal Service's procedure requiring individual to expressly waive subsection (e)(7) Privacy Act rights in order to allow agency to collect information regarding employee's exercise of religious beliefs so that accommodation could be established held not unreasonable); or

(3) pertinent to and within the scope of an authorized law enforcement activity.

Perhaps the leading precedent in the early case law on the "law enforcement activity" exception is Patterson v. FBI, 893 F.2d 595, 602-03 (3d Cir. 1990), a case that attracted national media attention because of its unusual factual background: An elementary school student, in the lawful exercise of his constitutional rights to write an encyclopedia of the world based upon requests to 169 countries for information, became the subject of an FBI national security investigation. The Court of Appeals for the Third Circuit, in affirming the dismissal of the student's subsection (e)(7) claim, ruled that a standard of "relevance" to a lawful law enforcement activity is "more consistent with Congress's intent and will prove to be a more manageable standard than employing one based on ad-hoc review." Id. at 603.

The "relevance" standard articulated in Patterson had earlier been recognized by the Court of Appeals for the Sixth Circuit in Jabara v. Webster, 691 F.2d 272, 279-80 (6th Cir. 1982), a case involving a challenge to the FBI's maintenance of investigative records regarding surveillance of the plaintiff's overseas communications. In Jabara, the Sixth Circuit vacated as "too narrow" the district court's ruling that the exception is limited to "investigation of past, present or future criminal activity." Id. It held that the exception applies where the record is "relevant to an authorized criminal investigation or to an authorized intelligence or administrative one." Id. at 280.

In MacPherson v. IRS, 803 F.2d at 482-85, the Court of Appeals for the Ninth Circuit ruled that the applicability of the exception could be assessed only on an "individual, case-by-case basis" and that a "hard and fast standard" was inappropriate. On the facts before it, however, the Ninth Circuit upheld the maintenance of notes and purchased tapes of a tax protester's speech as "necessary to give the IRS [and Justice Department] a complete and representative picture of the events," notwithstanding that no investigation of a specific violation of law was involved and no past, present or anticipated illegal conduct was revealed or even suspected. Id. The Ninth Circuit cautioned, though, that its holding was a narrow one tied to the specific facts before it. Id. at 485 n.9.

In Clarkson v. IRS, 678 F.2d at 1374-75--a case involving facts similar to MacPherson in that it likewise involved a challenge to the IRS's maintenance of records regarding surveillance of a tax protester's speech--the Court of Appeals for the Eleventh Circuit quoted with approval the standard set forth by the district court decision in Jabara (subsequently vacated and remanded by the Sixth Circuit) and held that the exception does not apply if the record is "unconnected to any investigation of past, present or anticipated violations of statutes [the agency] is authorized to enforce." On remand, the district court upheld the IRS's maintenance of the surveillance records as "connected to anticipated violations of the tax statutes" inasmuch as such records "provide information relating to suggested methods of avoiding tax liability" and aid in the "identification of potential tax violators." Clarkson v. IRS, No. C79-642A, slip op. at 6-10 (N.D. Ga. Dec. 27, 1984), aff'd per curiam, 811 F.2d 1396 (11th Cir. 1987); accord Tate v. Bindseil, 2 Gov't Disclosure Serv. (P-H) ¶ 82,114, at 82,427 (D.S.C. Aug. 4, 1981) ("[An] IRS investigation of activist organizations and individuals prominently associated with those organizations which advocate resistance to the tax laws by refusing to file returns or filing blank returns is a legitimate law enforcement activity.").

The Court of Appeals for the Seventh Circuit, although recognizing the "varying views" adopted by other courts of appeals, adopted what seems to be the most strict application of the law enforcement exception to date. The Seventh Circuit ordered the IRS to expunge information in a closed investigative file, based upon its determination, through in camera inspection, that it could not "be helpful in future enforcement activity." Becker v. IRS, 34 F.3d 398, 408-09 (7th Cir. 1994); cf. J. Roderick MacArthur Found. v. FBI, 102 F.3d 600, 607 (D.C. Cir. 1996) (Tatel, J., dissenting) (opining in favor of requirement that information be maintained only if pertinent to current law enforcement activity). In so ruling, the Seventh Circuit appeared to confusingly engraft the timeliness requirement of subsection (e)(5) onto subsection (e)(7). See Becker, 34 F.3d at 409 & n.28. Additionally, the Seventh Circuit appeared to confuse the district court's determination that the information was exempt from access under subsection (k)(2) with the district court's further ruling that the information also satisfied the requirements of subsection (e)(7). See id. at 407-08; see also Becker v. IRS, No. 91 C 1203, 1993 WL 114612, at *1 (N.D. Ill. Apr. 13, 1993).

Recently, the Court of Appeals for the District of Columbia Circuit was faced with interpreting the law enforcement exception in J. Roderick MacArthur Foundation v. FBI, 102 F.3d 600 (D.C. Cir. 1996). In MacArthur, the D.C. Circuit rejected the appellants' arguments, which were based on Becker, stating that "the court's analysis of § (e)(7) in Becker is neither clear nor compelling," and that the Seventh Circuit had "set out to determine the meaning 'of the "law enforcement purpose" phrase of § 552a(e)(7)' not realizing that the phrase used in the Privacy Act is 'authorized law enforcement activity'" and that it "appears to have confused § 552a(e)(7) with § 552a(k)(2)." 102 F.3d at 603. In MacArthur, the appellant did not challenge the FBI's having collected the information about him, but rather claimed that the FBI could not maintain or retain such information unless there was a "current law enforcement necessity to do so." Id. at 602. The D.C. Circuit, however, realizing that "[m]aterial may continue to be relevant to a law enforcement activity long after a particular investigation undertaken pursuant to that activity has been closed," id. at 602-03, ruled that "[i]nformation that was pertinent to an authorized law enforcement activity when collected does not later lose its

PRIVACY ACT OVERVIEW

pertinence to that activity simply because the information is not of current interest (let alone 'necessity') to the agency," id. at 603. The panel majority went on to hold:

> [T]he Privacy Act does not prohibit an agency from maintaining records about an individual's first amendment activities if the information was pertinent to an authorized law enforcement activity when the agency collected the information. The Act does not require an agency to expunge records when they are no longer pertinent to a current law enforcement activity.

Id. at 605. In its conclusion, the D.C. Circuit stated that subsection (e)(7) "does not by its terms" require an agency to show that information is pertinent to a "currently" authorized law enforcement activity, and that it found "nothing in the structure or purpose of the Act that would suggest such a reading." Id. at 607.

Several other courts have upheld the exception's applicability in a variety of contexts. See Doe v. FBI, 936 F.2d 1346, 1354-55, 1360-61 (D.C. Cir. 1991) (although holding that appellant was foreclosed from obtaining relief because he had "not suffered any adverse effect," stating that to extent appellant's argument as to violation of subsection (e)(7) was directed to underlying FBI records concerning investigation of appellant's "unauthorized possession of an explosive device" and reported advocacy of "violent overthrow of the Government," subsection (e)(7) was not violated as "'law enforcement activity' exception applies"); Wabun-Inini v. Sessions, 900 F.2d 1231, 1245-46 (8th Cir. 1990) (FBI maintenance of photographs seized with probable cause); Jochen v. VA, No. 88-6138, slip op. at 6-7 (9th Cir. Apr. 5, 1989) (VA evaluative report concerning operation of VA facility and job performance of public employee that contained remarks by plaintiff); Nagel v. HEW, 725 F.2d 1438, 1441 & n.3 (D.C. Cir. 1984) (citing Jabara with approval and holding that records describing statements made by employees while at work were properly maintained "for evaluative or disciplinary purposes"); Abernethy, 909 F. Supp. at 1566, 1570 (holding that maintenance of newspaper article that quoted plaintiff on subject of reverse discrimination and "Notice of Potential Class Action Complaint" were "relevant to and pertinent to authorized law enforcement activities" as they appeared in file pertaining to EEO complaint in which plaintiff was complainant's representative and was kept due to belief that a conflict of interest might exist through plaintiff's representation of complainant and, citing Nagel, holding that maintenance was also "valid" in files concerning possible disciplinary action against plaintiff); Maki v. Sessions, No. 1:90-CV-587, 1991 U.S. Dist. LEXIS 7103, at **27-28 (W.D. Mich. May 29, 1991) (holding that, although plaintiff claimed FBI investigation was illegal, the uncontested evidence was that plaintiff was the subject of an authorized investigation by FBI); Kassel v. VA, No. 87-217-S, slip op. at 27-28 (D.N.H. Mar. 30, 1992) (citing Nagel and Jabara, inter alia, and holding that information about plaintiff's statements to media fell within ambit of administrative investigation); Pacheco v. FBI, 470 F. Supp. 1091, 1108 n.21 (D.P.R. 1979) ("all investigative files of the FBI fall under the exception"); AFGE v. Schlesinger, 443 F. Supp. 431, 435 (D.D.C. 1978) (reasonable steps taken by agencies to prevent conflicts of interest are within exception); see also Felsen v. HHS, No. CCB-95-975, slip op. at 68-72 (D. Md. Sept. 30, 1998) (although not deciding whether report described First Amendment activity, finding no violation of subsection (e)(7) where report was relevant to authorized law enforcement activity of HHS and also was related to possible past violation of statute that HHS is empowered to enforce).

It should be noted that a finding that records are maintained in violation of subsection (e)(7) does not mean that those records must be disclosed. See Irons v. Bell, 596 F.2d 468, 470-71 & n.4 (1st Cir. 1979).

## H. 5 U.S.C. § 552a(e)(8)

"make reasonable efforts to serve notice on an individual when any record on such individual is made available to any person under compulsory legal process when such process becomes a matter of public record."

comment -- This provision becomes applicable when subsection (b)(11) "court order" disclosures occur. See, e.g., Moore v. United States Postal Serv., 609 F. Supp. 681, 682 (E.D.N.Y. 1985); see also OMB Guidelines, 40 Fed. Reg. 28,948, 28,965 (1975). By its terms, it requires notice not prior to the making of a legally compelled disclosure, but rather at the time that the disclosure becomes a matter of public record. Kassel v. VA, No. 87-217-S, slip op. at 30 (D.N.H. Mar. 30, 1992); see also Moore, 609 F. Supp. at 682 ("§552a(e)(8) does not speak of advance notice of release"); cf. Mangino v. Department of the Army, No. 94-2067, 1994 WL 477260, at **11-12 (D. Kan. Aug. 24, 1994) (citing Moore for proposition that subsection (e)(8) does not require advance notice, although finding no allegation that disclosure at issue was made "under compulsory legal process").

## I. 5 U.S.C. § 552a(e)(9)

"establish rules of conduct for persons involved in the design, development, operation, or maintenance of any system of records, or in maintaining any record, and instruct each such person with respect to such rules and the requirements of this section, including any other rules and procedures adopted pursuant to this section and the penalties for noncompliance."

comment -- For a discussion of this provision, see OMB Guidelines, 40 Fed. Reg. 28,948, 28,965 (1975).

PRIVACY ACT OVERVIEW

J. 5 U.S.C. § 552a(e)(10)

"establish appropriate administrative, technical and physical safeguards to insure the security and confidentiality of records and to protect against any anticipated threats or hazards to their security or integrity which could result in substantial harm, embarrassment, inconvenience, or unfairness to any individual on whom information is maintained."

comment -- This provision may come into play when documents are "leaked." See, e.g., Pilon v. United States Dep't of Justice, 796 F. Supp. 7, 13 (D.D.C. 1992) (because subsection (e)(10) is more specific than subsection (b), it governs with regard to allegedly inadequate safeguards that resulted in disclosure); Kostyu v. United States, 742 F. Supp. 413, 414-17 (E.D. Mich. 1990) (alleged lapses in IRS document-security safeguards were not willful and intentional). One district court has found that disclosures that are the result of "official decisions" by an agency, "cannot be the basis for a claim under subsection (e)(10)." Chasse v. United States Dep't of Justice, No. 1:98-CV-207, slip op. at 16-17 (D. Vt. Jan. 14, 1999) (magistrate's recommendation), adopted (D. Vt. Feb. 9, 1999), aff'd on other grounds sub nom. Devine v. United States, 202 F.3d 547 (2d Cir. 2000). For a further discussion of this provision, see OMB Guidelines, 40 Fed. Reg. 28,948, 28,966 (1975).

K. 5 U.S.C. § 552a(e)(11)

"at least 30 days prior to publication of information under paragraph (4)(D) of this subsection [routine uses], publish in the Federal Register notice of any new use or intended use of the information in the system, and provide an opportunity for interested persons to submit written data, views, or arguments to the agency."

comment -- For a discussion of this provision, see OMB Guidelines, 40 Fed. Reg. 28,948, 28,966 (1975).

## AGENCY RULES

To implement the Act, an agency that maintains a system of records "shall promulgate rules, in accordance with [notice and comment rulemaking, see 5 U.S.C. § 553]," which shall--

A. 5 U.S.C. § 552a(f)(1)

"establish procedures whereby an individual can be notified in response to his request if any system of records named by the individual contains a record pertaining to him."

comment -- For a discussion of this provision, see OMB Guidelines, 40 Fed. Reg. 28,948, 28,967 (1975).

B. 5 U.S.C. § 552a(f)(2)

"define reasonable times, places, and requirements for identifying an individual who requests his record or information pertaining to him before the agency shall make the record or information available to the individual."

comment -- For a discussion of this provision, see OMB Guidelines, 40 Fed. Reg. 28,948, 28,967 (1975).

## C. 5 U.S.C. § 552a(f)(3)

"establish procedures for the disclosure to an individual upon his request of his record or information pertaining to him, including special procedure, if deemed necessary, for the disclosure to an individual of medical records, including psychological records pertaining to him."

comment -- In the past, a typical regulation consistent with this provision would allow an agency to advise an individual requester that his medical records would be provided only to a physician, designated by the individual, who requested the records and established his identity in writing, and that the designated physician would determine which records should be provided to the individual and which should not be disclosed because of the possible harm to the individual or another person.

However, as a result of the opinion by the Court of Appeals for the District of Columbia Circuit in Benavides v. United States Bureau of Prisons, 995 F.2d 269 (D.C. Cir. 1993), such regulations are no longer valid. In Benavides, the D.C. Circuit held that subsection (f)(3) is "strictly procedural . . . merely authoriz[ing] agencies to devise the manner in which they will disclose properly requested non-exempt records" and that "[a] regulation that expressly contemplates that the requesting individual may never see certain medical records [as a result of the discretion of the designated physician] is simply not a special procedure for disclosure to that person." Id. at 272. The D.C. Circuit went on to state that the Justice Department's subsection (f)(3) regulation at issue, 28 C.F.R. § 16.43(d) (1992), "in effect, create[d] another substantive exemption" to Privacy Act access, and it accordingly held the regulation to be "ultra vires." 995 F.2d at 272-73.

Nevertheless, the D.C. Circuit in Benavides rejected the argument that the Privacy Act requires direct disclosure of medical records to the individual. Recognizing the "potential harm that could result from unfettered access to medical and psychological records," the court provided that "as long as agencies guarantee the ultimate disclosure of the medical records to the requesting individual . . . they should have freedom to craft special procedures to limit the potential harm." Id. at 273; cf. Waldron v. Social Sec. Admin., No. CS-92-334, slip op. at 9-10 (E.D. Wash. July 21, 1993) (holding claim not ripe because plaintiff had not designated representative and had not been denied information (only direct access), but stating that portion of regulation granting representative discretion in providing access to medical records "is troubling because it could be applied in such a manner as to totally deny an individual access to his medical records").

As a result of the Benavides decision, prior case law applying (and thus implicitly upholding) subsection (f)(3) regulations, such as the Justice Department's former regulation, is unreliable. See, e.g., Cowsen-El v. United States Dep't of Justice, 826 F. Supp. 532, 535-37 (D.D.C. 1992) (although recognizing that "the Privacy Act does not authorize government agencies to create new disclosure exemptions by virtue of their regulatory powers under the Privacy Act," nevertheless upholding Department of Justice regulation); Becher v. Demers, No. 91-C-99-S, 1991 WL 333708, at *4 (W.D. Wis. May 28, 1991) (where plaintiff failed to designate medical representative and agency determined that direct access would have adverse effect on plaintiff, request was properly denied); Sweatt v. United States Navy, 2 Gov't Disclosure Serv. (P-H) ¶ 81,038, at 81,102 (D.D.C. Dec. 19, 1980) (withholding of "raw psychological data" in accordance with regulation, on ground that disclosure would adversely affect requester's health, deemed not denial of request), aff'd per curiam, 683 F.2d 420 (D.C. Cir. 1982). But see Hill v. Blevins, No. 3-CV-92-0859, slip op. at 5-7 (M.D. Pa. Apr. 12, 1993) (finding Social Security Administration procedure requiring designation of representative other than family member for receipt and review of medical and psychological information valid), aff'd, 19 F.3d 643 (3d Cir. 1994) (unpublished table decision); Besecker v. Social Sec., No. 91-C-4818, 1992 WL 32243, at *2 (N.D. Ill. Feb. 18, 1992) (dismissal for failure to exhaust administrative remedies where plaintiff failed to designate representative to receive medical records), aff'd, 48 F.3d 1221 (7th Cir. 1995) (unpublished table decision); cf. Polewsky v. Social Sec. Admin., No. 95-6125, 1996 WL 110179, at **1-2 (2d Cir. Mar. 12, 1996) (affirming lower court decision which held that plaintiff's access claims were moot because he had ultimately designated representative to receive medical records and had been provided with them (even though prior to filing suit, plaintiff had refused to designate representative); stating further that plaintiff decided voluntarily to designate representative and thus although issue was "capable of repetition" it had "not been shown to evade review").

Although there is no counterpart provision qualifying a requester's independent right of access to his medical records under the FOIA, the D.C. Circuit found it unnecessary in Benavides to confront this issue. See 995 F.2d at 273. In fact, only two courts have addressed the matter of separate FOIA access and the possible applicability of 5 U.S.C. § 552a(t)(2) (addressing access interplay between Privacy Act and FOIA), one of which was the lower court in a companion case to Benavides. See Smith v. Quinlan, No. 91-1187, 1992 WL 25689, at *4 (D.D.C. Jan. 13, 1992) (court did "not find Section 552a(f)(3) as implemented [by 28 C.F.R. § 16.43(d)] and Section 552a(t)(2) to be incompatible"; reasoning that "if Congress had intended Section 552a(t) to disallow or narrow the scope of special pro-

PRIVACY ACT OVERVIEW

cedures that agencies may deem necessary in
releasing medical and psychological records, it
would have so indicated by legislation"), rev'd
& remanded sub nom. Benavides v. United States
Bureau of Prisons, 995 F.2d 269 (D.C. Cir.
1993); Waldron v. Social Sec. Admin., No. CS-92-
334, slip op. at 10-15 (E.D. Wash. June 1, 1993)
(same as Smith, but with regard to Social Security Administration regulation); cf. Hill, No.
3-CV-92-0859, slip op. at 7 (M.D. Pa. Apr. 12,
1993) (incorrectly interpreting subsection
(f)(3) as constituting an "exempting statute"
under FOIA).

For further discussion of this provision, see
OMB Guidelines, 40 Fed. Reg. 28,948, 28,957,
28,967 (1975), and the Report of the House Committee on Government Operations, H.R. Rep. No.
1416, 93d Cong., 2d Sess., at 16-17 (1974),
reprinted in Source Book at 309-10.

### D. 5 U.S.C. § 552a(f)(4)

"establish procedures for reviewing a request from an individual concerning the amendment of any record or information pertaining to the individual, for making a determination on the request, for an appeal within the agency of an initial adverse agency determination, and for whatever additional means may be necessary for each individual to be able to exercise fully his rights under [the Act]."

comment -- For a discussion of this provision, see OMB
Guidelines, 40 Fed. Reg. 28,948, 28,967 (1975).

### E. 5 U.S.C. § 552a(f)(5)

"establish fees to be charged, if any, to any individual
for making copies of his record, excluding the cost of any
search for and review of the record."

comment -- Unlike under the FOIA, search and review costs
are never chargeable under the Privacy Act. See
OMB Guidelines, 40 Fed. Reg. 28,948, 28,968
(1975).

Note also that subsection (f) provides that the
Office of the Federal Register shall biennially
compile and publish the rules outlined above and
agency notices published under subsection (e)(4)
in a form available to the public at low cost.

## CIVIL REMEDIES

The Privacy Act provides for four separate and distinct civil
causes of action, see 5 U.S.C. § 552a(g), two of which provide
for injunctive relief--amendment lawsuits under (g)(1)(A) and
access lawsuits under (g)(1)(B)--and two of which provide for
compensatory relief in the form of monetary damages--accuracy
lawsuits under (g)(1)(C) and lawsuits for other damages under
(g)(1)(D).

It is worth noting that several courts have stated that the remedies provided for by the Privacy Act are exclusive, in that a
violation of the Act does not provide for any relief in the
course of a federal criminal prosecution, see United States v.
Bressler, 772 F.2d 287, 293 (7th Cir. 1985) ("[E]ven if the defendant had made a sustainable argument [under 5 U.S.C.
§ 552a(e)(3)], the proper remedy is a civil action under Section

## PRIVACY ACT OVERVIEW

552a(g)(1) of the Privacy Act, not dismissal of the indictment."); United States v. Bell, 734 F.2d 1315, 1318 (8th Cir. 1984) (Even if appellant's (e)(3) argument was sufficiently raised at trial, "it cannot be a basis for reversing his conviction."); United States v. Gillotti, 822 F. Supp. 984, 989 (W.D.N.Y. 1993) ("[T]he appropriate relief for a violation of Section 552a(e)(7) is found in the statute and allows for damages as well as amendment or expungement of the unlawful records . . . there is nothing in the statute itself, nor in any judicial authority, which suggests that its violation may provide any form of relief in a federal criminal prosecution."), nor is failure to comply with the Privacy Act a proper defense to summons enforcement, see, e.g., United States v. McAnlis, 721 F.2d 334, 337 (11th Cir. 1983) (compliance with 5 U.S.C. § 552a(e)(3) not prerequisite to enforcement of summons); United States v. Berney, 713 F.2d 568, 572 (10th Cir. 1983) (Privacy Act "contains its own remedies for noncompliance"); United States v. Harris, No. 98-3117, 1998 WL 870351, at *2 (7th Cir. Dec. 11, 1998) (citing McAnlis and Berney and rejecting "irrelevant argument that . . . the Privacy Act . . . guarantee[s] [appellant] answers to his questions before he has to comply with the IRS summons"); Adams v. IRS, No. 2:98 MC 9, 1999 U.S. Dist. LEXIS 16018, at *15 (N.D. Ind. Sept. 29, 1999) (compliance with Privacy Act not prerequisite to enforcement of IRS summons); Reimer v. United States, 43 F. Supp. 2d 232, 237 (N.D.N.Y. 1999) (rejecting argument to quash summons on (e)(3) grounds because requirements of subsection (e)(3) "are not applicable to summons issued pursuant to 26 U.S.C. §§ 7602, 7609"); Connell v. United States, No. 1:98 CV 2094, 1998 U.S. Dist. LEXIS 20149, at *9 (N.D. Ohio Dec. 7, 1998) (citing McAnlis and stating: "That the Respondent did not comply with the Privacy Act, 5 U.S.C. § 552a (e)(3)(A)-(D), is not a basis upon which to quash the summonses at issue."); see also Phillips v. United States, No. 98-3128, 1999 WL 228585, at *2 (6th Cir. Mar. 10, 1999) (Privacy Act notice requirements inapplicable to issuance of IRS summons, as 26 U.S.C. § 7852(e) "plainly states that the provisions of the Privacy Act do not apply, directly or indirectly, to assessing the possibility of a tax liability"); Reimer v. United States, No. CV-F-99-5685, 1999 U.S. Dist. LEXIS 15282, at *10 (E.D. Cal. Sept. 8, 1999) (same); cf. Estate of Myers v. United States, 842 F. Supp. 1297, 1300-02 (E.D. Wash. 1993) (although ultimately applying § 7852(e)'s jurisdictional bar to dismiss Privacy Act claim, nevertheless recognizing applicability of subsection (e)(3) to IRS summons, and possibility "that a summons may be judicially enforceable yet not meet the disclosure requirements of the Privacy Act"). It has also been held that "[b]ecause the Privacy Act provides its own remedy for an agency's improper refusal to process a proper request for information, [a plaintiff] is not entitled to mandamus relief." Kotmair v. Netsch, No. 93-490, 1993 U.S. Dist. LEXIS 10781, at *5 (D. Md. July 21, 1993); cf. Graham v. Hawk, 857 F. Supp. 38, 41 (W.D. Tenn. 1994) ("[T]he existence of remedies under the Privacy Act [for alleged inaccuracy] preclude plaintiff's entitlement to mandamus, even though his claim under that act is substantively meritless."), aff'd, 59 F.3d 170 (6th Cir. 1995) (unpublished table decision).

In the context of civil remedies, the only court of appeals to consider the issue has held that the Privacy Act "does not limit the remedial rights of persons to pursue whatever remedies they may have under the [Federal Tort Claims Act]" for privacy violations consisting of record disclosures. O'Donnell v. United States, 891 F.2d 1079, 1084-85 (3d Cir. 1989); cf. Alexander v. FBI, 971 F. Supp. 603, 610-11 (D.D.C. 1997) (citing O'Donnell and holding that Privacy Act does not preempt causes of action under local or state law for common law invasion of privacy tort). But see Hager v. United States, No. 86-3555, slip op. at 7-8 (N.D. Ohio Oct. 20, 1987). However, several district courts have held that the Privacy Act's remedies do preclude an action against

PRIVACY ACT OVERVIEW

individual employees for damages under the Constitution in a "Bivens" suit. See, e.g., Downie v. City of Middleburg Heights, 76 F. Supp. 2d 794, 802-03 (N.D. Ohio 1999); Khalfani v. Secretary, Dep't of Veterans Affairs, No. 94-CV-5720, 1999 WL 138247, at *7 (E.D.N.Y. Mar. 10, 1999) (appeal pending); Fares v. INS, 29 F. Supp. 2d 259, 262 (W.D.N.C. 1998); Sullivan v. United States Postal Serv., 944 F. Supp. 191, 195-96 (W.D.N.Y. 1996); Hughley v. Federal Bureau of Prisons, No. 94-1048, slip op. at 5 (D.D.C. Apr. 30, 1996), aff'd sub nom. Hughley v. Hawks, No. 96-5159, 1997 WL 362725 (D.C. Cir. May 6, 1997); Blazy v. Woolsey, No. 93-2424, 1996 WL 43554, at *1 (D.D.C. Jan. 31, 1996), subsequent decision sub nom. Blazy v. Tenet, 979 F. Supp. 10, 27 (D.D.C. 1997), summary affirmance granted, No. 97-5330, 1998 WL 315583 (D.C. Cir. May 12, 1998); Williams v. VA, 879 F. Supp. 578, 585-87 (E.D. Va. 1995); Mangino v. Department of the Army, No. 94-2067, 1994 WL 477260, at *9 (D. Kan. Aug. 24, 1994); Mittleman v. United States Treasury, 773 F. Supp. 442, 454 (D.D.C. 1991); see also Patterson v. FBI, 705 F. Supp. 1033, 1045 n.16 (D.N.J. 1989) (to extent First Amendment claim involves damages resulting from maintenance of records, "such an action is apt to be foreclosed by the existence of the Privacy Act"), aff'd, 893 F.2d 595 (3d Cir. 1990). But see Doe v. United States Civil Serv. Comm'n, 483 F. Supp. 539, 564-75 (S.D.N.Y. 1980) (permitting Bivens claim, but relying on fact that plaintiff's claims related in part to events predating effective date of Privacy Act and, more significantly, so holding without benefit of subsequent Supreme Court precedent bearing on issue); see also Alexander, 971 F. Supp. at 610-11 (agreeing with outcome in Blazy and Mittleman, but concluding that their logic does not extend to prohibit recovery under local law for torts committed by individuals who, although government employees, were acting outside scope of their employment; holding that "Privacy Act does not preempt the common law invasion of privacy tort").

It also has been held that a court may order equitable relief in the form of the expungement of records either in an action under the Privacy Act or in a direct action under the Constitution. See, e.g., Doe v. United States Air Force, 812 F.2d 738, 741 (D.C. Cir. 1987); Smith v. Nixon, 807 F.2d 197, 204 (D.C. Cir. 1986); Hobson v. Wilson, 737 F.2d 1, 65-66 (D.C. Cir. 1984); Ezenwa v. Gallen, 906 F. Supp. 978, 986 (M.D. Pa. 1995); cf. Dickson v. OPM, 828 F.2d 32, 41 (D.C. Cir. 1987) (suggesting that it is not resolved "whether as a general proposition, the Privacy Act defines the scope of remedies available under the Constitution"). See also the discussion of expungement of records under "Amendment Lawsuits," below.

A. Amendment Lawsuits

"Whenever any agency . . . makes a determination under subsection (d)(3) . . . not to amend an individual's record in accordance with his request, or fails to make such review in conformity with that subsection [the individual may bring a civil action against the agency]." 5 U.S.C. § 552a(g)(1)(A).

-- Exhaustion of administrative remedies--through pursuit of an amendment request to the agency and a request for administrative review, see 5 U.S.C. § 552a(d)(2)-(3)--is a prerequisite to a civil action for amendment of records.

comment -- The exhaustion principle is well established in the case law. See, e.g., Jernigan v. Department of the Air Force, No. 97-35930, 1998 WL 658662, at *2 (9th Cir. Sept. 17, 1998); Quinn v. Stone, 978 F.2d 126, 137-38 (3d Cir. 1992); Hill v. United States Air Force, 795 F.2d 1067, 1069 (D.C. Cir. 1986) (per curiam); Nagel v. HEW, 725 F.2d 1438, 1441 (D.C. Cir.

1984); Blazy v. Tenet, 979 F. Supp. 10, 18-19 (D.D.C. 1997), summary affirmance granted, No. 97-5330, 1998 WL 315583 (D.C. Cir. May 12, 1998); Olivares v. NASA, 882 F. Supp. 1545, 1552 (D. Md. 1995), aff'd, 103 F.3d 119 (4th Cir. 1996) (unpublished table decision); Jerez v. United States Dep't of Justice, No. 94-100, slip op. at 8-9 (D. Ariz. Feb. 2, 1995); Hass v. United States Air Force, 848 F. Supp. 926, 930 (D. Kan. 1994); Gergick v. Austin, No. 89-0838-CV-W-2, 1992 U.S. Dist. LEXIS 7338, at **13-16 (W.D. Mo. Apr. 29, 1992), aff'd, No. 92-3210 (8th Cir. July 9, 1993); Simon v. United States Dep't of Justice, 752 F. Supp. 14, 23 & n.6 (D.D.C. 1990), aff'd, 980 F.2d 782 (D.C. Cir. 1992); Campbell v. United States Postal Serv., No. 86-3609, 1990 WL 36132, at *4 (E.D. La. Mar. 28, 1990); Green v. United States Postal Serv., No. 88-0539-CES, 1989 U.S. Dist. LEXIS 6846, at **7-8 (S.D.N.Y. June 19, 1989); Tracy v. Social Sec. Admin., No. 88-C-570-S, slip op. at 3-4 (W.D. Wis. Sept. 23, 1988); Ertell v. Department of the Army, 626 F. Supp. 903, 909-10 (C.D. Ill. 1986); Freude v. McSteen, No. 4-85-882, slip op. at 4-5 (D. Minn. Oct. 23, 1985), aff'd, 786 F.2d 1171 (8th Cir. 1986) (unpublished table decision); Beaver v. VA, No. 1-82-477, slip op. at 2 (E.D. Tenn. Apr. 6, 1983); Ross v. United States Postal Serv., 556 F. Supp. 729, 735 (N.D. Ala. 1983). One district court has even held that a plaintiff could not "boot-strap" an access claim under (g)(1)(B) into a (g)(1)(A) amendment violation, even though she argued that by denying her request for access the agency had prevented her from exercising her right to request amendment. See Smith v. Continental Assurance Co., No. 91 C 0963, 1991 WL 164348, at *2 (N.D. Ill. Aug. 22, 1991).

Although subsection (d)(2)(A) requires an agency to "acknowledge in writing such receipt" of an amendment request within ten working days, subsection (d)(2)(B) merely requires an agency to "promptly" make the requested correction or inform the individual of its refusal to amend. In construing this language, the Court of Appeals for the District of Columbia Circuit has held that "[t]he statute provides no exemption from administrative review when an agency fails, even by several months, to abide by a deadline, and none is reasonably implied." Dickson v. OPM, 828 F.2d 32, 40 (D.C. Cir. 1987) (requiring exhaustion of subsection (d)(3) administrative appeal remedy even when agency did not respond to initial amendment request for 90 days (citing Nagel, 725 F.2d at 1440-41)). But see Schaeuble v. Reno, 87 F. Supp. 2d 383, 389-90 (D.N.J. 2000) (not requiring further exhaustion of administrative remedies where plaintiff had requested amendment and agency had not responded for six months; stating that, "[a] six month delay is not a 'prompt' response" and "[m]oreover, not only has the [agency] not indicated that it will make a final determination . . . by any certain date, the Privacy Act does not bind the [agency] to any definite timeframe for administrative action, which weighs in favor of waiving the exhaustion requirement").

However, in contrast to subsection (d)(2)(B), subsection (d)(3) requires an agency to make a final determination on administrative appeal from an initial denial of an amendment request within 30 working days (unless, for good cause shown, the head of the agency extends this 30-day period). Thus, court jurisdiction exists as soon as an agency fails to comply with the time requirements of subsection (d)(3); "[t]o require further exhaustion would not only contradict the plain words of the statute but also would undercut [C]ongress's clear intent to provide speedy disposition of these claims." Diederich v. Department of the Army, 878 F.2d 646, 648 (2d Cir. 1989).

In Harper v. Kobelinski, 589 F.2d 721 (D.C. Cir. 1978) (per curiam), and Liguori v. Alexander, 495 F. Supp. 641 (S.D.N.Y. 1980), the agencies denied amendment requests but failed to inform the plaintiffs of their rights to administratively appeal those decisions. In light of the Act's requirement that agencies inform complainants whose amendment requests have been denied of the available administrative remedies, 5 U.S.C. § 552a(d)(2)(B)(ii), the courts in Harper and Liguori refused to penalize the plaintiffs for their failures to exhaust. Harper, 589 F.2d at 723; Liguori, 495 F. Supp. at 646-47; see also Germane v. Heckler, 804 F.2d 366, 369 (7th Cir. 1986) (discussing Harper and Liguori with approval); Mahar v. National Parks Serv., No. 86-0398, slip op. at 7-11 (D.D.C. Dec. 23, 1987) (same).

In White v. United States Civil Serv. Comm'n, 589 F.2d 713, 715-16 (D.C. Cir. 1978) (per curiam), the D.C. Circuit held that, notwithstanding any exhaustion of administrative remedies, an amendment action is "inappropriate and premature" where the individual had not yet sought judicial review (under the Administrative Procedure Act) of adverse employment decisions, because granting Privacy Act relief "would tend to undermine the established and proven method by which individuals . . . have obtained review from the courts." Cf. Douglas v. Farmers Home Admin., No. 91-1969, 1992 U.S. Dist. LEXIS 9159, at **4-5 (D.D.C. June 26, 1992) (damages action under Privacy Act dismissed where plaintiff had not sought review under Administrative Procedure Act of allegedly inaccurate property appraisal). But see Churchwell v. United States, 545 F.2d 59, 61 (8th Cir. 1976) (probationary employee need not pursue Privacy Act remedy prior to proceeding with due process claim for hearing).

-- Courts "shall determine the matter de novo." 5 U.S.C. § 552(g)(2)(A).

    comment -- "De novo review does not contemplate that the court will substitute its judgment for the [agency's], but rather that the court will undertake an independent determination of whether the amendment request should be denied." Nolan v. United States Dep't of Justice, No. 89-A-2035, 1991 WL 134803, at *3 (D. Colo. July 17, 1991), appeal dismissed in pertinent part on procedural grounds, 973 F.2d 843 (10th Cir. 1992); see also Doe v. United States, 821 F.2d 694, 697-98 (D.C. Cir. 1987) (holding that "[d]e novo means . . .a fresh, independent determination of 'the matter' at stake"). The applicable standards in amendment lawsuits are accuracy, relevancy, timeliness, and completeness. 5 U.S.C. § 552a(d)(2)(B)(i). But see Doe v. United States, 821 F.2d at 697 n.8, 699 (without explanation, stating that "whether the nature of the relief sought is injunctive or monetary, the standard against which the accuracy of the record is measured remains constant" and "[t]hat standard is found in 5 U.S.C. § 552a(e)(5) and reiterated in 5 U.S.C. § 552a(g)(1)(C)"). The burden of proof is on the individual. See Mervin v. FTC, 591 F.2d 821, 827 (D.C. Cir. 1978) (per curiam); Thompson v. Department of Transp. United States Coast Guard, 547 F. Supp. 274, 282 (S.D. Fla. 1982); OMB Guidelines, 40 Fed. Reg. 28,948, 28,969 (1975).

Note that in a unique statutory displacement action, Congress has expressly removed the jurisdiction of the district courts to order the amendment of IRS records concerning tax liability. 26 U.S.C. § 7852(e) (1994). See, e.g., Gogert v. IRS, No. 86-1674, slip op. at 3 (9th Cir. Apr. 7, 1987); England v. Commissioner, 798 F.2d 350, 351-52 (9th Cir. 1986); Singer v. IRS, No. 98-0024, 1998 U.S. Dist. LEXIS 13301, at **10-11 (E.D. Pa. Aug. 10, 1998); Chandler v. United States, No. 93-C-812A, 1994 WL 315759, at *1 (D. Utah Mar. 8, 1994); Fuselier v. IRS, No. 90-0300, slip op. at 1 (W.D. La. Oct. 25, 1990); Mallas v. Kolak, 721 F. Supp. 748, 751 (M.D.N.C. 1989); Schandl v. Heye, No. 86-6219, slip op. at 2 (S.D. Fla. Sept. 30, 1986); Dyrdra v. Commissioner, No. 85-0-41, slip op. at 2 (D. Neb. Oct. 28, 1985); Conklin v. United States, No. 83-C-587, slip op. at 2-3 (D. Colo. Feb. 26, 1985); Green v. IRS, 556 F. Supp. 79, 80 (N.D. Ill. 1982), aff'd, 734 F.2d 18 (7th Cir. 1984) (unpublished table decision); see also Gardner v. United States, No. 96-1467, 1999 U.S. Dist. LEXIS 2195, at *18 (D.D.C. Jan. 29, 1999) (finding that by virtue of § 7852(e) IRS is "exempt" from amendment provisions of Privacy Act), summary affirmance granted on other grounds, No. 99-5089, 1999 WL 728359 (D.C. Cir. Aug. 4, 1999).

Consistent with the OMB Guidelines, 40 Fed. Reg. at 28,958, 28,969, courts have routinely expressed disfavor toward litigants who attempt to invoke the subsection (g)(1)(A) amendment remedy as a basis for collateral attacks on judicial or quasi-judicial determinations recorded in agency records. See, e.g., Reinbold v. Evers, 187 F.3d 348, 361 (4th Cir. 1999) ("[T]he Privacy Act does not allow a court to alter records that accurately reflect an administrative decision, or the opinions behind that administrative decision."); Milhous v. EEOC, No. 97-5242, 1998 WL 152784, at *1 (6th Cir. Mar. 24, 1998) ("The Privacy Act may not be used to challenge unfavorable agency decisions. It is intended solely to be used to correct factual or historical errors."); Douglas v. Agricultural Stabilization & Conservation Serv., 33 F.3d 784, 785 (7th Cir. 1994) ("Privacy Act does not authorize relitigation of the substance of agency decisions"; "the right response . . . is to correct the disposition under the Administrative Procedure Act"); Bailey v. VA, No. 94-55092, 1994 WL 417423, at *1 (9th Cir. Aug. 10, 1994) (plaintiff may not use Privacy Act to collaterally attack grant or denial of benefits); Sugrue v. Derwinski, 26 F.3d 8, 11 (2d Cir. 1994) (Privacy Act may not be used "as a rhetorical cover to attack VA benefits determinations"); Edwards v. Rozzi, No. 92-3008, 1992 WL 133035, at *1 (6th Cir. June 12, 1992) ("[T]he Privacy Act may not be used to challenge unfavorable agency decisions."); Geurin v. Department of the Army, No. 90-16783, 1992 WL 2781, at *2 (9th Cir. Jan. 6, 1992) (doctrine of res judicata bars relitigation of claims under Privacy Act that had been decided against plaintiff by United States Claims Court in prior action under 28 U.S.C. § 1491); Pellerin v. VA, 790 F.2d 1553, 1555 (11th Cir. 1986) (amendment lawsuit challenging VA disability benefits determination dismissed on ground that 38 U.S.C. § 211(a) (later repealed, now see 38 U.S.C. § 511 (1994)) limits judicial review of VA's determinations; noting that Privacy Act "'may not be employed as a skeleton key for reopening consideration of unfavorable federal agency decisions'" (quoting Rogers v. United States Dep't of Labor, 607 F. Supp. 697, 699 (N.D. Cal. 1985))); Fields v. NRC, No. 98-1714, slip op. at 1-2, 5-7 (D.D.C. May 12, 1999) (stating that Privacy Act may not be used to collaterally attack NRC conclusion, as Act is not vehicle for amending judgments of federal officials); Gowan v. Department of the Air Force, No. 90-94, slip op. at 26, 33 (D.N.M. Sept. 1, 1995) (commenting that "Privacy Act, unfortunately, may not be used as a collateral attack on the improper preferral of charges [for court martial], nor may the Privacy Act be used as a method for the Court to oversee the activities of the armed services"), aff'd, 148 F.3d 1182 (10th Cir.), cert. denied, 525 U.S. 1042 (1998); Graham v. Hawk, 857 F. Supp. 38, 40-41 (W.D. Tenn. 1994) ("The Privacy Act is not a means of circumventing [habeas] exhaustion requirement."), aff'd, 59 F.3d 170 (6th Cir. 1995) (unpublished table decision); Williams v. McCausland, 90 Civ. 7563, 1994 WL 18510, at *17 (S.D.N.Y. Jan. 18, 1994) (MSPB properly denied plaintiff's request to supplement record of his administrative proceeding before MSPB because request "constitutes an attempt to contest the MSPB's determination on the merits of his request for a stay of his removal"); Smith v. VA, No. CV-93-B-2158-S, slip op. at 4-5 (N.D. Ala. Jan. 13, 1994) (following Pellerin and holding that plaintiff could not use Privacy Act to challenge dishonorable discharge or denial of VA disability benefits); Smith v. Continental Assurance Co., No. 91 C 0963, 1991 WL 164348, at *5 (N.D. Ill. Aug. 22, 1991) (plaintiff cannot use Privacy Act to collaterally attack agency decision regarding her Federal Employees Health Benefit Act claim); Rowan v. United States Postal Serv., No. 82-C-6550, 1984 U.S. Dist. LEXIS 17042, at *6 (N.D. Ill. May 2, 1984) (Privacy Act not "a means for all governmental employees to have unflattering appraisals removed from their personnel files or shaded according to their own whims or preferences"); Leib v. VA, 546 F. Supp. 758, 762 (D.D.C. 1982) ("The Privacy Act was not intended to be and should not be allowed to become a 'backdoor mechanism' to subvert the finality of agency determinations."); Lyon v. United States, 94 F.R.D. 69, 72 (W.D. Okla. 1982) (Privacy Act claim cannot be "a backdoor mechanism to subvert authority bestowed upon the Secretary of Labor to handle employee compensation claims"); Allen v. Henefin, 2 Gov't Disclosure Serv. (P-H) ¶ 81,056, at 81,147 (D.D.C. Dec. 10, 1980) (dismissing lawsuit seeking amendment of supervisor evaluation forms and comments, for failure to exhaust, but noting that "there is considerable doubt as to the permissibility of a Privacy Act suit to collaterally attack a final agency personnel determination of this type"); Weber v. Department of the Air Force, No. C-3-78-146, slip op. at 3-4 (S.D. Ohio Mar. 19, 1979) (Privacy Act not proper means "to arbitrate and determine a dispute over job classification"); Bashaw v. United States Dep't of the Treasury, 468 F. Supp. 1195, 1196-97 (E.D. Wis. 1979) (citing OMB Guidelines with approval and holding that amendment remedy is "neither a necessary nor an appropriate vehicle for resolving the merits of the plaintiff's [discrimination] claims"); Kennedy v. Andrus, 459 F. Supp. 240, 242 (D.D.C. 1978) (noting that OMB Guidelines "clearly forbid collateral attack in the case of final judicial or quasi-judicial actions" and observing that "the same considerations would seem to apply to agency personnel actions, such as the reprimand here, for collateral attack under the Privacy Act could undermine the effectiveness of agency grievance systems"), aff'd, 612 F.2d 586 (D.C. Cir. 1980) (unpublished table decision); cf. Doe v. HHS, 871 F. Supp. 808, 814-15 (E.D. Pa. 1994) ("[T]he specific reporting provisions encompassed in the [Health Care Quality Improvement] Act supersede[] any claims [plaintiff] might have under the Privacy Act."), aff'd, 66 F.3d 310 (3d Cir. 1995) (unpublished table decision).

It has even been held that the Civil Service Reform Act's (CSRA) comprehensive remedial scheme operates to deprive a court of subsection (g)(1)(A) jurisdiction to order the amendment of an allegedly inaccurate job description in a former federal employee's personnel file. See Kleiman v. Department of Energy, 956 F.2d 335, 338 (D.C. Cir. 1992) (refusing to allow

PRIVACY ACT OVERVIEW

exhaustive remedial scheme of CSRA to be "impermissibly frustrated" by granting review of personnel decisions under Privacy Act); see also Wills v. OPM, No. 93-2079, slip op. at 3-4 (4th Cir. Jan. 28, 1994) (alternative holding) (per curiam) (where challenge to merits of statement on SF-50 was actually complaint regarding adverse employment decision, jurisdiction was proper under CSRA); Vessella v. Department of the Air Force, No. 92-2195, 1993 WL 230172, at *2 (1st Cir. June 28, 1993) (citing Kleiman and holding that plaintiff could not "bypass the CSRA's regulatory scheme" by bringing Privacy Act claim for same alleged impermissible adverse personnel practices he challenged before MSPB, even though MSPB dismissed his claims as untimely).

Similarly, the D.C. Circuit has held that "[t]he proper means by which to seek a change to military records is through a proceeding before the . . . Board for Correction of Military Records," not under the Privacy Act. Glick v. Department of the Army, No. 91-5213, 1992 WL 168004, at *1 (D.C. Cir. June 5, 1992) (per curiam); see also Cargill v. Marsh, 902 F.2d 1006, 1007-08 (D.C. Cir. 1990) (per curiam) (affirming dismissal of Privacy Act claim; proper means to seek substantive change in military records is through proceeding before Army Board for Correction of Military Records under 10 U.S.C. § 1552(a) (1994)); Doe v. Department of the Navy, 764 F. Supp. 1324, 1327 (N.D. Ind. 1991) ("plaintiff is not free to choose to attempt amendment of his military records under the Privacy Act alone without resort to the records correction board remedy"); cf. Walker v. United States, No. 93-2728, 1998 WL 637360, at *14 (E.D. La. Sept. 16, 1998) (citing Cargill and finding plaintiff's claim "unavailing" to extent that he "is attempting to use the Privacy Act as a vehicle for his collateral attack on the Army's allegedly improper failure to correct his military records"), aff'd, 184 F.3d 816 (5th Cir. 1999) (unpublished table decision). But see Diederich v. Department of the Army, 878 F.2d 646, 647-48 (2d Cir. 1989) (holding that "Privacy Act claims were properly before the district court" and that plaintiff was not required to further exhaust administrative remedies before asserting claim for amendment of military records where his direct request to Army for correction had been stalled before appeals board for several months); see also Corrections of Military Records Under the Privacy Act, Defense Privacy Board Advisory Opinion 4 (reissued Apr. 8, 1992) (affording limited review under Privacy Act for factual matters).

It should be noted that several courts have ruled that statutes that provide other avenues of redress, such as the CSRA, can bar certain kinds of subsection (g)(1)(C) damages actions. These cases are discussed below under "Accuracy Lawsuits For Damages."

PRIVACY ACT OVERVIEW

- -- Courts can order an agency to amend records in accordance with a request "or in such other way as the court may direct." 5 U.S.C. § 552a(g)(2)(A).

    comment -- The Act contemplates "expungement [of inaccuracies] and not merely redress by supplement." R.R. v. Department of the Army, 482 F. Supp. 770, 774 (D.D.C. 1980); see also Smith v. Nixon, 807 F.2d 197, 204 (D.C. Cir. 1986); Hobson v. Wilson, 737 F.2d 1, 65-66 (D.C. Cir. 1984). In addition, several courts have concluded that judges have the equitable power, even apart from the Privacy Act, to order the expungement of records when the affected individual's privacy interest greatly outweighs the government's interest in maintaining the records. See, e.g., Doe v. United States Air Force, 812 F.2d 738, 740-41 (D.C. Cir. 1987); Fendler v. United States Parole Comm'n, 774 F.2d 975, 979 (9th Cir. 1985); Chastain v. Kelley, 510 F.2d 1232, 1235-38 (D.C. Cir. 1975); Ezenwa v. Gallen, 906 F. Supp. 978, 986 (M.D. Pa. 1995); NTEU v. IRS, 601 F. Supp. 1268, 1273 (D.D.C. 1985); cf. Johnson v. Sessions, No. 92-201, 1992 WL 212408, at *2 (D.D.C. Aug. 19, 1992) (refusing to invoke equitable powers to expunge plaintiff's arrest record because court did not have jurisdiction to order FBI to violate its own regulations which require FBI to wait for authorization from appropriate judicial authority before expunging arrest record). But see Scruggs v. United States, 929 F.2d 305, 307 (7th Cir. 1991) (questioning jurisdictional power of courts to order expungement of records that satisfy Privacy Act's requirements).

    Once an agency offers to destroy a record in response to an expungement request, the lawsuit is at an end and the agency cannot be compelled to affirmatively determine and announce that the challenged record violated the Act. See Reuber v. United States, 829 F.2d 133, 144-49 (D.C. Cir. 1987); see also Committee in Solidarity v. Sessions, 929 F.2d 742, 745 n.2 (D.C. Cir. 1991); Metadure Corp. v. United States, 490 F. Supp. 1368, 1375 (S.D.N.Y. 1980). But see Doe v. United States Civil Serv. Comm'n, 483 F. Supp. 539, 551 (S.D.N.Y. 1980).

B. Access Lawsuits

"Whenever any agency . . . refuses to comply with an individual request under subsection (d)(1) of this section [the individual may bring a civil action against the agency]." 5 U.S.C. § 552a(g)(1)(B).

- -- Courts can enjoin the agency from withholding records and order their production to the individual. See 5 U.S.C. § 552a(g)(3)(A).

    comment -- Just as under the FOIA, a requester must comply with agency procedures and exhaust all available administrative remedies--through pursuit of an access request to the agency--prior to bringing a subsection (g)(1)(B) action. See Taylor v. United States Treasury Dep't, 127 F.3d 470, 473-77 (5th Cir. 1997); Phillips v. Widnall, No. 96-2099, 1997 WL 176394, at *3

(10th Cir. Apr. 14, 1997); Fisher v. FBI, No. 3:99CV796, 2000 WL 502655, at *3 (D. Conn. Mar. 6, 2000); Haase v. Sessions, 893 F.2d 370, 373 (D.C. Cir. 1990); Biondo v. Department of the Navy, 928 F. Supp. 626, 630-33 (D.S.C. 1995), aff'd, 86 F.3d 1148 (4th Cir. 1996) (unpublished table decision); Reeves v. United States, No. 94-1291, 1994 WL 782235, at *2 (E.D. Cal. Nov. 16, 1994), aff'd, 108 F.3d 338 (9th Cir. 1997) (unpublished table decision); Guzman v. United States, No. S-93-1949, slip op. at 3-5 (E.D. Cal. Oct. 5, 1994); Hass v. United States Air Force, 848 F. Supp. 926, 930 (D. Kan. 1994); Gergick v. Austin, No. 89-0838-CV-W-2, 1992 U.S. Dist. LEXIS 7338, at **13-16 (W.D. Mo. Apr. 29, 1992), aff'd, No. 92-3210 (8th Cir. July 9, 1993); Wood v. IRS, No. 1:90-CV-2614, 1991 U.S. Dist. LEXIS 19707, at *8 (N.D. Ga. July 26, 1991); Searcy v. Social Sec. Admin., No. 91-C-26 J, slip op. at 8-11 (D. Utah June 25, 1991) (magistrate's recommendation), adopted (D. Utah Sept. 19, 1991), aff'd, No. 91-4181 (10th Cir. Mar. 2, 1992); Crooker v. Bureau of Prisons, 579 F. Supp. 309, 311 (D.D.C. 1984); Crooker v. United States Marshals Serv., 577 F. Supp. 1217, 1217-18 (D.D.C. 1983); Lilienthal v. Parks, 574 F. Supp. 14, 18 & n.7 (E.D. Ark. 1983); Gibbs v. Rauch, No. 77-59, slip op. at 2-3 (E.D. Ky. Feb. 9, 1978); Larsen v. Hoffman, 444 F. Supp. 245, 256 (D.D.C. 1977); cf. Walker v. Henderson, No. 98 C 3824, 1999 WL 39545, at *9 (N.D. Ill. Jan. 20, 1999) (finding request letters insufficient to comply with Postal Service regulations governing access to files covered by Privacy Act), appeal voluntarily dismissed, No. 99-1615 (7th Cir. May 27, 1999).

The Court of Appeals for the Fourth Circuit has also noted that an individual cannot "constructively exhaust" his administrative remedies under the Privacy Act, as "the Privacy Act contains no equivalent to FOIA's 'constructive exhaustion' provision[, 5 U.S.C. § 552(a)(6)(C)]." Pollack v. Department of Justice, 49 F.3d 115, 116 n.1 (4th Cir. 1995) (only FOIA claim was properly before district court); see also Anderson v. United States Postal Serv., 7 F. Supp. 2d 583, 586 n.3 (E.D. Pa. 1998) (citing Pollack for proposition that "Privacy Act contains no section equivalent to the 'constructive exhaustion' provision of the FOIA," but alternatively finding that access suit must be dismissed for failure to exhaust administrative remedies), aff'd, 187 F.3d 625 (3d Cir. 1999) (unpublished table decision); cf. Johnson v. FBI, No. 94-1741, slip op. at 6 (D.D.C. Aug. 31, 1995) (citing Pollack but determining that "since plaintiff has sought an action in equity, and has not exhausted his administrative remedies through administrative appeal . . . plaintiff is barred from seeking injunctive relief under the Privacy Act"). However, an agency's failure to comply with its own regulations can undercut an exhaustion defense. See Jonsson v. IRS, No. 90-2519, 1992 WL 115607, at *1 (D.D.C. May 4, 1992); Haldane v. Commissioner, No. 90-654M, 1990 U.S. Dist.

LEXIS 11612, at **4-6 (W.D. Wash. Aug. 23, 1990).

Several courts have recognized that jurisdiction to consider a Privacy Act access claim exists only if the government has failed to comply with a request for records; once a request is complied with and the responsive records have been disclosed, a Privacy Act access claim is moot. See Fisher v. FBI, No. 3:99CV796, 2000 WL 502655, at *3; Biondo, 928 F. Supp. at 631; Letscher v. IRS, No. 95-0077, 1995 WL 555476, at *1 (D.D.C. July 6, 1995); Polewsky v. Social Sec. Admin., No. 5:93-CV-200, slip op. at 9-10 (D. Vt. Mar. 31, 1995) (magistrate's recommendation), adopted (D. Vt. Apr. 13, 1995), aff'd, No. 95-6125, 1996 WL 110179, at *2 (2d Cir. Mar. 12, 1996); Smith v. Continental Assurance Co., No. 91 C 0963, 1991 WL 164348, at *3 (N.D. Ill. Aug. 22, 1991); see also Jacobs v. Reno, No. 3:97-CV-2698-D, 1999 U.S. Dist. LEXIS 3104, at **14-15 (N.D. Tex. Mar. 11, 1999) (dismissing access claim as moot where plaintiff had received access to records and finding no eligibility for award of attorney fees and costs based on plaintiff's assertion that his lawsuit may have caused agency to comply with Privacy Act when it would not otherwise have done so, "particularly when § 552a(d)(1) imposes no deadline for agency compliance and absent evidence of extended and unjustified delay"), aff'd, 208 F.3d 1006 (5th Cir. 2000) (unpublished table decision).

The Court of Appeals for the District of Columbia Circuit has ruled that "the specific provisions of [26 U.S.C.] § 6103 rather than the general provisions of the Privacy Act govern the disclosure of . . . tax information" and that "individuals seeking 'return information' . . . must do so pursuant to §6103 of the Internal Revenue Code, rather than the Privacy Act." Lake v. Rubin, 162 F.3d 113, 115-16 (D.C. Cir. 1998), cert. denied, 526 U.S. 1070 (1999). In reaching this conclusion, the D.C. Circuit looked to the legislative history of § 6103 and embraced an earlier ruling by the Court of Appeals for the Seventh Circuit, Cheek v. IRS, 703 F.2d 271 (7th Cir. 1983) (per curiam), that had similarly held that § 6103 "displaces" the Privacy Act and shields tax return information from release to a first-party requester, id. at 272; see also Paige v. IRS, No. 1P-85-64-C, slip op. at 3-4 (S.D. Ind. Jan. 13, 1986). Lake, 162 F.3d at 115-16. But cf. Sinicki v. United States Dep't of Treasury, No. 97 CIV. 0901, 1998 WL 80188, at **3-5 (S.D.N.Y. Feb. 24, 1998) (finding Cheek unpersuasive in context of wrongful disclosure claim and denying motion to dismiss Privacy Act claim, stating that "the language, structure, purpose and legislative history of Section 6103 do not make manifest and clear a legislative intent to repeal the Privacy Act as it applies to tax return information").

The Court of Appeals for the Ninth Circuit has confusingly interpreted 26 U.S.C. § 7852(e)

(1994) to likewise prevent Privacy Act access to records pertaining to tax liability. Jacques v. IRS, No. 91-15992, 1992 WL 185449, at *2 (9th Cir. Aug. 5, 1992); O'Connor v. United States, No. 89-15321, slip op. at 5 (9th Cir. June 4, 1991); see also Prince v. Commissioner, No. 98-17183, 1999 WL 511185, at *1 (9th Cir. July 15, 1999) (concluding that district court lacked subject matter jurisdiction over claim for attorney fees in Privacy Act suit for access to tax return records due to 26 U.S.C. § 7852(e)'s prohibition against application of subsection (g) of Privacy Act to determinations of tax liability); Weiss v. Sawyer, 28 F. Supp. 2d 1221, 1227-28 (W.D. Okla. 1997) (applying 26 U.S.C. § 7852 to prevent apparent access claim); cf. Baker v. Matson, No. 98 M 1675, 1998 U.S. Dist. LEXIS 21312, at **8-9 (D. Colo. Dec. 7, 1998) (ruling that court had no jurisdiction over Privacy Act access claim) (magistrate's recommendation), adopted (D. Colo. Jan. 12, 1999). The Ninth Circuit's interpretation of 26 U.S.C. § 7852(e), however, seems to go beyond that statute's objective of exempting determinations of tax liability from the Privacy Act's amendment provisions. Cf. Lake v. Rubin, 162 F.3d at 114-16 (discussing § 7852(e)--which had been interpreted by district court to deprive it of jurisdiction in access cases, see Maxwell v. Rubin, 3 F. Supp. 2d 45, 47-49 (D.D.C. 1998)--but affirming judgments of district court "not on the jurisdictional rationale contained in its opinions" but on basis of § 6103); Wood v. IRS, No. 1:90-CV-2614, 1991 U.S. Dist. LEXIS 19707, at *1, 8 (N.D. Ga. July 29, 1991) (denying plaintiff summary judgment on other grounds, but not barring Privacy Act request for access to records concerning plaintiff's tax liability).

Lastly, damages are not recoverable in an access case. See Benoist v. United States, No. 87-1028, slip op. at 3 (8th Cir. Nov. 4, 1987); Thurston v. United States, 810 F.2d 438, 447 (4th Cir. 1987); Haddon v. Freeh, 31 F. Supp. 2d 16, 22 (D.D.C. 1998); Vennes v. IRS, No. 5-88-36, slip op. at 6-7 (D. Minn. Oct. 14, 1988) (magistrate's recommendation), adopted (D. Minn. Feb. 14, 1989), aff'd, No. 89-5136MN (8th Cir. Oct. 13, 1989); Bentson v. Commissioner, No. 83-048-GLO-WDB, slip op. at 2 (D. Ariz. Sept. 14, 1984); see also Quinn v. HHS, 838 F. Supp. 70, 76 (W.D.N.Y. 1993) (citing Thurston in dictum).

-- Courts "shall determine the matter de novo." 5 U.S.C. § 552a(g)(3)(A).

-- Courts may review records in camera to determine whether any of the exemptions set forth in subsection (k) apply. See 5 U.S.C. § 552a(g)(3)(A).

## C. Accuracy Lawsuits for Damages

"Whenever any agency . . . fails to maintain any record concerning any individual with such accuracy, relevance, timeliness, and completeness as is necessary to assure fairness in any determination relating to the qualifications, character,

## PRIVACY ACT OVERVIEW

rights, or opportunities of, or benefits to the individual that may be made on the basis of such record, and consequently a determination is made which is adverse to the individual [the individual may bring a civil action against the agency]." 5 U.S.C. § 552a(g)(1)(C).

comment -- The standard of accuracy under this provision is the same as under subsection (e)(5), which requires agencies to maintain records used in making determinations about individuals "with such accuracy, relevance, timeliness, and completeness as is reasonably necessary to assure fairness to the individual in the determination."

As mentioned earlier, failure to comply with subsection (e)(5) gives rise to an amendment lawsuit under subsection (g)(1)(A), provided that administrative remedies (under subsections (d)(2)-(3)) have been exhausted. Note, however, that such exhaustion is not required prior to bringing a damages lawsuit under subsection (g)(1)(C) (or, for that matter, under subsection (g)(1)(D)). See Phillips v. Widnall, No. 96-2099, 1997 WL 176394, at **2-3 (10th Cir. Apr. 14, 1997); Diederich v. Department of the Army, 878 F.2d 646, 648 (2d Cir. 1989); Hubbard v. United States Envtl. Protection Agency, Adm'r, 809 F.2d 1, 7 (D.C. Cir.), vacated in nonpertinent part & reh'g en banc granted (due to conflict in circuit), 809 F.2d 1 (D.C. Cir. 1986), resolved on reh'g en banc sub nom. Spagnola v. Mathis, 859 F.2d 223 (D.C. Cir. 1988); Nagel v. HEW, 725 F.2d 1438, 1441 & n.2 (D.C. Cir. 1984); Gergick v. Austin, No. 89-0838-CV-W-2, 1992 U.S. Dist. LEXIS 7338, at **13-16 (W.D. Mo. Apr. 29, 1992), aff'd, No. 92-3210 (8th Cir. July 9, 1993); Doe v. FBI, No. 91-1252, slip op. at 8 (D.N.J. Feb. 26, 1992); Pope v. Bond, 641 F. Supp. 489, 500 (D.D.C. 1986). But see Olivares v. NASA, 882 F. Supp. 1545, 1546, 1552 (D. Md. 1995) (apparently confusingly concluding that plaintiff's failure to exhaust administrative remedies precludes damages claim under subsection (e)(5)), aff'd, 103 F.3d 119 (4th Cir. 1996) (unpublished table decision); Graham v. Hawk, 857 F. Supp. 38, 40 (W.D. Tenn. 1994) (heedlessly stating that "[e]ach paragraph of 5 U.S.C. § 552a(g) . . . requires as a prerequisite to any action that the agency refuse an individual's request to take some corrective action regarding his file"), aff'd, 59 F.3d 170 (6th Cir. 1995) (unpublished table decision).

In addition, de novo review is not provided for in (g)(1)(C) (or, for that matter, (g)(1)(D)) actions, see 5 U.S.C. § 552a(g)(4); rather, the court is to determine whether the standards articulated in subsection (g)(1)(C) have been met. See Sellers v. Bureau of Prisons, 959 F.2d 307, 312-13 (D.C. Cir. 1992); White v. OPM, 787 F.2d 660, 663 (D.C. Cir. 1986); Nolan v. United States Dep't of Justice, No. 89-A-2035, 1991 WL 134803, at *3 (D. Colo. July 17, 1991), appeal dismissed in pertinent part on procedural grounds, 973 F.2d 843 (10th Cir. 1992); see also Doe v. United States, 821 F.2d 694, 712 (D.C. Cir. 1987) (en banc) (Mikva, J., joined by Robinson and Edwards, JJ., dissenting.)

However, in order to bring a damages action under subsection (g)(1)(C), an individual has the burden of proving that (1) a defective record (2) proximately caused (3) an adverse determination concerning him. See, e.g., Deters v. United States Parole Comm'n, 85 F.3d 655, 657 (D.C. Cir. 1996); Rose v. United States, 905 F.2d 1257, 1259 (9th Cir. 1990); Johnston v. Horne, 875 F.2d 1415, 1422 (9th Cir. 1989); White v. OPM, 840 F.2d 85, 87 (D.C. Cir. 1988); Hubbard, 809 F.2d at 4-6; Hewitt v. Grabicki, 794 F.2d 1373, 1379 (9th Cir. 1986); Perry v. FBI, 759 F.2d 1271, 1275, rev'd en banc on other grounds, 781 F.2d 1294 (7th Cir. 1986); Molerio v. FBI, 749 F.2d 815, 826 (D.C. Cir. 1984); Clarkson v. IRS, 678 F.2d 1368, 1377 (11th Cir. 1982) (citing Edison v. Department of the Army, 672 F.2d 840, 845 (11th Cir. 1982)); Kellett v. United States, 856 F. Supp. 65, 70-71 (D.N.H. 1994), aff'd, 66 F.3d 306 (1st Cir. 1995) (unpublished table decision); McGregor v. Greer, 748 F. Supp. 881, 886 (D.D.C. 1990); Mobley v. Doyle, No. JH-87-3300, slip op. at 3-5 (D. Md. Nov. 8, 1988); Wirth v. Social Sec. Admin., No. JH-85-1060, slip op. at 6 (D. Md. Jan. 20, 1988); NTEU v. IRS, 601 F. Supp. 1268, 1271-72 (D.D.C. 1985); see also Gowan v. United States Dep't of the Air Force, 148 F.3d 1182, 1194 (10th Cir.) (no adverse effect from Air Force's informing Wyoming Bar of court martial charges preferred against plaintiff where plaintiff himself later informed Wyoming Bar without knowing Air Force had already done so), cert. denied, 525 U.S. 1042 (1998); Williams v. Bureau of Prisons, No. 94-5098, 1994 WL 676801, at *1 (D.C. Cir. Oct. 21, 1994) (appellant did not establish either that agency "maintained an inaccurate record or that it made a determination adverse to him in reliance on inaccurate information capable of verification, the statutory prerequisites to maintaining an action pursuant to the Privacy Act"); Hadley v. Moon, No. 94-1212, 1994 WL 582907, at **1-2 (10th Cir. Oct. 21, 1994) (plaintiff must allege actual detriment or adverse determination in order to maintain claim under Privacy Act); Hughley v. Federal Bureau of Prisons, No. 94-1048, slip op. at 4-5 (D.D.C. Apr. 30, 1996) (admitted inaccuracy in plaintiff's presentence investigation report regarding length of prior sentence did not result in "any cognizable injury that would give rise to an action under Section (g)(1)(C) because no adverse determination was made based on the inaccurate statement"; report correctly calculated plaintiff's criminal history points regardless of error), aff'd sub nom. Hughley v. Hawk, No. 96-5159, 1997 WL 362725 (D.C. Cir. May 6, 1997); Schwartz v. United States Dep't of Justice, No. 94 CIV. 7476, 1995 WL 675462, at **7-8 (S.D.N.Y. Nov. 14, 1995) (alleged inaccuracy in presentence report "cannot have caused an adverse determination" where sentencing judge was made aware of error and stated that fact at issue was not material for sentencing, nor did any omission of additional facts in report result in plaintiff's "not receiving a fair determination relating to his rights"), aff'd, 101 F.3d 686 (2d Cir. 1996) (unpublished table decision); Gowan v. Department of the Air Force, No. 90-94, slip op. at 34 (D.N.M. Sept. 1, 1995) (inaccuracy in report, i.e., listing of witnesses who were not interviewed, did not cause adverse agency action), aff'd, 148 F.3d 1182 (10th Cir.), cert. denied, 525 U.S. 1042 (1998). In addition, an agency must be found to have acted in an "intentional or willful" manner in order for a damages action to succeed. See 5 U.S.C. § 552a(g)(4). This standard is discussed below under "Intentional/Willful Standard and Actual Damages in Accuracy and Other Damages Lawsuits."

Just as in the amendment context (see the discussion above), many courts have expressed disfavor toward litigants who attempt to invoke the subsection (g)(1)(C) damages remedy as a basis for collateral attacks on judicial and quasi-judicial agency determinations, such as benefit and employment decisions. See, e.g., White v. United States Probation Office, 148 F.3d 1124, 1125-26 (D.C. Cir. 1998) (holding that Privacy Act claim for damages could not be brought "collaterally to attack" federal prisoner's sentence; "Because a judgment in favor of [plaintiff] on his challenge to the legal conclusions in his presentence report would necessarily imply the invalidity of his sentence, which has not been invalidated in a prior proceeding, his complaint for damages under the Privacy Act must be dismissed."); Compro-Tax v. IRS, No. H-98-2471, 1999 U.S. Dist. LEXIS 5972, at **11-12 (S.D. Tex. Apr. 9, 1999) (magistrate's recommendation) (finding no intentional or willful agency action and stating that the "Privacy Act may not be used to collaterally attack a final agency decision as 'inaccurate,' or 'incomplete' merely because the individual contests the decision"), adopted (S.D. Tex. May 12, 1999); Douglas v. Farmers Home Admin., No. 91-1969, 1992 U.S. Dist. LEXIS 9159, at **2-3 (D.D.C. June 26, 1992) (applying principles of White v. United States Civil Serv. Comm'n, 589 F.2d 713 (D.C. Cir. 1978) (per curiam) (amendment lawsuit), and holding that plaintiff not entitled to bring Privacy Act damages action for allegedly inaccurate appraisal of his property where he had not sought judicial review under APA); Thomas v. United States Parole Comm'n, No. 94-0174, 1994 WL 487139, at *6 (D.D.C. Sept. 7, 1994) (plaintiff should not be allowed to use Privacy Act "to collaterally attack the contents of his presentence report," as he "originally had the opportunity to challenge the accuracy . . . before the judge who sentenced him"); Castella v. Long, 701 F. Supp. 578, 584-85 (N.D. Tex.) ("collateral attack on correctness of the finding supporting the discharge decision" improper under Act), aff'd, 862 F.2d 872 (5th Cir. 1988) (unpublished table decision); Holmberg v. United States, No. 85-2052, slip op. at 2-3 (D.D.C. Dec. 10, 1985) (Privacy Act "cannot be used to attack the outcome of adjudicatory-type proceedings by alleging that the underlying record was erroneous"); see also Whitley v. Hunt, 158 F.3d 882, 889-90 (5th Cir. 1998) (affirming district court's conclusion that there was "no factual or legal basis" for claim that "prison officials abused their discretion by relying upon the sentence imposed against Whitley to determine his classification"; "Whitley is essentially claiming that his sentence itself was incorrectly entered. That is an issue that should have been resolved on direct appeal from his criminal conviction."); Hurley v. Bureau of Prisons, No. 95-1696, 1995 U.S. App. LEXIS 30148, at *4 (1st Cir. Oct. 24, 1995) (any alleged inaccuracy in plaintiff's presentence report, which agency relied on, "should have been brought to the attention of the district court at sentencing; or, at the very least, on appeal from his conviction and sentence"). The OMB Guidelines, 40 Fed. Reg. 28,948, 28,969 (1975), also address this issue.

As in the amendment context, 26 U.S.C. § 7852(e) (1994) (a provision of the Internal Revenue Code) also displaces the Privacy Act's damages remedy for inaccurate records in matters concerning tax liability. See, e.g., Ford v. United States, IRS, No. 91-36319, 1992 WL 387154, at *2 (9th Cir. Dec. 24, 1992); McMillen v. United States Dep't of Treasury, 960 F.2d 187, 188 (1st Cir. 1991); Sherwood v. United States, No. 96-2223, 1996 WL 732512, at *9 (N.D. Cal. Dec. 9, 1996).

In Hubbard v. United States Envtl. Protection Agency, Adm'r, the leading D.C. Circuit case concerning the causation requirement of subsection (g)(1)(C), the D.C. Circuit's finding of a lack of causation was heavily influenced by the Civil Service Reform Act's (CSRA) jurisdictional bar to district court review of government personnel practices. See 809 F.2d at 5. Although the D.C. Circuit stopped short of holding that the CSRA's comprehensive remedial scheme constitutes a jurisdictional bar to a subsection (g)(1)(C) action, it noted that "it would be anomalous to construe the pre-existing Privacy Act to grant the district court power to do indirectly that which Congress precluded directly: 'the Privacy Act was not intended to shield [federal] employees from the vicissitudes of federal personnel management decisions.'" Id. (quoting Albright v. United States, 732 F.2d 181, 190 (D.C. Cir. 1984)); cf. Biondo v. Department of the Navy, No. 2:92-0184-18, slip op. at 21-23 (D.S.C. June 29, 1993) (finding, based upon Hubbard, "that the 'collateral attack' argument complements the causation requirement of the Privacy Act"). The concurring opinion in Hubbard objected to this "canon of niggardliness" in construing subsection (g)(1)(C) and noted that circuit precedents since the passage of the CSRA have "without a hint of the majority's caution, reviewed the Privacy Act claims of federal employees or applicants embroiled in personnel disputes." 809 F.2d at 12-13 (Wald, J., concurring) (citing Molerio, 749 F.2d at 826, Albright, 732 F.2d at 188, and Borrell v. United States Int'l Communications Agency, 682 F.2d 981, 992-93 (D.C. Cir. 1982)).

Although Hubbard merely applied a strict causation test where a government personnel determination was being challenged, several more recent cases have extended Hubbard's reasoning and have construed the CSRA's comprehensive remedial scheme to constitute a jurisdictional bar to subsection (g)(1)(C) damages lawsuits challenging federal employment determinations. See Houlihan v. OPM, 909 F.2d 383, 384-85 (9th Cir. 1990) (per curiam); Henderson v. Social Sec. Admin., 908 F.2d 559,

560-61 (10th Cir. 1990), aff'g 716 F. Supp. 15, 16-17 (D. Kan. 1989)); Miller v. Hart, No. PB-C-91-249, slip op. at 6-8 (E.D. Ark. Feb. 25, 1993); Kassel v. VA, No. 87-217-S, slip op. at 7-8 (D.N.H. Mar. 30, 1992); Holly v. HHS, No. 89-0137, slip op. at 1 (D.D.C. Aug. 9, 1991), aff'd, 968 F.2d 92 (D.C. Cir. 1992) (unpublished table decision); Barhorst v. Marsh, 765 F. Supp. 995, 999 (E.D. Mo. 1991); Barkley v. United States Postal Serv., 745 F. Supp. 892, 893-94 (W.D.N.Y. 1990); McDowell v. Cheney, 718 F. Supp. 1531, 1543 (M.D. Ga. 1989); Holly v. HHS, No. 87-3205, slip op. at 4-6 (D.D.C. Aug. 22, 1988), aff'd, 895 F.2d 809 (D.C. Cir. 1990) (unpublished table decision); Tuesburg v. HUD, 652 F. Supp. 1044, 1049 (E.D. Mo. 1987); see also Phillips v. Widnall, No. 96-2099, 1997 WL 176394, at *3 (10th Cir. Apr. 14, 1997) (citing Henderson to hold that claim concerning alleged inaccuracies and omissions in appellant's employment file that formed basis of her claim for damages to remedy loss of promotion and other benefits of employment "is not a recognizable claim under the Privacy Act," as "CSRA provides the exclusive remedial scheme for review of [appellant's] claims related to her position as a nonappropriated fund instrumentality employee"); Vessella v. Department of the Air Force, No. 92-2195, 1993 WL 230172, at *2 (1st Cir. June 28, 1993) (citing Hubbard and Henderson for proposition that Privacy Act "cannot be used . . . to frustrate the exclusive, comprehensive scheme provided by the CSRA"); Pippinger v. Secretary of the United States Treasury, No. 95-CV-017, 1996 U.S. Dist. LEXIS 5485, at *15 (D. Wyo. Apr. 10, 1996) (citing Henderson and stating that to extent plaintiff challenges accuracy of his personnel records, action cannot be maintained because court does not have jurisdiction "to review errors in judgment that occur during the course of an employment/personnel decision where the CSRA precludes such review"), aff'd sub nom. Pippinger v. Rubin, 129 F.3d 519 (10th Cir. 1997); Edwards v. Baker, No. 83-2642, slip op. at 4-6 (D.D.C. July 16, 1986) (Privacy Act challenge to "employee performance appraisal system" rejected on ground that "plaintiffs may not use that Act as an alternative route for obtaining judicial review of alleged violations of the CSRA"). Other cases have declined to go that far. See Doe v. FBI, 718 F. Supp. 90, 100-01 n.14 (D.D.C. 1989) (rejecting contention that CSRA limited subsection (g)(1)(C) action), aff'd in part, reversed in part & remanded, on other grounds, 936 F.2d 1346 (D.C. Cir. 1991); see also Halus v. United States Dep't of the Army, No. 87-4133, 1990 WL 121507, at *5 n.8 (E.D. Pa. Aug. 15, 1990) ("court may determine whether a Privacy Act violation caused the plaintiff damage (here, the loss of his job)"); Hay v. Secretary of the Army, 739 F. Supp. 609, 612-13 (S.D. Ga. 1990) (similar).

As yet, the D.C. Circuit has declined to rule that the CSRA bars a Privacy Act claim for damages. See Kleiman v. Department of Energy, 956 F.2d 335, 337-39 & n.5 (D.C. Cir. 1992) (holding that Privacy Act does not afford relief where plaintiff did not contest that record accurately reflected his assigned job title, but rather challenged his position classification--a personnel decision judicially unreviewable under the CSRA--but noting that nothing in opinion "should be taken to cast doubt on Hubbard's statement that 'the Privacy Act permits a federal job applicant to recover damages for an adverse personnel action actually caused by an inaccurate or incomplete record'" (quoting Hubbard, 809 F.2d at 5)); Holly v. HHS, No. 88-5372, 1990 WL 13096, at *1 (D.C. Cir. Feb. 7, 1990) (declining to decide whether CSRA in all events precludes Privacy Act claim challenging federal employment determination; instead applying doctrine of "issue preclusion" to bar individual "from relitigating an agency's maintenance of challenged records where an arbitrator--in a negotiated grievance proceeding that included review of such records--had previously found that no "[agency] manager acted arbitrarily, capriciously or unreasonably in determining [that plaintiff] was not qualified"). But see Holly v. HHS, No. 89-0137, slip op. at 1 (D.D.C. Aug. 9, 1991) (citing Kleiman for proposition that court lacks subject matter jurisdiction in Privacy Act damages action in which plaintiff challenges a personnel action governed by CSRA), aff'd, 968 F.2d 92 (D.C. Cir. 1992) (unpublished table decision).

In Rosen v. Walters, 719 F.2d 1422, 1424-25 (9th Cir. 1983), the Court of Appeals for the Ninth Circuit held that 38 U.S.C. § 211(a) (later repealed, now see 38 U.S.C. § 511 (1994))--a statute that broadly precludes judicial review of VA disability benefit decisions--operated to bar a subsection (g)(1)(C) damages action. In Rosen, the plaintiff contended that the VA deliberately destroyed medical records pertinent to his disability claim, thereby preventing him from presenting all the evidence in his favor. Id. at 1424. The Ninth Circuit ruled that such a damages claim would "necessarily run counter to the purposes of § 211(a)" because it would require a determination as to whether "but for the missing records, Rosen should have been awarded disability benefits." Id. at 1425. Further, it declined to find that the Privacy Act "repealed by implication" 38 U.S.C. § 211(a). Id.; see also R.R. v. Department of the Army, 482 F. Supp. 770, 775-76 (D.D.C. 1980) (rejecting damages claim for lack of causation and noting that "[w]hat plaintiff apparently seeks to accomplish is to circumvent the statutory provisions making the VA's determinations of benefits final and not subject to judicial review"); cf. Kaswan v. VA, No. 81-3805, 1988 WL 98334, at *12 (E.D.N.Y. Sept. 15, 1988) (Privacy Act "not available to collaterally attack factual and legal decisions to grant or deny veterans benefits"), aff'd, 875 F.2d 856 (2d Cir. 1989) (unpublished table decision); Leib v. VA, 546 F. Supp. 758, 761-62 (D.D.C. 1982) ("The Privacy Act was not intended to be and should not be allowed to become a 'backdoor mechanism' to subvert the finality of agency determinations." (quoting Lyon v. United States, 94 F.R.D. 69, 72 (W.D. Okla. 1982))). Relying on Rosen, the District Court for the District of Idaho similarly held that the statutory scheme regarding the awarding of retirement benefits and "Congress's intent that OPM, MSPB and the Federal Circuit review decisions regarding the denial of disability retirement benefits" prohibited it from reviewing a Privacy Act damages claim where the plaintiff alleged that the VA's failure to maintain a file resulted in his being denied disability retirement benefits by OPM. Braun v. Brown, No. CV 97-0063-S, slip op. at 7-11 (D. Idaho June 22, 1998).

In Perry v. FBI, 759 F.2d at 1275, the Court of Appeals for the Seventh Circuit, without discussing subsection (g)(1)(C), adopted a comparatively narrower construction of subsection (e)(5), holding that "when one federal agency sends records to another agency to be used by the latter in making a decision about someone, the responsibility for ensuring that the information is accurate, relevant, timely, and complete lies with the receiving agency--the agency making 'the determination' about the person in question--not the sending agency."

Subsequently, though, in Dickson v. OPM, 828 F.2d 32, 36-40 (D.C. Cir. 1987), the D.C. Circuit held that a subsection (g)(1)(C) damages lawsuit is proper against any agency maintaining a record violating the standard of fairness mandated by the Act, regardless of whether that agency is the one making the adverse determination. See also Blazy v. Tenet, 979 F. Supp. 10, 19 (D.D.C. 1997) ("The adverse determination need not be made by the agency that actually maintains the record so long as it flowed from the inaccurate record." (citing Dickson)), summary affirmance granted, No. 97-5330, 1998 WL 315583 (D.C. Cir. May 12, 1998); Doe v. United States Civil Serv. Comm'n, 483 F. Supp. 539, 556 (S.D.N.Y. 1980) (applying subsection (e)(5) to agency whose records were used by another agency in making determination about individual); R.R. v. Department of the Army, 482 F. Supp. at 773 (same). In so holding, the D.C. Circuit noted that "the structure of the Act makes it abundantly clear that [sub]section (g) civil remedy actions operate independently of the obligations imposed on agency recordkeeping pursuant to [sub]section (e)(5)." Dickson, 828 F.2d at 38. In Dickson, the D.C. Circuit distinguished Perry on the grounds that "[a]ppellant is not proceeding under [sub]section (e)(5), Perry does not discuss [sub]section (g)(1)(C), and the construction of (e)(5) does not migrate by logic or statutory mandate to a separate [sub]section on civil remedies." 828 F.2d at 38; see also Doe v. FBI, 718 F. Supp. at 95 n.15 (noting conflict in cases but finding that Dickson's holding obviated need "to enter that thicket").

Assuming that causation is proven, "actual damages" sustained by the individual as a result of the failure--or $1000, whichever is greater--are recoverable. See 5 U.S.C. § 552a(g)(4)(A). The meaning of "actual damages" and the $1000 minimum recovery provision are discussed below under "Intentional/Willful Standard and Actual Damages in Accuracy and Other Damages Lawsuits."

PRIVACY ACT OVERVIEW

D.  Other Damages Lawsuits

"Whenever any agency . . . fails to comply with any other provision of this section, or any rule promulgated thereunder, in such a way as to have an adverse effect on an individual [the individual may bring a civil action]." 5 U.S.C. § 552a(g)(1)(D).

comment -- A complaint is subject to dismissal, for failure to state a subsection (g)(1)(D) damages claim, if no "adverse effect" is alleged. See, e.g., Quinn v. Stone, 978 F.2d 126, 135 (3d Cir. 1992) ("[T]he adverse effect requirement of (g)(1)(D) is, in effect, a standing requirement."); Doe v. Herman, No. 2:97CV00043, 1999 U.S. Dist. LEXIS 17302, at *38 (W.D. Va. Oct. 29, 1999) (magistrate's recommendation); Hass v. United States Air Force, 848 F. Supp. 926, 932 (D. Kan. 1994); Swenson v. United States Postal Serv., No. S-87-1282, 1994 U.S. Dist. LEXIS 16524, at *30 (E.D. Cal. Mar. 10, 1994); Green v. United States Postal Serv., No. 88-0539, 1989 U.S. Dist. LEXIS 6846, at **6-8 (S.D.N.Y. June 19, 1989); Tracy v. Social Sec. Admin., No. 88-C-570-S, slip op. at 4-5 (W.D. Wis. Sept. 23, 1988); Bryant v. Department of the Air Force, No. 85-4096, slip op. at 5 (D.D.C. Mar. 31, 1986); Harper v. United States, 423 F. Supp. 192, 196-97 (D.S.C. 1976); see also Crichton v. Community Servs. Admin., 567 F. Supp. 322, 324 (S.D.N.Y. 1983) (mere maintenance of allegedly "secret file" insufficient to warrant damages where no showing of adverse effect); Church v. United States, 2 Gov't Disclosure Serv. (P-H) ¶ 81,350, at 81,911 (D. Md. Jan. 5, 1981) (no adverse effect from failure to provide subsection (e)(3) notice).

An "adverse effect" includes not only monetary damages, but also nonpecuniary and nonphysical harm, such as mental distress, embarrassment, or emotional trauma. See Quinn, 978 F.2d at 135-36; Albright v. United States, 732 F.2d 181, 186 (D.C. Cir. 1984); Usher v. Secretary of HHS, 721 F.2d 854, 856 (1st Cir. 1983); Parks v. IRS, 618 F.2d 677, 682-83 & n.2 (10th Cir. 1980); Doe v. Herman, No. 2:97CV00043, 1999 U.S. Dist. LEXIS 17302, at *38; Romero-Vargas v. Shalala, 907 F. Supp. 1128, 1134 (N.D. Ohio 1995); see also Englerius v. VA, 837 F.2d 895, 897 (9th Cir. 1988).

For a novel interpretation of "adverse effect," see Bagwell v. Brannon, No. 82-8711, slip op. at 5-6 (11th Cir. Feb. 22, 1984), in which the Court of Appeals for the Eleventh Circuit found that no "adverse effect" was caused by the government's disclosure of an employee's personnel file (during cross-examination) while defending against the employee's tort lawsuit, because the "employee created the risk that pertinent but embarrassing aspects of his work record would be publicized" and "disclosure was consistent with the purpose for which the information was originally collected."

The threshold showing of "adverse effect," which typically is not difficult for a plaintiff to satisfy, should carefully be distinguished from

-777-

the conceptually separate requirement of "actual damages," discussed below.

A showing of causation--that the violation caused an adverse effect, and that the violation caused "actual damages," as discussed below--is also required. See, e.g., Quinn, 978 F.2d at 135; Hewitt v. Grabicki, 794 F.2d 1373, 1379 (9th Cir. 1986); Albright, 732 F.2d at 186-87; Edison v. Department of the Army, 672 F.2d 840, 842, 845 (11th Cir. 1982); Harmer v. Perry, No. 95-4197, 1998 WL 229637, at *3 (E.D. Pa. Apr. 28, 1998), aff'd, No. 98-1532 (3d Cir. Jan. 29, 1999); Swenson, No. S-87-1282, 1994 U.S. Dist. LEXIS 16524, at *30 (E.D. Cal. Mar. 10, 1994); Connelly v. Comptroller of the Currency, No. H-84-3783, slip op. at 4 (S.D. Tex. June 3, 1991); Rodgers v. Department of the Army, 676 F. Supp. 858, 862 (N.D. Ill. 1988); Tuesburg v. HUD, 652 F. Supp. 1044, 1048 (E.D. Mo. 1987); Ely v. Department of Justice, 610 F. Supp. 942, 946 (N.D. Ill. 1985), aff'd, 792 F.2d 142 (7th Cir. 1986) (unpublished table decision). But see Rickles v. Marsh, No. 3:88-100, slip op. at 8-9 (N.D. Ga. Jan. 10, 1990) (aberrational decision awarding minimum damages even in absence of causation).

In addition, an agency must be found to have acted in an "intentional or willful" manner in order for a damages action to succeed. See 5 U.S.C. § 552a(g)(4). This standard is discussed below under "Intentional/Willful Standard and Actual Damages in Accuracy and Other Damages Lawsuits."

Several district courts have held that various sections of the Internal Revenue Code prevent their exercise of subject matter jurisdiction over Privacy Act claims brought under subsection (g)(1)(D). See Gardner v. United States, No. 96-1467, 1999 U.S. Dist. LEXIS 2195, at **14-17 (D.D.C. Jan. 29, 1999) (discussing Sinicki, infra, but ruling that 26 U.S.C. § 6103 "is the exclusive remedy for alleged wrongful disclosures of returns and return information"), summary affirmance granted on other grounds, No. 99-5089, 1999 WL 728359 (D.C. Cir. Aug. 4, 1999); Berridge v. Heiser, 993 F. Supp. 1136, 1144-45 (S.D. Ohio 1997) (holding that 26 U.S.C. § 7431(a)(1), which provides mechanism for award of civil damages for unauthorized disclosure of tax return information (as defined in 26 U.S.C. § 6103), is "exclusive remedy by which [plaintiff] may bring a cause of action for improper disclosure of return information," and that 26 U.S.C. § 7852(e) prevented it from exercising jurisdiction over plaintiff's Privacy Act claims under subsections (e)(2), (5), and (6) related to tax liability); Government Nat'l Mortgage, Ass'n v. Lunsford, No. 95-273, 1996 U.S. Dist. LEXIS 1591, at *8 (E.D. Ky. Feb. 2, 1996) (dismissing Privacy Act claim for wrongful disclosure (presumably brought under (g)(1)(D)) and stating that "26 U.S.C. § 7852(e) precludes the maintenance of Privacy Act damages remedies in matters concerning federal tax liabilities"); Estate of Myers v. United States, 842 F. Supp. 1297, 1302-04 (E.D. Wash. 1993) (dismissing Privacy Act (g)(1)(D) damages claim and applying § 7852(e)'s jurisdictional bar to preclude Privacy

Act applicability to determination of foreign tax liability); cf. Smilde v. Richardson, Commissioner, No. 97-568, 1997 U.S. Dist. LEXIS 15050, at **6-7 (D. Minn. Aug. 28, 1997) (relying on limitation of Privacy Act applicability pursuant to sections 6103 and 7852(e) and finding that "Privacy Act does not support subject matter jurisdiction" to enjoin IRS from contracting out processing of tax returns), aff'd per curiam, 141 F.3d 1170 (8th Cir. 1998) (unpublished table decision); Trimble v. United States, No. 92-74219, 1993 WL 288295, at *1 (E.D. Mich. May 18, 1993) (citing 26 U.S.C. § 7852(e) for Privacy Act's inapplicability and dismissing unspecified Privacy Act claim), aff'd, 28 F.3d 1214 (6th Cir. 1994) (unpublished table decision).

The Court of Appeals for the Fifth Circuit has held that "[26 U.S.C.] § 6103 is a more detailed statute that should preempt the more general remedies of the Privacy Act, at least where . . . those remedies are in conflict." Hobbs v. United States, 209 F.3d 408, 412 (5th Cir. 2000) (finding § 6103 and Privacy Act to be "in conflict" where disclosure fell within one of exceptions in § 6103 and holding that "[t]o the extent that the Privacy Act would recognize a cause of action for unauthorized disclosure of tax return information even where § 6103 would provide an exception for the particular disclosure, § 6103 trumps the Privacy Act").

Nevertheless, one district court has specifically considered the issue and arrived at the conclusion that the Privacy Act's remedies are available for the wrongful disclosure of tax return information, see Sinicki v. United States Dep't of Treasury, No. 97 CIV. 0901, 1998 WL 80188, at **3-5 (S.D.N.Y. Feb. 24, 1998) (denying motion to dismiss Privacy Act wrongful disclosure claim and stating that "the language, structure, purpose and legislative history of Section 6103 do not make manifest and clear a legislative intent to repeal the Privacy Act as it applies to tax return information"). In addition, at least two courts of appeals, as well as the United States Tax Court, have readily applied the Privacy Act as well as the provisions of the tax code to disclosures of tax return information, see Scrimgeour v. Internal Revenue, 149 F.3d 318, 325-26 (4th Cir. 1998); Taylor v. United States, 106 F.3d 833, 835-37 (8th Cir. 1997); Stone v. Commissioner, No. 3812-97, 1998 WL 547043 (T.C. Aug. 31, 1998).

E. **Intentional/Willful Standard and Actual Damages in Accuracy and Other Damages Lawsuits**

"In any suit brought under the provisions of subsection (g)(1)(C) or (D) of this section in which the court determines that the agency acted in a manner which was intentional or willful, the United States shall be liable to the individual in an amount equal to the sum of . . . actual damages sustained by the individual as a result of the refusal or failure, but in no case shall a person entitled to recovery receive less than the sum of $1,000." 5 U.S.C. § 552a(g)(4).

comment -- In order for there to be any liability in a

(g)(1)(C) or (D) damages lawsuit, the agency must have acted in an "intentional or willful" manner. 5 U.S.C. § 552a(g)(4). It is important to understand that the words "intentional" and "willful" in subsection (g)(4) do not have their vernacular meanings; instead, they are "terms of art." White v. OPM, 840 F.2d 85, 87 (D.C. Cir. 1988) (per curiam). The Act's legislative history indicates that this unique standard is "[o]n a continuum between negligence and the very high standard of willful, arbitrary, or capricious conduct," and that it "is viewed as only somewhat greater than gross negligence." 120 Cong. Rec. 40,406 (1974), reprinted in Source Book at 862.

While not requiring premeditated malice, see Parks v. IRS, 618 F.2d 677, 683 (10th Cir. 1980), the voluminous case law construing this standard makes clear that it is a formidable barrier for a plaintiff seeking damages. See, e.g., Scrimgeour v. Internal Revenue, 149 F.3d 318, 326 (4th Cir. 1998) (plaintiff did not "demonstrate the higher standard of culpability required for recovery under the Privacy Act" where court had already determined that IRS's release of his tax returns did not meet lower standard of gross negligence for recovery under provision of Internal Revenue Code); Deters v. United States Parole Comm'n, 85 F.3d 655, 660 (D.C. Cir. 1996) (Parole Commission did not "'flagrantly disregard'" plaintiff's privacy when it supplemented his file with rebuttal quantity of drugs attributed to him in presentence investigation report (PSI) and offered inmate hearing concerning accuracy of disputed report and "[e]ven if the Commission inadvertently or negligently violated [plaintiff's] Privacy Act rights by not examining the accuracy of the PSI before preparing a preliminary assessment . . . such a violation (if any) could in no sense be deemed 'patently egregious and unlawful'" (quoting Albright and Laningham, infra)); Bailey v. Clay, No. 95-7533, 1996 WL 155160, at *1 (4th Cir. Mar. 29, 1996) (stating that because appellant had alleged mere negligence, he had not stated claim under Privacy Act); Nathanson v. FDIC, No. 95-1604, 1996 U.S. App. LEXIS 3111, at **3-6 (1st Cir. Feb. 22, 1996) (per curiam) (although declining to affirm district court opinion on basis that disclosure pursuant to routine use was proper given that published agency commentary conflicted with such routine use, nevertheless affirming on grounds that disclosure was not intentional and willful because routine use "afforded reasonable grounds for belie[f] that [agency employee's] conduct was lawful"); Kellett v. United States Bureau of Prisons, No. 94-1898, 1995 U.S. App. LEXIS 26746, at **8-10 (1st Cir. Sept. 18, 1995) (per curiam) (standard requires "showing that the agency acted without grounds for believing its action to be lawful, or in 'flagrant disregard' for rights under the Act" (quoting Wilborn v. HHS, infra)); Rose v. United States, 905 F.2d 1257, 1260 (9th Cir. 1990) ("conduct amounting to more than gross negligence" is required); Johnston v. Horne, 875 F.2d 1415, 1422-23 (9th Cir. 1989) (same); Scullion v. VA, No. 87-2405, slip op. at 4-8 (7th Cir. June 22, 1988) (no damages where agency relied upon apparently valid and unrevoked written con-

PRIVACY ACT OVERVIEW

sent to disclose records); <u>Andrews v. VA</u>, 838 F.2d 418, 424-25 (10th Cir. 1988) (standard "clearly requires conduct amounting to more than gross negligence" and that "must amount to, at the very least, reckless behavior"); <u>Reuber v. United States</u>, 829 F.2d 133, 144 (D.C. Cir. 1987) (standard not met as no evidence showed maintenance of record "was anything other than a good-faith effort to preserve an unsolicited and possibly useful piece of information"); <u>Laningham v. United States Navy</u>, 813 F.2d 1236, 1242-43 (D.C. Cir. 1987) (per curiam) (violation must be so "'patently egregious and unlawful'" that anyone undertaking the conduct "'should have known it unlawful'" (quoting <u>Wisdom v. HUD, infra</u>)); <u>Hill v. United States Air Force</u>, 795 F.2d 1067, 1070 (D.C. Cir. 1986) (per curiam) (no damages where no evidence of conduct greater than gross negligence); <u>Moskiewicz v. USDA</u>, 791 F.2d 561, 564 (7th Cir. 1986) (noting that "elements of recklessness often have been a key characteristic incorporated into a definition of willful and intentional conduct" (citing <u>Sorenson v. United States</u>, 521 F.2d 325 (9th Cir. 1975); <u>South v. FBI</u>, 508 F. Supp. 1104 (N.D. Ill. 1981))); <u>Dowd v. IRS</u>, 776 F.2d 1083, 1084 (2d Cir. 1985) (per curiam) ("mere administrative error" in negligently destroying files not a predicate for liability); <u>Chapman v. NASA</u>, 736 F.2d 238, 242-43 (5th Cir. 1984) (per curiam) (standard not met where agency "reasonably could have thought" untimely filing of evaluations was proper; "before our previous opinion 'timely' had no precise legal meaning in this circuit"); <u>Albright v. United States</u>, 732 F.2d 181, 189-90 (D.C. Cir. 1984) (standard requires that agency "act without grounds for believing it to be lawful, or by flagrantly disregarding others' rights under the Act"); <u>Wisdom v. HUD</u>, 713 F.2d 422, 424-25 (8th Cir. 1983) (good faith release of loan default records pursuant to unchallenged "Handbook" not willful violation of Act); <u>Perry v. Block</u>, 684 F.2d 121, 129 (D.C. Cir. 1982) (delayed disclosure of documents through administrative oversight not intentional or willful); <u>Edison v. Department of the Army</u>, 672 F.2d 840, 846 (11th Cir. 1982) (failure to prove agency acted "unreasonably" in maintaining records precludes finding intentional or willful conduct); <u>Bruce v. United States</u>, 621 F.2d 914, 917 (8th Cir. 1980) (standard not met where agency relied on regulations permitting disclosure of records pursuant to subpoena, as there were "at that time no regulations or other authority to the contrary"); <u>Mallory v. DOD</u>, No. 97-2377, slip op. at 9-14 (D.D.C. Sept. 30, 1999) (although DOD disclosure of record of plaintiff's rifle purchase to corporation was unlawful, intentional and willful standard was not met because statute gave DOD officials grounds to believe that transfer of such records was implicitly required by statute); <u>Wesley v. Don Stein Buick, Inc.</u>, 985 F. Supp. 1288, 1305-06 (D. Kan. 1997) (standard not met where, although disclosure was "unlawful," employee acted with belief that disclosure was proper, and it would have been proper if procedures set forth in routine use had been followed); <u>Armstrong v. United States Bureau of Prisons</u>, 976 F. Supp. 17, 22 (D.D.C. 1997) (standard not met where Bureau of Prisons refused to amend prison records to incorporate favorable information from inmate's prior incarceration in accordance with Bureau of Prisons guidelines), summary affirmance granted sub nom. Armstrong v. Federal Bureau of Prisons, No. 97-5208, 1998 WL 65543 (D.C. Cir. Jan. 30, 1998); Porter v. United States Postal Serv., No. CV595-30, slip op. at 10, 13, 21-22 (S.D. Ga. July 24, 1997) (concluding that Postal Service acted with "mere negligence" when it disclosed letter from plaintiff's attorney written as response to plaintiff's proposed termination to two union officials with belief that they had "a right and duty to know the disciplinary affairs of a fellow postal worker" even though plaintiff had not filed a grievance through union and "had specifically instructed the management that he did not want anyone from the [union] representing his interests"), aff'd, 166 F.3d 352 (11th Cir. 1998) (unpublished table decision); Harris v. USDA, No. 3:92CV-283-H, slip op. at 1-2, 4-5 (W.D. Ky. May 14, 1996) (standard not met where agency acted pursuant to Correspondence Management Handbook in maintaining supporting documentation for plaintiff's 1975 suspension), aff'd, 124 F.3d 197 (6th Cir. 1997) (unpublished table decision); Purrier v. HHS, No. 95-CV-6203, slip op. at 6-7 (W.D.N.Y. Mar. 15, 1996) ("given [defendant's] knowledge that she was subject to a grand jury subpoena," disclosure of limited information "even if [it] did violate the Act (which, with respect to plaintiff at least, [it] did not), fell far short of the kind of flagrant disregard of plaintiff's rights that is required"); Smith v. United States Bureau of Prisons, No. 94-1798, 1996 WL 43556, at *2 (D.D.C. Jan. 31, 1996) (standard not met where adverse determination had been rectified; fact that certain forms were corrected immediately, even though another form may not have been, "indicates that BOP officials did not intend to maintain plaintiff[']s records incorrectly"); Henson v. Brown, No. 95-213, slip op. at 5-7 (D. Md. June 23, 1995) (disclosure of medical records in response to subpoena signed by judge to attorney for plaintiff's ex-wife, rather than to court, did not "constitute an extreme departure from the standard of ordinary care"); Baitey v. VA, No. 8:CV89-706, slip op. at 8 (D. Neb. June 21, 1995) (standard not met where plaintiff failed to prove that VA acted in "flagrant or reckless disregard of [plaintiff's] rights under the Privacy Act" when it disclosed his medical records in response to incomplete and unsigned medical authorization); Olivares v. NASA, 882 F. Supp. 1545, 1549-50 (D. Md. 1995) (NASA's actions in contacting educational institutions to verify and correct discrepancies in plaintiff's record, even assuming initial consent to contact those institutions was limited, were not even negligent and do not "come close" to meeting standard), aff'd, 103 F.3d 119 (4th Cir. 1996) (unpublished table decision); Webb v. Magaw, 880 F. Supp. 20, 25 (D.D.C. 1995) (stating that even if court had found Privacy Act violation, agency conduct "at worst . . . would only amount to negligence . . . and would not amount to willful, intentional or even reckless disregard"); Sterling v. United States, 826 F. Supp. 570, 572 (D.D.C. 1993) (standard not met where agency's "efforts both before and after the release of

PRIVACY ACT OVERVIEW

information . . . indicate a sensitivity to the potential harm the release might cause and represent attempts to avert that harm"), summary affirmance granted, No. 93-5264 (D.C. Cir. Mar. 11, 1994); Dickson v. OPM, No. 83-3503, 1991 WL 423968, at **16-17 (D.D.C. Aug. 27, 1991) ("mere negligence" due to failure to follow internal guidelines not enough to show willfulness), summary affirmance granted, No. 91-5363 (D.C. Cir. Aug. 31, 1992); Stephens v. TVA, 754 F. Supp. 579, 582 (E.D. Tenn. 1990) (no damages where "some authority" existed for proposition that retrieval not initially and directly from system of records was not a "disclosure," and agency attempted to sanitize disclosed records); Brumley v. United States Dep't of Labor, No. 87-2220, 1990 WL 640002, at **2-3 (D.D.C. Dec. 5, 1990) (no damages for delayed response to amendment request); Alexander v. IRS, No. 86-0414, 1987 WL 13958, at *6 (D.D.C. June 30, 1987) (standard not met where agency relied on OMB Guidelines and internal manual in interviewing third parties prior to contacting plaintiff); Blanton v. United States Dep't of Justice, No. 82-0452, slip op. at 6-8 (D.D.C. Feb. 17, 1984) (unauthorized "leak" of record not intentional or willful agency conduct); Krohn v. United States Dep't of Justice, No. 78-1536, slip op. at 3-7 (D.D.C. Nov. 29, 1984) (standard not met where agency relied in good faith on previously unchallenged routine use to publicly file records with court); Daniels v. St. Louis VA Reg'l Office, 561 F. Supp. 250, 252 (E.D. Mo. 1983) (mere delay in disclosure due in part to plaintiff's failure to pay fees not intentional or willful); Doe v. GSA, 544 F. Supp. 530, 541-42 (D. Md. 1982) (disclosure not "wholly unreasonable" where "some kind of consent" given for release of psychiatric records and where agency employees believed that release was authorized under GSA's interpretation of its own guidelines, even though court concluded that such interpretation was erroneous).

While some district court decisions have found "intentional or willful" violations of the statute, see, e.g., Doe v. Herman, No. 2:97CV00043, 1999 U.S. Dist. LEXIS at **44-46 (W.D. Va. Oct. 29, 1999) (magistrate's recommendation); Stewart v. FBI, No. 97-1595, slip op. at 5-8 (D. Or. Mar. 12, 1999); Tomasello v. Rubin, No. 93-1326, slip op. at 17-19 (D.D.C. Aug. 19, 1997), aff'd on other grounds, 167 F.3d 612 (D.C. Cir. 1999); Porter, No. CV595-30, slip op. at 22-23 (S.D. Ga. July 24, 1997); Romero-Vargas v. Shalala, 907 F. Supp. 1128, 1133-34 (N.D. Ohio 1995); Swenson v. United States Postal Serv., No. S-87-1282, 1994 U.S. Dist. LEXIS 16524, at **33-45 (E.D. Cal. Mar. 10, 1994); Connelly v. Comptroller of the Currency, No. H-84-3783, slip op. at 25-27 (S.D. Tex. June 3, 1991); MacDonald v. VA, No. 87-544-CIV-T-15A, slip op. at 4, 7 (M.D. Fla. July 28, 1989); Fitzpatrick v. IRS, 1 Gov't Disclosure Serv. (P-H) ¶ 80,232, at 80,580 (N.D. Ga. Aug. 22, 1980), aff'd in part, vacated & remanded in part, on other grounds, 655 F.2d 327 (11th Cir. 1982); see also Louis v. VA, No. C95-5606, slip op. at 4-5 (W.D. Wash. Oct. 31, 1996) (awarding damages where agency conduct amounted to "reckless disregard" of

-783-

plaintiff's rights), as yet the only court of appeals to have found "intentional or willful" violations of the statute is the Court of Appeals for the Ninth Circuit, see Wilborn v. HHS, 49 F.3d 597, 602-03 (9th Cir. 1995); Covert v. Harrington, 876 F.2d 751, 756-57 (9th Cir. 1989).

In Wilborn, the plaintiff, an attorney who previously had been employed by the Department of Health and Human Services, sought damages under the Privacy Act for the disclosure of adverse personnel information about him that was disclosed in an opinion by an Administrative Law Judge before whom he had presented a case. 49 F.3d at 599-602. The court ruled that the "uncontroverted facts plainly establish that the ALJ disclosed the information . . . without any ground for believing it to be lawful and in flagrant disregard of the rights of Wilborn under the Privacy Act." Id. at 602. The Ninth Circuit noted that not only was the ALJ personally familiar with the Privacy Act and had advised his staff concerning the Act's disclosure prohibition, but further, that the ALJ had been informed by an agency attorney that the language at issue was "inappropriate and should not be included in the decision." Id. Particularly troubling in this case is the additional fact that all information pertaining to the adverse personnel record was required to, and in fact had been, removed from the system of records by the ALJ as a result of a grievance action filed by the plaintiff. Id.

In Covert, the Ninth Circuit ruled that the Department of Energy Inspector General's routine use disclosure of prosecutive reports, showing possible criminal fraud, to the Justice Department violated subsection (e)(3)(C) because, at the time of their original collection by another component of the agency, portions of those reports--consisting of personnel security questionnaires submitted by the plaintiffs--did not provide actual notice of the routine use. 876 F.2d 751, 754-57 (9th Cir. 1989). The Ninth Circuit held that the failure to comply with subsection (e)(3)(C) was "greater than grossly negligent" even though the Inspector General was relying on statutes, regulations and disclosure practices that appeared to permit disclosure, and no prior court had ever suggested that noncompliance with subsection (e)(3)(C) would render a subsequent subsection (b)(3) routine use disclosure improper. See id. Though it paid lip service to the correct standard, the Ninth Circuit in Covert actually applied a strict liability standard--one based upon the government's failure to anticipate its novel "linkage" between subsection (e)(3)(C) and subsection (b)(3)--a standard which markedly departs from settled precedent. Compare Covert, 876 F.2d at 756-57, with Chapman, 736 F.2d at 243, Wisdom, 713 F.2d at 424-25, and Bruce, 621 F.2d at 917. See also Doe v. Stephens, 851 F.2d 1457, 1462 (D.C. Cir. 1988) ("We cannot, in short, fairly predicate negligence liability on the basis of the VA's failure to predict the precise statutory interpretation that led this court in [Doe v. DiGenova, 779 F.2d 74, 79-85 (D.C. Cir. 1985)] to reject the agency's reliance on the [law indicating that a subpoena constituted a subsection (b)(11) court order].").

The Court of Appeals for the Third Circuit has held that the Privacy Act--with its stringent "greater than gross negligence" standard for liability--does not indicate a congressional intent to limit an individual's right under state law to recover damages caused by the merely <u>negligent</u> disclosure of a psychiatric report. See O'Donnell v. United States, 891 F.2d 1079, 1083-87 (3d Cir. 1989) (Federal Tort Claims Act case). But see Hager v. United States, No. 86-3555, slip op. at 7-8 (N.D. Ohio Oct. 20, 1987) (Privacy Act preempts FTCA action alleging wrongful disclosure); cf. Doe v. DiGenova, 642 F. Supp. 624, 629-30, 632 (D.D.C. 1986) (holding state law/FTCA claim preempted by Veterans' Records Statute, 38 U.S.C. §§ 3301-3302 (renumbered as 38 U.S.C. §§ 5701-5702 (1994))), <u>aff'd in pertinent part, rev'd in part & remanded sub nom.</u> Doe v. Stephens, 851 F.2d 1457 (D.C. Cir. 1988).

Assuming that a Privacy Act plaintiff can show: (1) a violation; (2) an adverse effect; (3) causation; and (4) intentional or willful agency conduct, then "actual damages sustained by the [plaintiff are recoverable] but in no case shall a person [who is] entitled to recovery receive less than the sum of $1,000." 5 U.S.C. § 552a(g)(4)(A).

The Court of Appeals for the District of Columbia Circuit recently ruled that a plaintiff was not entitled to $1000 for each copy of a letter that was disclosed in violation of the Privacy Act to 4500 individuals. See Tomasello v. Rubin, 167 F.3d 612, 617-18 (D.C. Cir. 1999). The D.C. Circuit stated that "[w]hile it may be linguistically possible to read the language [of § 552a(g)(4)] so as to forbid the aggregation of several more-or-less contemporaneous transmissions of the same record into one 'act[]' or 'failure [to comply with the Privacy Act],' the result [sought in this case] shows that such a reading defies common sense." Id. at 618. In reaching its determination "that each letter disclosure was not independently compensable," the D.C. Circuit also reasoned that as a waiver of sovereign immunity, subsection (g)(4) "'must be construed strictly in favor of the sovereign, and not enlarge[d] . . . beyond what the language requires.'" Id. (quoting United States v. Nordic Village, Inc., 503 U.S. 30, 34 (1992)).

The issue of what kinds of damages are recoverable under subsection (g)(4)(A) has engendered some confusing case law. The OMB Guidelines state that "[a]ctual damages <u>or</u> $1,000, whichever is greater," are/is recoverable. OMB Guidelines, 40 Fed. Reg. 28,948, 28,970 (1975) (emphasis added). Consistent with OMB's guidance, several courts have held that the statutory minimum damages amount of $1000 is recoverable for "proven injuries"--even in the absence of out-of-pocket expenses (pecuniary loss). See Fitzpatrick v. IRS, 665 F.2d 327-31 (11th Cir. 1982); Leverette v. Federal Law Enforcement Training Ctr., No. CV

280-136, slip op. at 2-5 (S.D. Ga. July 6, 1982); see also Doe v. Herman, No. 2:97CV00043, 1999 U.S. Dist. LEXIS 17302, at **49-52 (W.D. Va. Oct. 29, 1999) (magistrate's recommendation) (although "persuaded that a plaintiff should be able to recover the statutory damages . . . upon a showing that he has suffered emotional distress," interpreting the damages provision to "requir[e] a plaintiff to both plead and prove damages before being entitled to any recovery, including the statutory damages provided").

Two courts have seemed to take this even further by seemingly not requiring "proven injuries." See Wilborn, 49 F.3d at 603 (no need to remand to district court for determination of amount of damages because Wilborn had limited damages sought to statutory minimum of $1000 (citing Fitzpatrick)); Romero-Vargas, 907 F. Supp. at 1134 (stating that "emotional distress caused by the fact that the plaintiff's privacy has been violated is itself an adverse effect, and . . . statutory damages can be awarded without an independent showing of adverse effects"), motion to alter or amend denied, id. at 1135 (although defendant argued that court had made an error of law in awarding plaintiffs statutory damages in absence of specific findings of mental distress, finding that plaintiffs did present adequate evidence that they were adversely affected by disclosures); cf. Fitzpatrick, 665 F.2d at 330 (although confronted with a case in which appellant had "proved . . . that he suffered a general mental injury," stating that "$1,000 damage floor" was added as additional element of recovery "[t]o avoid a situation in which persons suffering injury had no provable damages and hence no incentive to sue"); Porter, No. CV595-30, slip op. at 15, 25 (S.D. Ga. July 24, 1997) (finding that because plaintiff had proven intentional and willful violation of his Privacy Act rights, he was entitled to recover statutory minimum of $1000 even though he had suffered no pecuniary loss and court did not discuss any nonpecuniary loss).

However, a few courts have held that even recovery of the statutory minimum damages amount of $1000 requires proof of "actual damages"--which, according to these courts, consist only of out-of-pocket expenses. See DiMura v. FBI, 823 F. Supp. 45, 48 (D. Mass. 1993); Nutter v. VA, No. 84-2392, slip op. at 6 n.2 (D.D.C. July 9, 1986); Houston v. United States Dep't of the Treasury, 494 F. Supp. 24, 30 (D.D.C. 1979); see also Mobley v. Doyle, No. JH-87-3300, slip op. at 6 (D. Md. Nov. 8, 1988) (congressional "intention to limit 'actual damages' to 'out of pocket' expenses"); Pope v. Bond, 641 F. Supp. 489, 500-01 (D.D.C. 1986) (plaintiff's recovery limited to "out-of-pocket" expenses).

With respect to damages beyond the $1000 level, "actual damages" must be proven. Although it is settled that actual damages include out-of-pocket expenses, there is a split of authority as to whether nonpecuniary damages for physical and mental injury--such as emotional trauma, anger, fear, or fright--are recoverable. Compare Johnson v. Department of the Treasury, IRS, 700 F.2d 971,

974-80 (5th Cir. 1983) (nonpecuniary damages recoverable), Parks, 618 F.2d at 682-83, 685 (stating that plaintiffs had "alleged viable claims for damages" where only alleged adverse effect was "psychological harm"), Dong v. Smithsonian Inst., 943 F. Supp. 69, 74-75 (D.D.C. Oct. 31, 1996) (following Johnson and awarding damages for injury to reputation), rev'd on grounds of statutory inapplicability, 125 F.3d 877 (D.C. Cir. 1997) (ruling that "Smithsonian is not an agency for Privacy Act purposes"), cert. denied, 524 U.S. 922 (1998); Louis, No. C95-5606, slip op. at 5 (W.D. Wash. Oct. 31, 1996) (awarding damages for "emotional suffering"), Swenson, No. S-87-1282, 1994 U.S. Dist. LEXIS 16524, at **46-52 (E.D. Cal. Mar. 10, 1994) (following Johnson), and Kassel v. VA, No. 87-217-S, slip op. at 38 (D.N.H. Mar. 30, 1992) (same), with Hudson v. Reno, 130 F.3d 1193, 1207 (6th Cir. 1997) (citing plaintiff's failure to show "actual damages" as additional basis for affirming district court decision and stating that "the weight of authority suggests that actual damages under the Privacy Act do not include recovery for 'mental injuries, loss of reputation, embarrassment or other non-quantifiable injuries'" (citing Fitzpatrick, Pope, and DiMura)), cert. denied, 525 U.S. 822 (1998); Fitzpatrick, 665 F.2d at 329-31 (damages for generalized mental injuries, loss of reputation, embarrassment or other nonquantifiable injuries not recoverable), Mallory v. DOD, No. 97-2377, slip op. at 15-16 n.3 (D.D.C. Sept. 30, 1999) (holding that actual damages limited to out-of-pocket losses); Gowan v. Department of the Air Force, No. 90-94, slip op. at 31 (D.N.M. Sept. 1, 1995) (adopting analysis of DiMura that emotional damages would not be recoverable), aff'd, 148 F.3d 1182 (10th Cir.), cert. denied, 525 U.S. 1042 (1998); DiMura, 823 F. Supp. at 47-48 ("'actual damages' does not include emotional damages"), Pope, 641 F. Supp. at 500-01 (only out-of-pocket expenses recoverable), and Houston, 494 F. Supp. at 30 (same).

The Court of Appeals for the District of Columbia Circuit has not expressly ruled on this issue. In Albright v. United States, 558 F. Supp. 260, 264 (D.D.C. 1982), the district court, citing Houston with approval, held that only out-of-pocket expenses--not damages for emotional trauma, anger, fright, or fear--are recoverable. On appeal, however, the D.C. Circuit affirmed on other grounds, expressly declining to decide whether "actual damages" include more than out-of-pocket expenses. Albright, 732 F.2d at 183, 185-86 & n.11; cf. Tomasello, 167 F.3d at 614, 618 n.6, 619 n.9 (declining to decide whether nonpecuniary damages were available under Privacy Act, given plaintiff's failure to raise issue below). In the absence of direction from the D.C. Circuit, the District Court for the District of Columbia on at least three other occasions has ruled that damages are limited to out-of-pocket expenses, see Mallory, No. 97-2377, slip op. at 15-16 n.3; Pope, 641 F. Supp. at 500-01; Houston, 494 F. Supp. at 30; and on one other occasion has awarded damages for nonpecuniary loss, see Dong, 943 F. Supp. at 74-75.

## PRIVACY ACT OVERVIEW

It is well settled that injunctive relief is available only under subsections (g)(1)(A) (amendment) and (g)(1)(B) (access)--both of which, incidentally, require exhaustion--and that it is not available under subsections (g)(1)(C) or (g)(1)(D). See, e.g., Locklear v. Holland, No. 98-6407, 1999 WL 1000835, at *1 (6th Cir. Oct. 28, 1999); Risley v. Hawk, 108 F.3d 1396, 1397 (D.C. Cir. 1997) (per curiam); Doe v. Stephens, 851 F.2d at 1463; Hastings v. Judicial Conference of the United States, 770 F.2d 1093, 1104 (D.C. Cir. 1985); Edison, 672 F.2d at 846; Hanley v. United States Dep't of Justice, 623 F.2d 1138, 1139 (6th Cir. 1980) (per curiam); Parks, 618 F.2d at 684; Cell Assocs. v. NIH, 579 F.2d 1155, 1161-62 (9th Cir. 1978); Purrier, No. 95-CV-6203, slip op. at 5 (W.D.N.Y. Mar. 15, 1996); AFGE v. HUD, 924 F. Supp. 225, 228 n.7 (D.D.C. 1996), rev'd on other grounds, 118 F.3d 786 (D.C. Cir. 1997); Robinson v. VA, No. 89-1156-B(M), slip op. at 2 (S.D. Cal. Dec. 14, 1989); Houston, 494 F. Supp. at 29; see also Word v. United States, 604 F.2d 1127, 1130 (8th Cir. 1979) (no "exclusionary rule" for subsection (b) violations; "No need and no authority exists to design or grant a remedy exceeding that established in the statutory scheme."); Shields v. Shetler, 682 F. Supp. 1172, 1176 (D. Colo. 1988) (Act "does not create a private right of action to enjoin agency disclosures"); 120 Cong. Rec. 40,406 (1974), reprinted in Source Book at 862. But see Florida Med. Ass'n v. HEW, 479 F. Supp. 1291, 1299 & n.8 (M.D. Fla. 1979) (aberrational decision construing subsection (g)(1)(D) to confer jurisdiction to enjoin agency's disclosure of Privacy Act-protected record).

There should be no reason for regarding this settled law as inapplicable where a subsection (e)(7) claim is involved. See Wabun-Inini v. Sessions, 900 F.2d 1234, 1245 (8th Cir. 1990); Clarkson v. IRS, 678 F.2d 1368, 1375 n.11 (11th Cir. 1982); Committee in Solidarity v. Sessions, 738 F. Supp. 544, 548 (D.D.C. 1990), aff'd, 929 F.2d 742 (D.C. Cir. 1991); see also Socialist Workers Party v. Attorney Gen., 642 F. Supp. 1357, 1431 (S.D.N.Y. 1986) (in absence of exhaustion, only damages remedy, rather than injunctive relief, is available for violation of subsection (e)(7)). In Haase v. Sessions, 893 F.2d 370, 373-75 (D.C. Cir. 1990), however, the D.C. Circuit, in dictum, suggested that its decision in Nagel v. HEW, 725 F.2d 1438, 1441 (D.C. Cir. 1984), could be read to recognize the availability of injunctive relief to remedy a subsection (e)(7) violation, under subsection (g)(1)(D); cf. Becker v. IRS, 34 F.3d 398, 409 (7th Cir. 1994) (finding that IRS had not justified maintenance of documents under subsection (e)(7) and stating that thus "the documents should be expunged"). Such a view is somewhat difficult to reconcile with the structure of subsection (g) and with the case law mentioned above.

There is a split of authority on the issue of whether destruction of a Privacy Act record gives rise to a damages action. Compare Tufts v. Department of the Air Force, 793 F.2d 259, 261-62 (10th Cir. 1986) (no), with Rosen v. Walters, 719 F.2d 1422, 1424 (9th Cir. 1983) (assuming action

PRIVACY ACT OVERVIEW

exists), and Waldrop v. United States Dep't of the Air Force, 3 Gov't Disclosure Serv. (P-H) ¶ 83,016, at 83,453 (S.D. Ill. Aug. 5, 1981) (yes); see also Dowd v. IRS, 776 F.2d 1083, 1084 (2d Cir. 1985) (per curiam) (expressly declining to decide issue).

## F. Principles Applicable to All Privacy Act Civil Actions

### 1. Attorney Fees and Costs

In amendment lawsuits brought under subsection (g)(1)(A), and access lawsuits brought under subsection (g)(1)(B), attorney fees and costs that are "reasonably incurred" are recoverable, in the court's discretion, if the plaintiff "has substantially prevailed." 5 U.S.C. § 552a(g)(2)(B) (amendment), (g)(3)(B) (access).

In damages lawsuits brought under subsection (g)(1)(C) or subsection (g)(1)(D), "the costs of the action together with reasonable attorney fees as determined by the court" are recoverable by the prevailing plaintiff. 5 U.S.C. § 552a(g)(4)(B). Such an award is not discretionary. See OMB Guidelines, 40 Fed. Reg. 28,948, 28,970 (1975).

comment -- The Privacy Act is one of approximately 100 federal statutes containing a "fee-shifting" provision allowing a prevailing plaintiff to recover attorney fees and costs from the government.

The Supreme Court has held that a pro se attorney may not recover attorney fees under the fee-shifting provision of 42 U.S.C. § 1988 (1994 & Supp. III 1997). See Kay v. Ehrler, 499 U.S. 432 (1991). The Court's reasoning in Kay calls into question the propriety of Cazalas v. United States Dep't of Justice, 709 F.2d 1051 (5th Cir. 1983), which addressed the award of attorney fees under the Privacy Act and held that a pro se attorney may recover attorney fees. 709 F.2d at 1052 n.3, 1057.

Although the Supreme Court in Kay did not expressly rule on the issue of the award of attorney fees to nonattorney pro se litigants, the Court recognized that "the Circuits are in agreement . . . that a pro se litigant who is not a lawyer is not entitled to attorney's fees" and was "satisfied that [those cases so holding] were correctly decided." 499 U.S. at 435. Furthermore, the Court's rationale in Kay would seem to preclude an award of fees to any pro se Privacy Act litigant, as the Court observed that "awards of counsel fees to pro se litigants-- even if limited to those who are members of the bar--would create a disincentive to employ counsel" and that "[t]he statutory policy of furthering the successful prosecution of meritorious claims is better served by a rule that creates an incentive to retain counsel in every such case." See id. at 438; see also Wilborn v. HHS, No. 91-538, slip op. at 14-16 (D. Or. Mar. 5, 1996) (rejecting argument that rationale in Kay should be construed as applying only to district court stage of litigation; "policy of the Privacy Act . . . would be better served by a rule that creates an incentive to retain counsel at all stages of the litigation, including appeals"), appeal voluntarily dismissed, No. 96-35569 (9th Cir. June 3, 1996).

Indeed, the Court of Appeals for the District of Columbia Circuit granted summary affirmance to a district court decision which held that a "nonattorney pro se litigant cannot recover attorney's fees under the Privacy Act." Sellers v. United States Bureau of Prisons, No. 87-2048, 1993 U.S. Dist. LEXIS 787, at *1 (D.D.C. Jan. 26, 1993), summary affirmance granted, No. 93-5090 (D.C. Cir. July 27, 1993). The district court in Sellers was "persuaded by the Fifth Circuit's opinion in Barrett v. Bureau of Customs, 651 F.2d 1087, 1089 (5th Cir. 1981)," an earlier Privacy Act decision also denying a nonattorney pro se litigant fees, and noted that "[t]he rationale utilized by the Supreme Court in Kay . . . is in accord." Sellers, No. 87-2048, 1993 U.S. Dist. LEXIS 787, at *1 (D.D.C. Jan. 26, 1993); see also Smith v. O'Brien, No. 94-41371, slip op. at 4 (5th Cir. June 19, 1995) (per curiam) (citing Barrett and stating: "Pro se litigants are not entitled to attorney fees under either the FOIA or the Privacy Act unless the litigant is also an attorney."); Westendorf v. IRS, No. 3:92-cv-761WS, 1994 WL 714011, at *2 (S.D. Miss. July 7, 1994) (citing Barrett and holding that nonattorney pro se plaintiff is not entitled to attorney fees), appeal dismissed, No. 94-60503, slip op. at 2-3 (5th Cir. Nov. 17, 1994) (stating that district court's holding is correct under Barrett). The D.C. Circuit has further ruled, however, that a plaintiff's pro se status does not preclude the recovery of fees for "consultations" with outside counsel. Blazy v. Tenet, 194 F.3d 90, 94 (D.C. Cir. 1999); see also id. at 98-99 (Sentelle, J., concurring but "writing separately only to distance [him]self from the majority's determination that a pro se litigant is entitled to recover counsel fees for consultations with attorneys not appearing or connected with appearances in the pro se litigation").

In addition, although under the FOIA it had previously been held that a fee enhancement as compensation for the risk in a contingency fee arrangement might be available in limited circumstances, see, e.g., Weisberg v. United States Dep't of Justice, 848 F.2d 1265, 1272 (D.C. Cir. 1988), the Supreme Court has clarified that such enhancements are not available under statutes authorizing an award of reasonable attorney fees to a prevailing or substantially prevailing party, City of Burlington v. Dague, 505 U.S. 557, 561-66 (1992) (prohibiting contingency enhancement in environmental fee-shifting statutes); see also King v. Palmer, 950 F.2d 771, 775 (D.C. Cir. 1991) (en banc) (pre-City of Burlington case anticipating result later reached by Supreme Court). In light of the Court's further observation that case law "construing what is a 'reasonable' fee applies uniformly to all [federal fee-shifting statutes]," there seems to be little doubt that the same principle also prohibits fee enhancements under the Privacy Act.

Attorney fees are not recoverable for services rendered at the administrative level. See Kennedy v. Andrus, 459 F. Supp. 240, 244 (D.D.C. 1978), aff'd, 612 F.2d 586 (D.C. Cir. 1980) (unpublished table decision).

The D.C. Circuit has held that attorney fees are not available in a subsection (g)(1)(A) amendment case unless the plaintiff has exhausted his administrative remedies. See Haase v. Sessions, 893 F.2d 370, 373-75 (D.C. Cir. 1990).

It has also been held that a plaintiff does not substantially prevail in an access case merely because the agency produced the records in question subsequent to the filing of the lawsuit. See Reinbold v. Evers, 187 F.3d 348, 363 (4th Cir. 1999) (upholding denial of interim fees where plaintiff had "not proved that his lawsuit was a catalyst for the [agency's] action," and evidence showed that delay was caused by staffing shortage); Jacobs v. Reno, No. 3:97-CV-2698-D, 1999 U.S. Dist. LEXIS 3104, at **14-15 (N.D. Tex. Mar. 11, 1999) (denying plaintiff's request for attorney fees and costs, and stating that plaintiff's argument was "too slim a reed on which to rest a § 552a(g)(1)(B) claim, particularly when § 552a(d)(1) imposes no deadline for agency compliance and absent evidence of extended and unjustified delay"), aff'd, 208 F.3d 1006 (5th Cir. 2000) (unpublished table decision).

Subsection (g)(3)(B) is similar to 5 U.S.C. § 552(a)(4)(E), the FOIA's attorney fees provision, and FOIA decisions concerning a plaintiff's eligibility for attorney fees may be consulted in this area. However, the Court of Appeals for the District of Columbia Circuit has expressly ruled that the FOIA's criteria for determining the additional factor of entitlement to attorney fees are inapplicable to a claim for fees under the Privacy Act. Blazy v. Tenet, 194 F.3d at 95-97 ("Even a cursory examination of these factors makes it clear that they have little or no relevance in the context of the Privacy Act."); see also Herring v. VA, No. 94-55955, 1996 WL 32147, at **5-6 (9th Cir. Jan. 26, 1996) (finding plaintiff to be "prevailing party" on access claim for her medical record with no mention or application of FOIA criteria). Nevertheless, two other courts of appeals have held the FOIA's entitlement criteria to be applicable to Privacy Act claims for attorney fees. See Gowan v. United States Dep't of the Air Force, 148 F.3d 1182, 1194-95 (10th Cir.) (applying FOIA's criteria and determining that plaintiff was not entitled to fees because his "suit was for his personal benefit rather than for the benefit of the public interest"), cert. denied, 525 U.S. 1042 (1998); Barrett v. Bureau of Customs, 651 F.2d 1087, 1088 (5th Cir. 1981) (stating that FOIA's guidelines apply to claims for attorney fees under Privacy Act); see also Reinbold v. Evers, 187 F.3d 348, 362 (4th Cir.

1999) (citing Gowan and stating in dicta that if determination is made that plaintiff substantially prevailed, court must evaluate FOIA factors to determine entitlement); Sweatt v. United States Navy, 683 F.2d 420, 423 (D.C. Cir. 1982) (stating in dicta that cases construing attorney fee provision in FOIA are apposite in Privacy Act context). For a discussion of current FOIA decisions, see the section of the "Justice Department Guide to the Freedom of Information Act" entitled "Litigation Considerations, Attorney Fees and Litigation Costs."

Litigation costs (if reasonably incurred) can be recovered by all plaintiffs who substantially prevail. See Parkinson v. Commissioner, No. 87-3219, 1988 WL 12121, at *3 (6th Cir. Feb. 17, 1988); Young v. CIA, No. 91-527-A, slip op. at 2 (E.D. Va. Nov. 30, 1992), aff'd, 1 F.3d 1235 (4th Cir. 1993) (unpublished table decision). Compare Herring v. VA, No. 94-55955, 1996 WL 32147, at **5-6 (9th Cir. Jan. 26, 1996) (although ruling in favor of VA on plaintiff's access claim, nonetheless finding that plaintiff was "a prevailing party with respect to her access claim" because "the VA did not provide her access to all her records until she filed her lawsuit"), with Abernethy v. IRS, 909 F. Supp. 1562, 1567-69 (N.D. Ga. 1995) ("[T]he fact that records were released after the lawsuit was filed, in and of itself, is insufficient to establish Plaintiff's eligibility for an award of attorneys' fees."), aff'd per curiam, No. 95-9489 (11th Cir. Feb. 13, 1997). Further, the D.C. Circuit has held that a pro se plaintiff's claim for litigation costs under the Privacy Act is not limited by 28 U.S.C. § 1920 (governing litigation costs generally). Blazy v. Tenet, 194 F.3d at 94-95 (embracing reasoning of Kuzma v. IRS, 821 F.2d 930 (2d Cir. 1987) (FOIA case)).

"Judgments, costs, and attorney's fees assessed against the United States under [subsection (g) of the Privacy Act] would appear to be payable from the public funds rather than from agency funds." OMB Guidelines, 40 Fed. Reg. 28,948, 28,968 (1975) (citing 28 U.S.C. § 2414 (1994 & Supp. III 1997); 31 U.S.C. § 724a (later replaced during enactment of revised Title 31, now see 31 U.S.C. § 1304 (1994 & Supp. III 1997) (first sentence of former § 724a) and 39 U.S.C. § 409(e) (1994) (last sentence of former § 724a)); and 28 U.S.C. § 1924 (1994)).

2. **Jurisdiction and Venue**

"An action to enforce any liability created under this section may be brought in the district court of the United States in the district in which the complainant resides, or has his principal place of business, or in which the agency records are situated, or in the District of Columbia." 5 U.S.C. § 552a(g)(5).

comment -- By its very terms, this section limits jurisdiction over Privacy Act matters to the federal district courts. 5 U.S.C. § 552a(g)(5); see also, e.g., Minnich v. MSPB, No. 94-3587, 1995

U.S. App. LEXIS 5768, at *3 (Fed. Cir. Mar. 21, 1995) (per curiam) (MSPB does not have jurisdiction over Privacy Act claims); Frasier v. United States, No. 94-5131, 1994 U.S. App. LEXIS 35392, at *3 (Fed. Cir. Dec. 6, 1994) ("U.S. Court of Federal Claims does not have jurisdiction over Privacy Act matters"); Strickland v. Commissioner, No. 9799-95, 2000 WL 274077 (T.C. Mar. 14, 2000) (Tax Court "do[es] not have the authority to address [Privacy Act] claim[].").

Because venue is always proper in the District of Columbia, the Privacy Act decisions of the Court of Appeals for the District of Columbia Circuit are of great importance.

For cases involving this provision, see Warg v. Reno, 19 F. Supp. 2d 776, 785 (N.D. Ohio 1998) ("find[ing] the Northern District of Ohio to be an improper venue" and transferring case to District of Columbia in interest of justice where plaintiff resided in Maryland and records were located in Washington, D.C.), Akutowicz v. United States, 859 F.2d 1122, 1126 (2d Cir. 1988) (venue proper only in District of Columbia for plaintiff who resided and worked continuously in France), Harton v. Bureau of Prisons, No. 97-0638, slip op. at 3, 6-7 (D.D.C. Nov. 12, 1997) (stating that "the fact that the Privacy Act provides for venue in the District of Columbia does not, by itself, establish that each and every Privacy Act claim involves issues of national policy," and granting agency's motion to transfer to jurisdiction where plaintiff was incarcerated, as complaint focused primarily on issues specific to plaintiff), and Finley v. National Endowment for the Arts, 795 F. Supp. 1457, 1467 (C.D. Cal. 1992) ("[I]n a multi-plaintiff Privacy Act action, if any plaintiff satisfies the venue requirement of 5 U.S.C. § 552a(g)(5), the venue requirement is satisfied as to the remaining plaintiffs.").

3. **Statute of Limitations**

"An action to enforce any liability created under this section may be brought . . . within two years from the date on which the cause of action arises, except that where an agency has materially and willfully misrepresented any information required under this section to be disclosed to an individual and the information so misrepresented is material to establishment of the liability of the agency to the individual under this section, the action may be brought at any time within two years after discovery by the individual of the misrepresentation. Nothing in this section shall be construed to authorize any civil action by reason of any injury sustained as the result of a disclosure of a record prior to September 27, 1975." 5 U.S.C. § 552a(g)(5).

comment -- The statute of limitations is jurisdictional in nature and must be strictly construed as it is an "'integral condition of the sovereign's consent to be sued under the Privacy Act.'" Bowyer v. United States Dep't of the Air Force, 875 F.2d 632, 635 (7th Cir. 1989) (quoting Diliberti v. United States, 817 F.2d 1259, 1262 (7th Cir. 1987)); accord Williams v. Reno, No.

95-5155, 1996 WL 460093, at *1 (D.C. Cir. Aug. 7, 1996); Akutowicz v. United States, 859 F.2d 1122, 1126 (2d Cir. 1988); Davis v. Gross, No. 83-5223, 1984 U.S. Dist. LEXIS 14279, at **2-3 (6th Cir. May 10, 1984); Mangino v. Department of the Army, 818 F. Supp. 1432, 1437 (D. Kan. 1993), aff'd, 17 F.3d 1437 (10th Cir. 1994) (unpublished table decision). Consequently, the plaintiff's failure to file suit within the specified time period "deprives the federal courts of subject matter jurisdiction over the action." Diliberti, 817 F.2d at 1262; accord Griffin v. United States Parole Comm'n, 192 F.3d 1081, 1082 (D.C. Cir. 1999); Bowyer, 875 F.2d at 635.

Amendment

In a subsection (g)(1)(A) amendment action, the limitations period begins when the agency denies the plaintiff's request to amend. See Englerius v. VA, 837 F.2d 895, 897-98 (9th Cir. 1988) (holding that the statute of limitations "commences at the time that a person knows or has reason to know that the request has been denied," rather than as of the date of the request letter); see also Blazy v. Tenet, 979 F. Supp. 10, 18 (D.D.C. 1997) (although ultimately finding plaintiff's amendment claim moot due to remedial action taken by CIA, citing Englerius and finding that claim for amendment of sexual harassment allegations in personnel file did not begin to run until employee discovered that FBI, where plaintiff had applied for employment, never received corrective letter from CIA, prior to which time plaintiff did not and could not have known of CIA's failure to amend), summary affirmance granted, No. 97-5330, 1998 WL 315583 (D.C. Cir. May 12, 1998). But see Wills v. OPM, No. 93-2079, slip op. at 2-3 (4th Cir. Jan. 28, 1994) (alternative holding) (per curiam) (holding that a cause of action triggers the statute of limitations when the plaintiff knows or should have known of the alleged violation, which in this case, was when the plaintiff sent his first letter requesting an amendment).

In determining what constitutes the agency's denial, it has been held that the agency's initial denial should govern, rather than the date of the agency's administrative appeal determination. See Quarry v. Department of Justice, 3 Gov't Disclosure Serv. (P-H) ¶ 82,407, at 83,020-21 (D.D.C. Feb. 2, 1982); see also Singer v. OPM, No. 83-1095, slip op. at 2 (D.N.J. Mar. 8, 1984) (rejecting claim that limitations period began on date plaintiff's appeal was dismissed as time-barred under agency regulation); cf. Shannon v. General Elec. Co., 812 F. Supp. 308, 320 & n.10 (N.D.N.Y. 1993) (finding that cause of action for damages claim arose when plaintiff's amendment request was partially denied and noting that "no caselaw can be found to support a finding that the pendency of the appeal has any affect upon the running of the statute of limitations").

In cases "[w]here the agency has not issued an express denial of the request, the question of when a person learns of the denial requires a factual inquiry and cannot ordinarily be decided on a motion to dismiss." Englerius, 837 F.2d at 897; see also Jarrell v. United States Postal Serv., 753 F.2d 1088, 1092 (D.C. Cir. 1985) (holding that issue of material fact existed and therefore summary judgment was inappropriate where agency contended that cause of action arose when it issued final denial of expungement request but requester argued that due to agency's excision of certain parts of documents, he was unaware of information until later point in time).

Access

The two-year statute of limitations set forth in subsection (g)(5) applies to the access provision of the Privacy Act as well. 5 U.S.C. § 552a(g)(5). However, because an individual's Privacy Act access request should be processed under the FOIA as well--see H.R. Rep. No. 98-726, pt. 2, at 16-17 (1984), reprinted in 1984 U.S.C.C.A.N. 3741, 3790-91 (regarding amendment of Privacy Act in 1984 to include subsection (t)(2) and stating: "Agencies that had made it a practice to treat a request made under either [the Privacy Act or the FOIA] as if the request had been made under both laws should continue to do so."); FOIA Update, Vol. VII, No. 1, at 6--and the FOIA is subject to the general six-year statute of limitations, see Spannaus v. Department of Justice, 824 F.2d 52, 55-56 (D.C. Cir. 1987) (applying 28 U.S.C. § 2401(a) to FOIA actions), the Privacy Act's "two-year bar" may be of little, if any, consequence. The ramifications of these arguably conflicting provisions have not been explored.

Indeed, only three decisions have addressed the Privacy Act's statute of limitations in the access context. See Biondo v. Department of the Navy, 928 F. Supp. 626, 632, 634-35 (D.S.C. 1995) (summarily stating that 1987 request "cannot serve as a basis for relief for a suit brought in 1992 because the Privacy Act has a two-year statute of limitations"; similar statements made as to undocumented requests for information in mid-80s and in 1976-77), aff'd, 86 F.3d 1148 (4th Cir. 1996) (unpublished table decision); Burkins v. United States, 865 F. Supp. 1480, 1496 (D. Colo. 1994) (cause of action "should not be time-barred" because it would have accrued when plaintiff knew his request for access had been denied); Mittleman v. United States Treasury, 773 F. Supp. 442, 448, 450-51 n.7 (D.D.C. 1991) (where claims are barred by statute of limitations, plaintiff "cannot attempt to resurrect" them by making subsequent request more than three years after she had first received information and almost six months after complaint had been filed), related subsequent case, Mittleman v. OPM, No. 92-158, slip op. at 1 n.1 (D.D.C. Jan. 18, 1995), summary affirmance granted, 76 F.3d 1240, 1242 (D.C. Cir. 1996).

-795-

### Damages

The statute of limitations for a damages cause of action begins when the plaintiff knew or should have known of the Privacy Act violation. See Williams v. Reno, No. 95-5155, 1996 WL 460093, at *1 (D.C. Cir. Aug. 7, 1996); Tijerina v. Walters, 821 F.2d 789, 797 (D.C. Cir. 1987); see also Bergman v. United States, 751 F.2d 314, 316-17 (10th Cir. 1984) (holding that limitations period for damages action under subsection (g)(1)(C) commences at time three conditions are met: (1) an error was made in maintaining plaintiff's records; (2) plaintiff was wronged by such error; and (3) plaintiff either knew or had reason to know of such error); cf. Bowyer v. United States Dep't of the Air Force, 875 F.2d 632, 636 (7th Cir. 1989) (applying stricter standard and holding that the limitations period begins to run when "plaintiff first knew or had reason to know that the private records were being maintained"); Diliberti v. United States, 817 F.2d 1259, 1262-64 (7th Cir. 1987) (same).

Some courts have held that once the plaintiff knows or has reason to know of a record's existence, even if based upon hearsay or rumors, the plaintiff has a "duty to inquire" into the matter--i.e., "two years from that time to investigate whether sufficient factual and legal bases existed for bringing suit." See Bowyer, 875 F.2d at 637; see also Diliberti, 817 F.2d at 1263-64 (stating that "the hearsay and rumors which the plaintiff described in his affidavit were enough to put him on notice" and "impose a duty to inquire into the veracity of those rumors"); Munson, No. 96-CV-70920-DT, slip op. at 2-3 (E.D. Mich. July 2, 1996); Strang v. Indahl, No. 93-97, slip op. at 2-4 (M.D. Ga. Apr. 13, 1995) ("The statute does not await confirmation or actual access to the records; hearsay and rumor are sufficient to begin running the statute of limitations."); Mangino, 818 F. Supp. at 1438 (quoting Diliberti); Rickard v. United States Postal Serv., No. 87-1212, slip op. at 5 (C.D. Ill. Feb. 16, 1990) (recognizing "duty to inquire" established by Diliberti, and stating that "[e]ven unsubstantiated hearsay and rumor suffice to give a plaintiff notice of alleged inaccuracies in a record").

Generally, the plaintiff knows or has reason to know of records in violation of the Privacy Act when the plaintiff suspects there is a violation rather than when the plaintiff actually possesses those records or when the government creates those records. See Dilberti, 817 F.2d at 1262 (stating that the "relevant fact is not when the plaintiff first had physical possession of the particular records, but rather when he first knew of the existence of the records"). If the plaintiff has constructive notice of the possible violation, the statute of limitations is triggered. See id. at 1262-63; see also Bowyer, 875 F. 2d at 632, 636 (stating that when agency employee confirmed that agency maintained private records on plaintiff relating to previous conflict with his supervisor, he had sufficient notice of possibly erroneous records). In the context of a damages action for wrongful disclosure, the D.C. Circuit rejected the government's argument that the limitations period commenced when the contested disclosure occurred, and observed that such an unauthorized disclosure "is unlikely to come to the subject's attention until it affects him adversely, if then." Tijerina, 821 F.2d at 797.

Other courts have similarly found that the statute of limitations began to run where the evidence or circumstances indicated that the plaintiff knew of the violation or had been affected by it. See Armstrong v. United States Bureau of Prisons, 976 F. Supp. 17, 21 (D.D.C. 1997) (following Tijerina and finding plaintiff's claim barred by statute of limitations where plaintiff had written letter over two and one-half years earlier indicating that her prison file was lacking favorable information), summary affirmance granted sub nom. Armstrong v. Federal Bureau of Prisons, No. 97-5208, 1998 WL 65543 (D.C. Cir. Jan. 30. 1998); Nwangoro v. Department of the Army, 952 F. Supp. 394, 397-98 (N.D. Tex. 1996) ("[T]he limitation period commences not when the plaintiff first obtains possession of the particular records at issue, but rather when he first knew of their existence."); Brown v. VA, No. 94-1119, 1996 WL 263636, at **1-2 (D.D.C. May 15, 1996) (Privacy Act claim barred by statute of limitations because plaintiff "knew or should have known that the Privacy Act may have been violated" when he submitted federal tort claim to VA concerning same matter "over two and a half years" before suit filed); Gordon v. Department of Justice, Fed. Bureau of Prisons, No. 94-2636, 1995 WL 472360, at *2 (D.D.C. Aug. 3, 1995) (statute of limitations ran from time of plaintiff's receipt of letter from sentencing judge rejecting information contained in presentencing report, at which point plaintiff "knew or . . . should have known what became inaccuracies in his presentencing report"); Rice v. Hawk, No. 94-1519, slip op. at 2-3 & n.1 (D.D.C. Dec. 30, 1994) (plaintiff knew of contents of presentence report at time he filed "Objection to Presentence Investigation Report," at which time statute of limitations began to run), summary affirmance granted, No. 95-5027, 1995 WL 551148 (D.C. Cir. Aug. 2, 1995); Szymanski, 870 F. Supp. at 378-79 (citing Bergman and Tijerina and stating that "[b]ecause plaintiff was given the opportunity to review the documents he now maintains contain incorrect information and waived that opportunity, the Court finds that he should have known about any errors at the time of this waiver" but that, additionally, plaintiff had complained about same information in his appeal to Parole Commission more than two years previously); Malewich v. United States Postal Serv., No. 91-4871, slip op. at 21-22 (D.N.J. Apr. 8, 1993) (statute began to run when plaintiff was aware that file was being used in investigation of plaintiff and when he was notified of proposed termination of employment), aff'd, 27 F.3d 557 (3d Cir. 1994) (unpublished table decision); Mangino, 818 F. Supp. at 1437-38 (applying Bergman, Bowyer, and Diliberti, and finding that cause of action accrued on date of letter in which plaintiff indicated knowledge of records being used by agency as basis for revoking his security clearance, rather than upon his receipt of records); Ertell v. Department of the Army, 626 F. Supp. 903, 908 (C.D. Ill. 1986) (limitations period commenced when plaintiff "knew" that there "had been negative evaluations in his file which may explain why he is not being selected," rather than upon actual discovery of such records); cf. Doe v. NSA, No. 97-2650, 1998 WL 743665, at **1-3 (4th Cir. Oct. 23, 1998) (per curiam) (citing Rose and Diliberti, and holding that appellant's wrongful disclosure claim was time-barred because in accordance with principles of agency law, Privacy Act action accrued from time her attorney received her records).

In contrast to the constructive notice theory adopted by many courts, some courts have suggested that the limitations period for a subsection (g)(1)(C) damages action would commence when a plaintiff actually receives his record -- i.e., when he actually discovers the inaccuracy. See Akutowicz v. United States, 859 F.2d 1122, 1126 (2d Cir. 1988) (holding that the limitations period "began to run, at the very latest, when the citizen received a copy of his records from the State Department"); see also Rose v. United States, 905 F.2d 1257, 1259 (9th Cir. 1990) (subsection (g)(1)(C) action accrues when reasonable person "knows or has reason to know of the alleged violation" and that period commenced when plaintiff received copy of her file); Lepkowski v. United States Dep't of the Treasury, 804 F.2d 1310, 1322-23 (D.C. Cir. 1986) (Robinson, J., concurring) (subsection (g)(1)(C) action "accrued no later than the date upon which [plaintiff] received IRS' letter . . . apprising him of destruction of the photographs and associated workpapers"); Harry v. United States Postal Serv., 867 F. Supp. 1199, 1205 (M.D. Pa. 1994) (although exact date when plaintiff should have known about alleged improper file maintenance was unclear, date of actual discovery was "sterling clear"--when plaintiff physically reviewed his files), aff'd sub nom. Harry v. Postal Serv. (United States), Marvin T. Runyon, 60 F.3d 815 (3d Cir. 1995) (unpublished table decision); Shannon, 812 F. Supp. at 319-20 (causes of action arose when plaintiff learned of wrongs allegedly committed against him which was when he received documents that were allegedly inaccurate or wrongfully maintained); Fiorella v. HEW, 2 Gov't Disclosure Serv. (P-H) ¶ 81,363, at 81,944 (W.D. Wash. Mar. 9, 1981); cf. Steele v. Cochran, No. 95-35373, 1996 WL 285651, at *1 (9th Cir. May 29, 1996) (citing Rose and holding that Privacy Act claim filed in 1994 was time-barred because plaintiff wrote letter to agency

**PRIVACY ACT OVERVIEW**

questioning validity of information disclosed to State Bar in 1991 and was formally informed by State Bar that he was denied admission in 1991).

One district court decision has also considered the statute of limitations in connection with a Privacy Act claim under subsection (e)(3) concerning the collection of information from individuals. Darby v. Jensen, No. 94-S-569, 1995 U.S. Dist. LEXIS 7007, at **7-8 (D. Colo. May 15, 1995). In that case, the court determined that the claim was time-barred, as more than two years had passed since the date upon which the plaintiff had received the request for information. Id.

Additionally, it has been held that "[a] Privacy Act claim is not tolled by continuing violations." Davis v. United States Dep't of Justice, 204 F.3d 723, 726 (7th Cir. 2000); see also Bergman, 751 F.2d at 316-17 (ruling that limitations period commenced when agency first notified plaintiff in writing that it would not reconsider his discharge or correct his job classification records and rejecting argument "that a new cause of action arose upon each and every subsequent adverse determination based on erroneous records"); Bowyer, 875 F.2d at 638 (citing Bergman and Diliberti and rejecting argument that continuing violation doctrine should toll statute of limitations); Diliberti, 817 F.2d at 1264 (citing Bergman for same proposition); Malewich, No. 91-4871, slip op. at 23-25 (D.N.J. Apr. 8, 1993) (same); Shannon, 812 F. Supp. at 319-20 (plaintiff "cannot revive a potential cause of action simply because the violation continued to occur; he can allege subsequent violations only if there are subsequent events that occurred in violation of the Privacy Act"); cf. Baker v. United States, 943 F. Supp. 270, 273 (W.D.N.Y. 1996) (citing Shannon with approval). But cf. Burkins v. United States, 865 F. Supp. 1480, 1496 (D. Colo. 1994) (citing Bergman and viewing plaintiff's harm as "continuing transaction").

Moreover, a plaintiff's voluntary pursuit of administrative procedures should not toll the running of the statute of limitations, because no administrative exhaustion requirement exists before a damages action can be brought. See Uhl v. Swanstrom, 876 F. Supp. 1545, 1560-61 (N.D. Iowa 1995), aff'd on other grounds, 79 F.3d 751 (8th Cir. 1996).

However, the limitations period is equitably tolled if the plaintiff belatedly discovers a material and willful misrepresentation by the agency. The statute's own terms provide that if the plaintiff remains unaware of his cause of action because of the agency's material and willful misrepresentations of information required by the statute to be disclosed to him and the information is material to establishment of the liability of the agency to the individual, then the limitations period runs from the date upon which the plaintiff discovers the misrepresentation. 5 U.S.C. § 552a(g)(5); _see also_ Lacey v. United States, 74 F. Supp. 2d 13, 15-16 (D.D.C. 1999) (concluding that defendants made material and willful misrepresentations to plaintiffs by telling them that they lacked evidence and should wait for agency to finish its own investigation of claim before bringing suit, which tolled statute of limitations until agency "confirmed that there was substance to plaintiffs' claim of violations"); Burkins, 865 F. Supp. at 1496 ("Accepting plaintiff's claims of agency misrepresentation as true, the statute may have been tolled."); Pope v. Bond, 641 F. Supp. 489, 500 (D.D.C. 1986) (holding that the FAA's actions constituted willful and material representation because of their repeated denials of plaintiff's request for access, which "prevents the statute of limitations from running until the misrepresentation is discovered"); cf. Marin v. United States Dep't of Defense, No. 95-2175, 1998 WL 779101, at *1 (D.D.C. Oct. 23, 1998) (denying defendants' motion to dismiss on ground that claim was time-barred and accepting plaintiff's claim regarding timing of agency misrepresentation), summary affirmance granted, No. 99-5102, 1999 WL 1006404 (D.C. Cir. Oct. 8, 1999); Munson, No. 96-CV-70920-DT, slip op. at 4-5 (E.D. Mich. July 2, 1996) (statement that agency could find no record of disclosure of report to state police but that it would check further "does not provide any evidence of a willful and material misrepresentation"); Strang v. Indahl, No. 93-97, slip op. at 2-4 (M.D. Ga. Apr. 13, 1995) (agency's denial of allegations in plaintiff's complaint did not equate as material misrepresentation; by voluntarily dismissing suit on belief that reliance on circumstantial evidence was insufficient, plaintiff "elected to forego the very lawsuit which would have . . . substantiated her suspicions").

Note that the Seventh Circuit has stated that this special relief provision is necessarily incorporated into tests, such as the one set forth in Bergman, which focus on when a plaintiff first knew or had reason to know of an error in maintaining his records. Diliberti, 817 F.2d at 1262 n.1; see also Malewich, No. 91-4871, slip op. at 25-27 (D.N.J. Apr. 8, 1993) (following Diliberti and precluding "the plaintiff from utilizing the discovery rule as a basis for extending the permissible filing date"). The government argued to the Court of Appeals for the District of Columbia Circuit in Tijerina v. Walters that subsection (g)(5) "makes sense only if Congress intended the normal statutory period to commence at the time of the alleged violation, regardless of whether the potential plaintiff is or should be aware of the agency's action." See 821 F.2d at 797-98. The D.C. Circuit, however, rejected that argument and stated that in order to ensure that the government cannot escape liability by purposefully misrepresenting information, "the Act allows the period to commence upon actual discovery of the misrepresentation, whereas . . . for other actions under the Act, the pe-

# PRIVACY ACT OVERVIEW

riod begins when the plaintiff knew or should have known of the violation . . . thus in no way affect[ing] the special treatment Congress provided for the particularly egregious cases of government misconduct singled out in the Act's statute of limitations." Id. at 798.

4. **Jury Trial**

The Act is silent on this point, but every court to have considered the issue has ruled that there is no right to a jury trial under the statute. See Harris v. USDA, No. 96-5783, 1997 WL 528498, at *3 (6th Cir. Aug. 26, 1997); Stewart v. FBI, No. 97-1595, 1999 U.S. Dist. LEXIS 18773, at **7-9 (D. Or. Sept. 29, 1999) (magistrate's recommendation), adopted, No. 97-1595, 1999 U.S. Dist. LEXIS 18785 (D. Or. Nov. 24, 1999); Flanagan v. Reno, 8 F. Supp. 2d 1049, 1053 n.3 (N.D. Ill. 1998); Clarkson v. IRS, No. 8:88-3036-3K, slip op. at 8 (D.S.C. May 10, 1990), aff'd, 935 F.2d 1285 (4th Cir. 1991) (unpublished table decision); Williams v. United States, No. H-80-249, slip op. at 13-14 (D. Conn. Apr. 10, 1984); Calhoun v. Wells, 3 Gov't Disclosure Serv. (P-H) ¶ 83,272, at 84,059 n.2 (D.S.C. July 30, 1980); Henson v. United States Army, No. 76-45-C5, 1977 U.S. Dist. LEXIS 16868, at *1 (D. Kan. Mar. 16, 1977). But cf. Tomasello v. Rubin, No. 93-1326, slip op. at 3-4, 19 (D.D.C. Aug. 19, 1997) ("guided by" advisory jury verdict in awarding Privacy Act damages), aff'd, 167 F.3d 612, 616-17 (D.C. Cir. 1999) (recounting fact of advisory jury verdict as to Privacy Act claims).

**CRIMINAL PENALTIES**

"Any officer or employee of an agency, who by virtue of his employment or official position, has possession of, or access to, agency records which contain individually identifiable information the disclosure of which is prohibited by this section or by rules or regulations established thereunder, and who knowing that disclosure of the specific material is so prohibited, willfully discloses the material in any manner to any person or agency not entitled to receive it, shall be guilty of a misdemeanor and fined not more than $5,000." 5 U.S.C. § 552a(i)(1).

"Any officer or employee of any agency who willfully maintains a system of records without meeting the notice requirements of subsection (e)(4) of this section shall be guilty of a misdemeanor and fined not more than $5,000." 5 U.S.C. § 552a(i)(2).

"Any person who knowingly and willfully requests or obtains any record concerning an individual from an agency under false pretenses shall be guilty of a misdemeanor and fined not more than $5,000." 5 U.S.C. § 552a(i)(3).

comment -- These provisions are solely penal and create no private right of action. See Jones v. Farm Credit Admin., No. 86-2243, slip op. at 3 (8th Cir. Apr. 13, 1987); Unt v. Aerospace Corp., 765 F.2d 1440, 1448 (9th Cir. 1985); McNeill v. IRS, No. 93-2204, 1995 U.S. Dist. LEXIS 2372, at **9-10 (D.D.C. Feb. 7, 1995); Lapin v. Taylor, 475 F. Supp. 446, 448 (D. Haw. 1979); see also FLRA v. DOD, 977 F.2d 545, 549 n.6 (11th Cir. 1992) (dictum); Beckette v. United States Postal Serv., No. 88-802, slip op. at 14 n.14 (E.D. Va. July 3, 1989); Kassel v. VA, 682 F. Supp. 646, 657 (D.N.H. 1988); Bernson v. ICC, 625 F. Supp. 10, 13 (D. Mass. 1984); cf. Thomas v. Reno, No. 97-1155, 1998 WL 33923, at *2 (10th Cir. Jan. 29, 1998) (finding that plaintiff's request for criminal sanctions did "not allege sufficient facts to raise the issue of whether there exists a private right of action to enforce the Privacy Act's provision for criminal penalties" and citing Unt and FLRA v. DOD).

There have been at least two criminal prosecutions for unlawful disclosure of Privacy Act-protected records. See United States v. Trabert, 978 F. Supp. 1368 (D. Colo. 1997) (defendant found not guilty; prosecution did not prove "beyond a reasonable doubt that defendant 'willfully disclosed' protected material," evidence presented constituted, "at best, gross negligence," and thus was "insufficient for purposes of prosecution under § 552a(i)(1)"); United States v. Gonzales, No. 76-132 (M.D. La. Dec. 21, 1976) (guilty plea entered). See generally In re Mullins (Tamposi Fee Application), 84 F.3d 1439, 1441 (D.C. Cir. 1996) (per curiam) (case concerning application for reimbursement of attorney fees where Independent Counsel found no prosecution was warranted under Privacy Act because there was no conclusive evidence of improper disclosure of information).

## TEN EXEMPTIONS

A. **One Special Exemption--5 U.S.C. § 552a(d)(5)**

"nothing in this [Act] shall allow an individual access to any information compiled in reasonable anticipation of a civil action or proceeding."

comment -- The subsection (d)(5) provision is sometimes mistakenly overlooked because it is not located with the other exemptions in sections (j) and (k). It is an exemption from only the access provision of the Privacy Act.

This exemption provision reflects Congress's intent to exclude civil litigation files from access under subsection (d)(1). See 120 Cong. Rec. 36,959-60 (1974), reprinted in Source Book at 936-38. Indeed, this Privacy Act provision has been held to be similar to the attorney work-product privilege, see, e.g., Martin v. Office of Special Counsel, 819 F.2d 1181, 1187-89 (D.C. Cir. 1987); Hernandez v. Alexander, 671 F.2d 402, 408 (10th Cir. 1982); Barber v. INS, No. 90-0067C, slip op. at 4-6 (W.D. Wash. May 15, 1990), and to extend even to information prepared by nonattorneys, see Varville v. Rubin, No. 3:96CV00629, 1998 U.S. Dist. LEXIS 14006, at **9-12 (D. Conn. Aug. 18, 1998) (citing Martin and Smiertka, infra, for proposition that courts "have interpreted the exemption in accordance with its plain language and have not read the requirements of the attorney work product doctrine into Exemption (d)(5)," and broadly construing subsection (d)(5) to protect report prepared pursuant to ethics inquiry into alleged hiring improprieties, finding "that the fact that the documents at issue were not prepared by or at the direction of an attorney is not determinative in deciding whether Exemption (d)(5) exempts the documents from disclosure"); Blazy v. Tenet, 979 F. Supp. 10, 24 (D.D.C. 1997) (broadly construing subsection (d)(5) to protect communications between CIA's Office of General Counsel and members of plaintiff's Employee Review Panel while panel was deciding whether to recommend retaining plaintiff), summary affirmance granted, No. 97-5330, 1998 WL 315583 (D.C. Cir. May 12, 1998); Smiertka v. United States Dep't of the Treasury, 447 F. Supp. 221, 227-28 (D.D.C. 1978) (broadly construing subsection (d)(5) to cover documents prepared by and at direction of lay agency staff persons during period prior to plaintiff's firing), remanded on other grounds, 604 F.2d 698 (D.C. Cir. 1979); see also Taylor v. United States Dep't of Educ., No. 91 N 837, slip op. at 3, 6 (D. Colo. Feb. 25, 1994) (applying subsection (d)(5) to private citizen's complaint letter maintained by plaintiff's supervisor in anticipation of plaintiff's termination); Government Accountability Project v. Office of Special Counsel, No. 87-0235, 1988 WL 21394, at *5 (D.D.C. Feb. 22, 1988) (subsection (d)(5) "extends to any records compiled in anticipation of civil proceedings, whether prepared by attorneys or lay investigators"); Crooker v. Marshals Serv., No. 85-2599, slip op. at 2-3 (D.D.C. Dec. 16, 1985) (subsection (d)(5) protects information "regardless of whether it was prepared by an attorney"); Barrett v. Customs Serv., No. 77-3033, slip op. at 2-3 (E.D. La. Feb. 22, 1979) (applying subsection (d)(5) to "policy recommendations regarding plaintiff['s] separation from the Customs Service and the possibility of a sex discrimination action").

This provision shields information that is compiled in anticipation of court proceedings or quasi-judicial administrative hearings. See, e.g., Martin, 819 F.2d at 1188-89; Frets v. Department of Transp., No. 88-0404-CV-W-9, slip op. at 11 (W.D. Mo. Dec. 14, 1988); see also OMB Guidelines, 40 Fed. Reg. 28,948, 28,960 (1975) ("civil proceeding" term intended to cover "quasi-judicial and preliminary judicial steps").

It should be noted, however, that this provision is in certain respects not as broad as Exemption 5 of the Freedom of Information Act, 5 U.S.C. § 552(b)(5) (1994 & Supp. IV 1998). For example, by its terms it does not cover information compiled in anticipation of criminal actions. (Of course, subsection (j)(2), discussed below, may provide protection for such information.) Also, subsection (d)(5) does not incorporate other Exemption 5 privileges, such as the deliberative process privilege. See, e.g., Savada v. DOD, 755 F. Supp. 6, 9 (D.D.C. 1991). But see Blazy, 979 F. Supp. at 24 (incorrectly stating that "FOIA Exemption 5 and Privacy Act Exemption (d)(5) permit the agency to withhold information that qualifies as attorney work product or falls under the attorney-client or deliberative process privilege"). This means that deliberative information regularly withheld under the FOIA can be required to be disclosed under the Privacy Act. See, e.g., Savada, 755 F. Supp. at 9; see also FOIA Update, Vol. XV, No. 2, at 5-6 (encouraging discretionary disclosure of attorney work-product information under FOIA Exemption 5).

Unlike all of the other Privacy Act exemptions discussed below, however, subsection (d)(5) is entirely "self-executing," inasmuch as it does not require an implementing regulation in order to be effective. Cf. Mervin v. Bonfanti, 410 F. Supp. 1205, 1207 (D.D.C. 1976) ("[A]n absolute prerequisite for taking advantage of [exemption (k)(5)] is that the head of the particular agency promulgate a rule.").

## B. Two General Exemptions--5 U.S.C. § 552a(j)

"The head of any agency may promulgate rules, in accordance with the requirements (including general notice) of sections 553(b)(1), (2), and (3), (c), and (e) of this title, to exempt any system of records within the agency from any part of this section except subsections (b), (c)(1) and (2), (e)(4)(A) through (F), (e)(6), (7), (9), (10), and (11), and (i) if the system of records is--

(1) maintained by the Central Intelligence Agency; or

(2) maintained by an agency or component thereof which performs as its principal function any activity pertaining to the enforcement of criminal laws, including police efforts to prevent, control, or reduce crime or to apprehend criminals, and the activities of prosecutors, courts, correctional, probation, pardon, or parole authorities, and which consists of

   (A) information compiled for the purpose of identifying individual criminal offenders and alleged offenders and consisting only of identifying data and notations of arrests, the nature and disposition of criminal charges, sentencing, confinement, release, and parole and probation status;

   (B) information compiled for the purpose of a criminal investigation, including reports of informants and investigators, and associated with an identifiable individual; or

   (C) reports identifiable to an individual compiled at any stage of the process of enforcement of the criminal laws from arrest or indictment through release from supervision.

At the time rules are adopted under this subsection, the agency shall include in the statement required under section 553(c) of this title, the reasons why the system of records is to be exempted from a provision of this section."

comment -- For cases involving subsection (j)(1), see Alford v. CIA, 610 F.2d 348, 348-49 (5th Cir. 1980), Blazy v. Tenet, 979 F. Supp. 10, 23-25 (D.D.C. 1997), summary affirmance granted, No. 97-5330, 1998 WL 315583 (D.C. Cir. May 12, 1998); Hunsberger v. CIA, No. 92-2186, slip op. at 2-3 (D.D.C. Apr. 5, 1995); Wilson v. CIA, No. 89-3356, 1991 WL 226682, at *1 (D.D.C. Oct. 15, 1991), Bryant v. CIA, No. 90-1163, 1991 U.S. Dist. LEXIS 8964, at *2 (D.D.C. June 28, 1991), and Anthony v. CIA, 1 Gov't Disclosure Serv. (P-H) ¶ 79,196, at 79,371 (E.D. Va. Sept. 19, 1979).

Subsection (j)(2)'s threshold requirement is that the system of records be maintained by "an agency or component thereof which performs as its principal function any activity pertaining to the enforcement of criminal laws." This requirement is usually met by such obvious law enforcement components as the FBI, DEA, and ATF. In addition, Department of Justice components such as the Federal Bureau of Prisons, see, e.g., Kellett v. United States Bureau of Prisons, No. 94-1898, 1995 U.S. App. LEXIS 26746, at **10-11 (1st Cir. Sept. 18, 1995) (per curiam); Duffin v. Carlson, 636 F.2d 709, 711 (D.C. Cir. 1980), the United States Attorney's Office, see, e.g., Hatcher v. United States Dep't of Justice Office of Info. & Privacy Act, 910 F. Supp. 1, 2-3 (D.D.C. 1995), and the Office of the Pardon Attorney, see, e.g., Binion v. United States Dep't of Justice, 695 F.2d 1189, 1191 (9th Cir. 1983), as well as the United States Parole Commission, see, e.g., Fendler v. United States Parole Comm'n, 774 F.2d 975, 979 (9th Cir. 1985); James v. Baer, No. 89-2841, 1990 U.S. Dist. LEXIS 5702, at *2 (D.D.C. May 11, 1990), a United States Postal Service component, the Postal Inspection Service, see Anderson v. United States Postal Serv., 7 F. Supp. 2d 583, 586 n.3 (E.D. Pa. 1998), aff'd, 187 F.3d 625 (3d Cir. 1999) (unpublished table decision); Dorman v. Mulligan, No. 92 C 3230 (N.D. Ill. Sept. 23, 1992), and the Air Force Office of Special Investigations, see, e.g., Gowan v. United States Dep't of the Air Force, 148 F.3d 1182, 1189-90 (10th Cir.), cert. denied, 525 U.S. 1042 (1998); Butler v. Department of the Air Force, 888 F. Supp. 174, 179 (D.D.C. 1995), aff'd per curiam, No. 96-5111 (D.C. Cir. May 6, 1997), also qualify to use subsection (j)(2).

However, it has been held that the threshold requirement is not met where only one of the principal functions of the component maintaining the system is criminal law enforcement. See Alexander v. IRS, No. 86-0414, 1987 WL 13958, at *4 (D.D.C. June 30, 1987) (IRS Inspection Service's internal "conduct investigation" system); Anderson v. United States Dep't of the Treasury, No. 76-1404, slip op. at 6-7 (D.D.C. July 19, 1977) (same). Two courts have held that an Inspector General's Office qualifies as a "principal function" criminal law enforcement component. See Taylor v. United States Dep't of Educ., No. 91 N 837, slip op. at 5 (D. Colo. Feb. 25, 1994); Von Tempske v. HHS, 2 Gov't Disclosure Serv. (P-H) ¶ 82,091, at 82,385 (W.D. Mo. Nov. 11, 1981) (IG's office qualifies to use subsection (j)(2), but records at issue did not fall within subsection (j)(2)(B) as they were compiled for "administrative" rather than "criminal" investigative purpose).

Once the threshold requirement is satisfied, it must be shown that the system of records at issue consists of information compiled for one of the criminal law enforcement purposes listed in subsection (j)(2)(A)-(C). Given the breadth of this exemption, an agency's burden of proof is generally less stringent than under the FOIA, at least in the access context. Indeed, several courts have observed that "the Vaughn rationale [requiring itemized indices of withheld records] is probably inapplicable to Privacy Act cases where a general exemption has been established." Restrepo v. United States Dep't of Justice, No. 5-86-294, slip op. at 6 (D. Minn. June 23, 1987) (citing Shapiro v. DEA, 721 F.2d 215, 218 (7th Cir. 1983), vacated as moot, 469 U.S. 14 (1984)); see also

PRIVACY ACT OVERVIEW

Miller v. Director of FBI, No. 77-C-3331, 1987 WL 18331, at *2 (N.D. Ill. Oct. 7, 1987); Welsh v. IRS, No. 85-1024, slip op. at 3-4 (D.N.M. Oct. 21, 1986). Moreover, in access cases the Act does not grant courts the authority to review the information at issue in camera to determine whether subsection (j)(2)(A)-(C) is applicable. See 5 U.S.C. § 552a(g)(3)(A) (in camera review only where subsection (k) exemptions are invoked); see also Exner v. FBI, 612 F.2d 1202, 1206 (9th Cir. 1980); Reyes v. Supervisor of DEA, 647 F. Supp. 1509, 1512 (D.P.R. 1986), vacated & remanded on other grounds, 834 F.2d 1093 (1st Cir. 1987). However, this may be a rather academic point in light of the FOIA's grant of in camera review authority under 5 U.S.C. § 552(a)(4)(B). See, e.g., Von Tempske v. HHS, 2 Gov't Disclosure Serv. at 82,385 (rejecting claim that "administrative inquiry" investigative file fell within subsection (j)(2)(B), following in camera review under FOIA).

An important requirement of subsection (j) is that an agency must state in the Federal Register "the reasons why the system of records is to be exempted" from a particular subsection of the Act. 5 U.S.C. § 552a(j) (final sentence); see also 5 U.S.C. § 552a(k) (final sentence). It is unclear whether an agency's stated reasons for exemption--typically, a list of the adverse effects that would occur if the exemption were not available--limit the scope of the exemption when it is applied to specific records in the exempt system in particular cases. See Exner, 612 F.2d at 1206 (framing issue but declining to decide it). As discussed below, a confusing mass of case law in this area illustrates the struggle to give legal effect to this requirement.

Most courts have permitted agencies to claim subsection (j)(2) as a defense in access and/or amendment cases--usually without regard to the specific records at issue or the regulation's stated reasons for the exemption. See, e.g., Castaneda v. Henman, 914 F.2d 981, 986 (7th Cir. 1990) (amendment); Wentz v. Department of Justice, 772 F.2d 335, 337-39 (7th Cir. 1985) (amendment); Fendler, 774 F.2d at 979 (amendment); Shapiro, 721 F.2d at 217-18 (access and amendment); Binion, 695 F.2d at 1192-93 (access); Duffin, 636 F.2d at 711 (access); Exner, 612 F.2d at 1204-07 (access); Ryan v. Department of Justice, 595 F.2d 954, 956-57 (4th Cir. 1979) (access); Anderson v. United States Marshals Serv., 943 F. Supp. 37, 39-40 (D.D.C. 1996) (access); Hatcher, 910 F. Supp. at 2-3 (access); Aquino v. Stone, 768 F. Supp. 529, 530-31 (E.D. Va. 1991) (amendment); aff'd, 957 F.2d 139 (4th Cir. 1992); Whittle v. Moschella, 756 F. Supp. 589, 595-96 (D.D.C. 1991) (access); Simon v. United States Dep't of Justice, 752 F. Supp. 14, 23 (D.D.C. 1990) (access), aff'd, 980 F.2d 782 (D.C. Cir. 1992); Bagley v. FBI, No. C88-4075, slip op. at 2-4 (N.D. Iowa Aug. 28, 1989) (access to accounting of disclosures); Anderson v. Department of Justice, No. 87-5959, 1988 WL 50372, at *1 (E.D. Pa. May 16, 1988) (amendment); Yon v. IRS, 671 F. Supp. 1344, 1347 (S.D. Fla. 1987) (access); Burks v. United States Dep't of Justice, No. 83-CV-189, slip op. at 2 n.1 (N.D.N.Y. Aug. 9,

1985) (access); Stimac v. Department of the Treasury, 586 F. Supp. 34, 35-37 (N.D. Ill. 1984) (access); Cooper v. Department of Justice (FBI), 578 F. Supp. 546, 547 (D.D.C. 1983) (access); Stimac v. FBI, 577 F. Supp. 923, 924-25 (N.D. Ill. 1984) (access); Turner v. Ralston, 567 F. Supp. 606, 607-08 (W.D. Mo. 1983) (access); Smith v. United States Dep't of Justice, No. 81-CV-813, 1983 U.S. Dist. Lexis 10878, at **15-20 (N.D.N.Y. Dec. 13, 1983) (amendment); Wilson v. Bell, 3 Gov't Disclosure Serv. (P-H) ¶ 83,025, at 83,471 (S.D. Tex. Nov. 2, 1982) (amendment); Nunez v. DEA, 497 F. Supp. 209, 211 (S.D.N.Y. 1980) (access); Bambulas v. Chief, United States Marshal, No. 77-3229, slip op. at 2 (D. Kan. Jan. 3, 1979) (amendment); Pacheco v. FBI, 470 F. Supp. 1091, 1107 (D.P.R. 1979) (amendment); Varona Pacheco v. FBI, 456 F. Supp. 1024, 1034-35 (D.P.R. 1978) (amendment). But cf. Mittleman v. United States Dep't of the Treasury, 919 F. Supp. 461, 469 (D.D.C. 1995) (finding subsection (k)(2) applicable and citing regulation's stated reasons for exemption of Department of Treasury Inspector General system of records from accounting of disclosures provision pursuant to subsections (j) and (k)(2)), aff'd in part & remanded in part on other grounds, 104 F.3d 410 (D.C. Cir. 1997).

Indeed, the Court of Appeals for the Seventh Circuit has gone so far as to hold that subsection (j)(2) "'does not require that a regulation's rationale for exempting a record from [access] apply in each particular case.'" Wentz, 772 F.2d at 337-38 (quoting Shapiro, 721 F.2d at 218). This appears also to be the view of the Court of Appeals for the First Circuit. See Irons v. Bell, 596 F.2d 468, 471 (1st Cir. 1979) ("None of the additional conditions found in Exemption 7 of the FOIA, such as disclosure of a confidential source, need be met before the Privacy Act exemption applies."); see also Reyes, 647 F. Supp. at 1512 (noting that "justification need not apply to every record and every piece of a record as long as the system is properly exempted" and that "[t]he general exemption applies to the whole system regardless of the content of individual records within it").

In contrast to these cases, a concurring opinion in the decision by the Court of Appeals for the Ninth Circuit in Exner v. FBI articulated a narrower view of subsection (j)(2). See 612 F.2d 1202, 1207-08 (9th Cir. 1980) (construing subsection (j)(2)(B) as "coextensive" with FOIA Exemption 7 and noting that "reason for withholding the document must be consistent with at least one of the adverse effects listed in the [regulation]"). This narrower view of the exemption finds support in two decisions--Powell v. United States Dep't of Justice, 851 F.2d 394, 395 (D.C. Cir. 1988) (per curiam), and Rosenberg v. Meese, 622 F. Supp. 1451, 1460 (S.D.N.Y. 1985). In Powell, the Court of Appeals for the District of Columbia Circuit ruled that "no legitimate reason" can exist for an agency to refuse to amend a record (in an exempt system of records) already made public with regard only to the requester's correct residence address, and that subsection (j)(2) does not permit an agency to refuse "disclosure or amendment of objective, noncontroversial information" such as race, sex, and correct addresses). 851 F.2d at 395. In <u>Rosenberg</u>, a district court ordered access to a sentencing transcript contained in the same exempt system of records on the ground that the "proffered reasons are simply inapplicable when the particular document requested is a matter of public record." 622 F. Supp. at 1460. The system of records at issue in both <u>Powell</u> and <u>Rosenberg</u> had been exempted from subsection (d), the Act's access and amendment provision. <u>Powell</u>, 851 F.2d at 395; <u>Rosenberg</u>, 622 F. Supp. at 1459-60. However, the agency's regulation failed to specifically state any reason for exempting the system from amendment and its reasons for exempting the system from access were limited. <u>Powell</u>, 851 F.2d at 395; <u>Rosenberg</u>, 622 F. Supp. at 1460. Apparently, because the contents of the particular records at issue were viewed as innocuous--i.e., they had previously been made public--each court found that the agency had lost its exemption (j)(2) claim. <u>Powell</u>, 851 F.2d at 395; <u>Rosenberg</u>, 622 F. Supp. at 1460.

The issue discussed above frequently arises when an agency's regulation exempts its system of records from subsection (g)--the Act's civil remedies provision. Oddly, the language of subsection (j) appears to permit this. <u>See</u> OMB Guidelines, 40 Fed. Reg. 28,948, 28,971 (1975). However, in <u>Tijerina v. Walters</u>, 821 F.2d 789, 795-97 (D.C. Cir. 1987), the D.C. Circuit held that an agency cannot insulate itself from a wrongful disclosure damages action (<u>see</u> 5 U.S.C. § 552a(b), (g)(1)(D)) in such a manner. It construed subsection (j) to permit an agency to exempt only a system of records--and not the agency itself--from other provisions of the Act. <u>See</u> 821 F.2d at 796-97. The result in <u>Tijerina</u> was heavily and understandably influenced by the fact that subsection (j) by its terms does not permit exemption from the subsection (b) restriction-on-disclosure provision. <u>Id.</u>; <u>see also</u> <u>Nakash v. United States Dep't of Justice</u>, 708 F. Supp. 1354, 1358-65 (S.D.N.Y. 1988) (agreeing with <u>Tijerina</u> after extensive discussion of case law and legislative history).

Other courts have indicated that agencies may employ subsection (j)(2) to exempt their systems of records from the subsection (g) civil remedies provision. However, all of these cases suggest that the regulation's statement of reasons for such exemption itself constitutes a limitation on the scope of the exemption. <u>See</u> <u>Fendler</u>, 846 F.2d at 553-54 & n.3 (declining to dismiss subsection (g)(1)(C) damages action--alleging violation of subsection (e)(5)--on ground that agency's "stated justification for exemption from subsection (g) bears no relation to subsection (e)(5)"); <u>Ryan</u>, 595 F.2d at 957-58 (dismissing access claim, but not wrongful disclosure claim, on ground that record system was exempt from subsection (g) because regulation mentioned only "access" as reason for exemption); <u>Nakash</u>, 708 F. Supp. at 1365 (declining to dismiss wrongful disclosure action for same reason) (alternative holding); <u>Kimberlin v. United States Dep't of Justice</u>, 605 F. Supp. 79,

82 (N.D. Ill. 1985) (same), aff'd, 788 F.2d 434 (7th Cir. 1986); Nutter v. VA, No. 84-2392, slip op. at 2-4 (D.D.C. July 9, 1985) (same); see also Alford, 610 F.2d at 349 (declining to decide whether agency may, by regulation, deprive district courts of jurisdiction to review decisions to deny access).

In contrast to the approach taken in these cases (and in Tijerina), other courts have construed subsection (j)(2) regulations to permit exemption of systems of records from provisions of the Act even where the stated reasons do not appear to be applicable in the particular case. See, e.g., Alexander v. United States, 787 F.2d 1349, 1351-52 & n.2 (9th Cir. 1986) (dismissing subsection (g)(1)(C) damages action--alleging violation of subsection (e)(5)--on ground that system of records was exempt from subsection (g) even though implementing regulation mentioned only "access" as rationale for exemption); Wentz, 772 F.2d at 336-39 (dismissing amendment action on ground that system of records was exempt from subsection (d) even though implementing regulation mentioned only "access" as rationale for exemption and record at issue had been disclosed to plaintiff). Note, however, that the Ninth Circuit's decision in Fendler v. United States Bureau of Prisons significantly narrowed the breadth of its earlier holding in Alexander. See 846 F.2d at 554 n.3 (observing that agency in Alexander "had clearly and expressly exempted its system of records from both subsection (e)(5) and subsection (g) . . . [but that for] some unexplained reason, the Bureau of Prisons, unlike the agency involved in Alexander, did not exempt itself from [subsection] (e)(5)").

Another important issue can arise with regard to the recompilation of information originally compiled for law enforcement purposes into a non-law enforcement record. The D.C. Circuit confronted this issue in Doe v. FBI, 936 F.2d 1346 (D.C. Cir. 1991), in which it applied the principles of a Supreme Court FOIA decision concerning recompilation, FBI v. Abramson, 456 U.S. 615 (1982), to Privacy Act-protected records. It held that "information contained in a document qualifying for subsection (j) or (k) exemption as a law enforcement record does not lose its exempt status when recompiled in a non-law enforcement record if the purposes underlying the exemption of the original document pertain to the recompilation as well." Doe, 936 F.2d at 1356. As was held in Abramson, the D.C. Circuit determined that recompilation does not change the basic "nature" of the information. Id.; accord OMB Guidelines, 40 Fed. Reg. at 28,971 ("The public policy which dictates the need for exempting records . . . is based on the need to protect the contents of the records in the system--not the location of the records. Consequently, in responding to a request for access where documents of another agency are involved, the agency receiving the request should consult the originating agency to determine if the records in question have been exempted.").

PRIVACY ACT OVERVIEW

C. Seven Specific Exemptions--5 U.S.C. § 552a(k)

"The head of any agency may promulgate rules, in accordance with the requirements (including general notice) of sections 553(b)(1), (2), and (3), (c), and (e) of this title, to exempt any system of records within the agency from subsections (c)(3), (d), (e)(1), (e)(4)(G), (H), and (I) and (f) of this section if the system of records is--

[The seven specific exemptions are discussed in order below.]

At the time rules are adopted under this subsection, the agency shall include in the statement required under section 553(c) of this title, the reasons why the system of records is to be exempted from a provision of this section."

comment -- As noted above, subsection (g)(3)(A) grants courts the authority to review requested records in camera when a subsection (k) exemption is invoked to deny access. Further, several courts have held that reasonable segregation is required under the Act whenever a subsection (k) exemption is invoked. See, e.g., May v. Department of the Air Force, 777 F.2d 1012, 1015-17 (5th Cir. 1985); Lorenz v. NRC, 516 F. Supp. 1151, 1153-55 (D. Colo. 1981); Nemetz v. Department of the Treasury, 446 F. Supp. 102, 105 (N.D. Ill. 1978).

1. 5 U.S.C. § 552a(k)(1)

"subject to the provisions of section 552(b)(1) of this title."

comment -- Subsection (k)(1) simply incorporates FOIA Exemption 1, 5 U.S.C. § 552(b)(1). See Keenan v. Department of Justice, No. 94-1909, slip op. at 2 n.2, 7-9 (D.D.C. Dec. 17, 1997); Blazy v. Tenet, 979 F. Supp. 10, 23-25 (D.D.C. 1997), summary affirmance granted, No. 97-5330, 1998 WL 315583 (D.C. Cir. May 12, 1998); Laroque v. United States Dep't of Justice, No. 86-2677, 1988 WL 28334, at *2 (D.D.C. Mar. 16, 1988); Moessmer v. CIA, No. 86-948C(1), slip op. at 3-5 (E.D. Mo. Feb. 19, 1987); Demetracopoulos v. CIA, 3 Gov't Disclosure Serv. (P-H) ¶ 82,508, at 83,279 (D.D.C. Oct. 8, 1982); see also OMB Guidelines, 40 Fed. Reg. 28,948, 28,972 (1975). The exemption has been construed to permit the withholding of classified records from an agency employee with a security clearance who seeks only private access to records about him. See Martens v. United States Dep't of Commerce, No. 88-3334, 1990 U.S. Dist. LEXIS 10351, at **10-11 (D.D.C. Aug. 6, 1990).

2. 5 U.S.C. § 552a(k)(2)

"investigatory material compiled for law enforcement purposes, other than material within the scope of subsection (j)(2) of this section: Provided, however, That if any individual is denied any right, privilege, or benefit that he would otherwise be entitled by Federal law, or for which he would otherwise be eligible, as a result of the maintenance of such material, such material shall be provided to such individual, except to the extent that the disclosure of such material would reveal the identity of a source who furnished information to the Government

PRIVACY ACT OVERVIEW

under an express promise that the identity of the source would be held in confidence, or, prior to the effective date of this section [9-27-75], under an implied promise that the identity of the source would be held in confidence."

comment -- This exemption covers: (1) material compiled for criminal investigative law enforcement purposes, by nonprincipal function criminal law enforcement entities; and (2) material compiled for other investigative law enforcement purposes, by any agency.

The material must be compiled for some investigative "law enforcement" purpose, such as a civil investigation or a criminal investigation by a nonprincipal function criminal law enforcement agency. See, e.g., Gowan v. United States Dep't of the Air Force, 148 F.3d 1182, 1188-89 (10th Cir.) (holding that fraud, waste, and abuse complaint to Inspector General is "the catalyst of the investigation and thus comes within the parameters of § 552a(k)(2)"), cert. denied, 525 U.S. 1042 (1998); Melius v. National Indian Gaming Comm'n, No. 98-2210, 1999 U.S. Dist. LEXIS 17537, at **14-15, 18-19 (D.D.C. Nov. 3, 1999) (recognizing Vymetalik, infra, and determining that exemption (k)(2) properly applied to law enforcement investigation into suitability of person involved in gaming contracts); Shewchun v. INS, No. 95-1920, slip op. at 3, 8-9 (D.D.C. Dec. 10, 1996), summary affirmance granted, No. 97-5044 (D.C. Cir. June 5, 1997); Viotti v. United States Air Force, 902 F. Supp. 1331, 1335 (D. Colo. 1995), aff'd, 153 F.3d 730 (10th Cir. 1998) (unpublished table decision); Jaindl v. Department of State, No. 90-1489, slip op. at 3 (D.D.C. Jan. 31, 1991), summary affirmance granted, No. 91-5034 (D.C. Cir. Jan. 8, 1992); Barber v. INS, No. 90-0067C, slip op. at 6-9 (W.D. Wash. May 15, 1990); Culver v. IRS, Nos. 85-242, 85-243, slip op. at 1-2 (N.D. Iowa June 5, 1990); Welsh v. IRS, No. 85-1024, slip op. at 2-3 (D.N.M. Oct. 21, 1986); Spence v. IRS, No. 85-1076, slip op. at 2 (D.N.M. Mar. 27, 1986); Jones v. IRS, No. 85-0-736, slip op. at 2-3 (D. Neb. Mar. 3, 1986); Nader v. ICC, No. 82-1037, 1983 U.S. Dist. LEXIS 11380, at *14 (D.D.C. Nov. 23, 1983); Heinzl v. INS, 3 Gov't Disclosure Serv. (P-H) ¶ 83,121, at 83,725 (N.D. Cal. Dec. 18, 1981); Lobosco v. IRS, No. 77-1464, 1981 WL 1780, at *3 (E.D.N.Y. Jan. 14, 1981); Utah Gas & Oil, Inc. v. SEC, 1 Gov't Disclosure Serv. (P-H) ¶ 80,038, at 80,114 (D. Utah Jan. 9, 1980); see also OMB Guidelines, 40 Fed. Reg. 28,948, 28,972-73 (1975).

Therefore, subsection (k)(2) does not include material compiled solely for the purpose of a routine background security investigation of a job applicant. See Vymetalik v. FBI, 785 F.2d 1090, 1093-98 (D.C. Cir. 1986) (noting applicability of narrower subsection (k)(5) to such material and ruling that "specific allegations of illegal activities" must be involved in order for subsection (k)(2) to apply); Bostic

-811-

v. FBI, No. 1:94 CV 71, slip op. at 7-8 (W.D. Mich. Dec. 16, 1994) (following Vymetalik). However, material compiled for the purpose of investigating agency employees for suspected violations of law can fall within subsection (k)(2). See Strang v. United States Arms Control & Disarmament Agency, 864 F.2d 859, 862-63 n.2 (D.C. Cir. 1989) ("Unlike Vymetalik, this case involves not a job applicant undergoing a routine check of his background and his ability to perform the job, but an existing agency employee investigated for violating national security regulations."); Cohen v. FBI, No. 93-1701, slip op. at 4-6 (D.D.C. Oct. 3, 1995) (applying Vymetalik and finding that particular information within background investigation file qualified as "law enforcement" information "withheld out of a legitimate concern for national security," thus "satisf[ying] the standards set forth in Vymetalik," which recognized that "'[i]f specific allegations of illegal activities were involved, then th[e] investigation might well be characterized as a law enforcement investigation'" and that "'[s]o long as the investigation was "realistically based on a legitimate concern that federal laws have been or may be violated or that national security may be breached" the records may be considered law enforcement records'" (quoting Vymetalik, 785 F.2d at 1098, in turn quoting Pratt v. Webster, 673 F.2d 408, 421 (D.C. Cir. 1982))); see also Croskey v. United States Office of Special Counsel, 9 F. Supp. 2d 8, 11 (D.D.C. 1998) (finding Office of Special Counsel Report of Investigation, which was developed to determine whether plaintiff had been fired for legitimate or retaliatory reasons, exempt from access and amendment provisions of Privacy Act pursuant to subsection (k)(2)), summary affirmance granted, No. 98-5346, 1999 WL 58614 (D.C. Cir. Jan. 12, 1999); Viotti, 902 F. Supp. at 1335 (concluding, "as a matter of law, that [Report of Inquiry] was compiled for a law enforcement purpose as stated in 5 U.S.C. § 552a(k)(2)" where "original purpose of the investigation . . . was a complaint to the [Inspector General] of fraud, waste and abuse," even though "complaint was not sustained and no criminal charges were brought," because "plain language of the exemption states that it applies to the purpose of the investigation, not to the result"); Mittleman v. United States Dep't of the Treasury, 919 F. Supp. 461, 469 (D.D.C. 1995) (finding that Inspector General's report "pertain[ing] to plaintiff's grievance against Treasury officials and related matters . . . falls squarely within the reach of exemption (k)(2)"), aff'd in part & remanded in part on other grounds, 104 F.3d 410 (D.C. Cir. 1997); Martens v. United States Dep't of Commerce, No. 88-3334, 1990 U.S. Dist. LEXIS 10351, at **18-20 (D.D.C. Aug. 6, 1990); Fausto v. Watt, 3 Gov't Disclosure Serv. (P-H) ¶ 83,217, at 83,929-30 (4th Cir. June 7, 1983); Frank v. United States Dep't of Justice, 480 F. Supp. 596, 597 (D.D.C. 1979).

However, in Doe v. United States Department of Justice, 790 F. Supp. 17, 19-21 (D.D.C. 1992), the District Court for the District of Columbia construed Vymetalik narrowly and determined that although subsection (k)(5) was "directly applicable," subsection (k)(2) also applied to records of an FBI background check on a prospective Department of Justice attorney. It determined that the Department of Justice, as "the nation's primary law enforcement and security agency," id. at 20, had a legitimate law enforcement purpose in ensuring that "officials like Doe . . . be 'reliable, trustworthy, of good conduct and character, and of complete and unswerving loyalty to the United States,'" id. (quoting Exec. Order No. 10,450, 18 Fed. Reg. 2489 (Apr. 29, 1953)). It seems to follow that subsection (k)(2) would likewise apply to background investigations of prospective FBI/DEA special agents. See Putnam v. United States Dep't of Justice, 873 F. Supp. 705, 717 (D.D.C. 1995) (finding subsection (k)(2) properly invoked to withhold information that would reveal identities of individuals who provided information in connection with former FBI agent's preemployment investigation).

More recently, though, the District Court for the District of Columbia, when faced with the same issue concerning subsection (k)(2)/(k)(5) applicability, relied entirely on the D.C. Circuit's opinion in Vymetalik, with no mention whatsoever of Doe v. United States Dep't of Justice. Cohen v. FBI, No. 93-1701 (D.D.C. Oct. 3, 1995). Nevertheless, the District Court found subsection (k)(2) to be applicable to one document in the background investigation file because that document was "withheld out of a legitimate concern for national security," and "satisfie[d] the standards set forth in Vymetalik," which recognized that "'[i]f specific allegations of illegal activities were involved, then th[e] investigation might well be characterized as a law enforcement investigation'" and that "'[s]o long as the investigation was "realistically based on a legitimate concern that federal laws have been or may be violated or that national security may be breached" the records may be considered law enforcement records.'" Cohen, No. 93-1701, slip op. at 3-6 (D.D.C. Oct. 3, 1995) (quoting Vymetalik, 785 F.2d at 1098, in turn quoting Pratt, 673 F.2d at 421). Another district court rejected Doe and, following the rationale in Vymetalik, held that "'law enforcement purposes' as that term is utilized in [subsection (k)(2) of] the Privacy Act, does not apply to documents and information gathered during a[n FBI agent applicant's] pre-employment background investigation." Bostic, No. 1:94 CV 71, slip op. at 7-8 (W.D. Mich. Dec. 16, 1994).

Unlike with Exemption 7(A) of the Freedom of Information Act, 5 U.S.C. § 552(b)(7)(A) (1994 & Supp. IV 1998), there is no temporal limitation on the scope of subsection (k)(2). See Irons v. Bell, 596 F.2d 468, 471 (1st Cir.

1979). But see Anderson v. United States Dep't of the Treasury, No. 76-1404, slip op. at 9-11 (D.D.C. July 19, 1977) (subsection (k)(2) inapplicable to investigatory report regarding alleged wrongdoing by IRS agent where investigation was closed and no possibility of any future law enforcement proceedings existed).

Although the issue has not been the subject of much significant case law, the OMB Guidelines explain that the "Provided, however" provision of subsection (k)(2) means that "[t]o the extent that such an investigatory record is used as a basis for denying an individual any right, privilege, or benefit to which the individual would be entitled in the absence of that record, the individual must be granted access to that record except to the extent that access would reveal the identity of a confidential source." OMB Guidelines, 40 Fed. Reg. at 28,973; cf. Guccione v. National Indian Gaming Comm'n, No. 98-CV-164, 1999 U.S. Dist. LEXIS 15475, at **11-12 (S.D. Cal. Aug. 5, 1999) (approving agency invocation of subsection (k)(2) to protect third-party names of individuals who had not been given express promises of confidentiality where plaintiff did not contend any denial of right, privilege, or benefit). The only decision that has discussed this provision in any depth is Viotti v. United States Air Force, 902 F. Supp. at 1335-36, in which the District Court for the District of Colorado determined that an Air Force Colonel's forced early retirement "resulted in a loss of a benefit, right or privilege for which he was eligible--the loss of six months to four years of the difference between his active duty pay and retirement pay," and "over his life expectancy . . . the difference in pay between the amount of his retirement pay for twenty-six years of active duty versus thirty years of active duty." Id. The court found that "as a matter of law, based on [a report of inquiry, plaintiff] lost benefits, rights, and privileges for which he was eligible" and thus he was entitled to an unredacted copy of the report "despite the fact that [it] was prepared pursuant to a law enforcement investigation." Id. It went on to find that "the 'express' promise requirement" of (k)(2) was not satisfied where a witness "merely expressed a 'fear of reprisal.'" Id. (citing Londrigan v. FBI, 670 F.2d 1164, 1170 (D.C. Cir. 1981)).

The Court of Appeals for the Tenth Circuit in affirming Viotti noted that subsection (k)(2)'s limiting exception applied only in the context of access requests and did not apply to limit the exemption's applicability with regard to amendment requests. Viotti v. United States Air Force, No. 97-1371, 1998 WL 453670, at *2 n.2 (10th Cir. Aug. 5, 1998). While the court's footnote in Viotti spoke in terms of the particular exempting regulations at issue, the more general proposition is in complete accord with the plain language of subsection (k)(2). See 5 U.S.C. § 552a(k)(2) (in provision limiting exemption's applicability requiring that "material shall be **provided** to [the] individual except to the extent that **disclosure** of such material would reveal the identity of a [confidential source]" (emphasis added)). Nevertheless, only a matter of weeks earlier, in its decision in Gowan v. United States Dep't of the Air Force, 148 F.3d 1182, 1189 (10th Cir.), cert. denied, 525 U.S. 1042 (1998), the Tenth Circuit, citing the Viotti district court decision in comparison, went through the exercise of determining whether the limiting exception applied in the context of the amendment claims before it. The Tenth Circuit stated that subsection (k)(2)'s limiting exception was inapplicable to an Inspector General complaint because "the charges contained in the complaint were deemed unworthy of further action." Gowan, 148 F.3d at 1189. Given the very limited case law interpreting subsection (k)(2)'s limiting exception and what constitutes denial of a "right, privilege, or benefit," it is worth noting the Tenth's Circuit's statement in Gowan, even though the court's subsequent footnote in Viotti certainly calls into question its relevance to the court's ultimate holding regarding subsection (k)(2)'s applicability.

In Doe v. United States Dep't of Justice, 790 F. Supp. at 21 n.4, 22, the court noted this provision of subsection (k)(2), but determined that it was not applicable because the plaintiff "ha[d] no entitlement to a job with the Justice Department." Inexplicably, the court did not discuss whether the denial of a federal job would amount to the denial of a "privilege" or "benefit." See id.; see also Jaindl, No. 90-1489, slip op. at 2 n.1 (D.D.C. Jan. 31, 1991) (noting that "[b]ecause there is no general right to possess a passport," application of (k)(2) was not limited in that case). Another court refused to address the provision's applicability where the plaintiff failed to raise the issue at the administrative level. Comer v. IRS, No. 85-10503-BC, slip op. at 3-5 (E.D. Mich. Mar. 27, 1986), aff'd, 831 F.2d 294 (6th Cir. 1987) (unpublished table decision).

It should be noted that information that originally qualifies for subsection (k)(2) protection should retain that protection even if it subsequently is recompiled into a non-law enforcement record. See Doe v. FBI, 936 F.2d 1346, 1356 (D.C. Cir. 1991) (discussed under subsection (j)(2), above); accord OMB Guidelines, 40 Fed. Reg. at 28,971 (same).

Finally, two courts have considered claims brought by individuals who allegedly provided information pursuant to a promise of confidentiality and sought damages resulting from disclosure of the information and failure to sufficiently protect their identities pursuant to subsection (k)(2). Bechhoefer v. United States Dep't of Justice, 934 F. Supp. 535, 538-39 (W.D.N.Y. 1996), vacated & remanded sub nom. Bechhoefer v. United States Dep't of

Justice Drug Enforcement Admin., 209 F.3d 57 (2d Cir. 2000) (finding that information at issue did qualify as "record" under Privacy Act); Sterling v. United States, 798 F. Supp. 47, 49 (D.D.C. 1992). In Sterling, the District Court for the District of Columbia stated that the plaintiff was "not barred from stating a claim for monetary damages [under (g)(1)(D)] merely because the record did not contain 'personal information' about him and was not retrieved through a search of indices bearing his name or other identifying characteristics," 798 F. Supp. at 49, but in a subsequent opinion the court ultimately ruled in favor of the agency, having been presented with no evidence that the agency had intentionally or willfully disclosed the plaintiff's identity. Sterling v. United States, 826 F. Supp. 570, 571-72 (D.D.C. 1993), summary affirmance granted, No. 93-5264 (D.C. Cir. Mar. 11, 1994). However, the District Court for the Western District of New York in Bechhoefer, when presented with an argument based on Sterling, stated that it did not "find the Sterling court's analysis persuasive." Bechhoefer, 934 F. Supp. at 538-39. Having already determined that the information at issue did not qualify as a record "about" the plaintiff, that court recognized that subsection (k)(2) "does not prohibit agencies from releasing material that would reveal the identity of a confidential source" but rather "allows agencies to promulgate rules to exempt certain types of documents from mandatory disclosure under other portions of the Act." Id. The court went on to state that "plaintiff's reliance on § 552a(k)(2) [wa]s misplaced," and that subsection (k) was "irrelevant" to the claim before it for wrongful disclosure. Id. at 539.

3. 5 U.S.C. § 552a(k)(3)

"maintained in connection with providing protective services to the President of the United States or other individuals pursuant to section 3056 of Title 18."

comment -- This exemption obviously is applicable to certain Secret Service record systems. For a discussion of this exemption, see OMB Guidelines, 40 Fed. Reg. 28,948, 28,973 (1975).

4. 5 U.S.C. § 552a(k)(4)

"required by statute to be maintained and used solely as statistical records."

comment -- For a discussion of this exemption, see OMB Guidelines, 40 Fed. Reg. 28,948, 28,973 (1975).

5. 5 U.S.C. § 552a(k)(5)

"investigatory material compiled solely for the purpose of determining suitability, eligibility, or qualifications for Federal civilian employment, military service, Federal contracts, or access to classified information, but only to the extent that the disclosure of such material would reveal the identity of a source who furnished information to the Government under an express promise that the identity of the source would be held in confidence, or, prior to the effective date of this section [9-27-75], under an implied promise that the identity of the source would be held in confidence."

comment -- This exemption is generally applicable to source-identifying material in background employment and personnel-type investigative files. See OMB Guidelines, 40 Fed. Reg. 28,948, 28,973-74 (1975); 120 Cong. Rec. 40,406, 40,884-85 (1974), reprinted in Source Book at 860, 996-97. The Court of Appeals for the District of Columbia Circuit has held that exemption (k)(5) is also applicable to source-identifying material compiled for determining eligibility for federal grants, stating that "the term 'Federal contracts' in Privacy Act exemption (k)(5) encompasses a federal grant agreement if the grant agreement includes the essential elements of a contract and establishes a contractual relationship between the government and the grantee." Henke v. United States Dep't of Commerce, 83 F.3d 1445, 1453 (D.C. Cir. 1996). In addition, exemption (k)(5) is applicable to information collected for continued as well as original employment. See Hernandez v. Alexander, 671 F.2d 402, 406 (10th Cir. 1982). In situations where "specific allegations of illegal activities" are being investigated, an agency may be able to invoke subsection (k)(2)--which is potentially broader in its coverage than subsection (k)(5). See, e.g., Vymetalik v. FBI, 785 F.2d 1090, 1093-98 (D.C. Cir. 1986).

Subsection (k)(5)--known as the "Erlenborn Amendment"--was among the most hotly debated of any the Act's provisions because it provides for absolute protection to those who qualify as confidential sources, regardless of the adverse effect that the material they provide may have on an individual. See 120 Cong. Rec. 36,655-58 (1974), reprinted in Source Book at 908-19.

That aside, though, subsection (k)(5) is still a narrow exemption in two respects. First, in contrast to Exemption 7(D) of the Freedom of Information Act, 5 U.S.C. § 552(b)(7)(D) (1994 & Supp. IV 1998), it requires an express promise of confidentiality for source material acquired after the effective date of the Privacy Act (September 27, 1975). Cf. Viotti v. United States Air Force, 902 F. Supp. 1331, 1336 (D. Colo. 1995) (finding that "'express' promise requirement" of subsection (k)(2) was not satisfied when witness "merely expressed a 'fear of reprisal'"), aff'd, 153 F.3d 730 (10th Cir. 1998) (unpublished table decision). For source material acquired prior to the effective date of the Privacy Act, an implied promise of confidentiality will suffice. See 5 U.S.C. § 552a(k)(5); cf. Londrigan v. FBI, 722 F.2d 840, 844-45 (D.C. Cir. 1983) (no "automatic exemption" for FBI background interviews prior to effective date of Privacy Act; however, inference drawn that interviewees were impliedly promised confidentiality where FBI showed that it had pursued "policy of confidentiality" to which interviewing agents conformed their conduct). See generally United States Dep't of Justice v. Landano, 508 U.S. 165 (1993) (setting standards for demonstrating implied confidentiality under FOIA Exemption 7(D)). Second, in contrast to the second clause of FOIA Exemption 7(D), subsection (k)(5) protects only source-identifying material, not all source-supplied material. Of course, where source-identifying material is exempt from Privacy Act access under subsection (k)(5), it typically is exempt under the broader exemptions of the FOIA as well. See, e.g., Keenan v. Department of Justice, No. 94-1909, slip op. at 16-17 (D.D.C. Mar. 25, 1997), subsequent decision, slip op. at 5-7 (D.D.C. Dec. 16, 1997); Bostic v. FBI, No. 1:94 CV 71, slip op. at 8-9, 12-13 (W.D. Mich. Dec. 16, 1994); Miller v. United States, 630 F. Supp. 347, 348-49 (E.D.N.Y. 1986); Patton v. FBI, 626 F. Supp. 445, 446-47 (M.D. Pa. 1985), aff'd, 782 F.2d 1030 (3d Cir. 1986) (unpublished table decision); Diamond v. FBI, 532 F. Supp. 216, 232 (S.D.N.Y. 1981), aff'd, 707 F.2d 75 (2d Cir. 1983). One court has held that subsection (k)(5) protects source-identifying material even where the identity of the source is known. See Volz v. United States Dep't of Justice, 619 F.2d 49, 50 (10th Cir. 1980). Another court has suggested to the contrary. Doe v. United States Civil Serv. Comm'n, 483 F. Supp. 539, 576-77 (S.D.N.Y. 1980) (aberrational decision holding addresses of three named persons "not exempt from disclosure under (k)(5) . . . because they didn't serve as confidential sources and the plaintiff already knows their identity").

Subsection (k)(5) is not limited to those sources who provide derogatory comments, see Londrigan v. FBI, 670 F.2d 1164, 1170 (D.C. Cir. 1981); see also Voelker v. FBI, 638 F. Supp. 571, 572-73 (E.D. Mo. 1986). It has also been held that the exemption is not limited to information that would reveal the identity of the source in statements made by those confidential sources, but also protects information that would reveal the source's identity in statements provided by third parties. See Haddon v. Freeh, 31 F. Supp. 2d 16, 21 (D.D.C. 1998). Also, the exemption's applicability is not diminished by the age of the source-identifying material. See Diamond, 532 F. Supp. at 232-33.

However, an agency cannot rely upon subsection (k)(5) to bar a requester's amendment request, as the exemption applies only to the extent that disclosure of information would reveal the identity of a confidential source. See Vymetalik, 785 F.2d at 1096-98; see also Doe v. FBI, 936 F.2d at 1356 n.12 (although documents at issue were not limited to exemption pursuant to subsection (k)(5), noting that subsection (k)(5) would not apply where FBI refused to amend information that had already been disclosed to individual seeking amendment); Bostic, No. 1:94 CV 71, slip op. at 9 (W.D. Mich. Dec. 16, 1994) (application of exemption (k)(5) in this access case is not contrary to, but rather consistent with, Vymetalik and Doe because in those cases exemption (k)(5) did not apply because relief sought was amendment of records).

Note also that OMB's policy guidance indicates that promises of confidentiality are not to be made automatically. 40 Fed. Reg. 28,948, 28,974 (1975). Consistent with the OMB Guidelines, the Office of Personnel Management has promulgated regulations establishing procedures for determining when a pledge of confidentiality is appropriate. See 5 C.F.R. § 736.102 (1999); see also Larry v. Lawler, 605 F.2d 954, 961 n.8 (7th Cir. 1978) (suggesting that finding of "good cause" is prerequisite for granting of confidentiality to sources).

Nevertheless, the District Court for the District of Columbia has held that in order to invoke exemption (k)(5) for sources that were in fact promised confidentiality, it is not necessary that the sources themselves affirmatively sought confidentiality, nor must the government make a showing that the sources would not have furnished information without a promise of confidentiality. Henke v. United States Dep't of Commerce, No. 94-0189, 1996 WL 692020, at **9-10 (D.D.C. Aug. 19, 1994). The court went on to state: "[T]he question of whether the reviewers expressed a desire to keep their identities confidential is wholly irrelevant to the Court's determination of whether they were in fact given promises of confidentiality." Id. at *10. On appeal, the Court of Appeals for the District of Columbia Circuit stated that while it "would not go quite that far," as agencies "must use subsection (k)(5) sparingly," agencies may make determinations that promises of confidentiality are necessary "categorically," as "[n]othing in either the statute or the case law requires that [an agency] apply subsection (k)(5) only to those particular reviewers who have expressly asked for an exemption and would otherwise have declined to participate in the peer review process." Henke v. United States Dep't of Commerce, 83 F.3d 1445, 1449 (D.C. Cir. 1996).

Finally, it should be noted that information that originally qualifies for subsection (k)(5) protection should retain that protection even if it subsequently is recompiled into a non-law enforcement record. See Doe v. FBI, 936 F.2d 1346, 1356 (D.C. Cir. 1991) (discussed under subsection (j)(2), above); accord OMB Guidelines, 40 Fed. Reg. at 28,971 (same).

6. **5 U.S.C. § 552a(k)(6)**

"testing or examination material used solely to determine individual qualifications for appointment or promotion in

PRIVACY ACT OVERVIEW

>  the Federal service the disclosure of which would compromise the objectivity or fairness of the testing or examination process."

>> comment -- It should be noted that material exempt from Privacy Act access under subsection (k)(6) is also typically exempt from FOIA access under FOIA Exemption 2. See Patton v. FBI, 626 F. Supp. 445, 447 (M.D. Pa. 1985), aff'd, 782 F.2d 1030 (3d Cir. 1986) (unpublished table decision); Oatley v. United States, 3 Gov't Disclosure Serv. (P-H) ¶ 83,274, at 84,065-66 (D.D.C. Aug. 16, 1983). For a discussion of this provision, see OMB Guidelines, 40 Fed. Reg. 28,948, 28,974 (1975).

### 7. 5 U.S.C. § 552a(k)(7)

> "evaluation material used to determine potential for promotion in the armed services, but only to the extent that the disclosure of such material would reveal the identity of a source who furnished information to the government under an express promise that the identity of the source would be held in confidence, or, prior to the effective date of this section [9-25-75], under an implied promise that the identity of the source would be held in confidence."

>> comment -- For an example of the application of this exemption, see May v. Department of the Air Force, 777 F.2d 1012, 1015-17 (5th Cir. 1985). For a further discussion of this provision, see OMB Guidelines, 40 Fed. Reg. 28,948, 28,974 (1975).

## SOCIAL SECURITY NUMBER USAGE

Section 7 of the Privacy Act (found at 5 U.S.C. § 552a note (Disclosure of Social Security Number)) provides that:

"It shall be unlawful for any Federal, State or local government agency to deny to any individual any right, benefit, or privilege provided by law because of such individual's refusal to disclose his social security account number." Sec. 7(a)(1).

> comment -- Note that although this provision applies beyond federal agencies, it does not apply to: (1) any disclosure which is required by federal statute; or (2) any disclosure of a social security number to any federal, state, or local agency maintaining a system of records in existence and operating before January 1, 1975, if such disclosure was required under statute or regulation adopted prior to such date to verify the identity of an individual. See Sec. 7(a)(2)(A)-(B).

> Note also that the Tax Reform Act of 1976, 42 U.S.C. § 405(c)(2)(C)(i), (iv) (1994 & Supp. III 1997), expressly exempts state agencies from this restriction to the extent that social security numbers are used "in the administration of any tax, general public assistance, driver's license, or motor vehicle registration law within its jurisdiction." See, e.g., Clauqus v. Roosevelt Island Hous. Management Corp., No. 96CIV8155, 1999 WL 258275, at *4 (S.D.N.Y. Apr. 29, 1999) (considering housing management corporation to be state actor for Privacy

-820-

Act purposes but finding that Privacy Act does not apply to income verification process for public housing program because of exception created by 42 U.S.C. § 405(c)(2)(C)(i)). Exemption from the Social Security number provisions of the Privacy Act is also provided for certain other state uses. See, e.g., 42 U.S.C. § 405(c)(2)(C)(ii) (authorizing state use of social security numbers in issuance of birth certificates and for purposes of enforcement of child support orders); 42 U.S.C. § 405(c)(2)(C)(iii) (authorizing use of social security numbers by Secretary of Agriculture in administration of Food Stamp Act of 1977 and by Federal Crop Insurance Corporation in administration of Federal Crop Insurance Act).

"Any Federal, State or local government agency which requests an individual to disclose his social security account number shall inform that individual whether that disclosure is mandatory or voluntary, by what statutory or other authority such number is solicited, and what uses will be made of it." Sec. 7(b).

comment -- Jurisdiction to enforce the social security number provision might appear questionable inasmuch as the Privacy Act does not expressly provide for a civil remedy against a nonfederal agency, or for injunctive relief outside of the access and amendment contexts. In fact, in a recent decision the Court of Appeals for the Ninth Circuit held that the Privacy Act provides no cause of action against a state licensing entity with regard to its requirement that individuals provide their social security number in order to obtain license renewal, inasmuch as the private right of civil action created by the Privacy Act "'is specifically limited to actions against agencies of the United States Government.'" Dittman v. California, 191 F.3d 1020, 1026 (9th Cir. 1999) (quoting Unt v. Aerospace Corp., 765 F.2d 1440, 1447 (9th Cir. 1981)).

However, other courts have recognized implied remedies for violations of this provision's requirements. See McKay v. Altobello, No. 96-3458, 1997 WL 266717, at **1-3, 5 (E.D. La. May 16, 1997); Yeager v. Hackensack Water Co., 615 F. Supp. 1087, 1090-92 (D.N.J. 1985); Wolman v. United States, 501 F. Supp. 310, 311 (D.D.C. 1980), remanded, 675 F.2d 1341 (D.C. Cir. 1982) (unpublished table decision), on remand, 542 F. Supp. 84, 85-86 (D.D.C. 1982); Greater Cleveland Welfare Rights Org. v. Bauer, 462 F. Supp. 1313, 1319-21 (N.D. Ohio 1978).

For other decisions construing the provision, see Crawford v. United States Trustee, 194 F.3d 954, 961-62 (9th Cir. 1999) (rejecting government's argument that because disclosure of plaintiff's social security number was expressly required by federal statute, section 7 was wholly inapplicable, stating that "§ 7(a)(2)(A)'s exclusion for federal statutes only pertains to the limitation recited in § 7(a)(1)"; holding that section 7(b) had no bearing on the public disclosure of plaintiff's social security number by the government, which was the only issue in dispute); Alcaraz v. Block, 746 F.2d 593, 608-09 (9th Cir. 1984) (Section 7(b)'s notice provision satisfied where agency informed "participants of the voluntariness of the disclosure, the source of authority for it and the possible uses to which the disclosed numbers may be put"); Brookens v. United States, 627 F.2d 494, 496-99 (D.C. Cir. 1980) (agency did not violate Privacy Act because it maintained system of records "before January 1, 1975 and disclosure of a social security number to identify individuals was required under [executive order]"); McElrath v. Califano, 615 F.2d 434, 440 (7th Cir. 1980) (because disclosure of social security number required by Aid to Families with Dependent Children program under 42 U.S.C. § 602(a)(25) (1994), regulations that give effect to that requirement are not violative of Privacy Act); Green v. Philbrook, 576 F.2d 440, 445-46 (2d Cir. 1978) (same); McKay v. Thompson, No. 1:98-CV-354, slip op. at 9-11 (E.D. Tenn. Oct. 29, 1999) (finding that Tennessee law requiring disclosure of social security number for voter registration fell within section 7(a)(2)'s exception for systems of records in existence prior to January 1, 1975, where disclosure was required under statute or regulation) (appeal pending); Russell v. Board of Plumbing Exam'rs, 74 F. Supp. 2d 339, 347 (S.D.N.Y. 1999) (finding violation of section 7 and ordering injunctive relief where defendants neither informed applicants that providing social security number was optional nor provided statutory authority by which number was solicited, and no statutory authority existed); Johnson v. Fleming, No. 95 Civ. 1891, 1996 WL 502410, at **1, 3-4 (S.D.N.Y. Sept. 4, 1996) (no violation of either section 7(a)(1) or section 7(b) where, during course of seizure of property from plaintiff, an unlicensed streetvendor, plaintiff refused to provide police officer with his social security number and officer "seized all of Plaintiff's records rather than only 'a bagful' as other officers allegedly had done" on previous occasions); In re Rausch, No. BK-S-95-23707, 1196 WL 333685, at *7 (Bankr. D. Nev. May 20, 1996) (Privacy Act "inapplicable" because 11 U.S.C. § 110 (1994) "requires placing the SSN upon 'documents for filing'"); In re Floyd, 193 B.R. 548, 552-53 (Bankr. N.D. Cal. 1996) (Bankruptcy Code, 11 U.S.C. § 110(c) (1994), required disclosure of social security number, thus section 7(a) inapplicable; further stating that section 7(b) also inapplicable "even assuming the [U.S. Trustee] or the clerk of the bankruptcy court were agencies" because no "request" had been made; rather, because disclosure of social security number is required by statute, "the [U.S. Trustee] is enforcing a Congressional directive, not 'requesting' anyone's SSN" and "[t]he clerk receives documents for filing but does not police their content or form or request that certain information be included"); Krebs v. Rutgers, 797 F. Supp. 1246, 1256 (D.N.J. 1992) (although state-chartered, Rutgers is not state agency or government-controlled corporation subject to Privacy Act); Greidinger v. Davis, 782 F. Supp. 1106, 1108-09 (E.D. Va. 1992) (Privacy Act violated where state did not provide timely notice in accordance with Section 7(b) when collecting social security number for voter registration), rev'd & remanded on other grounds, 988 F.2d 1344 (4th Cir. 1993); Libertarian Party v. Bremer Ehrler, Etc., 776 F. Supp. 1200, 1209 (E.D. Ky. 1991) (requirement that voter include social security number on signature petition violates Privacy Act); Ingerman v. IRS, No. 89-5396, slip op. at 3-5 (D.N.J. Apr. 3, 1991) (Section 7(b) not applicable to IRS request that taxpayers affix printed mailing label containing social security

# PRIVACY ACT OVERVIEW

number on tax returns; no new disclosure occurs because IRS already was in possession of taxpayers' social security numbers), aff'd, 953 F.2d 1380 (3d Cir. 1992) (unpublished table decision); Oakes v. IRS, No. 86-2804, slip op. at 2-3 (D.D.C. Apr. 16, 1987) (Section 7(b) does not require agency requesting individual to disclose his social security number to publish any notice in Federal Register); Doyle v. Wilson, 529 F. Supp. 1343, 1348-50 (D. Del. 1982) (Section 7(b)'s requirements are not fulfilled when no affirmative effort is made to disclose information required under 7(b) "at or before the time the number is requested"); Doe v. Sharp, 491 F. Supp. 346, 347-50 (D. Mass. 1980) (same as Green and McElrath regarding Section 7(a); Section 7(b) creates affirmative duty for agencies to inform applicant of uses to be made of social security numbers-- "after-the-fact explanations" not sufficient); and Chambers v. Klein, 419 F. Supp. 569, 580 (D.N.J. 1976) (same as Green, McElrath, and Doe regarding Section 7(a); Section 7(b) not violated where agency failed to notify applicants of use to be made of social security numbers as state had not begun using them pending full implementation of statute requiring their disclosure), aff'd, 564 F.2d 89 (3d Cir. 1977) (unpublished table decision). Cf. Doe v. Herman, No. 2:97CV00043, 1999 U.S. Dist. LEXIS 17302, at *30 (W.D. Va. Oct. 29, 1999) (magistrate's recommendation) (although not citing Section 7 with regard to issue, citing Doe v. Sharp and subsection (e)(3) for proposition that "when agency solicits a social security number it shall inform the individual of what use will be made of it").

## GOVERNMENT CONTRACTORS

"When an agency provides by a contract for the operation by or on behalf of the agency of a system of records to accomplish an agency function, the agency shall, consistent with its authority, cause the requirements of this section to be applied to such system. For purposes of subsection (i) of this section any such contractor and any employee of such contractor, if such contract is agreed to on or after the effective date of this section [9-27-75], shall be considered to be an employee of an agency." 5 U.S.C. § 552a(m)(1).

"A consumer reporting agency to which a record is disclosed under section 3711(e) of Title 31 shall not be considered a contractor for the purposes of this section." 5 U.S.C. § 552a(m)(2).

comment -- For guidance concerning this provision, see OMB Guidelines, 40 Fed. Reg. 28,948, 28,951, 28,975-76, (1975), and the legislative debate reported at 120 Cong. Rec. 40,408 (1974), reprinted in Source Book at 866. See generally Boggs v. Southeastern Tidewater Opportunity Project, No. 2:96cv196, U.S. Dist. LEXIS 6977, at *5 (E.D. Va. May 22, 1996) (subsection (m) inapplicable to community action agency that was not "in the business of keeping records for federal agencies").

The Federal Acquisition Regulation sets forth the language that must be inserted in solicitations and contracts "[w]hen the design, development, or operation of a system of records on individuals is required to accomplish an agency function." 48 C.F.R. § 24.104 (1999); see also id. § 52.224-1 to -2.

-823-

PRIVACY ACT OVERVIEW

Additionally, see the discussion regarding treatment of contractors as "employees" for purposes of subsection (b)(1) disclosures under "Conditions Of Disclosure To Third Parties," above.

Even when subsection (m) is applicable, the agency--not the contractor--remains the only proper party defendant in a Privacy Act lawsuit. See Campbell v. VA, 2 Gov't Disclosure Serv. (P-H) ¶ 82,076, at 82,355 (S.D. Iowa Dec. 21, 1981); see also Patterson v. Austin Med. Ctr., No. 97-1241, slip op. at 4-5 (D. Minn. Jan. 28, 1998) (Subsection (m) "does not create a private cause of action against a government contractor for violations of the Act."), aff'd, No. 98-1643, 1998 U.S. App. LEXIS 22371 (8th Cir. Sept. 11, 1998). But cf. Shannon v. General Elec. Co., 812 F. Supp. 308, 311-15 & n.5 (N.D.N.Y. 1993) (although subsection (m) not mentioned, stating that "GE is subject to the requirements of the Privacy Act, inasmuch as it falls within the definition of 'agency'"). See generally Adelman v. Discover Card Servs., 915 F. Supp. 1163, 1166 (D. Utah 1996) (with no mention of subsection (m), finding no waiver of sovereign immunity for action brought for alleged violation by state agency working as independent contractor to administer federal program for Social Security Administration, even though procedures and standards governing relationship between SSA and state agency explicitly stated that in event of alleged violation of Privacy Act concerning operation of system of records to accomplish agency function, civil action could be brought against agency).

**MAILING LISTS**

"An individual's name and address may not be sold or rented by an agency unless such action is specifically authorized by law. This provision shall not be construed to require the withholding of names and addresses otherwise permitted to be made public." 5 U.S.C. § 552a(n).

comment -- For a decision discussing this provision, see Disabled Officer's Ass'n v. Rumsfeld, 428 F. Supp. 454, 459 (D.D.C. 1977), aff'd, 574 F.2d 636 (D.C. Cir. 1978) (unpublished table decision). For a further discussion of this provision, see OMB Guidelines, 40 Fed. Reg. 28,948, 28,976 (1975).

**MISCELLANEOUS PROVISIONS**

Note that the Privacy Act also contains provisions concerning archival records, see 5 U.S.C. § 552a(l); see also OMB Guidelines, 40 Fed. Reg. 28,948, 28,974-75 (1975), reporting requirements for new record systems, see 5 U.S.C. § 552a(r), and a biennial report to Congress, see 5 U.S.C. § 552a(s).

# FREEDOM OF INFORMATION ACT

THE FREEDOM OF INFORMATION ACT

5 U.S.C. § 552

As Amended

§ 552. Public information; agency rules, opinions, orders, records, and proceedings

(a) Each agency shall make available to the public information as follows:

(1) Each agency shall separately state and currently publish in the Federal Register for the guidance of the public--

(A) descriptions of its central and field organization and the established places at which, the employees (and in the case of a uniformed service, the members) from whom, and the methods whereby, the public may obtain information, make submittals or requests, or obtain decisions;

(B) statements of the general course and method by which its functions are channeled and determined, including the nature and requirements of all formal and informal procedures available;

(C) rules of procedure, descriptions of forms available or the places at which forms may be obtained, and instructions as to the scope and contents of all papers, reports, or examinations;

(D) substantive rules of general applicability adopted as authorized by law, and statements of general policy or interpretations of general applicability formulated and adopted by the agency; and

(E) each amendment, revision, or repeal of the foregoing.

Except to the extent that a person has actual and timely notice of the terms thereof, a person may not in any manner be required to resort to, or be adversely affected by, a matter required to be published in the Federal Register and not so published. For the purpose of this paragraph, matter reasonably available to the class of persons affected thereby is deemed published in the Federal Register when incorporated by reference therein with the approval of the Director of the Federal Register.

(2) Each agency, in accordance with published rules, shall make available for public inspection and copying--

(A) final opinions, including concurring and dissenting opinions, as well as orders, made in the adjudication of cases;

(B) those statements of policy and interpretations which have been adopted by the agency and are not published in the Federal Register;

## FREEDOM OF INFORMATION ACT

(C) administrative staff manuals and instructions to staff that affect a member of the public;

(D) copies of all records, regardless of form or format, which have been released to any person under paragraph (3) and which, because of the nature of their subject matter, the agency determines have become or are likely to become the subject of subsequent requests for substantially the same records; and

(E) a general index of the records referred to under subparagraph (D);

unless the materials are promptly published and copies offered for sale. For records created on or after November 1, 1996, within one year after such date, each agency shall make such records available, including by computer telecommunications or, if computer telecommunications means have not been established by the agency, by other electronic means. To the extent required to prevent a clearly unwarranted invasion of personal privacy, an agency may delete identifying details when it makes available or publishes an opinion, statement of policy, interpretation, staff manual, instruction, or copies of records referred to in subparagraph (D). However, in each case the justification for the deletion shall be explained fully in writing, and the extent of such deletion shall be indicated on the portion of the record which is made available or published, unless including that indication would harm an interest protected by the exemption in subsection (b) under which the deletion is made. If technically feasible, the extent of the deletion shall be indicated at the place in the record where the deletion was made. Each agency shall also maintain and make available for public inspection and copying current indexes providing identifying information for the public as to any matter issued, adopted, or promulgated after July 4, 1967, and required by this paragraph to be made available or published. Each agency shall promptly publish, quarterly or more frequently, and distribute (by sale or otherwise) copies of each index or supplements thereto unless it determines by order published in the Federal Register that the publication would be unnecessary and impracticable, in which case the agency shall nonetheless provide copies of an index on request at a cost not to exceed the direct cost of duplication. Each agency shall make the index referred to in subparagraph (E) available by computer telecommunications by December 31, 1999. A final order, opinion, statement of policy, interpretation, or staff manual or instruction that affects a member of the public may be relied on, used, or cited as precedent by an agency against a party other than an agency only if--

(i) it has been indexed and either made available or published as provided by this paragraph; or

(ii) the party has actual and timely notice of the terms thereof.

(3)(A) Except with respect to the records made available under paragraphs (1) and (2) of this subsection, each agency, upon any request for records which (i) reasonably describes such records and (ii) is made in accordance with published rules stating the time, place, fees (if any), and procedures to be followed, shall make the records promptly available to any person.

## FREEDOM OF INFORMATION ACT

(B) In making any record available to a person under this paragraph, an agency shall provide the record in any form or format requested by the person if the record is readily reproducible by the agency in that form or format. Each agency shall make reasonable efforts to maintain its records in forms or formats that are reproducible for purposes of this section.

(C) In responding under this paragraph to a request for records, an agency shall make reasonable efforts to search for the records in electronic form or format, except when such efforts would significantly interfere with the operation of the agency's automated information system.

(D) For purposes of this paragraph, the term "search" means to review, manually or by automated means, agency records for the purpose of locating those records which are responsive to a request.

(4)(A)(i) In order to carry out the provisions of this section, each agency shall promulgate regulations, pursuant to notice and receipt of public comment, specifying the schedule of fees applicable to the processing of requests under this section and establishing procedures and guidelines for determining when such fees should be waived or reduced. Such schedule shall conform to the guidelines which shall be promulgated, pursuant to notice and receipt of public comment, by the Director of the Office of Management and Budget and which shall provide for a uniform schedule of fees for all agencies.

(ii) Such agency regulations shall provide that--

(I) fees shall be limited to reasonable standard charges for document search, duplication, and review, when records are requested for commercial use;

(II) fees shall be limited to reasonable standard charges for document duplication when records are not sought for commercial use and the request is made by an educational or noncommercial scientific institution, whose purpose is scholarly or scientific research; or a representative of the news media; and

(III) for any request not described in (I) or (II), fees shall be limited to reasonable standard charges for document search and duplication.

(iii) Documents shall be furnished without any charge or at a charge reduced below the fees established under clause (ii) if disclosure of the information is in the public interest because it is likely to contribute significantly to public understanding of the operations or activities of the government and is not primarily in the commercial interest of the requester.

(iv) Fee schedules shall provide for the recovery of only the direct costs of search, duplication, or review. Review costs shall include

# FREEDOM OF INFORMATION ACT

only the direct costs incurred during the initial examination of a document for the purposes of determining whether the documents must be disclosed under this section and for the purposes of withholding any portions exempt disclosure under this section. Review costs may not include any costs incurred in resolving issues of law or policy that may be raised in the course of processing a request under this section. No fee may be charged by any agency under this section--

(I) if the costs of routine collection and processing of the fee are likely to equal or exceed the amount of the fee; or

(II) for any request described in clause (ii)(II) or (III) of this subparagraph for the first two hours of search time or for the first one hundred pages of duplication.

(v) No agency may require advance payment of any fee unless the requester has previously failed to pay fees in a timely fashion, or the agency has determined that the fee will exceed $250.

(vi) Nothing in this subparagraph shall supersede fees chargeable under a statute specifically providing for setting the level of fees for particular types of records.

(vii) In any action by a requester regarding the waiver of fees under this section, the court shall determine the matter de novo, provided that the court's review of the matter shall be limited to the record before the agency.

(B) On complaint, the district court of the United States in the district in which the complainant resides, or has his principal place of business, or in which the agency records are situated, or in the District of Columbia, has jurisdiction to enjoin the agency from withholding agency records and to order the production of any agency records improperly withheld from the complainant. In such a case the court shall determine the matter de novo, and may examine the contents of such agency records in camera to determine whether such records or any part thereof shall be withheld under any of the exemptions set forth in subsection (b) of this section, and the burden is on the agency to sustain its action. In addition to any other matters to which a court accords substantial weight, a court shall accord substantial weight to an affidavit of an agency concerning the agency's determination as to technical feasibility under paragraph (2)(C) and subsection (b) and reproducibility under paragraph (3)(B).

(C) Notwithstanding any other provision of law, the defendant shall serve an answer or otherwise plead to any complaint made under this subsection within thirty days after service upon the defendant of the pleading in which such complaint is made, unless the court otherwise directs for good cause is shown.

(D) Repealed by Pub. L. 98-620, Title IV, 402(2), Nov. 8, 1984, 98

# FREEDOM OF INFORMATION ACT

Stat. 3335, 3357.

(E) The court may assess against the United States reasonable attorney fees and other litigation costs reasonably incurred in any case under this section in which the complainant has substantially prevailed.

(F) Whenever the court orders the production of any agency records improperly withheld from the complainant and assesses against the United States reasonable attorney fees and other litigation costs, and the court additionally issues a written finding that the circumstances surrounding the withholding raise questions whether agency personnel acted arbitrarily or capriciously with respect to the withholding, the Special Counsel shall promptly initiate a proceeding to determine whether disciplinary action is warranted against the officer or employee who was primarily responsible for the withholding. The Special Counsel, after investigation and consideration of the evidence submitted, shall submit his findings and recommendations to the administrative authority of the agency concerned and shall send copies of the findings and recommendations to the officer or employee or his representative. The administrative authority shall take the corrective action that the Special Counsel recommends.

(G) In the event of noncompliance with the order of the court, the district court may punish for contempt the responsible employee, and in the case of a uniformed service, the responsible member.

(5) Each agency having more than one member shall maintain and make available for public inspection a record of the final votes of each member in every agency proceeding.

(6)(A) Each agency, upon any request for records made under paragraph (1), (2), or (3) of this subsection, shall--

   (i) determine within twenty days (excepting Saturdays, Sundays, and legal public holidays) after the receipt of any such request whether to comply with such request and shall immediately notify the person making such request of such determination and the reasons therefor, and of the right of such person to appeal to the head of the agency any adverse determination; and

   (ii) make a determination with respect to any appeal within twenty days (excepting Saturdays, Sundays, and legal public holidays) after the receipt of such appeal. If on appeal the denial of the request for records is in whole or in part upheld, the agency shall notify the person making such request of the provisions for judicial review of that determination under paragraph (4) of this subsection.

(B)(i) In unusual circumstances as specified in this subparagraph, the time limits prescribed in either clause (i) or clause (ii) of subparagraph (A) may be extended by written notice to the person

## FREEDOM OF INFORMATION ACT

making such request setting forth the unusual circumstances for such extension and the date on which a determination is expected to be dispatched. No such notice shall specify a date that would result in an extension for more than ten working days, except as provided in clause (ii) of this subparagraph.

(ii) With respect to a request for which a written notice under clause (i) extends the time limits prescribed under clause (i) of subparagraph (A), the agency shall notify the person making the request if the request cannot be processed within the time limit specified in that clause and shall provide the person an opportunity to limit the scope of the request so that it may be processed within that time limit or an opportunity to arrange with the agency an alternative time frame for processing the request or a modified request. Refusal by the person to reasonably modify the request or arrange such an alternative time frame shall be considered as a factor in determining whether exceptional circumstances exist for purposes of subparagraph (C).

(iii) As used in this subparagraph, "unusual circumstances" means, but only to the extent reasonably necessary to the proper processing of the particular requests--

(I) the need to search for and collect the requested records from field facilities or other establishments that are separate from the office processing the request;

(II) the need to search for, collect, and appropriately examine a voluminous amount of separate and distinct records which are demanded in a single request; or

(III) the need for consultation, which shall be conducted with all practicable speed, with another agency having a substantial interest in the determination of the request or among two or more components of the agency having substantial subject matter interest therein.

(iv) Each agency may promulgate regulations, pursuant to notice and receipt of public comment, providing for the aggregation of certain requests by the same requestor, or by a group of requestors acting in concert, if the agency reasonably believes that such requests actually constitute a single request, which would otherwise satisfy the unusual circumstances specified in this subparagraph, and the requests involve clearly related matters. Multiple requests involving unrelated matters shall not be aggregated.

(C)(i) Any person making a request to any agency for records under paragraph (1), (2), or (3) of this subsection shall be deemed to have exhausted his administrative remedies with respect to such request if the agency fails to comply with the applicable time limit provisions of this paragraph. If the Government can show exceptional circumstances exist and that the agency is exercising due diligence in responding to the request, the court may retain jurisdiction and

## FREEDOM OF INFORMATION ACT

allow the agency additional time to complete its review of the records. Upon any determination by an agency to comply with a request for records, the records shall be made promptly available to such person making such request. Any notification of denial of any request for records under this subsection shall set forth the names and titles or positions of each person responsible for the denial of such request.

(ii) For purposes of this subparagraph, the term "exceptional circumstances" does not include a delay that results from a predictable agency workload of requests under this section, unless the agency demonstrates reasonable progress in reducing its backlog of pending requests.

(iii) Refusal by a person to reasonably modify the scope of a request or arrange an alternative time frame for processing the request (or a modified request) under clause (ii) after being given an opportunity to do so by the agency to whom the person made the request shall be considered as a factor in determining whether exceptional circumstances exist for purposes of this subparagraph.

(D)(i) Each agency may promulgate regulations, pursuant to notice and receipt of public comment, providing for multitrack processing of requests or records based on the amount of work or time (or both) involved in processing requests.

(ii) Regulations under this subparagraph may provide a person making a request that does not qualify for the fastest multitrack processing an opportunity to limit the scope of the request in order to qualify for faster processing.

(iii) This subparagraph shall not be considered to affect the requirement under subparagraph (C) to exercise due diligence.

(E)(i) Each agency shall promulgate regulations, pursuant to notice and receipt of public comment, providing for expedited processing of requests for records--

(I) in cases in which the person requesting the records demonstrates a compelling need; and

(II) in other cases determined by the agency.

(ii) Notwithstanding clause (i), regulations under this subparagraph must ensure--

(I) that a determination of whether to provide expedited processing shall be made, and notice of the determination shall be provided to the person making the request, within 10 days after the date of the request; and

(II) expeditious consideration of administrative appeals of

# FREEDOM OF INFORMATION ACT

such determinations of whether to provide expedited processing.

(iii) An agency shall process as soon as practicable any request for records to which the agency has granted expedited processing under this subparagraph. Agency action to deny or affirm denial of a request for expedited processing pursuant to this subparagraph, and failure by an agency to respond in a timely manner to such a request shall be subject to judicial review under paragraph (4), except that the judicial review shall be based on the record before the agency at the time of the determination.

(iv) A district court of the United States shall not have jurisdiction to review an agency denial of expedited processing of a request for records after the agency has provided a complete response to the request.

(v) For purposes of this subparagraph, the term "compelling need" means--

(I) that a failure to obtain requested records on an expedited basis under this paragraph could reasonably be expected to pose an imminent threat to the life or physical safety of an individual; or

(II) with respect to a request made by a person primarily engaged in disseminating information, urgency to inform the public concerning actual or alleged Federal Government activity.

(vi) A demonstration of a compelling need by a person making a request for expedited processing shall be made by a statement certified by such person to be true and correct to the best of such person's knowledge and belief.

(F) In denying a request for records, in whole or in part, an agency shall make a reasonable effort to estimate the volume of any requested matter the provision of which is denied, and shall provide any such estimate to the person making the request, unless providing such estimate would harm an interest protected by the exemption in subsection (b) pursuant to which the denial is made.

(b) This section does not apply to matters that are--

(1)(A) specifically authorized under criteria established by an Executive order to be kept secret in the interest of national defense or foreign policy and (B) are in fact properly classified pursuant to such Executive order;

(2) related solely to the internal personnel rules and practices of an agency;

(3) specifically exempted from disclosure by statute (other than section

# FREEDOM OF INFORMATION ACT

552b of this title), provided that such statute (A) requires that the matters be withheld from the public in such a manner as to leave no discretion on the issue, or (B) establishes particular criteria for withholding or refers to particular types of matters to be withheld;

(4) trade secrets and commercial or financial information obtained from a person and privileged or confidential;

(5) inter-agency or intra-agency memorandums or letters which would not be available by law to a party other than an agency in litigation with the agency;

(6) personnel and medical files and similar files the disclosure of which would constitute a clearly unwarranted invasion of personal privacy;

(7) records or information compiled for law enforcement purposes, but only to the extent that the production of such law enforcement records or information (A) could reasonably be expected to interfere with enforcement proceedings, (B) would deprive a person of a right to a fair trial or an impartial adjudication, (C) could reasonably be expected to constitute an unwarranted invasion of personal privacy, (D) could reasonably be expected to disclose the identity of a confidential source, including a State, local, or foreign agency or authority or any private institution which furnished information on a confidential basis, and, in the case of a record or information compiled by a criminal law enforcement authority in the course of a criminal investigation or by an agency conducting a lawful national security intelligence investigation, information furnished by a confidential source, (E) would disclose techniques and procedures for law enforcement investigations or prosecutions, or would disclose guidelines for law enforcement investigations or prosecutions if such disclosure could reasonably be expected to risk circumvention of the law, or (F) could reasonably be expected to endanger the life or physical safety of any individual;

(8) contained in or related to examination, operating, or condition reports prepared by, on behalf of, or for the use of an agency responsible for the regulation or supervision of financial institutions; or

(9) geological and geophysical information and data, including maps, concerning wells.

Any reasonably segregable portion of a record shall be provided to any person requesting such record after deletion of the portions which are exempt under this subsection. The amount of information deleted shall be indicated on the released portion of the record, unless including that indication would harm an interest protected by the exemption in this subsection under which the deletion is made. If technically feasible, the amount of the information deleted shall be indicated at the place in the record where such deletion is made.

(c)(1) Whenever a request is made which involves access to records described in subsection (b)(7)(A) and--

>(A) the investigation or proceeding involves a possible violation of

## FREEDOM OF INFORMATION ACT

criminal law; and

(B) there is reason to believe that (i) the subject of the investigation or proceeding is not aware of its pendency, and (ii) disclosure of the existence of the records could reasonably be expected to interfere with enforcement proceedings, the agency may, during only such time as that circumstance continues, treat the records as not subject to the requirements of this section.

(2) Whenever informant records maintained by a criminal law enforcement agency under an informant's name or personal identifier are requested by a third party according to the informant's name or personal identifier, the agency may treat the records as not subject to the requirements of this section unless the informant's status as an informant has been officially confirmed.

(3) Whenever a request is made which involves access to records maintained by the Federal Bureau of Investigation pertaining to foreign intelligence or counterintelligence, or international terrorism, and the existence of the records is classified information as provided in subsection (b)(1), the Bureau may, as long as the existence of the records remains classified information, treat the records as not subject to the requirements of this section.

(d) This section does not authorize the withholding of information or limit the availability of records to the public, except as specifically stated in this section. This section is not authority to withhold information from Congress.

(e)(1) On or before February 1 of each year, each agency shall submit to the Attorney General of the United States a report which shall cover the preceding fiscal year and which shall include--

(A) the number of determinations made by the agency not to comply with requests for records made to such agency under subsection (a) and the reasons for each such determination;

(B)(i) the number of appeals made by persons under subsection (a)(6), the result of such appeals, and the reason for the action upon each appeal that results in a denial of information; and

(ii) a complete list of all statutes that the agency relies upon to authorize the agency to withhold information under subsection (b)(3), a description of whether a court has upheld the decision of the agency to withhold information under each such statute, and a concise description of the scope of any information withheld;

(C) the number of requests for records pending before the agency as of September 30 of the preceding year, and the median number of days that such requests had been pending before the agency as of that date;

(D) the number of requests for records received by the agency and the number of requests which the agency processed;

# FREEDOM OF INFORMATION ACT

(E) the median number of days taken by the agency to process different types of requests;

(F) the total amount of fees collected by the agency for processing requests; and

(G) the number of full-time staff of the agency devoted to processing requests for records under this section, and the total amount expended by the agency for processing such requests.

(2) Each agency shall make each such report available to the public including by computer telecommunications, or if computer telecommunications means have not been established by the agency, by other electronic means.

(3) The Attorney General of the United States shall make each report which has been made available by electronic means available at a single electronic access point. The Attorney General of the United States shall notify the Chairman and ranking minority member of the Committee on Government Reform and Oversight of the House of Representatives and the Chairman and ranking minority member of the Committees on Governmental Affairs and the Judiciary of the Senate, no later than April 1 of the year in which each such report is issued, that such reports are available by electronic means.

(4) The Attorney General of the United States, in consultation with the Director of the Office of Management and Budget, shall develop reporting and performance guidelines in connection with reports required by this subsection by October 1, 1997, and may establish additional requirements for such reports as the Attorney General determines may be useful.

(5) The Attorney General of the United States shall submit an annual report on or before April 1 of each calendar year which shall include for the prior calendar year a listing of the number of cases arising under this section, the exemption involved in each case, the disposition of such case, and the cost, fees, and penalties assessed under subparagraphs (E), (F), and (G) of subsection (a)(4). Such report shall also include a description of the efforts undertaken by the Department of Justice to encourage agency compliance with this section.

(f) For purposes of this section, the term--

(1) "agency" as defined in section 551(1) of this title includes any executive department, military department, Government corporation, Government controlled corporation, or other establishment in the executive branch of the Government (including the Executive Office of the President), or any independent regulatory agency; and

(2) "record" and any other term used in this section in reference to information includes any information that would be an agency record subject to the requirements of this section when maintained by an agency in any format, including an electronic format.

## FREEDOM OF INFORMATION ACT

(g) The head of each agency shall prepare and make publicly available upon request, reference material or a guide for requesting records or information from the agency, subject to the exemptions in subsection (b), including--

(1) an index of all major information systems of the agency;

(2) a description of major information and record locator systems maintained by the agency; and

(3) a handbook for obtaining various types and categories of public information from the agency pursuant to chapter 35 of title 44, and under this section.

# PRIVACY ACT

## THE PRIVACY ACT OF 1974

## 5 U.S.C. § 552a

## As Amended

§ 552a. Records maintained on individuals

(a) Definitions

For purposes of this section--

(1) the term "agency" means agency as defined in section 552[(f)] of this title;

(2) the term "individual" means a citizen of the United States or an alien lawfully admitted for permanent residence;

(3) the term "maintain" includes maintain, collect, use or disseminate;

(4) the term "record" means any item, collection, or grouping of information about an individual that is maintained by an agency, including, but not limited to, his education, financial transactions, medical history, and criminal or employment history and that contains his name, or the identifying number, symbol, or other identifying particular assigned to the individual, such as a finger or voice print or a photograph;

(5) the term "system of records" means a group of any records under the control of any agency from which information is retrieved by the name of the individual or by some identifying number, symbol, or other identifying particular assigned to the individual;

(6) the term "statistical record" means a record in a system of records maintained for statistical research or reporting purposes only and not used in whole or in part in making any determination about an identifiable individual, except as provided by section 8 of Title 13;

(7) the term "routine use" means, with respect to the disclosure of a record, the use of such record for a purpose which is compatible with the purpose for which it was collected;

(8) the term "matching program"--

    (A) means any computerized comparison of--

        (i) two or more automated systems of records or a system of records with non-Federal records for the purpose of–

            (I) establishing or verifying the eligibility of, or continuing compliance with statutory and regulatory requirements by,

# PRIVACY ACT

applicants for, recipients or beneficiaries of, participants in, or providers of services with respect to, cash or in-kind assistance or payments under Federal benefit programs, or

(II) recouping payments or delinquent debts under such Federal benefit programs, or

(ii) two or more automated Federal personnel or payroll system of records or a system of Federal personnel or payroll records with non-Federal records,

(B) but does not include--

(i) matches performed to produce aggregate statistical data without any personal identifiers;

(ii) matches performed to support any research or statistical project, the specific data of which may not be used to make decisions concerning the rights, benefits, or privileges of specific individuals;

(iii) matches performed, by an agency (or component thereof) which performs as its principal function any activity pertaining to the enforcement of criminal laws, subsequent to the initiation of a specific criminal or civil law enforcement investigation of a named person or persons for the purpose of gathering evidence against such person or persons;

(iv) matches of tax information (I) pursuant to section 6103(d) of the Internal Revenue Code of 1986, (II) for purposes of tax administration as defined in section 6103(b)(4) of such Code, (III) for the purpose of intercepting a tax refund due an individual under authority granted by section 404(e), 464, or 1137 of the Social Security Act; or (IV) for the purpose of intercepting a tax refund due an individual under any other tax refund intercept program authorized by statute which has been determined by the Director of the Office of Management and Budget to contain verification, notice, and hearing requirements that are substantially similar to the procedures in section 1137 of the Social Security Act;

(v) matches--

(I) using records predominantly relating to Federal personnel, that are performed for routine administrative purposes (subject to guidance provided by the Director of the Office of Management and Budget pursuant to subsection (v)); or

(II) conducted by an agency using only records from systems of records maintained by that agency;

if the purpose of the match is not to take any adverse financial, personnel, disciplinary, or other adverse action against Federal personnel; or

**PRIVACY ACT**

> (vi) matches performed for foreign counterintelligence purposes or to produce background checks for security clearances of Federal personnel or Federal contractor personnel;
>
> (vii) matches performed incident to a levy described in section 6103(k)(8) of the Internal Revenue Code of 1986; or
>
> (viii) matches performed pursuant to section 202(x)(3) or 1611(e)(1) of the Social Security Act (42 U.S.C. 402(x)(3), 1382(e)(1));

(9) the term "recipient agency" means any agency, or contractor thereof, receiving records contained in a system of records from a source agency for use in a matching program;

(10) the term "non-Federal agency" means any State or local government, or agency thereof, which receives records contained in a system of records from a source agency for use in a matching program;

(11) the term "source agency" means any agency which discloses records contained in a system of records to be used in a matching program, or any State or local government, or agency thereof, which discloses records to be used in a matching program;

(12) the term "Federal benefit program" means any program administered or funded by the Federal Government, or by any agent or State on behalf of the Federal Government, providing cash or in-kind assistance in the form of payments, grants, loans, or loan guarantees to individuals; and

(13) the term "Federal personnel" means officers and employees of the Government of the United States, members of the uniformed services (including members of the Reserve Components), individuals entitled to receive immediate or deferred retirement benefits under any retirement program of the Government of the United States (including survivor benefits).

(b) Conditions of disclosure

No agency shall disclose any record which is contained in a system of records by any means of communication to any person, or to another agency, except pursuant to a written request by, or with the prior written consent of, the individual to whom the record pertains, unless disclosure of the record would be--

> (1) to those officers and employees of the agency which maintains the record who have a need for the record in the performance of their duties;
>
> (2) required under section 552 of this title;
>
> (3) for a routine use as defined in subsection (a)(7) of this section and described under subsection (e)(4)(D) of this section;

# PRIVACY ACT

(4) to the Bureau of the Census for purposes of planning or carrying out a census or survey or related activity pursuant to the provisions of Title 13;

(5) to a recipient who has provided the agency with advance adequate written assurance that the record will be used solely as a statistical research or reporting record, and the record is to be transferred in a form that is not individually identifiable;

(6) to the National Archives and Records Administration as a record which has sufficient historical or other value to warrant its continued preservation by the United States Government, or for evaluation by the Archivist of the United States or the designee of the Archivist to determine whether the record has such value;

(7) to another agency or to an instrumentality of any governmental jurisdiction within or under the control of the United States for a civil or criminal law enforcement activity if the activity is authorized by law, and if the head of the agency or instrumentality has made a written request to the agency which maintains the record specifying the particular portion desired and the law enforcement activity for which the record is sought;

(8) to a person pursuant to a showing of compelling circumstances affecting the health or safety of an individual if upon such disclosure notification is transmitted to the last known address of such individual;

(9) to either House of Congress, or, to the extent of matter within its jurisdiction, any committee or subcommittee thereof, any joint committee of Congress or subcommittee of any such joint committee;

(10) to the Comptroller General, or any of his authorized representatives, in the course of the performance of the duties of the General Accounting Office;

(11) pursuant to the order of a court of competent jurisdiction; or

(12) to a consumer reporting agency in accordance with section 3711(e) of Title 31.

(c) Accounting of certain disclosures

Each agency, with respect to each system of records under its control, shall--

(1) except for disclosures made under subsections (b)(1) or (b)(2) of this section, keep an accurate accounting of--

(A) the date, nature, and purpose of each disclosure of a record to any person or to another agency made under subsection (b) of this section; and

(B) the name and address of the person or agency to whom the dis-

# PRIVACY ACT

closure is made;

(2) retain the accounting made under paragraph (1) of this subsection for at least five years or the life of the record, whichever is longer, after the disclosure for which the accounting is made;

(3) except for disclosures made under subsection (b)(7) of this section, make the accounting made under paragraph (1) of this subsection available to the individual named in the record at his request; and

(4) inform any person or other agency about any correction or notation of dispute made by the agency in accordance with subsection (d) of this section of any record that has been disclosed to the person or agency if an accounting of the disclosure was made.

(d) Access to records

Each agency that maintains a system of records shall--

(1) upon request by any individual to gain access to his record or to any information pertaining to him which is contained in the system, permit him and upon his request, a person of his own choosing to accompany him, to review the record and have a copy made of all or any portion thereof in a form comprehensible to him, except that the agency may require the individual to furnish a written statement authorizing discussion of that individual's record in the accompanying person's presence;

(2) permit the individual to request amendment of a record pertaining to him and--

(A) not later than 10 days (excluding Saturdays, Sundays, and legal public holidays) after the date of receipt of such request, acknowledge in writing such receipt; and

(B) promptly, either--

(i) make any correction of any portion thereof which the individual believes is not accurate, relevant, timely, or complete; or

(ii) inform the individual of its refusal to amend the record in accordance with his request, the reason for the refusal, the procedures established by the agency for the individual to request a review of that refusal by the head of the agency or an officer designated by the head of the agency, and the name and business address of that official;

(3) permit the individual who disagrees with the refusal of the agency to amend his record to request a review of such refusal, and not later than 30 days (excluding Saturdays, Sundays, and legal public holidays) from the date on which the individual requests such review, complete such review and make a final determination unless, for good cause shown, the head of the agency extends such 30-day period; and if, after his review,

## PRIVACY ACT

the reviewing official also refuses to amend the record in accordance with the request, permit the individual to file with the agency a concise statement setting forth the reasons for his disagreement with the refusal of the agency, and notify the individual of the provisions for judicial review of the reviewing official's determination under subsection (g)(1)(A) of this section;

(4) in any disclosure, containing information about which the individual has filed a statement of disagreement, occurring after the filing of the statement under paragraph (3) of this subsection, clearly note any portion of the record which is disputed and provide copies of the statement and, if the agency deems it appropriate, copies of a concise statement of the reasons of the agency for not making the amendments requested, to persons or other agencies to whom the disputed record has been disclosed; and

(5) nothing in this section shall allow an individual access to any information compiled in reasonable anticipation of a civil action or proceeding.

(e) Agency requirements

Each agency that maintains a system of records shall--

(1) maintain in its records only such information about an individual as is relevant and necessary to accomplish a purpose of the agency required to be accomplished by statute or by Executive order of the President;

(2) collect information to the greatest extent practicable directly from the subject individual when the information may result in adverse determinations about an individual's rights, benefits, and privileges under Federal programs;

(3) inform each individual whom it asks to supply information, on the form which it uses to collect the information or on a separate form that can be retained by the individual--

(A) the authority (whether granted by statute, or by Executive order of the President) which authorizes the solicitation of the information and whether disclosure of such information is mandatory or voluntary;

(B) the principal purpose or purposes for which the information is intended to be used;

(C) the routine uses which may be made of the information, as published pursuant to paragraph (4)(D) of this subsection; and

(D) the effects on him, if any, of not providing all or any part of the requested information;

(4) subject to the provisions of paragraph (11) of this subsection, publish in the Federal Register upon establishment or revision a notice of the

# PRIVACY ACT

existence and character of the system of records, which notice shall include--

(A) the name and location of the system;

(B) the categories of individuals on whom records are maintained in the system;

(C) the categories of records maintained in the system;

(D) each routine use of the records contained in the system, including the categories of users and the purpose of such use;

(E) the policies and practices of the agency regarding storage, retrievability, access controls, retention, and disposal of the records;

(F) the title and business address of the agency official who is responsible for the system of records;

(G) the agency procedures whereby an individual can be notified at his request if the system of records contains a record pertaining to him;

(H) the agency procedures whereby an individual can be notified at his request how he can gain access to any record pertaining to him contained in the system of records, and how he can contest its content; and

(I) the categories of sources of records in the system;

(5) maintain all records which are used by the agency in making any determination about any individual with such accuracy, relevance, timeliness, and completeness as is reasonably necessary to assure fairness to the individual in the determination;

(6) prior to disseminating any record about an individual to any person other than an agency, unless the dissemination is made pursuant to subsection (b)(2) of this section, make reasonable efforts to assure that such records are accurate, complete, timely, and relevant for agency purposes;

(7) maintain no record describing how any individual exercises rights guaranteed by the First Amendment unless expressly authorized by statute or by the individual about whom the record is maintained or unless pertinent to and within the scope of an authorized law enforcement activity;

(8) make reasonable efforts to serve notice on an individual when any record on such individual is made available to any person under compulsory legal process when such process becomes a matter of public record;

(9) establish rules of conduct for persons involved in the design, devel-

# PRIVACY ACT

opment, operation, or maintenance of any system of records, or in maintaining any record, and instruct each such person with respect to such rules and the requirements of this section, including any other rules and procedures adopted pursuant to this section and the penalties for noncompliance;

(10) establish appropriate administrative, technical and physical safeguards to insure the security and confidentiality of records and to protect against any anticipated threats or hazards to their security or integrity which could result in substantial harm, embarrassment, inconvenience, or unfairness to any individual on whom information is maintained;

(11) at least 30 days prior to publication of information under paragraph (4)(D) of this subsection, publish in the Federal Register notice of any new use or intended use of the information in the system, and provide an opportunity for interested persons to submit written data, views, or arguments to the agency; and

(12) if such agency is a recipient agency or a source agency in a matching program with a non-Federal agency, with respect to any establishment or revision of a matching program, at least 30 days prior to conducting such program, publish in the Federal Register notice of such establishment or revision.

(f) Agency rules

In order to carry out the provisions of this section, each agency that maintains a system of records shall promulgate rules, in accordance with the requirements (including general notice) of section 553 of this title, which shall--

(1) establish procedures whereby an individual can be notified in response to his request if any system of records named by the individual contains a record pertaining to him;

(2) define reasonable times, places, and requirements for identifying an individual who requests his record or information pertaining to him before the agency shall make the record or information available to the individual;

(3) establish procedures for the disclosure to an individual upon his request of his record or information pertaining to him, including special procedure, if deemed necessary, for the disclosure to an individual of medical records, including psychological records, pertaining to him;

(4) establish procedures for reviewing a request from an individual concerning the amendment of any record or information pertaining to the individual, for making a determination on the request, for an appeal within the agency of an initial adverse agency determination, and for whatever additional means may be necessary for each individual to be able to exercise fully his rights under this section; and

# PRIVACY ACT

(5) establish fees to be charged, if any, to any individual for making copies of his record, excluding the cost of any search for and review of the record.

The Office of the Federal Register shall biennially compile and publish the rules promulgated under this subsection and agency notices published under subsection (e)(4) of this section in a form available to the public at low cost.

(g)(1) Civil remedies

Whenever any agency

(A) makes a determination under subsection (d)(3) of this section not to amend an individual's record in accordance with his request, or fails to make such review in conformity with that subsection;

(B) refuses to comply with an individual request under subsection (d)(1) of this section;

(C) fails to maintain any record concerning any individual with such accuracy, relevance, timeliness, and completeness as is necessary to assure fairness in any determination relating to the qualifications, character, rights, or opportunities of, or benefits to the individual that may be made on the basis of such record, and consequently a determination is made which is adverse to the individual; or

(D) fails to comply with any other provision of this section, or any rule promulgated thereunder, in such a way as to have an adverse effect on an individual,

the individual may bring a civil action against the agency, and the district courts of the United States shall have jurisdiction in the matters under the provisions of this subsection.

(2)(A) In any suit brought under the provisions of subsection (g)(1)(A) of this section, the court may order the agency to amend the individual's record in accordance with his request or in such other way as the court may direct. In such a case the court shall determine the matter de novo.

(B) The court may assess against the United States reasonable attorney fees and other litigation costs reasonably incurred in any case under this paragraph in which the complainant has substantially prevailed.

(3)(A) In any suit brought under the provisions of subsection (g)(1)(B) of this section, the court may enjoin the agency from withholding the records and order the production to the complainant of any agency records improperly withheld from him. In such a case the court shall determine the matter de novo, and may examine the contents of any agency records in camera to determine whether the records or any portion thereof may be withheld under any of the exemptions set forth in subsection (k) of this section, and the burden is on the agency to sustain its action.

# PRIVACY ACT

(B) The court may assess against the United States reasonable attorney fees and other litigation costs reasonably incurred in any case under this paragraph in which the complainant has substantially prevailed.

(4) In any suit brought under the provisions of subsection (g)(1)(C) or (D) of this section in which the court determines that the agency acted in a manner which was intentional or willful, the United States shall be liable to the individual in an amount equal to the sum of--

(A) actual damages sustained by the individual as a result of the refusal or failure, but in no case shall a person entitled to recovery receive less than the sum of $1,000; and

(B) the costs of the action together with reasonable attorney fees as determined by the court.

(5) An action to enforce any liability created under this section may be brought in the district court of the United States in the district in which the complainant resides, or has his principal place of business, or in which the agency records are situated, or in the District of Columbia, without regard to the amount in controversy, within two years from the date on which the cause of action arises, except that where an agency has materially and willfully misrepresented any information required under this section to be disclosed to an individual and the information so misrepresented is material to establishment of the liability of the agency to the individual under this section, the action may be brought at any time within two years after discovery by the individual of the misrepresentation. Nothing in this section shall be construed to authorize any civil action by reason of any injury sustained as the result of a disclosure of a record prior to September 27, 1975.

(h) Rights of legal guardians

For the purposes of this section, the parent of any minor, or the legal guardian of any individual who has been declared to be incompetent due to physical or mental incapacity or age by a court of competent jurisdiction, may act on behalf of the individual.

(i)(1) Criminal penalties

Any officer or employee of an agency, who by virtue of his employment or official position, has possession of, or access to, agency records which contain individually identifiable information the disclosure of which is prohibited by this section or by rules or regulations established thereunder, and who knowing that disclosure of the specific material is so prohibited, willfully discloses the material in any manner to any person or agency not entitled to receive it, shall be guilty of a misdemeanor and fined not more than $5,000.

(2) Any officer or employee of any agency who willfully maintains a system of records without meeting the notice requirements of subsection (e)(4) of this section shall be guilty of a misdemeanor and fined not more than $5,000.

**PRIVACY ACT**

(3) Any person who knowingly and willfully requests or obtains any record concerning an individual from an agency under false pretenses shall be guilty of a misdemeanor and fined not more than $5,000.

(j) General exemptions

The head of any agency may promulgate rules, in accordance with the requirements (including general notice) of sections 553(b)(1), (2), and (3), (c), and (e) of this title, to exempt any system of records within the agency from any part of this section except subsections (b), (c)(1) and (2), (e)(4)(A) through (F), (e)(6), (7), (9), (10), and (11), and (i) if the system of records is--

(1) maintained by the Central Intelligence Agency; or

(2) maintained by an agency or component thereof which performs as its principal function any activity pertaining to the enforcement of criminal laws, including police efforts to prevent, control, or reduce crime or to apprehend criminals, and the activities of prosecutors, courts, correctional, probation, pardon, or parole authorities, and which consists of (A) information compiled for the purpose of identifying individual criminal offenders and alleged offenders and consisting only of identifying data and notations of arrests, the nature and disposition of criminal charges, sentencing, confinement, release, and parole and probation status; (B) information compiled for the purpose of a criminal investigation, including reports of informants and investigators, and associated with an identifiable individual; or (C) reports identifiable to an individual compiled at any stage of the process of enforcement of the criminal laws from arrest or indictment through release from supervision.

At the time rules are adopted under this subsection, the agency shall include in the statement required under section 553(c) of this title, the reasons why the system of records is to be exempted from a provision of this section.

(k) Specific exemptions

The head of any agency may promulgate rules, in accordance with the requirements (including general notice) of sections 553(b)(1), (2), and (3), (c), and (e) of this title, to exempt any system of records within the agency from subsections (c)(3), (d), (e)(1), (e)(4)(G), (H), and (I) and (f) of this section if the system of records is--

(1) subject to the provisions of section 552(b)(1) of this title;

(2) investigatory material compiled for law enforcement purposes, other than material within the scope of subsection (j)(2) of this section: Provided, however, That if any individual is denied any right, privilege, or benefit that he would otherwise be entitled by Federal law, or for which he would otherwise be eligible, as a result of the maintenance of such material, such material shall be provided to such individual, except to the extent that the disclosure of such material would reveal the identity of a source who furnished information to the Government under an express promise that the identity of the source would be held in con-

## PRIVACY ACT

fidence, or, prior to the effective date of this section, under an implied promise that the identity of the source would be held in confidence;

(3) maintained in connection with providing protective services to the President of the United States or other individuals pursuant to section 3056 of Title 18;

(4) required by statute to be maintained and used solely as statistical records;

(5) investigatory material compiled solely for the purpose of determining suitability, eligibility, or qualifications for Federal civilian employment, military service, Federal contracts, or access to classified information, but only to the extent that the disclosure of such material would reveal the identity of a source who furnished information to the Government under an express promise that the identity of the source would be held in confidence, or, prior to the effective date of this section, under an implied promise that the identity of the source would be held in confidence;

(6) testing or examination material used solely to determine individual qualifications for appointment or promotion in the Federal service the disclosure of which would compromise the objectivity or fairness of the testing or examination process; or

(7) evaluation material used to determine potential for promotion in the armed services, but only to the extent that the disclosure of such material would reveal the identity of a source who furnished information to the Government under an express promise that the identity of the source would be held in confidence, or, prior to the effective date of this section, under an implied promise that the identity of the source would be held in confidence.

At the time rules are adopted under this subsection, the agency shall include in the statement required under section 553(c) of this title, the reasons why the system of records is to be exempted from a provision of this section.

(1)(1) Archival records

Each agency record which is accepted by the Archivist of the United States for storage, processing, and servicing in accordance with section 3103 of Title 44 shall, for the purposes of this section, be considered to be maintained by the agency which deposited the record and shall be subject to the provisions of this section. The Archivist of the United States shall not disclose the record except to the agency which maintains the record, or under rules established by that agency which are not inconsistent with the provisions of this section.

(2) Each agency record pertaining to an identifiable individual which was transferred to the National Archives of the United States as a record which has sufficient historical or other value to warrant its continued preservation by the United States Government, prior to the effective date of this section, shall, for the purposes of this section, be considered to be maintained by the National Archives and shall not be subject to the

**PRIVACY ACT**

provisions of this section, except that a statement generally describing such records (modeled after the requirements relating to records subject to subsections (e)(4)(A) through (G) of this section) shall be published in the Federal Register.

(3) Each agency record pertaining to an identifiable individual which is transferred to the National Archives of the United States as a record which has sufficient historical or other value to warrant its continued preservation by the United States Government, on or after the effective date of this section, shall, for the purposes of this section, be considered to be maintained by the National Archives and shall be exempt from the requirements of this section except subsections (e)(4)(A) through (G) and (e)(9) of this section.

(m) Government contractors

(1) When an agency provides by a contract for the operation by or on behalf of the agency of a system of records to accomplish an agency function, the agency shall, consistent with its authority, cause the requirements of this section to be applied to such system. For purposes of subsection (i) of this section any such contractor and any employee of such contractor, if such contract is agreed to on or after the effective date of this section, shall be considered to be an employee of an agency.

(2) A consumer reporting agency to which a record is disclosed under section 3711(e) of Title 31 shall not be considered a contractor for the purposes of this section.

(n) Mailing lists

An individual's name and address may not be sold or rented by an agency unless such action is specifically authorized by law. This provision shall not be construed to require the withholding of names and addresses otherwise permitted to be made public.

(o) Matching agreements-- (1) No record which is contained in a system of records may be disclosed to a recipient agency or non-Federal agency for use in a computer matching program except pursuant to a written agreement between the source agency and the recipient agency or non-Federal agency specifying--

(A) the purpose and legal authority for conducting the program;

(B) the justification for the program and the anticipated results, including a specific estimate of any savings;

(C) a description of the records that will be matched, including each data element that will be used, the approximate number of records that will be matched, and the projected starting and completion dates of the matching program;

(D) procedures for providing individualized notice at the time of application, and notice periodically thereafter as directed by the Data

**PRIVACY ACT**

Integrity Board of such agency (subject to guidance provided by the Director of the Office of Management and Budget pursuant to subsection (v)), to--

(i) applicants for and recipients of financial assistance or payments under Federal benefit programs, and

(ii) applicants for and holders of positions as Federal personnel, that any information provided by such applicants, recipients, holders, and individuals may be subject to verification through matching programs;

(E) procedures for verifying information produced in such matching program as required by subsection (p);

(F) procedures for the retention and timely destruction of identifiable records created by a recipient agency or non-Federal agency in such matching program;

(G) procedures for ensuring the administrative, technical, and physical security of the records matched and the results of such programs;

(H) prohibitions on duplication and redisclosure of records provided by the source agency within or outside the recipient agency or the non-Federal agency, except where required by law or essential to the conduct of the matching program;

(I) procedures governing the use by a recipient agency or non-Federal agency of records provided in a matching program by a source agency, including procedures governing return of the records to the source agency or destruction of records used in such program;

(J) information on assessments that have been made on the accuracy of the records that will be used in such matching program; and

(K) that the Comptroller General may have access to all records of a recipient agency or a non-Federal agency that the Comptroller General deems necessary in order to monitor or verify compliance with the agreement.

(2)(A) A copy of each agreement entered into pursuant to paragraph (1) shall--

(i) be transmitted to the Committee on Governmental Affairs of the Senate and the Committee on Government Operations of the House of Representatives; and

(ii) be available upon request to the public.

(B) No such agreement shall be effective until 30 days after the date on which such a copy is transmitted pursuant to subparagraph (A)(i).

**PRIVACY ACT**

(C) Such an agreement shall remain in effect only for such period, not to exceed 18 months, as the Data Integrity Board of the agency determines is appropriate in light of the purposes, and length of time necessary for the conduct, of the matching program.

(D) Within 3 months prior to the expiration of such an agreement pursuant to subparagraph (C), the Data Integrity Board of the agency may, without additional review, renew the matching agreement for a current, on-going matching program for not more than one additional year if--

(i) such program will be conducted without any change; and

(ii) each party to the agreement certifies to the Board in writing that the program has been conducted in compliance with the agreement.

(p) Verification and opportunity to contest findings

(1) In order to protect any individual whose records are used in a matching program, no recipient agency, non-Federal agency, or source agency may suspend, terminate, reduce, or make a final denial of any financial assistance or payment under a Federal benefit program to such individual, or take other adverse action against such individual, as a result of information produced by such matching program, until--

(A)(i) the agency has independently verified the information; or

(ii) the Data Integrity Board of the agency, or in the case of a non-Federal agency the Data Integrity Board of the source agency, determines in accordance with guidance issued by the Director of the Office of Management and Budget that--

(I) the information is limited to identification and amount of benefits paid by the source agency under a Federal benefit program; and

(II) there is a high degree of confidence that the information provided to the recipient agency is accurate;

(B) the individual receives a notice from the agency containing a statement of its findings and informing the individual of the opportunity to contest such findings; and

(C)(i) the expiration of any time period established for the program by statute or regulation for the individual to respond to that notice; or

(ii) in the case of a program for which no such period is established, the end of the 30-day period beginning on the date on which notice under subparagraph (B) is mailed or otherwise provided to the individual.

# PRIVACY ACT

(2) Independent verification referred to in paragraph (1) requires investigation and confirmation of specific information relating to an individual that is used as a basis for an adverse action against the individual, including where applicable investigation and confirmation of--

(A) the amount of any asset or income involved;

(B) whether such individual actually has or had access to such asset or income for such individual's own use; and

(C) the period or periods when the individual actually had such asset or income.

(3) Notwithstanding paragraph (1), an agency may take any appropriate action otherwise prohibited by such paragraph if the agency determines that the public health or public safety may be adversely affected or significantly threatened during any notice period required by such paragraph.

(q) Sanctions

(1) Notwithstanding any other provision of law, no source agency may disclose any record which is contained in a system of records to a recipient agency or non-Federal agency for a matching program if such source agency has reason to believe that the requirements of subsection (p), or any matching agreement entered into pursuant to subsection (o), or both, are not being met by such recipient agency.

(2) No source agency may renew a matching agreement unless--

(A) the recipient agency or non-Federal agency has certified that it has complied with the provisions of that agreement; and

(B) the source agency has no reason to believe that the certification is inaccurate.

(r) Report on new systems and matching programs

Each agency that proposes to establish or make a significant change in a system of records or a matching program shall provide adequate advance notice of any such proposal (in duplicate) to the Committee on Government Operations of the House of Representatives, the Committee on Governmental Affairs of the Senate, and the Office of Management and Budget in order to permit an evaluation of the probable or potential effect of such proposal on the privacy or other rights of individuals.

(s) Biennial report

The President shall biennially submit to the Speaker of the House of Representatives and the President pro tempore of the Senate a report--

(1) describing the actions of the Director of the Office of Management and Budget pursuant to section 6 of the Privacy Act of 1974 during the

# PRIVACY ACT

preceding two years;

(2) describing the exercise of individual rights of access and amendment under this section during such years;

(3) identifying changes in or additions to systems of records;

(4) containing such other information concerning administration of this section as may be necessary or useful to the Congress in reviewing the effectiveness of this section in carrying out the purposes of the Privacy Act of 1974.

(t) Effect of other laws

(1) No agency shall rely on any exemption contained in section 552 of this title to withhold from an individual any record which is otherwise accessible to such individual under the provisions of this section.

(2) No agency shall rely on any exemption in this section to withhold from an individual any record which is otherwise accessible to such individual under the provisions of section 552 of this title.

(u) Data Integrity Boards

(1) Every agency conducting or participating in a matching program shall establish a Data Integrity Board to oversee and coordinate among the various components of such agency the agency's implementation of this section.

(2) Each Data Integrity Board shall consist of senior officials designated by the head of the agency, and shall include any senior official designated by the head of the agency as responsible for implementation of this section, and the inspector general of the agency, if any. The inspector general shall not serve as chairman of the Data Integrity Board.

(3) Each Data Integrity Board--

(A) shall review, approve, and maintain all written agreements for receipt or disclosure of agency records for matching programs to ensure compliance with subsection (o), and all relevant statutes, regulations, and guidelines;

(B) shall review all matching programs in which the agency has participated during the year, either as a source agency or recipient agency, determine compliance with applicable laws, regulations, guidelines, and agency agreements, and assess the costs and benefits of such programs;

(C) shall review all recurring matching programs in which the agency has participated during the year, either as a source agency or recipient agency, for continued justification for such disclosures;

(D) shall compile an annual report, which shall be submitted to the

**PRIVACY ACT**

head of the agency and the Office of Management and Budget and made available to the public on request, describing the matching activities of the agency, including--

(i) matching programs in which the agency has participated as a source agency or recipient agency;

(ii) matching agreements proposed under subsection (o) that were disapproved by the Board;

(iii) any changes in membership or structure of the Board in the preceding year;

(iv) the reasons for any waiver of the requirement in paragraph (4) of this section for completion and submission of a cost-benefit analysis prior to the approval of a matching program;

(v) any violations of matching agreements that have been alleged or identified and any corrective action taken; and

(vi) any other information required by the Director of the Office of Management and Budget to be included in such report;

(E) shall serve as a clearinghouse for receiving and providing information on the accuracy, completeness, and reliability of records used in matching programs;

(F) shall provide interpretation and guidance to agency components and personnel on the requirements of this section for matching programs;

(G) shall review agency recordkeeping and disposal policies and practices for matching programs to assure compliance with this section; and

(H) may review and report on any agency matching activities that are not matching programs.

(4)(A) Except as provided in subparagraphs (B) and (C), a Data Integrity Board shall not approve any written agreement for a matching program unless the agency has completed and submitted to such Board a cost-benefit analysis of the proposed program and such analysis demonstrates that the program is likely to be cost effective.

(B) The Board may waive the requirements of subparagraph (A) of this paragraph if it determines in writing, in accordance with guidelines prescribed by the Director of the Office of Management and Budget, that a cost-benefit analysis is not required.

(C) A cost-benefit analysis shall not be required under subparagraph (A) prior to the initial approval of a written agreement for a matching program that is specifically required by statute. Any subsequent written agreement for such a program shall not be approved by the

**PRIVACY ACT**

Data Integrity Board unless the agency has submitted a cost-benefit analysis of the program as conducted under the preceding approval of such agreement.

(5)(A) If a matching agreement is disapproved by a Data Integrity Board, any party to such agreement may appeal the disapproval to the Director of the Office of Management and Budget. Timely notice of the filing of such an appeal shall be provided by the Director of the Office of Management and Budget to the Committee on Governmental Affairs of the Senate and the Committee on Government Operations of the House of Representatives.

(B) The Director of the Office of Management and Budget may approve a matching agreement notwithstanding the disapproval of a Data Integrity Board if the Director determines that--

(i) the matching program will be consistent with all applicable legal, regulatory, and policy requirements;

(ii) there is adequate evidence that the matching agreement will be cost-effective; and

(iii) the matching program is in the public interest.

(C) The decision of the Director to approve a matching agreement shall not take effect until 30 days after it is reported to committees described in subparagraph (A).

(D) If the Data Integrity Board and the Director of the Office of Management and Budget disapprove a matching program proposed by the inspector general of an agency, the inspector general may report the disapproval to the head of the agency and to the Congress.

(6) In the reports required by paragraph (3)(D), agency matching activities that are not matching programs may be reported on an aggregate basis, if and to the extent necessary to protect ongoing law enforcement or counterintelligence investigations.

(v) Office of Management and Budget responsibilities

The Director of the Office of Management and Budget shall--

(1) develop and, after notice and opportunity for public comment, prescribe guidelines and regulations for the use of agencies in implementing the provisions of this section; and

(2) provide continuing assistance to and oversight of the implementation of this section by agencies.

**The following section was enacted as part of the Privacy Act, but was not codified; it may be found at § 552a (note).**

# PRIVACY ACT

Sec. 7 (a)(1) It shall be unlawful for any Federal, State or local government agency to deny to any individual any right, benefit, or privilege provided by law because of such individual's refusal to disclose his social security account number.

> (2) the provisions of paragraph (1) of this subsection shall not apply with respect to--
>
>> (A) any disclosure which is required by Federal statute, or
>>
>> (B) any disclosure of a social security number to any Federal, State, or local agency maintaining a system of records in existence and operating before January 1, 1975, if such disclosure was required under statute or regulation adopted prior to such date to verify the identity of an individual.

(b) Any Federal, State or local government agency which requests an individual to disclose his social security account number shall inform that individual whether that disclosure is mandatory or voluntary, by what statutory or other authority such number is solicited, and what uses will be made of it.

**The following sections were enacted as part of Pub.L. 100-503, the Computer Matching and Privacy Protection Act of 1988; they may be found at § 552a (note).**

Sec. 6 Functions of the Director of the Office of Management and Budget.

> (b) Implementation Guidance for Amendments-- The Director shall, pursuant to section 552a(v) of Title 5, United States Code, develop guidelines and regulations for the use of agencies in implementing the amendments made by this Act not later than 8 months after the date of enactment of this Act.

Sec. 9 Rules of Construction.

> Nothing in the amendments made by this Act shall be construed to authorize--
>
>> (1) the establishment or maintenance by any agency of a national data bank that combines, merges, or links information on individuals maintained in systems of records by other Federal agencies;
>>
>> (2) the direct linking of computerized systems of records maintained by Federal agencies;
>>
>> (3) the computer matching of records not otherwise authorized by law; or
>>
>> (4) the disclosure of records for computer matching, except to a Federal, State, or local agency.

Sec. 10 Effective Dates.

**PRIVACY ACT**

(a) In General-- Except as provided in subsection (b), the amendments made by this Act shall take effect 9 months after the date of enactment of this Act.

(b) Exceptions-- The amendment made by sections 3(b) [Notice of Matching Programs - Report to Congress and the Office of Management and Budget], 6 [Functions of the Director of the Office of Management and Budget], 7 [Compilation of Rules and Notices] and 8 [Annual Report] of this Act shall take effect upon enactment.

The Attorney General has determined that the publication of this periodical is necessary to the transaction of the public business of the Department of Justice, as required by law.

**Date Due**

| | | |
|---|---|---|
| JUN 0 5 2006 | | |
| | | |
| | | |
| | | |
| | | |
| | | |
| | | |
| | | |
| | | |
| | | |
| | | |